Engineering Graphics with AutoCAD 2013

James D. Bethune

PHI Learning Private Limited
Delhi-110092
2013

This Indian Reprint—₹ 695.00
(Original U.S. Edition—₹ 6976.00)

ENGINEERING GRAPHICS WITH AUTOCAD® 2013
by James D. Bethune

Original edition, entitled *Engineering Graphics with AutoCAD® 2013* by James D. Bethune, published by Pearson Education, Inc., publishing as Pearson Prentice Hall.

ISBN-978-81-203-4697-0

Indian edition published by PHI Learning Private Limited.

This edition is manufactured in India, and is authorized for sale in India, Pakistan, Sri Lanka, Bhutan, Bangladesh, Nepal and the Maldives only.

Published by Asoke K. Ghosh, PHI Learning Private Limited, Rimjhim House, 111, Patparganj Industrial Estate, Delhi-110092 and Printed by Rajkamal Electric Press, Plot No. 2, Phase IV, HSIDC, Kundli-131028, Sonepat, Haryana.

Preface

This book teaches technical drawing and uses AutoCAD® 2013 as its drawing instrument. Although it follows the general format of many technical drawing texts and presents much of the same material about drawing conventions and practices, the emphasis is on creating accurate, clear drawings. For example, the book shows how to locate dimensions on a drawing so that they completely define the object in accordance with ASME Y14.5-2009 national standards, but the presentation centers on the AutoCAD's **Dimensions** panel and its associated tools and options. The standards and conventions are presented and their applications are shown by the use of AutoCAD® 2013. This integrated teaching concept is followed throughout the book.

Most chapters include design problems. The design problems are varied in scope and are open-ended, which means that there are several correct solutions. This is intended to encourage student creativity and increase their problem-solving abilities.

Chapters 1 through 3 cover AutoCAD **Draw** and **Modify** panels and other commands needed to set up and start drawings. The text starts with simple **Line** commands and proceeds through geometric constructions. The final sections of Chapter 3 describe how to bisect a line and how to draw a hyperbola, a parabola, a helix, and an ogee curve. Redrawing many of the classic geometric shapes will help students learn how to use the **Draw** and **Modify** panels, and other associated commands with accuracy and creativity.

Chapter 4 presents freehand sketching. Simply stated, there is still an important place for sketching in technical drawing. Many design ideas start as freehand sketches and are then developed on the computer. This chapter now includes extensive exercise problems associated with object orientation.

Chapter 5 presents orthographic views. Students are shown how to draw three views of an object by using AutoCAD 2013. The discussion includes projection theory, hidden lines, compound lines, oblique surfaces, rounded surfaces, holes, irregular surfaces, castings, and thin-walled objects. The chapter ends with several intersection problems. These problems serve as a good way to pull together orthographic views and projection theory. Several new, more difficult, exercise problems have been added to this edition.

Chapter 6 presents sectional views and introduces the **Hatch** and **Gradient** commands. The chapter includes multiple, broken-out, and partial sectional views and shows how to draw an S-break for a hollow cylinder.

Chapter 7 covers auxiliary views and shows how to use the **Snap, Rotate** command to create axes aligned with slanted surfaces. Secondary auxiliary views are also discussed. Solid modeling greatly simplifies the determination of the true shape of a line or plane, but a few examples of secondary auxiliary views help students refine their understanding of orthographic views and, eventually, the application of UCSs.

Chapter 8 shows how to dimension both two-dimensional shapes and orthographic views. The **Dimension** command and its associated commands are demonstrated, and examples of how to use the **Dimension Styles** tool are included. The commands are presented as needed to create required dimensions. The conventions demonstrated are in compliance with ANSI Y14.5-2009.

Chapter 9 introduces tolerances. The chapter shows how to draw dimensions and tolerances by using the **Dimension** and **Tolerance** commands, among others. The chapter ends with an explanation of fits and shows how to use the tables included in the Appendix to determine the maximum and minimum tolerances for matching holes and shafts.

Chapter 10 discusses the use of geometric tolerances and explains how AutoCAD® 2013 can be used to create geometric tolerance symbols directly from dialog boxes. Both profile and positional tolerances are explained. The overall intent of the chapter is to teach students how to make parts fit together. Fixed and floating fastener applications are discussed, and design examples are given for both conditions.

Chapter 11 covers how to draw and design with the use of standard fasteners, including bolts, nuts, machine screws, washers, hexagon heads, square heads, setscrews, rivets, and springs. Students are shown how to create wblocks of the individual thread representations and how to use them for different size requirements.

Chapter 12 discusses assembly drawings, detail drawings, and parts lists. Instructions for drawing title blocks, tolerance blocks, release blocks, and revision blocks, and for inserting drawing notes are also included to give students better preparation for industrial practices. New exercise problems have been added.

Chapter 13 presents gears, cams, and bearings. The chapter teaches how to design by using gears selected from manufacturers' catalogs and websites. The chapter shows how to select bearings to support gear shafts and how to tolerance holes in support plates to maintain the desired center distances of meshing gears. It also explains how to create a displacement diagram and then draw the appropriate cam profile. Two new assembly problems involving gears have been added.

Chapter 14 introduces AutoCAD 3D capabilities. Both parallel (isometric) and perspective grids, as well as the WCS and UCS coordinate systems are demonstrated so students learn the fundamentals of 3D drawings before drawing objects.

Chapter 15 shows how to draw three-dimensional solid models. It includes examples of both parallel and perspective grids drawn using all of the different **Visual Style** options. The chapter shows how to union primitive shapes to create more complex models and orthographic views from those models. New complex exercise problems have been added.

Chapter 16 is completely revised. The discussion on descriptive geometry has been replaced with two project problems on milling vise and tennon jig that can be used for group or individual projects. Both problems include extensive dimensions and tolerances requirements. So much work in industry is done in groups that it seemed natural to include problems that require students to work in groups.

Features New to This Edition

1. Uses panels and tabs rather than toolbars.
2. Explores new applications of 3D and solid commands.
3. Defines the use of panels and their flyouts to access commands.
4. Explores the new applications of the **Layer, Block,** and **Attributes** commands.
5. Includes a completely revised Chapter 16 that includes two project problems that can be used as group projects or individual term projects.

Online Supplementary Materials

To access supplementary materials online, instructors need to register at **www.pearsonhighered.com/irc** and request an instructor access code. Within 48 hours after registering, you will receive a confirming e-mail, including an instructor access code. Once you have received your code, go to the site and log on for full instructions on downloading the materials that you wish to use.

Acknowledgments

Thanks to Sara Eilert, Brian Baker, Alicia Ritchey, and Mohinder Singh; also thanks to David, Maria, Randy, Hannah, Wil, Madison, Jack, Luke, Sam, and Ben for their continued support. A special thanks to Cheryl.

James D. Bethune

Contents

chapter one
Getting Started

1-1 Introduction

The figure on the previous page shows the initial AutoCAD drawing screen. It will appear when the program is first accessed. If you are a new AutoCAD user, it is suggested that you view the Getting Started Videos. They are very helpful. If you have worked with AutoCAD before, take a few minutes and look through What's New in 2013.

To Start a New Drawing

1 Click the **New** icon on the Welcome screen.

A listing of available templates will appear on the **Select template** dialog box. See Figure 1-1. Various templates will be used throughout the book, but for a start, we will use the **acad** template. The **acad** template defines inches as its primary units.

Figure 1-1

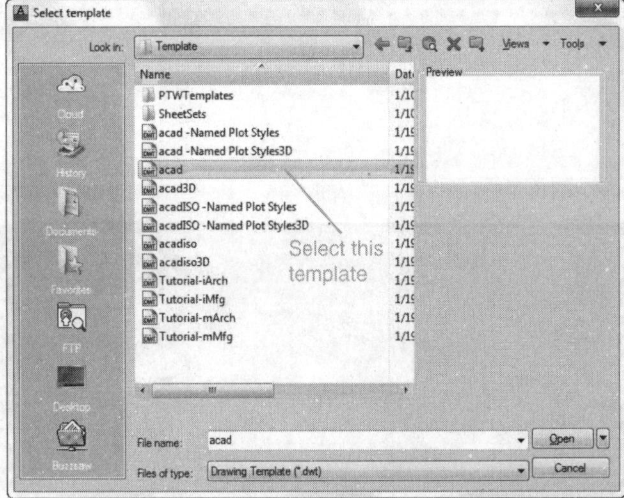

2 Click **acad** on the **Select template.**

The drawing screen will appear. See Figure 1-2. Note that the screen uses the **Drafting & Annotation** format. There are other formats available. Figure 1-3 shows the **AutoCAD Classic** screen. This screen uses toolbars, whereas the **Drafting & Annotation** format uses tabs and panels. The **Drafting & Annotation** format will be used in this book.

An Alternative Method to Starting a New Drawing

1 Click the large A, the **Menu Browser,** in the upper left corner of the drawing screen to access the **Command Headings** box.

A listing of command headings will appear. See Figure 1-4.

2 Click the **New** command.

The **Select template** dialog box will appear. See Figure 1-4.

3 Select the **acad** template by double-clicking the **acad** option.

The **2D Drafting & Annotation** screen will appear. See Figure 1-5. A grouping of tabs and panels will appear across the top of the screen. The tabs are used to access other groups of panels. Panels contain commands.

Figure 1-2

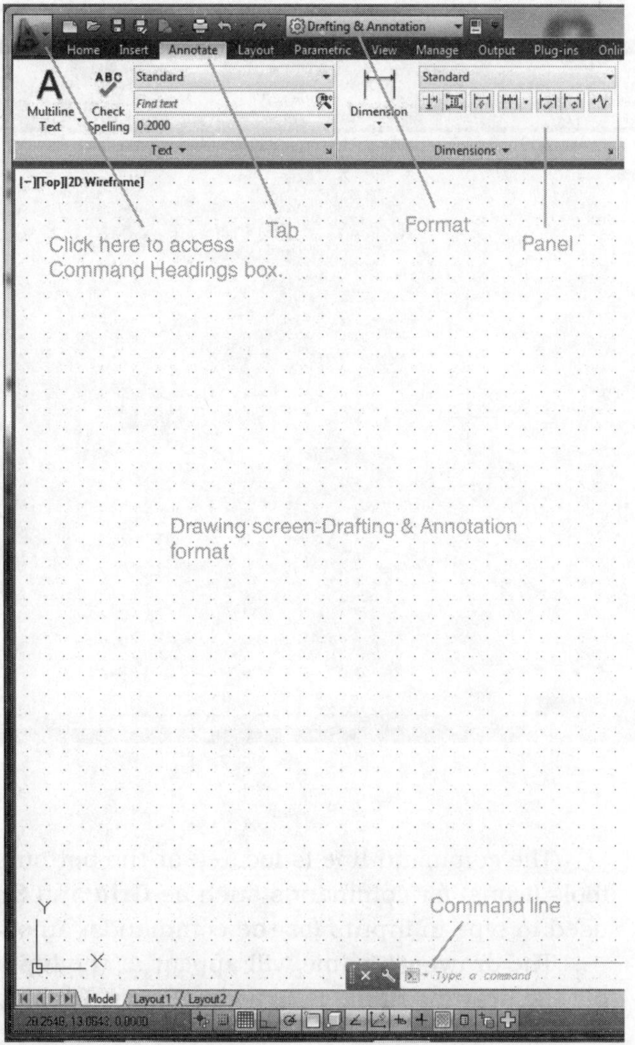

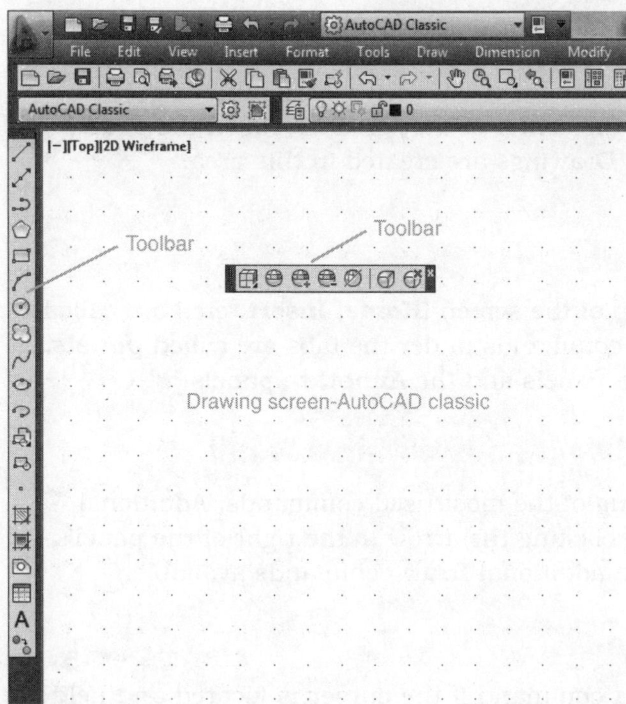

Figure 1-3

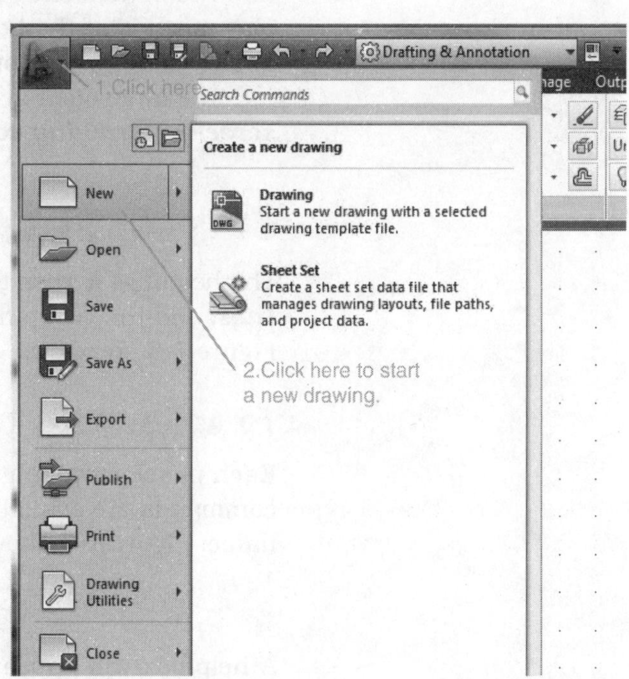

Figure 1-4

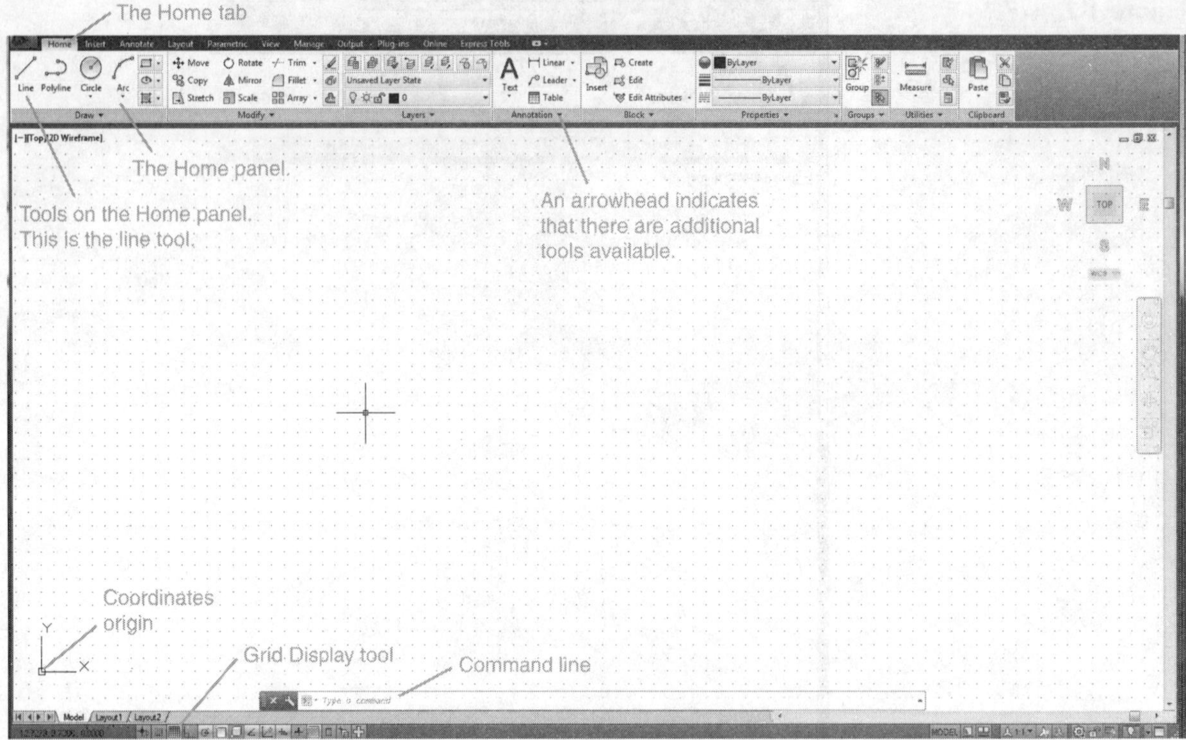

Figure 1-5

The command line is located at the bottom of the screen, as are other tools (icons) for commands such as **Grid** and **Snap.** The command line is used to type in inputs for the commands, among other uses.

The drawing's name will appear at the top of the screen. In this example the drawing name is **Drawing1.dwg.** This is a default name created by AutoCAD. If a drawing name had been entered, it would appear where the **Drawing1.dwg** title currently appears.

The bottom left corner of the drawing screen shows the coordinate display position of the horizontal, vertical crosshairs in terms of an X,Y coordinate value, whose origin is the lower left corner of the drawing screen.

The large open area in the center of the screen is called the ***drawing screen*** or ***drawing editor.*** Drawings are created in this area.

1-2 Tabs and Panels

The headings across the top of the screen (**Home, Insert,** etc.) are called ***tabs,*** and the groupings of commands under the tabs are called ***panels.*** Figure 1-6 shows the **Home** panels and the **Annotate** panels.

To Access Additional Commands Within a Panel

Each panel shows a grouping of the most used commands. Additional commands are available by clicking the arrow to the right of the panel's name. Figure 1-7 shows the additional **Draw** commands available.

Help Boxes for Commands

A help box will appear for a command if the cursor is located and held on the command's icon. See Figure 1-7. Initially, when a cursor is located on

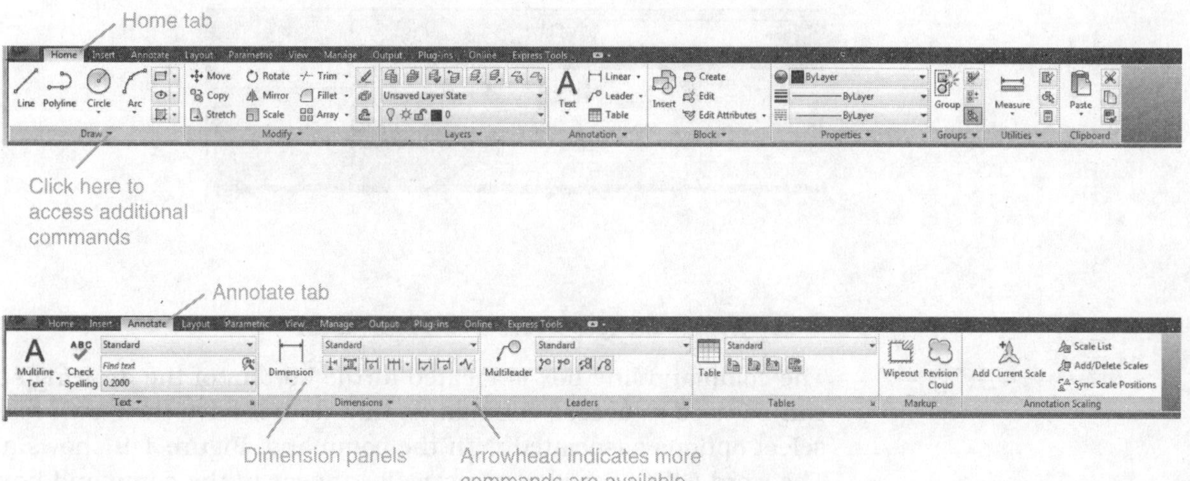

Figure 1-6

Figure 1-7

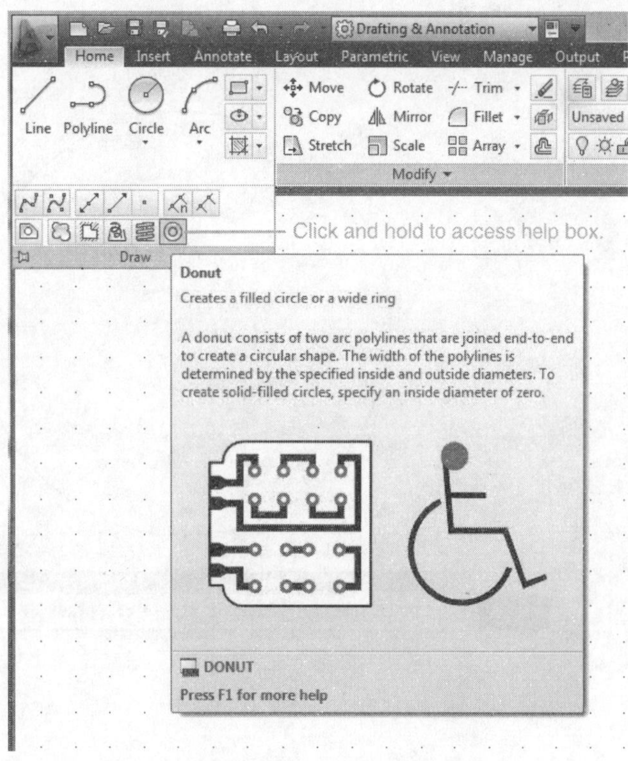

a command icon, but not clicked, an identifying box will appear identifying the command. After a few seconds the box will expand to define the command.

To Access Other Help Information

If you cannot find a command or need further instructions for operating a particular command, use the **InfoCenter** located at the top right section of the screen. See Figure 1-8. Type in the name of what you are seeking, and click the binocular icon just to the right of the **InfoCenter** box.

Figure 1-8

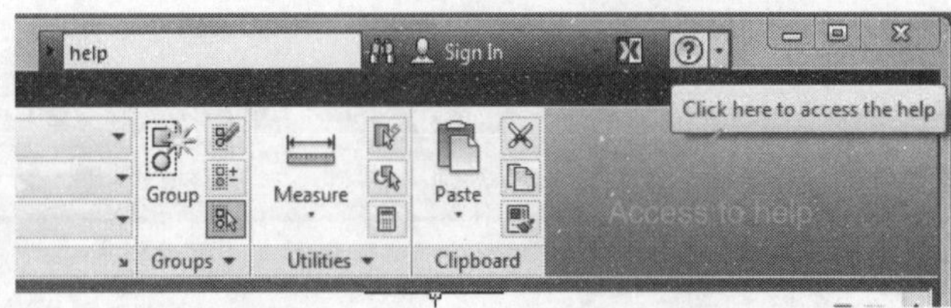

1-3 The Command Line Box

The command line box is located at the bottom of the drawing screen. It can be used to access commands that do not have their own icons, or to select options associated with the command. Figure 1-9 shows a circle. The word CIRCLE will automatically appear in the command box when the **Circle** command is clicked on the **Draw** panel. As presented, the circle will be defined by using a radius value. A radius value is entered into the radius box with the blue background.

Figure 1-9

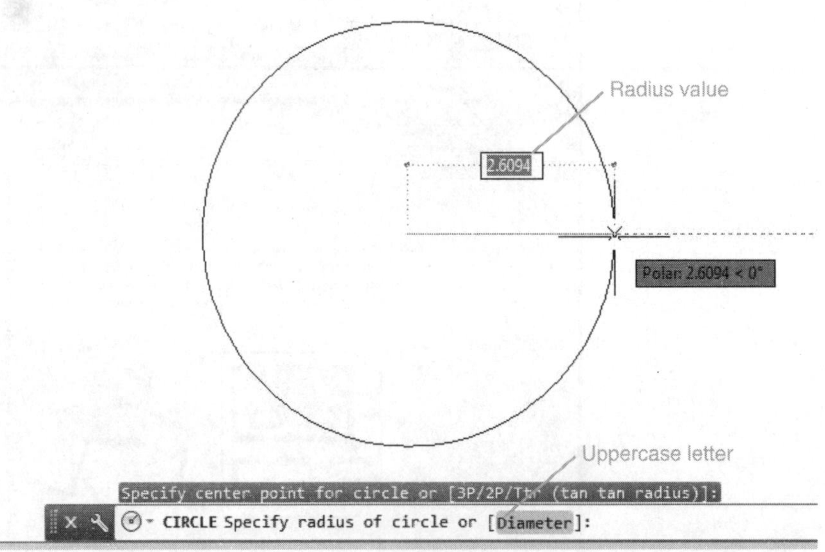

The command line shows the word Diameter in brackets: [Diameter]. This means that there is a diameter option.

To Enter a Diameter Value

1. Click the command line box.
2. Type **d;** press **Enter.**

   The system is now set for a diameter value for the circle.

3. Enter a value for the diameter of the circle; press **Enter.**

   The options shown in the command line box will always include one uppercase letter. It may not always be the first letter. Type that letter and press **Enter** to access the option.

1-4 Command Tools

A ***tool*** is a picture (icon) that represents an AutoCAD command. Most commands have equivalent tools.

To Determine the Command That a Tool Represents

See Figure 1-10.

Figure 1-10

1 Locate the cursor arrow on the selected tool (icon).

In the example shown, the **Line** command tool within the **Draw** panel was selected.

2 Hold the arrow still without pressing any mouse buttons.

The command name will appear below the tool. This name is referred to as a ***tooltip.***

If you continue to keep the cursor arrow on the tool box, a help box will appear.

1-5 Starting a New Drawing

When a new drawing is started, a drawing name is assigned, the drawing units are specified, the drawing limits are modified, if needed, and **Grid** and **Snap** values are defined. The following four sections will show how to start a new drawing.

1-6 Naming a Drawing

Any combination of letters and numbers may be used as a file name. Either uppercase or lowercase letters may be used, since AutoCAD file names are not case sensitive. The symbols $, -, and _ (underscore) may also be used. Other symbols, such as % and *, may not be used. See Figure 1-11.

Figure 1-11

Correct drawing names:

FIRST EK-131-1 PA1-1a

Incorrect drawing names:

100% *.*

To locate a file on a the C: drive:

C:FIRST

All AutoCAD drawing files will automatically have the extension .dwg added to the given file name. If you name a drawing **FIRST,** it will appear in the files as **FIRST.dwg.** Other extensions can be used, but the .dwg is the default setting. (A default setting is one that AutoCAD will use unless specifically told to use some other value.)

If you want to locate a file on another drive, specify the drive letter followed by a colon in front of the drawing name. For example, in Figure 1-11 the file specified **C:FIRST** will locate the drawing file **FIRST** on the C: drive.

To Start a New Drawing

There are three ways to access the **Create New Drawing** dialog box that is used to name a new drawing:

1. Select the **New** tool from the **Command Headings** box. (See Figure 1-12.)

Figure 1-12

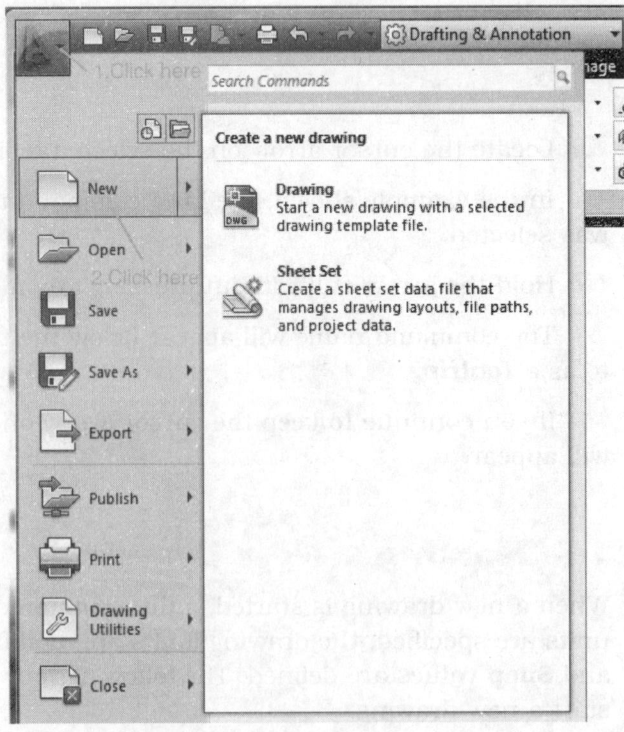

2. Type the word **new** in response to a command prompt.

3. Hold down the **<Ctrl>** key and press **N.**

Any of these methods will cause the **Select template** dialog box to appear on the screen. See Figure 1-13. The **acad** template will set up a drawing with inch values and ANSI style dimensions. The **acadiso** template will set up a drawing with millimeter values and ISO style dimensions.

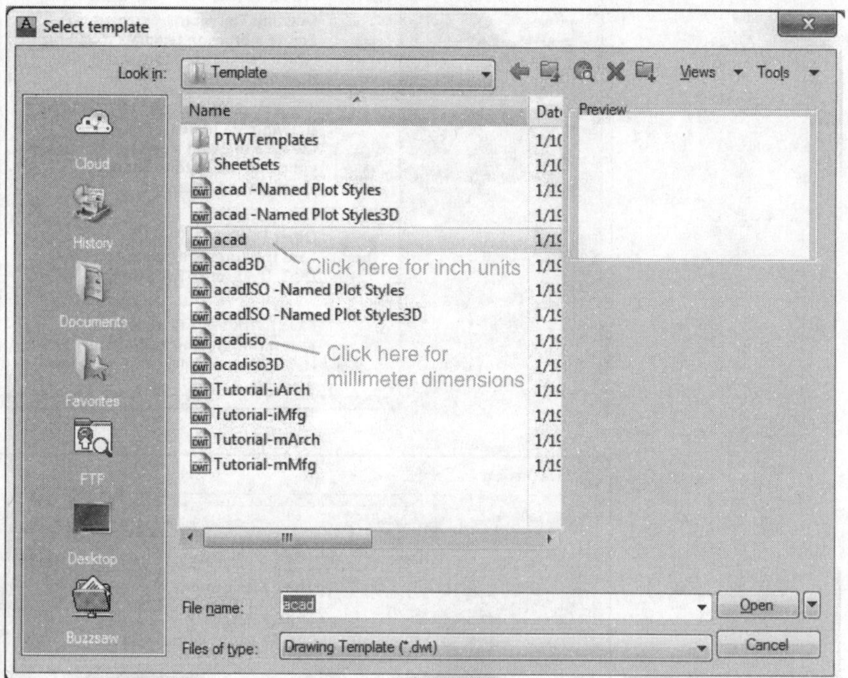

Figure 1-13

To Save a New Drawing File

A drawing name is entered as a file name by using the **Save As** option located in the **Command Headings** box. See Figure 1-14. It is recommended that a drawing name be assigned before a new drawing is started.

1. Click the large A in the upper left corner of the screen.

2. Select the **Save As** tool.

The **Save Drawing As** dialog box will appear. See Figure 1-15.

The **Save Drawing As** dialog box will list all existing drawings. Click on the thumbnail option to change the list to thumbnail drawings.

3. Enter the drawing name.

In this example, the drawing name **First** was used.

4. Select **OK.**

The name of the drawing will appear at the top of the screen. See Figure 1-16.

Figure 1-14

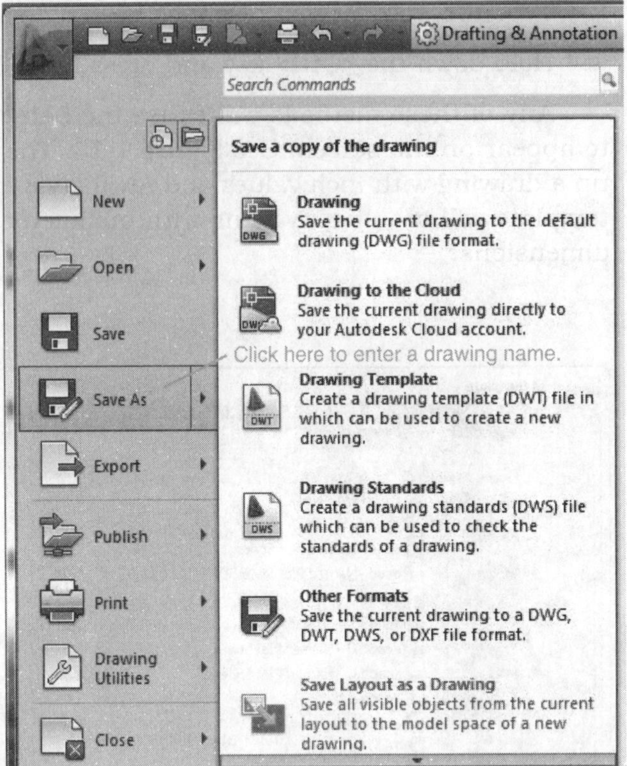

Figure 1-15

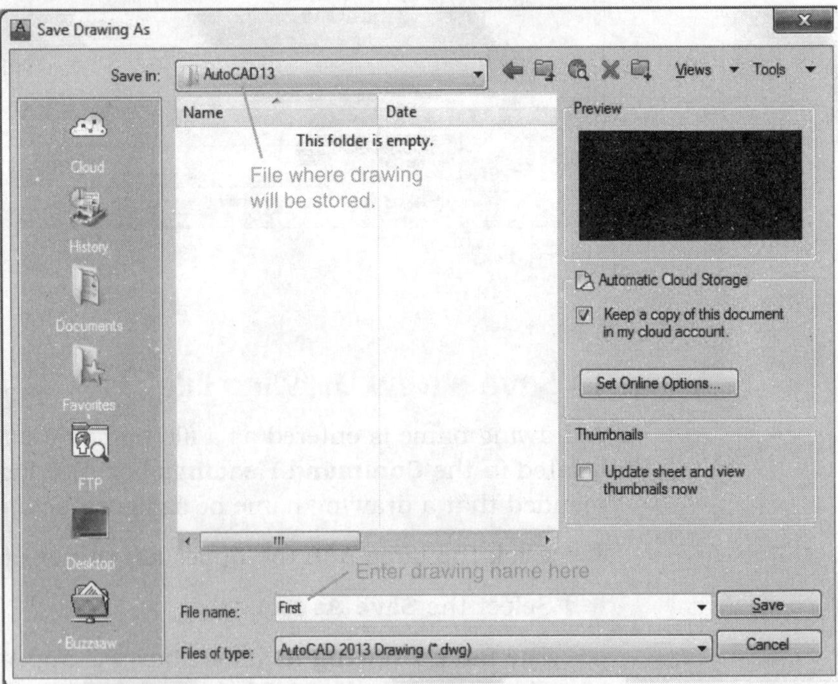

Figure 1-16

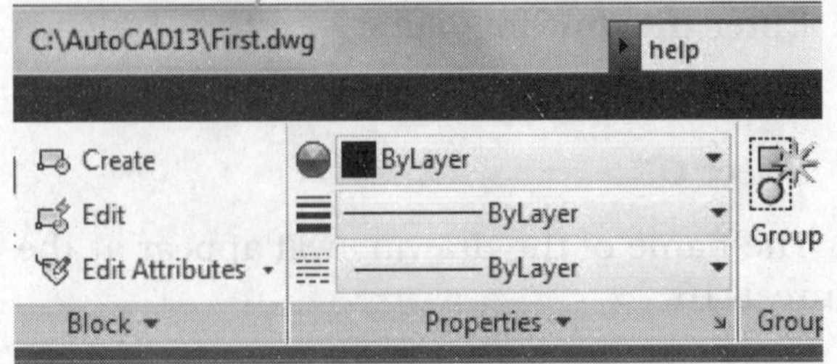

1-7 Drawing Units

AutoCAD 2013's **Drawing Units** dialog box allows for either English or metric units to be used as default values; however, AutoCAD can work in any of five different unit systems: scientific, decimal, engineering, architectural, or fractional. The default system is the decimal system and can be applied to either English values (inches) or metric values (millimeters). See Figure 1-17.

Figure 1-17

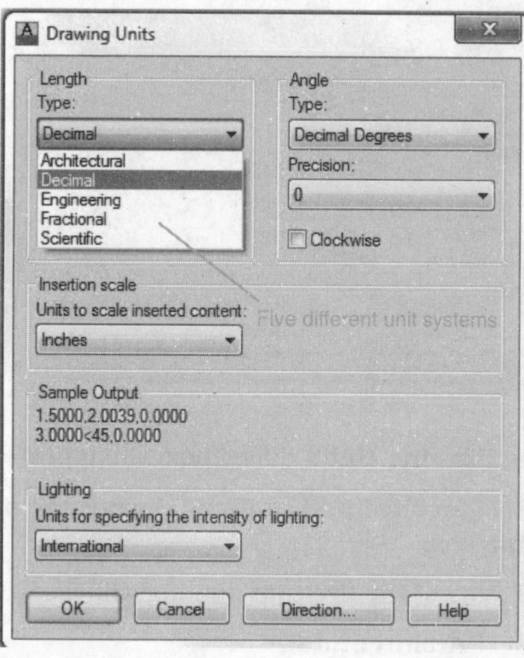

To Specify or to Change the Drawing Units

1. Select the **Drawing Utilities** heading in the **Command Headings** box.
2. Select **Units.** (See Figure 1-18.)

Figure 1-18

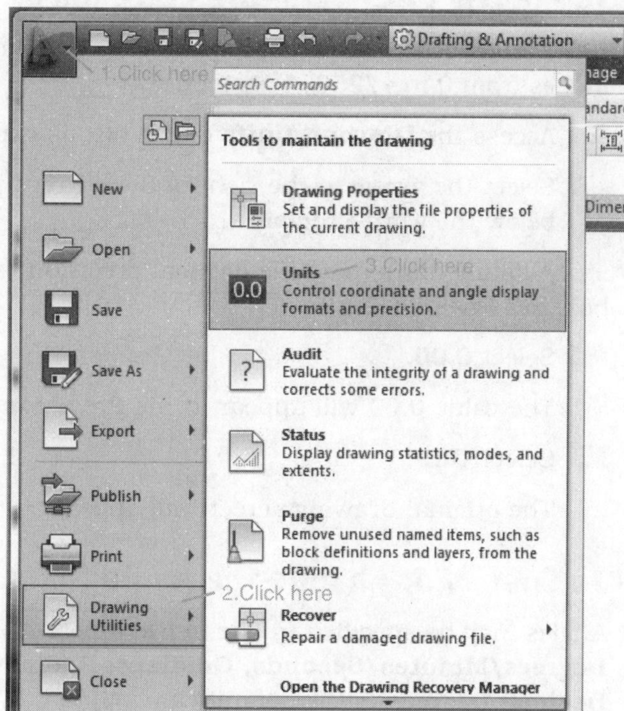

Figure 1-19

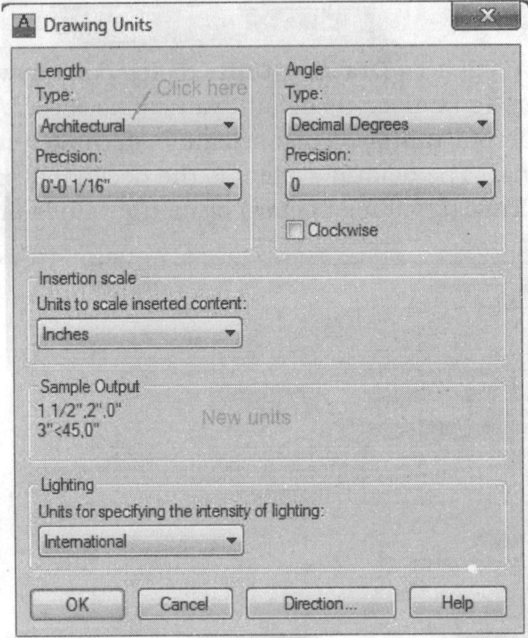

The **Drawing Units** dialog box will appear. See Figure 1-19.

3 Select architectural units by clicking the arrow to the right of the **Type** box.

A listing of the five unit options will cascade down.

4 Select **Architectural.**

Note that the **Sample Output,** located slightly below the center of the **Drawing Units** box, is in fractional inches.

5 Repeat the procedure, and set the units back to **Decimal.**

To Specify or Change the Precision of the Units System

Unit values can be expressed with decimal places from zero to eight or in inches from 0 to 1/256 of an inch.

1 Access the **Drawing Units** dialog box as explained previously.

2 Select the arrow to the right of the current precision value display box below the word **Precision.**

A listing of the possible decimal precision values will cascade from the box. See Figure 1-20.

3 Select **0.00.**

The value 0.00 will appear in the **Precision** box.

4 Select **OK.**

The original drawing screen will appear.

To Specify or Change the Angle Units Value

Angles may be specified in one of five different units: **Decimal Degrees, Degrees/Minutes/Seconds, Gradians, Radians,** or **Surveyor** units. **Decimal Degrees** is the default value.

Figure 1-20

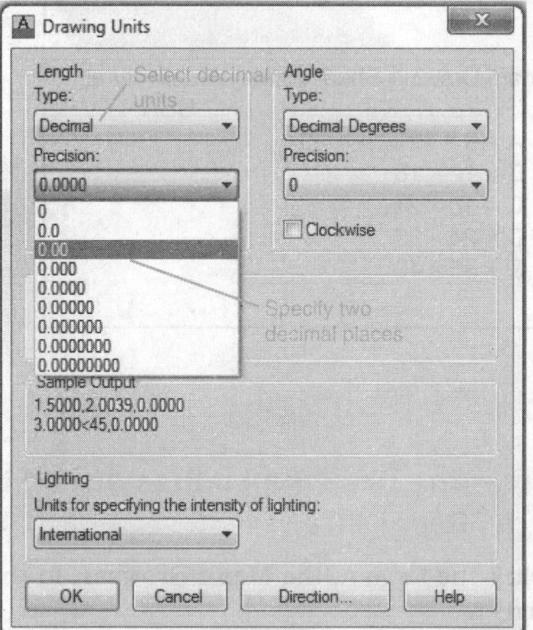

Change the angle units by selecting the desired units in the cascade menu under **Angle Type.** The precision of the angle units is changed as specified for linear units.

1-8 Drawing Limits

Drawing limits are used to set the boundaries of the drawing. The drawing boundaries are usually set to match the size of a sheet of drawing paper. This means that when the drawing is plotted and a hard copy is made, it will fit on the drawing paper.

Figure 1-21 shows a listing of standard flat-size drawing papers for engineering applications, Figure 1-22 shows standard metric sizes, and Figure 1-23 shows standard architectural sizes.

A standard 8.5″ × 11″ letter-size sheet of paper as used by most printers is referred to as an ***A-size*** sheet of drawing paper.

NOTE

A sheet of paper can be sized to match standard sheet sizes by the capabilities of the printer or plotter. Many printers and plotters have built-in scaling features, and some list standard sheet sizes that can be applied to a drawing.

Standard Drawing Sheet Sizes—Inches

A = 8.5 × 11
B = 11 × 17
C = 17 × 22
D = 22 × 34
E = 34 × 44

Figure 1-21

Standard Drawing Sheet Sizes—Millimeters

A4 = 210 × 297
A3 = 297 × 420
A2 = 420 × 594
A1 = 594 × 841
A0 = 841 × 1189

Figure 1-22

Standard Drawing Sheet Sizes—Architectural
USA

A = 9 × 12
B = 12 × 18
C = 18 × 24
D = 24 × 36
E = 36 × 48

Figure 1-23

To Align the Drawing Limits with a Standard A3 (Metric) Paper Size

1. Click the large A, the **Menu Browser,** in the upper left corner of the screen.
2. Click the **Print** command, and then click the **Page Setup** option.

   See Figure 1-24. The **Page Setup Manager** dialog box will appear.
3. Click the **Modify . . .** option.

   See Figure 1-25. The **Page Setup - Model** dialog box will appear.
4. Click the arrow to the right of the **Paper size** box.

   A listing of available paper sizes will cascade down. See Figure 1-26.

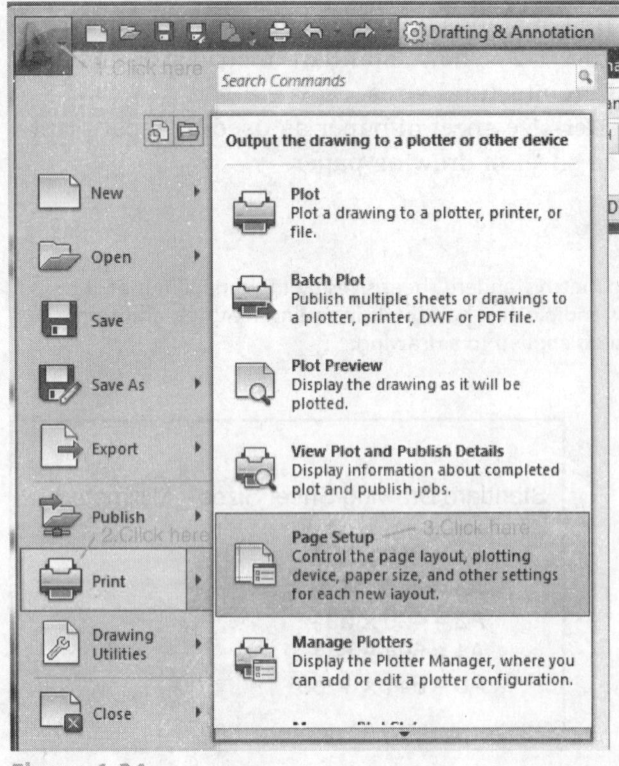

Figure 1-24

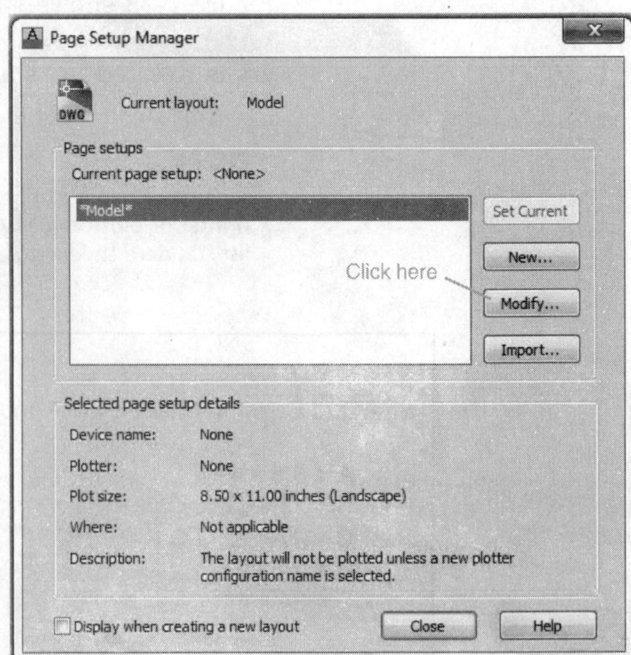

Figure 1-25

Figure 1-26

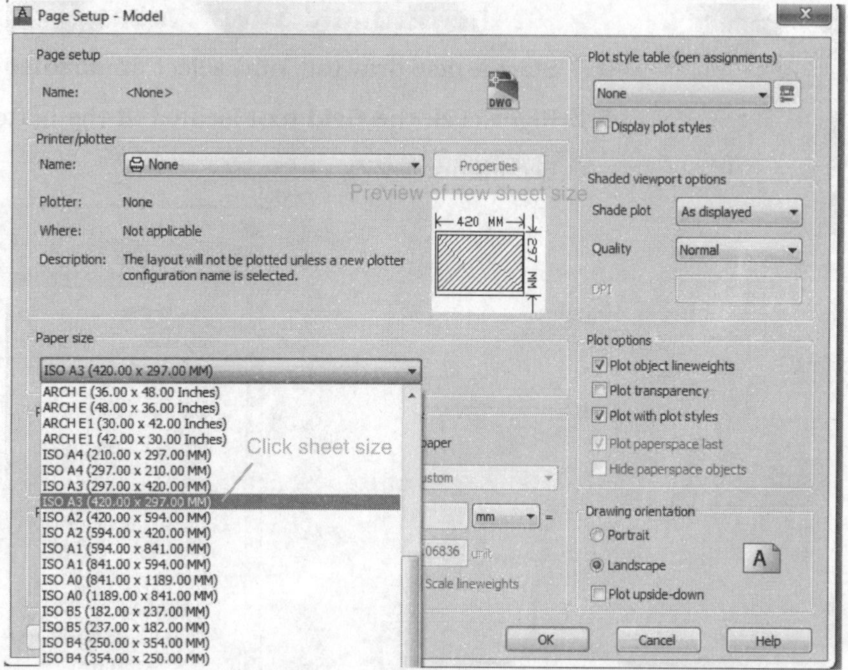

5 Select the **ISO A3 (420.00 × 297.00)** size.

The dimensions in the preview box in the **Printer/Plotter** dialog box will change to the selected values.

6 Click **OK.**

The drawing screen is now sized to the 297 × 420 A3 dimensions.

NOTE

The sheet size may also be set with the **Drawing Limits** command. Type **drawing limits** in response to a command prompt, and define the drawing limits. If the new limits exceed the current screen limits, type **zoom.** Then, all the new drawing limits will match the screen size. The default sheet size for an acad template is 8.5 × 11 (ansi a), and for an acadiso template it is 210 × 297 (iso a4).

1-9 Grid and Snap

The **Grid** command is used to place a grid background on the drawing screen. This background grid is helpful for establishing visual reference points for sizing and for locating points and lines.

The **Snap** command limits the movement of the cursor to predefined points on the screen. For example, if the **Snap** command values are set to match the **Grid** values, the cursor will snap from intersection to intersection on the grid.

The default **Grid** and **Snap** setting for the acad template is **.50** inch, and the default setting for **Grid** and **Snap** for the acadiso template is **10** millimeters.

NOTE

The **Grid** function can be toggled off and on with the **<F7>** key, and the **Snap** function can be toggled with the **<F9>** key.

To Set the Grid and Snap Values

1. Start a new drawing, and select an **acadiso** template.
2. Right-click the **Grid** tool located at the bottom left of the screen.

   See Figure 1-27.

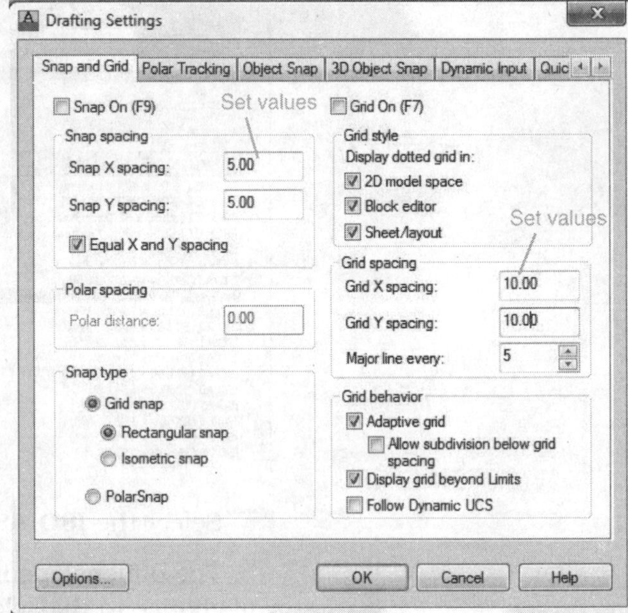

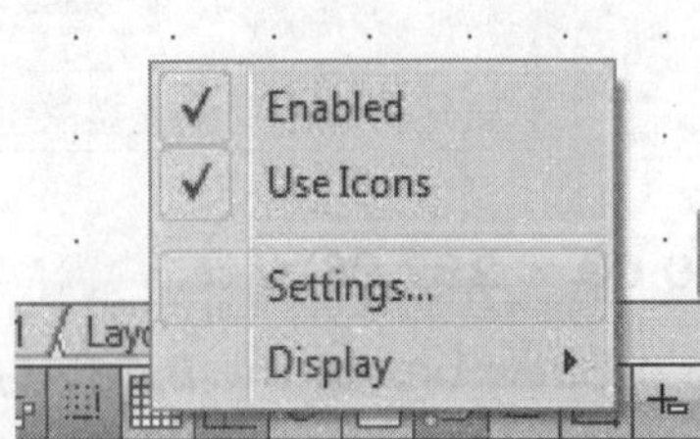

Figure 1-27

The **Drafting Settings** dialog box will appear. See Figure 1-27. If necessary, click the **Snap and Grid** tab.

3. Click on the **Grid On** and **Snap On** boxes. A check mark will appear in the boxes.
4. Place the cursor on the **Snap X spacing** box to the right of the given value under the **Snap On** heading.

   A vertical flashing cursor will appear.
5. Backspace out the existing value and type in **5**.
6. Click the **Snap Y spacing** box.

The Y spacing will automatically be made equal to the X spacing value. Rectangular grid spacing can be created by specifying different X and Y spacing values.

7. Select the **Grid X spacing** box under the **Grid spacing** heading.
8. Backspace out the existing value and type in **10** if needed.
9. Click the **Grid Y spacing** box to make the X and Y values equal.
10. Select **OK.**

See Figure 1-28. Since the **Snap** values have been set to exactly half of the **Grid** values, the cursor can be located either directly on grid intersections or halfway between them.

The grid can be turned on and off either by double-clicking the **Grid** icon at the bottom of the screen or by pressing the **<F7>** key on the keyboard. Snap can be turned on and off by double-clicking the **Snap** icon at the bottom of the screen or by pressing the <F9> key on the keyboard. **Grid** and **Snap** can also be activated by the tools on the status bar located at bottom of the screen. See Figure 1-28.

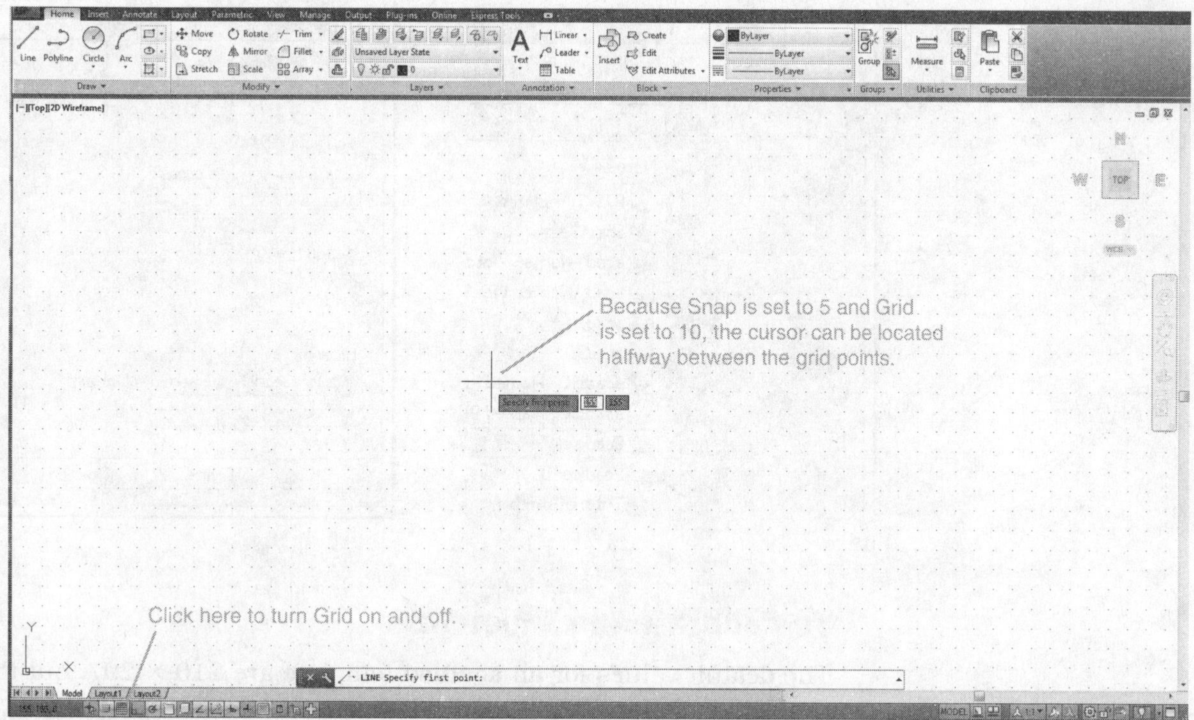

Figure 1-28

1-10 Sample Problem SP1-1

Set up a drawing that will use millimeter dimensions and the following parameters:

Sheet size = **297,420(A3)**

Grid = **10** spacing

Snap = **5** spacing

Whole-number precision

To Specify the Drawing Units

1. Click the **Menu Browser** in the upper left corner of the drawing screen, and select the **File** command, then the **New** option.

   The **Select template** dialog box will appear. See Figure 1-29.

2. Select the **acadiso** template, then **Open.**

To Define the Drawing Precision

1. Click the **Menu Browser** in the upper left corner of the drawing screen, and select the **Drawing Utilities** command, then the **Units** option.

   The **Drawing Units** dialog box will appear. See Figure 1-30. In this example only whole numbers will be used, so the **0** option is selected.

2. Select the **0** precision, then **OK.**

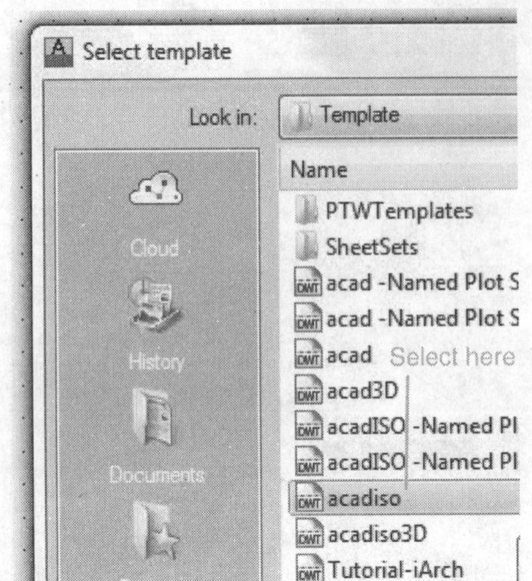

Figure 1-29

Figure 1-30

To Calibrate the Sheet Size

The default values for an **acadiso** template are 210 × 297, but this sample problem calls for 297,420, an A3 sheet size.

1. Click the **Menu Browser,** and select the **Print option,** then the **Page Setup** option.

   The **Page Setup Manager** dialog box will appear.

2. Click the **Modify** box.

   The **Page Setup – Model** dialog box will appear. See Figure 1-31.

Figure 1-31

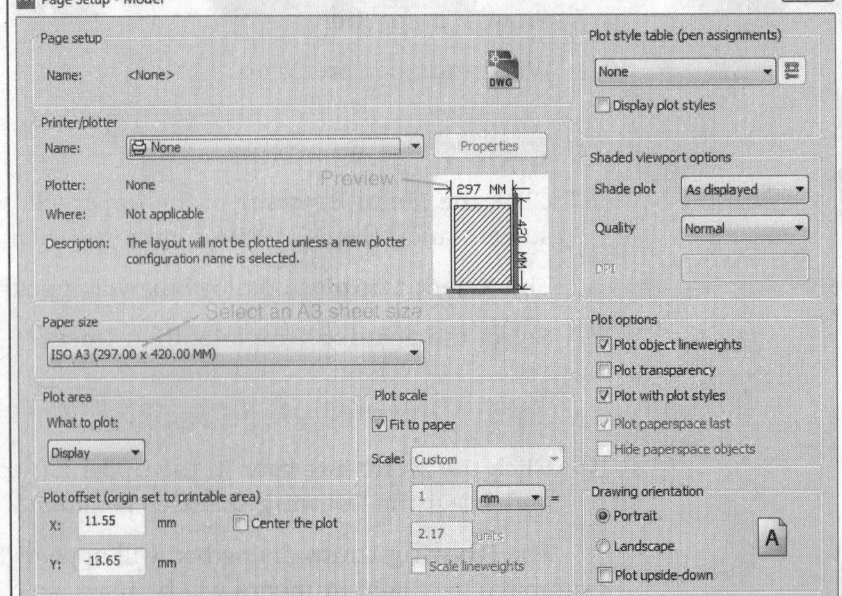

3. Scroll down the available **Paper size** options and select the **ISO A3 (297.00 × 420.00)** option.
4. Click **OK.**

To Set the Grid and Snap Values

1. Right-click the **Grid** icon at the bottom of the screen.
2. Click the **Settings** option.

   The **Drafting Settings** dialog box will appear. See Figure 1-32.

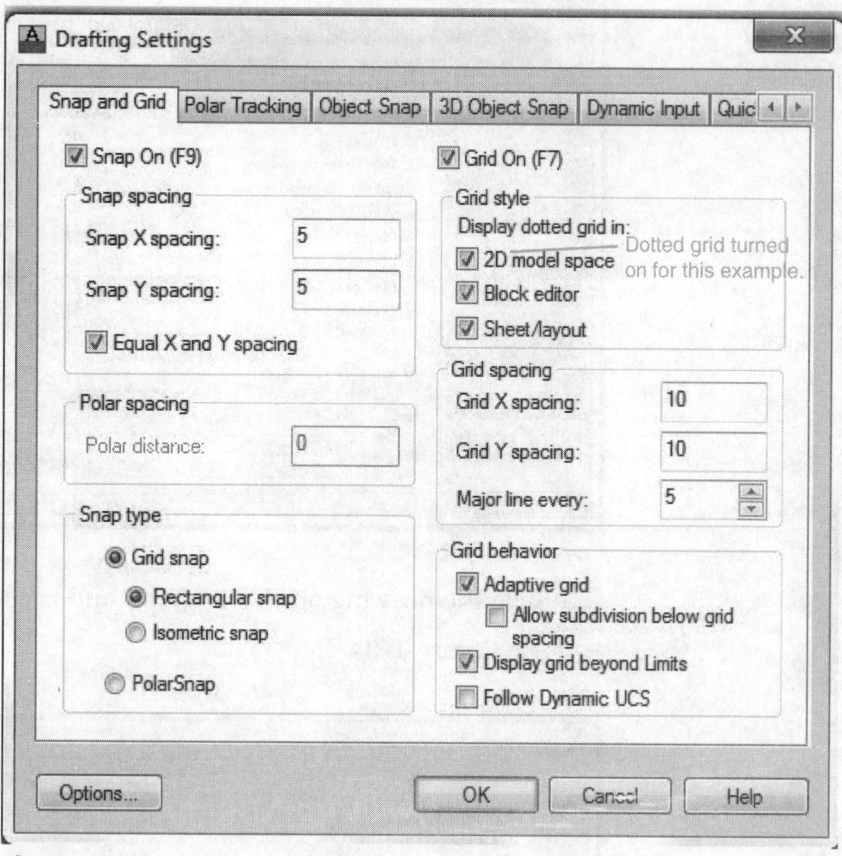

Figure 1-32

3. Turn the **Grid** and **Snap** commands on, and set the snap spacing for **5** and the grid spacing for **10.**
4. Type the word **zoom** in response to a command prompt. Then type **A;** press **Enter.**

   The screen is now ready for starting a drawing by using millimeter values. Note that the display dotted grid options have been turned on, generating a dotted rather than a lined grid.

1-11 Save and Save As

The **Save** and **Save As** commands are used to save a drawing.

To Use the Save and Save As Commands

1 Click the **Menu Browser** in the upper left corner of the drawing screen, and select the **Save As** option.

The **Save Drawing As** dialog box will appear. See Figure 1-33. In this example the file name **Drawing3.dwg** appears. This is the default name that was created automatically when a new drawing was created.

Figure 1-33

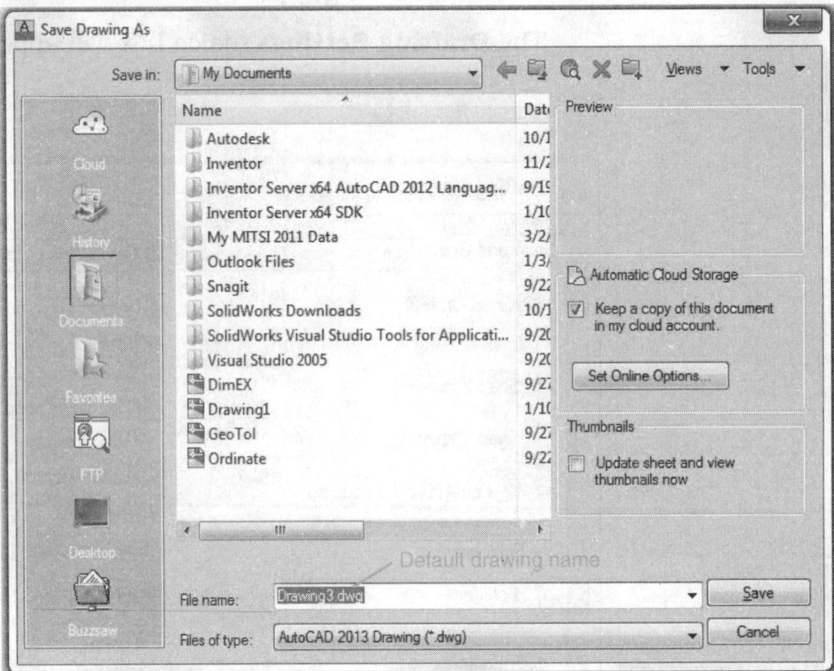

2 Save the drawing on the C: drive, and enter a new file name, **Box.**

See Figure 1-34.

Figure 1-34

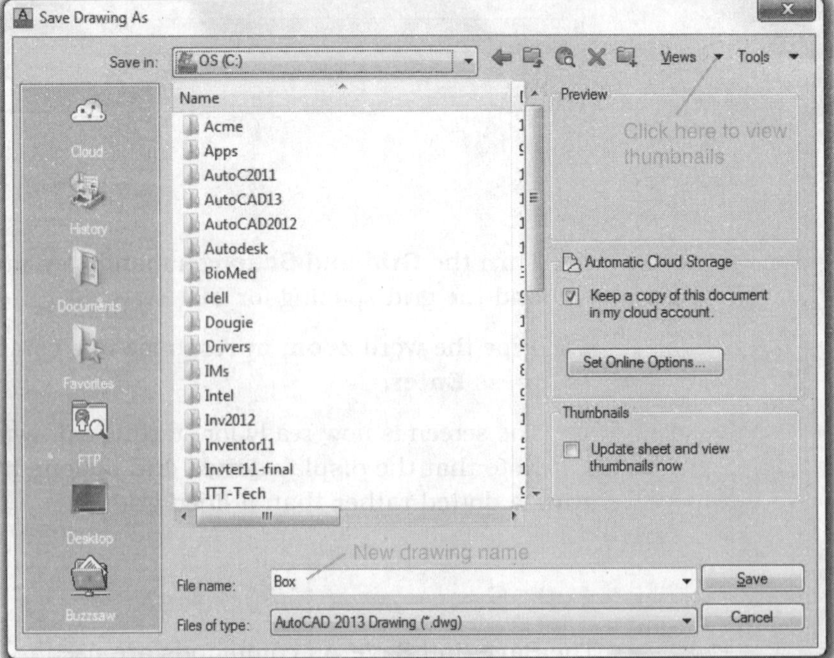

NOTE

The **Open** option can also be accessed by pressing **<Ctrl>** + **<o>**.

3 Click the **Save** box.

1-12 Open

The **Open** command is used to call up an existing drawing so that you may continue working on it or revise it.

To Use the Open Command

The **Open** command may be accessed in one of two ways:

1 Click the **Menu Browser** in the upper left corner of the drawing screen, and then select **Open.**

The **Select File** dialog box will appear. See Figure 1-35.

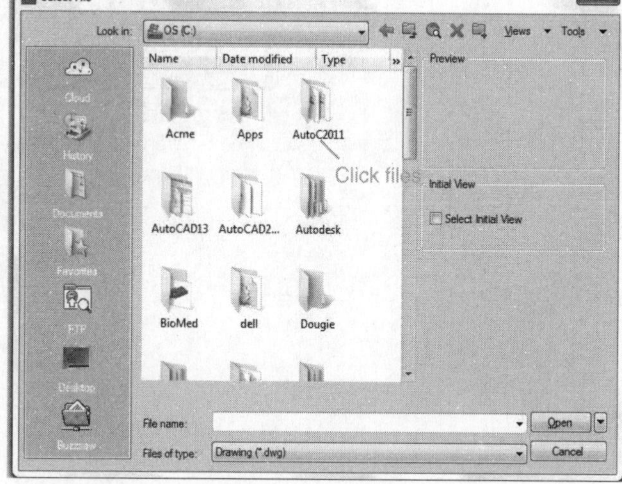

Figure 1-35

2 Click the **Views** option at the top of the **Select File** dialog box, and click the **Thumbnails** and **Preview** options.

Thumbnails of the drawing files will appear.

3 Click the desired file.

A preview will appear.

4 Click the **Open** box.

1-13 Close

The **Close** command allows you to close the current drawing.

1 Click the **Menu Browser,** click **Close,** and then click **Current Drawing.** See Figure 1-36. The system will exit the AutoCAD program.

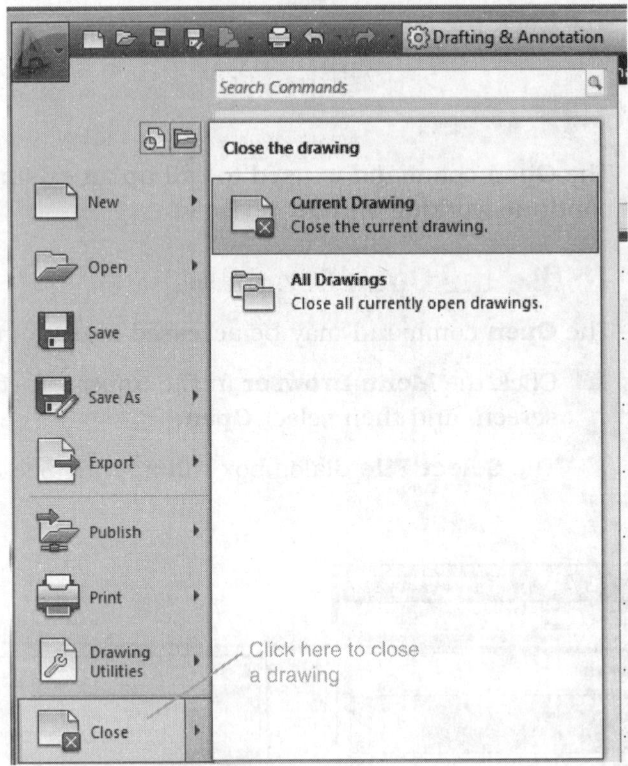

Figure 1-36

1-14 EXERCISE PROBLEMS

EX1-1

Create a drawing screen as shown in Figure EX1-1. Use the **Drafting & Annotation** format, select an **acadiso** template, turn on the **Grid** and **Snap** functions, and set the grid spacing for **10** and snap spacing for **5.** Set the sheet size for **A3 (247.00 × 210.00).** Name the drawing **Screen 1.**

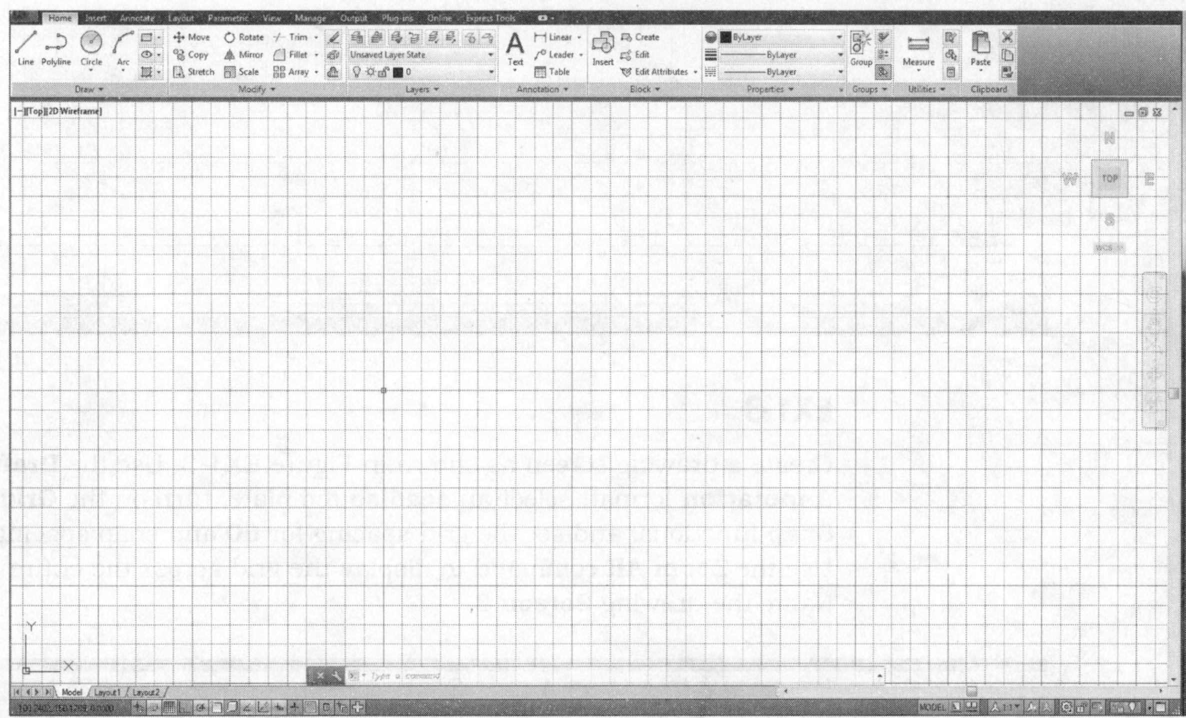

EX1-2

Create a drawing screen as shown in Figure EX1-2. Use the **Drafting & Annotation** format, select an **acad** template, turn on the **Grid** and **Snap** functions, and set the grid spacing for **0.50** and snap spacing for **0.25.** Locate the origin in the lower left corner of the drawing screen. Name the drawing **Screen 2.**

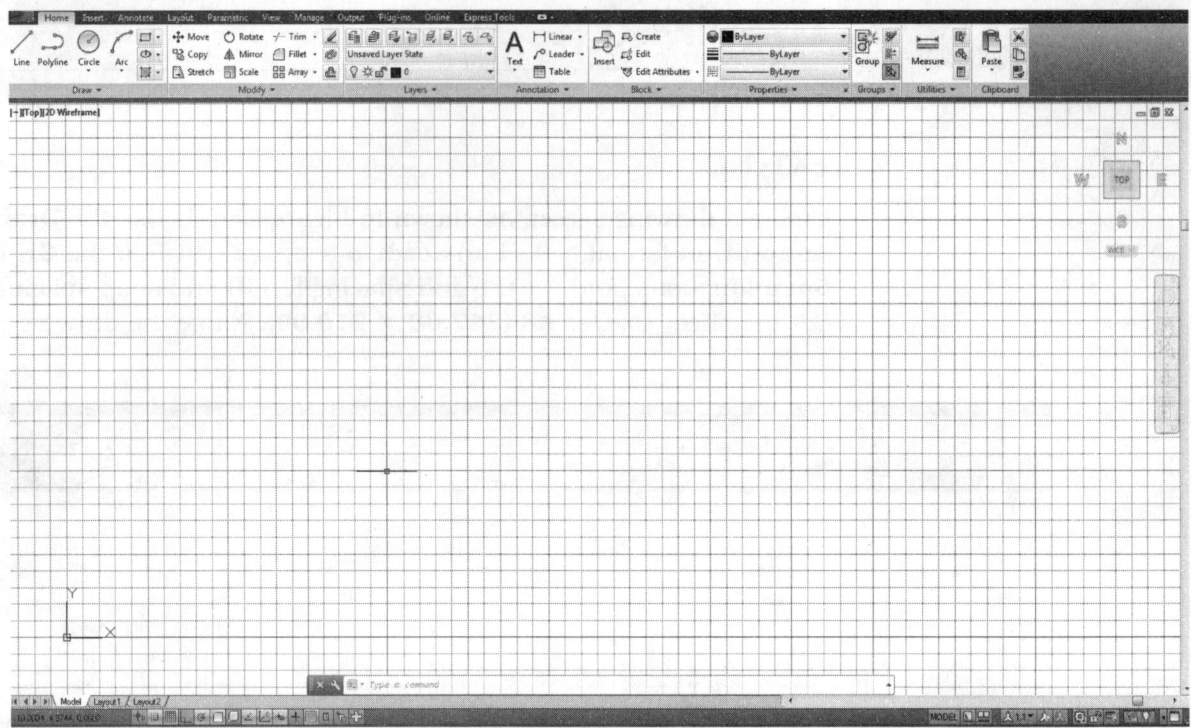

EX1-3

Create a drawing screen as shown in Figure EX1-3. Use the **Drafting & Annotation** format, select an **acadiso** template, turn on the **Grid** and **Snap** functions, and set the grid spacing for **50** and snap spacing for **10.** Use the **Zoom All** command to display the grid across the entire screen. Name the drawing **Screen 3.**

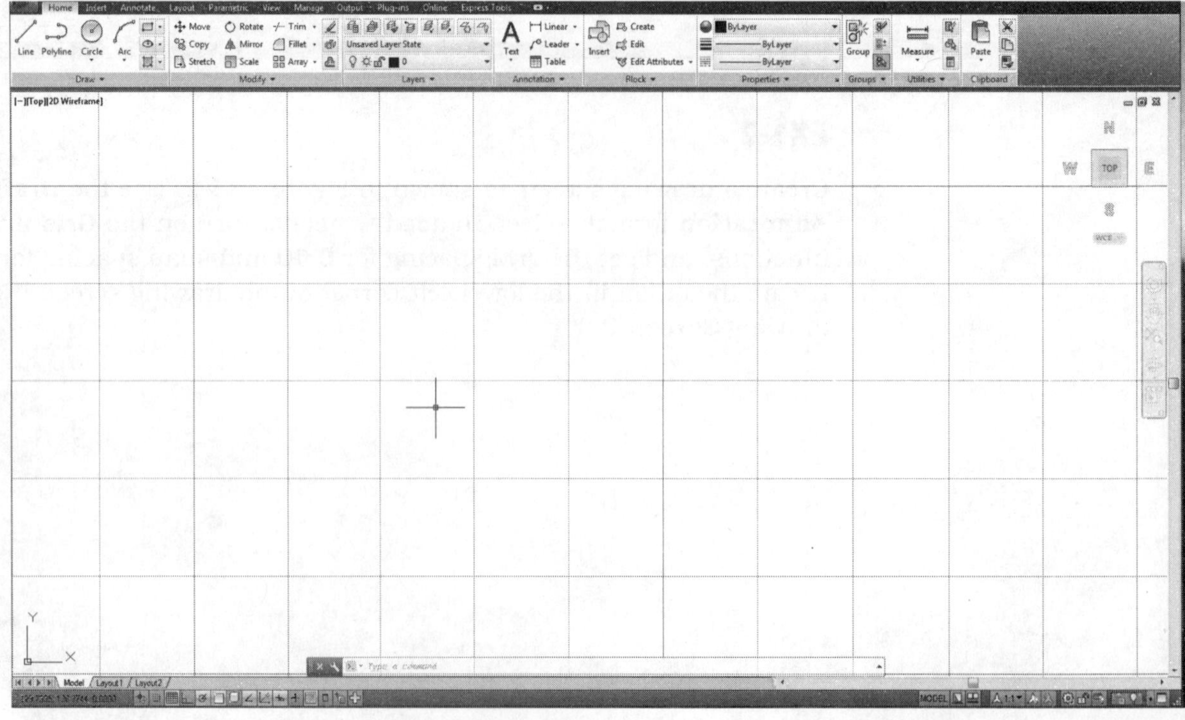

EX1-4

Create a drawing screen as shown in Figure EX1-4. Use the **Drafting & Annotation** format, select an **acadiso3D** template, turn on the **Grid** and **Snap** functions, and set the grid spacing for **20** and snap spacing for **5.** Use the **Zoom All** command to display the grid across the entire screen. Name the drawing **Screen 4-3D.**

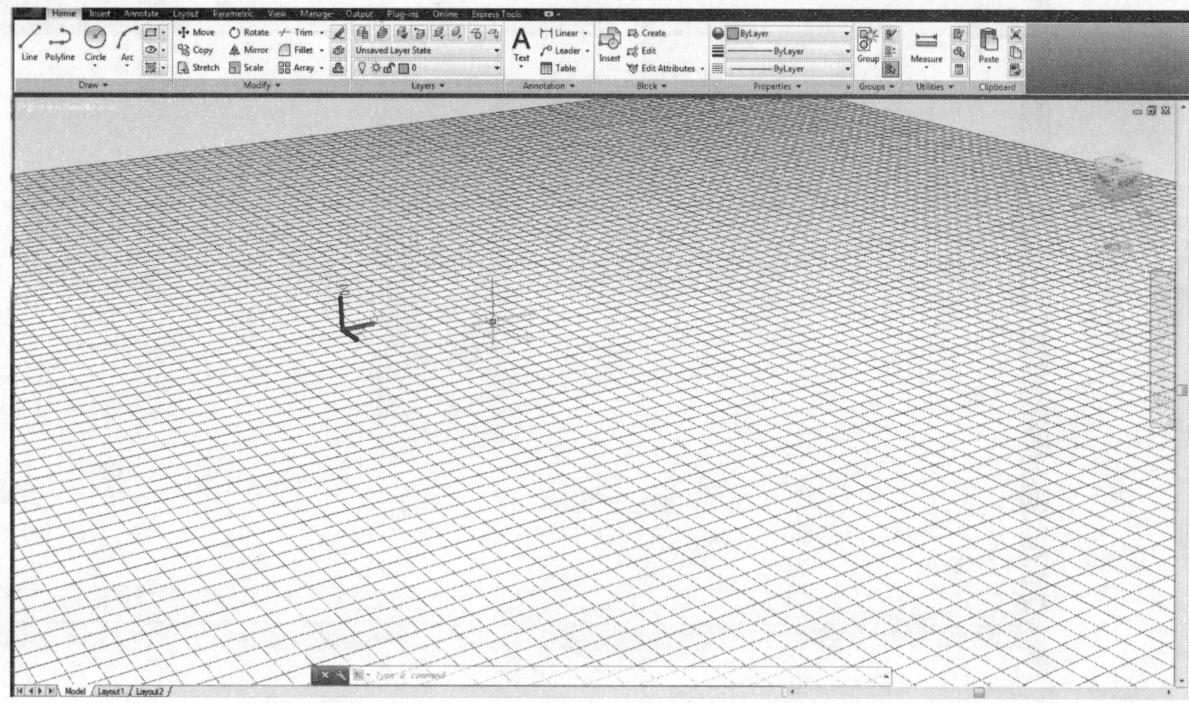

EX1-5

Create a drawing screen as shown in Figure EX1-5. Select an **acad** template. Select the **AutoCAD Classic** format. Set the grid spacing for **1.00** and the snap spacing for **0.50.** Use the **Zoom All** command to display the grid. Name the drawing **Screen Classic.**

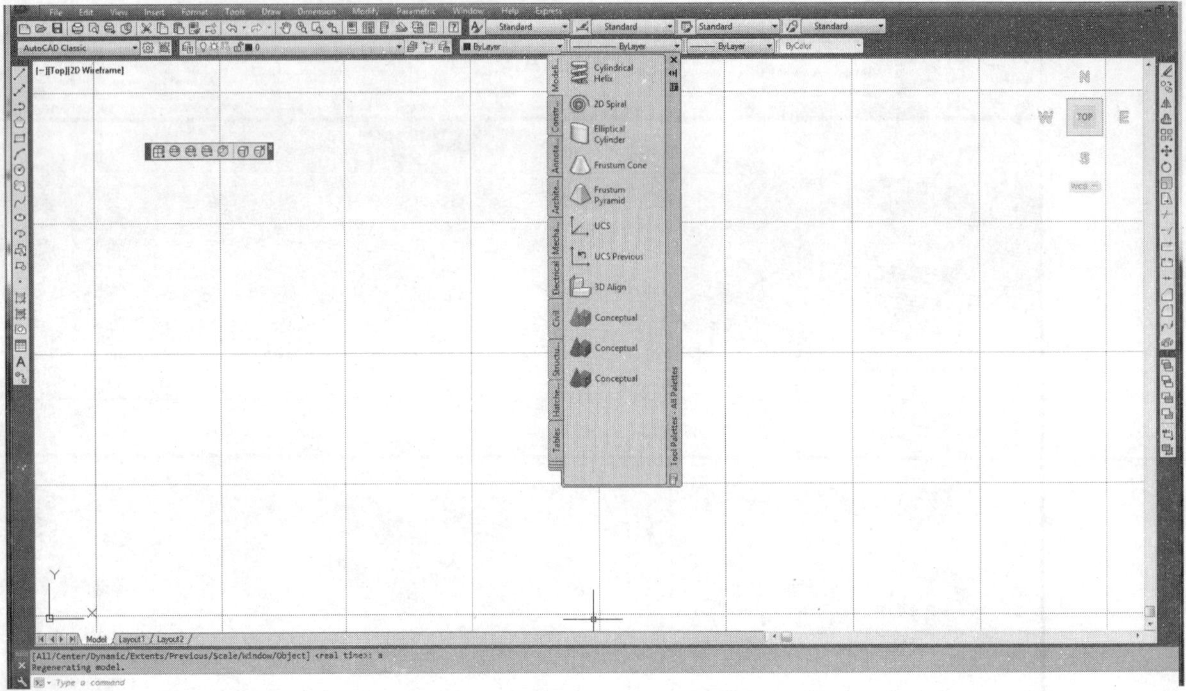

chapter two

2 Fundamentals of 2D Construction

2-1 Introduction

This chapter demonstrates how to work with AutoCAD commands. AutoCAD commands are executed by using command tools and a series of prompts. The prompts appear in the command line box and ask the user for a selection or numeric input so that a command sequence can be completed. The **Line** command was chosen to demonstrate the various input and prompt sequences that are typical with AutoCAD commands.

Most of the commands contained in the **Draw** and **Modify** panels will be demonstrated in this chapter. The purpose is to present enough commands for the reader to be able to create simple 2D shapes. The next chapter will present more advanced applications for these commands and will present some new commands as well.

2-2 Line—Random Points

The **Line** command is used to draw straight lines between two defined points. Figure 2-1 shows the **Line** tool on the **Draw** panel.

There are four ways to define the length and location of a line: (1) randomly select points; (2) set a specific value for the **Snap** function, and select points with the **Snap** spacing values; (3) enter the coordinate values for the start and end points; (4) and use relative inputs and specify the starting point, the length, and the direction of the line.

To Randomly Select Points (See Figure 2-2.)

1 Select the **Line** tool on the **Draw** panel under the **Home** tab.

You can also access the **Line** command by typing the word **line** in response to a command prompt.

Figure 2-1

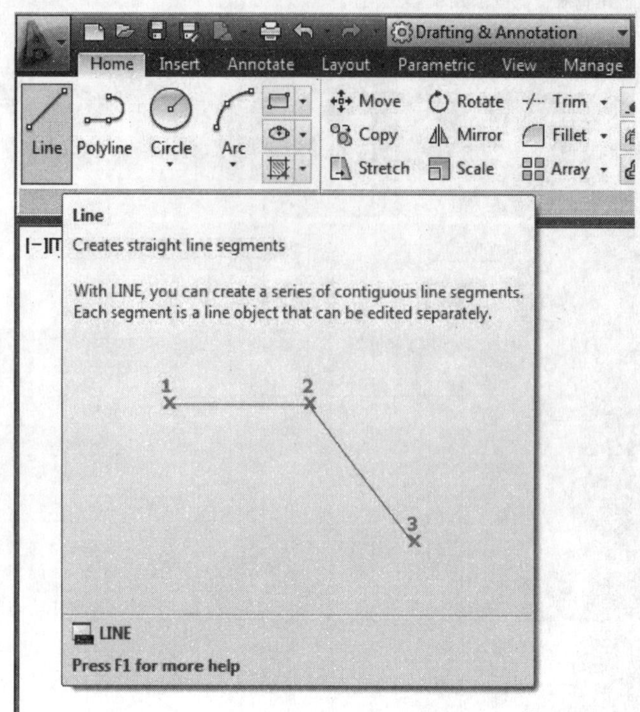

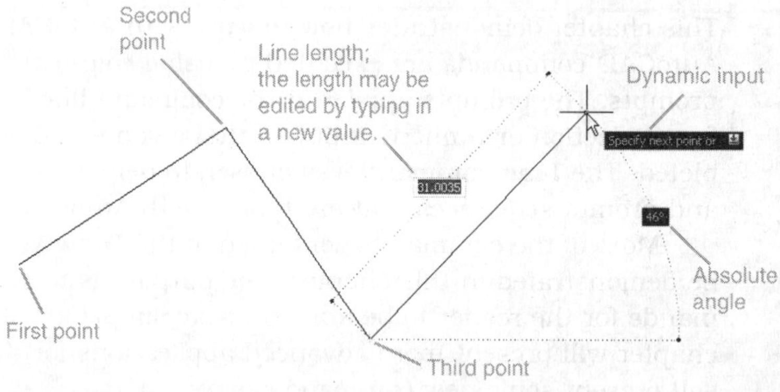

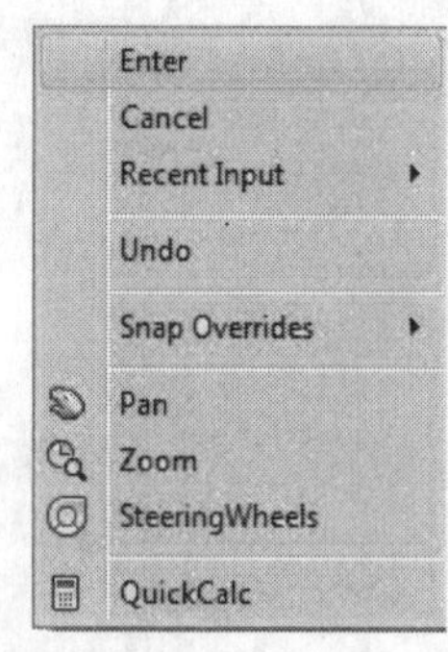

Figure 2-2

The following command sequence will appear in the command line box:

Command: _line Specify first point:

2 Place the cursor anywhere on the drawing screen, and press the left mouse button.

Specify next point or [Undo]:

As you move the cursor from point to point, dynamic inputs will appear on the screen. See Figure 2-2. Dynamic inputs include an absolute angle and length change box. Dynamic inputs will be discussed in Section 2-5.

3 Pick another random point on the screen.

Specify next point or [Undo]:

AutoCAD will keep asking for another point until you press either the **Enter** key or the right mouse button.

4. When the right mouse button is pressed, a small dialog box will appear. See Figure 2-2.

5. Click the **Enter** option to end the **Line** command sequence.

The **Line** command may be reactivated by pressing the right mouse button immediately after selecting the **Enter** option. A dialog box will appear. See Figure 2-3. Select the **Repeat LINE** option to restart the **Line** command.

To Exit a Command Sequence

If, as you work, you need to exit a command sequence, press the **<Esc>** key, which will return you to a command prompt. The **<Esc>** key allows you to exit almost all AutoCAD commands.

To Create a Closed Area (See Figure 2-4.)

1. Select the **Line** tool from the **Draw** panel.

   Command: _line Specify first point:

Figure 2-3

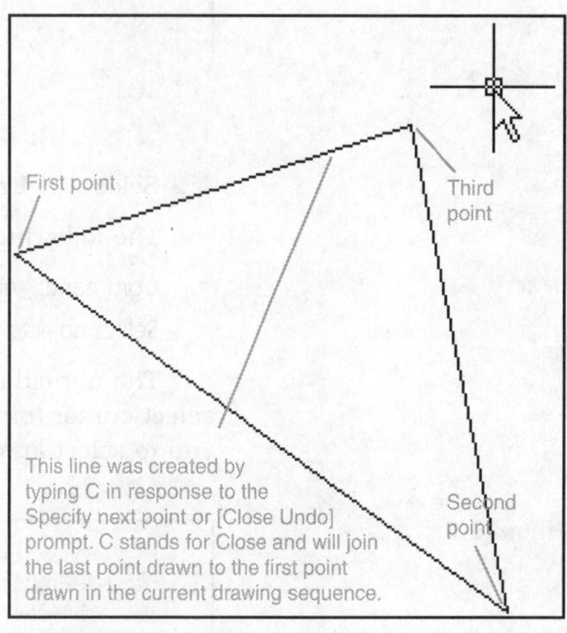

Figure 2-4

2. Select a random point.

   Specify next point or [Undo]:

3. Select a second random point.

   Specify next point or [Undo]:

4. Select a third random point.

   Specify next point or [Close Undo]:

5. Type **c,** and then press **Enter** to activate the **Close** option.

A line will be drawn from the third point to the starting point, creating a closed area. An enclosed area can also be created by using the **Object**

Snap Endpoint option. As you move the cursor toward a line, a box will appear at the line's endpoint. Clicking within the endpoint box will attach the line to that endpoint. Right-click the **Object Snap** icon at the bottom of the screen for a listing of other **Snap** options.

2-3 Erase

You can erase any line by using the **Erase** command. There are two ways to erase lines: Select individual lines, or window a group of lines. The **Erase** tool is located on the **Modify** panel under the **Home** tab. See Figure 2-5.

Figure 2-5

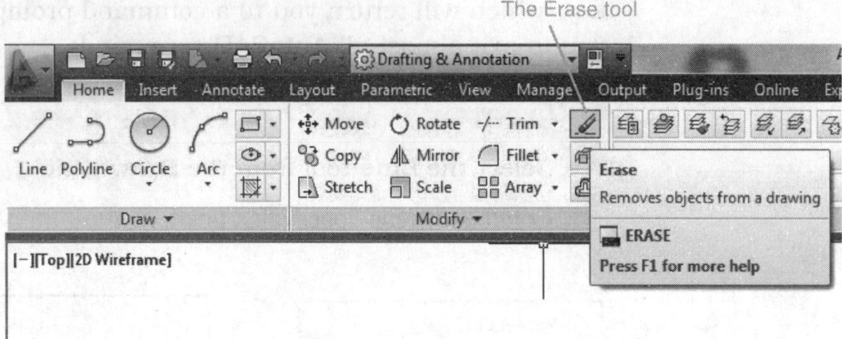

To Erase Individual Lines

1 Select the **Erase** tool on the **Modify** panel.

The following prompt will appear in the command line box:

Command: _erase

Select objects:

The normal cursor will be replaced by a rectangular cursor. This is the select cursor (*pickbox*). Any time that you see this cursor, AutoCAD expects you to select an entity—in this example, a line. See Figure 2-6.

Figure 2-6

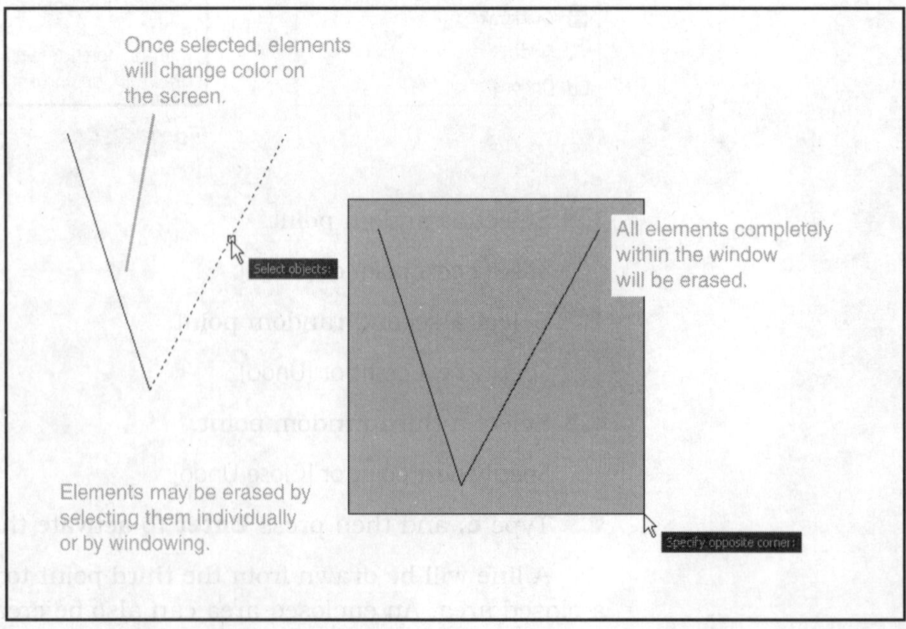

If you change your mind and do not want to erase anything, select the next command that you want to use, and the **Erase** command will be terminated.

2 Select the two open lines by placing the rectangular cursor on each line, one at a time, and pressing the left mouse button.

The lines will change color from solid black to a broken gray pattern. This color change indicates that the line has been selected. The selection is confirmed by a change in the prompt.

Select objects: 1 found
Select objects:

3 Press the right mouse button or the **Enter** key to complete the **Erase** sequence.

The two lines should disappear from the screen.

To Erase a Group of Lines Simultaneously (See Figure 2-6.)

1 Select the **Erase** tool.

Command: _erase
Select objects:

2 Place the rectangular select cursor above and to the left of the lines to be erased, and press the left mouse button.

3 Move the mouse, and a shaded window will drag from the selected first point.

4 When all the lines to be erased are completely within the window, press the left mouse button.

All of the lines completely within the window will be selected and will change to broken gray lines. The number of lines selected will be referenced in the command line box.

5 Press the right mouse button or the **Enter** key to complete the command sequence.

The lines will disappear from the screen. The **Undo** tool will return all of the lines, if needed. If the **Erase** window is created from right to left, any line even partially within the **Erase** window will be erased.

2-4 Line—Snap Points

Lines can be drawn by using calibrated snap spacing. This technique is similar to drawing points randomly, but because the cursor is limited to specific points, the length of lines can be determined accurately. See Figure 2-7.

Problem: Draw a 3″ × 5″ Rectangle

1 Set the grid spacing for **.5** and the snap spacing for **.50,** and turn both commands on. Zoom the grid in or out to fit the screen.

Figure 2-7

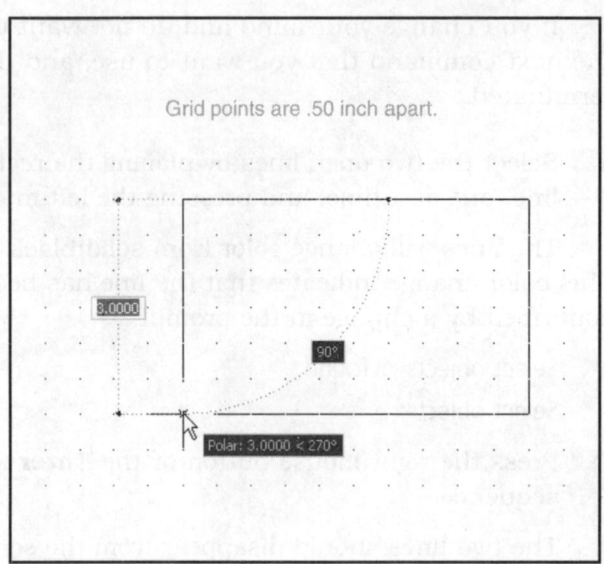

NOTE

See Section 1-9 for instructions on how to operate the **Grid** and **Snap** functions.

2. Select the **Line** tool from the **Draw** panel.

   Command: _line Specify first point:

3. Select a grid point.

   Specify next point or [Undo]:

4. Move the cursor horizontally to the right **10** grid spaces, and press the left mouse button.

   The grid spacing has been set at .5, so 10 spaces equals 5 units. Watch the dynamic input readings as you move the cursor. The X value should increase by 5, and the Y value should stay the same.

   Specify next point or [Undo]:

5. Move the cursor vertically **6** spaces, and press the left mouse button.

   Specify next point or [Close Undo]:

6. Move the cursor horizontally to the left **10** spaces, and press the left mouse button.

   Specify next point or [Close Undo]:

7. Type **c**; press **Enter,** or place the endpoint of the left vertical line on the starting point of the first line. Right-click the mouse, and select the **Enter** option.

   Save or erase the drawing as desired.

2-5 Line—Dynamic Inputs

The **Dynamic Input** command allows both angular and distance values to be added to a drawing by the use of screen prompts.

To Create Lines by Using Dynamic Input

This example was created by using inch values.

1. Click the **Line** command tool on the **Draw** panel, and select a starting point.

   Figure 2-8 shows the dynamic input for the selected first point.

Figure 2-8

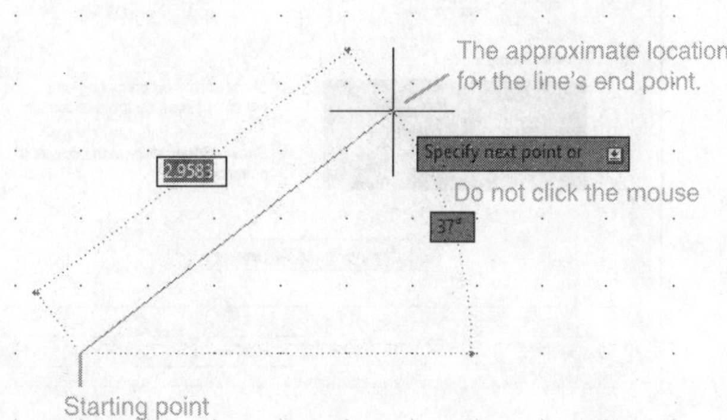

2. Move the cursor to the approximate location of the second line point.

   The distance and angular values for this new point will be displayed in boxes. Do not click the mouse.

   Angular values assume that 0° is a horizontal line to the right of the first line point.

3. Move the cursor to the command line box, and type in the desired distance value.

   Use the format @ Distance < angle. In this example, an input of @ 3.50 < 45 was entered. See Figure 2-9.

Figure 2-9

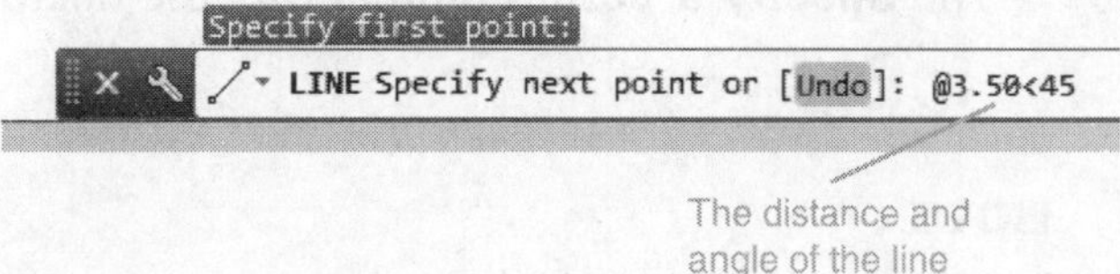

4. Type **Enter.**

   The angular value will be applied to the line, and the **Dynamic Input** command will prepare for the next line point input.

5. Complete the desired shape; press **Enter.**

To Access the Dynamic Input Settings

See Figure 2-10.

1. Right-click the **Dynamic Input** tool at the bottom of the screen, and click the **Settings** option.

   The **Drafting Settings** dialog box will appear.

Figure 2-10

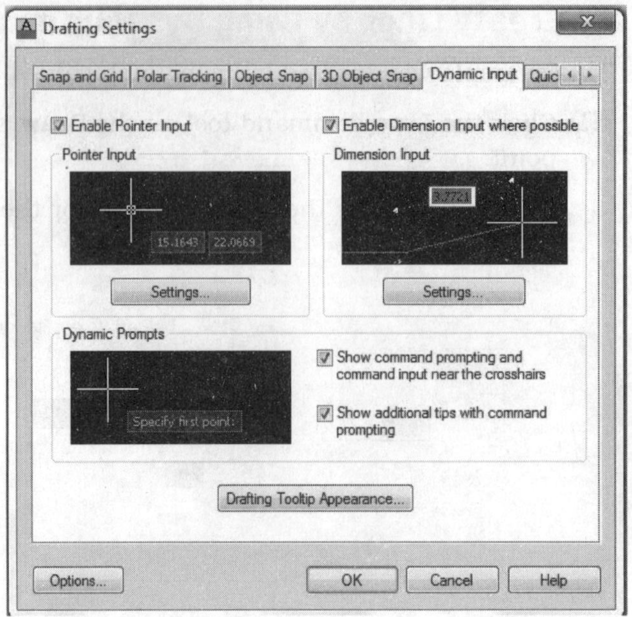

The **Dynamic Inputs** dialog box is used to control the **Pointer Input, Dimension Input,** and **Dynamic Prompts** aspects of dynamic input. The default values will be used throughout the book.

2-6 Construction Line

The **Construction Line** command is used to draw lines of infinite length. Construction lines are very helpful during the initial layout of a drawing. They can be trimmed during the creation of the drawing as needed.

1 Select the **Construction Line** tool from the **Draw** panel. See Figure 2-11.

Command:_ xline Specify a point or [Hor Ver Ang Bisect Offset]:

The **Specify a point** command is the default setting.

NOTE

The **Construction Line** tool is located on a flyout from the **Draw** panel. Click the arrow next to the word **Draw** to access the additional panel.

2 Select or define a starting point.

You can position the direction of the line by moving the cursor or by using dynamic input, as defined in Section 2-5, to define the line's direction.

3 Select or use dynamic input to define a through point.

Specify through point:

A line will pivot about the designated starting point and extend an infinite length in a direction through the cursor. You can position the direction of the line by moving the cursor. See Figure 2-12.

Figure 2-11

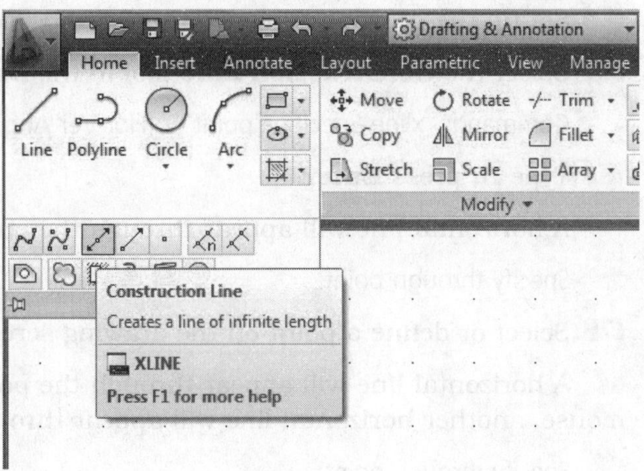

4 Select or define a through point.

An infinitely long line will be drawn through the two designated points.

Specify through point:

Another infinite line will appear through the starting point through the cursor.

5 Press **Enter.**

This ends the **Construction Line** command sequence. The sequence may be reactivated and another construction line drawn by pressing the **Enter** key a second time.

Other Construction Line Commands: Hor Ver Ang

The lines shown in Figure 2-12 were created by using the **Hor** (horizontal), **Ver** (vertical), and **Ang** (angular) options. A grid was created, and the **Snap** option was turned on so that the lines could be drawn through known points. Figure 2-12 was created as follows:

Figure 2-12

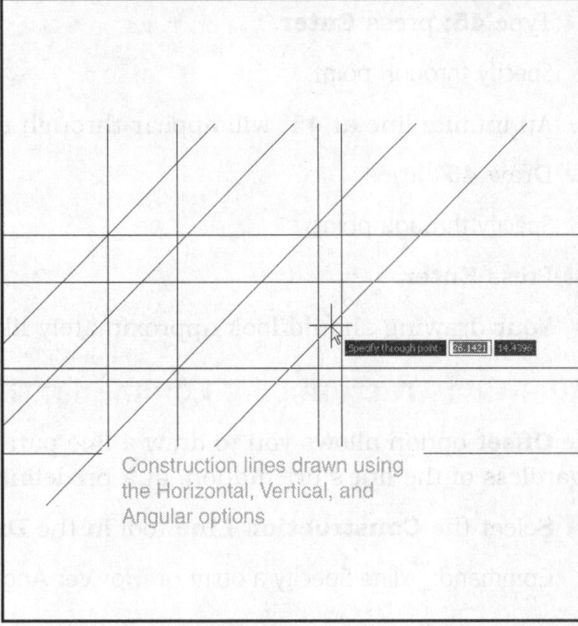

1. Set up the drawing screen with grid and snap spacings of **.5.**
2. Select the **Construction Line** tool in the **Draw** panel.

   Command:_ xline Specify a point or [Hor Ver Ang Bisect Offset]:

3. Type **H;** press **Enter.**

   A horizontal line will appear through the cursor.

   Specify through point:

4. Select or define a point on the drawing screen.

   A horizontal line will appear through the point. As you move the mouse, another horizontal line will appear through the cursor.

   Specify through point:

5. Select or define a second point.

   Specify through point:

6. Select or define a third point.

   Specify through point:

7. Double-click the right mouse button, and select the **Repeat Construction Line** option from the dialog box that appears on the screen.

   Command:_ xline Specify a point or [Hor Ver Ang Bisect Offset]:

8. Type **V;** press **Enter.**

   Specify through point:

9. Draw vertical lines, and then double-click the **Enter** key and select the **Repeat Construction Line** option.

   Command:_ xline Specify a point or [Hor Ver Ang Bisect Offset]:

10. Type **A;** press **Enter.**

    Enter angle of xline (0) or [Reference]:

11. Type **45;** press **Enter.**

    Specify through point:

    An infinite line at 45° will appear through the crosshairs.

12. Draw **45°** lines.

    Specify through point:

13. Press **Enter.**

    Your drawing should look approximately like Figure 2-12.

Other Construction Line Command: Offset

The **Offset** option allows you to draw a line parallel to an existing line, regardless of the line's orientation, at a predefined distance. See Figure 2-13.

1. Select the **Construction Line** tool in the **Draw** panel.

   Command:_ xline Specify a point or [Hor Ver Ang Bisect Offset]:

Figure 2-13

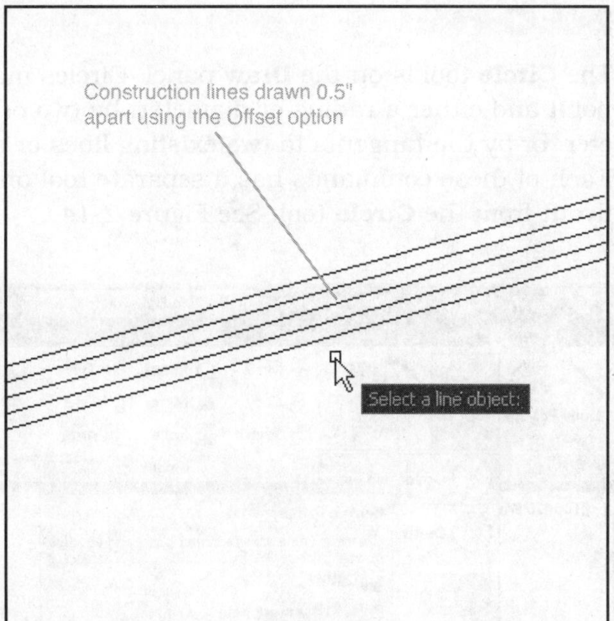

2 Draw a line approximately **15°** to the horizontal.

Specify through point:

3 Double-click the **Enter** key to restart the **Construction Line** command sequence.

Command:_ xline Specify a point or [Hor Ver Ang Bisect Offset]:

4 Type **O;** press **Enter.**

The O will appear in the dynamic input box.

Offset distance or through <Through>:

5 Type **.5;** press **Enter.**

Select a line object:

6 Select the line.

Select side to offset:

7 Select a point above the line.

Select a line object:

8 Select the line just created by the **Offset** option.

Select side to offset:

9 Again select a point above the selected line.

Select a line object:

10 Draw several more lines below the original line.

Select a line object:

11 Press the right mouse button.

This will end the **Offset** command sequence and return a command prompt to the command prompt line.

2-7 Circle

The **Circle** tool is on the **Draw** panel. Circles may be defined by a center point and either a radius or diameter, by two or three points on the diameter, or by the tangents to two existing lines or arcs and a radius value. Each of these commands has a separate tool on the **Draw** panel that is a flyout from the **Circle** tool. See Figure 2-14.

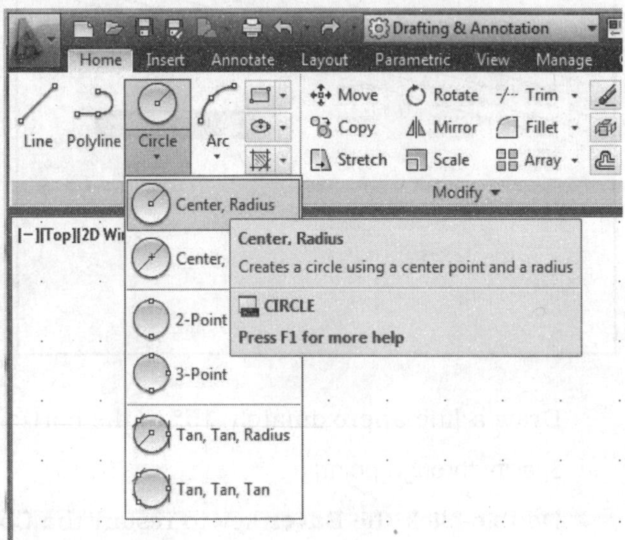

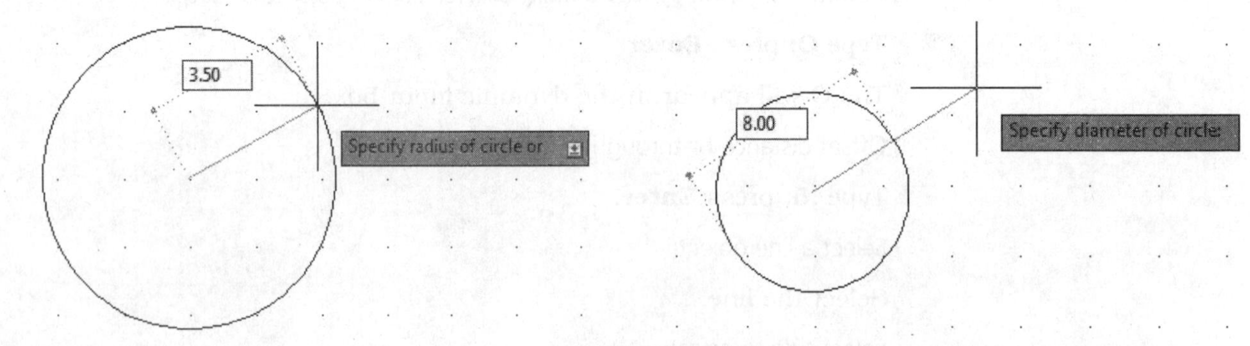

Figure 2-14

To Draw a Circle—Radius (See Figure 2-14.)

1. Click the **Center, Radius** tool on the **Draw** panel.

   Command: _circle Specify a center point for circle or [3P 2P Ttr (tan tan radius)]:

2. Select or use dynamic input to define a center point.

   Specify radius of circle or [Diameter]:

3. Type **3.50;** press **Enter.**

   The radius value will appear in the dynamic input box.

To Draw a Circle—Diameter (See Figure 2-14.)

1. Click the **Center, Diameter** tool on the **Draw** panel.

   Command: _circle Specify a center point for circle or [3P 2P Ttr (tan tan radius)]:

2 Select or define a center point.

Specify radius of circle or [Diameter]:

3 Type **8.00;** press **Enter.**

To Draw a Circle—2 Points (See Figure 2-15.)

1 Click the **2-Point** tool on the **Draw** panel.

Command: _circle Specify a center point for circle or [3P 2P Ttr (tan tan radius)]:

Specify first end point of circle's diameter:

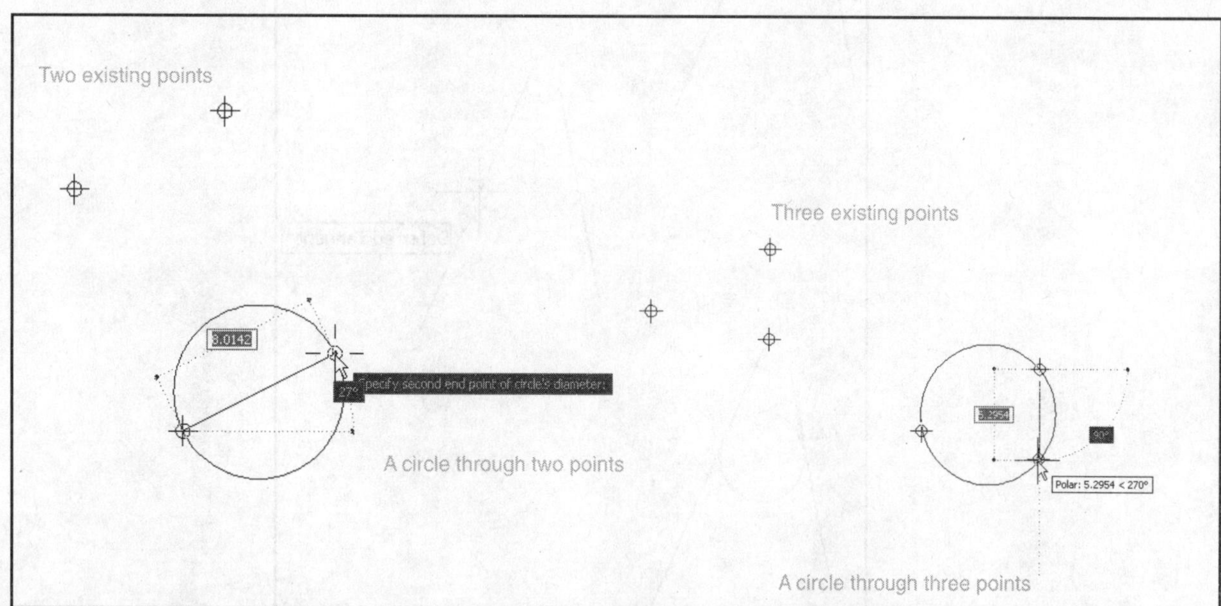

Figure 2-15

2 Select or define a first point.

Select second end point of circle's diameter:

3 Select or define a second point.

The circle will automatically be drawn through the first and second points.

To Draw a Circle—3 Points (See Figure 2-15.)

1 Click the **3-Point** tool on the **Draw** panel.

Command: _circle Specify a center point for circle or [3P 2P Ttr (tan tan radius)]:

Specify first point on circle:

2 Select or define a first point.

Specify second point on circle:

3 Select or define a second point.

Specify third point on circle:

4 Select or define a third point.

To Draw a Circle—Tangent Tangent Radius

The **tangent tangent radius** option allows you to draw a circle tangent to two other entities. Figure 2-16 shows a circle drawn tangent to two lines.

Figure 2-16

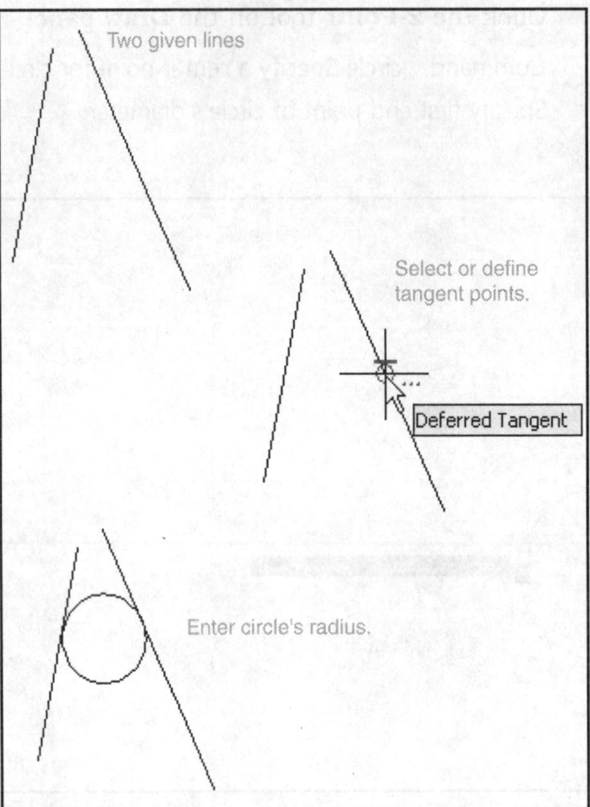

1. Click the **Tan, Tan, Radius** tool on the **Draw** panel.

   Command: _circle Specify a center point for circle or [3P 2P Ttr (tan tan radius)]:

   Specify point on object for first tangent of circle:

2. Select an entity.

   Specify point on object for second tangent of circle:

3. Select the other entity.

   Specify radius of circle <value>:

4. Type a radius value; press **Enter.**

Quadrant-Sensitive Applications

The circle **TTR** option is quadrant-sensitive; that is, the final location of the tangent circle will depend on the location of the tangent spec points. In Figure 2-17, the **TTR** option was applied to two circles, and in both examples the tangent circle was created by using the same radius. Note the difference in results depending on the circle's quadrants selected.

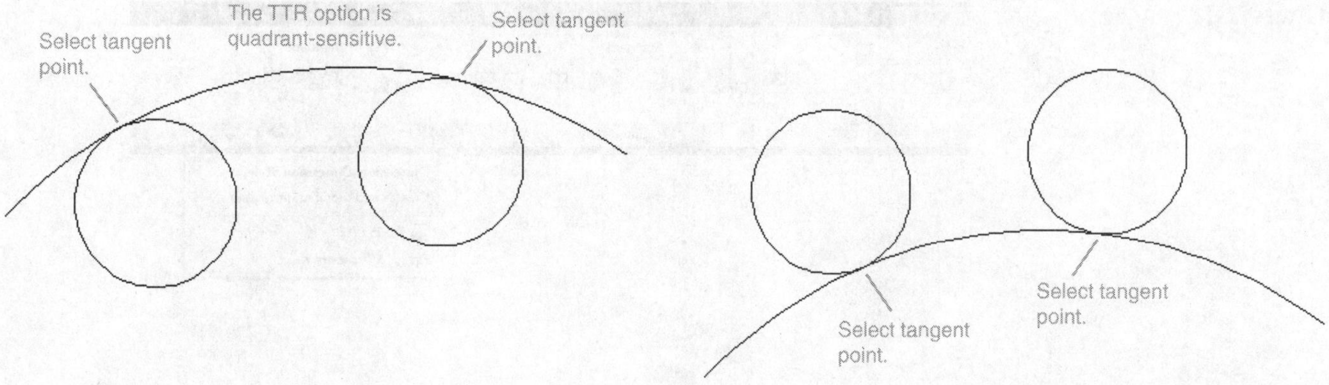

Figure 2-17

2-8 Circle Centerlines

It is standard drawing convention to include centerlines with all circles. Circles usually represent holes. The circle's center point is used to locate the hole and, during manufacture, serves as the location point for a drill. There are two ways to set up AutoCAD to add centerlines easily to a given circle: Redefine the **Dimcen** system variable, or use the **Center Mark** option found on the **Dimensions** panel of the **Annotate** tab.

To Change the Dimcen System Variable

There are no icons for **Dimcen;** the change is made by keyboard input entirely.

1. Type **setvar** next to the command prompt; press **Enter.**

   Enter variable name or? [?]

2. Type **dimcen;** press **Enter.**

   New value for DIMCEN <0.0900>:

3. Type **–.1** for inch units or **–2** for metric units; press **Enter.**

   Command:

   The system variable is now changed, but must be applied to the circle.

4. Type **dim;** press **Enter.**

   Dim:

5. Type **center;** press **Enter.**

   Select arc or circle:

6. Select the given circle.

   A centerline and center point will be added as shown in Figure 2-18.

7. Press the **<Esc>** key to exit the **dim** command.

To Use the Center Mark Tool

1. Click the **Annotate** tab at the top of the screen.

   A new set of panels will appear.

Figure 2-18

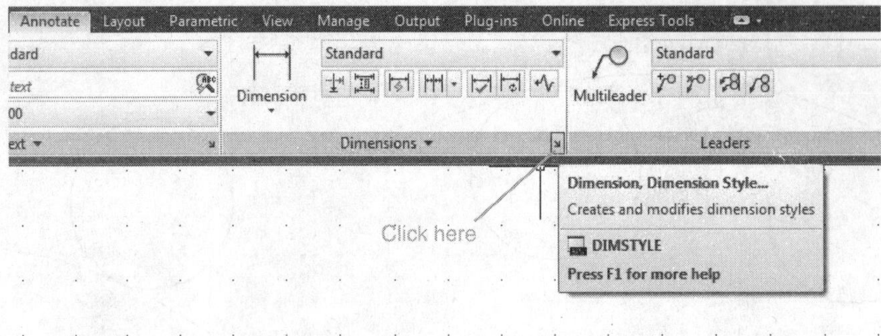

2 Click the arrow in the lower right corner of the **Dimensions** panel.

See Figure 2-18.

The **Dimension Style Manager** dialog box will appear. See Figure 2-19.

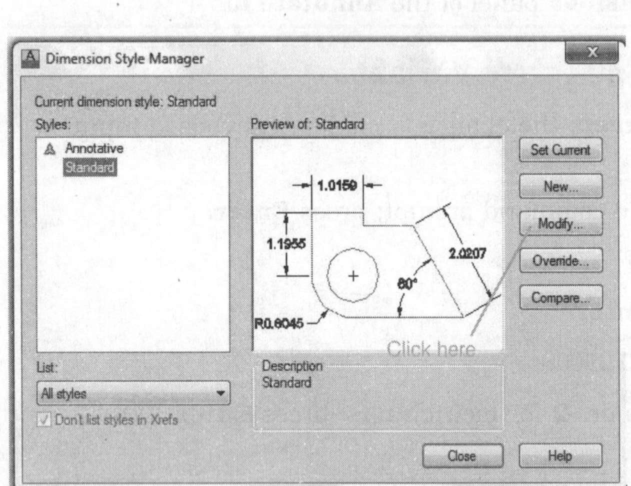

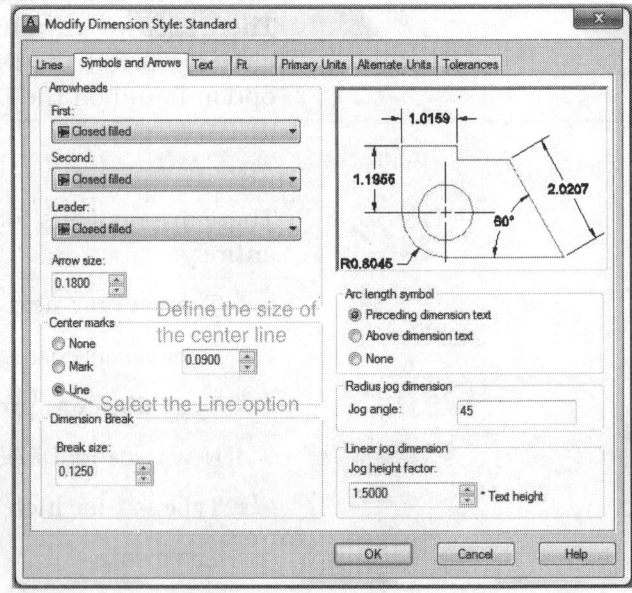

Figure 2-19

3 Select the **Modify** box.

The **Modify Dimension Style: Standard** dialog box will appear.

4 Select the **Symbols and Arrows** tab, then the **Center marks Line** option.

The preview screen will display centerlines.

5 Select **OK,** and return to the drawing screen.

Change the size value to create a clear center point and lines.

6 Click the **Center Mark** tool on the **Dimensions** panel, and then click the given circle.

Centerlines will appear on the circle.

2-9 Polyline

A ***polyline*** is a line made from a series of individual, connected line segments that act as a single entity. Polylines are used to generate curves and splines and can be used in three-dimensional applications to produce solid objects.

Polylines can be entered by using dynamic input. See Section 2-5.

To Draw a Polyline (See Figure 2-20.)

1. Select the **Polyline** tool from the **Draw** panel.

   Command: _pline
   Specify start point:

Figure 2-20

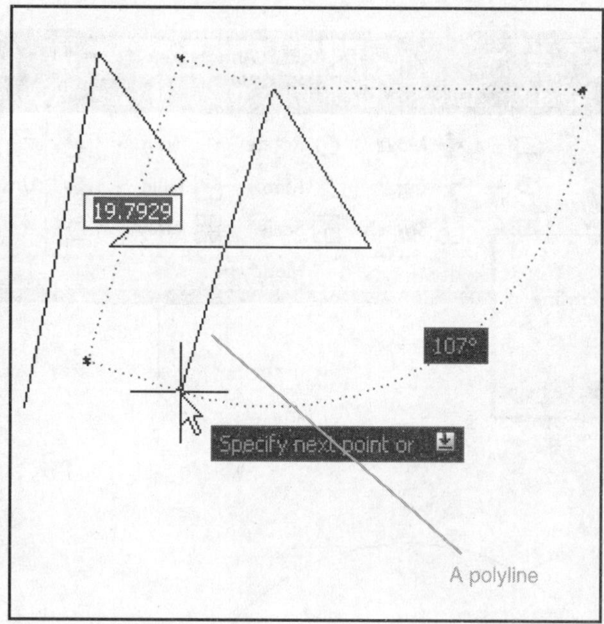

2. Select or define a start point.

   Specify next point or [Arc Close Halfwidth Length Undo Width]:

3. Select or define a second point.

   Specify next point or [Arc Close Halfwidth Length Undo Width]:

4. Select or define several more points.

   Specify next point or [Arc Close Halfwidth Length Undo Width]:

5. Press the right mouse button, and then select **Enter.**

To Verify That a Polyline is a Single Entity

Figure 2-20 shows a polyline.

1. Select the **Erase** tool from the **Modify** panel, or type the word **erase.**

   Select objects:

2. Select any one of the line segments in the polyline.

   Select objects:

The entire polyline, not just the individual line segment, will be selected because in AutoCAD the polyline is a single entity.

3 Press **Enter.**

The entire polyline will disappear.

4 Select the **Undo** tool from the **Standard** panel.

The object will reappear.

To Draw a Polyline: Arc (See Figure 2-21.)

1 Select the **Polyline** tool from the **Draw** panel.

Specify start point:

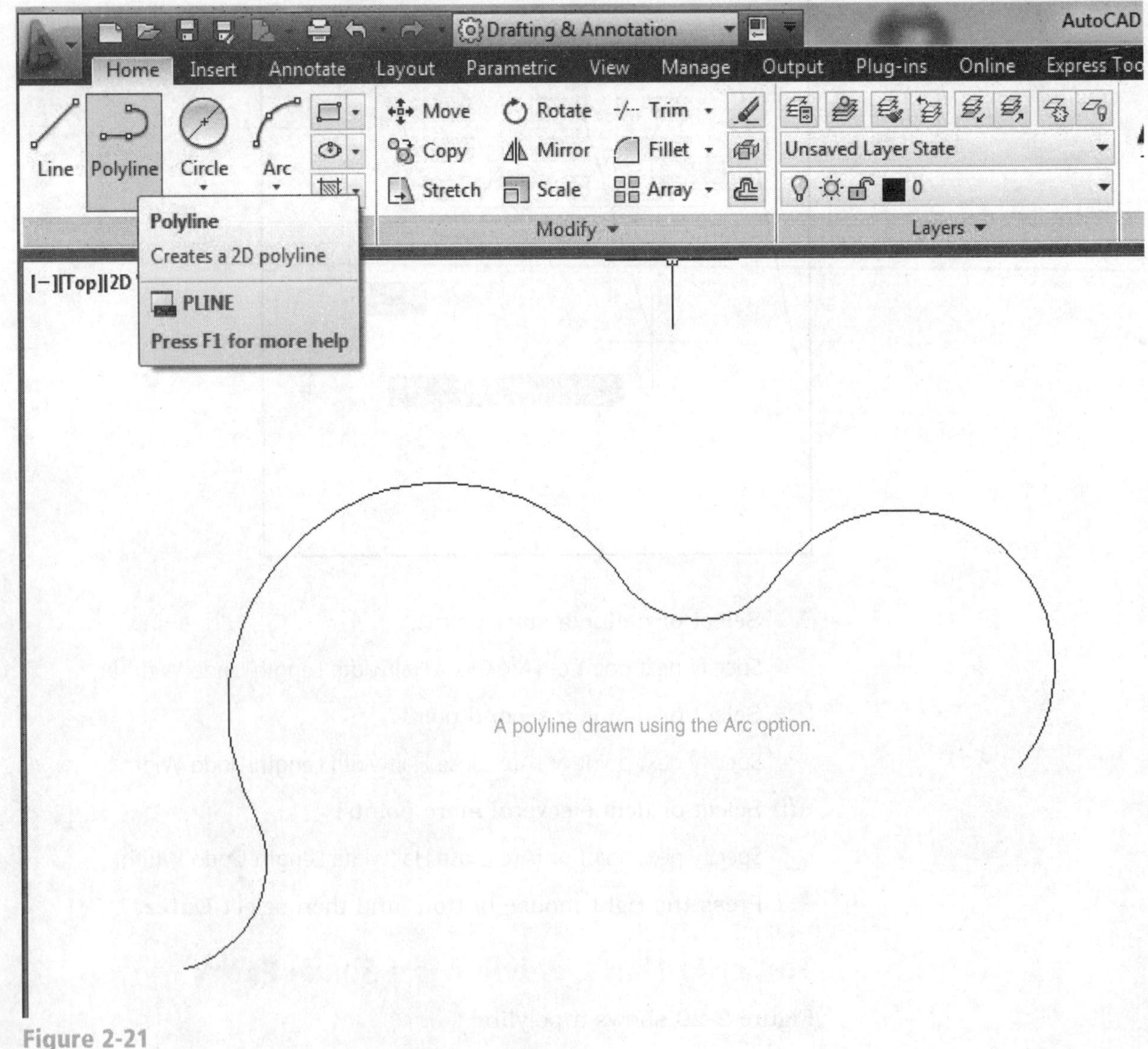

Figure 2-21

2 Select or define a start point.

Specify next point or [Arc Close Halfwidth Length Undo Width]:

3 **Type A; press Enter.**

Specify endpoint of arc or [Angle CEnter Direction Halfwidth Line Radius Second pt Undo Width]:

4 **Select or define another point.**

Specify endpoint of arc or [Angle CEnter Direction Halfwidth Line Radius Second pt Undo Width]:

5 **Select or define another point.**

6 **Press the right mouse button, and then select Enter.**

Other Options with a Polyline Arc

Figure 2-22 shows example of Polyline Arc options.

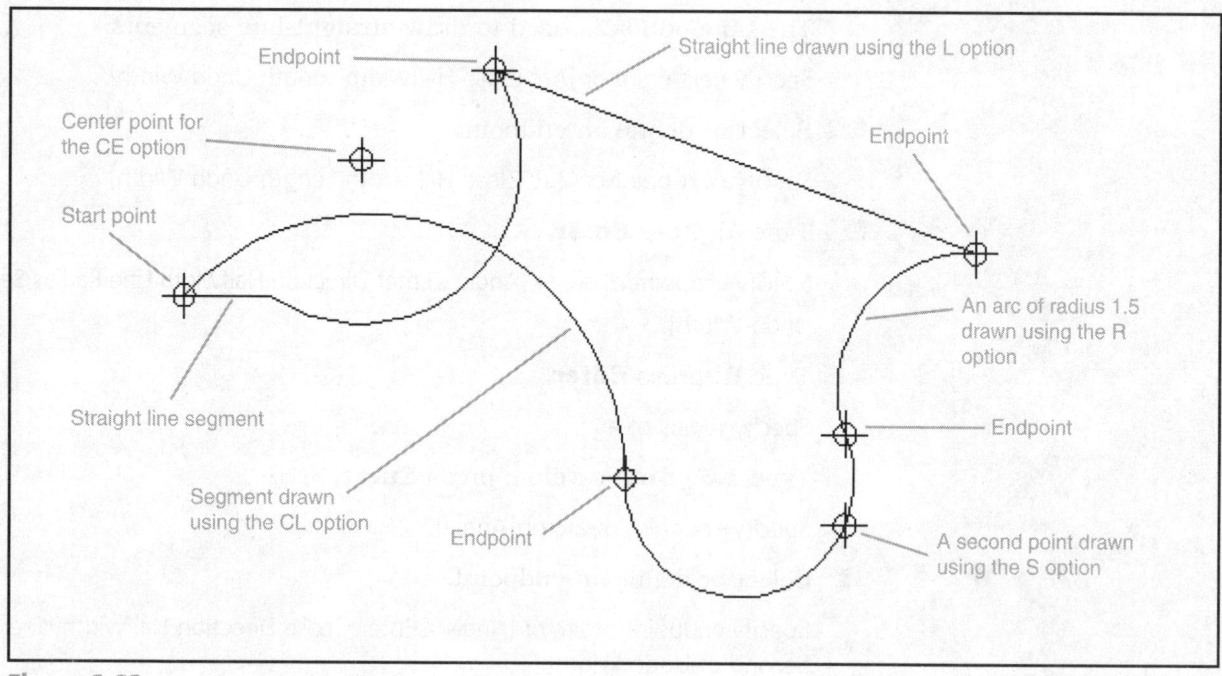

Figure 2-22

1 **Select the Polyline tool from the Draw panel.**

Command: _pline
Specify start point:

2 **Select or define a start point.**

Specify next point or [Arc Halfwidth Length Undo Width]:

3 **Draw a short horizontal line segment.**

Specify next point or [Arc Close Halfwidth Length Undo Width]:

4 Type **A;** press **Enter.**

Specify endpoint of arc or [Angle CEnter CLose Direction Halfwidth Line Radius Second pt Undo Width]:

5 Type **CE;** press **Enter.**

CE activates the **Center** option. You can now define an arc that will be part of the polyline by defining the arc's center point and its angle, chord length, or endpoint.

Specify center point of arc:

6 Select or define a center point.

Specify endpoint of arc or [Angle Width]:

7 Select or define an endpoint.

Specify endpoint of arc or [Angle CEnter Direction Halfwidth Line Radius Second pt Undo Width]:

8 Type **L;** press **Enter.**

The **Line** option is used to draw straight-line segments.

Specify next point or [Arc Close Halfwidth Length Undo Width]:

9 Select or define an endpoint.

Specify next point or [Arc Close Halfwidth Length Undo Width]:

10 Type **A;** press **Enter.**

Specify endpoint of arc or [Angle CEnter Direction Halfwidth Line Radius Second pt Undo Width]:

11 Type **R;** press **Enter.**

Specify radius of arc:

12 Type **1.5** or other value; press **Enter.**

Specify endpoint of arc or [Angle]:

13 Select or define an endpoint.

Specify endpoint of arc or [Angle CEnter CLose Direction Halfwidth Line Radius Second pt Undo Width]:

14 Type **S;** press **Enter.**

Specify second point on arc:

15 Select or define a point.

Specify endpoint of arc:

16 Select or define an endpoint.

Specify endpoint of arc or [Angle CEnter CLose Direction Halfwidth Line Radius Second pt Undo Width]:

17 Type **CL;** press **Enter.**

The **CL** (close) option will join the last point drawn to the first point of the polyline by use of an arc.

To Draw Different Line Thicknesses (See Figure 2-23.)

1. Select the **Polyline** tool from the **Draw** panel.

   Specify start point:

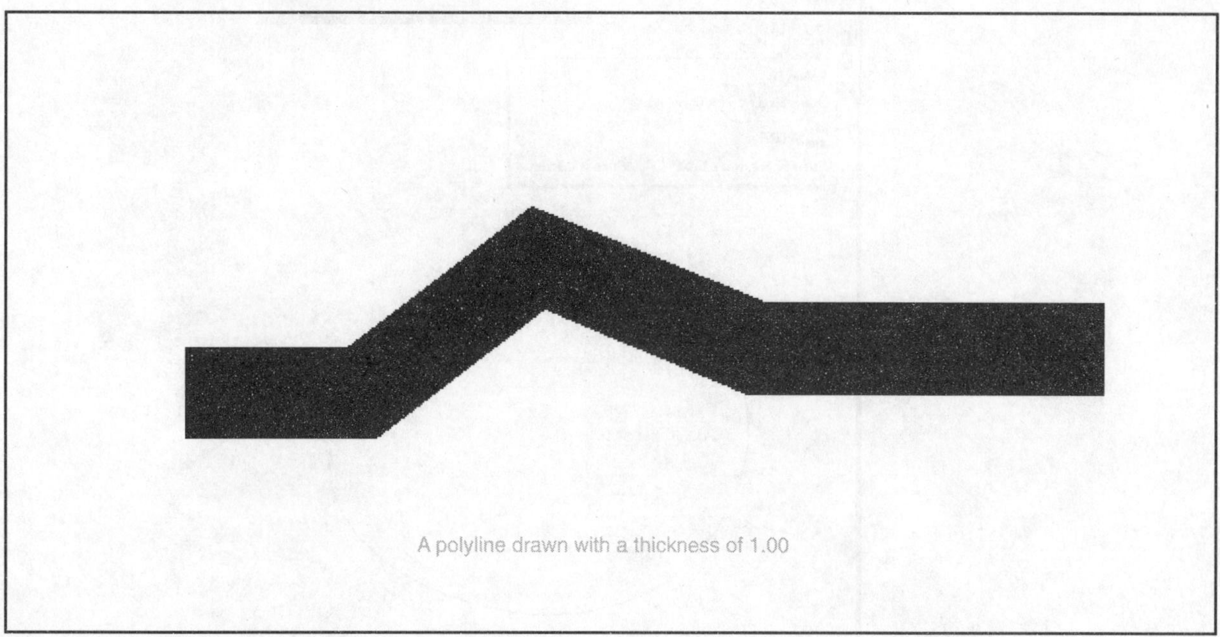

Figure 2-23

2. Select or define a start point.

   Specify next point or [Arc Close Halfwidth Length Undo Width]:

3. Type **W;** press **Enter.**

   The **Width** option is used to define the width of a line. The **Halfwidth** option is used to define half of the width of a line.

   Specify starting width <0.0000>:

4. Type **1.00;** press **Enter.**

   Specify ending width <1.0000>:

5. Press **Enter.**

   Specify next point or [Arc Close Halfwidth Length Undo Width]:

6. Draw several line segments.

2-10 Spline

A ***spline*** is a curved line created through a series of predefined points. If the curve forms an enclosed area, it is called a ***closed spline.*** Curved lines that do not enclose an area are called ***open splines.*** See Figure 2-24.

1. Select the **Spline Fit** tool from the **Draw** panel.

   Command: _spline

   Specify first point or [Method Knots Object]:

Figure 2-24

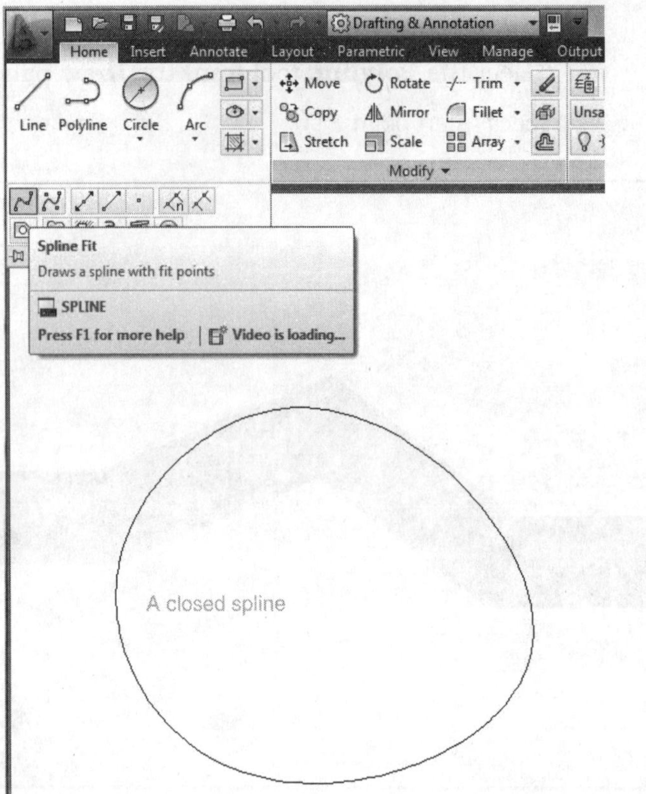

2 Select or define a start point.

Specify next point:

3 Select or define a second point.

Specify next point or [Close Fit tolerance] <start tangent>:

4 Select or define two more points.

Specify next point or [Arc Close Halfwidth Length Undo Width]:

5 Type **C;** press **Enter.**

Specify tangent.

6 Select or define a point.

Note how the shape of the spline changes as you move the cursor to locate the tangent point. These changes are based on your selection of a tangent point, which, in turn, affects the mathematical calculations used to create the curve.

2-11 Ellipse

There are three options associated with the **Ellipse** tool. These three options allow you to define an ellipse by using the lengths of its major and minor axes, an included angle, or an angle of rotation about the major axis.

To Draw an Ellipse—Axis Endpoint (See Figure 2-25.)

1 Click the **Ellipse – Axis, End** tool on the **Draw** panel.

Specify axis endpoint of ellipse or [Arc Center]:

Figure 2-25

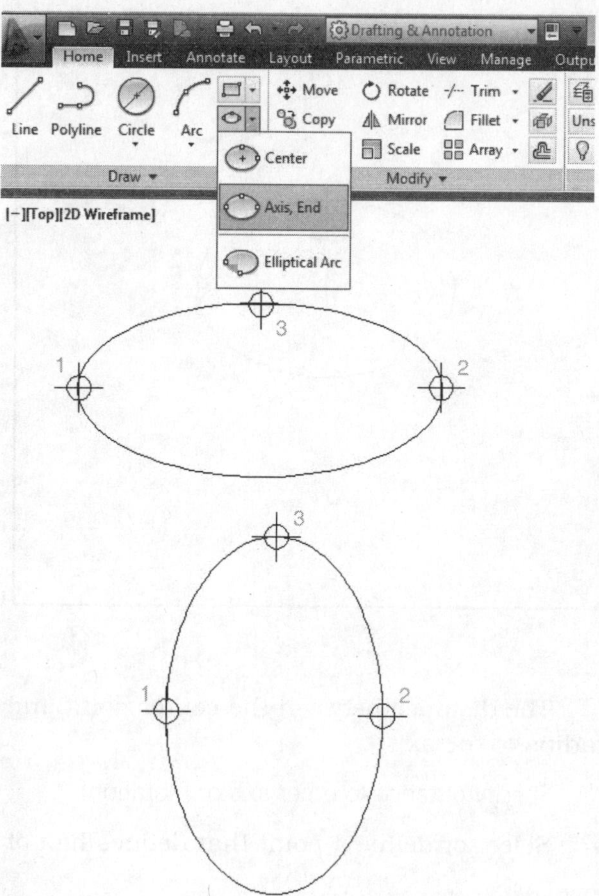

2 Select or define a start point for one of the axes.

Specify other endpoint of axis:

3 Select or define an endpoint that defines the length of the axis.

Specify distance to other axis or [Rotation]:

4 Select or define a point that defines half of the length of the other axis.

This distance is the radius of the axis. In the example shown, points 1 and 2 were used to define the major axes, and point 3 defines the minor axis. The bottom figure in Figure 2-25 shows an object in which points 1 and 2 were used to define the minor axes, and point 3 the major axis.

To Draw an Ellipse—Center (See Figure 2-26.)

1 Click the **Ellipse - Center** tool on the **Draw** panel.

Specify axis endpoint of ellipse or [Arc Center]:
Specify center of ellipse:

2 Select or define the center point of the ellipse.

Specify axis endpoint:

3 Select or define one of the endpoints of one of the axes.

Figure 2-26

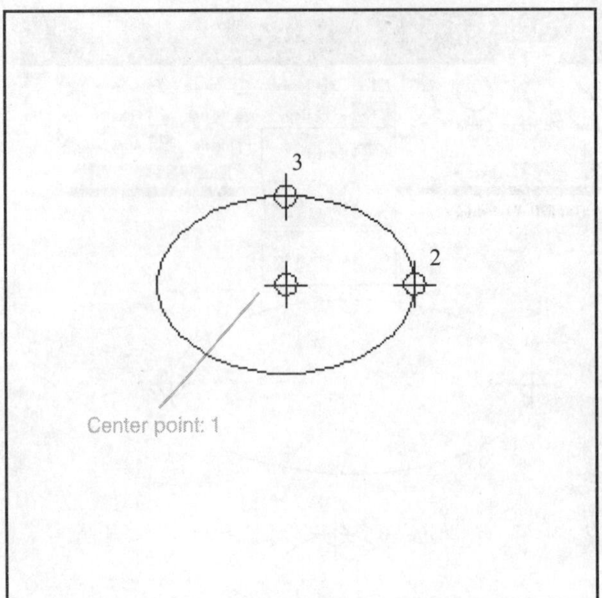

The distance between the center point and the endpoint is equal to the radius of the axis.

Specify distance to other axis or [Rotation]:

4. Select or define a point that defines half of the length of the other axis.

To Draw an Ellipse—Arc (See Figure 2-27.)

1. Click the **Ellipse - Elliptical Arc** tool on the **Draw** panel.

   Specify axis endpoint of ellipse or [Arc Center]:

   Specify axis endpoint of elliptical arc or [Center]:

2. Select or define a point.

   Specify other endpoint of axis:

Figure 2-27

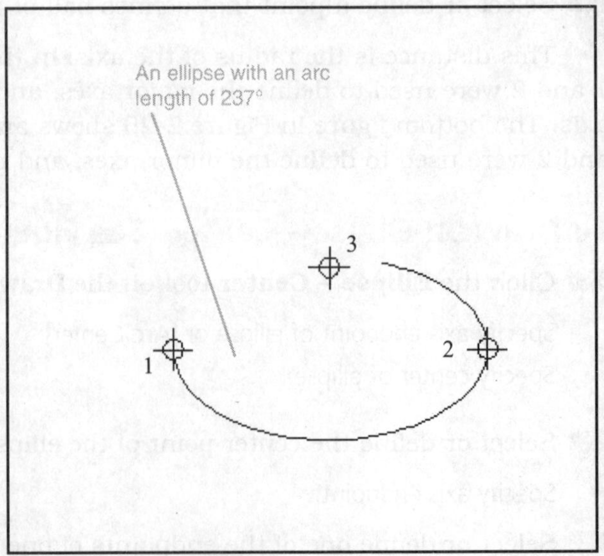

3 Select or define a point.

The distance between points 1 and 2 defines the length of the major axis.

Specify distance to other axis or [Rotation]:

4 Select or define a point that defines the minor axis.

Specify start angle or [Parameter]:

5 Type **0;** press **Enter.**

Specify end angle or [Parameter Included angle]:

6 Type **237;** press **Enter.**

An ellipse may also be defined in terms of its angle of rotation about the major axis. An ellipse with 0° rotation is a circle, an ellipse of constant radius. An ellipse with 90° rotation is a straight line, an end view of an ellipse. See Figure 2-28.

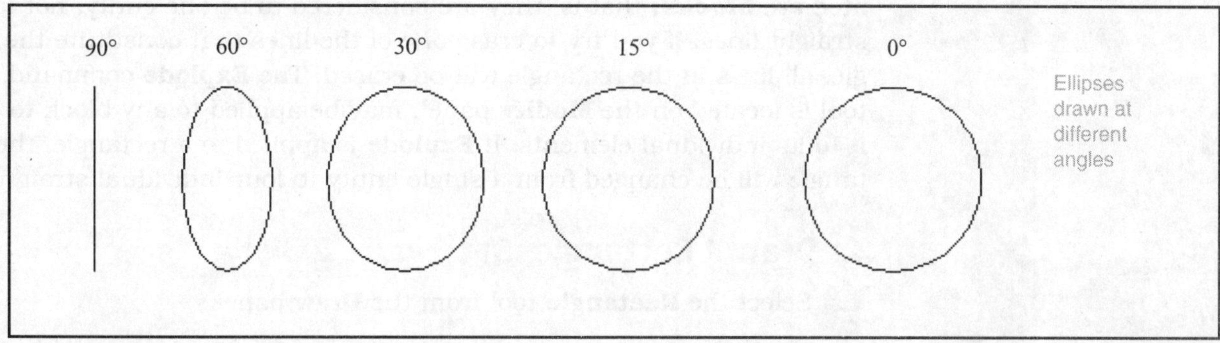

Figure 2-28

To Draw an Ellipse by Defining Its Angle of Rotation About the Major Axis (See Figure 2-29.)

1 Click the **Ellipse – Center** tool on the **Draw** panel.

Specify axis endpoint of ellipse or [Arc Center]:

Figure 2-29

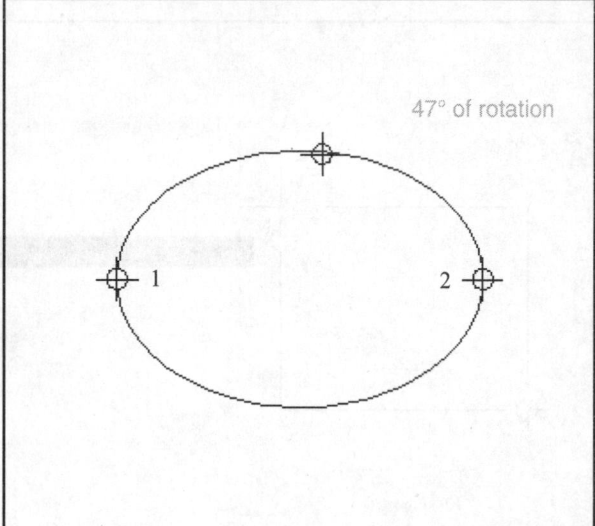

2. Select or define an endpoint of the major axis.

Specify other endpoint of axis:

3. Select or define the other endpoint of the major axis.

Specify distance to other axis or [Rotation]:

4. Type **R;** press **Enter.**

Specify rotation around major axis:

5. Type **47;** press **Enter.**

The same sequence of commands could have been applied by using the **Ellipse Center** tool option. The distance between points 1 and 2 determined with the **Center** option is half of the distance of the major axis.

2-12 Rectangle

The **Rectang** command is used to draw rectangles. The rectangles generated are ***blocks;*** that is, they are considered to be one entity, not four straight lines. If you try to erase one of the lines that constitute the rectangle, all lines in the rectangle will be erased. The **Explode** command, whose tool is located on the **Modify** panel, may be applied to any block to reduce it to its individual elements. If **Explode** is applied to a rectangle, the rectangle will be changed from a single entity to four individual straight lines.

To Draw a Rectangle (See Figure 2-30.)

1. Select the **Rectangle** tool from the **Draw** panel.

Specify first corner point or [Chamfer Elevation Fillet Thickness Width]:

2. Select or define a starting point.

Specify other corner point:

3. Select or define a point.

The distance between the two points is the diagonal distance across the rectangle's corners. In this example, a distance of 20 was defined by the use of dynamic input.

Figure 2-30

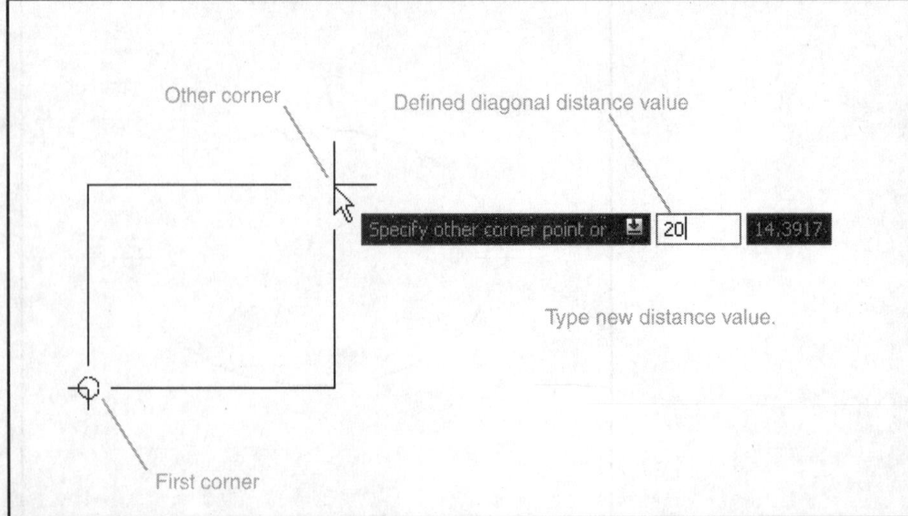

To Explode a Rectangle (See Figure 2-30.)

1 Select the **Explode** tool from the **Modify** panel.

Select object:

2 Select the rectangle.

Select object:

3 Press **Enter.**

There is no visible change in the rectangle, but it is now composed of four individual straight lines. As a test, use the **Erase** command to remove one of the lines.

2-13 Polygon

A ***polygon*** is a closed figure bounded by straight lines. The **Polygon** command will draw only regular polygons, in which all sides are equal. A regular polygon with four equal sides is a square. A six-sided polygon, or hexagon, will be drawn in this example.

To Draw a Polygon—Center Point (See Figure 2-31.)

1 Select the **Polygon** tool from the **Draw** panel.

Command: _polygon

Enter number of sides <4>:

2 Type **6;** press **Enter.**

Specify center of polygon or [Edge]:

3 Select or define a center point.

Enter an option [Inscribed in circle Circumscribed about circle] <I>:

4 Type **C;** press **Enter.**

Specify radius of circle:

5 Type a value; press **Enter.**

The **Circumscribe** option was selected because the diameter of the designated circle will equal the distance across the flats of the hexagon. The distance across the flats is often used to specify hexagon head bolt sizes and the wrench sizes used to fit them. The **Inscribe** option is used in a similar manner.

To Draw a Polygon—Edge Distance (See Figure 2-31.)

1 Select the **Polygon** tool from the **Draw** panel.

Command: _polygon

Enter number of sides <4>:

2 Type **6;** press **Enter.**

Specify center of polygon or [Edge]:

3 Type **E;** press **Enter.**

Specify first endpoint of edge:

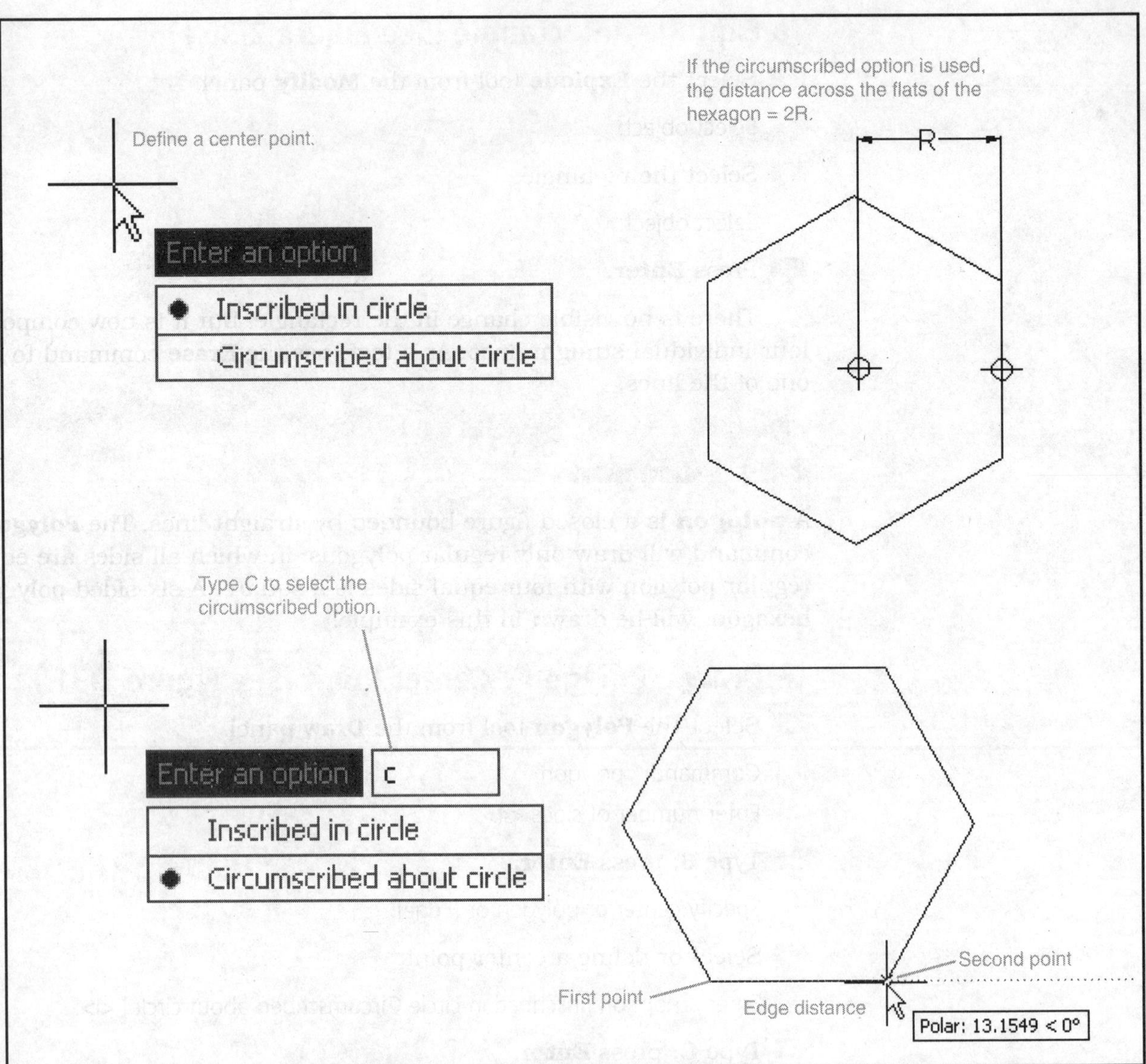

Figure 2-31

4 Select or define a point.

Specify second endpoint of edge:

5 Select or define a point.

2-14 Point

The **Point** command is used to draw points on a drawing. The default setting for a point's shape is a small dot, the kind used to display background grids. Other point shapes are available. See Figure 2-32. The default small dot point shape is listed as 0. Note that shape 1 is a void. The five available shapes can be enhanced by adding the numbers 32, 64, and 96 to the point's assigned value. For example, shape 2 is crossed horizontal and vertical lines. Shape 34 is shape 2 with a circle around it, shape 66 is shape 2 with a square overlay, and shape 98 is shape 2 with both a circle and a square around it.

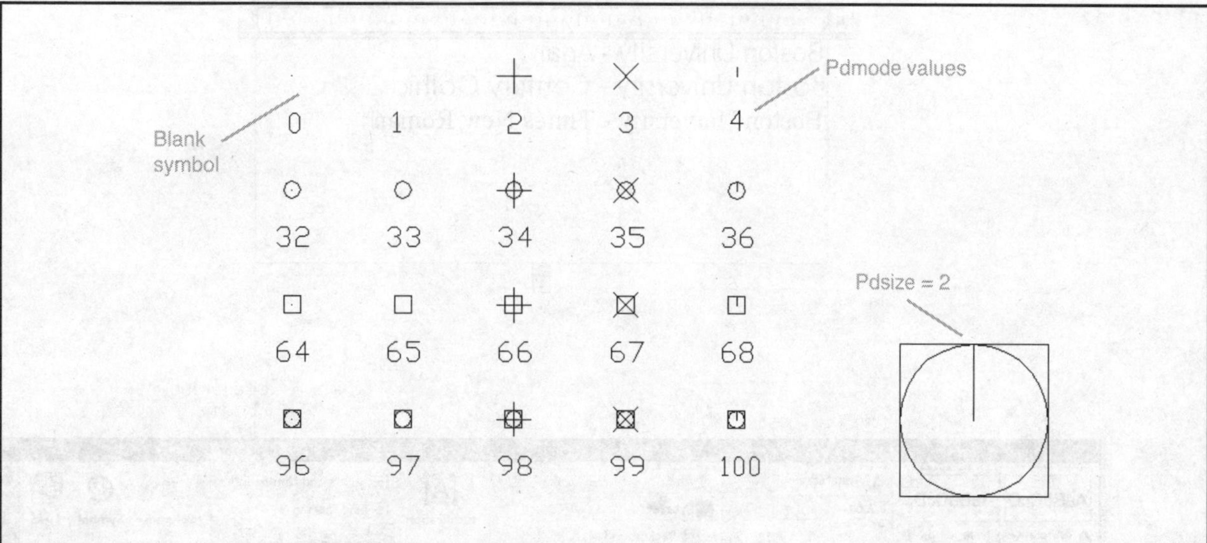

Figure 2-32

To Change the Shape of a Point (See Figure 2-32.)

Start with the cursor at the command prompt. Do not click the **Point** tool.

1. Type **pdmode** on the command line, and press **Enter.**

   Command: _pdmode

   Enter new value for PDMODE<0>:

2. Type **2;** press **Enter.**

   A type 2 point will appear on the screen.

3. Click the **Point** tool, and add several points to the screen.

4. Press the **<Esc>** key to exit the **Point** tool.

To Change the Size of a Point (See Figure 2-32.)

1. Type **pdsize** in response to a command prompt.

   Command: _pdsize

   Enter new value for PDSIZE<0.0000>:

2. Type **2;** press **Enter.**

   If you change the **pdsize** value, all points on the screen and all new points added will be drawn according to the new **pdsize** value.

2-15 Text

Text is added to a drawing by the **Multiline Text** tool found on the **Annotation** panel. The **Annotation** panel is located under the **Home** tab.

To Use the Multiline Text Tool (See Figures 2-33 Through 2-39.)

The **Multiline Text** command is used to enter text. First, the area in which the text is to be entered is defined. Text is typed into the dialog box, just

Figure 2-33

Figure 2-34

Figure 2-35

Figure 2-36

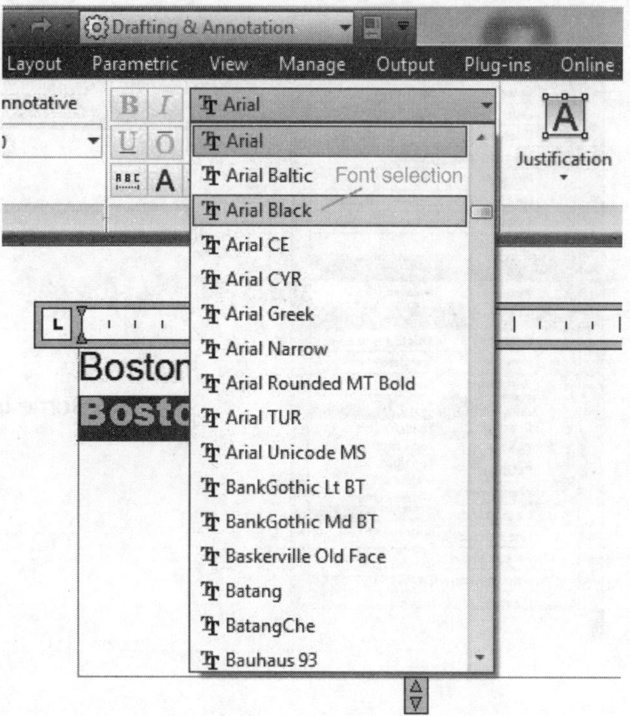

Figure 2-37

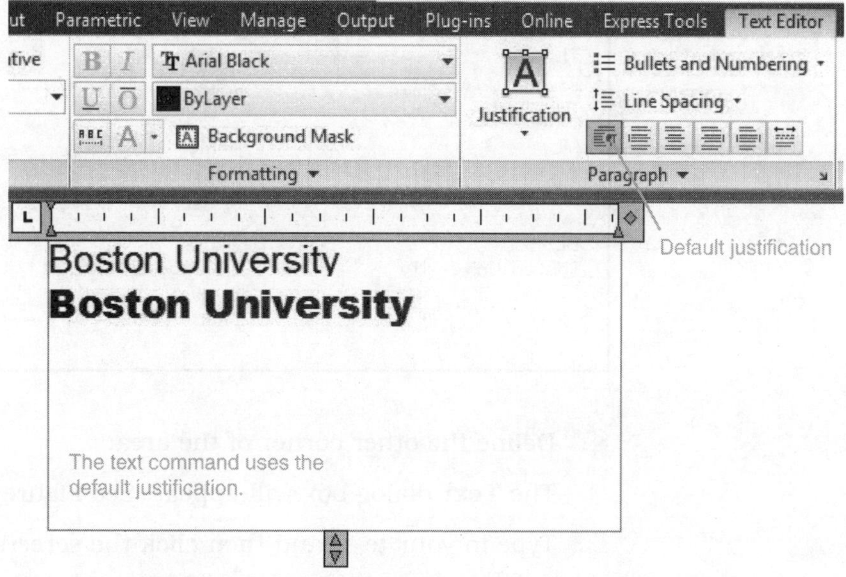

as with word processing programs, and then transferred back to the drawing screen. Text can be moved to different locations on the drawing screen by use of the **Move** command.

1 Select the **Multiline Text** tool from the **Annotation** panel.

Specify first corner:

2 Select or define a point.

The area that you are about to define is for the entire text entry, but it can be modified. See Figure 2-33. Text can be created with different fonts.

Specify opposite corner or [Height Justify Line spacing Rotation Style Width]:

Figure 2-38

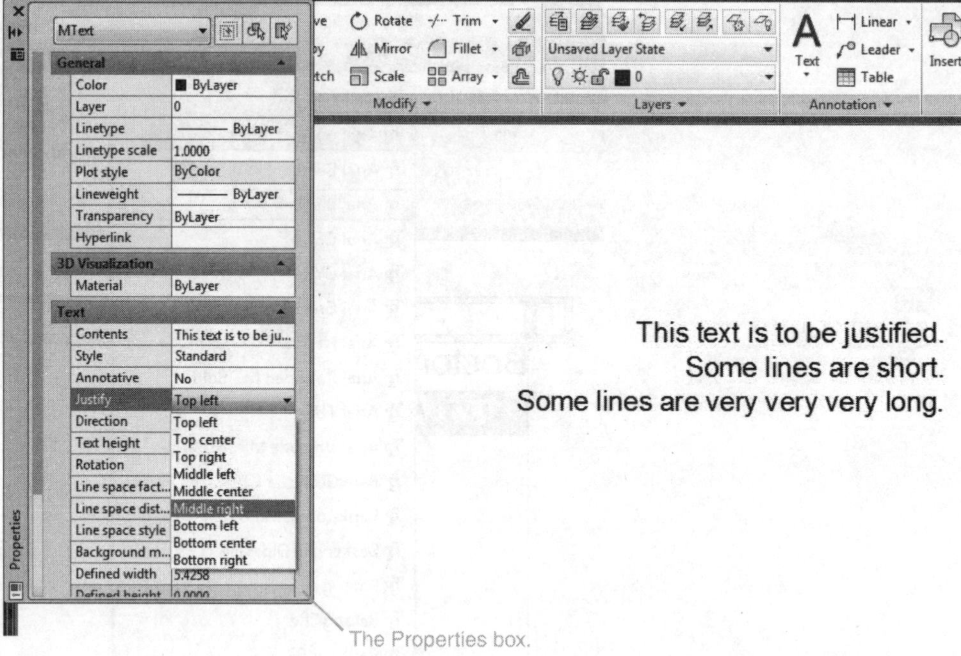

The Properties box.

Figure 2-39

The justification options created using AutoCAD's standard text font

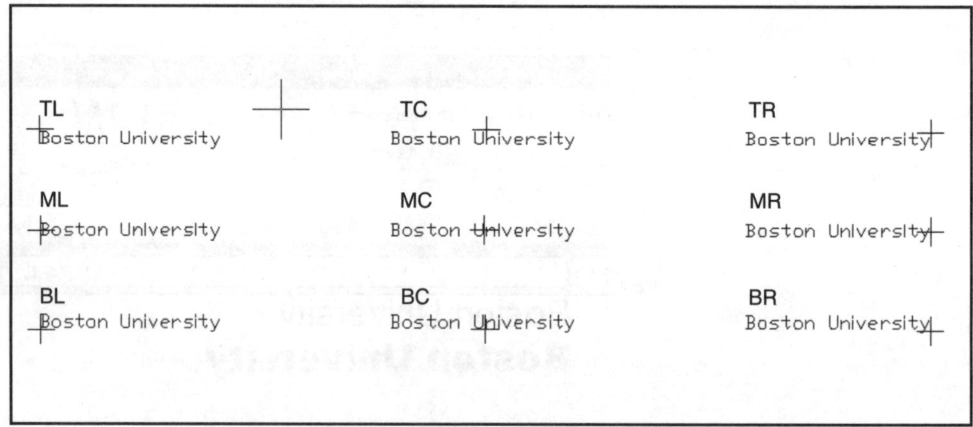

3. Define the other corner of the area.

   The **Text** dialog box will appear. See Figure 2-33.

4. Type in your text, and then click the screen outside of the text box.

   The text will be located on the drawing screen within the specified area. See Figure 2-33.

The Text Editor Panel

The **Text Editor** panel is used to change the text height, color, and font style, and the text justification.

To Access the Text Editor

1. Click the **Annotate** tab.

   The **Multiline Text** tool is also available on the **Text** panel of the **Annotate** tab.

2 Click the **Multiline Text** tool.

3 Define an area for text.

The **Text Editor** tab and its panels will appear. See Figure 2-34. The **Text Editor** tab is not normally visible. It appears only in concert with the **Multiline Text** command.

To Change Text Height

1 Use the **Multiline Text** tool, and type the desired text.

2 Access the **Text Editor** panels.

3 Highlight the text.

4 Click and highlight the **Text Height** box, and type in a new text height.

5 Press **Enter.**

See Figure 2-35.

To Change the Text Font

1 Use the **Multiline Text** tool, and type the desired text.

2 Highlight the text.

3 Access the **Font** box under the **Text Editor** tab.

4 Click the arrow on the right side of the box, scroll down the listing, and select the **Arial Black** font.

The font of the selected text will change when the new font is selected. See Figure 2-36.

Figure 2-37 shows two lines of text, one typed in Arial font and the other in Arial Black font.

To Justify Text

AutoCAD will justify text to the left unless otherwise specified. Figure 2-37 shows text created with the default left justification.

To Justify the Text to the Right

1 Window the given three lines of text.

The **Mtext Properties** dialog box will appear. See Figure 2-38.

2 Right-click the mouse and select the **Properties** option.

3 Click the **Justify** box, and then click the arrowhead on the right side of the box.

4 Scroll down the **Justify** box, and click the **Middle right** option.

The text will justify to the right. Note that the justification is dynamic—that is, as you scroll, the lines of text will change.

Figure 2-38 shows a listing of other possible justifications available. Figure 2-39 shows examples of the nine possible justifications listed in the **Mtext** box. Figure 2-40 and Figure 2-41 are examples of center and distribute justifications.

Figure 2-40

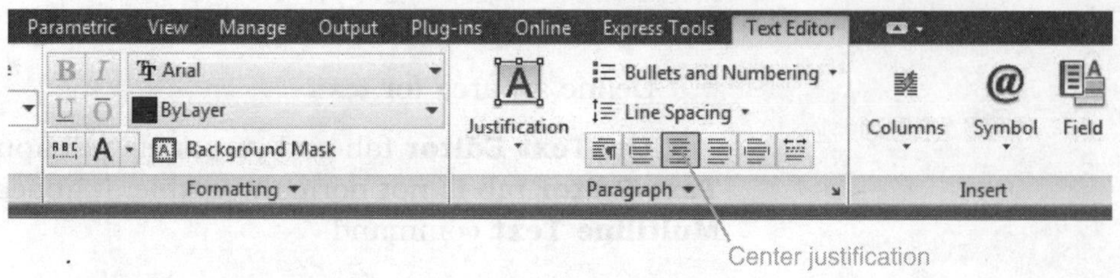

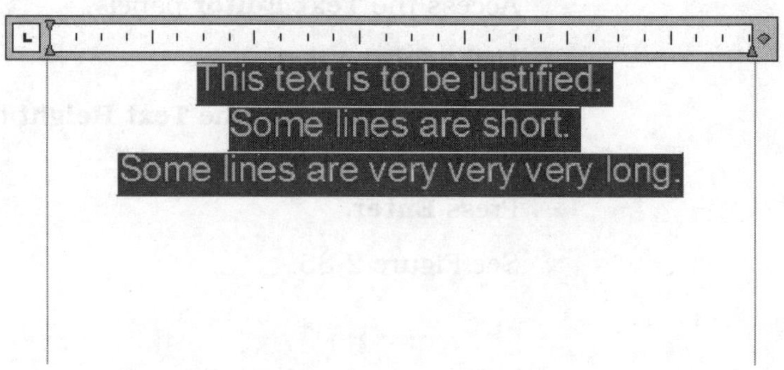

Figure 2-41

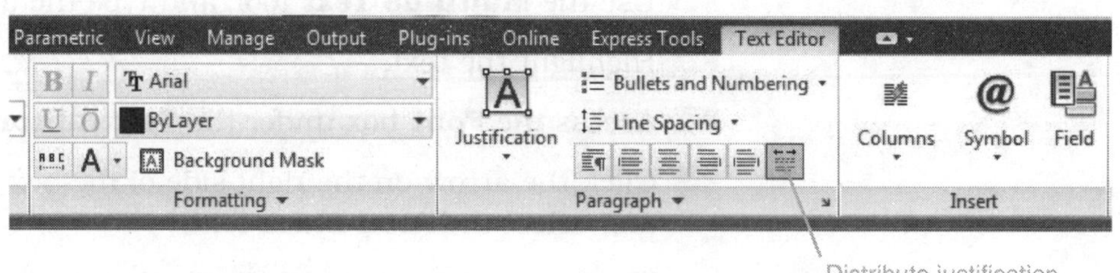

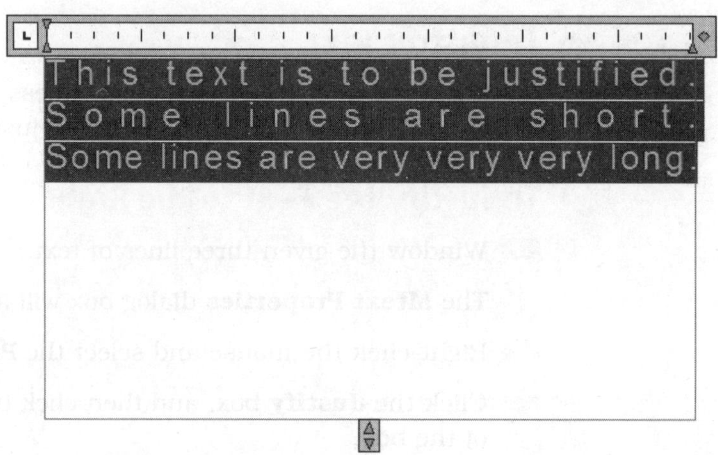

The Symbol Options

AutoCAD has three symbol commands:

%%C = ∅

%%P = ±

%%D = °

A symbol will initally appear in the %% form in the **Text Editor** tab, but will change to the equivalent symbol when the text is transferred to the drawing.

Symbols may also be created by using the **Windows Character** chart, as follows:

ALT + 0216 = ∅

ALT + 0177 = ±

ALT + 0176 = °

Text Color

The color of a text input may be changed through the **Color** option located on the **Text Editor** tab. See Figure 2-42. Select the scroll arrow to the right of the **Color** box, and a listing of available colors will scroll down.

Figure 2-42

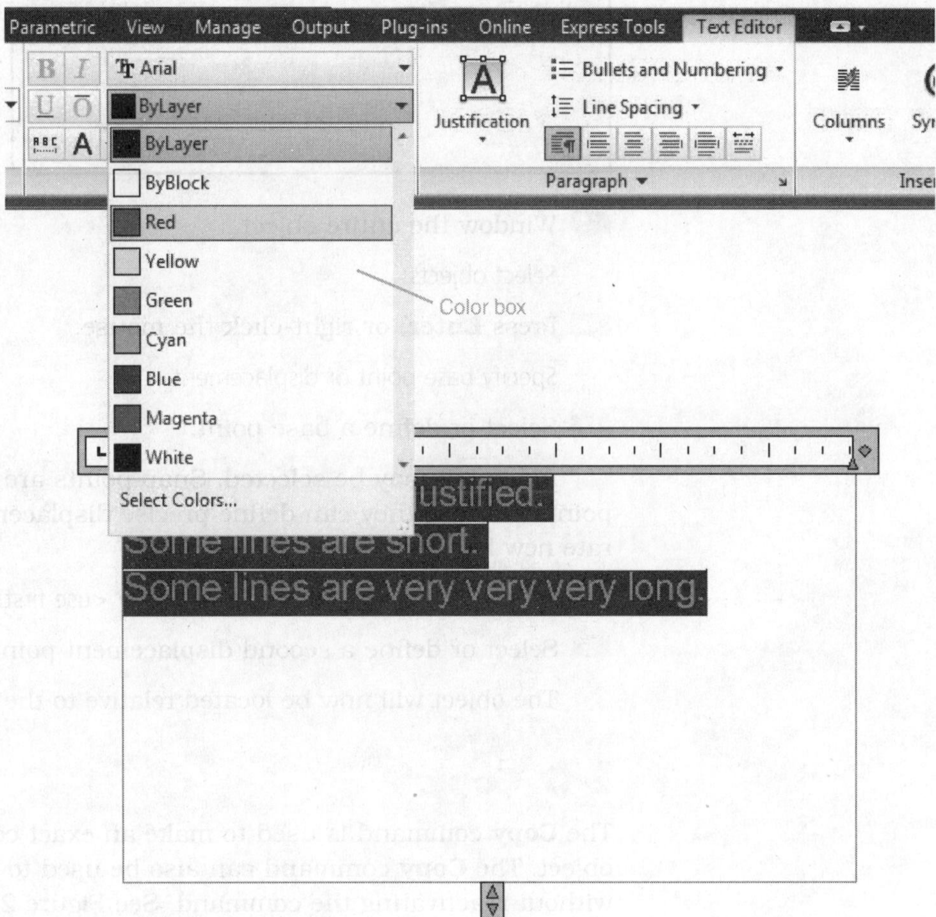

2-16 Move

The **Move** command is used to move a line or object to a new location on the drawing. See Figure 2-43.

To Move an Object

1. Select the **Move** tool from the **Modify** panel under the **Home** tab.

   Select objects:

Figure 2-43

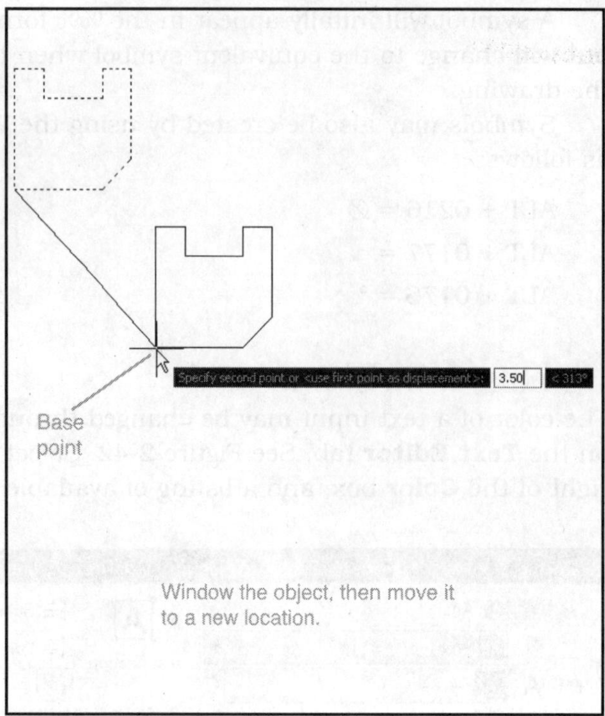

2 Window the entire object.

Select objects:

3 Press **Enter,** or right-click the mouse.

Specify base point or displacement:

4 Select or define a base point.

Any point may be selected. Snap points are usually used as base points because they can define precise displacement distances and accurate new locations.

Specify second point of displacement or <use first point of displacement>:

5 Select or define a second displacement point.

The object will now be located relative to the second displacement point.

2-17 Copy

The **Copy** command is used to make an exact copy of an existing line or object. The **Copy** command can also be used to create more than one copy without reactivating the command. See Figure 2-44.

To Copy an Object

1 Select the **Copy** tool from the **Modify** panel.

Select objects:

2 Window the entire object.

Select objects:

3 Press **Enter,** or right-click the mouse.

Specify base point:

4 Select or define a base point.

In the example shown in Figure 2-43, the lower left corner of the object was selected as the base point.

Specify second point of displacement or <use first point as displacement>:

5 Select or define a second displacement point.

The original object will remain in its original location, and a new object will appear at the second displacement point.

6 Right-click the mouse to enter the copied object.

To Draw Multiple Copies (See Figure 2-45.)

AutoCAD will continue to make copies of a selected object until all of the copied objects are entered. After each copy appears the prompt

Select a second displacement point:

Move the cursor to a new base point, or right-click the mouse to enter the objects.

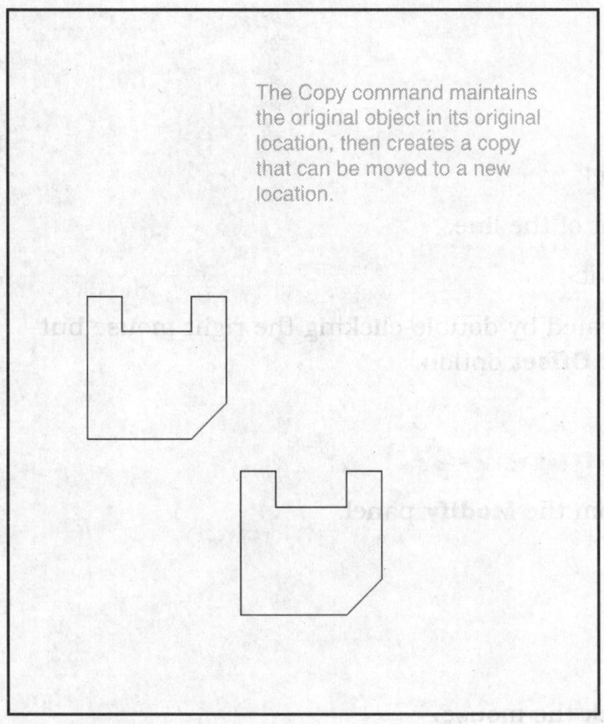

Figure 2-44

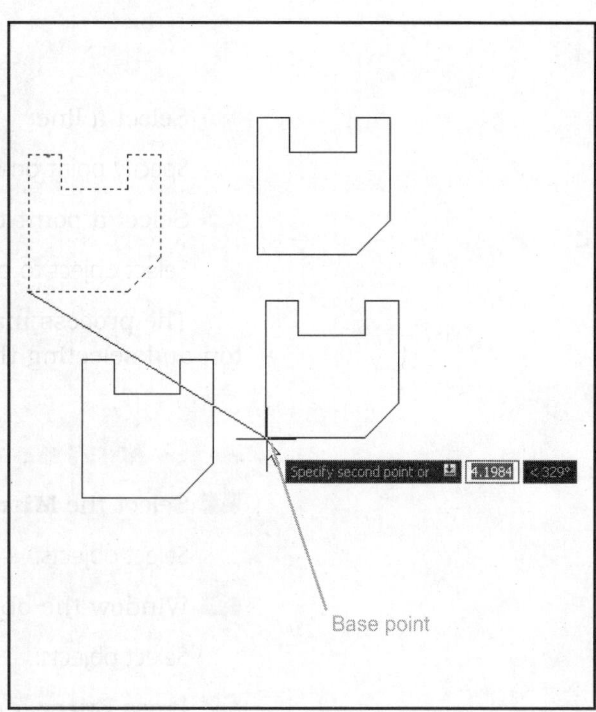

Figure 2-45

2-18 Offset (See Figure 2-46.)

1 Select the **Offset** tool from the **Modify** panel.

Specify offset distance or [Through Erase Layer] <Through>:

2 Specify the offset distance by typing a value; press **Enter.**

In this example, a distance of **.25** was selected.

Select object to offset or <exit>:

Figure 2-46

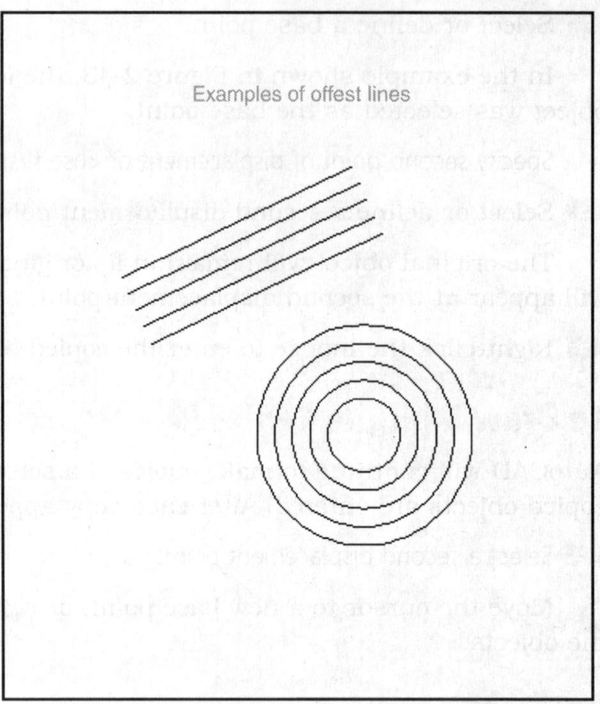

3. Select a line.

   Specify point on side to offset:

4. Select a point to the right of the line.

   Select object to offset or <exit>:

The process may be repeated by double-clicking the right mouse button and selecting the **Repeat Offset** option.

2-19 Mirror (See Figure 2-47.)

1. Select the **Mirror** tool from the **Modify** panel.

   Select objects:

2. Window the object.

   Select objects:

3. Press **Enter,** or right-click the mouse.

   Specify first point of mirror line:

4. Select a point on the mirror line.

   Specify second point of mirror line:

5. Select a second point on the mirror line.

   Delete source object? [Yes No]<N>:

6. Press **Enter,** or right-click the mouse.

Any line may be used as a mirror line, including lines within the object. Figure 2-48 shows an object mirrored about one of its edge lines.

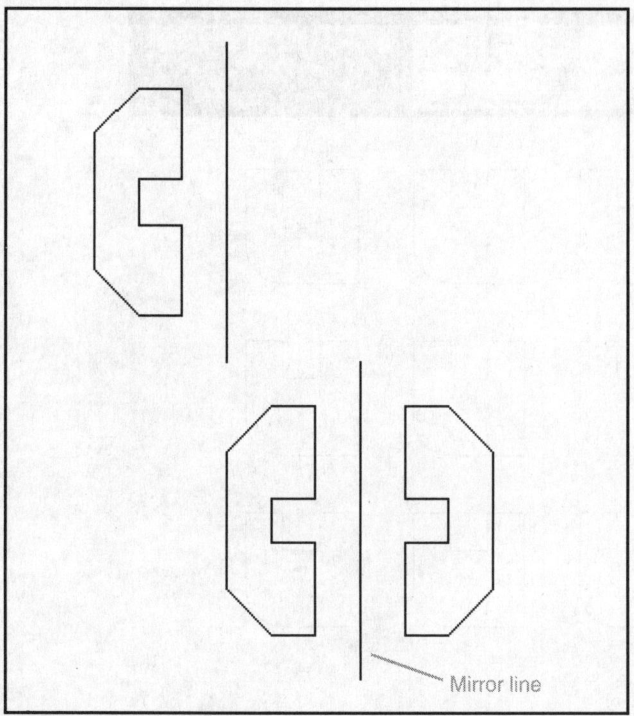

Figure 2-47

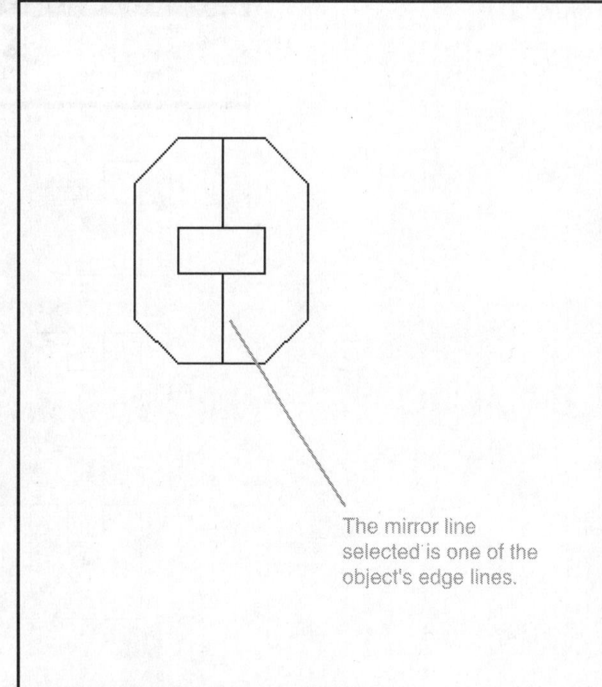

Figure 2-48

The **Mirror** command is very useful when drawing symmetrical objects. Only half of the object need be drawn. The second half can be created by using the **Mirror** command.

2-20 Array

Objects may be arrayed through either the **Rectangular** or the **Polar** option. The **Rectangular** option is demonstrated in Figure 2-49.

To Use the Rectangular Array Option

1. Select the **Rectangular Array** tool from the **Modify** panel.
2. Select the given object.

   The screen will change. The **Array Creation** panels will appear under the **Array Creation** tab. See Figure 2-49. The default setting is for a 4-by-3 array. The default array can be edited by using the panels under the **Array Creation** tab. In this example, a 5-by-2 array was created.
3. Enter the array values.
4. Right-click the mouse and select the **Enter** option.

To Use the Polar Array Option

Objects may also be arrayed through the **Polar Array** option. The **Polar Array** option will array objects about a defined center point at a given radius. See Figure 2-50.

1. Select the **Polar Array** tool from the **Modify** panel.

Figure 2-49

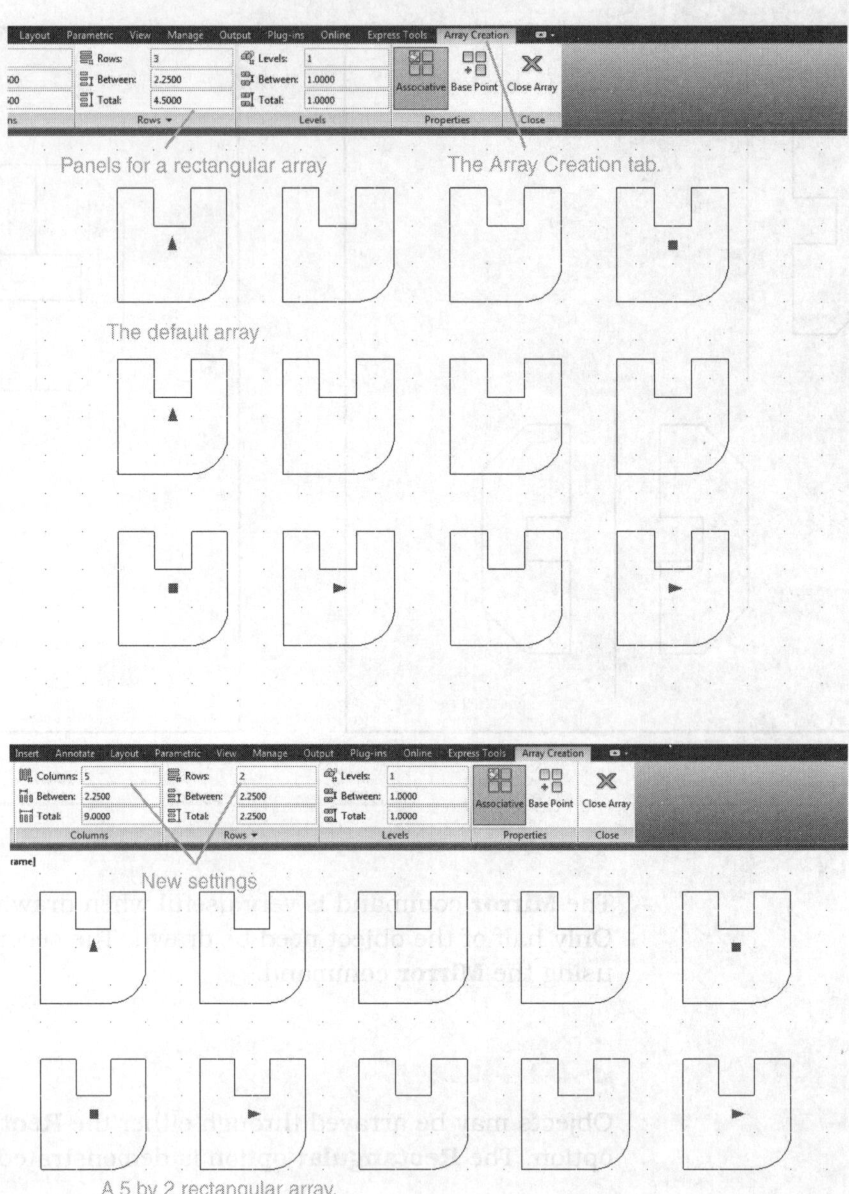

2. Select the given object.

Specify center point of Array or [Base point Axis of rotation]:

3. Select a center point for the array.

The screen will change. The **Array Creation** panels will appear under the **Array Creation** tab. See Figure 2-50. The default setting is for 6 items in the array. The default array can be edited by using the panels under the **Array Creation** tab. In this example, 8 items were selected and the direction command box was activated. Note that all the items in the array are orientated in the same direction.

4. Enter the array values.

5. Right-click the mouse and select the **Enter** option.

Figure 2-50

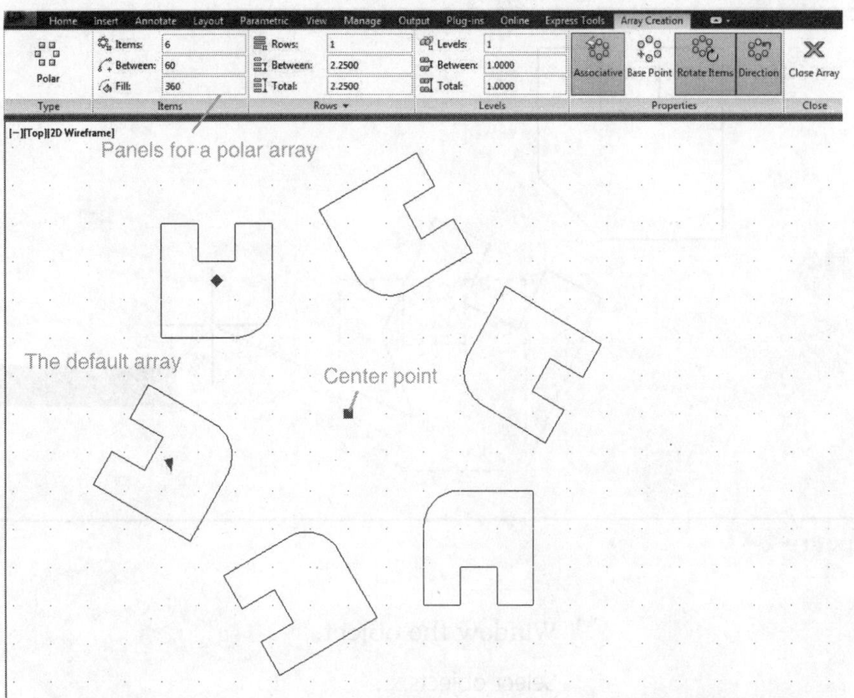

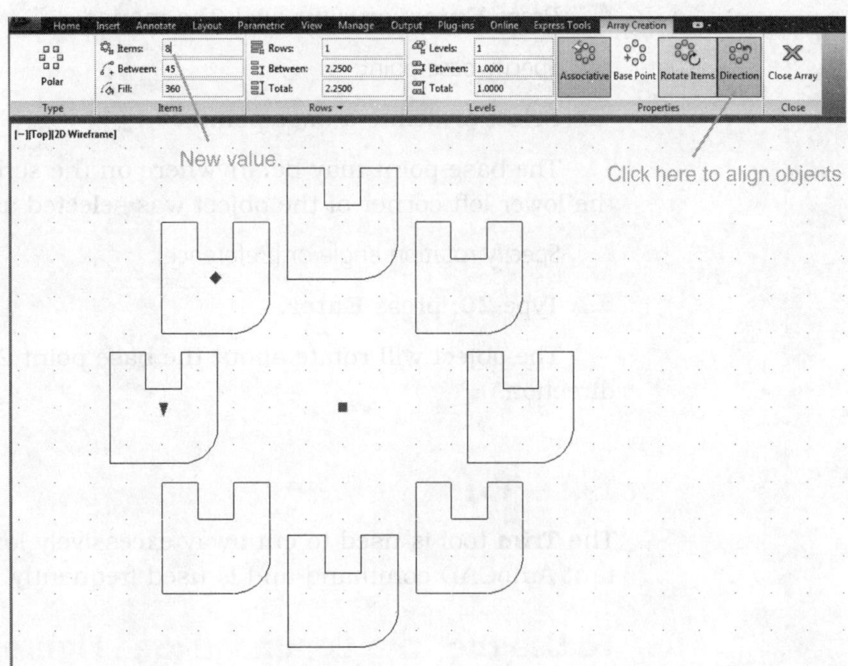

2-21 Rotate

The **Rotate** tool is used to rotate an object about a specified base point. The **3D Rotate** command will be covered later in the book. See Figure 2-51.

AutoCAD defines a horizontal line to the right as **0°.** Angles in the counterclockwise direction are positive angles.

To Rotate an Object (See Figure 2-51.)

1. Select the **Rotate** tool from the **Modify** panel.

   Select objects:

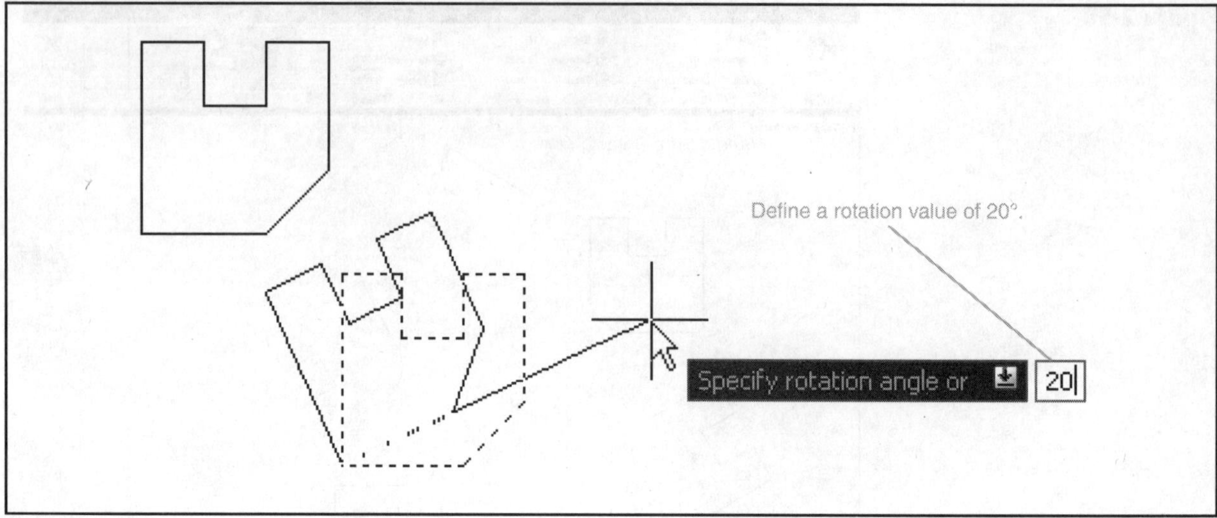

Figure 2-51

2 Window the object.

Select objects:

3 Press **Enter,** or right-click the mouse.

Specify base point:

4 Select or define a base point.

The base point may be anywhere on the screen. In the example shown, the lower left corner of the object was selected as the base point.

Specify rotation angle or [Reference]:

5 Type **20;** press **Enter.**

The object will rotate about the base point 20° in the counterclockwise direction.

2-22 Trim

The **Trim** tool is used to cut away excessively long lines. It is a very important AutoCAD command and is used frequently.

To Use the Trim Command (See Figure 2-52.)

1 Select the **Trim** tool from the **Modify** panel.

Select cutting edges:

Select objects:

2 Select the circle.

Select objects:

3 Press **Enter,** or right-click the mouse.

Select object to trim or [Project Edge Undo]:

4 Select the center portions of the lines within the circle.

5 Press **Enter.**

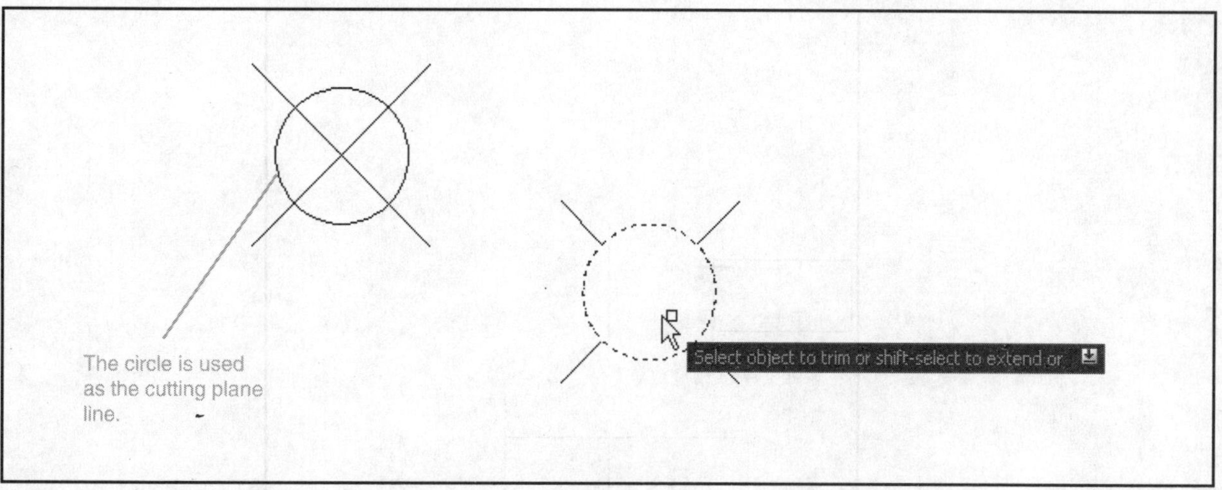

Figure 2-52

The lines within the circle will disappear. Figure 2-53 shows an example similar to that presented in Figure 2-52, but in this example the lines were selected as the cutting edges and portions of the circle were trimmed.

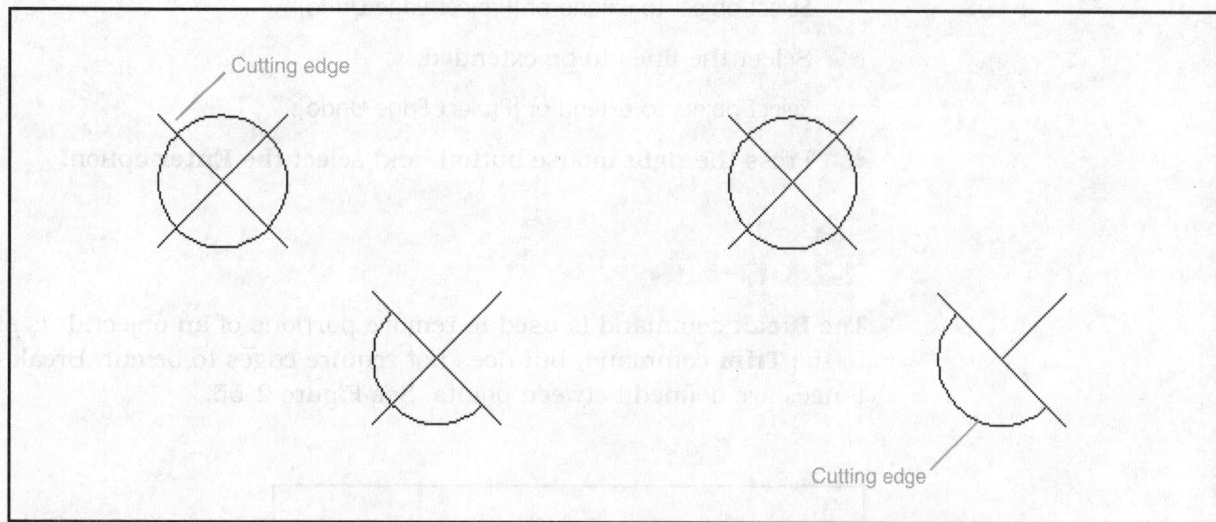

Figure 2-53

2-23 Extend

The **Extend** command allows given lines to be extended to new lengths. See Figure 2-54.

1. Select the **Extend** tool from the **Modify** panel.

   Select boundary edges:
   Select objects:

2. Select a line that can be used as a boundary edge.

A boundary line must be positioned so that all of the lines to be extended will intersect it. If you have an object that you want to make longer, draw a boundary line. Or you can use the **Move** command and

Figure 2-54

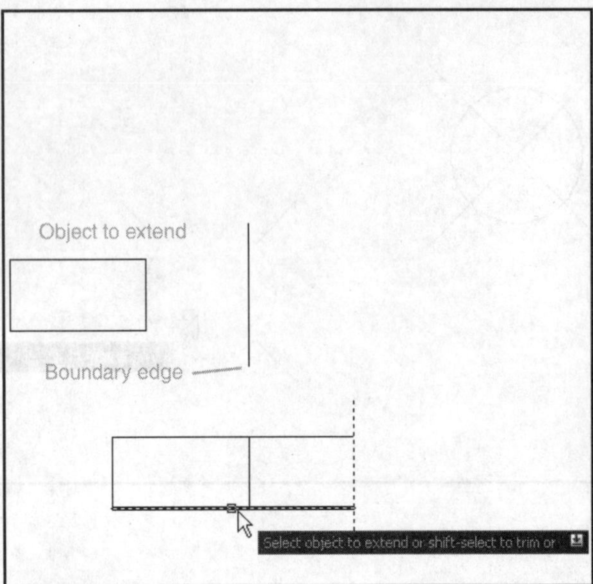

move one of the object's edge lines to the new position and use it as a boundary line.

Select object to extend or [Project Edge Undo]:

3 Select the lines to be extended.

Select object to extend or [Project Edge Undo]:

4 Press the right mouse button, and select the **Enter** option.

2-24 Break

The **Break** command is used to remove portions of an object. It is similar to the **Trim** command, but does not require edges to be cut. Break distances are defined between points. See Figure 2-55.

Figure 2-55

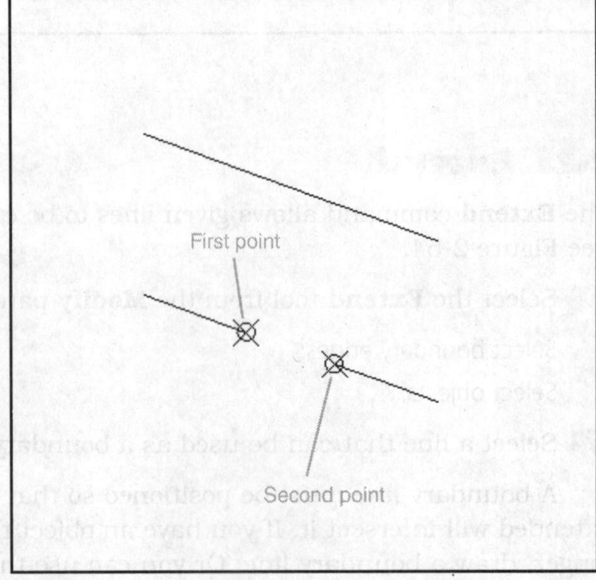

To Use the Break Command

1. Select the **Break** tool from the **Modify** panel.

   Select object:

2. Select a point on the line.

   If necessary, press the **<Shift>** key and right mouse button simultaneously to access the **Object Snap** screen menu. Select the **Clear all** option to eliminate the default snap function.

   Specify second break point or [First point]:

3. Select a second point.

   The length of the break will be equal to the distance between the two selected points.

   The **Break at point** tool is used to change a line into two parts. It does not remove part of the line, but simply breaks the line into two parts.

To Use the First Point Option

The **F,** or **First point,** option allows you to first select the line and then define the size of the break. This means that unlike the original **Break** command sequence, as just described, the first selection captures only the line, not the line and the first break point.

1. Select the **Break** tool from the **Modify** panel.

   Select object:

2. Select the line.

   Specify second break point or [First point]:

3. Type **F;** press **Enter.**

   Specify first break point:

4. Select or define the first point of the break.

   Specify second break point:

5. Select or define the second point of the break.

2-25 Chamfer

A ***chamfer*** is a straight-line corner cut, usually cut at 45°. Other angles may be used. See Figure 2-56.

To Create a Chamfer

1. Select the **Chamfer** tool from the **Modify** panel.

   (TRIM mode) Current chamfer Dist1 = 0.0000, Dist2 = 0.0000

   Select first line or [Polyline Distance Angle Trim Method]<Select first line>:

2. Type **D;** press **Enter.**

   Specify first chamfer distance <0.0000>:

3. Type **.75;** press **Enter.**

   Specify second chamfer distance <0.7500>:

Figure 2-56

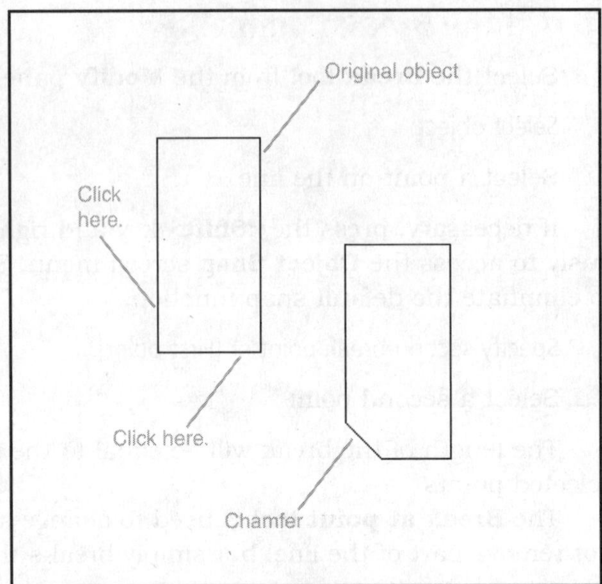

AutoCAD assumes that the chamfer will be at 45° and automatically sets the second distance equal to the first.

4 Press **Enter.**

Command:

The chamfer has now been set for a 45° chamfer of length .75. The chamfer can now be applied to the rectangular figure in Figure 2-56 by clicking the two lines involved in the chamfer. In this example, the left vertical line and the bottom horizontal line were selected.

2-26 Fillet

A ***fillet*** is a rounded corner. See Figure 2-57.

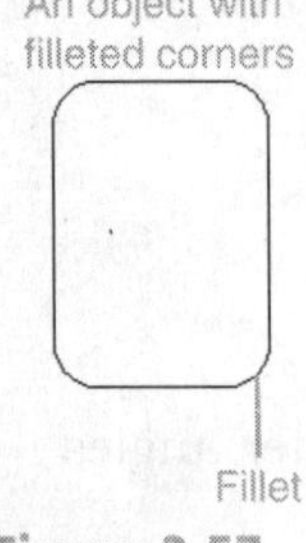

Figure 2-57

To Draw a Fillet

1 Select the **Fillet** tool from the **Modify** panel.

Current settings: Mode = Trim, Radius = 0.5000
Select first object or [Polyline Radius Trim]:

2 Type **R;** press **Enter.**

Specify fillet radius <0.0000>:

3 Type **1.25;** press **Enter.**

Command:
Select first object or [Polyline Radius Trim Multiple]:

4 Select a line.

Select second object:

5 Select a second line.

6 Press **Enter.**

Fillets can also be drawn between circles. See Figure 2-58. The **Fillet** command is location sensitive, meaning that the location of the selection points will affect the shape of the resulting fillet. Figure 2-59 shows a line and an arc. Note the different shapes that are created when fillets are drawn between the line and arc from different points on each.

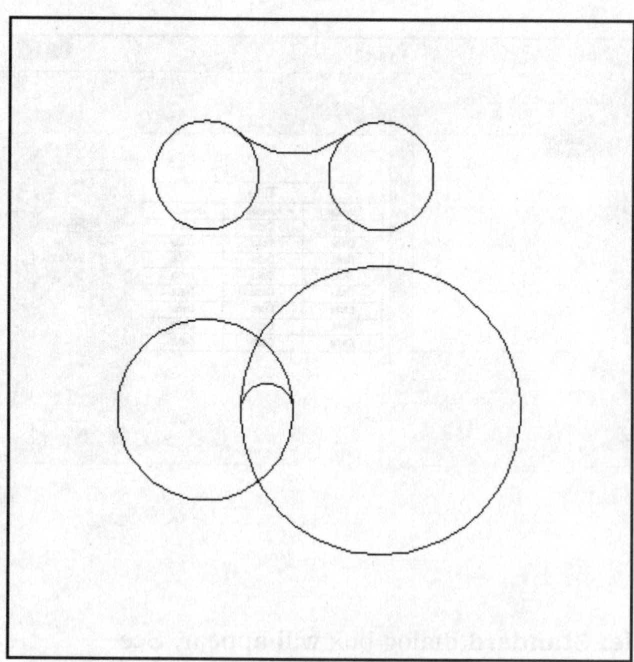

Some examples of the Fillet command applied to circles

Figure 2-58

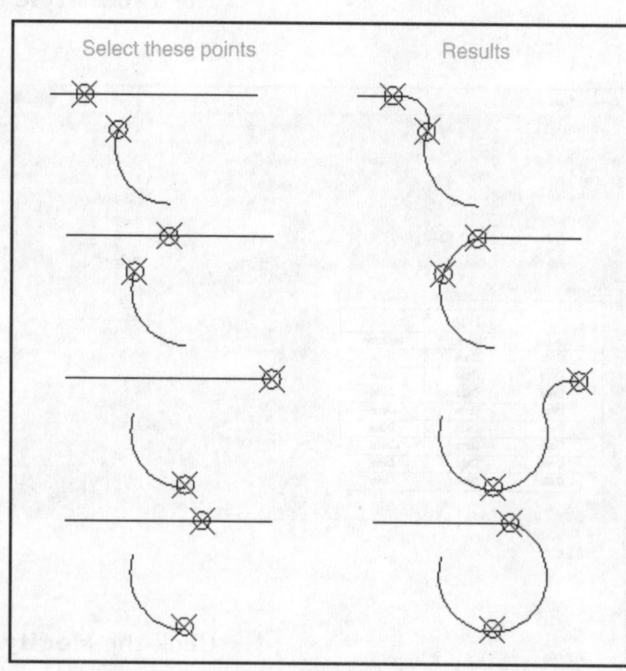

The Fillet command is location sensitive. The final shape of the fillet will depend on the location of your selection points. Here are four examples of fillets drawn from the same initial arc line setup.

Figure 2-59

2-27 Table

The **Table** command is used to create tables such as the one shown in Figure 2-60. Tables are used on drawings to define multiple hole dimensions, to define coordinate data, and to create parts lists, among other uses.

Created using the Table tool

LOCATION	X-DIM	Y-DIM	Ø
A1	15.00	85.00	20.00
A2	15.00	15.00	20.00
A3	145	85.00	20.00
A4	145	15.00	20.00
B1	55	70.00	30.00
B2	110	70.00	30.00
C1	80	30.00	40.00

Figure 2-60

To Create a Table

1. Click the **Table** command tool on the **Annotation** panel.

   The **Insert Table** dialog box will appear. See Figure 2-61.

2. Click the **Table style** button.

   The **Table Style** dialog box will appear. See Figure 2-62.

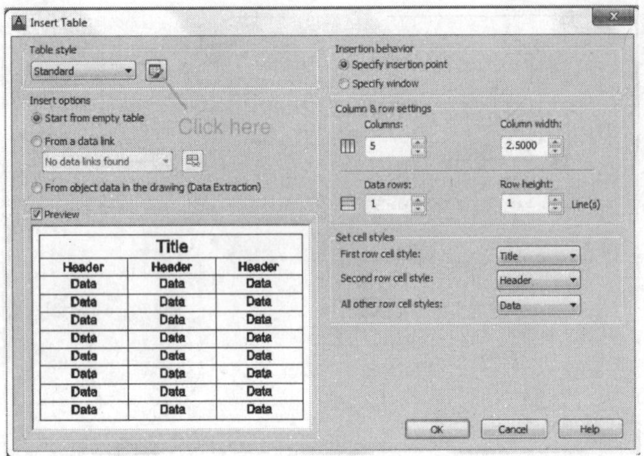

Figure 2-61

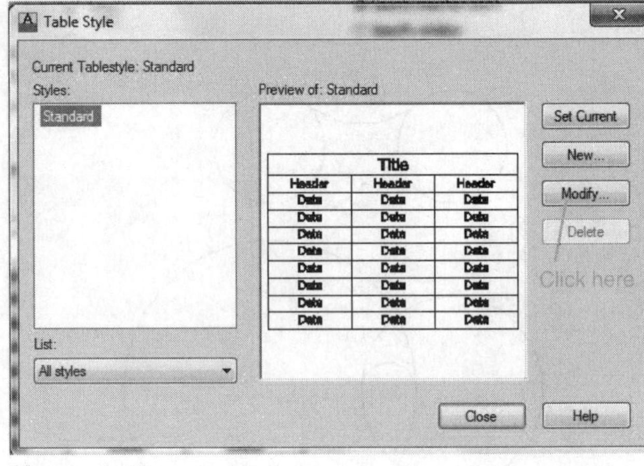

Figure 2-62

3. Click the **Modify** box.

   The **Modify Table Style: Standard** dialog box will appear. See Figure 2-63.

4. Click the **Text** tab under the **Cell styles** heading.

   The word **Data** indicates that the modifications will be made on the text used in the data cells.

5. Click the box to the right of **Text style: Standard,** as shown in Figure 2-64.

   The **Text Style** dialog box will appear. See Figure 2-65.

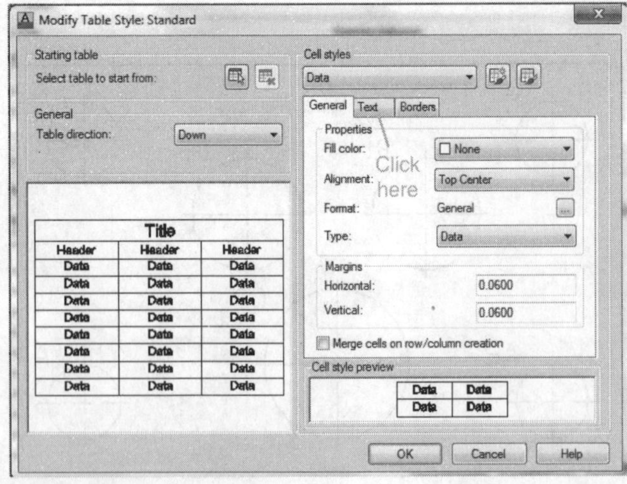

Figure 2-63

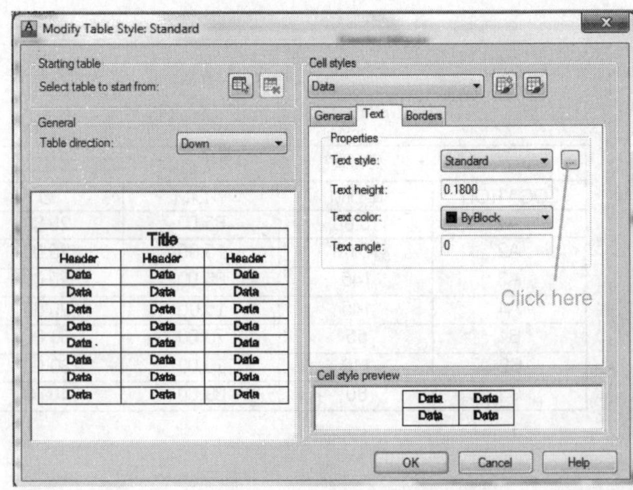

Figure 2-64

Figure 2-65

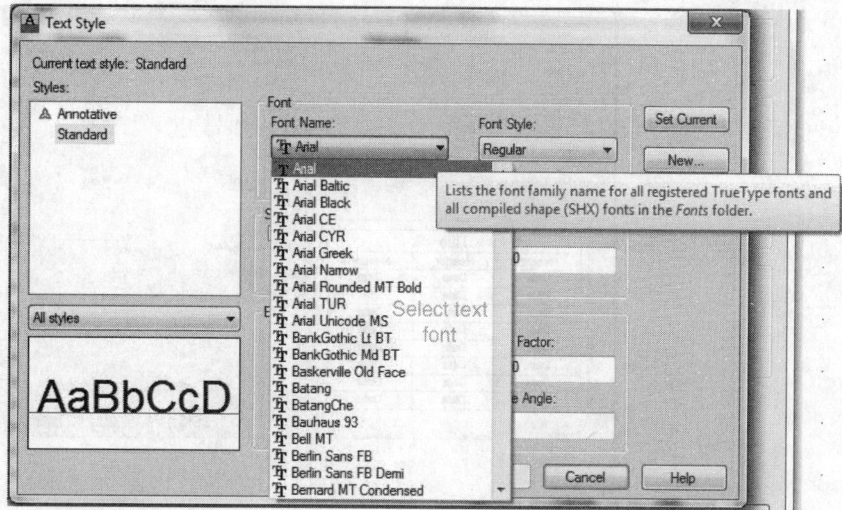

6 Select the **Arial** font, and set the height for **0.25.** Then click **Apply** and **Close.**

The **Modify Table Style: Standard** dialog box will appear. See Figure 2-66.

Figure 2-66

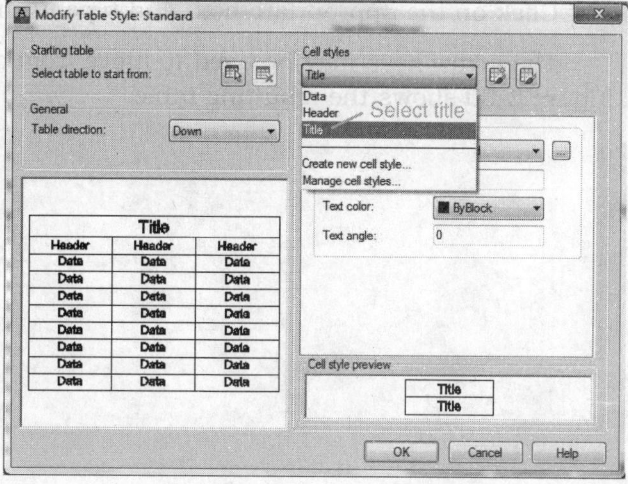

7 Click the arrow to the right of **Data** under **Cell styles,** and select the **Title** option.

The table's title can now be modified.

8 Return to the **Text Style** dialog box, and set the text font for **Arial** and the text height for **0.375.** Click **Apply** and **Close.**

9 Return to the **Insert Table** dialog box, and set the number of data rows and columns and the size of boxes; then click **OK.** See Figure 2-67.

Note that the number of data rows does not include the column headings.

A blank table will appear on the screen. See Figure 2-68.

Figure 2-67

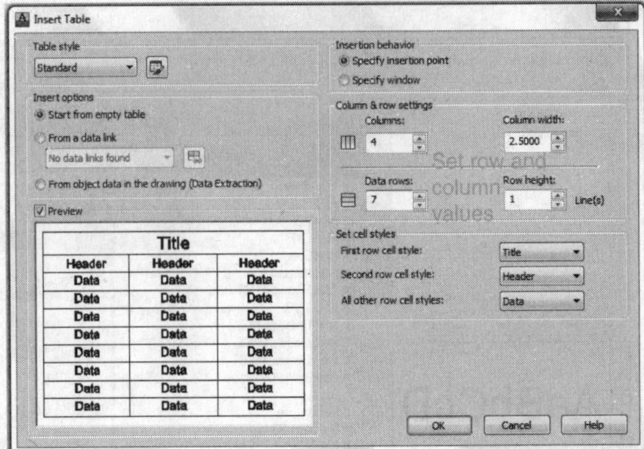

Figure 2-68

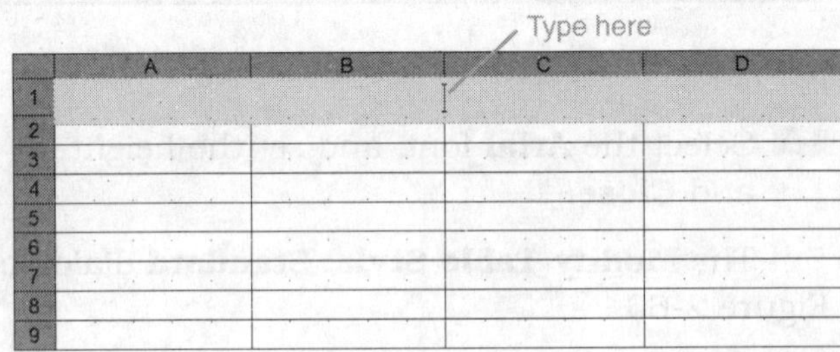

10 Click on the appropriate box, and type in the required data.

The arrow keys may be used to move from one box to another. Figure 2-60 shows the resulting table.

2-28 EXERCISE PROBLEMS

Redraw the figures that follow. Do not include dimensions. Dimensional values are as indicated.

EX2-1 Inches

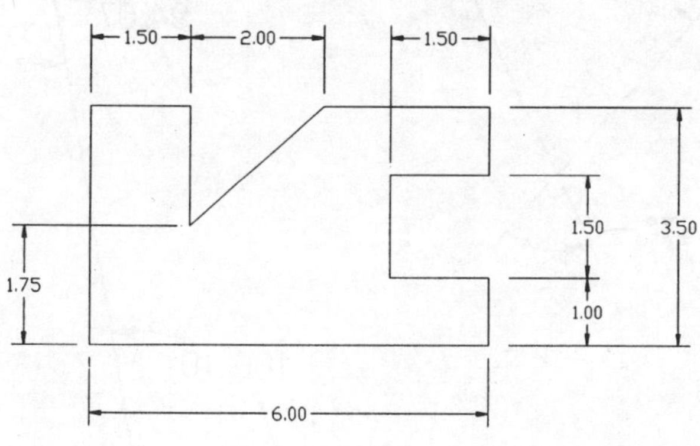

EX2-2 Inches

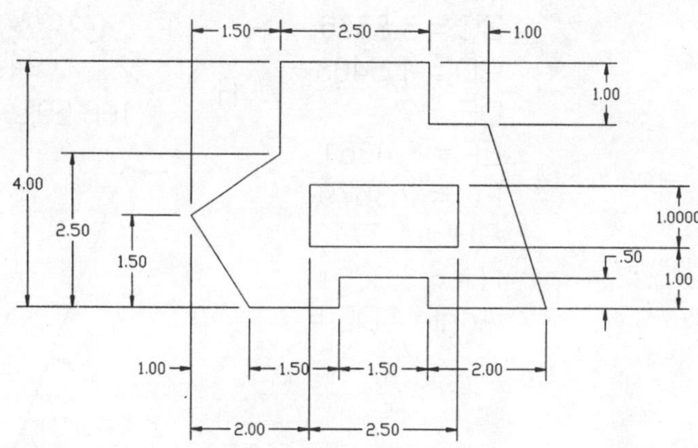

EX2-3 Millimeters

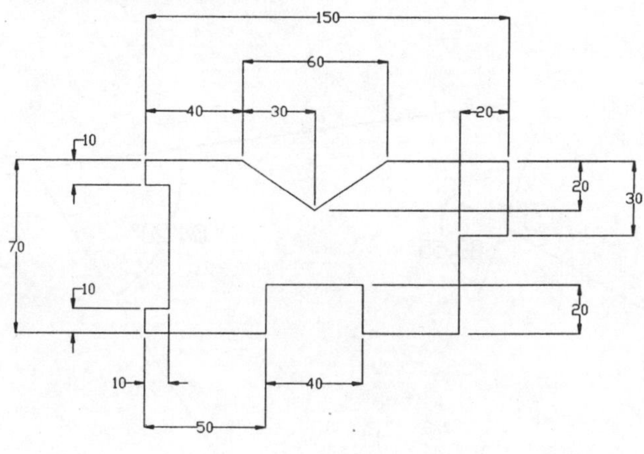

EX2-4 Millimeters

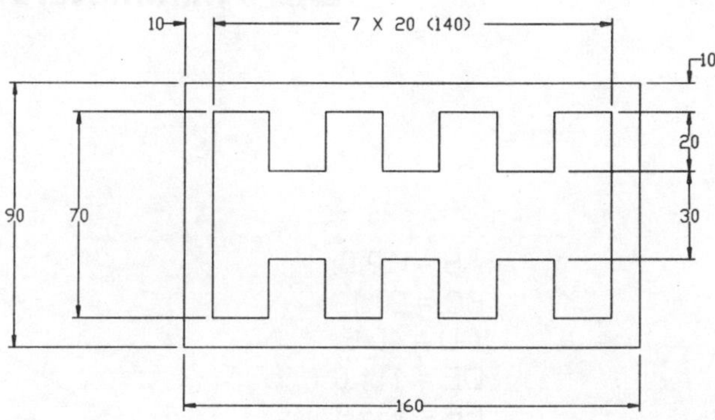

EX2-5 Inches

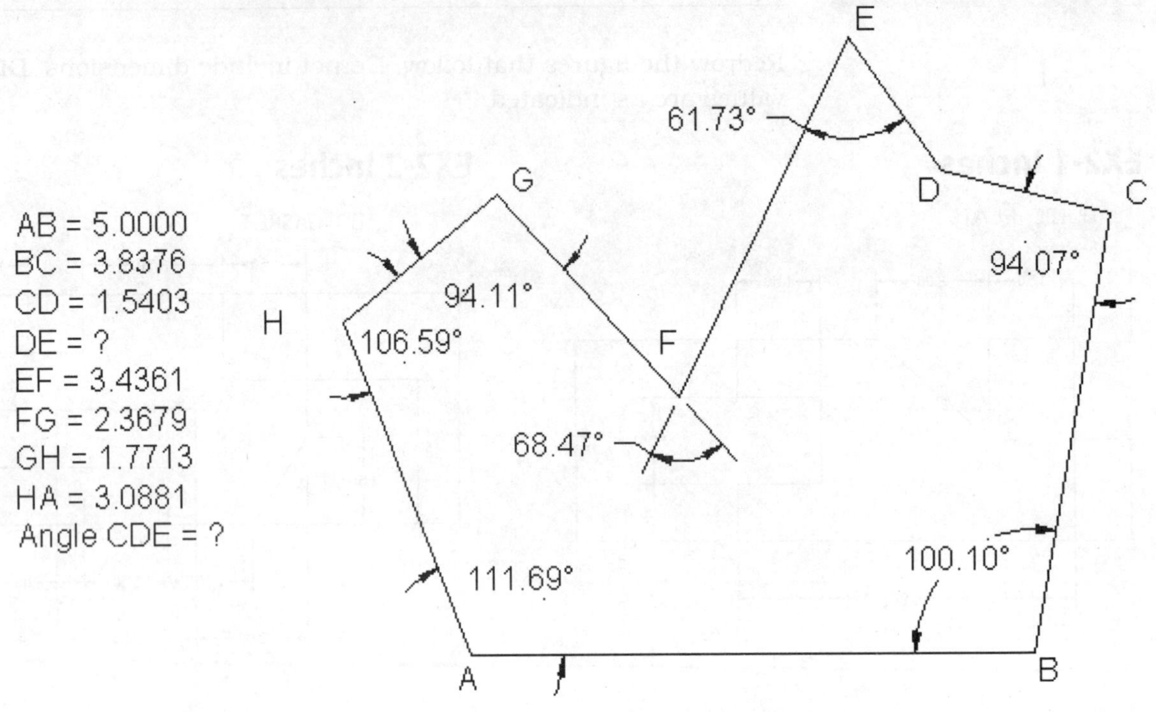

EX2-6 Millimeters

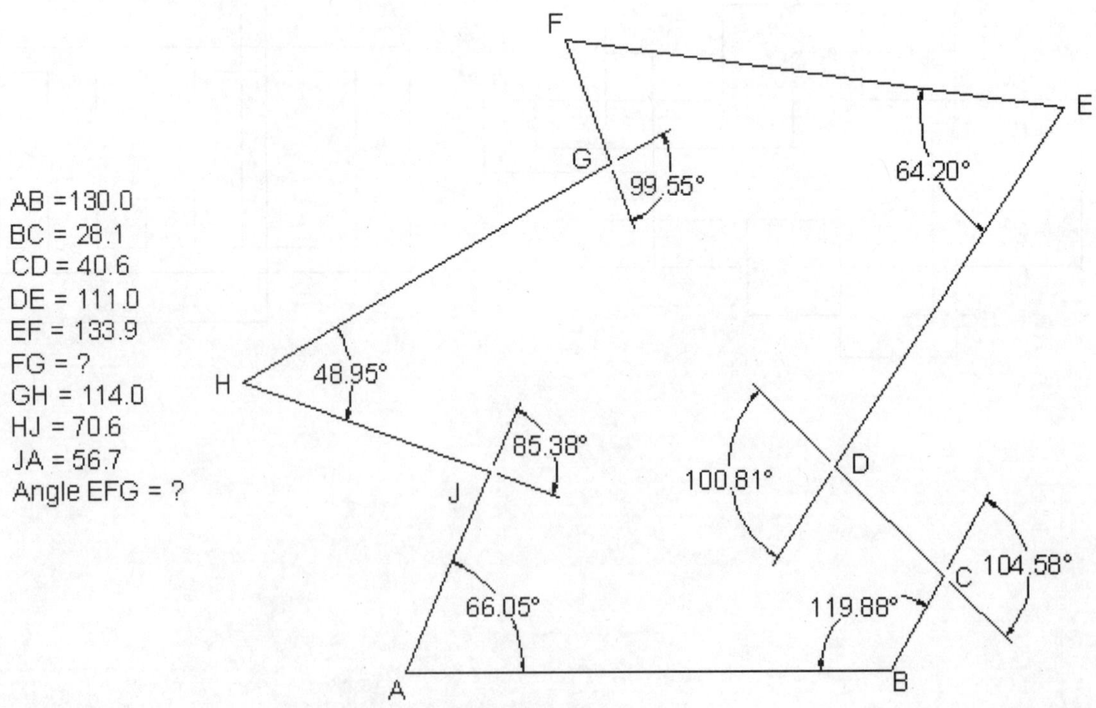

EX2-7 Inches

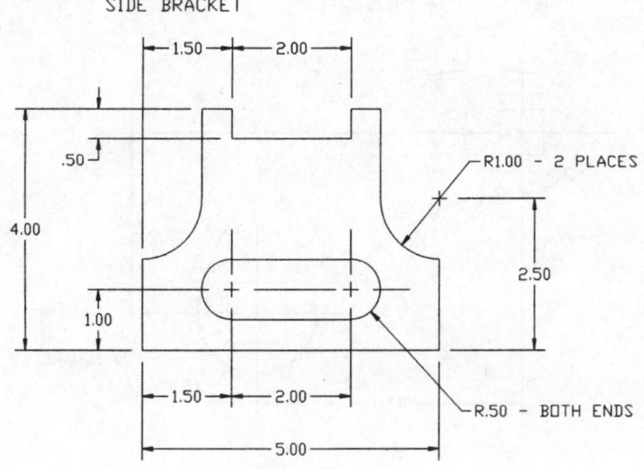

EX2-8 Inches

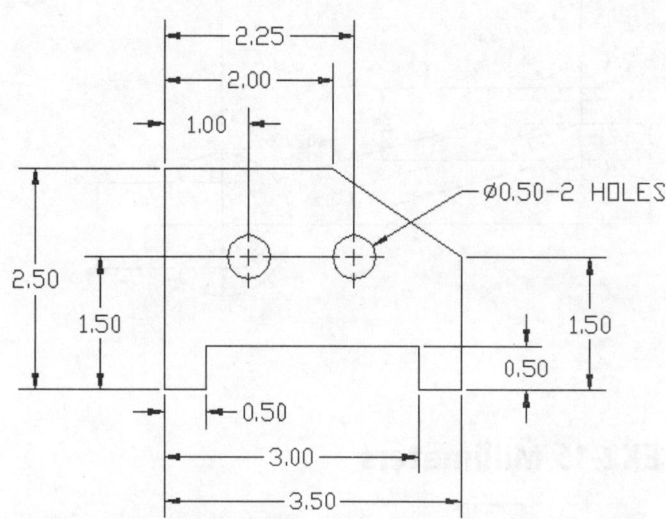

EX2-9 Millimeters

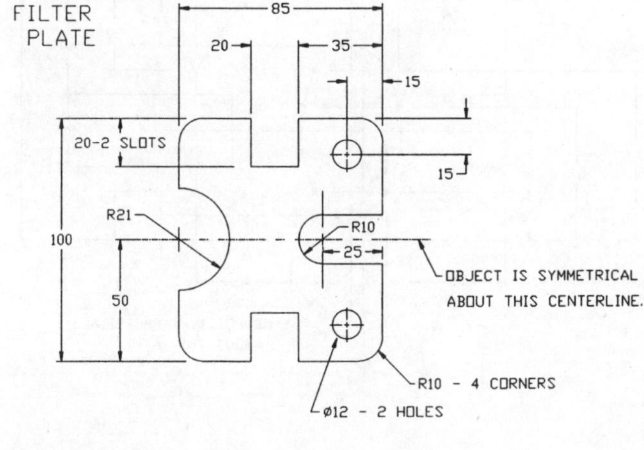

EX2-10 Inches

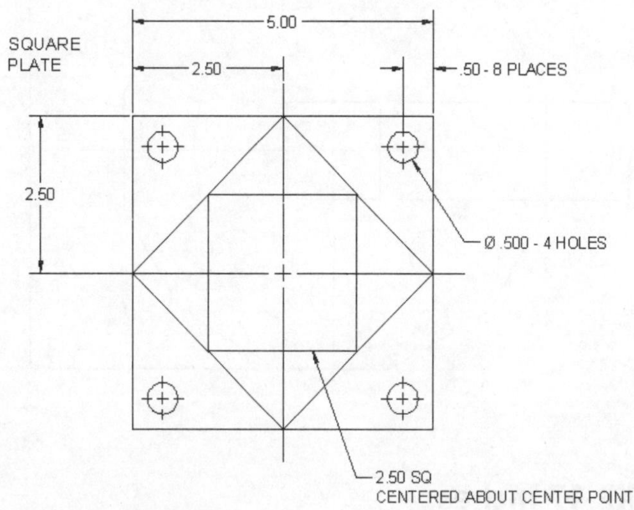

EX2-11 Inches

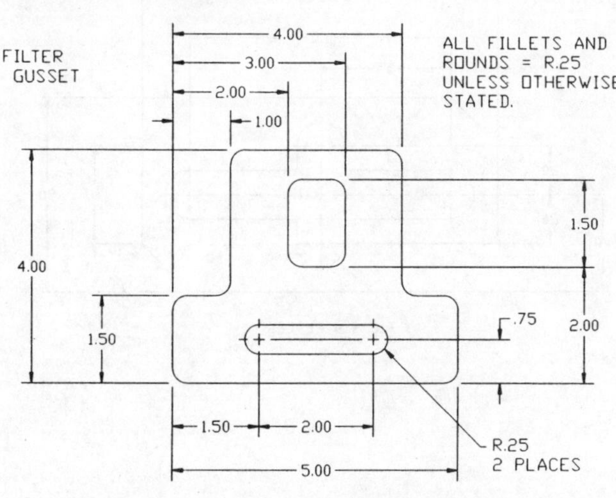

EX2-12 Millimeters

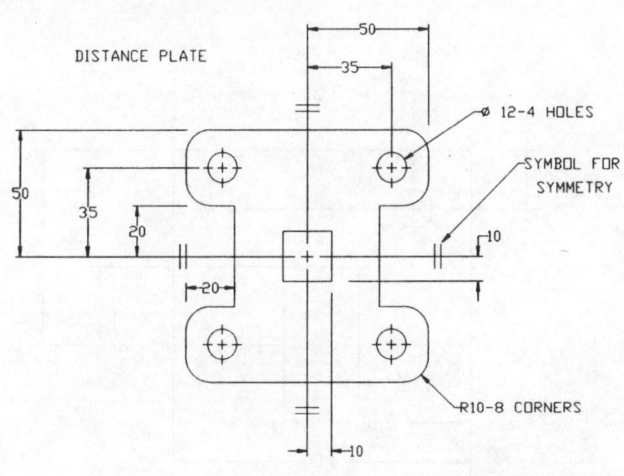

EX2-13 Millimeters

METRIC WRENCH

130

R3

ø40

25

10

35

30

R3

ø50

EX2-14 Inches

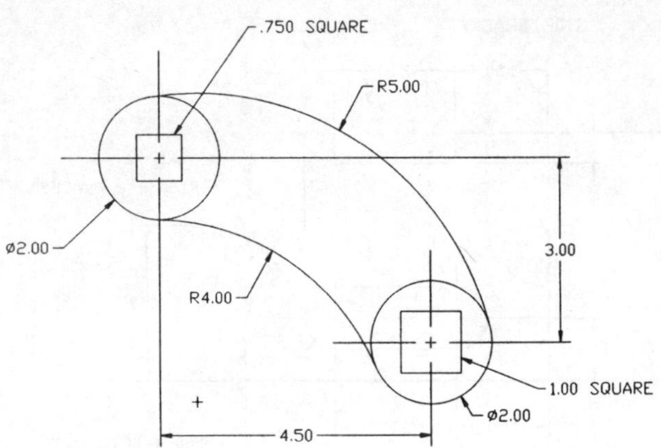

EX2-15 Millimeters

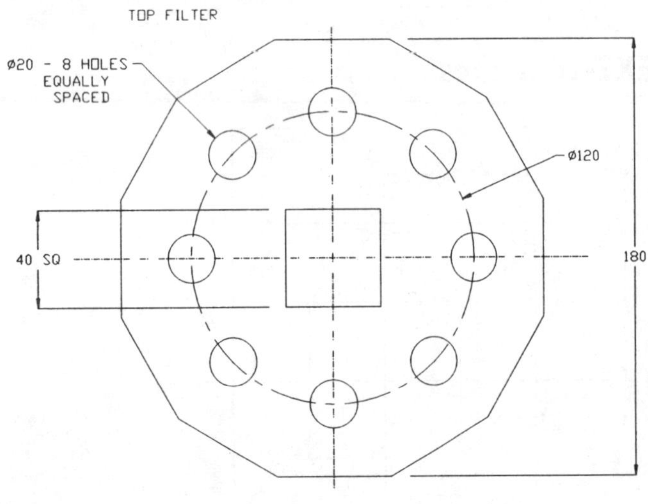

EX2-16 Millimeters

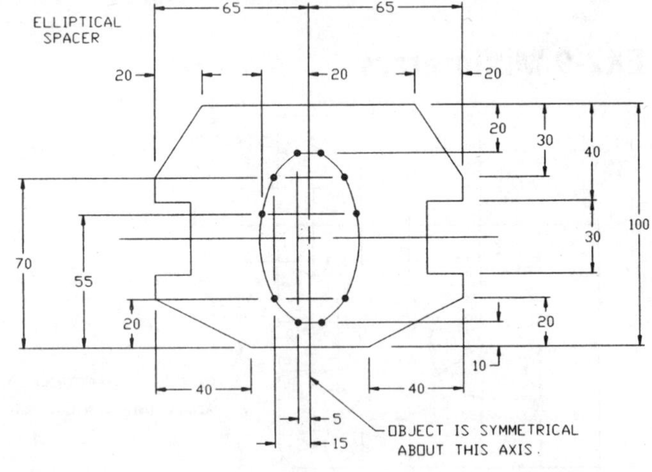

EX2-17 Inches

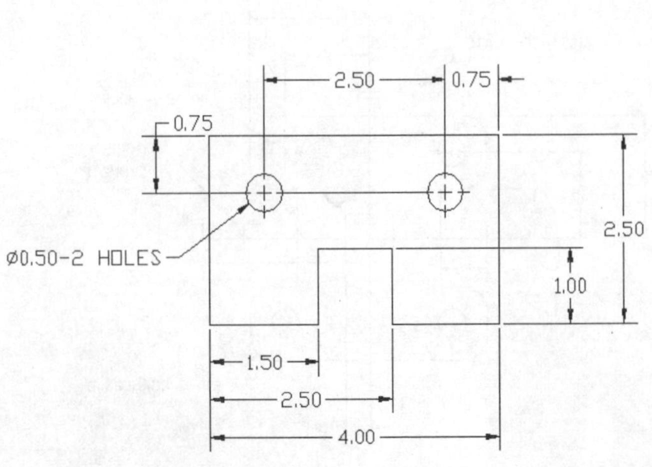

EX2-18 Millimeters

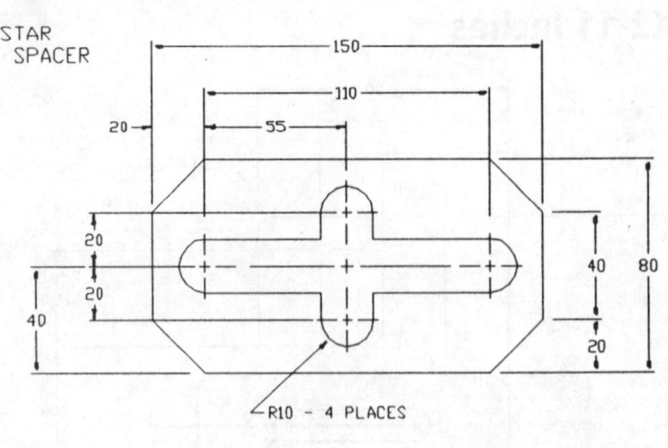

EX2-19 Inches

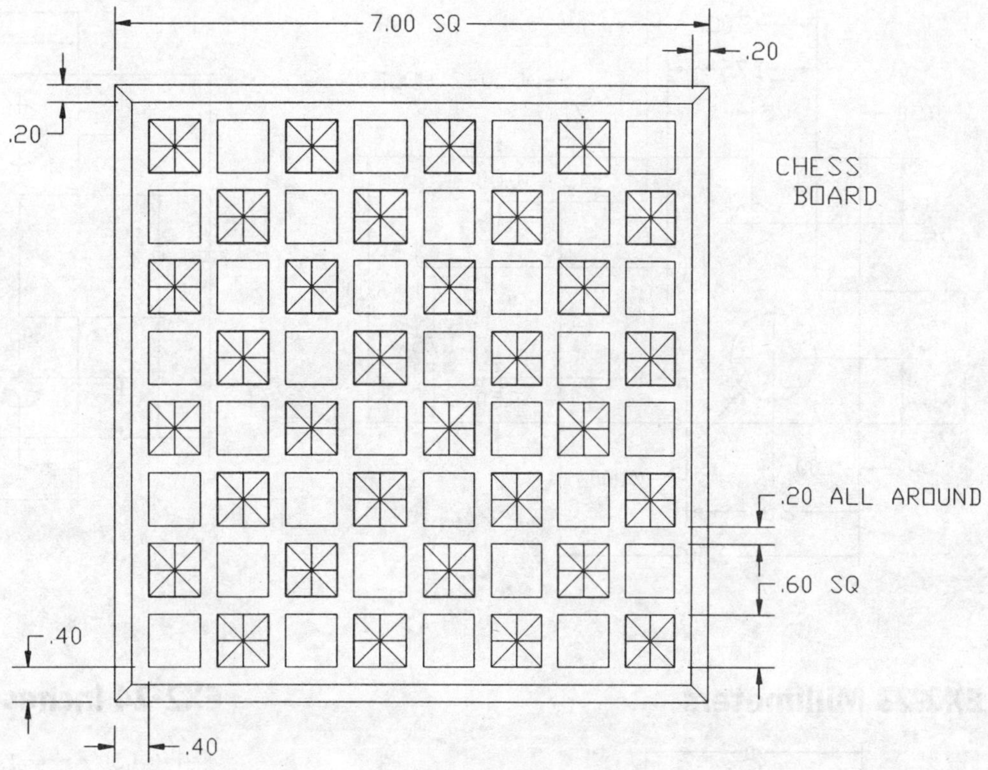

EX2-20 Millimeters

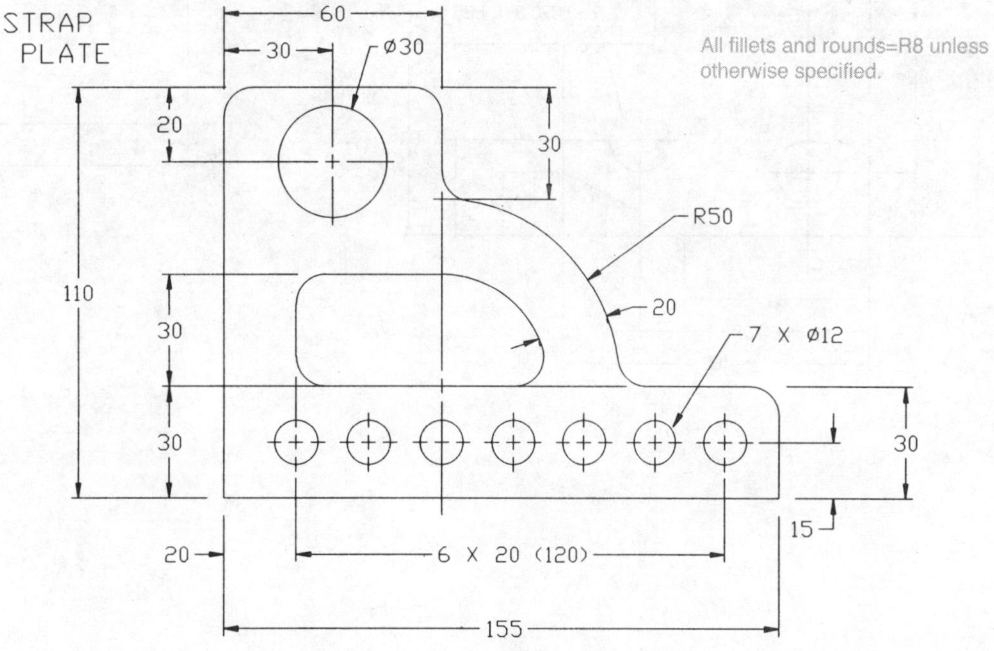

EX2-21 Inches

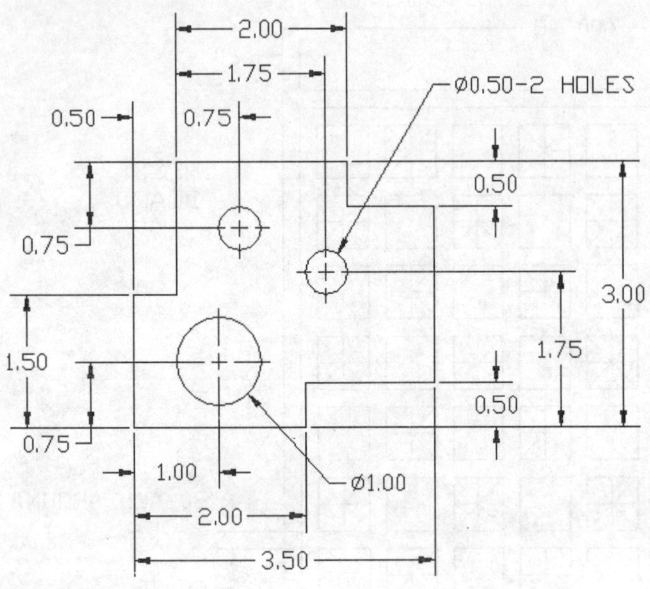

EX2-22 Millimeters

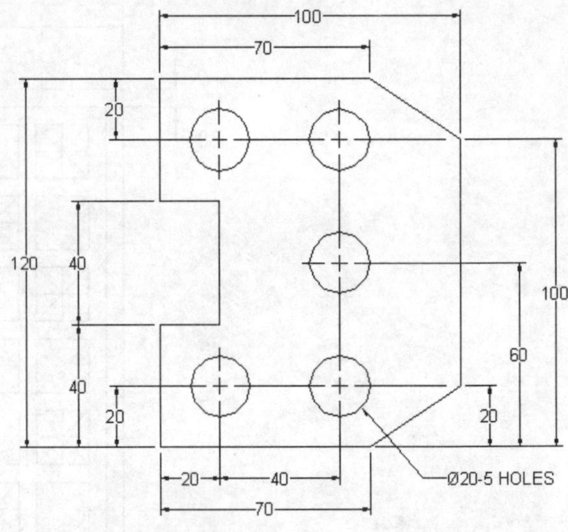

EX2-23 Millimeters

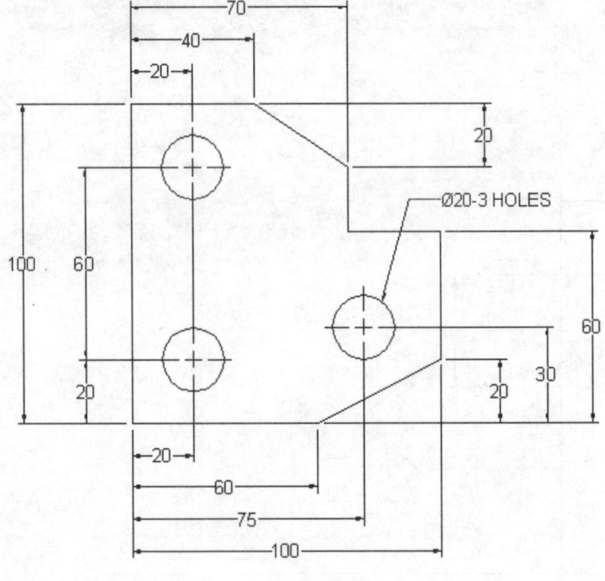

EX2-24 Inches

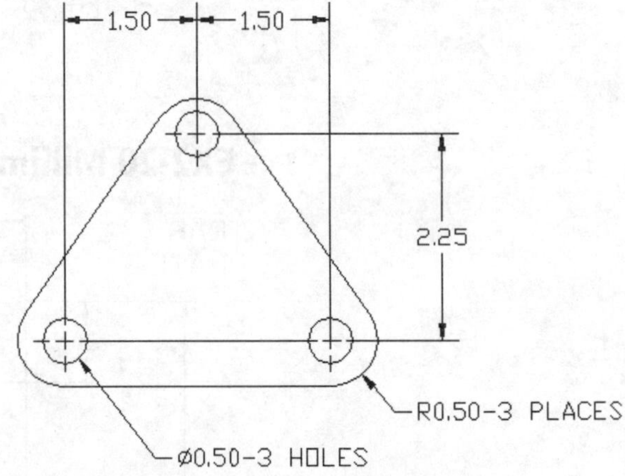

EX2-25 Millimeters

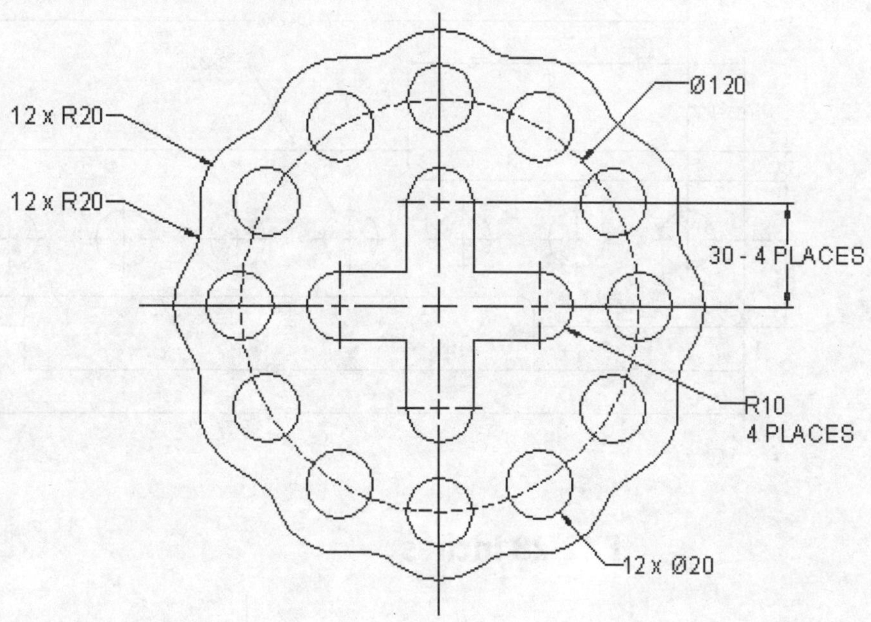

EX2-26 Millimeters

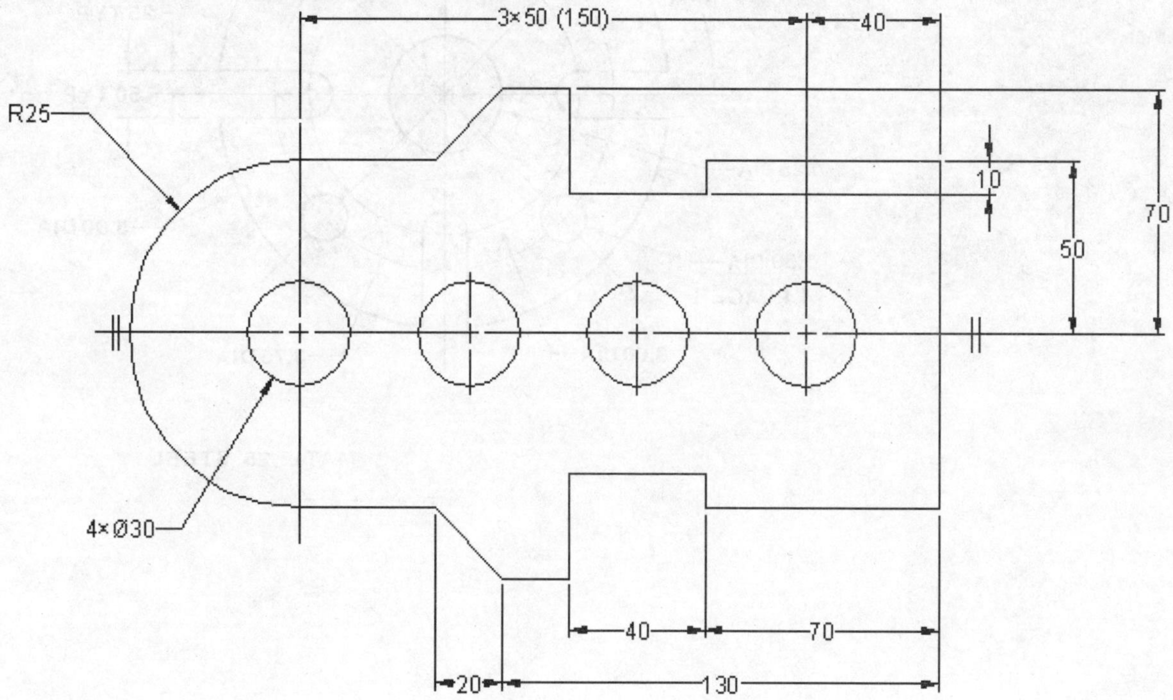

EX2-27 Millimeters

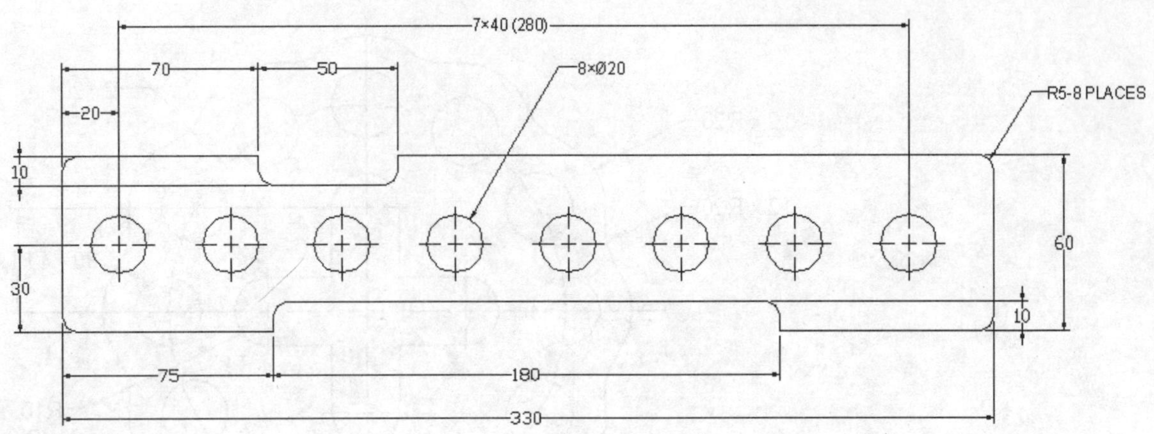

EX2-28 Inches

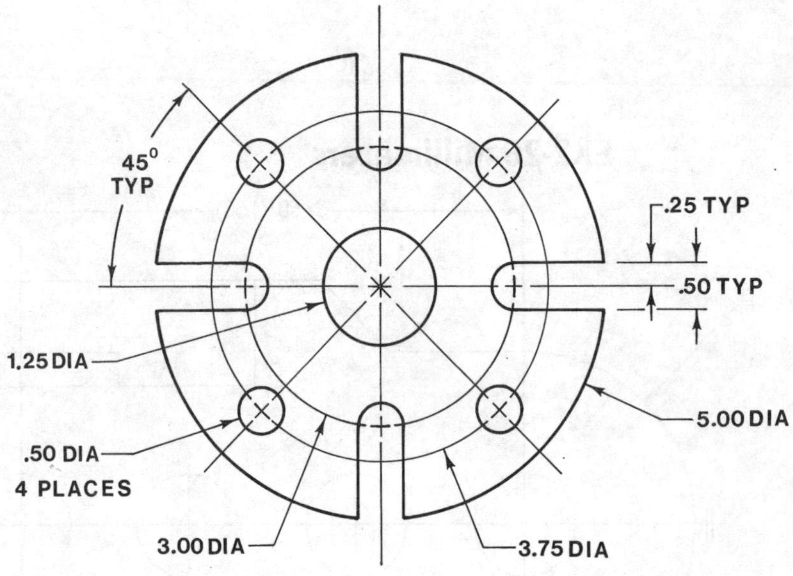

EX2-29 Millimeters

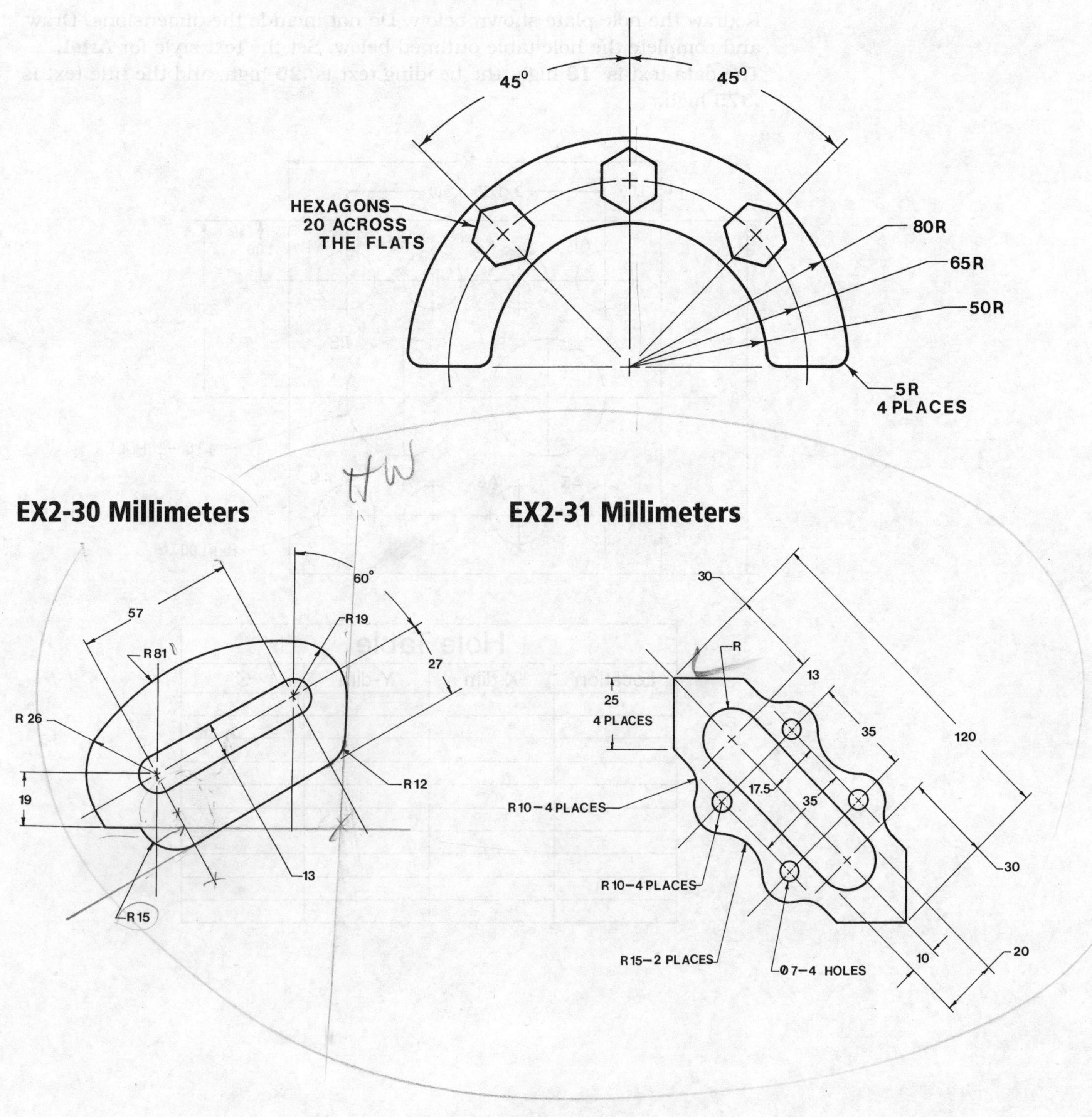

EX2-30 Millimeters

EX2-31 Millimeters

EX2-32 Inches

Redraw the hole plate shown below. Do not include the dimensions. Draw and complete the hole table outlined below. Set the text style for **Arial.** The data text is **.18** high, the heading text is **.25** high, and the title text is **.375** high.

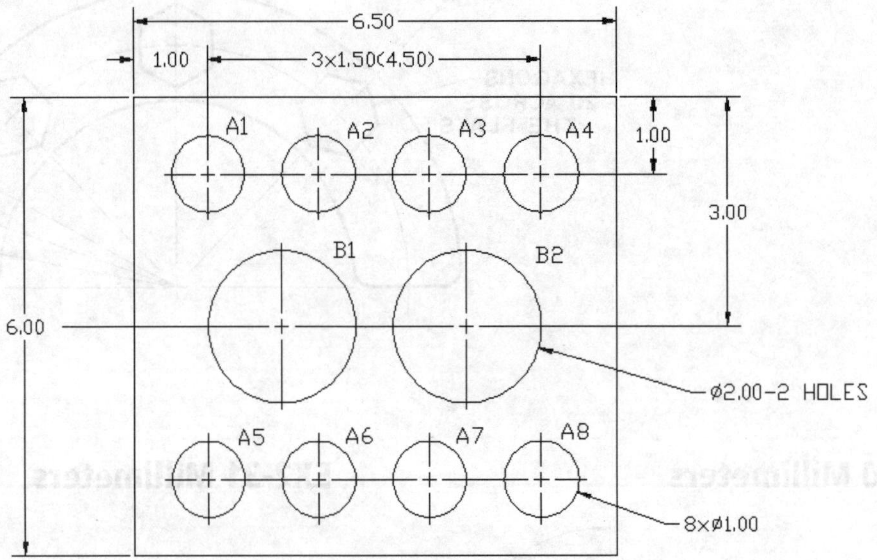

Hole Table			
Location	X-dim	Y-dim	Ø
A1			

EX2-33 Millimeters

Redraw the Hole Plate shown below. Do not include the dimensions. Draw and complete the hole table outlined below. Set the text style for **Arial.** The data text is **5** high, the heading text is **10** high, and the title text is **15** high.

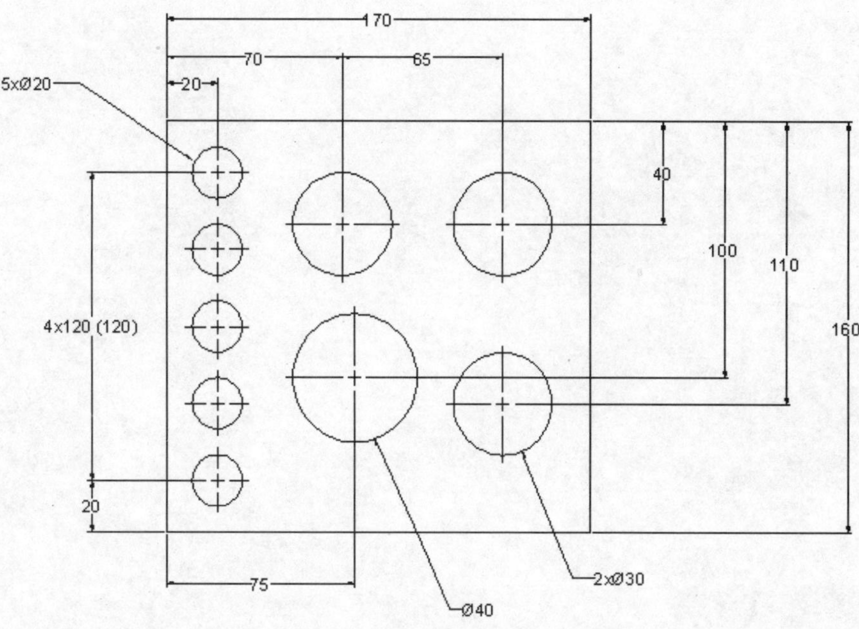

Hole Table			
Location	X-dim	Y-dim	Ø
A1			

← %%c

chapter three

Advanced Commands

3-1 Introduction

This chapter explains how to use some of the more advanced AutoCAD commands. Included are the **Osnap, Grips, Layer, Block,** and **Attribute** commands.

3-2 Osnap

The **Object Snap** command allows you to snap to entities on the drawing screen rather than just to points, as does the **Snap** command. **Osnap** can snap to the endpoint of a line, to the intersection of two lines, or to the center point of a circle, as well as to other items. The **Osnap** dialog box allows you to access the various **Osnap** commands.

To Access the Osnap Commands

1. Locate the cursor on the **Osnap** tool located at the bottom of the screen.
2. Right-click the mouse.

   A listing of **Osnap** commands will appear. See Figure 3-1.

Osnap can also be accessed by holding down the **<Ctrl>** key and pressing the right mouse button. This feature can be activated during any command sequence. A dialog box will appear on the screen listing the **Osnap** options. See Figure 3-2.

The **Osnap Settings** tool allows you to access the **Osnap Settings** dialog box. See Figure 3-2. The **Osnap Settings** dialog box can be used to turn an **Osnap** option on permanently; that is, the option will remain on until you turn it off. If the **Endpoint** option is on, the cursor will snap to the nearest endpoint every time a point selection is made. Turning an

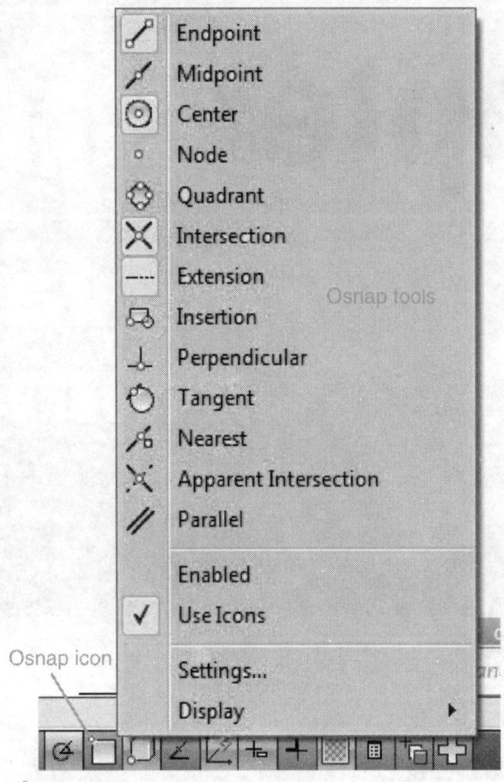

Figure 3-1

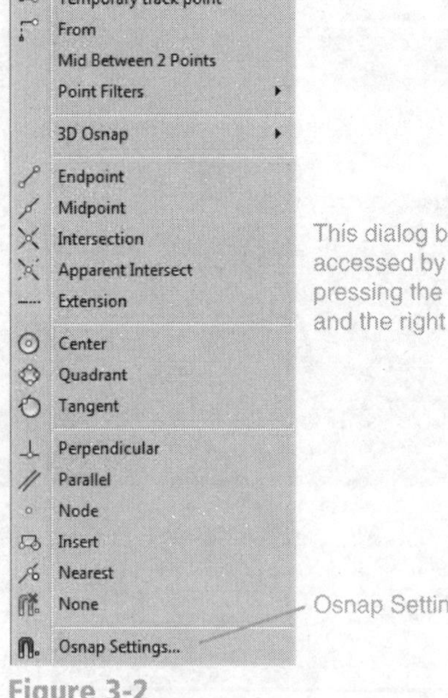

Figure 3-2

Osnap option on is very helpful when you know that you are going to select several points of the same type; however, in most cases, it is more practical to activate an **Osnap** option as needed by using the **Osnap** tool or the **Osnap** menu.

To Turn Osnap On

1. You can access the **Object Snap** dialog box in one of two ways: Right-click the **Object Snap** icon at the bottom of the screen and click the **Settings** option, or hold down the **<Ctrl>** key, right-click the mouse, and click the **Osnap Settings** option.

   The **Drafting Settings** dialog box will appear. See Figure 3-3.

2. Click the box to the left of the command that you wish to activate.

   A check mark will appear, indicating that the command is active.

3. Close the **Drafting Settings** dialog box.

   The **Options** box on the **Drafting Settings** dialog box allows you to access the **Options** dialog box, which can be used to change the color of the cursor box used to identify osnap points.

To Change the Size of the Osnap Cursor Box

The **Options** dialog box also contains an **Aperture Size** option. This option allows you to change the size of the rectangular box on the cursor. A larger box makes it easier to grab objects, but too large a box may grab more than one object or the wrong object.

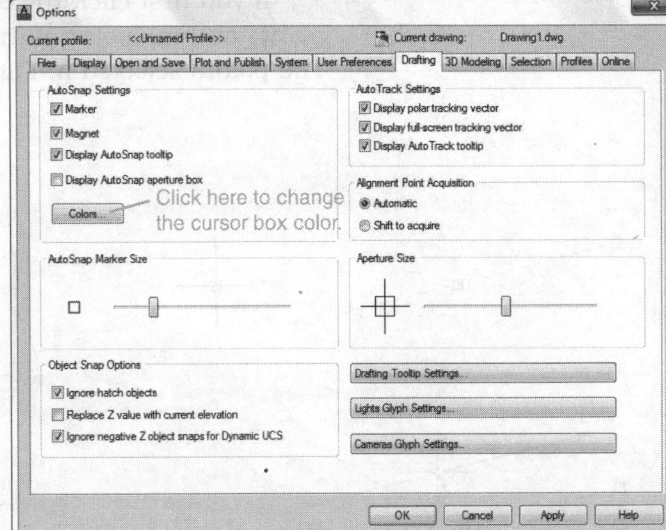

Figure 3-3

3-3 Osnap—Endpoint

The **Endpoint** option is used to snap to the endpoint of an existing entity. Figure 3-4 shows an existing line.

Figure 3-4

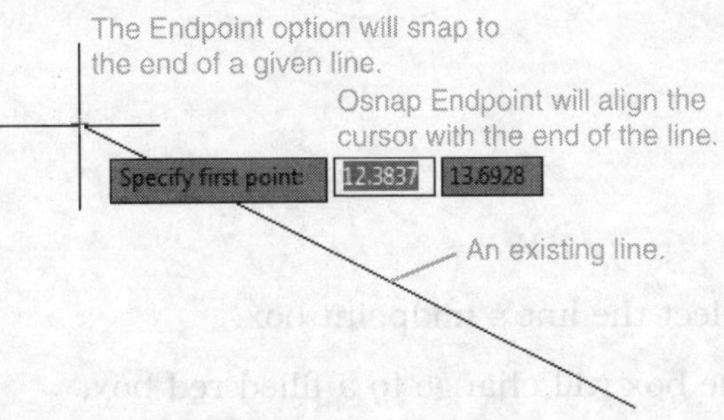

To Snap to the Endpoint of an Existing Line

1. Select the **Line** tool from the **Draw** panel.

   Command: _line Specify first point:

2. Select the **Endpoint** tool from the **Object Snap** dialog box.

   Specify next point or [Undo]: _endp of

Most of the **Osnap** options do not work independently, but in conjunction with other commands. In this example, the **Line** command must be activated first, then the **Osnap** command. Note that a box will appear around the endpoint of the line, indicating that the **Osnap Endpoint** command has selected the line's endpoint. The **Endpoint** command also works with arcs, mlines, and 3D applications.

3-4 Osnap—Snap From

The **Snap From** option allows you to grab the line directly, without having to enter another command. See Section 3-15, Grips.

If you first click the **Snap From** option and then select a line, the endpoints and midpoint of the line will be defined by boxes. See Figure 3-5. The points selected in Figure 3-5 are selected at random locations.

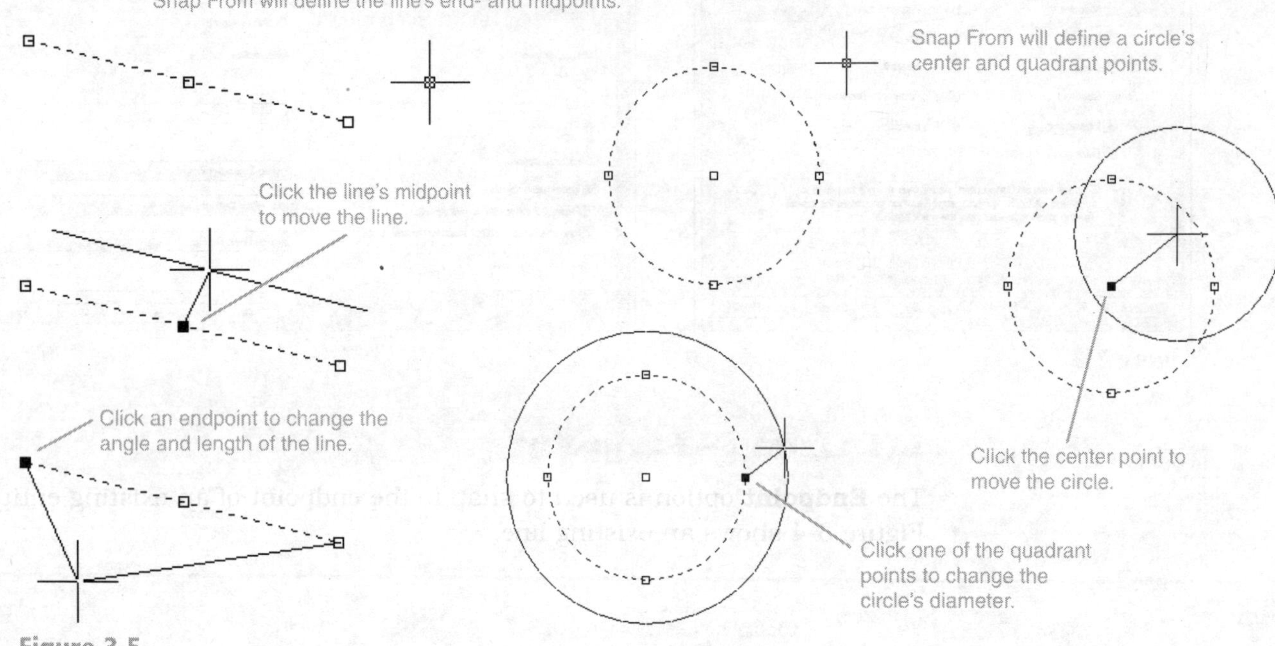

Figure 3-5

To Move a Line

1. Select the line's midpoint box.

   The box will change to a filled red box.

2. Move the cursor, and the line moves with the cursor.
3. Select a new location for the line.

To Change the Angle and Length of a Line

1. Select one of the designated endpoint boxes created from the **Snap From** option.

   The box will change to a filled red box.

2. Move the cursor, and the line's endpoint will move with the cursor.
3. Select a new angle and length for the line.

To Apply the Snap From Option to a Circle

1. Select the **Snap From** option, then the circle.

   The four quadrant points and the circle's midpoint are defined by boxes. See Figure 3-5.

2. Select the circle's center point to move the circle, or select one of the quadrant points to change the circle's diameter.

3-5 Osnap—Midpoint

The **Midpoint** option is used to snap to the midpoint of an existing entity. In the example presented in Figure 3-6, a circle is to be drawn with its center point at the midpoint of the line.

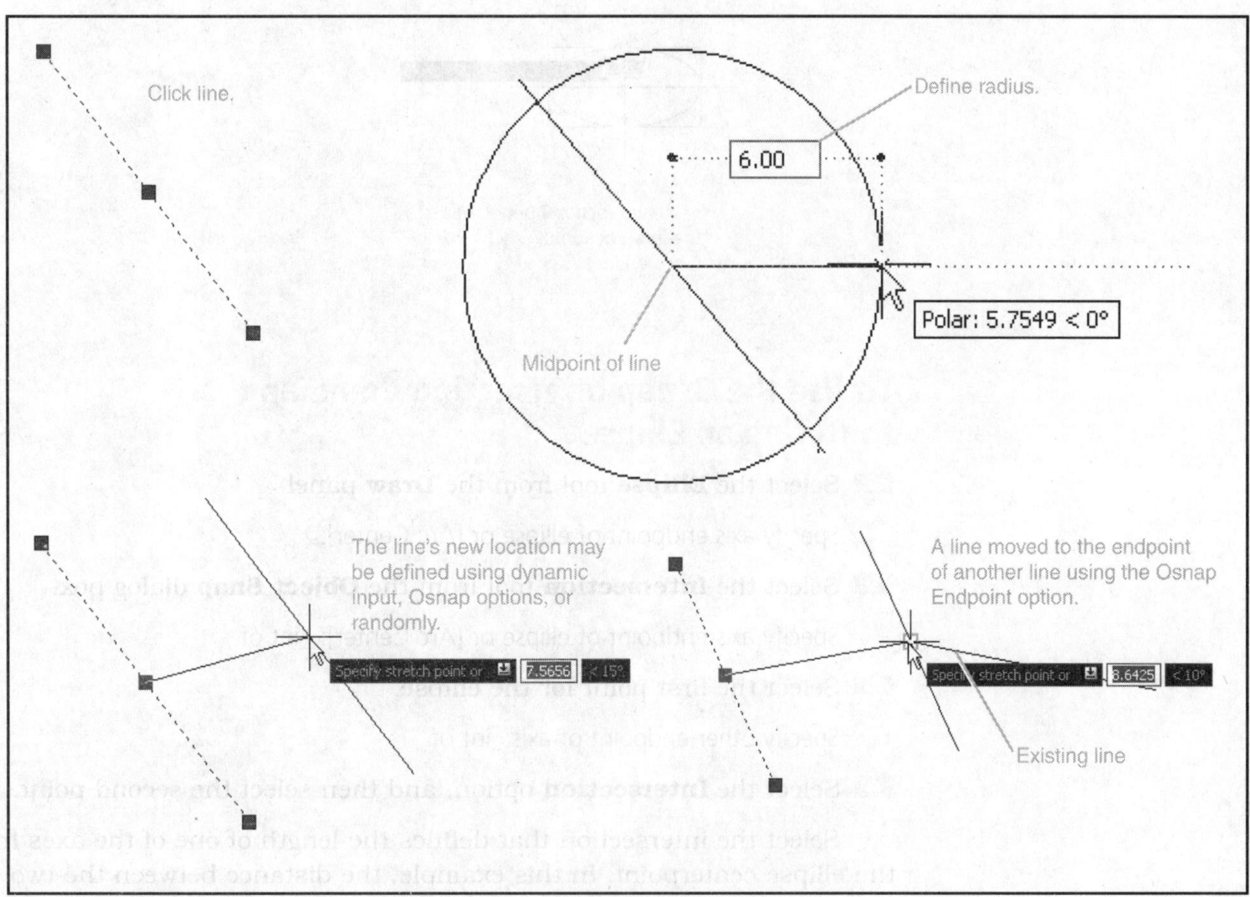

Figure 3-6

To Draw a Circle About the Midpoint of a Line

1. Select the **Circle** tool from the **Draw** panel.

   Command:_circle Specify center point for circle or [3P 2P Ttr (tan tan radius)]:

2. Select the **Snap to Midpoint** tool from the **Object Snap** dialog box.

   Command:_circle Specify center point for circle or [3P 2P Ttr (tan tan radius)]:_mid of

3. Select the line.

   Specify radius of circle or [Diameter]:

4. Select a radius value.

3-6 Osnap—Intersection

The **Intersection** option is used to snap to the intersection of two or more entities. Figure 3-7 shows a set of projection lines that are to be used to define an ellipse.

Figure 3-7

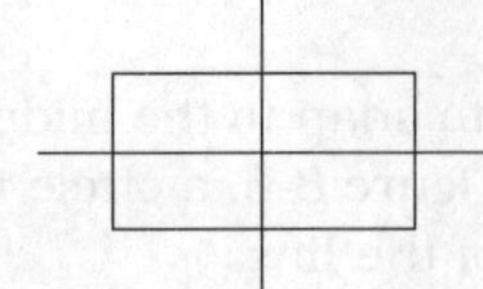

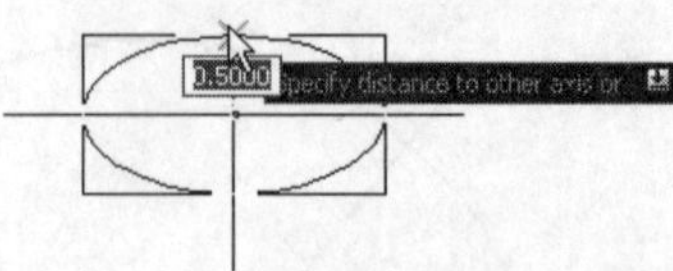

The Intersection option snaps to the intersection of any two or more entities.

To Use the Osnap Intersection Command to Define an Ellipse

1. Select the **Ellipse** tool from the **Draw** panel.

   Specify axis endpoint of ellipse or [Arc Center]:

2. Select the **Intersection** tool from the **Object Snap** dialog box.

   Specify axis endpoint of ellipse or [Arc Center]: _int of

3. Select the first point for the ellipse.

   Specify other endpoint of axis:_int of

4. Select the **Intersection** option, and then select the second point.

   Select the intersection that defines the length of one of the axes from the ellipse centerpoint. In this example, the distance between the two points selected equals the length of the major axis of the ellipse.

   Specify distance to other axis or [Rotation]:_int of

5. Select the **Intersection** tool from the **Object Snap** dialog box, and select the intersection that defines the other axis length.

3-7 Osnap—Apparent Intersection

The **Apparent Intersection** option is used to snap to an intersection that would be created if the two entities were extended to create an intersection. Figure 3-8 shows two lines that do not intersect, but if continued, would intersect.

To Draw a Circle Centered About an Apparent Intersection

1. Select the **Circle** tool from the **Draw** panel.

   Command: _circle Specify center point for circle or [3P 2P Ttr (tan tan radius)]:

2. Select the **Apparent Intersection** tool from the **Object Snap** dialog box.

   Command: _circle Specify center point for circle or [3P 2P Ttr (tan tan radius)]: _appint of

Figure 3-8

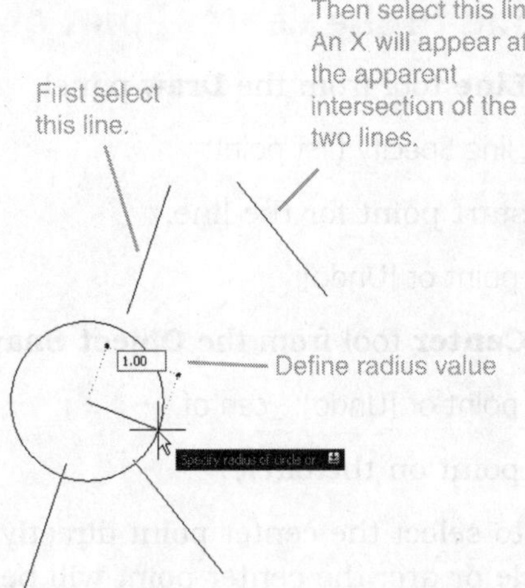

The circle's center point will be located on the apparent intersection of the two lines.

3 Select one of the lines.

Command: _circle Specify center point for circle or [3P 2P Ttr (tan tan radius)]: _appint of

4 Select the other line.

Specify radius of circle or [Diameter]:

5 Define a radius value for the circle.

3-8 Osnap—Center

The **Center** option is used to draw a line from a given point directly to the center point of a circle. See Figure 3-9.

Figure 3-9

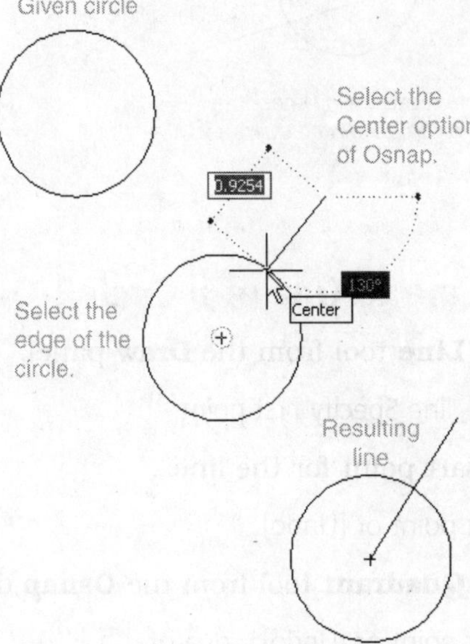

The Center option will snap to the center of a given circle.

To Draw a Line to the Center Point of a Circle

1. Select the **Line** tool from the **Draw** panel.

   Command: _line Specify first point:

2. Select the start point for the line.

   Specify next point or [Undo]:

3. Select the **Center** tool from the **Object Snap** dialog box.

   Specify next point or [Undo]: _cen of

4. Select any point on the circle.

   Do *not* try to select the center point directly. Select any point on the edge of the circle or arc; the center point will be calculated automatically.

3-9 Osnap—Quadrant

The **Quadrant** option is used to snap directly to one of the quadrant points of an arc or circle. Figure 3-10 shows the quadrant points for an arc and a circle.

Figure 3-10

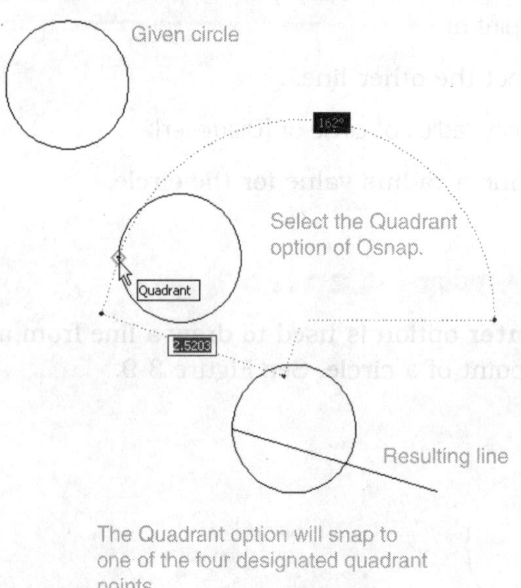

To Draw a Line to One of a Circle's Quadrant Points

1. Select the **Line** tool from the **Draw** panel.

   Command: _line Specify first point:

2. Select a start point for the line.

   Specify next point or [Undo]:

3. Select the **Quadrant** tool from the **Osnap** dialog box.

   Specify next point or [Undo]: _qua of

4. Select a point on the circle near the desired quadrant point.

3-10 Osnap—Perpendicular

The **Perpendicular** option is used to draw a line perpendicular to an existing entity. See Figure 3-11.

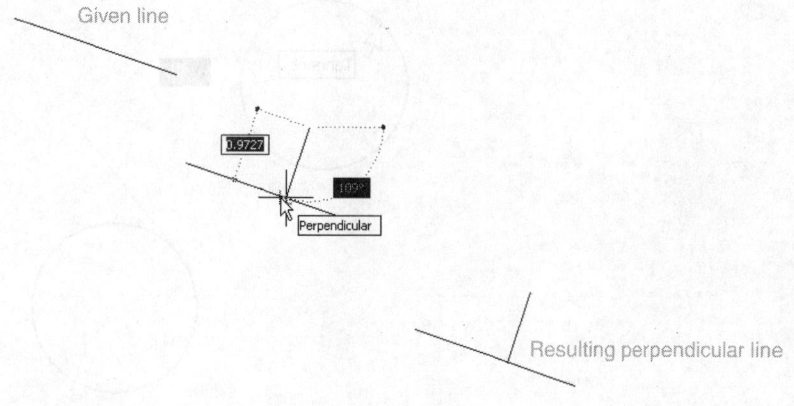

Figure 3-11

To Draw a Line Perpendicular to a Line

1. Select the **Line** tool from the **Draw** panel.

   Command: _line Specify first point:

2. Select a start point for the line.

   Specify next point or [Undo]:

3. Select the **Perpendicular** tool on the **Osnap** dialog box.

   Specify next point or [Undo]: _per to

4. Select the line or entity that will be perpendicular to the drawn line.

3-11 Osnap—Tangent

The **Tangent** option is used to draw lines tangent to existing circles and arcs. See Figure 3-12.

To Draw a Line Tangent to a Circle

1. Select the **Line** tool from the **Draw** panel.

   Command: _line Specify first point:

2. Select the start point for the line.

   Specify next point or [Undo]:

3. Select the **Tangent** tool from the **Osnap** dialog box.

   Specify next point or [Undo]: _tan to

4. Select the circle.

Figure 3-12

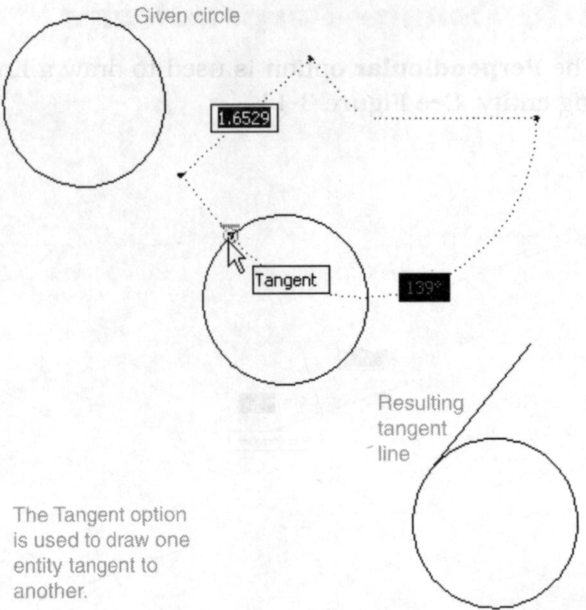

3-12 Osnap—Nearest

The **Nearest** option is used to snap to the nearest available point on an existing entity. See Figure 3-13.

Figure 3-13

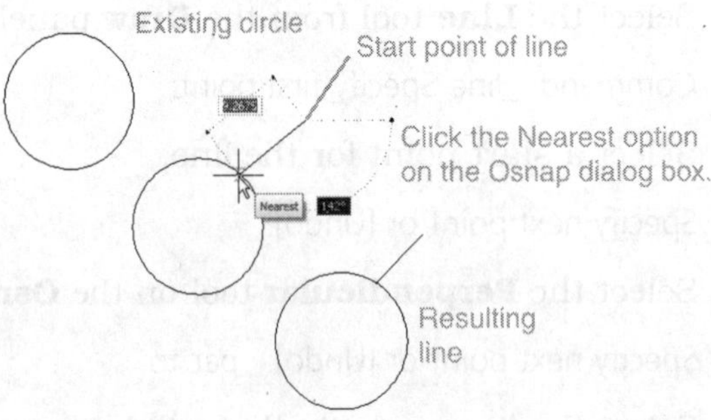

To Draw a Line from a Point to the Nearest Selected Point on an Existing Line

1. Select the **Line** tool from the **Draw** panel.

   Command: _line Specify first point:

2. Select a start point for the line.

   Specify next point or [Undo]:

3. Select the **Nearest** tool from the **Osnap** dialog box.

   Specify next point or [Undo]: _nea to

4. Select the existing line.

   The existing line need be only within the rectangular box on the cursor. The line endpoint will be snapped to the nearest available point on the line.

3-13 Sample Problem SP3-1

Redraw the object shown in Figure 3-14. Do *not* include dimensions. Use **Osnap** commands whenever possible.

1. Create a new drawing called **SP3-1.**

2. Drawing setup:

   Limits: lower left = **<0.0000,0.0000>**

   Limits: upper right = **297,210**

   Zoom All

   Grid = **10**

   Snap = **5**

3. Draw an **83.9** × **56.5** rectangle. Use dynamic input values to draw the rectangle's edge lines. See Figure 3-15.

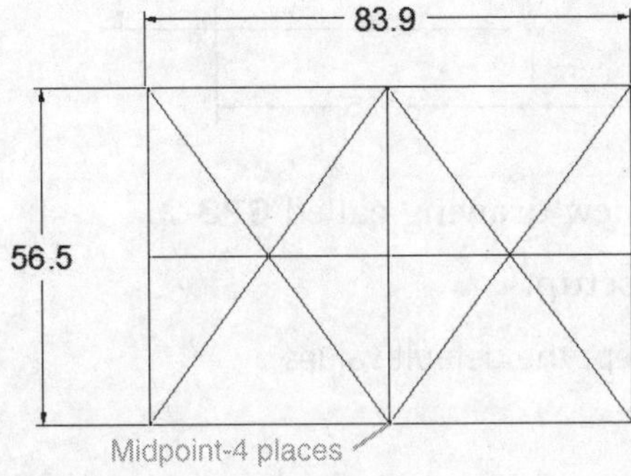

Figure 3-14

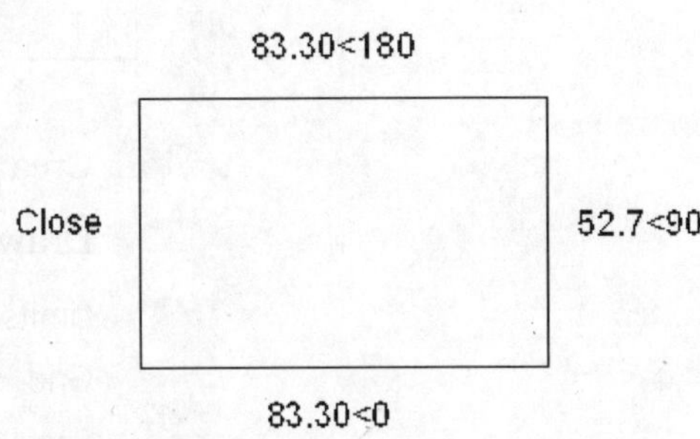

Figure 3-15

4. Draw line **A–B–C.** Point **A** is a grid snap point, so it may be selected directly. Point **B** is selected by using **Osnap Midpoint,** and point **C** is selected by using **Osnap Endpoint** (or **Intersection**). See Figure 3-16.

5. Draw line **D–E–F** by using **Endpoint, Midpoint,** and **Endpoint,** respectively.

6. Draw line **B–E** by using **Intersection.** See Figure 3-17.

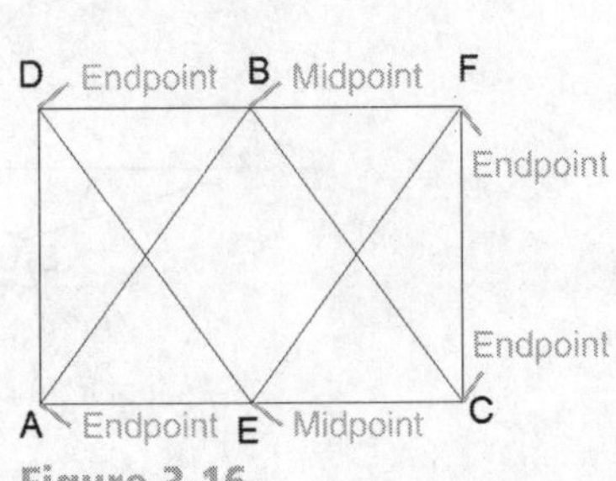

Figure 3-16

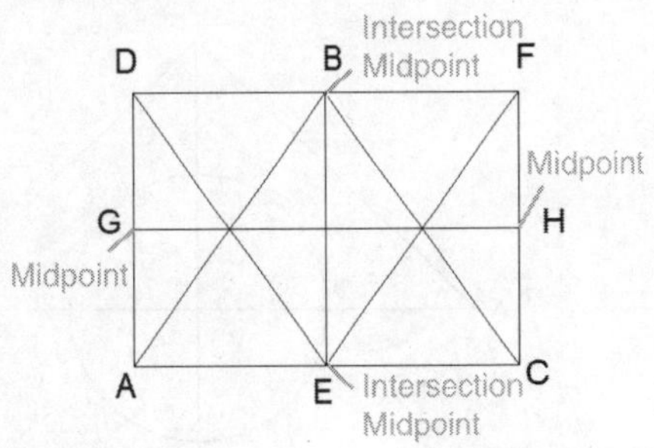

Figure 3-17

7. Draw line **G–H** by using **Midpoint.**

8. Save the drawing if desired.

3-14 Sample Problem—SP3-2

Redraw the object shown in Figure 3-18. Do not include dimensions.

Figure 3-18

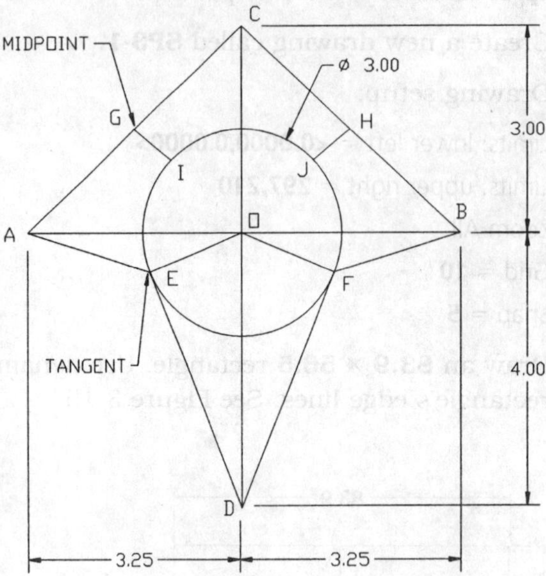

1. Create a new drawing called **SP3-2.**
2. Drawing setup:

   Limits: Accept the default values

   Grid = **.50**

   Snap = **.25**
3. Draw lines **A–B, C–D, A–C,** and **C–B.** The endpoint of each of these lines is located on a grid snap point, so the points may be selected directly.
4. Draw circle **O.** See Figure 3-19. Respond to the center point prompt by selecting **Intersection** from the **Osnap** pop-up menu.
5. Draw lines **G–I** and **H–J,** using **Midpoint** and **Nearest.** See Figure 3-20.

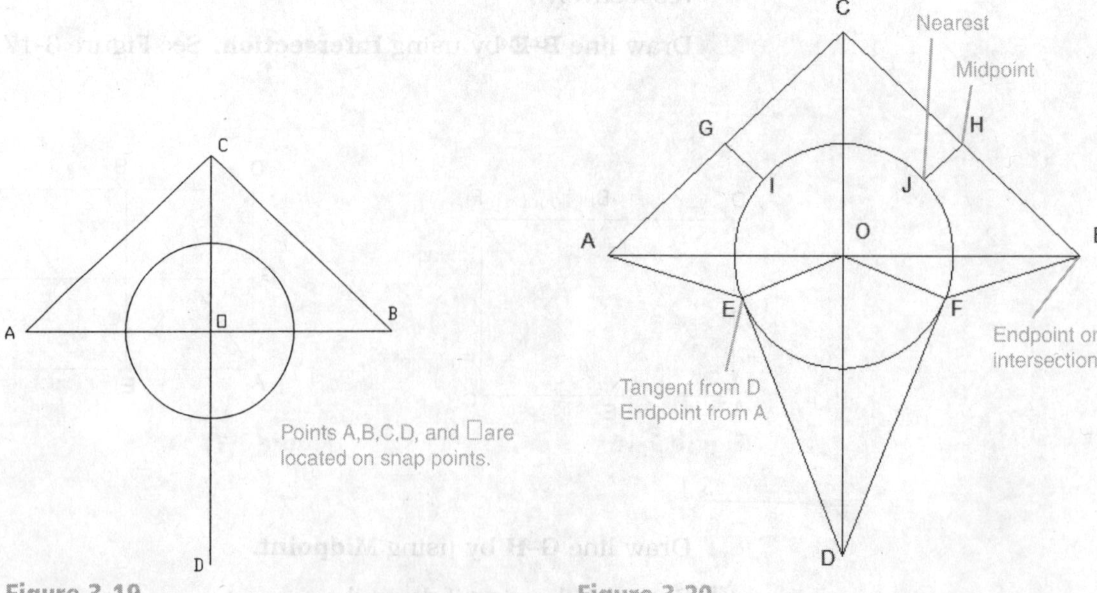

Figure 3-19

Figure 3-20

6. Draw lines **D–E** and **D–F**, using **Tangent.** Draw lines **A–E** and **A–F**, using **Endpoint.** Points **A, B,** and **D** are grid snap points and also are endpoints.
7. Save the drawing if desired.

3-15 Grips

The **Grips** function is used to quickly identify and lock onto convenient points on entities such as the endpoints of lines or the center point of a circle. Figure 3-21 shows some examples of grip points.

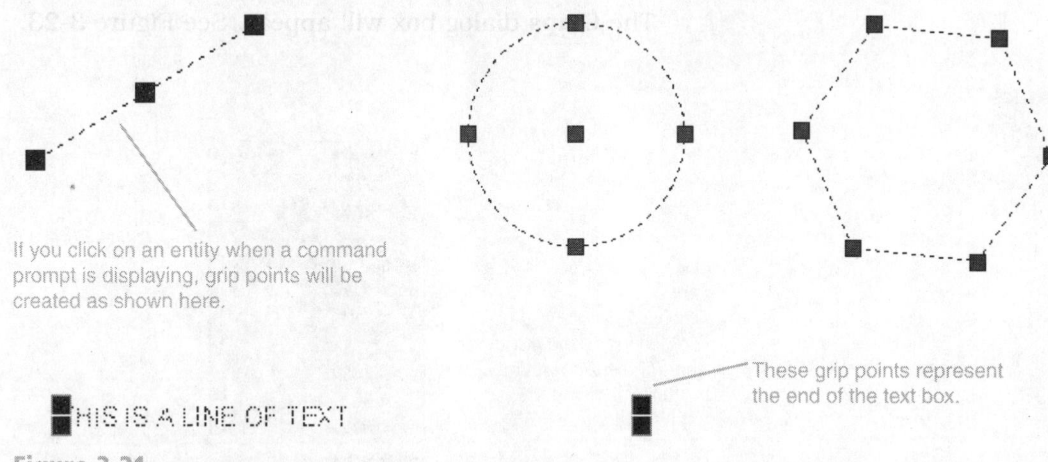

Figure 3-21

Grips are helpful when using some **Modify** commands. For example, if a line is to be rotated about its center point, a grip can be used to first identify the line's center point (pickbox) and then lock onto it as the center point (basepoint) for the rotation. The center point of a circle can be used to move the circle to a new location.

To Turn the Grips Function Off

By default, the **Grips** command is automatically on. The **Grips** command may be turned off as follows:

1. Type **Grips** in response to a command prompt.

   Enter new value for GRIPS <1>:

   There are two possible values: 1 and 0. The **1** value turns the **Grips** command on. The **0** value turns the **Grips** command off. See Figure 3-22.

2. Type **0;** press **Enter.**

   The **Grips** command is now off.

Figure 3-22

THE DEFAULT GRIPS VALUE IS 1.

1 = GRIPS ON

0 = GRIPS OFF

To Access the Grips Dialog Box

1 Grip an existing line; that is, place the cursor on the line, and press the left mouse button.

A line is gripped when a command prompt is displayed and no other command sequence is active.

2 Click on one of the grip points.

In this example, the lower endpoint was selected.
<Stretch to point>/Basepoint/Copy/Undo/eXit:

3 Press the right mouse button.

The **Grips** dialog box will appear. See Figure 3-23.

Figure 3-23

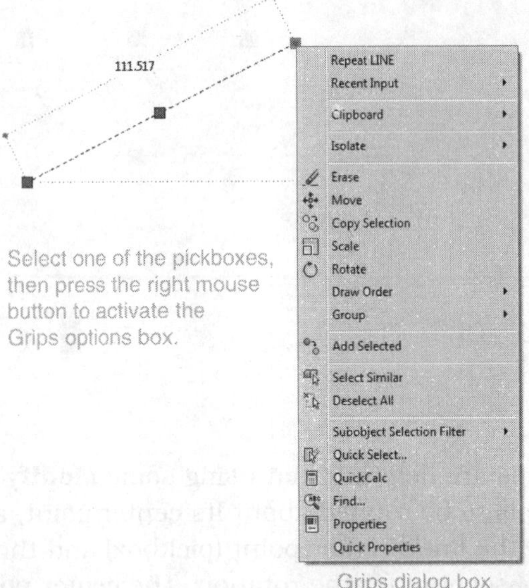

3-16 Grips—Extend

To Extend the Length of a Line (See Figure 3-24.)

Given a line, extend it 1.25 inches.

1 Draw an angled line as shown; then draw a circle of radius **1.25** centered on one of the line's endpoints.

Figure 3-24

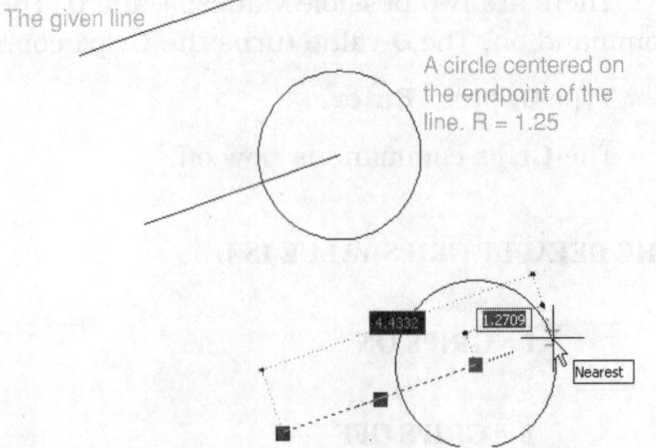

2. Press the **<Esc>** key to ensure a command prompt.
3. Select the line.

Blue pickboxes should appear at the two endpoints and at the midpoint.

4. Select the endpoint that also serves as the circle's center point.

The blue pickbox should change to a solid-red square box.

5. Press the right mouse button, and select the **Stretch** option from the **Grips** menu.

STRETCH

Specify stretch point or [Base point Copy Undo eXit]:

Stretch the endpoint of the line to the edge of the 1.25 circle by accessing the **Osnap** menu (press the **<Ctrl>** key and right mouse button) and selecting the **Nearest** option.

6. Select a point on the circle that aligns the line through the three grip points; then press the left button.
7. Erase the circle.

3-17 Grips—Move

To Move an Object by Using Grips (See Figure 3-25.)

Move the given circle to a new location on the drawing.

1. Press the **<Esc>** key to ensure a command prompt.
2. Select any point on the circle.

Figure 3-25

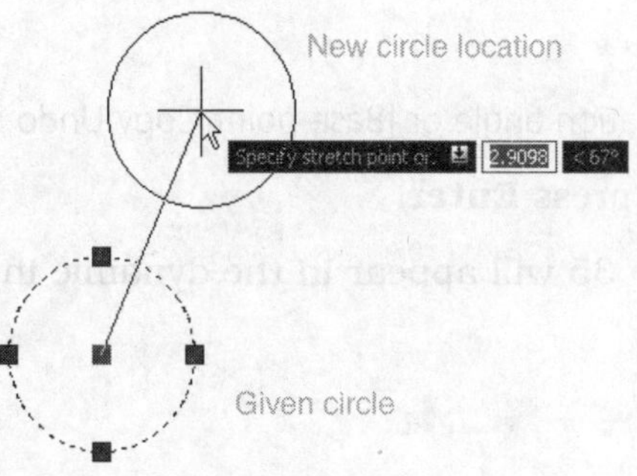

Blue pickboxes should appear at circle **O**'s center point and at each of the quadrant points.

3. Select the circle's center point.

The center point pickbox should change to a solid-red square box.

STRETCH

Specify stretch point or [Base_point Copy Undo eXit]:

4. Move the circle to a new location, and press the left mouse button.

The circle's new location can be located by using dynamic input.

3-18 Grips—Rotate

To Rotate an Object by Using Grips (See Figure 3-26.)

Given a line, rotate it 35° about its midpoint.

1. Press the **<Esc>** key to ensure a command prompt.
2. Select the line.

Figure 3-26

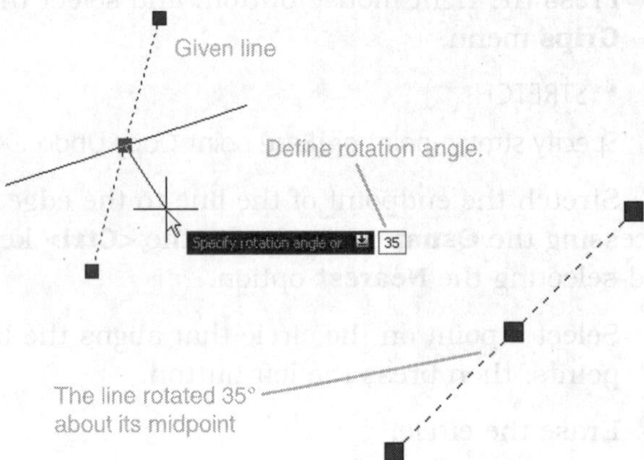

Blue pickboxes should appear at the line's two endpoints and at its midpoint.

3. Select the line's midpoint.

The blue pickbox at the midpoint should change to a solid-red square box.

4. Press the right mouse button; then select **Rotate** from the **Grips** dialog box.

ROTATE

Specify rotation angle or [Base point Copy Undo eXit]:

5. Type **35;** press **Enter.**

The value 35 will appear in the dynamic input box.

3-19 Grips—Scale

To Change the Scale of an Object (See Figure 3-27.)

Given an object, reduce it to half of its original size.

1. Press the **<Esc>** key to ensure a command prompt.
2. Select the object by first windowing it, then pressing the left mouse button.

Blue pickboxes should appear all around the object.

3. Select any one of the pickboxes.

The selected pickbox should change to a solid-red square box.

4. Press the right mouse button to activate the **Grips** options box.

Figure 3-27

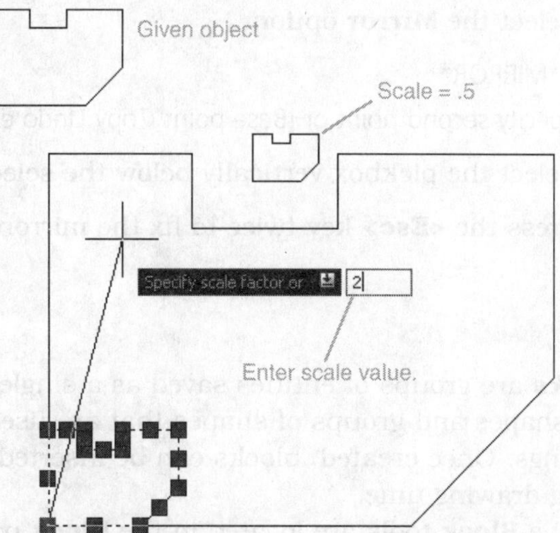

5 Select **Scale** from the menu.

SCALE

Specify scale factor or [Base point Copy Undo Reference eXit]:

6 Type **.5**; press **Enter.**

Figure 3-27 also shows the same object scaled to twice its original size—that is, a scale factor of 2.

3-20 Grips—Mirror

To Mirror an Object (See Figure 3-28.)

Given an object, draw a mirror image of the object.

1 Press the **<Esc>** key to ensure a command prompt.

2 Window the object; then press the left mouse button.

Blue pickboxes should appear at each corner intersection of the hexagon.

3 Select the upper right pickbox.

The selected pickbox should change to a solid-red square box.

4 Press the right mouse button to activate the **Grips** options box.

Figure 3-28

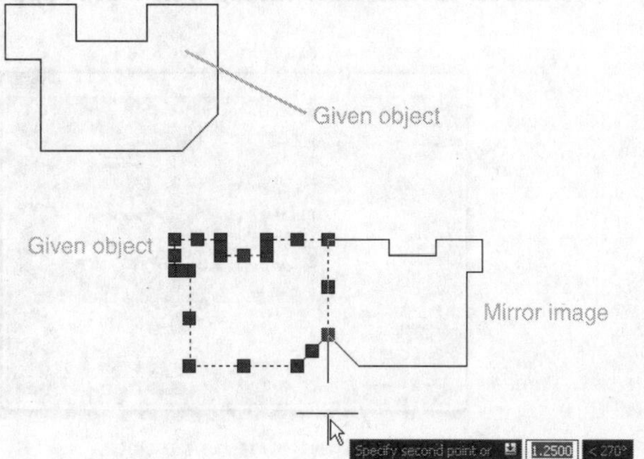

5 Select the **Mirror** option.

MIRROR

Specify second point or [Base point Copy Undo eXit]:

6 Select the pickbox vertically below the selected upper-right pickbox.

7 Press the **<Esc>** key twice to fix the mirrored object.

3-21 Blocks

Blocks are groups of entities saved as a single unit. Blocks are used to save shapes and groups of shapes that are used frequently when creating drawings. Once created, blocks can be inserted into the drawings, thereby saving drawing time.

The **Block** tools are located in the **Block** panel under the **Home** tab. Blocks are first created by using the **Block** tool. They are then saved and, when needed, inserted into a drawing by use of the **Insert** tool. Blocks can be edited after they are created. See Figure 3-29.

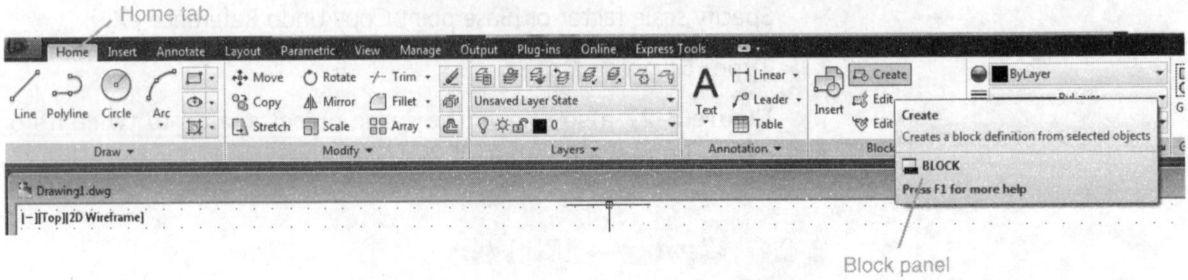

Figure 3-29

To Create a Block

Figure 3-30 shows an object. A block can be made from this existing drawing as follows:

1 Select the **Create** tool from the **Block** panel.

The **Block Definition** dialog box appears. See Figure 3-30.

2 Click the **Select objects** box.

Select objects:

3 Window the object; press **Enter.**

The **Block Definition** dialog box will reappear.

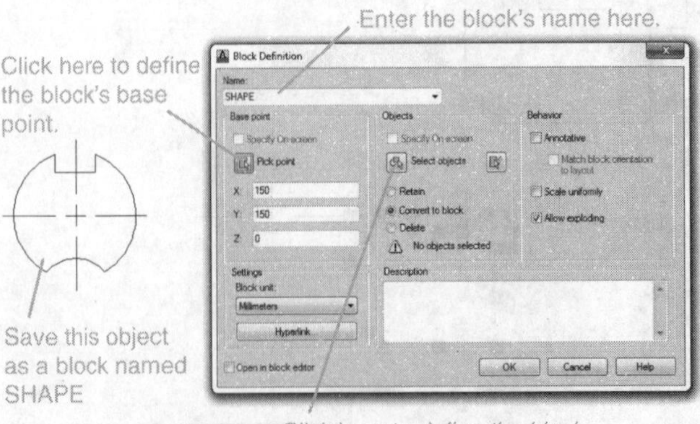

Figure 3-30

4 Type **SHAPE** in the **Name** box.

Block names may contain up to 31 characters.

5 Click the **Pick point** box.

6 Define the centerline insertion as the base point for the block.

The **Block Definition** dialog box will reappear. **Osnap** may be used to locate an insertion point. The values listed in the **Block Definition** dialog box are XYZ values relative to the current origin.

The insertion base point will be a point on the object that will align with the screen cursor during the block insertion process.

In this example, the **Osnap** tool was used to define the intersection of the shape's centerlines as the insertion point.

7 Select the **OK** box.

To Insert a Block

1 Select **Insert** from the **Block** panel.

The **Insert** dialog box will appear. See Figure 3-31.

2 Select the **Name** box.

A cascade menu will appear. See Figure 3-32.

3 Select **SHAPE.**

The word **SHAPE** will appear in the **Name** box.

4 Select **OK.**

The **Insert** dialog box will reappear with the word **SHAPE** in the **Name** box.

5 Select **OK.**

The **SHAPE** block will appear on the screen, with its insertion point aligned with the cursor. The shape will move as you move the crosshairs.

Specify insertion point or [Basepoint Scale X Y Z Rotate]:

6 Select an insertion point for the shape.

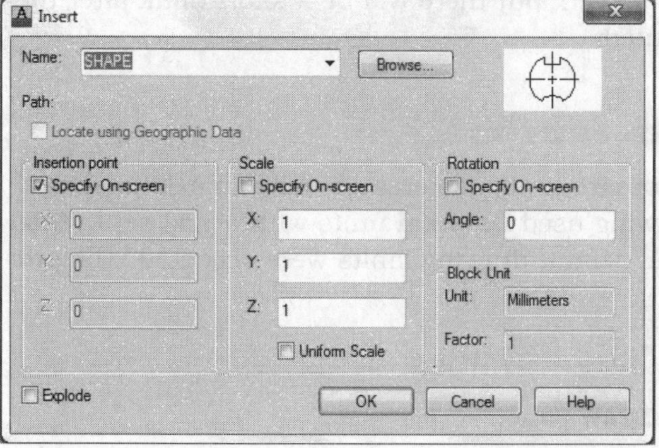

Figure 3-31

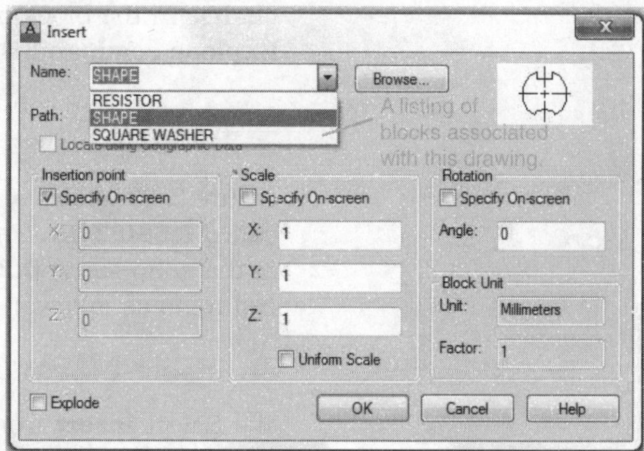

Figure 3-32

The default scale factor is 1. This means that if you accept the default value by pressing **Enter,** the shape will be redrawn at its original size. The shape of the object may be changed by using the options available at the **Insert** prompt.

To Change the Scale of a Block

1. Select **Insert** from the **Block** panel.
2. Select the **SHAPE** block.

   Specify insertion point or [Basepoint Scale X Y Z Rotate]:
3. Type **S;** press **Enter.**

   Specify scale factor for XYZ axes:
4. Type **2;** press **Enter.**

   Specify insertion point:
5. Select a point.

The **Rotation** option is used to rotate a block about its insertion point. AutoCAD assumes that a horizontal line to the right of the insertion point is 0° and that counterclockwise is the positive angular direction.

The block is now part of the drawing; however, the block in its present form may not be edited. Blocks are treated as a single entity and not as individual lines. You can verify this by trying to erase any one of the lines in the block. The entire object will be erased. The object can be returned to the screen by clicking the **Undo** tool. A block must first be exploded before it can be edited.

To Explode a Block

1. Select the **Explode** tool from the **Modify** panel.

   Command: _explode

   Select objects:
2. Window the entire object.

   Select objects:
3. Press **Enter.**

The object is now exploded and can be edited. There is no visible change in the block on the screen, but there will be a short blink after the **Explode** command is executed.

3-22 Working with Blocks

Figure 3-33 shows a resistor circuit. It was created from an existing block called **RESISTOR**. The drawing used **Decimal** units with a grid set to **0.5** and a snap set to **0.25.** The default drawing limits were accepted. The procedure is as follows:

To Insert Blocks at Different Angles

1. Select **Insert** from the **Draw** panel.

   The **Insert** dialog box will appear.

2 Select the cascade menu on the right side of the **Name** box.

3 Figure 3-34 shows **RESISTOR** in the **Name** box. Select the **RESISTOR** block.

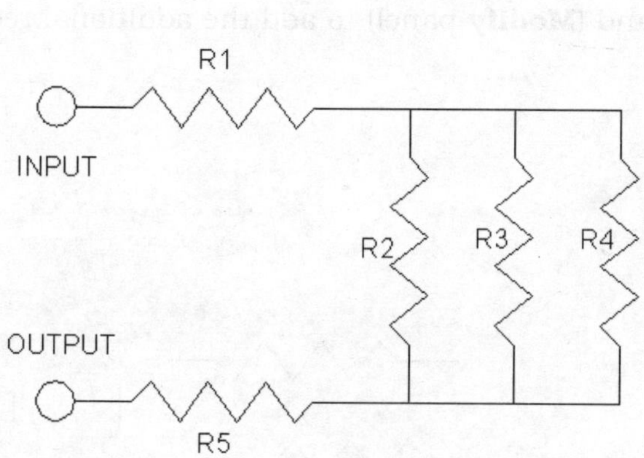

Figure 3-33

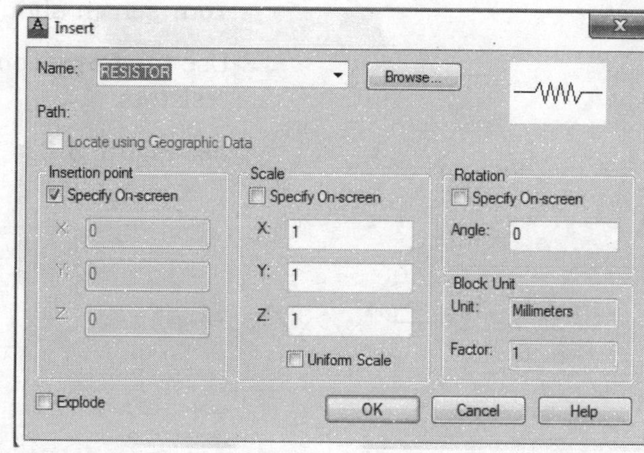

Figure 3-34

4 Select **OK** to return to the drawing screen.

The **RESISTOR** block will appear attached to the crosshairs at the predefined insertion point. See Figure 3-35.

Figure 3-35

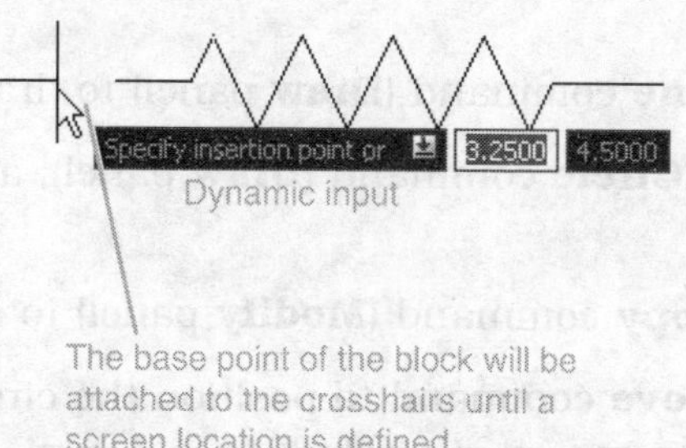

The resistor is too large for the drawing, so a reduced scale will be used to generate the appropriate size.

Specify insertion point or [Basepoint Scale X Y Z Rotate]:

5 Type **S;** press **Enter.**

Specify scale factor for XYZ axes:

6 Type **0.50;** press **Enter.**

Specify insertion point:

Locate the resistor on the screen.

7 Press the right mouse button, and select the **Repeat Insert** option.

8 Select the **RESISTOR** block again, and set the X, Y, Z scale factors for **.50.**

Specify insertion point or [Scale X Y Z Rotate PScale PX PY PZ PRotate]:

9 Type **R;** press **Enter.**

Specify rotation angle:

10. Type **90;** press **Enter.**

Specify insertion point:

11. Select an insertion point as shown in Figure 3-36.

Your screen should look like Figure 3-36.

12. Use the **Copy** command (**Modify** panel) to add the additional required resistors.

See Figure 3-37.

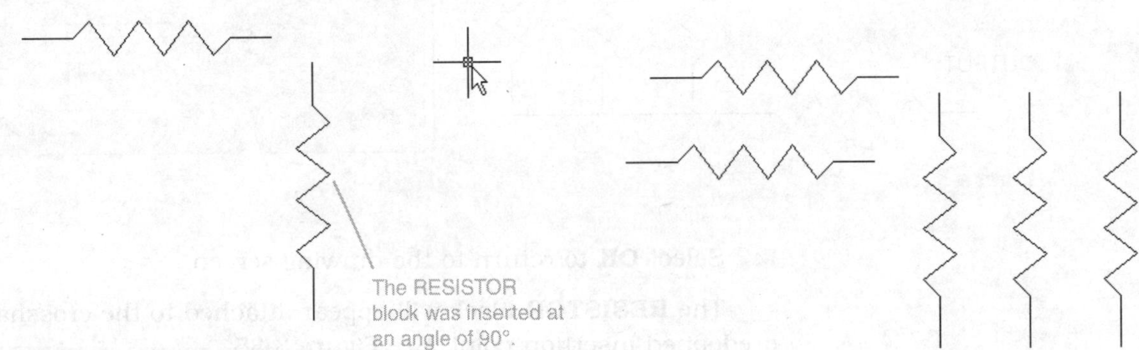

Figure 3-36

Figure 3-37

13. Use the **Line** command (**Draw** panel) to draw the required lines.

14. Select the **Circle** command (**Draw** panel), and draw a circle of diameter **0.250.**

15. Use the **Copy** command (**Modify** panel) to create a second circle.

16. Use the **Move** command to position the circles so that they touch the edges of the two open circles.

17. Use the **Dtext** command to add the appropriate text.

The drawing should now look like the diagram presented in Figure 3-33.

To Insert Blocks with Different Scale Factors

Figure 3-38 shows four different-sized threads, all created from the same block. The block labeled A used the default scale factor of 1, so it is exactly the same size as the original drawing used to create the block. The block labeled B was created with an X scale factor equal to 1, and a Y scale factor equal to 2. The procedure is as follows:

1. Select the **Insert** tool from the **Draw** panel.

2. Select the **THREAD** block.

The **THREAD** block is not an AutoCAD creation. **THREAD** was created specifically for this example.

Specify insertion point or [Scale X Y Z Rotate PScale PX PY PZ PRotate]:

3. Type **X;** press **Enter.**

Specify X scale factor:

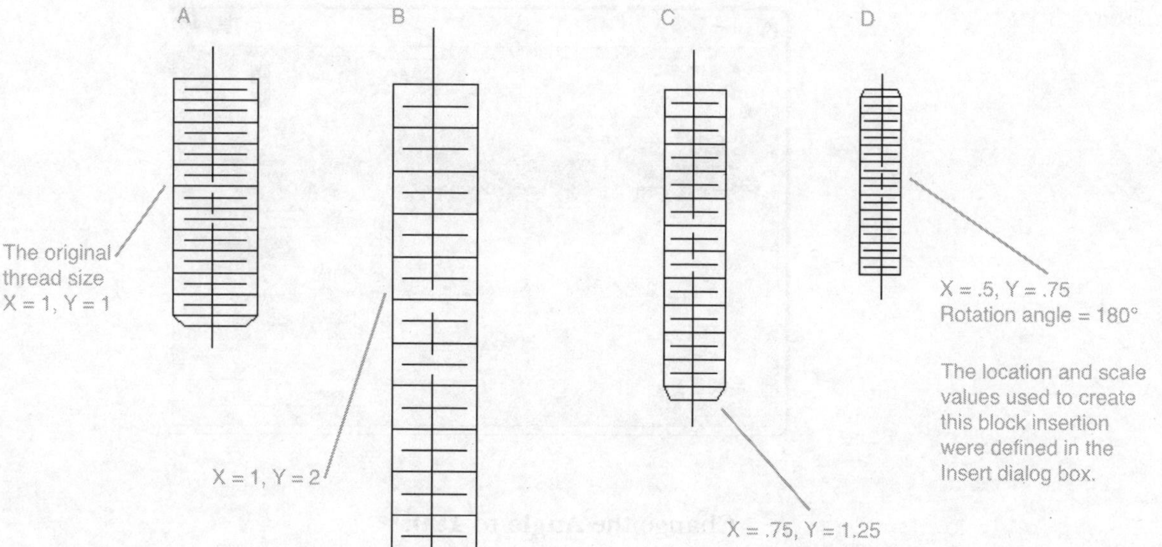

Figure 3-38

4. Type **1;** press **Enter.**

   Specify insertion point:

5. Type **Y;** press **Enter.**

   Specify Y scale factor:

6. Type **2;** press **Enter.**

   Specify insertion point:

7. Specify a point.

   The thread labeled C has an X scale factor of 0.75 and a Y scale factor of 1.25. The thread labeled D has an X scale factor of 0.5, a Y scale factor of 0.75, and a rotation angle of 180°.

To Use the Insert Dialog Box to Change the Shape of a Block

The D thread scale factors and rotation angle were defined through the **Insert** dialog box. The procedure is as follows:

1. Select the **Insert** tool.

   The **Insert** dialog box will appear. See Figure 3-39.

2. Click the box to the left of the words **Specify On-screen.**

   The click should remove the checkmark in the box, indicating that the option has been turned off. When the checkmark has been removed, the options labeled **Insertion Point, Scale,** and **Rotation** should change from gray to black in the dialog box.

3. Place the cursor arrow inside the **X Scale** box, backspace to remove the existing value, and type **.50.**

4. Change the **Y Scale** factor to **.75.**

Figure 3-39

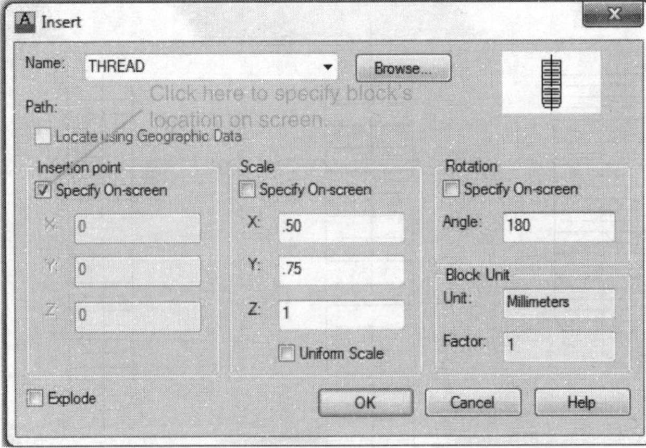

5 Change the **Angle** to **180.**

See Figure 3-39. The insertion point was defined on screen.

To Combine Blocks

Figure 3-40 shows a hex head screw that was created from two blocks. The threaded portion of the screw was created first; then the head portion was added. Note in Figure 3-40 that when the hex head block was created, the insertion point was deliberately selected so that it could easily be aligned with the centerline and the top surface of the thread block.

Figure 3-40

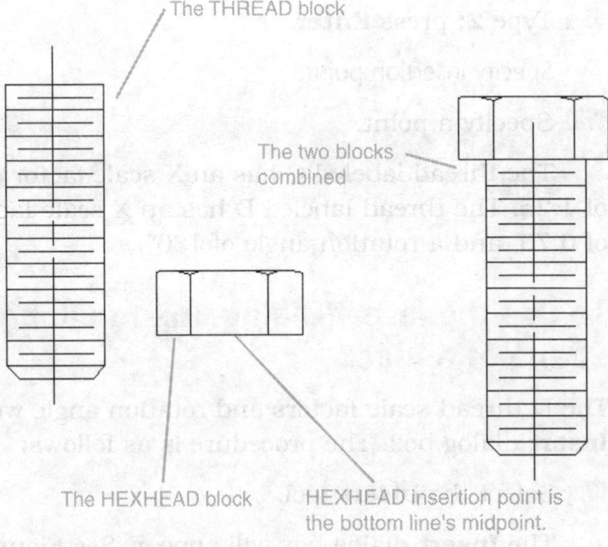

3-23 Wblock

Wblocks are blocks that can be entered into any drawing. When a block is created, it is unique to the drawing on which it was defined. This means that if you create a block on a drawing, then save and exit the drawing, the block is saved with the drawing, but cannot be used on another drawing. If you start a new drawing, the saved block will not be available.

Any block can be defined and saved, however, as a wblock. Wblocks are saved as individual drawing files and can be inserted into any drawing.

To Create a Wblock

This section shows how to create a wblock for the block called **SHAPE-1** shown in Figure 3-30. A wblock may be created directly from an object shown on the screen.

1. Open the **SHAPE** drawing.
2. At a command prompt, type **Wblock;** press **Enter**.

The **Write Block** dialog box appears. See Figure 3-41. There is no Wblock icon.

Ensure that the **Objects** radio button is on.

Figure 3-41

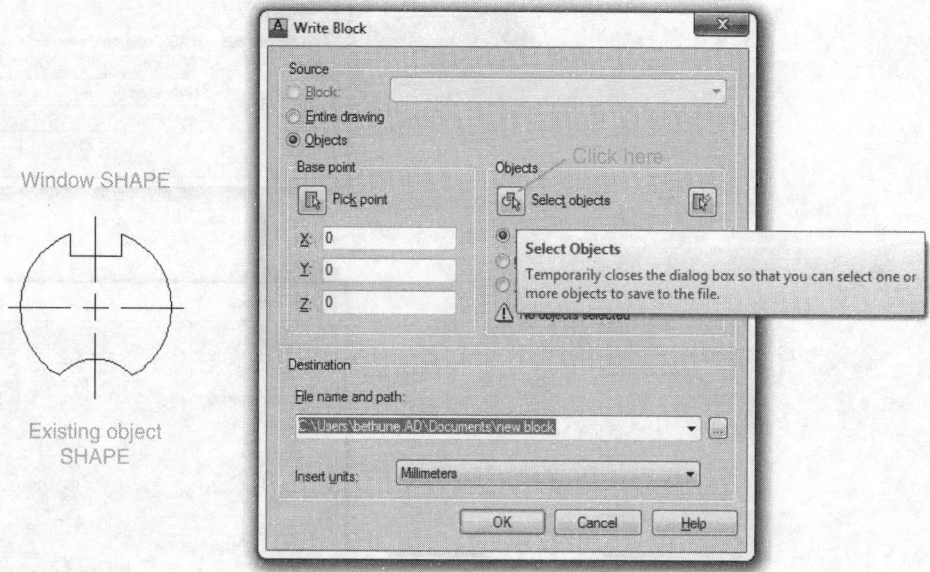

3. Click the **Select objects** box.

The **Write Block** dialog box will vanish.

4. Select the **SHAPE;** press **Enter**.
5. Click the **Pick point** box.

See Figure 3-42.

6. Select the base point for the **Wblock.**
7. Enter a new file name for the Wblock.

In this example, the name **SHAPE-1** was entered. See Figure 3-43.

8. Click **OK.**

To Verify that a Wblock Has Been Created

1. Select the **Insert** tool from the **Block** panel.

The **Insert** dialog box will appear. See Figure 3-44.

2. Click the **Browse** box.

The **Select Drawing File** dialog box will appear.

3. Scroll down the file listing to locate the **SHAPE-1** file; then click it.

Figure 3-42

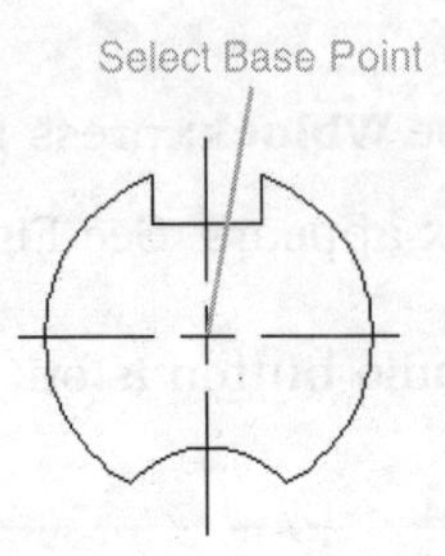

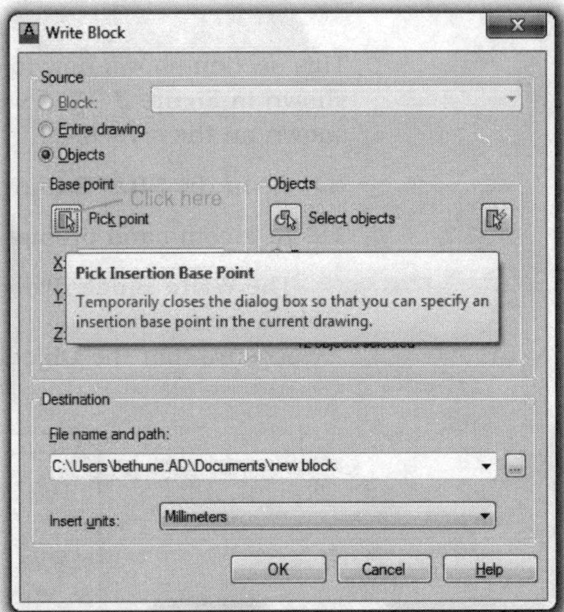

Figure 3-43

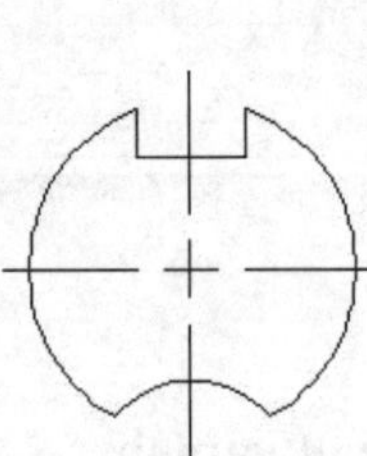

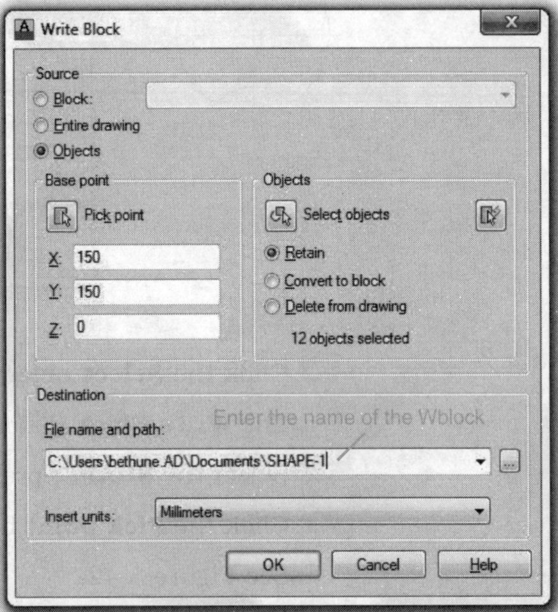

Figure 3-44

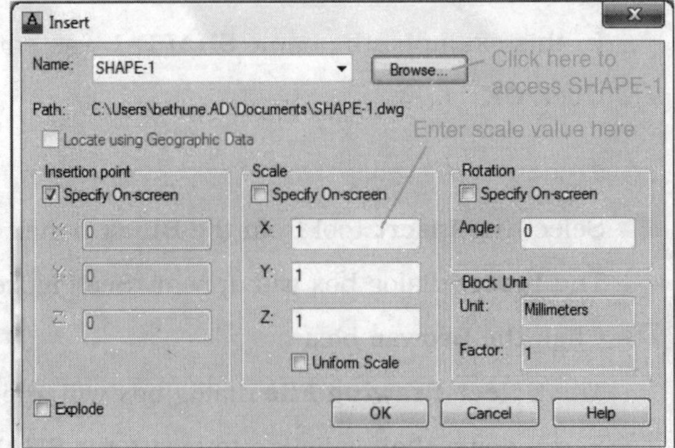

4 Click the **Open** box, then the **OK** box.

The **Insert** dialog box will reappear.

To Change the Size of a Wblock

1 Select the **Insert** tool from the **Draw** panel.

The **Insert** dialog box will appear.

2 Select the **Browse** option.

3 Select the **SHAPE-1** wblock file, and then click the **Open** box.

The **Insert** dialog box will appear.

4 Set the **Scale** values.

In this example, the *x* and *y* values were set at **2.**

5 Select **OK.**

See Figure 3-45.

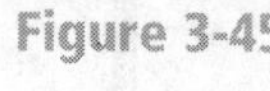

Figure 3-45

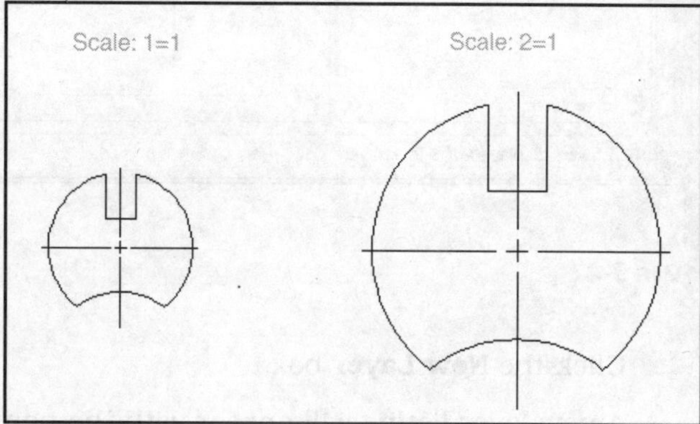

3-24 Layers

A ***layer*** is like a clear piece of paper that you can lay directly over the drawing. You can draw on the layer and see through it to the original drawing. Layers can be made invisible, and information can be transferred between layers.

In the example shown, a series of layers will be created, and then a group of lines will be moved from the initial **0** layer to the other layers.

The **Layers** panel is located under the **Home** tab. See Figure 3-46. There are five indicators shown on the **Layers** panel that serve to indicate the status of some of the layer options. For example, the open padlock indicates that layer **0** is open. If the padlock were closed, it would indicate that the layer was locked.

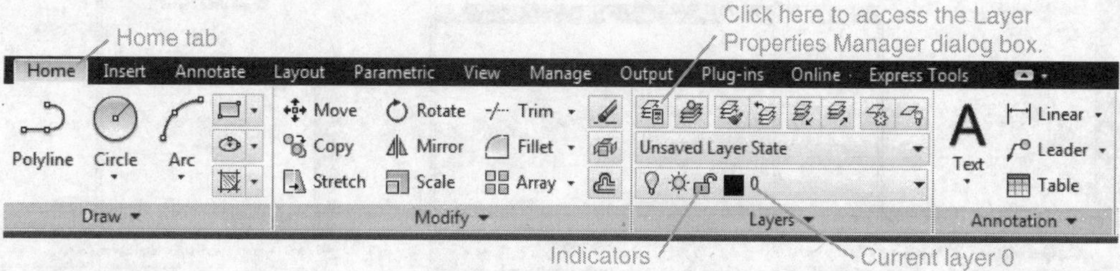

Figure 3-46

To Create New Layers

This exercise will create two new layers: **Hidden** and **Center.**

1. Click the **Layer Properties** tool on the **Layers** panel.

   The **Layer Properties Manager** dialog box will appear along the left side of the screen. See Figure 3-47.

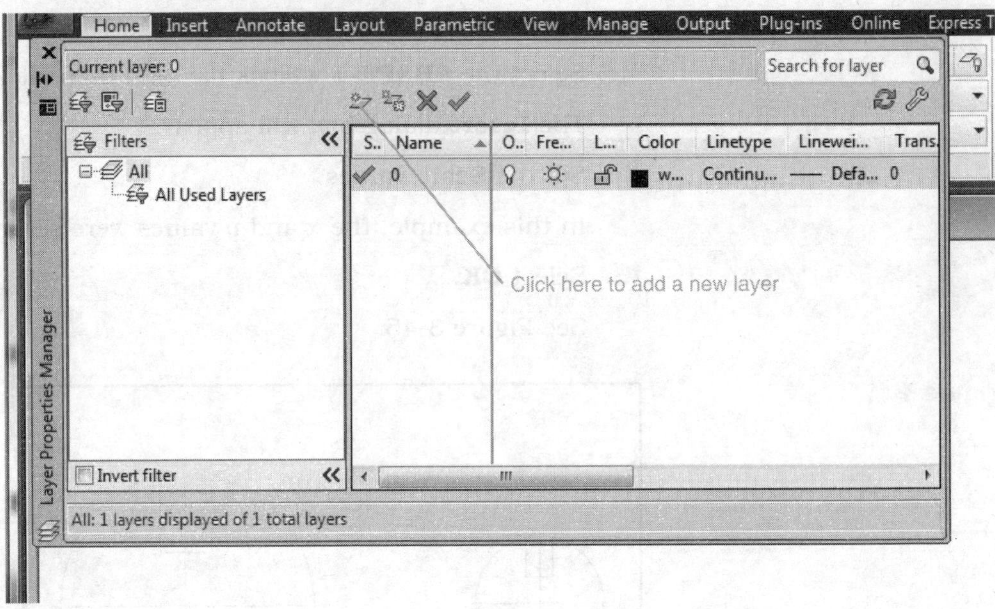

Figure 3-47

2. Click the **New Layer** box.

   A new layer listing will appear with the name **Layer1.** See Figure 3-48.

3. Type **Hidden** in place of the **Layer1** name.

   The name **Hidden** should appear under the **0** layer heading in the **Name** column.

4. Click the **New Layer** box again, and add another new layer named **Center.**

   The name **Center** will appear in the **Name** column. There are now three layers associated with the drawing. See Figure 3-49. The **0** layer is the current layer, as indicated by the 0 to the right of the **Current layer** box.

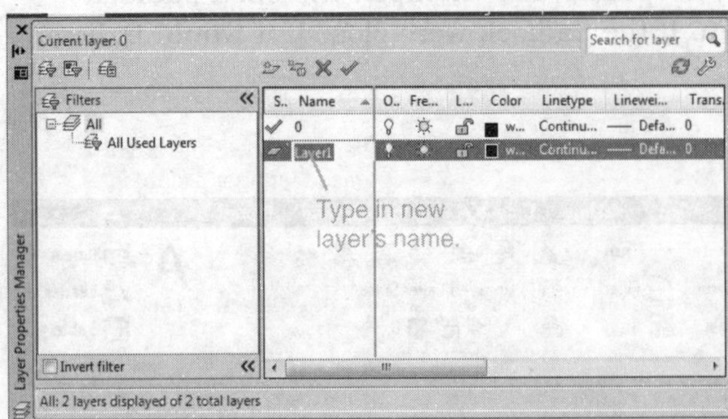

Figure 3-48

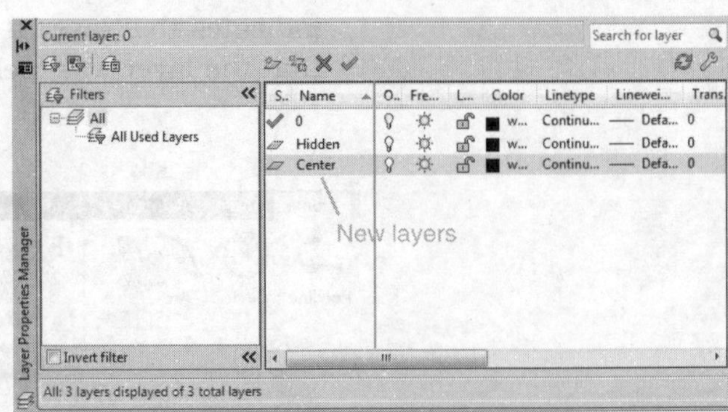

Figure 3-49

To Change the Color and Linetype of a Layer

1. Scroll across the **Layer Properties Manager** to the **Color** heading.
2. Locate the cursor on the **w . . .** notation on the **Hidden** layer line.

The word **white** will appear, indicating that the layer's color is white. See Figure 3-50.

Figure 3-50

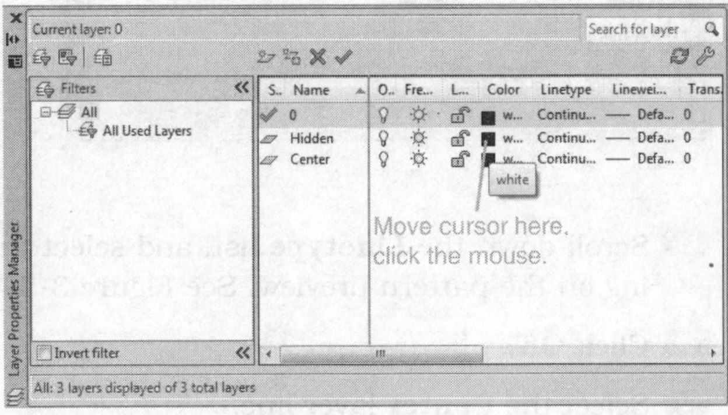

The **Select Color** dialog box will appear. See Figure 3-51.

3. Select the color **blue;** then click **OK.**

All lines drawn on the **Hidden** layer will now be blue. The color box for the **Hidden** layer will be blue.

4. Click the word **Continuous** on the **Hidden** layer line under the **Linetype** heading.

The **Select Linetype** dialog box will change. See Figure 3-52.

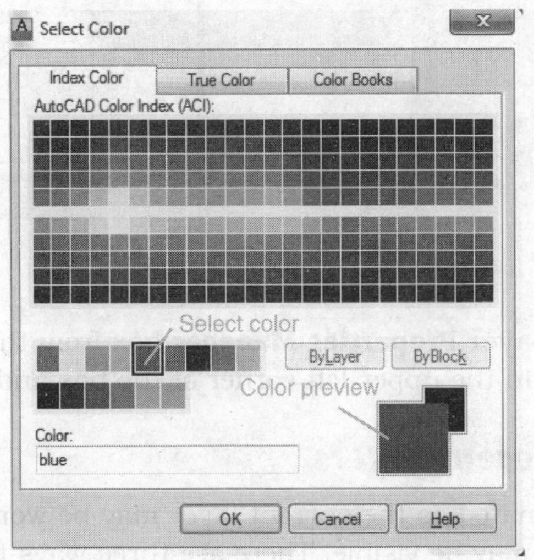

Figure 3-51

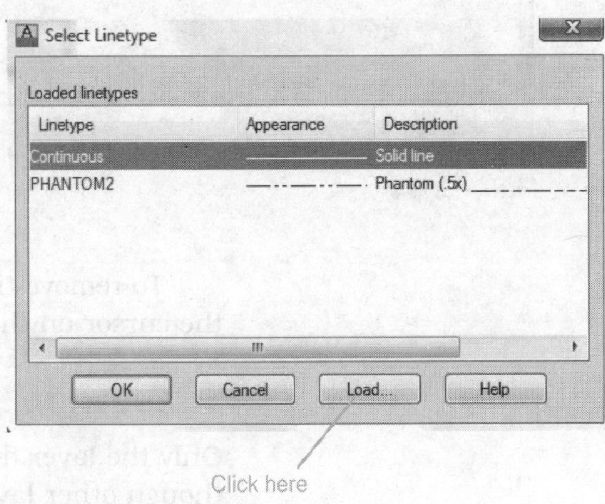

Figure 3-52

5. Click the **Load** button.

The **Load or Reload Linetypes** dialog box will appear. See Figure 3-53.

Figure 3-53

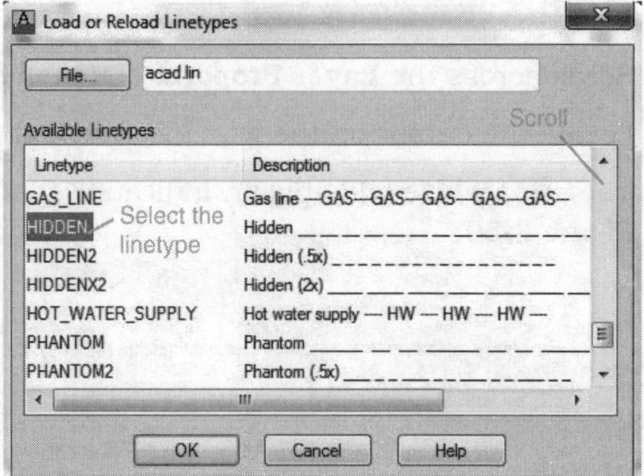

6. Scroll down the **Linetype** list, and select the **HIDDEN** pattern by clicking on the pattern preview. See Figure 3-54.
7. Click **OK.**
8. Select the **Center** layer line.

   The line will be highlighted.
9. Change the **Center** layer's line color to **red** and its linetype to **CENTER.**

   The **Layer Properties Manager** dialog box should look like Figure 3-55.

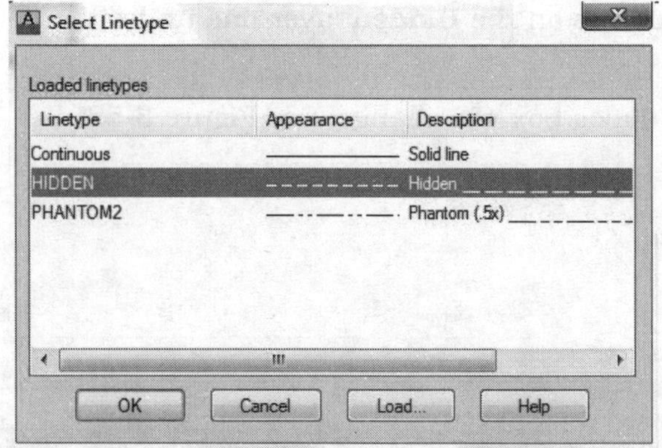

Figure 3-54

Figure 3-55

To remove the **Layer Properties Manager** box from the screen, locate the cursor on the **X** in the upper-left corner of the box and click the mouse.

To Draw on Different Layers

Only the layer designated as the current layer may be worked on, even though other layers may be visible. There are three ways to make a layer the current layer. See Figure 3-56.

1. Use the **Layer** located on the **Layers** panel under the **Home** tab. Click a layer's name. The layer will become the current layer. The current layer is the name displayed in the **Layer control** box after the cascade disappears.

Figure 3-56

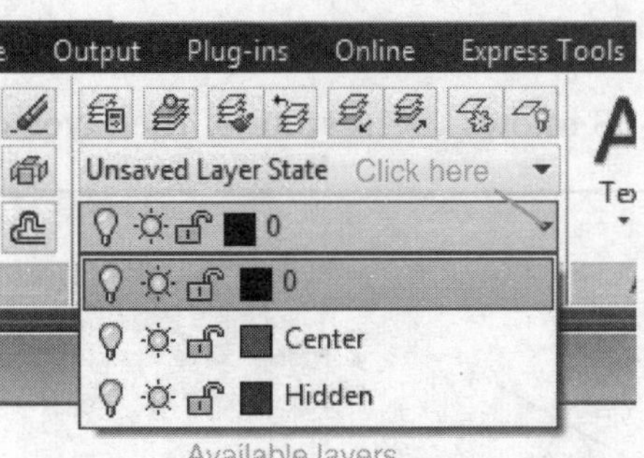

2 Use the **Layer Properties Manager** tool to access the **Layer Properties Manager** dialog box. Click on a layer name, click the current box, and then click **OK.** The layer name will appear in the **Layer control** box, indicating that it is the current layer.

3 Use the **Make Object's Layer Current** tool by clicking an entity on the screen. The entity's layer will become the current layer.

Once a current layer has been established, objects may be drawn and modified on that layer.

To Change Layers

An object may be drawn on one layer, then moved to another layer. This feature is helpful when designing; for example, an original layout may be created in a single layer and then lines may be transferred to different layers as needed. As a line changes layers, it assumes the color and linetype of the new layer. Figure 3-57 shows a circle and a line drawn on the **0** layer. Change the line to a centerline and the circle to a hidden line by moving the objects to the appropriate layer.

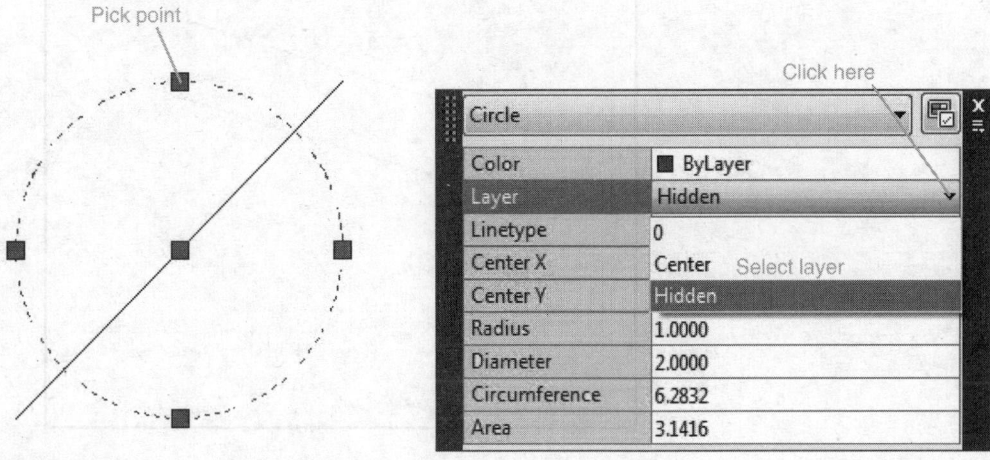

Figure 3-57

1 Click the circle, and right-click one of the grip pickboxes. Then click the **Quick Properties** option.

The **Circle properties** dialog box will appear.

2 Click the **Layer** line, and scroll down and click the **Hidden** option.

The circle's color will turn blue, and the linetype will change to a hidden pattern.

3 Transfer the line to the **Center** layer by the same procedure.

Figure 3-58 shows the results of the layer changes.

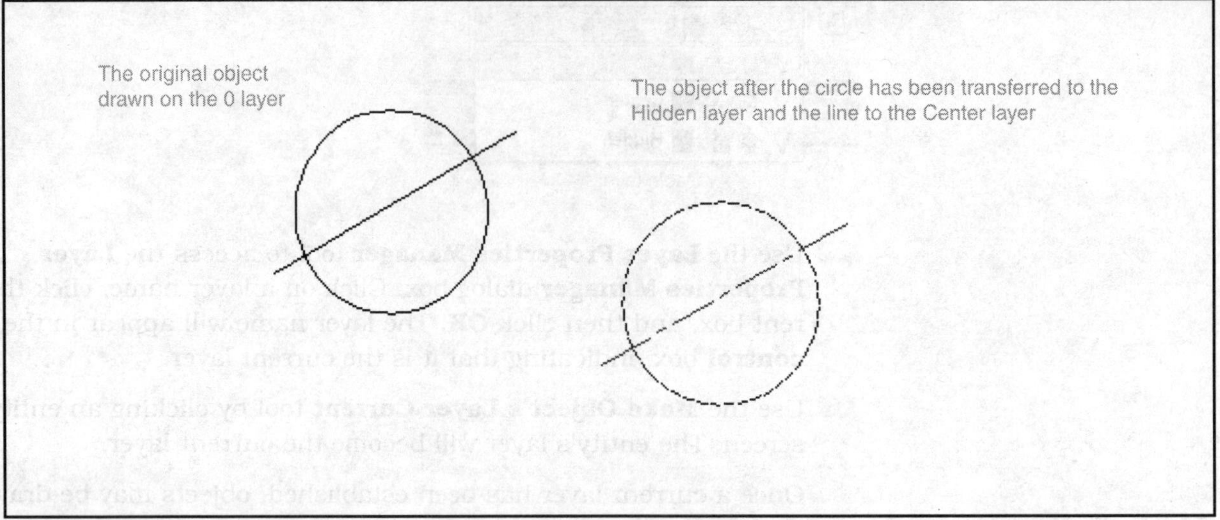

Figure 3-58

To Change the Scale of a Linetype

Figure 3-59 shows two parallel lines drawn on the **Hidden** layer.

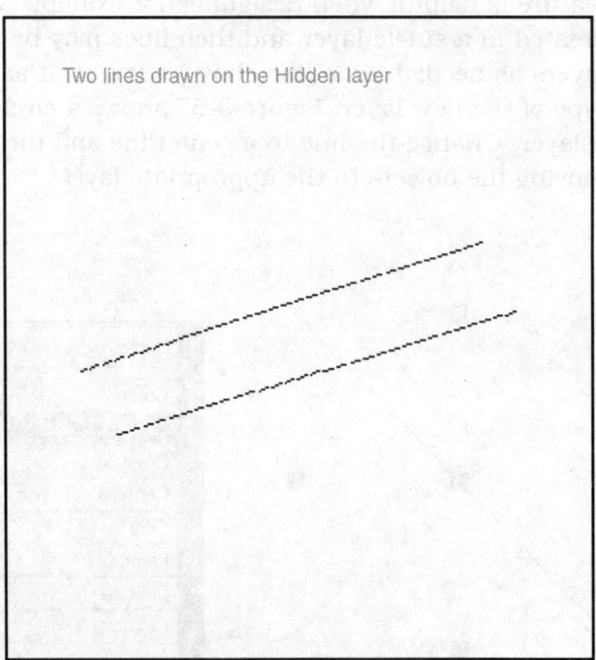

Figure 3-59

1 Click the lower line.

The grip points will appear on the line.

2 Right-click one of the pick points.

A dialog box will appear.

3 Click the **Properties** option.

The **Properties** dialog box will appear. See Figure 3-60.

4 Change the **Linetype scale** to **3.0000.**

Figure 3-60

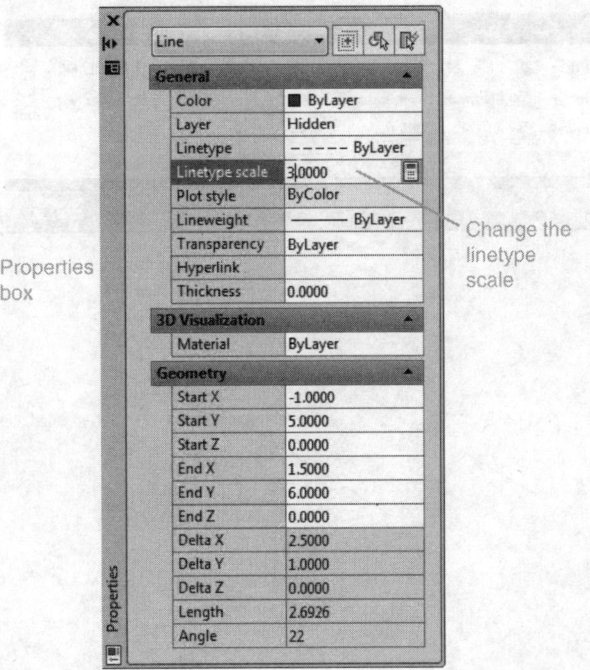

5 Close the **Properties** dialog box by clicking the **X** in the upper left corner of the box, and press the **<Esc>** key.

Figure 3-61 shows the resulting changes in the lower line. The new line has a different linetype scale and therefore different spacing.

Figure 3-61

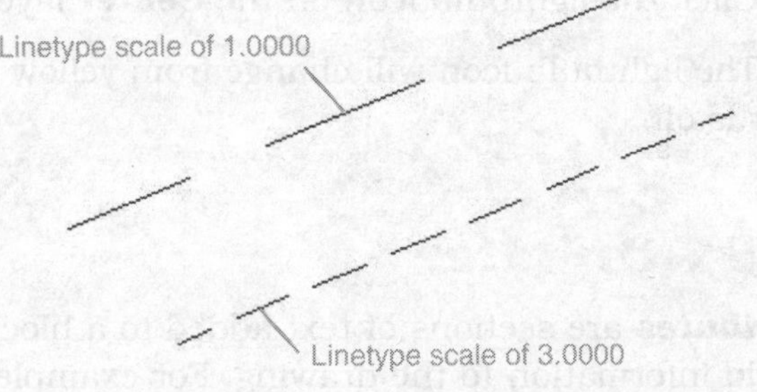

To Use the Match Tool

Figure 3-62 shows two lines. The upper line is on the **Center** layer, and the lower line is on the **0** layer. The **Match** tool is used to change the layer of lower line (**0** layer) to the layer of another object (**Center** layer).

1 Click the **Match** tool.

Select objects to changed:

Select objects:

2 Click the line on the **0** layer, the lower line.

Select object:

3 Right-click the mouse.

Select object on destination layer or [Name]:

Figure 3-62

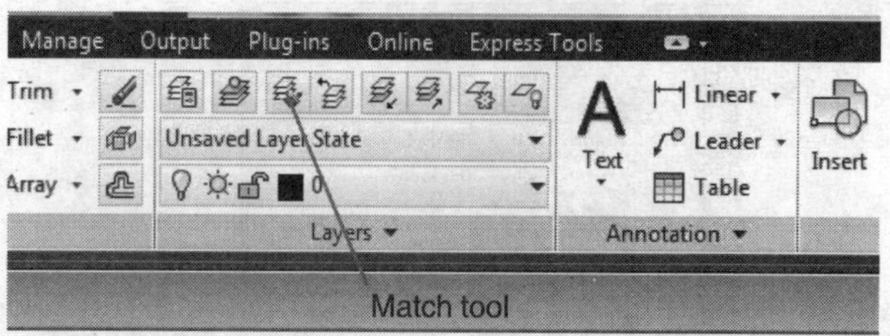

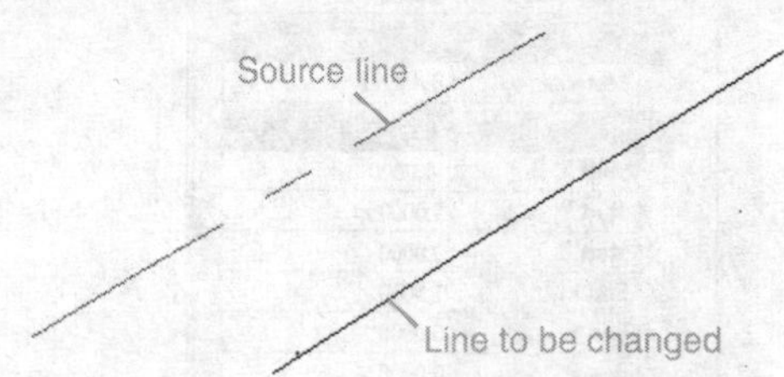

4 Click the line on the **Center** layer, the upper line.

The lines are both on the **Center** layer.

To Turn Layers Off

1 Select the **Layer Properties** tool.

A list of current layers will cascade from the box.

2 Click the lightbulb icon on the **Center** layer.

The lightbulb icon will change from yellow to blue, indicating that the layer is off.

3-25 Attributes

Attributes are sections of text added to a block that prompt the drawer to add information to the drawing. For example, a title block may have an attribute that prompts the illustrator to add the date to the title block as it is inserted into a drawing. Attributes can be found on the **Attributes** panel on the **Insert** tab.

To Add an Attribute to a Block

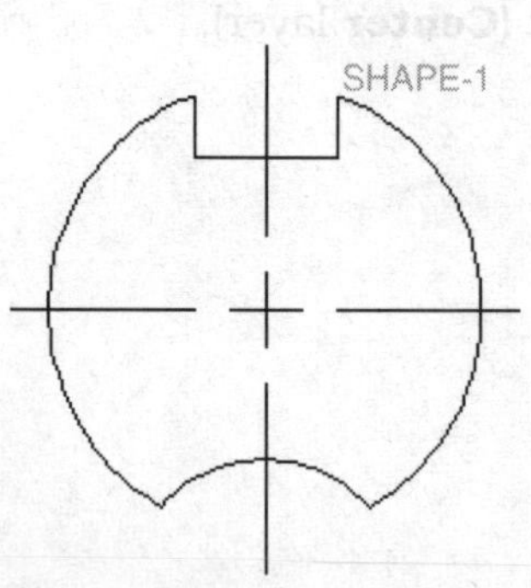

Figure 3-63

Figure 3-63 shows a block named **SHAPE-1**. It was added to a new drawing by using the closest command on the **Block** panel. This example will add attributes that request information about the product's part number, material, quantity, and finish.

1 Access the **Block** panel under the **Home** tab, and click the arrow to the right of the word **Block.**

The **Attribute** tools will appear.

2 Click the **Define Attributes** tool.

The **Attribute Definition** dialog box will appear. See Figure 3-64.

Figure 3-64

3 Type **Number** in the **Tag** box.

A ***tag*** is the name of an attribute and is used for filing and reference purposes. Tag names must be one word with no spaces.

4 Select the **Prompt** box, and type **Define the part number.**

The prompt line will eventually appear at the bottom of the screen when a block containing an attribute is inserted into a drawing. If you do not define a prompt, the tag name will be used as a prompt.

5 Leave the **Default** box empty.

The **Value** box entry will be the default value if none is entered when the prompt appears. Based on the defined prompt and value inputs, the following prompt line will appear when the attribute is combined with a block:

Define the part number <>:

6 Select **Specify on-screen;** click **OK.**

The drawing will appear with crosshairs. Select a location for the attribute tag by moving the crosshairs; then press the left mouse button.

Figure 3-65 shows the attribute tag applied to a drawing. Figures 3-66 and 3-67 show three more **Attribute Definition** dialog boxes. Note that the **Align below previous attribute definition** box is turned on by clicking the box. Figure 3-68 shows the resulting drawing.

Figure 3-65

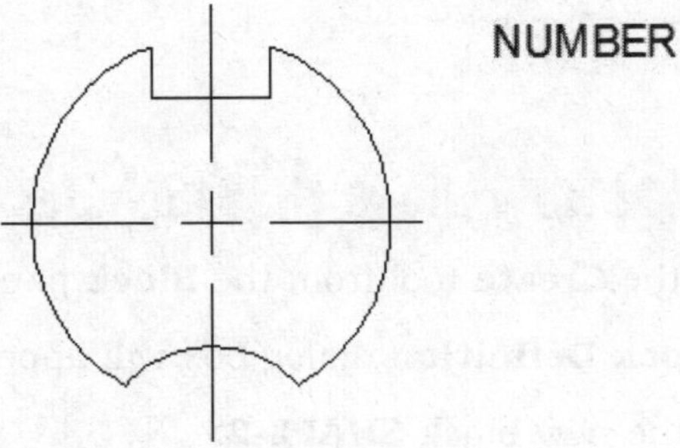

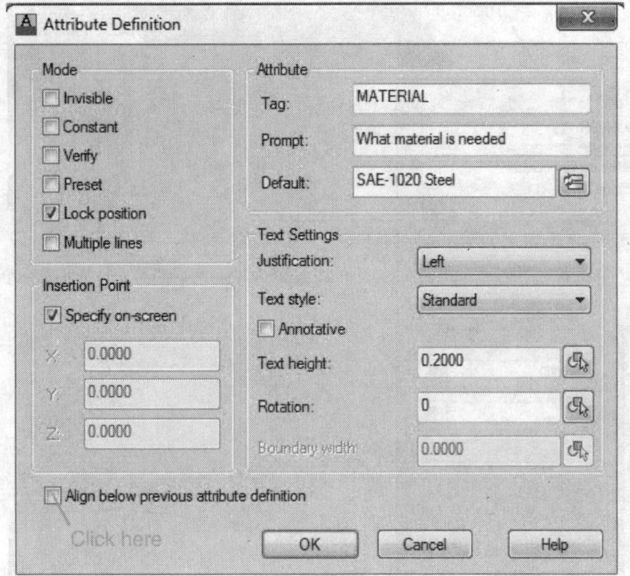

Figure 3-66

Figure 3-67

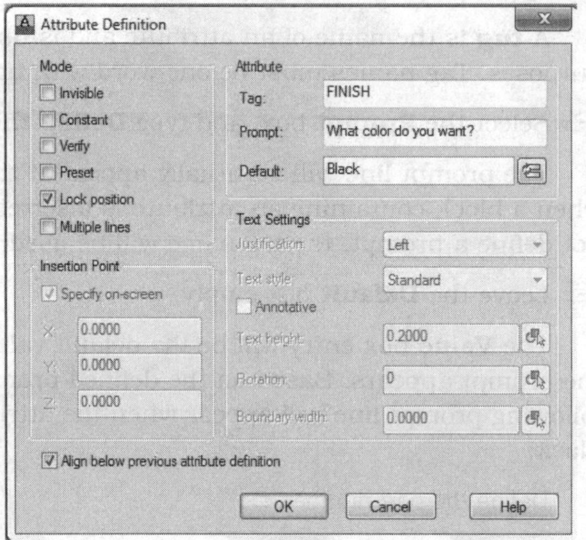

Figure 3-68

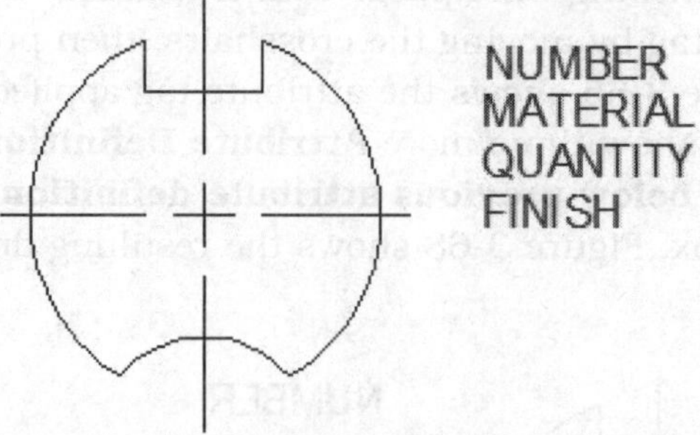

To Create a New Block that Includes Attributes

1. Select the **Create** tool from the **Block** panel.

   The **Block Definition** dialog box will appear.

2. Name the new block **SHAPE-2.**

3. Select a base point.

   In this example, the center point was selected.

4. Select the object by windowing the block and all the attribute tags.
5. Select **OK.**
6. The **Edit Attributes** dialog box will appear. If all entries are correct, select **OK.**

   See Figure 3-69.

   Figure 3-70 shows the resulting block.

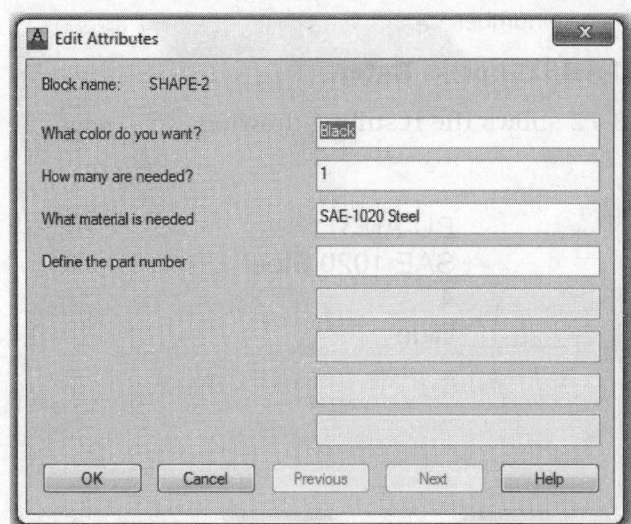

Figure 3-69

SAE-1020 Steel
1
Black

Figure 3-70

To Insert an Exisiting Block with Attributes

1. Select the **Insert** tool on the **Draw** panel.

   The **Insert** dialog box will appear. See Figure 3-71.

2. Select **SHAPE-2,** and then click **OK.**

   Specify the insertion point or [Scale X Y Z Rotate PScale PX PY PZ PRotate]:

3. Select an insertion point.

   Enter attribute values What material is needed? <Steel>:

Figure 3-71

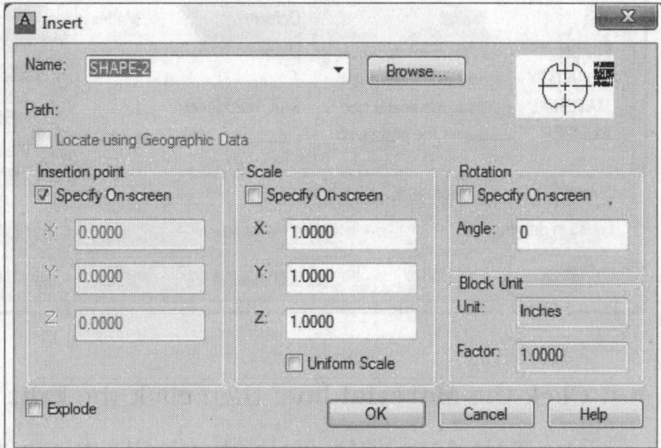

4 Press **Enter.**

What color do you want? <Black>:

5 Select a different color by typing **Blue;** press **Enter.**

How many are needed?

6 Type **4;** press **Enter.**

What material is needed?

7 Press **Enter**.

(The default value **Steel** is acceptable.)

Define the part number <>:

8 Type **BU-AM311;** press **Enter.**

Figure 3-72 shows the resulting drawing.

Figure 3-72

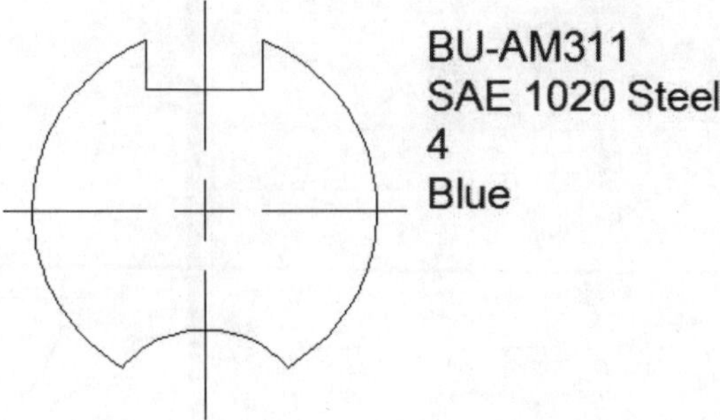

To Edit an Existing Attribute

Once a block has been created that includes attributes, it may be edited by using the **Manage Attributes** command. The procedure is as follows. The block to be edited must be on the drawing screen.

1 Click the **Manage Attributes** tool on the **Block** panel.

The **Block Attribute Manager** dialog box will appear. See Figure 3-73.

Figure 3-73

2 Click the **Material** line; then click the **Edit** box.

The **Edit Attribute** dialog box will appear. See Figure 3-74.

3. Replace the words **SAE 1020 Steel** with the word **Aluminum.**

4. Click **OK.**

Figure 3-75 shows the resulting changes.

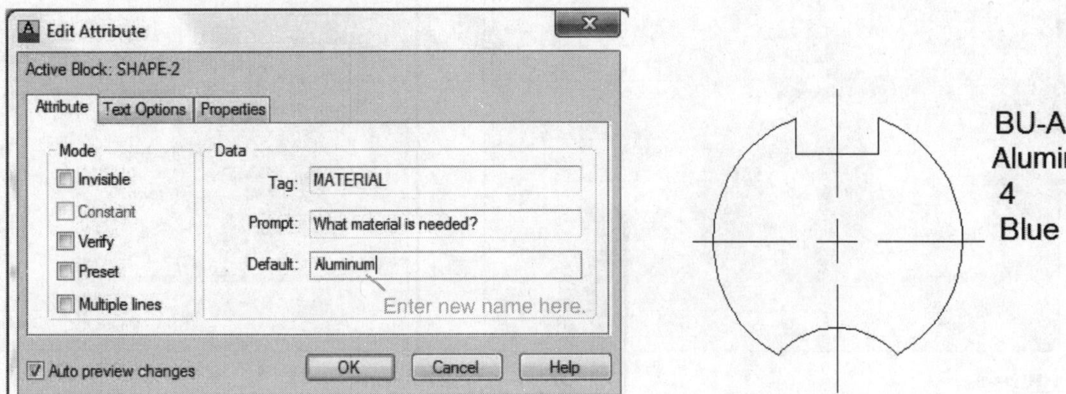

Figure 3-74

Figure 3-75

3-26 Title Blocks with Attributes

Figure 3-76 shows a title block that has been saved as a block. It would be helpful to add attributes to the block so that when it is called up to a drawing, the drawer will be prompted to enter the required information.

Figure 3-76

Boston University
110 Cummington Street
Boston, MA 02215

TITLE:

PART NO:

REV:

SCALE:

DATE:

Note that text may be added to an AutoCAD template by use of the **Mtext** command. Create the desired text, and use the **Move** command to position it within the title block. The title block shown in Figure 3-76 was custom drawn for a special application.

Figures 3-77, 3-78, 3-79, 3-80, and 3-81 show the five **Attribute Definition** dialog boxes used to define the title block attributes. Note that the text height in Figures 3-77 through 3-81 may be varied if desired. Also note that no attribute defaults were assigned. This means that the space on the drawing will be left blank if no prompt value is entered. Figure 3-82 shows the resulting title block with the attribute tags in place.

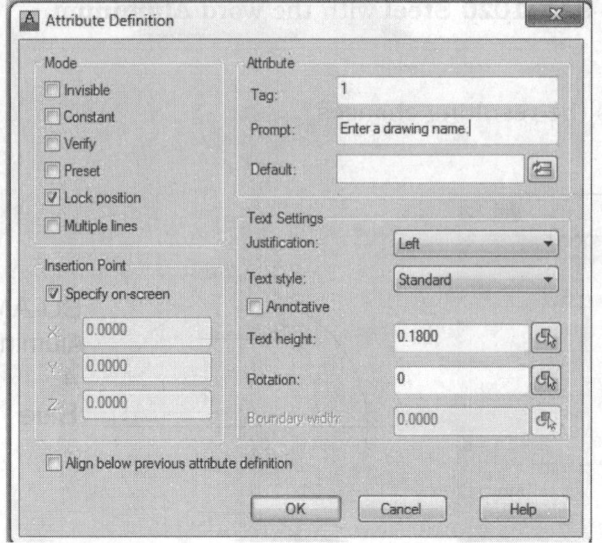

Figure 3-77

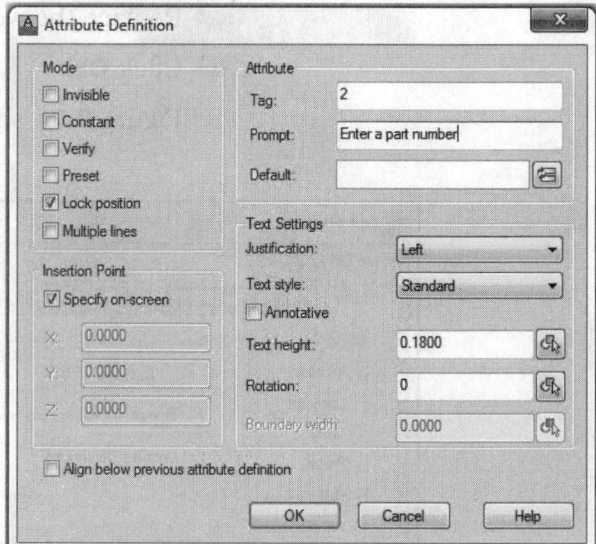

Figure 3-78

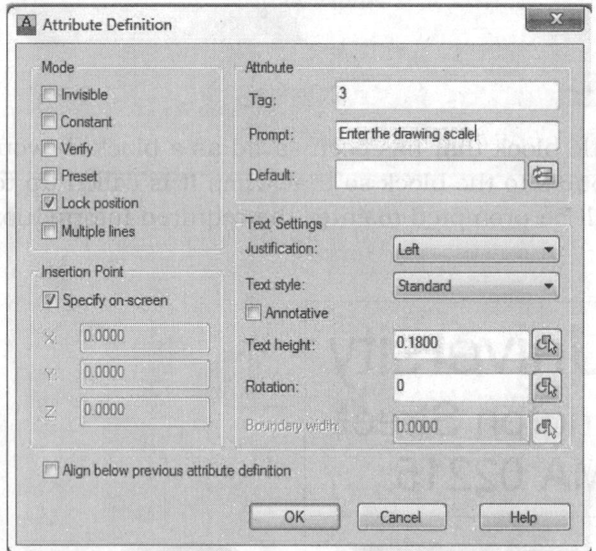

Figure 3-79

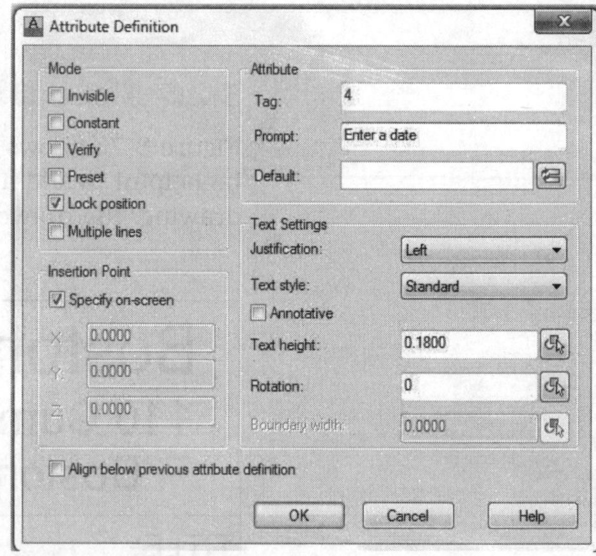

Figure 3-80

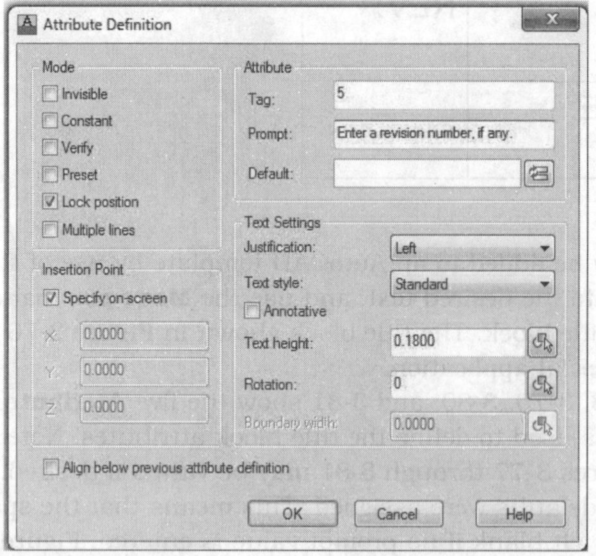

Figure 3-81

Boston University
110 Cummington Street
Boston, MA 02215

TITLE: 1

PART NO: 2

REV: 5

SCALE: 3

DATE: 4

Figure 3-82

The new block with attributes was saved as **TITLE-A** by using the **Block** command. It can now be saved as a wblock and used on future drawings. Figure 3-83 shows a possible title block created from the **TITLE-A** block.

Figure 3-83

3-27 Edit Polyline

The **Edit Polyline** tool, on the **Modify** panel under the **Home** tab, is used to change the shape of a given polyline. In the example shown in Figure 3-84, the **Edit Polyline** command was used to create a spline from a given polyline. The **Edit Polyline** tool is discussed further in Section 16-17.

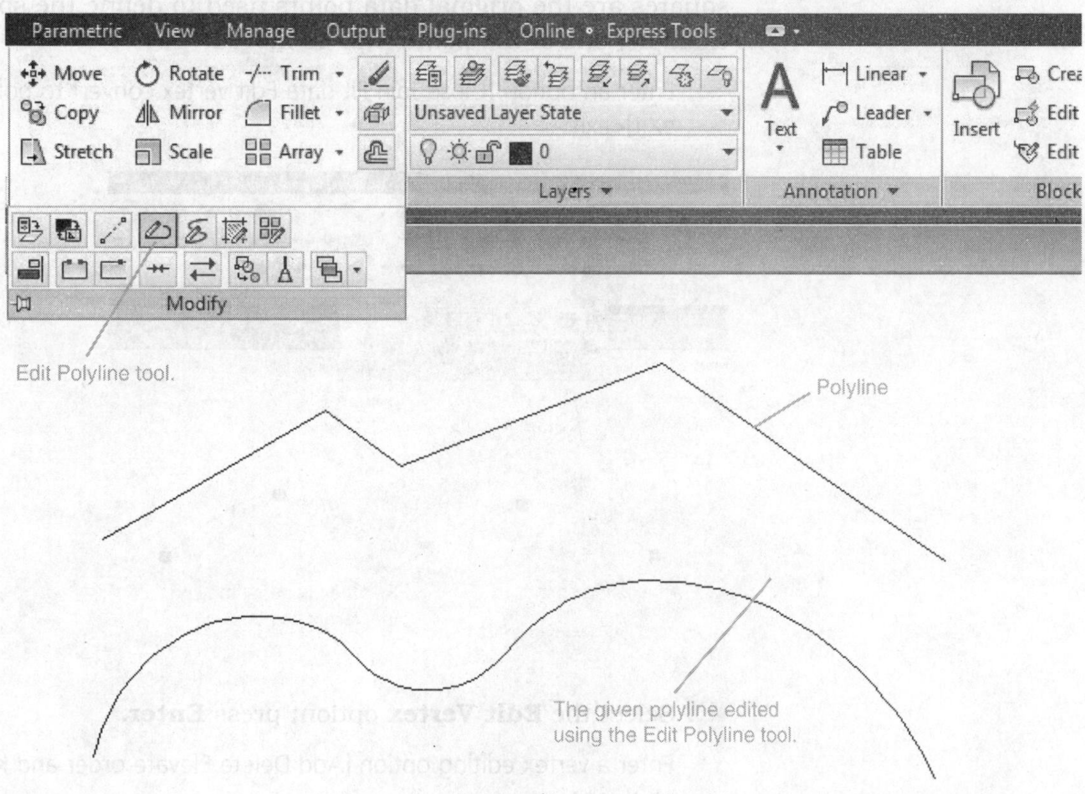

Figure 3-84

To Create a Spline from a Given Polyline

1. Draw a polyline, using the **Polyline** tool on the **Draw** panel.
2. Select the **Edit Polyline** tool from the **Modify** panel.

   Command: _pedit Select polyline:

3. Select the polyline.

   Select an option [Close Join Width Edit vertex Fit Spline Decurve Ltype gen Undo]:

4. Select the **Spline** option.
5. Select the **Fit** option; press **Enter.**

   Figure 3-84 shows the edited polyline.

3-28 Edit Spline

The **Edit Spline** tool, found on the **Modify** panel under the **Home** tab, is used to change the shape of a given spline.

To Edit a Spline

1. Select the **Edit Spline** tool from the **Modify** panel.

   Command: _splinedit
   Select spline:

2. Select the given spline.

   A series of squares will appear on the screen. See Figure 3-85. These squares are the original data points used to define the spline. In this example, one of the points will be moved.

   Enter an option [Close Join Fit data Edit vertex convert to polyline Reverse Undo eXit]<exit>:

Figure 3-85

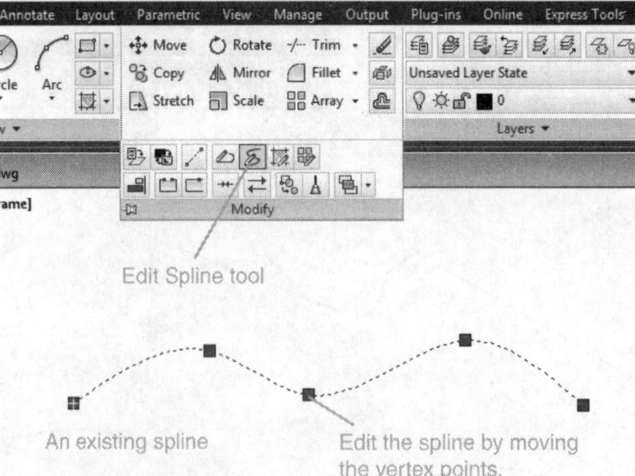

3. Select the **Edit Vertex** option; press **Enter.**

   Enter a vertex editing option [Add Delete Elevate order and Kink Move Weight eXit]<exit>:

4. Select the **Move** option; press **Enter.**

The first square data point will change colors, and a rubber-band-type line will extend from the point. An **x** will appear within the point. See Figure 3-86.

5 Select a new location for the point, and click the mouse; then right-click the mouse, and select the **Exit** option.

Figure 3-87 shows the edited spline. The chosen location will become the new location for the first point. If a point other than the first point needs to be moved, press **Enter** when the **X** appears, and the **Edit** command will advance to the next point. Every time the **Enter** key is pressed, the **Edit** command will advance to the next point. Only the **X** option will allow you to exit the command sequence.

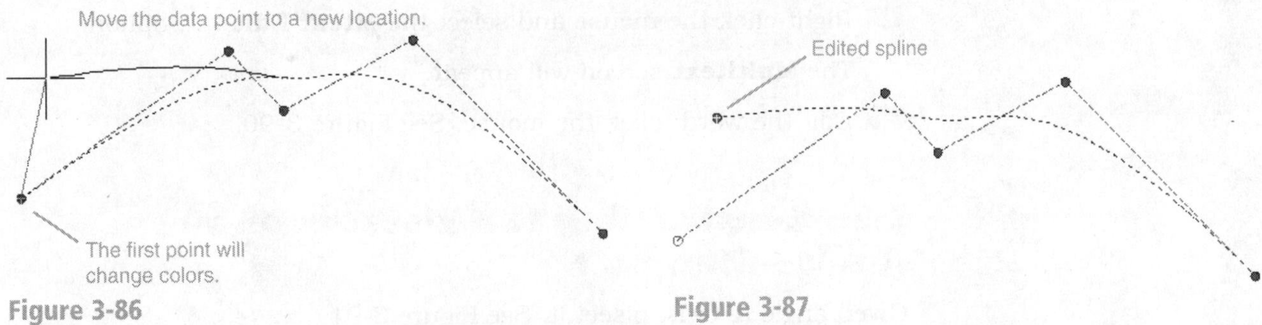

Figure 3-86

Figure 3-87

3-29 Edit Text

Figure 3-88 shows a line of text that contains a typing error. When the word *word* was typed, the <f> key was struck by mistake.

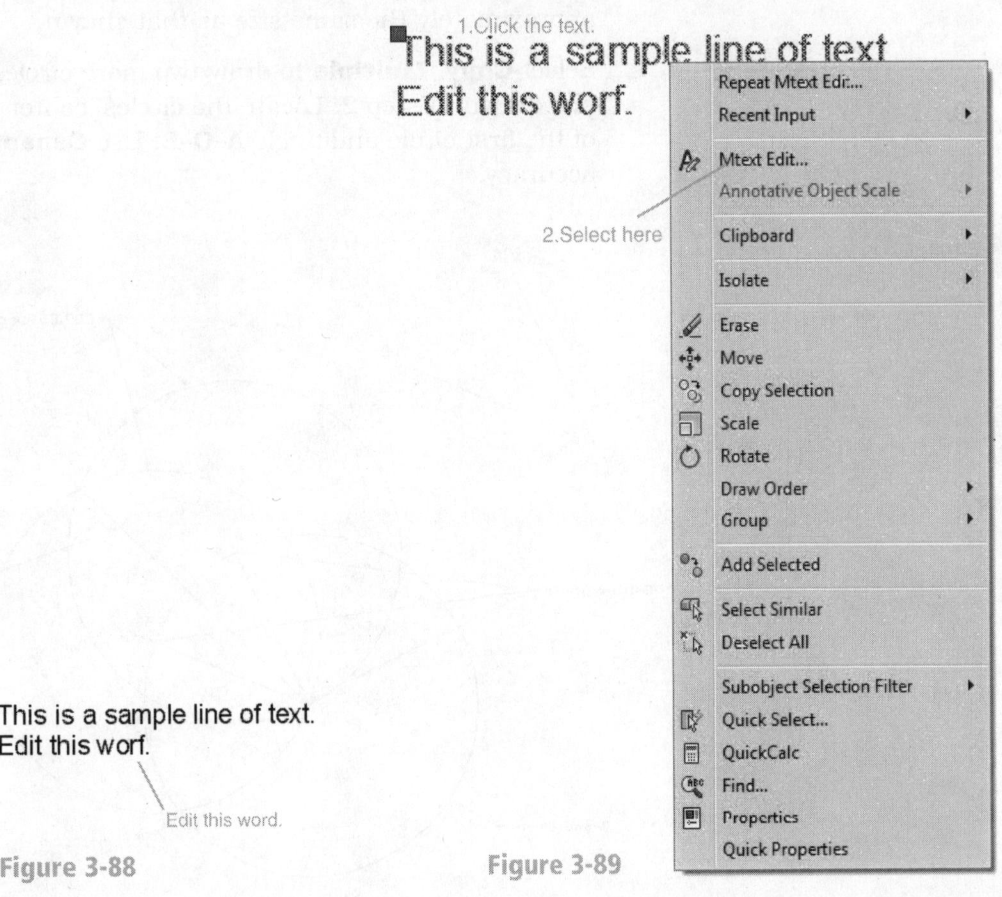

Figure 3-88

Figure 3-89

Figure 3-90

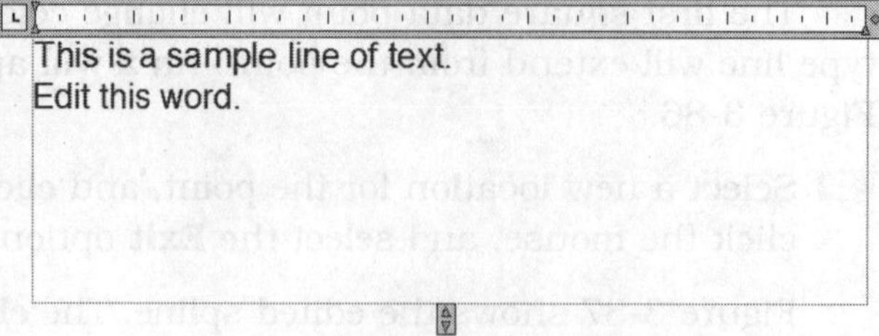

To Change Existing Text

1. Click the existing text. See Figure 3-89.

   Blue indicator marks will appear.

2. Right-click the mouse and select the **Mtext Edit . . .** option.

   The **Multitext** screen will appear.

3. Edit the word; click the mouse. See Figure 3-90.

3-30 Constructing the Bisector of an Angle—Method I

Given angle **A–O–B,** bisect it. See Figure 3-91.

1. Select **Draw, Circle.**
2. Draw a circle with a center point located at point **O.** The circle may be of any radius. This is an excellent place to take advantage of AutoCAD's **Drag** mode. Move the cursor until the circle appears to be approximately the same size as that shown.
3. Select **Copy, Multiple** to draw two more circles equal in radius to the one drawn in step 2. Locate the circles' center points on intersections of the first circle and angle **A–O–B.** Use **Osnap Intersection** to ensure accuracy.

Figure 3-91

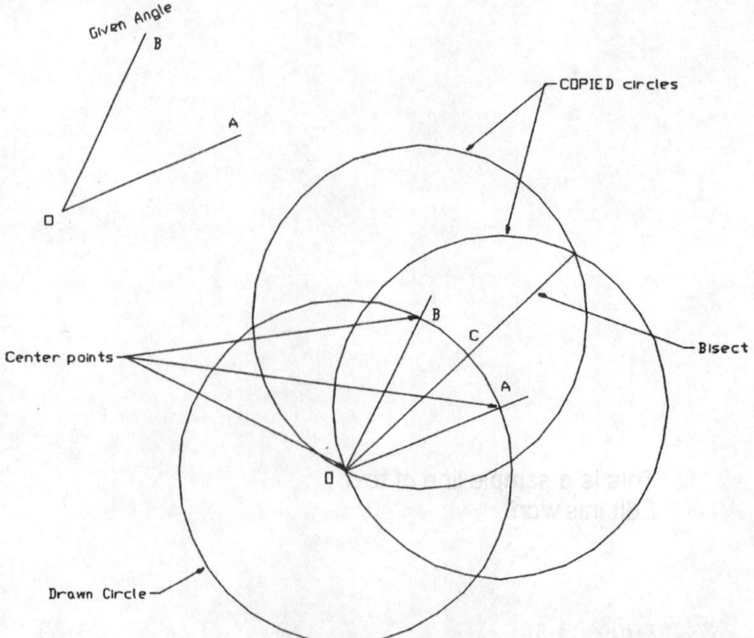

4. Draw a line from point **O** to intersection **C** as shown. Use **Osnap Intersection** to ensure accuracy.

3-31 Constructing the Bisector of an Angle—Method II

Given angle **A–O–B,** bisect it. See Figure 3-92.

1. Draw a circle with a center point located at point **O.** The circle may be of any radius. This is an excellent place to take advantage of AutoCAD's **Drag** mode. Move the cursor until the circle appears to be approximately the same size as that shown.

Figure 3-92

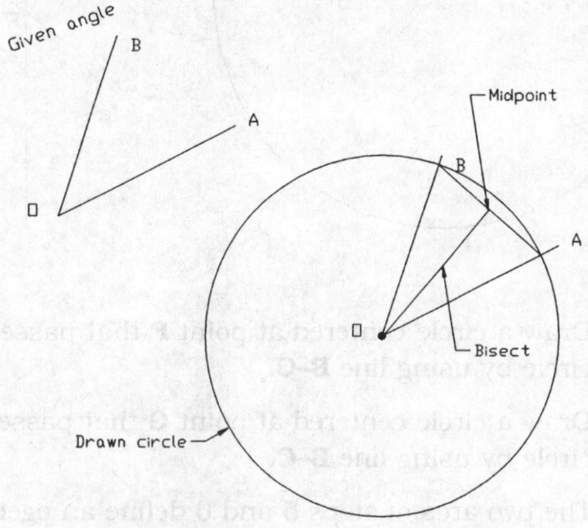

2. Draw a line between the intersection point created by the circle and angle **A–O–B.** Use **Osnap Intersection** to ensure accuracy.

3. Draw a line between point **O** and the midpoint of the line. Use **Osnap Midpoint** to ensure accuracy.

3-32 Constructing an Ogee Curve (S-Curve) with Equal Arcs

Given points **B** and **C,** construct an ogee curve between them. See Figure 3-93.

1. Draw a straight line between points **B** and **C.** Use **Osnap Endpoint** to ensure accuracy.

2. Draw lines perpendicular to lines **A–B** and **C–D** as shown.

Use **Osnap Endpoint** to accurately start the lines on points **B** and **C,** respectively. Use relative coordinates to draw the lines. The lines may be of any length greater than the perpendicular distance between lines **A–B** and **C–D.**

3. Construct a perpendicular bisector of line **B–C.**

4. Define the intersections of the perpendicular lines drawn in step 2 with the perpendicular bisector of **B–C** at points **F** and **G.**

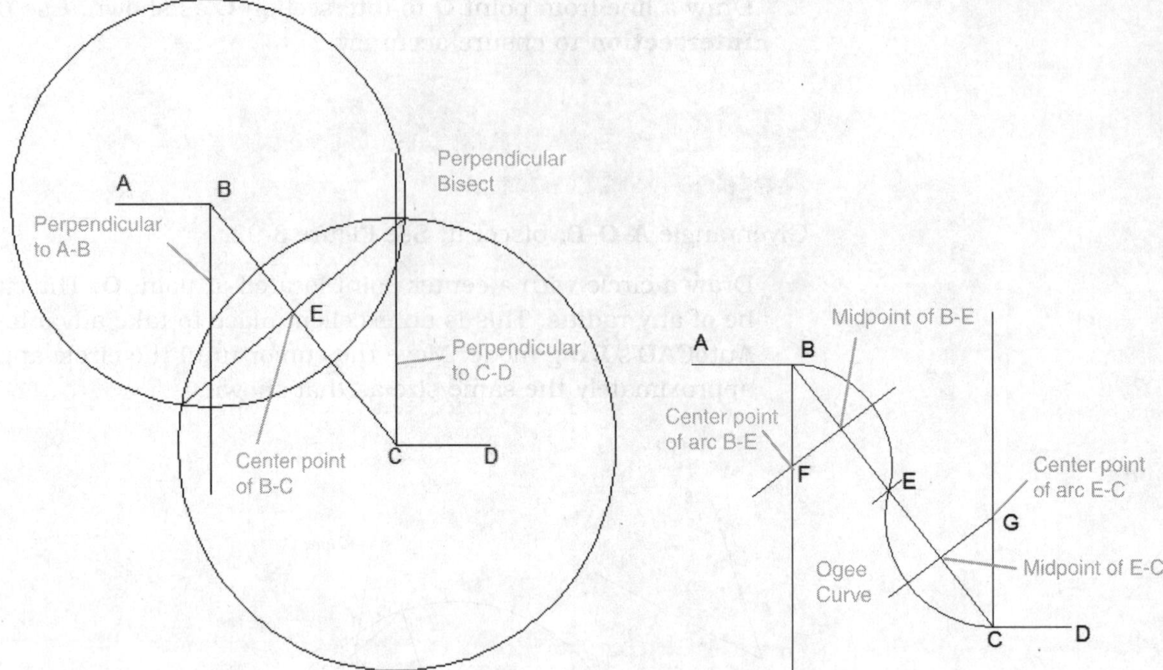

Figure 3-93

5 Draw a circle centered at point **F** that passes points **B** and **E.** Trim the circle by using line **B–C.**

6 Draw a circle centered at point **G** that passes points **C** and **E.** Trim the circle by using line **B–C.**

The two arcs of steps 5 and 6 define an ogee curve by equal arcs. Figure 3-94 shows the construction of an ogee curve with unequal arcs. The construction techniques are similar to those presented previously.

Figure 3-94

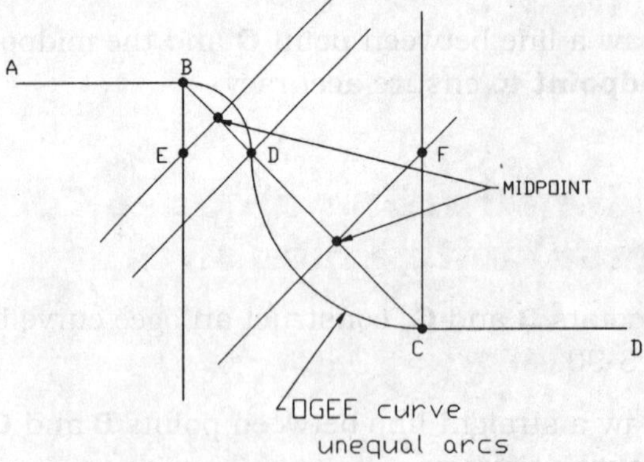

3-33 Constructing a Parabola

Definition: A ***parabola*** is the loci of points such that the distances between a fixed point, the ***focus,*** and a fixed line, the ***directrix,*** are always equal.

Given a focus point **A** and a directrix **B–C,** construct a parabola. See Figure 3-95.

1 Draw a line parallel to **B–C** so that it intersects the midpoint between line **B–C** and point **A.** Use **Offset.**

Figure 3-95

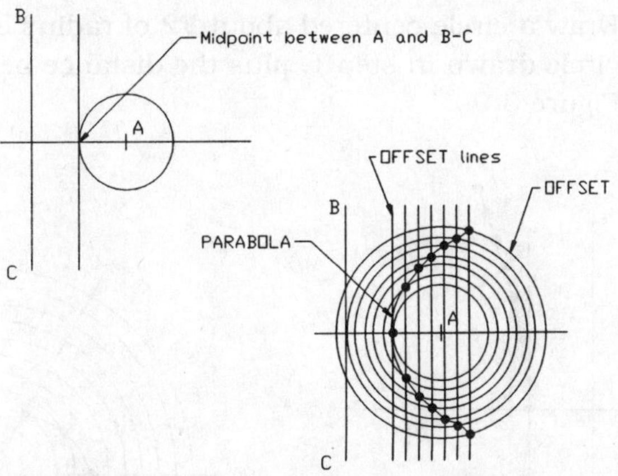

2. Draw a circle centered about point **A** whose radius is equal to half of the distance between line **B–C** and point **A.**

3. Offset lines and a circle **0.2 inch** from the parallel line and the circle created in steps 1 and 2.

4. Identify the intersections of the lines and circles created in step 3. In this example, filled circles were used to identify the points.

5. Draw a polyline connecting all the intersection points.

6. Use the **Edit Polyline, Fit** option to change the polyline to a parabolic curve.

3-34 Constructing a Hyperbola

Definition: A ***hyperbola*** is the loci of points equidistant between two fixed foci.

Given foci points F1 and F2 equidistant from a vertical line and two other vertical lines drawn through points **A** and **B,** draw a hyperbola. See Figures 3-96, 3-97, and 3-98.

1. Draw a circle of arbitrary radius, using point **F2** as the center. If possible, set the drawing up so that both points **F1** and **F2** are on snap points. If this is not possible, draw a vertical line through point **F2** so that the **Osnap Intersection** option may be used to locate the center accurately.

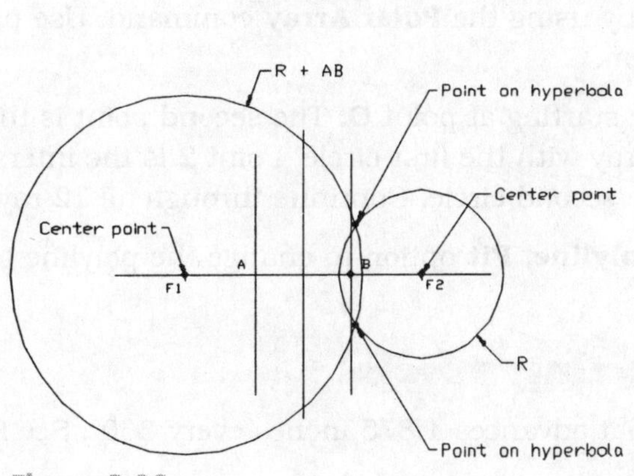

Figure 3-96

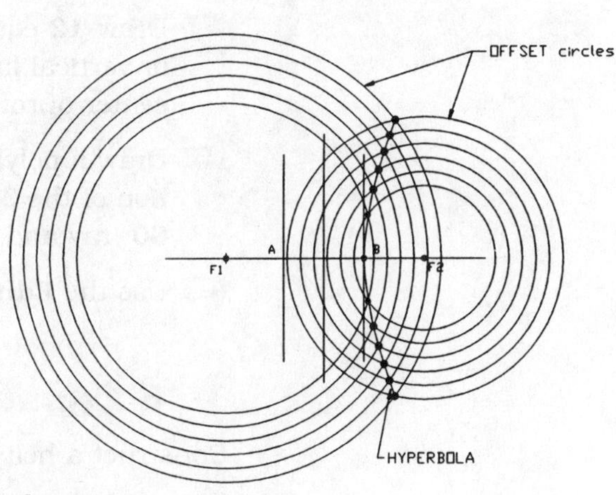

Figure 3-97

2. Draw a circle centered about **F2** of radius equal to the radius of the circle drawn in step 1, plus the distance between points **A** and **B.** See Figure 3-99.

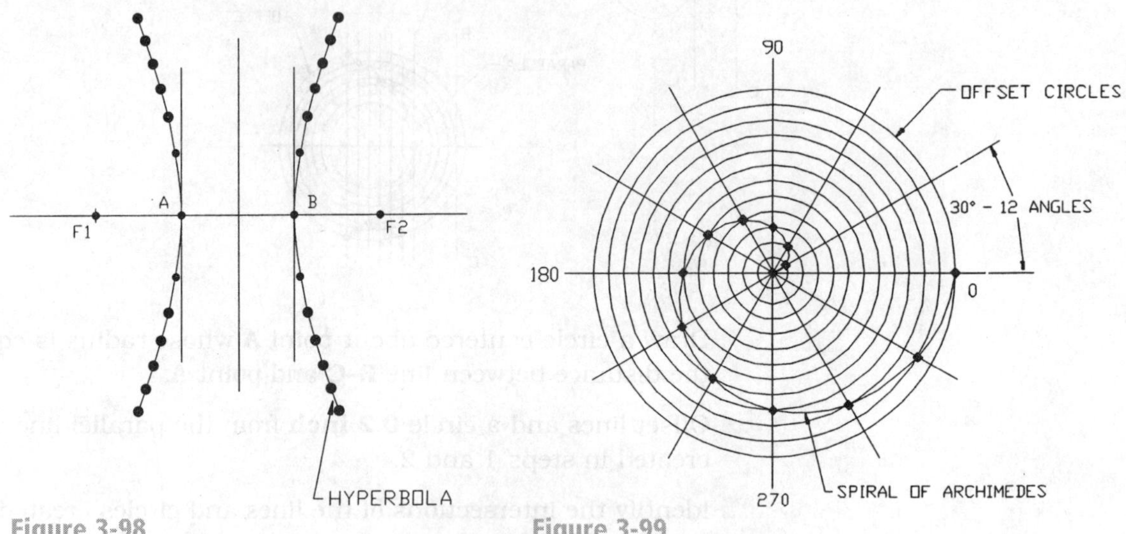

Figure 3-98

Figure 3-99

3. Draw concentric circles around the circles centered about **F1** and **F2.** The distance between all the circles should be equal. Use **Offset.**
4. Mark the intersections between the smaller and larger circles, as shown in Figure 3-97. Use filled circles to define the points.
5. Draw a polyline connecting points 1 through 12.
6. Use the **Edit Polyline, Fit** option to draw the hyperbola.
7. Use **Mirror** to create the opposing hyperbola. See Figure 3-98.

3-35 Constructing a Spiral

Construct a spiral of Archimedes. See Figure 3-99.

1. Draw a set of perpendicular centerlines as shown.
2. Draw **12** concentric circles about center point **O.** Use **Offset** to draw circles.
3. Draw **12** equally spaced ray lines as shown. Array either the horizontal or vertical line by using the **Polar Array** command. Use point **O** as the center of rotation.
4. Draw a polyline starting at point **O.** The second point is the intersection of the **30**° ray with the first circle. Point 2 is the intersection of the **60**° ray and the second circle. Continue through all 12 rays and circles.
5. Use the **Edit Polyline, Fit** option to change the polyline to a spiral.

3-36 Constructing a Helix

Construct a helix that advances 1.875 inches every 360°. See Figure 3-100.

1. Draw a vertical line **1.875** inches long and a horizontal line, as shown.

Figure 3-100

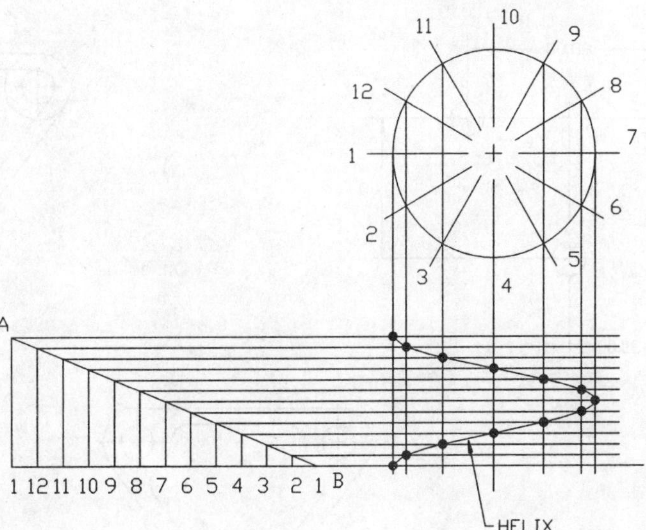

2. Draw a horizontal line that can easily be divided into **12** equal spaces. The length of the horizontal line is arbitrary. Set up a grid so that the 12 equal spaces can easily be identified.
3. Draw a circle as shown. Use **Array,** and divide the circle by **12** equally spaced rays. Use the **Polar Array** command with the circle's center point as the center of rotation.
4. Draw line **A–B** as shown. Draw **12** vertical, equally spaced lines between the horizontal line and line **A–B.**
5. Label both the circle and the horizontal line as shown. The number of divisions must be the same for both the circle and the horizontal line.
6. Draw vertical lines from the intersections of the 12 equally spaced rays and the circle's circumference as shown in Figure 3-100. Use the **Osnap Intersection** option to ensure accuracy.
7. Draw horizontal lines from the intersections on line **A–B** so that they intersect the vertical lines from step 6. Use the **Osnap Intersection** option to ensure accuracy.
8. Mark the intersections of the lines from steps 6 and 7 as shown.
9. Use a polyline to connect the horizontal and vertical intersections as shown.
10. Use the **Edit Polyline, Fit** option to draw the helix.

3-37 Designing by Using Shape Parameters

An elementary design problem often faced by beginning designers is to create a shape based on a given set of parameters. This section presents two examples of this type of design problem.

Design Problem DP3-1

Design a shape that will support the hole pattern shown in Figure 3-101, subject to the given parameters. Design for the minimum amount of material. All dimensions are in millimeters.

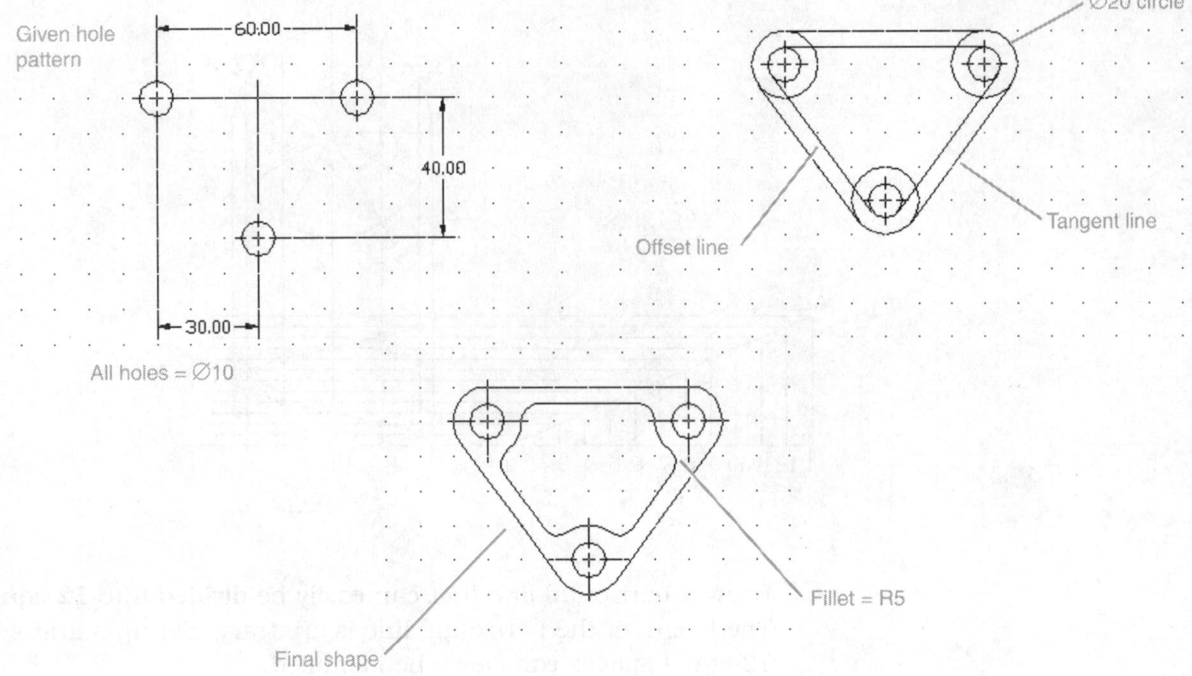

Figure 3-101

1. The edge of the material may be no closer to the center of a hole than a distance equivalent to the radius of the hole.
2. The minimum distance from any cutout to the edge of the part may not be less than the smallest distance calculated in step 1.
3. The minimum inside radius for a cutout is R = **5** millimeters.

The solution is as follows:

1. Calculate the minimum edge distances for the holes.

In this problem, the three holes are all the same diameter: 10 millimeters. Given the parameter that an edge may be no closer to the center of the hole than a distance equivalent to the size of the hole's diameter, the distance from the outside edge of the hole to the edge of the part must be no less than 5 millimeters, or a circular shape of diameter 20 millimeters.

2. Draw **Ø20** circles, using the existing circle's center point, as shown in Figure 3-101.
3. Draw outside tangent lines between the Ø20 circles.

The second parameter limits the minimum edge distance to the minimum edge distance calculated in step 2, or 5 millimeters.

4. Use the **Offset** command to draw lines **5** millimeters from the outside tangent lines drawn in step 3 to define the internal cutout.
5. Use the inside radius parameter of **5** millimeters, and add fillets to the internal cutout.
6. Erase any excess lines.

Figure 3-101 shows the final shape.

Design Problem DP3-2

Design a shape that will support the hole pattern shown in Figure 3-102. Support the center hole with four perpendicular webs. All dimensions are in inches.

Figure 3-102

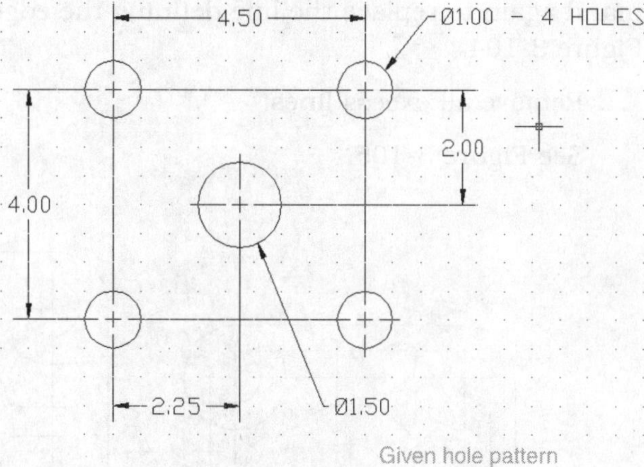

Given hole pattern

1. The edge of the material may be no closer to the center of a hole than a distance equivalent to the radius of the hole.
2. The minimum distance from any cutout to the edge of the part may not be less than the smallest distance calculated in step 1.
3. The minimum inside radius for a cutout is R = **.125** inch.

The solution is as follows:

1. Calculate the minimum edge distances for the holes.

   In this example, the hole diameters are 1.00 and 1.50 inches.

2. Add circles of radius **2.00** and **3.00** as shown. See Figure 3-103.

Figure 3-103

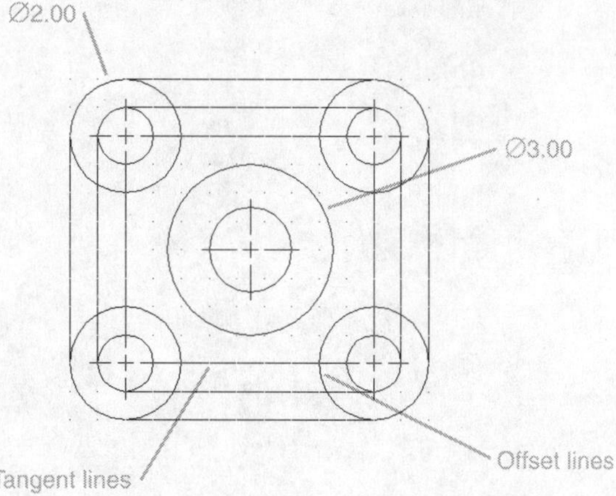

The minimum edge distance based on the Ø1.00 of the smaller hole equals 0.50 inch.

3. Use the minimum edge distance, and define the inside edge of the internal cutouts.

4 Use the minimum edge distance to define the four supporting webs for the center hole.

5 Add the inside bend radii.

The inside bend radii were added by using the **Fillet** command. This will cause a portion of the internal edge to disappear. Use the **Offset** command again to replace the line defining the edge of the internal cutout. See Figure 3-104.

6 Remove all excess lines.

See Figure 3-105.

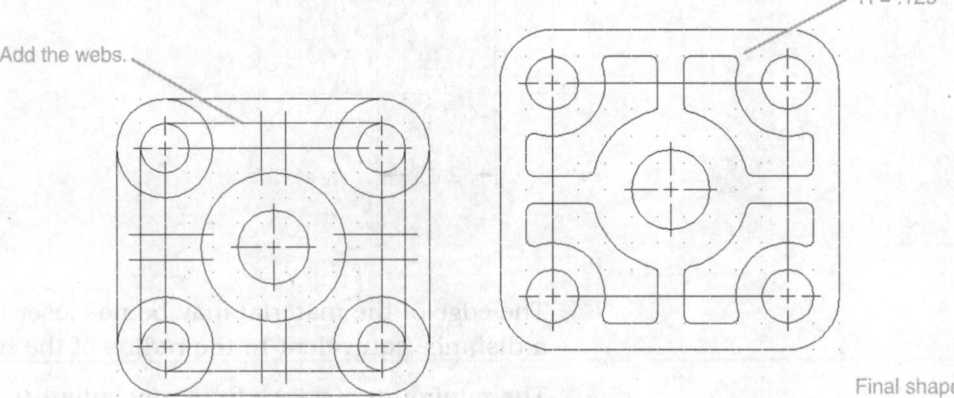

Figure 3-104

Figure 3-105

3-38 EXERCISE PROBLEMS

Redraw to scale the figures that follow, using the given dimensions. Do not include dimensions on the drawing.

EX3-1 Inches (Hint: Use Osnap)

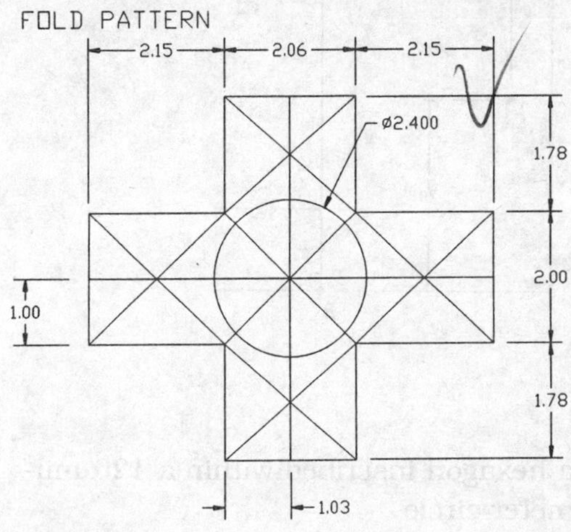

EX3-2 Millimeters (Hint: Use Osnap)

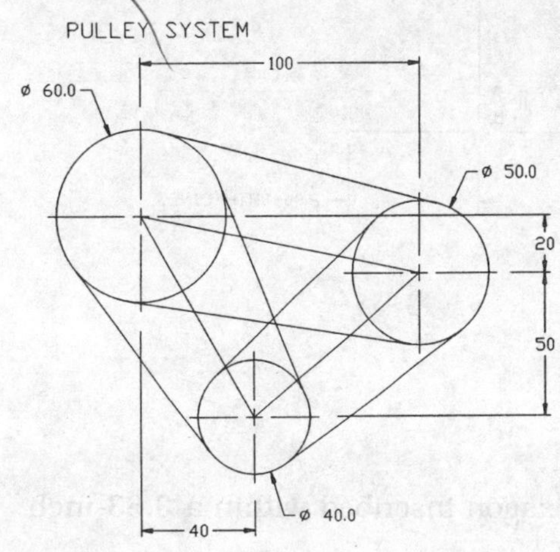

EX3-3 Millimeters (Hint: Use Osnap)

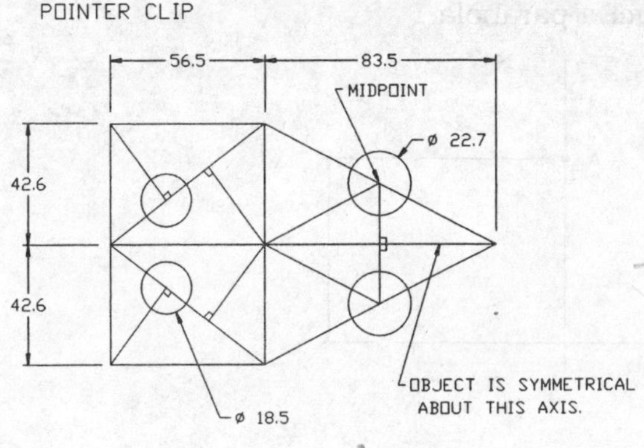

EX3-4 Millimeters (Hint: Use Osnap)

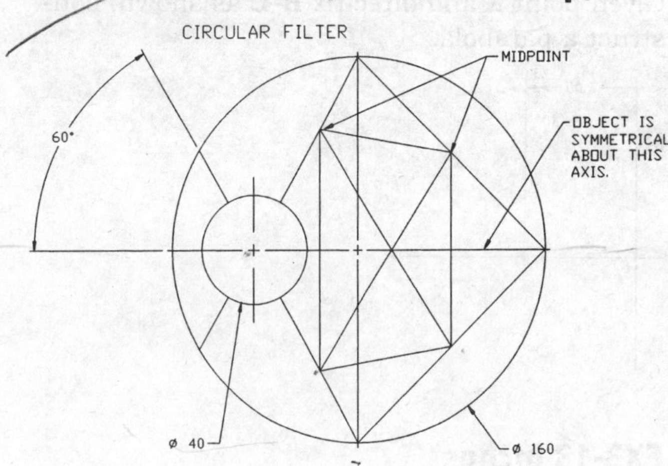

EX3-5

Draw a 54° angle; construct the bisector.

EX3-6

Draw an 89.33° angle; construct the bisector.

EX3-7 Inches

Given points **A** and **B** as shown next, construct an ogee curve of equal arcs.

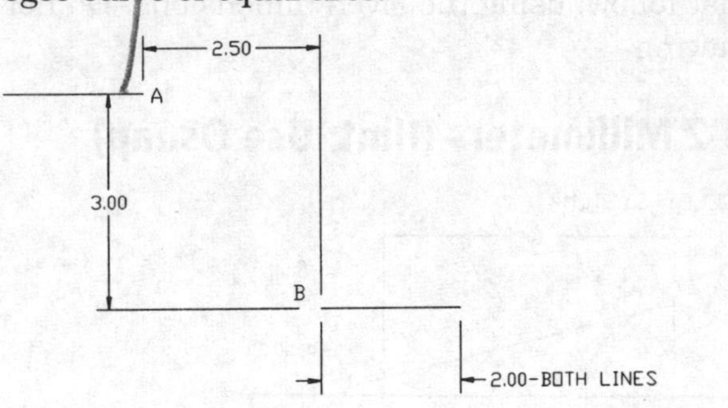

EX3-8 Millimeters

Given points **A, B, C,** as shown next, construct an ogee curve that starts at point **A,** passes through point **C,** and ends at point **B.**

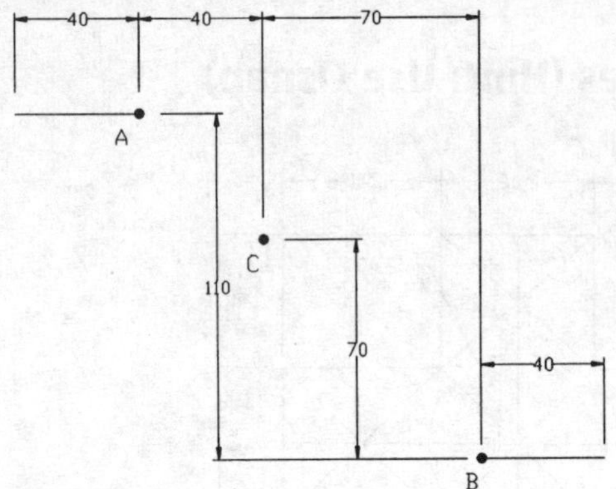

EX3-9

Construct a hexagon inscribed within a 3.63-inch diameter circle.

EX3-10

Construct a hexagon inscribed within a 120-millimeter diameter circle.

EX3-11 Inches

Given point **A** and directrix **B–C** as shown, construct a parabola.

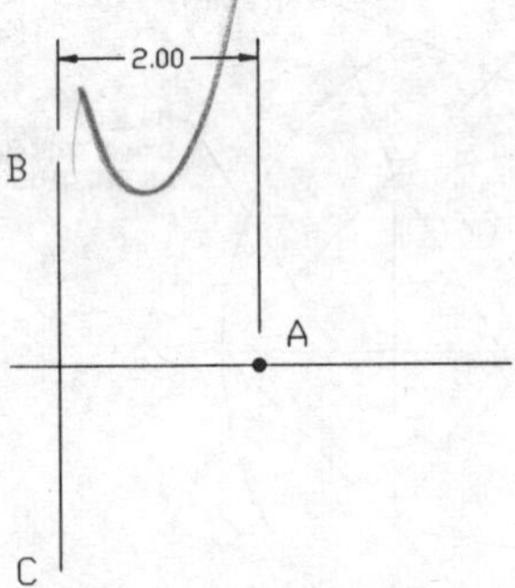

EX3-12 Millimeters

Given point **A** and directrix **B–C** as shown next, construct a parabola.

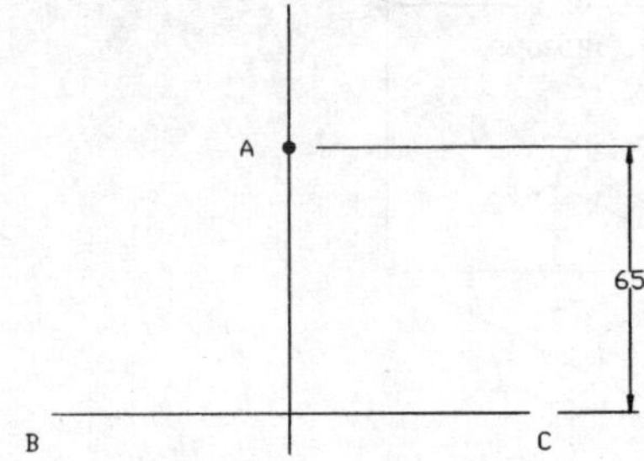

EX3-13 Inches

Given foci **F1** and **F2** as shown next, draw a hyperbola.

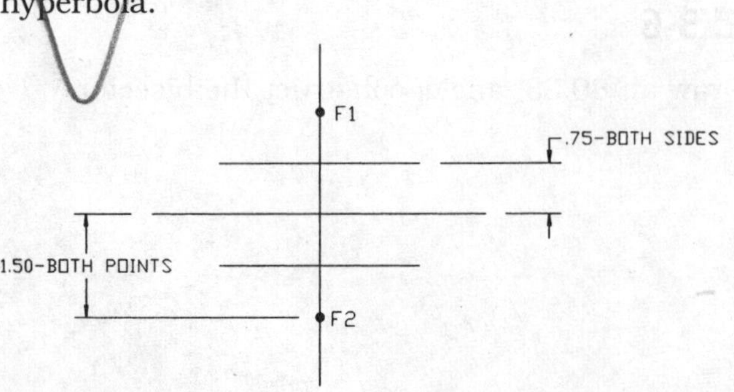

EX3-14 Millimeters

Given foci **F1** and **F2** as shown next, draw a hyperbola.

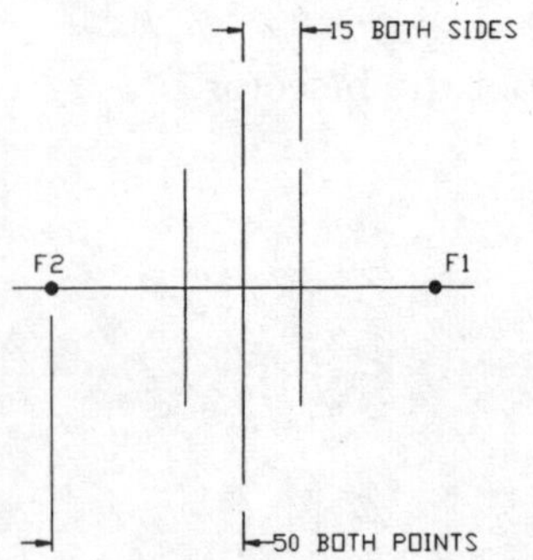

EX3-15 Inches

Given the concentric circles and rays shown next, construct a spiral.

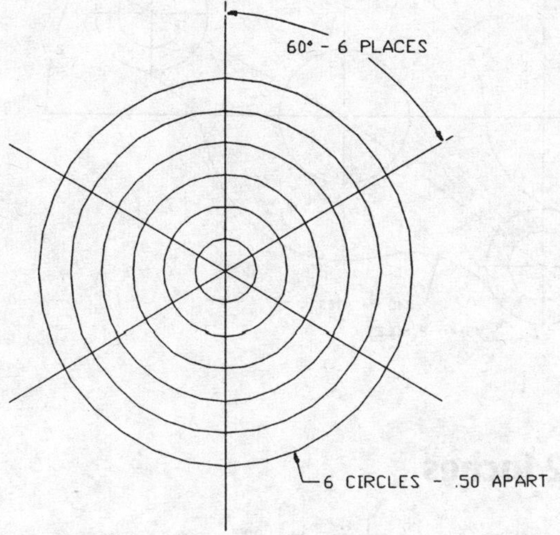

EX3-16 Millimeters

Given the concentric circles and rays shown next, construct a spiral.

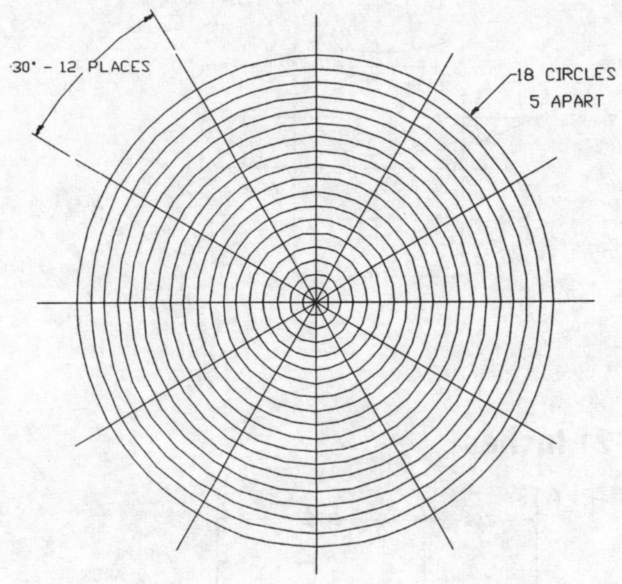

EX3-17 Inches

Given the setup shown next, construct a helix.

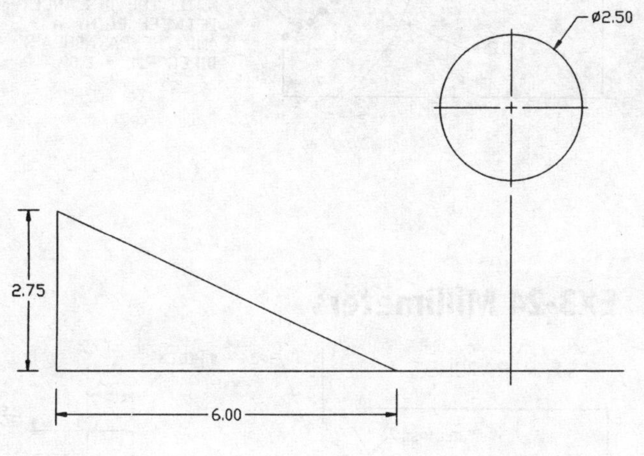

EX3-18 Millimeters

Given the setup shown next, construct a helix.

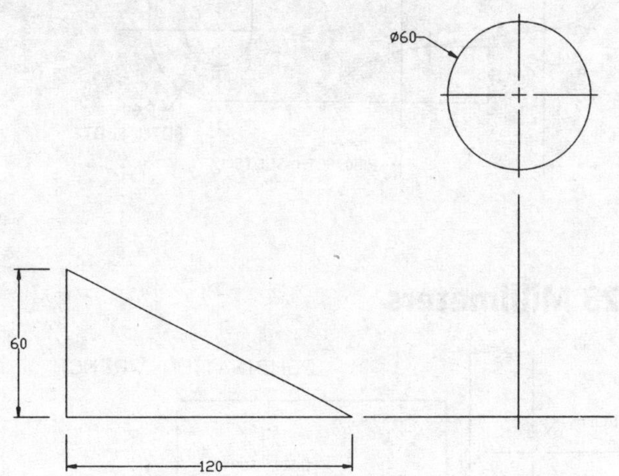

Redraw the following objects based on the given dimensions:

EX3-19 Millimeters

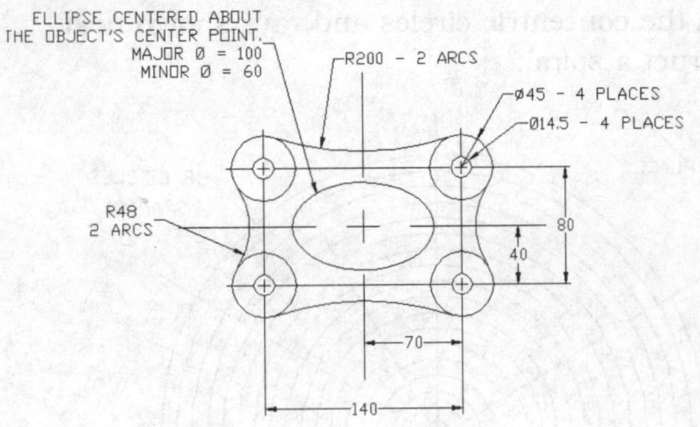

EX3-20 Millimeters

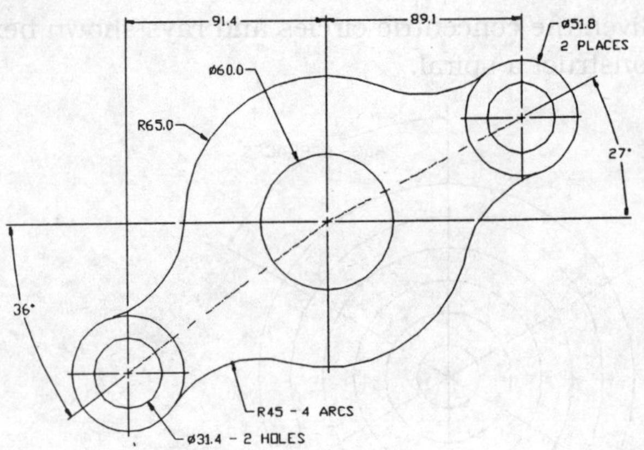

EX3-21 Inches

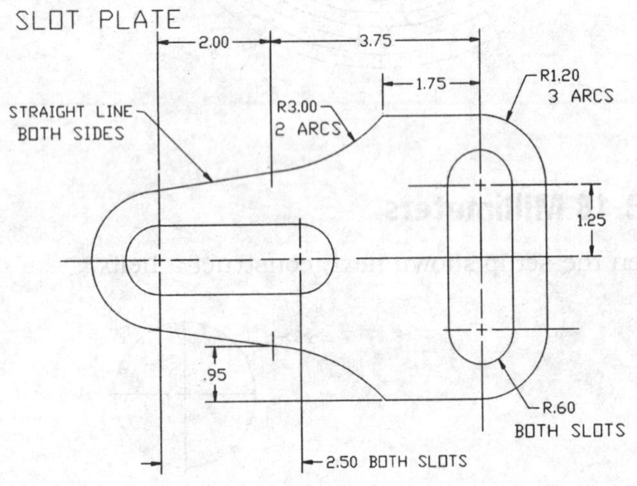

EX3-22 Inches

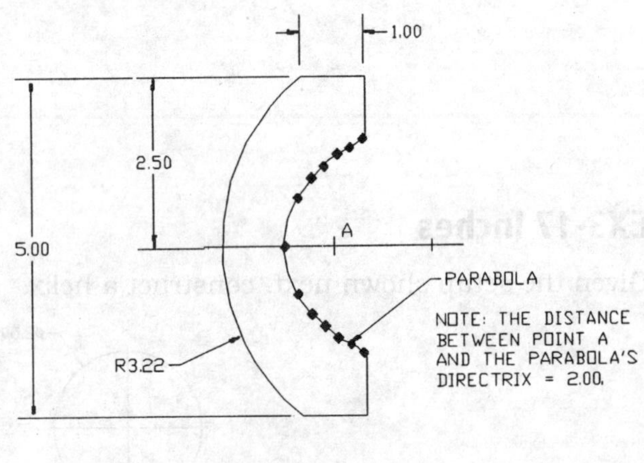

EX3-23 Millimeters

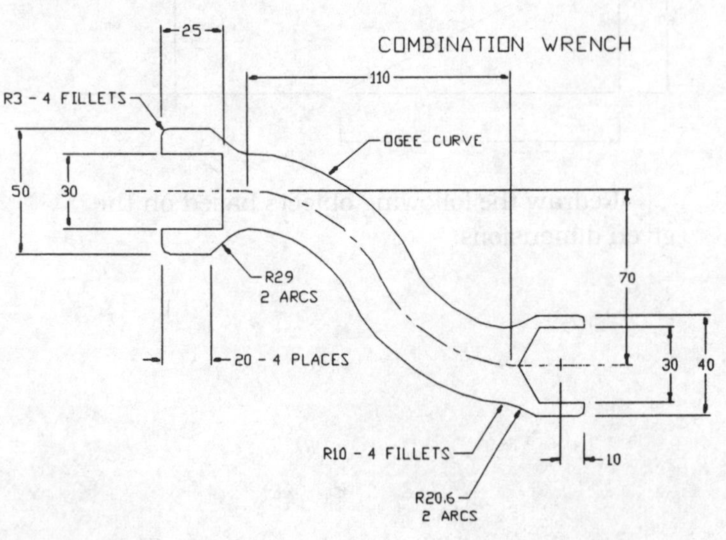

EX3-24 Millimeters

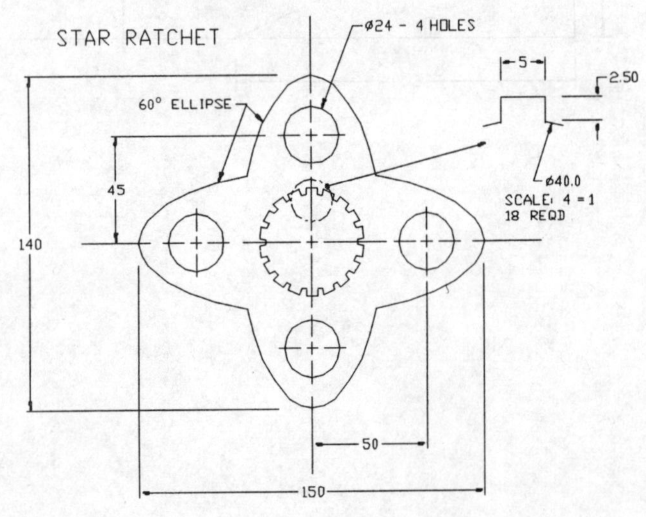

EX3-43

Draw a circle, mark off 24 equally spaced points, and then connect each point with every other point by using only straight lines.

EX3-44 Millimeters

A. Create a block of the drawing layout that follows.
B. Add the following attributes:

Tag = **DATE**
Prompt = Enter today's date
Value = (leave blank)

Tag = **DRAWING**
Prompt = Enter the drawing number
Value = (leave blank)

Tag = **NAME**
Prompt = Enter your name
Value = (leave blank)

Align the attribute tags on the drawing.

DRAWING LAYOUT - 2(MILLIMETERS)

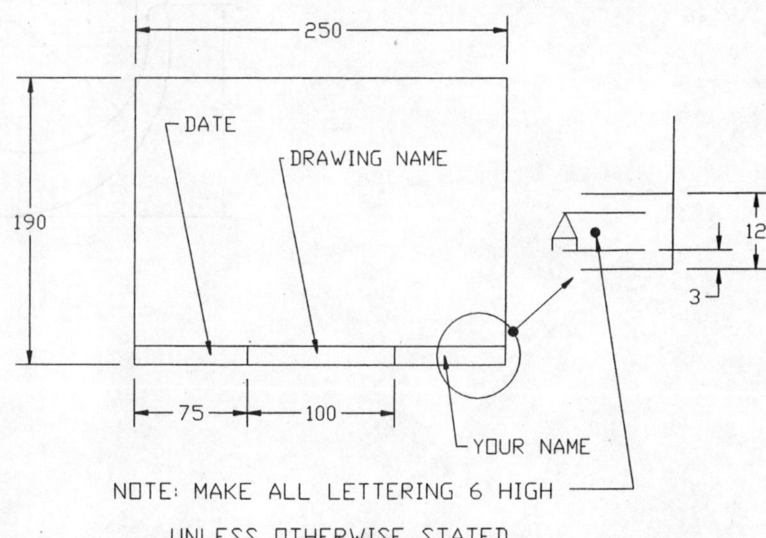

EX3-45 Millimeters

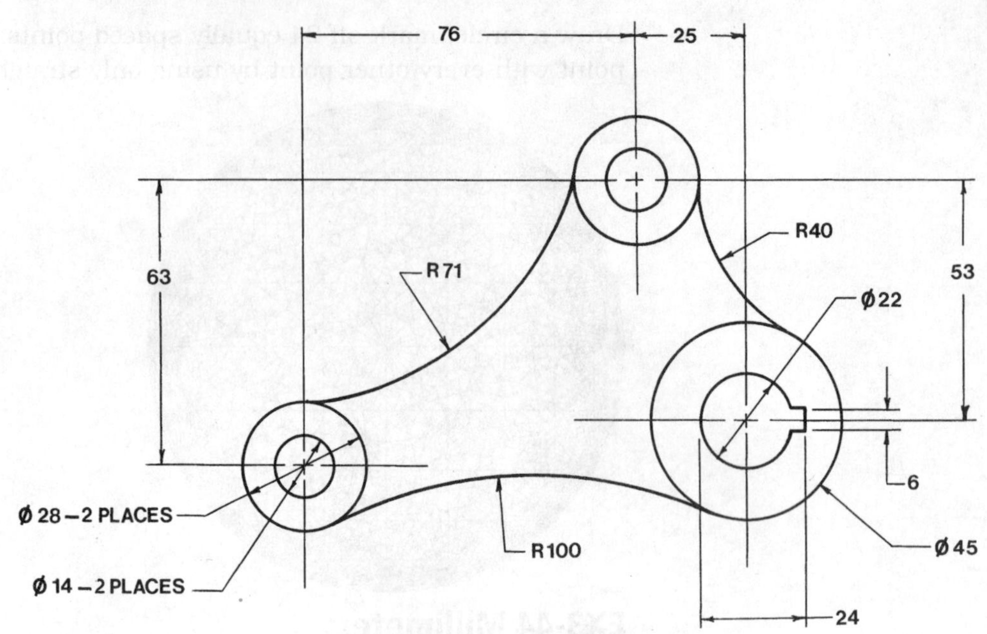

EX3-46 Millimeters

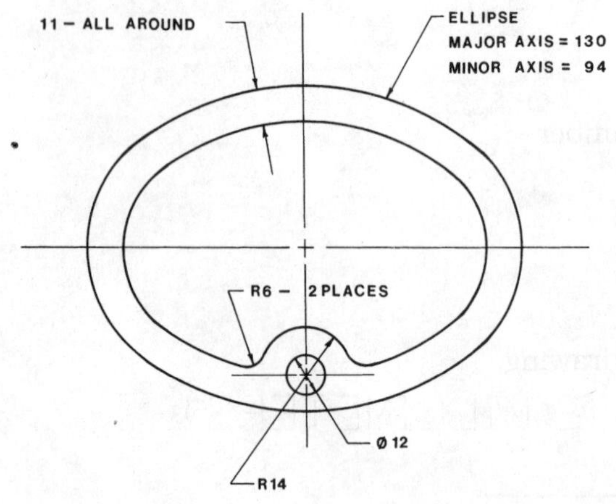

EX3-47 Millimeters

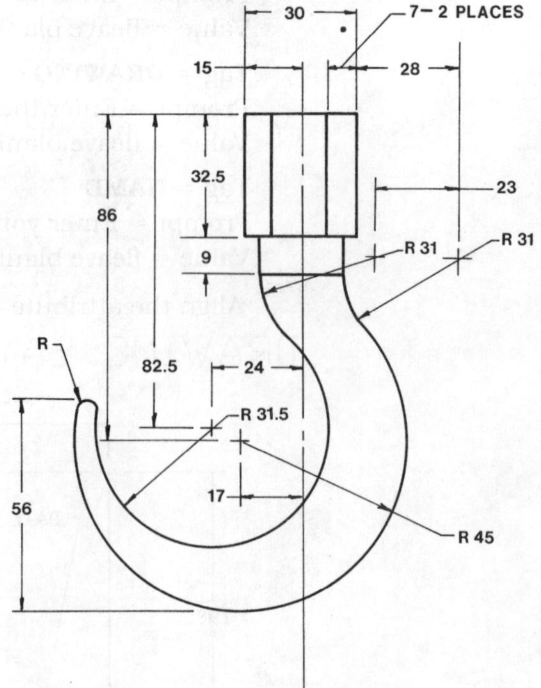

EX3-48 Inches

Create a block for the standard tolerance blocks shown.

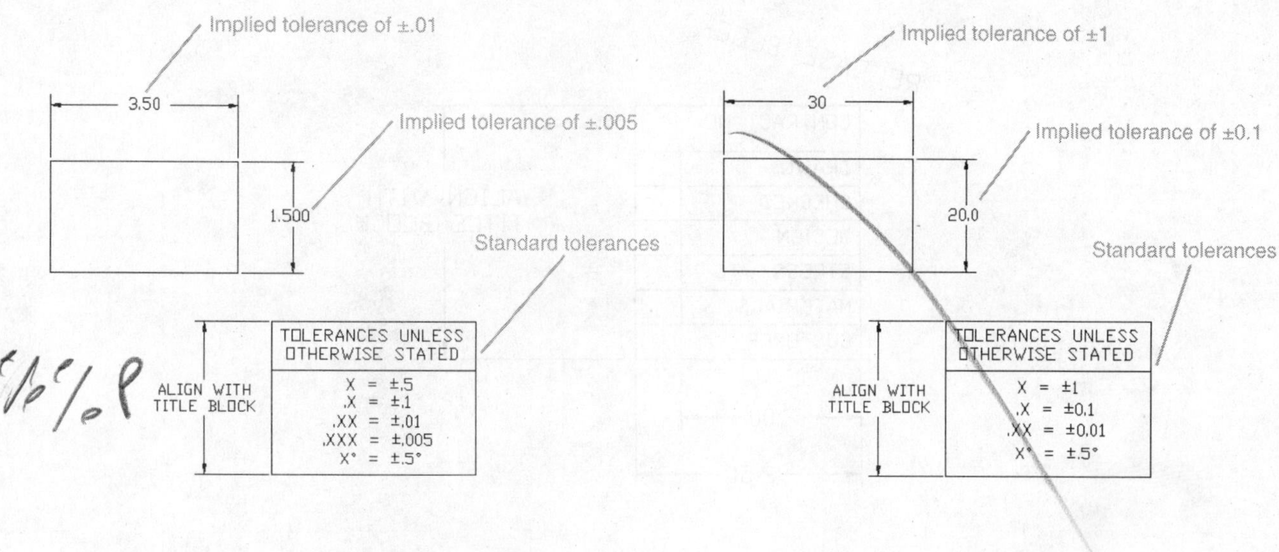

EX3-49 Inches

A. Create a block for one of the title blocks shown. A sample completed title block is also shown.

B. Add attributes that will help the user to complete the title block satisfactorily.

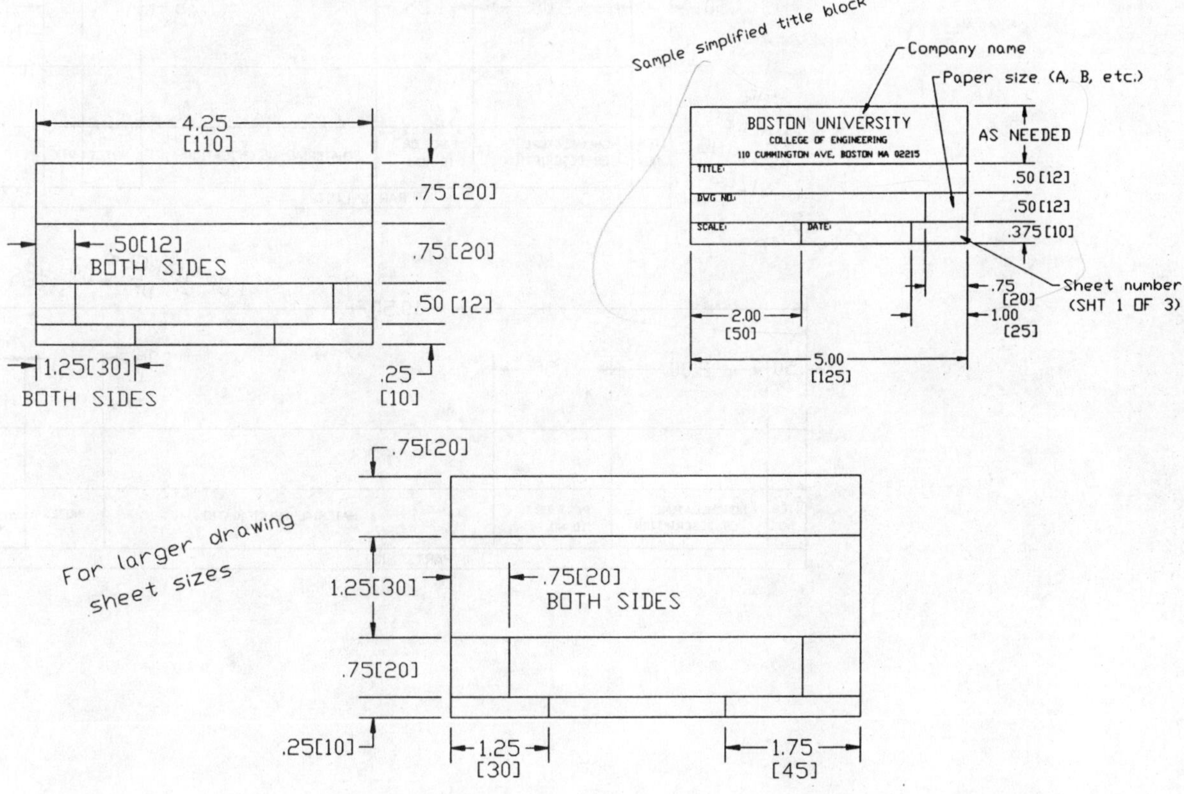

EX3-50 Inches

Create a block of the following release block:

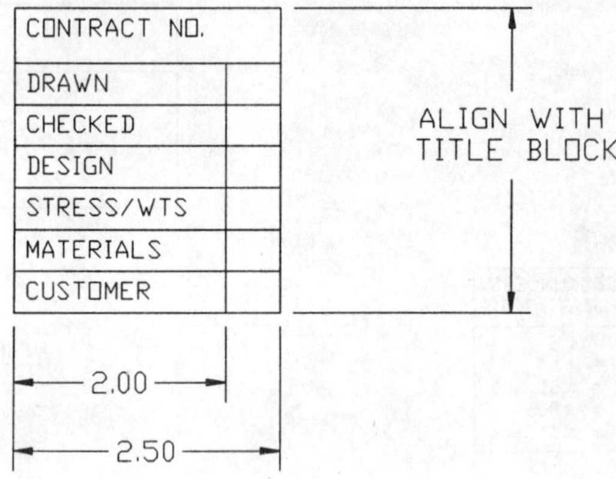

EX3-51 Inches

Create blocks for the parts list formats that follow. Add the appropriate attributes.

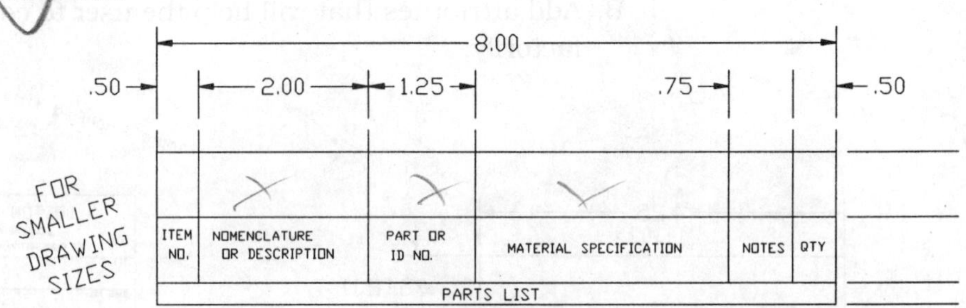

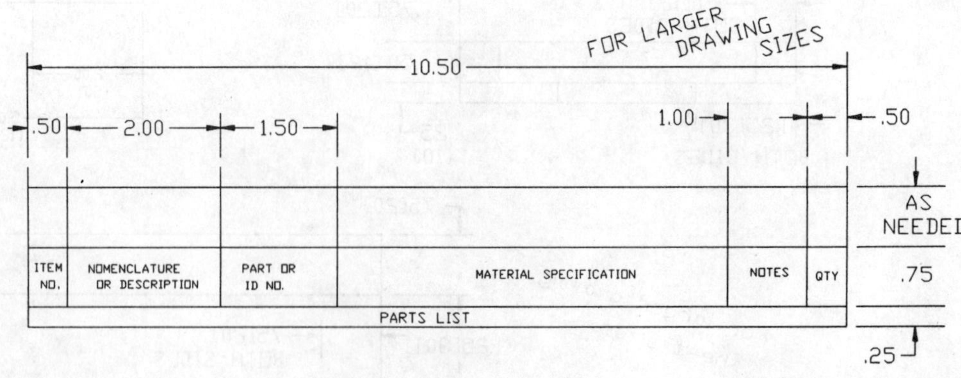

EX3-52

Create blocks for the given revision block formats. The dimensions within the dimension lines are inches; the dimensions within the brackets are millimeters.

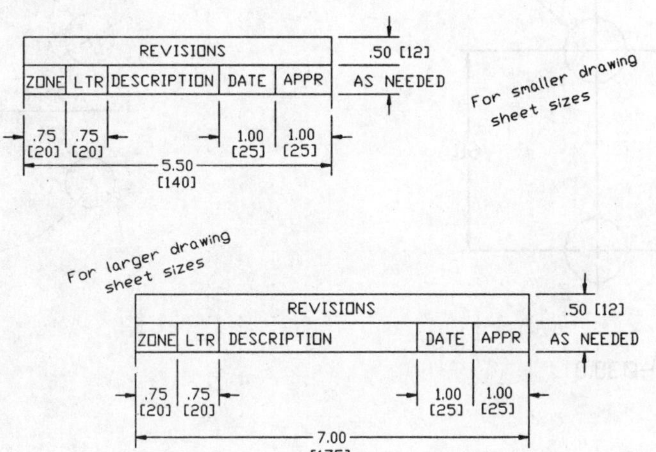

Design a shape that will support the hole patterns shown in Exercises EX3-53 through EX3-57. Design for a minimum amount of material and to satisfy the following parameters:

1. The edge distance of the material may be no closer to the center of a hole than a distance equal to the radius of the hole.
2. The minimum edge distance from any internal cutout to the edge of the part may be no less than the distance calculated in step 1.
3. The minimum inside radius for a cutout is 5 millimeters, or 0.125 inch.

EX3-53 Inches

HW

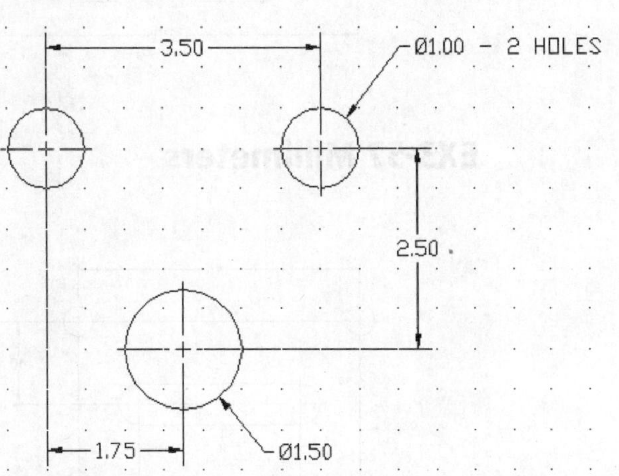

EX3-54 Millimeters

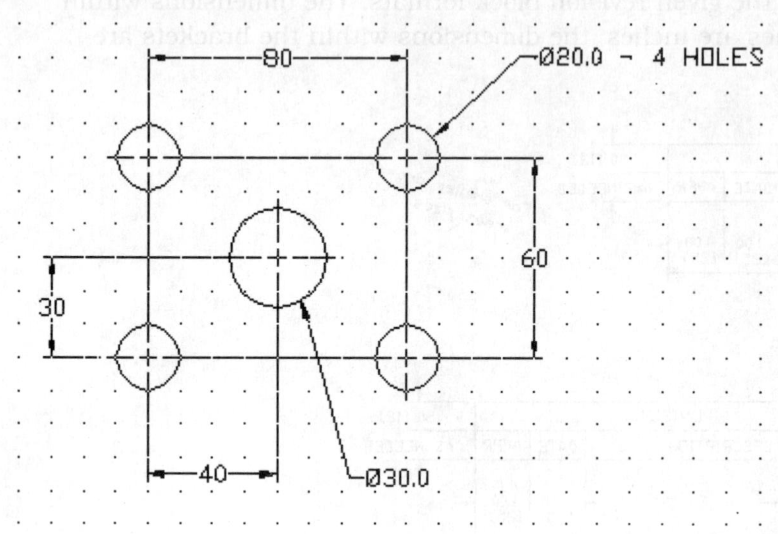

EX3-55 Millimeters

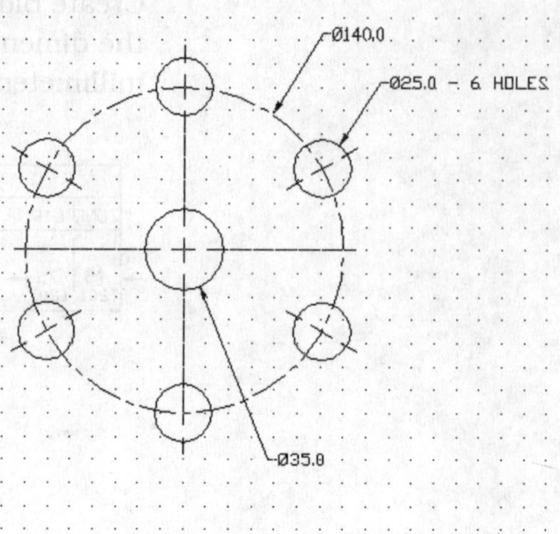

EX3-56 Millimeters

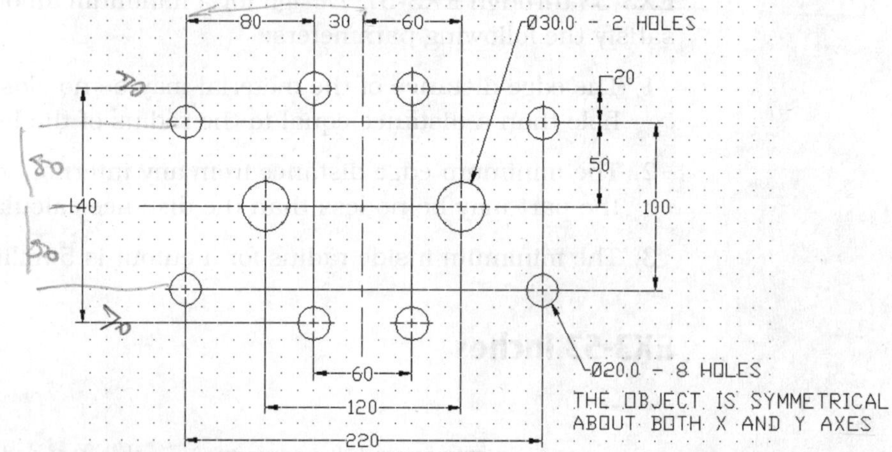

EX3-57 Millimeters

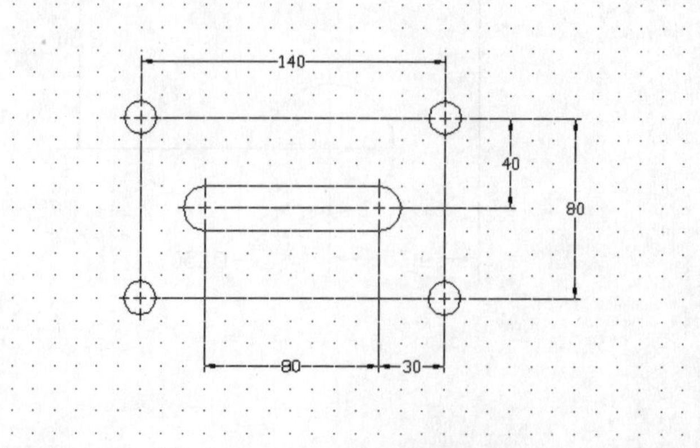

chapterfour
Sketching

4-1 Introduction

The ability to create freehand sketches is an important skill for engineers and designers to acquire. The old joke about engineers' and designers' not being able to talk without a pencil in their hand is not far from the truth. Many design concepts and ideas are very difficult to express verbally, so they must be expressed visually. Sketches can be created quickly and used as a powerful aid in communicating technical ideas.

This chapter presents the fundamentals of freehand sketching as applied to technical situations. It includes both two-dimensional and three-dimensional sketching. Like any skill, freehand sketching is best learned by lots of practice.

4-2 Establishing Your Own Style

As you learn how to sketch and practice sketching, you will find that you develop your own way of doing things, your own style. This is very acceptable, as there is no absolutely correct method for sketching, but only recommendations.

The most important requirement of freehand sketching is that you be comfortable. As you practice and experiment, you may find that you prefer a certain pencil lead hardness, a certain angle for your paper, and a certain way to make your lines, both straight and curved. You may find that you prefer to use oblique sketches rather than isometric sketches when sketching three-dimensional objects. Eventually, you will develop a style that is comfortable for you and that you can consistently use to create good-quality sketches.

It is recommended that you try all the types of sketches presented in the chapter. Only after you have tried and practiced all of the different types will you be able to settle on a technique and style that works best for you.

4-3 Graph Paper

Graph paper is very helpful when preparing freehand sketches. It helps you to sketch straight lines, allows you to set up guide points for curved lines, and can be used to establish proportions. It is recommended that you start by doing all two-dimensional sketches on graph paper. As your sketching becomes more proficient, you may sketch on plain paper, but because most technical sketching requires some attention to correct proportions, grid paper will always be helpful.

Graph paper is available in many different scales and in both inch and metric units. Some graph paper is printed with light-blue lines, since many copying machines cannot easily reproduce blue lines. This means that copies of the sketches done on light-blue guidelines will appear to have been drawn on plain paper and will include only the sketch.

4-4 Pencils

Pencils are made with many grades of lead hardness. See Figure 4-1. Hard leads can produce thin, light lines and are well suited for the accuracy requirements of board-type drawings, but are usually too light for sketching. The soft leads produce broad, dark lines, but tend to smudge easily if handled too much.

Figure 4-1

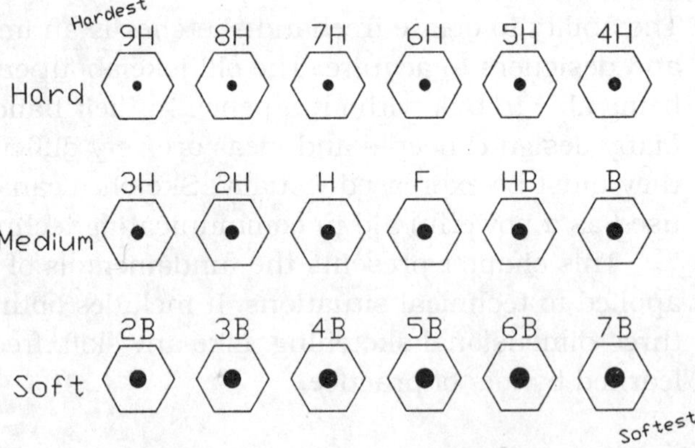

The choice of lead hardness is a personal one. Some designers use 3H leads very successfully; others use HB leads with equally good results. You are probably used to a 2H lead, as this is the most commonly available. Start sketching with a 2H lead, and if the lines are too light, try a softer lead; if they are too dark, try a harder lead until you are satisfied with your work. Pencils with different grades of lead hardness are available at most stationery and art supply stores.

Most sketching is done in pencil because it can easily be erased and modified. If you want the very dark lines that ink produces, it is recommended that you first prepare the drawing in pencil and then use a pen to trace over the lines that you want to emphasize.

4-5 Lines

Straight lines are sketched by one of two methods: by drawing a series of short lines—called *feathering*—or by drawing a series of line segments. The line segments should be about 1 to 2 inches or 25 to 50 millimeters long.

It is very difficult to keep the line segments reasonably straight if they are much longer. As you practice you will develop a comfortable line segment length. See Figure 4-2.

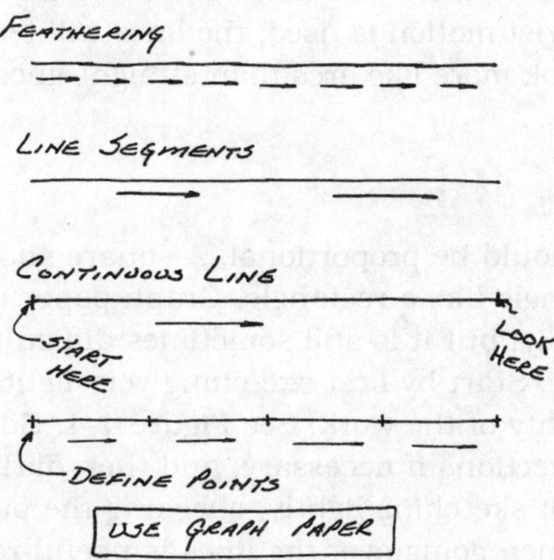

Figure 4-2

Lines may also be sketched as long, continuous lines. First, locate the pencil at the line's starting point; then, look at the endpoint as you sketch. This will help you develop straighter long lines. Continuous lines are best sketched on graph paper because the graph lines will serve as an additional guide for keeping the lines straight.

Long lines can be created by a series of shorter lines, and very long lines can be sketched by first defining a series of points, then using short segments to connect the points.

It is usually more comfortable to turn the paper slightly when sketching, as shown in Figure 4-3. Right-handers turn the paper counterclockwise, and left-handers, clockwise.

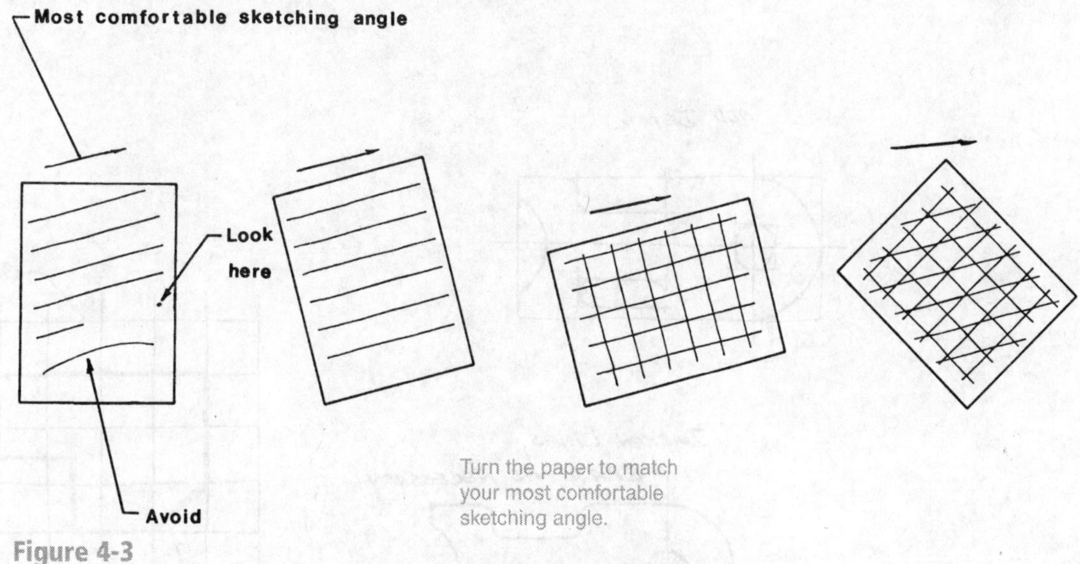

Figure 4-3

It is also easier to sketch all lines in the same direction—that is, with your hand motion always the same. Rather than change your hand position for lines of different angles, simply change the position of the paper and sketch the lines as before. Horizontal and vertical lines are sketched by using exactly the same motion; the paper is just turned 90°. Straight lines of any angle can be sketched in the same manner.

Sketch lines by using a gentle, easy motion. Don't squeeze the pencil too hard. Sketch lines with more of an arm motion than a wrist motion. If too much wrist motion is used, the lines will tend to curve down at the ends and look more like arcs than straight lines.

4-6 Proportions

Sketches should be proportional. A square should look like a square, and a rectangle like a rectangle. Graph paper is very helpful in sketching proportionally, but it is still sometimes difficult to be accurate even with graph paper. Start by first sketching very lightly and then checking the proportionality of the work. See Figure 4-4. Go back over the lines, making corrections if necessary, and then darken in the lines. The technique of first sketching lightly, checking the proportions, making corrections, and then going over the lines is useful regardless of the type of paper used.

It is often helpful to sketch a light grid background based on the unit values of the object being sketched. This is true even if you are working on graph paper because it helps to emphasize the unit values you need. See Figure 4-5.

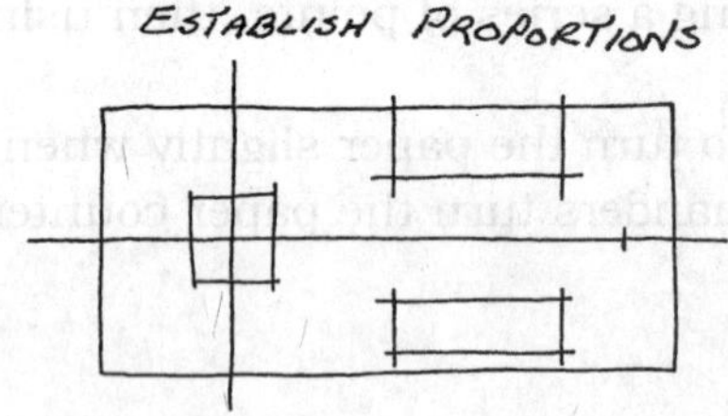

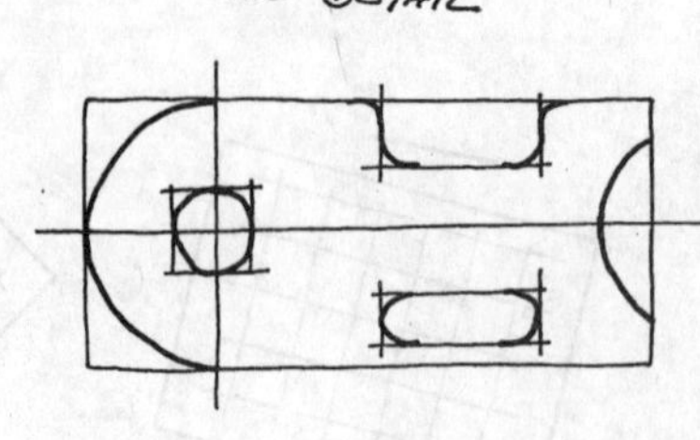

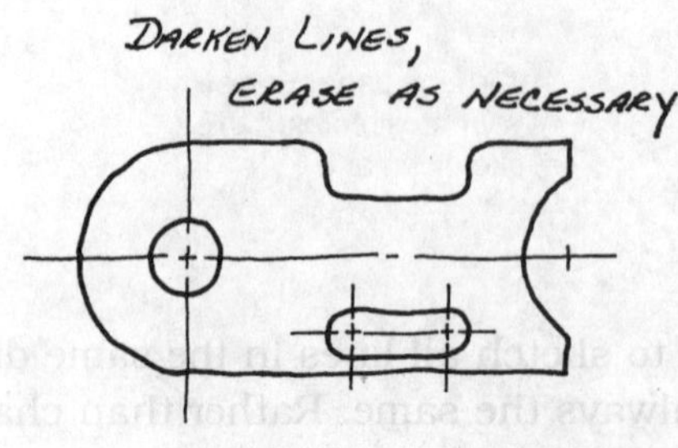

Figure 4-4

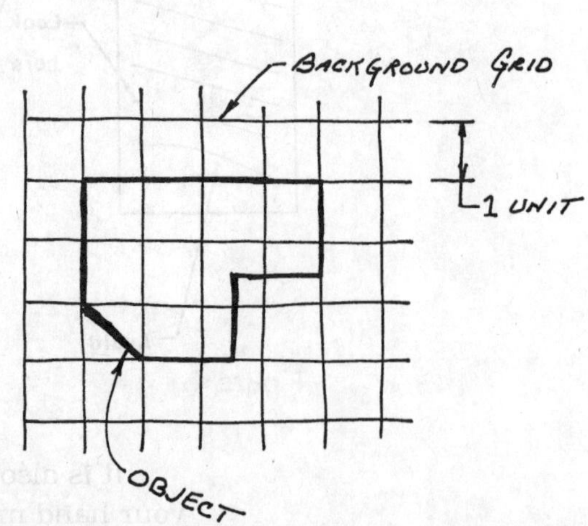

Figure 4-5

The exact proportions of an object are not always known. A simple technique to approximately measure an object is to use the sketching pencil. See Figure 4-6. Hold the pencil at arm's length and sight the object. Move your thumb up the pencil so that the distance between the end of the pencil and your thumb represents a distance on the object. Transfer the distance to the sketch. Continue taking measurements and transferring them to the sketch until reasonable proportions have been created.

Figure 4-6

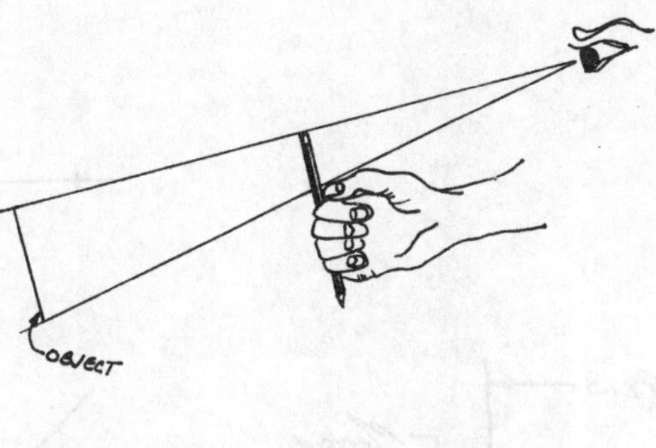

4-7 Curves

Curved shapes are best sketched by first defining points along the curve, then lightly sketching the curve between the points. See Figure 4-7. Evaluate the accuracy and smoothness of the curve, make any corrections necessary, and then darken in the curve.

Circles can be sketched by sketching perpendicular centerlines and marking off four points equally spaced from the center point along the centerlines. The distance between the center point and the points on the centerlines should be approximately equal to the circle's radius. See Figure 4-8.

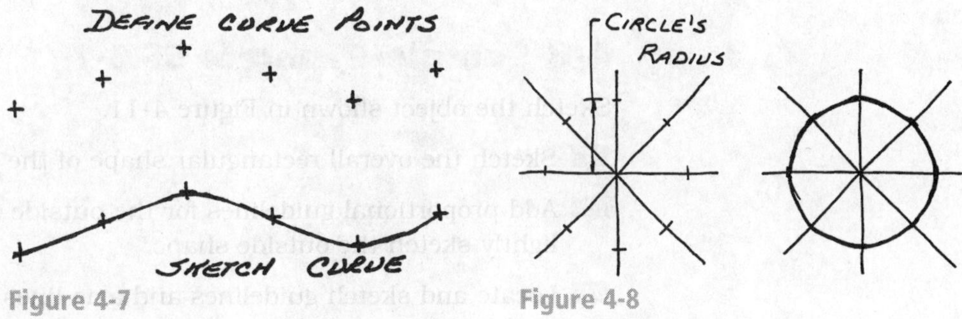

Figure 4-7 Figure 4-8

Draw a second set of perpendicular centerlines approximately 45° to the first. Again mark four points approximately equal to the radius of the circle. Sketch a light curve through the eight points, and check the curve for accuracy and smoothness. Make any corrections necessary, and darken in the circle.

An ellipse can be sketched by first sketching a perpendicular axis, and then locating four marks on the centerlines that are approximately equal to major and minor axis distances. Sketch a light curve, make any corrections necessary, and darken in the elliptical shape. See Figure 4-9.

Figure 4-10 shows how to sketch a slot. To sketch the slot, centerlines for the two end semicircles are located and sketched. Two additional radius points are added, and then the overall shape of the slot is lightly sketched. Corrections are made, and the final lines are darkened.

The triangular object is first sketched as a triangle, guidelines and axis are added for the curved sections, and the final shape of the object is sketched.

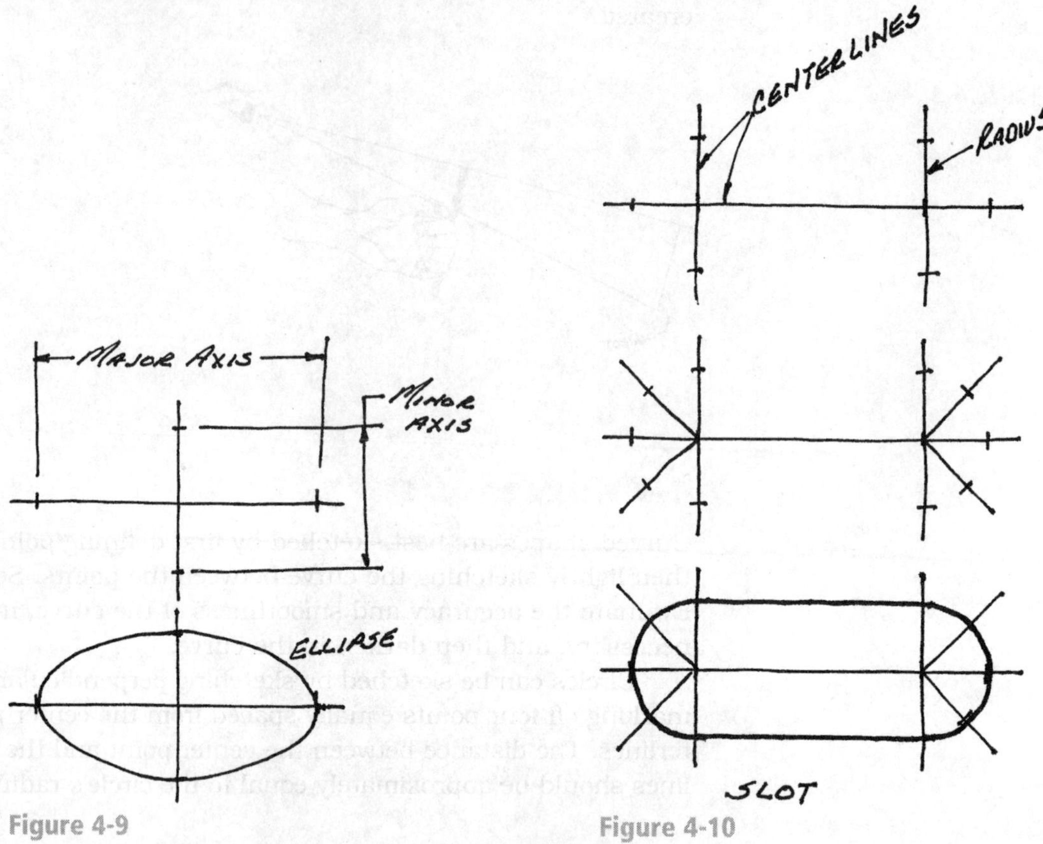

Figure 4-9

Figure 4-10

4-8 Sample Problem SP4-1

Sketch the object shown in Figure 4-11.

1. Sketch the overall rectangular shape of the object. See Figure 4-12.
2. Add proportional guidelines for the outside shape of the object, and lightly sketch the outside shape.
3. Locate and sketch guidelines and axis lines for the other features.
4. Lightly sketch the object, and make any corrections necessary.
5. Darken the final lines.

Figure 4-11

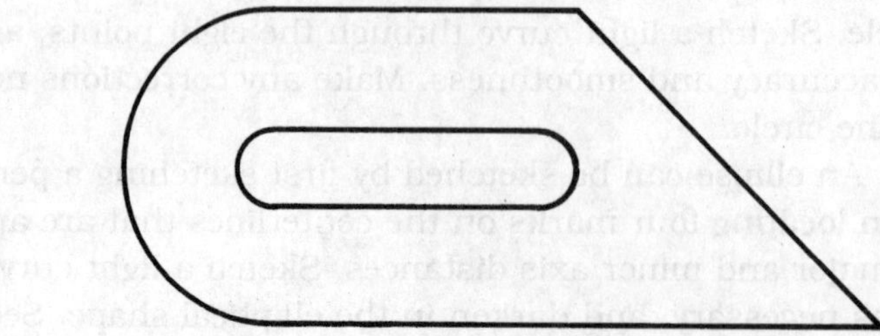

Figure 4-12

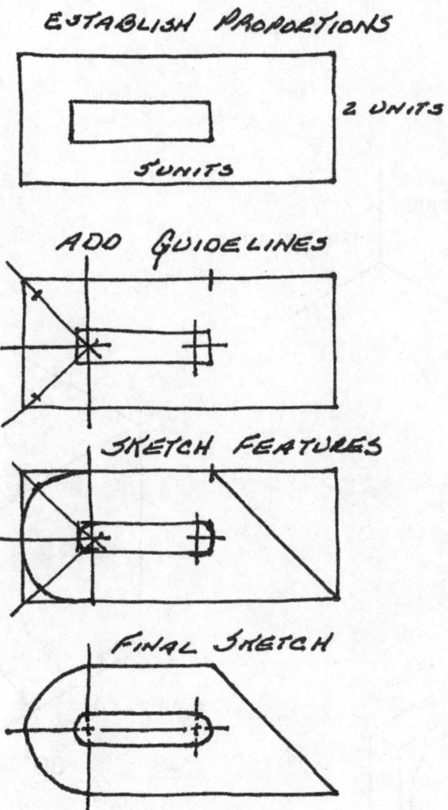

4-9 Isometric Sketches

Isometric sketches are based on an isometric axis that contains three lines, 120° apart. See Figure 4-13. The isometric axis can also be drawn in a modified form that contains a vertical line and two 30° lines. The modified axis is more convenient for sketching and is the more commonly used form. See Figure 4-14.

The receding lines of an isometric sketch are parallel. This is not visually correct, as the human eye naturally sees objects farther away as smaller than those closer. In reality, railroad tracks appear to converge; however, it is easier to draw objects with parallel receding lines, and if the object is not too big, the slight visual distortion is acceptable. See Section 4-12 for an explanation of perspective drawings whose receding lines are not parallel, but convergent.

The three planes of an isometric axis are defined as the left, right, and top planes, respectively. See Figure 4-14. When creating isometric sketches, it is best to start with the three planes drawn as if the object were a rectangular prism or cube. Think of creating the sketch from these planes as working with a piece of wood, and trim away the unnecessary areas. Figure 4-15 shows an example of an isometric sketch. In the example, the overall proportions of the object were used to define the boundaries of the object, and then other surfaces were added as necessary.

Isometric sketches may be sketched in different orientations. Figure 4-16 shows six possible orientations. Note how orientation 1 makes the object look as if it is below you, and orientation 6 makes it look as if it is above you. Orientation can also serve to show features that would otherwise be hidden from view. The small cutout is clearly visible in only

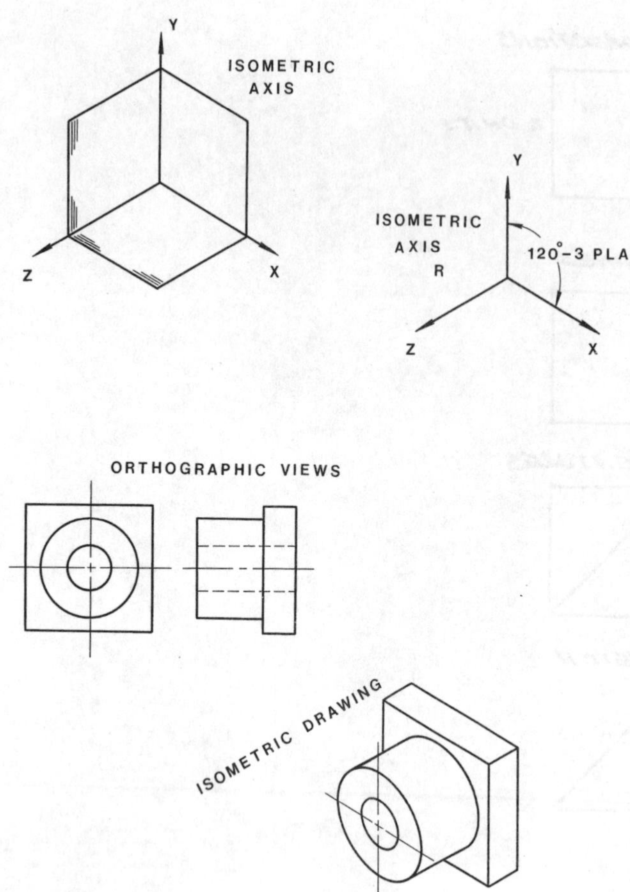

Figure 4-13

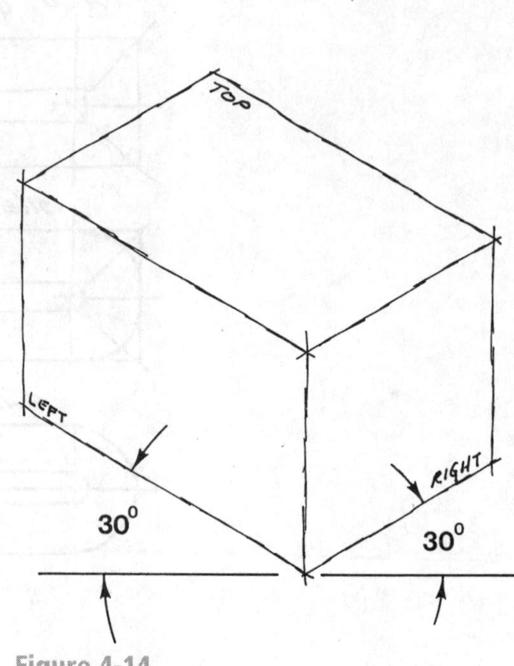

Figure 4-14

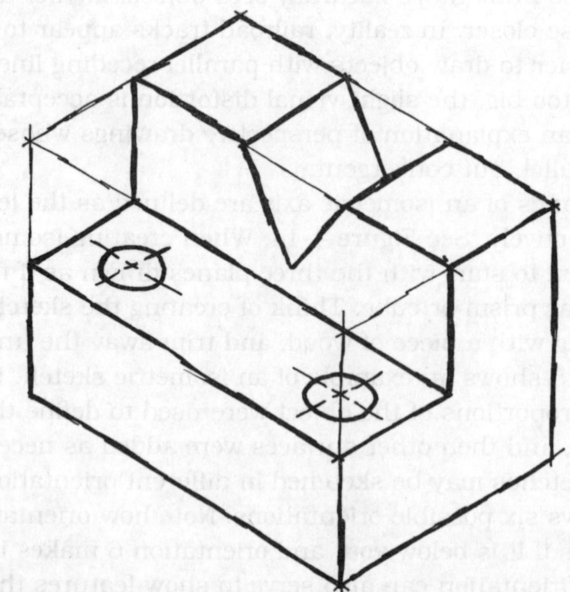

Figure 4-15

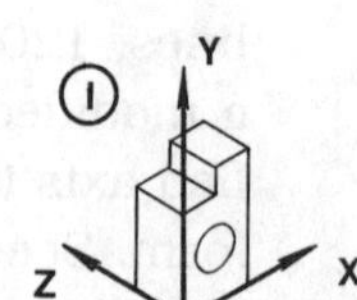
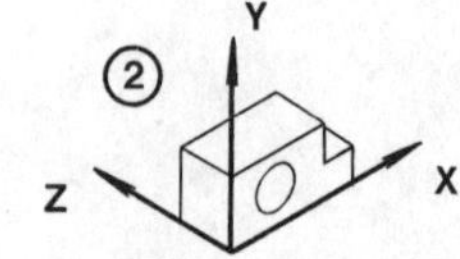
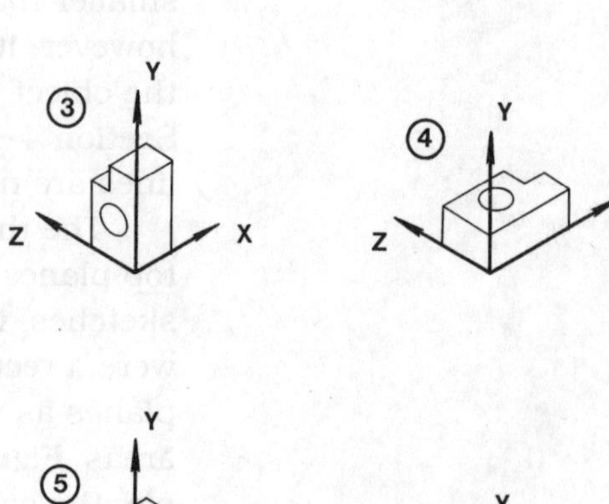
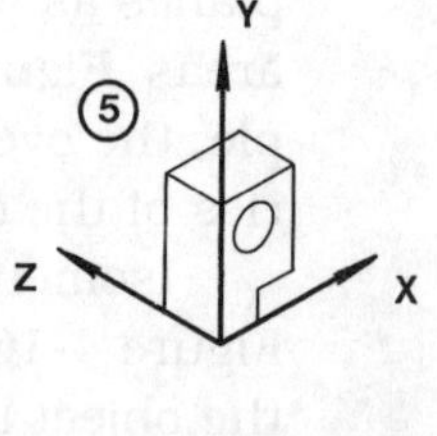
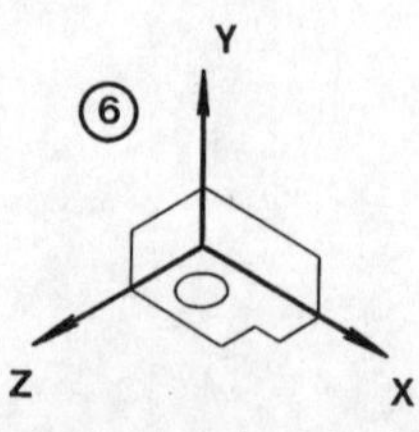

Figure 4-16

one of the orientations. Always try to orient the isometric sketch so that it shows as many of the object's features as possible.

Figure 4-17 shows an isometric drawing of a cube that has a hole in the top plane. The hole must be sketched as an ellipse to appear visually correct in the isometric drawing. The axis lines for the ellipse are parallel to the edge lines of the plane. The proportions of the ellipse are defined by four points equidistant from the ellipse center point along the axis lines. The ellipse is then sketched lightly, checked for accuracy, and darkened.

Figure 4-17

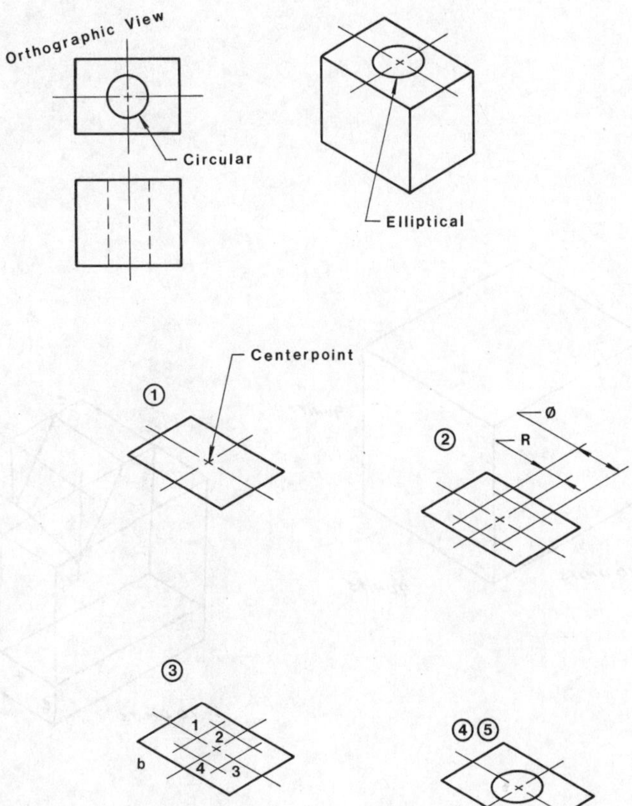

4-10 Sample Problem SP4-2

Sketch the object shown in Figure 4-18. Do not include dimensions, but keep the object proportional.

1. Use the overall dimensions of the object to sketch a rectangular prism of the correct proportions. This is a critical step. If the first attempt is not proportionally correct, erase it and sketch again until a satisfactory result is achieved. See Figure 4-19.
2. Sketch the cutout.
3. Sketch the rounded surfaces. Note how axis lines are sketched and the elliptical shape added. Tangency lines are added, and visually incorrect lines are erased.
4. Sketch the holes. The holes are located by locating their centerlines and then sketching the required ellipses.

Figure 4-18

Figure 4-19

4-11 Oblique Sketches

Oblique sketches are based on an axis system that contains one perpendicular set of axis lines and one receding line. See Figure 4-20. The front plane of an oblique axis is perpendicular, so the front face of a cube will appear as a square and the front face of a cylinder as a circle. The receding lines can be at any angle, but 30° is most common.

The receding lines of oblique sketches are parallel. As with isometric sketches, this causes some visual distortions, but unless the object is very large, these distortions are acceptable.

Holes in the front plane of an oblique sketch may be sketched as circles, but holes in the other two planes are sketched as ellipses. See Figure 4-21. The axis lines for the ellipse are parallel to the edge lines of the plane. The proportions of the ellipses are determined by points equidistant from the center point along the axis.

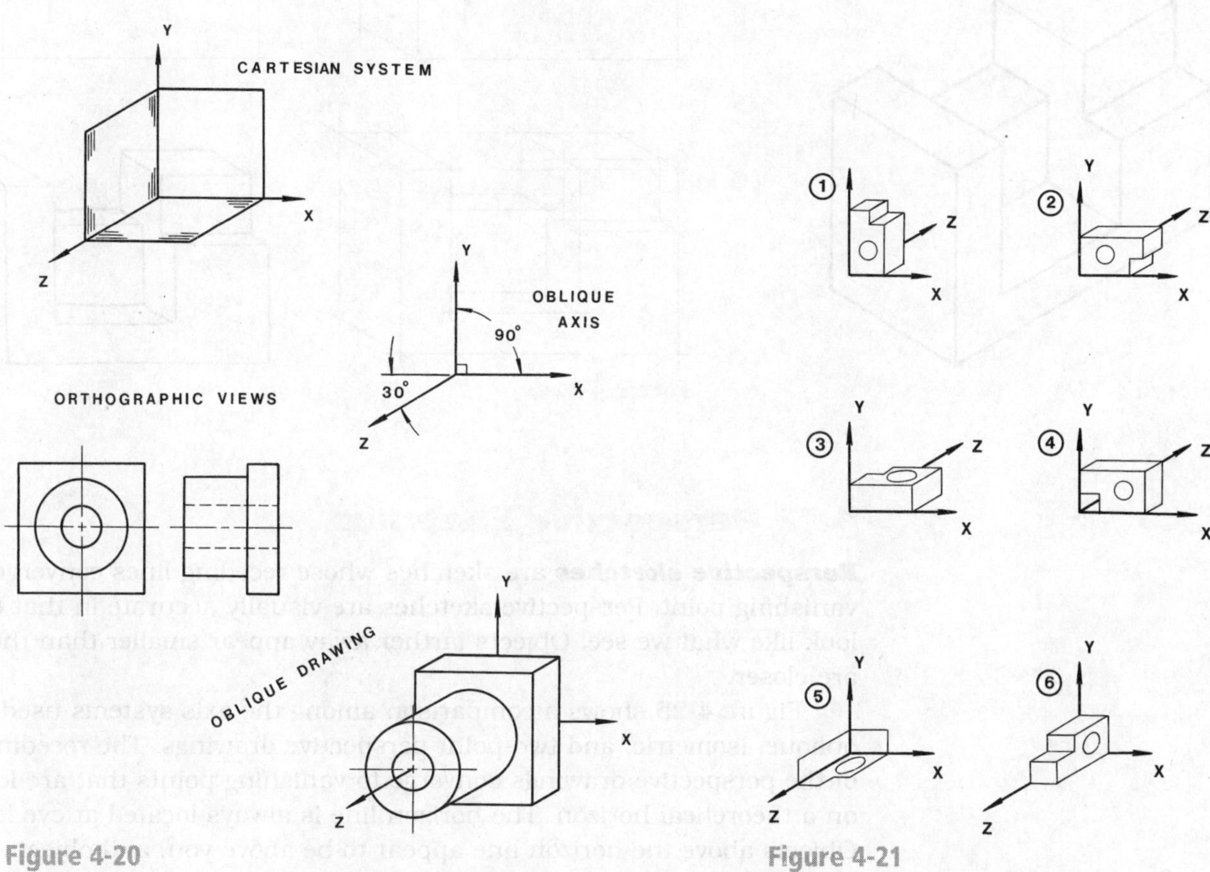

Figure 4-20

Figure 4-21

Figure 4-22 shows an example of a circular object sketched as an oblique sketch. Oblique sketches are particularly useful in sketching circular objects because they allow circles in the frontal planes to be sketched as circles rather than the elliptical shapes required by isometric sketches.

Figure 4-22

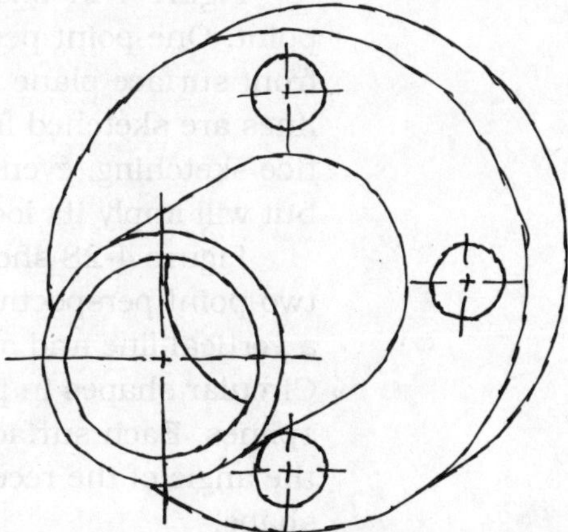

Figure 4-23 shows an object. Figure 4-24 shows how an oblique sketch of the object was developed.

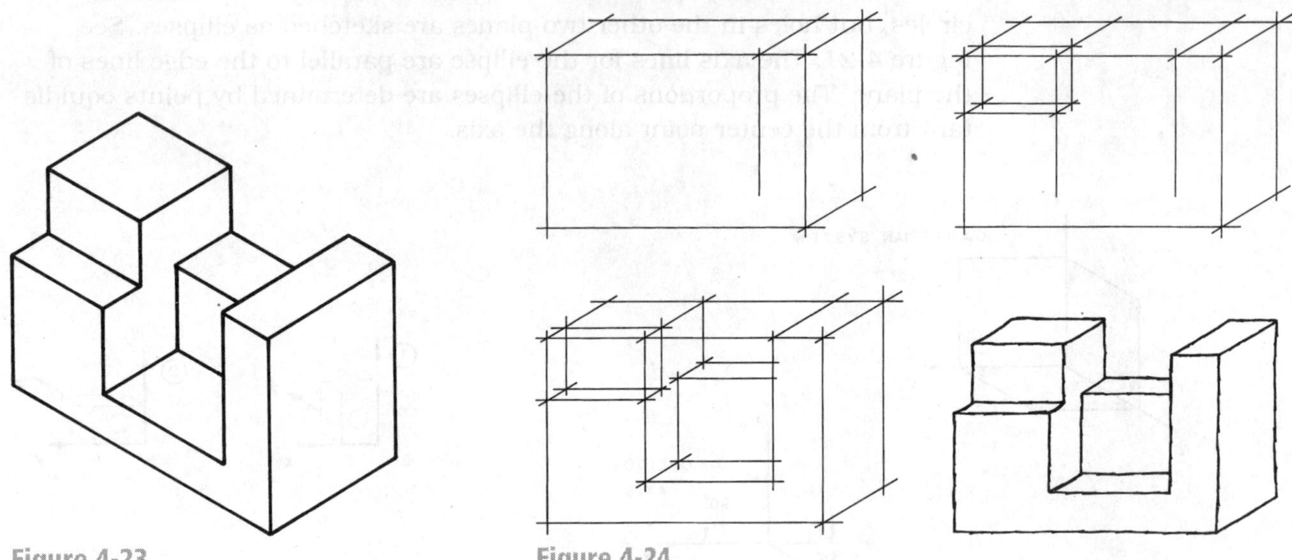

Figure 4-23

Figure 4-24

4-12 Perspective Sketches

Perspective sketches are sketches whose receding lines converge to a vanishing point. Perspective sketches are visually accurate in that they look like what we see: Objects farther away appear smaller than those that are closer.

Figure 4-25 shows a comparison among the axis systems used for oblique, isometric, and two-point perspective drawings. The receding lines of the perspective drawings converge to vanishing points that are located on a theoretical horizon. The horizon line is always located at eye level. Objects above the horizon line appear to be above you, and objects below the horizon appear to be below you.

Perspective drawings are often referred to as *pictorial drawings.* Figure 4-26 shows an object drawn twice: once as an isometric drawing and again as a pictorial, or two-point, perspective. Note how much more lifelike the pictorial drawing looks in comparison with the isometric drawing.

Figure 4-27 shows a perspective sketch based on only one vanishing point. One-point perspective sketches are similar to oblique sketches. The front surface plane is sketched by using a 90° axis, and then receding lines are sketched from the front plane to a vanishing point. As you practice sketching, eventually you will not need to include a vanishing point, but will imply its location.

Figure 4-28 shows how to sketch circular shapes in one- and two-point perspective sketches. In each style, the axis lines consist of a vertical line and a line that is aligned with the receding edge lines. Circular shapes in perspective drawings are not elliptical, but are irregular splines. Each surface will require a slightly different shape, depending on the angle of the receding lines, to produce a visually accurate circular shape.

CARTESIAN (OBLIQUE)

ISOMETRIC

Parallel Receding Lines

Parallel Receding Lines

TWO-POINT PERSPECTIVE

Vanishing Point Left

Horizon

Vanishing Point Right

Receding Lines NOT Parallel

Figure 4-25

Pictorial

Isometric

Figure 4-26

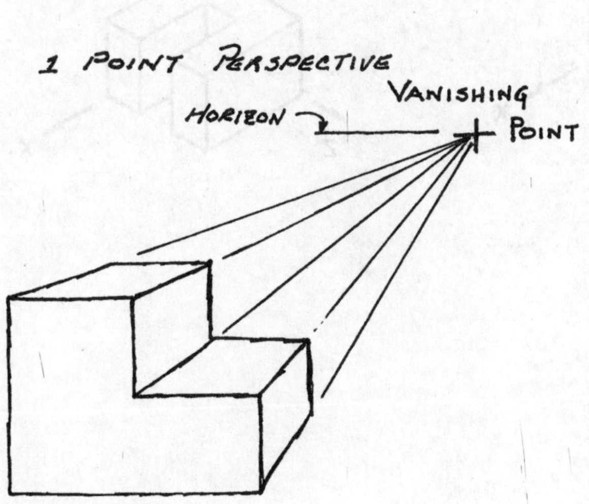

Figure 4-27

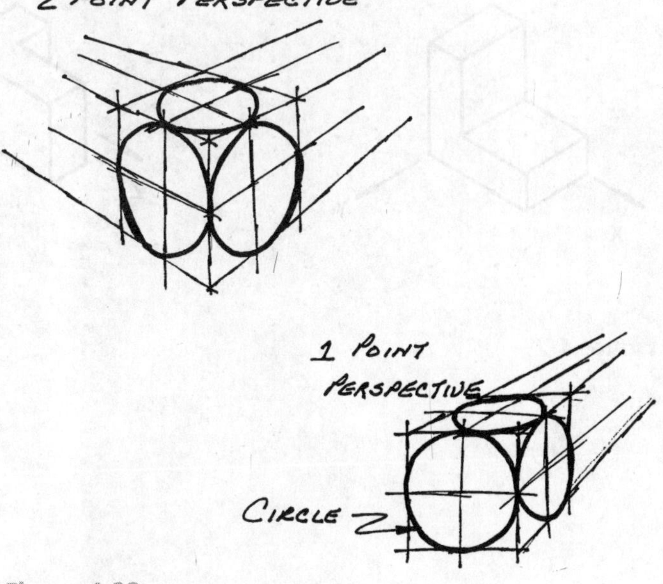

Figure 4-28

4-13 Working in Different Orientations

It is important for a designer to be able to sketch an object in different orientations in order to present a clear representation of all of the design's different facets.

Figure 4-29 shows three different objects sketched in three different orientations. Each sketch used an isometric format. Proportions for each object were determined by using the dot grid background.

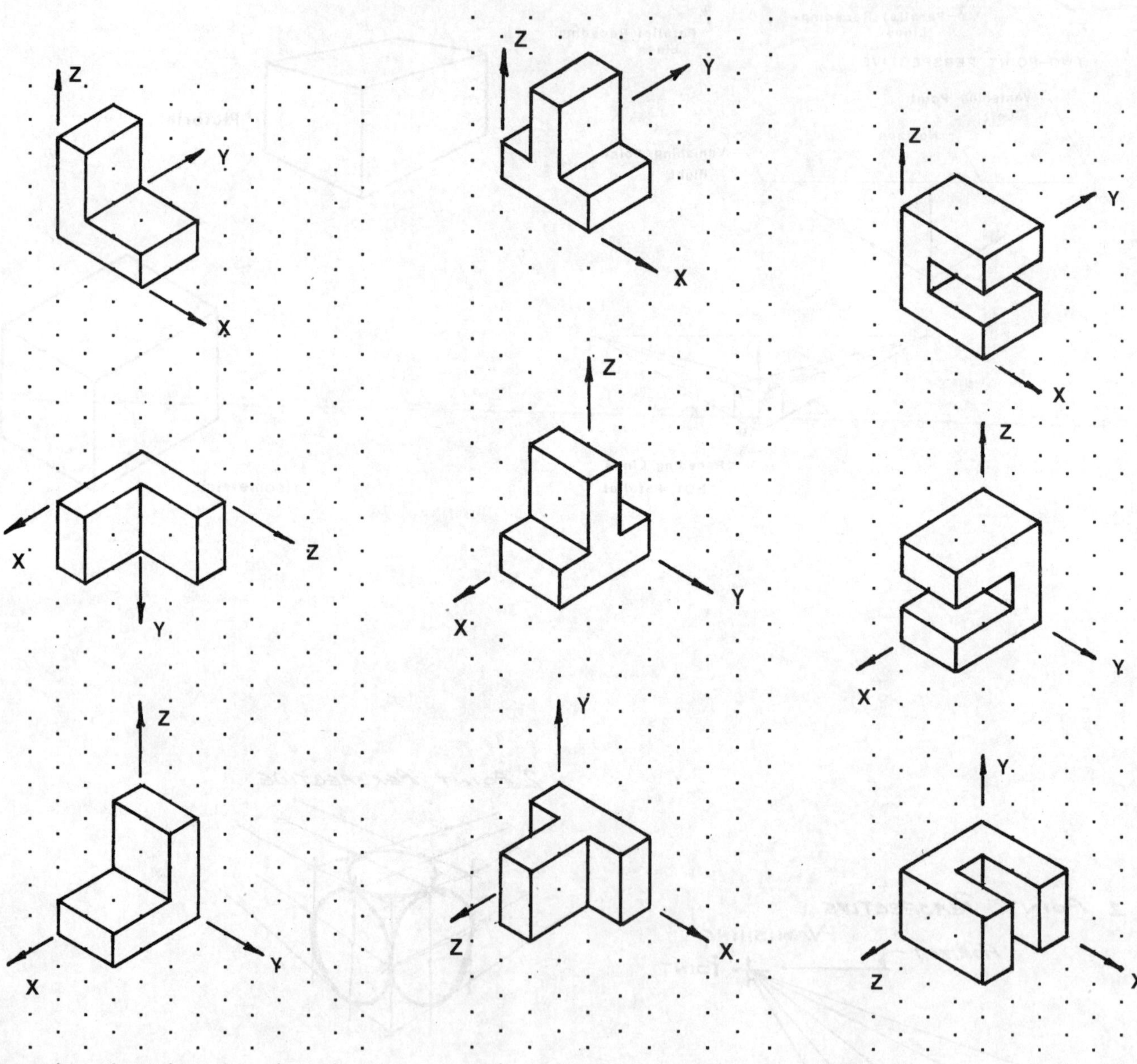

Figure 4-29

4-14 EXERCISE PROBLEMS

Sketch the shapes in Exercise Problems EX4-1 through EX4-6. Measure the shapes to determine their dimensions.

EX4-1

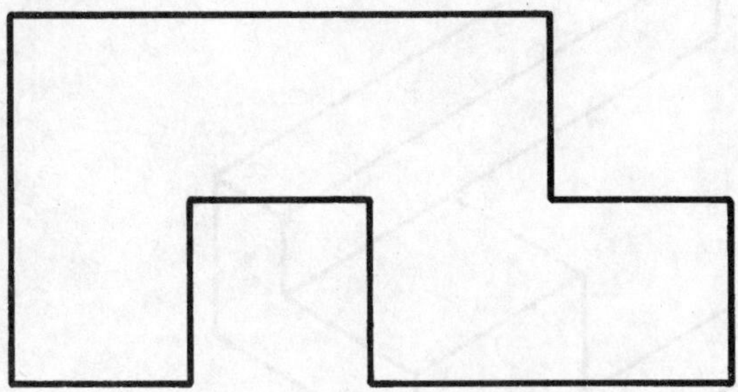

EX4-2

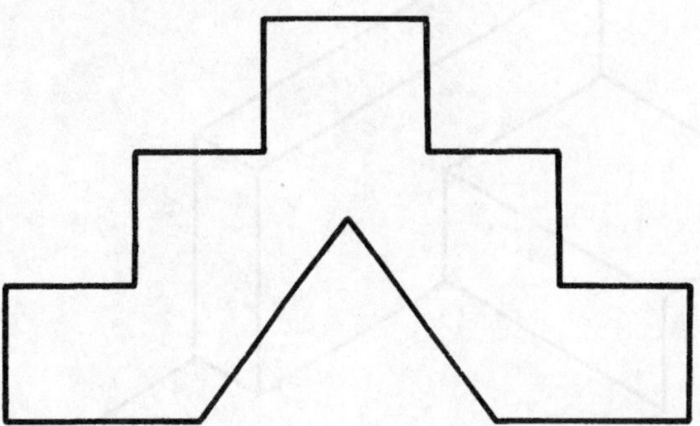

EX4-3

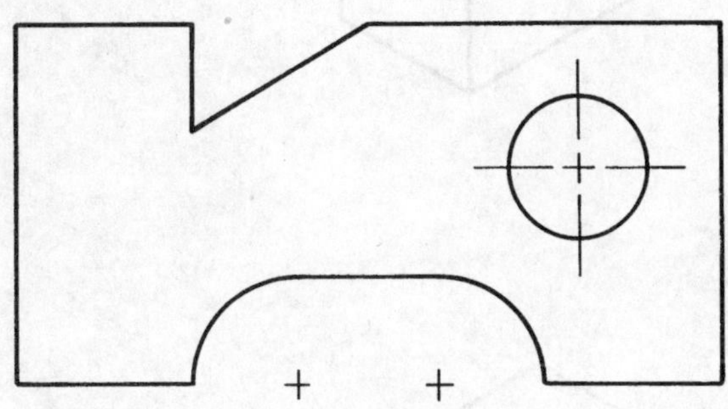

EX4-4

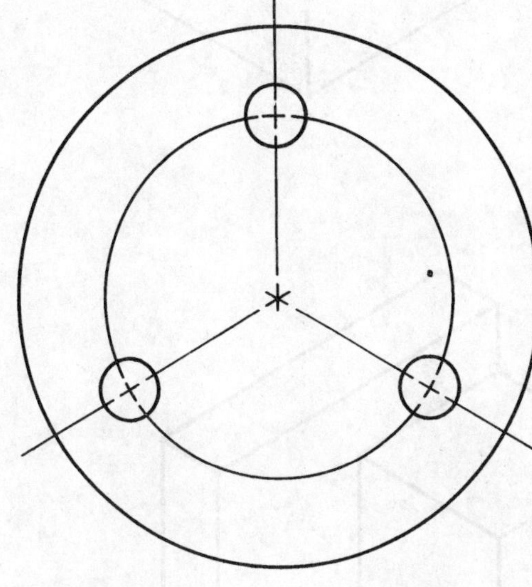

EX4-5

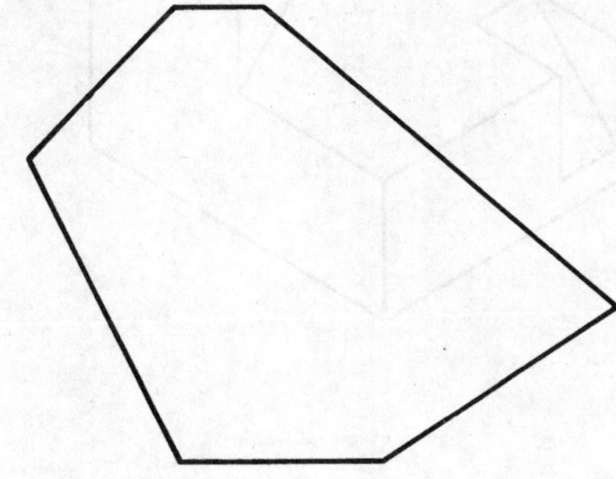

EX4-6

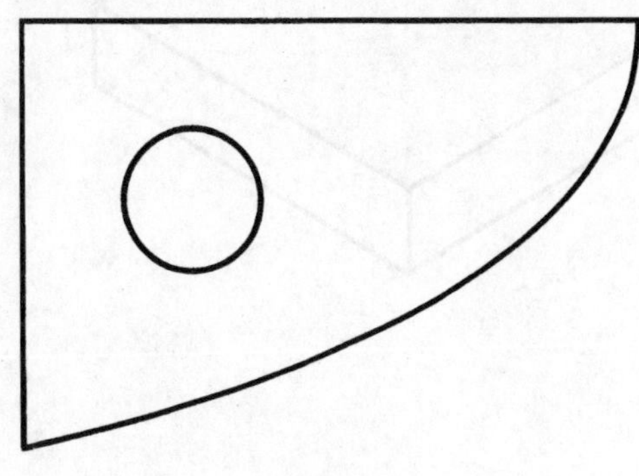

Prepare isometric or perspective sketches of the objects shown in Exercise Problems EX4-7 through EX4-18. Measure the objects to determine their dimensions.

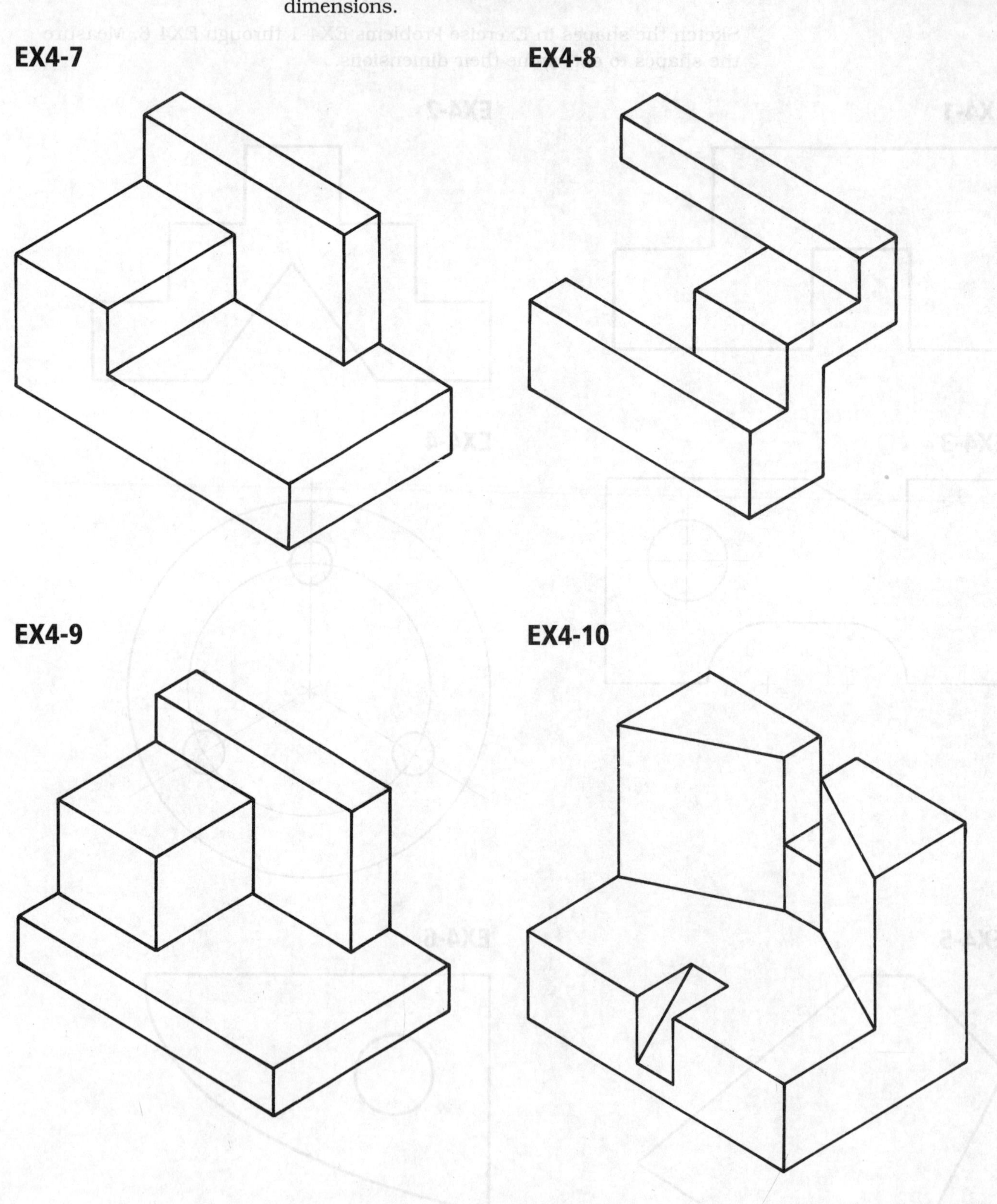

EX4-11

EX4-12

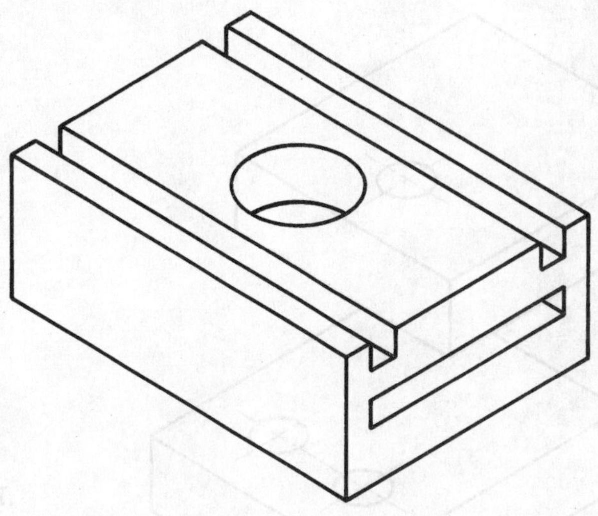

EX4-13

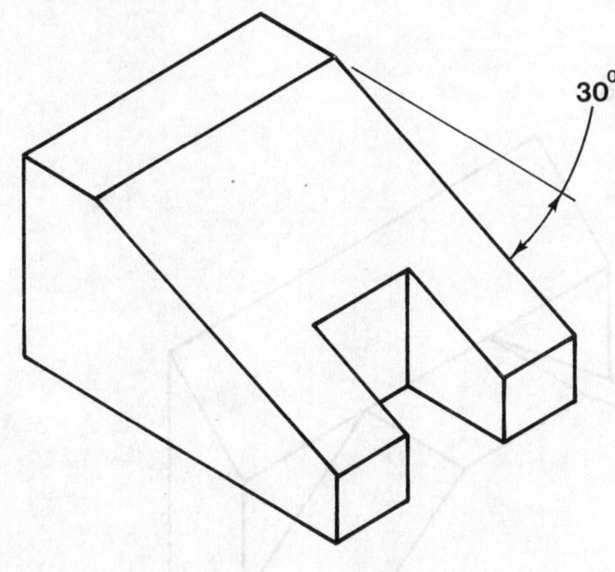

EX4-14

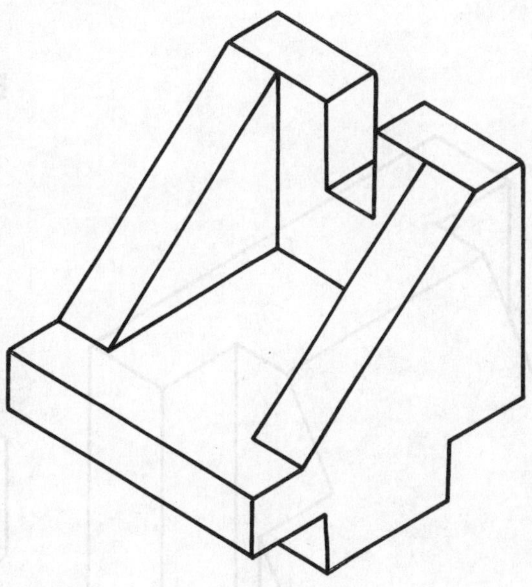

EX4-15

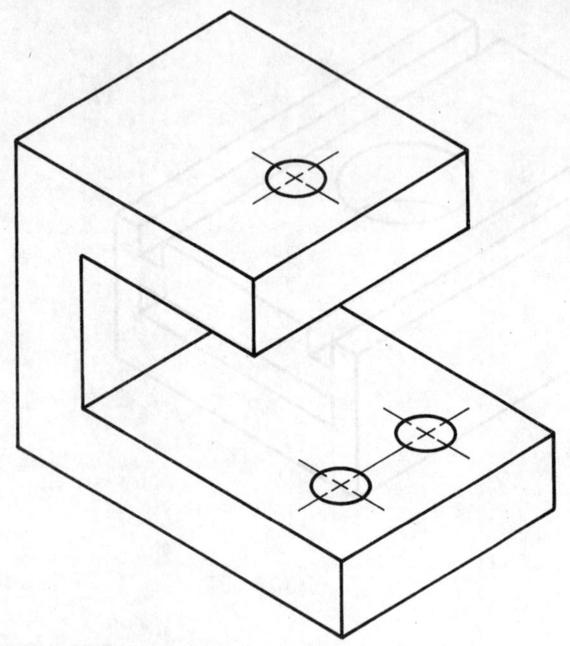

EX4-16

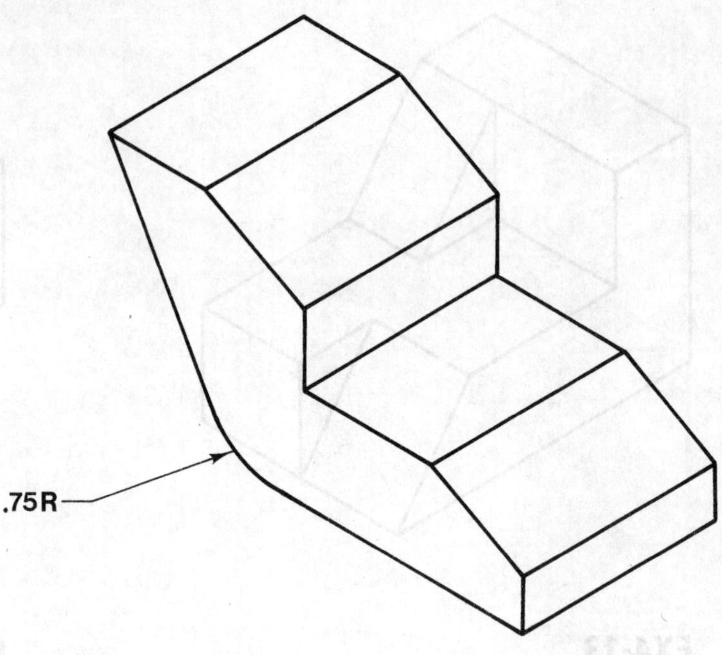

EX4-17

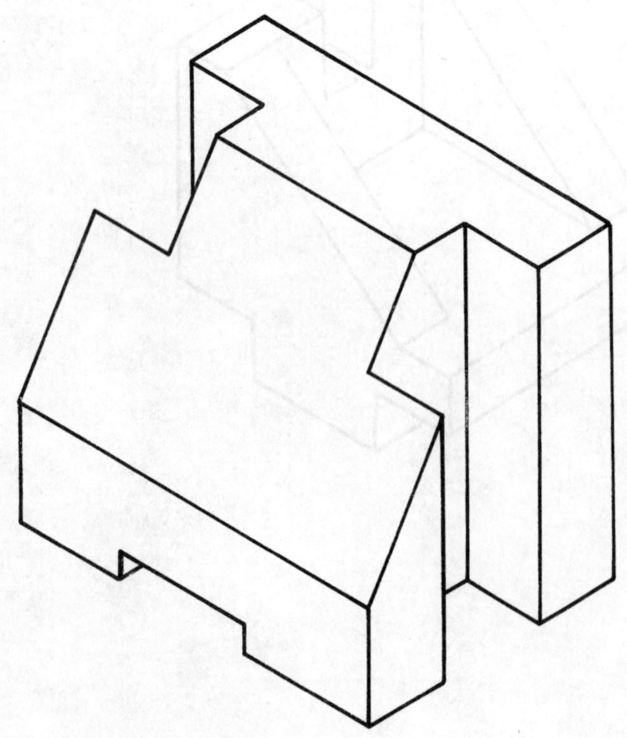

EX4-18

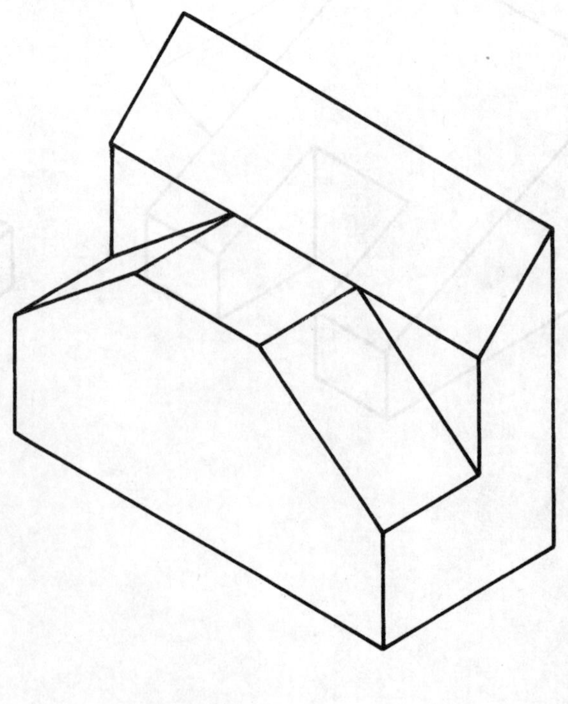

Prepare oblique or perspective sketches of the objects shown in Exercise Problems EX4-19 through EX4-22. Measure the objects to determine their dimensions.

EX4-19

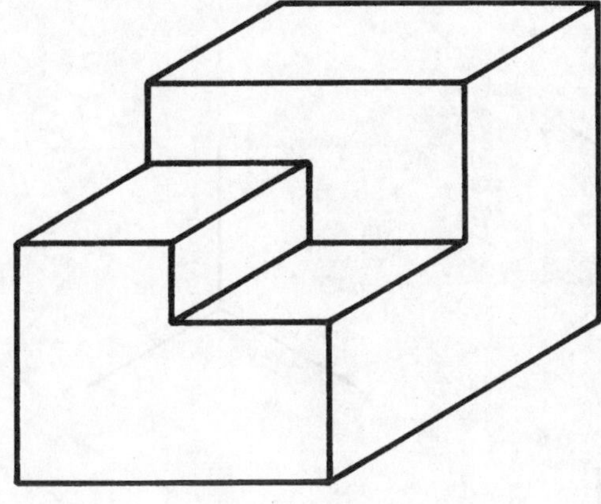

EX4-20

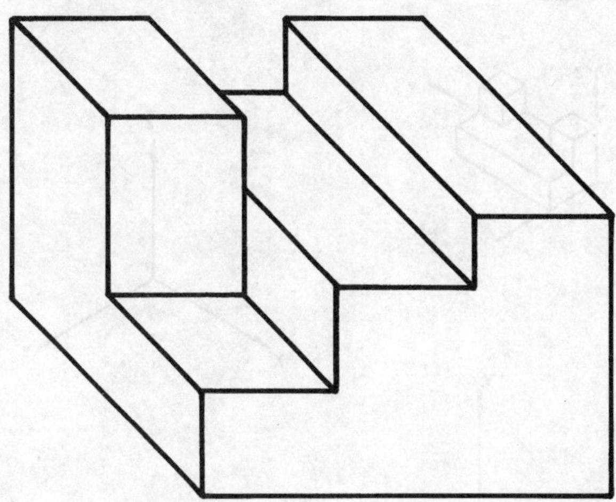

EX4-21

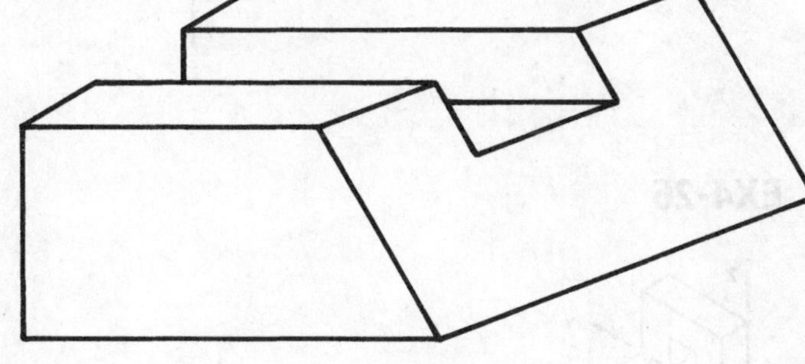

EX4-22

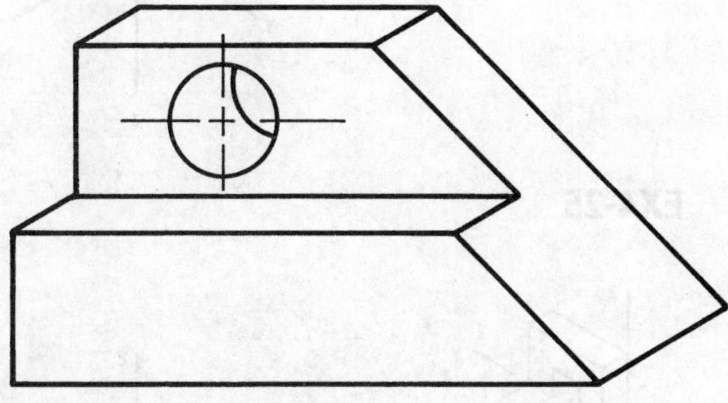

Prepare isometric sketches of the shapes that follow, each in the given orientation, and then sketch the objects in the three different orientations defined by the X,Y,Z axes. Assume that the spacing between dots in the background grid is approximately 0.25 inch, or 10 millimeters.

EX4-23

EX4-24

EX4-25

EX4-26

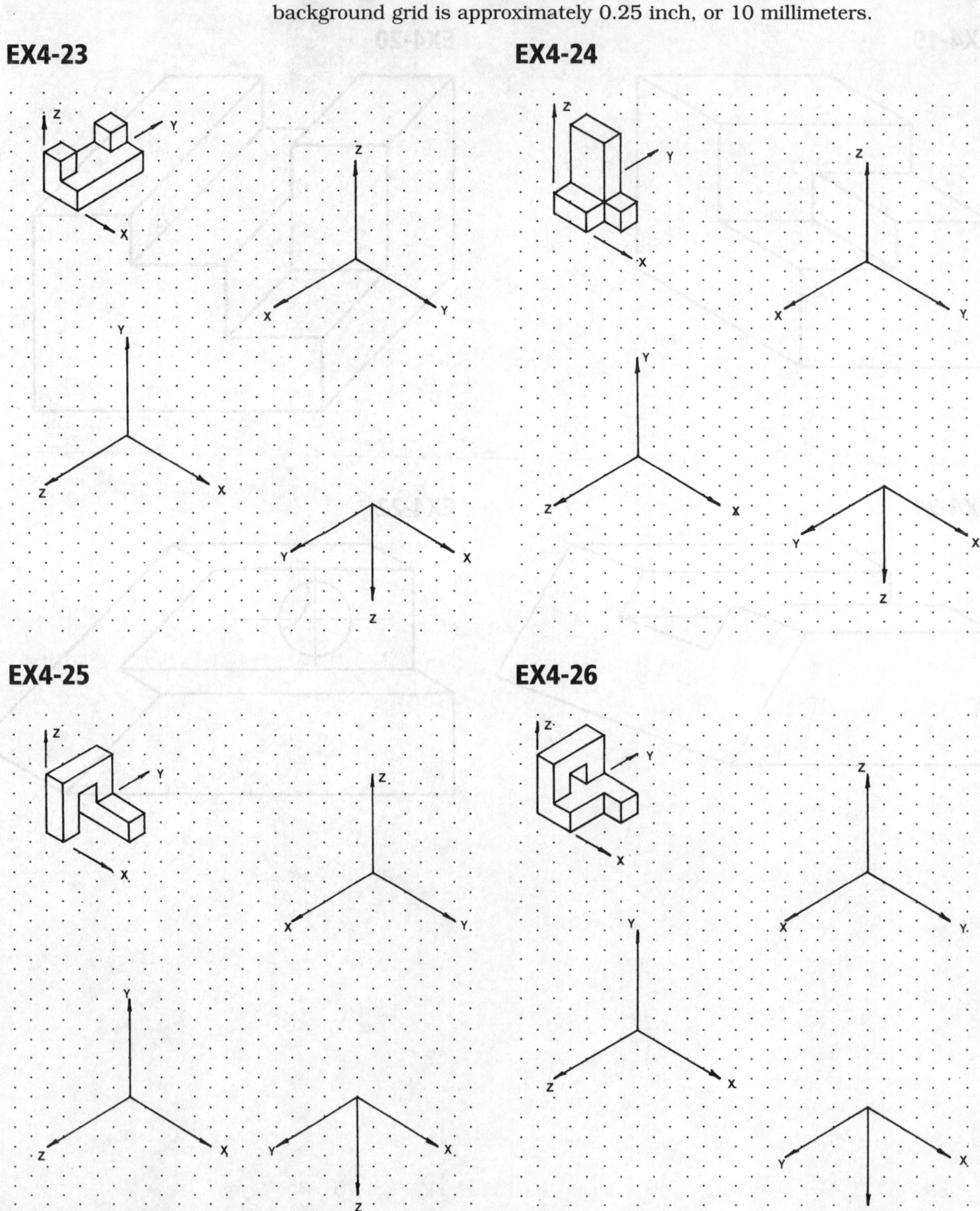

EX4-27

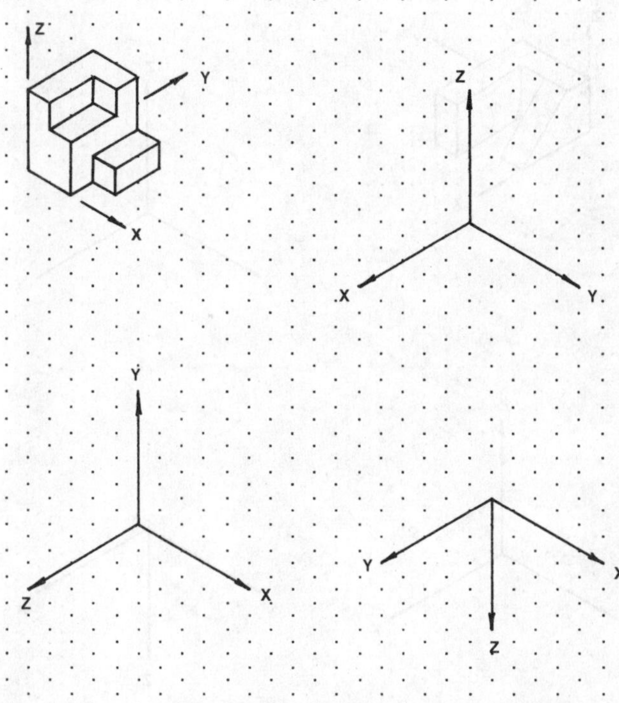

EX4-28

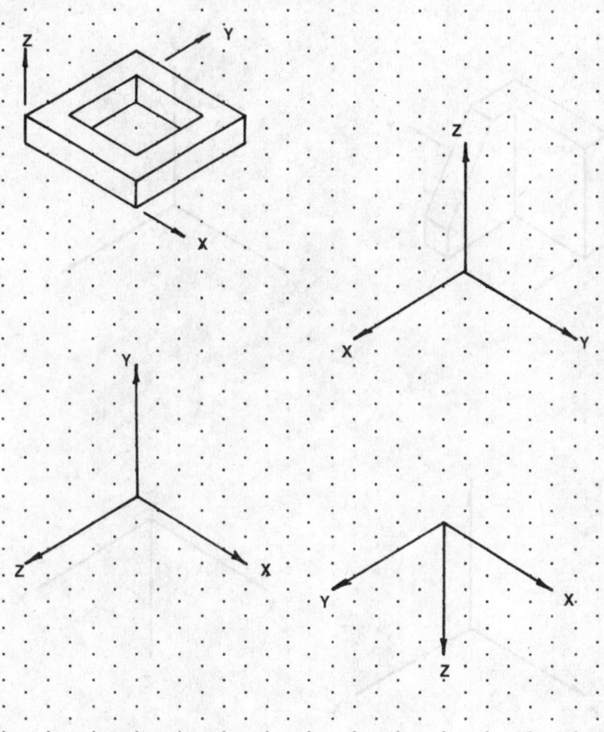

EX4-29

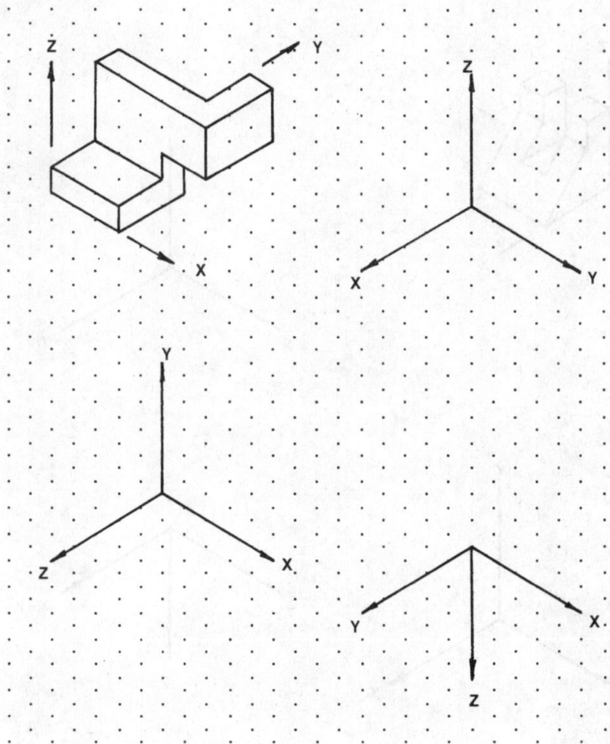

EX4-30

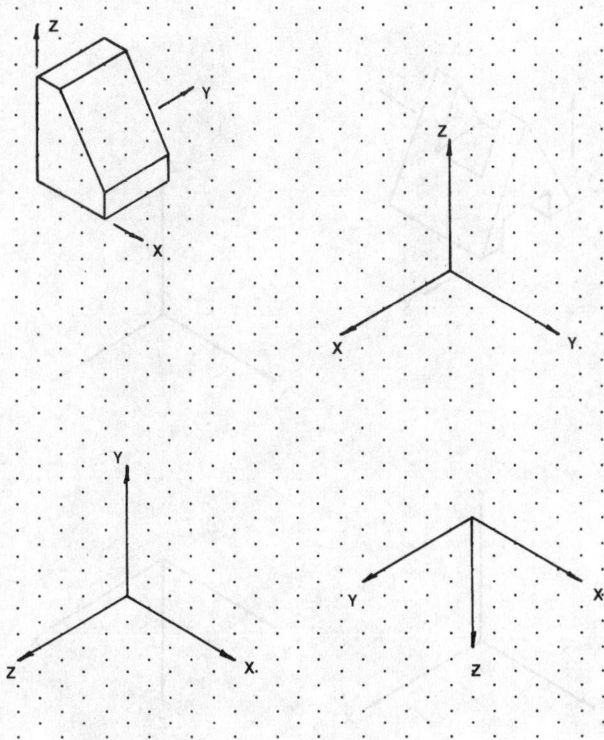

EX4-31

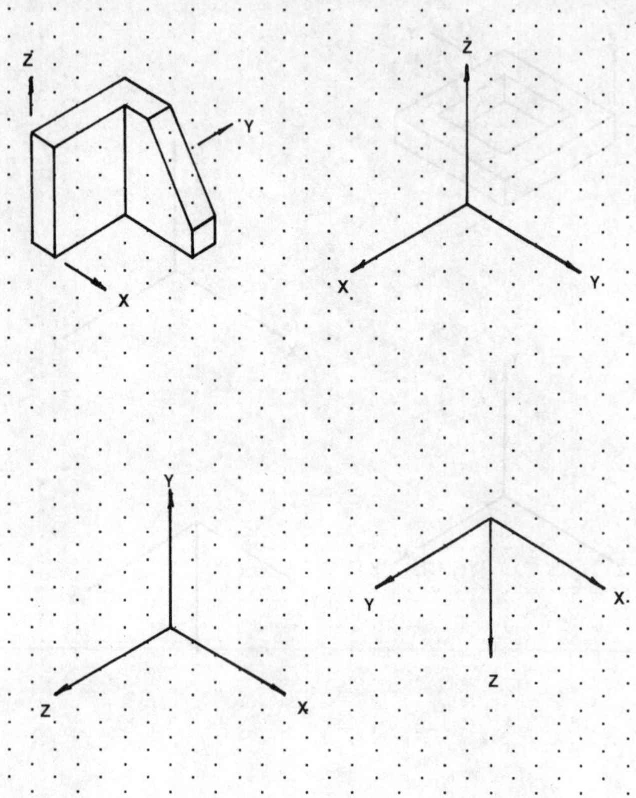

EX4-32

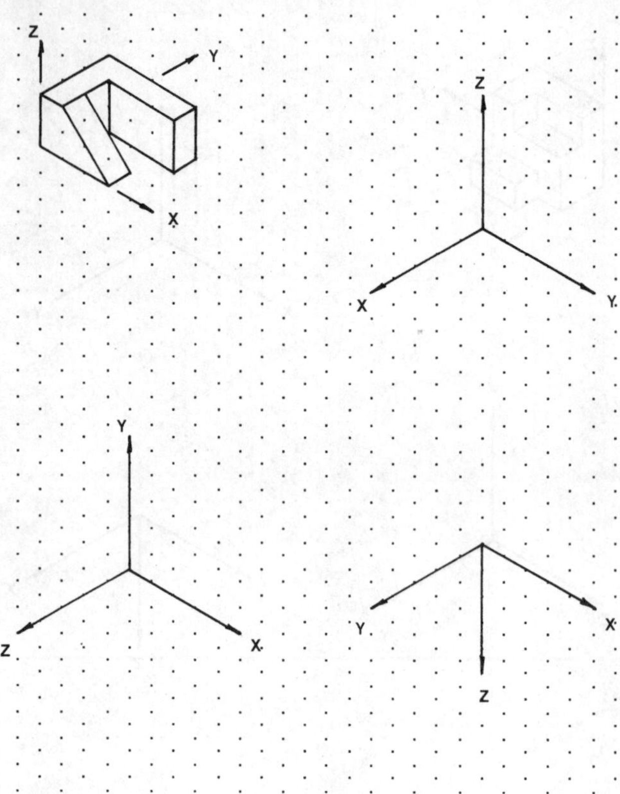

EX4-33

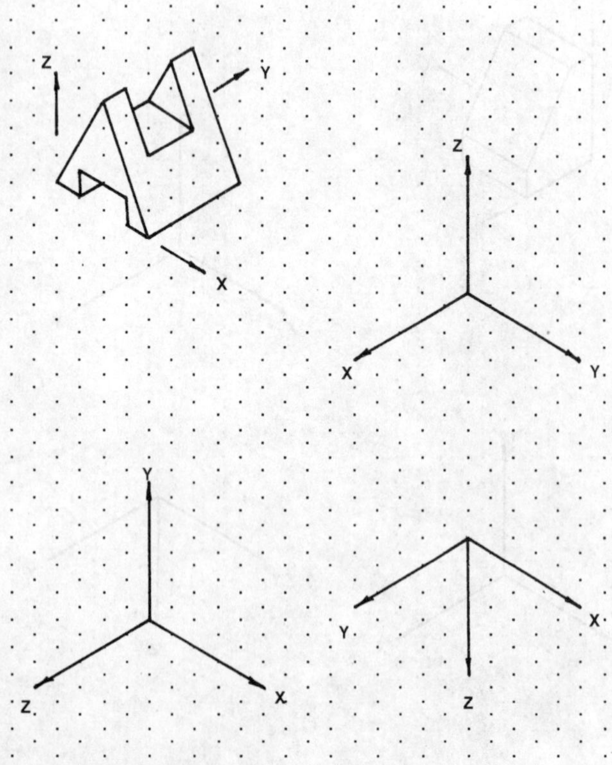

EX4-34

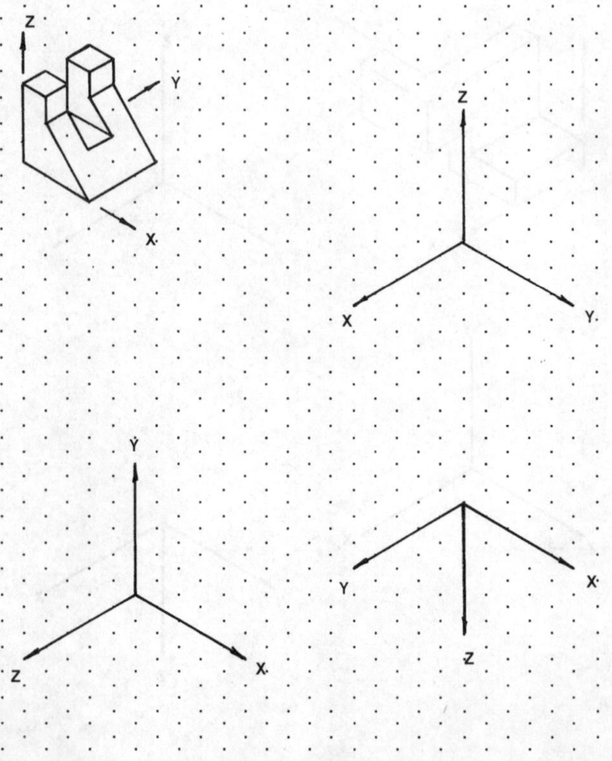

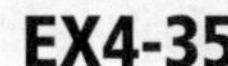

EX4-35

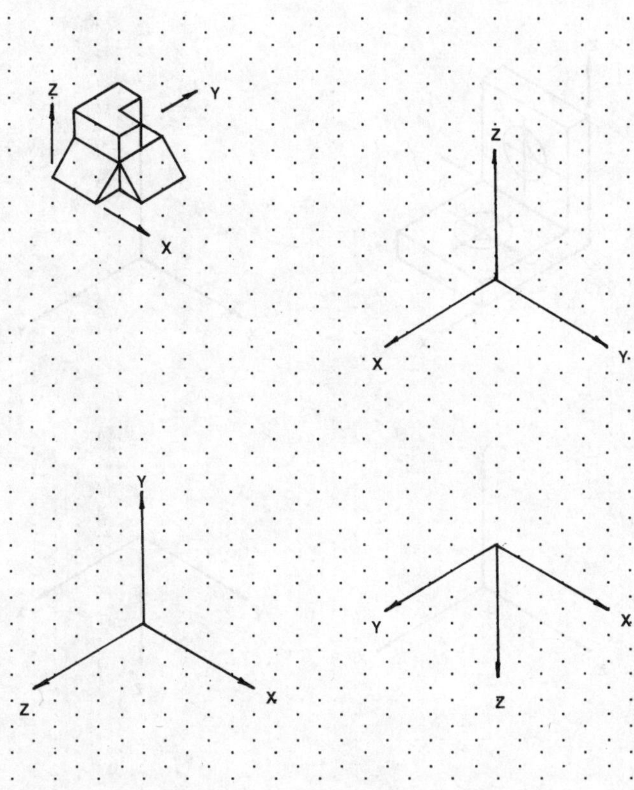

EX4-36

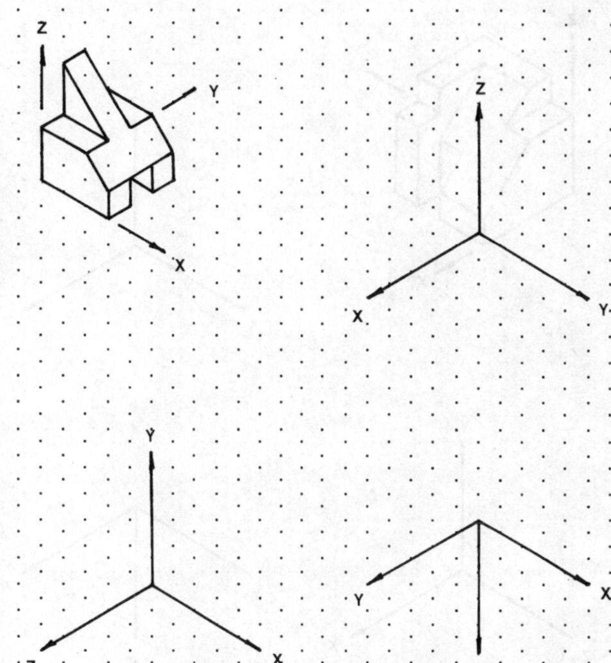

EX4-37

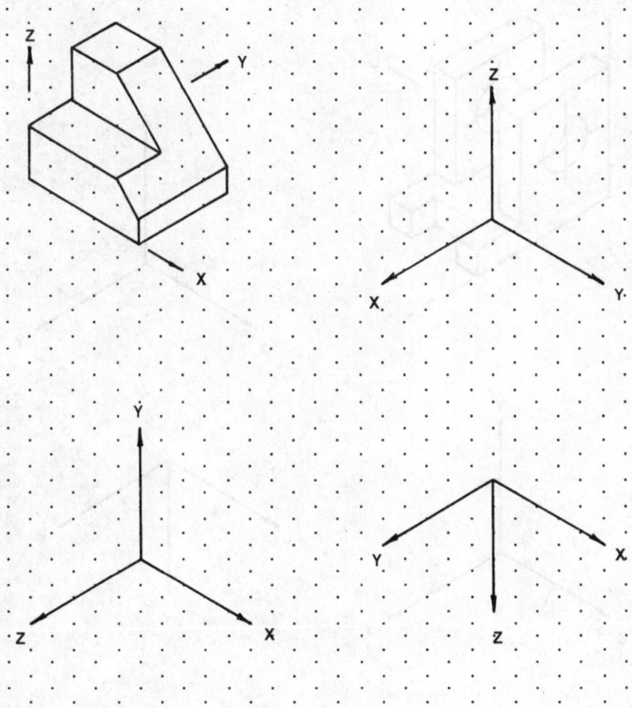

EX4-38

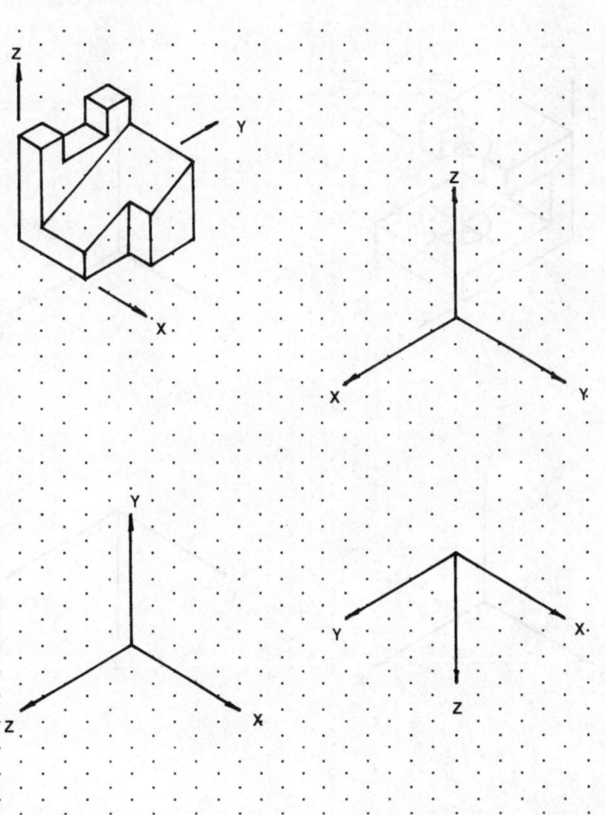

EX4-39

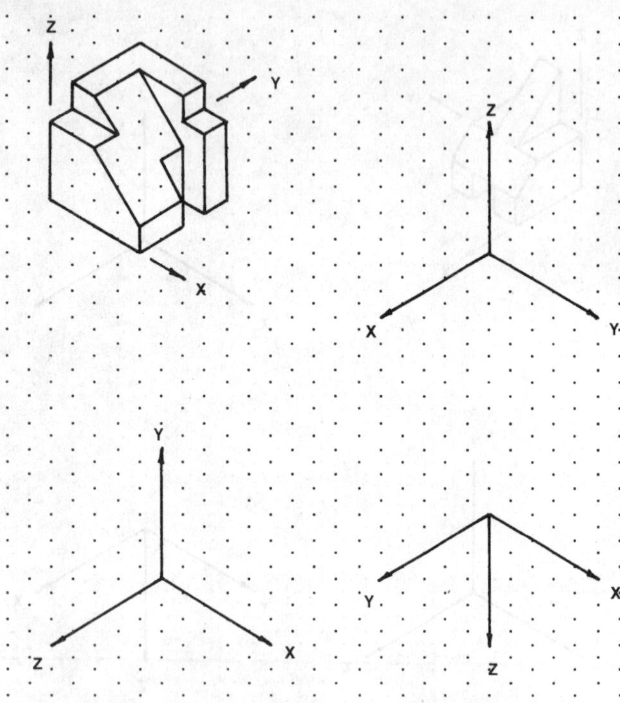

EX4-40

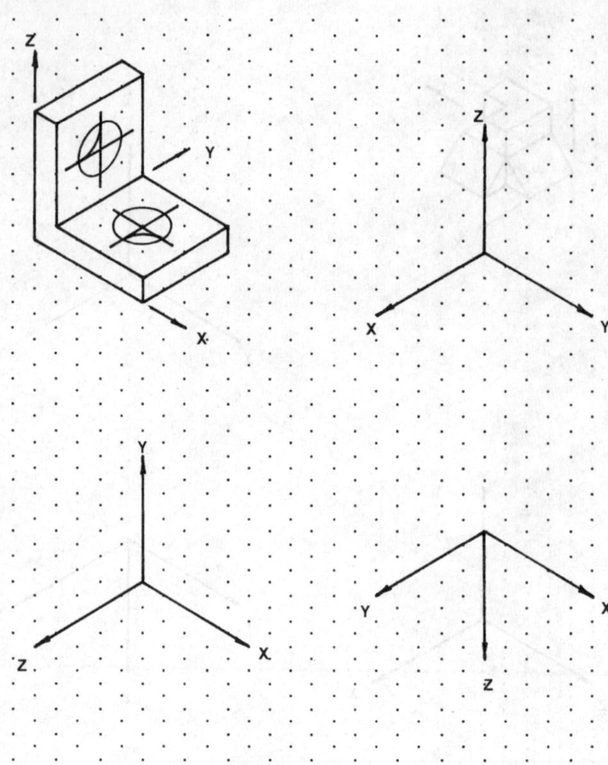

EX4-41

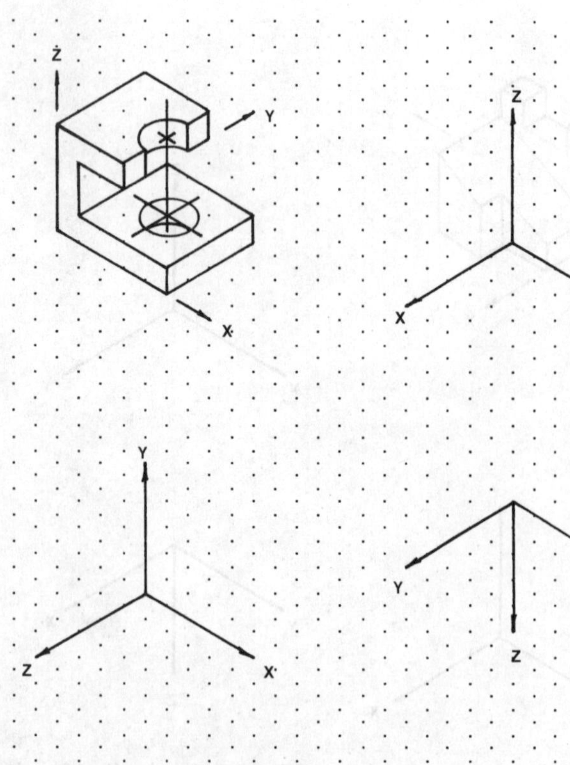

EX4-42

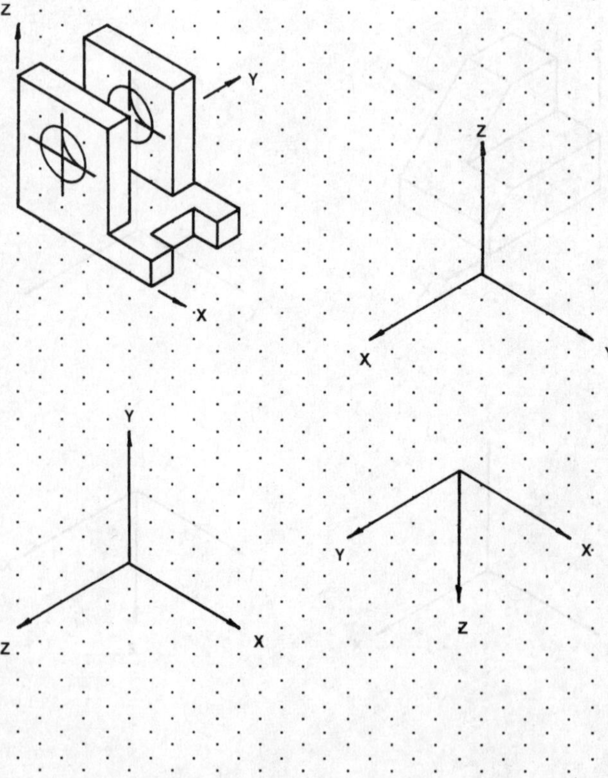

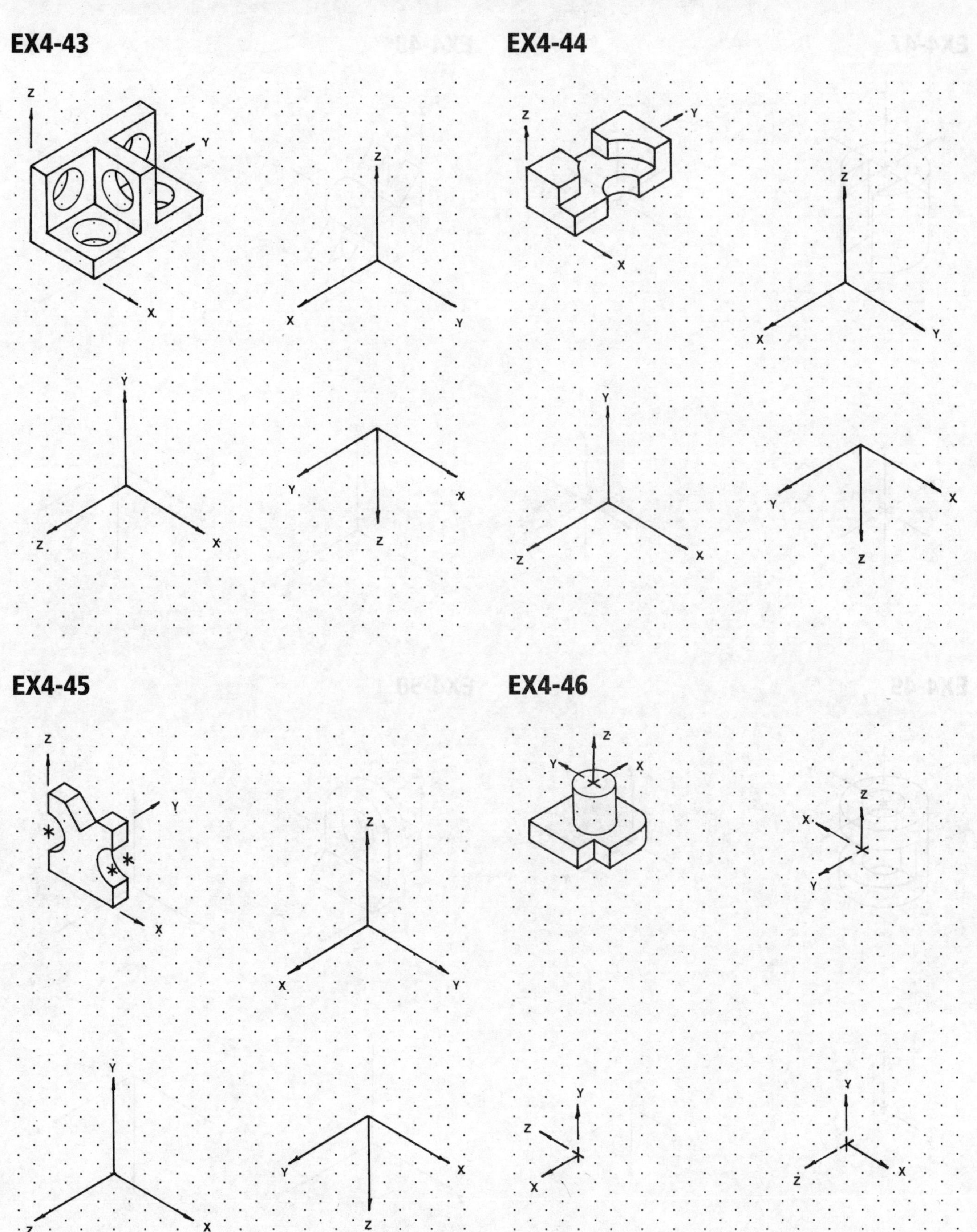
EX4-43
Z
Y
X
EX4-44
Z
Y
X
EX4-45
Z
Y
X
EX4-46
Z
Y
X

EX4-47

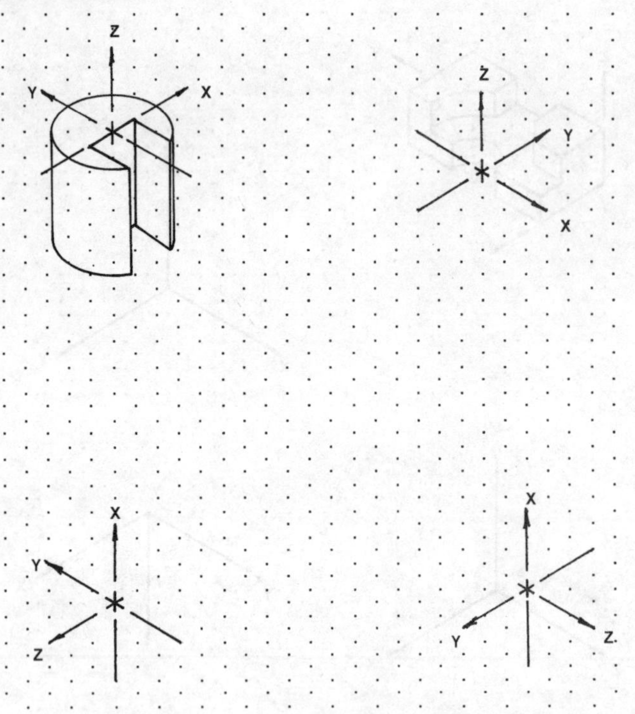

EX4-48

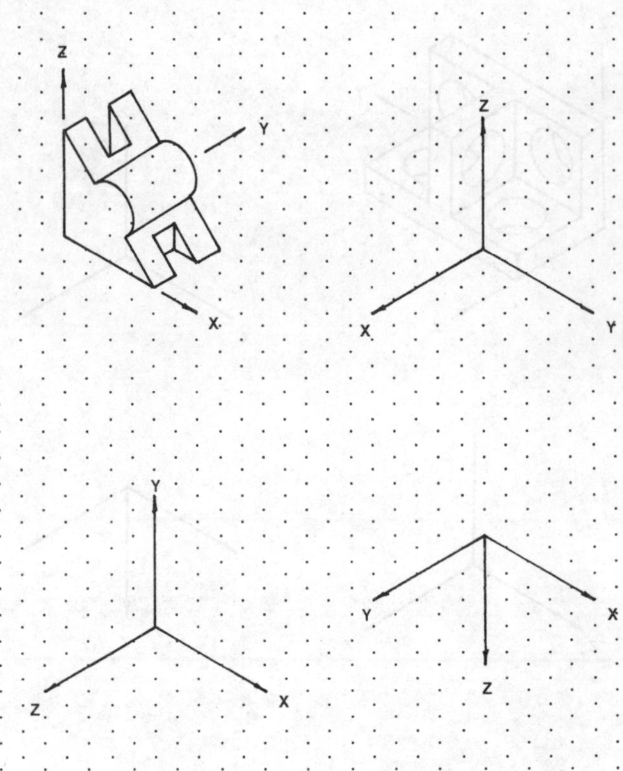

EX4-49

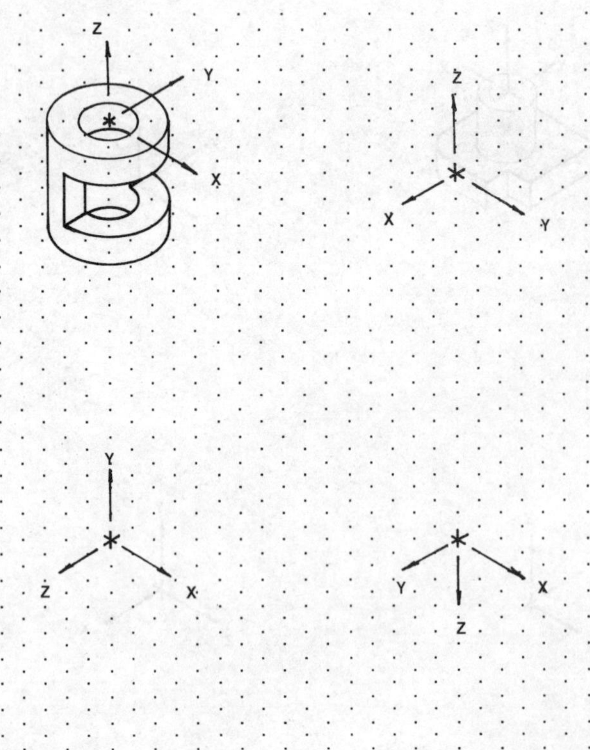

EX4-50

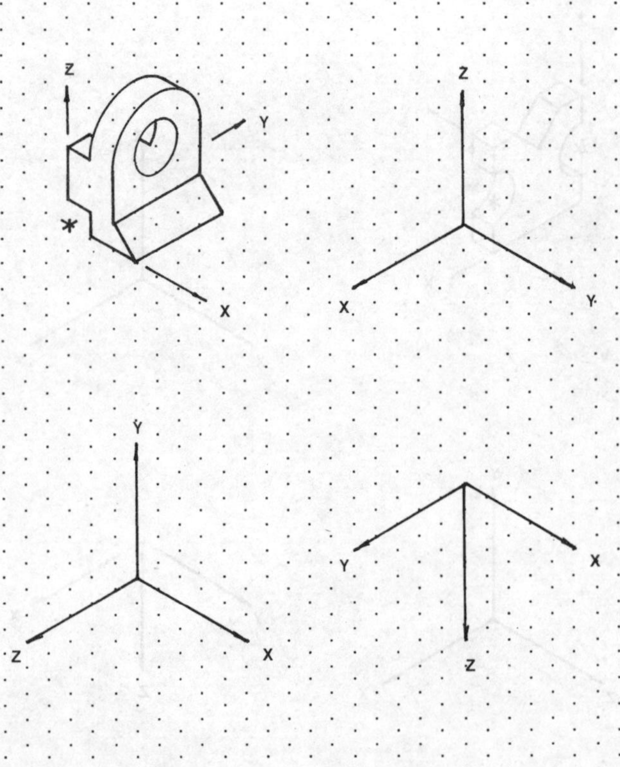

EX4-51

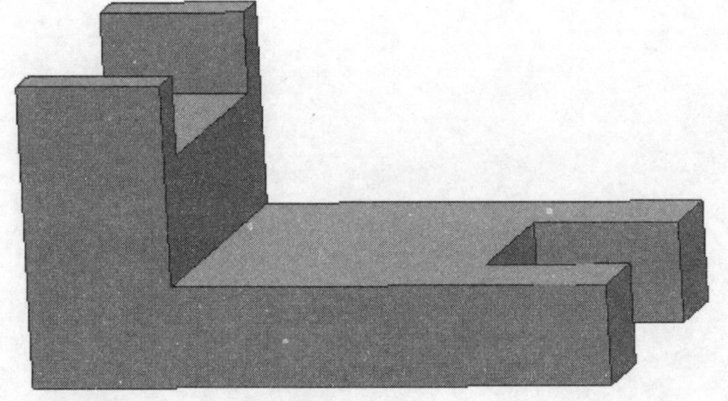

EX4-52

EX4-53

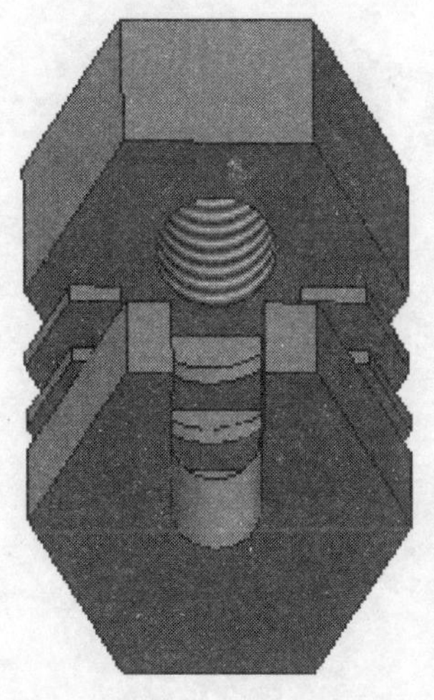

EX4-54

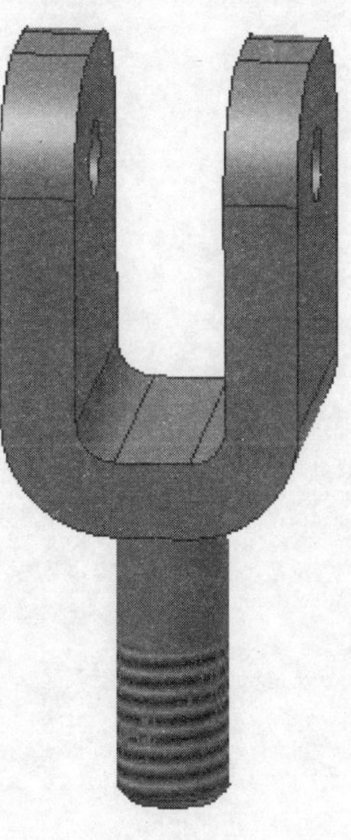

5 chapter five
Orthographic Views

5-1 Introduction

This chapter introduces orthographic views. ***Orthographic views*** are two-dimensional views of three-dimensional objects. Orthographic views are created by projecting a view of an object onto a plane which is usually positioned so that it is parallel to one of the planes of the object. See Figure 5-1.

Figure 5-1

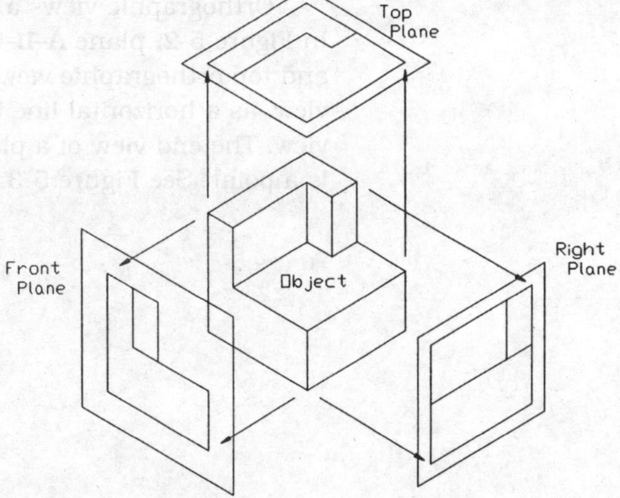

Orthographic projection planes may be positioned at any angle relative to an object, but in general, the six views parallel to the six sides of a rectangular object are used. See Figure 5-2. Technical drawings usually include only the front, top, and right-side orthographic views because together they are considered sufficient to completely define an object's shape.

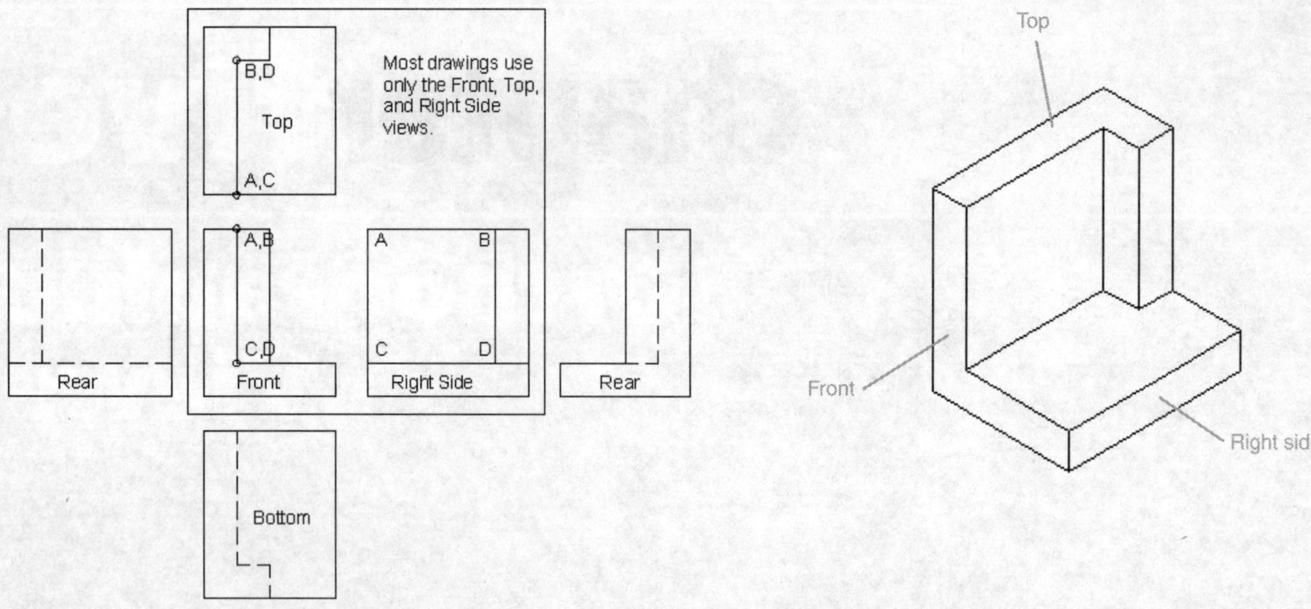

Figure 5-2

5-2 Three Views of an Object

Orthographic views are positioned on a technical drawing so that the top view is located directly over the front view, and the side view is directly to the right side of the front view. See Figure 5-2.

The locations of the front, top, and right-side views relative to each other are critical. Correct relative positioning of views allows information to be projected between the views. Vertical lines are used to project information between the front and top views, and horizontal lines are used to project information between the front and right-side views.

Orthographic views are two-dimensional, so they cannot show depth. In Figure 5-2, plane **A–B–C–D** appears as a straight line in both the front and top orthographic views. Edge **A–B** appears as a vertical line in the top view, as a horizontal line in the side view, and as point **AB** in the front view. The end view of a plane is a straight line, and the end view of a line is a point. See Figure 5-3.

Figure 5-3

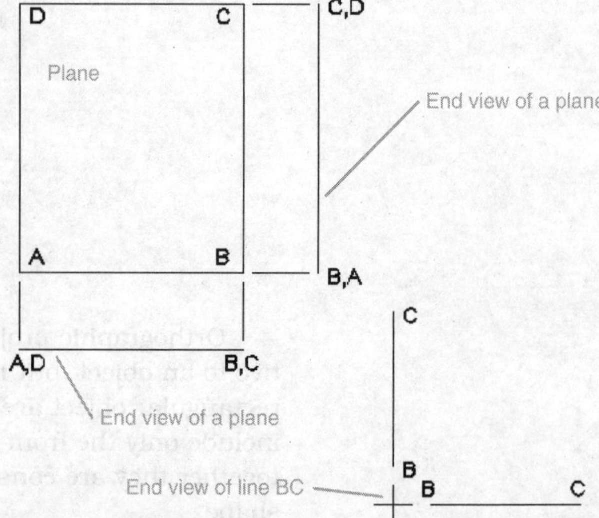

Figure 5-4 shows an object and the front, top, and right-side orthographic views of the object. Plane **A–B–C–D** appears as a rectangle in the front view and as a line in both the top and right-side views.

To help you better understand the relationship between orthographic views and, in particular, the front, top, and side views of an object, place a book on a table as shown in Figure 5-5. Note how the front, top, and side views were projected and then arranged to create a technical drawing of the book.

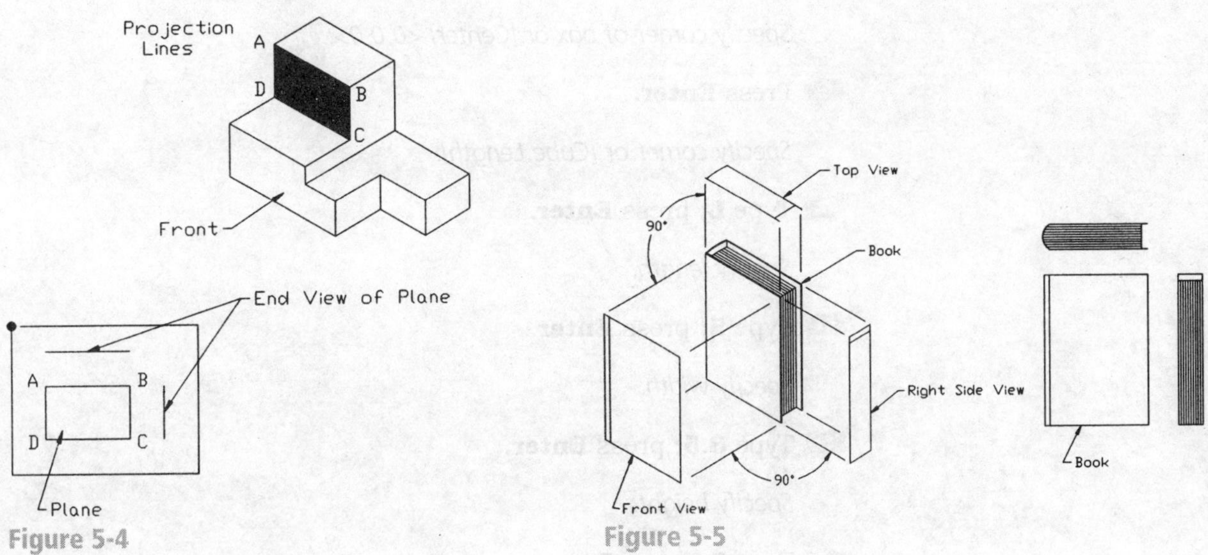

Figure 5-4

Figure 5-5

5-3 Visualization

Visualization is the ability to look at a three-dimensional object and mentally see the appropriate three orthographic views.

It is an important skill for a designer and an engineer to develop. Visualization also includes the ability to look at two-dimensional orthographic views and mentally picture the three-dimensional object that the views represent.

Figure 5-6 shows a 5 × 3.5 × 2-inch box and three orthographic views of the box. The creation of three-dimensional object drawings is explained in detail in Chapters 14, 15, and 16. This section presents a short exercise to help you better understand how orthographic views are related to three-dimensional objects.

Figure 5-6

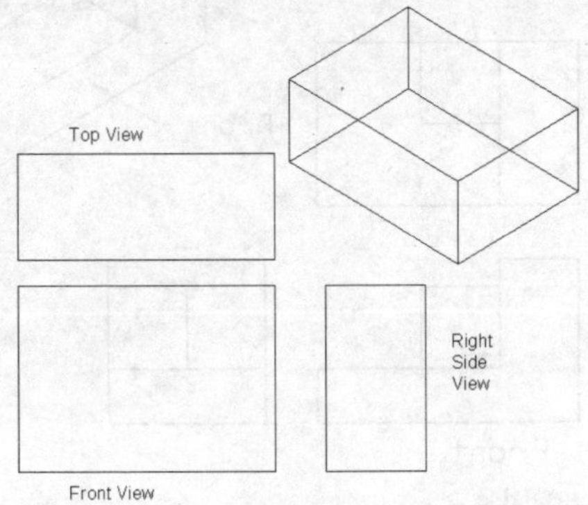

To Draw a Three-Dimensional Box

1. Set the AutoCAD drawing screen for **inches,** and then select the **3D View** command from the **View** menu accessed by clicking first the **Menu Browser** in the upper-left corner of the screen, then **SE Isometric.**

   The origin axis reference icon will change to the 3D alignment.

2. Type the word **box** to a command prompt.

   Specify corner of box or [Center] <0,0,0>:

3. Press **Enter.**

   Specify corner or [Cube Length]:

4. Type **L; press Enter.**

   Specify length:

5. Type **5; press Enter.**

   Specify width:

6. Type **3.5; press Enter.**

   Specify height:

7. Type **2; press Enter.**

   A box will appear on the screen.

8. Select the **3D Orbit** command from the **View** menu. Move the cursor around the drawing screen, holding the left mouse button down. Position the box so as to create each of the three orthographic views shown in Figure 5-6.

Figures 5-7 and 5-8 show two additional objects and their orthographic views.

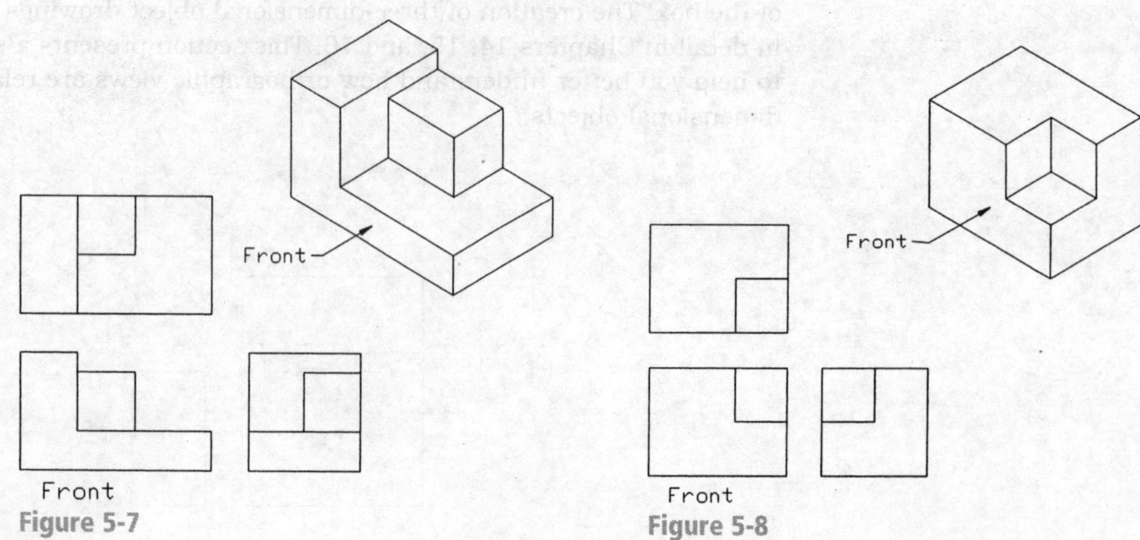

Figure 5-7 **Figure 5-8**

5-4 Hidden Lines

Hidden lines are used to represent surfaces that are not directly visible in an orthographic view. Figure 5-9 shows an object that contains a surface that is not visible in the right side view. A hidden line is used to represent the end view of the surface.

Figure 5-10 shows an object and three views of the object. The top and side views of the object contain hidden lines.

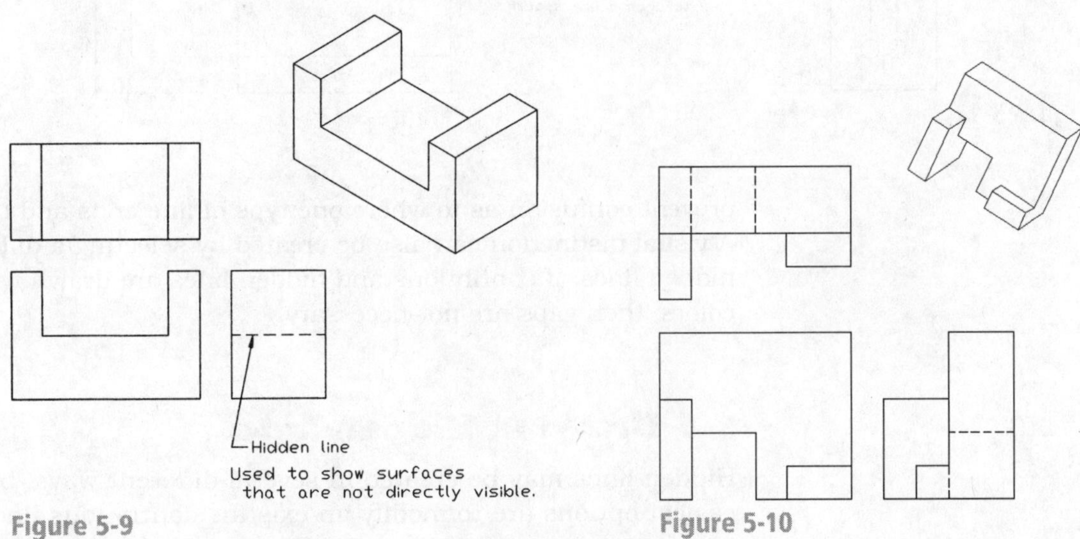

Figure 5-9

Figure 5-10

Figure 5-11 shows an object that contains an edge line **A–B.** In the top view of the object, line **A–B** is partially hidden and partially visible. When the line is directly visible through the square hole, it is drawn as a continuous line; when it is not directly visible, it is drawn as a hidden line.

Figure 5-11

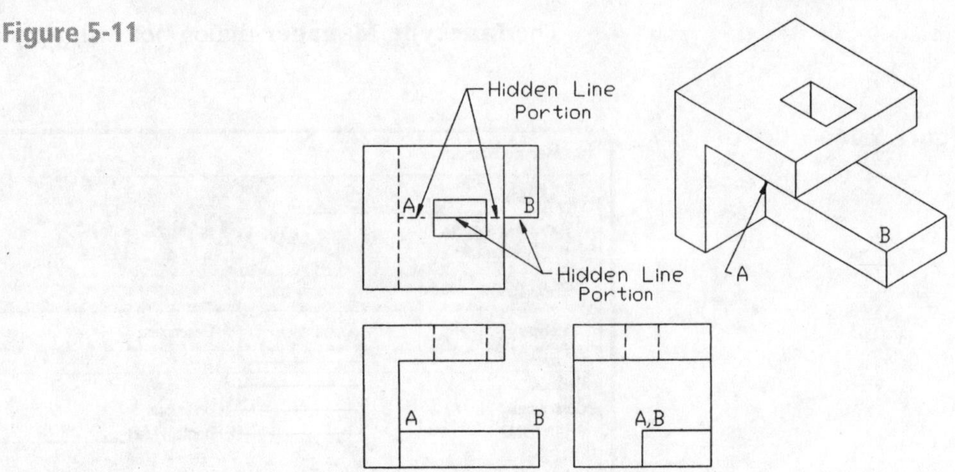

5-5 Hidden Line Conventions

Figure 5-12 shows several conventions associated with drawing hidden lines. Whenever possible, show intersections of hidden lines as touching lines, not as open gaps. Corners should also be shown as touching lines.

Figure 5-13 shows two hidden lines and a continuous line that are aligned. A small gap should be included between the two types of lines to

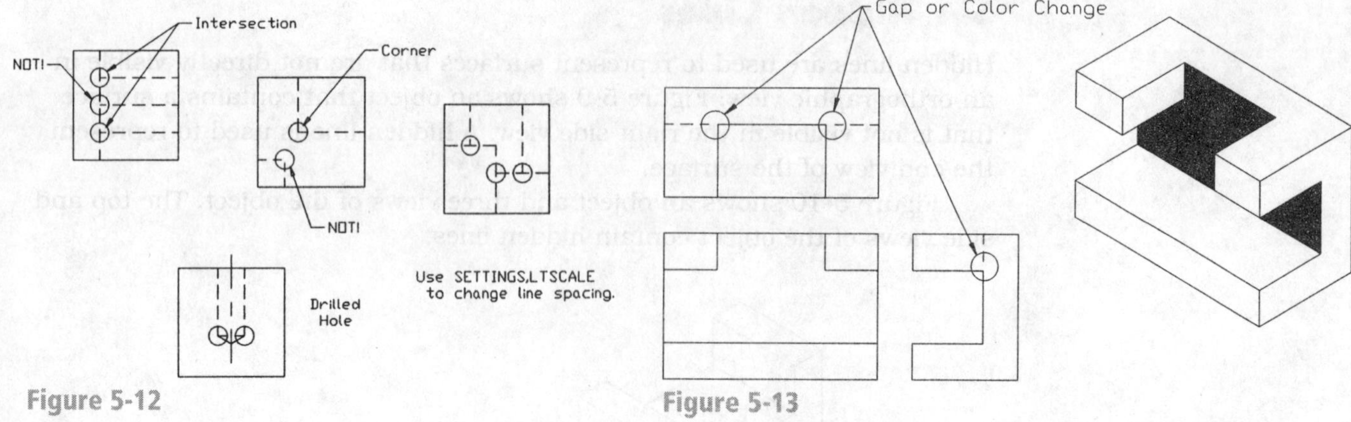

Figure 5-12

Figure 5-13

prevent confusion as to where one type of line ends and the other begins. A visual distinction can also be created by selecting a different color for hidden lines. If continuous and hidden lines are drawn with different colors, then gaps are not necessary.

5-6 Drawing Hidden Lines

Hidden lines may be created in several different ways, but two of the easiest options are to modify an existing continuous line or to transfer an existing continuous line to a layer created specifically for hidden lines. In the examples presented, both linetype and line color will be changed.

To Add Hidden Linetypes to the Drawing

 Type the word **Linetype** in response to a command prompt.

The **Linetype Manager** dialog box will appear. See Figure 5-14.

Figure 5-14

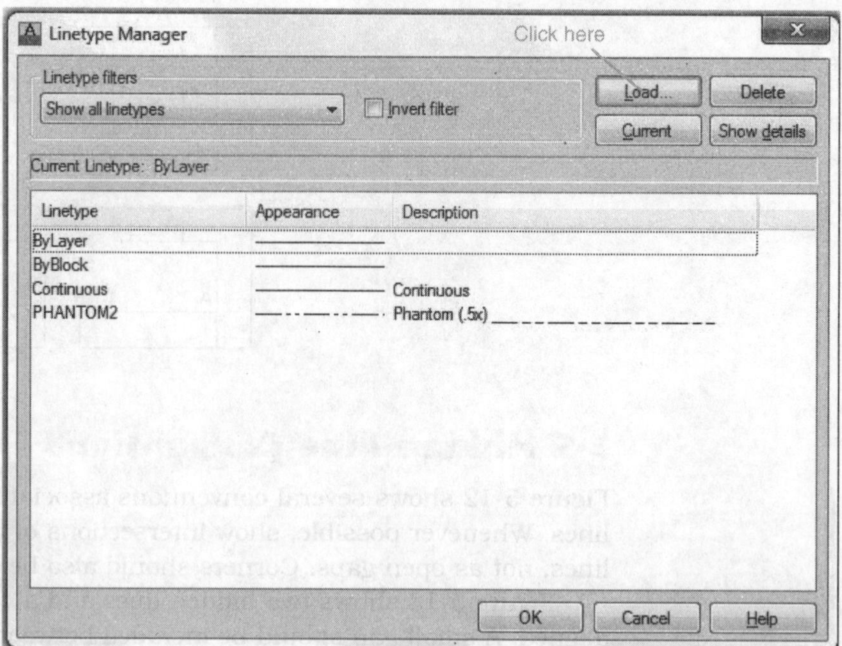

2. Click the **Load** box on the **Linetype Manager.**

The **Load or Reload Linetypes** dialog box will appear. See Figure 5-15.

Figure 5-15

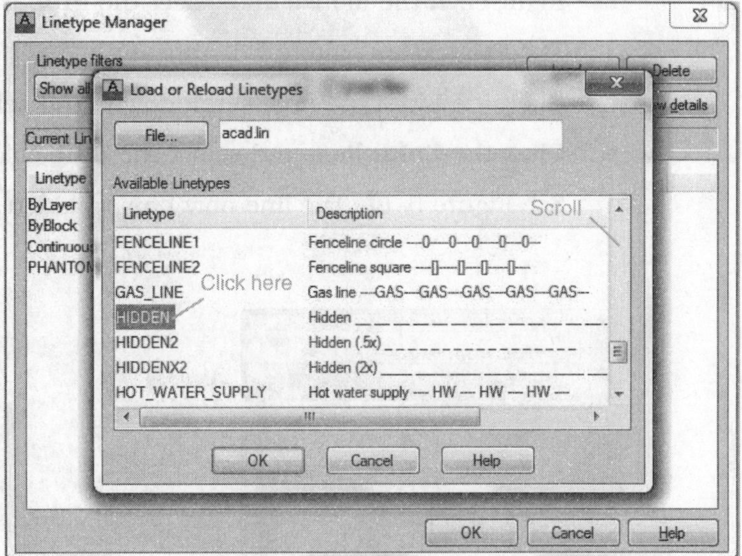

3. Scroll down the linetypes, and select **HIDDEN** linetype.

4. Click **OK,** and **OK** again to return to the drawing screen.

The **HIDDEN** line should appear in the **Linetype Manager** box.

5. Draw a line as shown in Figure 5-16.

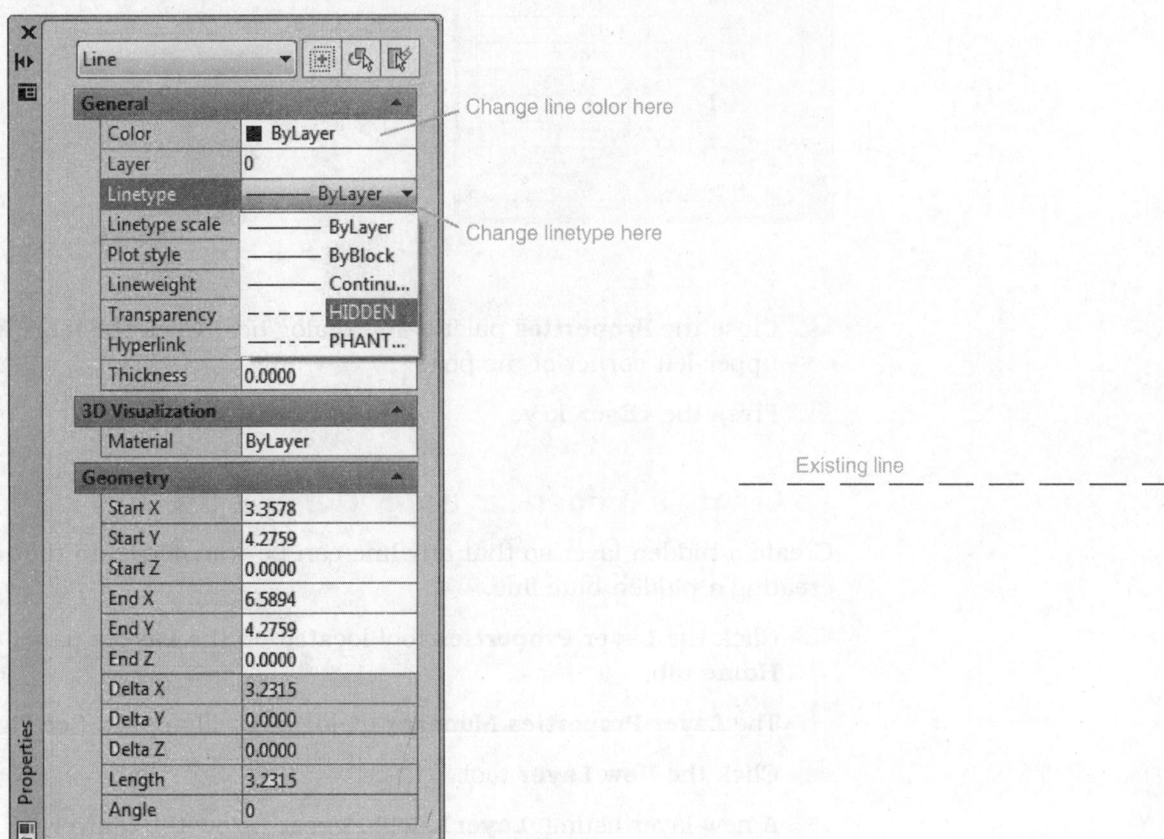

Figure 5-16

6. Click the line.

   Grip points will appear on the line, along with a dialog box.

7. Right-click the mouse and select the **Properties** option.

   The **Properties** palette will appear.

8. Click the **Linetype** line, scroll down, and select the **HIDDEN** linetype.

9. Click the **Color** line, and select the **Blue** color.

   See Figure 5-17. The line now has a hidden linetype and is blue.

Figure 5-17

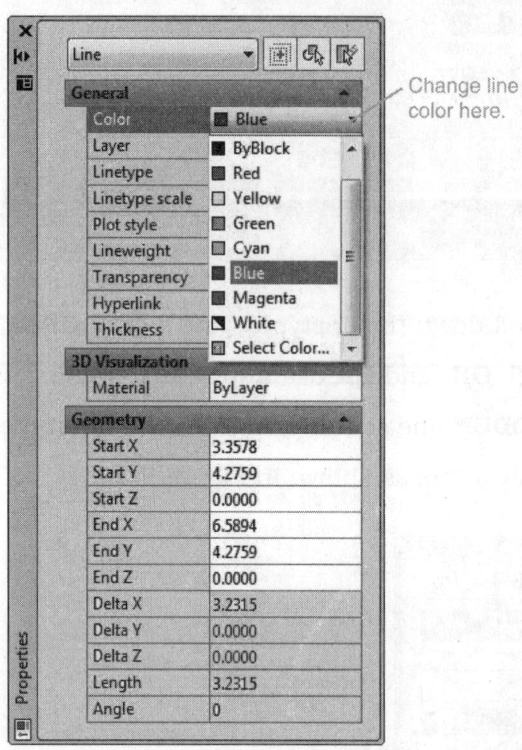

10. Close the **Properties** palette and dialog box. Click the large **X** in the upper-left corner of the box.

11. Press the **<Esc>** key.

To Create a Hidden Layer for General Use

Create a hidden layer so that any line can be transferred to that layer, creating a hidden blue line.

1. Click the **Layer Properties** tool located on the **Layers** panel under the **Home** tab.

   The **Layer Properties Manager** dialog box will appear. See Figure 5-18.

2. Click the **New Layer** tool.

   A new layer listing, **Layer1,** will appear below the **0** layer.

3. Change the **Layer1** name to **Hidden.**

Figure 5-18

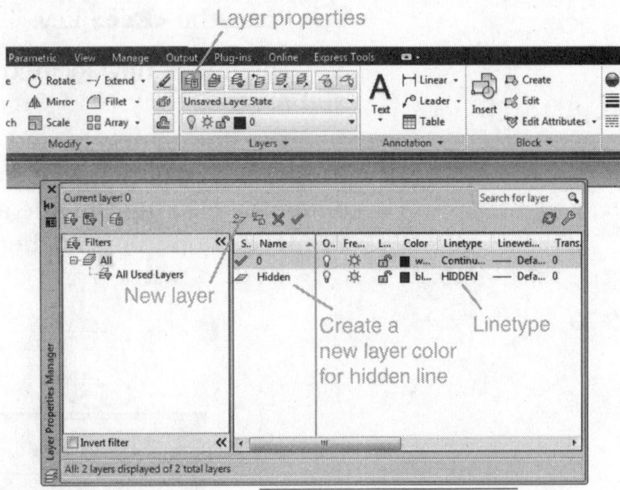

4. Scroll across the **Hidden** layer line, and click the word **Continuous** under the **Linetype** heading.

   The **Select Linetype** dialog box will appear.

5. Click the **Hidden** line on the **Select Linetype** dialog box, and click **OK.**

6. Repeat the procedure, and change the hidden line's color to blue.

7. Close the **Layer Properties Manager.**

To Change Layers

Figure 5-19 shows a continuous line drawn on the **0** layer.

1. Click the line.

2. Click the **Layer** tool and scroll down, selecting the **Hidden** layer.

   See Figure 5-19.

Figure 5-19

1. Click the existing line

3 Press the **<Esc>** key.

The line is now located on the **Hidden** layer, has a hidden linetype, and is blue.

The line's linetype and color could have been changed by the **Quick Properties** option shown in Figure 5-20. Access the **Quick Properties** option by clicking the line and then right-clicking the mouse. **The Quick Properties** option is at the bottom of the dialog box.

Figure 5-20

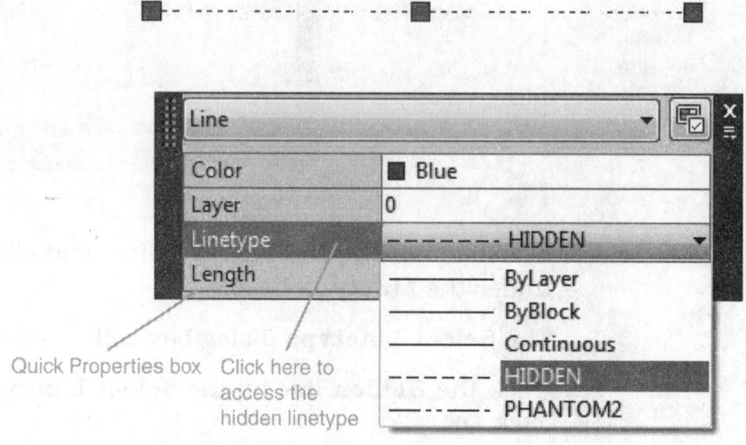

Figures 5-21 and 5-22 show an object and three views of that object. There are hidden lines in several of the orthographic views.

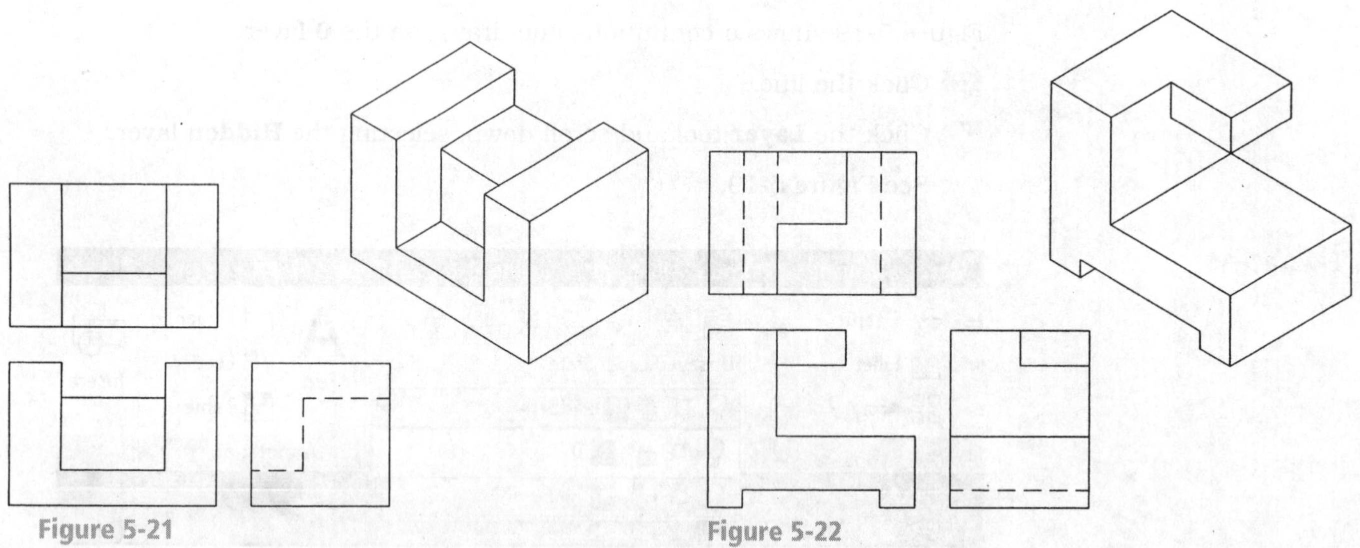

Figure 5-21

Figure 5-22

5-7 Precedence of Lines

When orthographic views are prepared, it is not unusual for one type of line to be drawn over another type—a continuous line over a centerline, for example. See Figure 5-23. Drawing convention has established a precedence of lines: A continuous line takes precedence over a hidden line, and a hidden line takes precedence over a centerline.

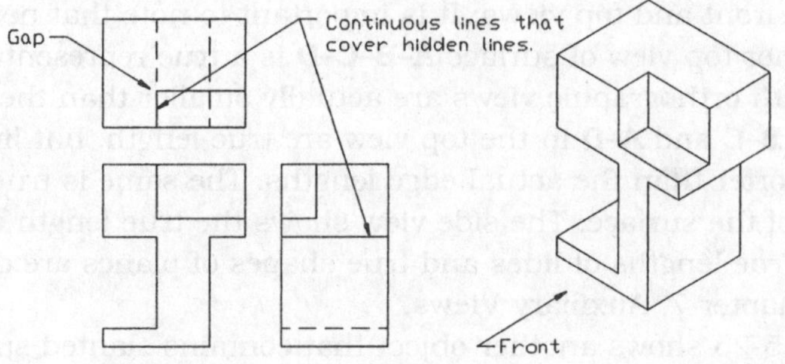

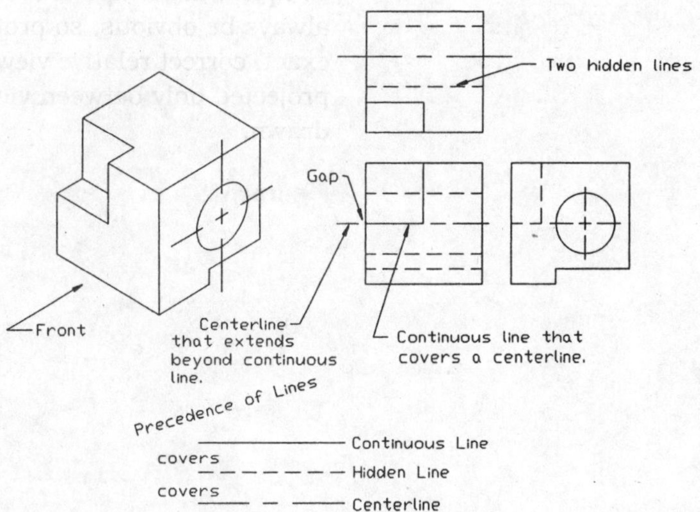

Figure 5-23

If different linetypes are of different lengths, include a gap where the line changes from continuous to either hidden or center in order to create a visual distinction between the lines. Color changes may also be used to create visual distinctions between lines.

5-8 Slanted Surfaces

Slanted surfaces are surfaces that are not parallel to either the horizontal or vertical axis. Figure 5-24 shows a slanted surface **A–B–C–D.** Slanted surface **A–B–C–D** appears as a straight line in the side view and as a plane

Figure 5-24

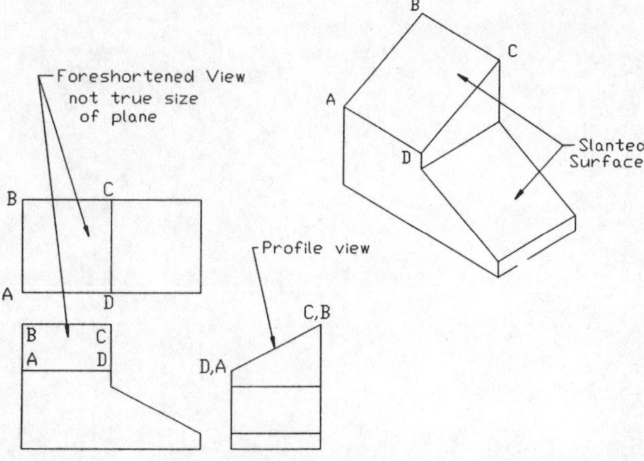

in both the front and top views. It is important to note that neither the front view nor top view of surface **A–B–C–D** is a true representation of the surface. Both orthographic views are actually smaller than the actual surface. Lines **B–C** and **A–D** in the top view are true length, but lines **A–B** and **C–D** are shorter than the actual edge lengths. The same is true for the front view of the surface. The side view shows the true length of lines **A–B** and **D–C.** True lengths of lines and true shapes of planes are discussed again in Chapter 7, Auxiliary Views.

Figure 5-25 shows another object that contains slanted surfaces. Note how projection lines are used between the views. As objects become more complex, the shape of a surface or the location of an edge line will not always be obvious, so projecting information between views—and therefore, exact, correct relative view location—becomes critical. Information can be projected only between views that are correctly positioned and accurately drawn.

Figure 5-25

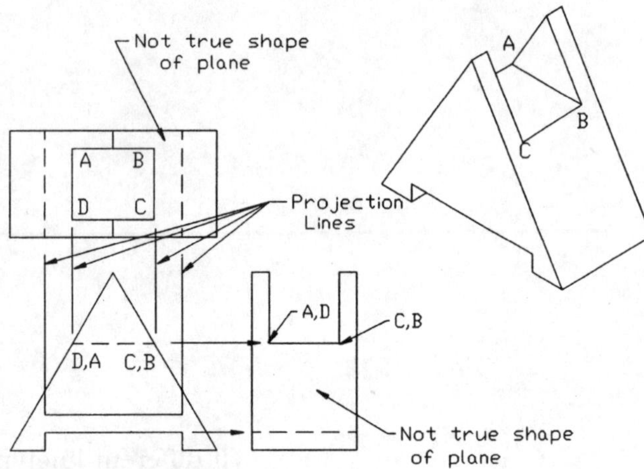

5-9 Projection Between Views

Information is projected between the front and side views by using horizontal lines, and between the front and top views by using vertical lines. Information can be projected between the top and side views by using a combination of horizontal and vertical lines that intersect a 45° miter line. See Figure 5-26.

Figure 5-26

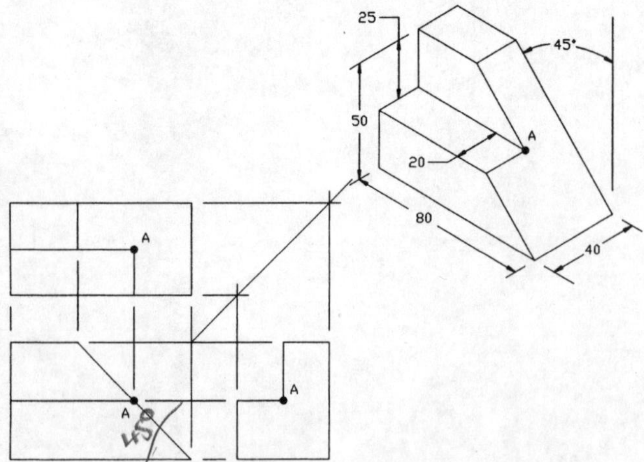

A 45° miter line is constructed between the top and side views. This line allows the project lines to change direction, turn a corner, and change from horizontal to vertical lines. To go from the top view to the side view, horizontal projection lines are constructed from the top view so that they intersect the miter line. Vertical lines are constructed from the intersection points on the miter line into the side view. The reverse process is used to go from the side view to the top view.

The following sample problem shows how projection lines can be used to create orthographic views through AutoCAD.

5-10 Sample Problem SP5-1

Draw the front, top, and right-side orthographic views of the object shown in Figure 5-26. Set up the drawing as follows:

1 Create a separate layer for hidden lines.

Limits = **297** × **210** (Metric setup)

Grid = **10**

Snap = **5**

Ortho = **ON** (F8)

Layer = **HIDDEN** (LType = **HIDDEN**, Color = **Green**)

2 Use the overall dimensions (length = **80,** height = **50,** and depth = **40**) to define the overall size requirements of the three orthographic views. See Figure 5-27. The **20** spacing between the views is arbitrary. The distance between the front and top views does not have to equal the distance between the front and side views. In this example, the two distances are equal.

3 Draw a **45°** miter line starting from the upper-right corner of the front view. This step is possible only if the distances between the views are equal. If the distances are not equal, draw the front and top views, add the miter line, and project the overall size of the side view from the front and top views.

3a. (Optional) Trim away the excess lines to clearly define the areas of the front, top, and side views.

3b. (Optional) The **Layer** tool may be used to create a layer for construction lines and another layer for final drawing lines. The lines for the final drawing may then be transferred to the final drawing layer, and the construction layer turned off. This method eliminates the need for extensive erasing or trimming.

4 Draw the **45°** slanted surface in the front view as shown in Figure 5-27. Project the intersection of the slanted surface and the top edge of the front view into the top view. Add a horizontal line across the front and right-side views **25** from the bottom edge line. The 25 value comes from the given dimension. Label the intersection of the slanted line and the horizontal line as point **A.**

5 Draw a horizontal line in the top view **20** from the top edge as shown in Figure 5-27. Continue the line so that it intersects the miter line. Project the line into the side view. Use **Osnap Intersection** with **Ortho** on to ensure an accurate projection. Label point **A** in the side view.

Figure 5-27

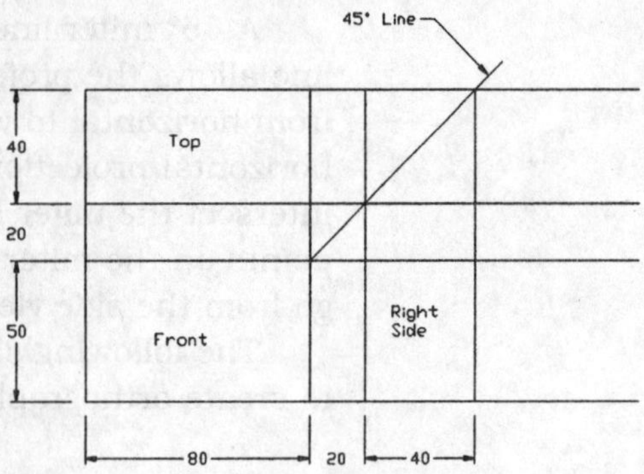

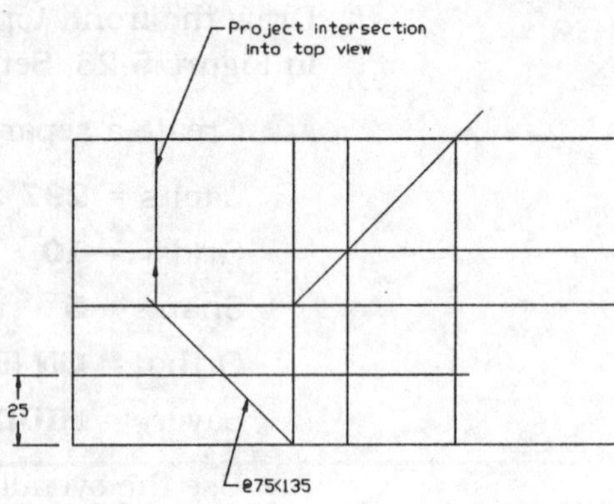

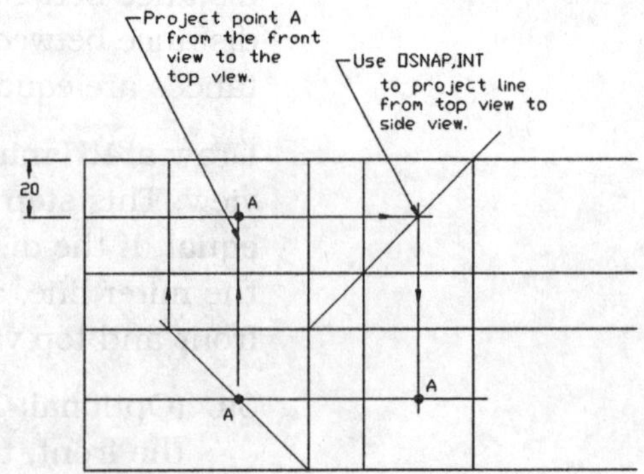

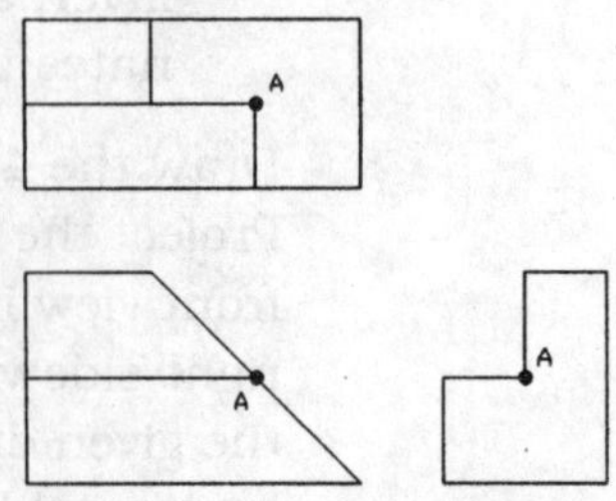

6 Project point **A** in the front view into the top view (vertical line). Label the intersection of the projection line and the horizontal line in the top view as point **A.**

7 Use **Erase** and **Trim** to remove the excess lines.

8 Save the drawing if desired.

5-11 Compound Lines

A ***compound line*** is formed when two slanted surfaces intersect. See Figure 5-28. The true length of a compound line is not shown in the front, top, or side views.

Figure 5-29 shows another object that contains compound lines. The three orthographic views of a compound line are sometimes difficult to visualize, making it more important to be able to project information accurately between views. Usually, part of an object can be visualized and part of the orthographic views created. The remainder of the drawing can be added by projecting from the known information.

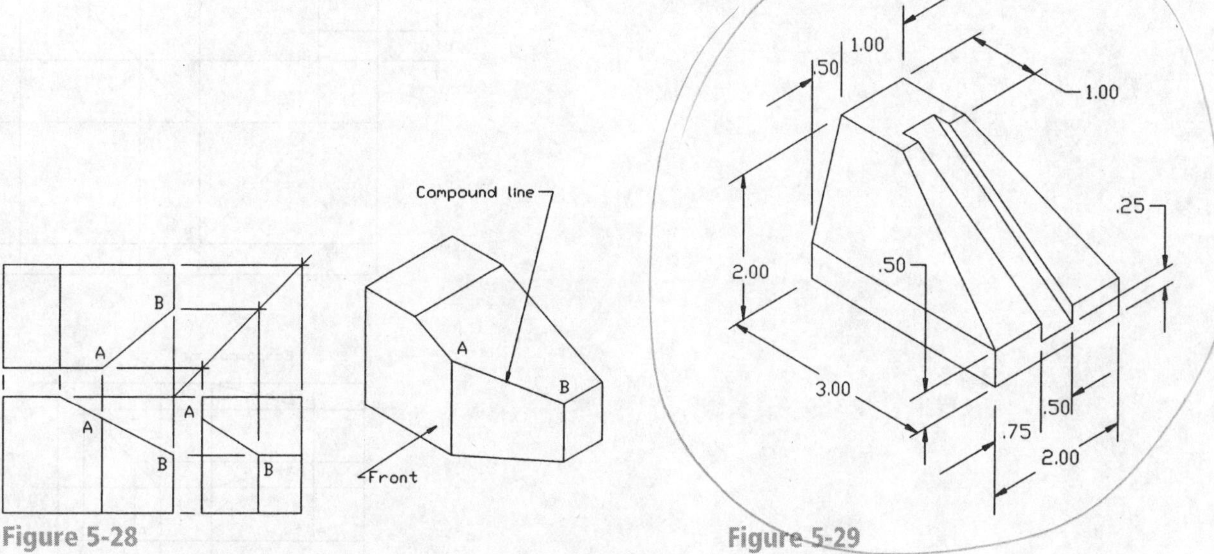

Figure 5-28

Figure 5-29

5-12 Sample Problem SP5-2

Figure 5-30 shows how the front, top, and side views of the object shown in Figure 5-29 were created by projecting information. The procedure is as follows:

1 Set the drawing up as follows:

Limits = **Default**

Grid = **.5**

Snap = **.25**

2 Use the overall dimensions to define the space and location requirements for the views. Draw the **45°** miter line.

3 Use the given dimensions to define the starting and end points on the compound lines in the top and front views. One of the lines has been labeled **A–B.**

Figure 5-30

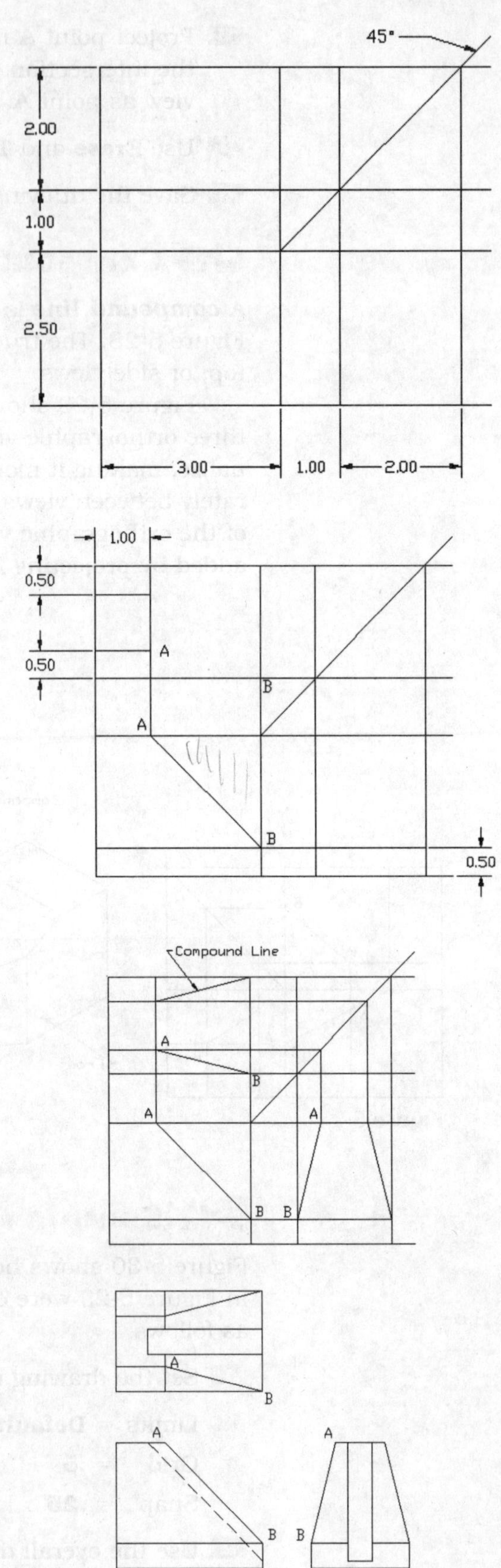

4. Draw the compound line in the top view, and then project it into the side view, using information from both the top and front views.
5. Add the dovetailed shape, using the given dimensions. Draw the appropriate hidden lines for the dovetail.
6. Erase and trim the excess lines.
7. Save the drawing if desired.

Figure 5-31 shows the three orthographic views and pictorial view of another example of an object that includes compound lines. Some of the projection lines have also been included.

Figure 5-31

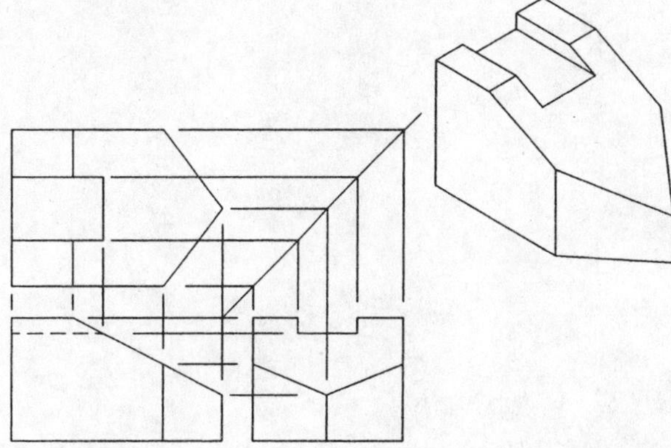

5-13 Oblique Surfaces

Oblique surfaces are surfaces that do not appear correctly shaped in the front, top, or side views. Figure 5-32 shows an object that contains oblique surface **A–B–C–D.** Figure 5-32 also shows three views of just surface **A–B–C–D.** Oblique surfaces are projected by first projecting their corner points and then joining the points with straight lines. The orthographic views of oblique surfaces are sometimes visually abstract. This makes the development of their orthographic views more dependent on projection than other types of surfaces.

Figure 5-33 shows another object that contains an oblique surface. Figure 5-34 shows how the three orthographic views were developed. The oblique surface is defined by using only two angles, but this is sufficient to

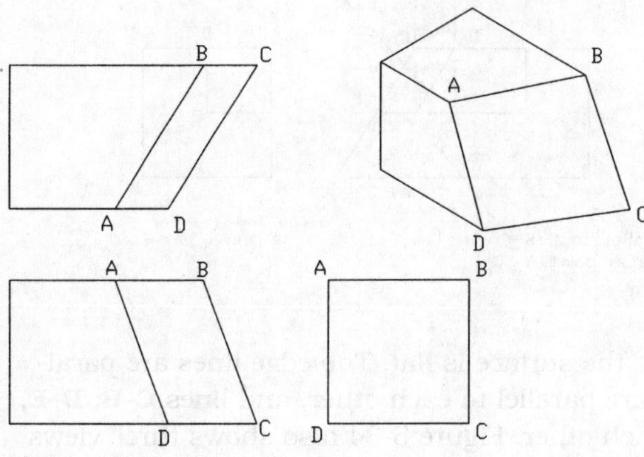

Figure 5-32

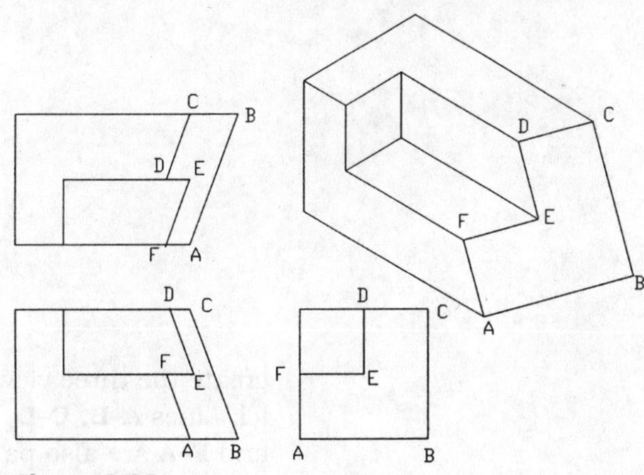

Figure 5-33

Figure 5-34

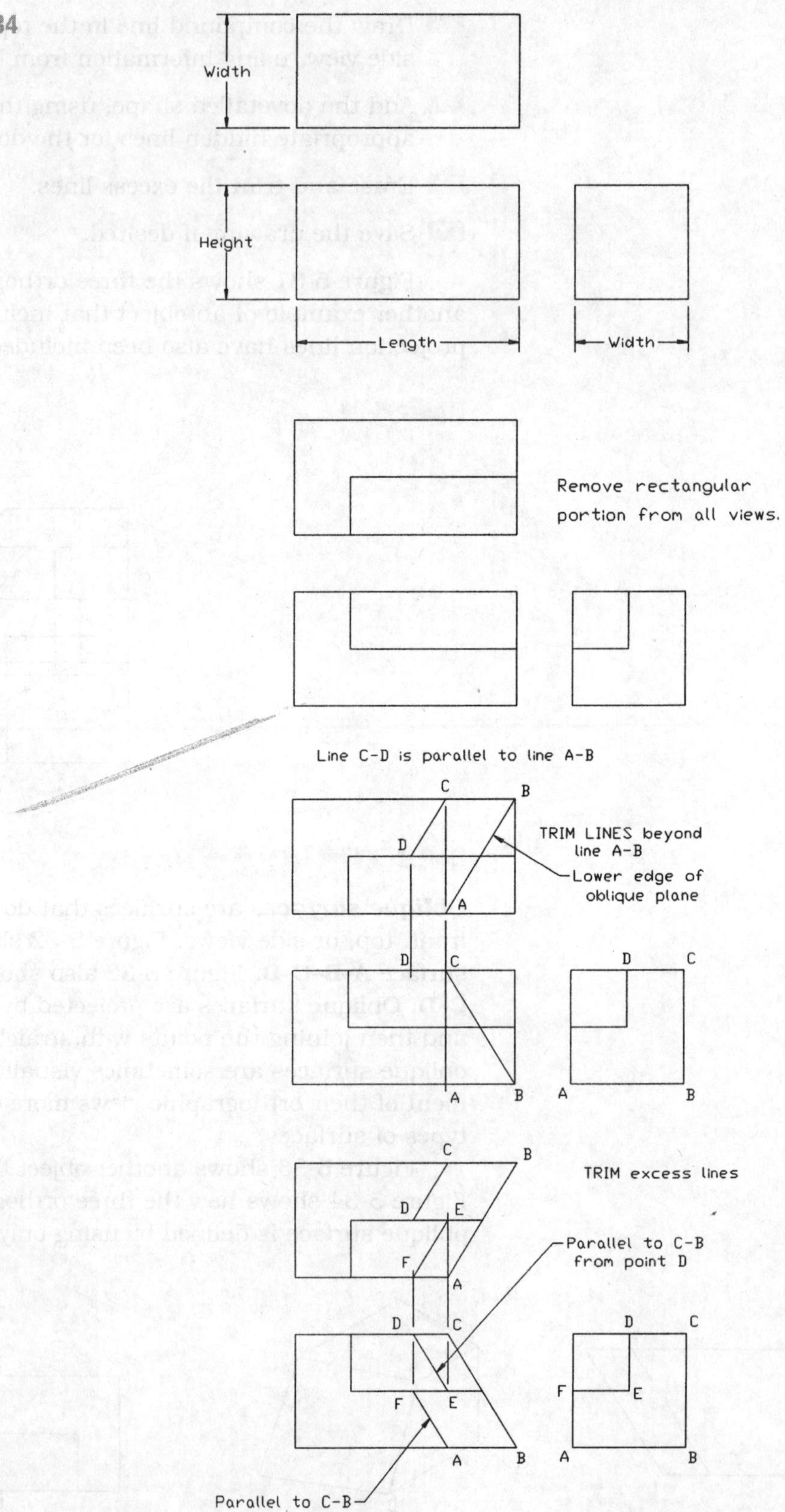

create the three views because the surface is flat. The edge lines are parallel. Lines **A–B, C–D,** and **E–F** are parallel to each other, and lines **C–B, D–E,** and **F–A** are also parallel to each other. Figure 5-34 also shows three views of just the oblique surface, along with the appropriate projection lines.

5-14 Sample Problem SP5-3

The three views of the object shown in Figure 5-35A may be drawn as follows. (The given dimensions are in millimeters.)

1. Use the **Line** and the **Offset** commands to set up the sizes and locations of the three views. Use **Osnap Intersection** to draw the projection lines. See Figure 5-35B.

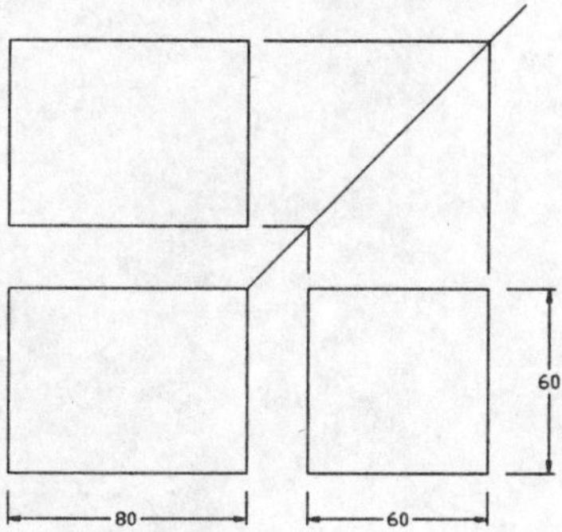

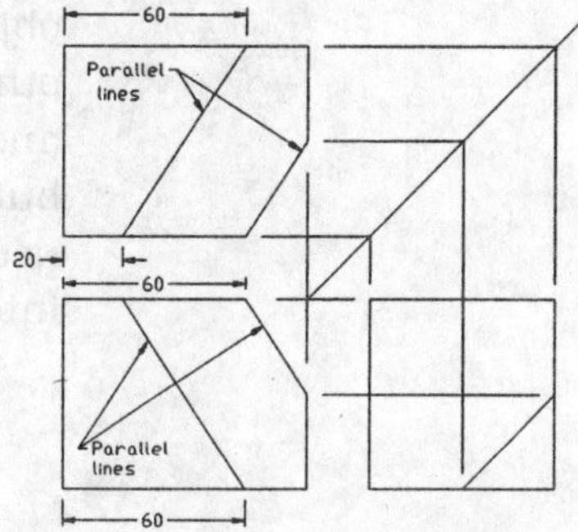

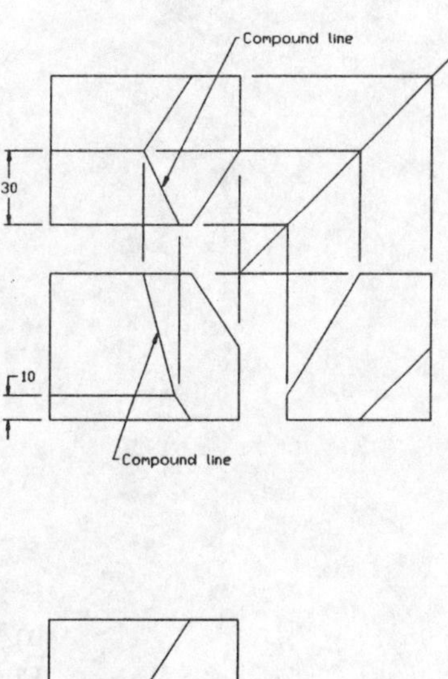

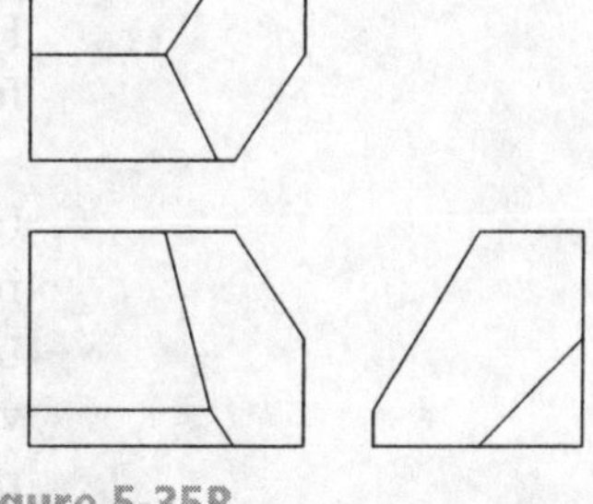

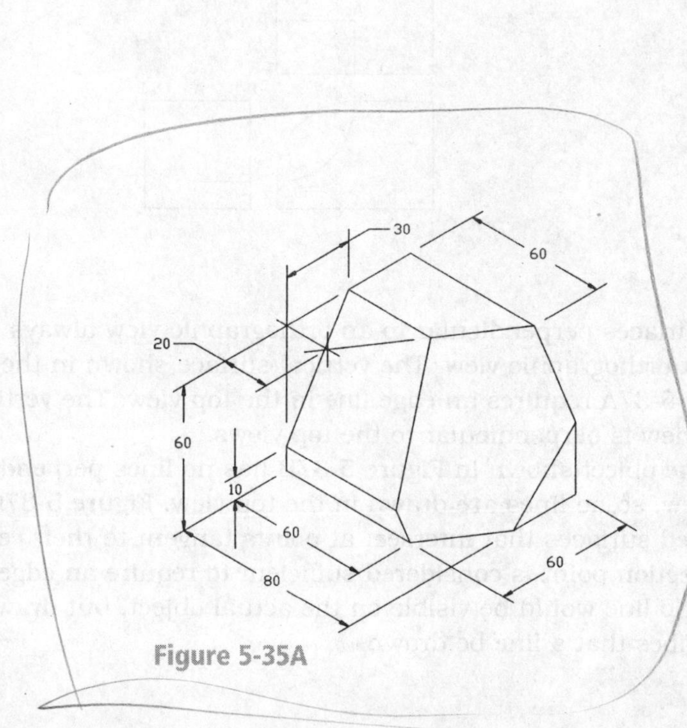

Figure 5-35A

Figure 5-35B

2. Draw an oblique surface based on the given dimensions. The edge lines of the oblique surface are parallel.
3. Draw the slanted surface in the side view, and project the surface into the other views. Use the intersection between the slanted surface and flat sections on the top and side of the object to determine the shape of the oblique surface.
4. Use **Erase** and **Trim** to remove any excess lines. Save the drawing if desired.

5-15 Rounded Surfaces

Rounded surfaces are surfaces that have constant radii, such as arcs or circles. Surfaces that do not have constant radii are classified as irregular surfaces. See Section 5-24.

Figure 5-36 shows an object with rounded surfaces. Surface **A–B–C–D** is tangent to both the top and side surfaces of the object, so no edge line is drawn. This means that the top and side orthographic views of the object are ambiguous. If only the top and side views are considered, then other interpretations of the views are possible. Figure 5-36 shows another object that generates the same top and side orthographic views, but does not include rounded surface **A–B–C–D.** The front view is needed to define the rounded surfaces and limit the views to only one interpretation.

Figure 5-36

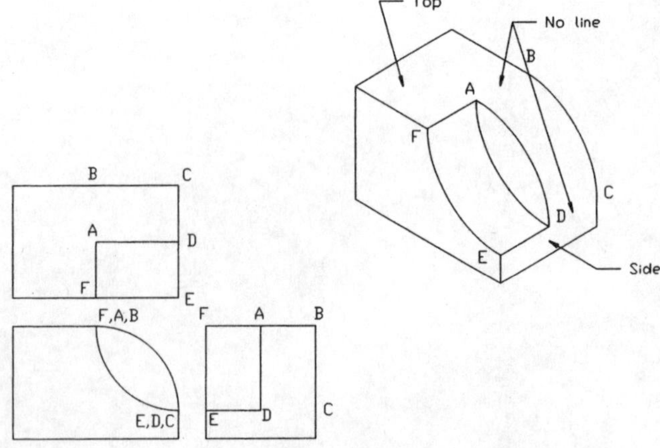

Surfaces perpendicular to an orthographic view always produce lines in that orthographic view. The vertical surface shown in the front view of Figure 5-37A requires an edge line in the top view. The vertical line in the front view is perpendicular to the top views.

The object shown in Figure 5-37B has no lines perpendicular to the top view, so no lines are drawn in the top view. Figure 5-37C shows two rounded surfaces that intersect at points tangent to their centerlines. The intersection point is considered sufficient to require an edge line in the top view. No line would be visible on the actual object, but drawing convention prescribes that a line be drawn.

Figure 5-37

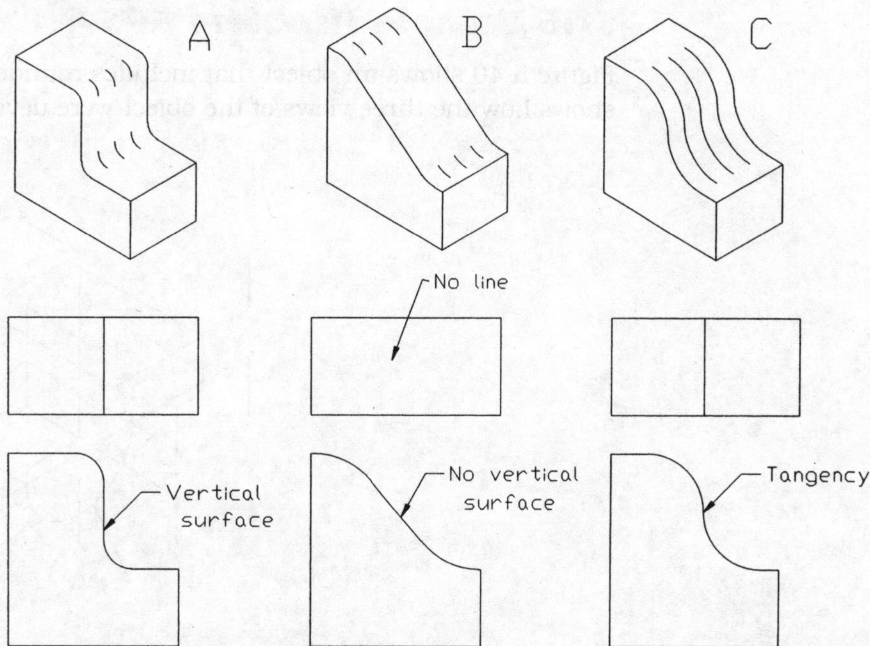

Figure 5-38 shows an object that contains two semicircular surfaces. Note how lines representing the widest and deepest point of the surfaces generate lines in the top view. No line would actually appear on the object. Figure 5-39 shows further examples of objects with curved surfaces.

Tangency line

Tangency line

Figure 5-38

Runout

Figure 5-39

5-16 Sample Problem SP5-4

Figure 5-40 shows an object that includes rounded surfaces, and Figure 5-41 shows how the three views of the object were developed.

Figure 5-40

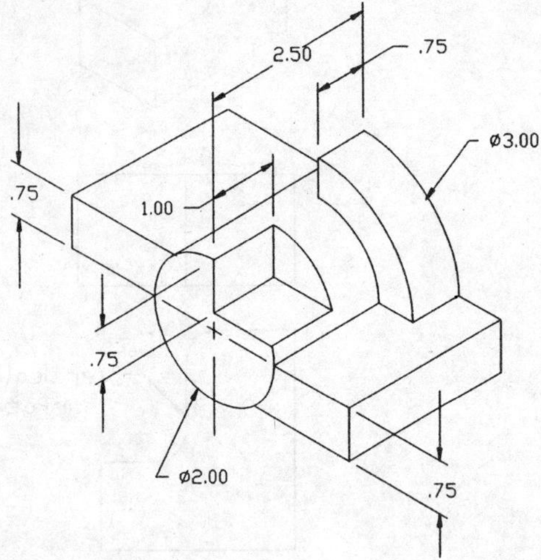

Figure 5-41

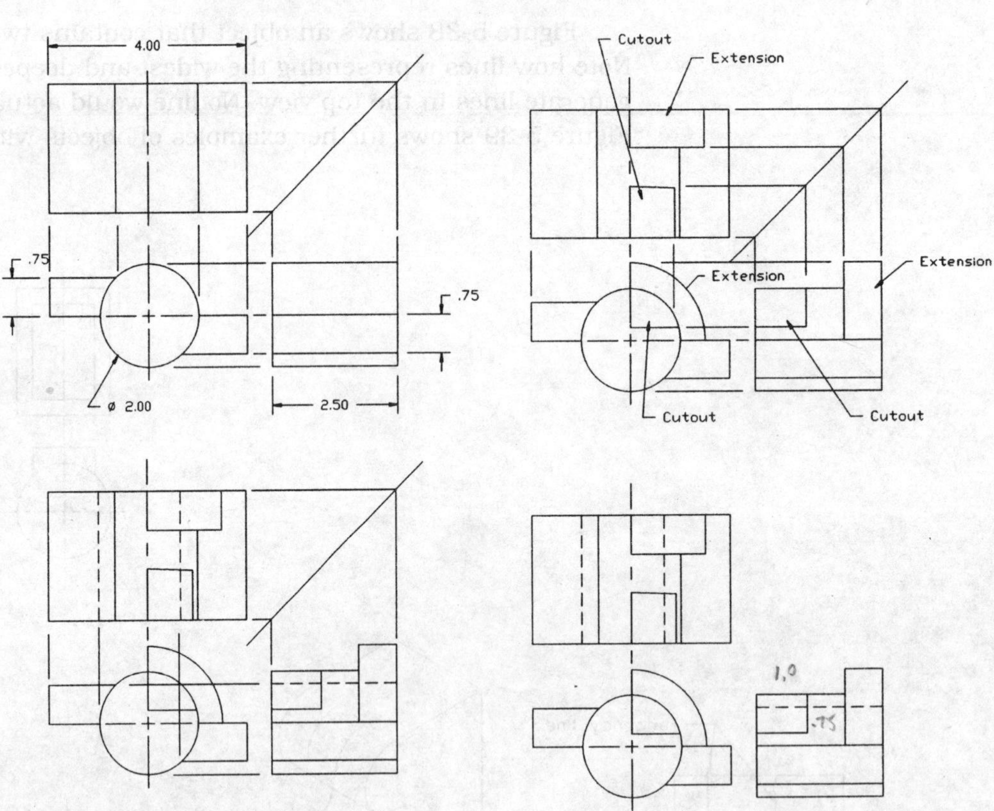

The procedure is as follows:

1. Use the given overall dimensions to lay out the size and location of the three views.
2. Draw in the external details, the cutout, and the circular extension in all three views.
3. Add the appropriate hidden lines. Either use the **Modify Properties** option or create a layer for hidden lines.
4. Erase and trim any excess lines, and save the drawing if desired.

5-17 Holes

Holes are represented in orthographic views by circles and parallel hidden lines. All views of a hole always include centerlines. See Figure 5-42. It is suggested that a layer entitled **Center** be added to any drawing being created. Specify the linetype **Center** and the color **Red.**

Figure 5-42

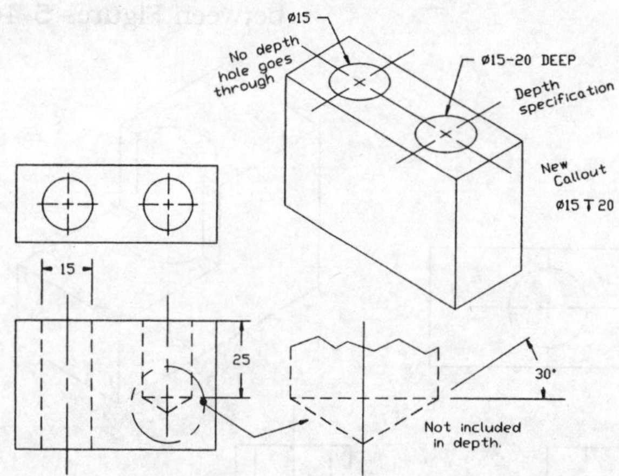

Holes that go completely through an object are dimensioned by the use of only a diameter. The notation **THRU** may be added to the diameter specification for clarity.

Holes that do not go completely through an object include a depth specification in their dimension. The depth specification is interpreted as shown in Figure 5-42. Holes that do not go completely through an object must include a conical point. The conical point is not included in the depth specification. Conical points must be included because most holes are produced by using a twist drill with conically shaped cutting edges.

The cutting angles of twist drills vary, but they are always represented by a 30° angle, as shown.

Figure 5-43 shows an object that contains two through holes and one hole with a depth specification. Note how these holes are represented

Figure 5-43

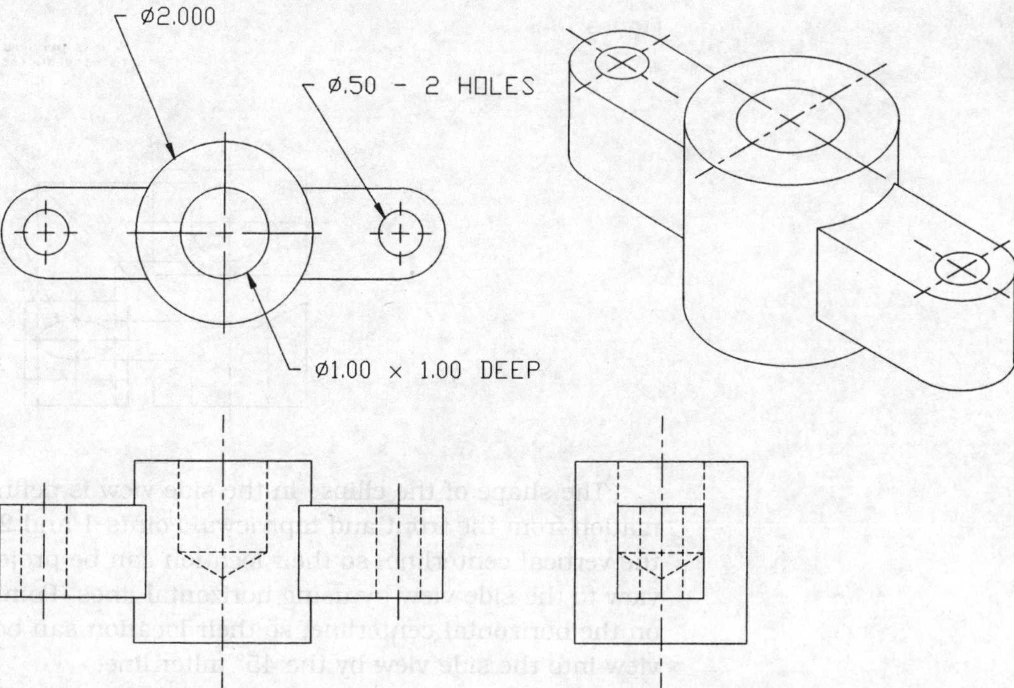

in the orthographic views and how centerlines are used in the different views.

Figure 5-44 is another example of an object that includes a hole. The hole is centered about the edge line between the two normal surfaces. Figure 5-45 shows the same object with the hole's center point offset from the edge line between the two normal surfaces. Compare the differences between Figures 5-44 and 5-45.

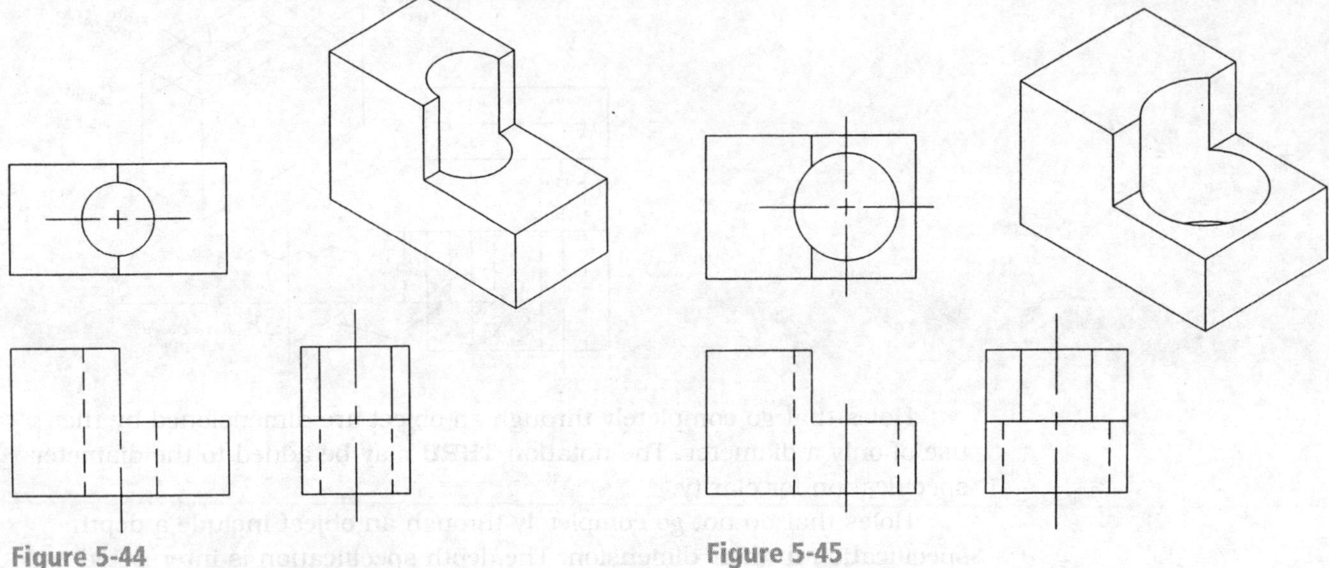

Figure 5-44 Figure 5-45

5-18 Holes in Slanted Surfaces

Figure 5-46 shows a hole that penetrates a slanted surface. The hole is perpendicular to the bottom surface of the object. The top view of the hole appears as a circle because we are looking straight down into it. The side view shows a distorted view of the circle and is represented by an ellipse.

Figure 5-46

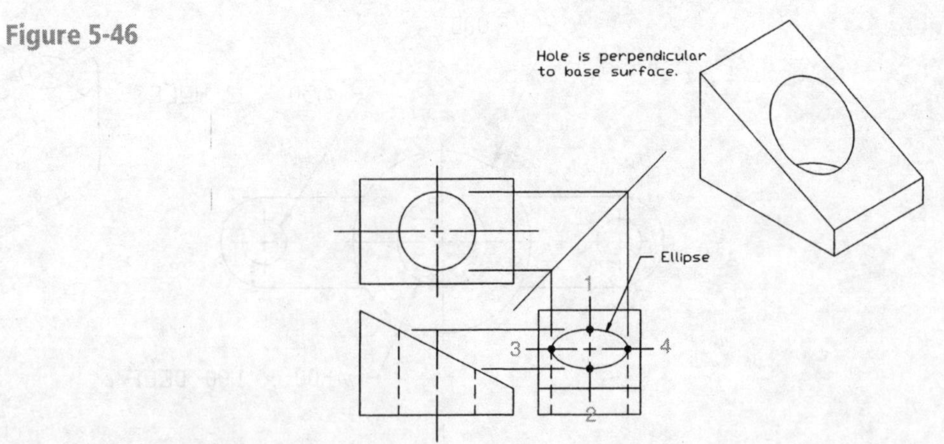

The shape of the ellipse in the side view is defined by projecting information from the front and top views. Points 1 and 2 are known to be on the vertical centerline, so their location can be projected from the front view to the side view by using horizontal lines. Points 3 and 4 are located on the horizontal centerline, so their location can be projected from the top view into the side view by the 45° miter line.

The elliptical shape of the hole in the side view is drawn, connecting the projected points, by using the **Ellipse** command.

To Draw an Ellipse Representing a Projected Hole

See Figure 5-47.

Figure 5-47

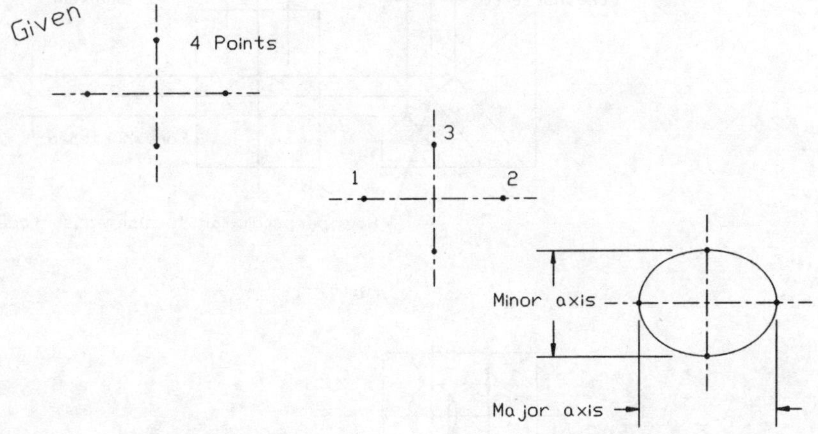

1. Define the **first point** as one of the points at which the major axis intersects one of the centerlines.
2. Define the **second point** as the other point on the major axis that intersects the same centerline.
3. Define the **third point** as one of the points on the minor axis that intersects the centerline perpendicular to the centerline used in steps 1 and 2.

To Draw Three Views of a Hole in a Slanted Surface

Figure 5-48 shows an object that includes a hole drilled perpendicular to the slanted surface. The hole is 1.00 unit in diameter. The hidden lines in the front view that represent the edges of the hole are drawn parallel to the centerline at a distance of 0.50. The horizontal and vertical centerlines of the hole are located in the top and right views. The intersection of the hole edges with the slanted surface shown in the front view is projected into the top and side views as shown.

The slanted surface shown in Figure 5-48 appears as a straight line in the front view. This means that the hole representations in the top and side views are rotated about only one axis. This, in turn, means that the hole representation is foreshortened in only one direction. The other direction—the other axis length—remains at the original diameter distance on 1.00. The four points needed to define the projected elliptical shape can be defined by the projection lines and the measured 1.00 distance.

The hole also penetrates the bottom surface, forming a different-sized ellipse. The hole's penetration can be shown in the side view by hidden lines parallel to the given centerline. The elliptical shape in the top view is defined by drawing horizontal parallel lines from the intersection of the hole's projected shape with the vertical centerline, and by projection lines from the front view that define the hole's length.

Figure 5-48

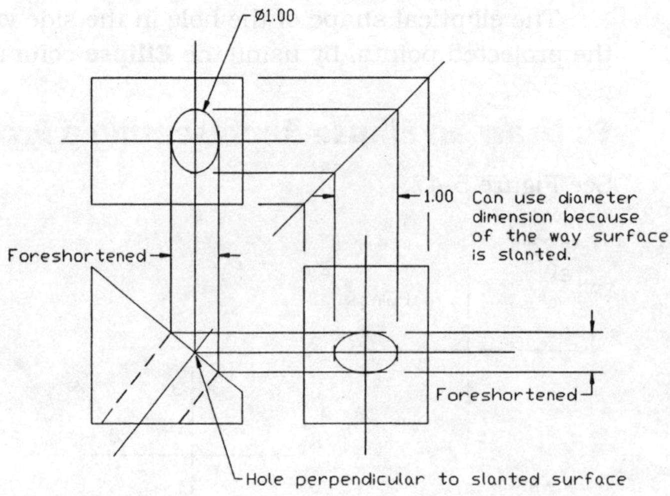

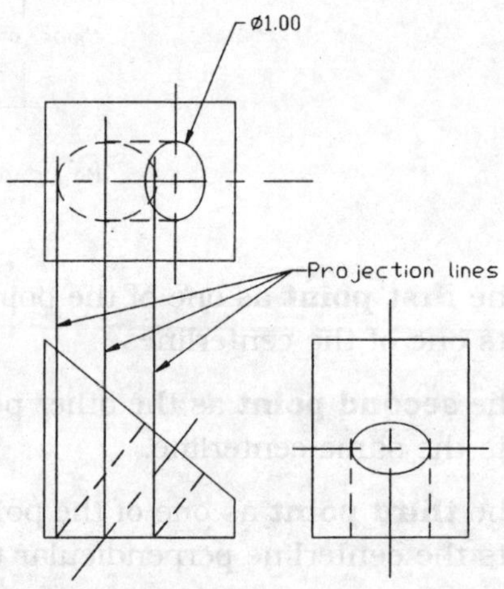

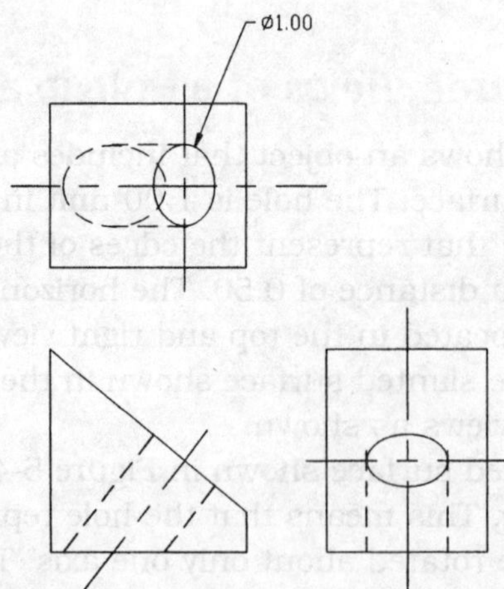

To Draw Three Views of a Hole Through an Oblique Surface

Figure 5-49A shows a hole drilled horizontally through the exact center of an oblique surface of an object. The oblique surface means that both axes in the top and front views will be foreshortened. The procedure used to create the hole's projection in the front and top views is as follows. (See Figure 5-49B.)

1. Draw the hole in the side view. The hole will appear as a circle because it is drilled horizontally.

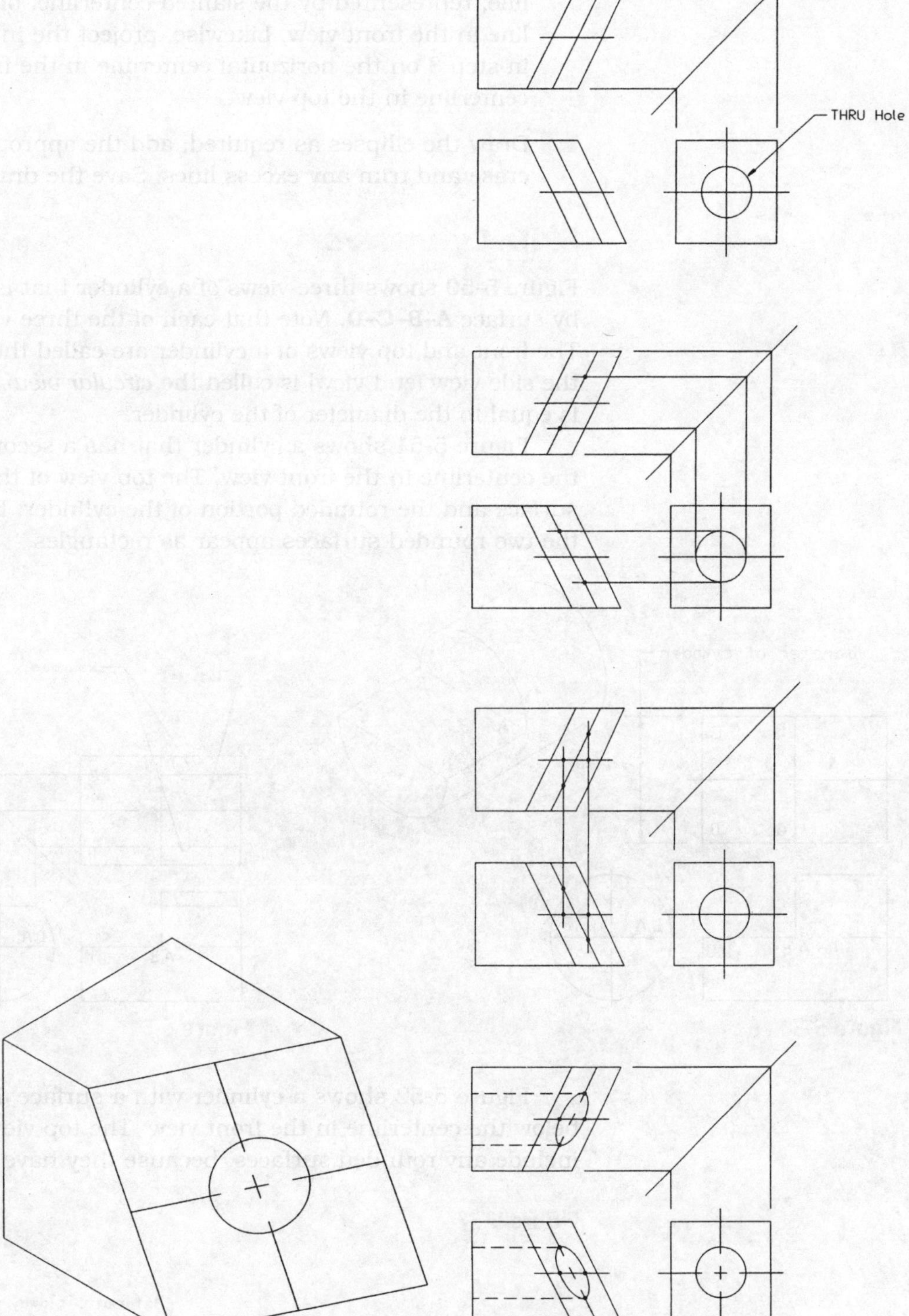

Figure 5-49A

Figure 5-49B

2 Draw the hole's centerlines in the front and top views. The hole is located exactly in the center of the oblique surface, so lines parallel to the surface's edge lines located midway across the surface may be drawn.

3 Project the intersection of the hole and the horizontal centerline into the top view, and project the intersection of the hole with the vertical centerline into the front view.

4 Project the intersections created in step 3 with the horizontal centerline, represented by the slanted centerline, onto the horizontal centerline in the front view. Likewise, project the intersection points created in step 3 on the horizontal centerline in the front view to the slanted centerline in the top view.

5 Draw the ellipses as required, add the appropriate hidden lines, and erase and trim any excess lines. Save the drawing if desired.

5-19 Cylinders

Figure 5-50 shows three views of a cylinder that is cut along the centerline by surface **A–B–C–D.** Note that each of the three views includes centerlines. The front and top views of a cylinder are called the *rectangular views,* and the side view (end view) is called the *circular view.* The width of the top view is equal to the diameter of the cylinder.

Figure 5-51 shows a cylinder that has a second surface located above the centerline in the front view. The top view of the cylinder shows the flat surface and the rounded portion of the cylinder. Both the flat surface and the two rounded surfaces appear as rectangles.

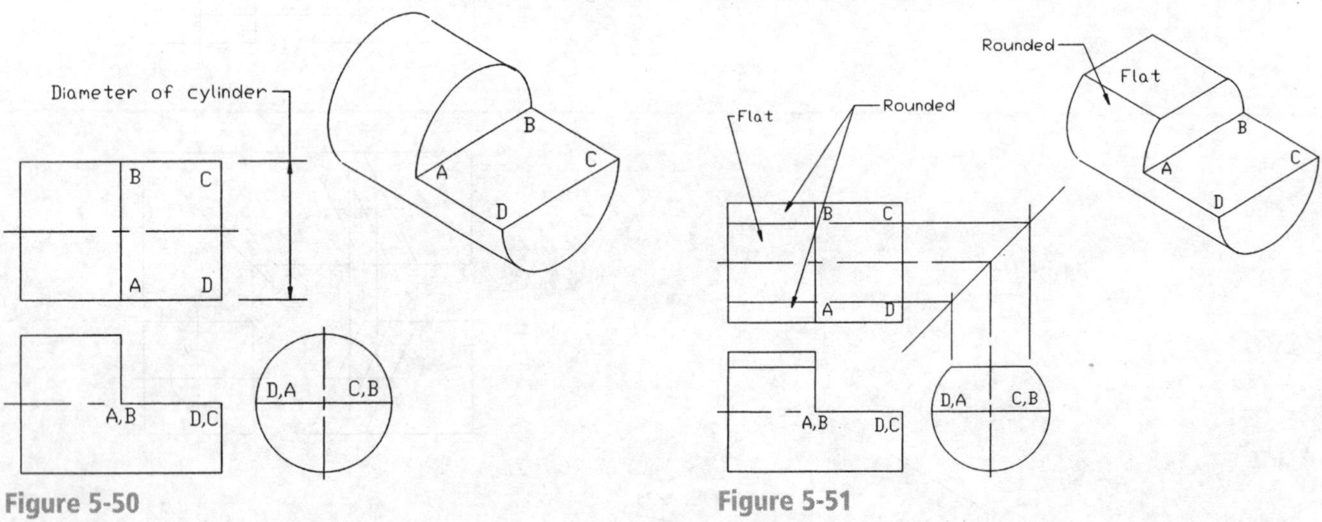

Figure 5-50

Figure 5-51

Figure 5-52 shows a cylinder with a surface **J–K–L–M** that is located below the centerline in the front view. The top view of this surface does not include any rounded surfaces, because they have been cut away.

Figure 5-52

5-20 Sample Problem SP5-5

Figure 5-53 shows a cylindrically shaped object that has three surface cuts: one above the centerline, one below the centerline, and one directly on the centerline. Figure 5-54 shows how the three views of the object were developed. The procedure is as follows:

1 **Use the given overall length of the cylinder and its diameter to create the two rectangular top and front views and the circular end views.**

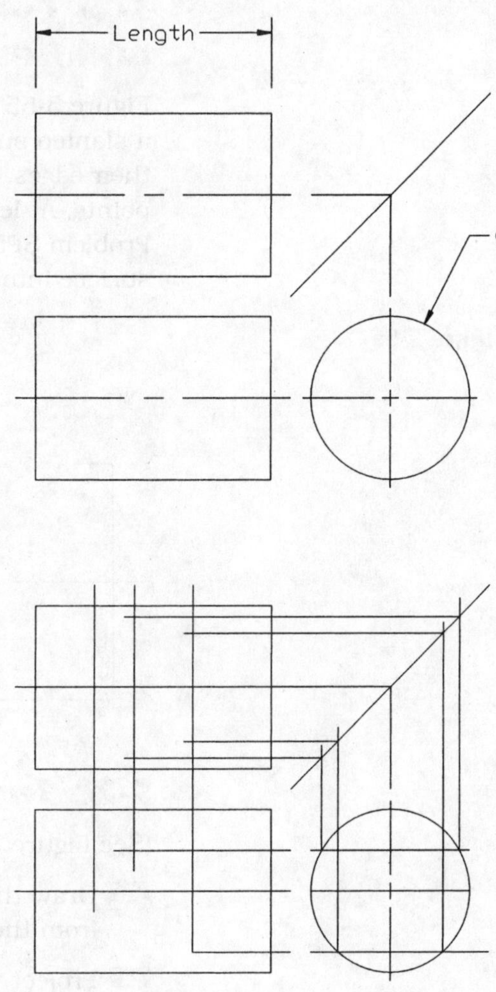

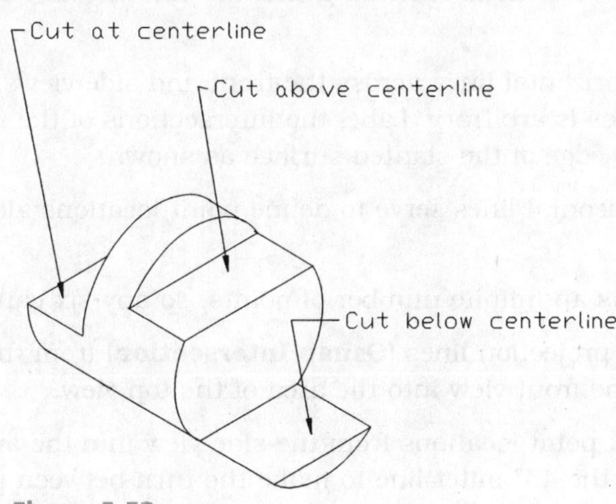

Figure 5-53

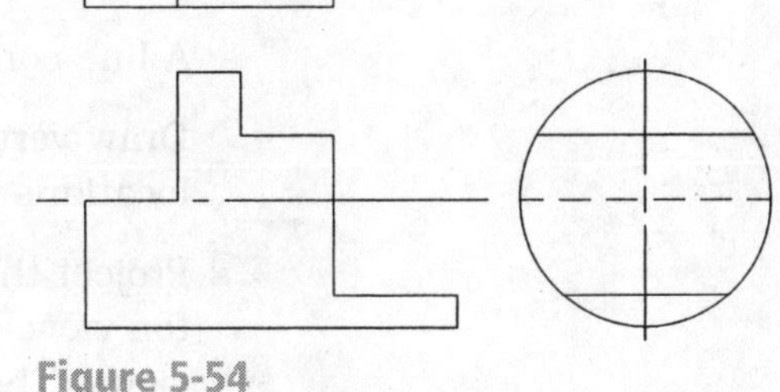

Figure 5-54

2. Draw horizontal lines in the side view that define the end views of the three surfaces. Project the size and location of the surfaces into the front and top views. Use **Osnap Intersection,** with **Ortho** on, for accurate projection.
3. Erase and trim the excess lines.
4. Save the drawing if desired.

5-21 Cylinders with Slanted and Rounded Surfaces

Figure 5-55 shows a front and side view of a cylindrical object that includes a slanted surface. Slanted surfaces are projected by defining points along their edges in known orthographic views and then projecting the edge points. At least two known views are needed for accurate projection. Sample Problem SP5-6 shows how to define and project a slanted cylindrical surface into the top view, given the front and side views.

Figure 5-55

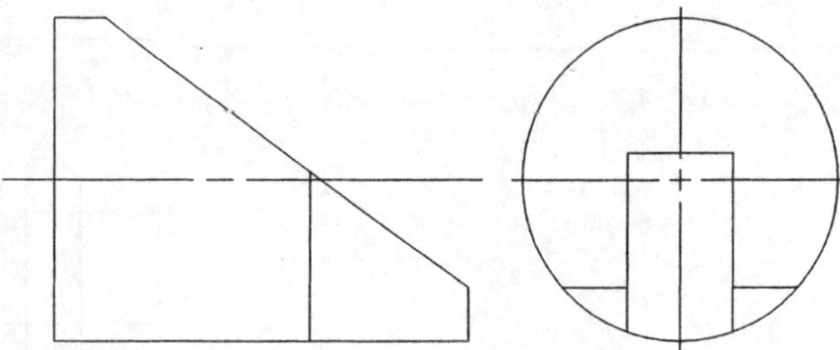

5-22 Sample Problem SP5-6

(See Figure 5-56.)

1. Draw the rectangular shape of the top view by projecting the length from the front view and the width from the side view.
2. Project the centerlines, and label points 1, 2, and 3 in the front and side views. The locations of these points are known from the given information.
3. Draw three horizontal lines across the front and side views. The location of the lines is arbitrary. Label the intersections of the horizontal lines with the edge of the slanted surface as shown.
4. The three horizontal lines serve to define point locations along the surface's edge.

   A line contains an infinite number of points, so any six can be used.
5. Draw vertical projection lines (**Osnap Intersection**) from the six point locations in the front view into the area of the top view.
6. Project the six point locations from the side view into the area of the top view. Use the 45° miter line to make the turn between the two views. The intersection of the vertical projection lines of step 2 and the

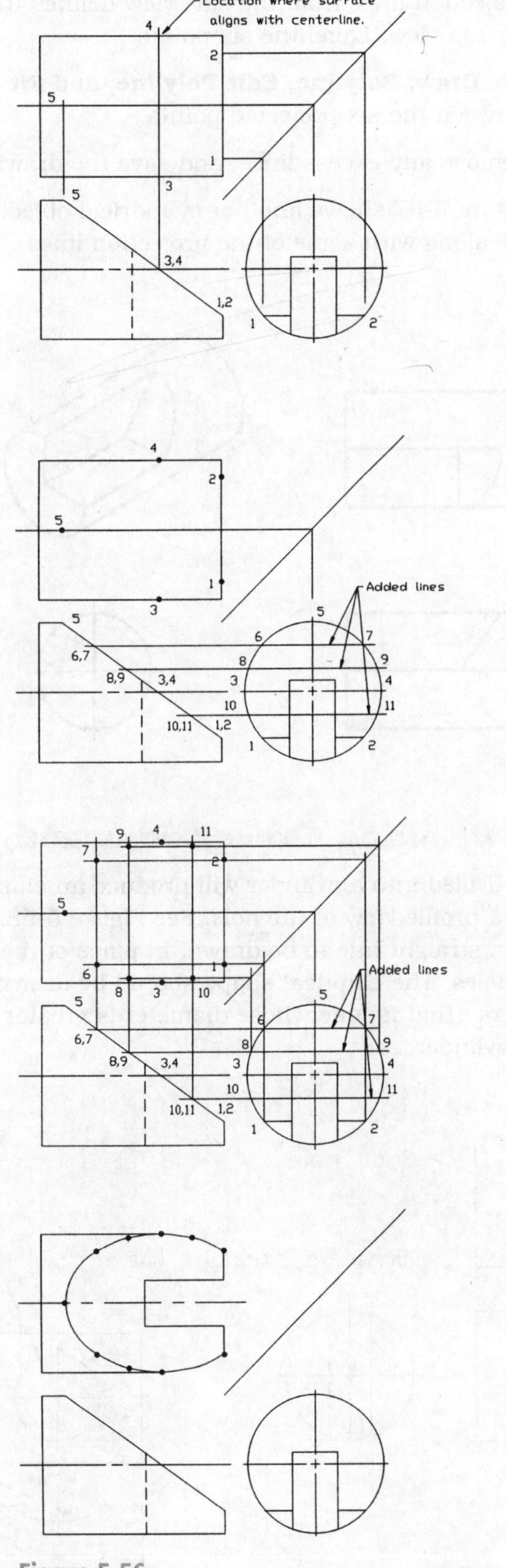

Figure 5-56

projection lines from the side view defines the location of the points in the top view. Label the six points.

7 Use **Draw, Polyline, Edit Polyline,** and **Fit** to create a smooth line between the six projected points.

8 Remove any excess lines, and save the drawing if desired.

Figure 5-57 shows another cylindrical object that contains a slanted surface along with some of the projection lines.

Figure 5-57

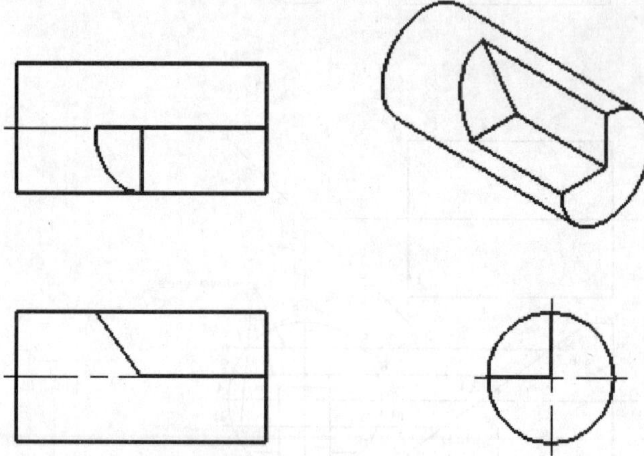

5-23 Drawing Conventions and Cylinders

A hole drilled into a cylinder will produce an elliptically shaped edge line in a profile view of the hole. See Figure 5-58. Drawing convention allows a straight line to be drawn, in place of the elliptical shape, for small holes. The elliptical shape should be drawn for large holes in cylinders—that is, one whose diameter is greater than half the diameter of the cylinder.

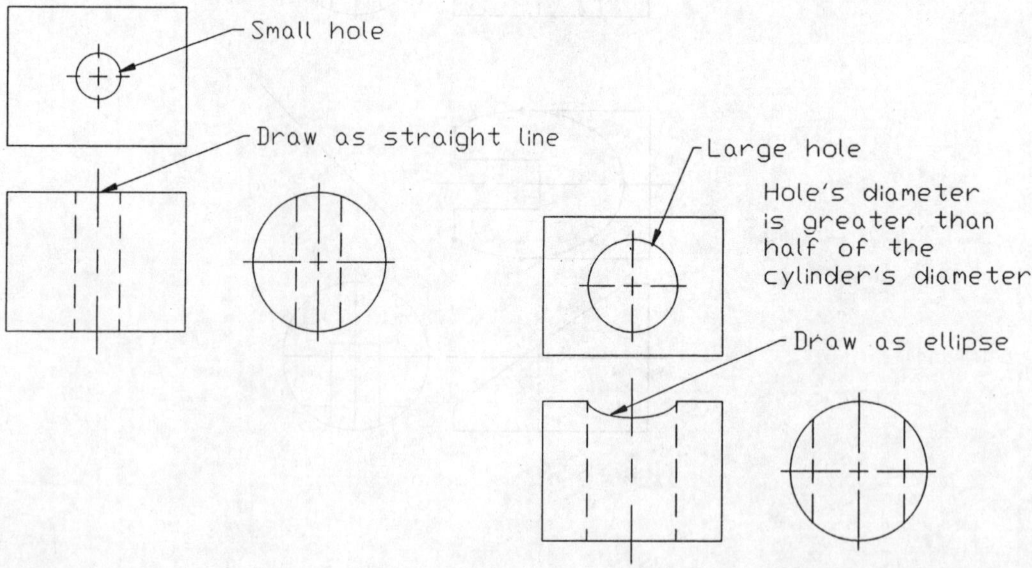

Figure 5-58

Drawing convention also permits straight lines to be drawn for the profile view of a keyway cut into a cylinder. See Figure 5-59. As with holes, if a keyway is large relative to a cylinder, the correct offset shape should be drawn. A keyway is considered large if its width is greater than half of the diameter of the cylinder.

Figure 5-59

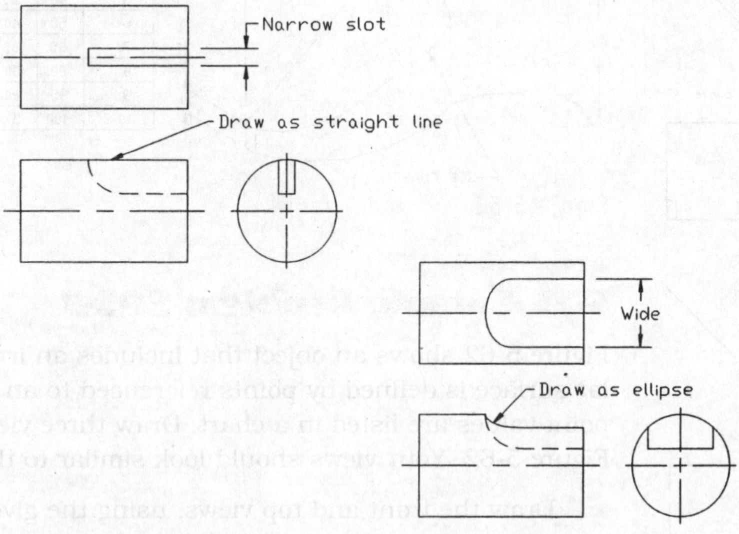

5-24 Irregular Surfaces

Irregular surfaces are curved surfaces that do not have constant radii. See Figures 5-60 and 5-61. Irregular surfaces are defined by the X,Y coordinates of points located on the edge of the surface. The points may be dimensioned directly on the view, but are often presented in chart form, as shown in Figure 5-61. Figure 5-61 also shows a wing surface defined relative to a given X,Y coordinate system.

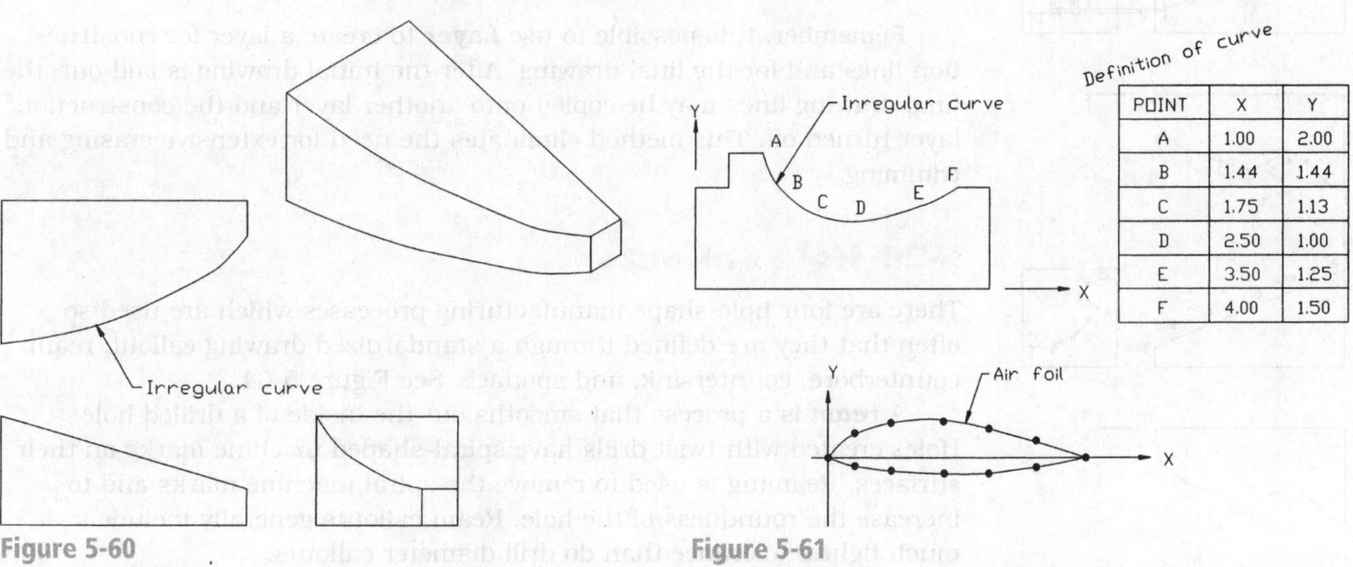

POINT	X	Y
A	1.00	2.00
B	1.44	1.44
C	1.75	1.13
D	2.50	1.00
E	3.50	1.25
F	4.00	1.50

Figure 5-60 **Figure 5-61**

Irregular surfaces are projected by defining points along their edges and then projecting the points. At least two known views are needed for accurate projection. The more points used to define the curve, the more accurate the final curve shape will be.

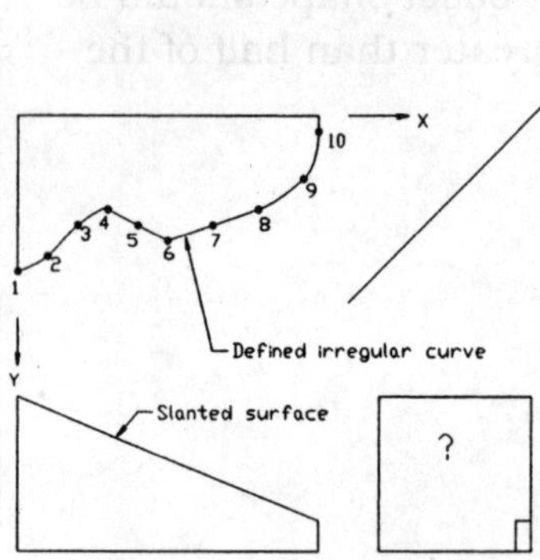

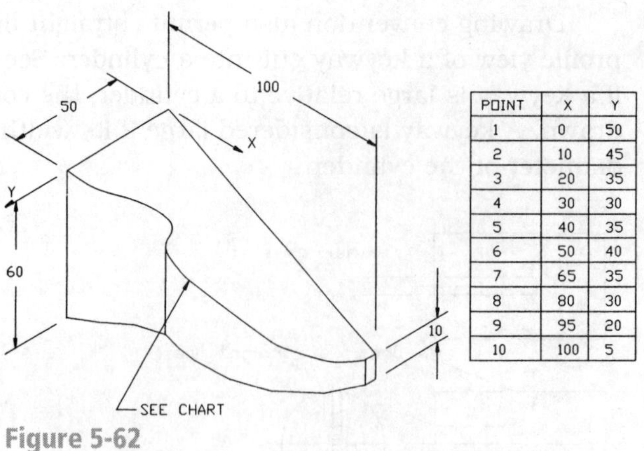

POINT	X	Y
1	0	50
2	10	45
3	20	35
4	30	30
5	40	35
6	50	40
7	65	35
8	80	30
9	95	20
10	100	5

Figure 5-62

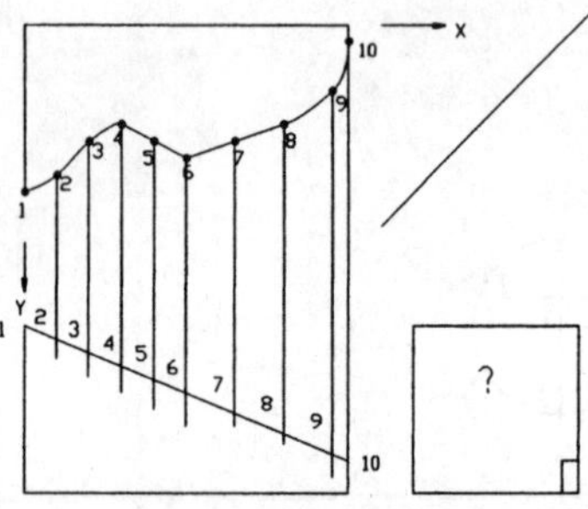

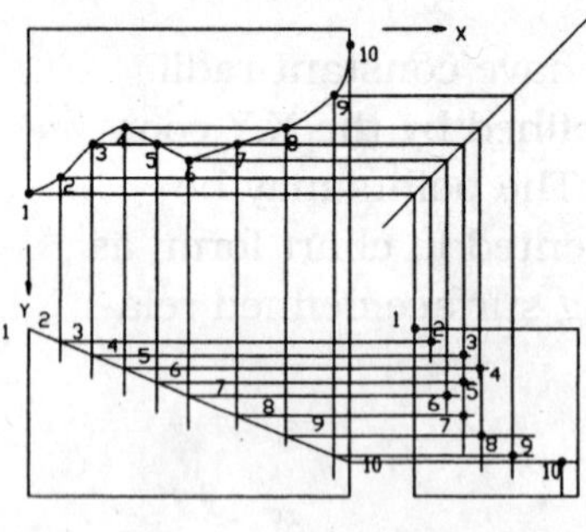

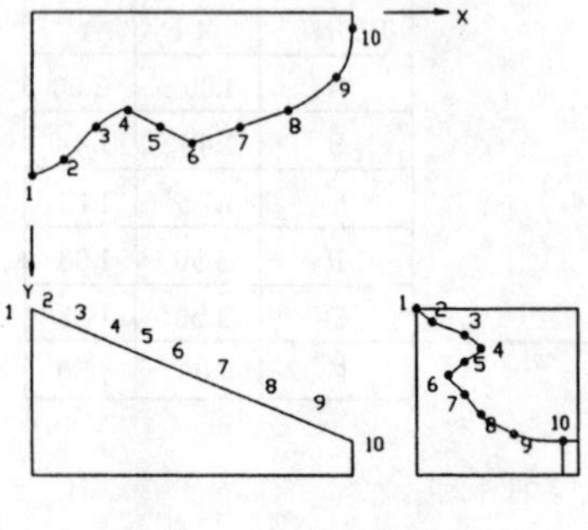

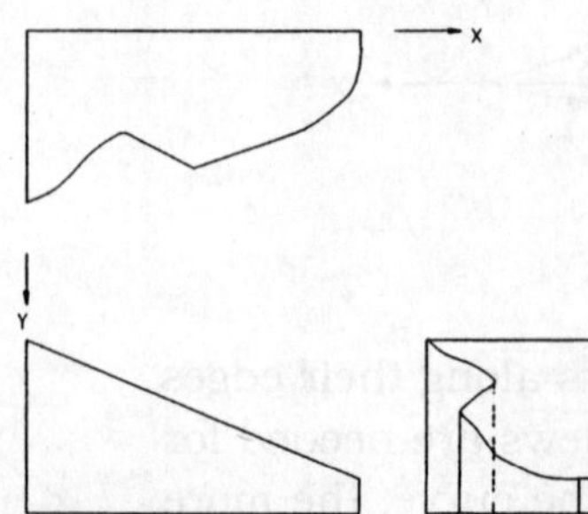

Figure 5-63

5-25 Sample Problem SP5-7

Figure 5-62 shows an object that includes an irregular surface. The irregular surface is defined by points referenced to an X,Y coordinate system. The point values are listed in a chart. Draw three views of the object shown in Figure 5-62. Your views should look similar to those in Figure 5-63.

1. Draw the front and top views, using the given dimensions and chart values. Draw the outline of the side view, using the given dimensions.

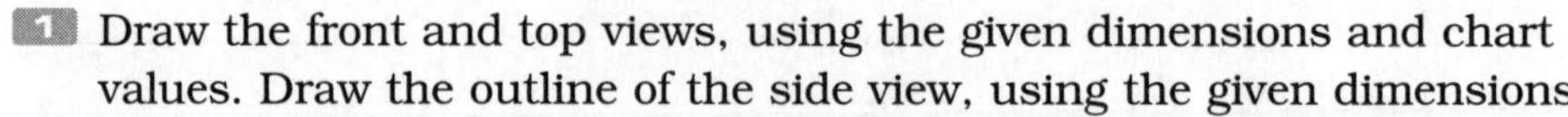

2. Project the points that define the irregular curve in the top view into the front view. Label the points.

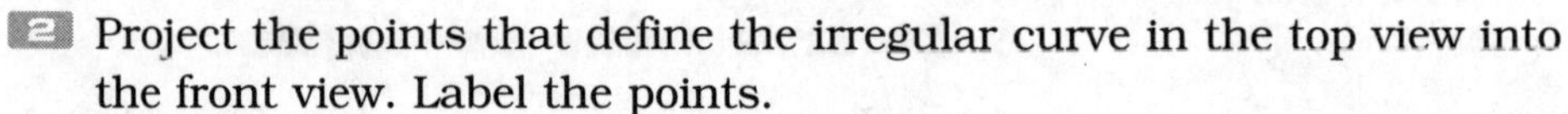

3. Project the points for the curve from both the top and front views into the side view. Label the intersection points.

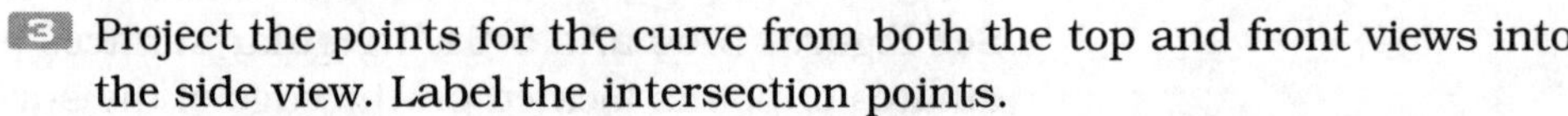

4. Use **Polyline, Edit Polyline,** and **Fit** to create a curve that represents the side view of the irregular surface.

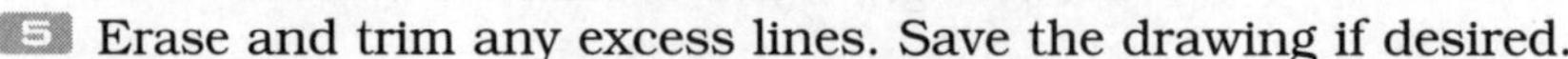

5. Erase and trim any excess lines. Save the drawing if desired.

Remember, it is possible to use **Layer** to create a layer for construction lines and for the final drawing. After the initial drawing is laid out, the final drawing lines may be copied onto another layer and the construction layer turned off. This method eliminates the need for extensive erasing and trimming.

5-26 Hole Callouts

There are four hole-shape manufacturing processes which are used so often that they are defined through a standardized drawing callout: ream, counterbore, countersink, and spotface. See Figure 5-64.

A ***ream*** is a process that smooths out the inside of a drilled hole. Holes created with twist drills have spiral-shaped machine marks on their surfaces. Reaming is used to remove the spiral machine marks and to increase the roundness of the hole. Ream callouts generally include a much tighter tolerance than do drill diameter callouts.

A ***counterbore*** consists of two holes drilled along the same centerline. Counterbores are used to allow fasteners or other objects to be recessed, thus keeping the top surface uniform in height.

A counterbore drawing callout specifies the diameter of the small hole, the diameter of the large hole, and the depth of the large hole.

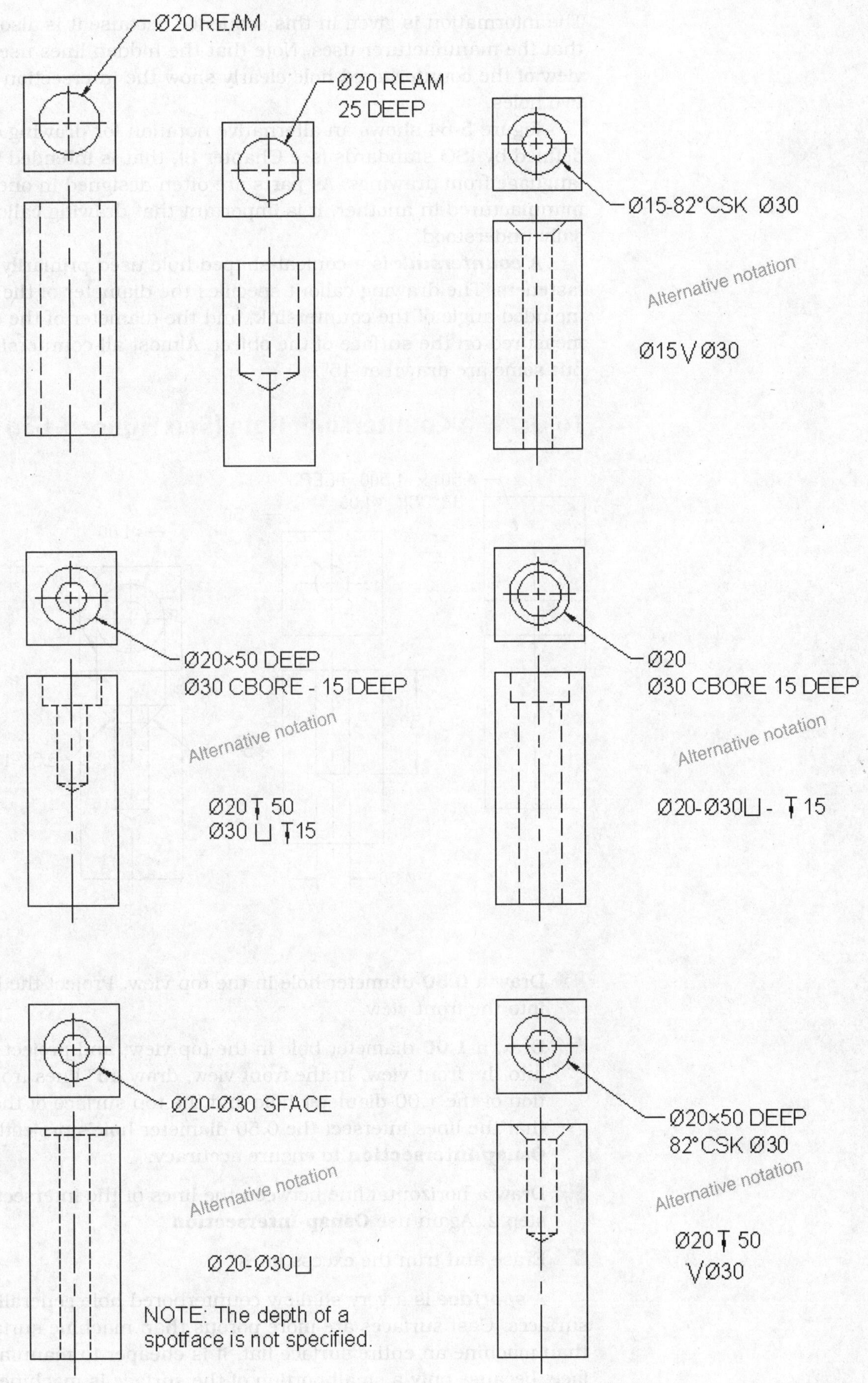

Figure 5-64

The information is given in this sequence because it is also the sequence that the manufacturer uses. Note that the hidden lines used in the front view of the counterbored hole clearly show the intersection between the two holes.

Figure 5-64 shows an alternative notation for drawing callouts, as defined by ISO standards (see Chapter 8), that is intended to remove language from drawings. As parts are often designed in one country and manufactured in another, it is important that drawing callouts be universally understood.

A ***countersink*** is a conical-shaped hole used primarily for flat-head fasteners. The drawing callout specifies the diameter of the hole, the included angle of the countersink, and the diameter of the countersink as measured on the surface of the object. Almost all countersinks are 82°, but some are drawn at 45°.

To Draw a Countersunk Hole (See Figure 5-65.)

Figure 5-65

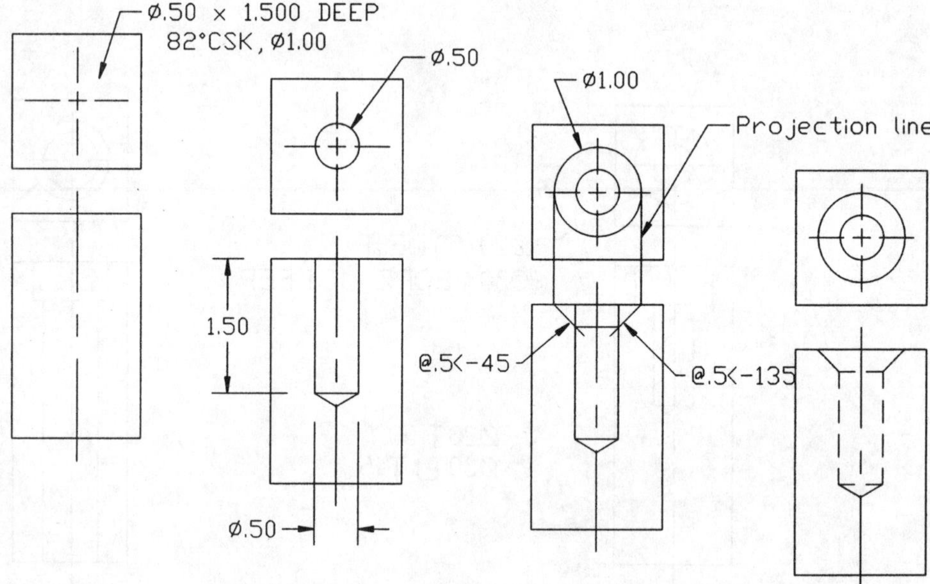

1. Draw a **0.50**-diameter hole in the top view. Project the hole's diameter into the front view.
2. Draw a **1.00**-diameter hole in the top view, and project its diameter into the front view. In the front view, draw **45**° lines from the intersection of the 1.00-diameter hole and the top surface of the front view so that the lines intersect the 0.50-diameter hole's projection lines. Use **Osnap Intersection** to ensure accuracy.
3. Draw a horizontal line between the lines of the intersection created in step 2. Again use **Osnap Intersection.**
4. Erase and trim the excess lines.

A ***spotface*** is a very shallow counterbored hole generally used on cast surfaces. Cast surfaces are more porous than machine surfaces. Rather than machine an entire surface flat, it is cheaper to manufacture a spotface, because only a small portion of the surface is machined. Spotfaces are usually used for bearing surfaces of fasteners.

A spotface callout defines the diameter of the hole and the diameter of the spotface. A depth need not be given. When machining was done mostly by hand, the machinist would make the spotface just deep enough to produce a shiny surface (most cast surfaces are more gray in color), so no depth was needed. Automated machines require a spotface depth specification. Usually, the depth is very shallow.

5-27 Castings

Casting is one of the oldest manufacturing processes. Metal is heated to liquid form, then poured into molds and allowed to cool. The resulting shapes usually include many rounded edges and surface tangencies because it is very difficult to cast square edges. Concave edges are called ***rounds,*** and convex edges are called ***fillets.*** See Figure 5-66. A runout is used to indicate that two rounded surfaces have become tangent to one another. A ***runout*** is a short arc of arbitrary radius—that is, arbitrary as long as the runout is visually clear.

Figure 5-66

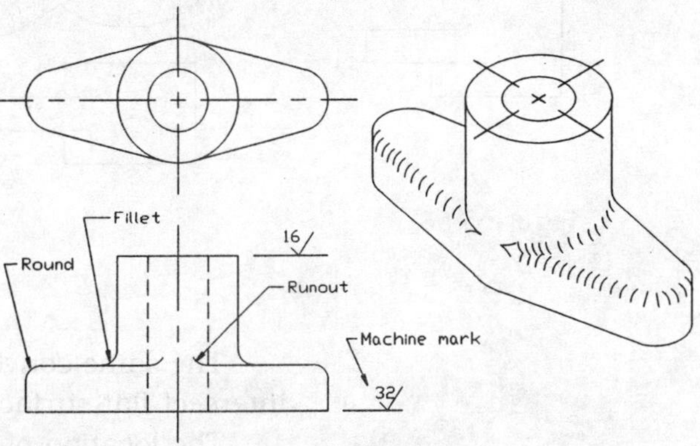

Cast objects are often partially machined to produce flatter surfaces than can be produced by the casting process. Machined surfaces are defined by the use of machine marks (checkmarks), as shown in Figure 5-66. The numbers within the machine marks specify the flatness requirements in terms of microinches or micrometers. Machine marks are explained in greater detail in Section 9-26.

A ***boss*** is a turretlike shape that is often included on castings to localize and minimize machining. A boss is defined by its diameter and its height. The sides of a boss are rounded and defined by a radius that is usually equal to the height of the boss. See Figure 5-67.

Figure 5-67

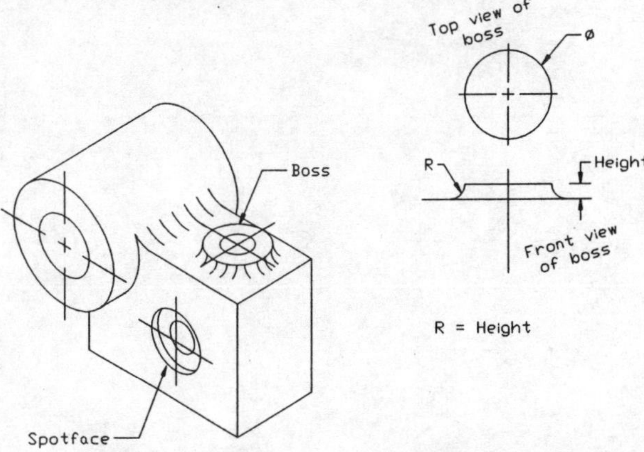

Spotfacing is a machine process often associated with castings. As with bosses, spotfaces help to localize and minimize machining requirements. Spotfaces were defined in Section 5-26.

The direction of runouts is determined by the shape of the two surfaces involved. Flat surfaces intersecting rounded surfaces generate runouts that turn out. Rounded surfaces that intersect rounded surfaces generate runouts that turn in. See Figure 5-68.

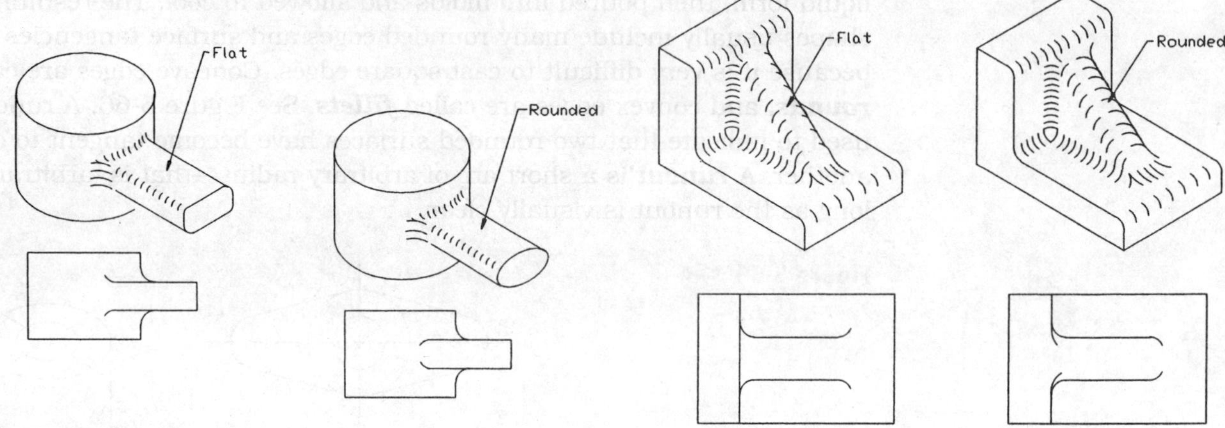

Figure 5-68

The same convention is followed for flat and rounded surfaces that intersect flat surfaces.

The location of a runout is determined by the location of the tangent that it represents. See Figure 5-69. The location of a tangency point can be determined by first drawing the top view of the tangency line by using **Osnap Tangent.** A line can then be drawn from the center point of the circular top view to the end of the tangency line by using **Osnap Endpoint.** The point of tangency can then be projected from the top view to the front view by using **Osnap Intersection** with **Ortho** on.

Figure 5-69

Drawn using OSNAP,TAN
Drawn using OSNAP,END
Point of tangency
Drawn using OSNAP, INT, with ORTHO on.

Use **Arc** (type the word **arc** in response to a command prompt) to draw runouts. Any convenient radius may be used, providing that the runout is clearly visible and visually distinct from the straight line. Figure 5-70 shows some further examples of cast surfaces that include runouts.

Figure 5-70

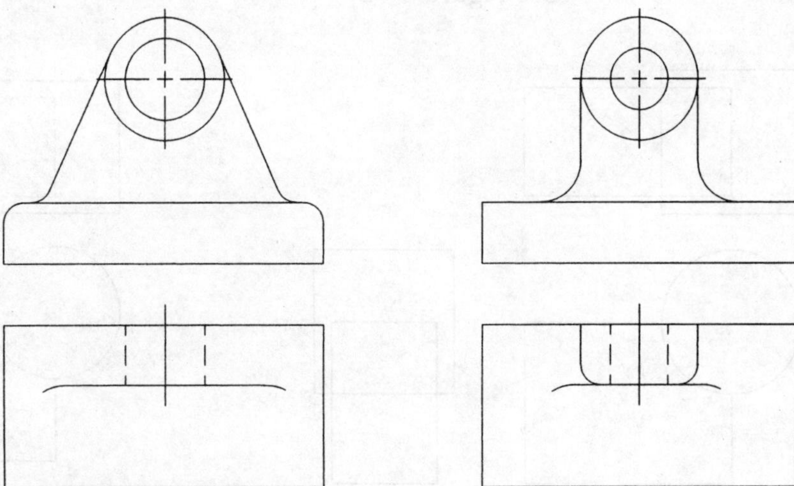

5-28 Sample Problem SP5-8

Draw three views of the object shown in Figure 5-71. The solution was drawn as follows:

1. Use the given overall dimensions, and draw the outline of the front, top, and side views.
2. Modify the appropriate lines to hidden lines. Draw the fillets and rounds. The **Fillet** command may erase needed lines. This cannot always be avoided, so simply redraw the needed lines after the fillet or round is complete.
3. Draw the spotface and boss in each of the views. The hole in the boss is **0.500** deep. Clearly show the bottom of the hole, including the conical point. Draw the hole in the front view, and use **Copy** to copy the hole into the side view.

Figure 5-71

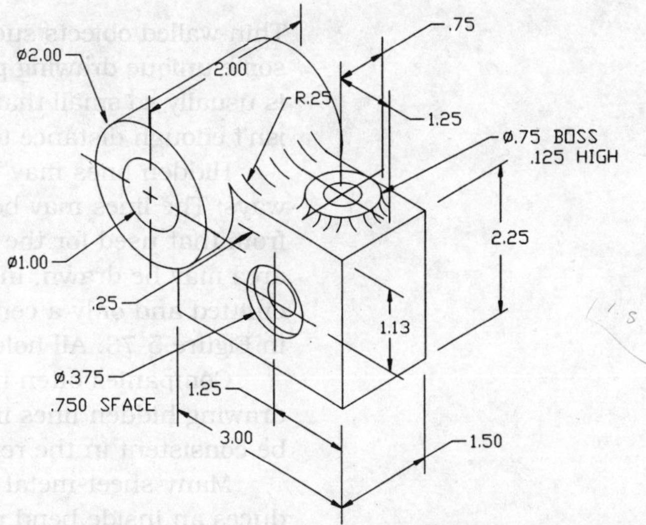

4 Use **Draw, Circle** to draw the **1.00**-diameter hole in the front view. Draw the appropriate hidden and centerlines in the other views.

5 Save the drawing if desired.

See Figure 5-72.

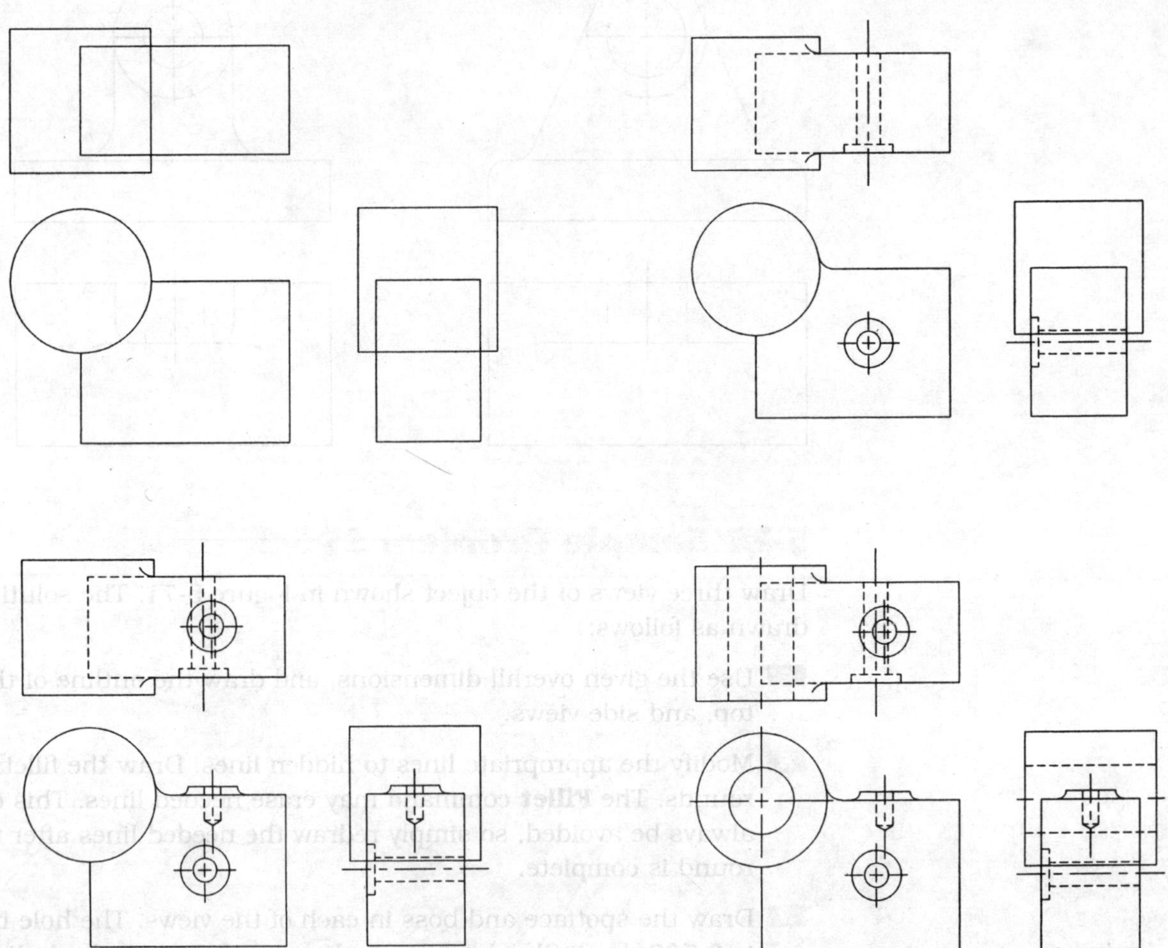

Figure 5-72

5-29 Thin-Walled Objects

Thin-walled objects such as parts made from sheet metal or tubing present some unique drawing problems. For example, the distance between surfaces is usually so small that hidden lines can't be used to define holes, and there isn't enough distance to draw a broken-line pattern. See Figure 5-73.

Hidden lines may be applied to thin-walled objects in one of three ways: The lines may be drawn as continuous lines, but in a different color from that used for the actual continuous lines; an enlarged detail of the area may be drawn, including the hidden lines; or the hidden lines may be omitted and only a centerline included. Each of these techniques is shown in Figure 5-73. All holes must include a centerline.

Companies often have a drawing manual that states their policy on drawing hidden lines in thin-walled objects. The most important goal is to be consistent in the representation.

Many sheet-metal parts are manufactured by bending. Bending produces an inside bend radius and an outside bend radius. The inside bend

Figure 5-73

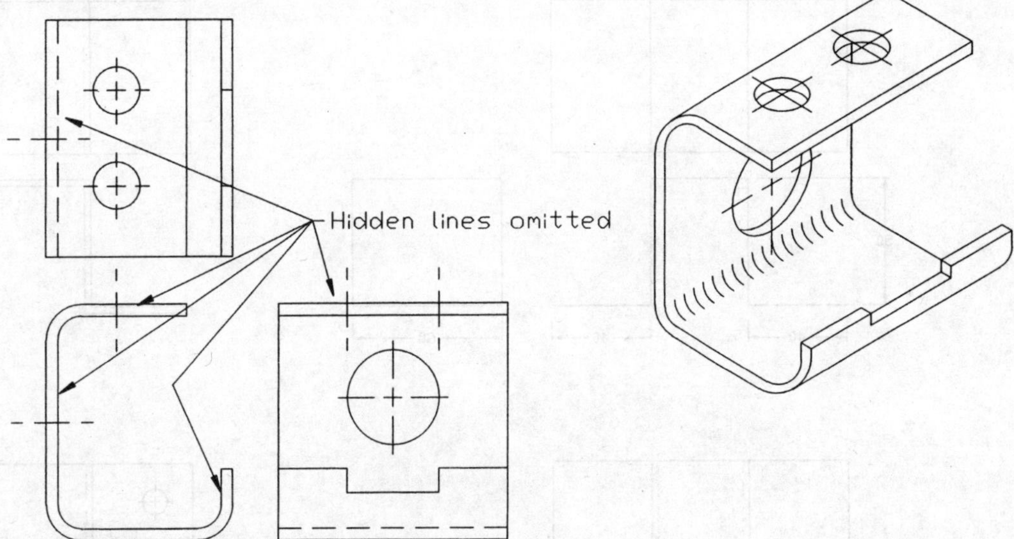

radius plus the material thickness should equal the outside bend radius. See Figure 5-74. The same radius should not be used for both the inside and the outside bends.

Figure 5-74

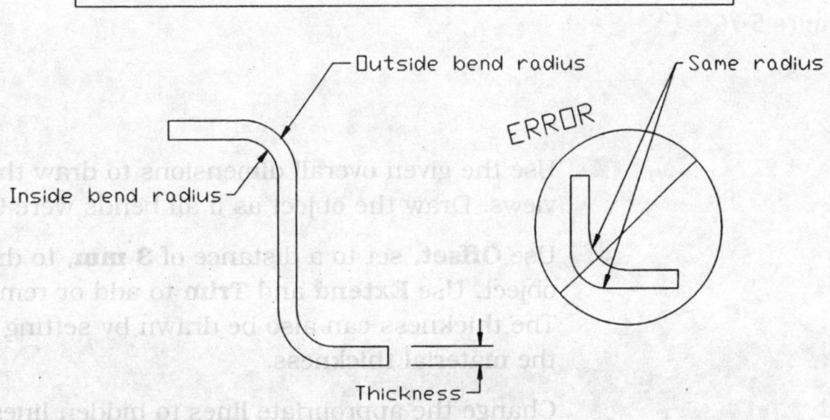

5-30 Sample Problem SP5-9

Draw three views of the object shown in Figure 5-75. Figure 5-76 shows how the three views were developed.

Figure 5-75

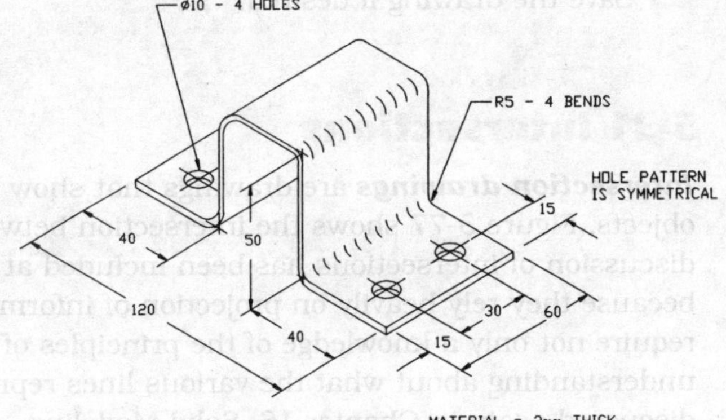

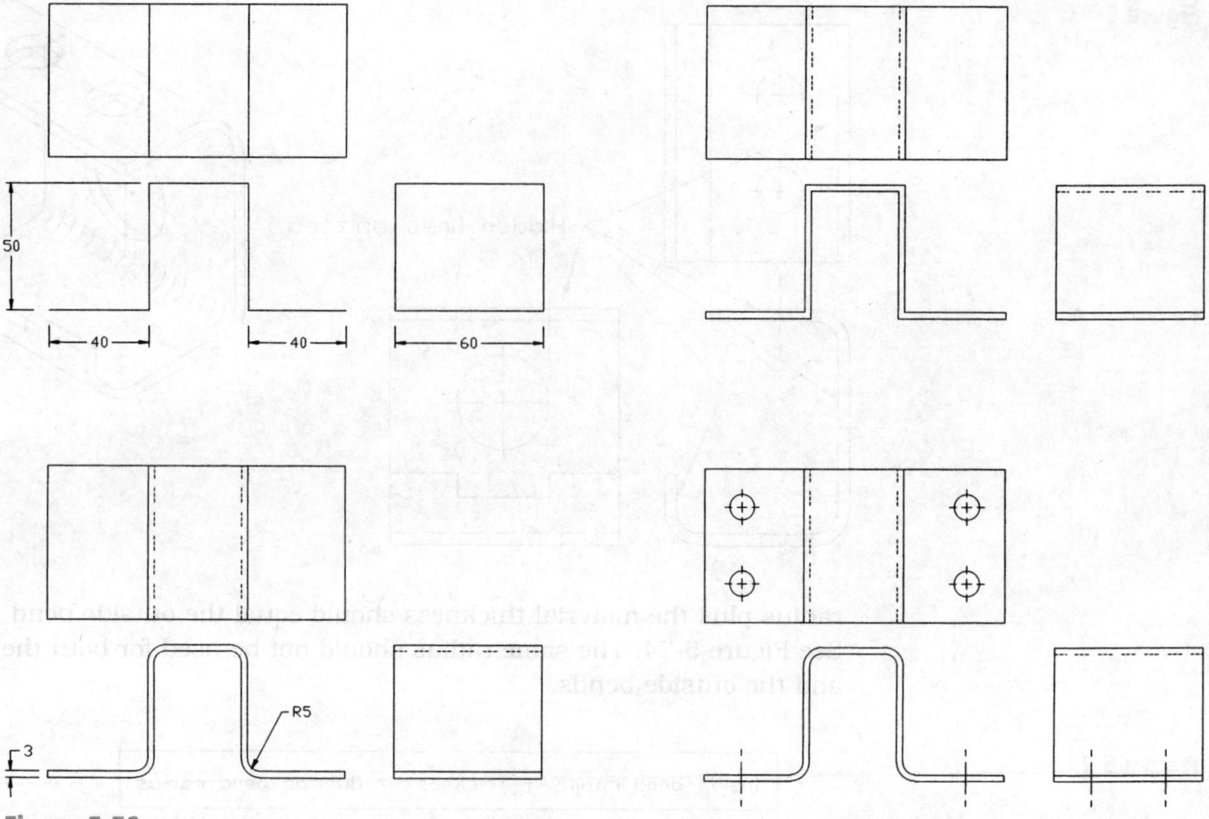

Figure 5-76

1. Use the given overall dimensions to draw the outline of the three views. Draw the object as if all bends were 90°.

2. Use **Offset,** set to a distance of **3 mm,** to draw the thickness of the object. Use **Extend** and **Trim** to add or remove lines as needed. The thickness can also be drawn by setting the snap spacing equal to the material thickness.

   Change the appropriate lines to hidden lines.

3. Draw fillets, using a radius of **5 mm** for the inside bend radii and **8 mm** for the outside bend radii.

4. Use **Draw, Circle** to draw the holes in the appropriate view and add centerlines as shown.

5. Save the drawing if desired.

5-31 Intersections

Intersection drawings are drawings that show the intersection of two objects. Figure 5-77 shows the intersection between two offset squares. A discussion of intersections has been included at this point in the book because they rely heavily on projection of information between views. They require not only a knowledge of the principles of projection, but also an understanding about what the various lines represent. Intersections will be discussed again in Chapter 16, Solid Modeling.

Figure 5-77

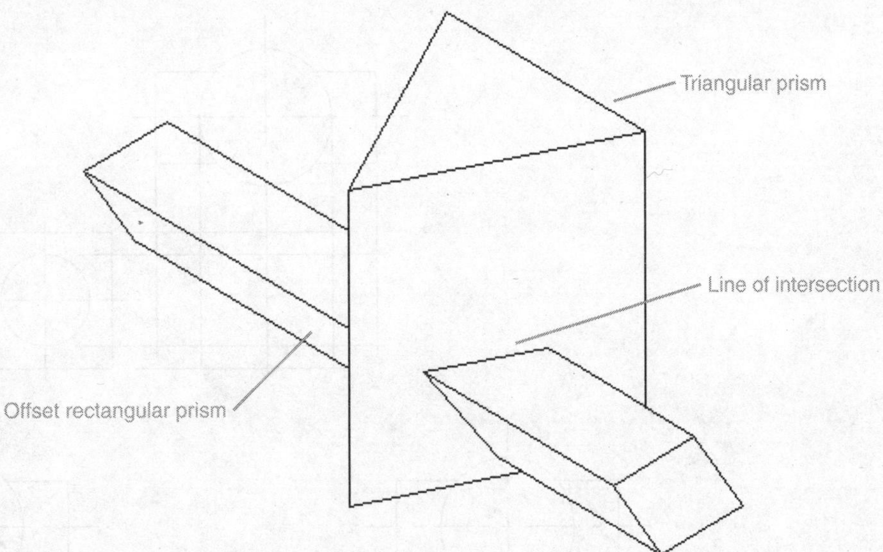

Three intersection problems are presented in the following three sample problems.

5-32 Sample Problem SP5-10

Given the side and top views of a smaller circle intersecting a larger circle, as shown in Figure 5-78, draw the front view. All dimensions are in inches. Because the object is symmetrical, the intersection for one side will be developed and then mirrored.

Figure 5-78

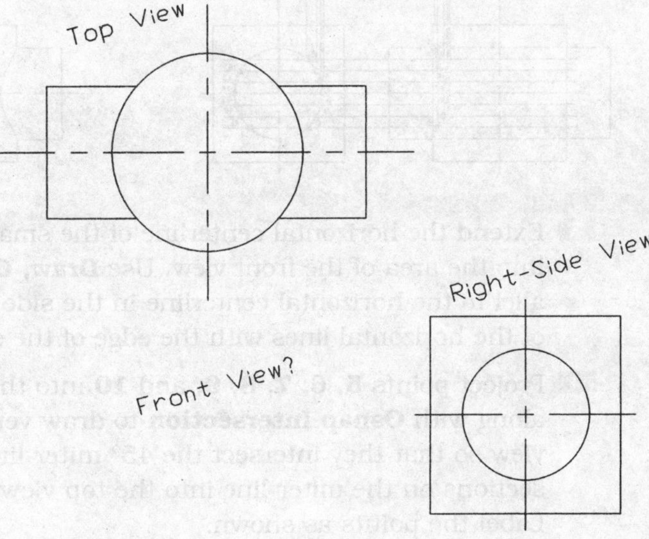

1. Draw the outline of the front view by projecting lines from the given top and front views. See Figure 5-79.

2. Define points on the edge of the smaller circle. In this example, 17 points were defined.

Figure 5-79

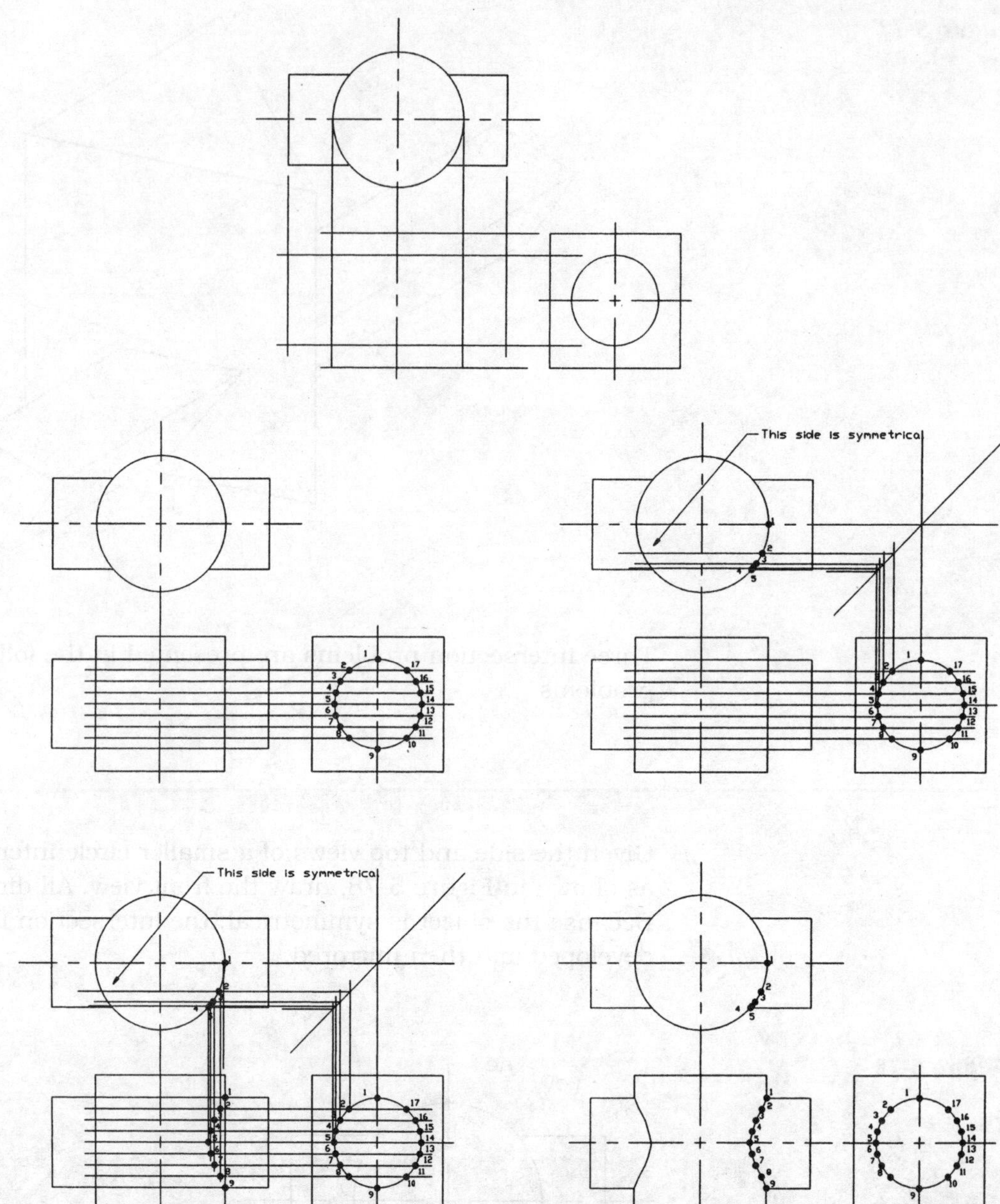

3 Extend the horizontal centerline of the smaller circle in the side view into the area of the front view. Use **Draw, Offset,** and add six lines parallel to the horizontal centerline in the side view. Label the intersection of the horizontal lines with the edge of the smaller circle as shown.

4 Project points **5, 6, 7, 8, 9,** and **10** into the top view. Use **Draw, Line** along with **Osnap Intersection** to draw vertical lines from the side view so that they intersect the 45° miter line. Then, project the intersections on the miter line into the top view by using horizontal lines. Label the points as shown.

5 Project points **5, 6, 7, 8, 9,** and **10** from the top view into the area of the front view so that they intersect the horizontal lines from the side view. Label the points as shown. Use **Draw, Polyline, Edit Polyline,** and **Fit** to draw the curve that represents the intersection.

6 Add the lines needed to complete the front view, remove all excess lines, and save the drawing if desired.

5-33 Sample Problem SP5-11

Figure 5-80 shows the top and right-side views of a triangular-shaped piece intersecting a hexagonal-shaped piece. What is the shape of the front view?

Figure 5-80

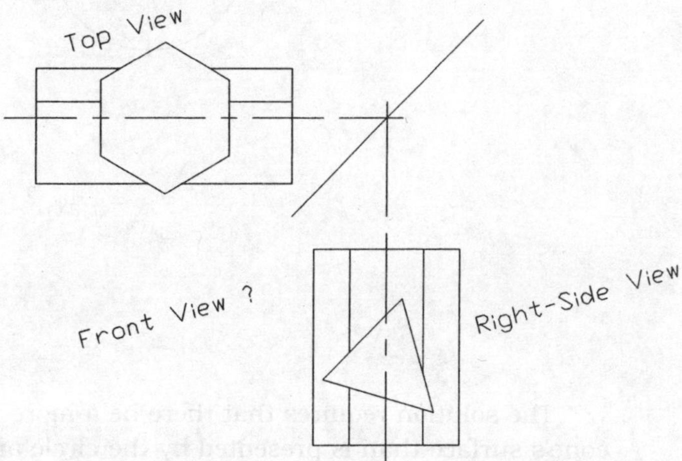

Figure 5-81 shows the solution obtained by projecting lines from the two given views into the front view and shows an enlargement of the intersecting surfaces. Using a straightedge, verify the location of each labeled point by projecting horizontal lines from the front view and vertical lines from the top view into the front view.

Figure 5-81

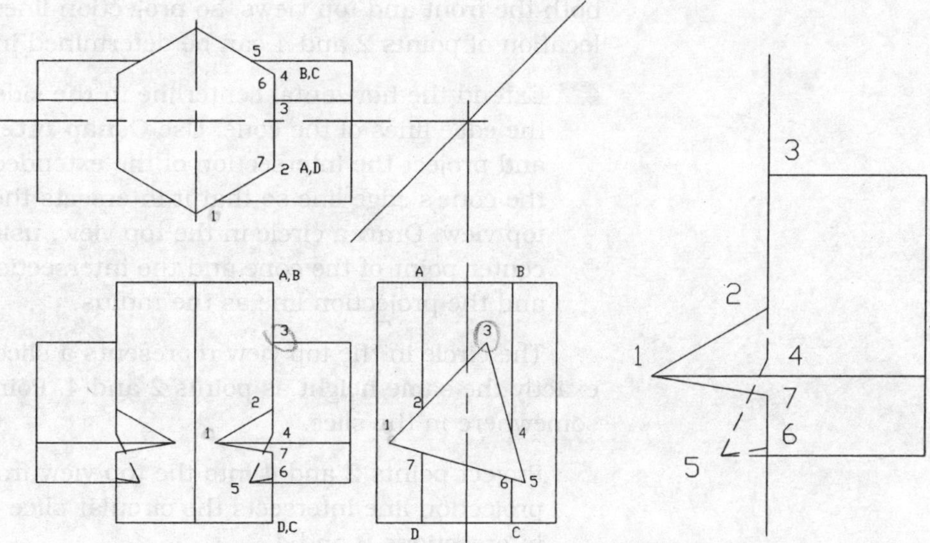

5-34 Sample Problem SP5-12

Given the side and top views of a circle intersecting a cone, as shown in Figure 5-82, draw the front view.

As in the previous sample problems, the problem is solved by defining intersection points in the given two views and then projecting them into the front view. The cone, however, presents a unique problem because it is both round and tapered. There are few edge lines to work with.

Figure 5-82

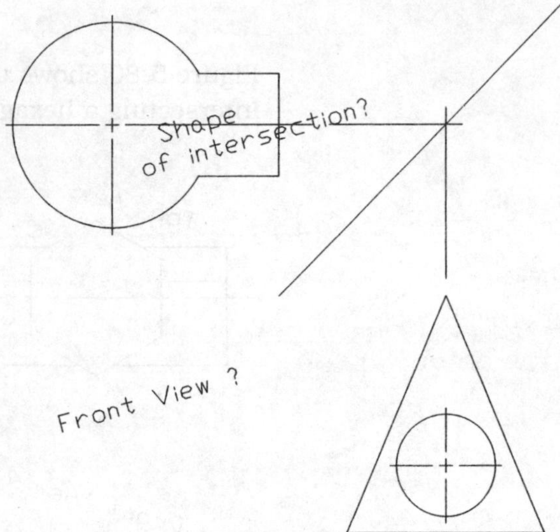

The solution requires that there be a more precise definition of the cone's surface than is presented by the circle and centerlines in the top view and the profile front view.

1 Figure 5-83, step 1, shows how points **1** and **3,** located on the vertical centerline of the cylinder, are projected from the side view to the front view and then to the top view. The vertical centerline is aligned with the right-side profile line of the cone so that it can be used for projection.

This is not true for points 2 and 4, located on the horizontal centerline in the side view. Currently, the location of points 2 and 4 is unknown in both the front and top views, so projection lines cannot be drawn. The location of points 2 and 4 can be determined in the front and top views.

2 Extend the horizontal centerline in the side view so that it intersects the edge lines of the cone. Use **Osnap Intersection,** with **Ortho** on, and project the intersection of the extended horizontal centerline and the cone's edge line so that it intersects the vertical centerline in the top view. Draw a circle in the top view, using the distance between the center point of the cone and the intersection of the vertical centerline and the projection line as the radius.

The circle in the top view represents a slice of the cone located at exactly the same height as points 2 and 4. Points 2 and 4 must be located somewhere in the slice.

3 Project points **2** and **4** into the top view from the side view so that the projection line intersects the circular slice drawn in step 2. Label the intersections **2** and **4.**

4 Project the locations of points **2** and **4** in the top view into the front view, using a vertical line. Project the locations of the points from the side view into the front view, using a horizontal line. The intersection of the vertical and horizontal projection lines defines the locations of points 2 and 4 in the front view.

5 Expand the procedure explained in steps 2, 3 and 4 by drawing a series of horizontal projection lines between the front and side views, as shown. Use **Draw** for the first line and **Offset** for the other lines. The location of these additional lines is random.

Step 1

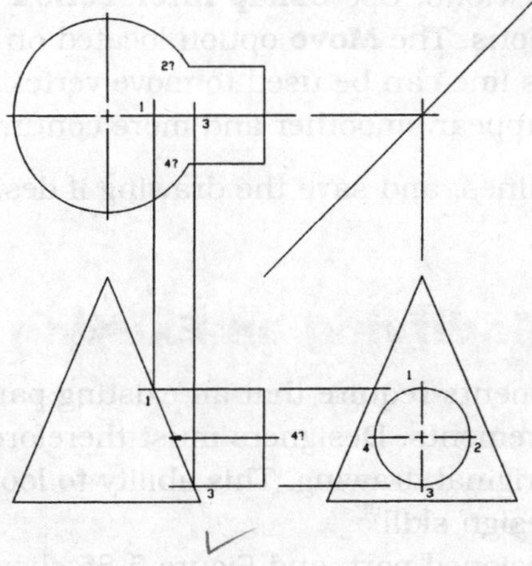

Step 2

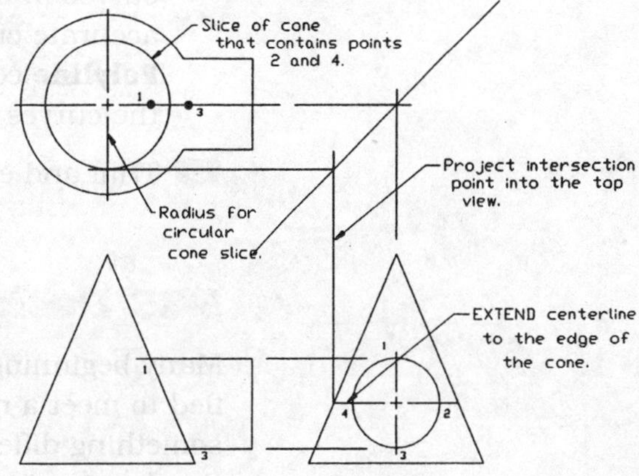

Step 3

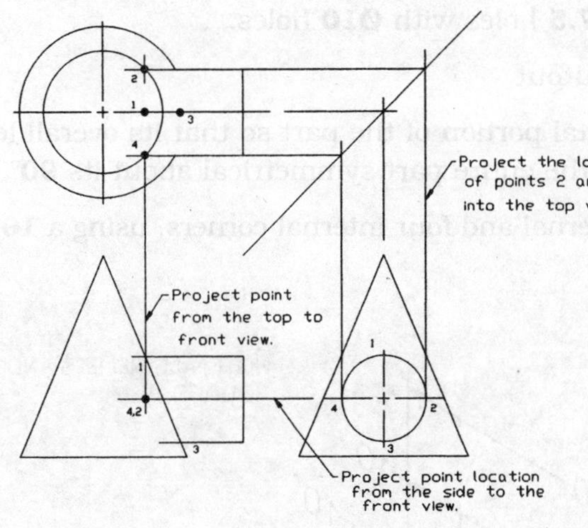

Step 4

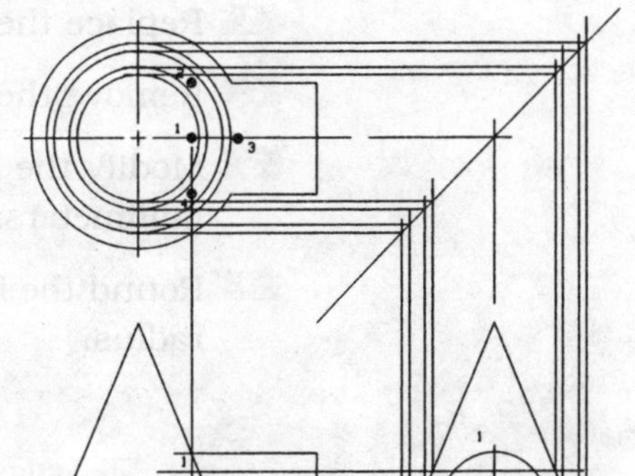

Step 5

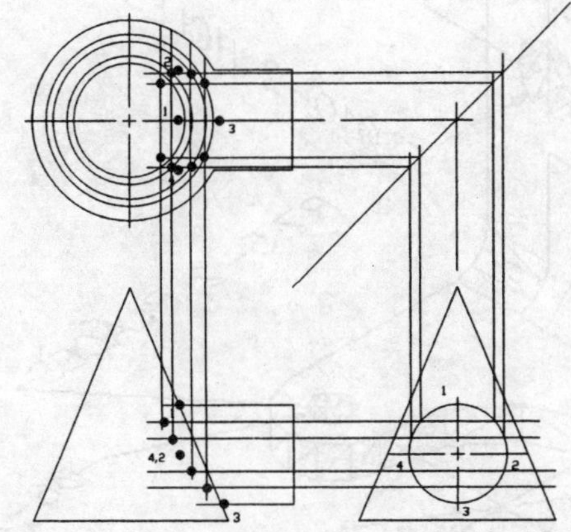

Step 6

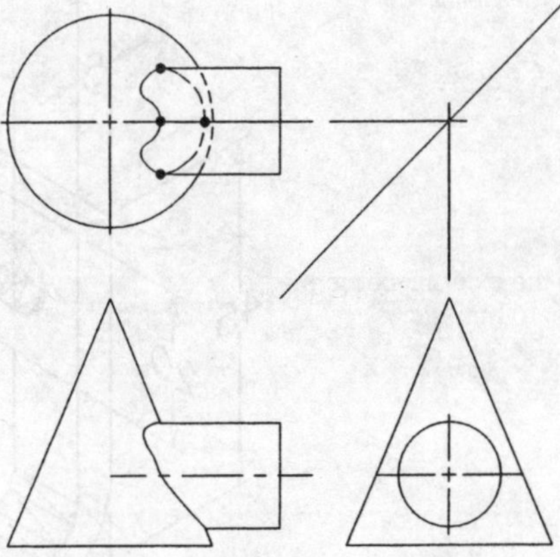

Figure 5-83

Use **Osnap Intersection,** with **Ortho** on, to project the intersections of the horizontal lines with the cone's edge lines in the top view.

6 Draw circles, using the distance between the cone's center point and the projection lines' intersections with the vertical centerline as radii. Use **Osnap Intersection** to locate the circles' center point and radii distances.

7. Use **Draw, Polyline, Edit Polyline,** and **Fit** to draw the required curves in the top and front views. Use **Osnap Intersection** to ensure accurate curve point locations. The **Move** option located on the **Edit Polyline** command options line can be used to move vertex points on the curves to make them appear smoother and more continuous.

8. Trim and erase all excess lines, and save the drawing if desired.

5-35 Designing by Modifying an Existing Part

Many beginning design assignments require that an existing part be modified to meet a new set of requirements. Designers must therefore create something different from the original drawing. This ability to look beyond the drawing is an important design skill.

Figure 5-84 shows a dimensioned part, and Figure 5-85 shows the three orthographic views of the part. The part is to be redesigned as follows:

1. Replace the two **Ø7.5** holes with **Ø10** holes.
2. Remove the **R20** cutout.
3. Modify the horizontal portion of the part so that its overall length is **45** millimeters; make the entire part symmetrical about its **90°** axis.
4. Round the four external and four internal corners, using a **10**-millimeter radius.

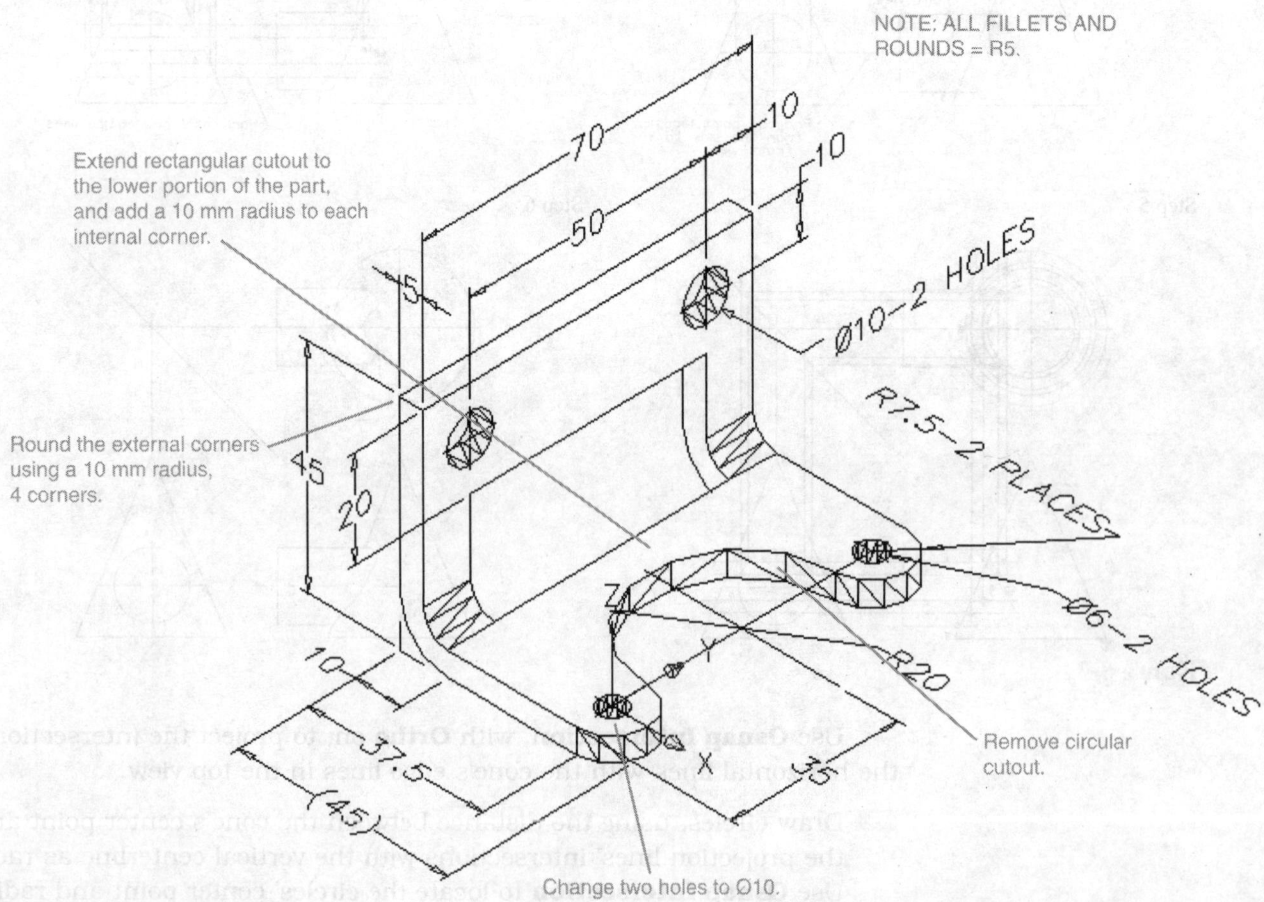

Figure 5-84

Figure 5-85

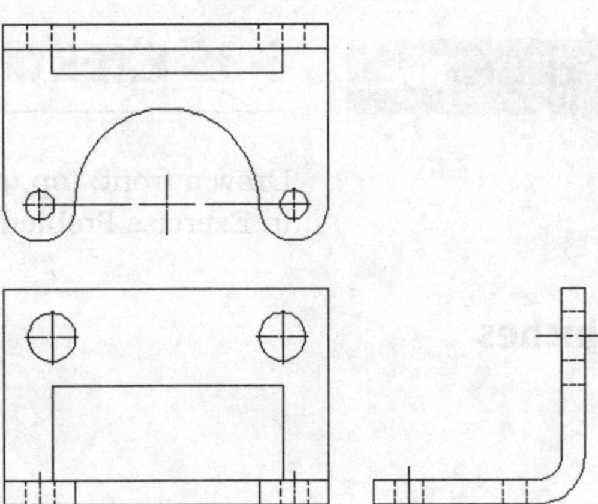

Figure 5-86 shows the resulting three orthographic views.

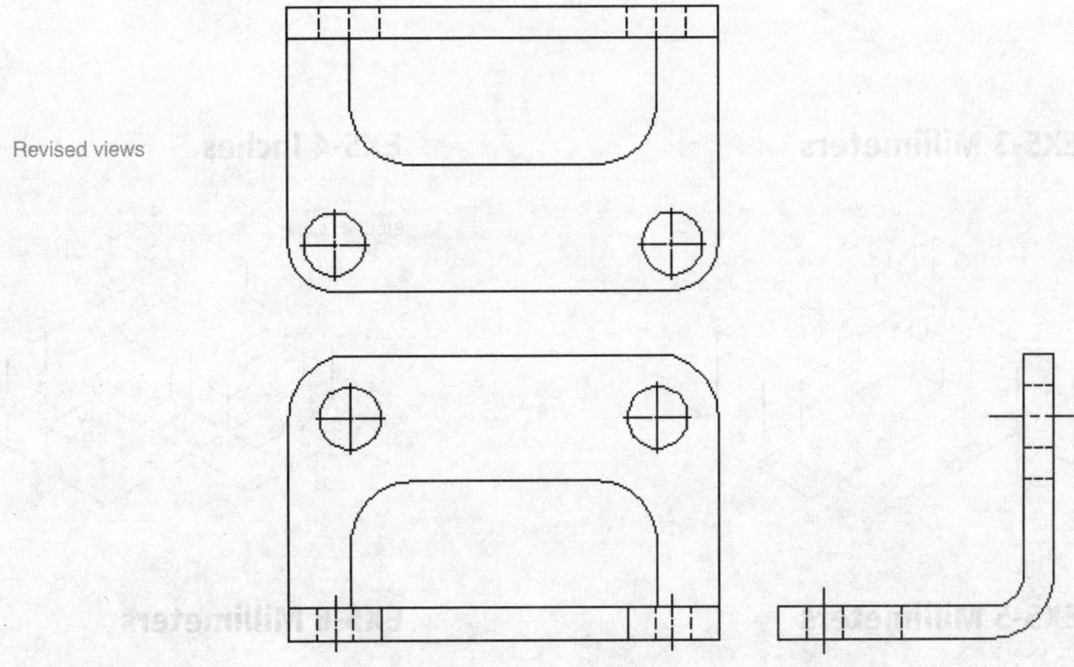

Figure 5-86

5-36 EXERCISE PROBLEMS

Draw a front, top, and right-side orthographic view of each of the objects in Exercise Problems EX5-1 through EX5-94. Do not include dimensions.

EX5-1 Inches

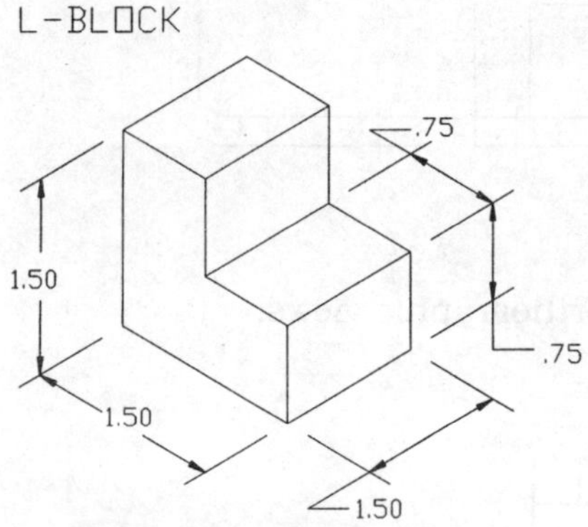

EX5-2 Millimeters

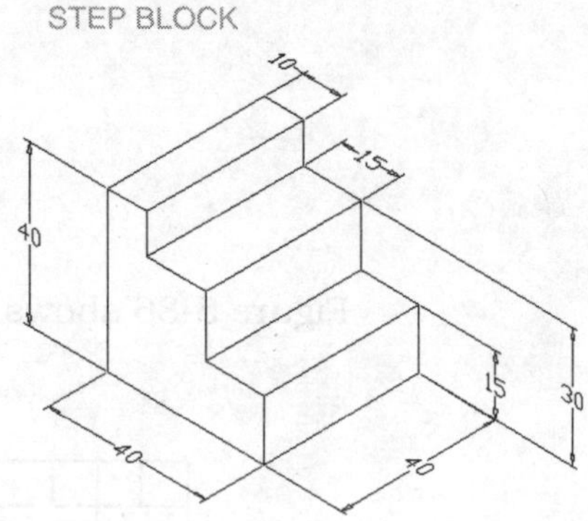

EX5-3 Millimeters

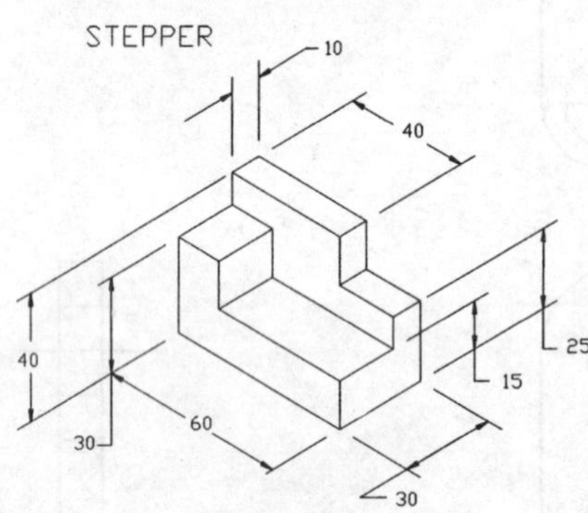

EX5-4 Inches

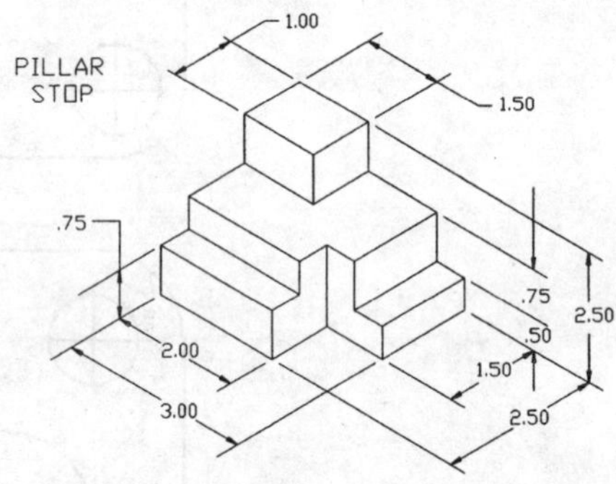

EX5-5 Millimeters

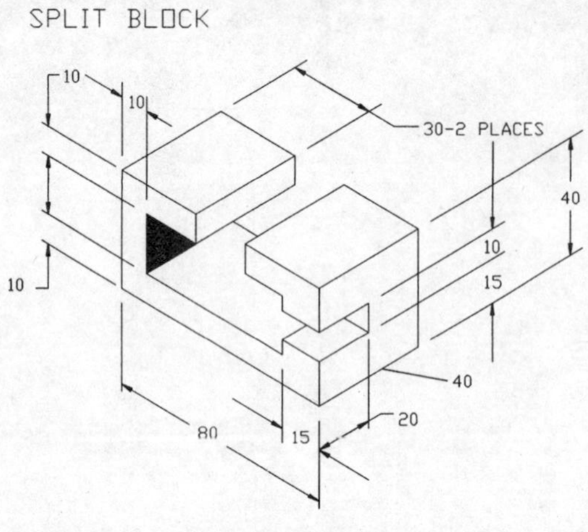

EX5-6 Millimeters

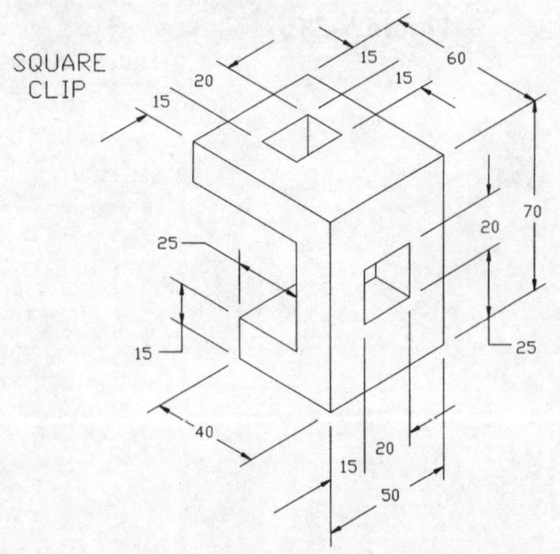

EX5-7 Millimeters

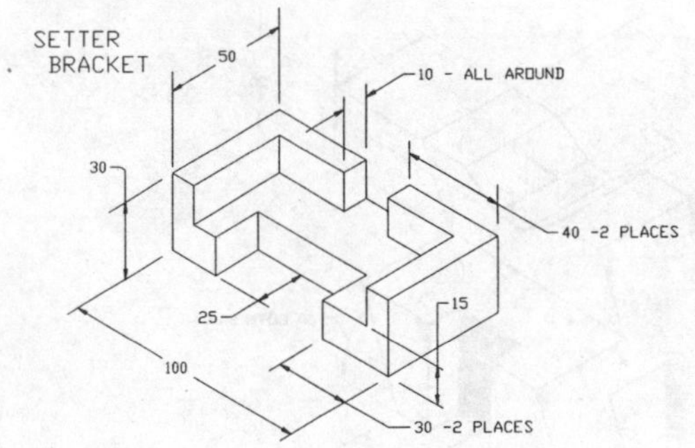

EX5-8 Millimeters

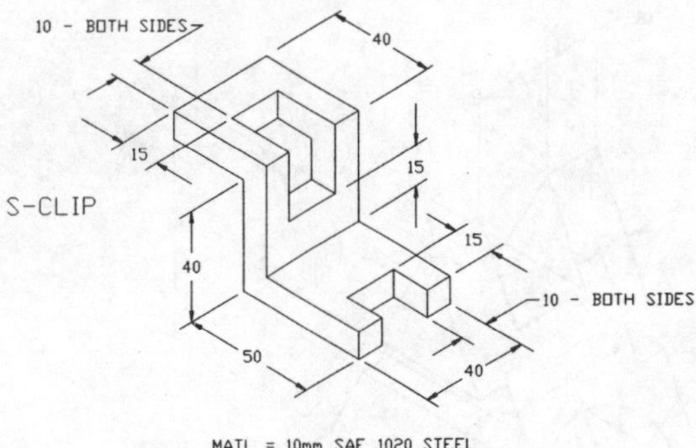

EX5-9 Inches

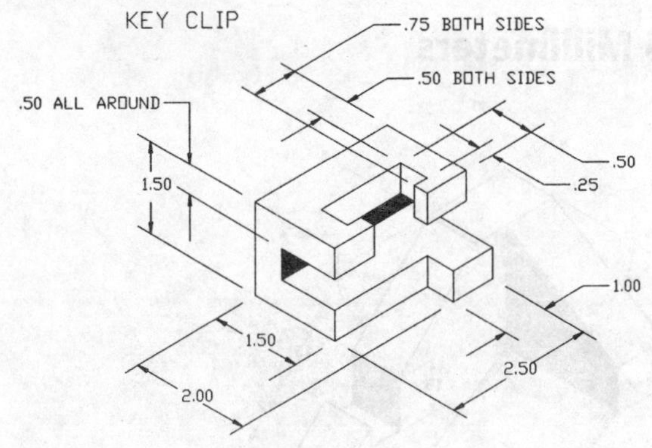

EX5-10 Millimeters

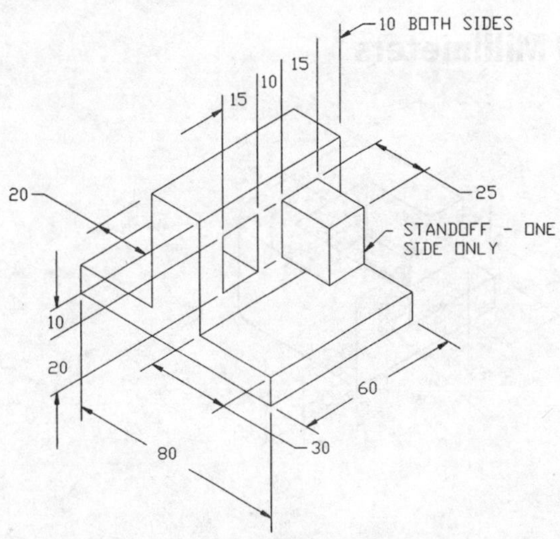

EX5-11 Millimeters

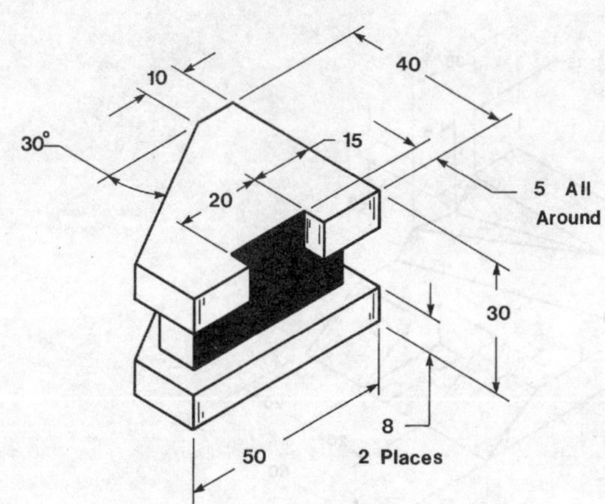

EX5-12 Inches

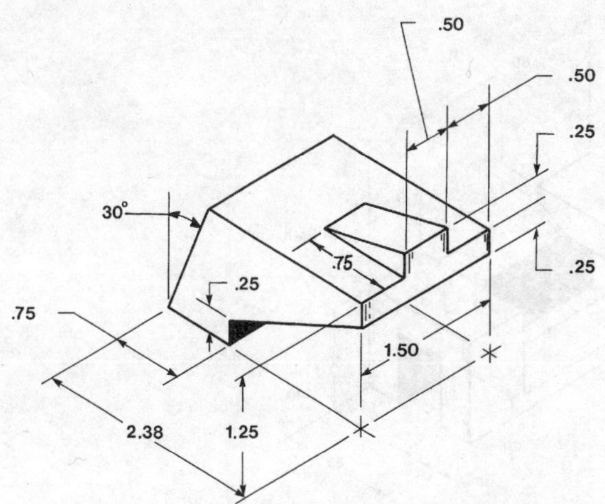

EX5-13 Millimeters

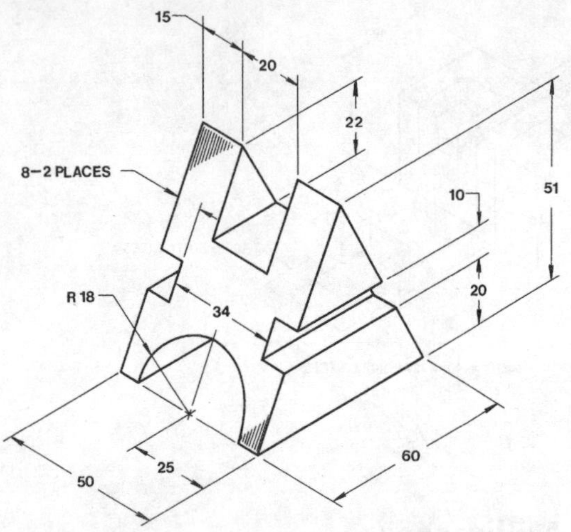

EX5-14 Millimeters

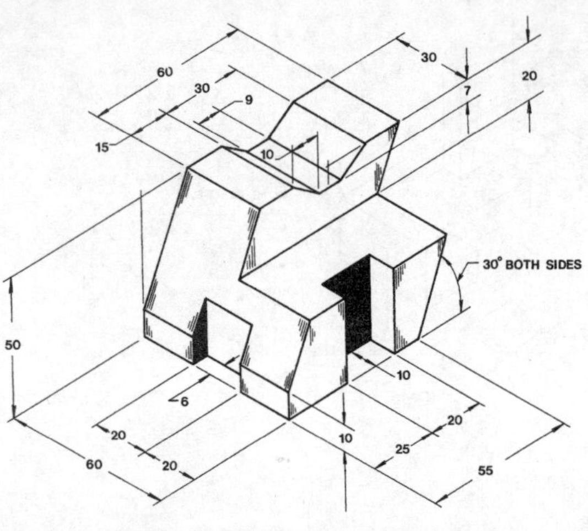

EX5-15 Millimeters

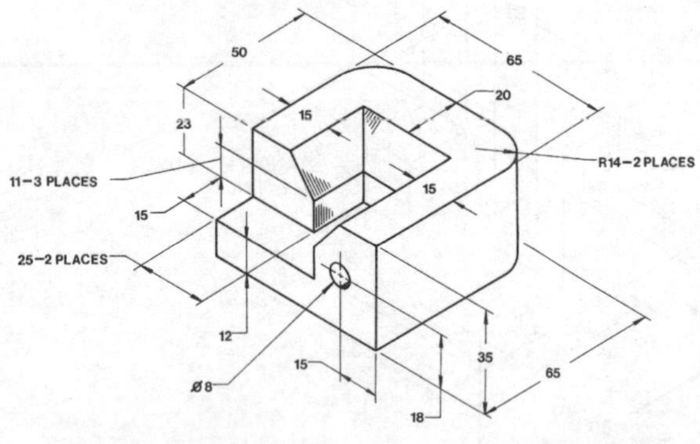

EX5-16 Millimeters

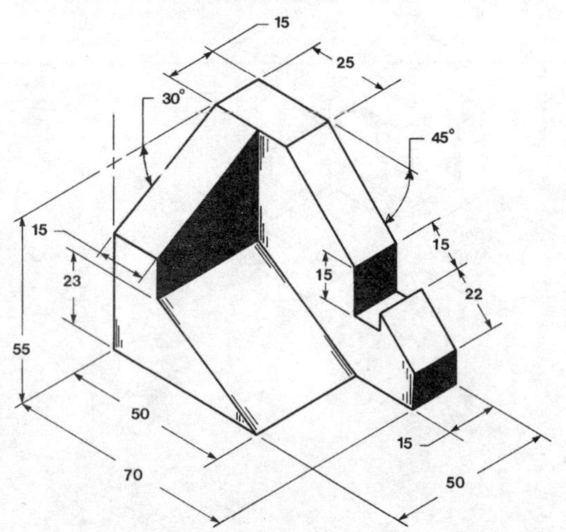

EX5-17 Millimeters

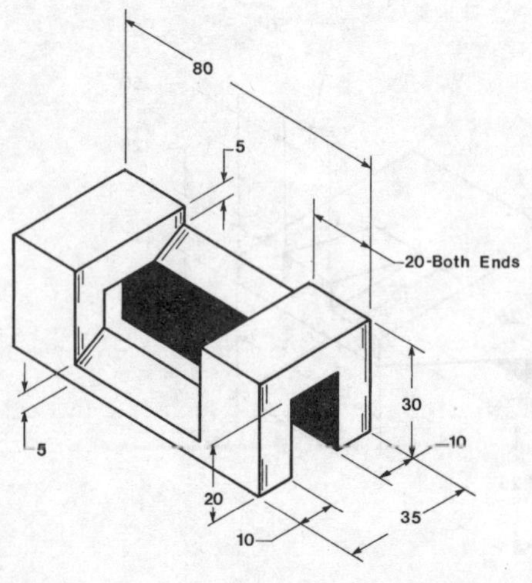

EX5-18 Millimeters

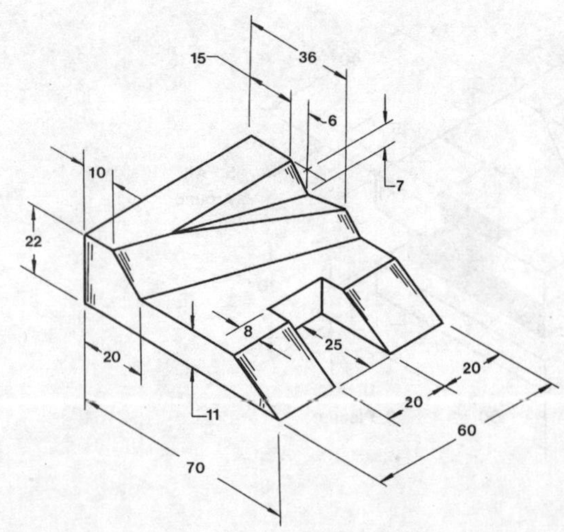

EX5-19 Millimeters

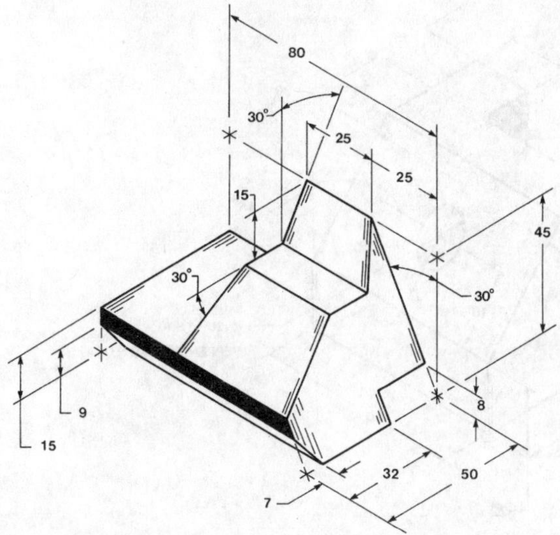

EX5-20 Millimeters

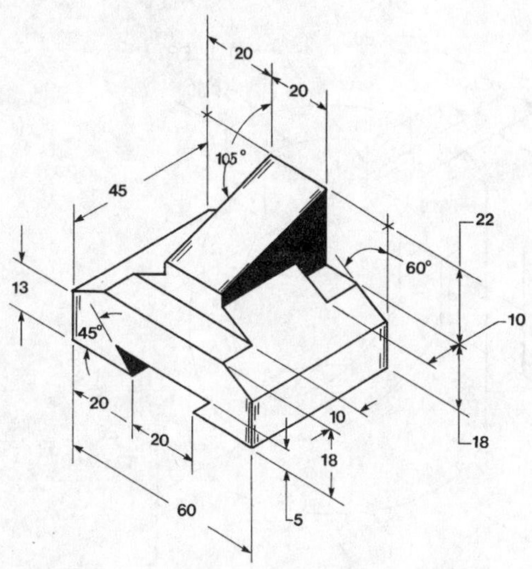

EX5-21 Inches

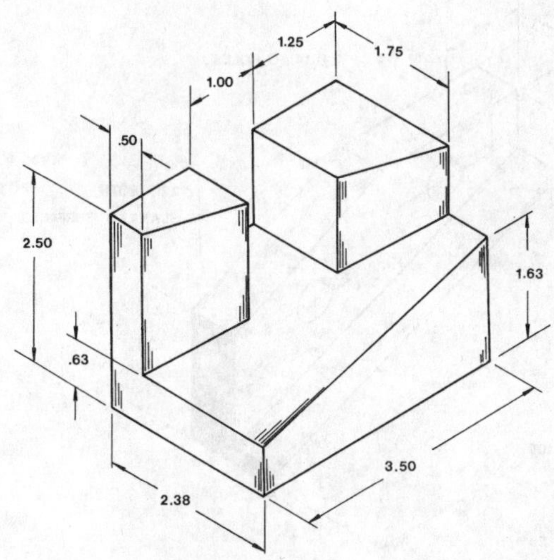

EX5-22 Millimeters

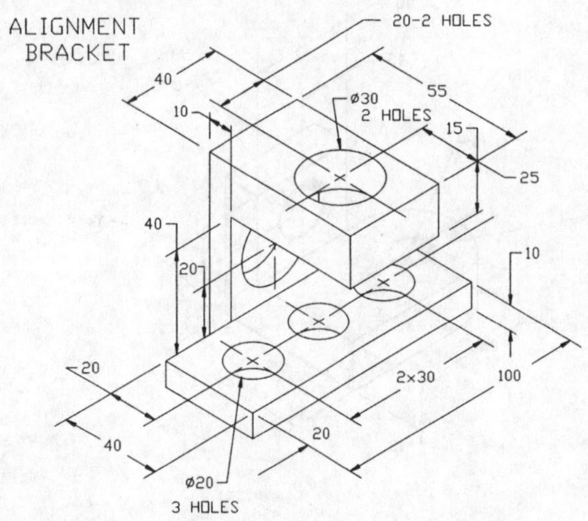

EX5-23 Millimeters

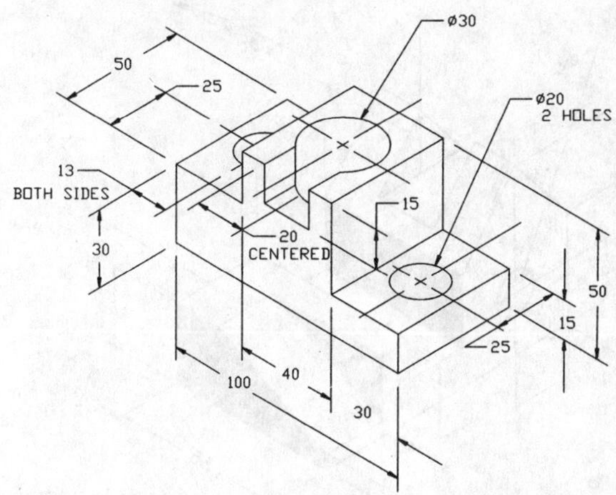

EX5-24 Inches

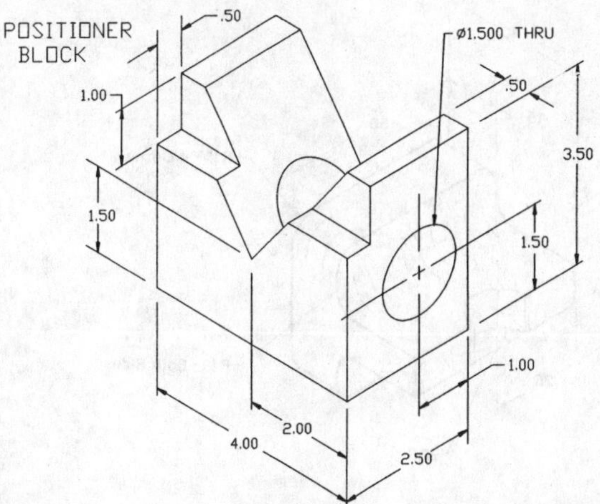

EX5-25 Millimeters

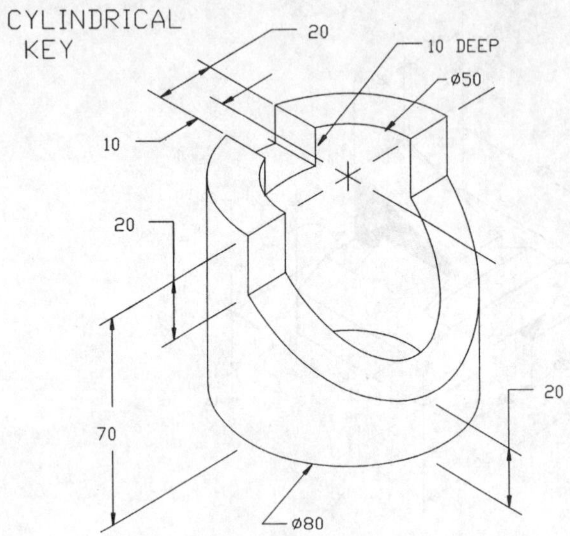

EX5-26 Millimeters

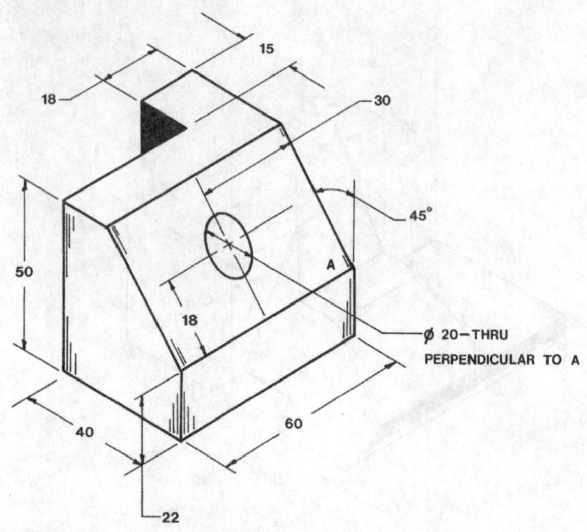

EX5-27 Millimeters

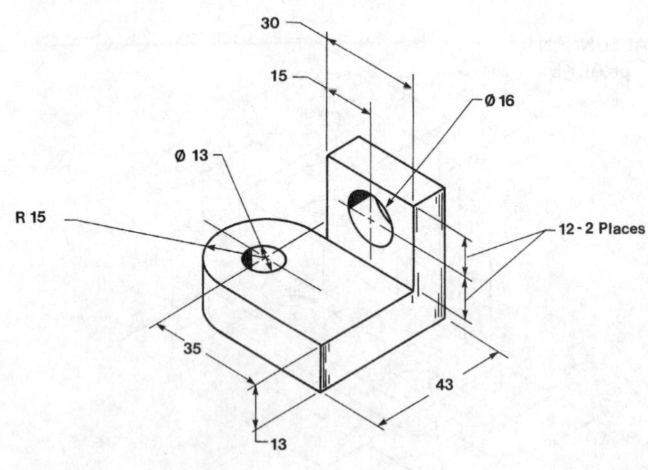

EX5-28 Millimeters

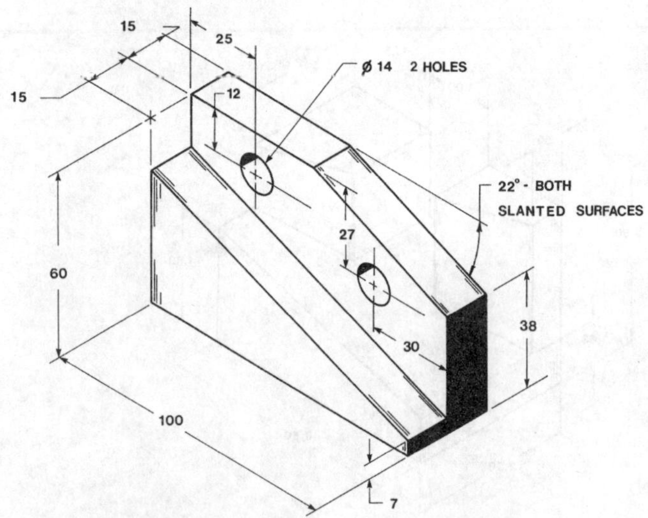

EX5-29 Millimeters

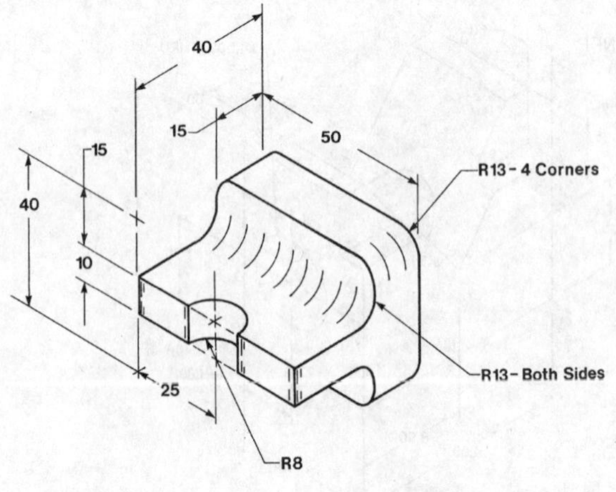

EX5-30 Millimeters

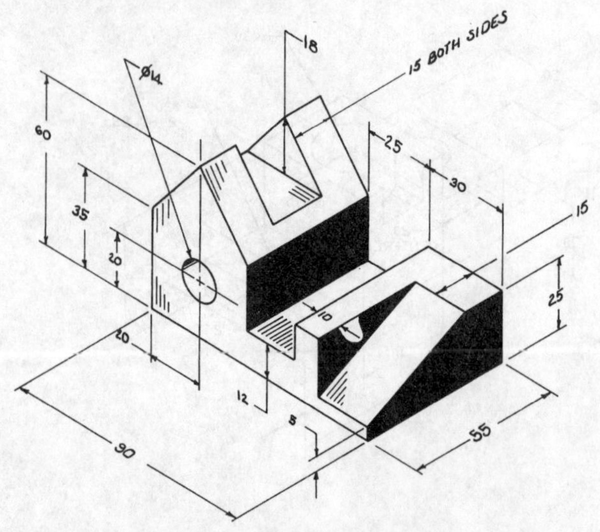

EX5-31 Inches

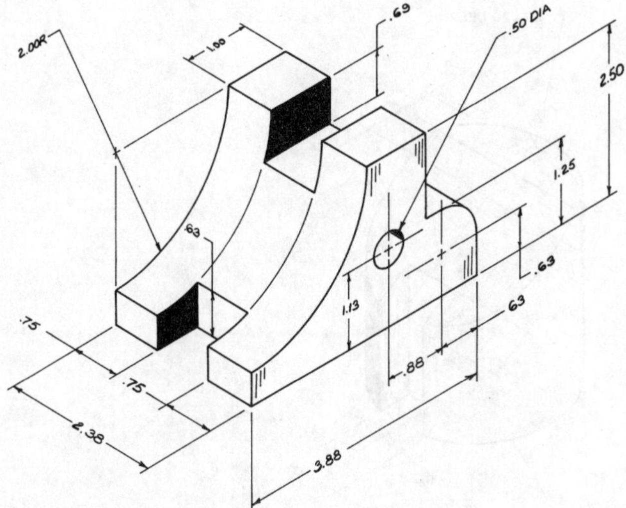

EX5-32 Millimeters

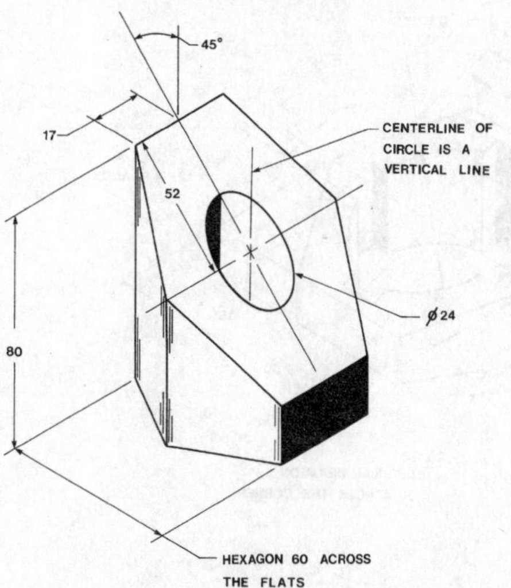

EX5-33 Inches

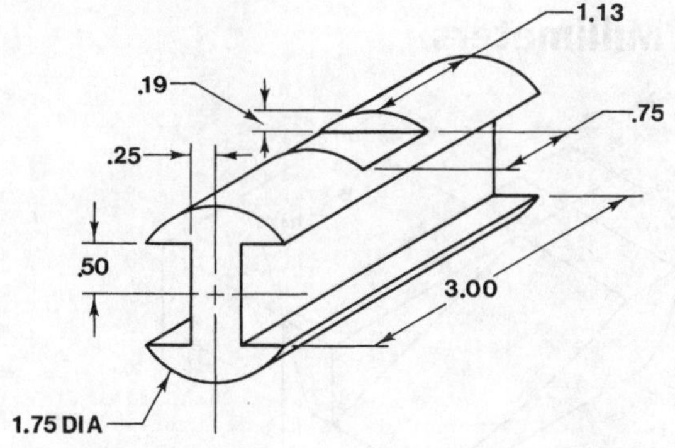

EX5-34 Millimeters

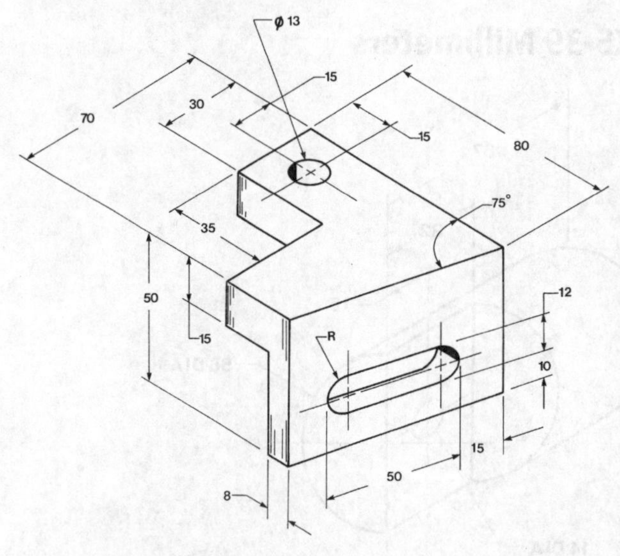

EX5-35 Millimeters

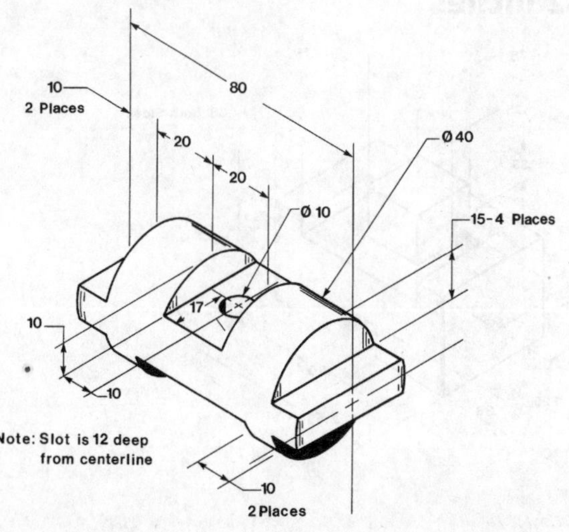

EX5-36 Inches

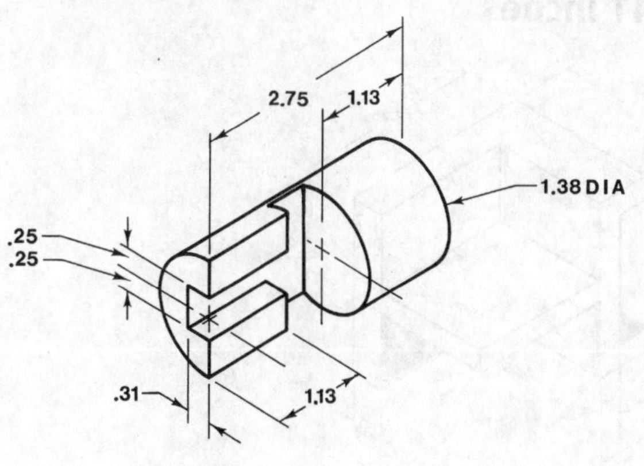

EX5-37 Millimeters

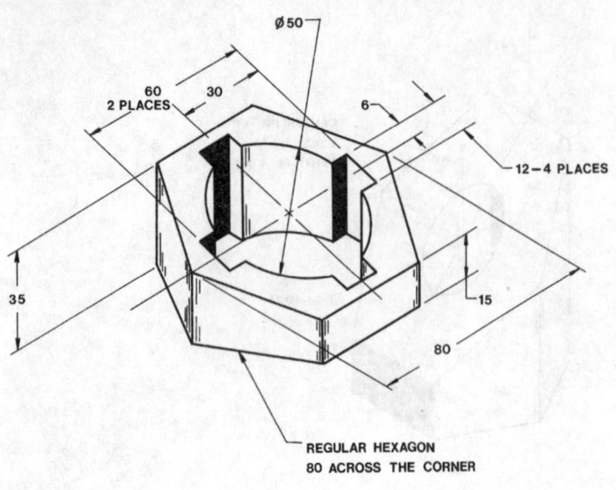

EX5-38 Millimeters

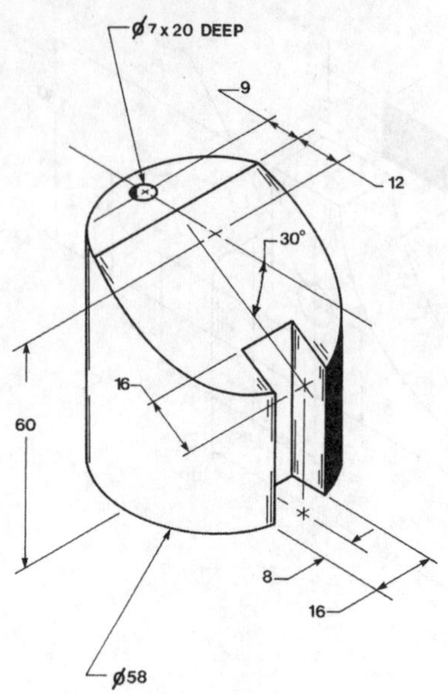

EX5-39 Millimeters

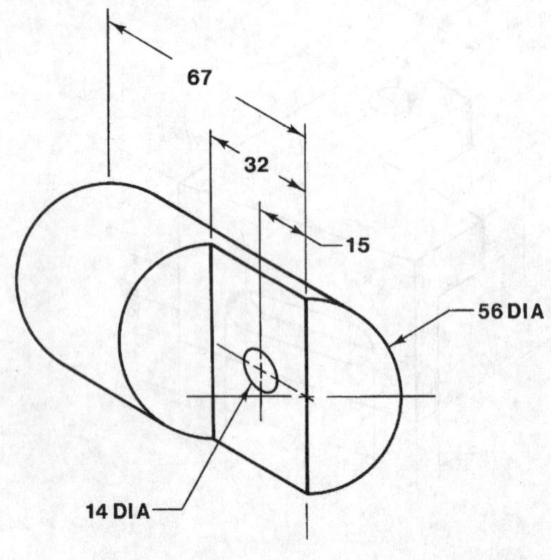

EX5-40 Millimeters

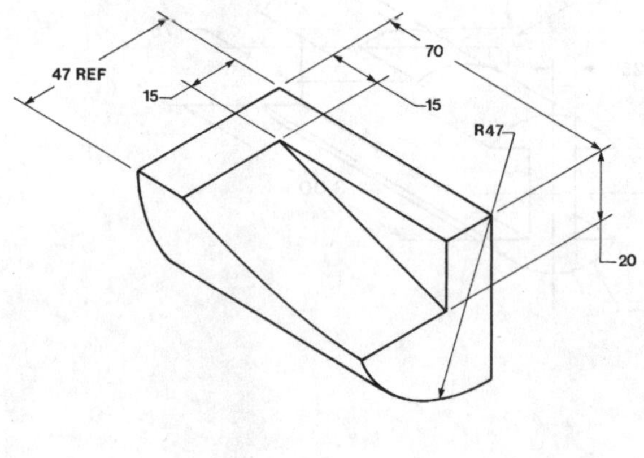

EX5-41 Inches

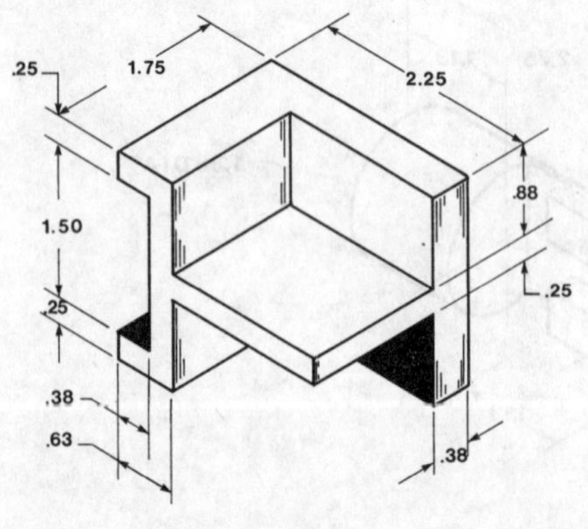

EX5-42 Inches

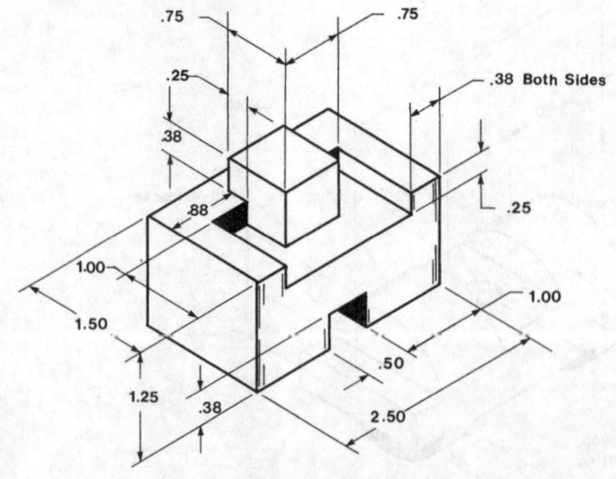

EX5-43 Millimeters

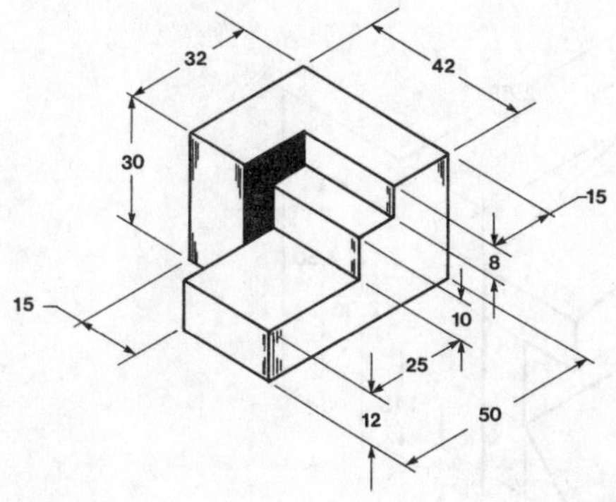

EX5-44 Millimeters

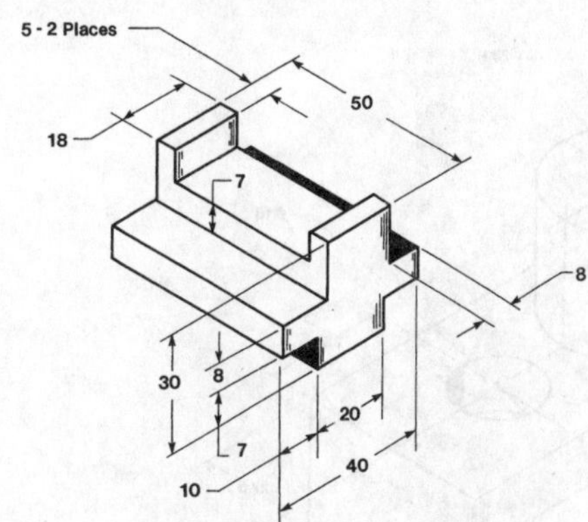

EX5-45 Millimeters

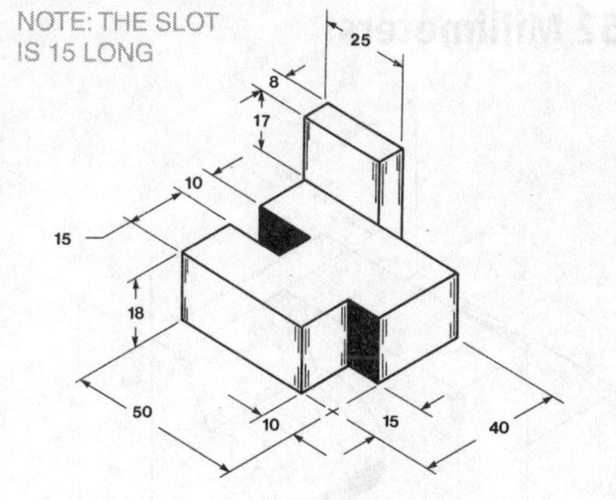

EX5-46 Millimeters

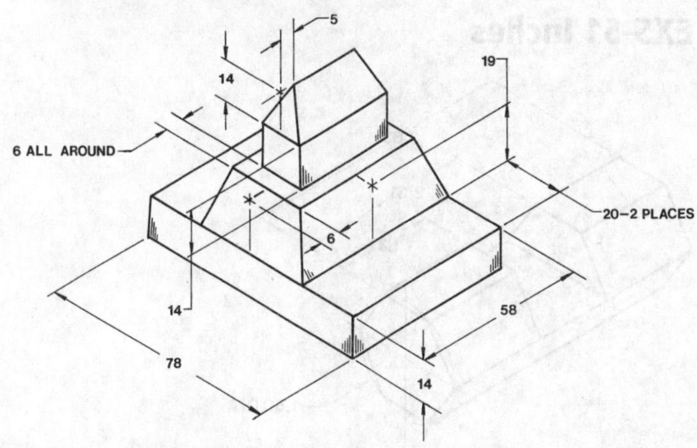

EX5-47 Inches

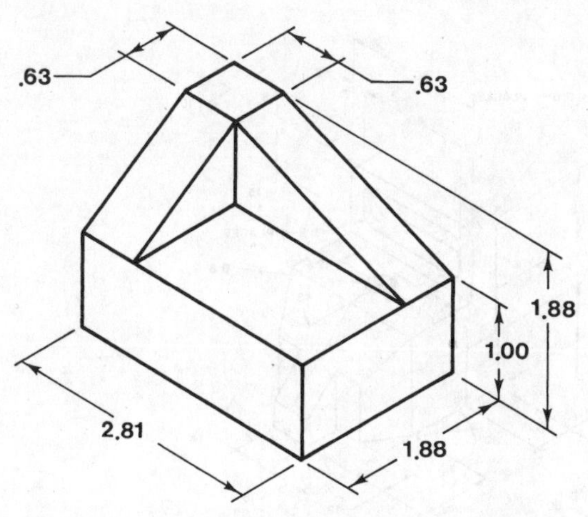

EX5-48 Inches

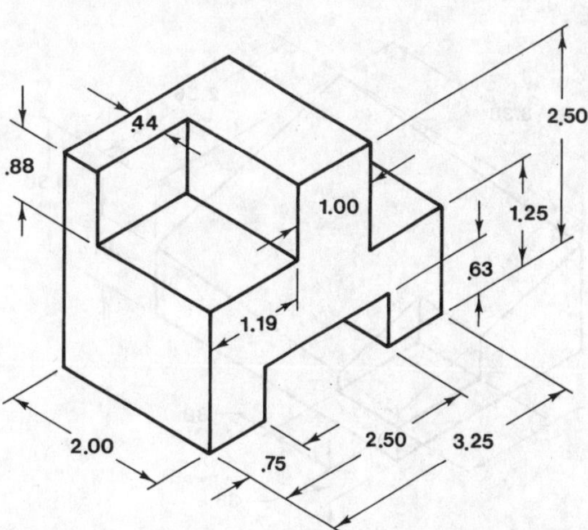

EX5-49 Millimeters

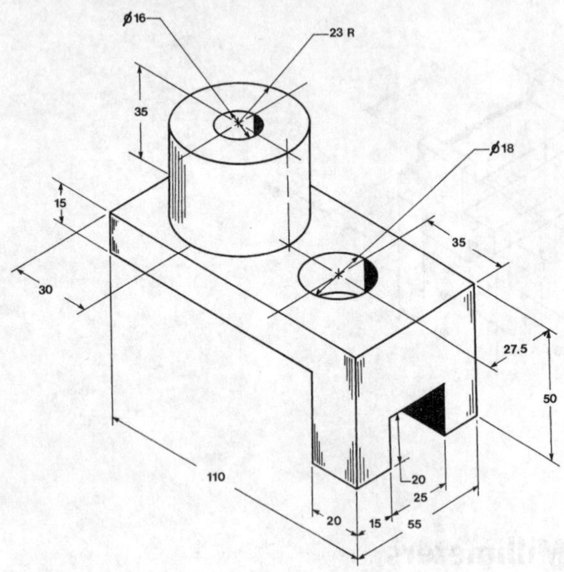

EX5-50 Inches

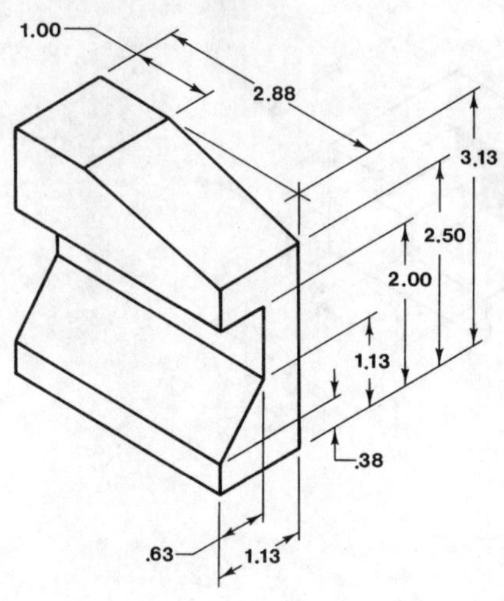

EX5-51 Inches

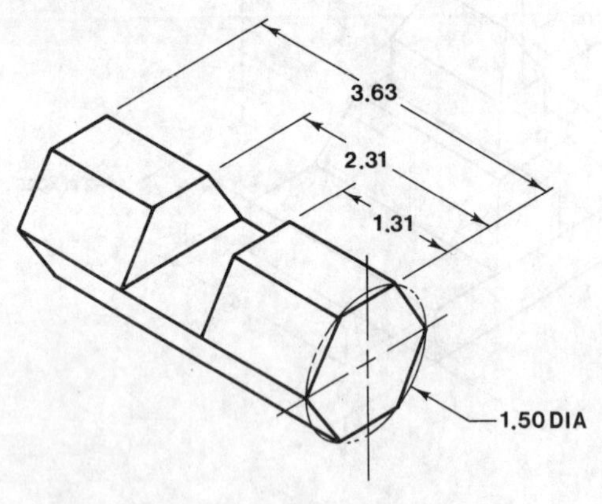

EX5-52 Millimeters

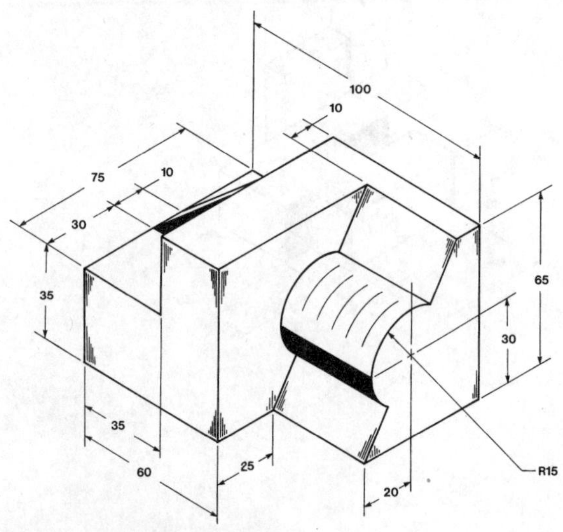

EX5-53 Inches

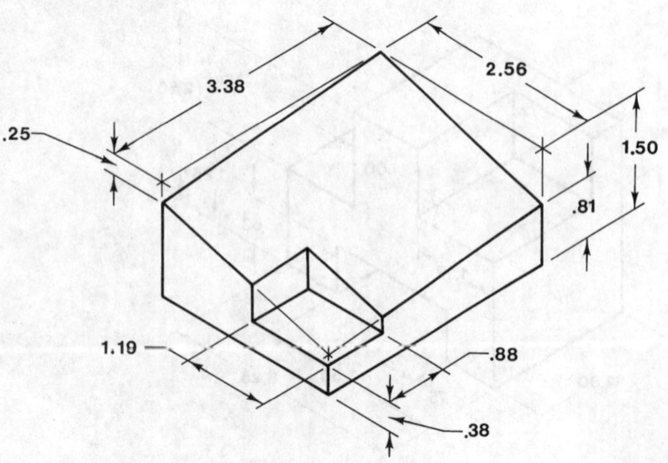

EX5-54 Millimeters

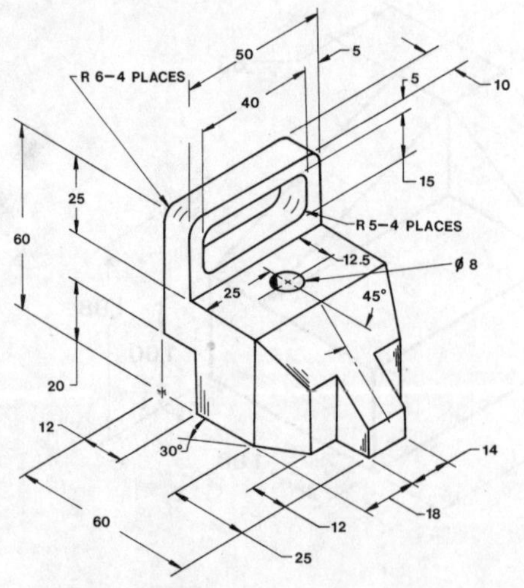

EX5-55 Millimeters

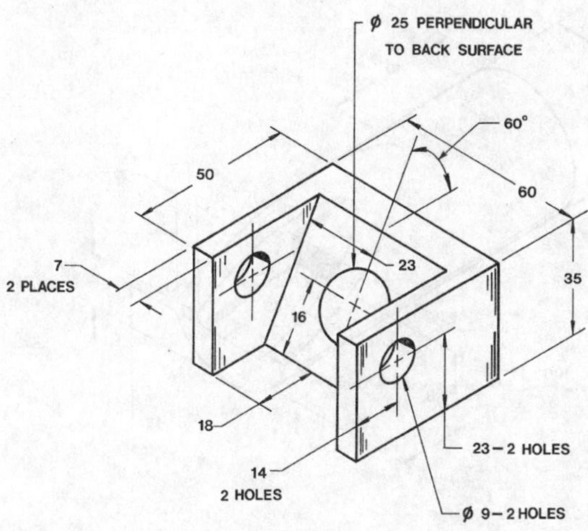

EX5-56 Millimeters

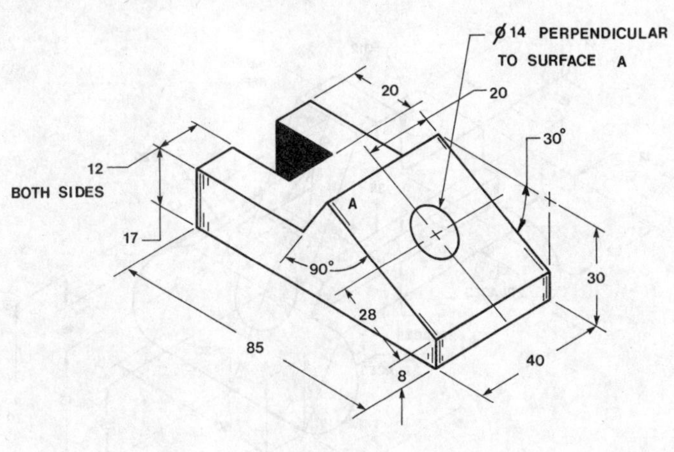

EX5-57 Millimeters

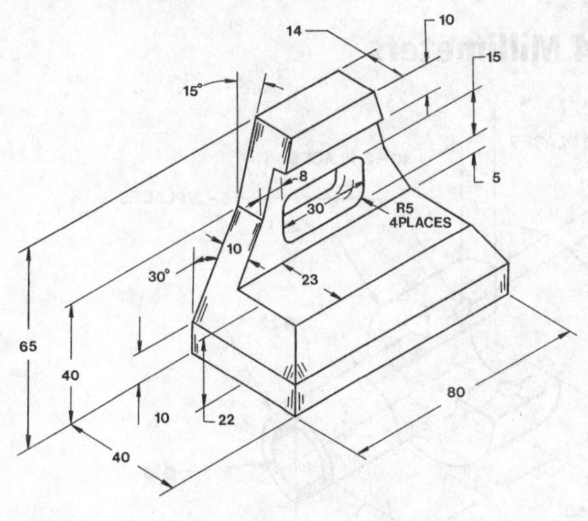

EX5-58 Millimeters

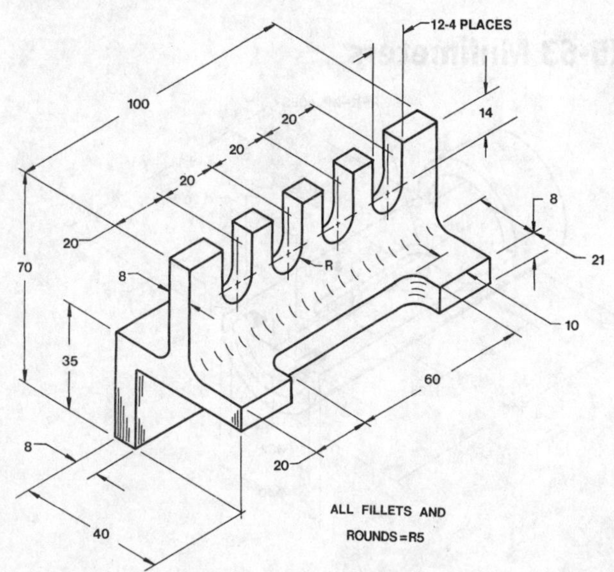

EX5-59 Millimeters

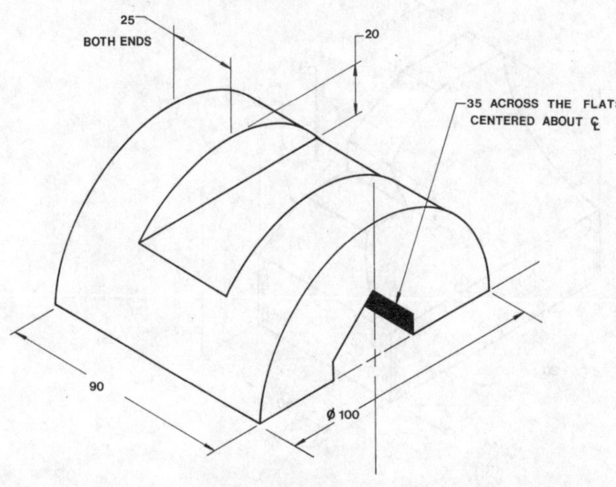

EX5-60 Inches

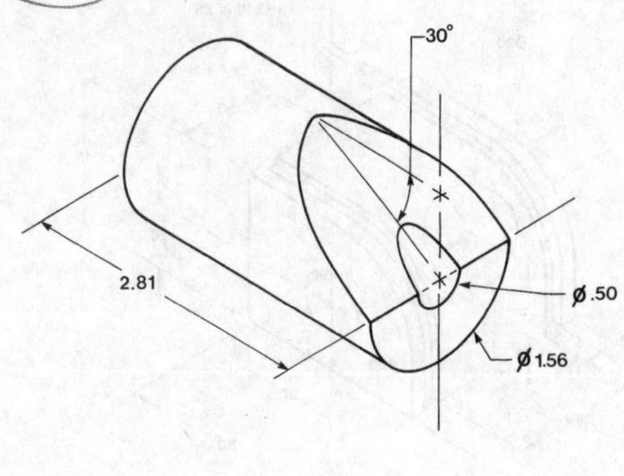

EX5-61 Millimeters

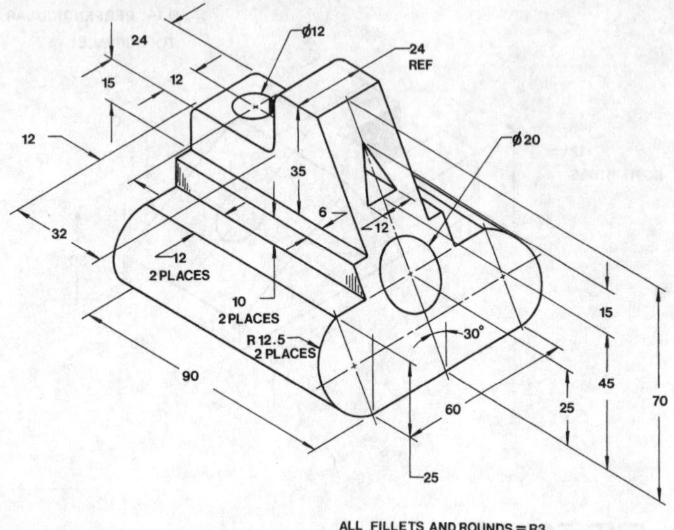

EX5-62 Millimeters

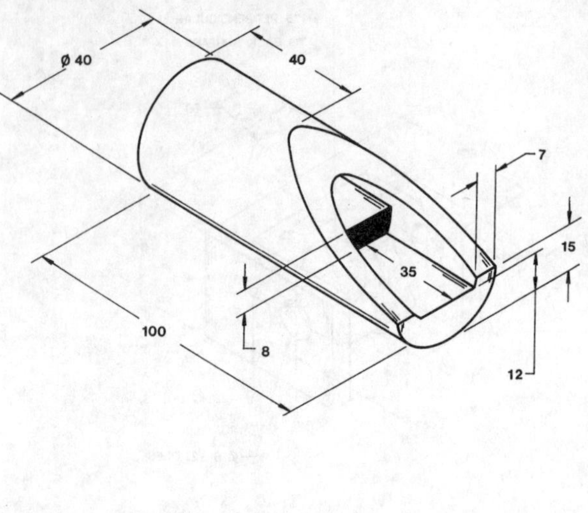

EX5-63 Millimeters

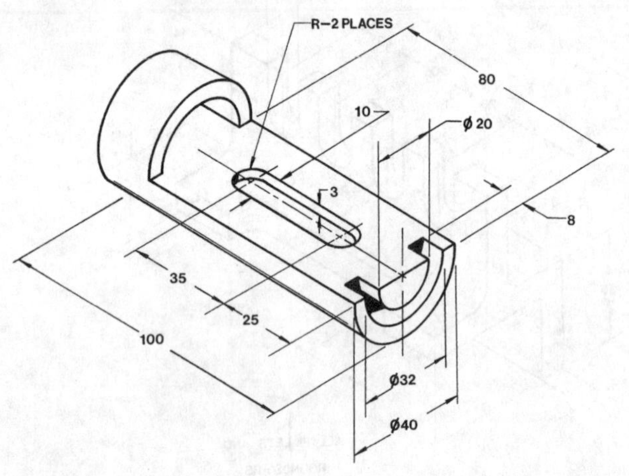

EX5-64 Millimeters

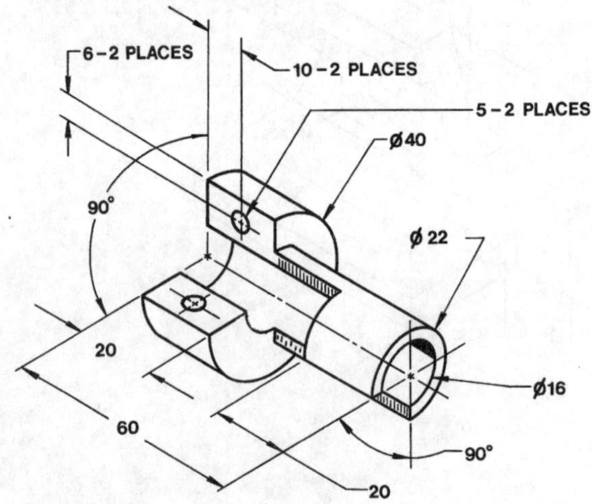

EX5-65 Millimeters

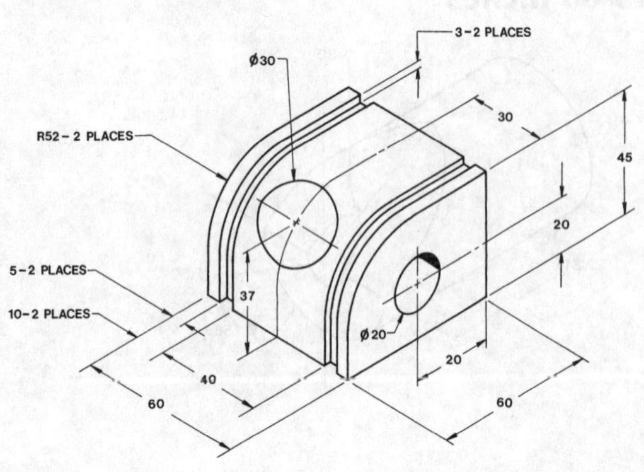

EX5-66 Millimeters

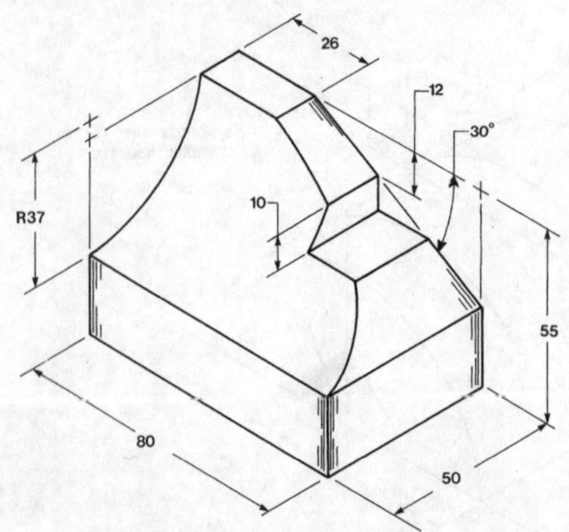

EX5-67 Millimeters

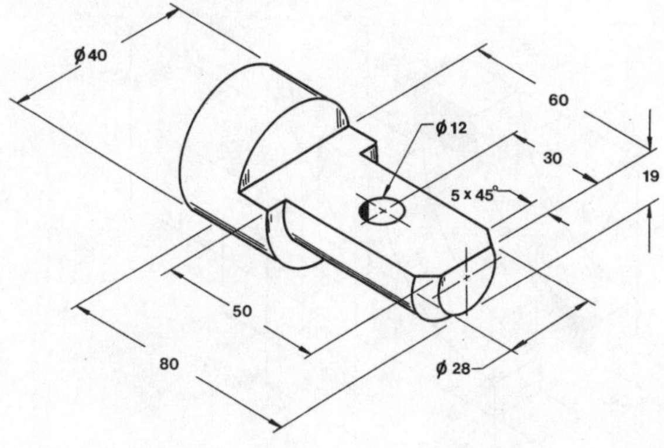

EX5-68 Millimeters

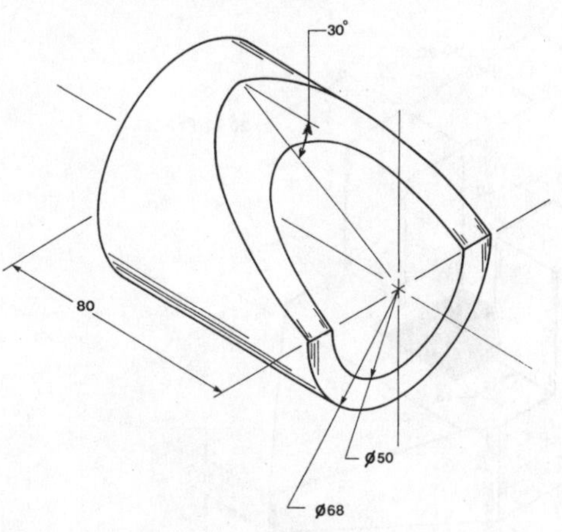

EX5-69 Millimeters

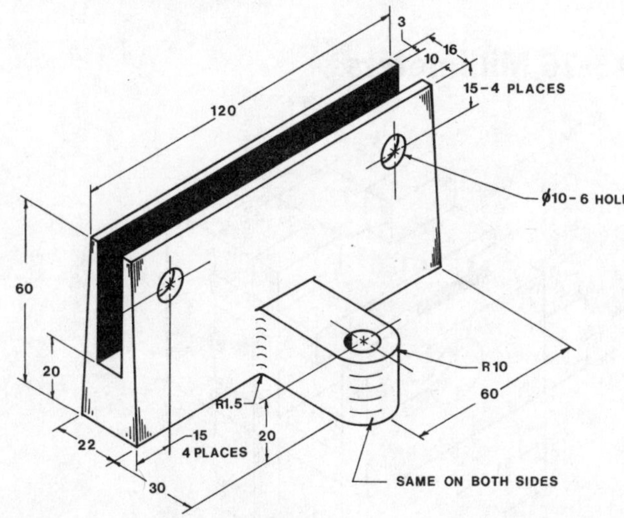

EX5-70 Millimeters

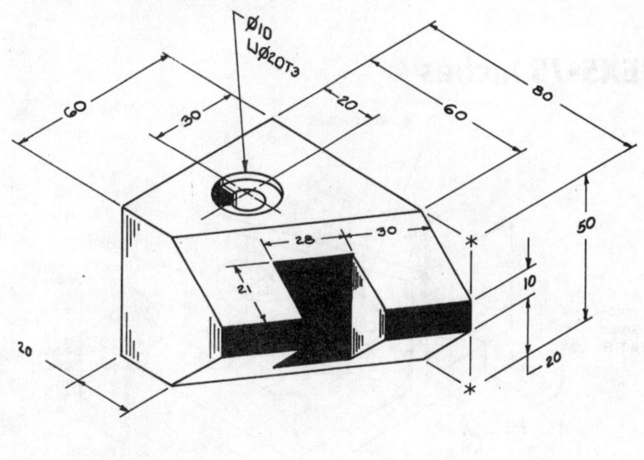

EX5-71 Millimeters

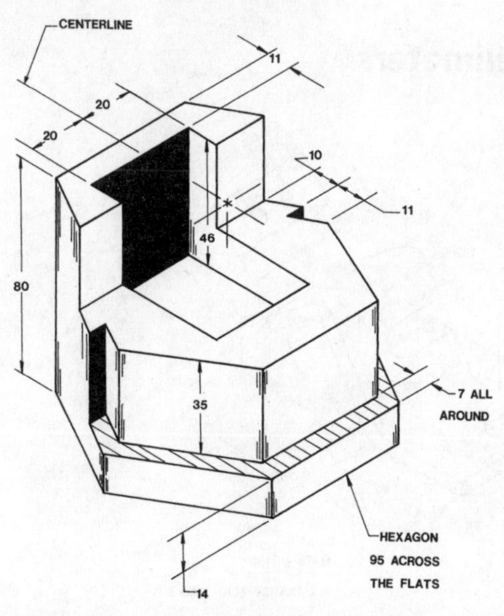

EX5-72 Millimeters

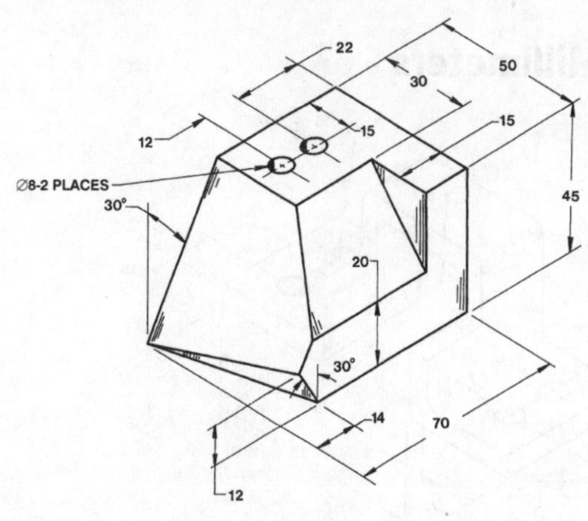

EX5-73 Millimeters

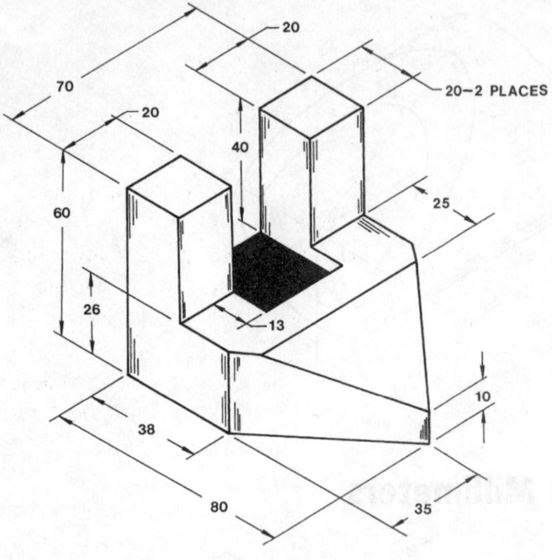

EX5-74 Inches

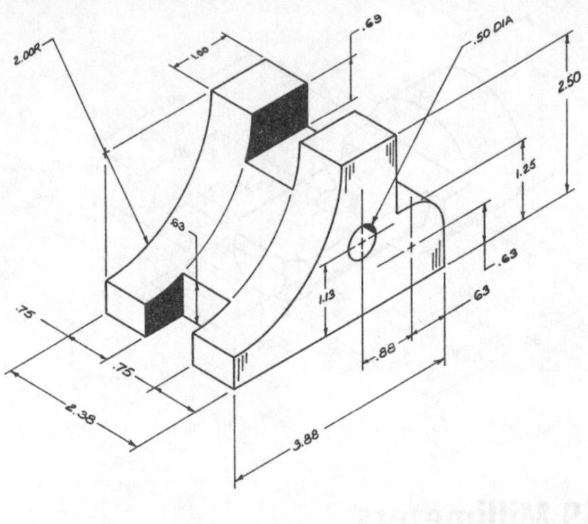

EX5-75 Inches

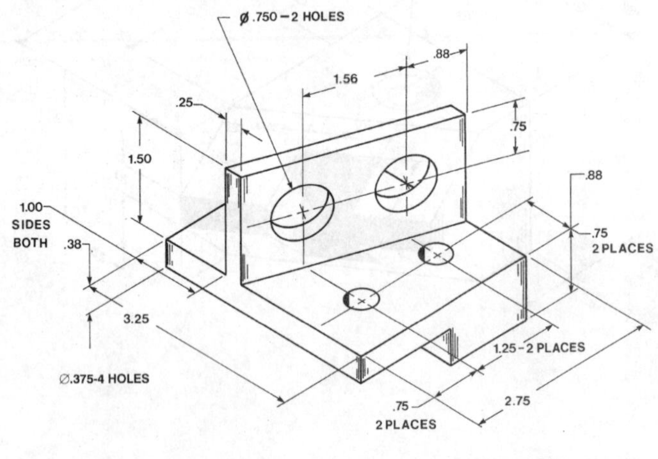

EX5-76 Millimeters

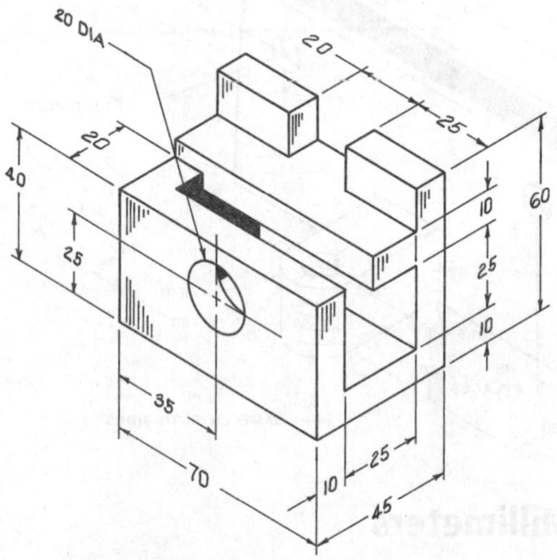

EX5-77 Millimeters

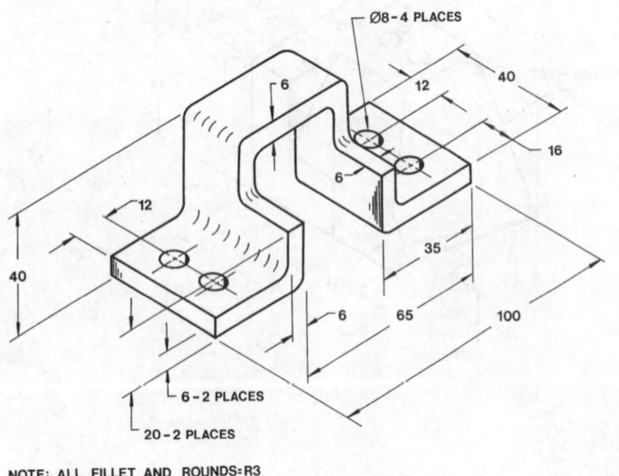

NOTE: ALL FILLET AND ROUNDS=R3

EX5-78 Millimeters

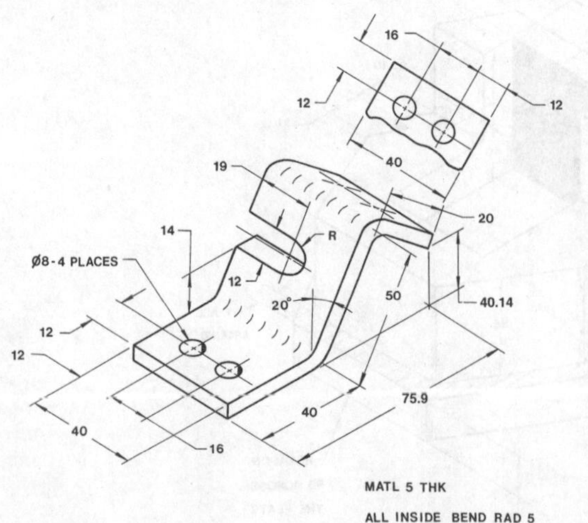

MATL 5 THK
ALL INSIDE BEND RAD 5

EX5-79 Millimeters

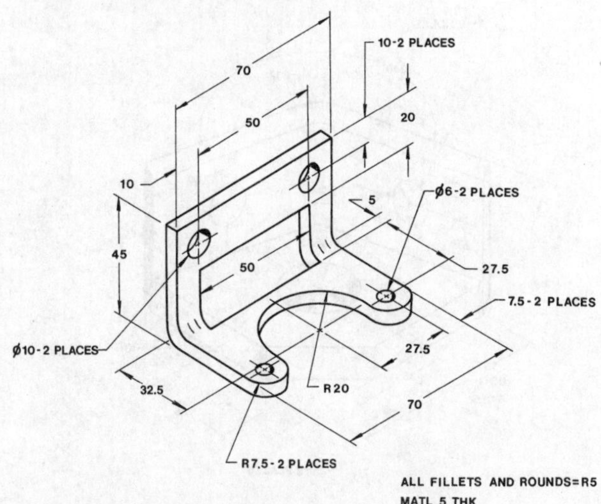

EX5-80 Millimeters

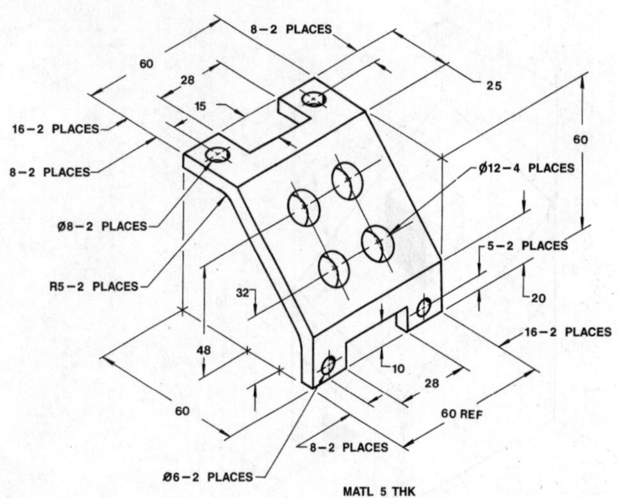

EX5-81 Millimeters

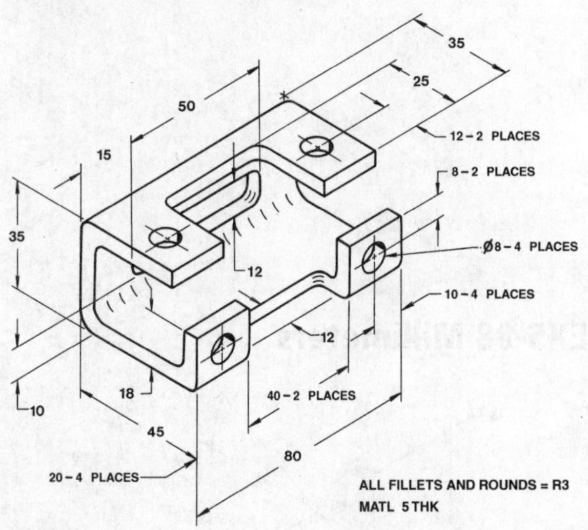

EX5-82 Millimeters

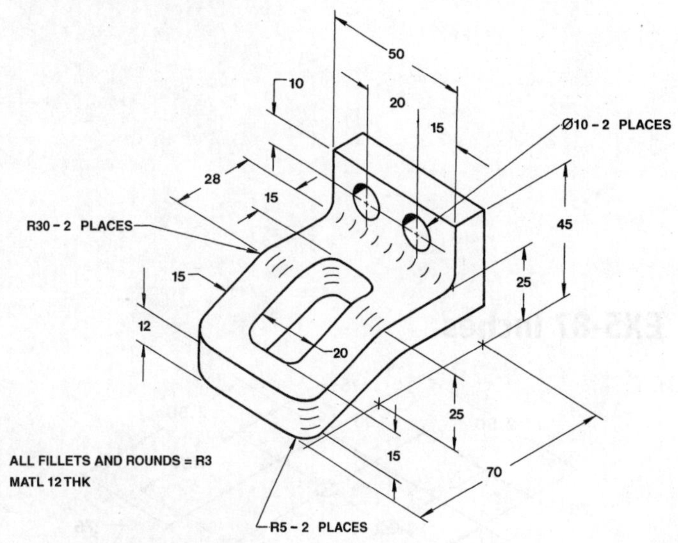

EX5-83 Millimeters

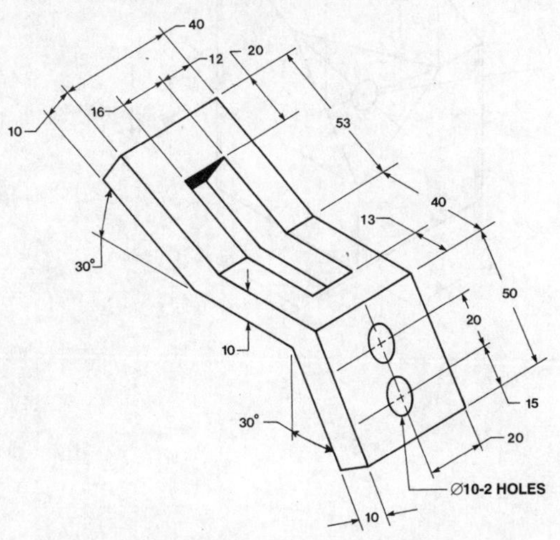

EX5-84 Inches

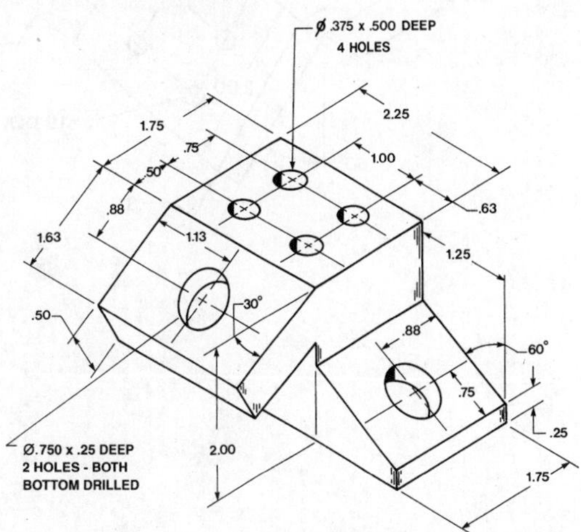

EX5-85 Millimeters

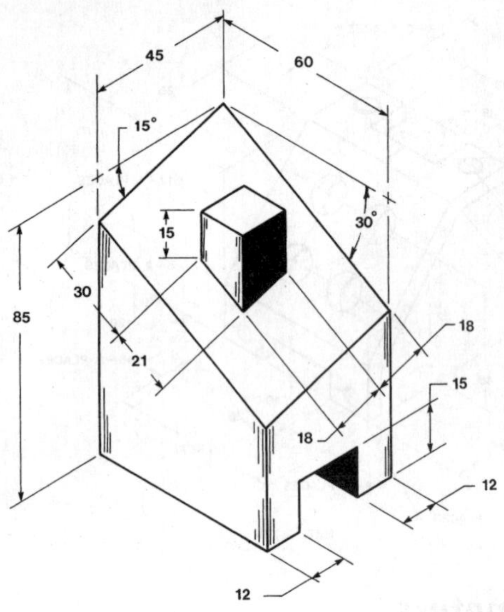

EX5-86 Millimeters

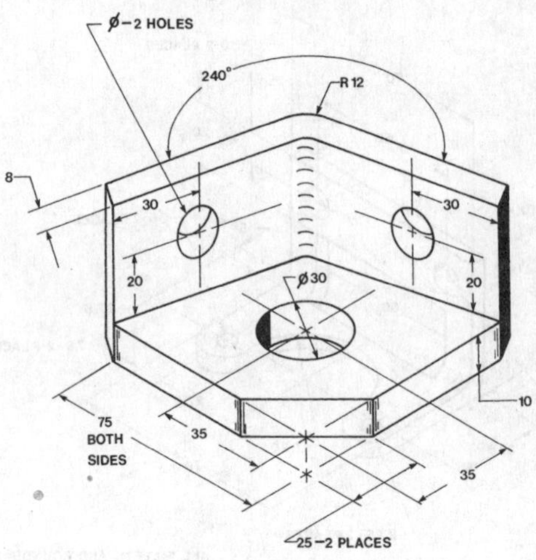

EX5-87 Inches

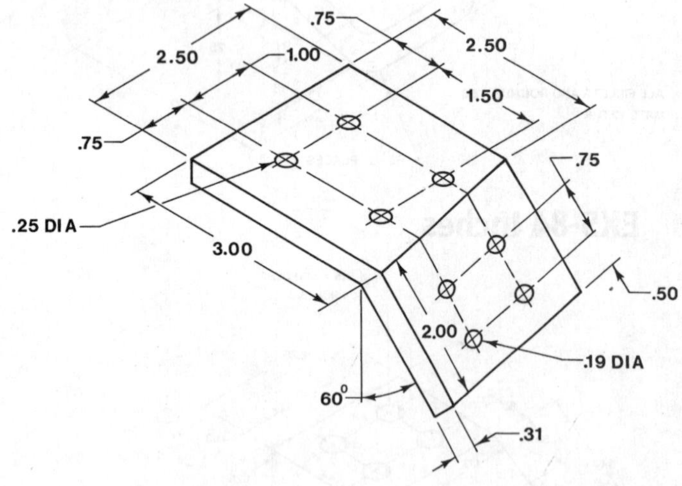

EX5-88 Millimeters

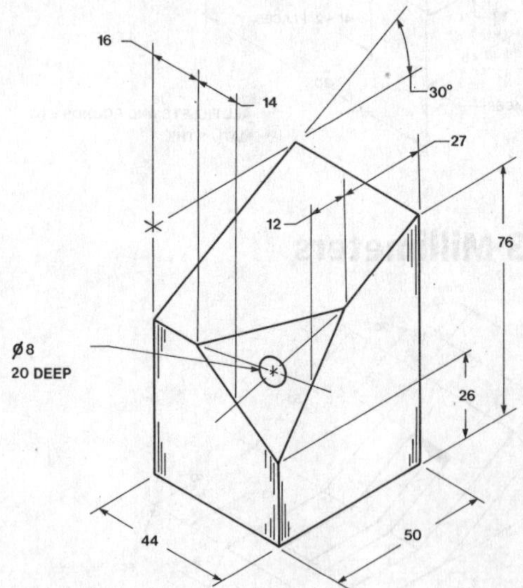

EX5-89 Millimeters

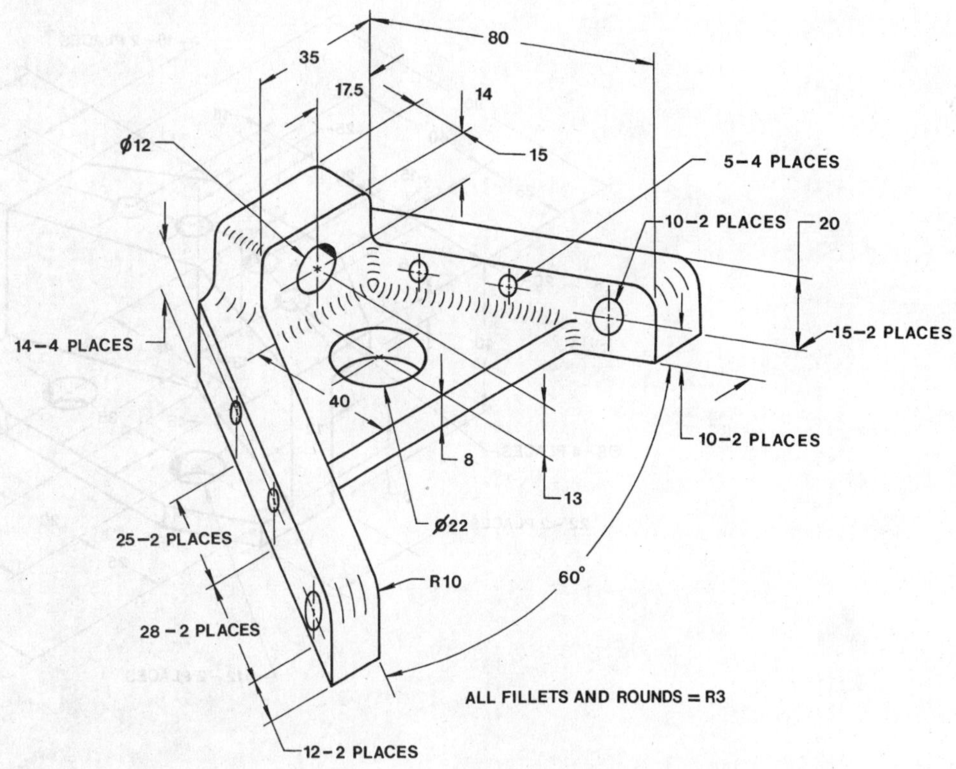

EX5-90 Millimeters

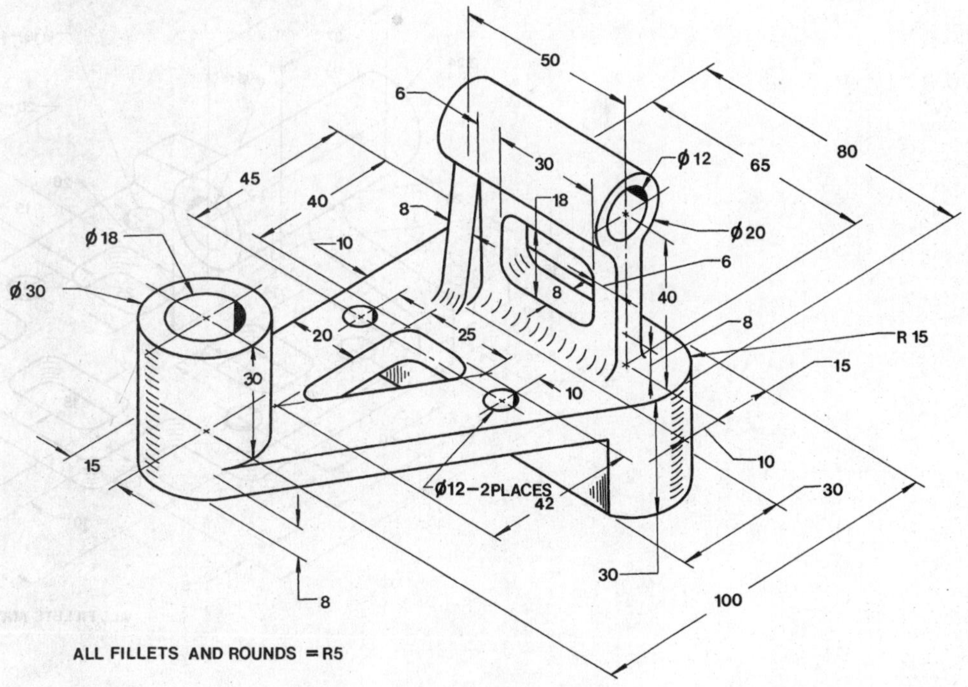

EX5-91 Millimeters

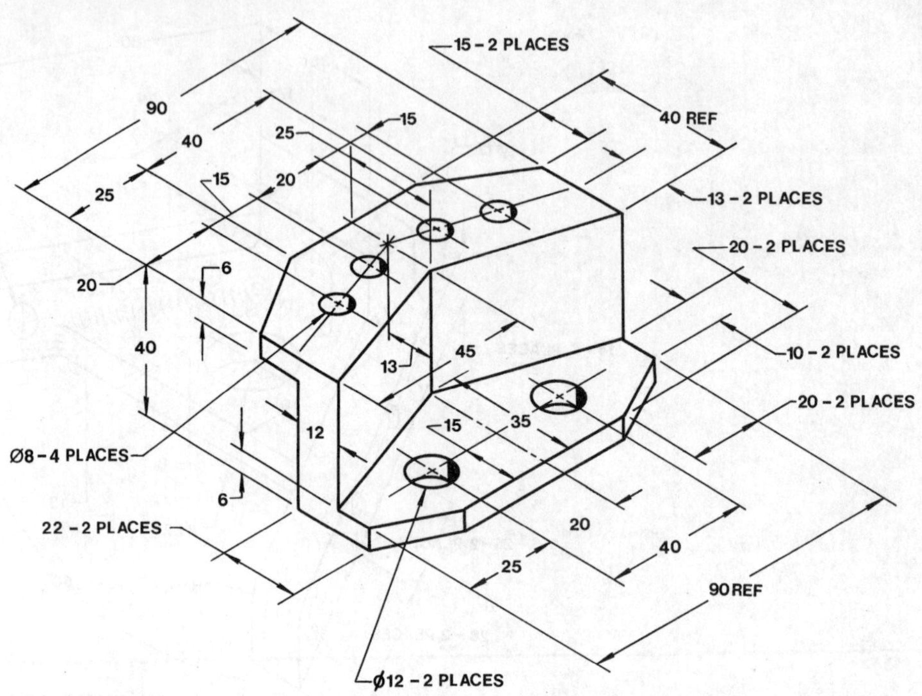

EX5-92 Millimeters

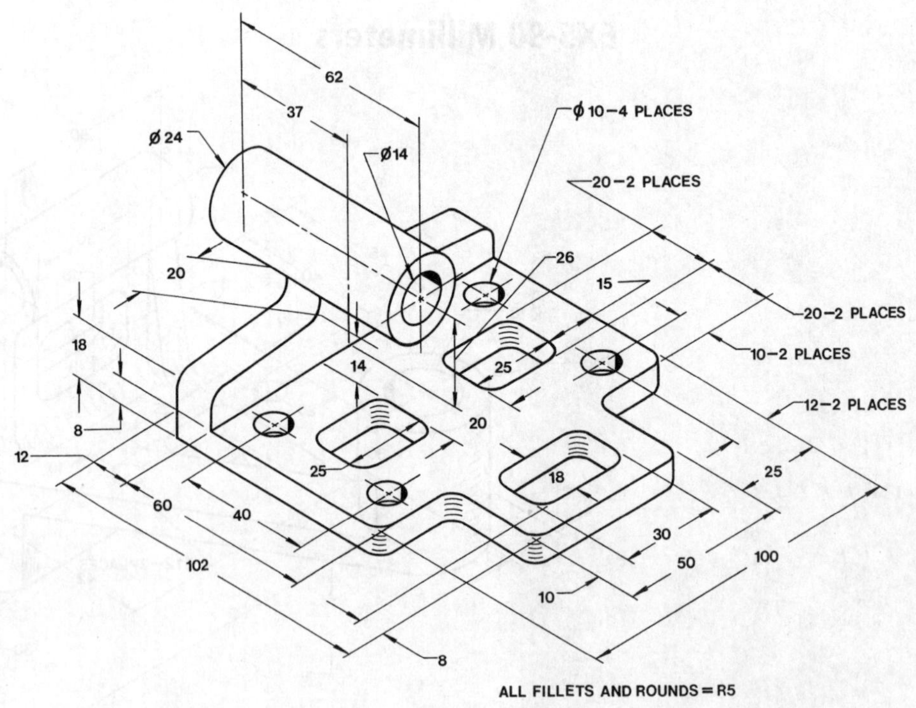

EX5-93 Millimeters

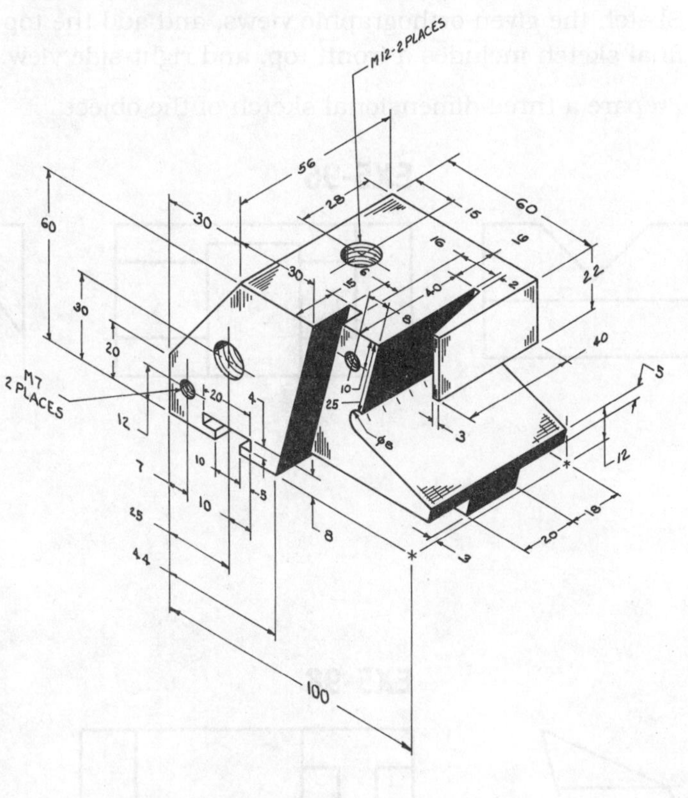

EX5-94 Millimeters

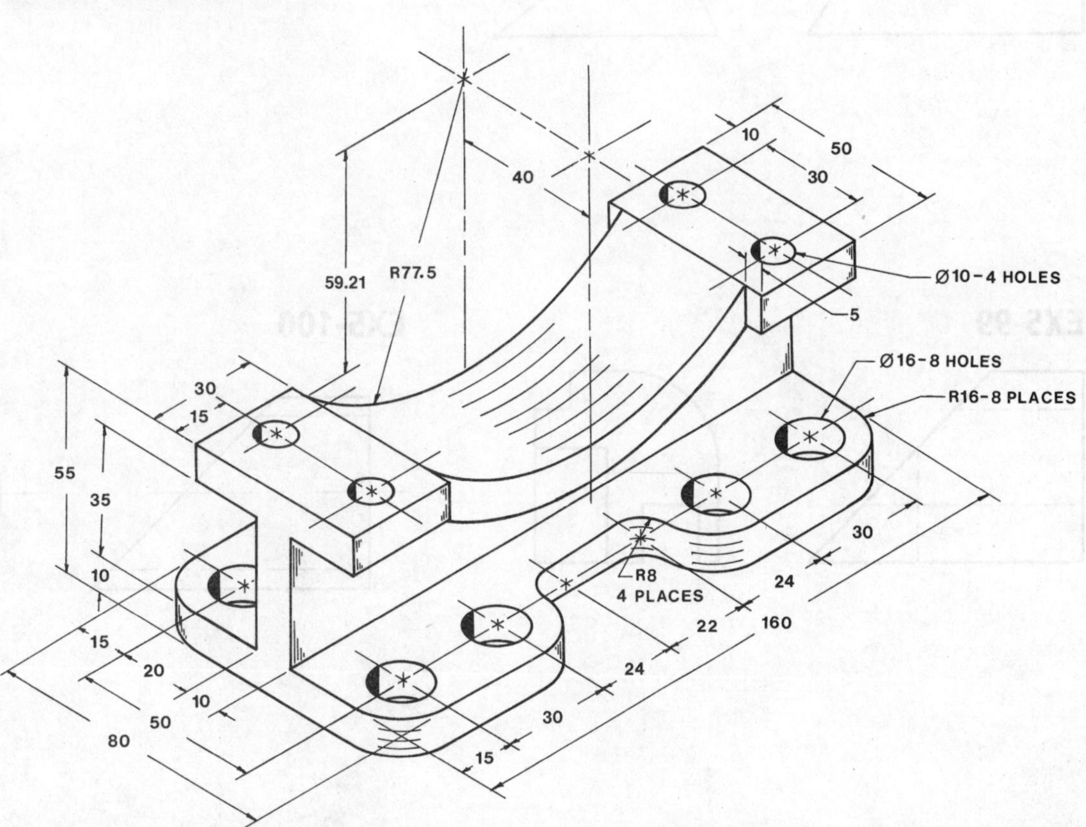

For Exercises EX5-95 through EX5-100:

A. Sketch the given orthographic views, and add the top view so that the final sketch includes a front, top, and right-side view.

B. Prepare a three-dimensional sketch of the object.

EX5-95

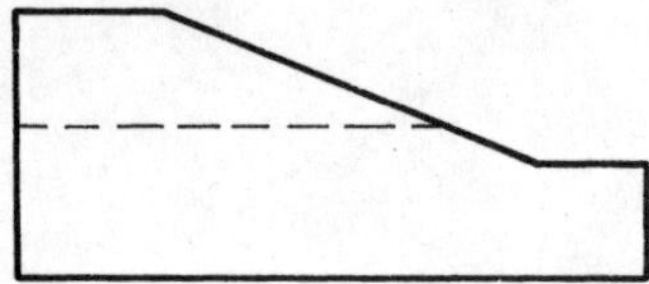

EX5-96

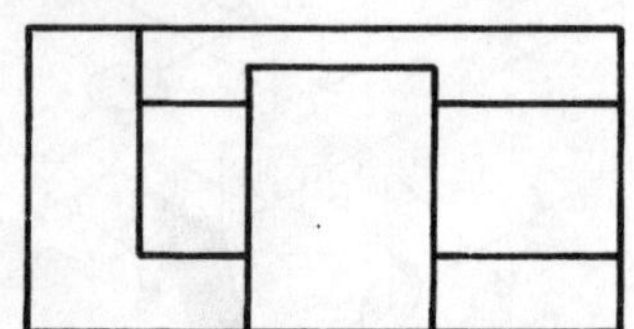

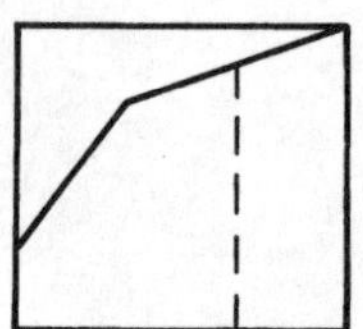

EX5-97

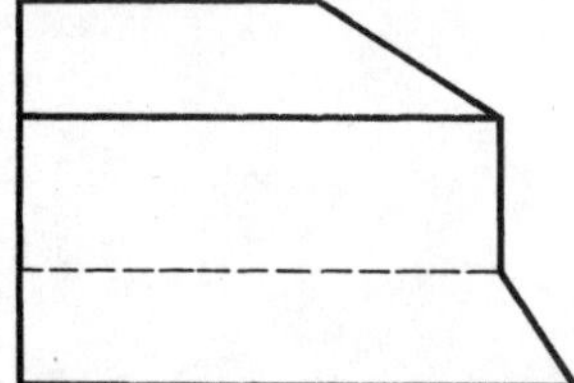

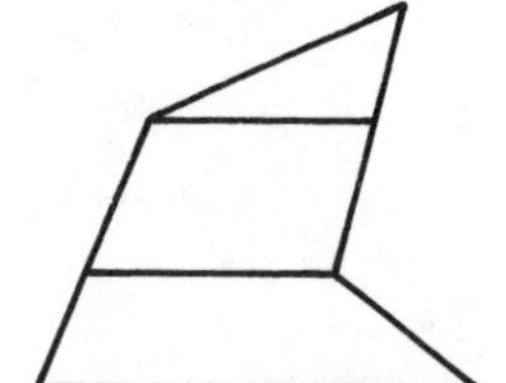

EX5-98

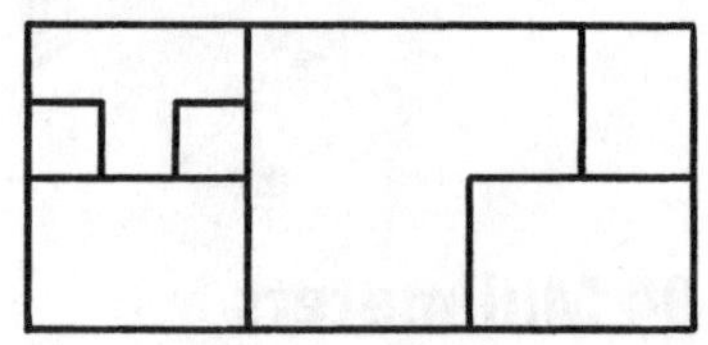

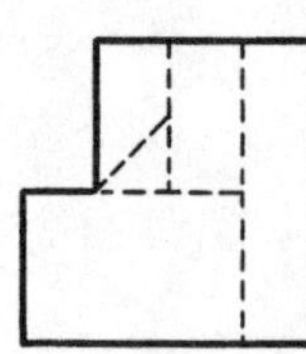

EX5-99

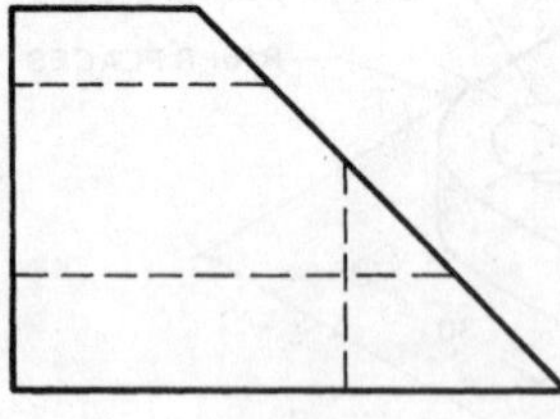

EX5-100

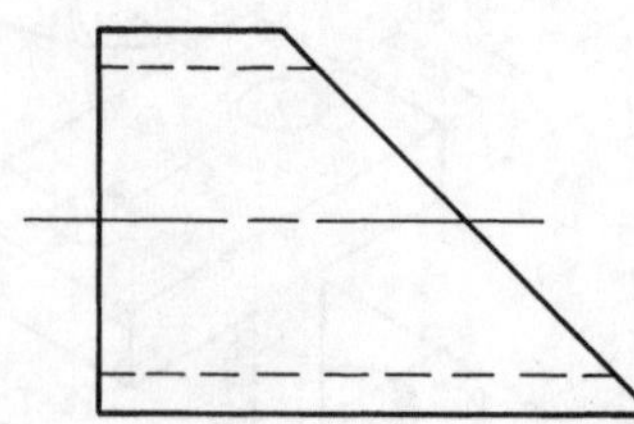

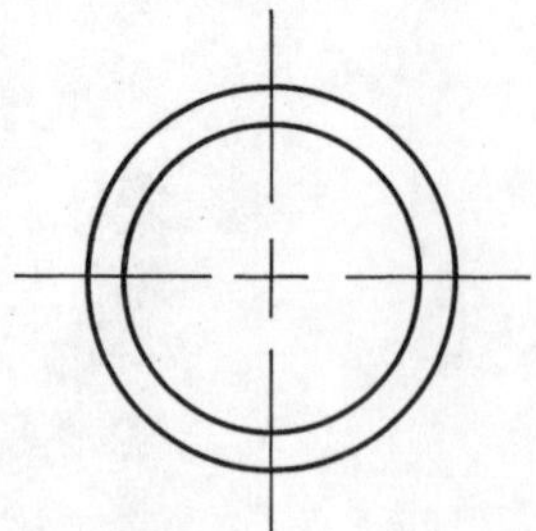

For Exercise Problems EX5-101 through EX5-128:

A. Redraw the given views, and draw the third view.

B. Prepare a three-dimensional sketch of the object.

EX5-101 Inches

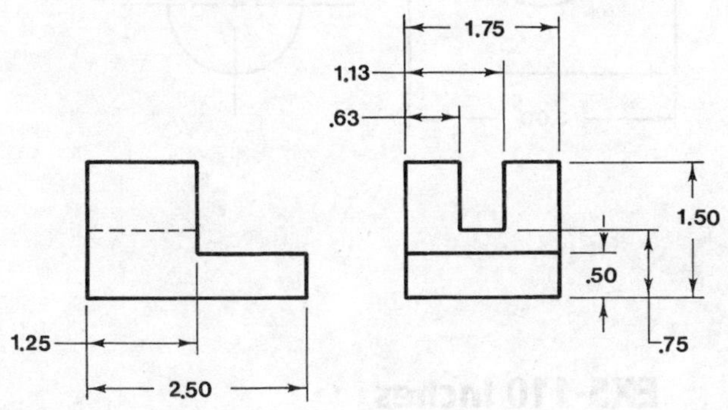

EX5-102 Inches

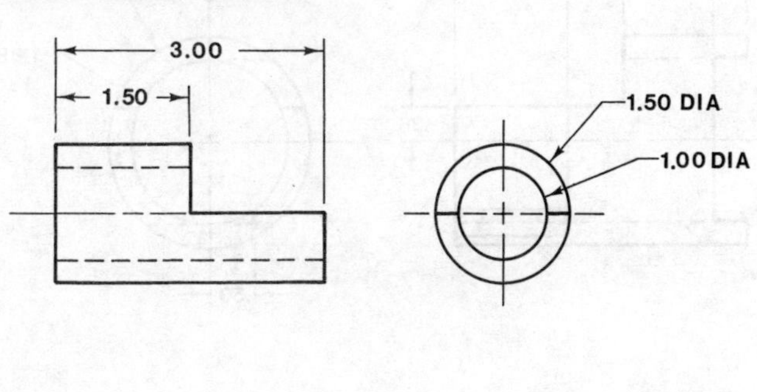

EX5-103 Inches

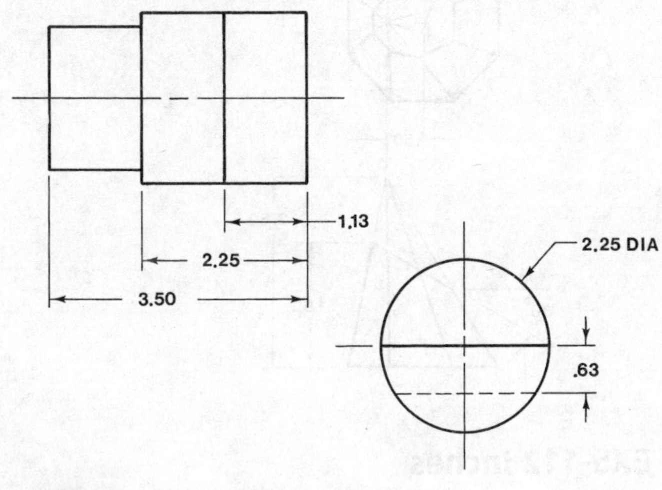

EX5-104 Inches

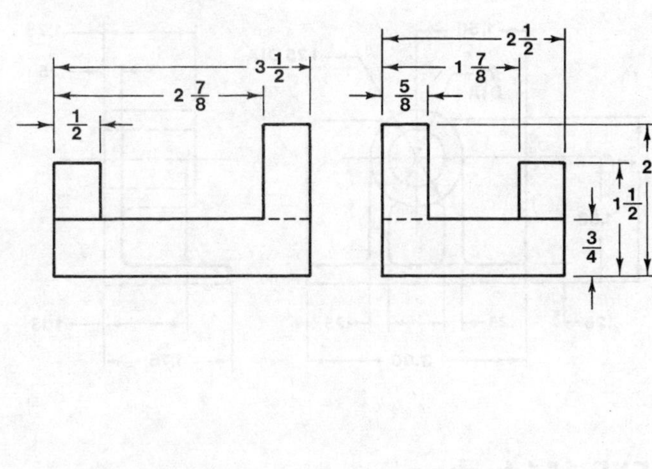

EX5-105 Inches

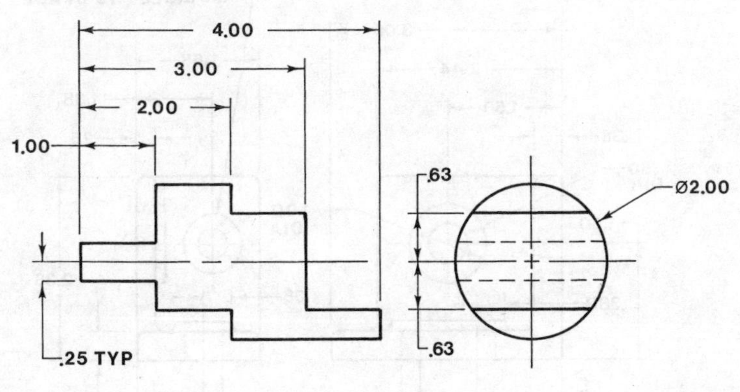

EX5-106 Inches

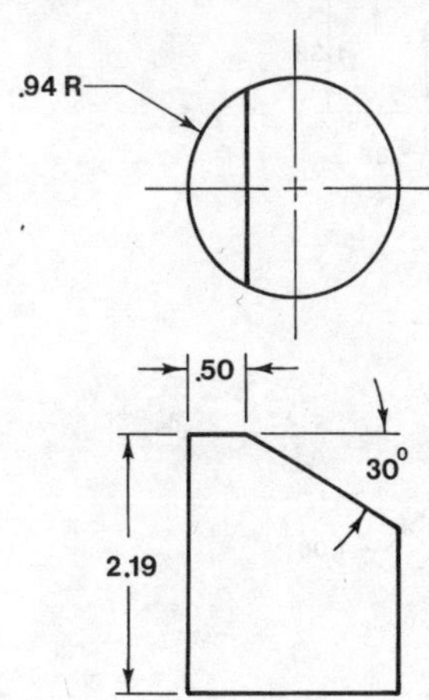

EX5-107 Inches

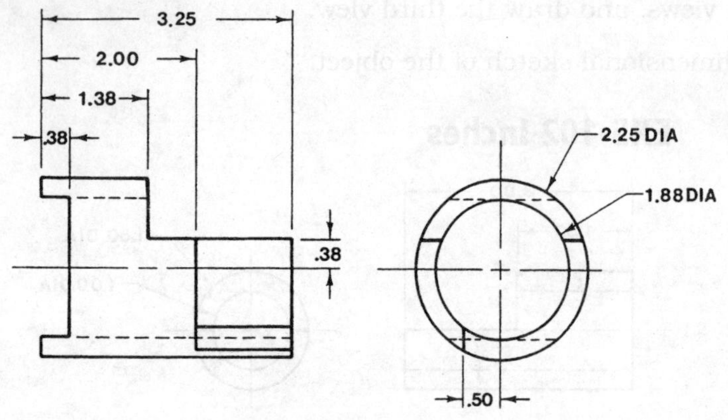

EX5-108 Inches

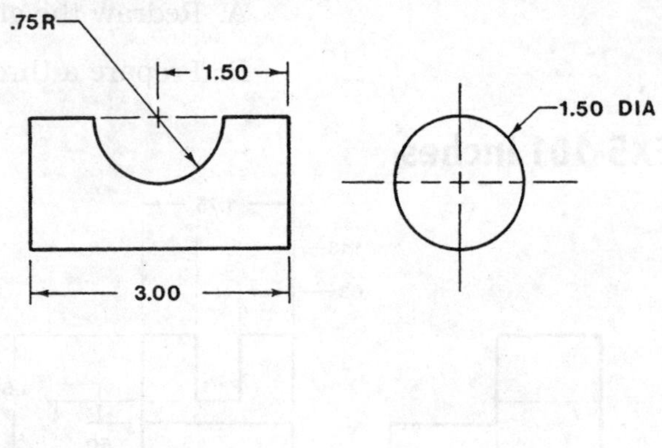

EX5-109 Inches

All fillets and rounds = $\frac{1}{8}$R

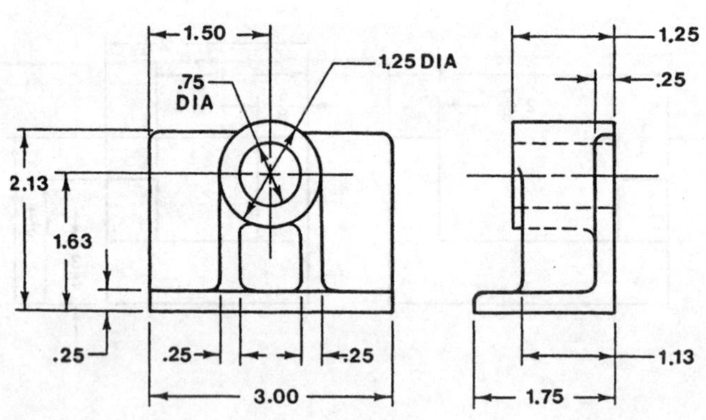

EX5-110 Inches

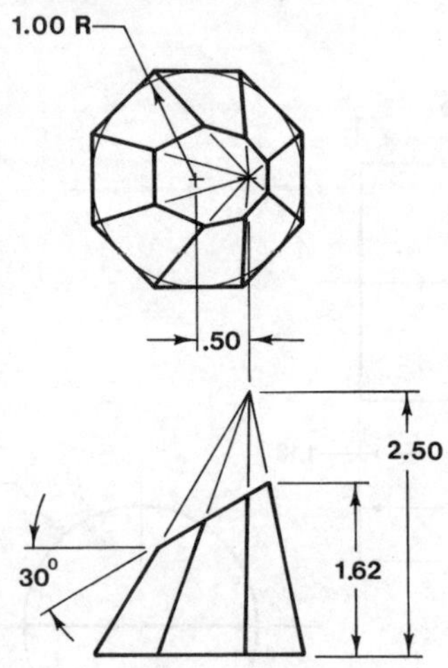

EX5-111 Inches

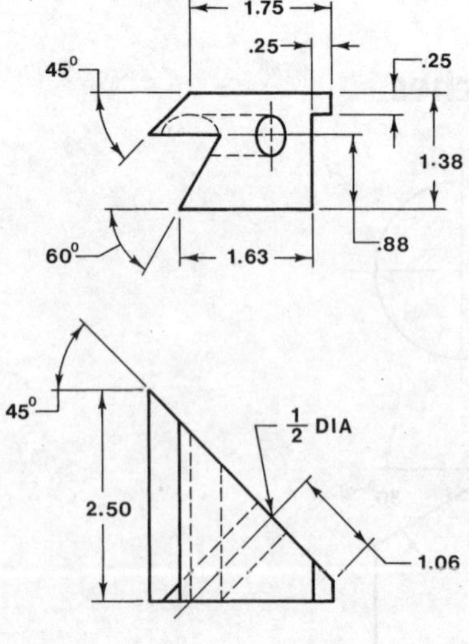

EX5-112 Inches

All fillets and rounds = $\frac{1}{8}$R

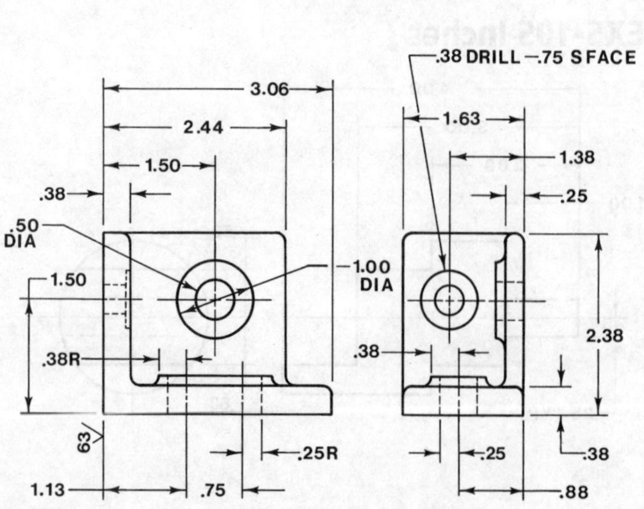

Each exercise on this page is presented on a 10 × 10-mm grid.

EX5-113

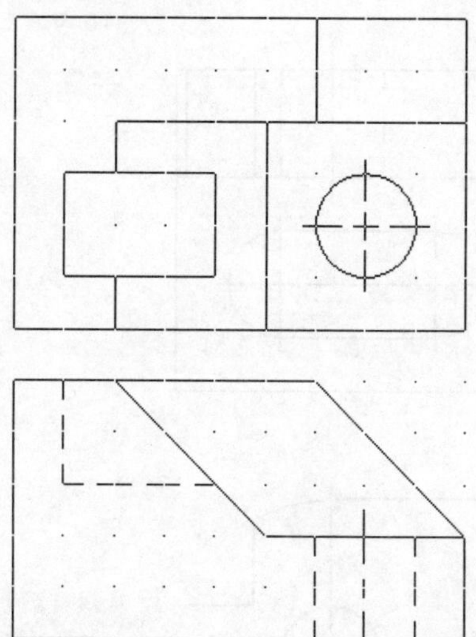

EX5-114

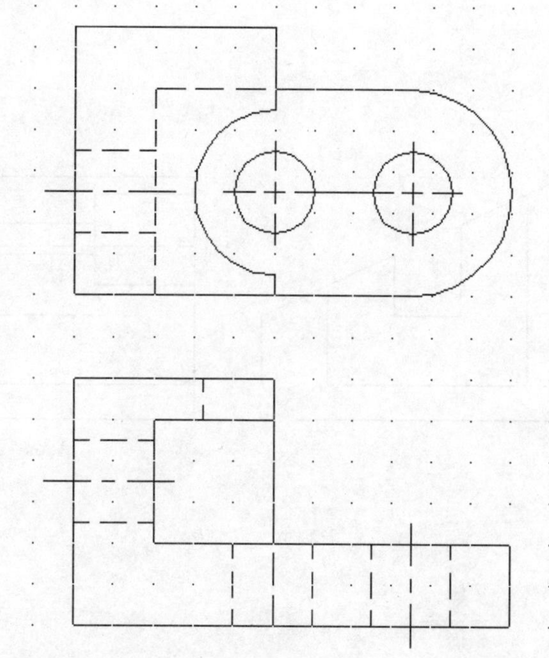

EX5-115

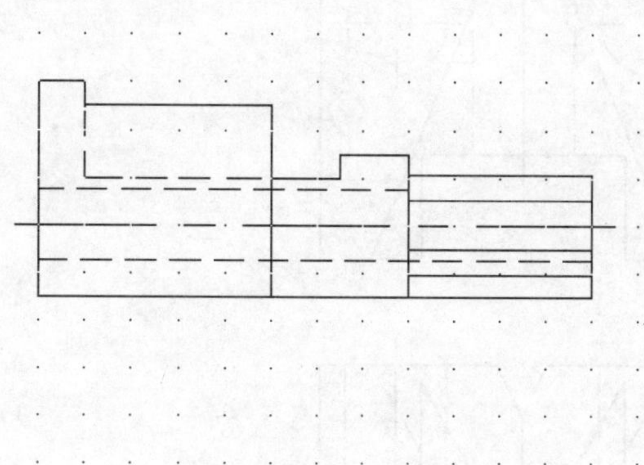

EX5-116

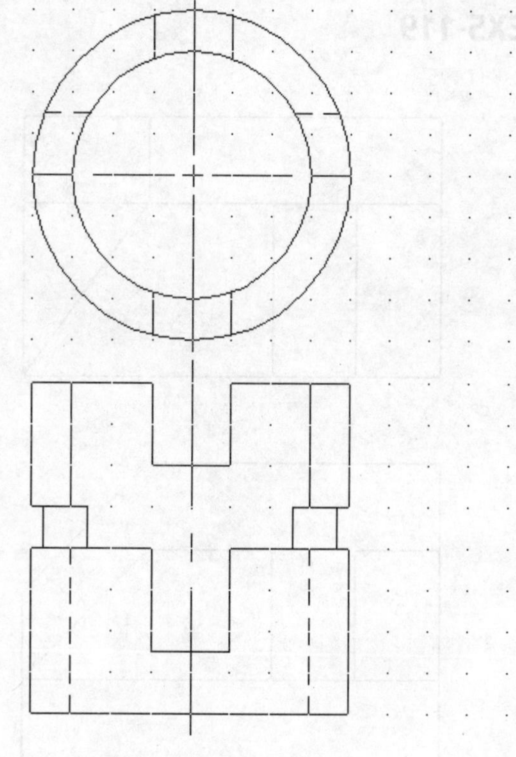

Each exercise on this page is presented on a .50″ × .50″ grid.

EX5-117

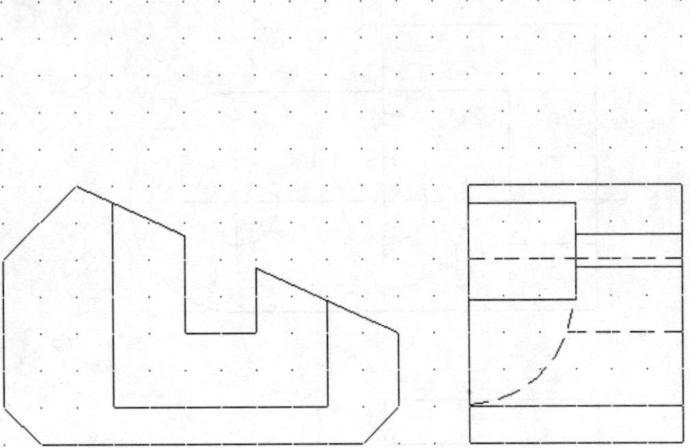

EX5-118

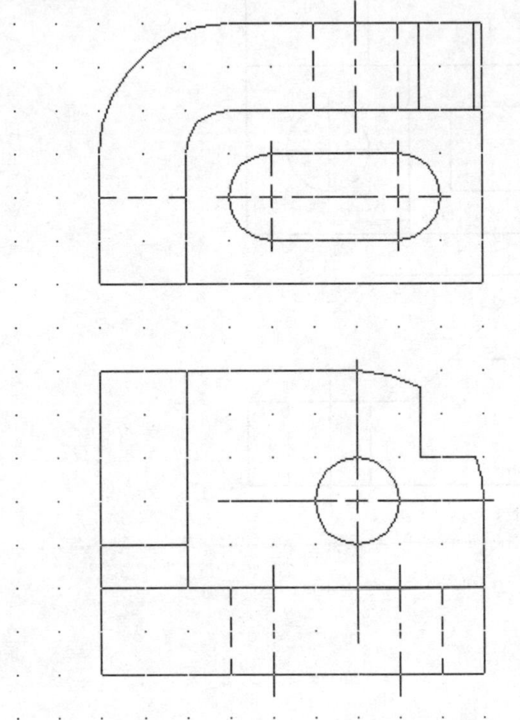

EX5-119

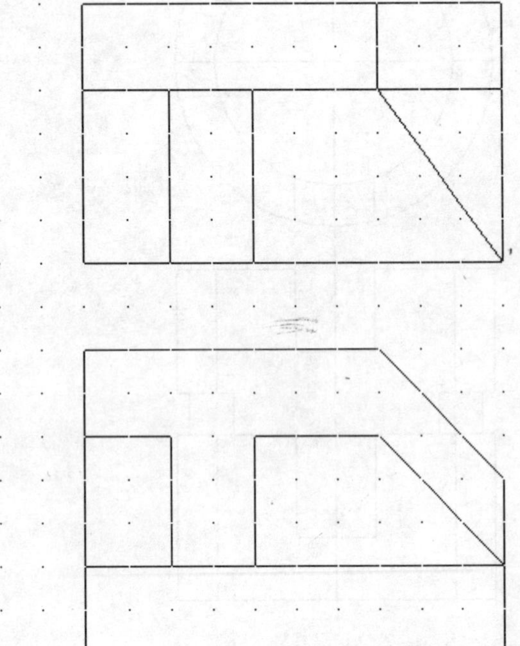

EX5-120

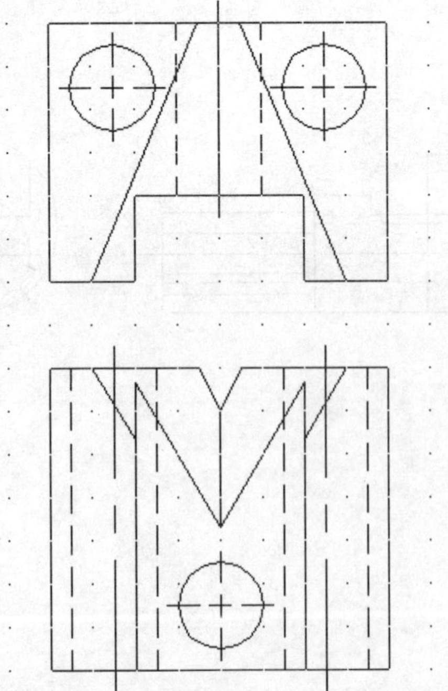

Each exercise on this page is presented on a 0.50″ × 0.50″ grid.

EX5-121

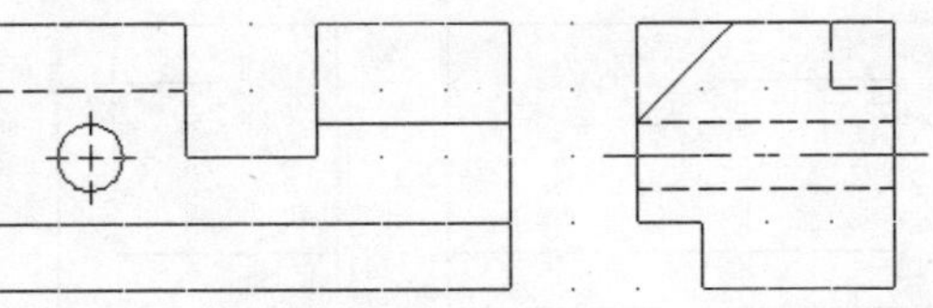

EX5-122

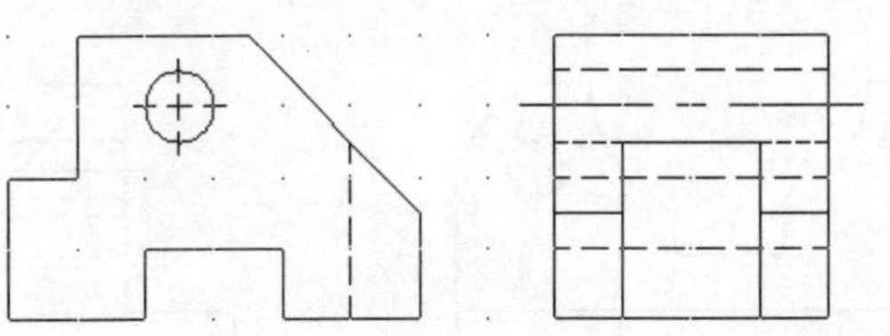

EX5-123

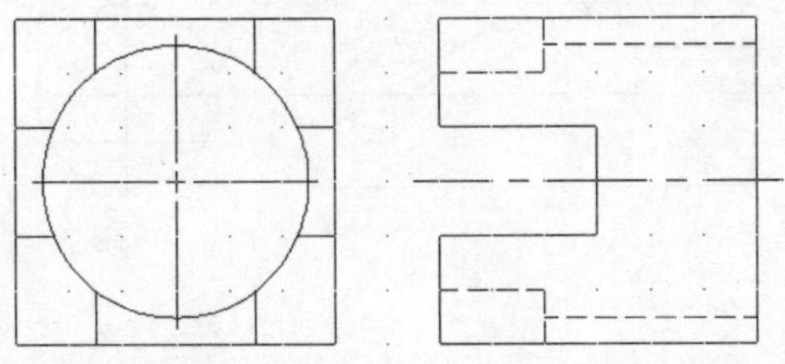

EX5-124

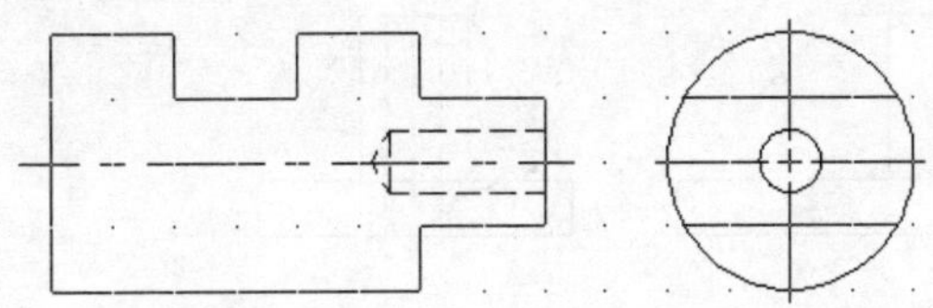

Each exercise on this page is presented on a 10 × 10-mm grid.

EX5-125

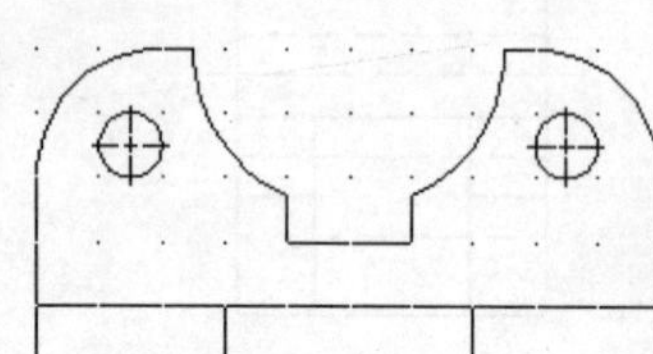

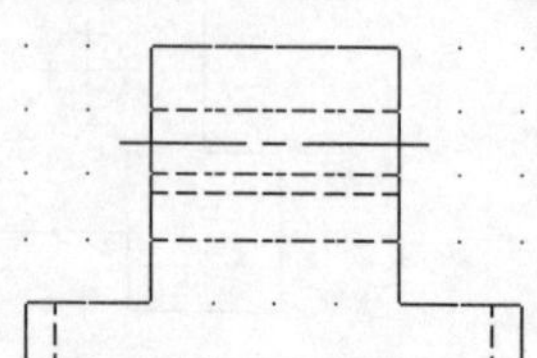

EX5-126

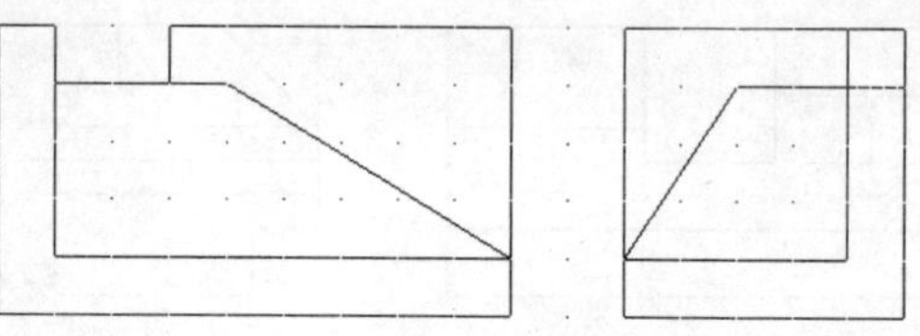

EX5-127

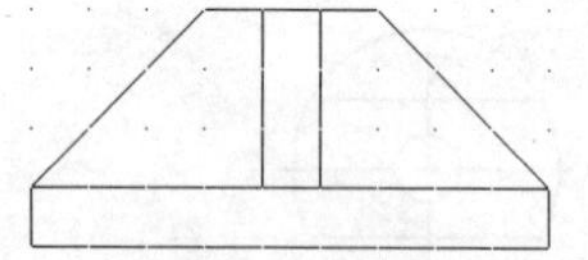

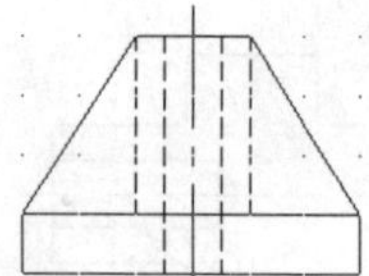

EX5-128

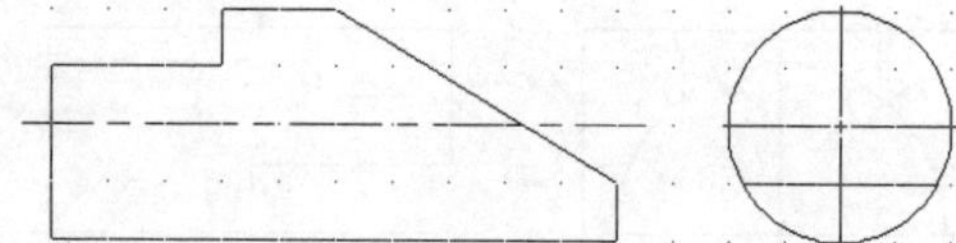

Draw the complete front, top, and side views of the two intersecting objects given in Exercise Problems EX5-129 through EX5-134 on the basis of the given complete and partially complete orthographic views.

EX5-129 Millimeters

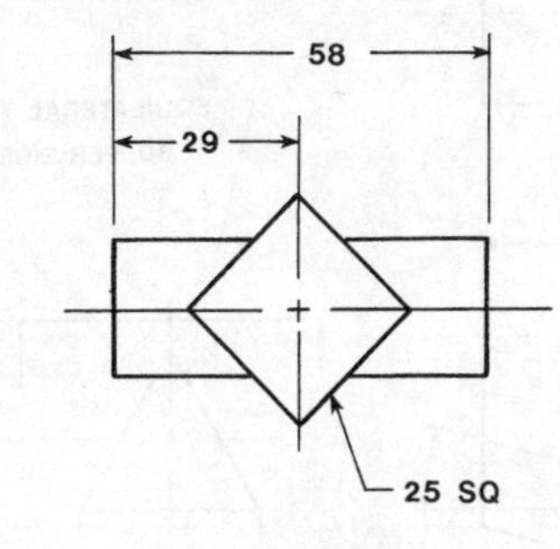

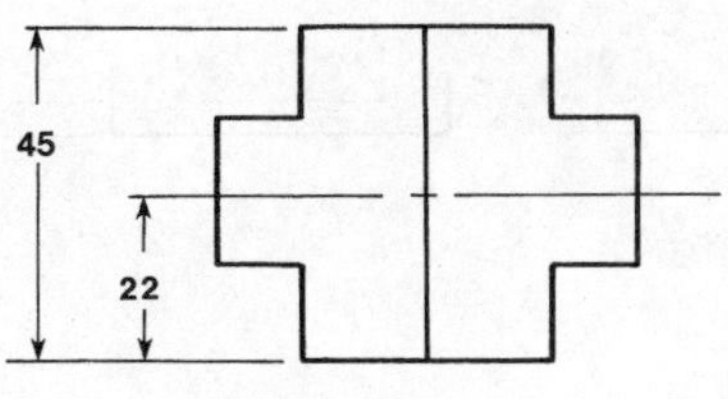

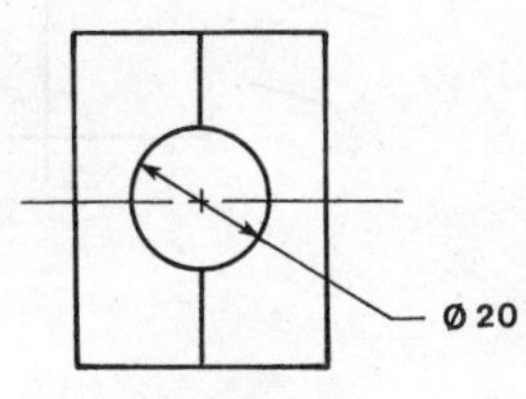

EX5-130 Millimeters

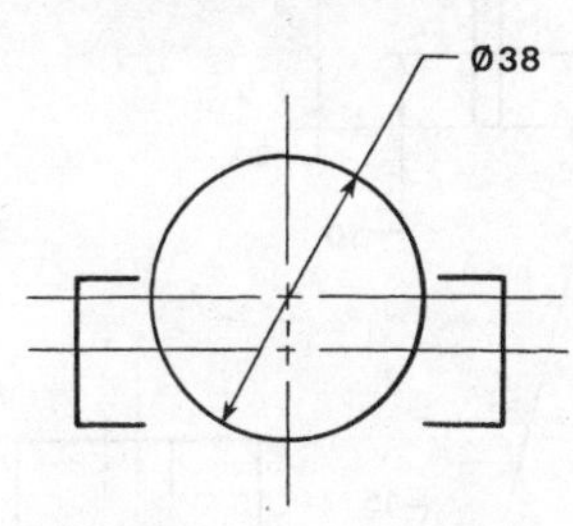

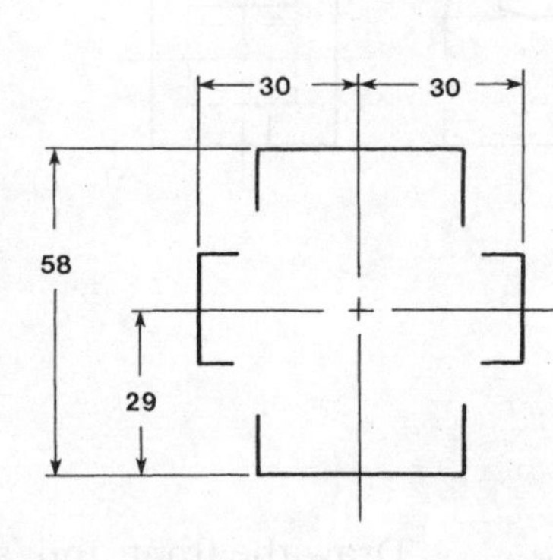

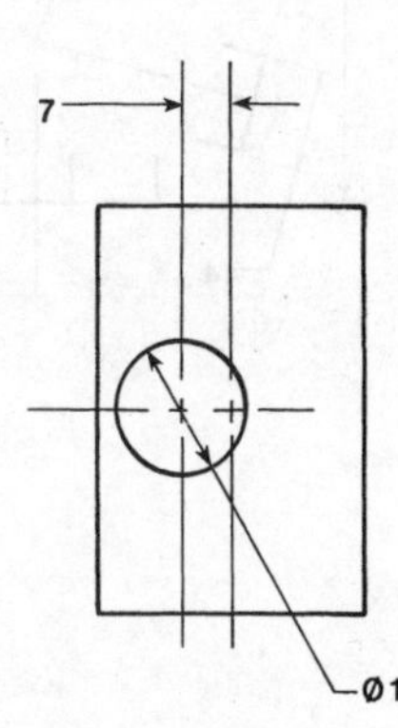

EX5-131 Inches

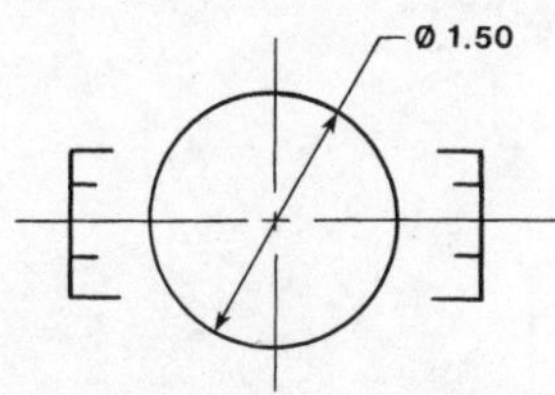

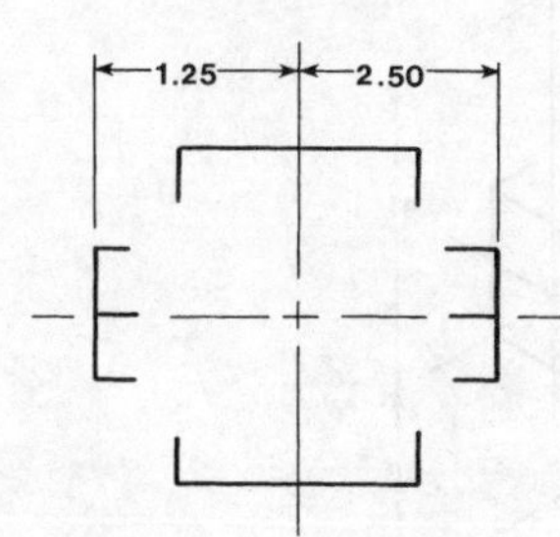

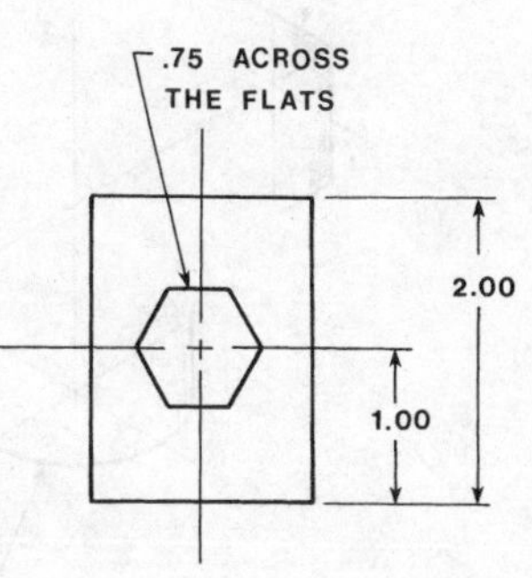

EX5-132 Inches

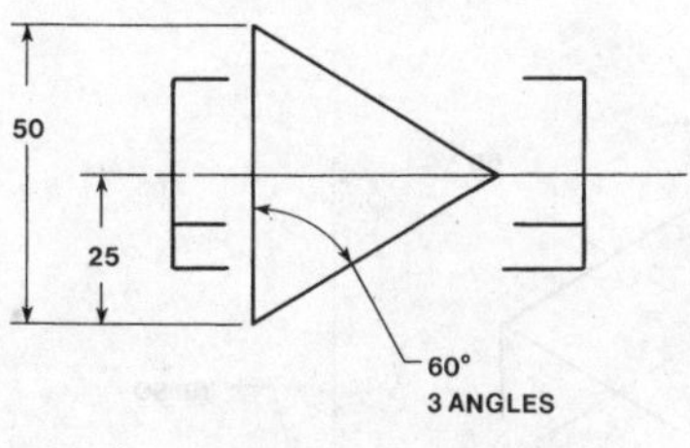

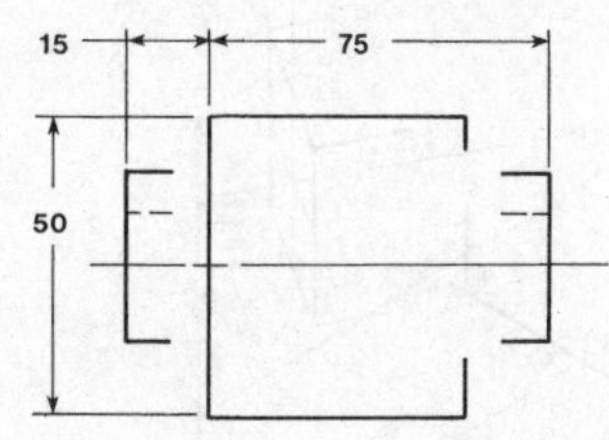

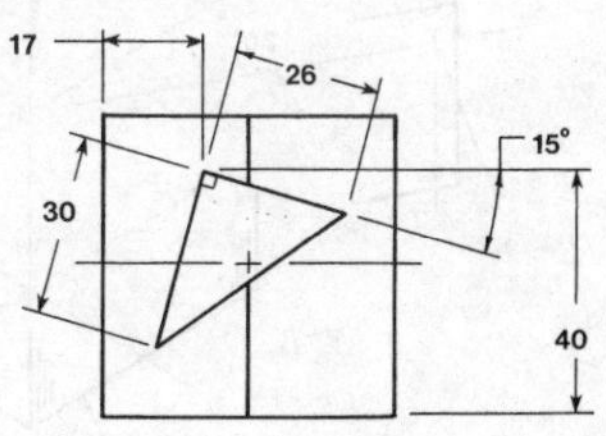

EX5-133 Millimeters

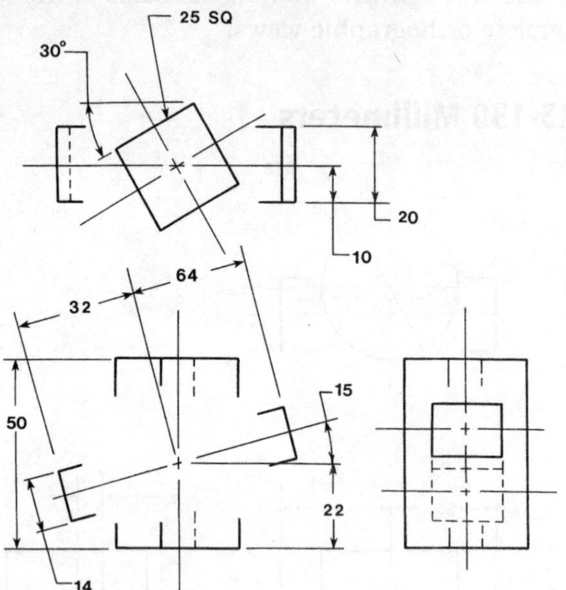

EX5-134 Millimeters

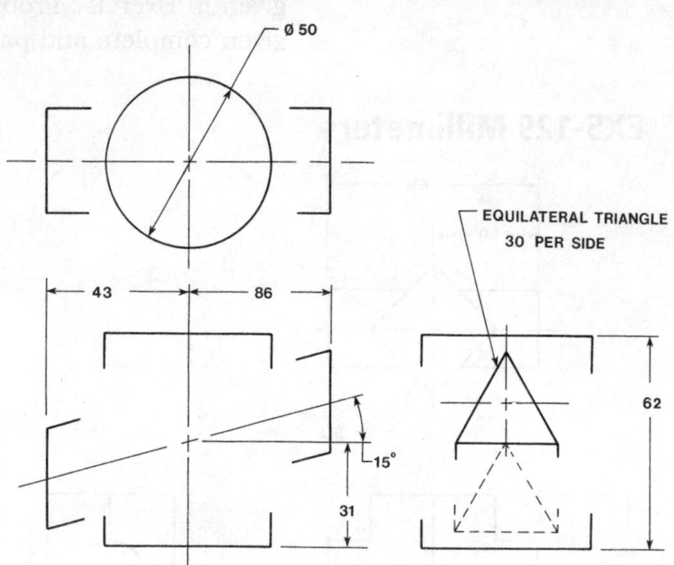

Draw the front, top, and side orthographic views of the objects given in Exercise Problems EX5-135 through EX5-138 on the basis of the partially complete isometric drawings.

EX5-135 Millimeters

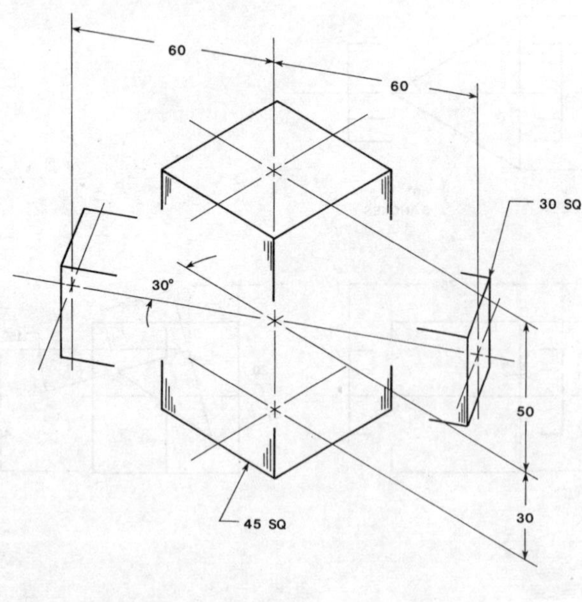

EX5-136 Millimeters

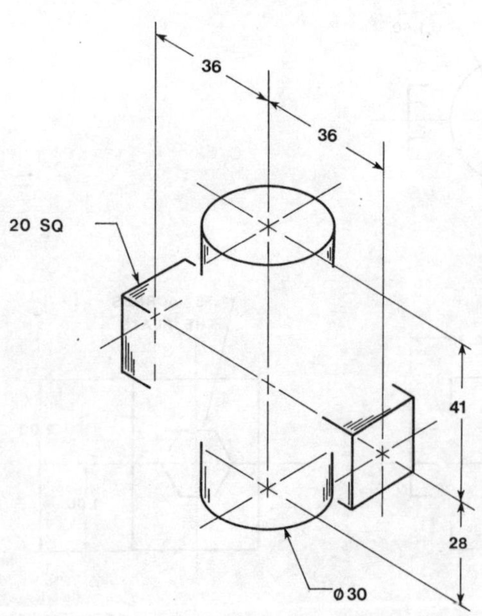

EX5-137 Inches

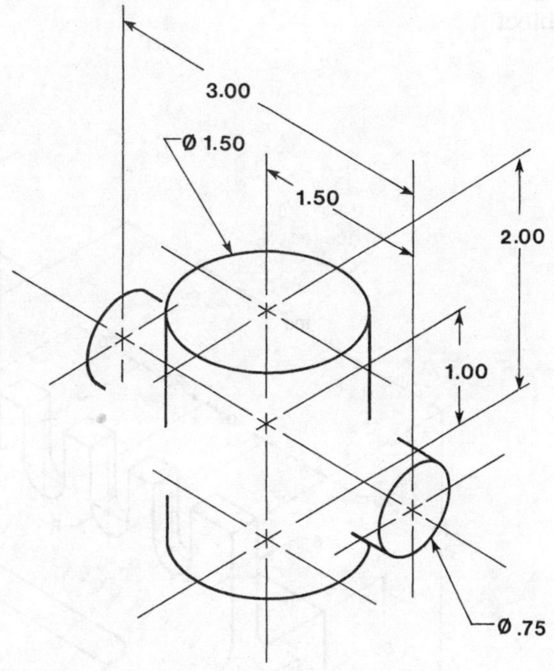

EX5-138 INCHES (SCALE: 5=1)

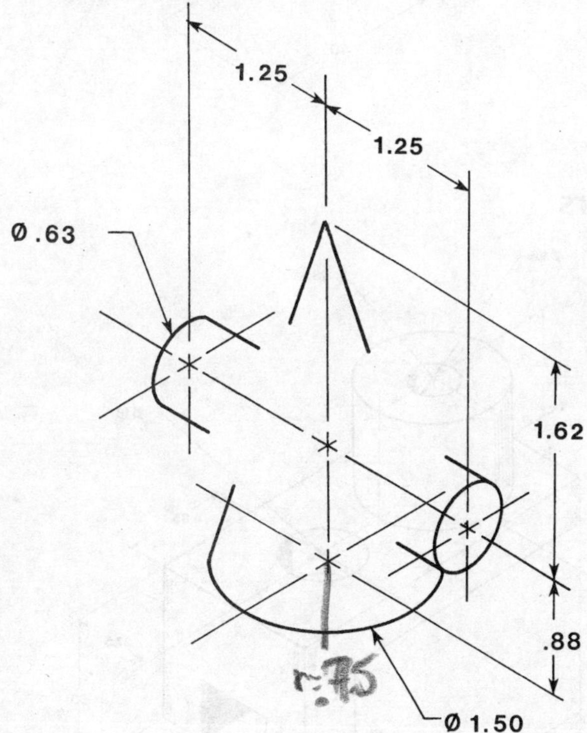

Redesign the existing objects as indicated in Exercise Problems EX5-139 through EX5-142, and then prepare a front, top, and right-side view of the object.

EX5-139 Millimeters

1. Replace the four existing 12-wide slots with seven slots 16 wide.
2. Increase the distance between the slots from 20 to 24.
3. Modify the overall length as needed.
4. Increase the size of the 60 slot so that it is 20 from both ends.

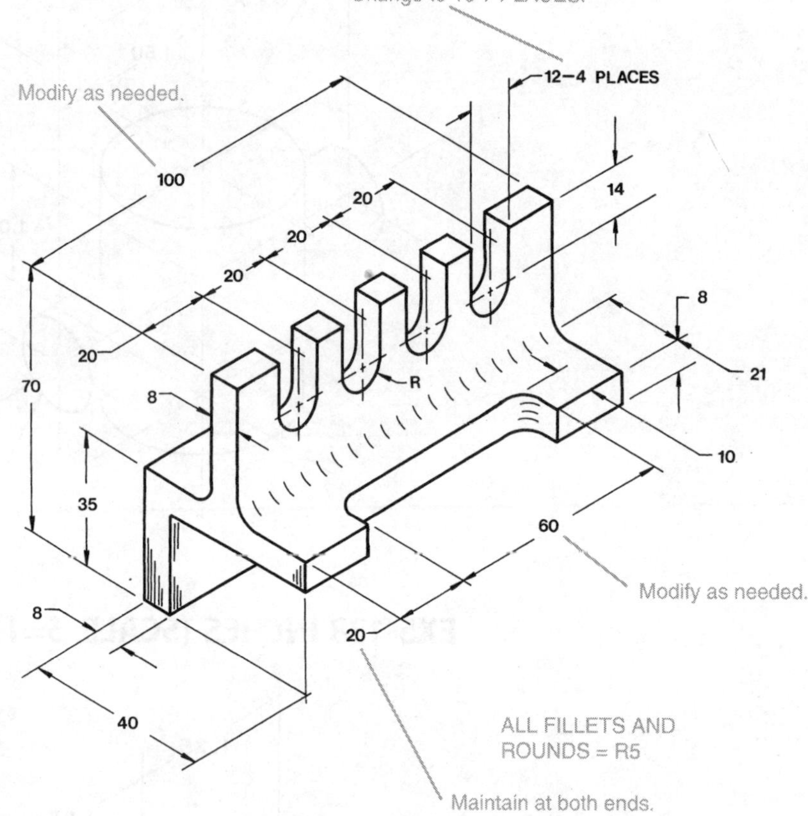

EX5-140 Millimeters

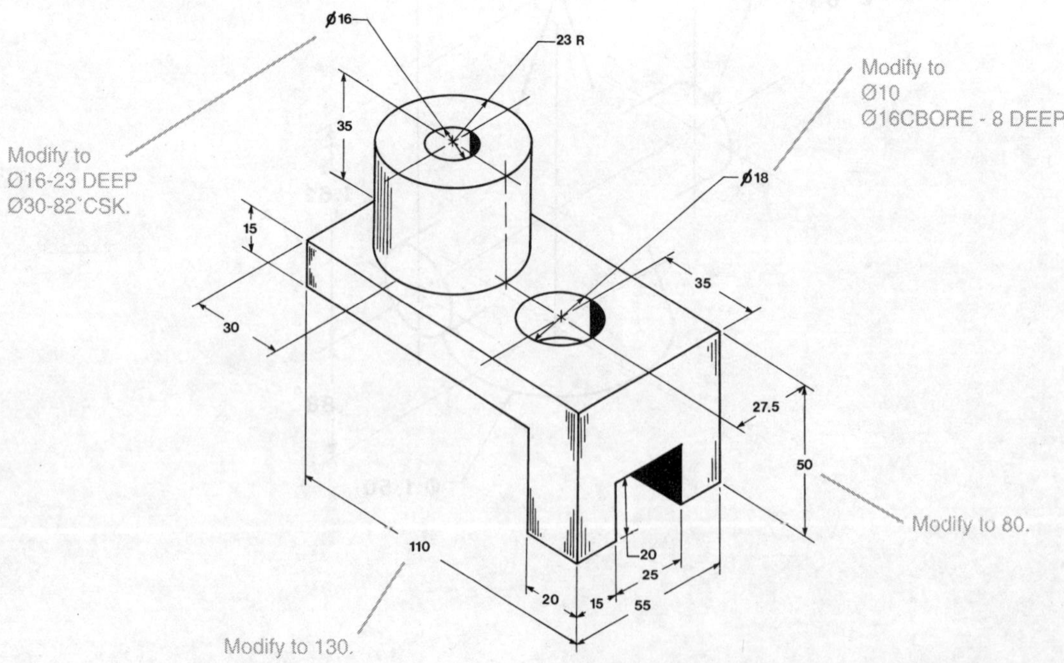

EX5-141 Millimeters

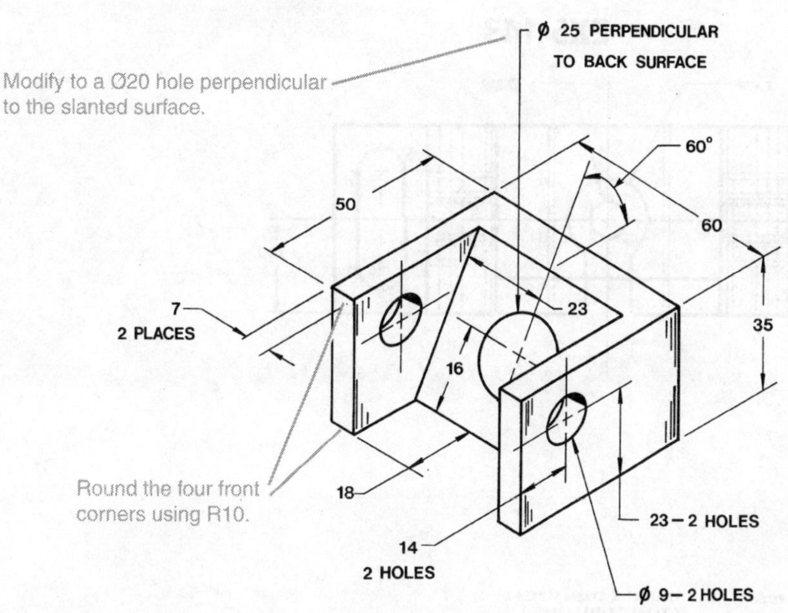

EX5-142 Millimeters

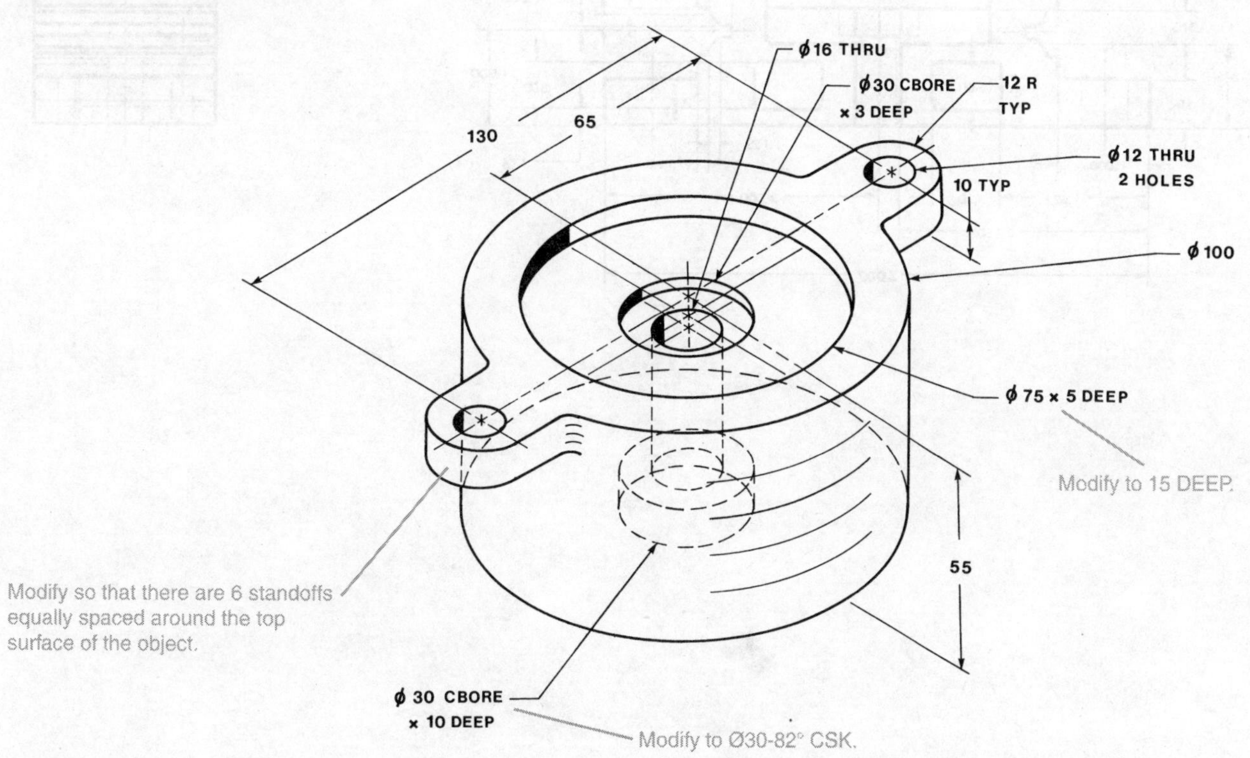

Given the following orthographic views, create a 3D model of the object:

EX5-143

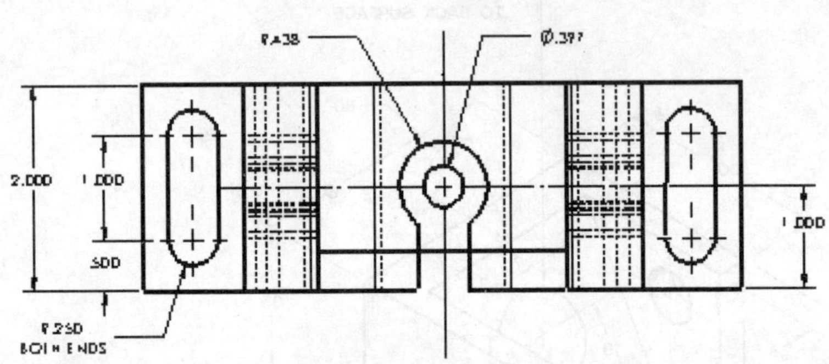

Front, Top, and Side Orthographic Views

All dimensions are in inches.

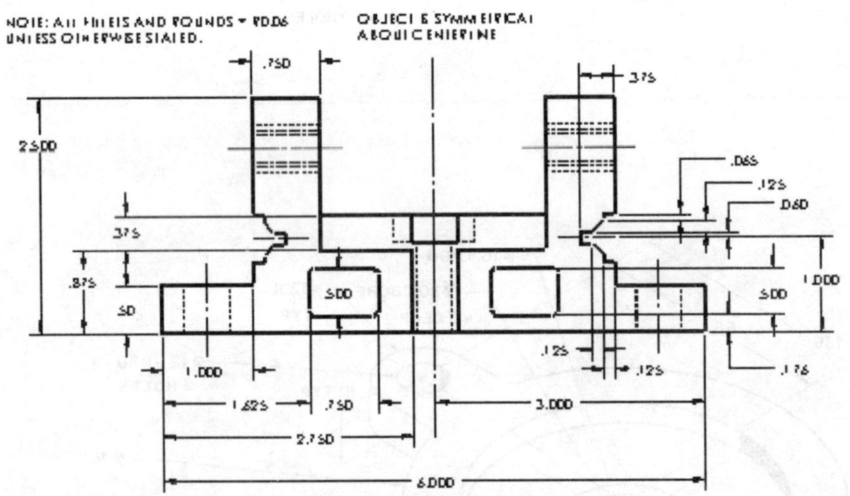

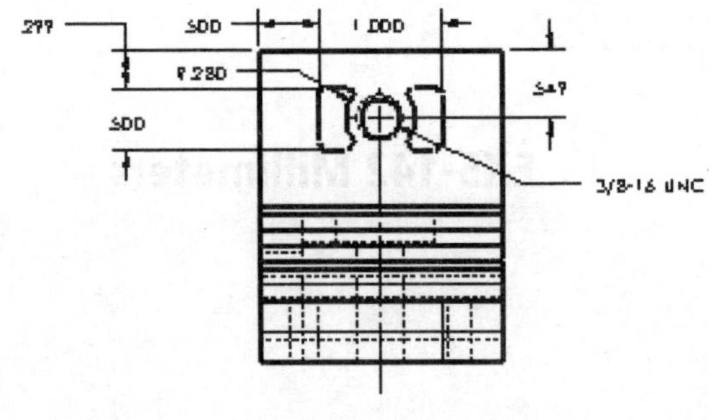

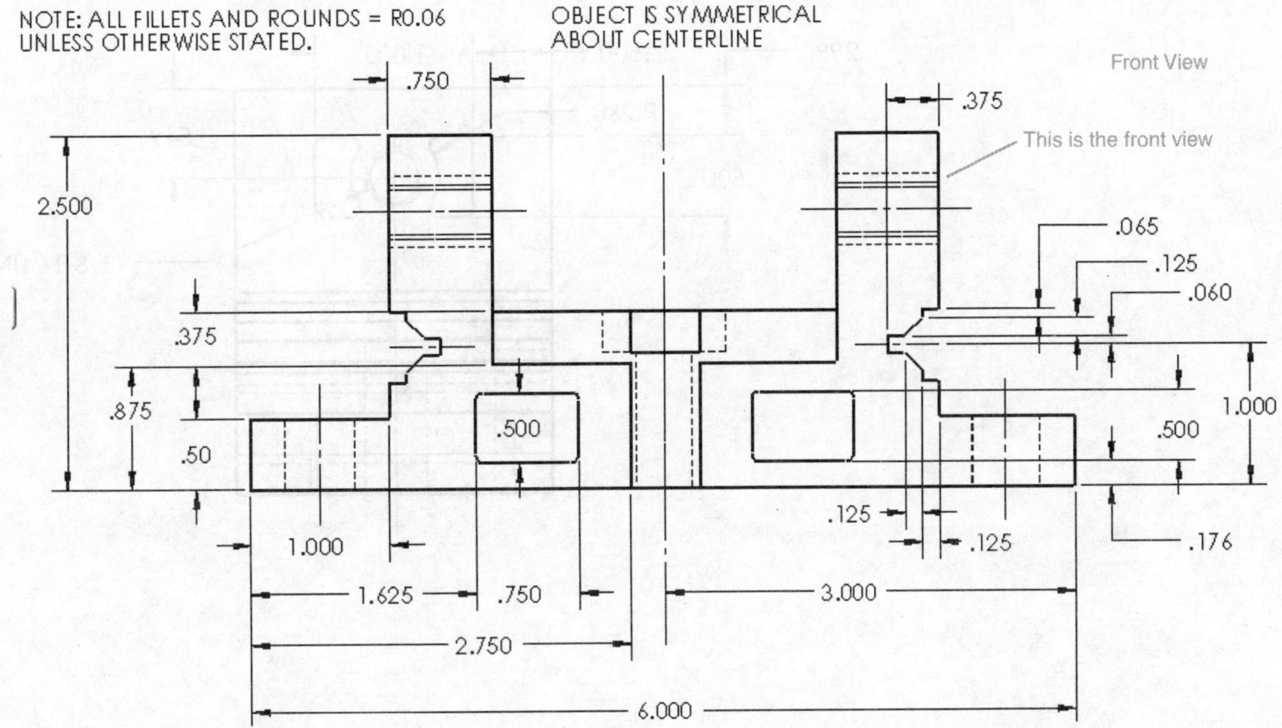

Top View

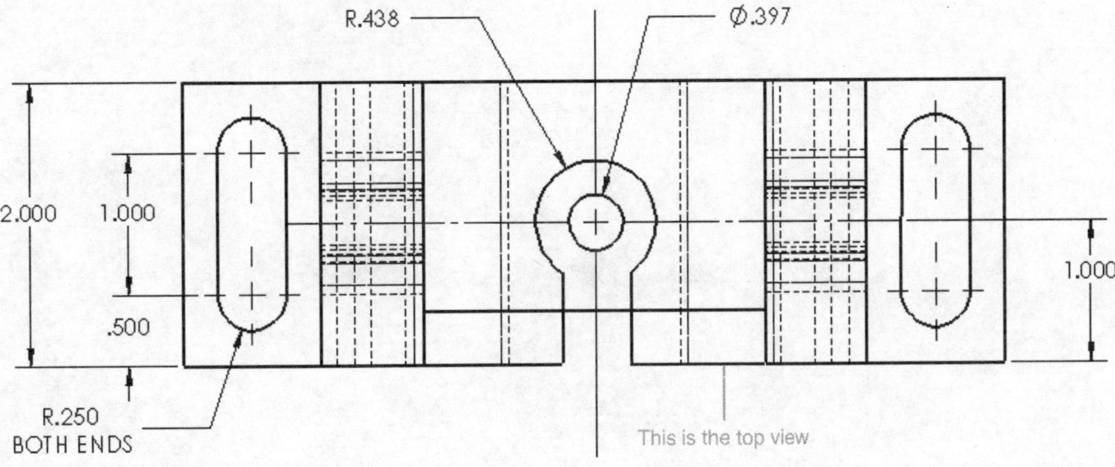

Side View

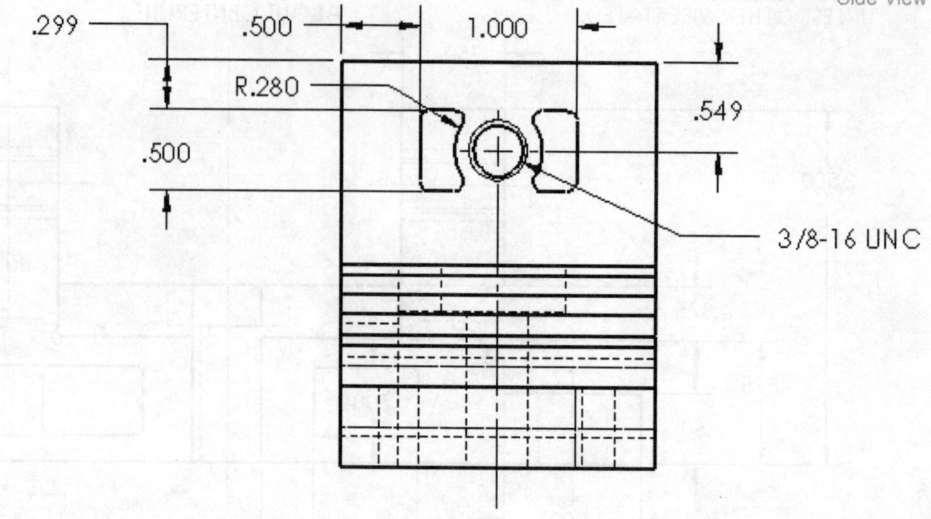

chapter six

Sectional Views

6-1 Introduction

Sectional views are used in technical drawing to expose internal surfaces. They serve to present additional orthographic views of surfaces that appear as hidden lines in the standard front, top, and side orthographic views.

Figure 6-1A shows an object intersected by a cutting plane. Figure 6-1B shows the same object, with its right side and the cutting plane removed. Hatch lines are drawn to represent the location on the surfaces where the cutting plane passed through solid material. Also shown are the front and right-side orthographic views and a sectional view. Note the similarity between the sectional view and the cut pictorial view.

Figure 6-1A

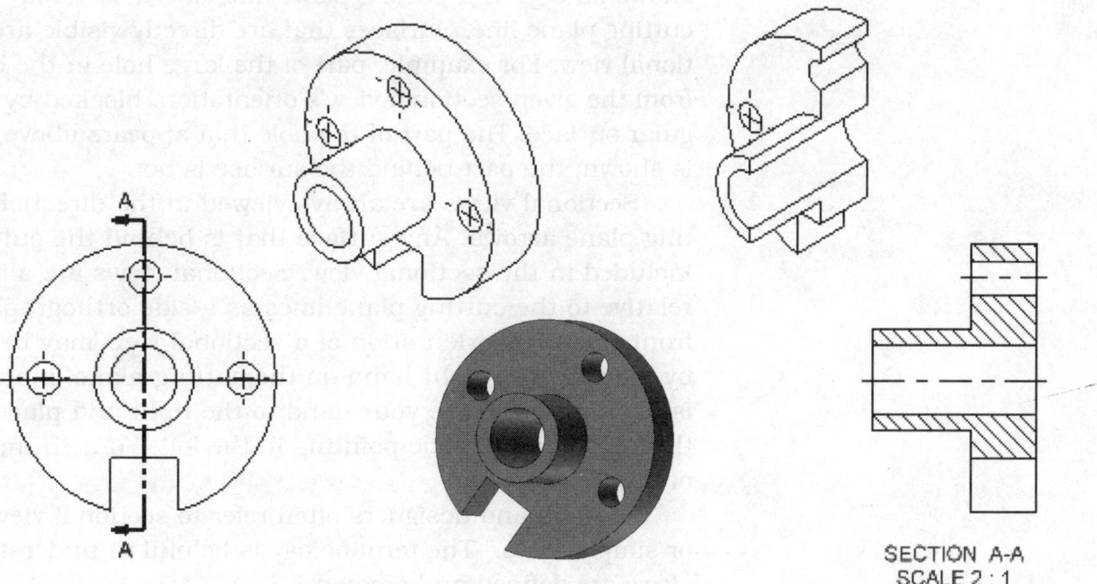

Figure 6-1B

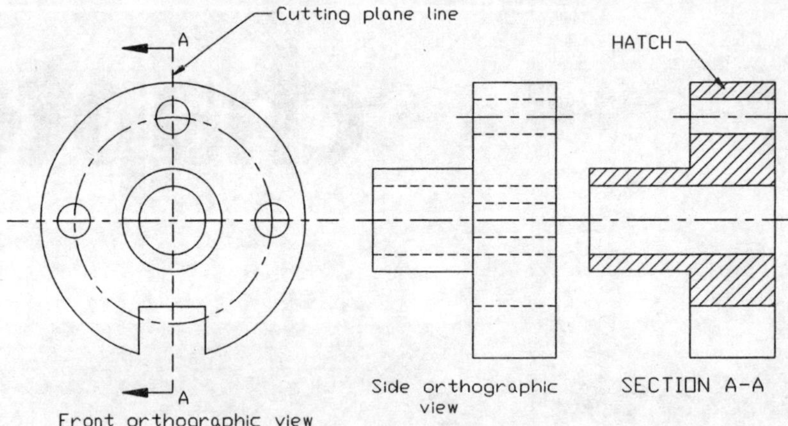

Sectional views do not contain hidden lines, so they are used to clarify orthographic views that are difficult to understand because of excessive hidden lines. Figure 6-2 shows an object with a complex internal shape. The standard right view contains many hidden lines and is difficult to follow. Note how much easier it is to understand the object's internal shape when it is presented as a sectional view.

Figure 6-2

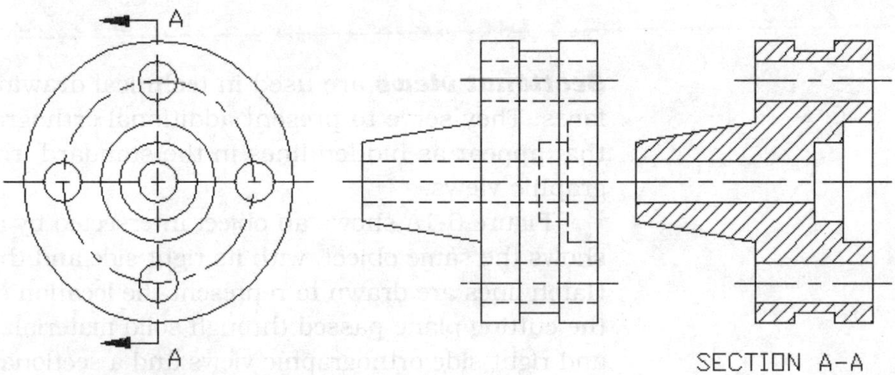

Sectional views *do* include all lines that are directly visible. Figure 6-3 shows an object, a cutting plane line, and a sectional view taken along the cutting plane line. Surfaces that are directly visible are shown in the sectional view. For example, part of the large hole in the back left surface is, from the given sectional view's orientation, blocked by the shorter rectangular surface. The part of the hole that appears above the blocking surface is shown; the part behind the surface is not.

Sectional views are always viewed in the direction defined by the cutting plane arrows. Any surface that is behind the cutting plane is not included in the sectional view. Sectional views are aligned and oriented relative to the cutting plane lines as a side orthographic view is to the front view. The orientation of a sectional view may be better understood by placing your right hand on the cutting plane line so that your thumb is pointing up. Move your hand to the right and place it palm down. Your thumb should now be pointing to the left. Your thumb indicates the top of the view.

Drafters and designers often refer to sectional views as "sectional cuts" or simply "cuts." The terminology is helpful in understanding how sectional views are defined and created.

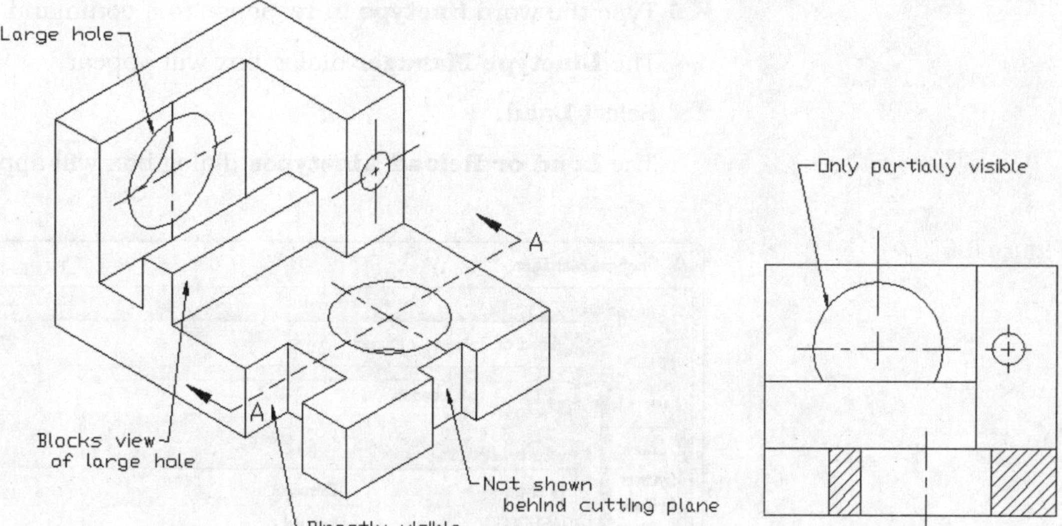

Figure 6-3

6-2 Cutting Plane Lines

Cutting plane lines are used to define the location for the sectional view's cutting plane. An object is "cut" along a cutting plane line.

Figure 6-4 shows two linetype patterns for cutting plane lines. Either pattern is acceptable, although some companies prefer to use only one linetype for all drawings to ensure a uniform appearance in all of their drawings. The dashed-line pattern will be used throughout this book.

The two patterns shown in Figure 6-4 are included in AutoCAD's linetype library as **Dashed** and **Phantom** styles. The arrow portion of the cutting plane line is created by the use of the **Multileader** tool, found on the **Leaders** panel under the **Annotate** tab or on the **Annotation** panel under the **Home** tab.

To Draw a Cutting Plane Line—Method I

Change a given continuous line, **A–A,** to a cutting plane line. See Figure 6-5. The **Dashed** linetype must first be added to the listing of available linetypes.

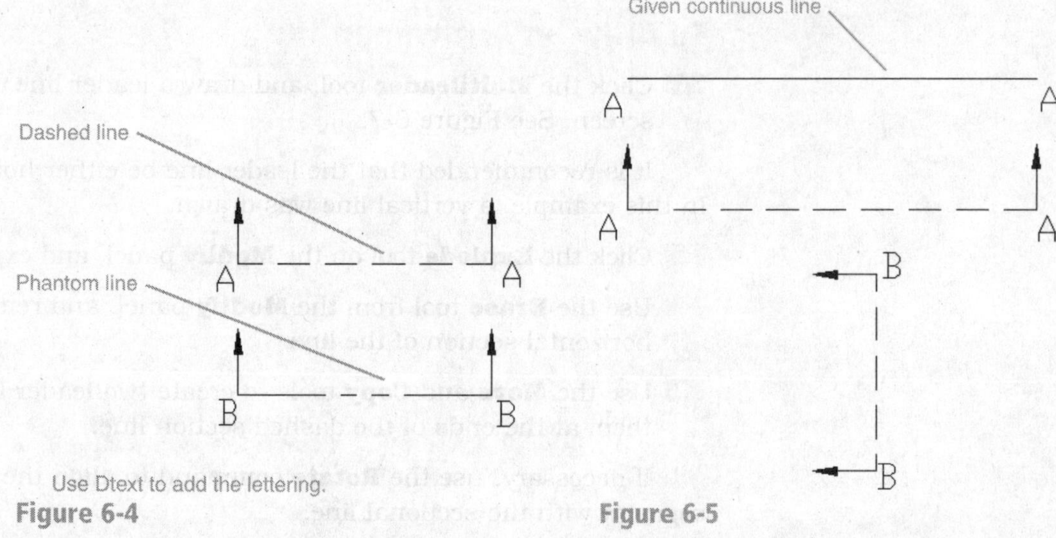

Figure 6-4

Figure 6-5

1. Type the word **linetype** in response to a command prompt.

   The **Linetype Manager** dialog box will appear.

2. Select **Load.**

   The **Load or Reload Linetypes** dialog box will appear. See Figure 6-6.

Figure 6-6

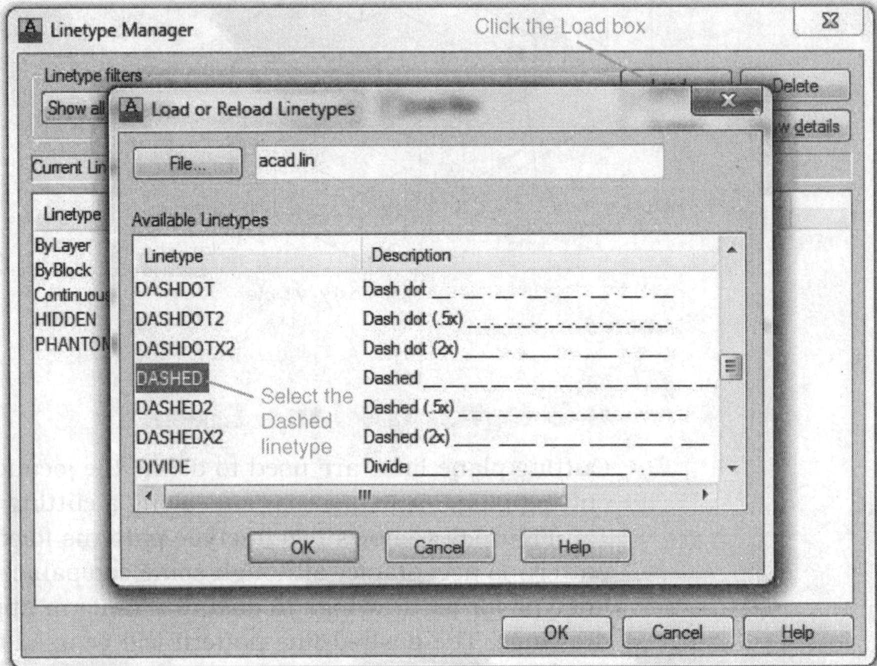

3. Select **Dashed** and **Phantom;** then return to the drawing screen.
4. Click line **A–A.**

   A **Properties** dialog box will appear.

5. Select the **Linetype** line on the **Properties** dialog box.
6. Scroll down the linetype listing, and select the **DASHED** option.
7. Close the **Properties** dialog box, and press the **<Esc>** key.

To Draw an Arrowhead

1. Click the **Multileader** tool, and draw a leader line on the drawing screen. See Figure 6-7.

   It is recommended that the leader line be either horizontal or vertical. In this example, a vertical line was drawn.

2. Click the **Explode** tool on the **Modify** panel, and explode the leader line.
3. Use the **Erase** tool from the **Modify** panel, and remove the short horizontal section of the line.
4. Use the **Move** and **Copy** tools to create two leader lines, and position them at the ends of the dashed section line.

   If necessary, use the **Rotate** command to align the arrowhead and line segment with the sectional line.

Figure 6-7

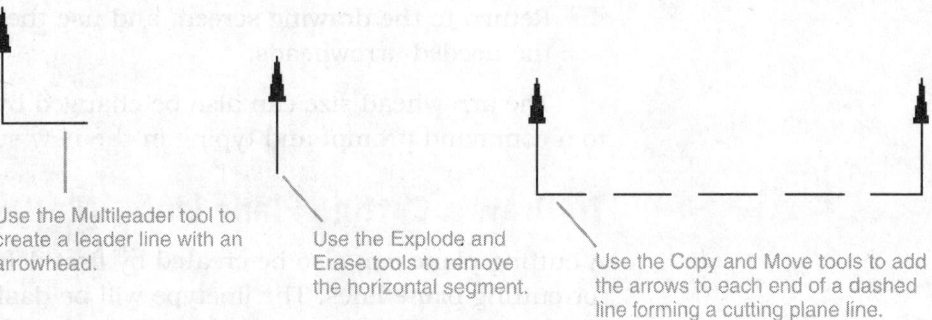

To Change the Size of an Arrowhead

Arrowheads used for cutting plane lines are usually drawn larger than arrowheads used for dimension lines. This serves to make them more distinctive and easier to find. The normal arrowhead scale factor is 0.19. In this example, the scale factor is 0.375.

1. Select the **Dimension Style Manager** from the **Dimensions** panel under the **Annotate** tab.

   The manager is accessed by clicking the arrow in the lower right corner of the **Dimensions** panel.

2. Select **Modify.**

   The **Modify Dimension Style: Standard** dialog box will appear. See Figure 6-8.

Figure 6-8

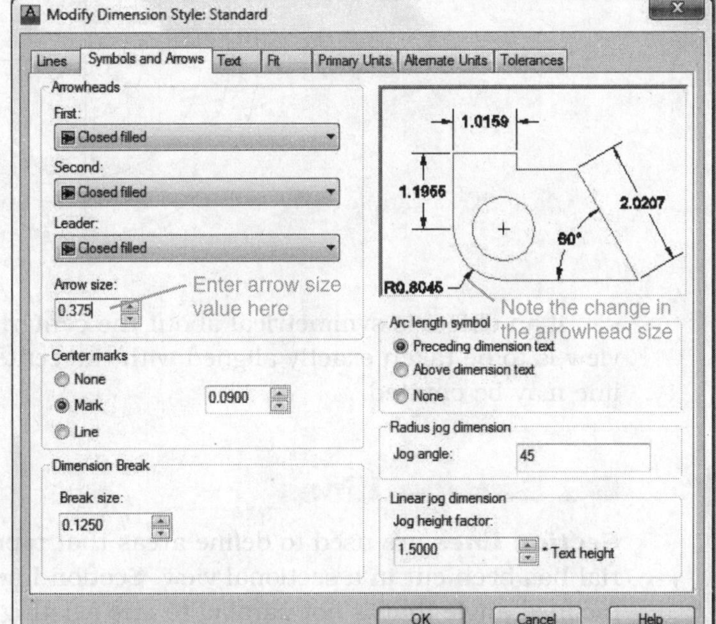

3. Select the **Symbols and Arrows** tab, and use the **Arrow size** box within the **Arrowheads** portion of the dialog box to change the arrowhead's scale factor (change to **0.3750**); click **OK.**

4 Return to the drawing screen, and use the **Multileader** tool to create the needed arrowheads.

The arrowhead size can also be changed by typing **dimasz** in response to a command prompt and typing in the new scale factor.

To Draw a Cutting Plane Line—Method II

A cutting plane can also be created by first defining a separate layer setup for cutting plane lines. The linetype will be dashed or phantom, and a color can be assigned if desired. Section 3-24 described how to create and work with layers.

To Draw Cutting Plane Lines

Cutting plane lines should extend beyond the edges of the object. See Figures 6-1, 6-2, and 6-3. A cutting plane line should extend far enough beyond the edges of the object so that there is a clear gap between the arrowhead and the edge of the object.

> **NOTE**
>
> If a cutting plane line is located directly on a centerline, it may be omitted. See Figure 6-9.

Figure 6-9

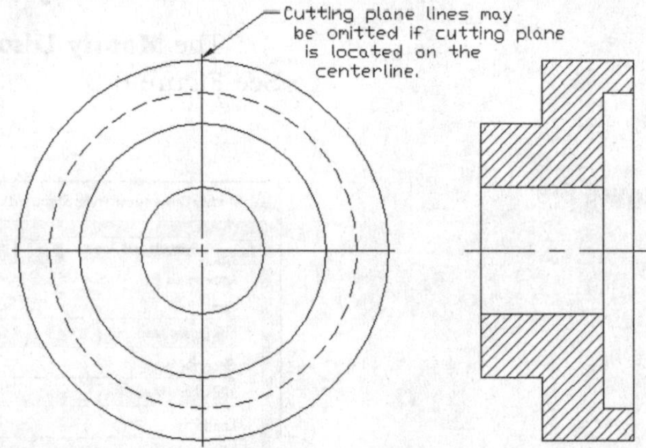

If an object is symmetrical about the centerline and only one sectional view is to be taken exactly aligned with the centerline, the cutting plane line may be omitted.

6-3 Section Lines

Section lines are used to define areas that represent where solid material has been cut in a sectional view. Section lines are evenly spaced at any inclined angle that is not parallel to any existing edge line and should be visually distinct from the continuous lines that define the boundary of the sectional view.

Figure 6-10 shows an area that includes uniform section lines evenly spaced at 45°. The other area shown in Figure 6-10 includes a 45° edge line; therefore, the section lines cannot be drawn at 45°. Lines at 135° (0° is horizontal to the right) were drawn instead.

Figure 6-11 shows an object that contains edge lines at both 45° and 135°. The section lines within this area were drawn at 60°.

If two or more parts are included within the same sectional view, each part must have visually different section lines. Figure 6-12 shows a sectional view that contains two parts. Part one's section lines were spaced 3 millimeters apart at 45°; part two's were spaced 3 millimeters apart at 135° (–45).

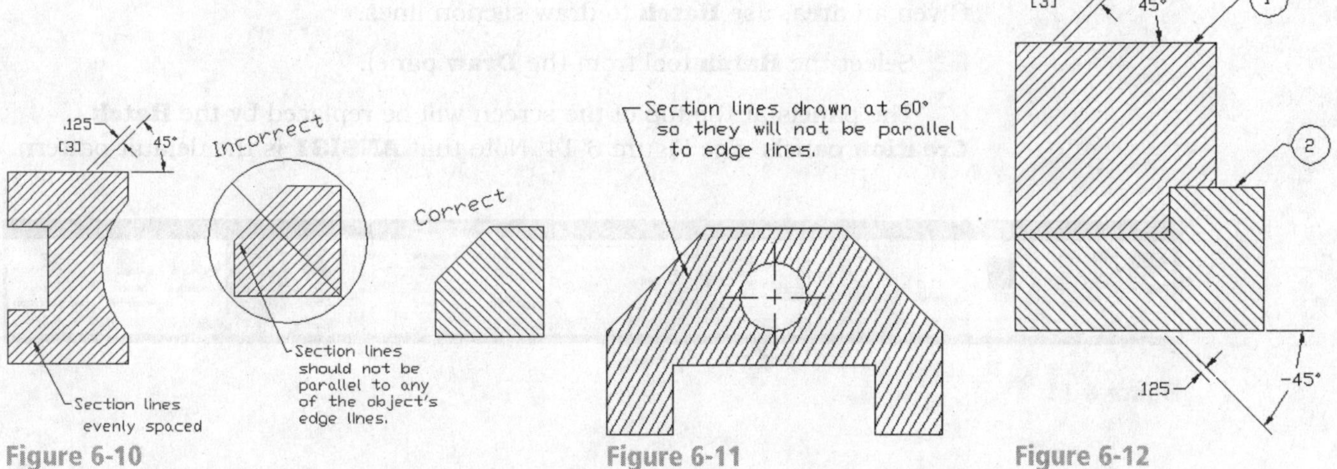

Figure 6-10

Figure 6-11

Figure 6-12

The recommended spacing for sectional lines is 0.125 inch or 3 millimeters, but smaller areas may use section lines spaced closer together than larger areas. See Figure 6-13. Section lines should never be spaced so close together as to look blurry or be so far apart that they are not clearly recognizable as section lines.

Figure 6-13

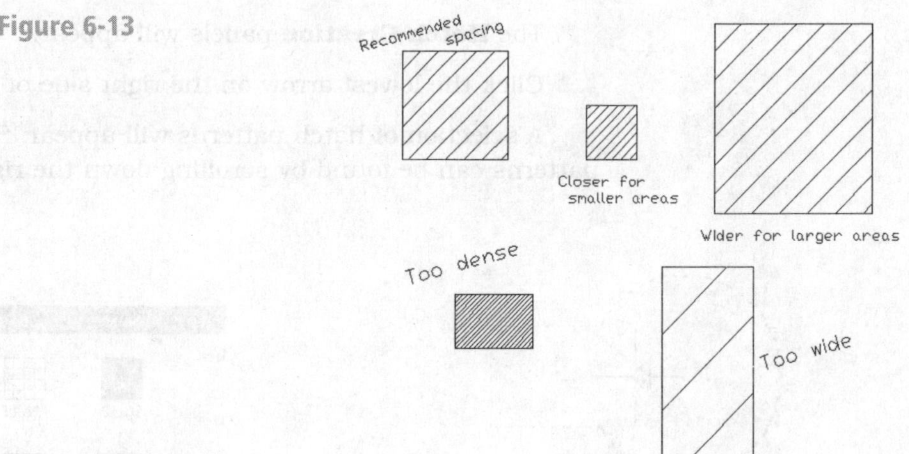

Evenly spaced sectional line patterns drawn at 45° are called *general* or *uniform* patterns; other patterns are available. Different section line patterns are used to help distinguish different materials. The different patterns allow the drawing reader to see what materials are used in a design without having to refer to the drawing's parts list. It should be noted that not all companies use different patterns to define material differences. When you are in doubt, the general pattern is usually acceptable.

How to draw different section line patterns is explained in Section 6-4.

6-4 Hatch

Section lines are drawn in AutoCAD by use of the **Hatch** tool, located on the **Draw** panel under the **Home** tab. The **Hatch** tool offers many different hatch patterns and spacings. The general pattern of evenly spaced lines at 45° is defined as pattern ANSI31 and is the default setting for the **Hatch** tool.

To Hatch a Given Area

Given an area, use **Hatch** to draw section lines.

1. Select the **Hatch** tool from the **Draw** panel.

The panels at the top of the screen will be replaced by the **Hatch Creation** panels. See Figure 6-14. Note that **ANSI31** is the default pattern.

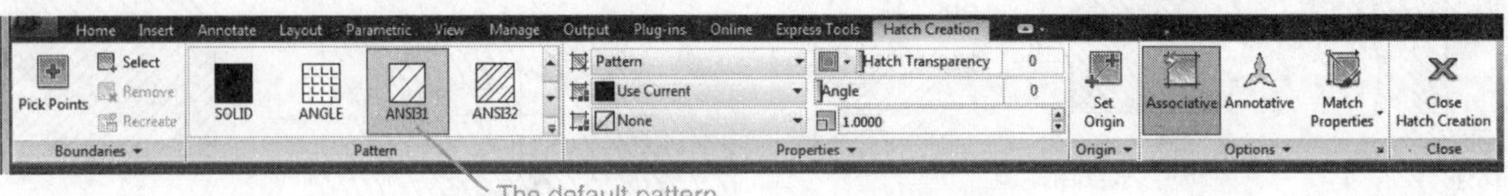

Figure 6-14

2. Select a point within the area to be hatched, and click the mouse.
3. Right-click the mouse, and select the **Enter** option.

The area will be hatched. See Figure 6-15.

To Change Hatch Patterns

1. Select the **Hatch** tool from the **Draw** panel.

The **Hatch Creation** panels will appear.

2. Click the lowest arrow on the right side of the **Pattern** panel.

A selection of hatch patterns will appear. See Figure 6-16. Additional patterns can be found by scrolling down the right side of the panel.

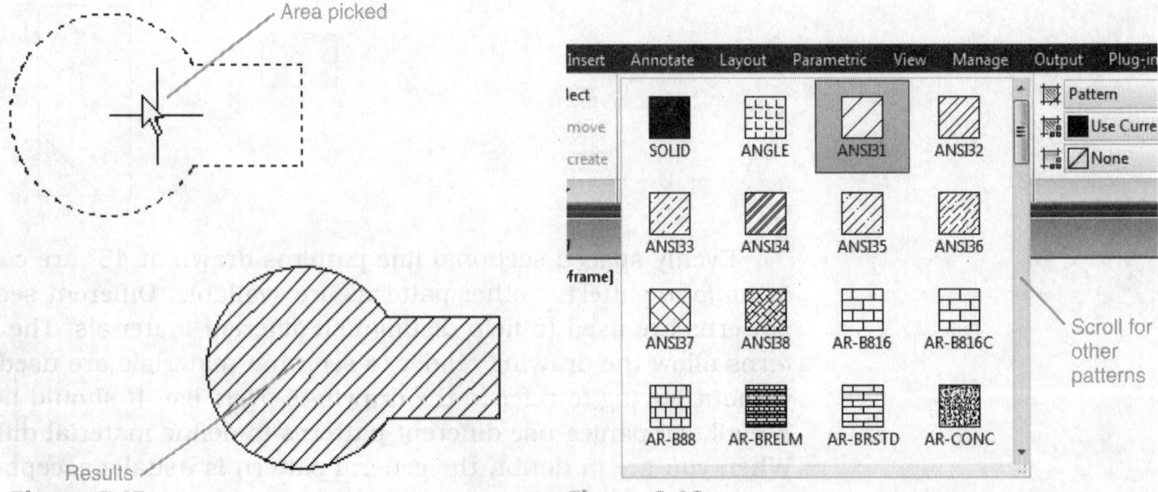

Figure 6-15 Figure 6-16

3. Select the desired pattern, and apply it as described previously.

Figure 6-17 shows three areas with three different hatch patterns applied.

Figure 6-17

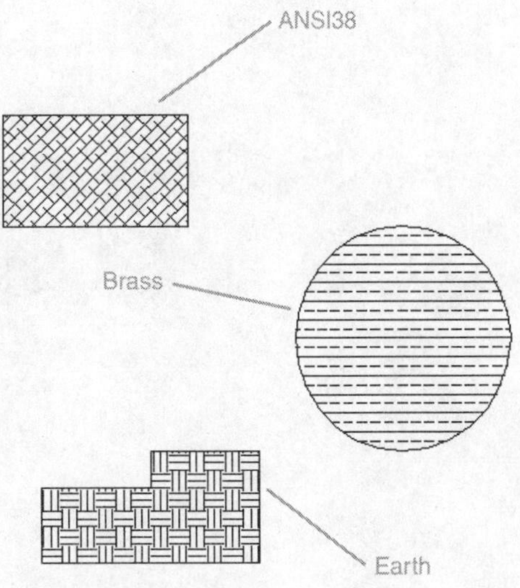

To Change the Spacing and Angle of a Hatch Pattern

1. Select the **Hatch** tool from the **Draw** panel.

The **Hatch Creation** panels will appear. See Figure 6-18. The **Angle** and **Scale** option boxes are located on the **Properties** panel.

2. Change the **Angle** to **15** and the **Scale** to **2.**

Figure 6-19 shows a comparison between an ANSI31 pattern created with the default values of 1 and 0°, and the adjusted pattern of 2 and 15°.

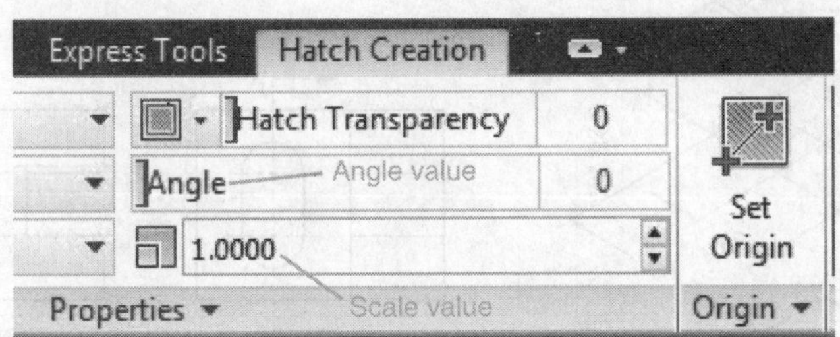

Figure 6-18

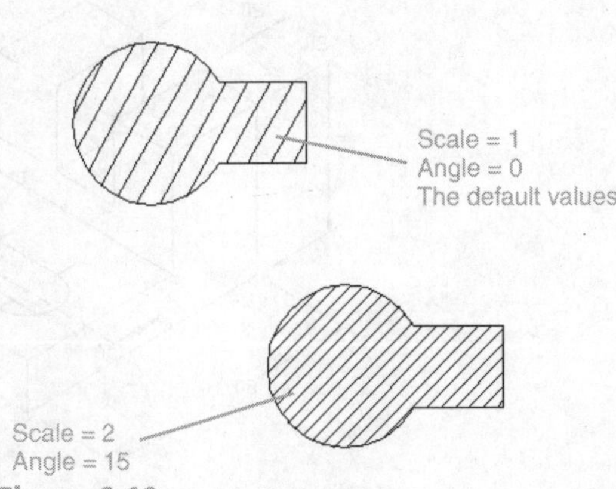

Figure 6-19

6-5 Sample Problem SP6-1

Figure 6-20 shows an object with a cutting plane line. Figure 6-21 shows how a front view and a sectional view of the object are created.

1 Draw the front orthographic view of the object, and lay out the height and width of the object on the basis of the given dimensions. Sectional

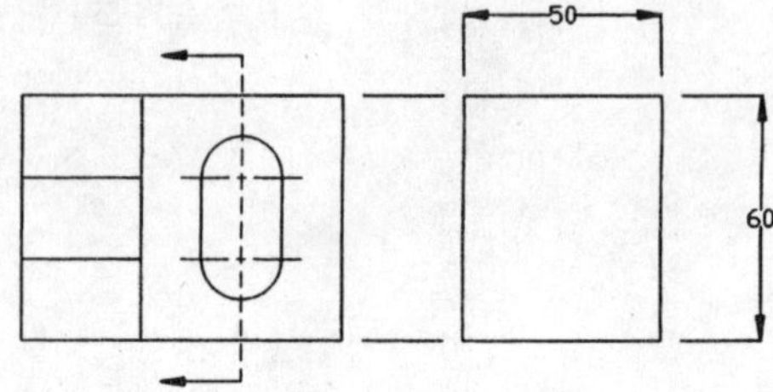

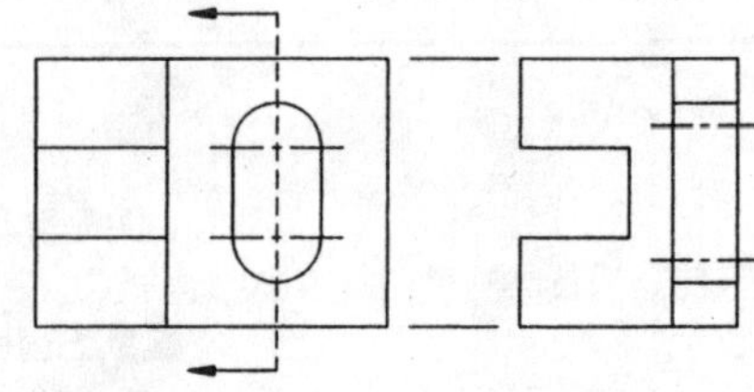

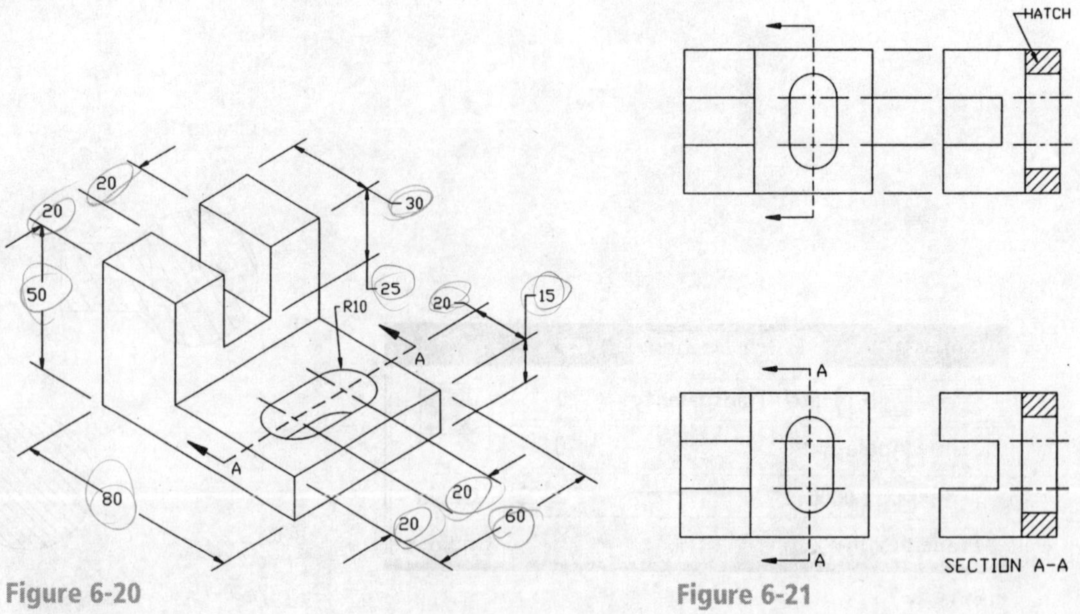

Figure 6-20

Figure 6-21

views must be directly aligned with the angle of the cutting plane line. Sectional views are, in fact, orthographic views that are based on the angle of the cutting plane line. Information is projected to sectional views as it was projected to top and side views. In this example, the cutting plane line is a vertical line, so horizontal projection lines are used to draw the sectional view.

2. Draw the object features. No hidden lines are drawn.

3. Use **Hatch** to draw sectional lines within the appropriate areas.

4. Erase or trim any excess lines.

5. Modify the color of the sectional lines if desired.

6. Save the drawing if desired.

6-6 Styles of Section Lines

AutoCAD has more than 50 different hatch patterns. The different patterns can be previewed in the **Swatch** option in the **Hatch Creation** panels.

Most of the available options are for architectural use. The patterns can be used to create elevation drawings and to add texture patterns to drawings of houses, buildings, and other structures. Technical drawings usually refer to objects made from steel, aluminum, or a composite material. There are hundreds of variations of each of these materials.

In general, if you decide to assign a particular pattern to a material, clearly state which pattern has been assigned to which material on the drawing. This is best done by including a note on the drawing that includes a picture of the pattern and the material that it is to represent. Figure 6-22 shows a drawing note for a hatch pattern used to represent SAE 1040 steel. The representation is unique for the drawing shown.

Figure 6-22

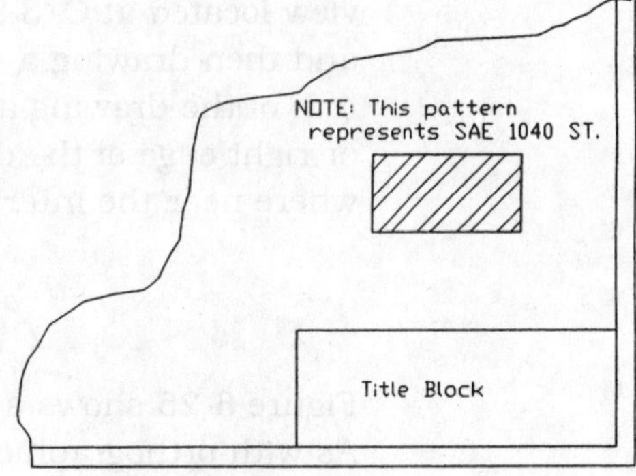

6-7 Sectional View Location

Sectional views should be located on a drawing behind the arrows. The arrows represent the viewing direction for the sectional view. See Figure 6-23. If it is impossible to locate sectional views behind the arrows, they may be located above or below, but still behind, the arrowed portion of the cutting plane line. Sectional views should never be located in front of the arrows.

Sectional views located on a different drawing sheet than the cutting plane line must be cross referenced to the appropriate cutting plane line. See Figure 6-24. The boxed notation C/3 SHT2 next to the cutting plane line means that the sectional view may be found in zone C/3 on sheet 2 of the drawing.

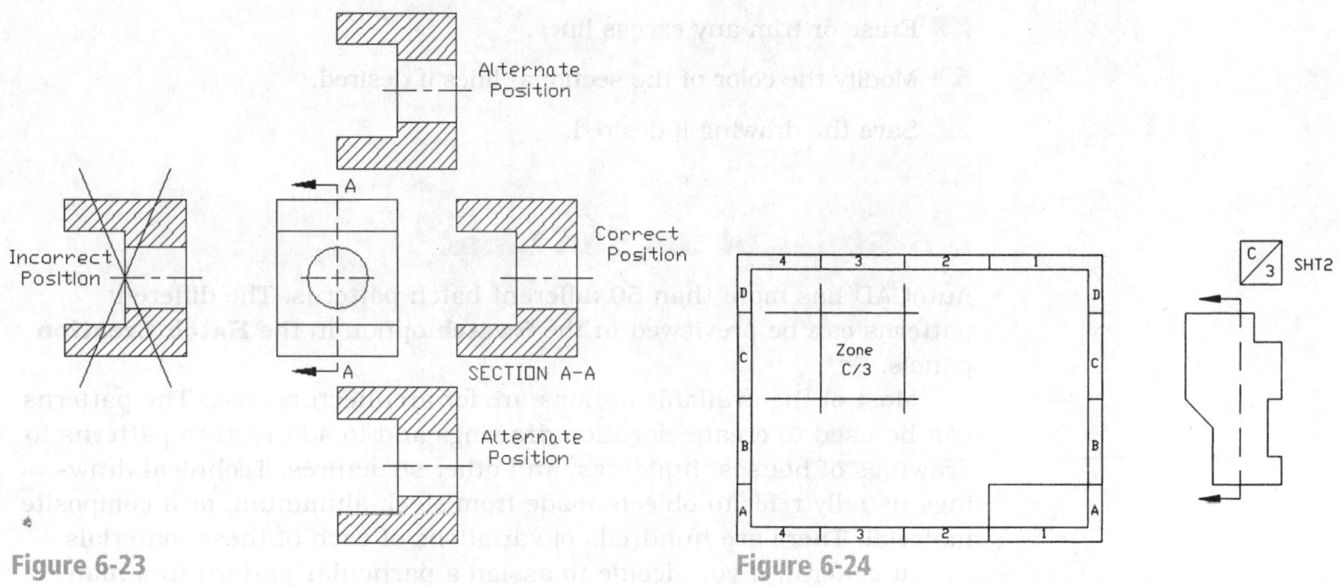

Figure 6-23

Figure 6-24

The location of the sectional view must be referenced to the cutting plane line if the view's location is not near the cutting plane. The notation C/3 SHT2 defines the location of the cutting plane line for the sectional view.

The reference numbers and letters are based on a drawing area charting system similar to that used for locating features on maps. A sectional view located at C/3 SHT2 can be found by going to sheet 2 of the drawing and then drawing a vertical line from the box marked 3 at the top or bottom of the drawing and a horizontal line from the box marked C on the left or right edge of the drawing. The sectional view should be located somewhere near the intersection of the two lines.

6-8 Holes in Sections

Figure 6-25 shows a sectional view of an object that contains three holes. As with orthographic views, a conical point must be included on holes that do not completely penetrate the object.

A common mistake is to omit the back edge of a hole when drawing a sectional view. Figure 6-25 shows a hole drilled through an object. Note that the sectional view includes a straight line across the top and bottom edges of the view that represents the back edges of the hole.

Figure 6-26 shows a countersunk hole, a counterbored hole, a spotface, and a hole through a boss. Again, any hole that does not completely penetrate the object must include a conical point.

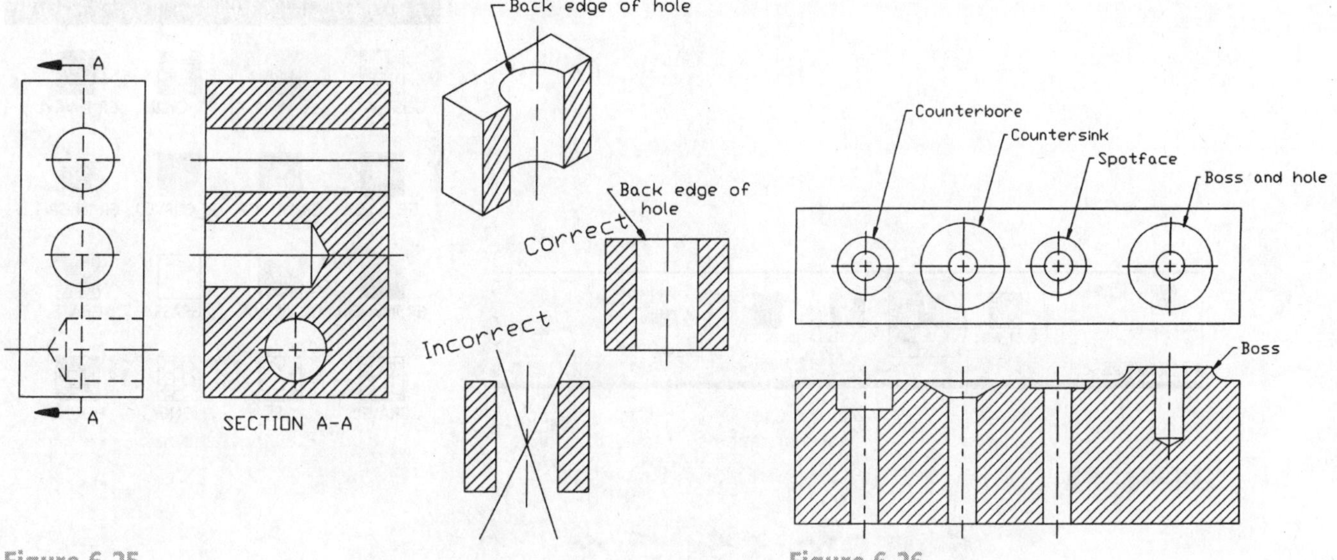

Figure 6-25

Figure 6-26

6-9 Gradients

In AutoCAD, a ***gradient*** is shading that varies in intensity. Figure 6-27 shows a rectangular shape with two internal circles. The figure also shows the same shape with various gradients added.

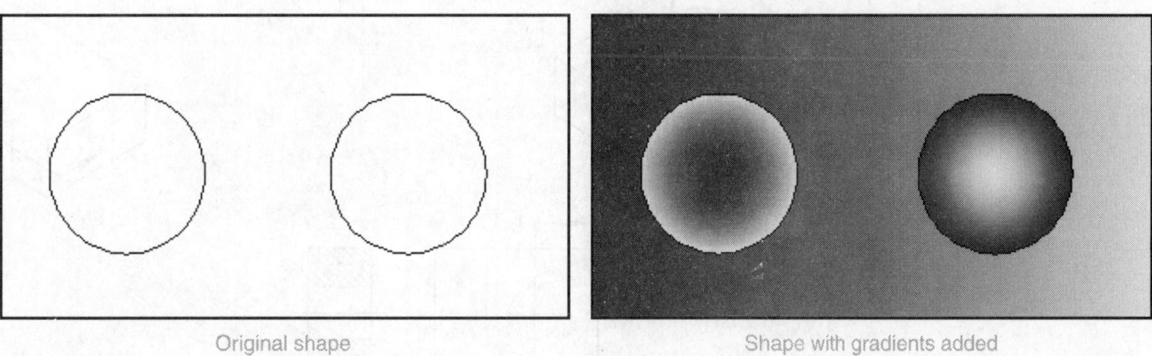

Figure 6-27

To Create a Gradient

1. Select the **Gradient** tool from the **Draw** panel.

   The **Hatch Creation** panels will appear. See Figure 6-28.

2. Click a point within the area to which to apply the gradient.

3. Right-click the mouse, and select the **Enter** option.

The gradient's pattern, color, angle, and density, among other properties, are controlled through the **Hatch Creation** panels. Figure 6-28 shows some additional patterns available.

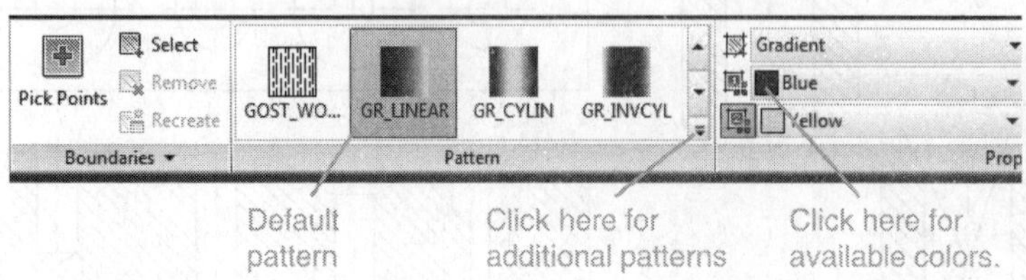

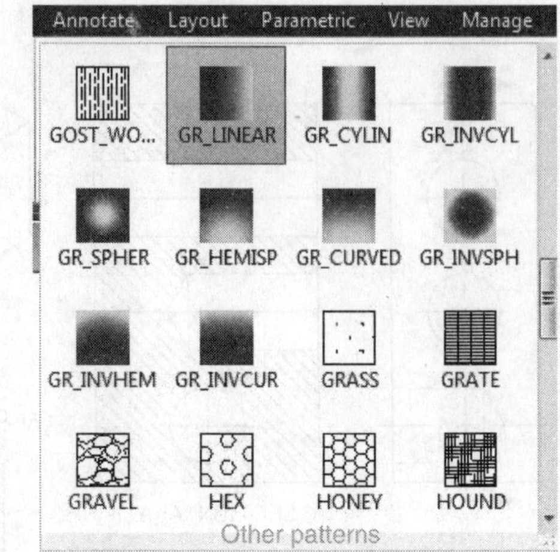

Figure 6-28

6-10 Offset Sections

Cutting plane lines need not be drawn as straight lines across the surface of an object. They may be stepped so that more features can be included in the sectional view. See Figure 6-29. In the object shown in Figure 6-29, the cutting plane line crosses two holes and a directly visible open surface that contains a hole. There is no indication in the sectional view that the cutting plane line has been offset.

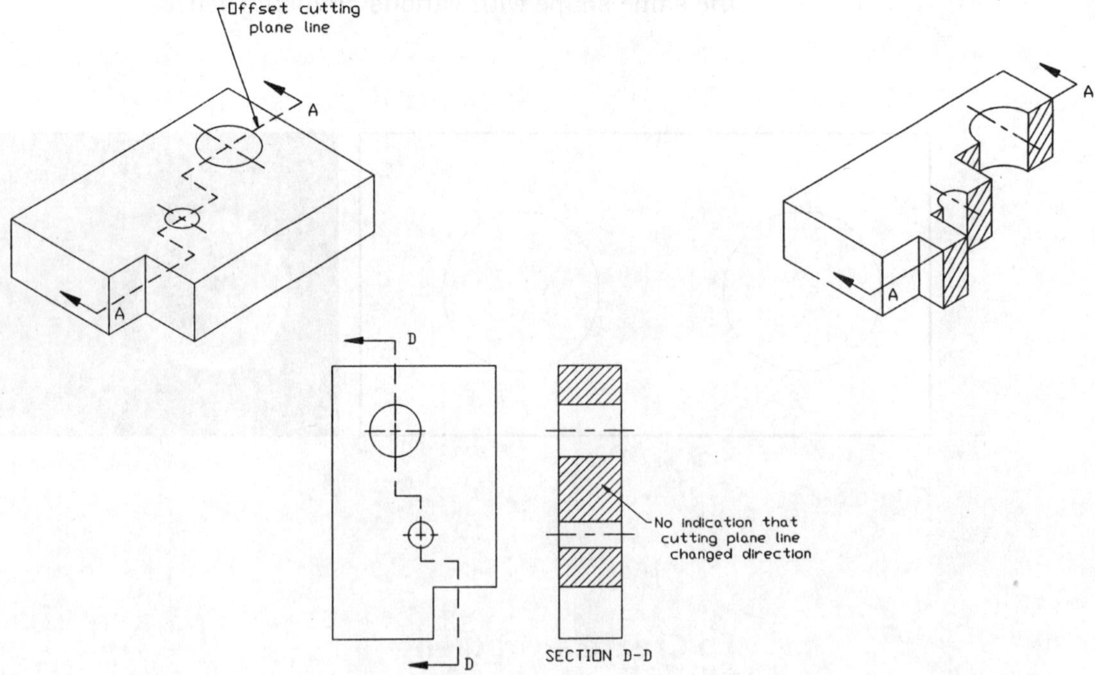

Figure 6-29

Cutting plane lines should be placed to include as many features as possible without causing confusion. The intent of using sectional views is to simplify views and to clarify the drawing. Several features can be included on the same cutting plane line so that fewer views are used, giving the drawing a less cluttered look and making it easier for the reader to understand the shape of the object's features.

Figure 6-30 shows another example of an offset cutting plane line.

Figure 6-30

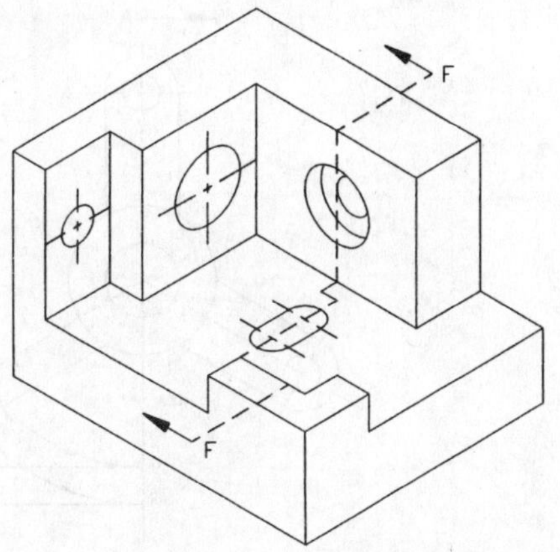

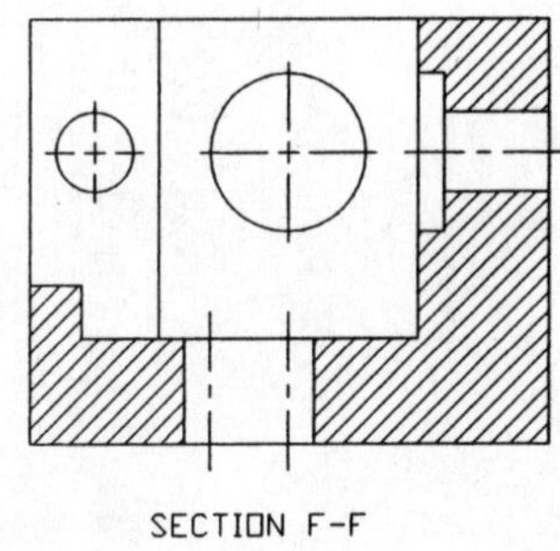

6-11 Multiple Sections

More than one sectional view may be taken from the same orthographic view. Figure 6-31 shows a drawing that includes three sectional views, all taken from a front view. Each cutting plane line is labeled with a letter. The letters, in turn, are used to identify the appropriate sectional view. Identifying letters are also placed at the ends of the cutting plane lines, behind the arrowheads. Identifying letters are also placed below the sectional view and written in the format SECTION A-A, SECTION B-B, and so on. The abbreviation SECT may also be used: SECT A-A, SECT B-B.

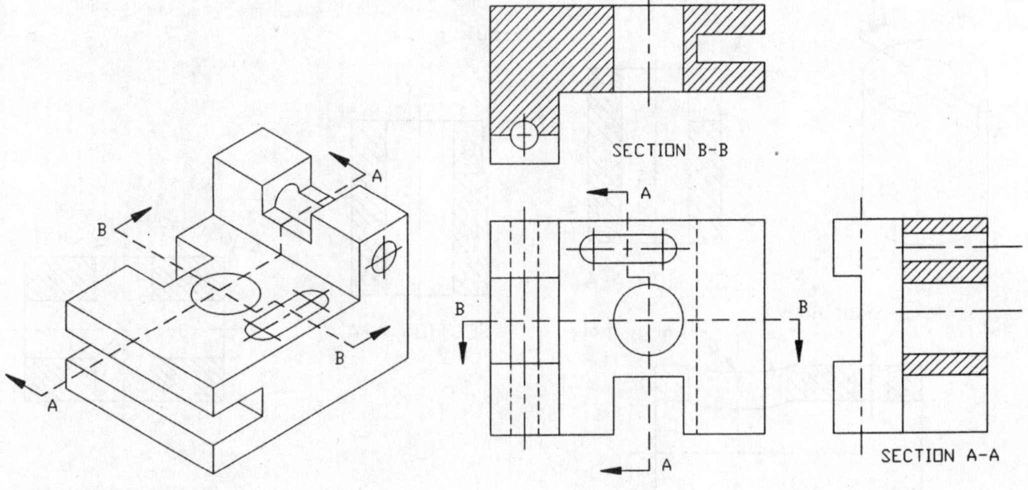

Figure 6-31

The letters I, O, and X are generally not used to identify sectional views, because they can easily be misread. If more than 23 sectional views are used, the lettering starts again with double letters: AA-AA, BB-BB, and so on.

6-12 Aligned Sections

Cutting plane lines taken at angles on circular shapes may be aligned, as shown in Figure 6-32. Aligning the sectional views prevents the foreshortening that would result if the view were projected from the original cutting plane line location. A foreshortened view would not present an accurate picture of the object's surfaces.

Figure 6-32

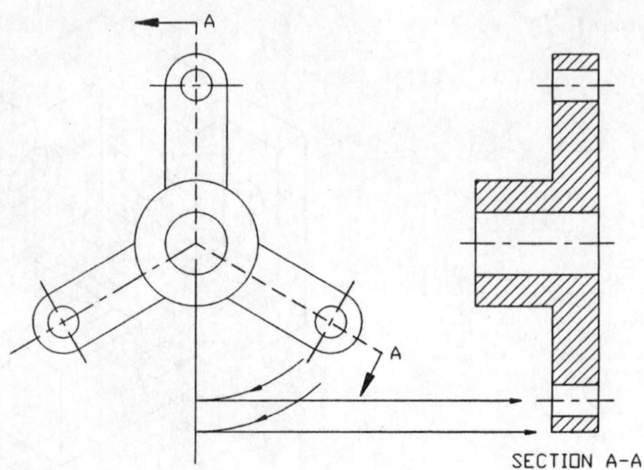

6-13 Drawing Conventions in Sections

Slots and small holes that penetrate cylindrical surfaces may be drawn as straight lines, as shown in Figure 6-33. Larger holes—that is, holes whose diameters are greater than the radii of their cylinders—should be drawn showing an elliptical curvature.

Intersecting holes are represented by crossed lines, as shown in Figure 6-34. The crossed lines are drawn from the intersecting corners of the holes.

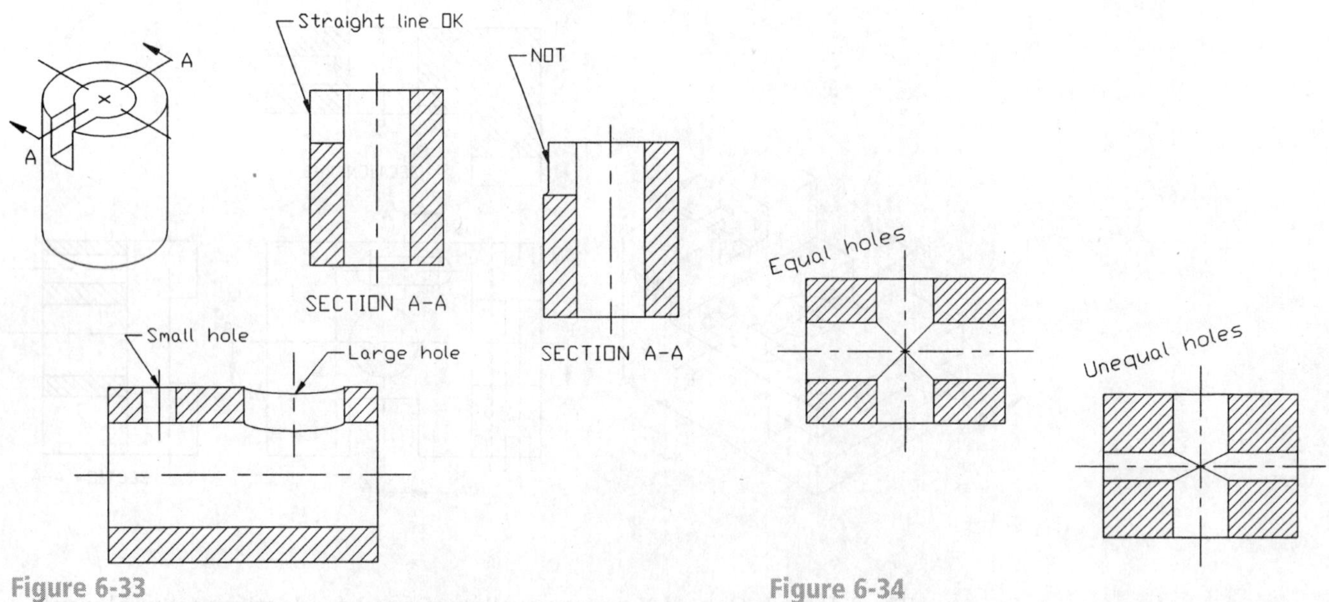

Figure 6-33

Figure 6-34

6-14 Half, Partial, and Broken-Out Sectional Views

Half and partial sectional views allow a designer to show an object by an orthographic view and a sectional view within one view. A half-sectional view is shown in Figure 6-35. Half of the view is a sectional view; the other half is a normal orthographic view including hidden lines. The cutting plane line is drawn as shown and includes an arrowhead at only one end of the line.

Figure 6-36 shows a partial sectional view. It is similar to a half-sectional view, but the sectional view is taken at a location other than directly on a centerline or one defined by a cutting plane line. A broken line is used to separate the sectional view from the orthographic view. A broken line is a freehand line drawn through the **Sketch** command.

Broken-out sectional views are like small partial views. They are used to show only small internal portions of an object. Figure 6-37 shows a broken-out sectional view. Broken lines are used to separate the broken-out section from the rest of the orthographic views.

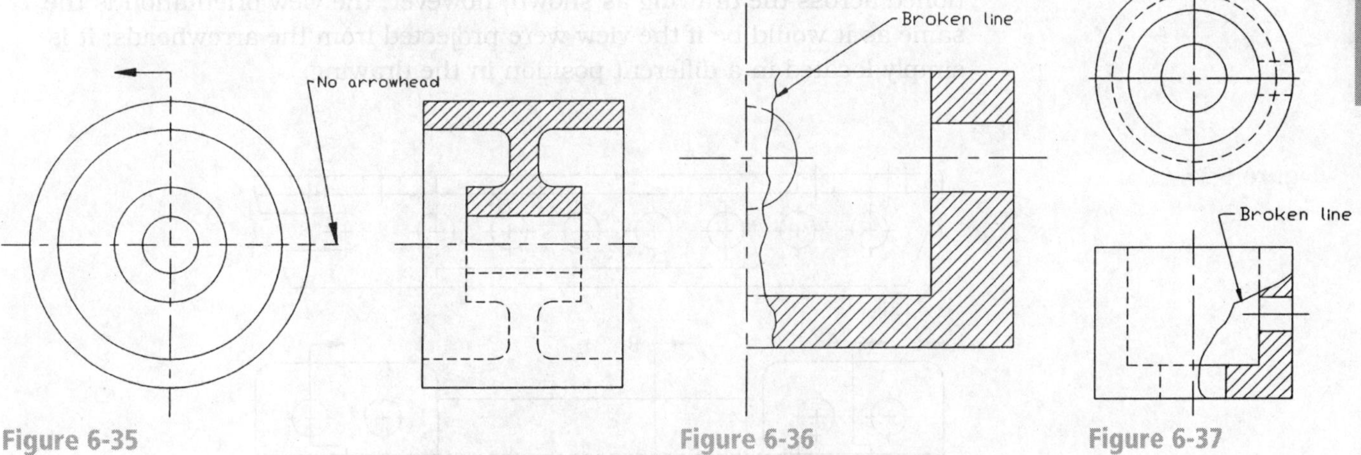

Figure 6-35

Figure 6-36

Figure 6-37

To Draw a Broken Line

1 Type **Sketch** in response to a command prompt.

Command:_sketch

Record Increment <0.1000>:

2 Press **Enter**.

Sketch. Pen eXit Quit Record Erase Connect:

3 Press the left mouse button.

<Pen down>

4 Move the cursor across the screen. A green freehand line will emerge from the crosshairs as it is moved.

5 Press the left mouse button again.

<Pen up>

The crosshairs can now be moved without producing a sketched line.

6 Select **RECORD** from the menu.

23 lines recorded

The number of lines generated and recorded will depend on the length of the line and the size of the line increment.

7 Select **eXit** from the menu.

Command:

Do *not* use the right mouse button to exit the **Sketch** command. If the right mouse button is pressed, a line will be drawn from the end of the sketched line to the present location of the crosshairs. Use **eXit** to end the **Sketch** command.

6-15 Removed Sectional Views

Removed sectional views are used to show how an object's shape changes over its length. Removed sectional views are most often used with long objects whose shape changes continuously over its length. See Figure 6-38. The sectional views are not positioned behind the arrowheads, but are positioned across the drawing as shown; however, the view orientation is the same as it would be if the view were projected from the arrowheads; it is simply located in a different position in the drawing.

Figure 6-38

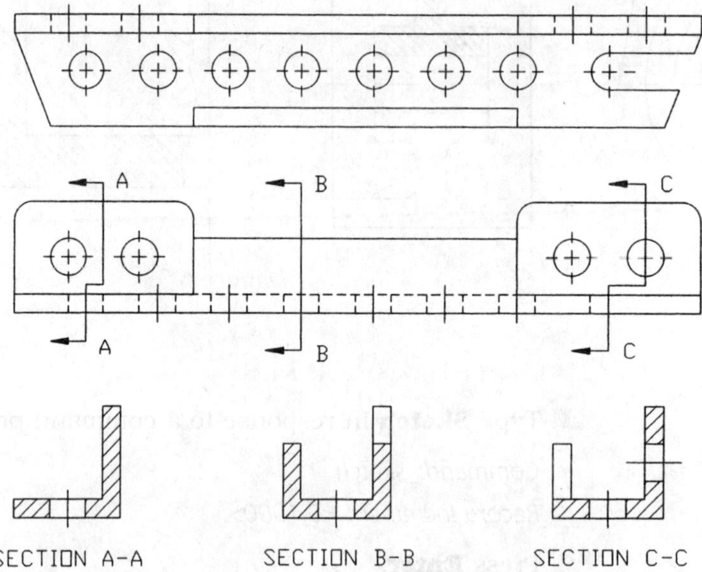

It is good practice to identify the cutting plane lines and the sectional views in alphabetical order. This will make it easier for the drawing's readers to find the sectional views.

6-16 Breaks

It is often convenient to break long continuous shapes so that they take up less drawing space. There are two drawing conventions used to show breaks: *freehand lines* used for rectangular shapes, and *S-breaks* used for cylindrical shapes. See Figure 6-39. Freehand break lines are drawn by use of the **Sketch** command as explained in Section 6-14. Instructions for drawing S-breaks follow.

To Draw an S-Break (See Figure 6-40.)

1. Draw a rectangular view of the cylindrical object, and draw a construction line where the break is to be located. The rectangular view should include a centerline.

Figure 6-39

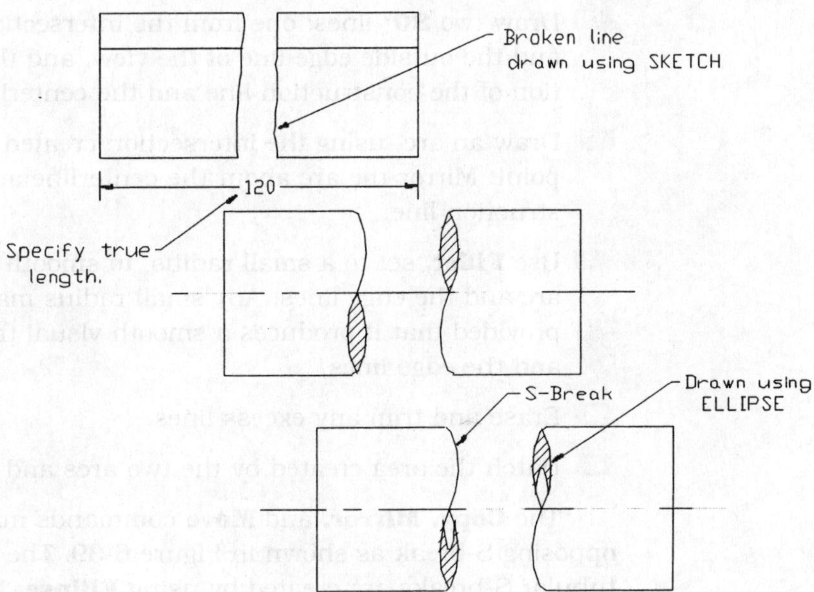

Figure 6-40

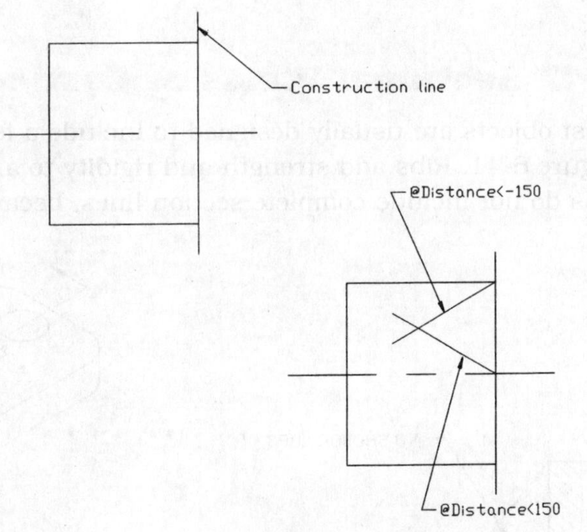

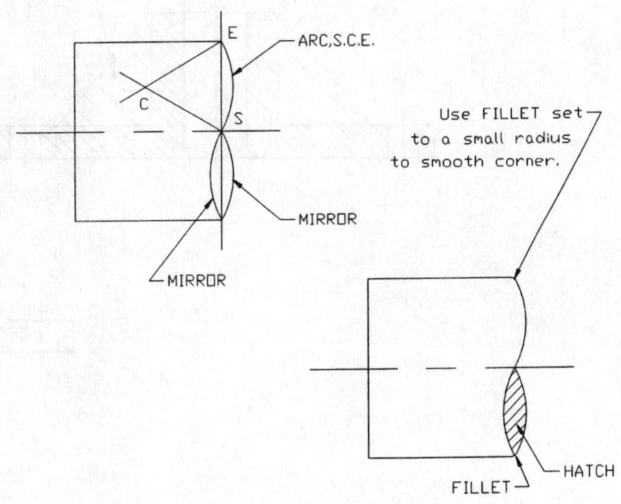

2. Draw two **30°** lines: one from the intersection of the construction line and the outside edge line of the view, and the other from the intersection of the construction line and the centerline as shown.

3. Draw an arc, using the intersection created in step 2 as the center point. Mirror the arc about the centerline and then about the construction line.

4. Use **Fillet,** set to a small radius, to smooth the corners between the arc and the edge lines. Any small radius may be used for the fillet, provided that it produces a smooth visual transition between the arc and the edge lines.

5. Erase and trim any excess lines.

6. Hatch the area created by the two arcs and fillet as shown.

The **Copy, Mirror,** and **Move** commands may be used to create the opposing S-break as shown in Figure 6-39. The internal shapes of the tubular S-breaks are created by using **Ellipse.** Position the end of the ellipse according to the thickness specifications, and determine the elliptical shape by eye. Trim the sectional lines from the inside of the ellipse.

6-17 Sectional Views of Castings

Cast objects are usually designed to include a feature called a ***rib.*** See Figure 6-41. Ribs add strength and rigidity to an object. Sectional views of ribs do not include complete section lines, because this is considered mis-

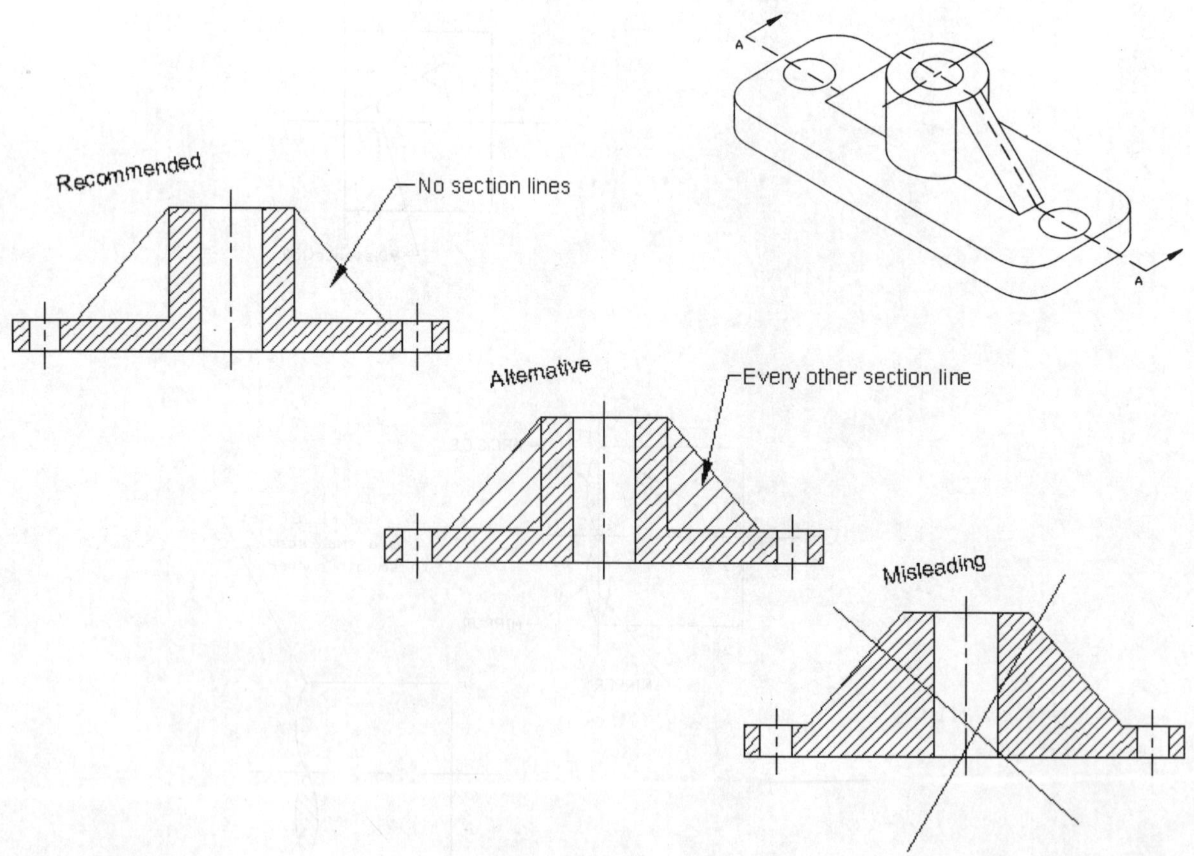

Figure 6-41

leading to the reader. Ribs are usually narrow, and a large sectioned area gives the impression of a denser and stronger area than is actually on the casting.

There are two conventions used to present sectional views of cast ribs: one that does not draw any section lines on the ribs, and one that puts every other section line on the rib. Sectional views of castings that do not include section lines on ribs are created by using **Hatch** for those areas that are to be hatched.

Chapter 6

6-18 EXERCISE PROBLEMS

Draw a complete front view and a sectional view of the objects in Exercise Problems EX6-1 through EX6-4. The cutting plane line is located on the vertical centerline of the object.

EX6-1 Millimeters

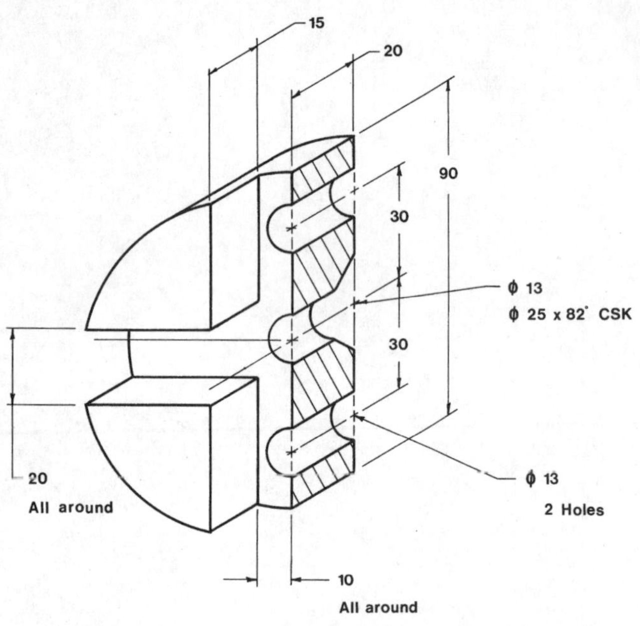

EX6-2 Millimeters

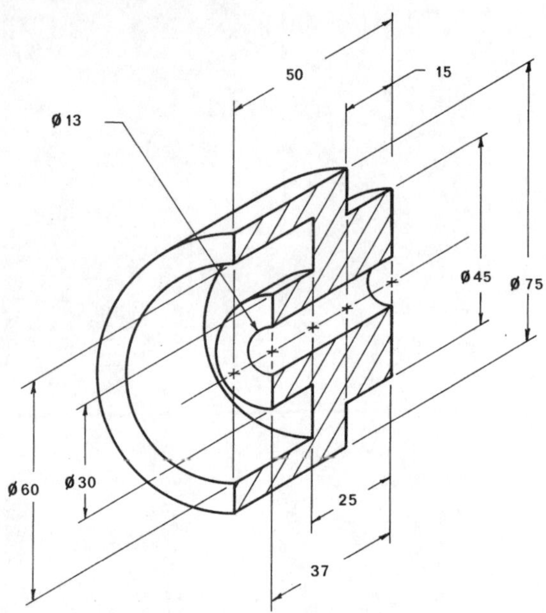

EX6-3 Inches

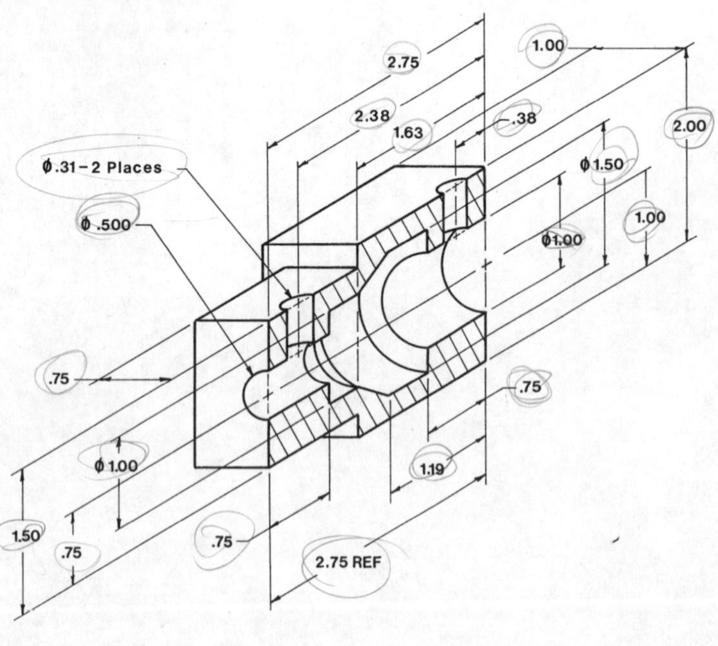

EX6-4 Millimeters

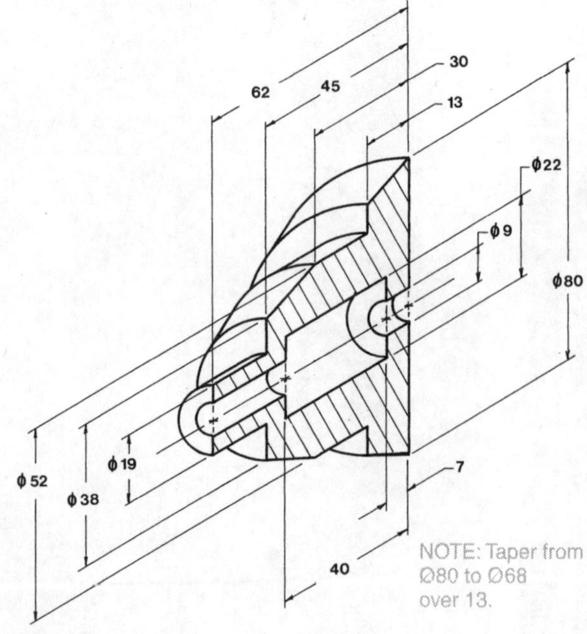

Draw the following sectional views, using the given dimensions:

EX6-5

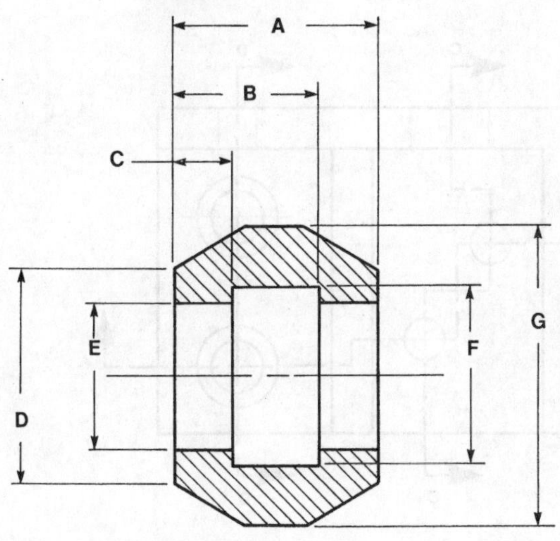

DIMENSIONS	INCHES	mm
A	.50	12
B	1.25	32
C	1.75	44
D	Ø1.75	44
E	Ø1.25	32
F	Ø1.50	38
G	Ø2.50	64

EX6-6

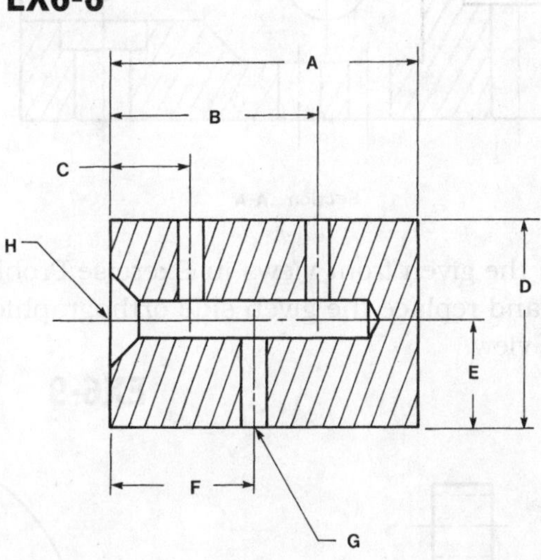

DIMENSIONS	INCHES	mm
A	3.00	72
B	2.00	48
C	.75	18
D	2.00	48
E	1.00	24
F	1.38	33
G	Ø.25	6
H	Ø.375 X 2.50 DEEP Ø.875 X 82° CSINK	Ø10 X 60 DEEP Ø24 X 82° CSINK

Resketch the given top view and Section A-A; then sketch Sections B-B, C-C, and D-D.

EX6-7

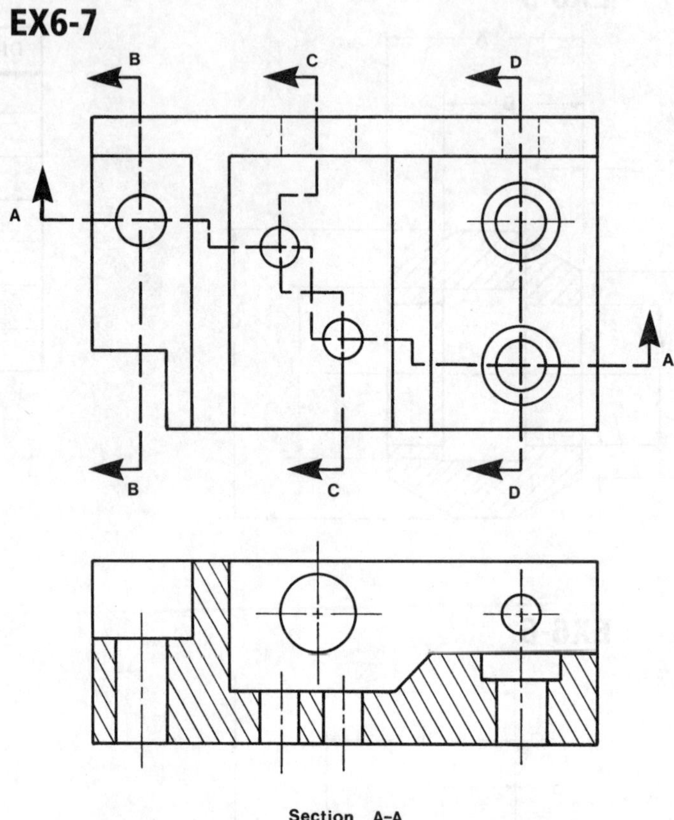

Section A-A

Resketch the given front views in Exercise Problems EX6-8 through EX6-11, and replace the given side orthographic view with the appropriate sectional view.

EX6-8

EX6-9

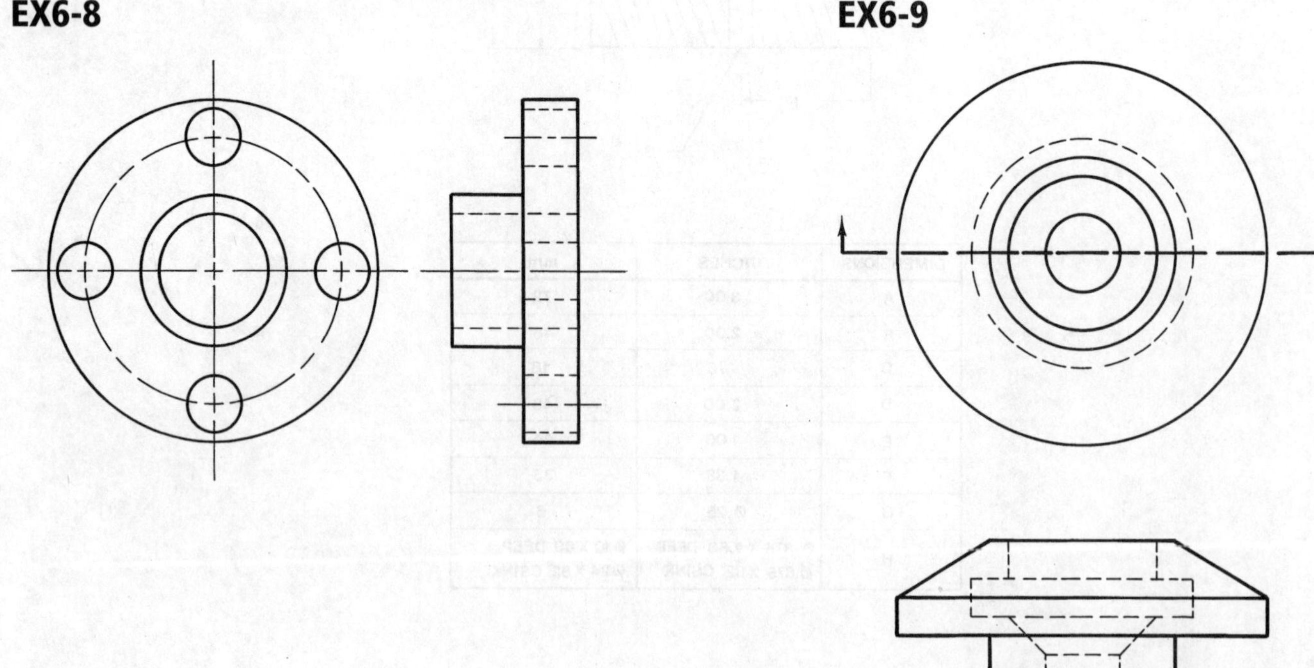

EX6-10 Inches

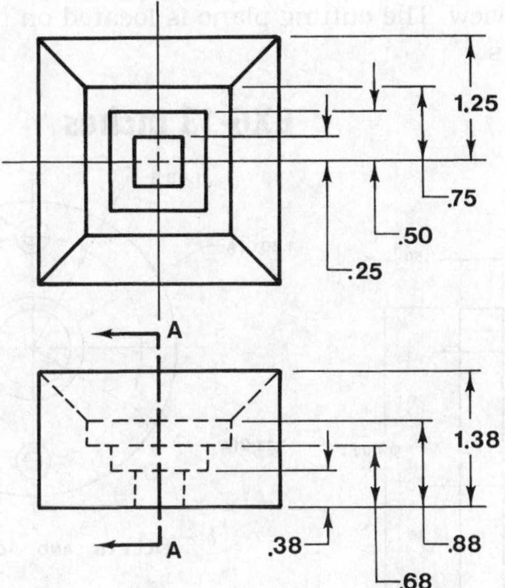

Object is symmetrical about both centerlines

EX6-11

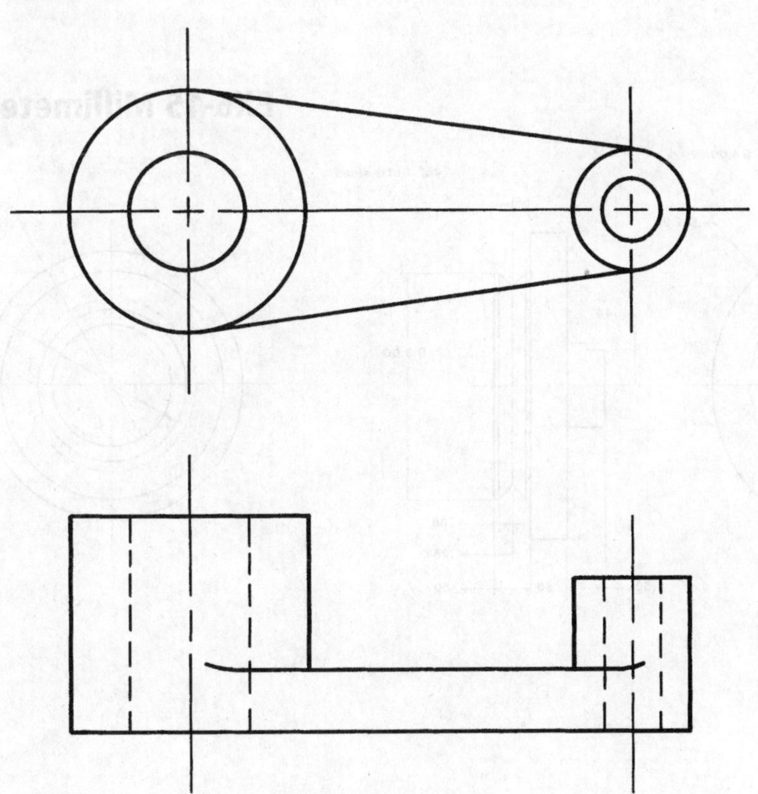

Redraw the given front views in Exercise Problems EX6-12 through EX6-15, and replace the given side orthographic view with the appropriate sectional view. The cutting plane is located on the vertical centerlines of the objects.

EX6-12 Inches

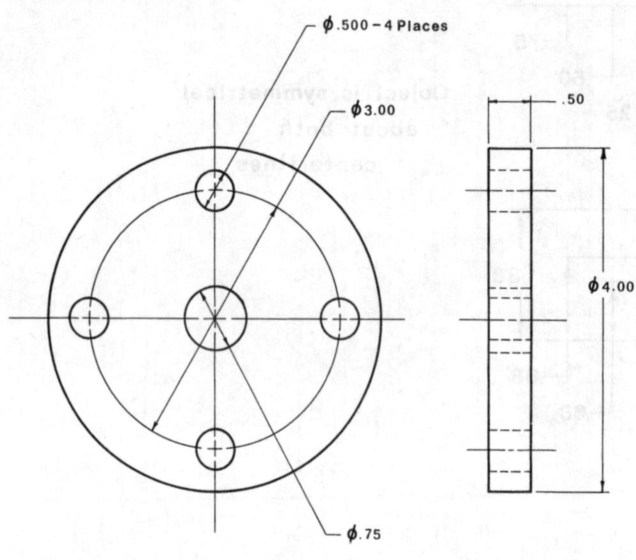

EX6-13 Inches

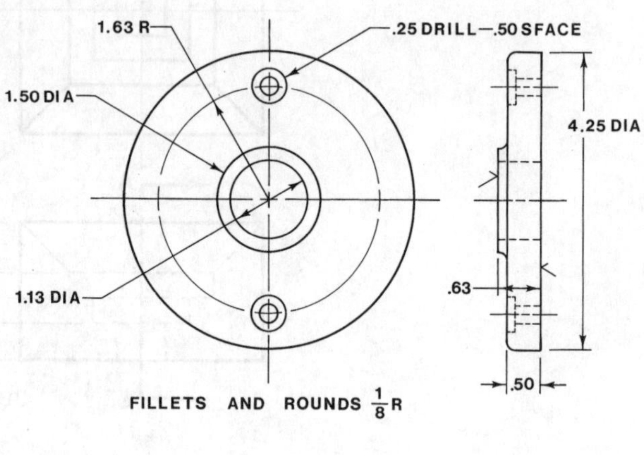

EX6-14 Inches

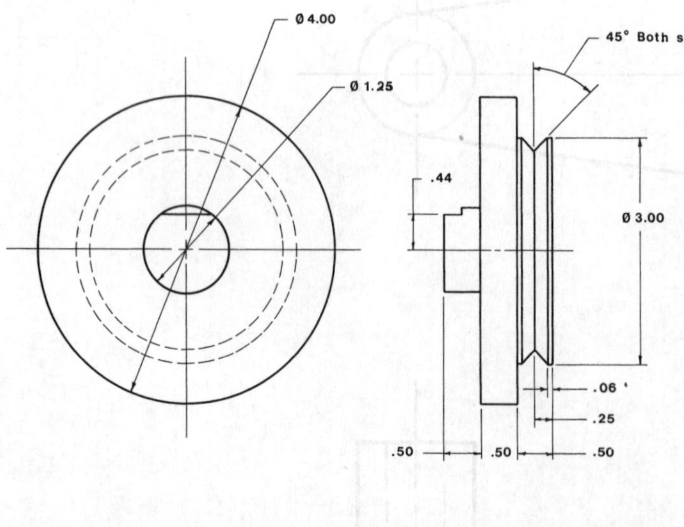

EX6-15 Millimeters

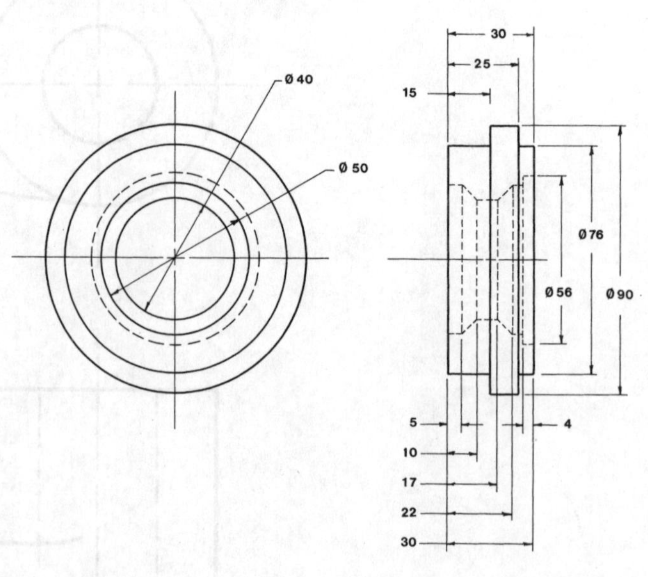

Draw the top orthographic view and the indicated sectional view.

EX6-16 Millimeters

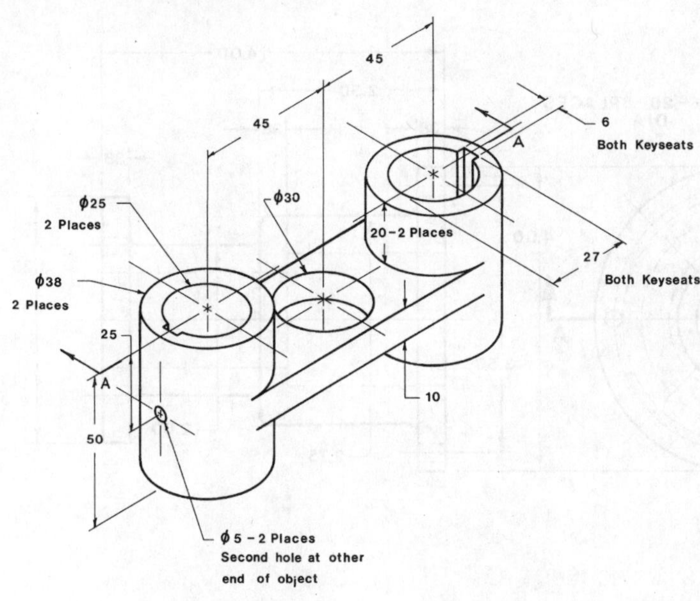

EX6-17 Inches

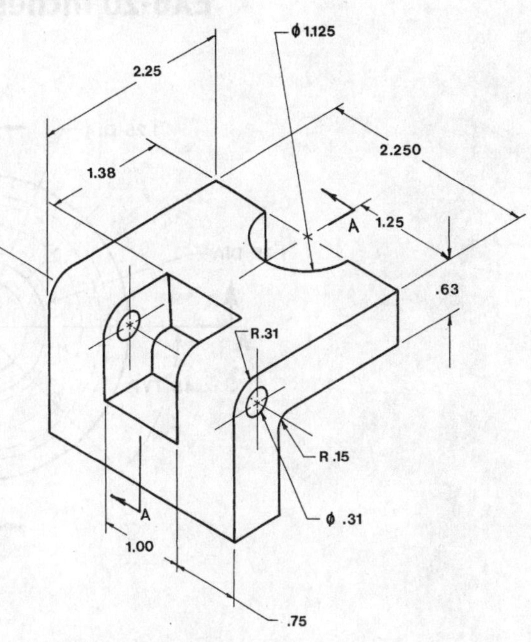

EX6-18 Millimeters

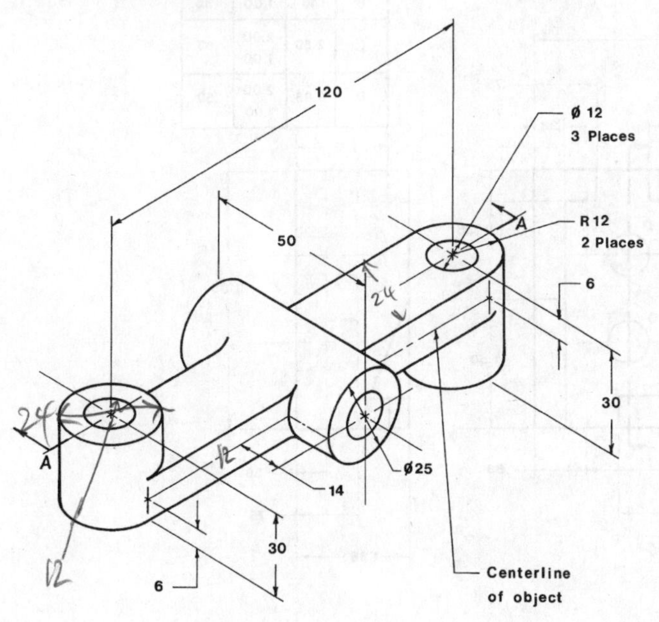

EX6-19 Millimeters

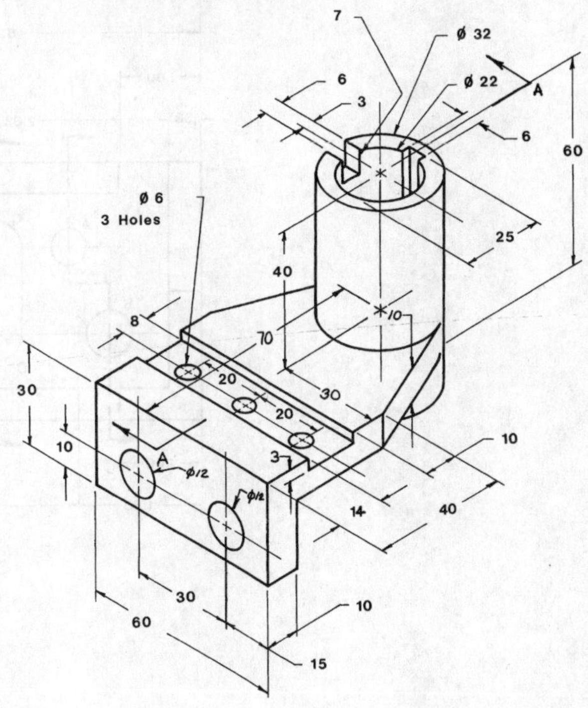

Redraw the given views, and add the specified sectional views in Exercise Problems EX6-20 through EX6-34.

EX6-20 Inches

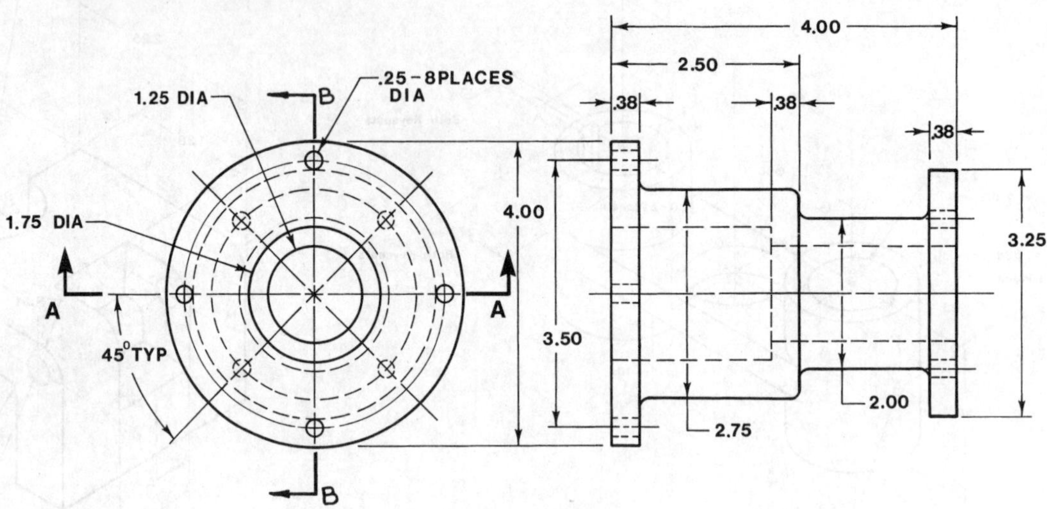

ALL FILLETS AND ROUNDS = R.125

EX6-21 Inches

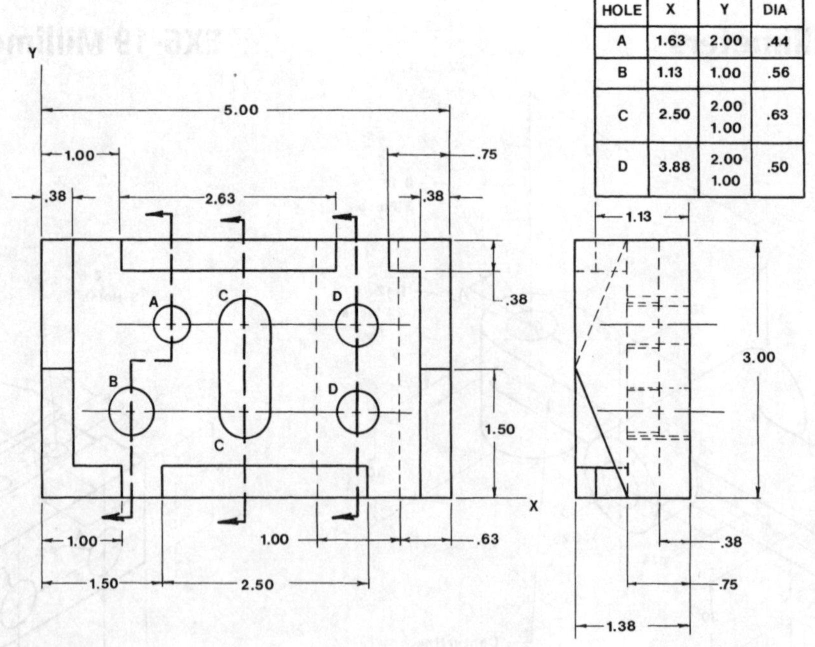

HOLE	X	Y	DIA
A	1.63	2.00	.44
B	1.13	1.00	.56
C	2.50	2.00 1.00	.63
D	3.88	2.00 1.00	.50

EX6-22 Inches

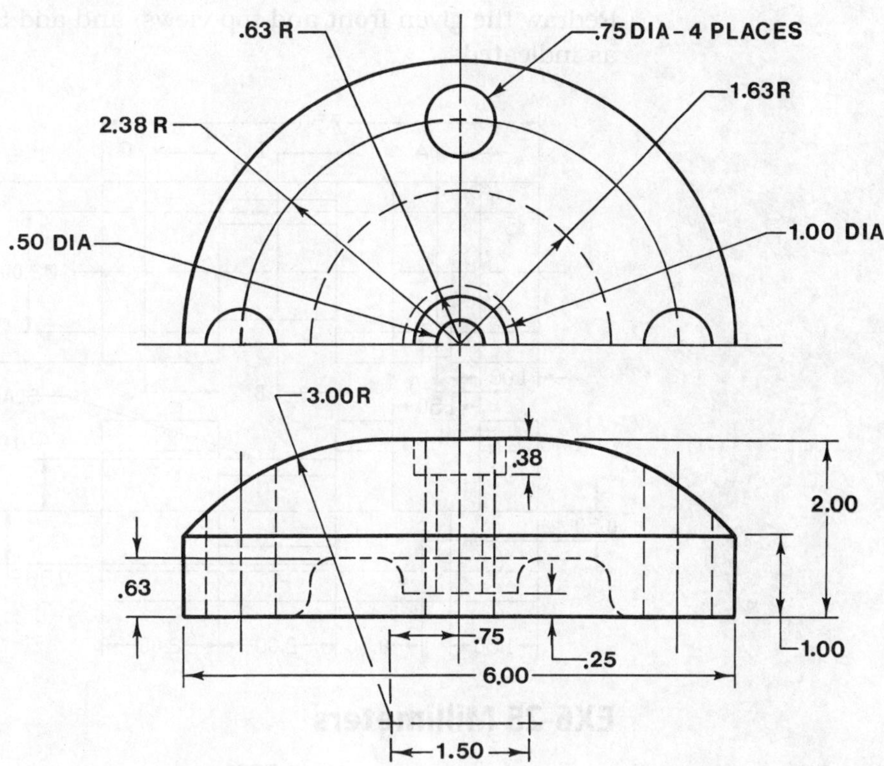

EX6-23 Inches

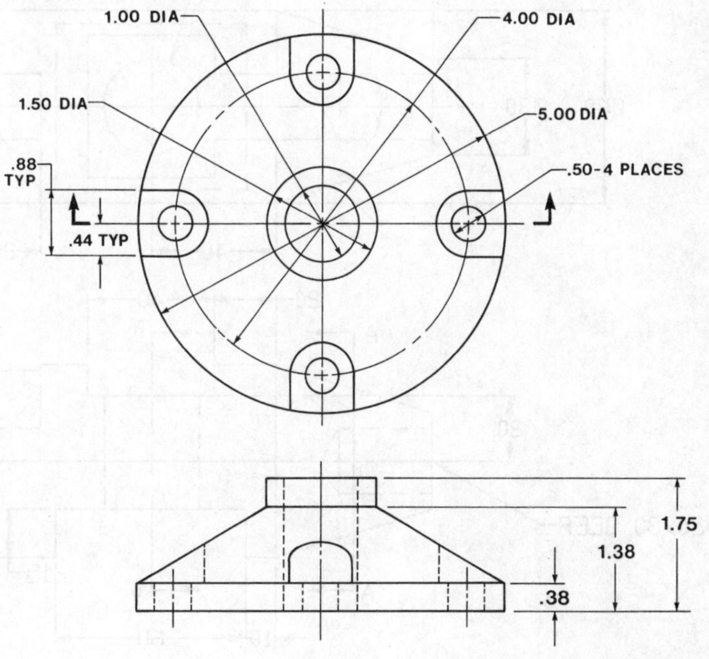

EX6-24 Inches

Redraw the given front and top views, and add Sections A-A, B-B, and C-C as indicated.

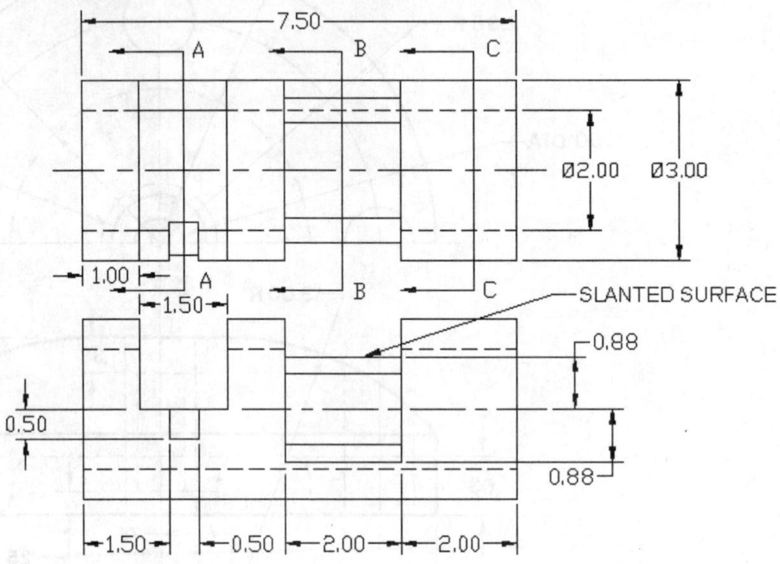

EX6-25 Millimeters

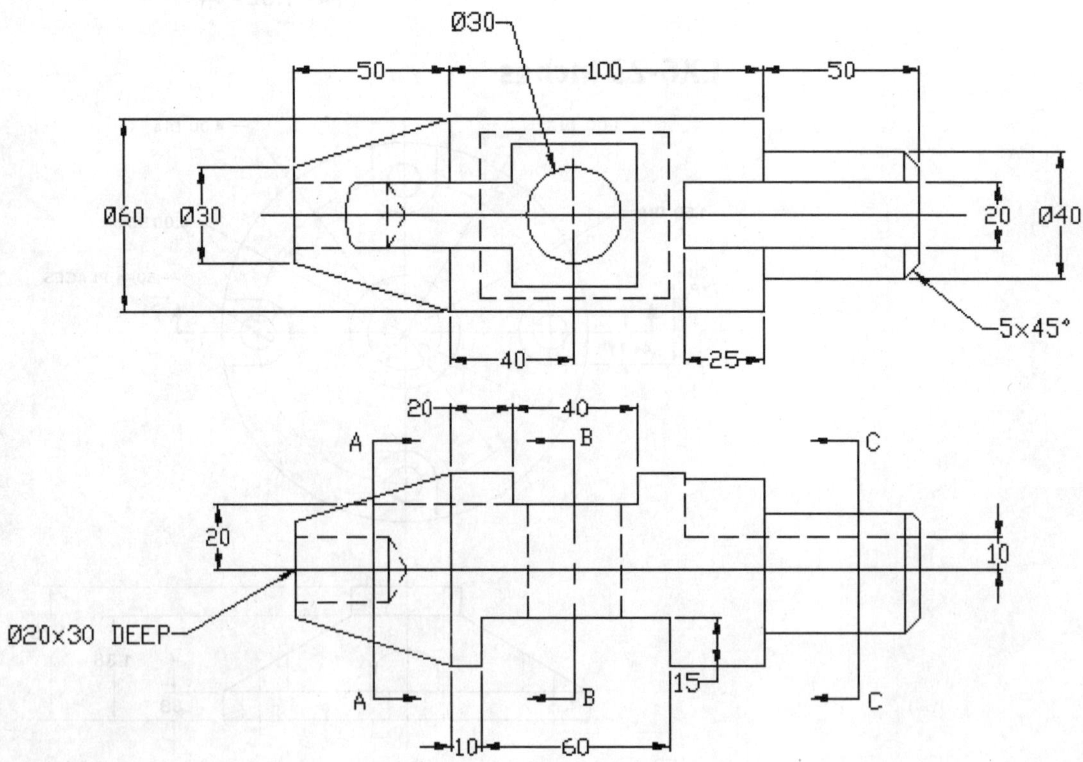

EX6-26 Inches

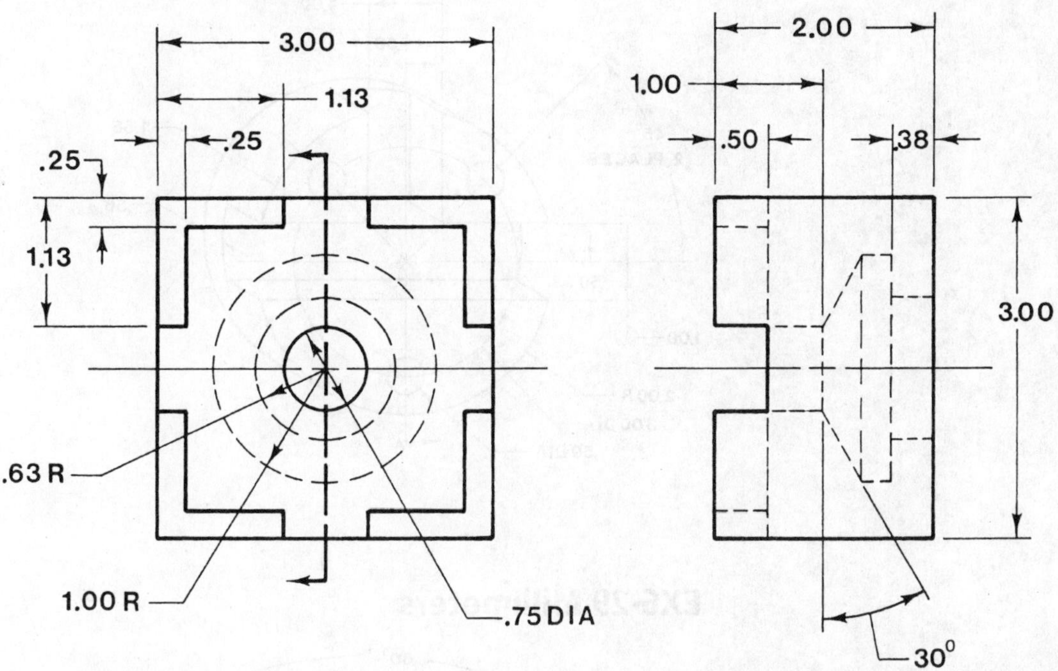

EX6-27 Inches

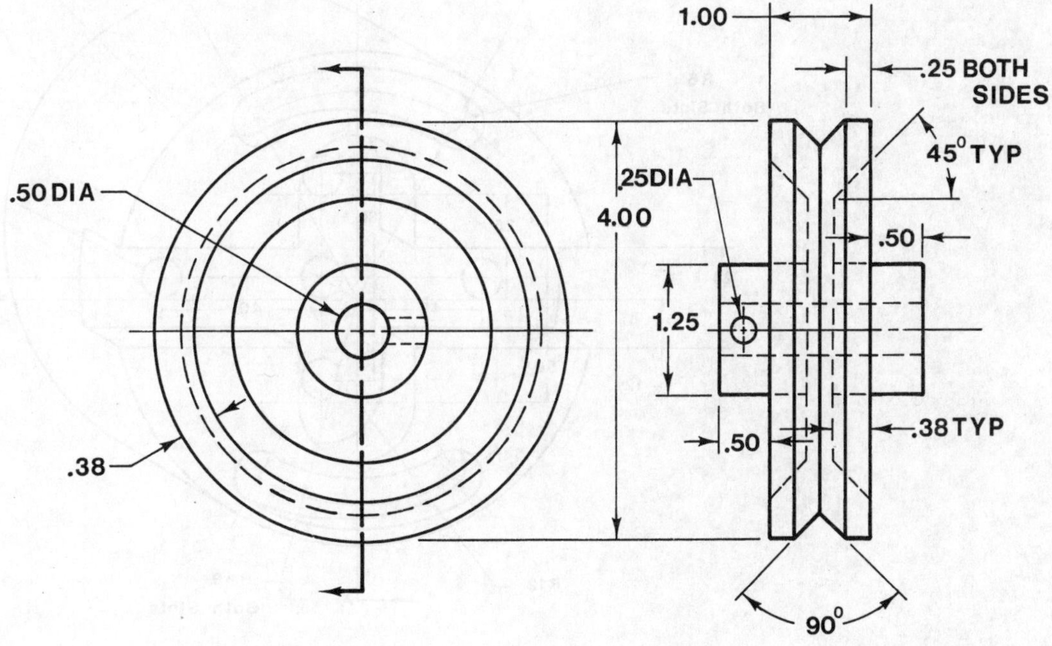

EX6-28 Inches

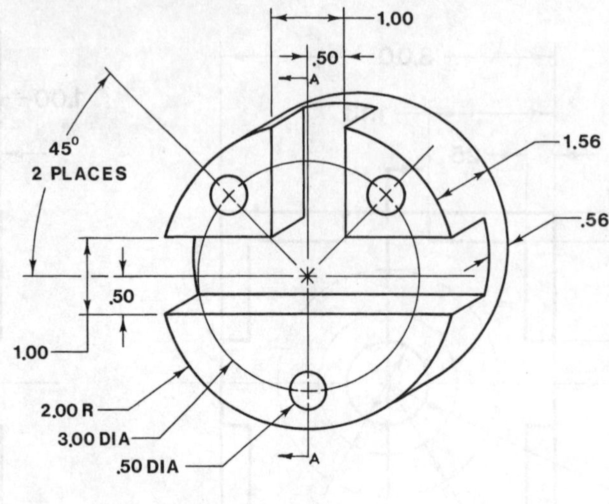

EX6-29 Millimeters

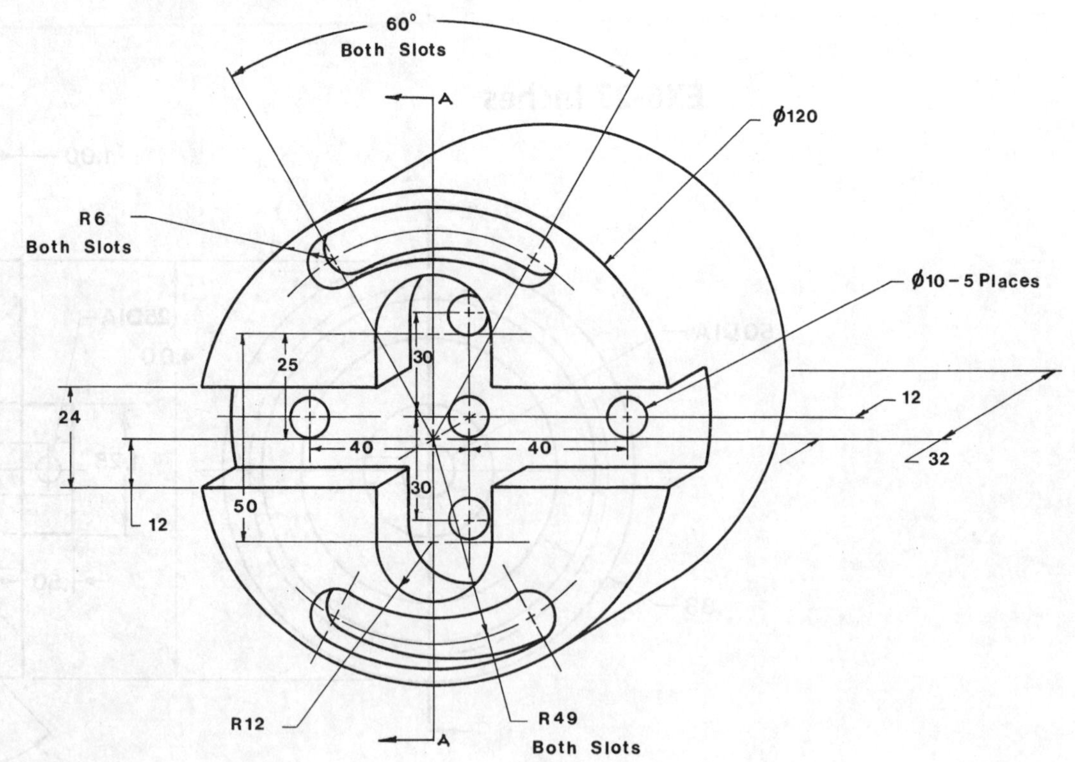

EX6-30 Millimeters

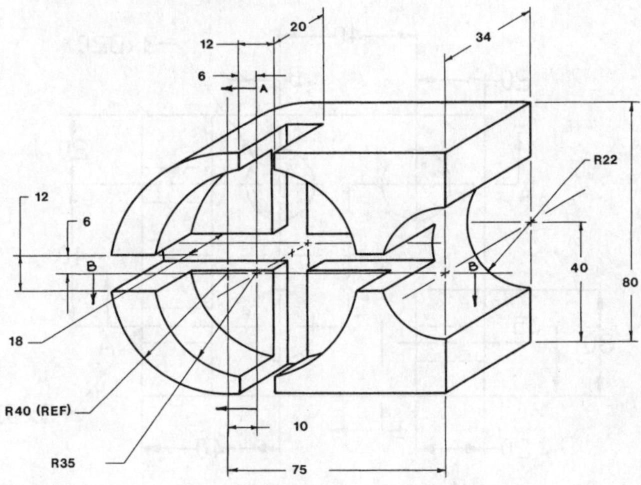

EX6-31 Millimeters

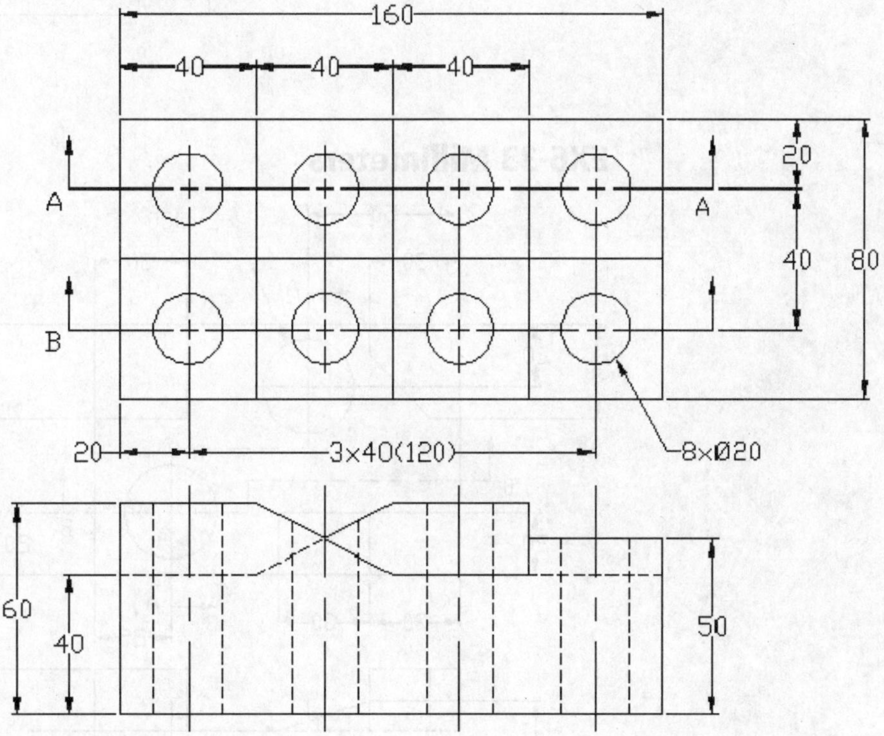

EX6-32 Millimeters

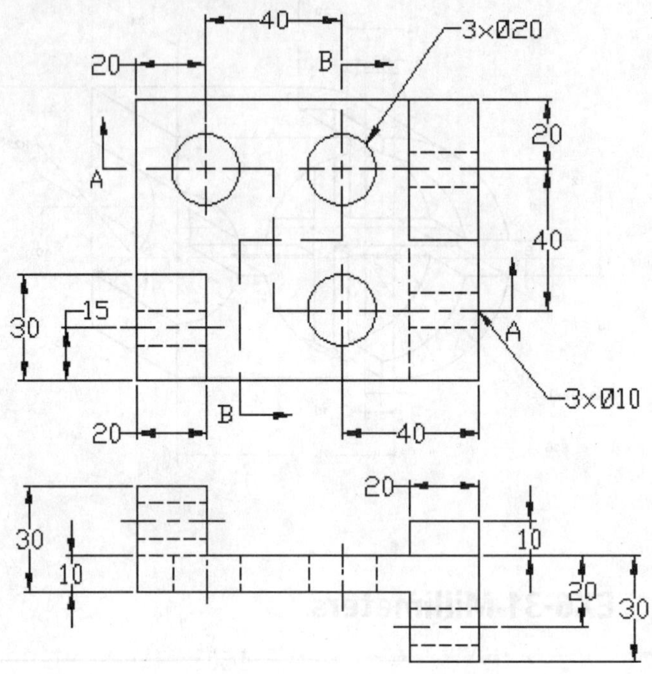

EX6-33 Millimeters

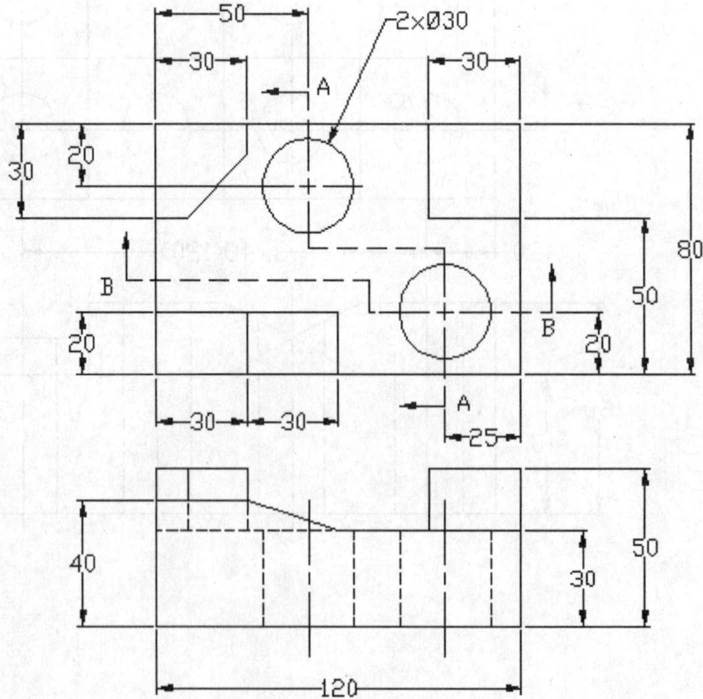

EX6-34 Inches

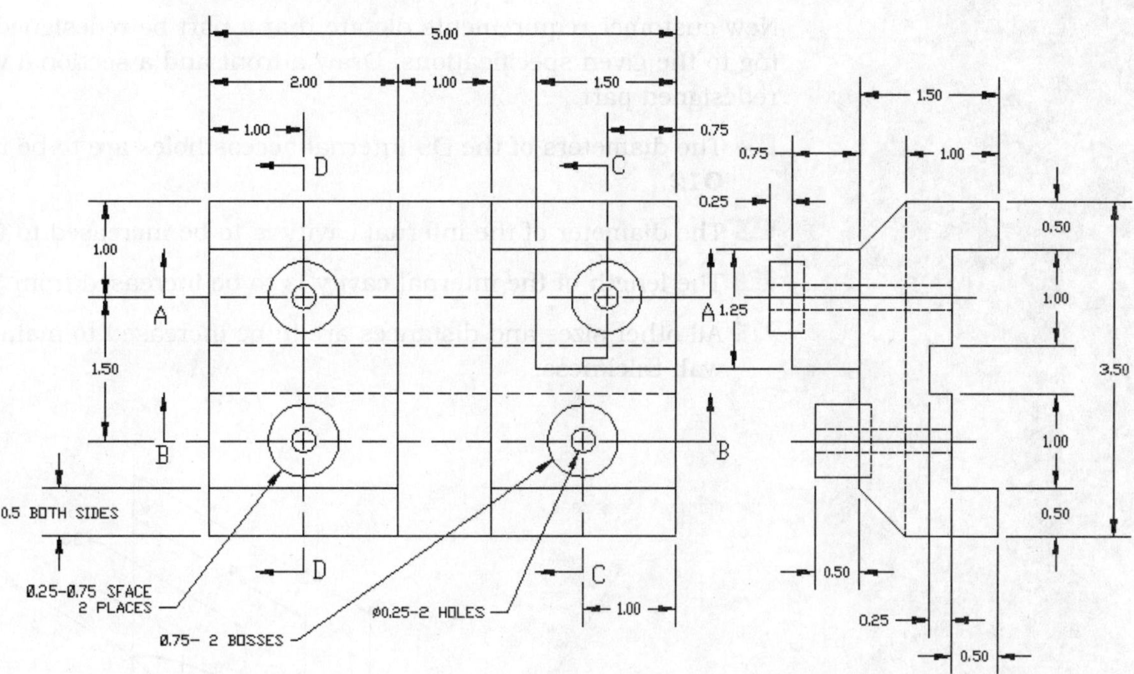

EX6-35

New customer requirements dictate that a part be redesigned according to the given specifications. Draw a front and a sectional view of the redesigned part.

1. The diameters of the Ø9 internal access holes are to be increased to **Ø12.**
2. The diameter of the internal cavity is to be increased to **Ø30.**
3. The length of the internal cavity is to be increased from 33 to **50.**
4. All other sizes and distances are to be increased to maintain the same wall thickness.

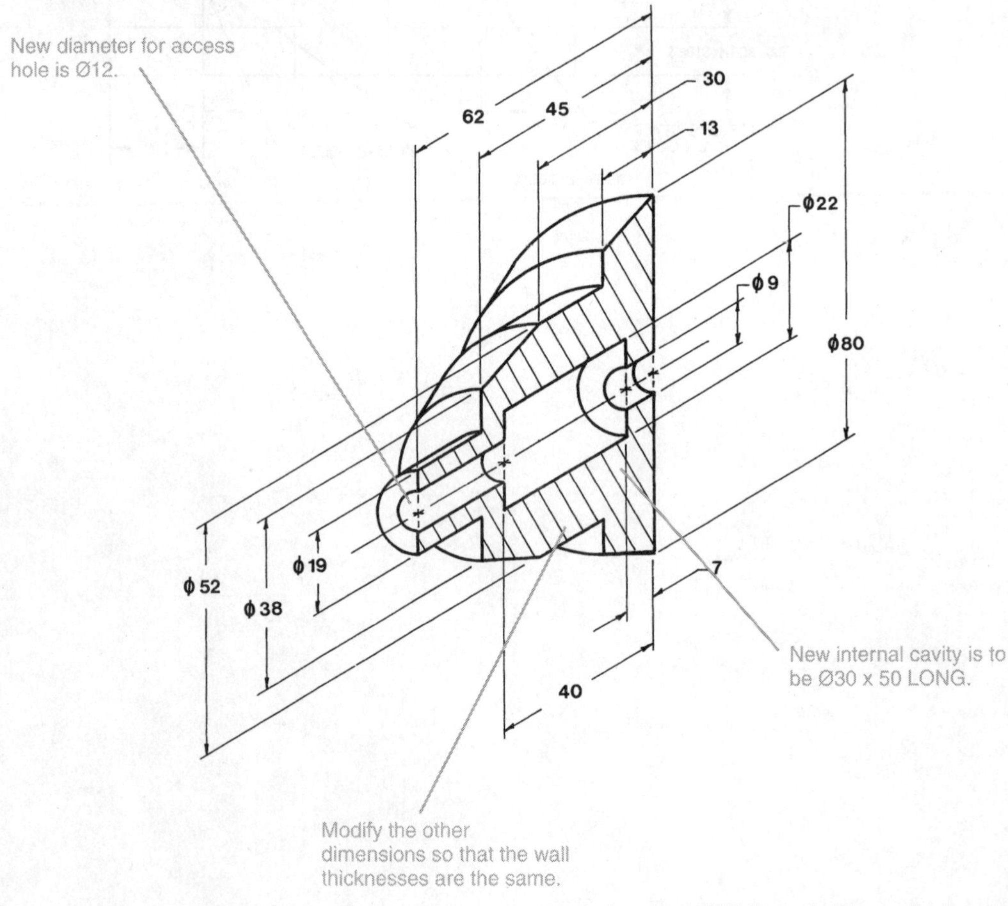

EX6-36

An object is to be redesigned as follows:

1. Extend the 1.00-inch vertical slot all the way through the object, creating four corner sections.
2. Locate countersunk holes in each of the four corner sections. Note that two of the corner sections presently have Ø.50 holes. The countersink specifications are Ø.50 - 82°, Ø.75.
3. Locate a Ø.625 hole in the center of the object.

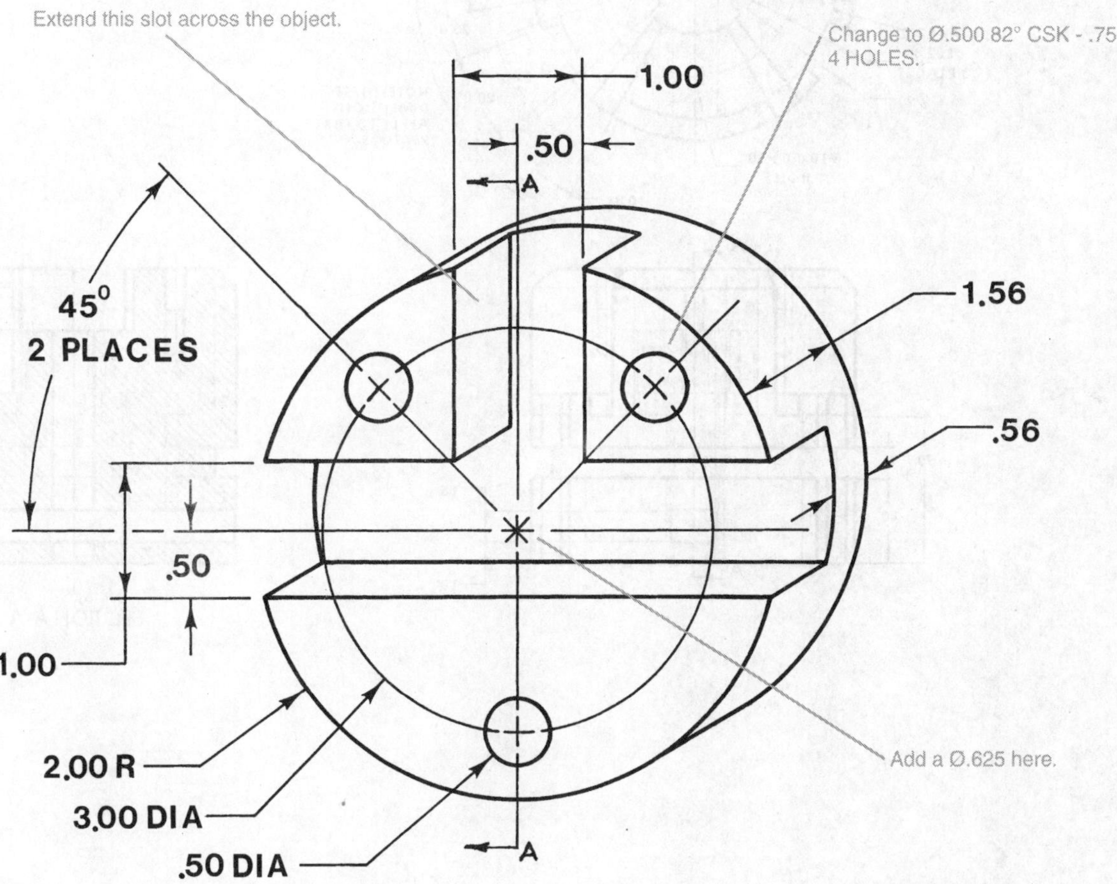

EX6-37

Given the following front, top, and sectional views, create a 3D model of the object:

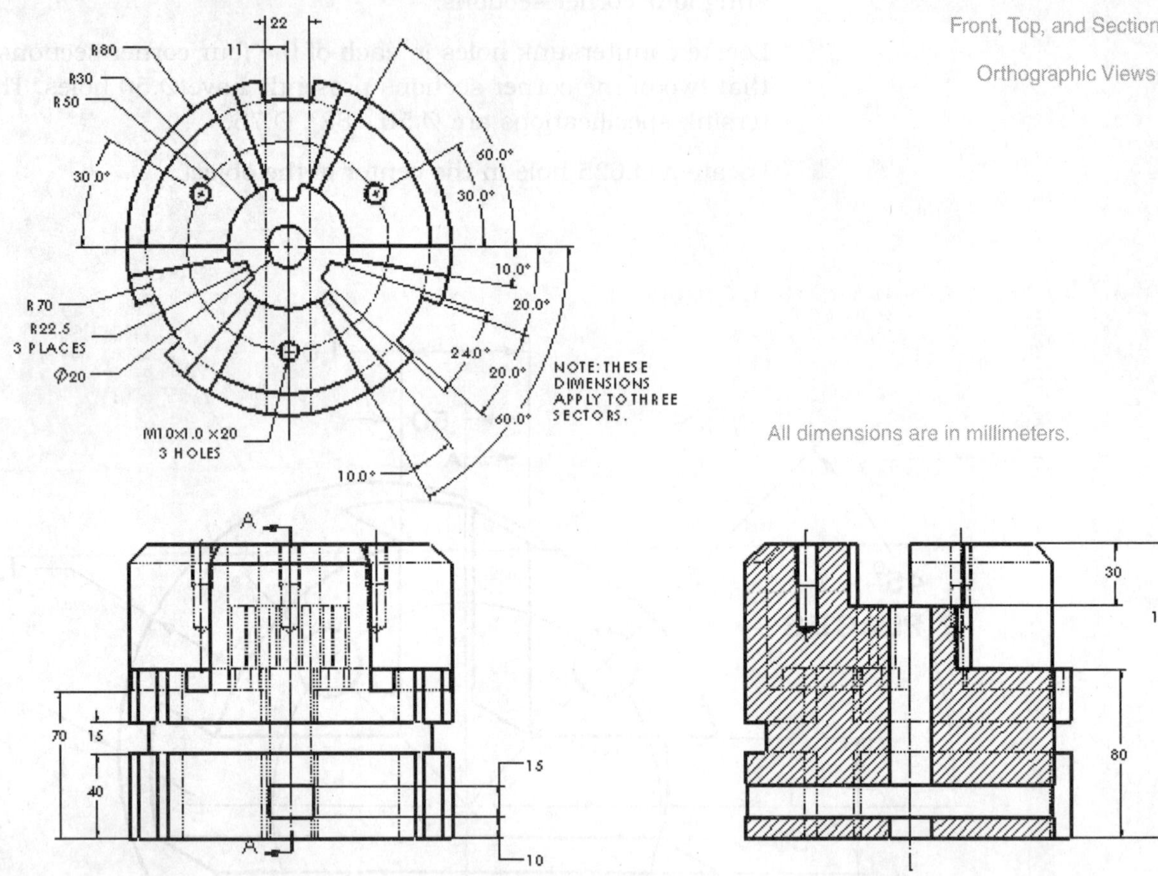

Front, Top, and Sectional Orthographic Views

All dimensions are in millimeters.

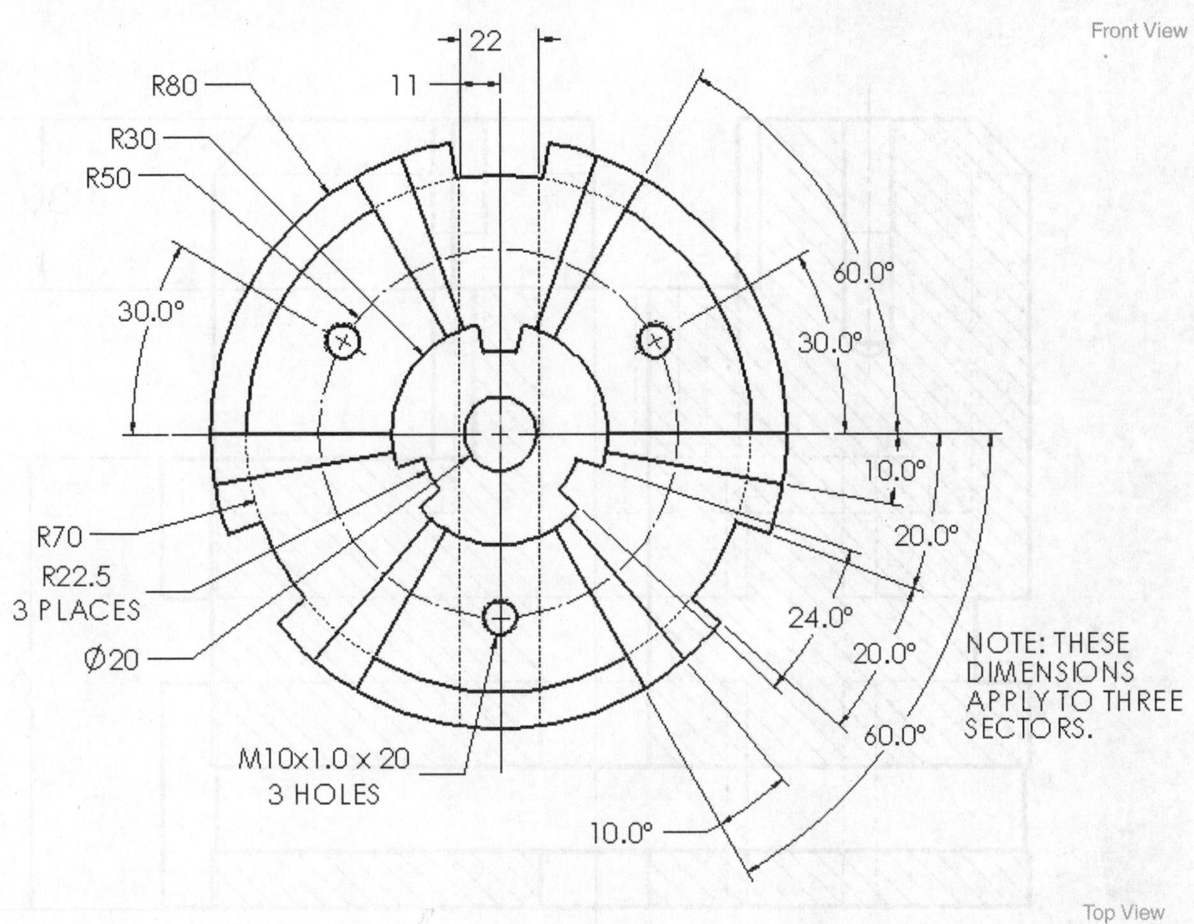
Front View
22
11
R80
R30
R50
30.0°
60.0°
30.0°
10.0°
20.0°
R70
R22.5
3 PLACES
Ø20
24.0°
20.0°
NOTE: THESE
DIMENSIONS
APPLY TO THREE
SECTORS.
60.0°
M10x1.0 x 20
3 HOLES
10.0°

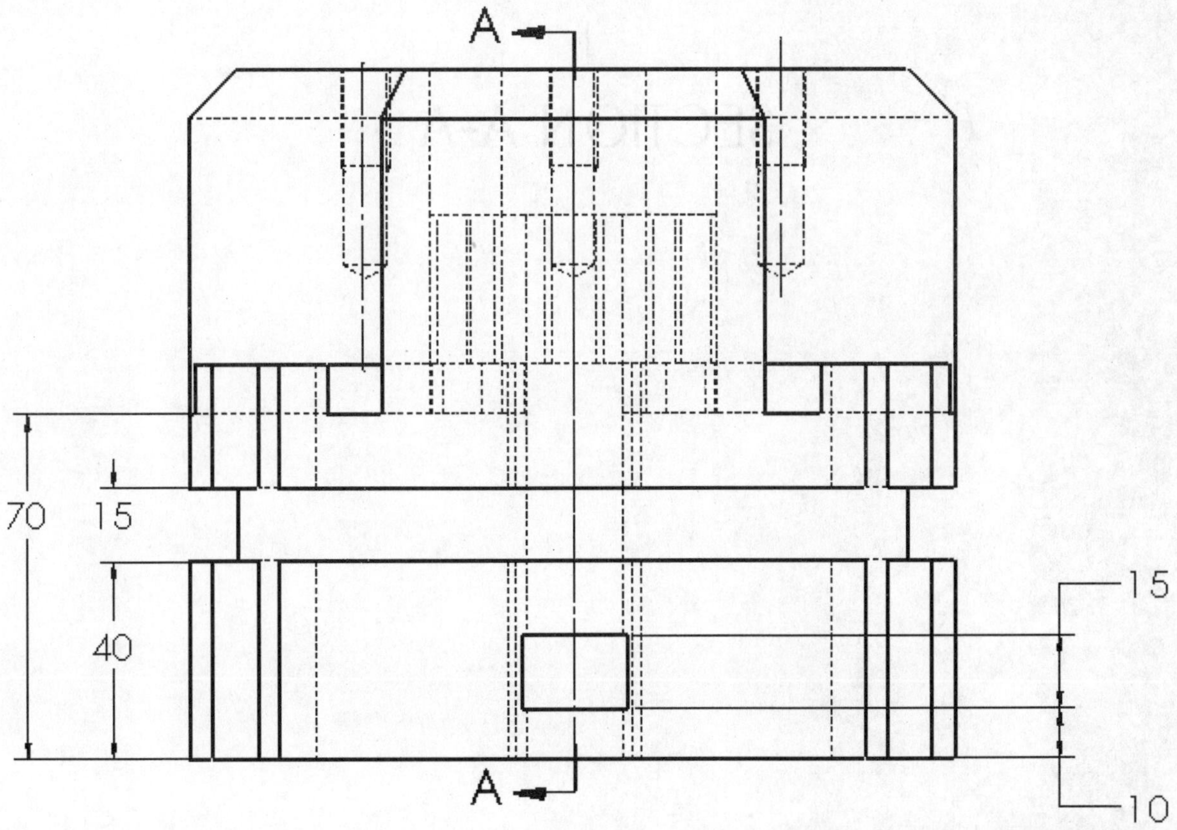
Top View
A
70
15
40
15
10
A

This section includes hidden lines for clarity.

30

140

80

SECTION A-A

chapterseven
Auxiliary Views

7-1 Introduction

Auxiliary views are orthographic views used to present true-shaped views of slanted and oblique surfaces. Slanted and oblique surfaces appear foreshortened or as edge views in normal orthographic views. Holes in the surfaces are elliptical, and other features are also distorted.

Figure 7-1 shows an object with a slanted surface that includes a hole drilled perpendicular to that surface. Note how the slanted surface is foreshortened in both the normal top and side views, and note that the hole appears as an ellipse in both of these views. The hole appears as an edge view with hidden lines in the front view, so none of the normal views show the hole as a circle.

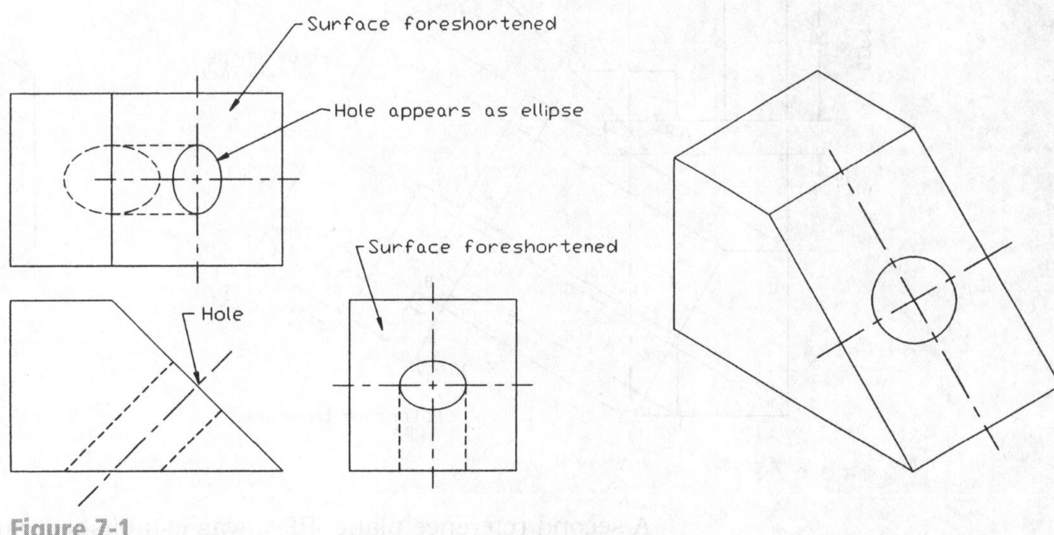

Figure 7-1

Figure 7-2 shows the same object shown in Figure 7-1. The front and side views are the same, but the top view is replaced with an auxiliary view. The auxiliary view shows the true shape of the slanted surface, and the hole appears as a circle.

The auxiliary view in Figure 7-2 shows the true shape of the slanted surface, but a foreshortened view of surface **A–B–C–D.** Positioning the auxiliary view to generate the true shape of the slanted surface foreshortened the other surfaces.

Figure 7-2

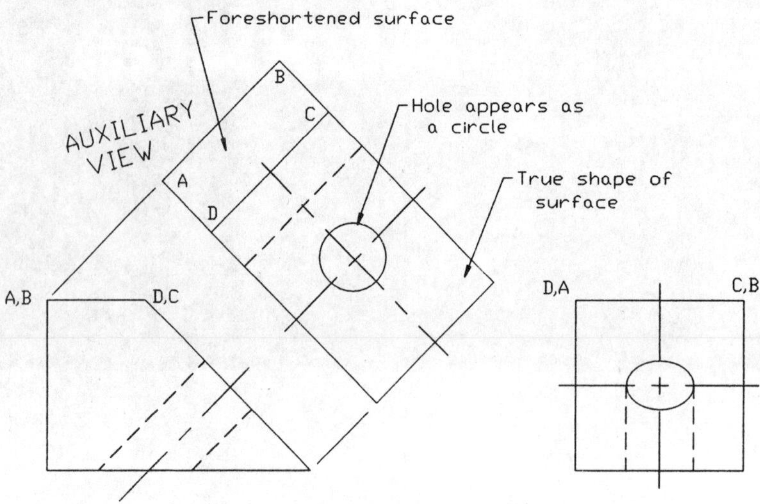

7-2 Projection Between Normal and Auxiliary Views

Information about an object's features can be projected between the normal views and any additional auxiliary views by establishing reference planes. A reference plane RPT is located between the top and front views of Figure 7-3. The plane appears as a horizontal line, and its location is arbitrary. In the example shown, the plane was located 10 millimeters from the top view.

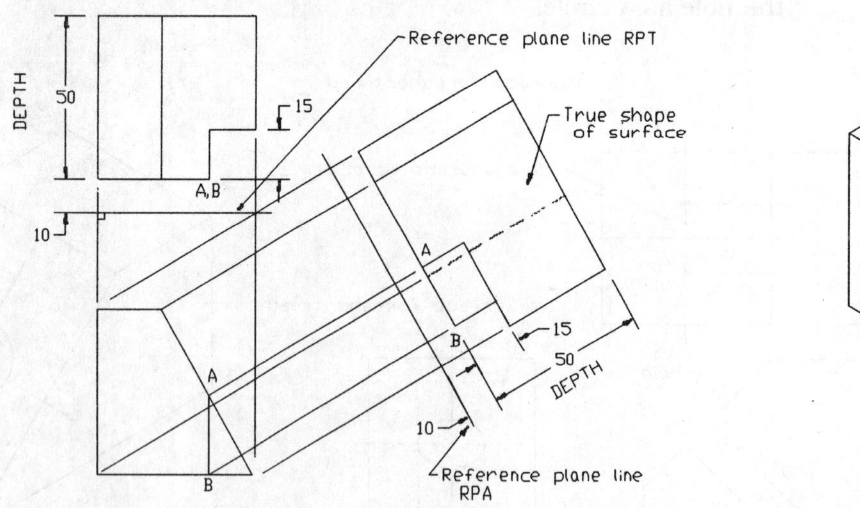

Figure 7-3

A second reference plane, RPA, was established parallel to the slanted surface at a location that prevents the auxiliary view from interfering with the top view. The **Move** command can be used to move the top view farther away from the front view if necessary.

Information was projected from the front view into the auxiliary view by projection lines perpendicular to reference plane RPA.

The depth of the object was transferred from the top view to the auxiliary view. Figure 7-3 shows the 50-millimeter depth and 15-millimeter slot depth dimensioned in both the top and auxiliary views.

Figure 7-4 shows information projected from given front and side views into an auxiliary view. Reference planes RPS and RPA were located 10 millimeters from, and parallel to, the side and auxiliary views, and information was projected from the front view into the auxiliary view by lines perpendicular to plane RPA. The depth information was transferred from the side view to the auxiliary view.

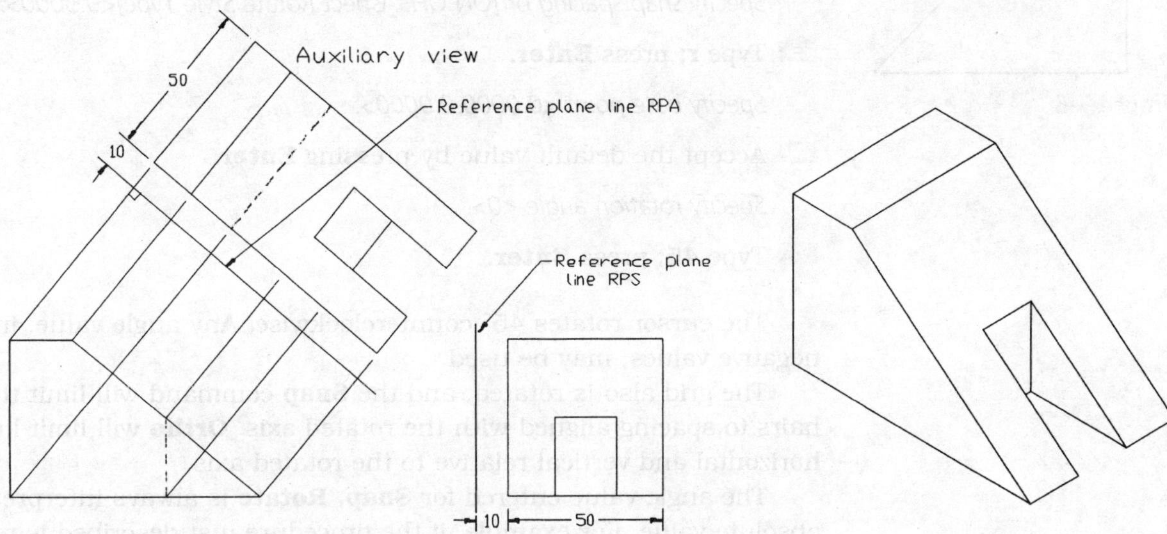

Figure 7-4

Figure 7-5 shows an object that has a slanted surface in the top view. The reference plane line, RPA, for the auxiliary view was located parallel to the slanted surface, and another reference plane, RPF (horizontal line), was established between the front and top views. Information was projected from the top view into the auxiliary view by lines perpendicular to RPA. The 30-millimeter height measurement was transferred from the front view into the auxiliary view.

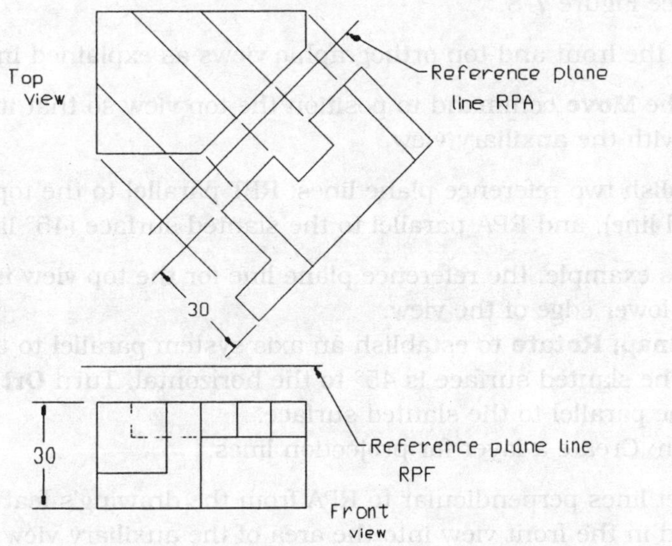

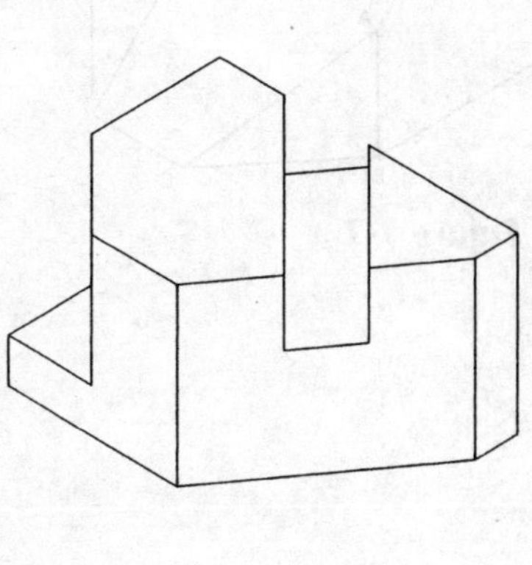

Figure 7-5

Reference plane lines and projection lines drawn perpendicular to them are best drawn by rotating the drawing's axis system, indicated by the crosshairs, so that it is parallel to the slanted surface. A separate layer may be created for projection lines.

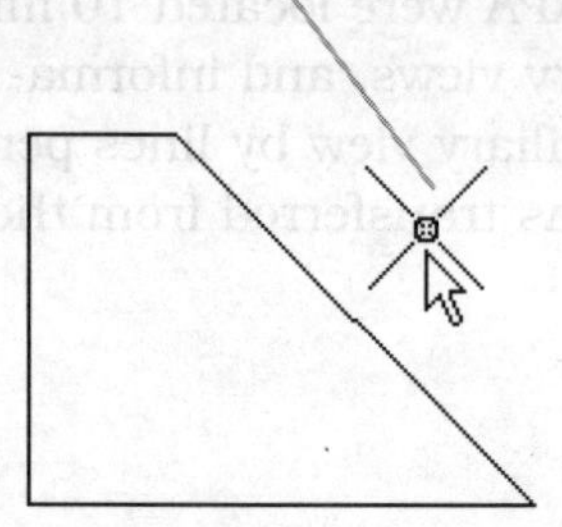

Figure 7-6

To Rotate the Drawing's Axis System (See Figure 7-6.)

1. Type **Snap** in response to a command prompt.

   The command prompts are as follows:

   Command: _snap

   Specify snap spacing or [ON OFF Aspect Rotate Style Type]<0.5000>:

2. Type **r;** press **Enter.**

   Specify base point <0.0000,0.0000>:

3. Accept the default value by pressing **Enter.**

   Specify rotation angle <0>:

4. Type **45;** press **Enter.**

The cursor rotates 45° counterclockwise. Any angle value, including negative values, may be used.

The grid also is rotated, and the **Snap** command will limit the crosshairs to spacing aligned with the rotated axis. **Ortho** will limit lines to horizontal and vertical relative to the rotated axis.

The angle value entered for **Snap, Rotate** is always interpreted as an absolute value. For example, if the procedure just described is repeated and a value of 60 entered, the crosshairs will advance only 15° from their present location, or 60° from the system's absolute 0° axis system.

7-3 Sample Problem SP7-1

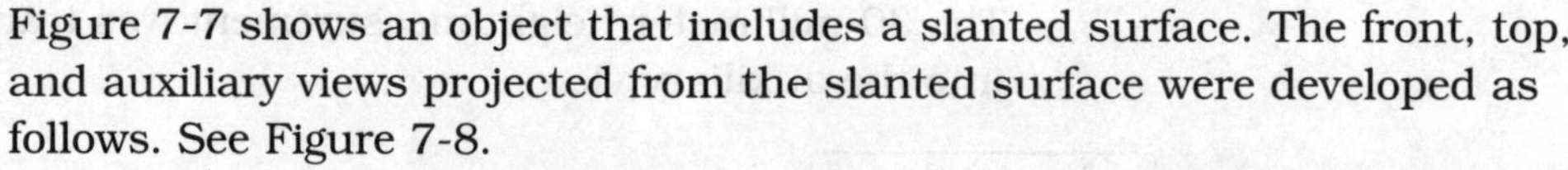

Figure 7-7 shows an object that includes a slanted surface. The front, top, and auxiliary views projected from the slanted surface were developed as follows. See Figure 7-8.

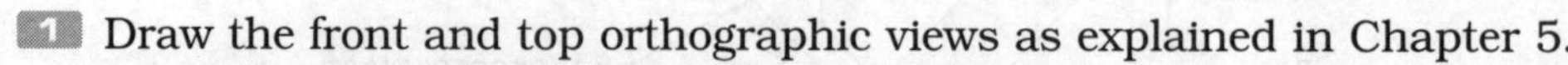

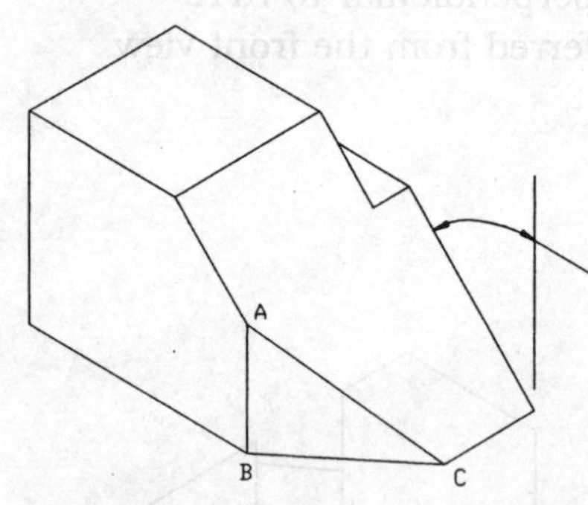

Figure 7-7

1. Draw the front and top orthographic views as explained in Chapter 5.

Use the **Move** command to position the top view so that it will not interfere with the auxiliary view.

2. Establish two reference plane lines: RPT parallel to the top view (horizontal line), and RPA parallel to the slanted surface (45° line).

In this example, the reference plane line for the top view is located along the lower edge of the view.

Use **Snap, Rotate** to establish an axis system parallel to the slanted surface. The slanted surface is 45° to the horizontal. Turn **Ortho** on, and draw a line parallel to the slanted surface.

Option: Create a layer for projection lines.

3. Project lines perpendicular to RPA from the drawing's feature presented in the front view into the area of the auxiliary view. Use **Osnap Intersection** to ensure accuracy.

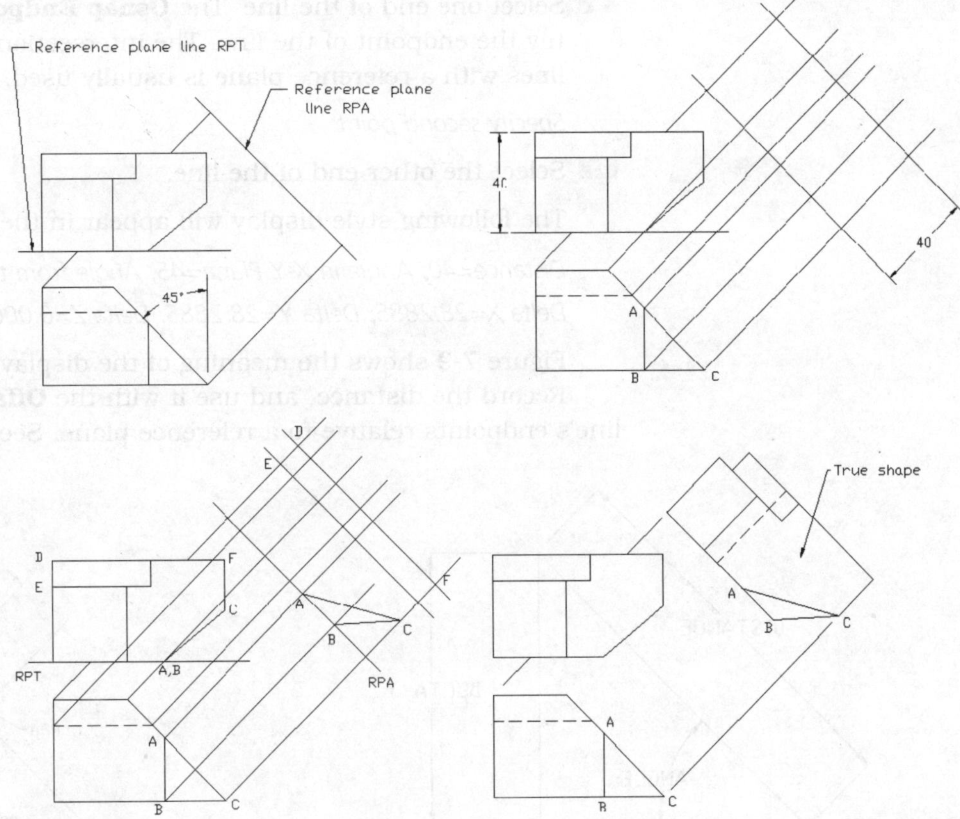

Figure 7-8

4 Type **Dist** in response to a command prompt to determine the distance from the reference plane line, RPT, to the object's features.

5 Use **Offset** to draw a line parallel to RPA at a distance equal to the distances of the object's features.

6 Erase and trim any excess lines, and save the drawing if desired.

7-4 Transferring Lines Between Views

Objects are often dimensioned so that only some of their edge lines are dimensioned. This means that **Offset** may not be used to transfer distances to auxiliary views until the line length is known. There are three possible methods that can be used to transfer an edge line of unknown length: Measure the line length by using **Dist,** and then use the determined distance with the **Offset** command; use grips, and rotate and move the line; or use **Copy, Modify, Rotate,** and relocate the line. The procedures are as follows:

To Measure the Length of a Line

1 Type **Dist** in response to a command prompt.

The command prompts are as follows:

Command: Dist

Specify first point:

2. Select one end of the line. The **Osnap Endpoint** option will help identify the endpoint of the line. The intersection of one of the projection lines with a reference plane is usually used.

   Specify second point:

3. Select the other end of the line.

   The following style display will appear in the screen's prompt area:

   Distance=40, Angle in X-Y Plane=45, Angle from the X-Y Plane=0

   Delta X=28.2885, Delta Y=28.2885, Delta Z=0.0000

   Figure 7-9 shows the meaning of the displayed distance information. Record the distance, and use it with the **Offset** command to locate the line's endpoints relative to a reference plane. See Figure 7-9.

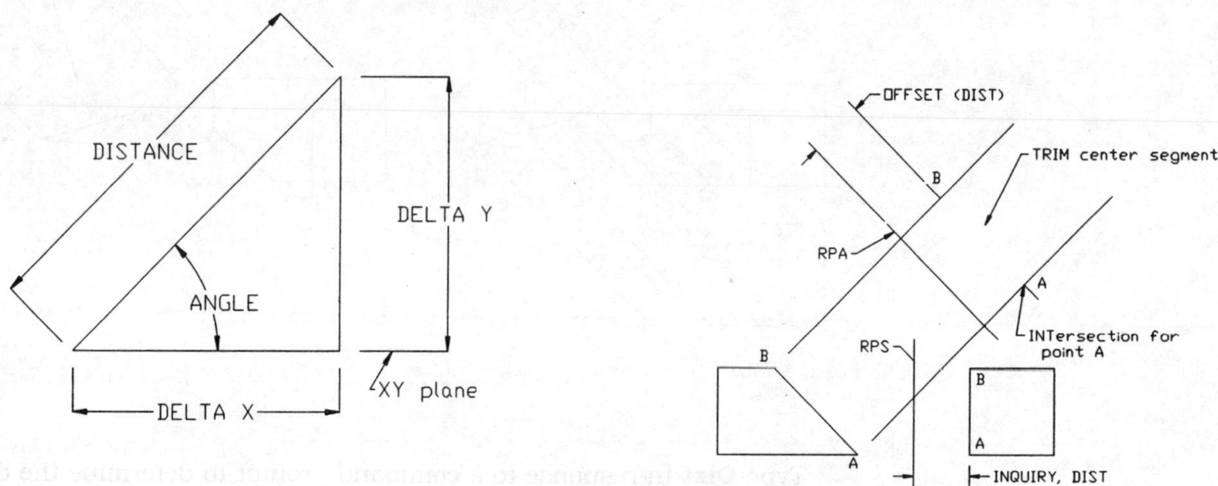

Figure 7-9

To Grip and Move a Line (See Figure 7-10.)

1. Copy the line, and move the copy to an open area of the drawing.
2. Click the line to highlight its grip points. See Section 3-15.
3. Select the line's lower endpoint; press the right mouse button.

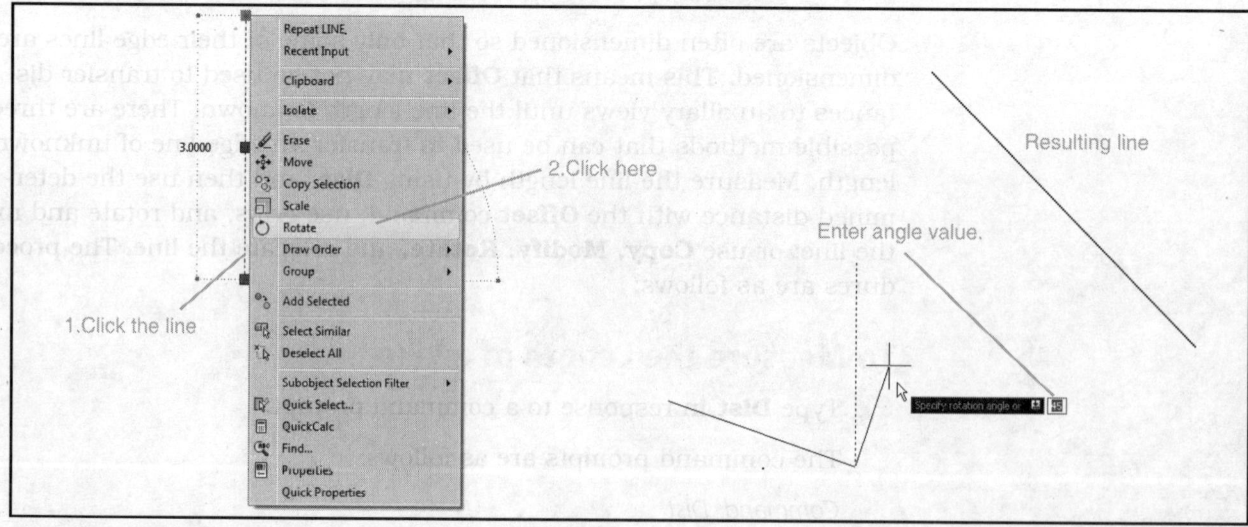

Figure 7-10

4. Select the **Rotate** option from the menu.

   ROTATE

   Specify rotation angle or [Base point Copy Undo Reference eXit]:

5. Select the endpoint as the base point.
6. Type **45;** press **Enter.**

The **Dist** command can also be used to determine the angle of a slanted surface if it is not known.

7. Select the line's lower endpoint again.
8. Select **Move** from the menu.
9. Select the lower line point as the base point.
10. Move the line to a new location, or use dynamic input to define a new location.

To Rotate and Move a Line

1. Copy the line, and move the line to an open area of the drawing.
2. Select the **Rotate** tool from the **Modify** panel, and rotate the line **45**°. See Section 3-15.
3. Select **Move** from the **Modify** panel, and relocate the line to the auxiliary view. Use **Osnap** if necessary to ensure accuracy.

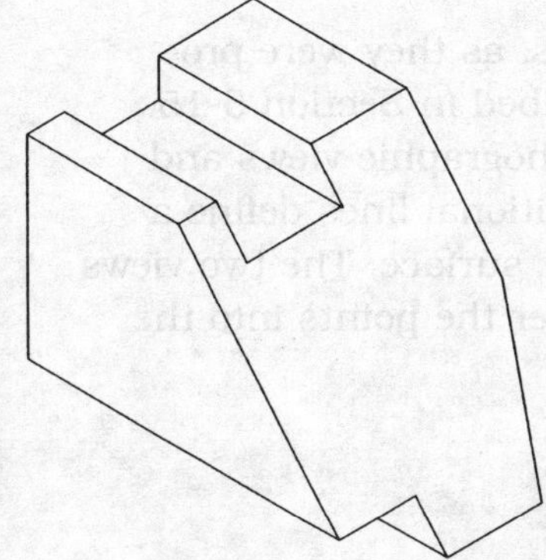

Figure 7-11

7-5 Sample Problem SP7-2

Figure 7-11 shows an object that contains two slanted surfaces and two cutouts. Draw a front and right-side orthographic view, and an auxiliary view. See Figure 7-12.

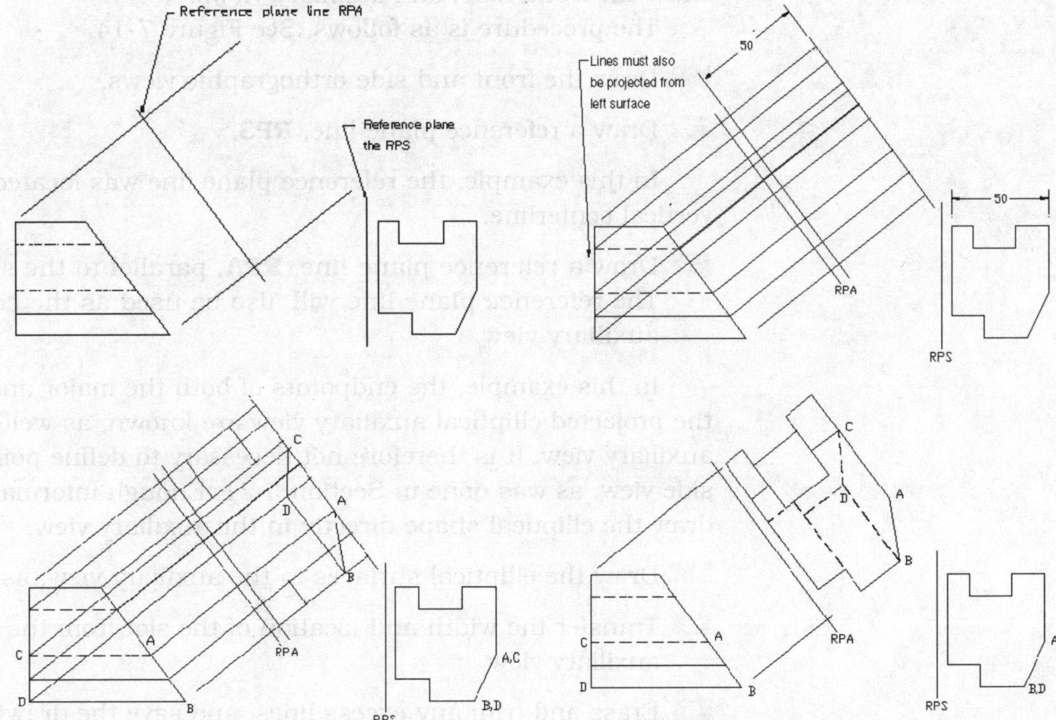

Figure 7-12

1. Draw the front and side orthographic views as described in Chapter 5.
2. Define a reference plane, **RPS**, between the front and side views.
3. Use **Snap, Rotate (37.5)** to align the crosshairs with the slanted surface. The 37.5° value was determined by use of the **Dist** command.
4. Draw a reference plane line, **RPA**, parallel to the slanted surface, and project the features of the object into the auxiliary view area.
5. Transfer the distance measurements from RPS and the side view into the auxiliary view.

   Label the various points as needed.
6. Erase and trim any excess lines, and save the drawing if desired.

7-6 Projecting Rounded Surfaces

Rounded surfaces are projected into auxiliary views, as they were projected into the normal orthographic views as described in Section 5-15. Additional lines are added to one of the normal orthographic views and then projected into the other normal view. The additional lines define a series of points that define the outside shape of the surface. The two views with the added lines are used to project and transfer the points into the auxiliary view.

7-7 Sample Problem SP7-3

Figure 7-13 shows a cylindrical object that includes a slanted surface. Draw the front, side, and auxiliary views.

The procedure is as follows. See Figure 7-14.

1. Draw the front and side orthographic views.
2. Draw a reference plane line, **RPS.**

In this example, the reference plane line was located on the side view's vertical centerline.

3. Draw a reference plane line, **RPA,** parallel to the slanted surface. The reference plane line will also be used as the centerline for the auxiliary view.

In this example, the endpoints of both the major and minor axes of the projected elliptical auxiliary view are known, as well as the angle of the auxiliary view. It is therefore not necessary to define points in the circular side view, as was done in Section 5-21. Enough information is present to draw the elliptical shape directly in the auxiliary view.

4. Draw the elliptical surfaces in the auxiliary view, as shown.
5. Transfer the width and location of the slot from the side view to the auxiliary view.
6. Erase and trim any excess lines, and save the drawing if desired.

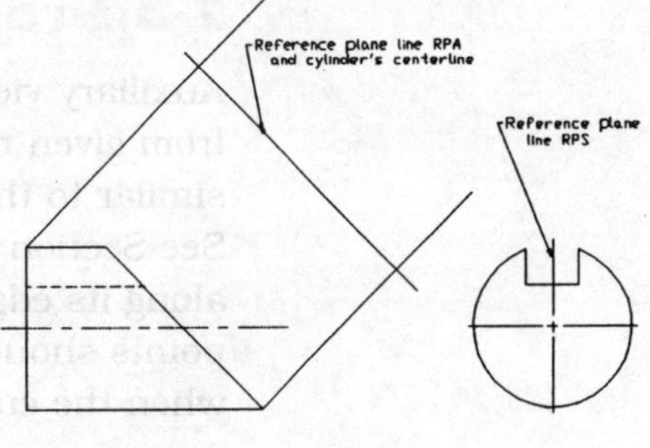

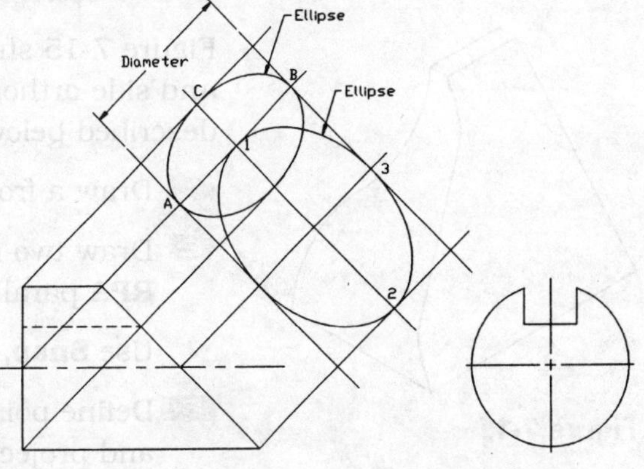

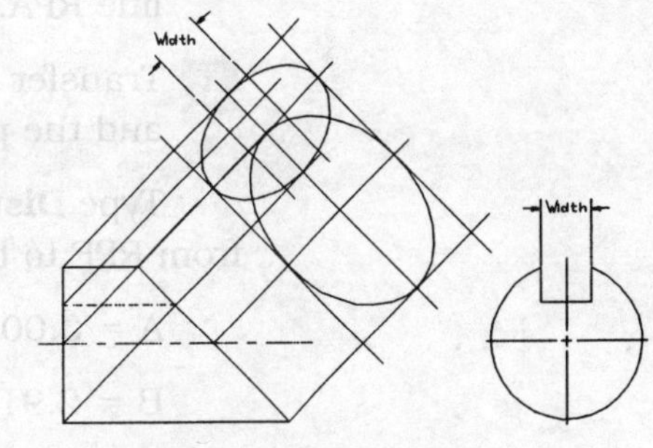

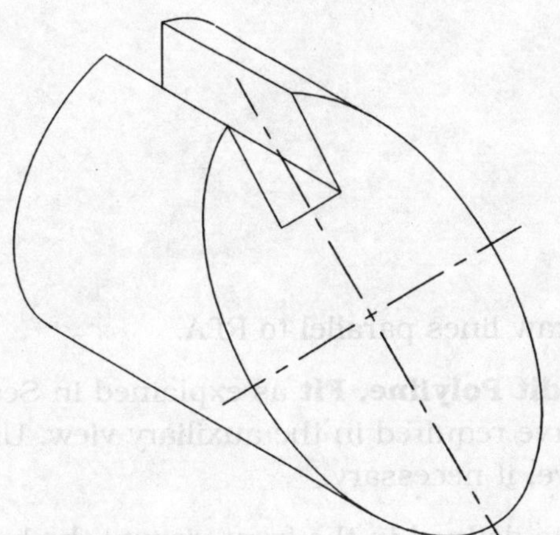

Figure 7-13

Figure 7-14

7-8 Projecting Irregular Surfaces

Auxiliary views of irregular surfaces are created by projecting information from given normal orthographic views into the auxiliary views in a manner similar to the way information was projected between orthographic views. See Section 5-28. The irregular surface is defined by a series of points along its edge line. The location of the points is random, although more points should be used when the curve's shape is changing sharply than when the curve tends to be smoother.

7-9 Sample Problem SP7-4

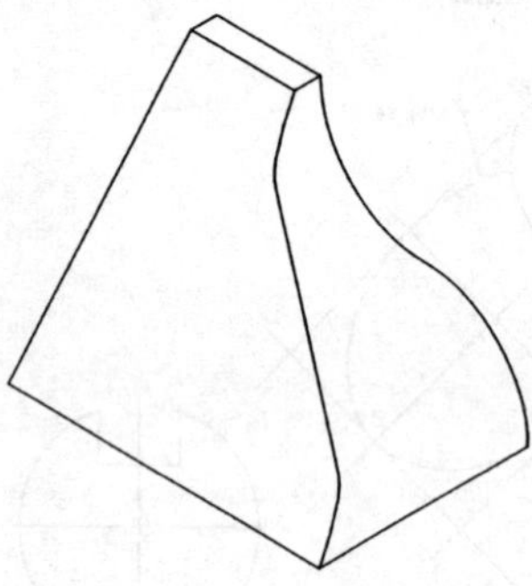
Figure 7-15

Figure 7-15 shows an object that includes an irregular surface. Draw front and side orthographic and auxiliary views of the object. The procedure is described below. See Figure 7-16.

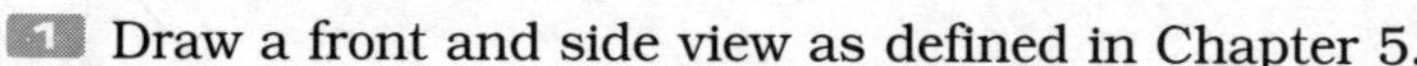
1 Draw a front and side view as defined in Chapter 5.

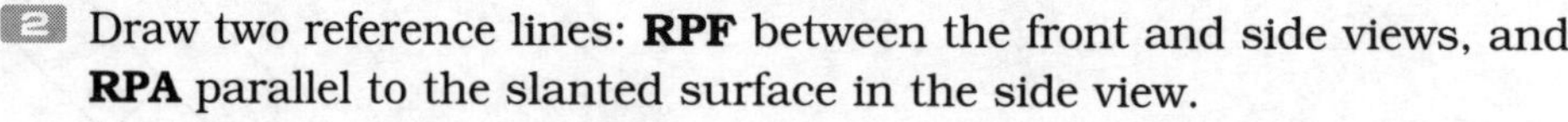
2 Draw two reference lines: **RPF** between the front and side views, and **RPA** parallel to the slanted surface in the side view.

Use **Snap, Rotate** to align the crosshairs with the slanted surface.

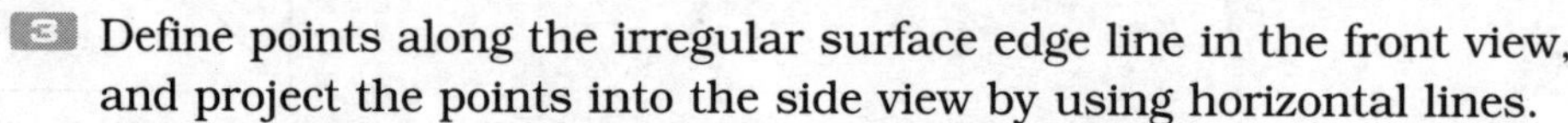
3 Define points along the irregular surface edge line in the front view, and project the points into the side view by using horizontal lines.

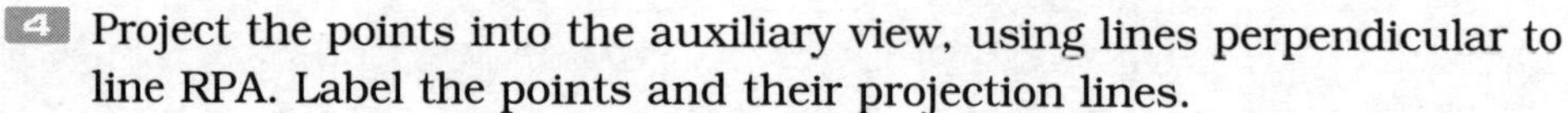
4 Project the points into the auxiliary view, using lines perpendicular to line RPA. Label the points and their projection lines.

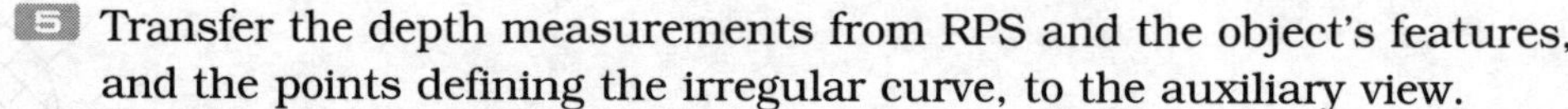
5 Transfer the depth measurements from RPS and the object's features, and the points defining the irregular curve, to the auxiliary view.

Type **Dist** in response to a command prompt to determine the distance from RPF to the points. Record the distances.

A = 3.00

B = 2.91

C = 2.62

D = 1.50

E = 0.30

F = 0.09

G = 0

Use **Offset** to draw lines parallel to RPA.

6 Use **Polyline, Edit Polyline, Fit** as explained in Section 5-26 to draw the irregular curve required in the auxiliary view. Use **Edit Vertex** to smooth the curve, if necessary.

7 Project the points defined in the front view to the back surface (far right vertical line) in the side view, and project the points into the auxiliary view.

8 Use **Polyline, Edit Polyline, Fit** to draw the required irregular curve.

9 Erase and trim any excess lines, and save the drawing if desired.

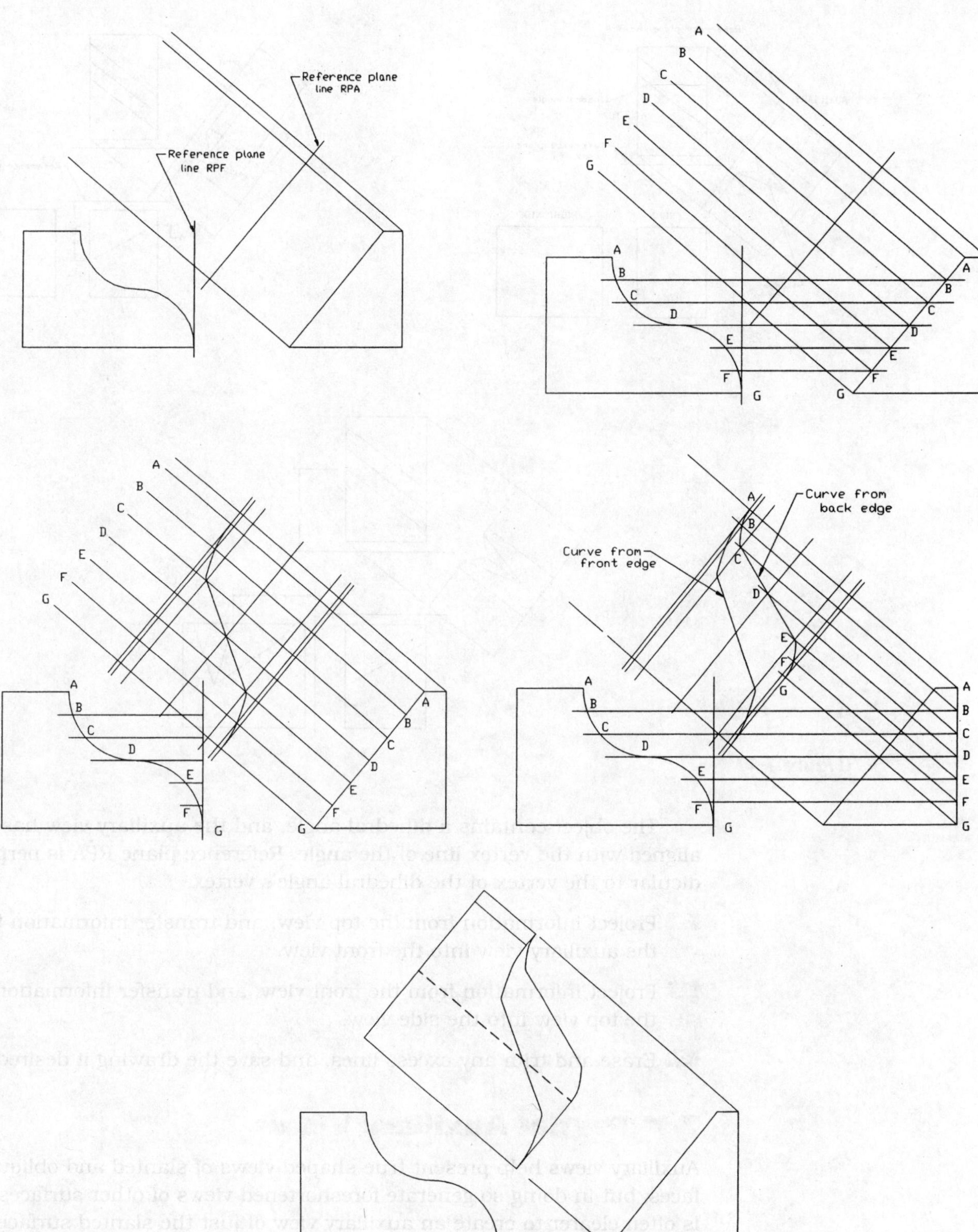

Figure 7-16

7-10 Sample Problem SP7-5

Figure 7-17 shows a top view and an auxiliary view of an object. Redraw the given views, and add the front and right-side views. The procedure is described as follows.

1 Draw a reference plane line, **RPA**, parallel to the auxiliary view and a reference plane line, **RPT**, a horizontal line.

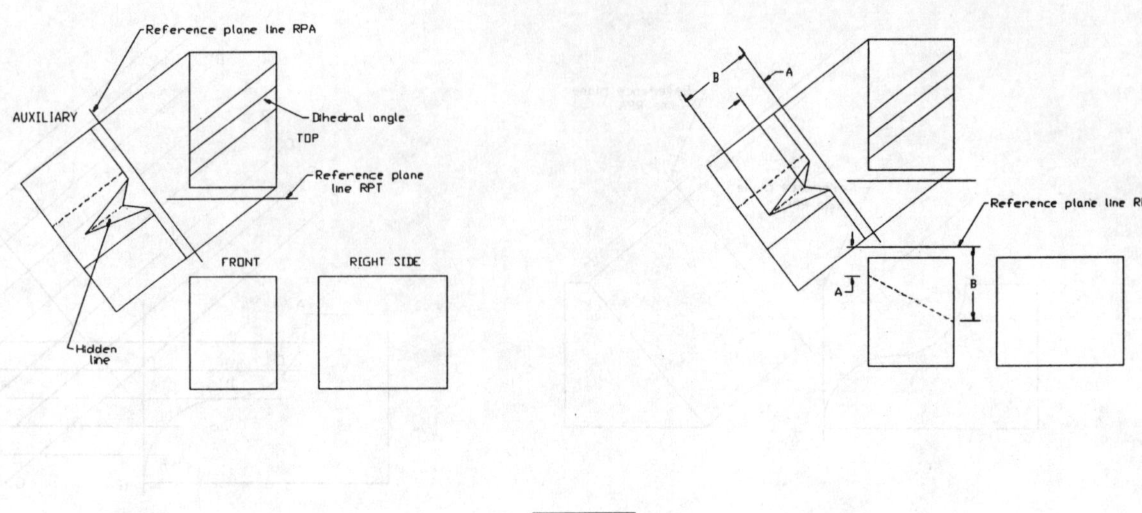

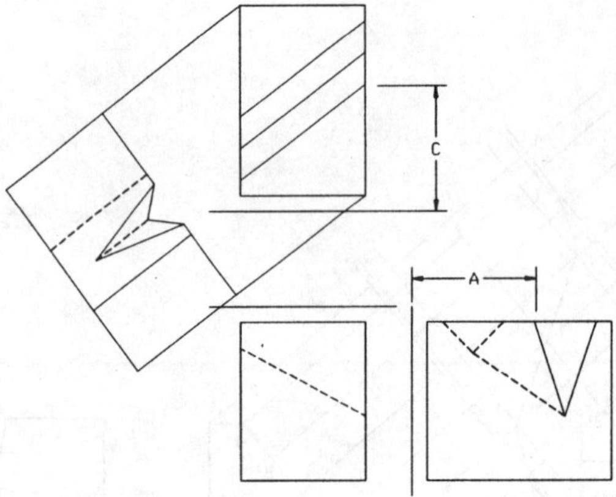

Figure 7-17

The object contains a dihedral angle, and the auxiliary view has been aligned with the vertex line of the angle. Reference plane RPA is perpendicular to the vertex of the dihedral angle's vertex.

2. Project information from the top view, and transfer information from the auxiliary view into the front view.

3. Project information from the front view, and transfer information from the top view into the side view.

4. Erase and trim any excess lines, and save the drawing if desired.

7-11 Partial Auxiliary Views

Auxiliary views help present true-shaped views of slanted and oblique surfaces, but in doing so generate foreshortened views of other surfaces. It is often clearer to create an auxiliary view of just the slanted surface and omit the surfaces that would be foreshortened. Auxiliary views that show only one surface of an object are called ***partial auxiliary views.***

Figure 7-18 shows a front view and three partial views of the object: a partial top view and two partial auxiliary views. A broken line (see Section 6-14) may be used to show that the partial auxiliary view is part of a larger view that has been omitted. Likewise, hidden lines may or may not be included. Figure 7-19 shows a front, side, and two partial auxiliary views of an object. Both the hidden lines and broken lines were omitted. If you are unsure about the interpretation of a view with hidden lines

Figure 7-18

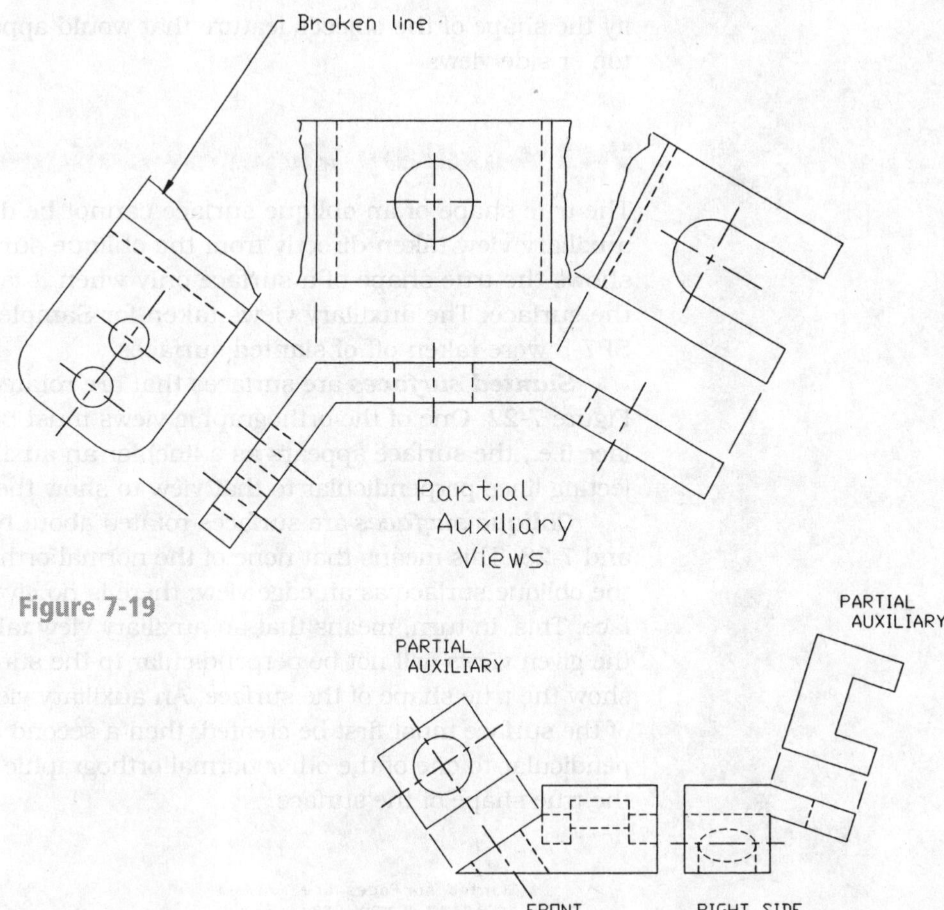

Figure 7-19

omitted, add a note to the drawing next to the partial views that says, "ALL HIDDEN LINES OMITTED FOR CLARITY."

7-12 Sectional Auxiliary Views

Sectional views may also be drawn as auxiliary views. Figure 7-20 shows an auxiliary sectional view. The cutting plane line is positioned across the object. A reference plane line is drawn parallel to the cutting plane line, and information is projected into the auxiliary sectional view by use of lines perpendicular to the cutting plane line.

Figure 7-21 shows front, partial auxiliary, and auxiliary sectional views of an object. In this example, the partial sectional view was used to help clar-

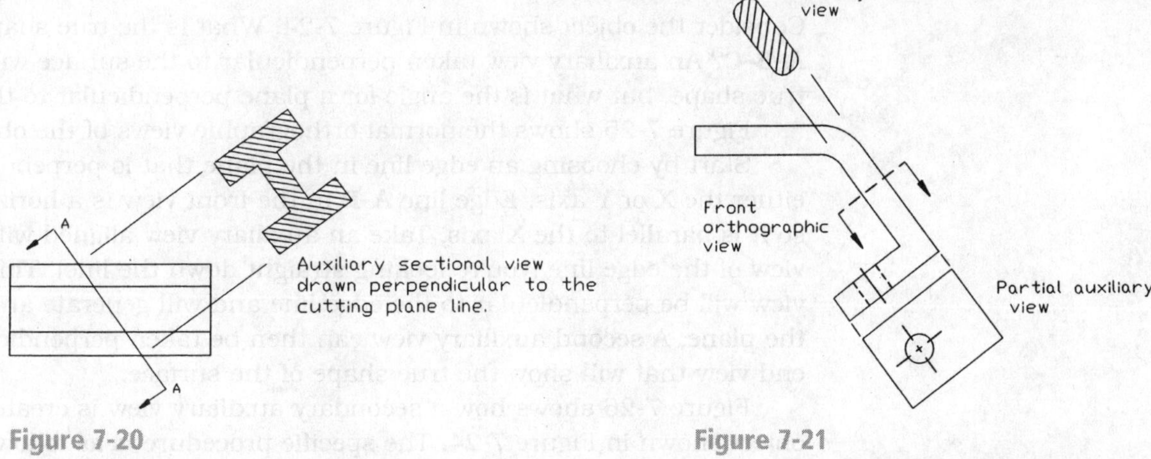

Figure 7-20

Figure 7-21

ify the shape of the object's feature that would appear vague in the normal top or side views.

7-13 Auxiliary Views of Oblique Surfaces

The true shape of an oblique surface cannot be determined by a single auxiliary view taken directly from the oblique surface. An auxiliary view shows the true shape of a surface only when it is taken at exactly 90° to the surface. The auxiliary views taken for Sample Problems SP7-1 through SP7-5 were taken off of slanted surfaces.

Slanted surfaces are surfaces that are rotated about only one axis. See Figure 7-22. One of the orthographic views must be an edge view of the surface (i.e., the surface appears as a line) for an auxiliary view created by projecting lines perpendicular to that view to show the true shape of the surface.

Oblique surfaces are surfaces rotated about two axes. See Figures 7-22 and 7-23. This means that none of the normal orthographic views will show the oblique surface as an edge view; there is no given end view of the surface. This, in turn, means that an auxiliary view taken directly from one of the given views will not be perpendicular to the surface and therefore will not show the true shape of the surface. An auxiliary view that shows an edge view of the surface must first be created; then a second auxiliary view taken perpendicular to one of the other normal orthographic views is needed to show the true shape of the surface.

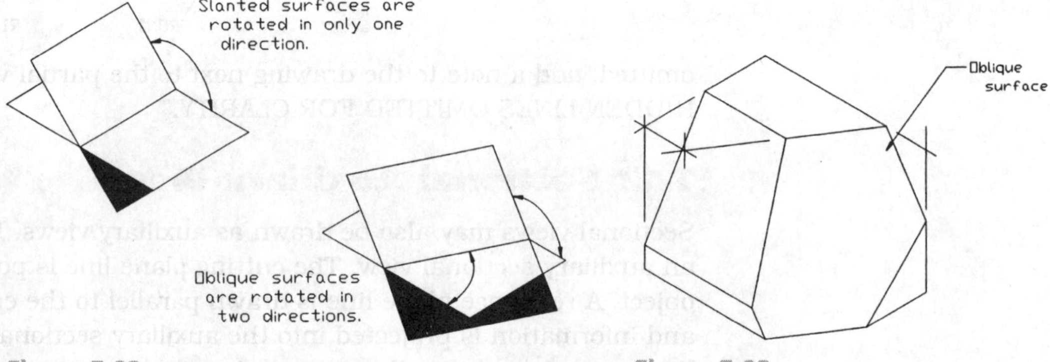

Figure 7-22 **Figure 7-23**

7-14 Secondary Auxiliary Views

Consider the object shown in Figure 7-24. What is the true shape of surface **A–B–C**? An auxiliary view taken perpendicular to the surface will show its true shape, but what is the angle for a plane perpendicular to the surface?

Figure 7-25 shows the normal orthographic views of the object.

Start by choosing an edge line in the plane that is perpendicular to either the X or Y axis. Edge line **A–B** in the front view is a horizontal line, so it is parallel to the X axis. Take an auxiliary view aligned with the top view of the edge line (you're looking straight down the line). This auxiliary view will be perpendicular to the edge line and will generate an end view of the plane. A second auxiliary view can then be taken perpendicular to the end view that will show the true shape of the surface.

Figure 7-26 shows how a secondary auxiliary view is created for the object shown in Figure 7-24. The specific procedure is as follows:

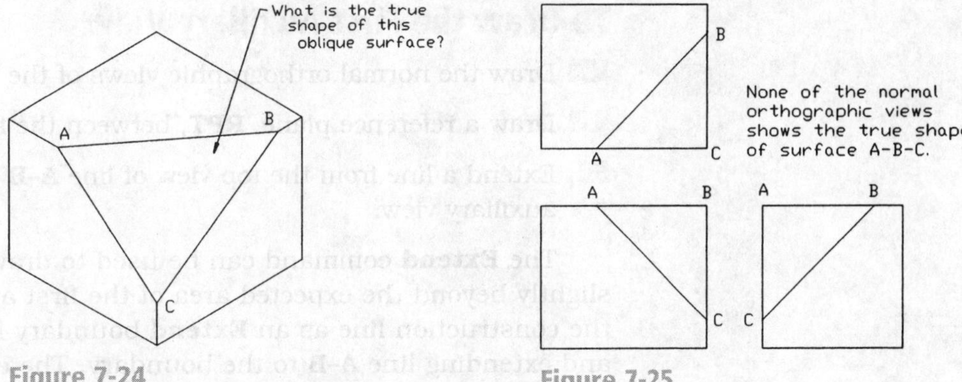

Figure 7-24

Figure 7-25

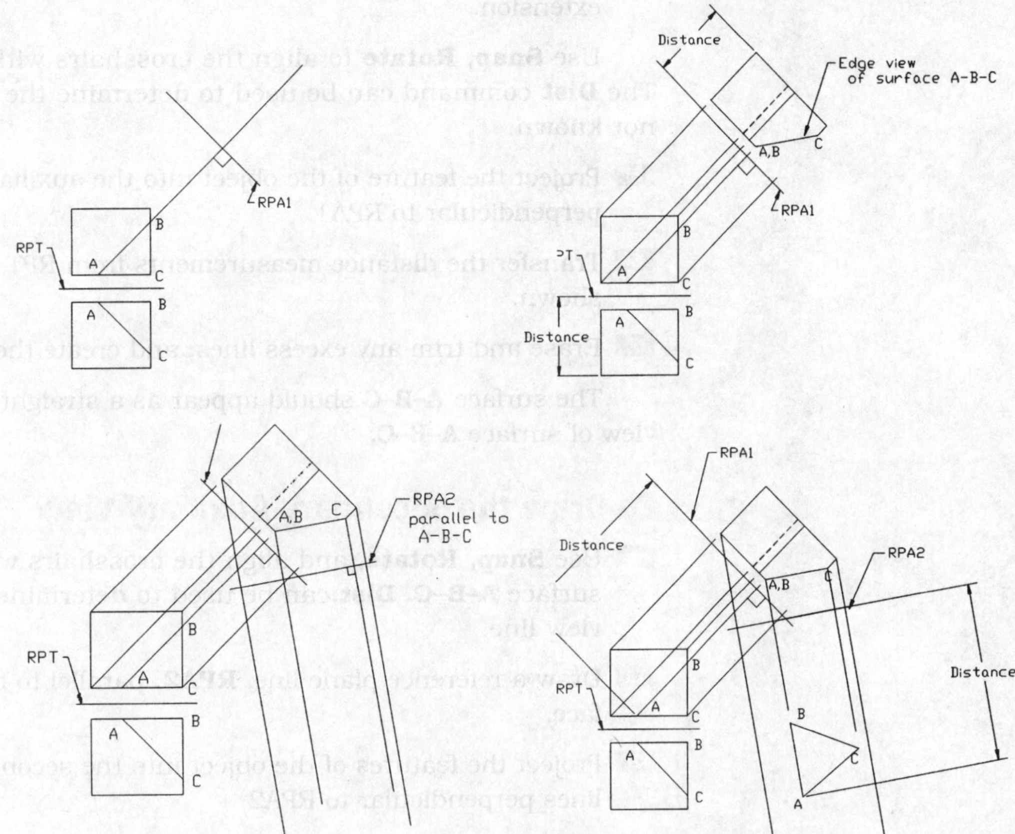

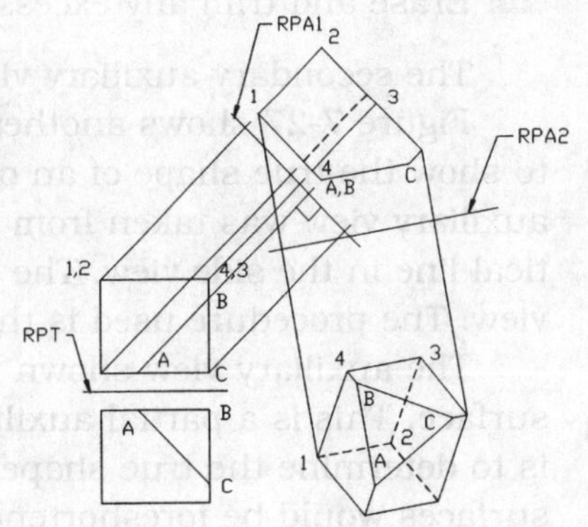

Figure 7-26

To Draw the First Auxiliary View

1. Draw the normal orthographic views of the object.
2. Draw a reference plane, **RPT,** between the front and top views.
3. Extend a line from the top view of line **A–B** in the area for the first auxiliary view.

The **Extend** command can be used to draw a construction line slightly beyond the expected area of the first auxiliary view, then using the construction line as an **Extend** boundary line (see Section 2-24), and extending line **A–B** to the boundary. The construction line can then be erased.

4. Draw a reference plane line, **RPA1,** perpendicular to the line **A–B** extension.

Use **Snap, Rotate** to align the crosshairs with the extension line. The **Dist** command can be used to determine the line's angle if it is not known.

5. Project the feature of the object into the auxiliary view by using lines perpendicular to RPA1.
6. Transfer the distance measurements from RPT and the front view as shown.
7. Erase and trim any excess lines, and create the first auxiliary view.

The surface **A–B–C** should appear as a straight line. This is an edge view of surface **A–B–C.**

To Draw the Secondary Auxiliary View

1. Use **Snap, Rotate,** and align the crosshairs with the end view of surface **A–B–C. Dist** can be used to determine the angle of the edge view line.
2. Draw a reference plane line, **RPA2,** parallel to the edge view of the surface.
3. Project the features of the object into the second auxiliary view, using lines perpendicular to RPA2.
4. Transfer the distance measurements from RPA1 and the top view as shown.
5. Erase and trim any excess lines, and save the drawing if desired.

The secondary auxiliary view shows the true shape of surface **A–B–C.**

Figure 7-27 shows another example of a secondary auxiliary view used to show the true shape of an oblique surface. In this example, the first auxiliary view was taken from line **F–A** in the front view because it is a vertical line in the side view. The distance measurements came from the top view. The procedure used is the same as described previously.

The auxiliary view shown in Figure 7-27 includes only the oblique surface. This is a partial auxiliary view. The purpose of the auxiliary view is to determine the true shape of the oblique surface. All of the other surfaces would be foreshortened, not their true shape, if included in the auxiliary views.

Figure 7-27

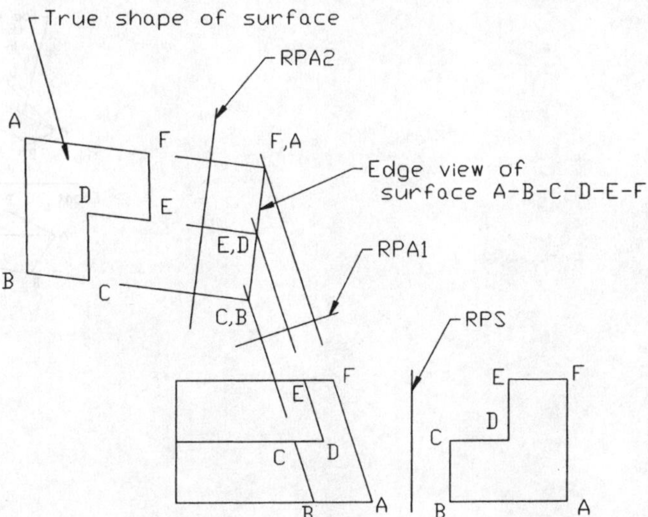

7-15 Sample Problem SP7-6

What is the true shape of the plane shown in Figure 7-28?

None of the edge lines are horizontal or vertical lines, so a line must be defined within the plane that is either horizontal or vertical. The added line can then be used to generate the two auxiliary views needed to define the true shape of the plane.

The procedure is as follows. See Figure 7-29.

1 Draw a horizontal line from point **A** in the front view.

Use **Osnap Intersection** with **Ortho** on, and draw the line across the view. Use **Trim** to remove the excess portion of the line.

2 Define the intersection of the new line with one of the plane's edge lines **(D–C)** as **x.**

3 Project line **A–x** into the top view.

Option: Create a layer for projection lines.

The location of point **A** is already known in the top view. The location of point **x** in the top view can be found by drawing a vertical line from point **x** in the front view so that the line intersects line **D–C** in the top view. Use **Osnap Intersection, Ortho** on, to ensure accuracy.

4 Extend line **A–x** into the area for the first auxiliary view.

Draw a construction line to use as a boundary line for the **Extend** command.

5 Draw two reference plane lines: **RPT** between the front and top views, and **RPA1** perpendicular to the extension of line **A–x.**

Use **Snap, Rotate** to align the crosshairs with the extension of line **A–x.**

6 Project the plane's corner points into the area of the first auxiliary view from the top view. Transfer the distance measurements from RPT and the front view.

Use **Dist** to determine the distance from RPF and the corner points of the surface. Use **Offset** to transfer the point distance from RPF to RPA1. Use **Trim** to remove the internal portion of the offset lines. This will help clarify

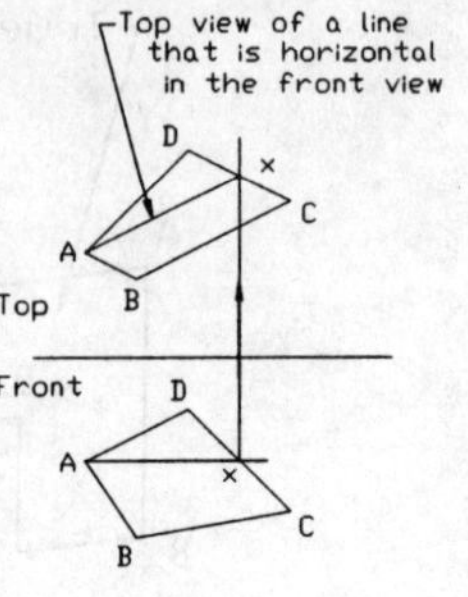

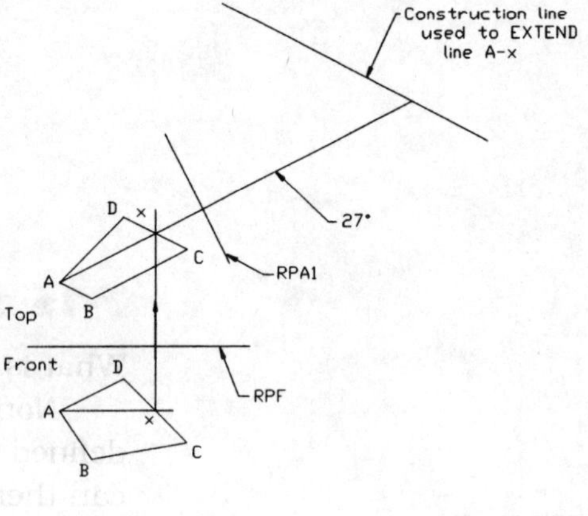

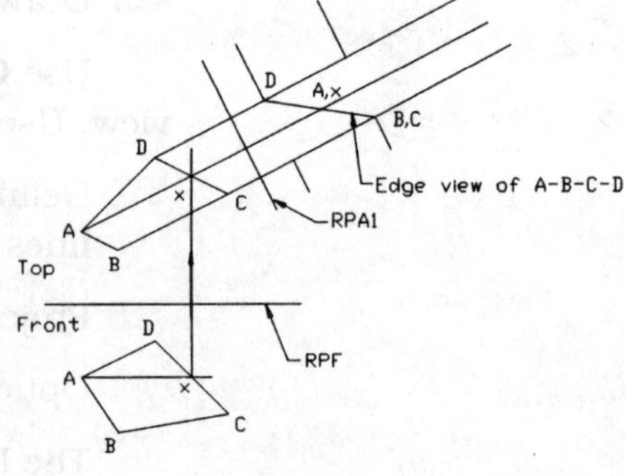

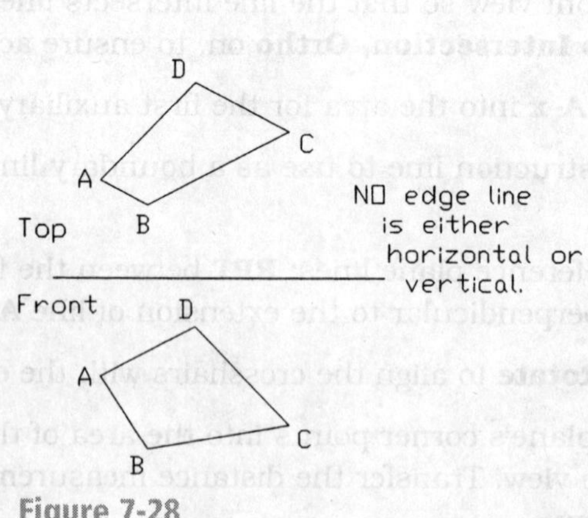

Figure 7-28

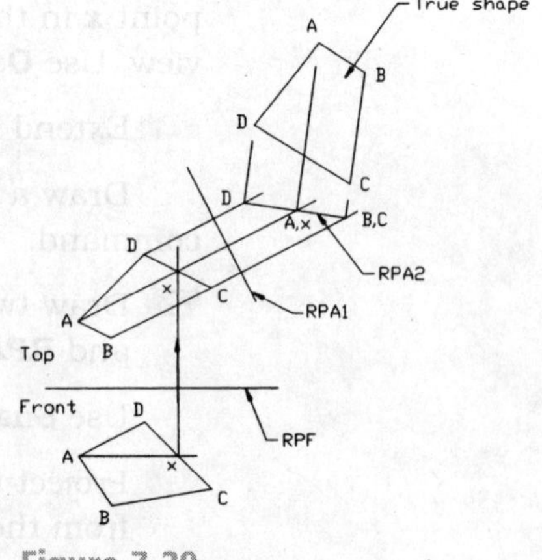

Figure 7-29

the drawing by removing excess lines from the auxiliary view, but will retain intersection points needed to draw lines by using **Osnap Intersection.**

The plane should appear as a straight line, the end view of the plane.

7. Draw a third reference plane line, **RPA2,** parallel to the end view of the plane, and project the plane's corner points into the secondary auxiliary view area.
8. Transfer the depth distances from RPA1 and the top view to RPA2 and the secondary auxiliary view.
9. Erase and trim any excess lines, and save the drawing if desired.

The secondary auxiliary view shows the true shape of surface **A–B–C–D.**

7-16 Secondary Auxiliary View of an Ellipse

Figure 7-30 shows the front and side views of an oblique surface and includes a foreshortened view of a hole—that is, an ellipse. Also included are two auxiliary views, the second of which shows the hole as a circle.

Figure 7-30

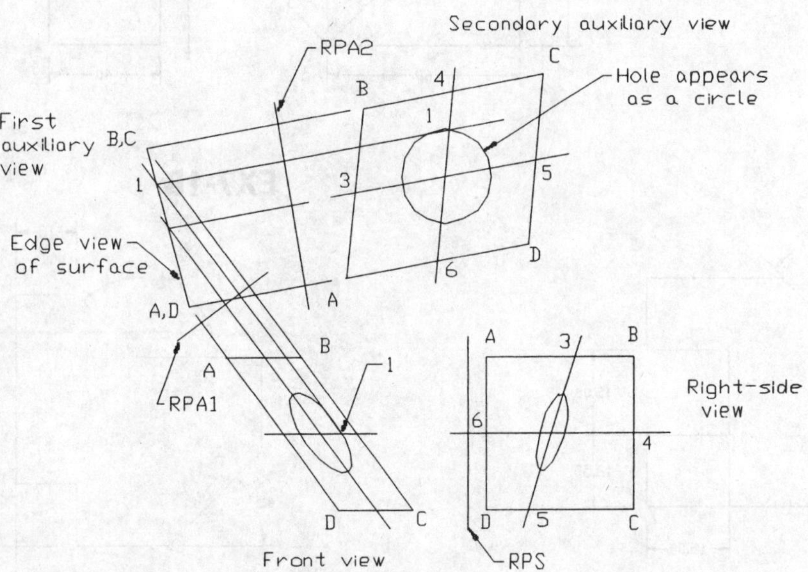

The ellipse is projected by first determining the correct projection angle that will produce an edge view of surface **A–B–C–D.** In this example, line **B–C** appears as a vertical line in the side view, so its front view can be used to project the required edge view.

It is known that the secondary view of the surface will show the hole as a circle, so only a radius value need be carried between the views. In this example, point 1 in the front view was projected into the first auxiliary view and then into the second auxiliary view, thereby defining the radius of the circle.

The hole is located at the center of the surface, which means that its centerlines are located on the midpoints of the edge lines in the secondary auxiliary views. If the hole's center point was not in the center of the surface, the intersections of the hole's centerlines with the surface's edge lines would also have to be projected into the secondary auxiliary view to accurately locate the hole.

7-17 EXERCISE PROBLEMS

Given the outlines for front, side, and auxiliary views as shown, substitute one of the side views shown in Exercise Problems EX7-1A through EX7-1D and complete the front and auxiliary views. All dimensions are in millimeters.

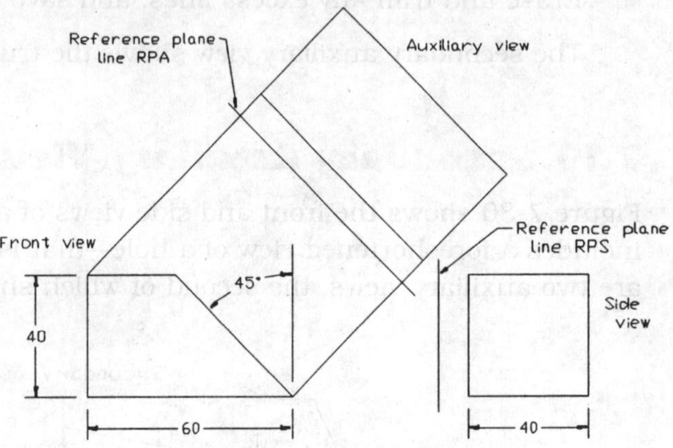

EX7-1A

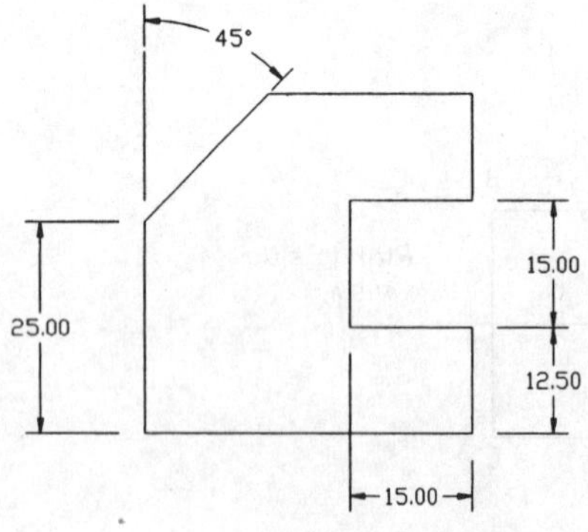

EX7-1B

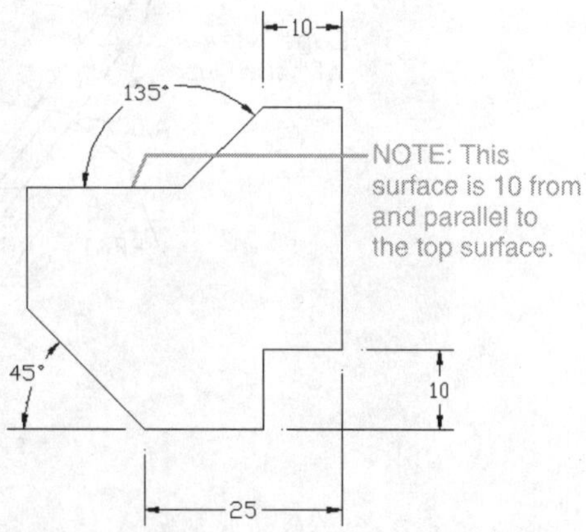

EX7-1C

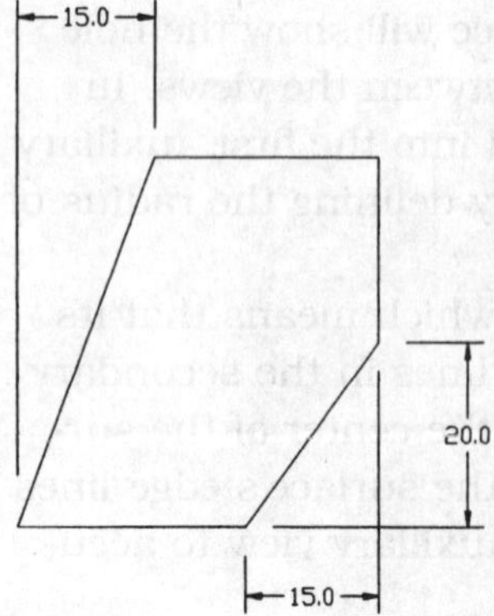

EX7-1D

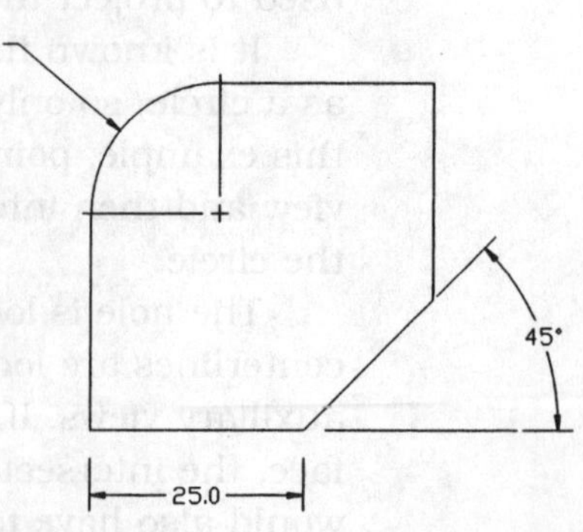

Given the outlines for front, side, and auxiliary views as shown, substitute one of the side views shown in Exercise Problems EX7-2A through EX7-2D and complete the front and auxiliary views. All dimensions are in millimeters.

Draw two orthographic views and an auxiliary view for each of the objects shown.

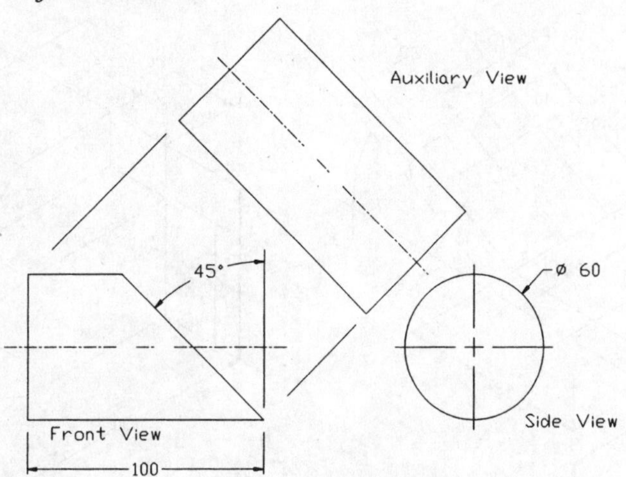

EX7-2A

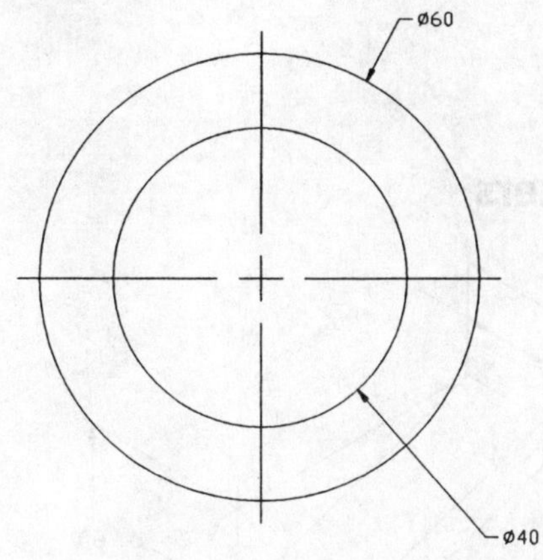

EX7-2B

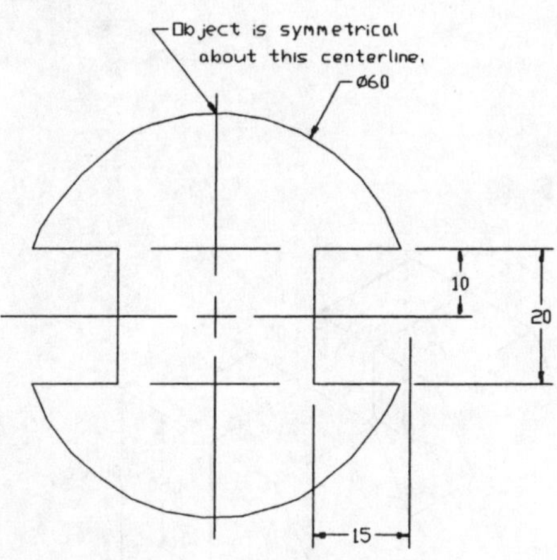

EX7-2C

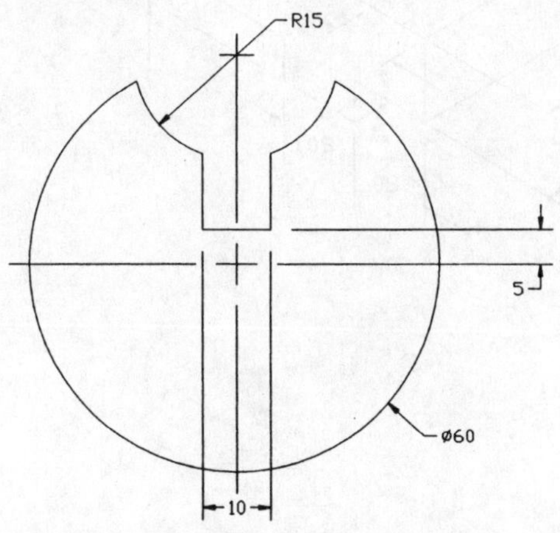

EX7-2D

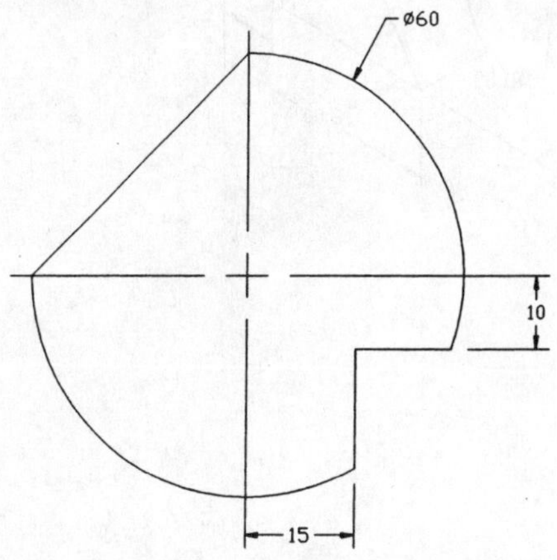

Draw two orthographic views and an auxiliary view for each of the objects in Exercise Problems EX7-3 through EX7-6.

EX7-3 Millimeters

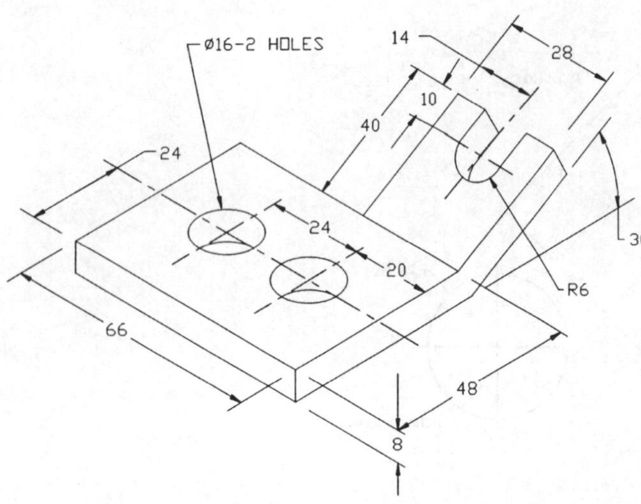

EX7-4 Millimeters

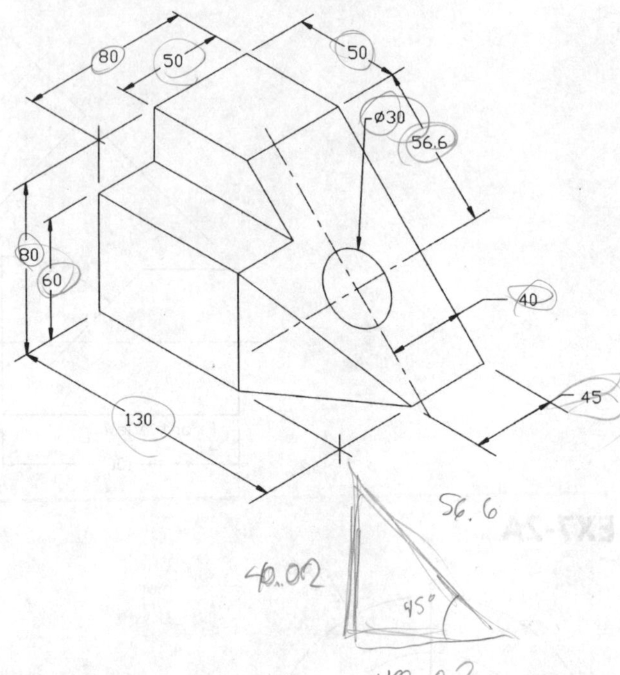

EX7-5 Inches

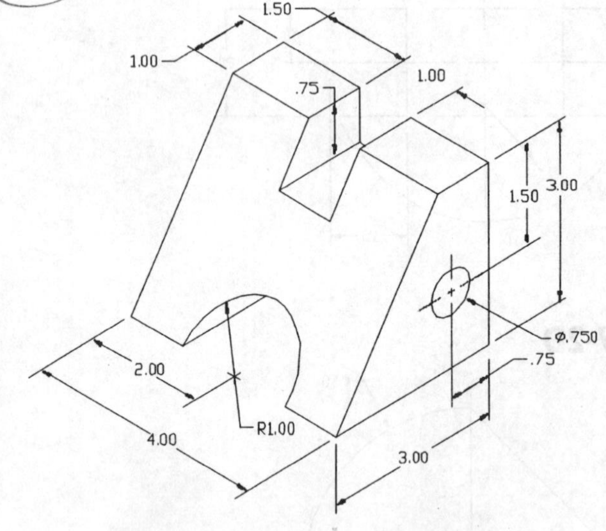

EX7-6 Millimeters

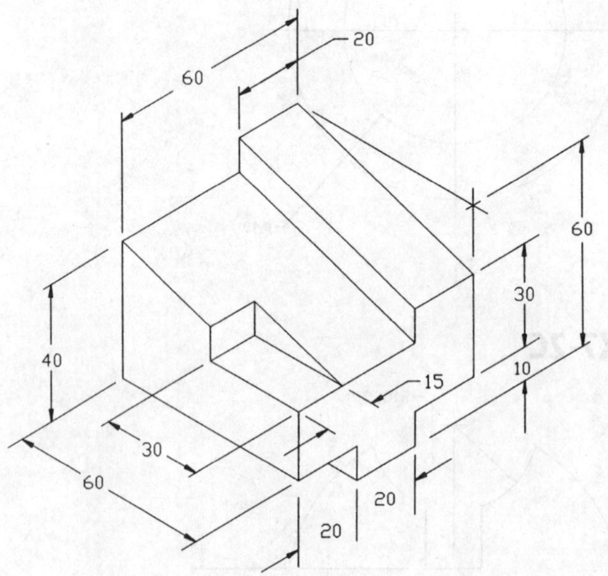

Redraw the given orthographic views in Exercise Problems EX7-7 through EX7-10, and add the appropriate auxiliary view.

EX7-7 Millimeters

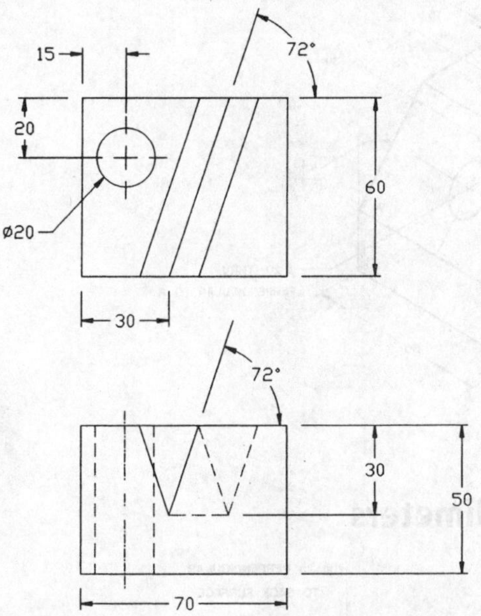

EX7-8 Millimeters

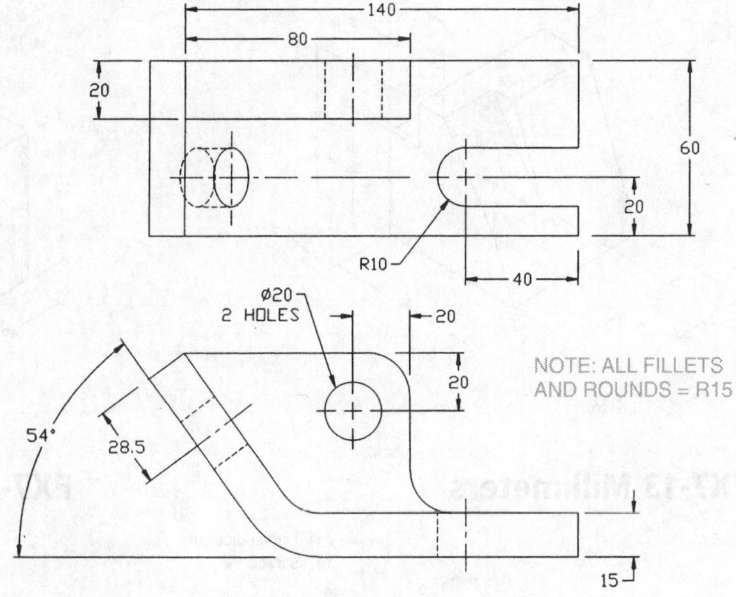

EX7-9 Inches

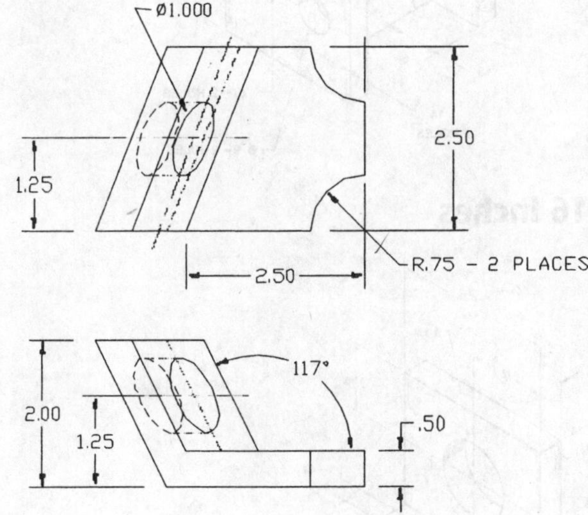

EX7-10 Millimeters

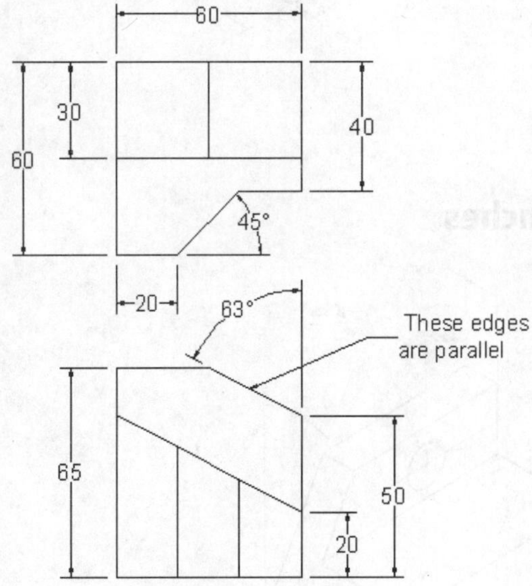

Draw two orthographic views and an auxiliary view for each of the objects in Exercise Problems EX7-11 through EX7-40.

EX7-11 Millimeters

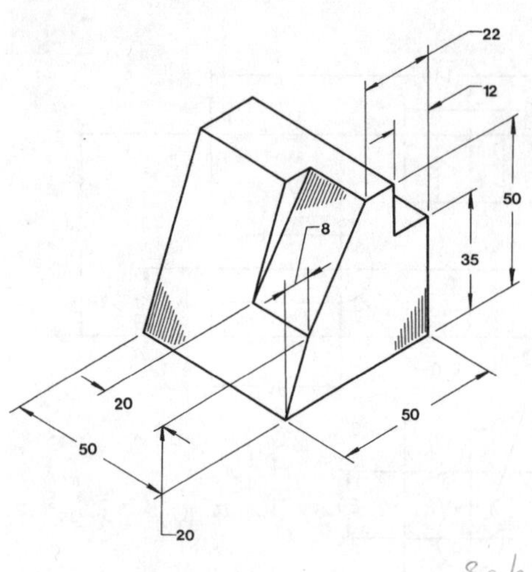

EX7-12 Millimeters

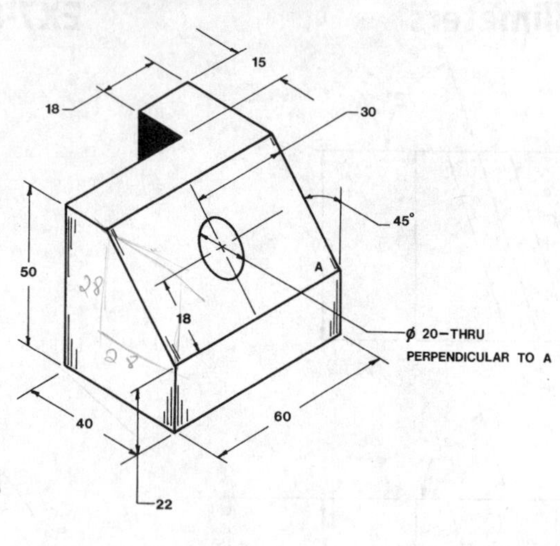

EX7-13 Millimeters

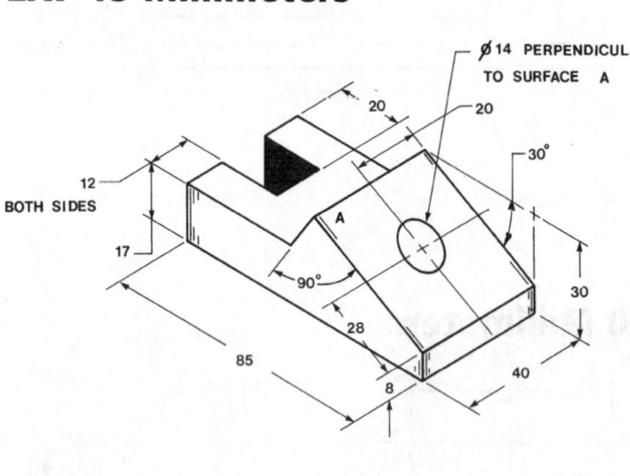

EX7-14 Millimeters

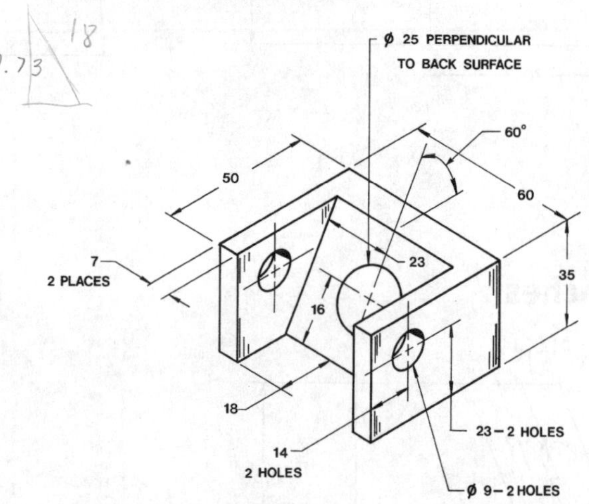

EX7-15 Inches

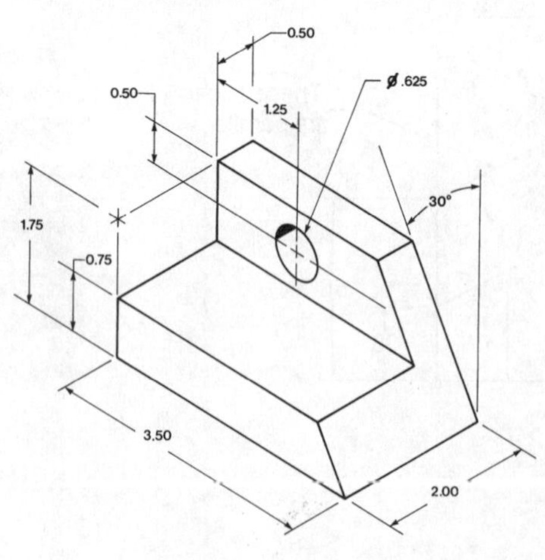

EX7-16 Inches

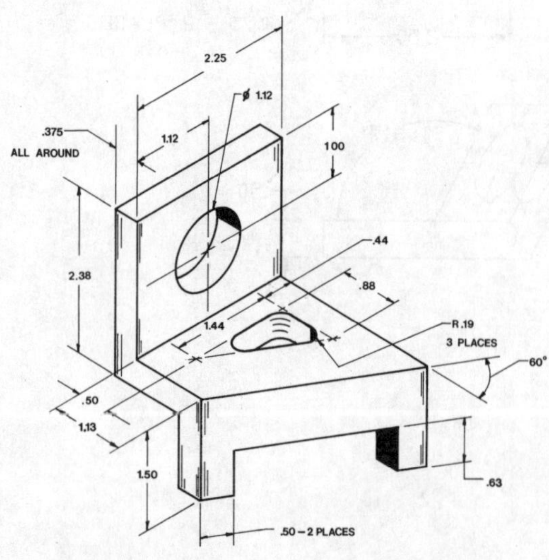

EX7-17 Millimeters

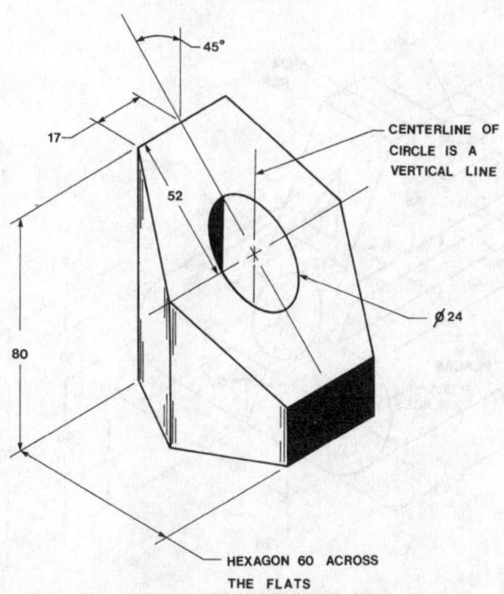

EX7-18 Millimeters

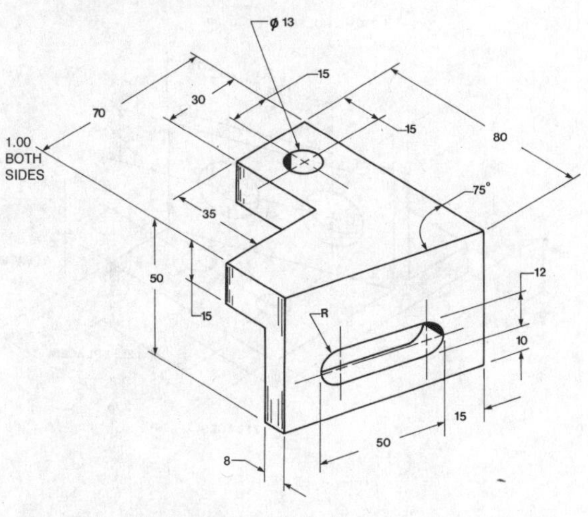

EX7-19 Millimeters

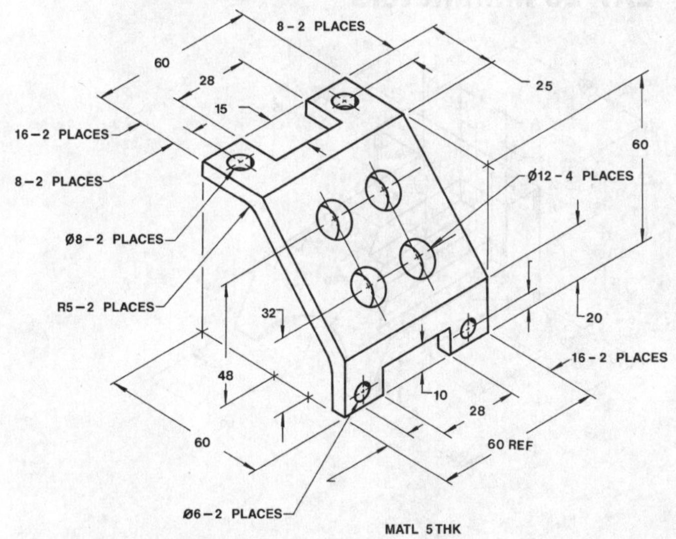

EX7-20 Inches

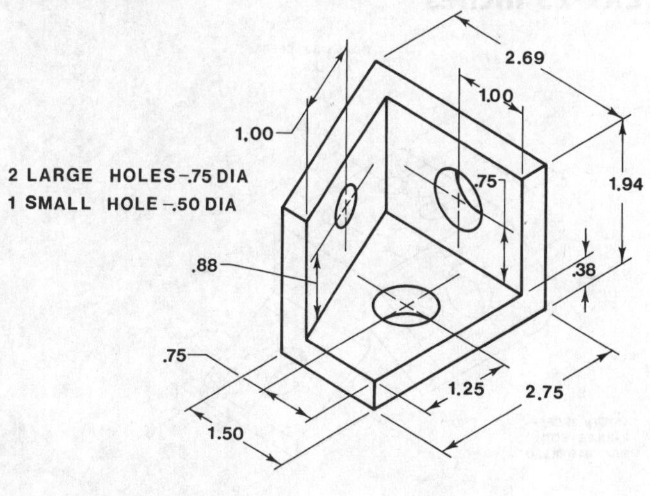

EX7-21 Millimeters

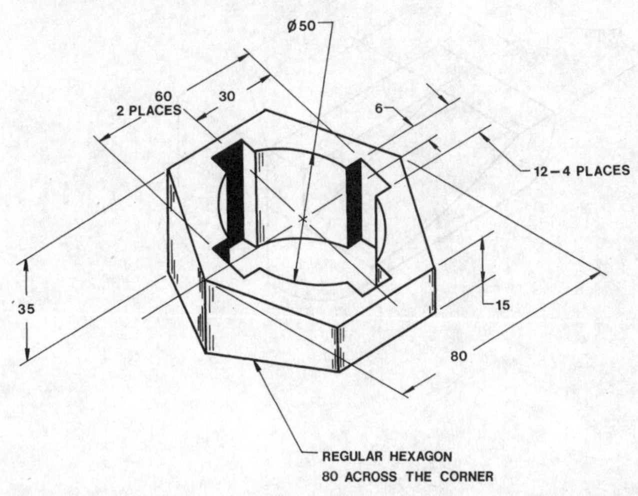

EX7-22 Millimeters

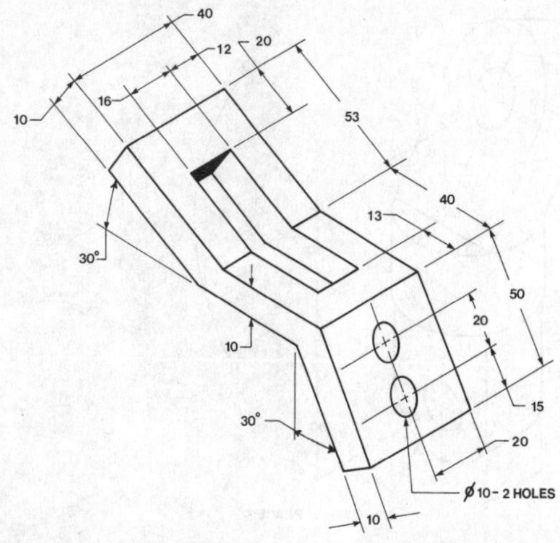

EX7-23 Inches

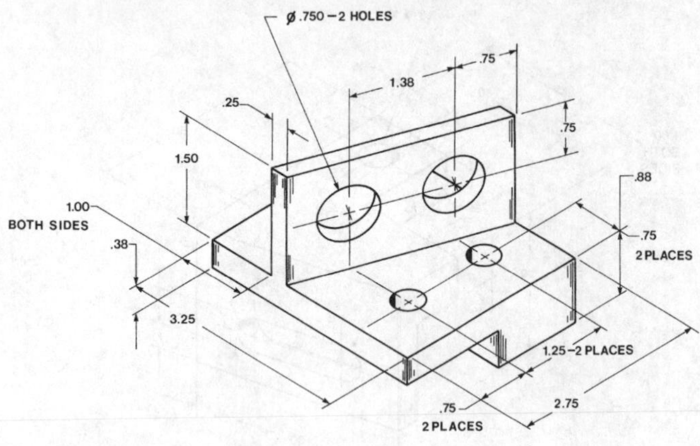

EX7-24 Millimeters

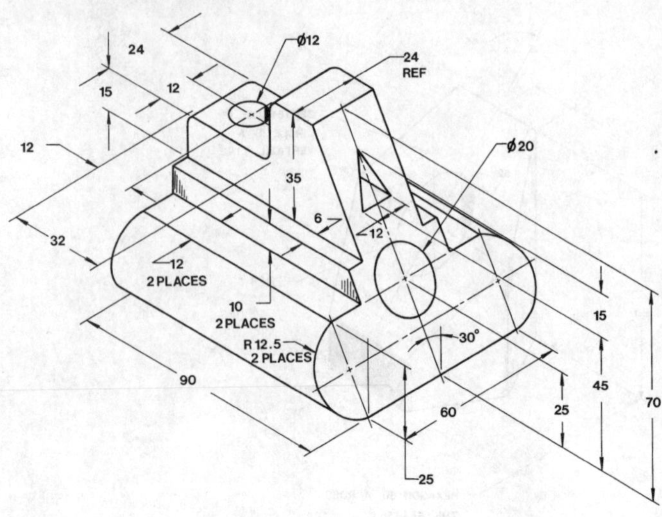

EX7-25 Inches

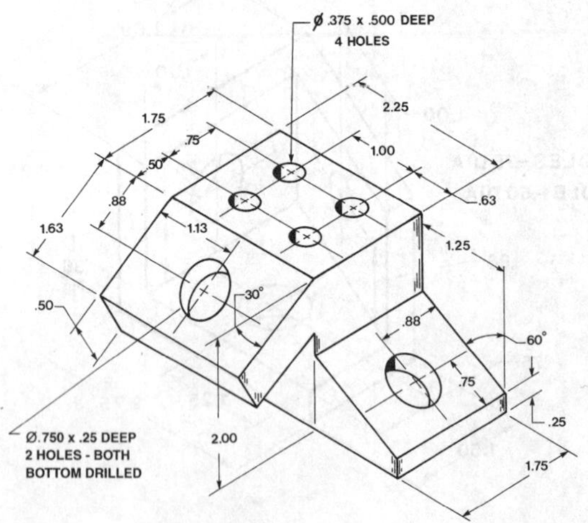

EX7-26 Millimeters

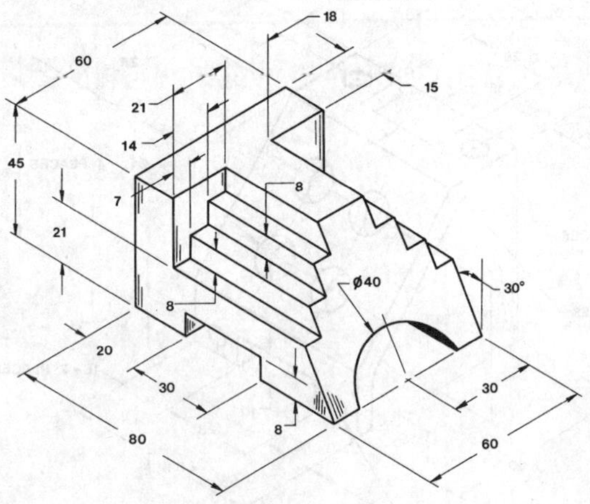

EX7-27 Millimeters

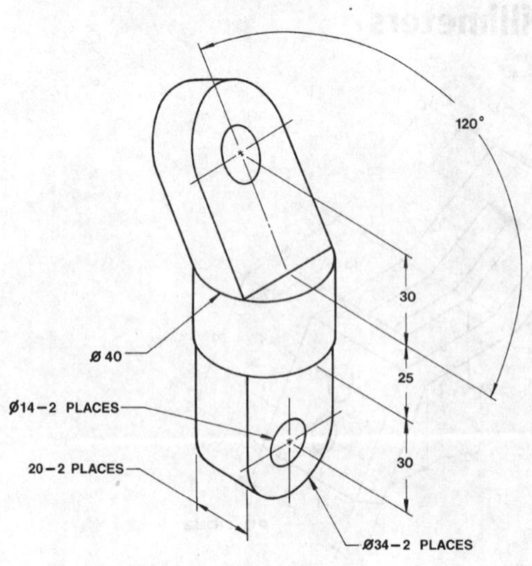

EX7-28 Millimeters

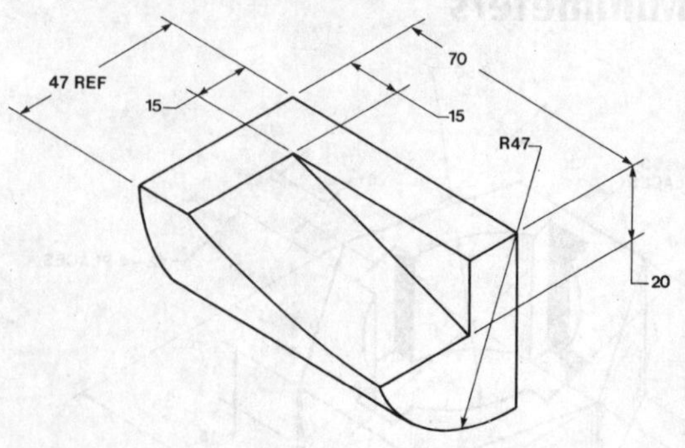

EX7-29 Millimeters

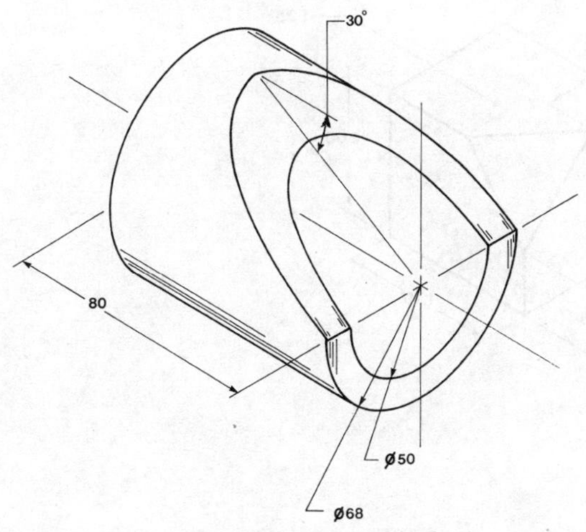

EX7-30 Millimeters

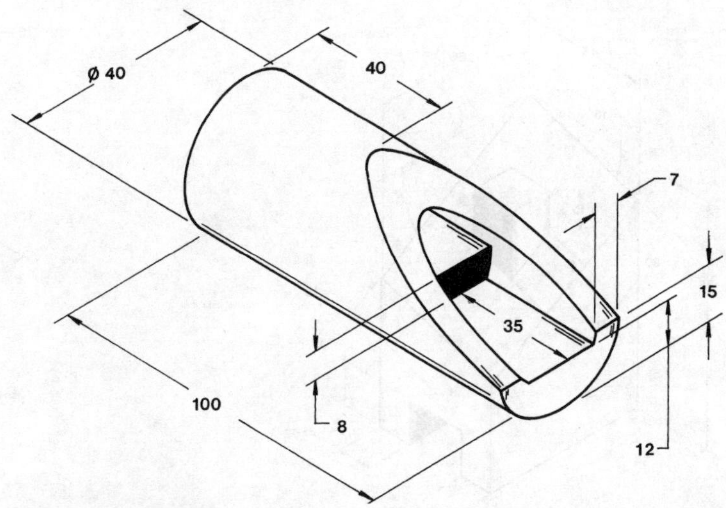

EX7-31 Inches

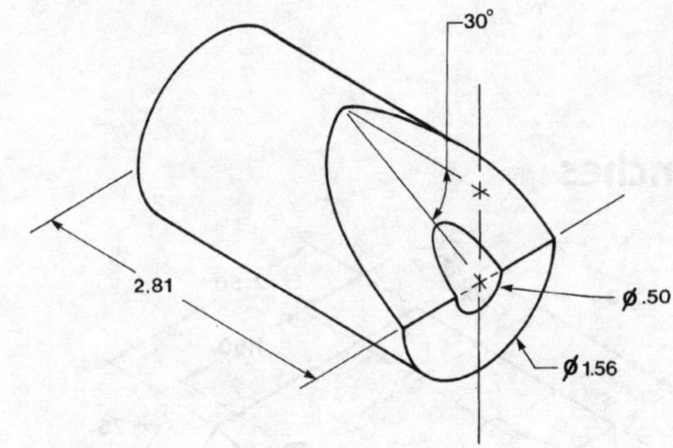

EX7-32 Millimeters

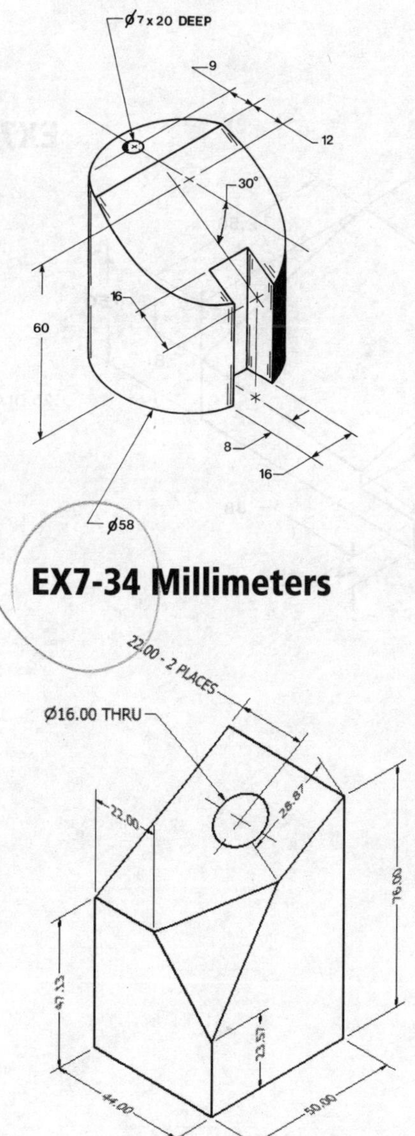

EX7-33 Millimeters

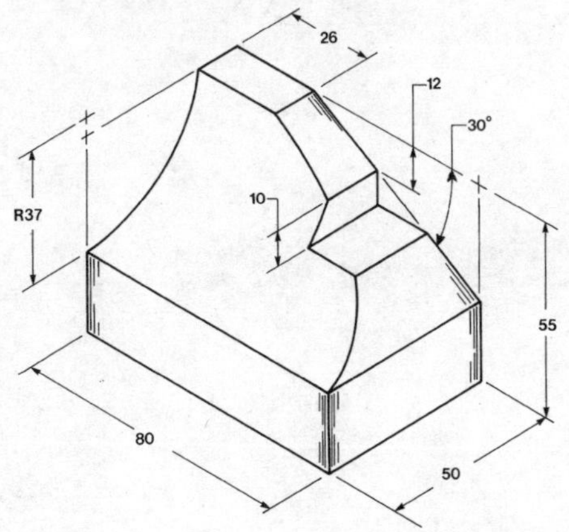

EX7-34 Millimeters

EX7-35 Millimeters

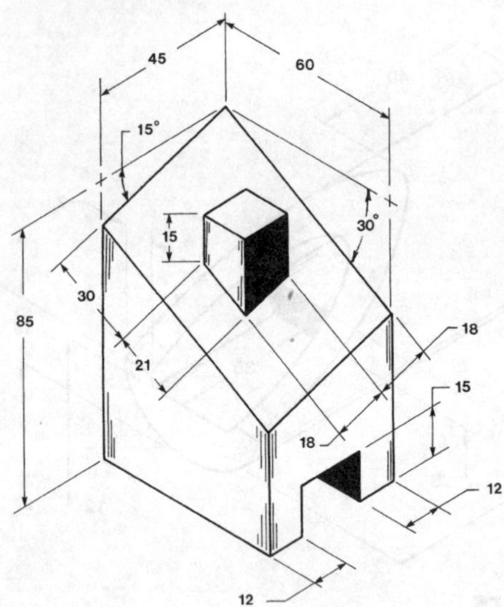

EX7-36 Inches

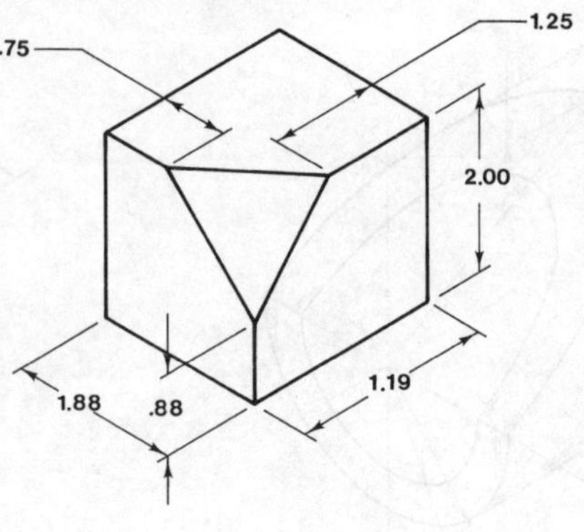

EX7-37 Inches

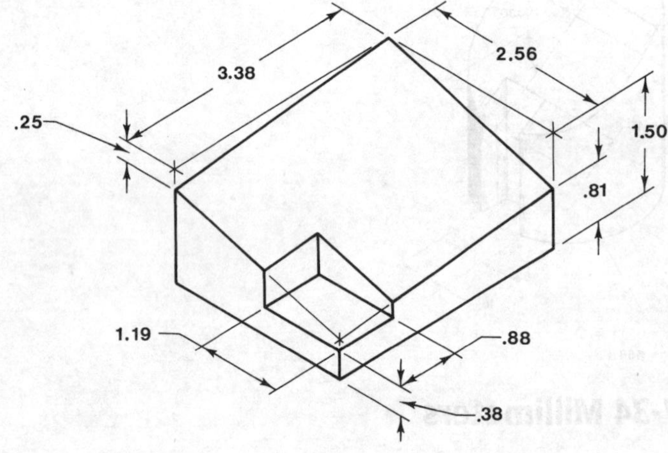

EX7-38 Inches

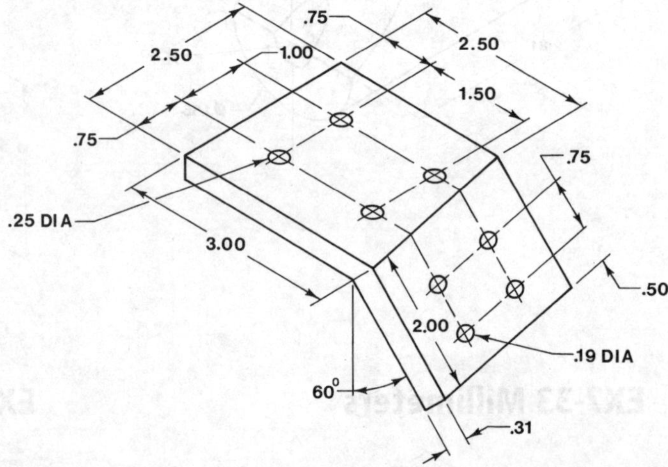

EX7-39 Millimeters

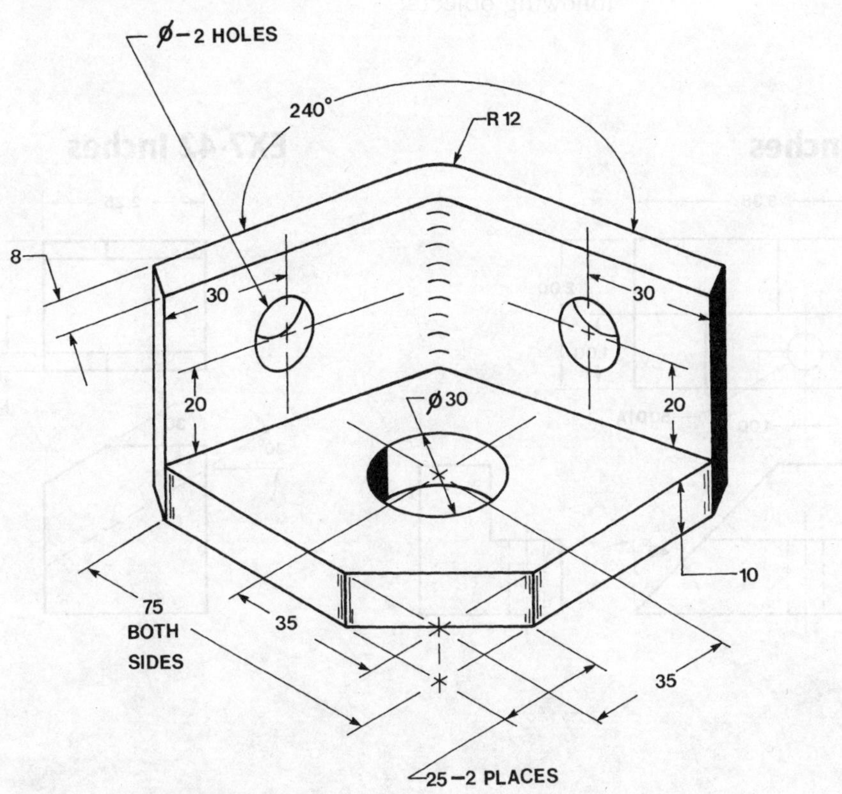

EX7-40 Millimeters

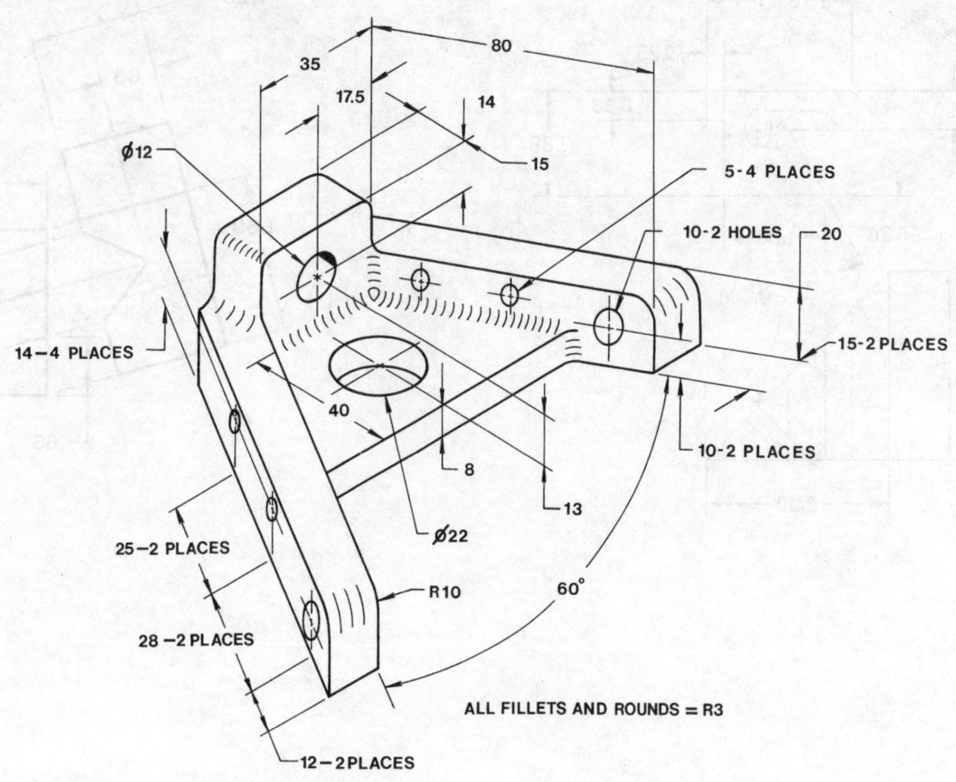

Draw at least two orthographic views and one auxiliary view for each of the following objects:

EX7-41 Inches

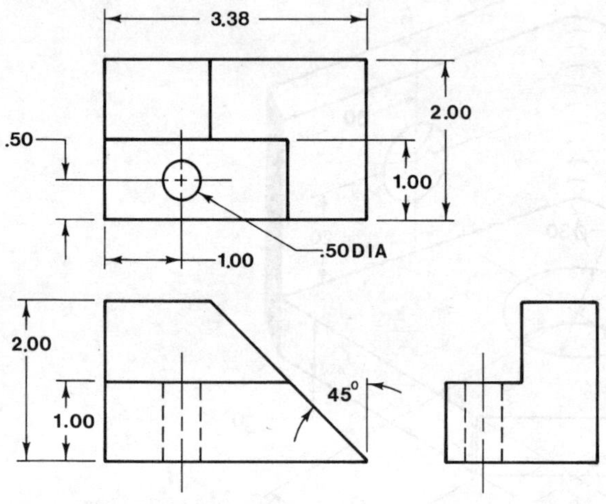

EX7-42 Inches

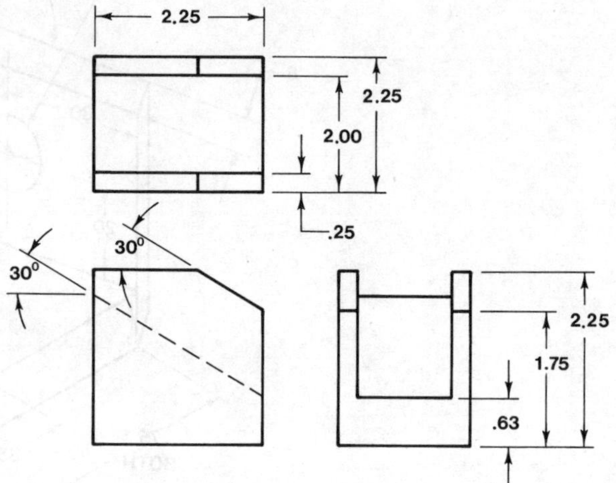

EX7-43 Inches

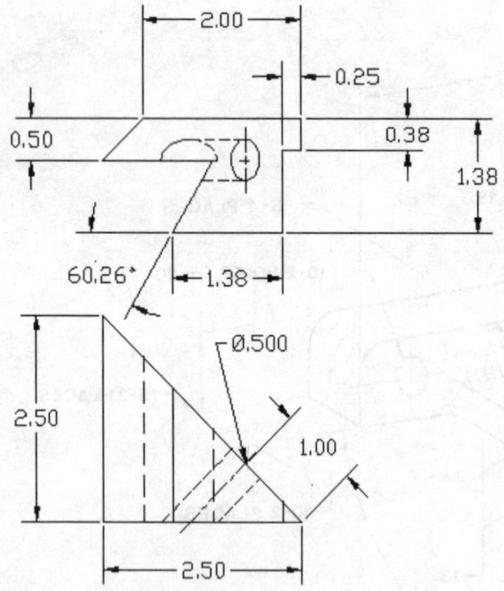

EX7-44 Inches

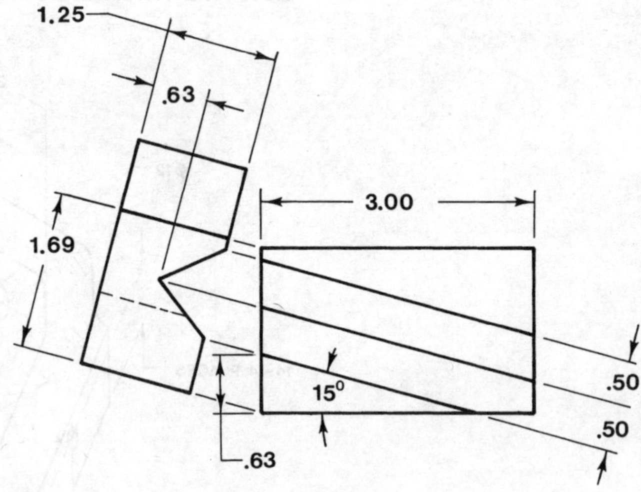

Use a secondary auxiliary view to find the true shape of the planes in Exercise Problems EX7-45 through EX7-50.

EX7-45 Millimeters

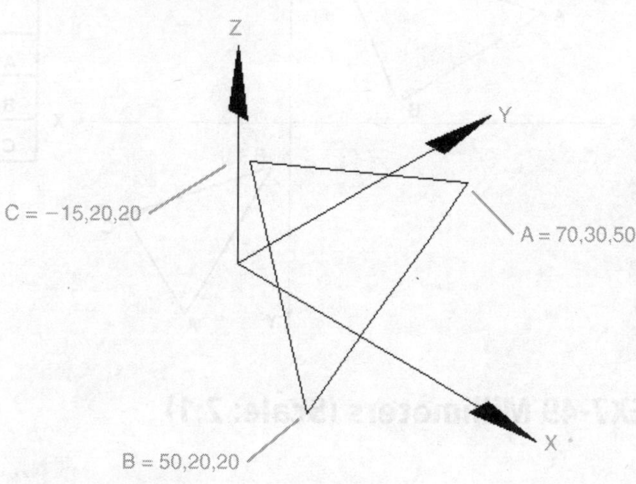

EX7-46 Millimeters

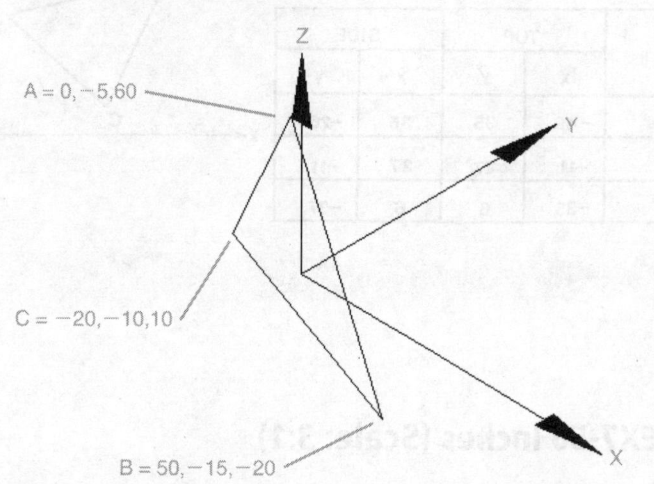

EX7-47 Millimeters

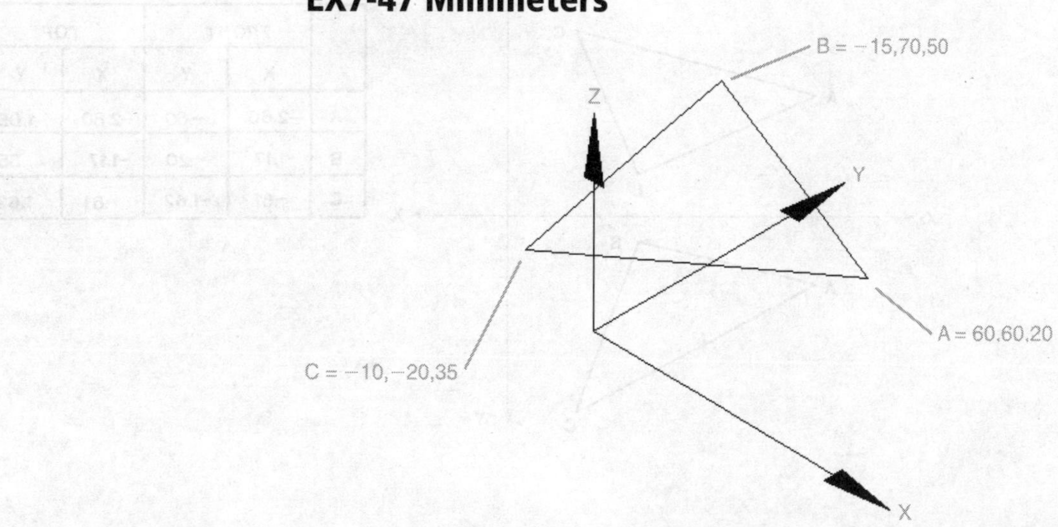

EX7-48 Inches (Scale: 4:1)

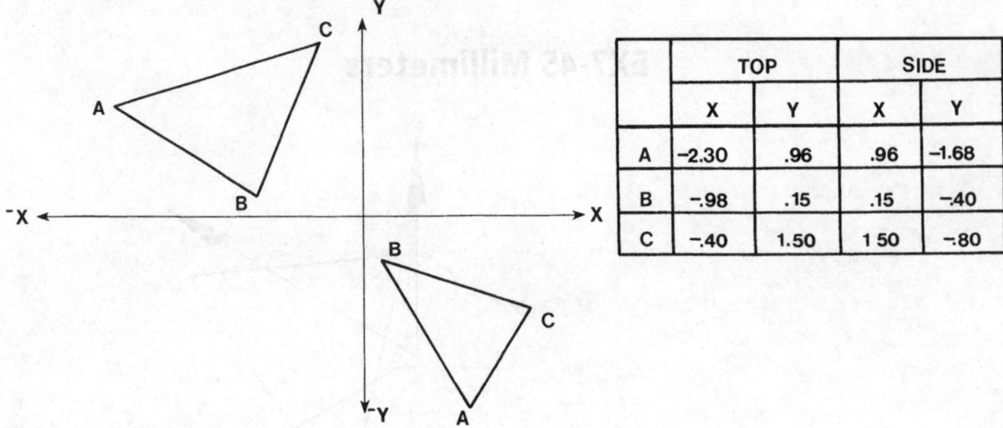

	TOP		SIDE	
	X	Y	X	Y
A	–2.30	.96	.96	–1.68
B	–.98	.15	.15	–.40
C	–.40	1.50	1.50	–.80

EX7-49 Millimeters (Scale: 2:1)

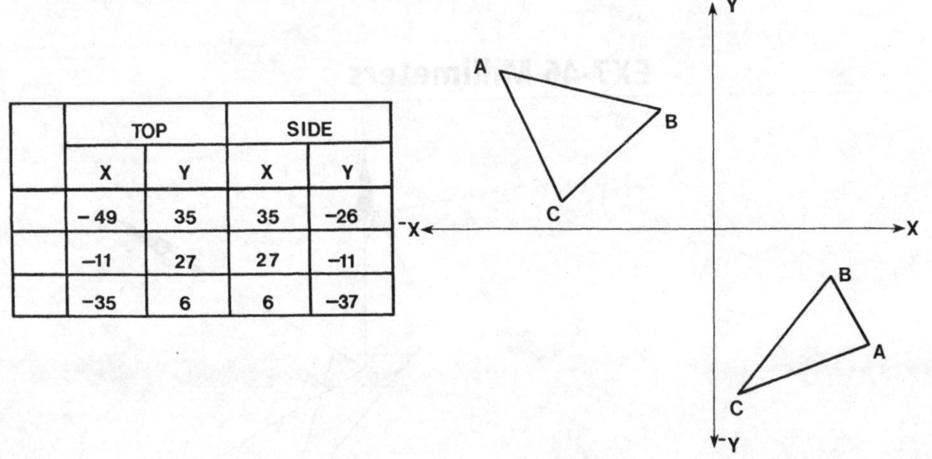

	TOP		SIDE	
	X	Y	X	Y
	– 49	35	35	–26
	–11	27	27	–11
	–35	6	6	–37

EX7-50 Inches (Scale: 3:1)

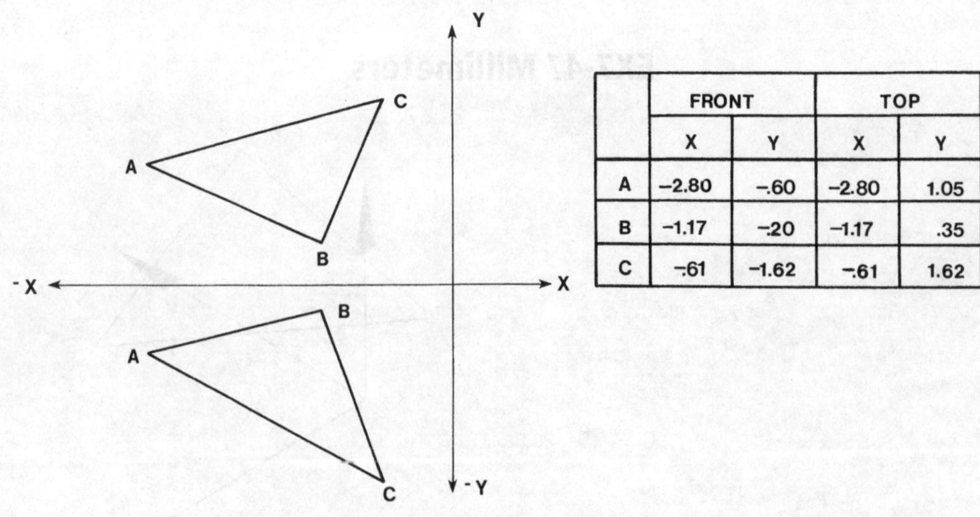

	FRONT		TOP	
	X	Y	X	Y
A	–2.80	–.60	–2.80	1.05
B	–1.17	–.20	–1.17	.35
C	–.61	–1.62	–.61	1.62

EX7-51 Millimeters

Redesign the given object to include two Ø10 holes in the slanted surface. The holes should be centered along the longitudinal axis, and spaced so that the distance between the holes' centers equals the distance from the holes' centers to the upper and lower edges of the slanted surface. The holes should be perpendicular to the slanted surface.

Draw the front, top, and side views of the object, plus an auxiliary view of the slanted surface.

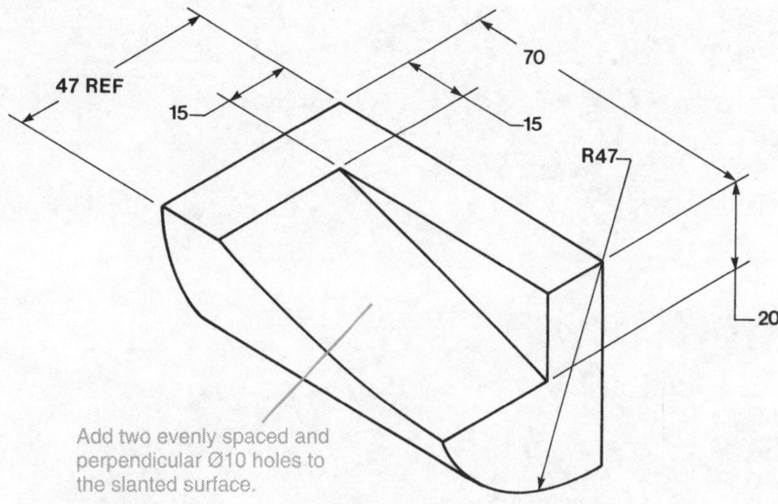

EX7-52 Millimeters

Redesign the given object so that the outside shape is a regular heptagon (seven-sided polygon) 80 across the flats, and the inside Ø50 hole is intersected by six evenly spaced slots each 12 wide. Draw front and top orthographic views and an auxiliary view of the object.

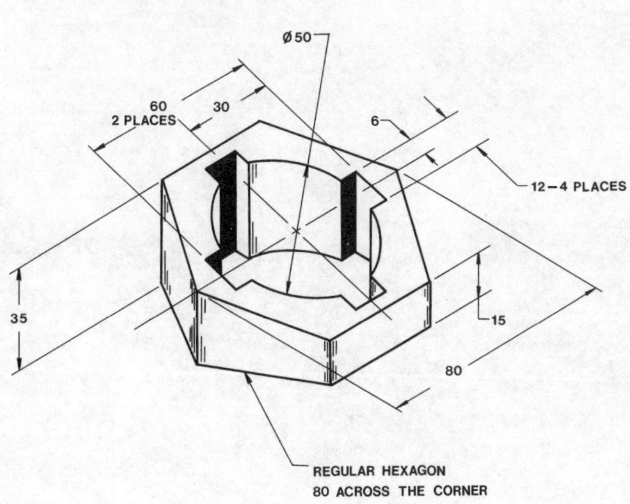

EX7-53 Millimeters

Calculate the area of the given plane. Redesign the plane so that the new plane is congruent to the original, but has an area equal to 1.5 times the original area. Draw and label the true shape of the new plane relative to the X, Y, Z axes.

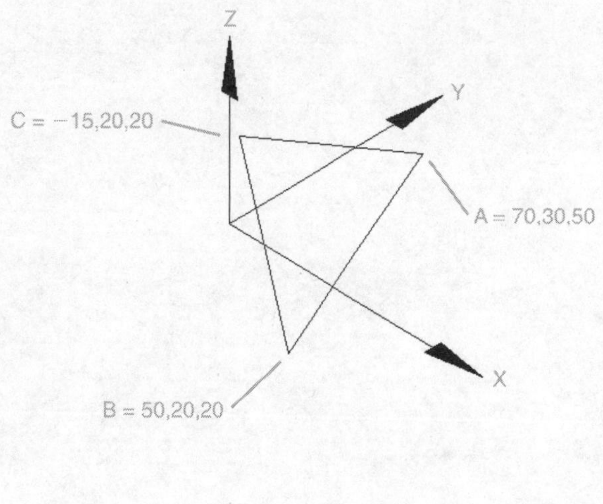

8 chapter eight

Dimensioning

8-1 Introduction

This chapter explains the **Dimensions** panel located under the **Annotate** tab. See Figure 8-1. The chapter first explains dimensioning terminology and conventions, and then presents an explanation of each tool within the **Dimensions** panel. The chapter also demonstrates how dimensions are applied to drawings and gives examples of standard drawing conventions and practices.

Figure 8-1

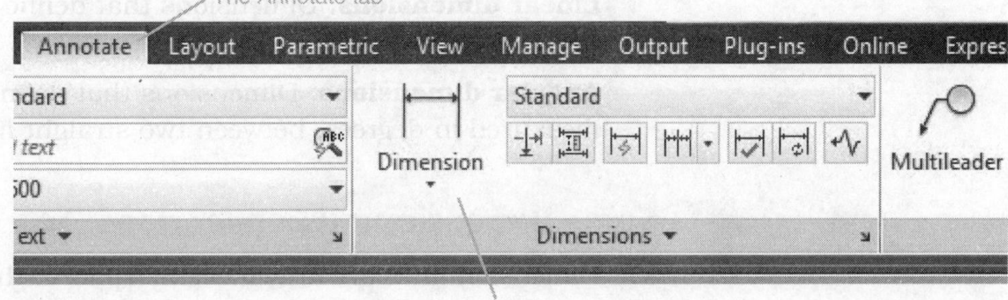

8-2 Terminology and Conventions

Some Common Terms (See Figure 8-2.)

Dimension lines: Mechanical drawings contain lines between extension lines that end with arrowheads and include a numerical dimensional value located within the line; these are dimension lines. Architectural drawings contain lines between extension lines that end with tick marks and include a numerical dimensional value above the line; these also are dimension lines.

Extension lines: Lines that extend away from an object and allow dimensions to be located off of the surface of an object.

Figure 8-2

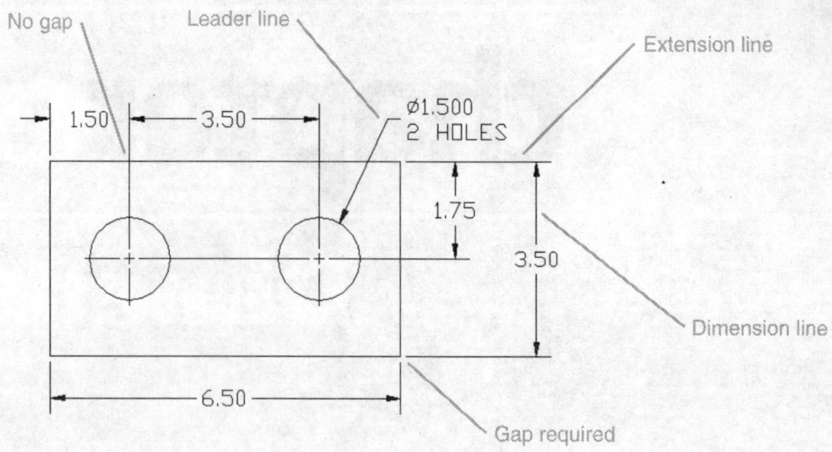

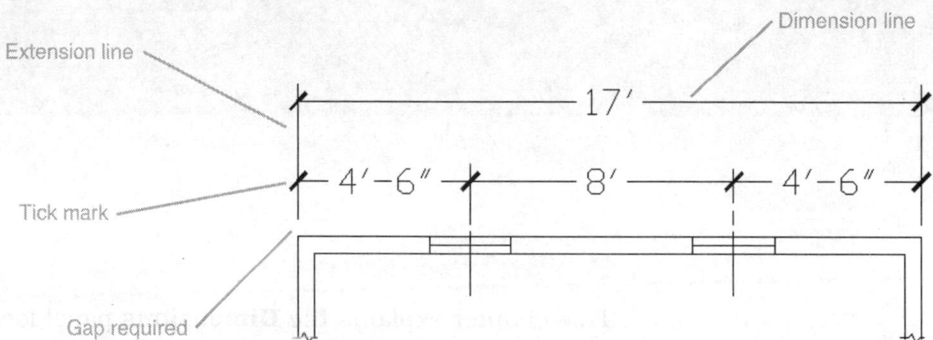

Leader lines: Lines drawn at an angle, not horizontal or vertical, that are used to dimension specific shapes such as holes. The start point of a leader line includes an arrowhead. Numerical values are drawn at the end opposite the arrowhead.

Linear dimensions: Dimensions that define the straight-line distance between two points.

Angular dimensions: Dimensions that define the angular value, measured in degrees, between two straight lines.

Some Dimensioning Conventions (See Figure 8-3.)

1. Dimension lines are drawn evenly spaced; that is, the distance between dimension lines is uniform. A general rule of thumb is to locate dimension lines about 1/2 inch, or 15 millimeters, apart.
2. There should be a noticeable gap between the edge of a part and the beginning of an extension line. This serves as a visual break between the object and the extension line. The visual difference between the linetypes can be emphasized by using different colors for the two types of lines.
3. Leader lines are used to define the size of holes and should be positioned so that the arrowhead points at the center of the hole.
4. Centerlines may be used as extension lines. No gap is used when a centerline is extended beyond the edge lines of an object.
5. Dimension lines should be aligned whenever possible to give the drawing a neat, organized appearance.

Figure 8-3

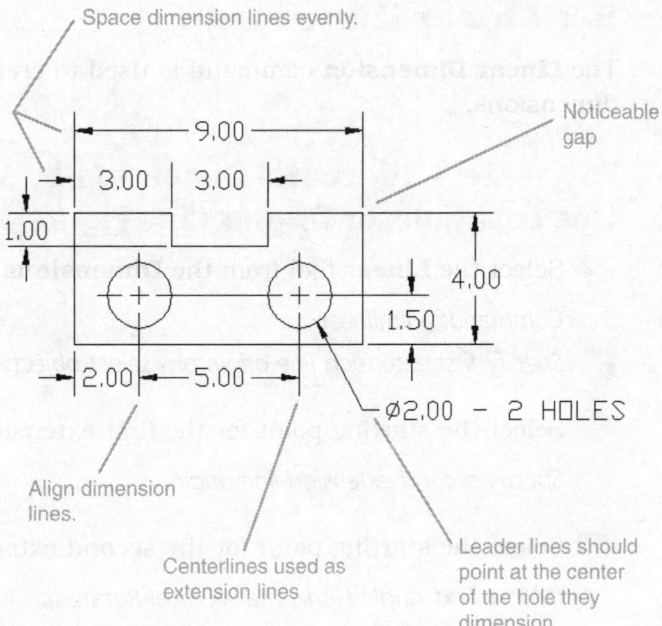

Some Common Errors to Avoid (See Figure 8-4.)

1. Avoid crossing extension lines. Place longer dimensions farther away from the object than shorter dimensions.
2. Do not locate dimensions within cutouts; always use extension lines.
3. Do not locate any dimension too close to the object. Dimension lines should be at least 1/2 inch, or 15 millimeters, from the edge of the object.
4. Avoid long extension lines. Locate dimensions in the same general area as the feature being defined.

Figure 8-4

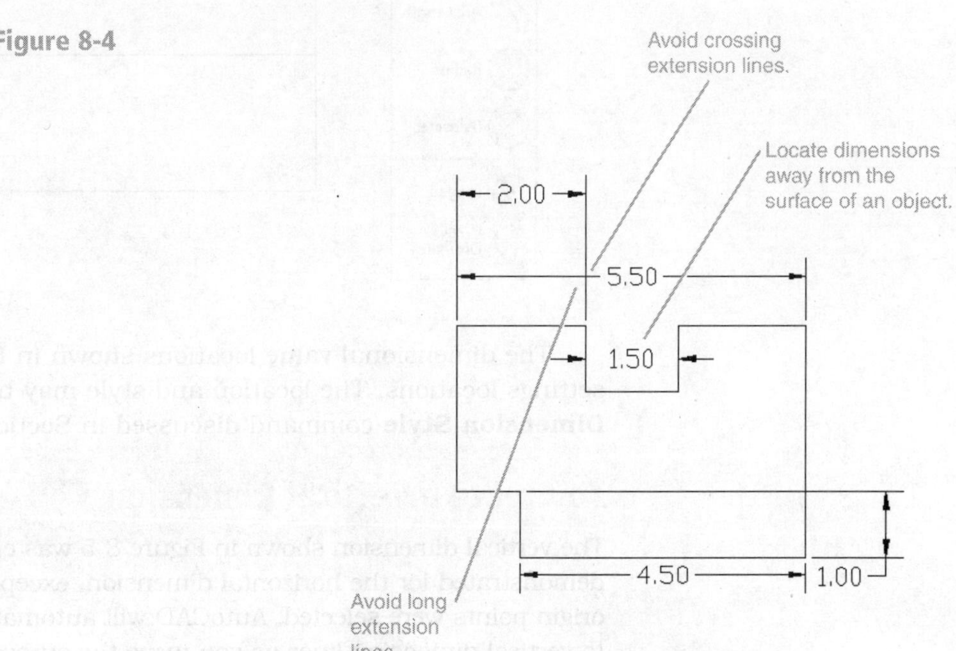

8-3 Linear Dimension

The **Linear Dimension** command is used to create horizontal and vertical dimensions.

To Create a Horizontal Dimension by Selecting Extension Line Locations or Origins (See Figure 8-5.)

1. Select the **Linear** tool from the **Dimensions** panel.

   Command: _dimlinear

   Specify first extension line origin or <select object>:

2. Select the starting point for the first extension line.

   Specify second extension line origin:

3. Select the starting point for the second extension line.

   [MText Text Angle Horizontal Vertical Rotated]:

4. Locate the dimension line by moving the crosshairs to the desired location.

5. Press the left mouse button to place the dimension.

Figure 8-5

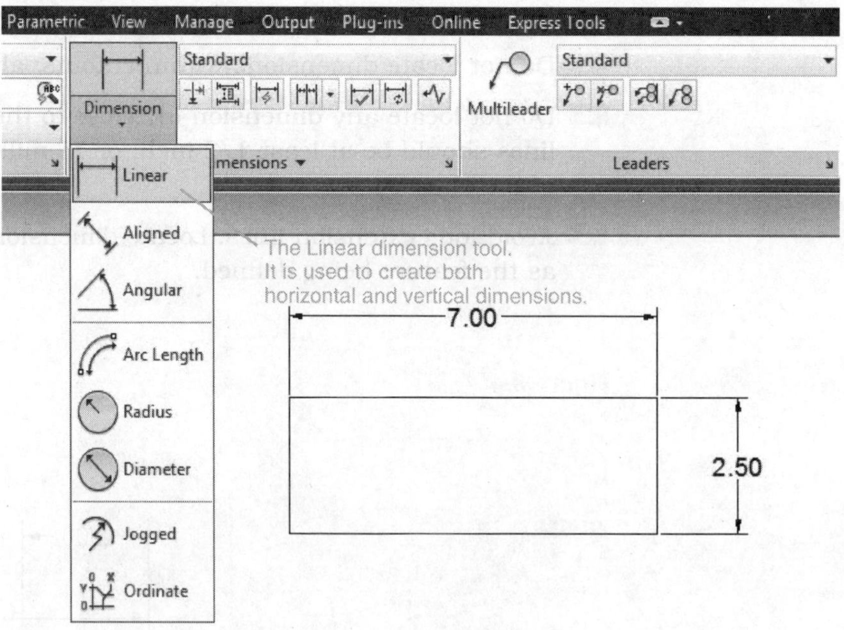

The dimensional value locations shown in Figure 8-5 are the default settings locations. The location and style may be changed by using the **Dimension Style** command discussed in Section 8-4.

To Create a Vertical Dimension

The vertical dimension shown in Figure 8-5 was created by the same procedure demonstrated for the horizontal dimension, except that different extension line origin points were selected. AutoCAD will automatically switch from horizontal to vertical dimension lines as you move the cursor around the object.

If there is confusion between horizontal and vertical lines when adding dimensions—that is, you don't seem to be able to generate a vertical line—type **V** and press **Enter** in response to the following prompt:

[MText Text Angle Horizontal Vertical Rotated]:

The system will now draw vertical dimension lines.

To Create a Horizontal Dimension by Selecting the Object to Be Dimensioned (See Figure 8-6.)

1. Select the **Linear** tool from the **Dimensions** panel.

   Command: _dimlinear

   Specify first extension line origin or <select object>:

2. Press the right mouse button.

   Select object to Dimension:

3. Select the line to be dimensioned.

Figure 8-6

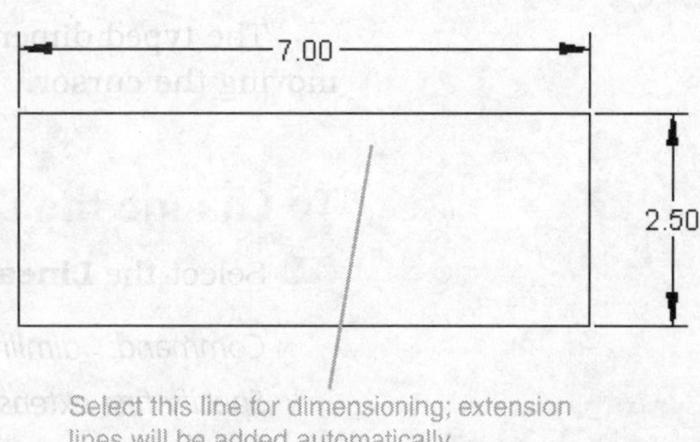

This option allows you to select the distance to be dimensioned directly. The option applies only to horizontal and vertical lengths. Aligned dimensions, although linear, are created by using the **Aligned** tool.

To Change the Default Dimension Text—Text Option

AutoCAD will automatically create a text value for a given linear distance. A different value or additional information may be added, as follows. See Figure 8-7.

Figure 8-7

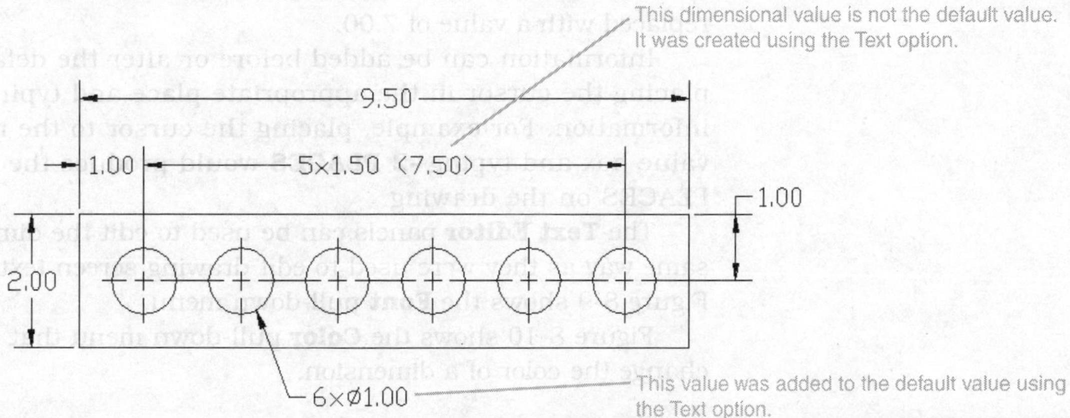

1. Select the **Linear** tool from the **Dimensions** panel.

   Command: _dimlinear

   Specify first extension line origin or <select object>:

2. Select the starting point for the first extension line.

   Specify second extension line origin:

3. Select the starting point for the second extension line.

   [MText Text Angle Horizontal Vertical Rotated]:

4. Type **t;** press **Enter.**

   Enter dimension text <7.50>:

   The value given will be the linear value of the distance selected. In this example, more information is required, so the default distance value must be modified.

5. Type **5 × 1.50 (7.50);** press **Enter.**

   The typed dimension will appear on the screen and can be located by moving the cursor.

To Change the Default Dimension Text—Mtext Option

1. Select the **Linear** tool from the **Dimensions** panel.

   Command: _dimlinear

   Specify first extension line origin or <select object>:

2. Select the starting point for the first extension line.

   Specify second extension line origin:

3. Select the starting point for the second extension line.

   [MText Text Angle Horizontal Vertical Rotated]:

4. Type **m;** press **Enter.**

   The **Text Editor** panels will appear. See Figure 8-8. The text value will appear in a box below the **Text Editor** panels. To remove the existing text, highlight the text and press the **<Del>** key. You can then type new text into the box. In the example shown, the default value of 7.0000 was replaced with a value of 7.00.

   Information can be added before or after the default text by placing the cursor in the appropriate place and typing the additional information. For example, placing the cursor to the right of the text value box and typing **-2 PLACES** would produce the text 7.00 - 2 PLACES on the drawing.

   The **Text Editor** panels can be used to edit the dimension text in the same way as they were used to edit drawing screen text (Section 2-15). Figure 8-9 shows the **Font** pull-down menu.

   Figure 8-10 shows the **Color** pull-down menu that may be used to change the color of a dimension.

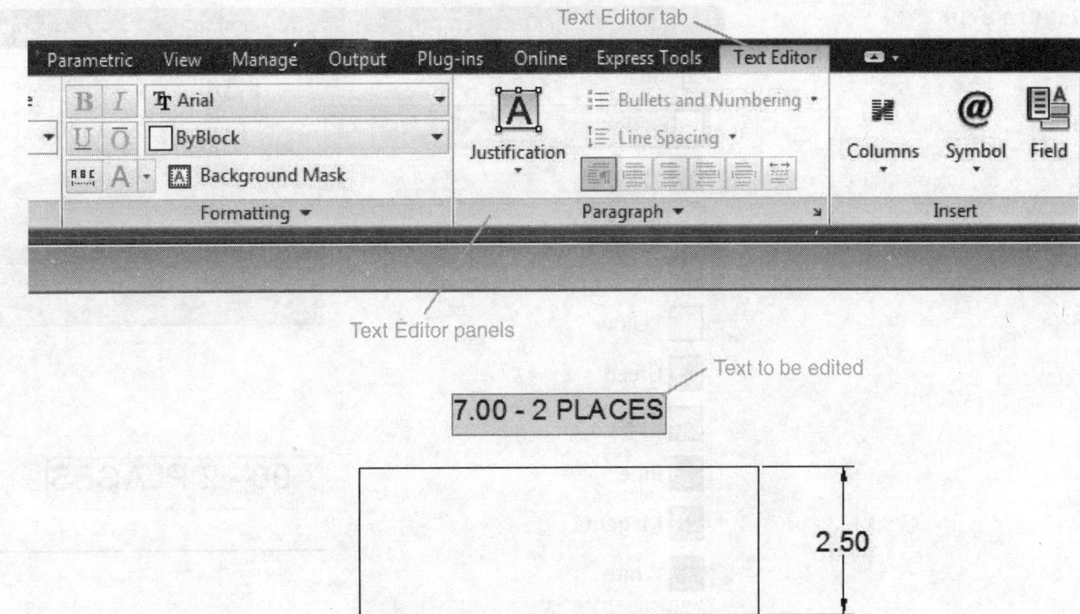

Figure 8-8

Figure 8-9

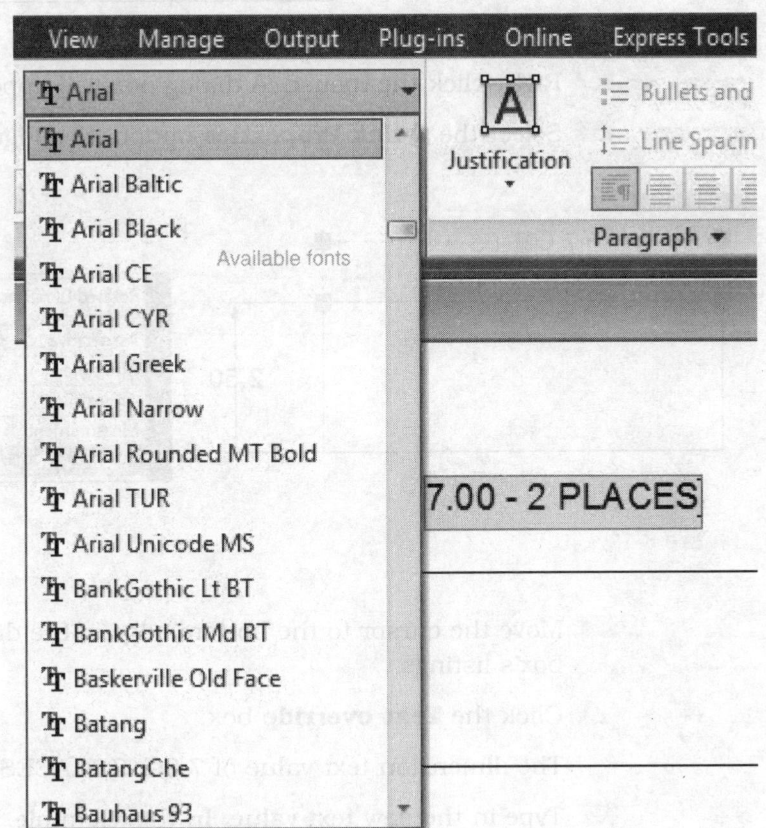

To Edit an Existing Dimension

Figure 8-8 shows a figure with an existing 7.00 -2 PLACES dimension.

1. Click the existing dimension.

   Blue boxes will appear.

Figure 8-10

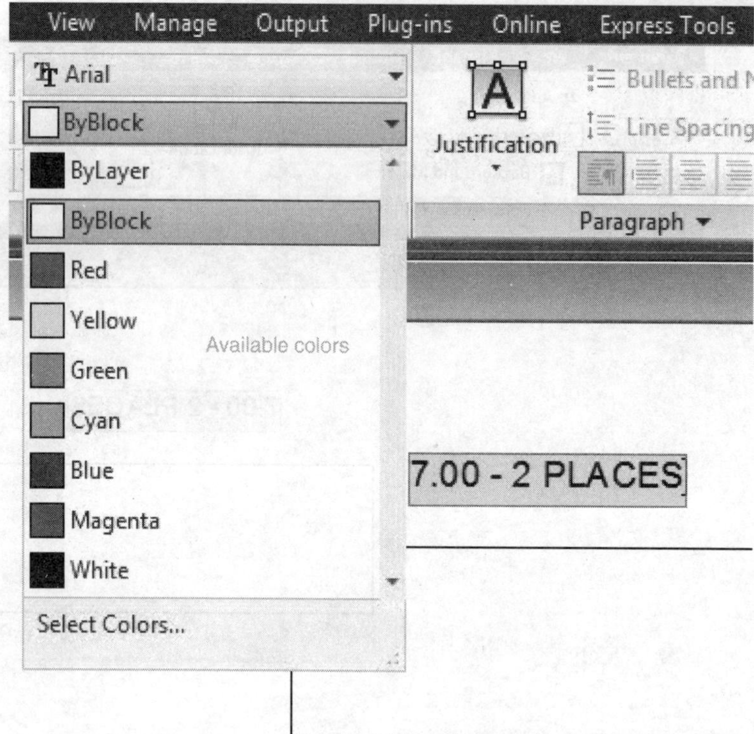

2. Right-click the mouse. A dialog box will appear.
3. Select the **Quick Properties** option. See Figure 8-11.

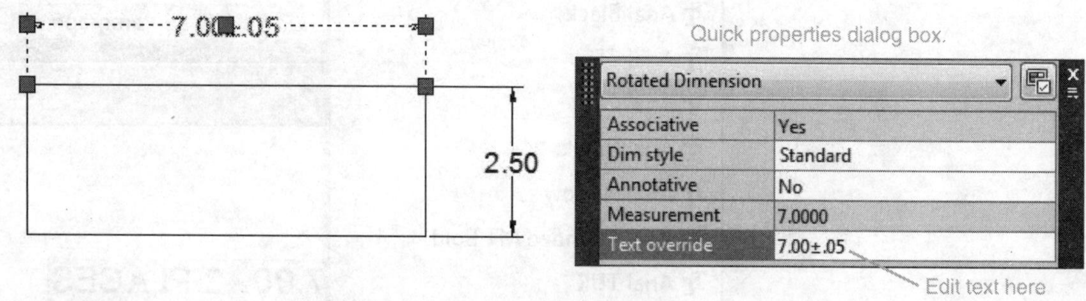

Figure 8-11

4. Move the cursor to the bottom edge of the dialog box to expand the box's listings.
5. Click the **Text override** box.

   The dimension text value of 7.00 -2 PLACES will be highlighted.

6. Type in the new text value. In this example, 7.00 ± 0.05 was entered.

   The ± sign was created by pressing and holding the **<Alt>** key and typing **0177.**

7. Delete the dialog box, and press the **<Esc>** key.

   Figure 8-12 shows the edited dimension.

Dimension text can also be edited with the **Properties** dialog box. Access the **Properties** dialog box by clicking the dimension, right-clicking

Figure 8-12

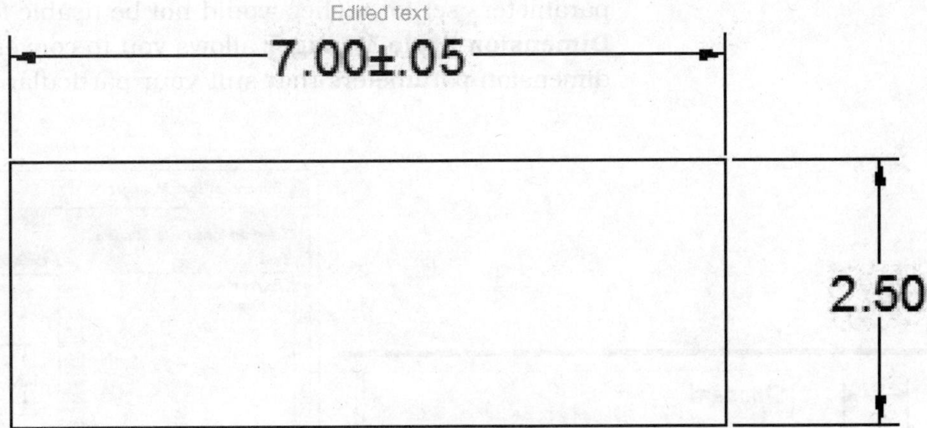

the mouse, and selecting the **Propertied** option. Scroll down the box to the **Text override** box, and enter the new values. Note: The **Text Editor** may also be accessed by double-clicking the existing dimension.

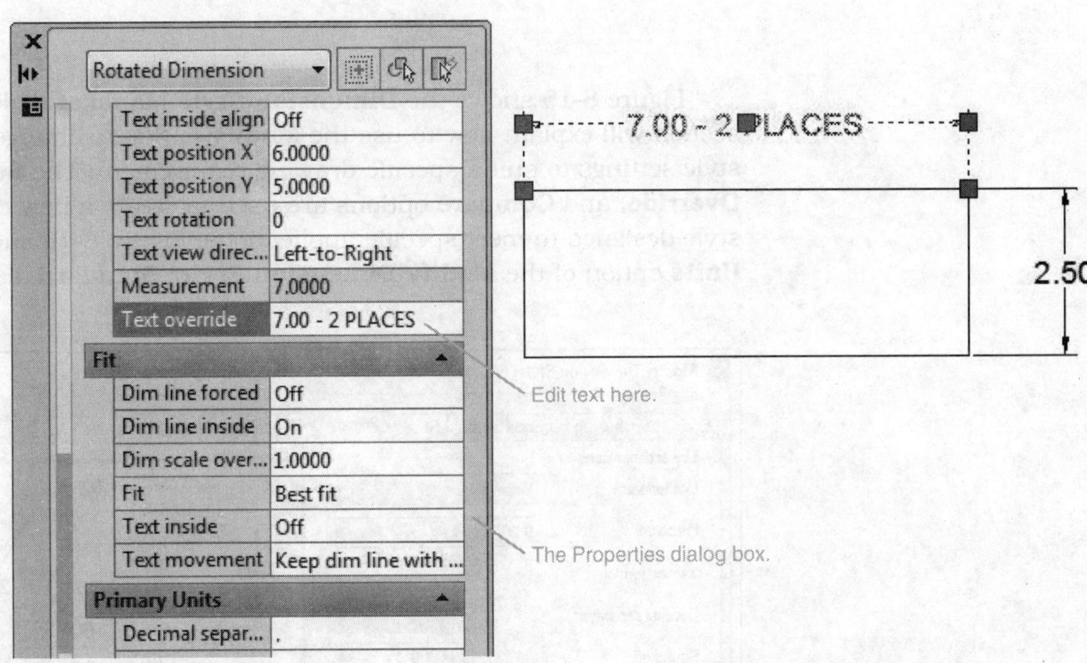

Figure 8-13

8-4 Dimension Styles

The **Dimension Style Manager** is used to control the appearance and format of dimensions. The **Dimension Style Manager** is accessed by clicking the arrow in the lower-right corner of the **Dimensions** panel under the **Annotate** tab. See Figure 8-14.

A great variety of styles are used to create technical drawings. The style difference may be the result of different drawing conventions. For example, architects locate dimensions above the dimension lines, and mechanical engineers locate the dimensions within the dimension lines. AutoCAD works in decimal units for both millimeters and inches, so parameters set for inches would not be usable for millimeter drawings. The **Dimension Style Manager** allows you to conveniently choose and set dimension parameters that suit your particular drawing requirements.

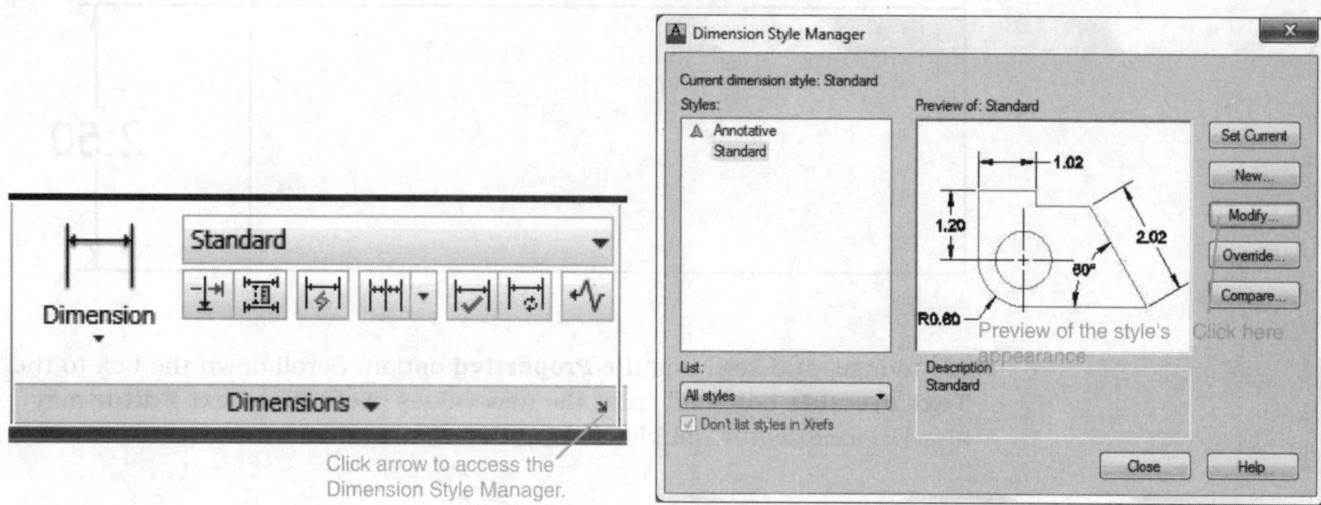

Figure 8-14

Figure 8-15

Figure 8-15 shows the **Dimension Style Manager** dialog box. This section will explain how to use the **Modify** option to change the **Standard** style settings to suit a specific drawing requirement. The **Set Current, New, Override,** and **Compare** options are used to create a new custom dimension style designed to meet specific applications. Figure 8-16 shows the **Primary Units** option of the **Modify Dimension Style: Standard** dialog box.

Figure 8-16

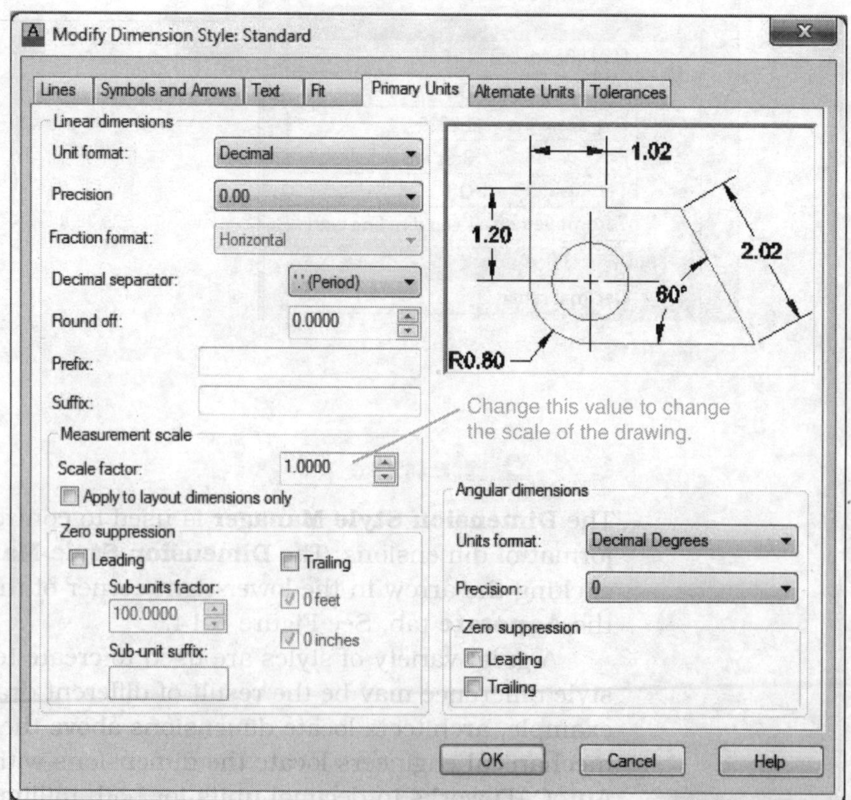

To Change the Scale of a Drawing

Drawings are often drawn to scale because the actual part is either too big to fit on a sheet of drawing paper or too small to be seen. For example, a microchip circuit must be drawn at several thousand times its actual size in order to be seen.

Drawing scales are written according to the following formats:

SCALE: 1 = 1

SCALE: FULL

SCALE: 1000 = 1

SCALE: .25 = 1

In each example, the value on the left indicates the scale factor. A value greater than 1 indicates that the drawing is larger than actual size. A value less than 1 indicates that the drawing is smaller than actual size.

Regardless of the drawing scale selected, the dimension values must be true size. Figure 8-17 shows the same rectangle drawn at two different scales. The top rectangle is drawn at a scale of 1 = 1, or its true size. The bottom rectangle is drawn at a scale of 2 = 1, or twice its true size. In both examples, the 3.00 dimension remains the same.

The **Measurement scale** box on the **Primary Units** option on the **Modify Dimension Style: Standard** dialog box is used to change the dimension values to match different drawing scales. Figure 8-18 shows the measurement scale set to a factor of 0.5000. If the drawing scale is 2 = 1, as shown in Figure 8-17, then the scale factor for the **Measurement scale** must be 0.5000. Compare the preview in Figure 8-16 with the preview in Figure 8-18, in which the scale factor has been changed.

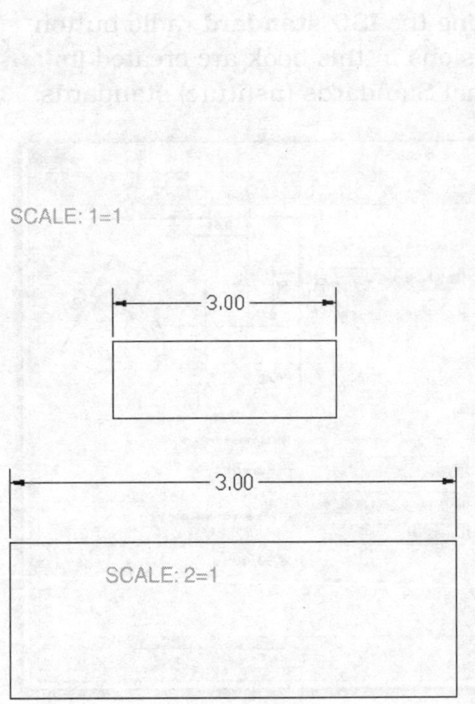

Figure 8-17

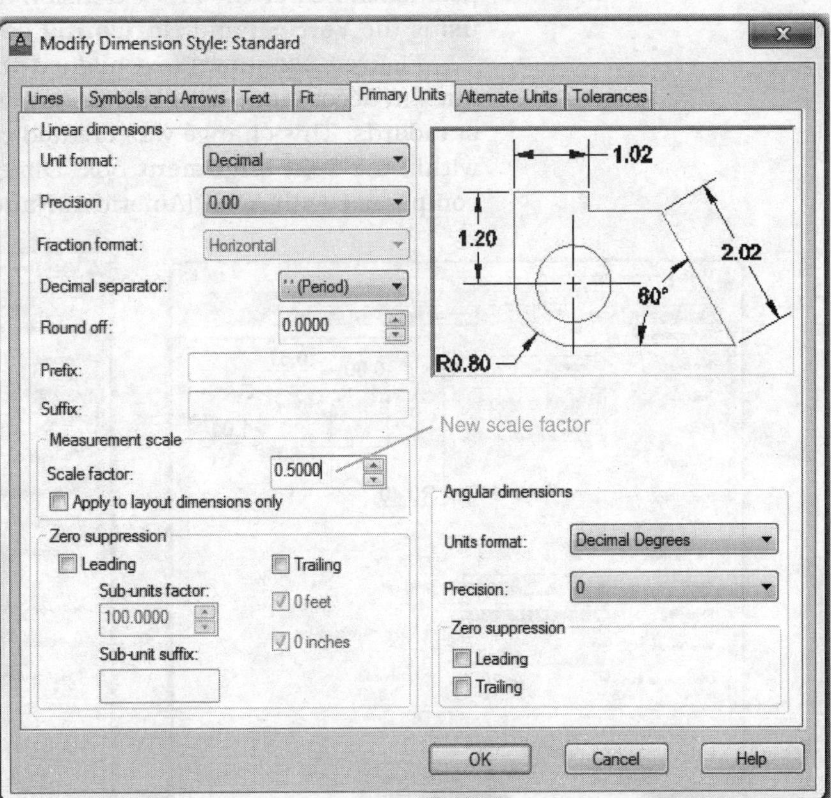

Figure 8-18

To Use the Text Option

Figure 8-19 shows the **Text** option on the **Modify Dimension Style: Standard** dialog box. This option can be used to change the height of dimension text or the text placement. In Figure 8-20, the text height was changed from the default value of 0.1800 to a value of 0.3500. The preview box shows the resulting changes in both the text and how it will be positioned on the drawing.

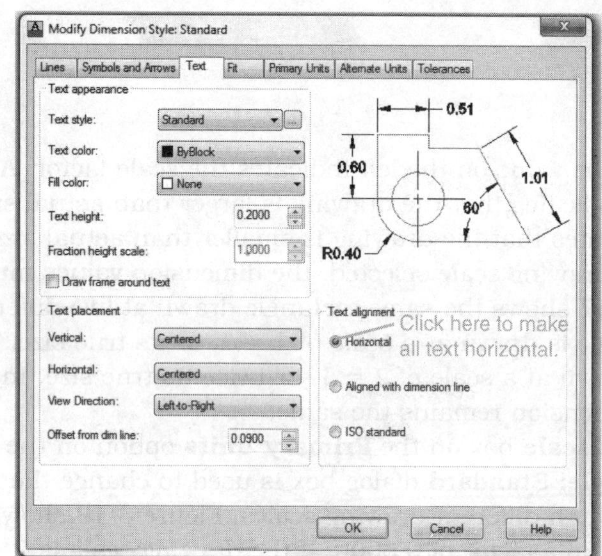

Figure 8-19

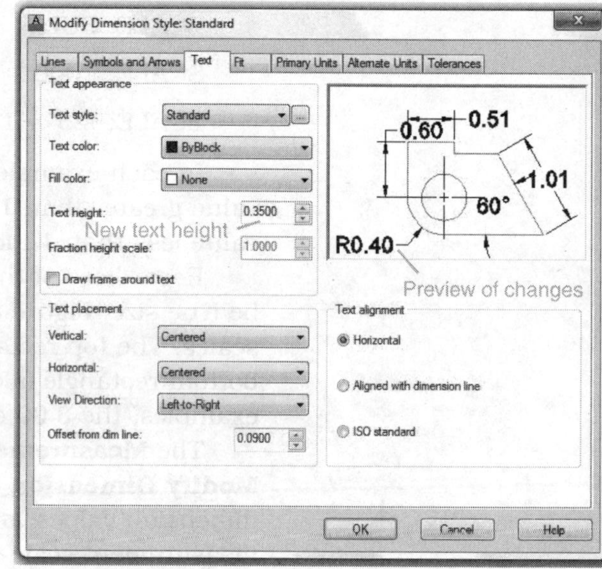

Figure 8-20

Figure 8-21 shows text located above the dimension lines and positioned nearer the first extension line. These changes were created by using the **Vertical** and **Horizontal** options within the **Text placement** box.

Figure 8-22 shows text aligned with the direction of the dimension lines in accordance with ISO (International Standard Organization) standards. This change was created using the **ISO standard** radio button within the **Text alignment** box. Dimensions in this book are created in compliance with ANSI (American National Standards Institute) standards.

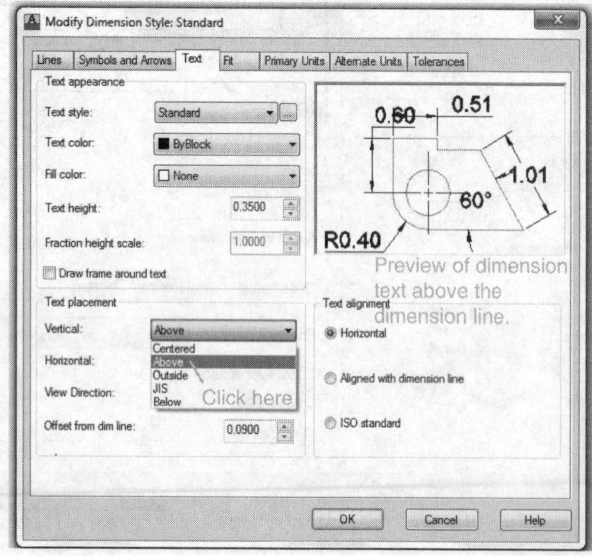

Figure 8-21

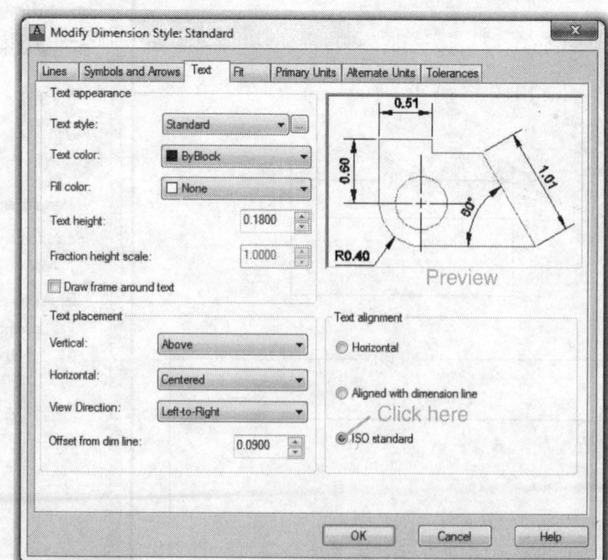

Figure 8-22

8-5 Units

It is important to understand that dimensional values are not the same as mathematical units. Dimensional values are manufacturing instructions and always include a tolerance, even if the tolerance value is not stated. Manufacturers use a predefined set of standard dimensions that are applied to any dimensional value that does not include a written tolerance. Standard tolerance values differ from organization to organization. Figure 8-23 shows a chart of standard tolerances.

In Figure 8-24, a distance is dimensioned twice: once as 5.50 and a second time as 5.5000. Mathematically, these two values are equal, but they are not equal according to the same manufacturing instruction. The 5.50 value could, for example, have a standard tolerance of ±0.01, whereas the 5.5000 value could have a standard tolerance of ±0.0005. A tolerance of ±0.0005 is more difficult and therefore more expensive to manufacture than a tolerance of ±0.01.

STANDARD TOLERANCES
X = ±1 X.X = ±0.1 X.XX = ±0.01 X.XXX = ±0.001 X.XXXX = ±0.0005
X° = ±0.1°
THESE TOLERANCES APPLY UNLESS OTHERWISE STATED.

Figure 8-23

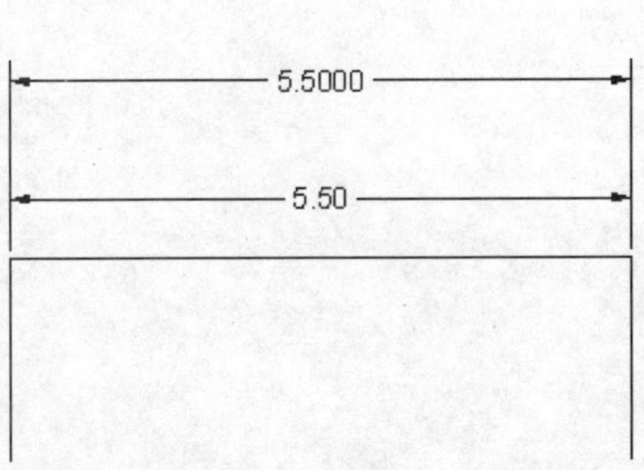

Figure 8-24

Figure 8-25 shows examples of units expressed in millimeters, decimal inches, and architectural units. A zero is not required to the left of the decimal point for decimal inch values less than one. Millimeter values do not require zeros to the right of the decimal point. Architectural units should always include the feet (′) and inch (″) symbols. Millimeter and decimal inch values never include symbols; the units will be defined in the title block of the drawing.

Figure 8-25

MILLIMETERS — Zero required

0.25　0.5　0.033

32　1.45　3

INCHES — No zero required

.25　.5　.003

32.00　145.0　3.000

ARCHITECTURAL UNITS (feet and inches)

0″-0 1/2″　8″　2′-8″

To Prevent a 0 from Appearing to the Left of the Decimal Point

1. Access the **Dimension Style Manager.**

   The **Dimension Style** dialog box will appear.

2. Select **Modify.**

   The **Modify Dimension Style: Standard** dialog box will appear.

3. Select the **Primary Units** option.

   The **Primary Units** dialog box will appear. See Figure 8-26.

Figure 8-26

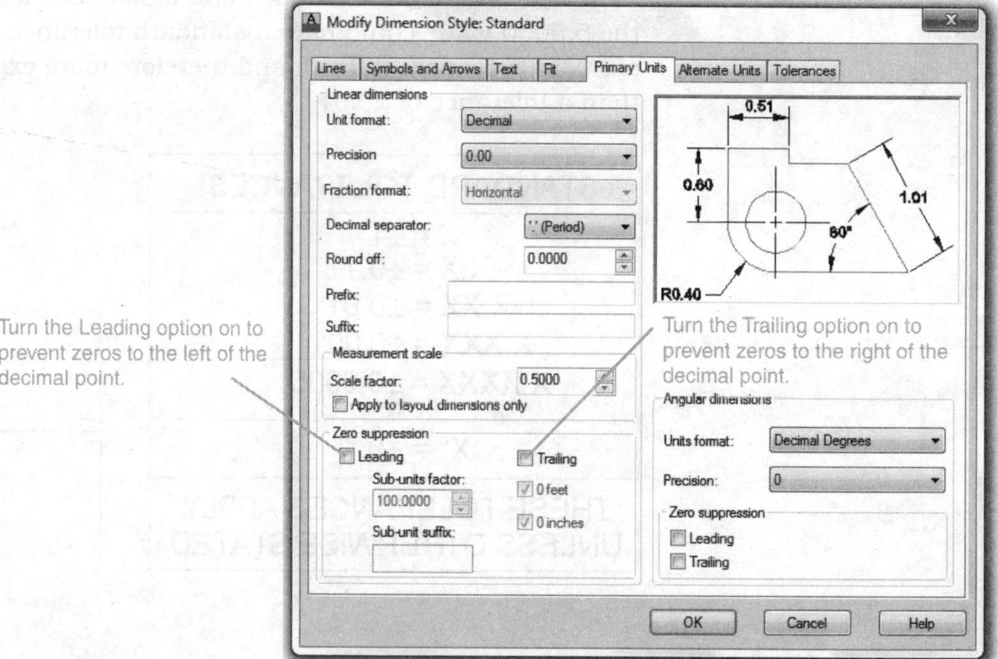

4. Click the box to the left of the word **Leading** within the **Zero suppression** box.

   A checkmark will appear in the box, indicating that the function is on.

5. Select **OK** to return to the drawing.

   Save the change if desired. You can now dimension by using any of the dimension commands; no zeros will appear to the left of the decimal point. Figure 8-27 shows the results.

To Change the Number of Decimal Places in a Dimension Value

1. Access the **Dimension Style Manager.**

   The **Dimension Style Manager** dialog box will appear.

2. Select **Modify**.

   The **Modify Dimension Style: Standard** dialog box will appear.

3. Select the **Primary Units** option.

4. Select the arrow to the right of the **Precision** box.

   A list of precision options will cascade down. See Figure 8-28.

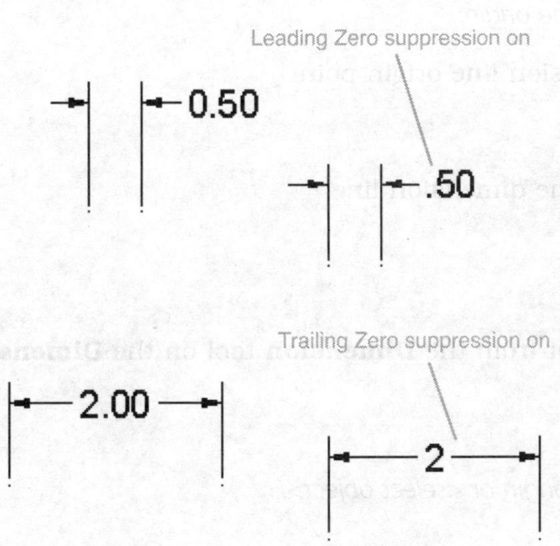

Figure 8-27

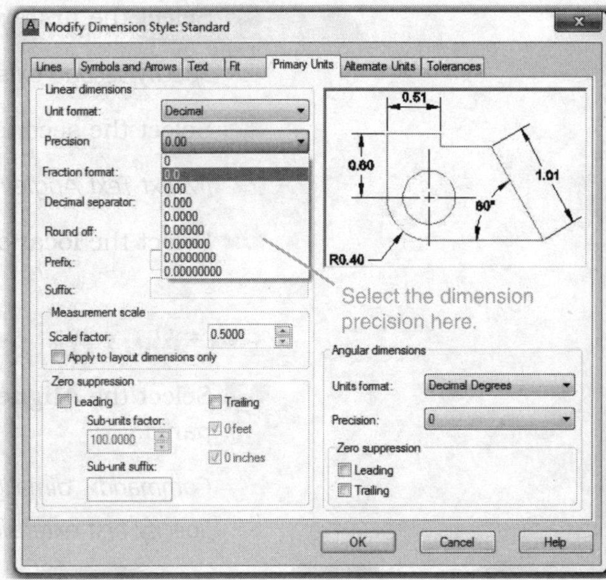

Figure 8-28

5. Select the desired value.

Save the changes if desired. You can now dimension by using any of the dimension commands, and the resulting values will be expressed with the selected precision.

8-6 Aligned Dimensions (See Figures 8-29 and 8-30.)

To Create an Aligned Dimension

1. Select the **Aligned** tool, which is a flyout from the **Dimension** tool on the **Dimensions** panel under the **Annotate** tab.

Command: _dimaligned

Specify first extension line origin or <select object>:

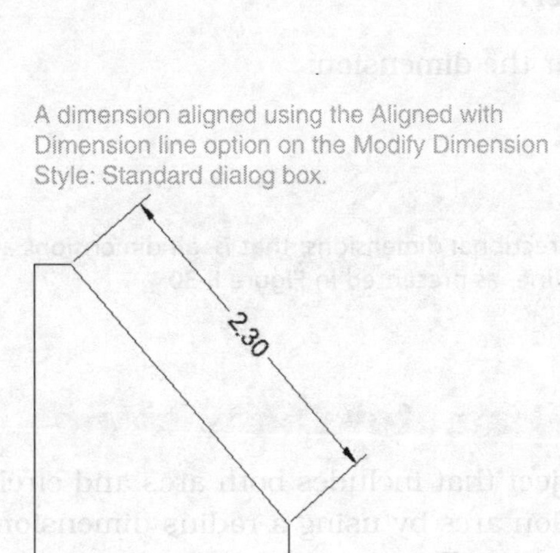

Figure 8-29

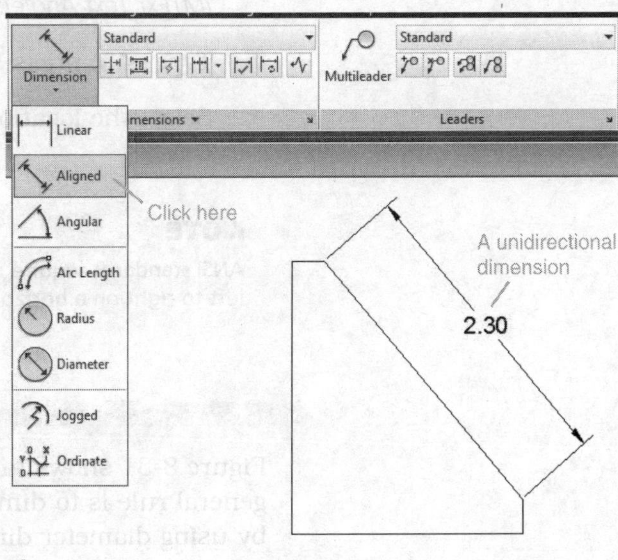

Figure 8-30

2. Select the first extension line origin point.

Specify second extension line origin:

3. Select the second extension line origin point.

[Mtext Text Angle]:

4. Select the location for the dimension line.

The Select Object Option

1. Select the **Aligned** flyout from the **Dimension** tool on the **Dimensions** panel.

Command: _dimaligned

Specify first extension line origin or <select object>:

2. Press **Enter.**

Select object to dimension:

3. Select the line.

[Mtext Text Angle]:

4. Select the dimension line location.

A response of **M** to the last prompt line will activate the **Multiline Text** option. The **Text Editor** dialog box will appear. The **Text** option can be used to replace or supplement the default text generated by AutoCAD. The **Multiline Text** option is discussed in Section 2-15.

A response of **A** to the prompt will activate the **Angle** option. The **Angle** option allows you to change the angle of the text within the dimension line. See Figure 8-30. The default angle value is **0°**, or horizontal. The example shown in Figure 8-29 used an angle of –45°. The prompt responses are as follows:

Specify angle of dimension text:

[MTExt Text Angle]:

1. Type **–45;** press **Enter.**

2. Select the location for the dimension.

NOTE

ANSI standards require unidirectional dimensions; that is, all dimensions are read from left to right on a horizontal line, as presented in Figure 8-30.

8-7 Radius and Diameter Dimensions

Figure 8-31 shows an object that includes both arcs and circles. The general rule is to dimension arcs by using a radius dimension, and circles by using diameter dimensions. This convention is consistent with the tooling required to produce the feature shape. Any arc greater than 180° is considered a circle and is dimensioned by using a diameter.

Figure 8-31

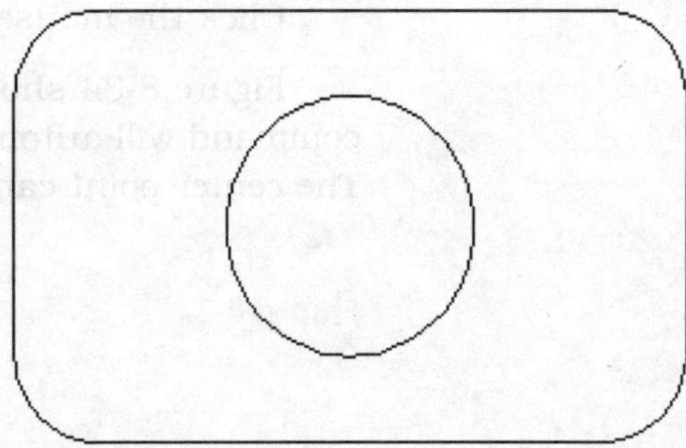

To Create a Radius Dimension

1. Select the **Radius** tool, which is a flyout from the **Dimension** tool on the **Dimensions** panel under the **Annotate** tab.

   Command: _dimradius
   Select arc or circle:

2. Select the arc to be dimensioned.

   Specify dimension line location or [Mtext Text Angle]:

3. Position the radius dimension so that its leader line is neither horizontal nor vertical.

Figure 8-32 shows the resulting dimension. The dimension text can be altered by clicking the text. A dialog box will appear. See Figure 8-33. Highlight the existing text and type in the new text. Close the dialog box, and press the <Esc> key.

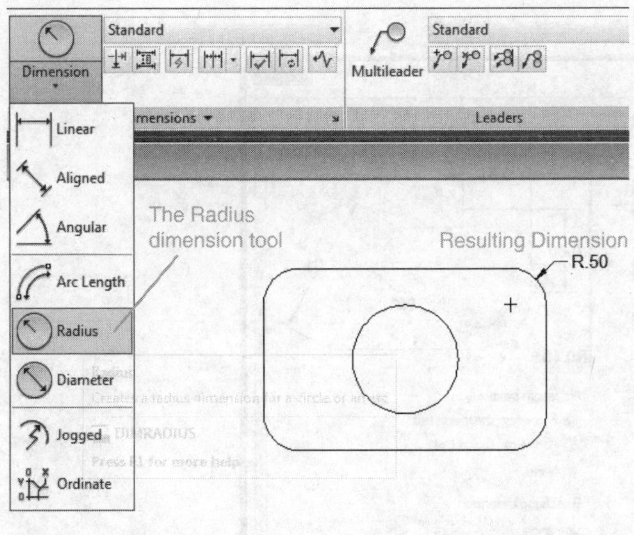

Figure 8-32

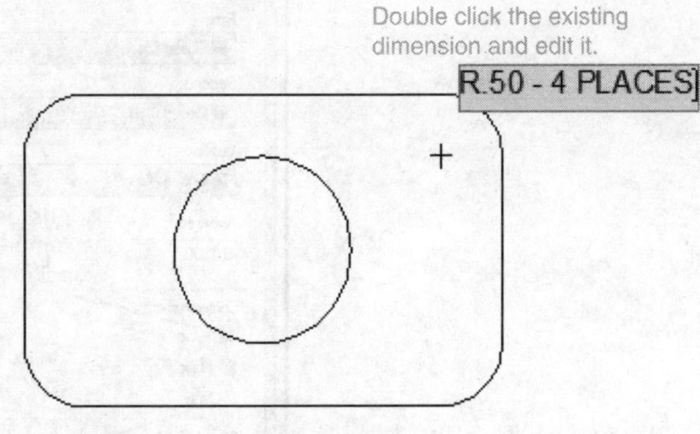

Figure 8-33

To Alter the Default Dimension

1. Double-click the dimension.

The dimension will be enclosed in a shaded box.

2. Use the **Delete** key to remove the existing dimension.

3. Type in the new dimension.

4. Click the mouse.

Figure 8-34 shows the resulting dimension. The **Radius** dimension command will automatically include a center point with the dimension. The center point can be excluded from the dimension as follows.

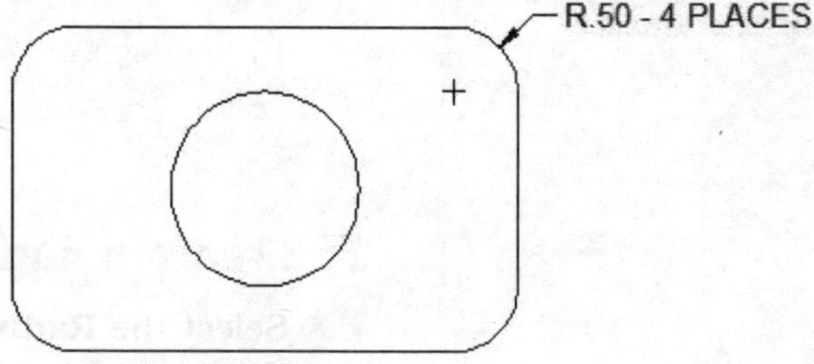

Figure 8-34

To Remove the Center Mark from a Radius Dimension

1. Access the **Dimension Style Manager.**

   The **Dimension Style Manager** dialog box will appear.

2. Select **Modify.**

   The **Modify Dimension Style: Standard** dialog box will appear.

3. Select the **Symbols and Arrows** option.

4. Select the **None** radio button in the **Center marks** area.

   A solid circle will appear in the preview box, indicating that it is on. See Figure 8-35.

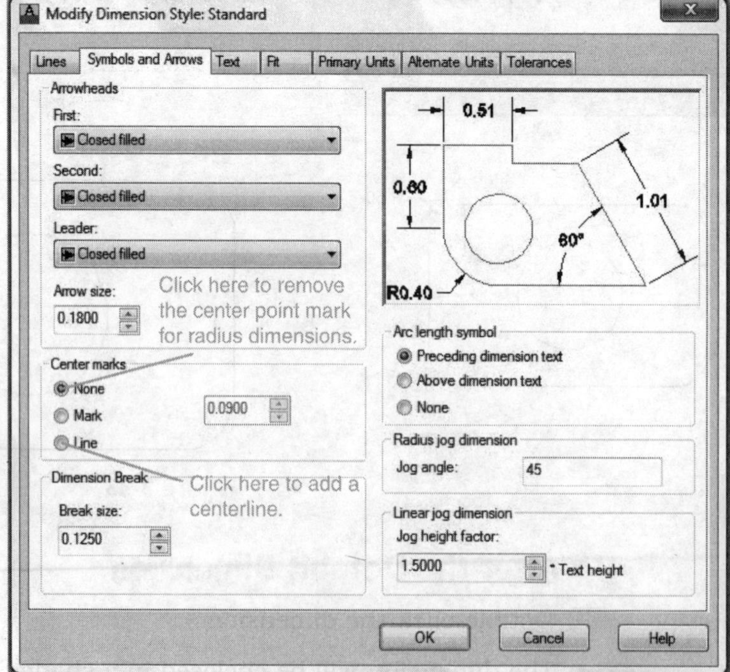

Figure 8-35

5 Select **OK** to return to the drawing.

You will have to redimension the arc, including the text alteration. Figure 8-36 shows the results.

Figure 8-36

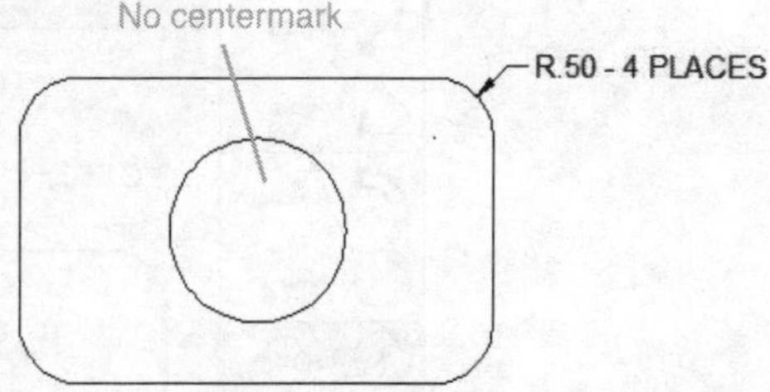

To Create a Diameter Dimension

Circles require three dimensions: a diameter value, plus two linear dimensions used to locate the circle's center point. AutoCAD can be configured to automatically add horizontal and vertical centerlines as follows:

1 Access the **Dimension Style Manager.**

The **Dimension Style Manager** dialog box will appear.

2 Select **Modify.**

The **Modify Dimension Style: Standard** dialog box will appear.

3 Select the **Symbols and Arrows** option.

4 Select the **Line** option from the **Center marks** box.

5 Select **OK** to return to the drawing.

Centerlines will be added to the existing radius dimension.

6 Explode the radius dimension; then erase the radius centerlines.

7 Select the **Diameter** tool, which is a flyout from the **Dimension** tool on the **Dimensions** panel under the **Annotate** tab.

Command: _dimdiameter

Select arc or circle:

8 Select the circle.

Specify dimension line location or [MText Text Angle]:

9 Locate the dimension away from the object so that the leader line is neither horizontal nor vertical.

Figure 8-37 shows the results.

To Add Linear Dimensions to Given Centerlines

1 Select the **Linear** flyout from the **Dimension** tool on the **Dimensions** panel.

Command: _dimlinear

Specify first extension line origin or <select object>:

2 Select the lower endpoint of the circle's vertical centerline.

Specify second extension line origin:

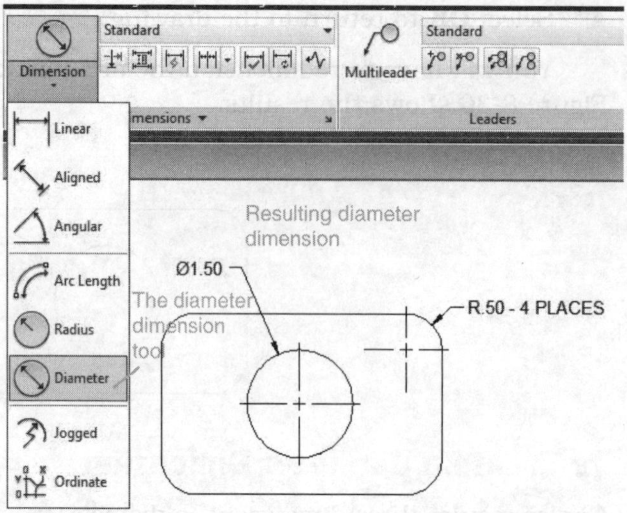

Figure 8-37

3. Select the endpoint of the vertical edge line (the endpoint that joins with the corner arc).

   Figure 8-38 shows the results.

4. Repeat the previous procedure to add the vertical dimension needed to locate the circle's center point.

5. Add the overall dimensions, using the **Linear** dimension tool.

   Figure 8-39 shows the results. Radius and diameter dimensions are usually added to a drawing after the linear dimensions because they are less restricted in their locations. Linear dimensions are located close to the distance that they are defining, whereas radius and diameter dimensions can be located farther away and use leader lines to identify the appropriate arc or circle.

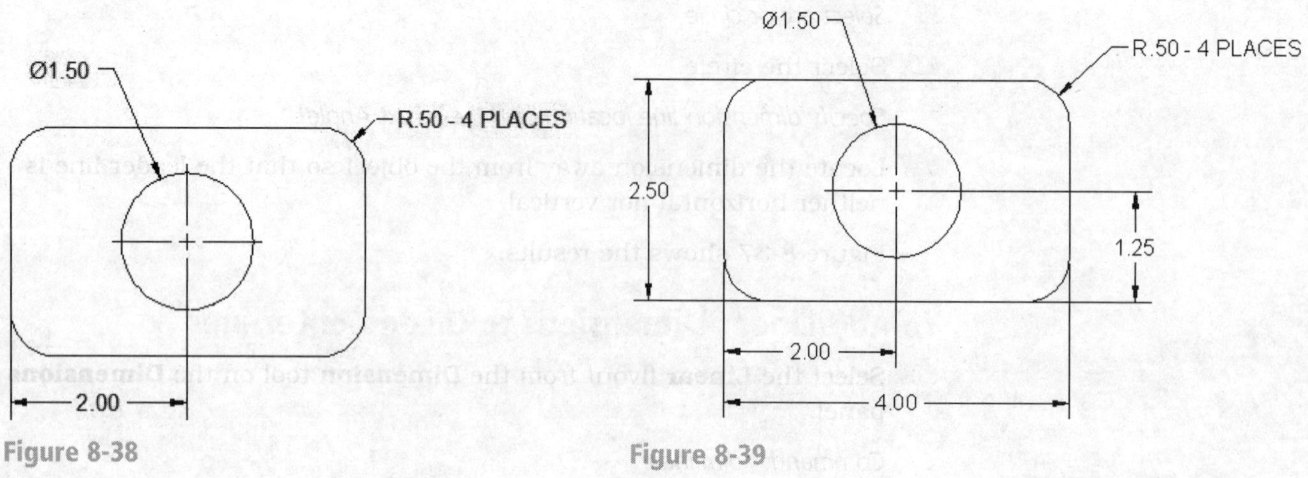

Figure 8-38

Figure 8-39

Avoid crossing extension and dimension lines with leader lines. See Figure 8-40.

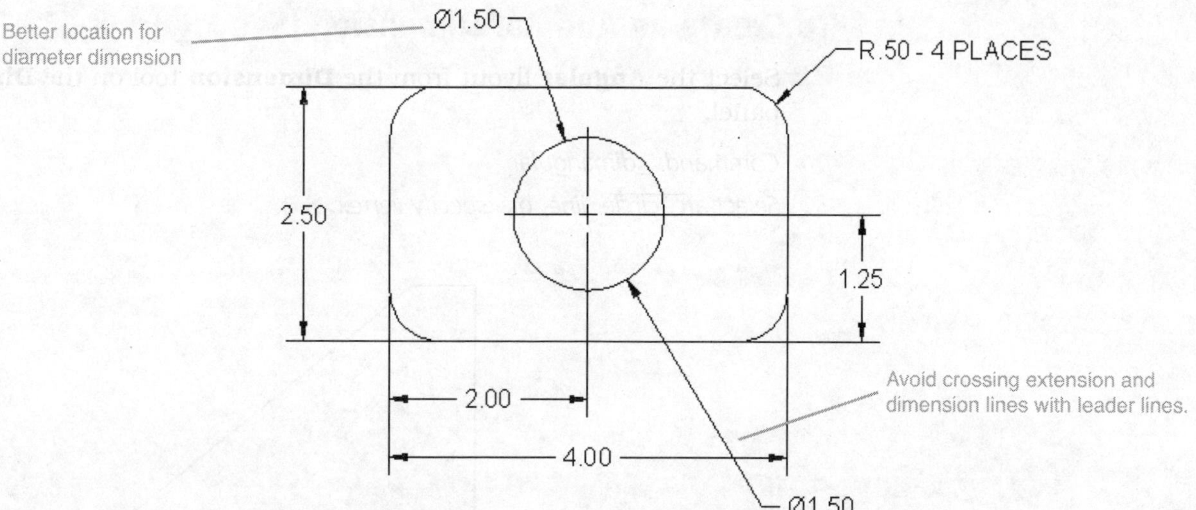

Figure 8-40

NOTE

The diameter symbol Ø can be added when creating text by typing **%%c.** The characters **%%c** will appear on the **Text Formatting** screen, but will be converted to the diameter symbol Ø when the text is applied to the drawing.

8-8 Angular Dimensions

Figure 8-41 shows four possible angular dimensions that can be created by use of the **Angular** tool, which is a flyout from the **Dimension** tool on the **Dimensions** panel. The extension lines and degree symbol will be added automatically.

Figure 8-41

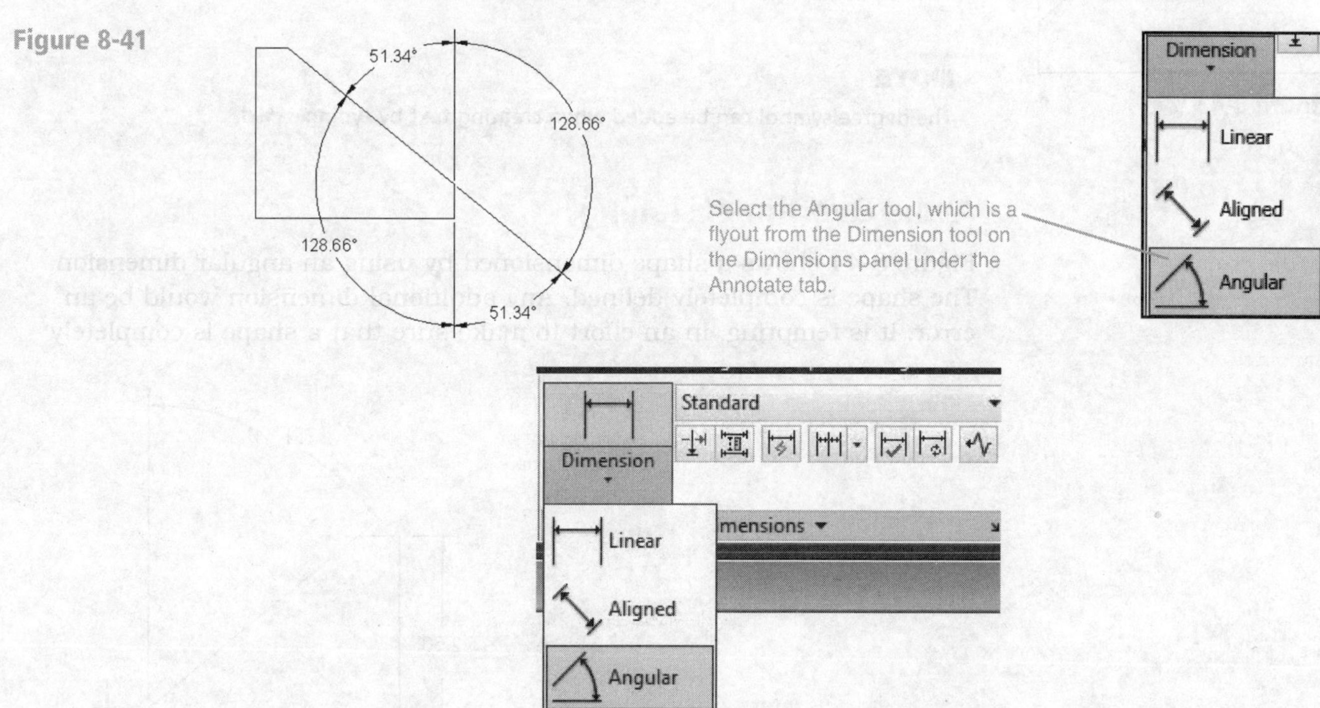

To Create an Angular Dimension (See Figure 8-42.)

1. Select the **Angular** flyout from the **Dimension** tool on the **Dimensions** panel.

Command: _dimangular

Select arc, circle, line, or <specify vertex>:

Figure 8-42

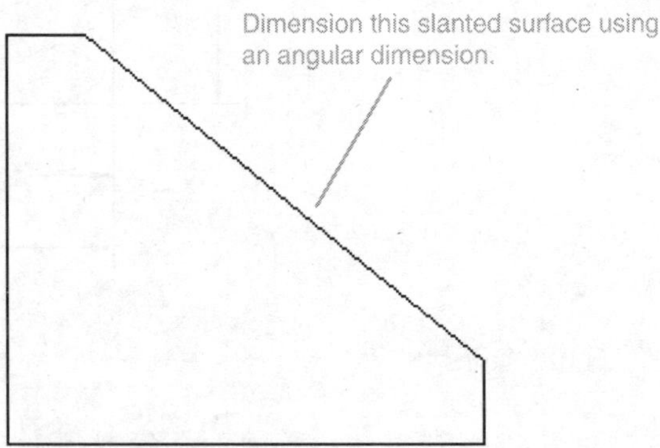

2. Select the short vertical line on the lower right side of the object.

Select second line:

3. Select the slanted line.

Specify dimension arc line location [MText Text Angle]:

4. Locate the text away from the object.

Figure 8-43 shows the results. It is considered better to use two extension lines for angular dimensions and to not have an arrowhead touch the surface of the part.

51.34°

Figure 8-43

> **NOTE**
>
> The degree symbol can be added when creating text by typing **%%d**.

Avoid Overdimensioning

Figure 8-44 shows a shape dimensioned by using an angular dimension. The shape is completely defined. Any additional dimension would be an error. It is tempting, in an effort to make sure that a shape is completely

Figure 8-44

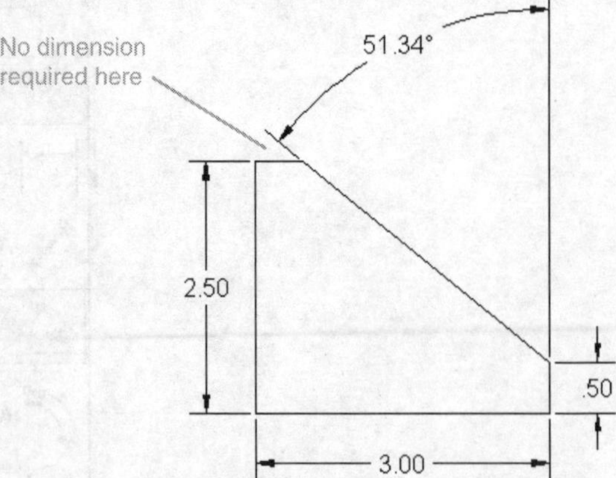

defined, to add more dimensions such as a horizontal dimension for the short horizontal edge at the top of the shape. This dimension is not needed and is considered double dimensioning.

8-9 Ordinate Dimensions

Ordinate dimensions are dimensions based on an X,Y coordinate system. Ordinate dimensions do not include extension, or dimension, lines or arrowheads, but simply horizontal and vertical leader lines drawn directly from the features of the object. Ordinate dimensions are particularly useful when dimensioning an object that includes many small holes.

Figure 8-45 shows an object that is to be dimensioned by use of ordinate dimensions. Ordinate dimensions are automatically calculated from the X, Y origin or, in this example, the lower left corner of the screen. If the object had been drawn with its lower left corner on the origin, you could proceed directly to the **Ordinate** tool, which is a flyout from the **Dimension** tool on the **Dimensions** panel. However, the lower left corner of the object is not located on the origin. First move the origin to the corner of the object, and then use the **Ordinate** dimension tool.

To Move the Origin and the Origin Icon (See Figure 8-46.)

1. Move the cursor onto the origin icon.
2. Right-click the mouse.

   A listing of options will appear.
3. Select the **Origin** option.

   The cursor will become attached to the origin.

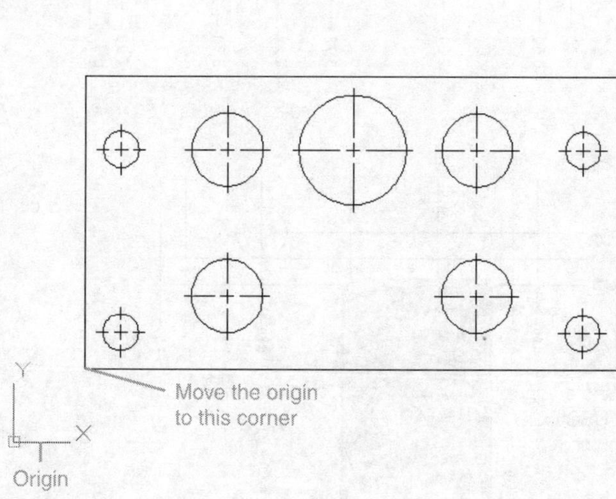

Figure 8-45

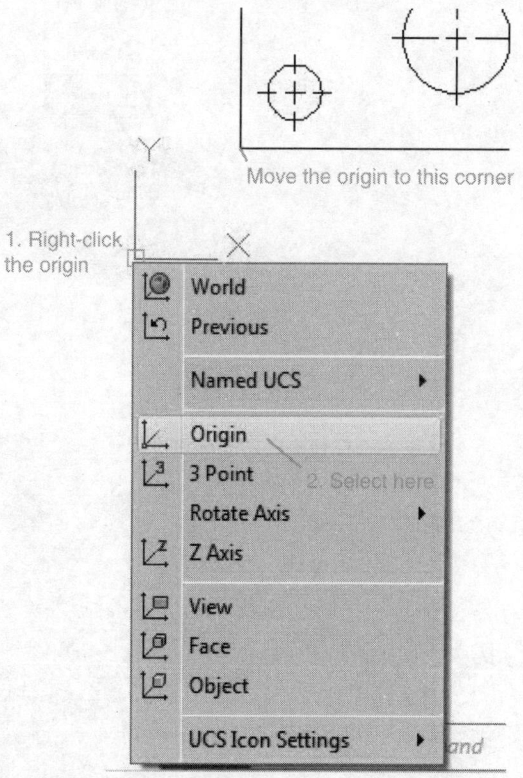

Figure 8-46

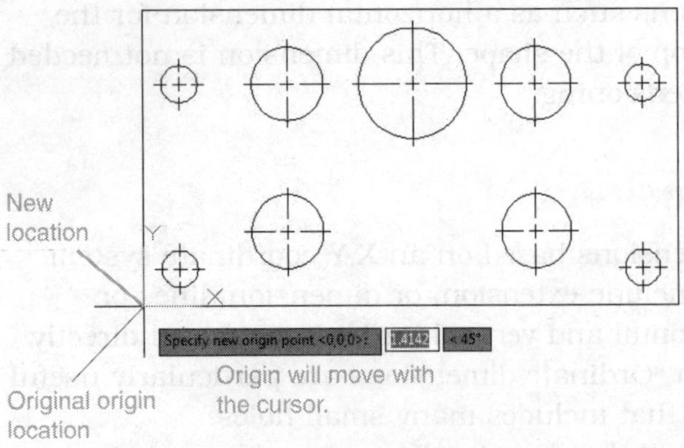

Figure 8-47

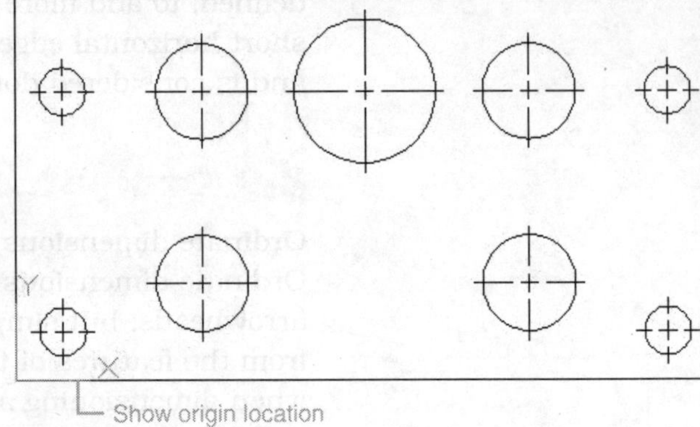

Figure 8-48

4 Move the origin to the desired location.

5 Click the mouse. See Figures 8-47 and 8-48.

To Add Ordinate Dimensions to an Object

The following procedure assumes that you have already used the **Dimension Style Manager** (Section 8-4) to set the desired dimension style and that you have moved the origin to the lower left corner of the object as shown:

1 Turn the **Ortho Mode** command on. (Click the **Ortho Mode** box at the bottom of the screen.) See Figure 8-49.

Figure 8-49

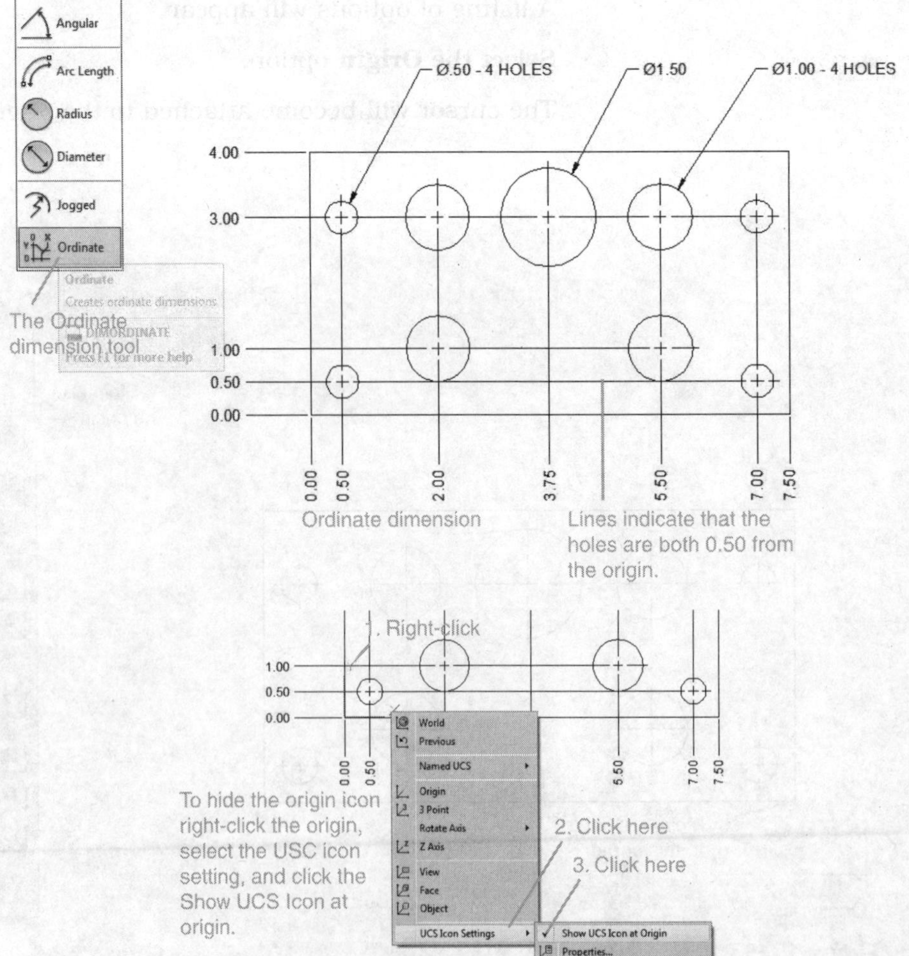

2 Select the **Ordinate** tool flyout from the **Dimension** tool on the **Dimensions** panel.

Command: _dimordinate

Select feature location:

3 Select the lower endpoint of the first circle's vertical centerline.

Specify leader endpoint or [Xdatum Ydatum MText Text Angle]:

4 Select a point along the X axis directly below the vertical centerline of the circle.

The ordinate value of the point will be added to the drawing. This point should have a **0.50** value. The text value may be modified by using either the **MText** or **Text** option, or by using the **Dimension Style Manager** dialog box to define the precision of the text.

5 Press the right mouse button to restart the command, and dimension the object's other features.

6 Extend the centerlines across the object, and add the diameter dimensions for the holes.

Figure 8-49 shows the completed drawing. The **Text** option of the prompt shown in step 3 can be used to modify or remove the default text value.

8-10 Baseline Dimensions

Baseline dimensions are a series of dimensions that originate from a common baseline or datum line. Baseline dimensions are very useful because they help eliminate tolerance buildup associated with chain-type dimensions.

The **Baseline** tool can be used only after an initial dimension has been drawn. AutoCAD will define the first extension line origin of the initial dimension selected as the baseline for all baseline dimensions.

To Use the Baseline Dimension Tool (See Figure 8-50.)

1 Select the **Linear** tool flyout from the **Dimension** tool on the **Dimensions** panel.

Command: _dimlinear

Specify first extension line origin or <select object>:

2 Select the upper left corner of the object.

This selection determines the baseline.

Specify second extension line origin:

Figure 8-50

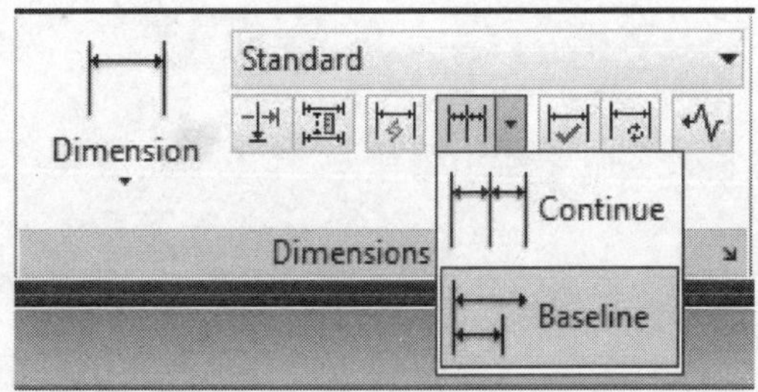

3 Select the endpoint of the first circle's vertical centerline.

Specify dimension line location or [Text Angle Horizontal Vertical Rotated]:

4 Select a location for the dimension line.

Command:

5 Select the **Baseline** tool on the **Dimensions** panel.

Specify a second extension line origin or [Undo Select] <Select>:

6 Select the endpoint of the next circle's vertical centerline.

Specify a second extension line origin or [Undo Select] <Select>:

7 Continue to select the circle centerlines until all circles are located.

Specify a second extension line origin or [Undo Select] <Select>:

8 Select the upper right corner of the object.

9 Press the right mouse button, and then press **Enter.** This will end the **Baseline** dimension command.

10 Repeat the preceding procedure for the vertical baseline dimensions.

11 Add the circles' diameter values.

The **Baseline** dimension option can also be used with the **Angular** dimension option.

8-11 Continue Dimension

The **Continue** tool on the **Dimensions** panel is used to create chain dimensions based on an initial linear, angular, or ordinate dimension. The second extension line's origin becomes the first extension line origin for the continued dimension.

To Use the Continue Dimension Command (See Figure 8-51.)

1 Select the **Linear** tool flyout from the **Dimension** tool on the **Dimensions** panel.

Command: dimcontinue

Specify first extension line origin or <select object>:

2 Select the upper left corner of the object.

Specify second extension line origin:

Figure 8-51

The second extension line of the previous dimension becomes the first extension line of the next dimension.

2.00 2.50 3.00 2.50

3 Select the right endpoint of the uppermost horizontal line.

Dimension line location (Text Angle Horizontal Vertical Rotated):

4 Select a dimension line location.

Command:

5 Select the **Continue** tool on the **Dimensions** panel.

Command: _dimcontinue

Specify a second extension line origin or [Undo Select] <Select>:

6 Select the next linear distance to be dimensioned.

Specify a second extension line origin or [Undo Select] <Select>:

7 Continue until the object's horizontal edges are completely dimensioned.

AutoCAD will automatically align the dimensions. Figure 8-52 shows how the **Continue** tool dimensions distances that are too small for both the arrowhead and dimension value to fit within the extension lines.

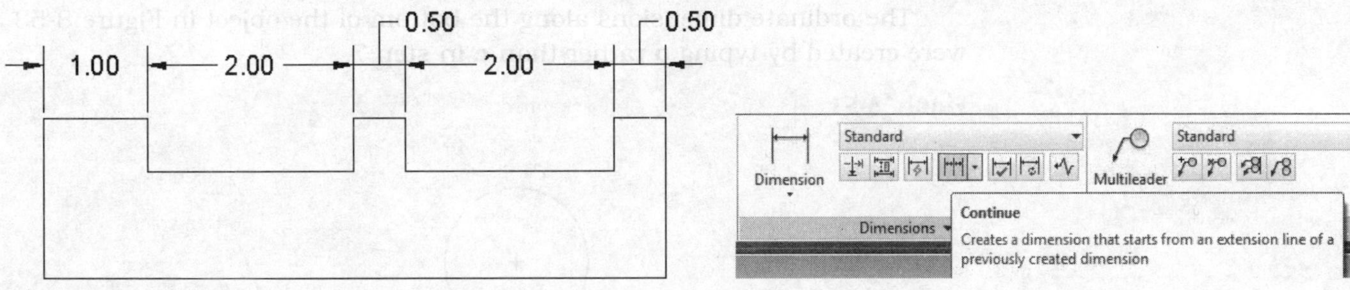

Figure 8-52

8-12 Quick Dimension

The **Quick Dimension** tool is used to add a series of dimensions. See Figure 8-53.

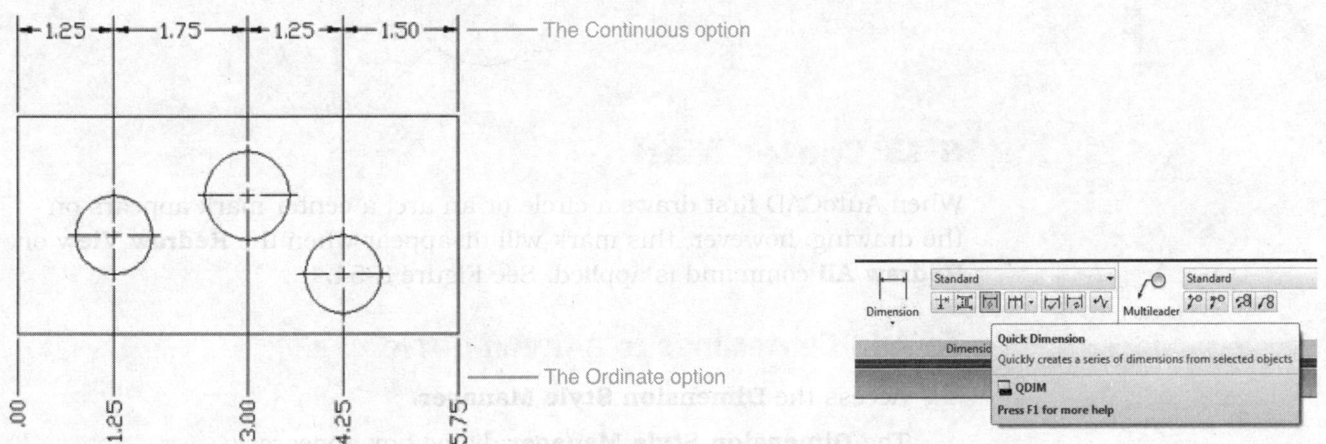

Figure 8-53

To Use the Quick Dimension Command

1 Select the **Quick Dimension** tool from the **Dimensions** panel.

Command: _qdim

Select geometry to dimension:

2. Select the left vertical edge line of the object to be dimensioned; press **Enter.**

   Specify dimension line position, or [Continuous Staggered Baseline Ordinate Radius Diameter datumPoint Edit seTtings]<Baseline>:

3. Select the vertical centerline of the first hole.
   Select geometry to dimension:

4. Select the vertical centerline of the second hole.
   Select geometry to dimension:

5. Select the vertical centerline of the third hole.

6. Press the right mouse button.
   Specify dimension line position, or [Continuous Staggered Baseline Ordinate Radius Diameter datumPoint Edit seTtings]<Baseline>:

7. Type **c;** press **Enter.**

8. Position the dimension lines, press the right mouse button, and enter the position.

   The ordinate dimensions along the bottom of the object in Figure 8-53 were created by typing **o** rather than **c** in step 7.

Figure 8-54

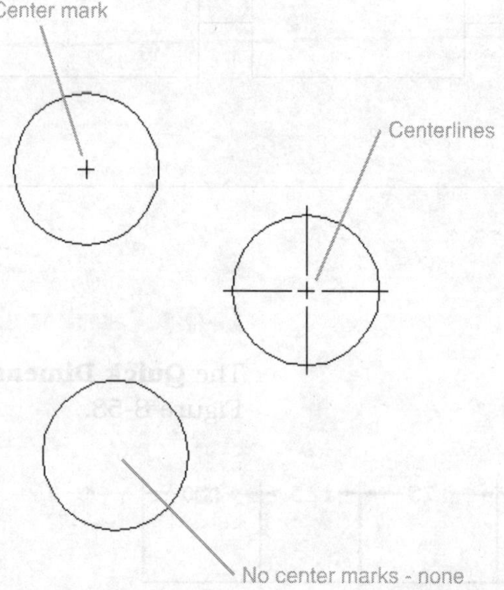

8-13 Center Mark

When AutoCAD first draws a circle or an arc, a center mark appears on the drawing; however, this mark will disappear when the **Redraw View** or **Redraw All** command is applied. See Figure 8-54.

To Add Centerlines to a Given Circle

1. Access the **Dimension Style Manager.**

   The **Dimension Style Manager** dialog box appears.

2. Select **Modify,** then the **Symbols and Arrows** option.

   The **Modify Dimension Style: Standard** dialog box will appear.

3. Select the **Line** option.

   The preview display will show a horizontal and a vertical centerline.

4. Select **OK** to return to the drawing.
5. Select the **Center Mark** tool located on the **Dimensions** panel.

Select arc or circle:

6. Select the circle.

Horizontal and vertical centerlines will appear. The size of the center mark can be controlled by using the **Size** box in the **Center marks** box. If the centerline's size appears to be unacceptable, try different sizes until you get an acceptable size.

8-14 MLEADER and QLEADER

Leader lines are slanted lines that extend from notes or dimensions to a specific feature or location on the surface of a drawing. They usually end with an arrowhead or a dot. The **Radius** and **Diameter** tools, flyouts from the **Dimension** tool on the **Dimensions** panel, automatically create a leader line. The **MLEADER** and **QLEADER** commands can be used to add leader lines not associated with radius and diameter dimensions.

To Create a Leader Line with Text

1. Type **qleader** in response to a command prompt.

Command: _qleader
Specify first leader point, or [Settings]<Settings>:

2. Select the starting point for the leader line.

This is the point at which the arrowhead will appear. In the example shown in Figure 8-55, the upper right corner of the object was selected.

Specify next point:

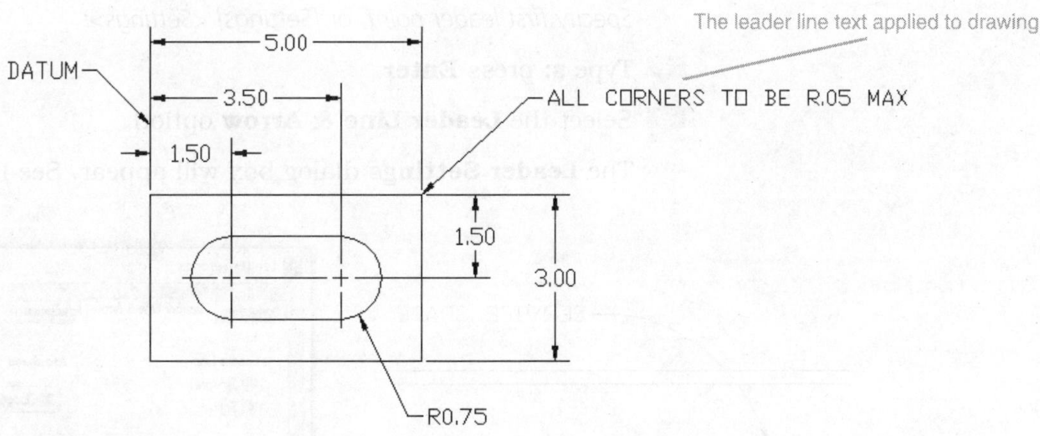

Figure 8-55

3. Select the location of the endpoint of the slanted line segment.

Specify next point:

4. Draw a short horizontal line segment; press **Enter.**

Specify text width <0.0000>:

5 Press **Enter.**

Enter first line of annotation text <MText>:

6 Press **Enter.**

7 Use the cursor, and extend the text box as needed.

8 Type the desired text. See Figure 8-56.

Figure 8-56

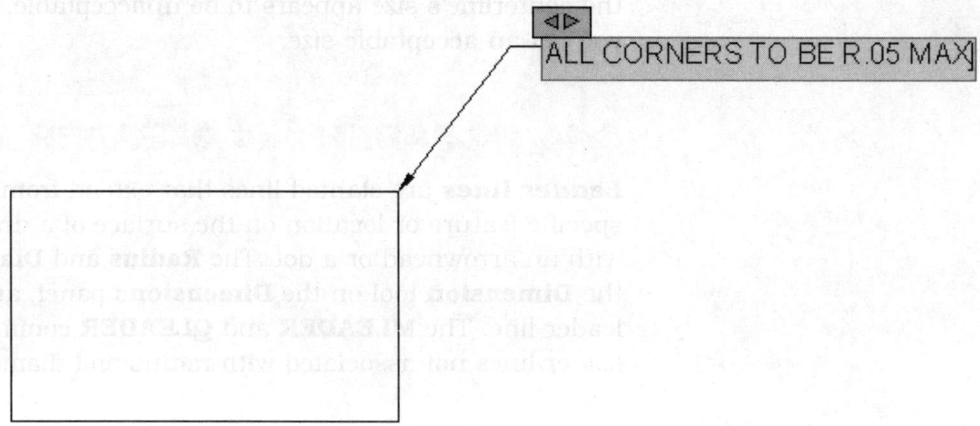

9 Click the **OK** button.

The text will appear next to the horizontal line segment of the leader line.

To Draw a Curved Leader Line

The **Leader** command can be used to draw curved leader lines and leader lines that end with dots. See Figure 8-57.

1 Type **qleader** in response to a command prompt.

Command: _qleader

Specify first leader point, or [Settings] <Settings>:

2 Type **s;** press **Enter.**

3 Select the **Leader Line & Arrow** option.

The **Leader Settings** dialog box will appear. See Figure 8-58.

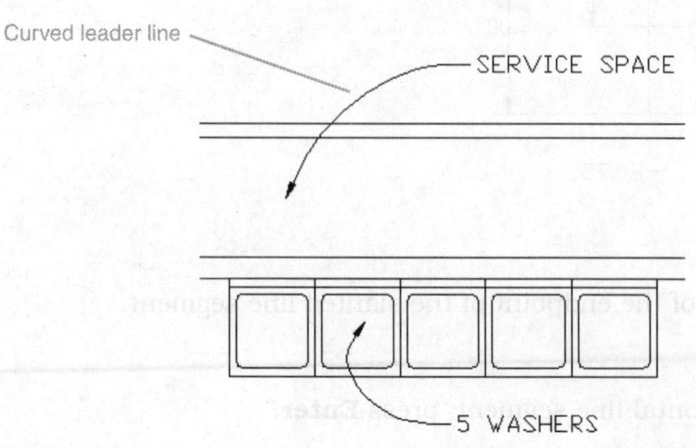

Figure 8-57

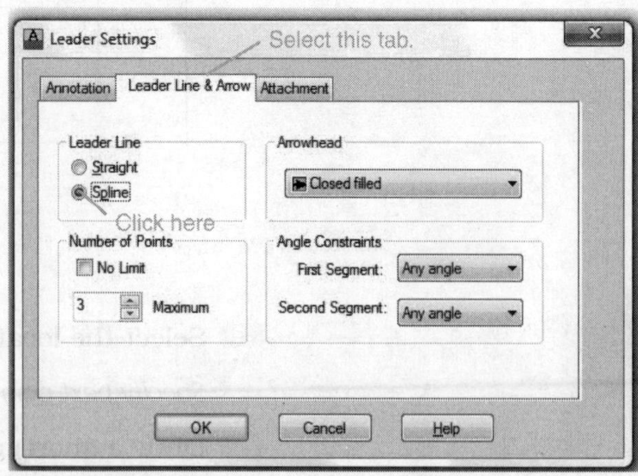

Figure 8-58

4 Select the **Spline** option in the **Leader Line** box, and then click **OK.**

Specify first leader point, or [Settings] <Settings>:

5 Select the starting point for the leader line.

At this point the arrowhead will appear.

Specify next point:

6 Select the next point.

Select next point:

AutoCAD will shift to the **Drag** mode, which allows you to move the cursor around and watch the changes in shapes of the leader line. More than one point may be selected to define the shape.

7 Complete the leader line, as explained previously.

To Draw a Leader Line with a Dot at Its End

1 Click the arrow in the lower left corner of the **Leaders** panel located under the **Annotate** tab.

The **Multileader Style Manager** dialog box will appear. See Figure 8-59.

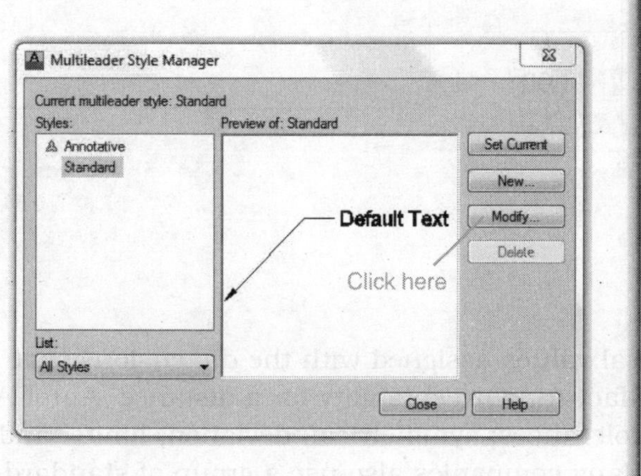

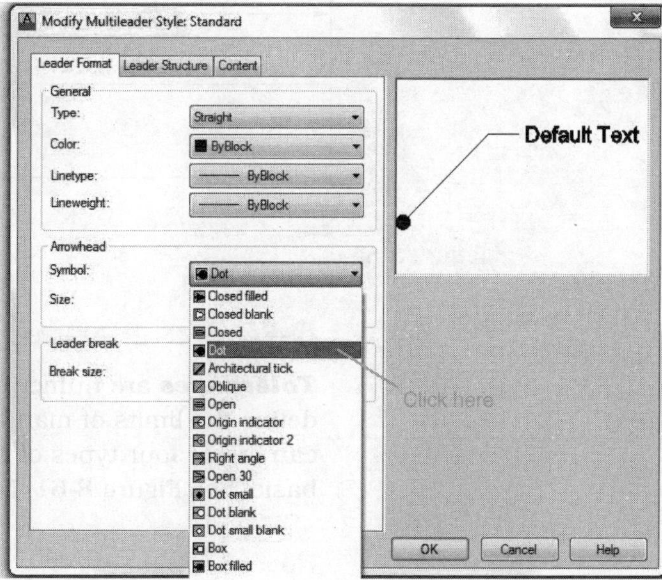

Figure 8-59

2 Click the **Modify** option.

The **Modify Multileader Style: Standard** dialog box will appear. See Figure 8-59.

3 Click the arrow on the right end of the **Symbol** box under the **Arrowhead** heading.

4 Select the **Dot** option.

5 Click **OK.**

8-15 Text Angle

To Change the Angle of a Dimension Text

The **Text Angle** tool is used to change the angle of an existing dimension text.

1. Click the **Text Angle** tool on the **Dimensions** panel.

   Select dimension:

2. Select the dimension text.

   Select new location for dimension or [Left Right Center Home Angle]: _a

   Specify angle for dimension text:

3. Type **90;** press **Enter.**
   See Figure 8-60.

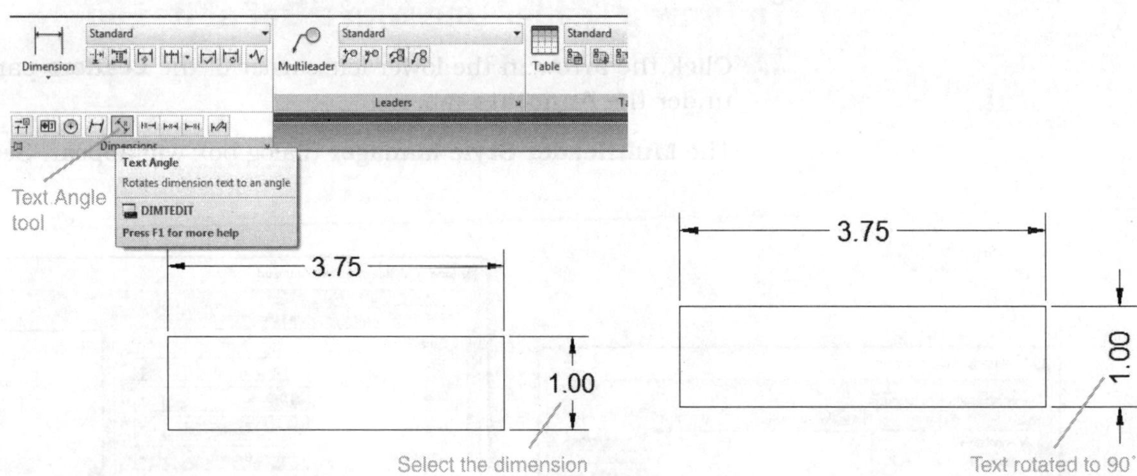

Figure 8-60

8-16 Tolerances

Tolerances are numerical values assigned with the dimensions that define the limits of manufacturing acceptability for a distance. AutoCAD can create four types of tolerances: symmetrical, deviation, limits, and basic. See Figure 8-61. Many companies also use a group of standard

Figure 8-61

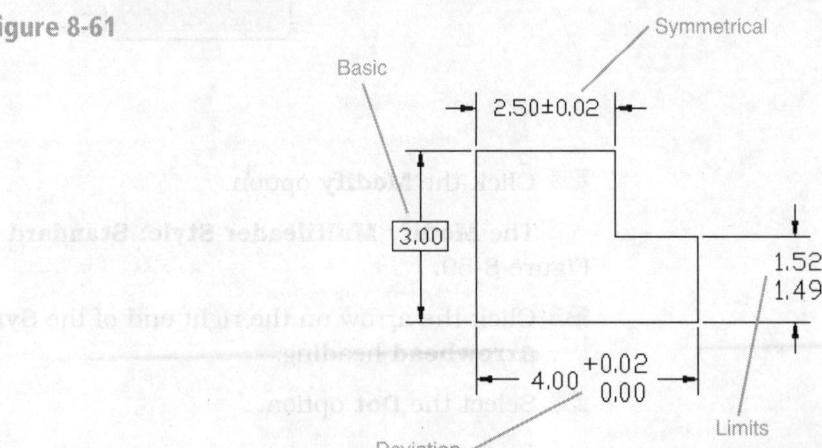

tolerances that are applied to any dimensional value that is not assigned a specific tolerance. See Figure 8-23. Tolerances for numerical values expressed in millimeters are applied by a different convention than that used for inches. Tolerances are discussed in Chapters 9 and 10. The discussion of the appropriate dimensioning tools will be covered in those chapters.

8-17 Dimensioning Holes

Holes are dimensioned by stating their diameter and depth, if any. The symbol **Ø** is used to represent diameter. It is considered good practice to dimension a hole by using a diameter value, because the tooling used to produce the hole is also defined in terms of diameter values. A notation like 12 DRILL is considered less desirable, because it specifies a machining process. Manufacturing processes should be left, whenever possible, to the discretion of the shop.

To Dimension Individual Holes

Figure 8-62 shows three different methods that can be used to dimension a hole that does not go completely through an object. If the hole goes completely through, only the diameter need be specified. The **Radius** and **Diameter** dimension tools were covered in Section 8-7. Depth values may be added by selecting the **Single Line** option of the **Multitext** tool.

Figure 8-63 shows two methods of dimensioning holes in sectional views. The single-line note version is the preferred method.

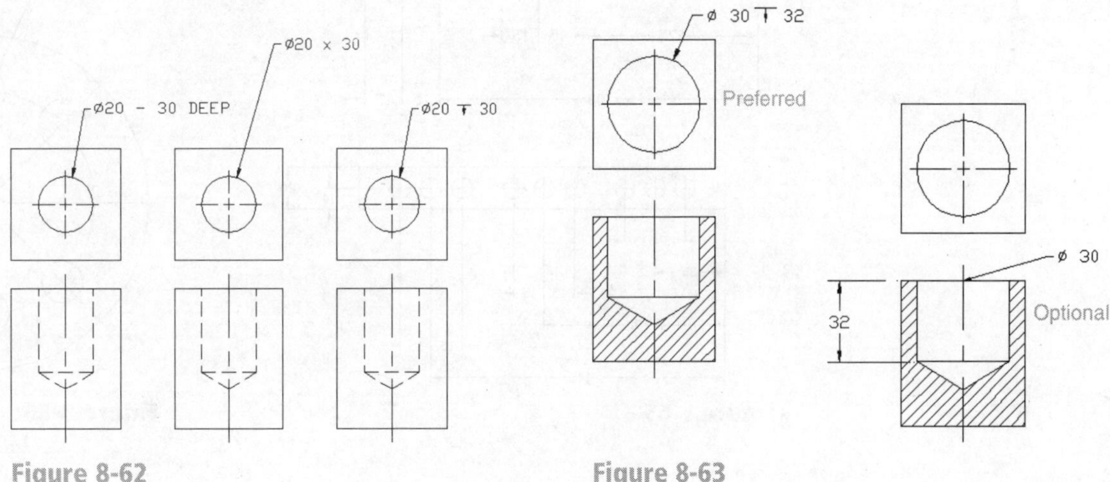

Figure 8-62

Figure 8-63

To Dimension Hole Patterns

Figure 8-64 shows two different hole patterns dimensioned. The circular pattern includes the note **Ø10-4 HOLES.** This note serves to define all four holes within the object.

Figure 8-64 also shows a rectangular object that contains five holes of equal diameter, equally spaced from one another. The notation **5** × **Ø10** specifies five holes of 10 diameter. The notation **4** × **20 (**=**80)** means 4 equal spaces of 20. The notation (=**80)** is a reference dimension and is included for convenience. Reference dimensions are explained in Chapter 9.

Figure 8-64

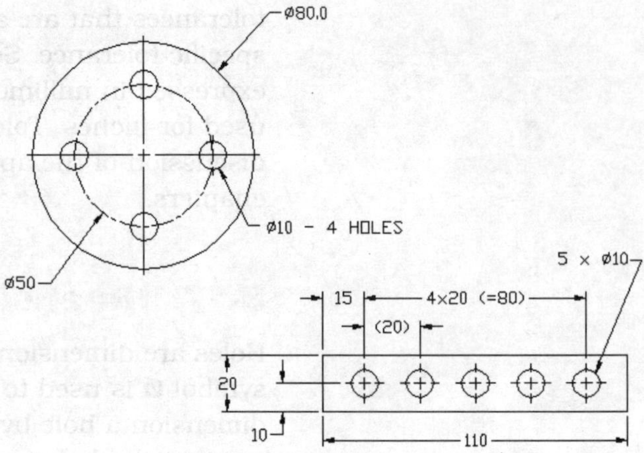

Figure 8-65 shows two additional methods for dimensioning repeating hole patterns. Figure 8-66 shows a circular hole pattern that includes two different hole diameters. The hole diameters are not noticeably different and could be confused. One group is defined by indicating letter (A); the other is dimensioned in a normal manner.

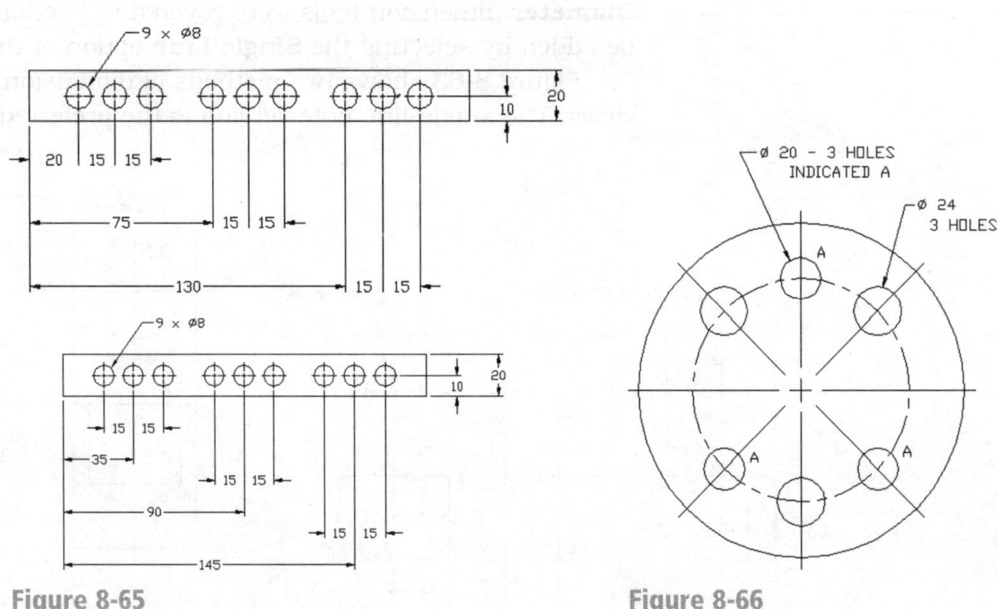

Figure 8-65

Figure 8-66

8-18 Placing Dimensions

There are several general rules concerning the placement of dimensions. See Figure 8-67.

1. Place dimensions near the features that they are defining.
2. Do not place dimensions on the surface of the object.
3. Align and group dimensions so that they are neat and easy to understand.
4. Avoid crossing extension lines.

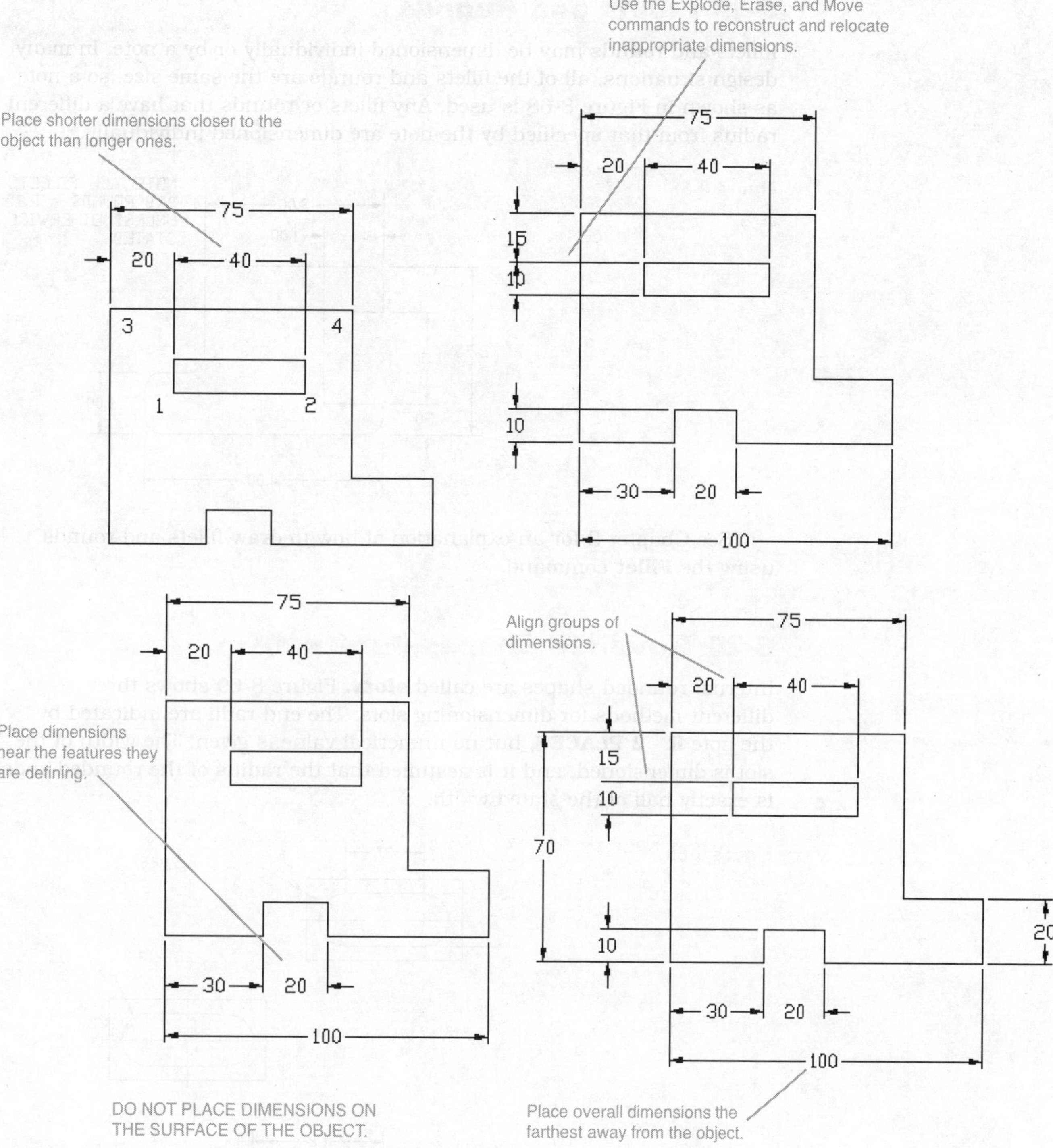

Figure 8-67

Sometimes, it is impossible not to cross extension lines because of the complex shape of the object, but whenever possible, avoid crossing extension lines.

5 Place shorter dimensions closer to the object than longer ones.

6 Always place overall dimensions the farthest away from the object.

7 Do not dimension the same distance twice. This is called *double dimensioning.* Double dimensioning will be discussed in Chapter 9.

8-19 Fillets and Rounds

Fillets and rounds may be dimensioned individually or by a note. In many design situations, all of the fillets and rounds are the same size, so a note as shown in Figure 8-68 is used. Any fillets or rounds that have a different radius from that specified by the note are dimensioned individually.

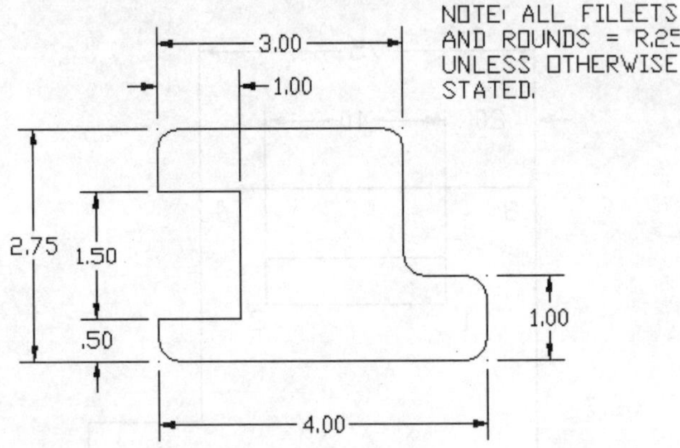

Figure 8-68

See Chapter 2 for an explanation of how to draw fillets and rounds using the **Fillet** command.

8-20 Rounded Shapes (Internal)

Internal rounded shapes are called ***slots.*** Figure 8-69 shows three different methods for dimensioning slots. The end radii are indicated by the note **R - 2 PLACES,** but no numerical value is given. The width of the slot is dimensioned, and it is assumed that the radius of the rounded ends is exactly half of the stated width.

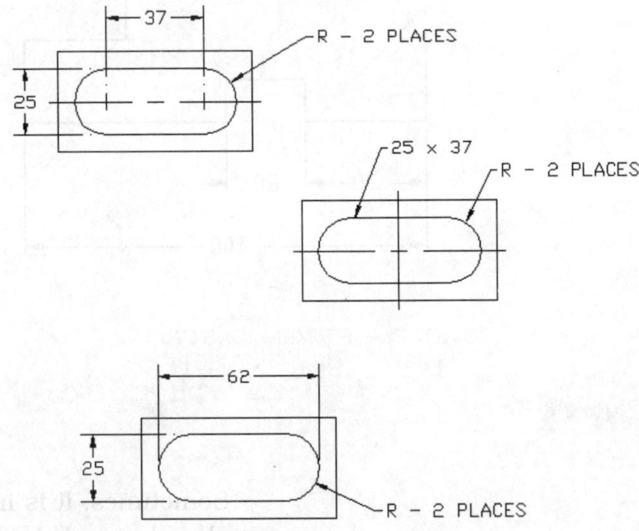

Figure 8-69

8-21 Rounded Shapes (External)

Figure 8-70 shows two example shapes with external rounded ends. As with internal rounded shapes, the end radii are indicated, but no value is given. The width of the object is given, and the radius of the rounded end is assumed to be exactly half of the stated width.

Figure 8-70

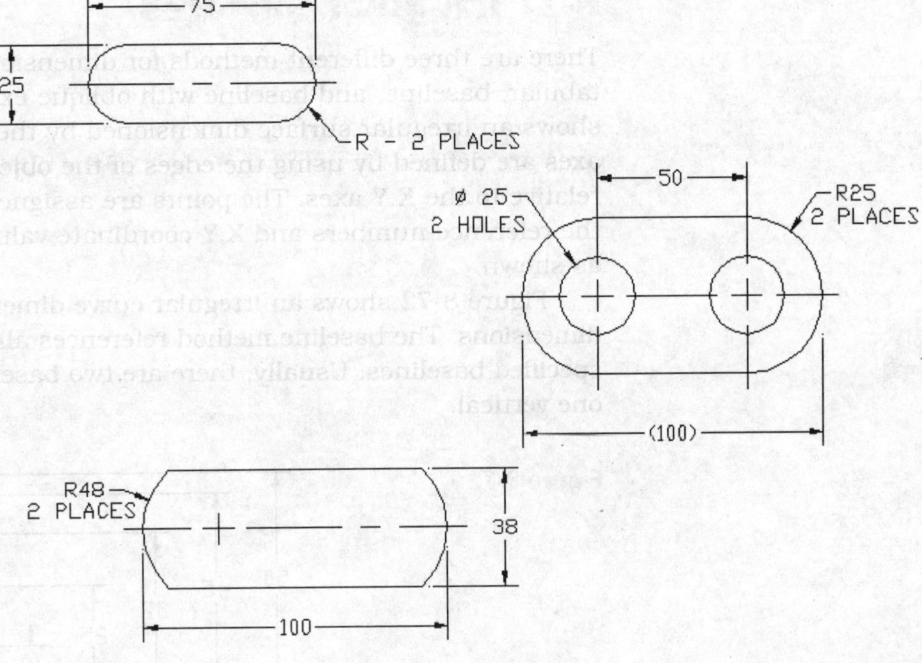

The second example shown in Figure 8-71 shows an object dimensioned by using the object's centerline. This type of dimensioning is used when the distance between the holes is more important than the overall length of the object; that is, the tolerance for the distance between the holes is more exact than the tolerance for the overall length of the object.

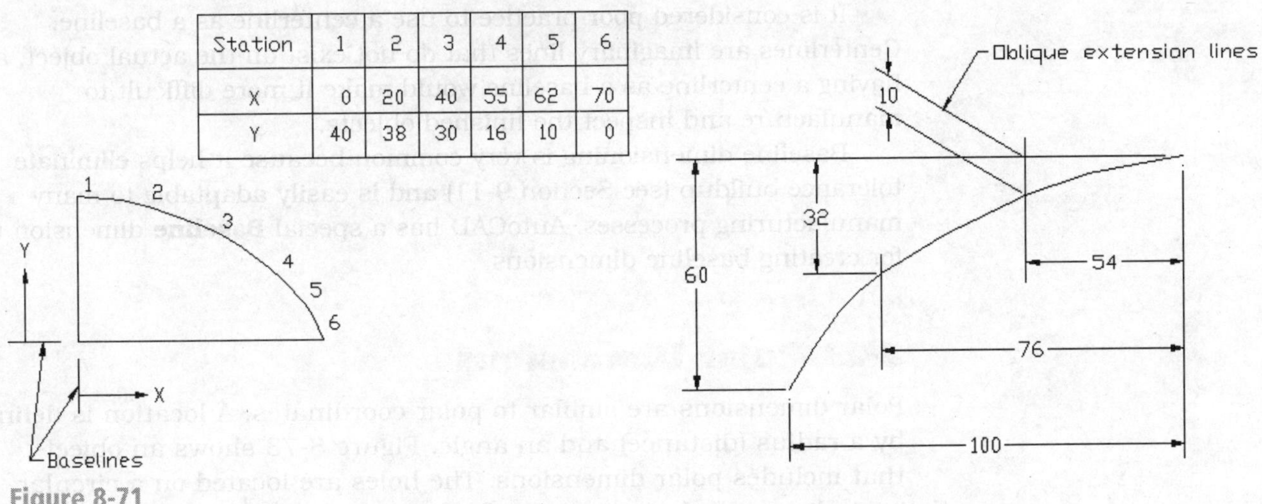

Station	1	2	3	4	5	6
X	0	20	40	55	62	70
Y	40	38	30	16	10	0

Figure 8-71

The overall length of the object is given as a reference dimension (100). This means that the object will be manufactured on the basis of other dimensions and the 100 value will be used only for reference.

Objects with partially rounded edges should be dimensioned as shown in Figure 8-71. The radii of the end features are dimensioned. The center point of the radii is implied to be on the object centerline. The overall dimension is given; it is not referenced unless specific radii values are included.

8-22 Irregular Surfaces

There are three different methods for dimensioning irregular surfaces: tabular, baseline, and baseline with oblique extension lines. Figure 8-71 shows an irregular surface dimensioned by the tabular method. The X,Y axes are defined by using the edges of the object. Points are then defined relative to the X,Y axes. The points are assigned reference numbers, and the reference numbers and X,Y coordinate values are listed in chart form as shown.

Figure 8-72 shows an irregular curve dimensioned by using baseline dimensions. The baseline method references all dimensions back to specified baselines. Usually, there are two baselines, one horizontal and one vertical.

Figure 8-72

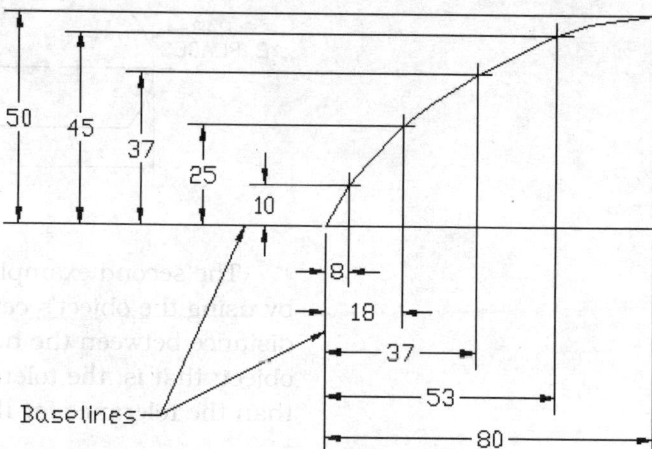

It is considered poor practice to use a centerline as a baseline. Centerlines are imaginary lines that do not exist on the actual object, and having a centerline as a baseline would make it more difficult to manufacture and inspect the finished objects.

Baseline dimensioning is very common because it helps eliminate tolerance buildup (see Section 9-11) and is easily adaptable to many manufacturing processes. AutoCAD has a special **Baseline** dimension tool for creating baseline dimensions.

8-23 Polar Dimensions

Polar dimensions are similar to polar coordinates. A location is defined by a radius (distance) and an angle. Figure 8-73 shows an object that includes polar dimensions. The holes are located on a circular centerline, and their positions from the vertical centerline are specified by angles.

Figure 8-74 shows an example of a hole pattern dimensioned by using polar dimensions.

8-24 Chamfers

Chamfers are angular cuts made on the edges of objects. They are usually used to make it easier to fit two parts together. They are most often made at 45° angles, but may be made at any angle. Figure 8-75

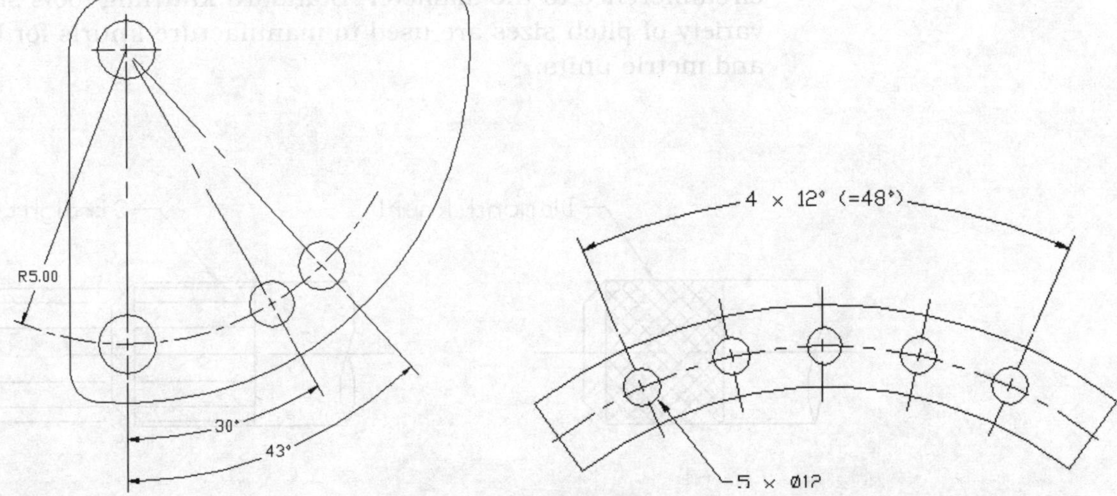

Figure 8-73

Figure 8-74

shows two objects with chamfers between surfaces 90° apart, and two examples between surfaces that are not 90° apart. Either of the two types of dimensions shown for the 45° dimension may be used. If an angle other than 45° is used, the angle and setback distance must be specified.

Figure 8-76 shows two examples of internal chamfers. Both define the chamfers by using an angle and diameter. Internal chamfers are very similar to countersunk holes. See Section 5-26.

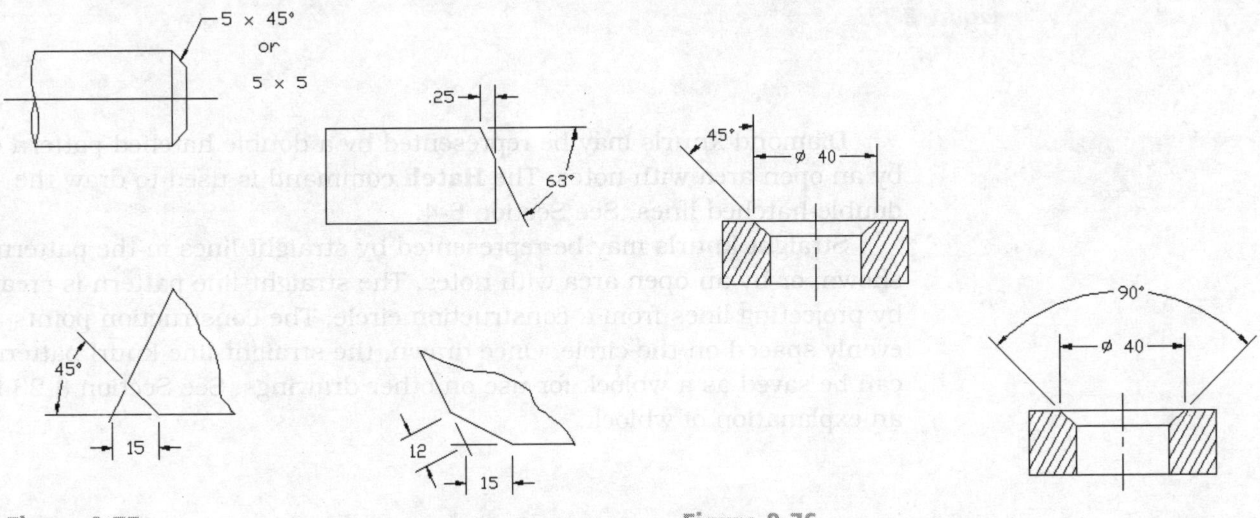

Figure 8-75

Figure 8-76

8-25 Knurling

Knurls are used to make it easier to grip a shaft, or to roughen a surface before it is used in a press fit. There are two types of knurls: diamond and straight.

Knurls are defined by their pitch and diameter. See Figure 8-77. The *pitch* of a knurl is the ratio of the number of grooves on the circumference to the diameter. Standard knurling tools sized to a variety of pitch sizes are used to manufacture knurls for both English and metric units.

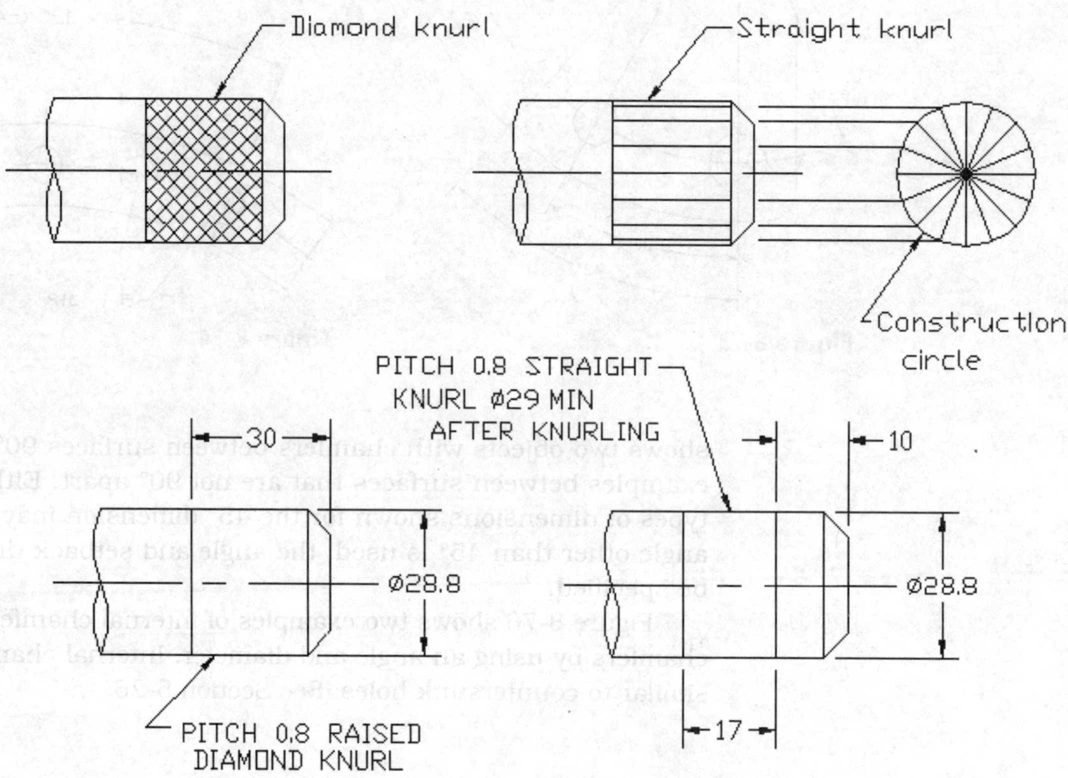

Figure 8-77

Diamond knurls may be represented by a double hatched pattern or by an open area with notes. The **Hatch** command is used to draw the double-hatched lines. See Section 6-4.

Straight knurls may be represented by straight lines in the pattern shown, or by an open area with notes. The straight-line pattern is created by projecting lines from a construction circle. The construction points are evenly spaced on the circle. Once drawn, the straight-line knurl pattern can be saved as a wblock for use on other drawings. See Section 3-23 for an explanation of wblock.

8-26 Keys and Keyseats

Keys are small pieces of material used to transmit power. For example, Figure 8-78 shows how a key can be fitted between a shaft and a gear so that the rotary motion of the shaft can be transmitted to the gear.

There are many different styles of keys. The key shown in Figure 8-78 has a rectangular cross section and is called a square key. Keys fit into grooves called ***keyseats,*** or ***keyways.***

Keyways are dimensioned from the bottom of the shaft, or hole, as shown.

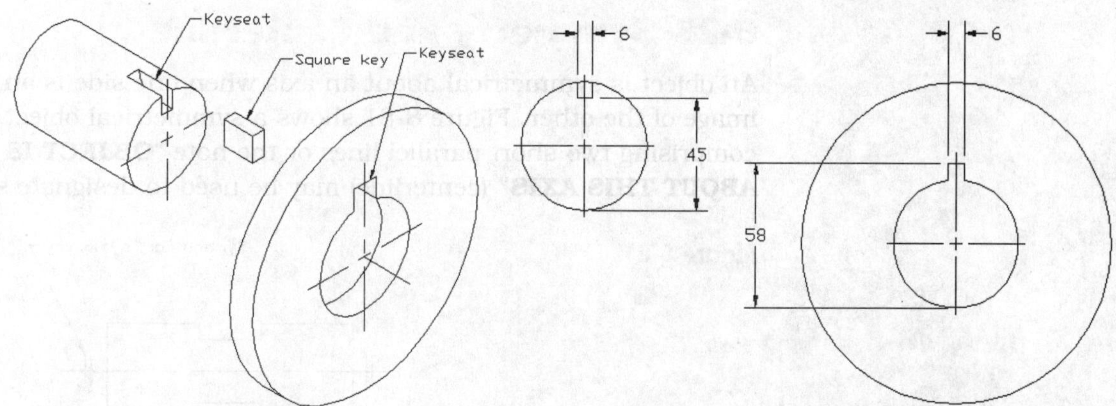

Figure 8-78

8-27 Symbols and Abbreviations

Symbols are used in dimensioning to help accurately display the meaning of the dimension. Symbols also help eliminate language barriers when reading drawings. Figure 8-79 shows a list of dimensioning symbols and their meanings. The height of a symbol should be the same as the text height.

Figure 8-79

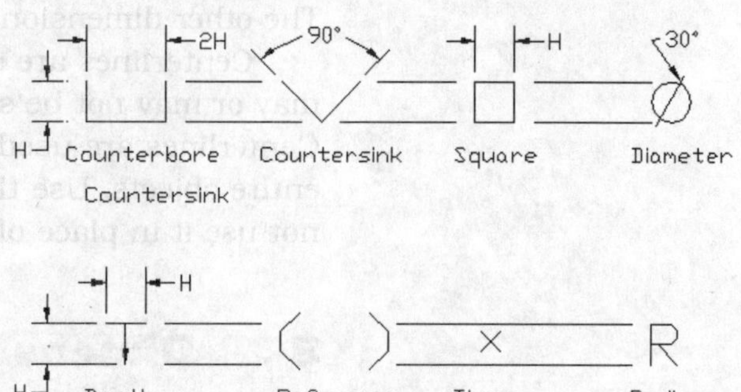

Abbreviations should be used very carefully on drawings. Whenever possible, write out the full word, including correct punctuation. Figure 8-80 shows several standard abbreviations used on technical drawings.

Figure 8-80

AL = Aluminum
C'BORE = Counterbore
CRS = Cold Rolled Steel
CSK = Countersink
DIA = Diameter
EQ = Equal
HEX = Hexagon
MAT'L = Material
R = Radius
SAE = Society of Automotive Engineers
SFACE = Spotface
ST = Steel
SQ = Square
REQD = Required

8-28 Symmetry and Centerline

An object is symmetrical about an axis when one side is an exact mirror image of the other. Figure 8-81 shows a symmetrical object. The symbol comprising two short parallel lines or the note "**OBJECT IS SYMMETRICAL ABOUT THIS AXIS**" (centerline) may be used to designate symmetry.

Figure 8-81

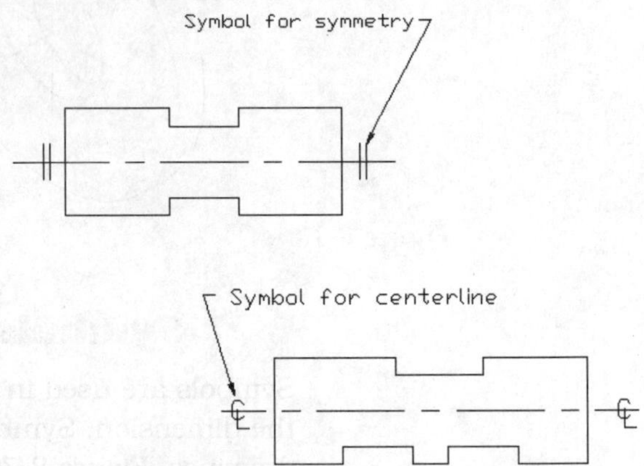

If an object is symmetrical, only half of the object need be dimensioned. The other dimensions are implied by the symmetry note or symbol.

Centerlines are slightly different from the axis of symmetry. An object may or may not be symmetrical about its centerline. See Figure 8-81. Centerlines are used to define the center of both individual features and entire objects. Use the centerline symbol when a line is a centerline, but do not use it in place of the symmetry symbol.

8-29 Dimensioning to Points

Curved surfaces can be dimensioned by using theoretical points. See Figure 8-82. There should be a small gap between the surface of the object and the lines used to define the theoretical point. The point should be defined by the intersection of at least two lines.

Figure 8-82

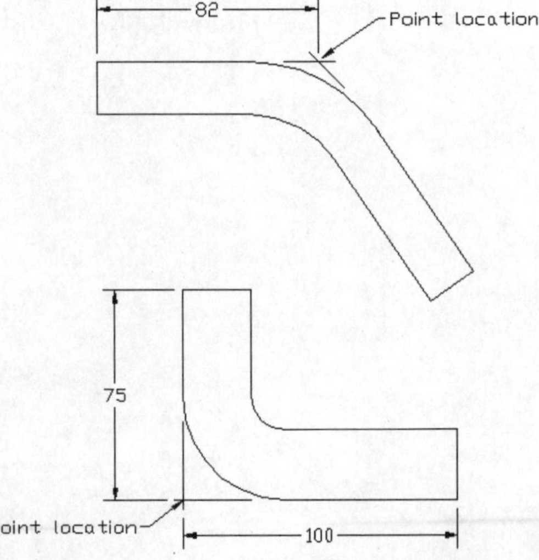

There should also be a small gap between the extension lines and the theoretical point used to locate the point.

8-30 Coordinate Dimensions

Coordinate dimensions are used for objects that contain many holes. Baseline dimensions can also be used, but when there are many holes, baseline dimensions can create a confusing appearance and will require a large area on the drawing. Coordinate dimensions use charts that simplify the appearance, use far less space on the drawing, and are easy to understand.

Figure 8-83 shows an object that has been dimensioned by using coordinate dimensions without dimension lines. Holes are identified on the drawing by letters. Holes of equal diameter use the same letter. The hole diameters are presented in chart form.

Figure 8-83

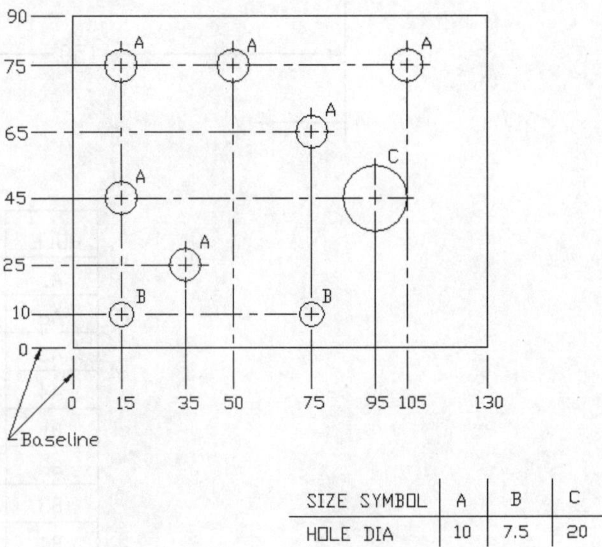

SIZE SYMBOL	A	B	C
HOLE DIA	10	7.5	20

Hole locations are defined by a series of centerlines referenced to baselines. The distance from the baseline to the centerline is written below the centerline, as shown.

Figure 8-84 shows an object that has been dimensioned by using coordinate dimensions in tabular form. Each hole is assigned both a letter and a number. Holes of equal diameter are assigned the same letter. A chart is used to define the diameter values for each hole letter.

Hole locations are defined relative to X,Y axes. A Z axis is used for depth dimensions. A chart lists each hole by its letter–number designation and specifies its distance from the X, Y, or Z axis. The overall dimensions are given by using extension and dimension lines.

The side view does not show any hidden lines because if all of the lines were shown, it would be too confusing to understand. A note **"THIS VIEW LEFT BLANK FOR CLARITY"** may be added to the drawing.

8-31 Sectional Views

Sectional views are dimensioned, as are orthographic views. See Figure 8-85. The sectional lines should be drawn at an angle that allows the viewer to clearly distinguish between the sectional lines and the extension lines.

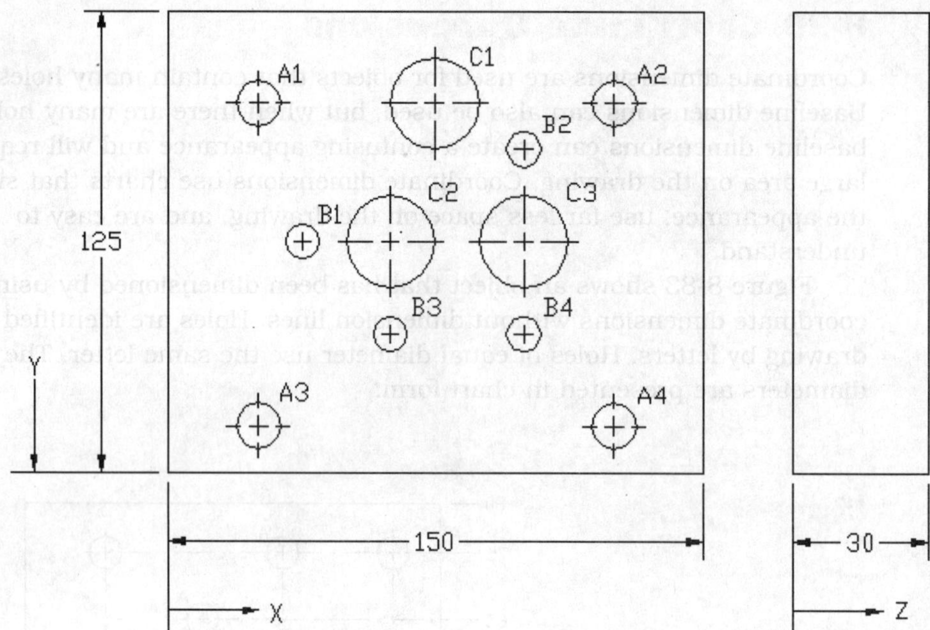

HOLE	FROM	X	Y	Z
A1	XY	15	65	THRU
A2	XY	80	65	THRU
A3	XY	15	10	THRU
A4	XY	80	10	THRU
B1	XY	25	40	12
B2	XY	65	56	12
B3	XY	40	25	12
B4	XY	65	25	12
C1	XY	48	65	THRU
C2	XY	40	40	THRU
C3	XY	65	40	THRU

HOLE	DESCRIPTION	QTY
A	Ø8	4
B	Ø5	4
C	Ø16	3

Figure 8-84

Figure 8-85

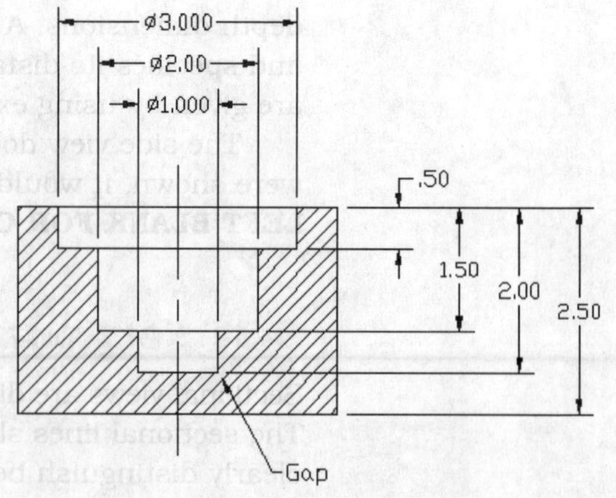

8-32 Orthographic Views

Dimensions should be added to orthographic views where the features appear in contour. Holes should be dimensioned in their circular views. Figure 8-86 shows three views of an object that has been dimensioned.

The hole dimensions are added to the top view where the hole appears circular. The slot is also dimensioned in the top view because it appears in contour. The slanted surface is dimensioned in the front view.

The height of surface A is given in the side view rather than run along extension lines across the front view. The length of surface A is given in the front view. This is a contour view of the surface.

It is considered good practice to keep dimensions in groups. This makes it easier for the viewer to find dimensions.

Be careful not to double-dimension a distance. A distance should be dimensioned only once per view. If a 30 dimension were added above the 25 dimension on the right-side view, it would be an error. The distance would be double-dimensioned: once with the 25 + 30 dimension, and again with the 55 overall dimension. The 25 + 30 dimensions are mathematically equal to the 55 overall dimension, but there is a distinct difference in how they affect the manufacturing tolerances. Double dimensions are explained more fully in Chapter 9.

Figure 8-87 shows an object dimensioned from its centerline. This type of dimensioning is used when the distances between the holes relative to one another are critical.

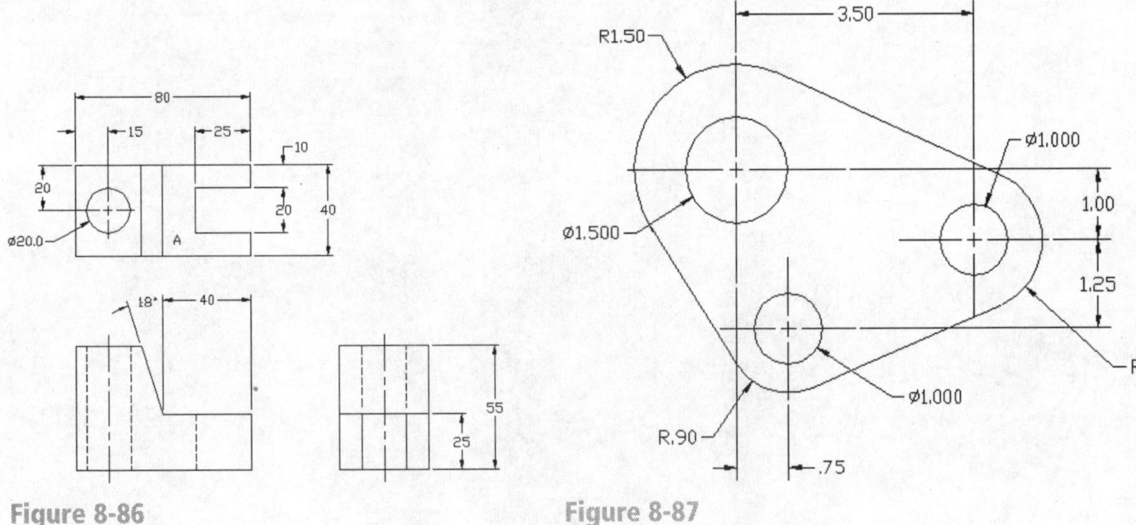

Figure 8-86

Figure 8-87

8-33 Very Large Radii

Some radii are so large that it is not practical to draw the leader for the radius dimension at full size. Figure 8-88 shows an example of an object that uses foreshortened leader lines.

To Create a Radius for Large Radii

1 Click the **Jogged** tool on the **Dimensions** panel.

Select arc or circle:

Figure 8-88

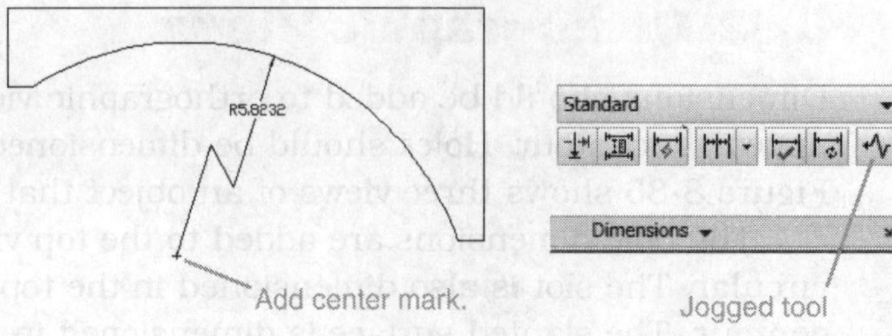

2 Click the large arc.

Specify center location override:

3 Select a center point for the dimension.

The point selected is not the arc's true center point, as that is probably off of the screen. The **Jogged** tool will override the true center point location and substitute the one selected. See Figure 8-88.

4 Right-click the mouse, and click **Enter.**

5 Select a text location by moving the cursor and then clicking the left mouse button.

Add a center mark to the end of the leader line.

8-34 EXERCISE PROBLEMS

Redraw the shapes shown in Exercise Problems EX8-1 through EX8-6. Locate the dimensions and tolerances as shown.

EX8-1 Inches

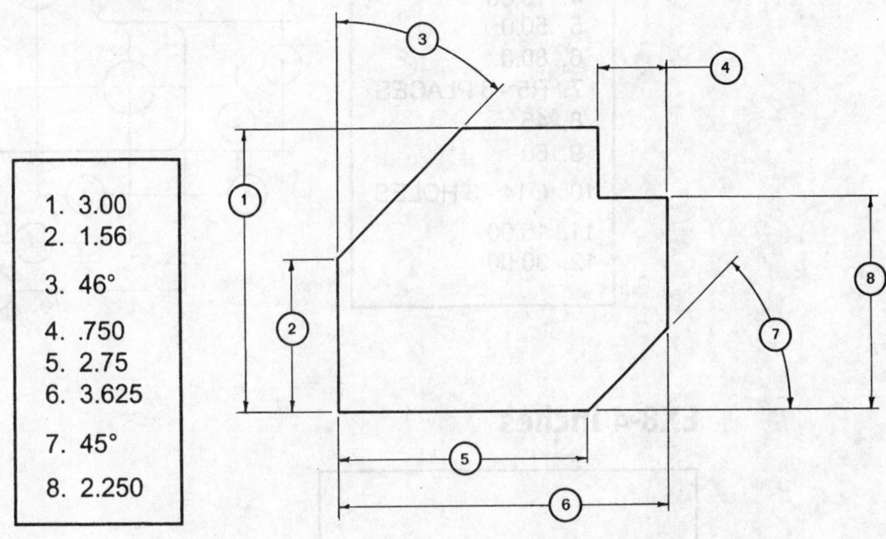

EX8-2 Millimeters

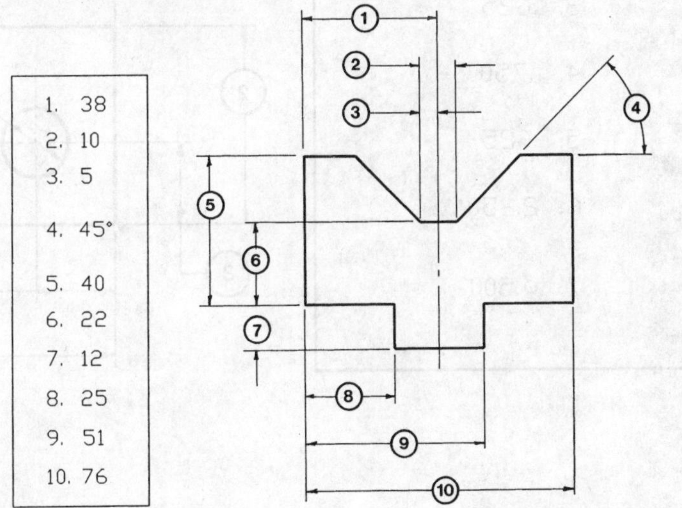

EX8-3 Millimeters

1. 34.0
2. 17.0
3. 25.0
4. 15.00
5. 50.0
6. 80.0
7. R5 - 8 PLACES
8. 45
9. 60
10. Ø14 - 3 HOLES
11. 15.00
12. 30.00

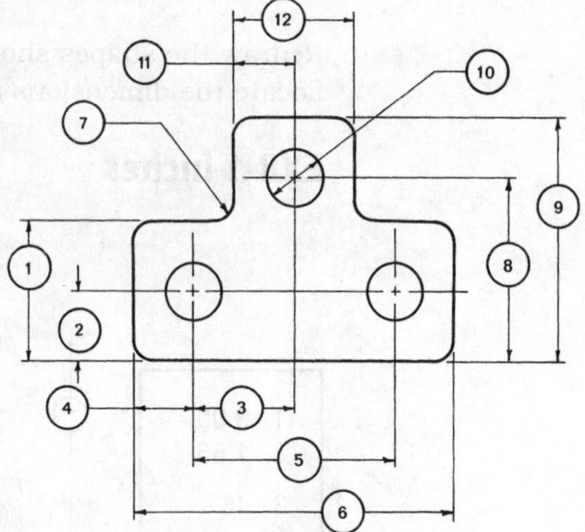

EX8-4 Inches

1. 1.50
2. 1.50
3. .625
4. .750
5. .625
6. 2.250
7. ø.500

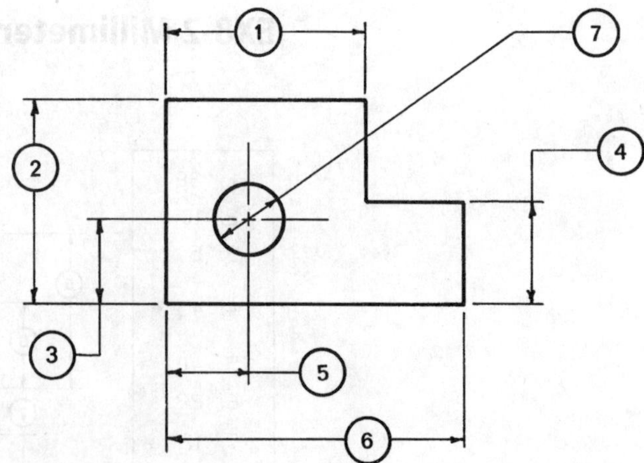

EX8-5 Millimeters

1. Ø30.0
2. Ø15.00
3. 10.0
4. 20.0
5. 66.2
6. 15.1
7. 35.02
8. 70.00

NOTE: ALL FILLETS AND ROUNDS = R5.0 UNLESS OTHERWISE STATED.

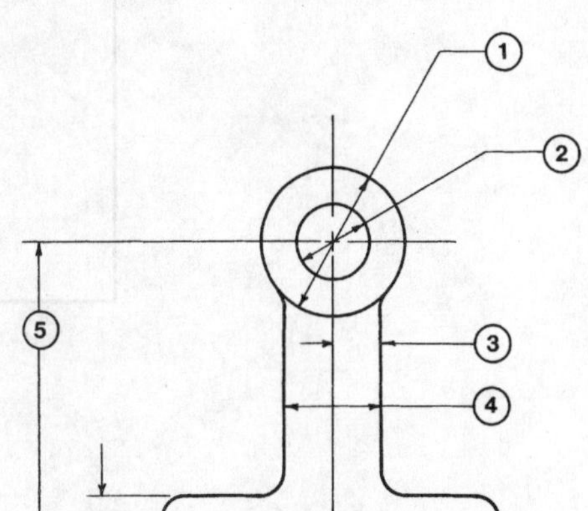

EX8-6 Millimeters

1. 184.5	7. 28.0	13. 83.2	19. 120.0
2. 91.5	8. 16.00	14. 63.00	20. (184.0)
3. 44.2	9. 16.00	15. 50.00	21. 12 × 31
4. 22.00	10. 28.0	16. 28.5	R – 3 SLOTS
5. 13.00	11. 12.5	17. 32.0	22. 6.00
6. 6.51	12. ø6.00	18. 76.0	23. 6.00

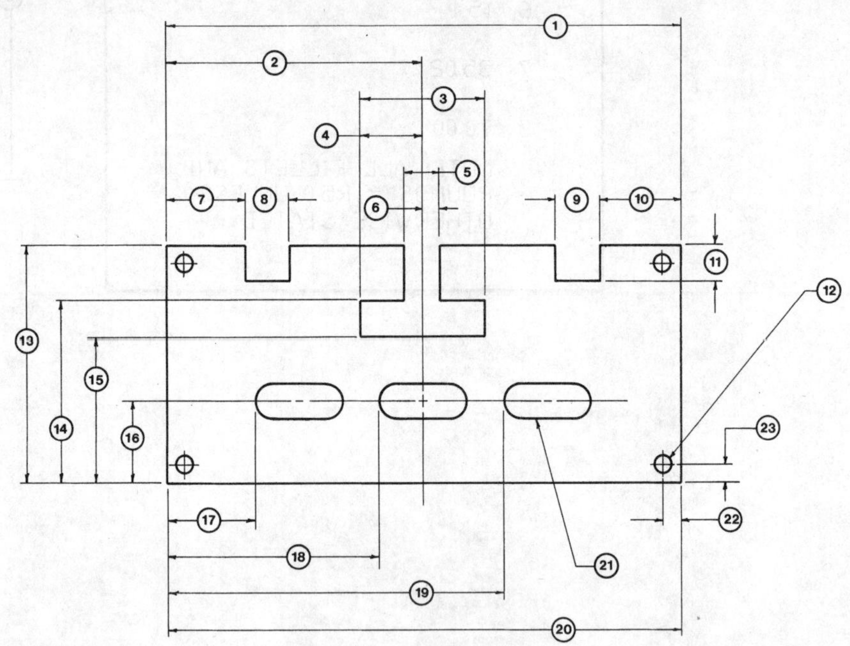

Measure and redraw the shapes in Exercise Problems EX8-7 through EX8-53. Add the appropriate dimensions. Specify the units and scale of the drawing. The dotted grid background has either 0.50-inch or 10-millimeter spacing.

EX8-7

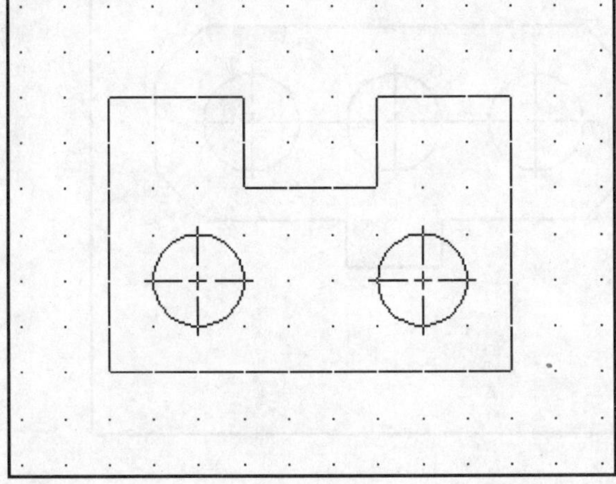

EX8-8

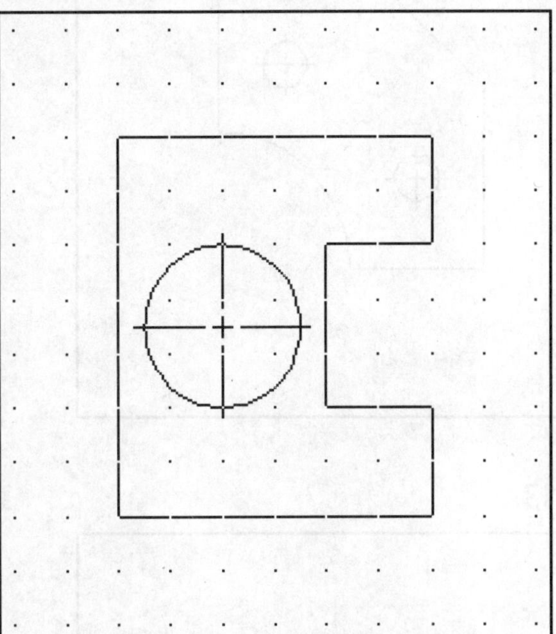

EX8-9

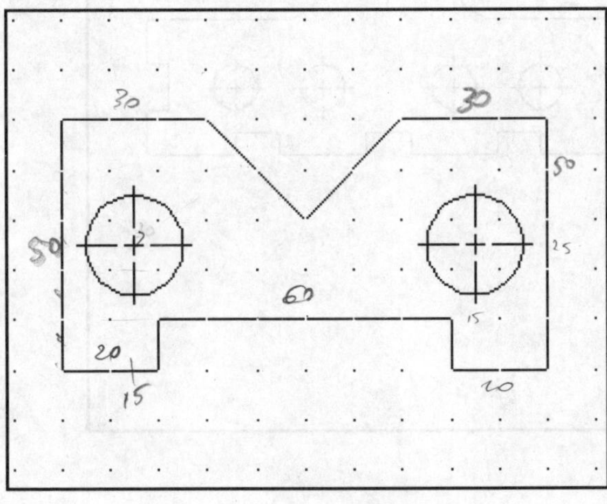

EX8-10

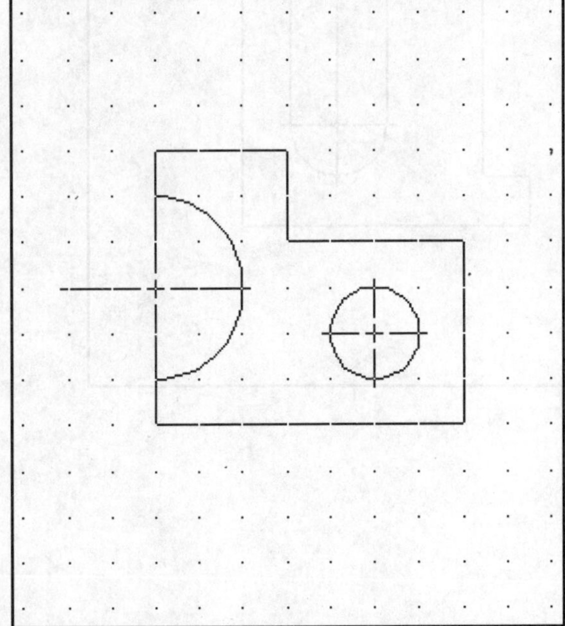

EX8-11

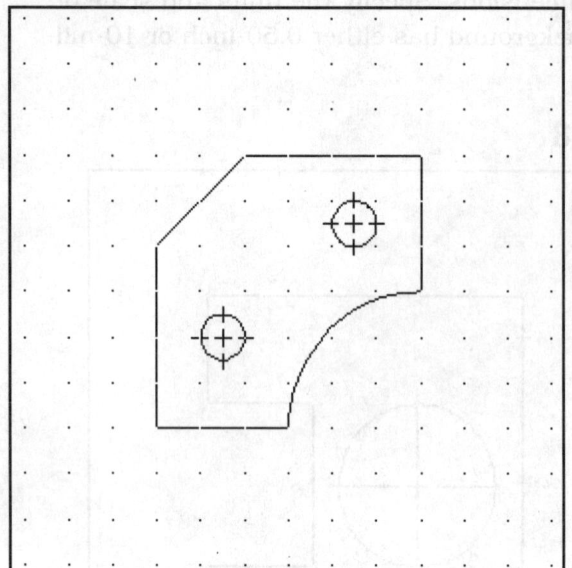

EX8-12

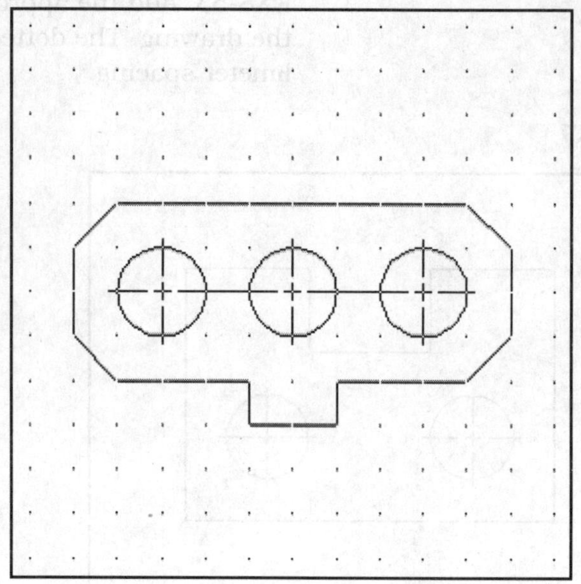

EX8-13

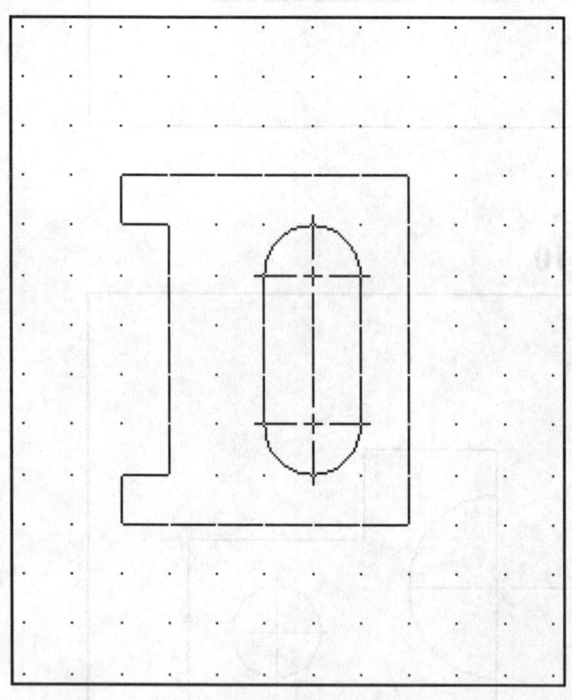

EX8-14

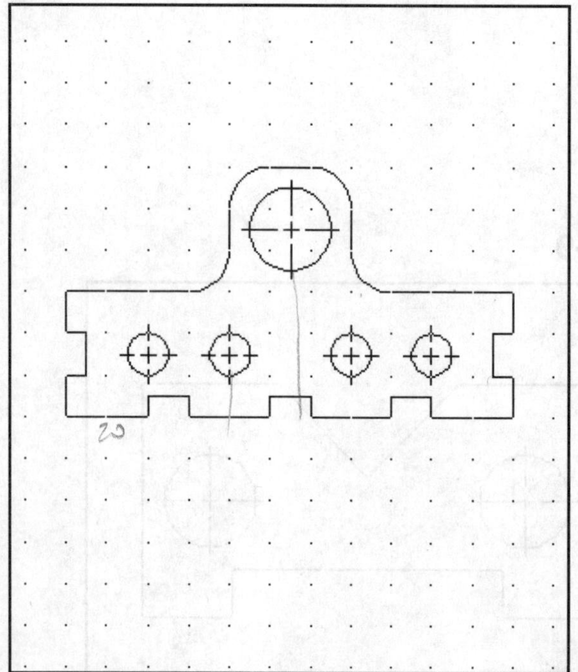

EX8-15

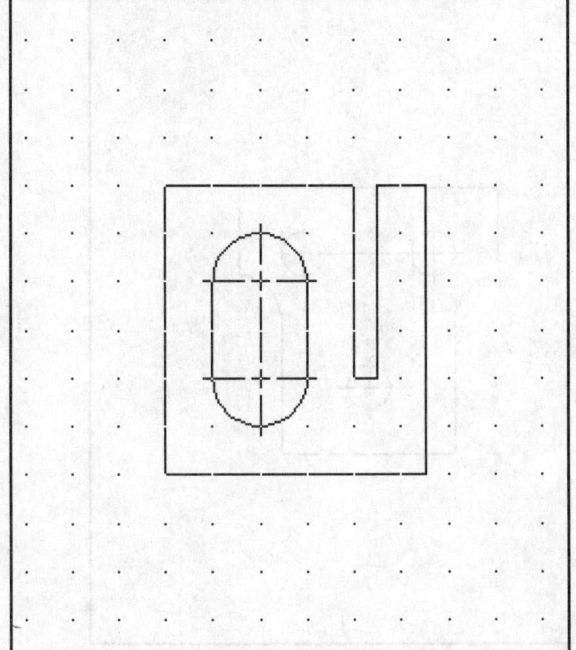

EX8-16

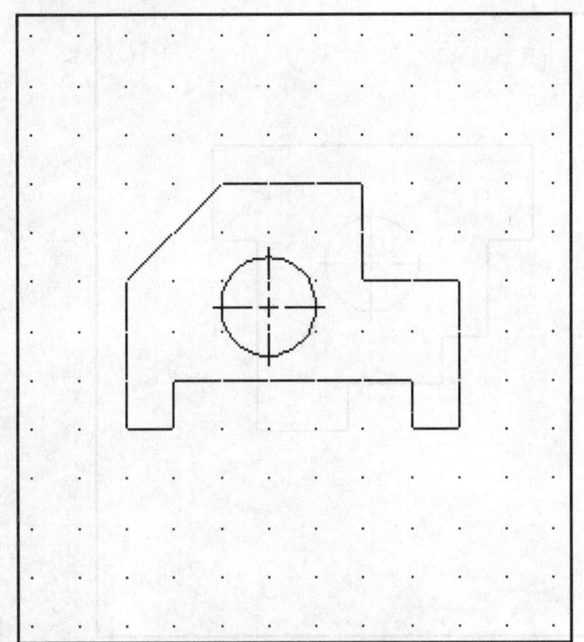

EX8-17

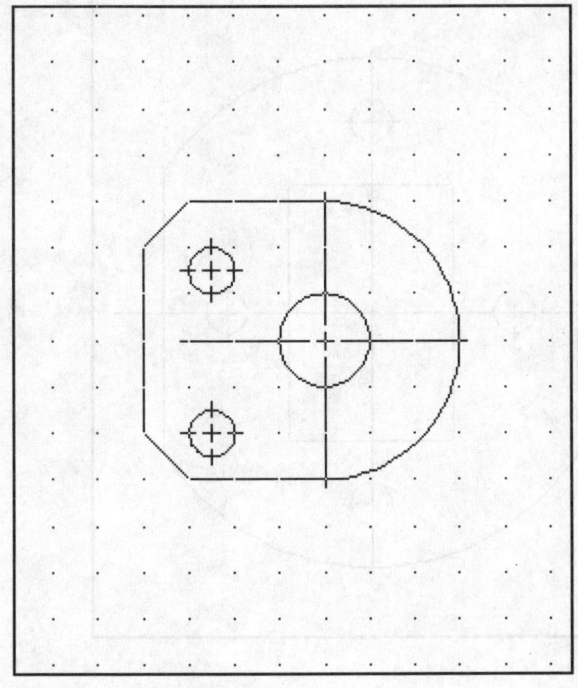

EX8-18

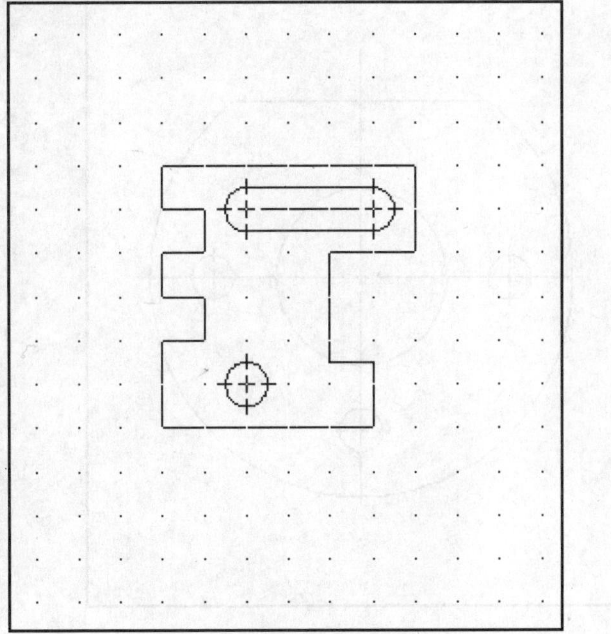

EX8-19

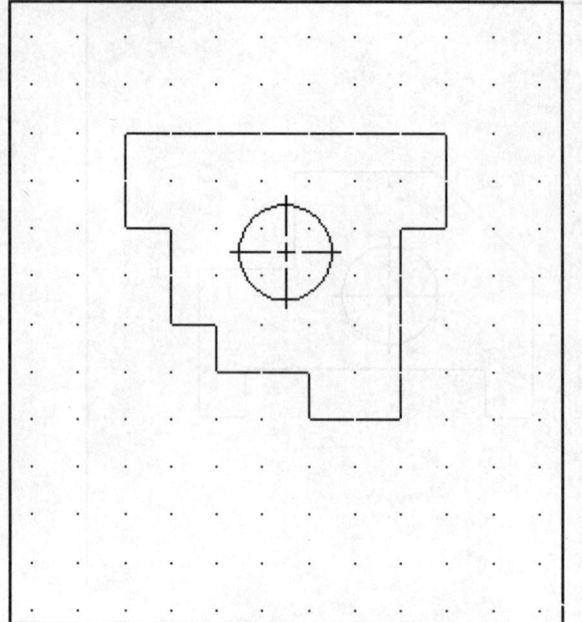

EX8-20

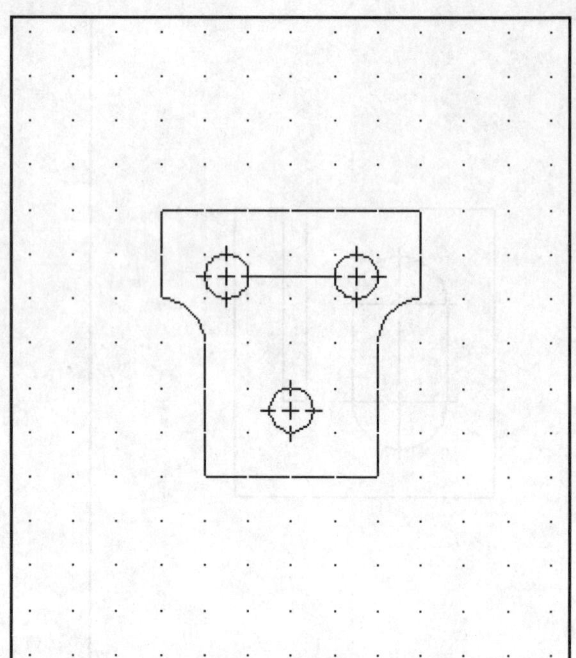

EX8-21

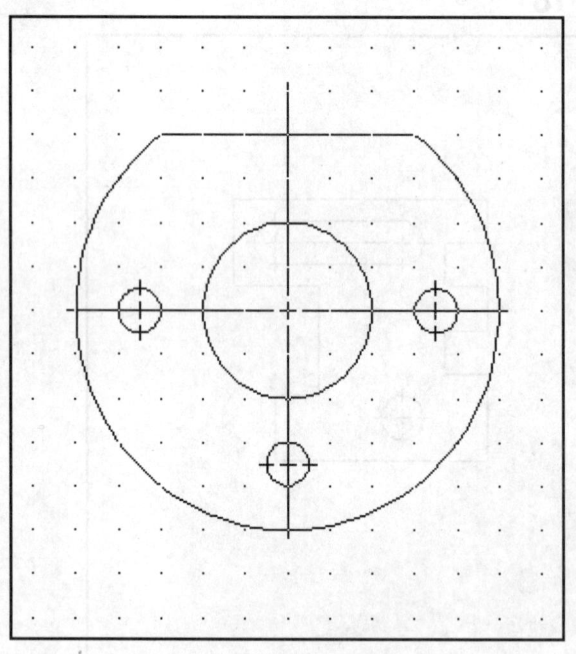

EX8-22

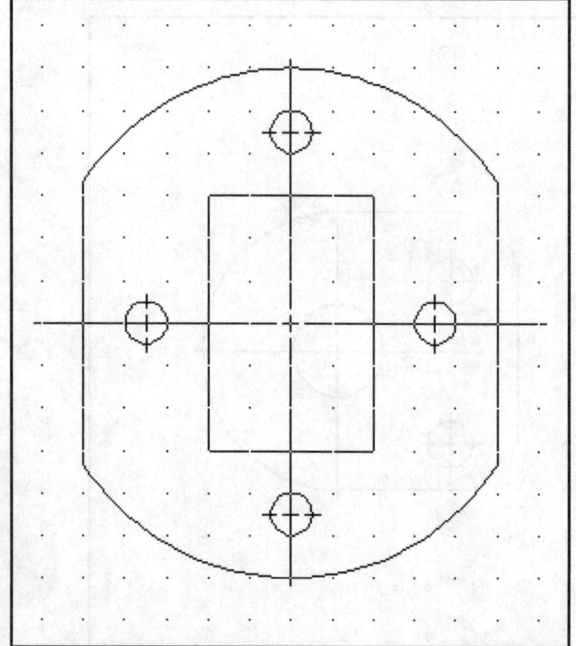

EX8-23

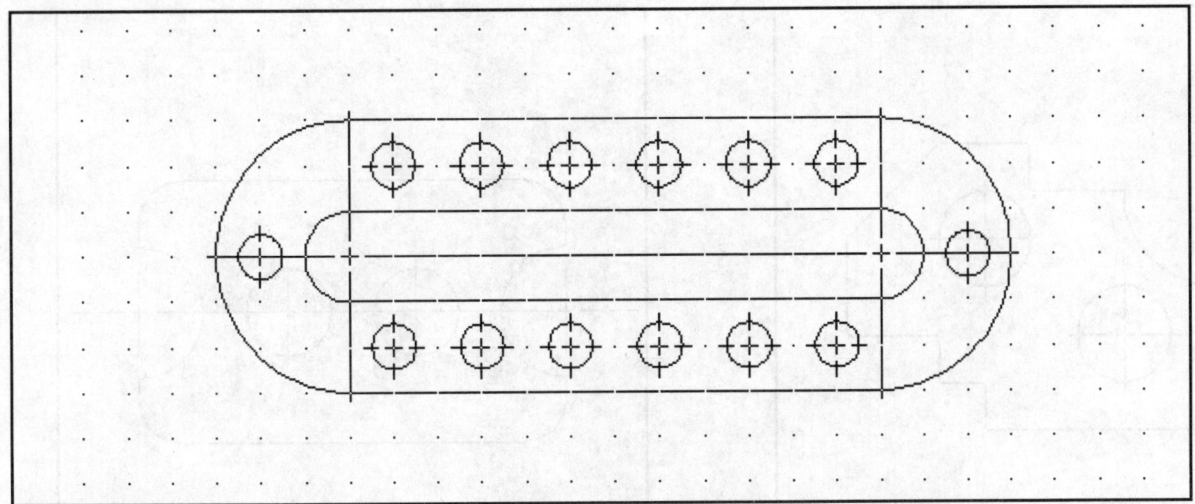

EX8-24

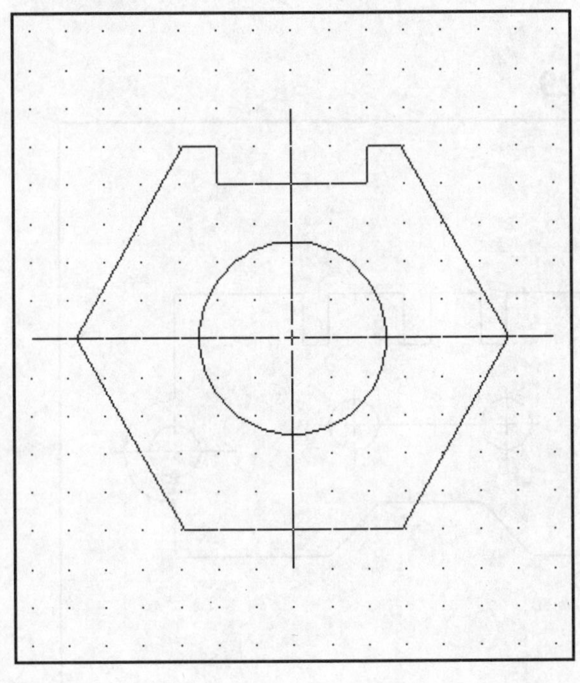

EX8-25

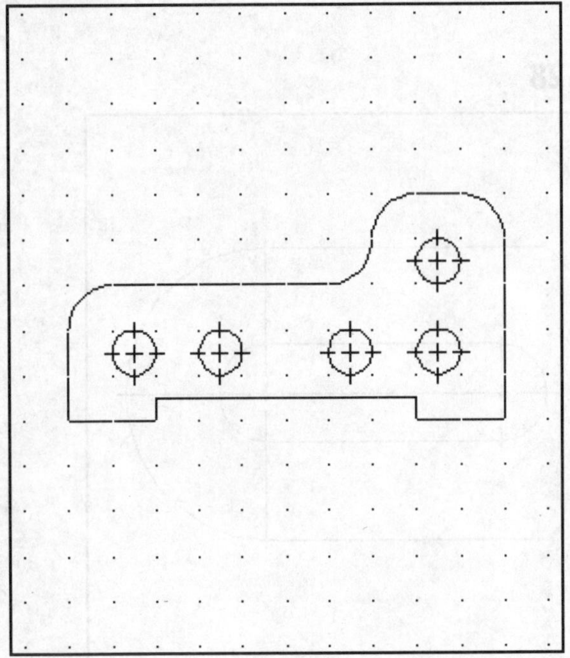

EX8-26

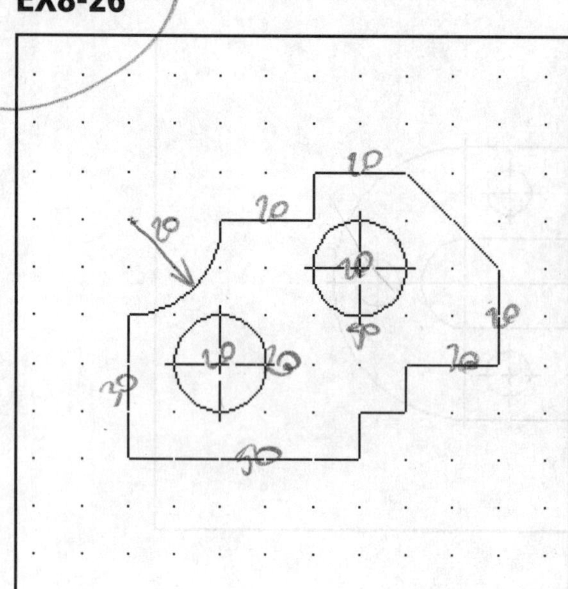

EX8-27

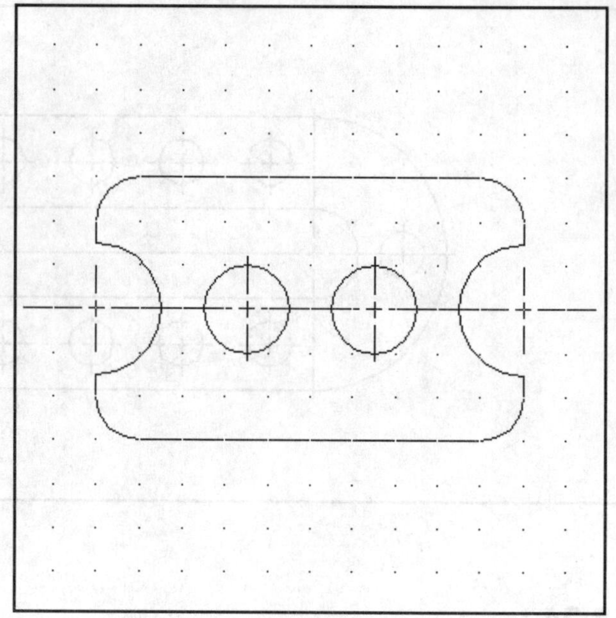

EX8-28

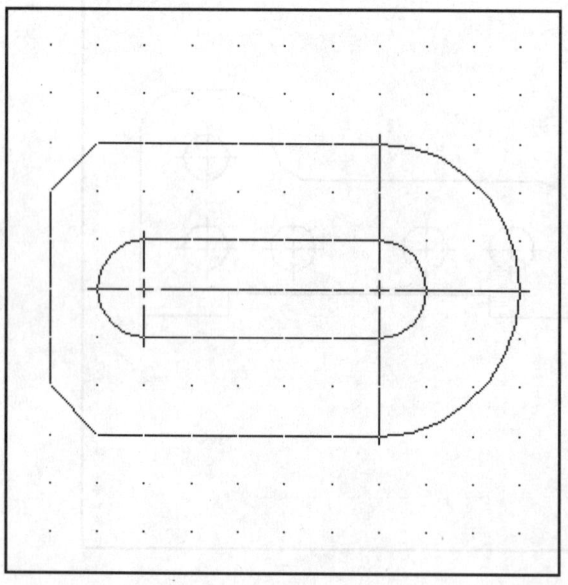

EX8-29

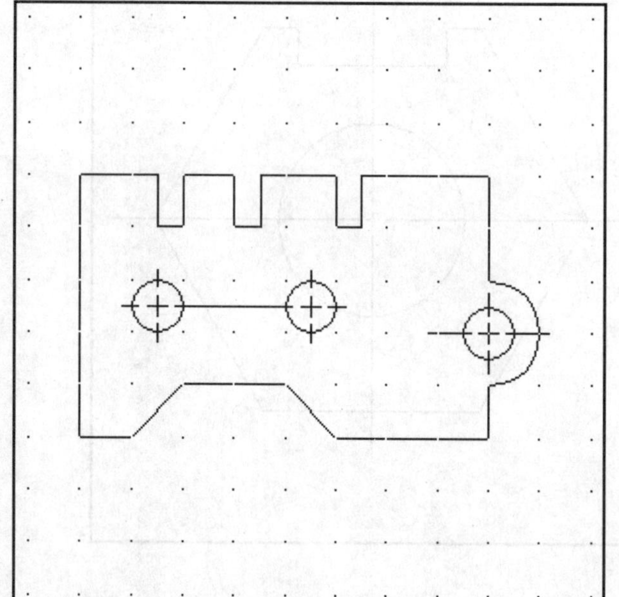

EX8-30

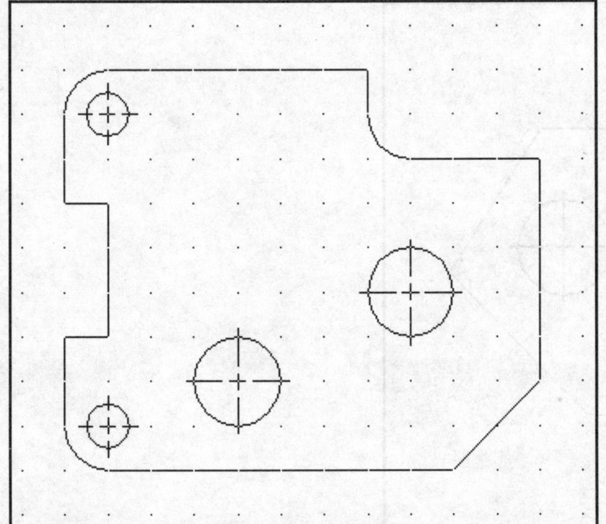

EX8-31

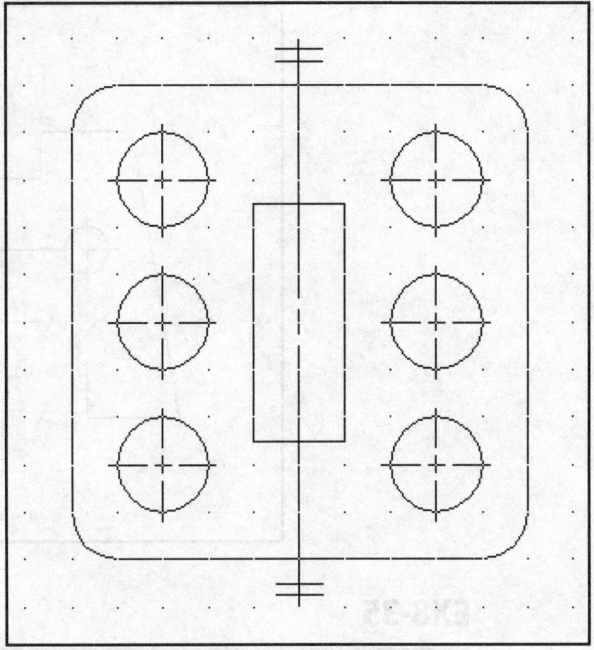

EX8-32

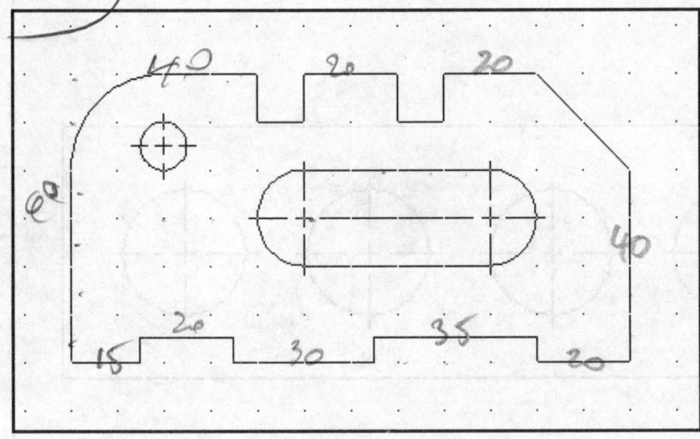

EX8-33

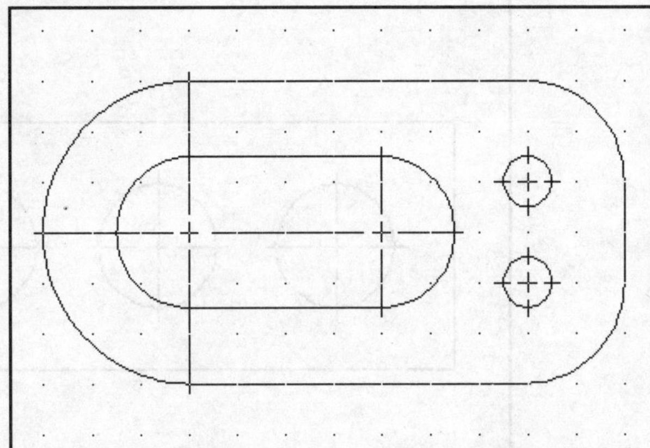

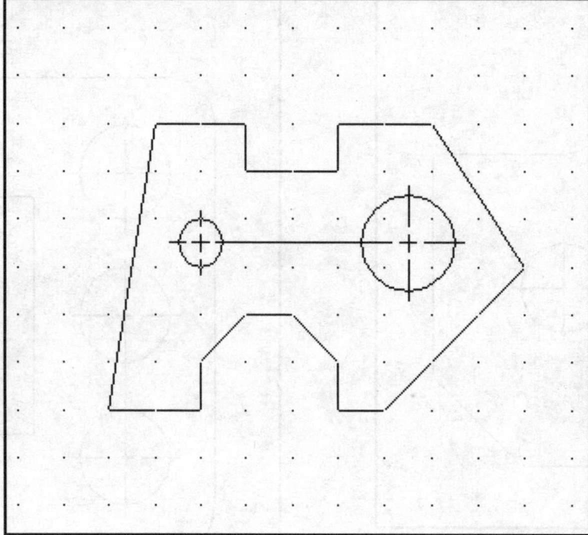

EX8-35

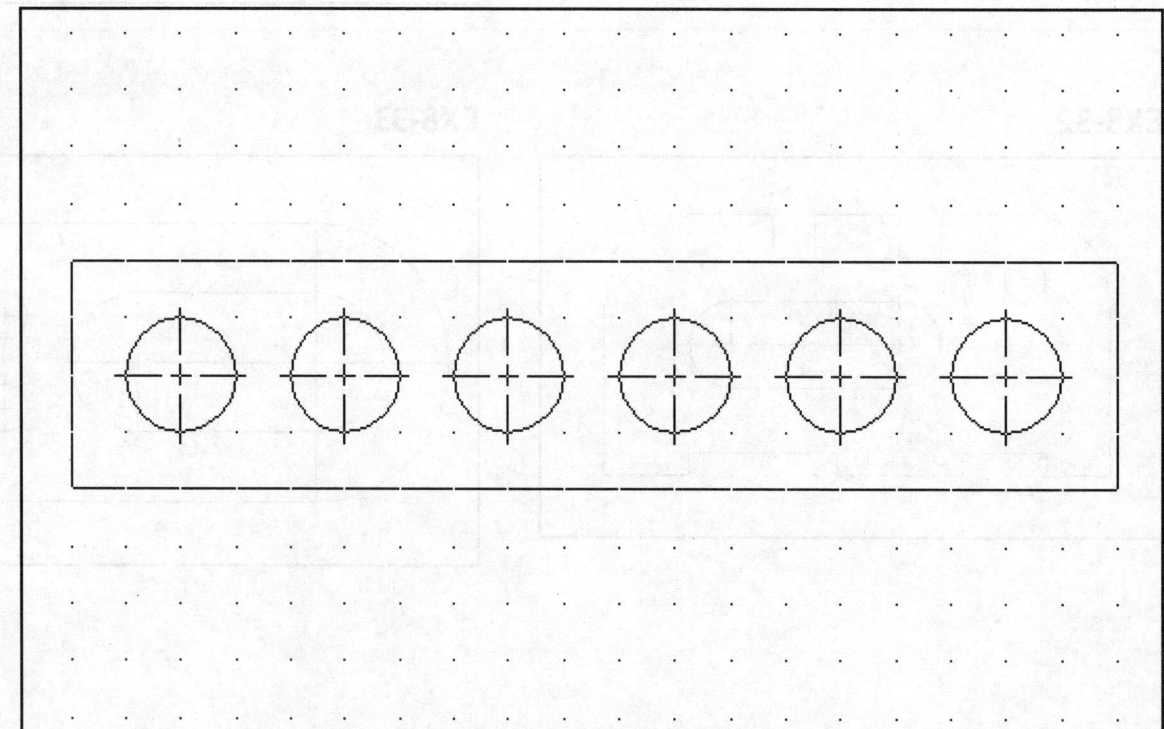

EX8-36

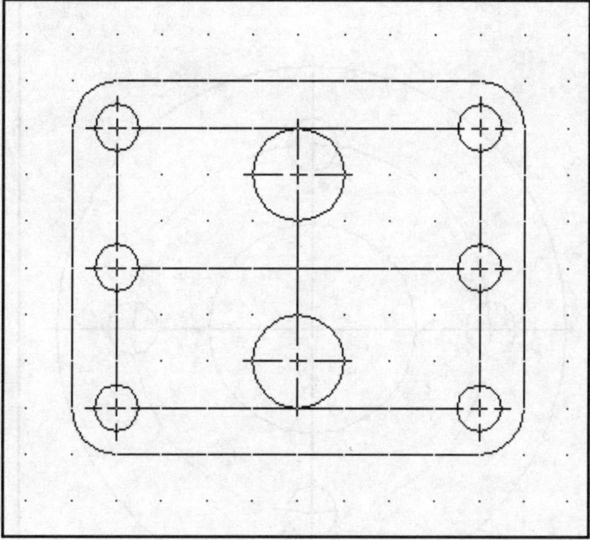

EX8-37

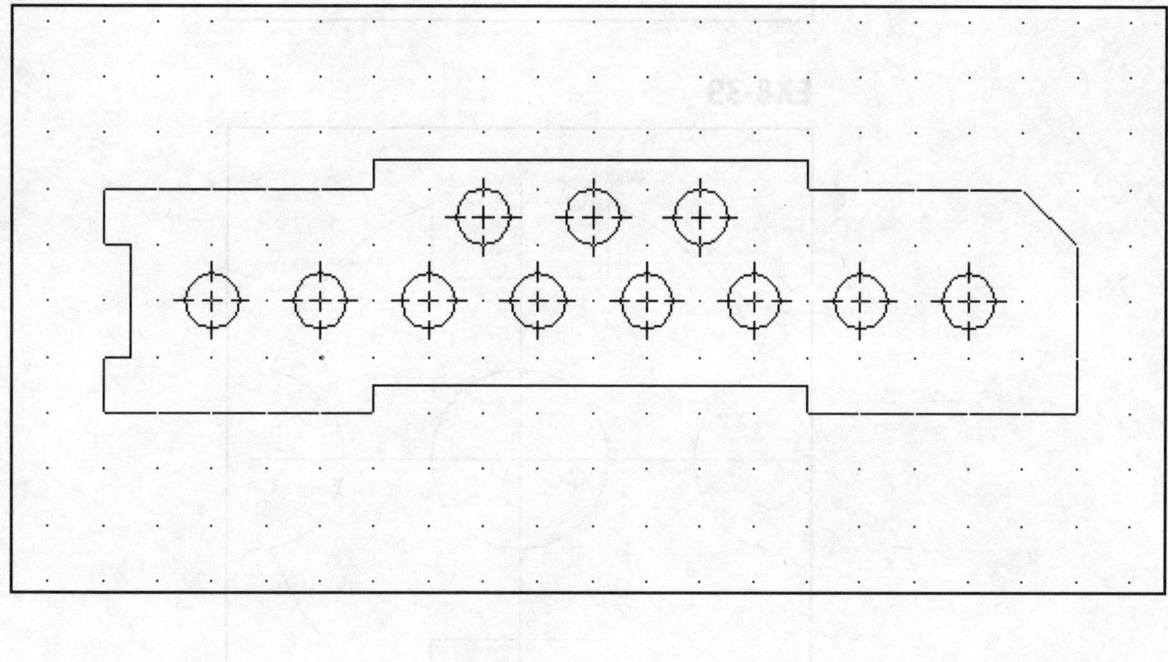

EX8-38

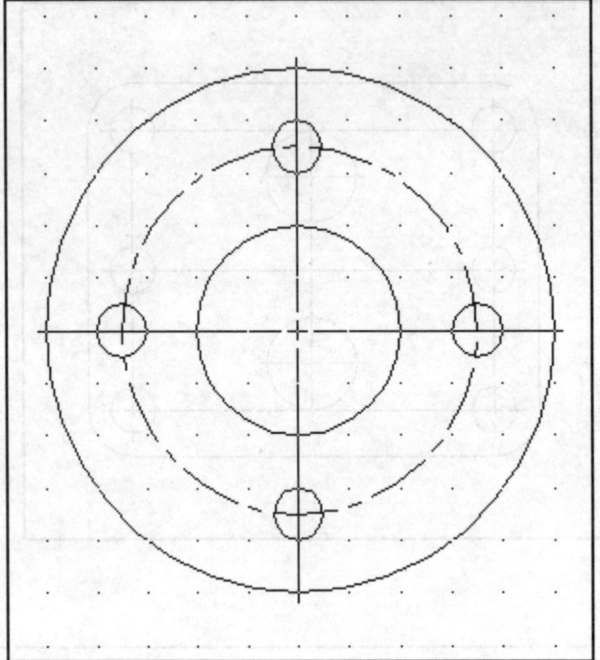

EX8-39

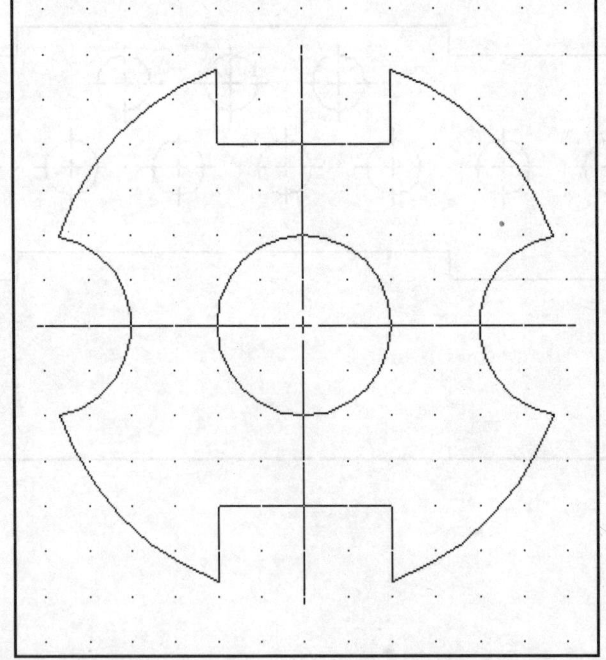

EX8-40

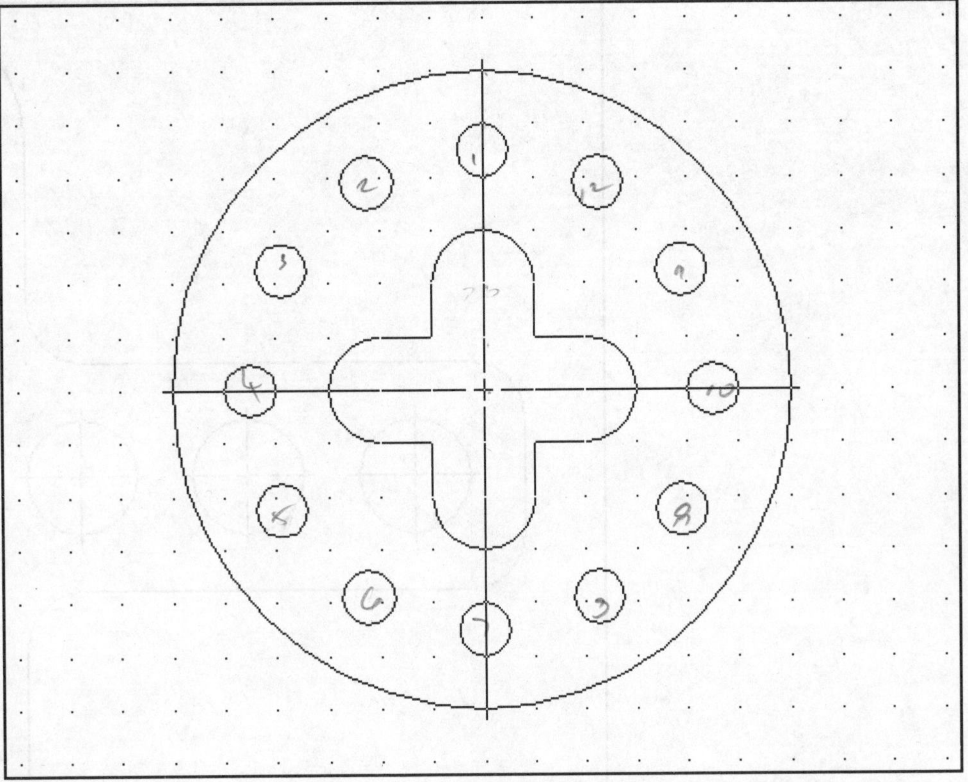

EX8-41

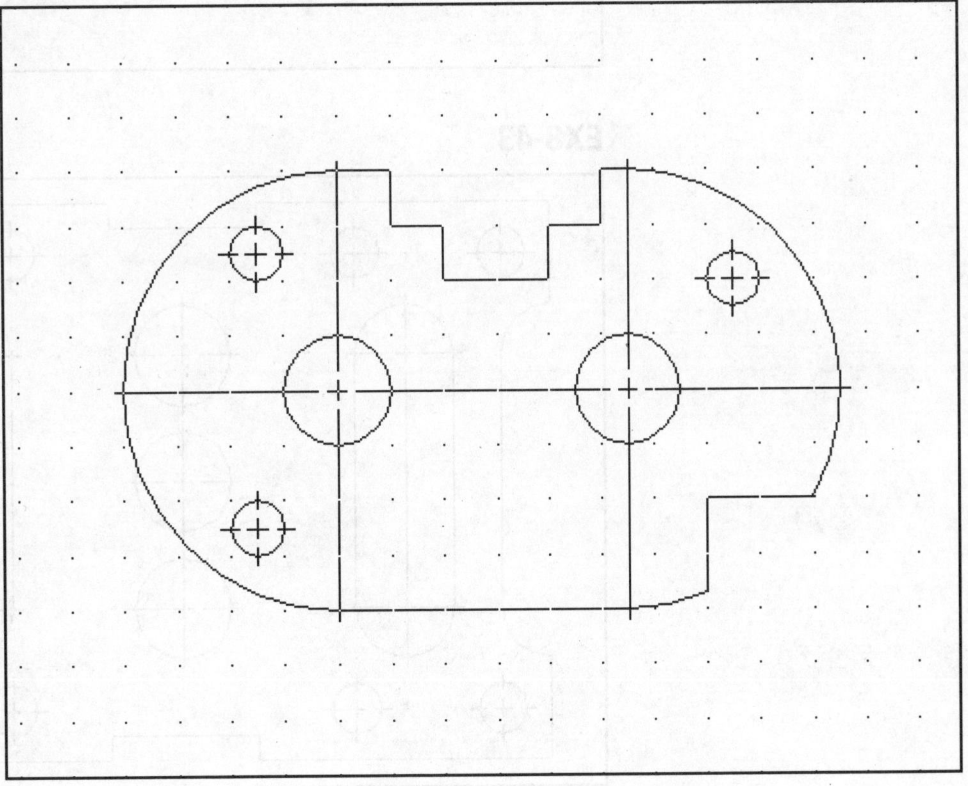

EX8-42

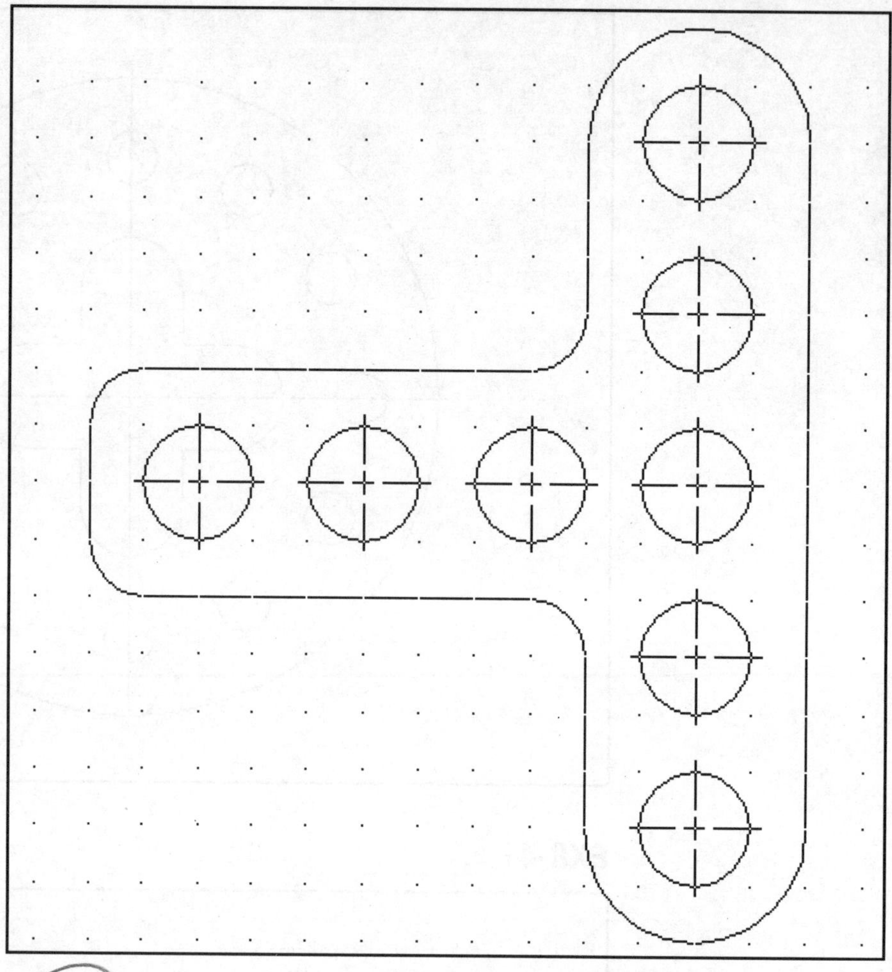

EX8-43

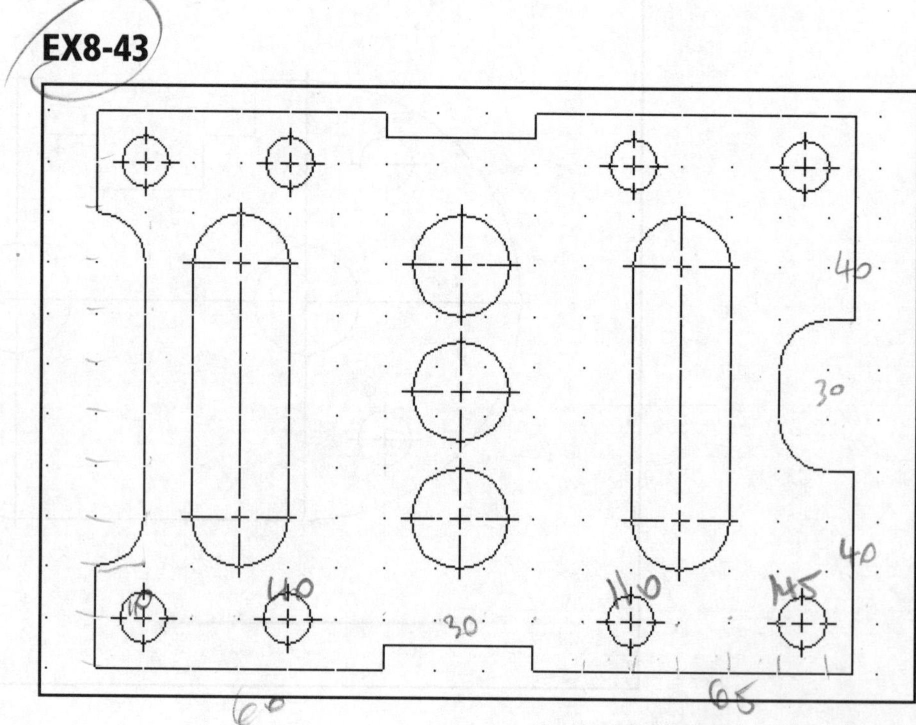

EX8-44

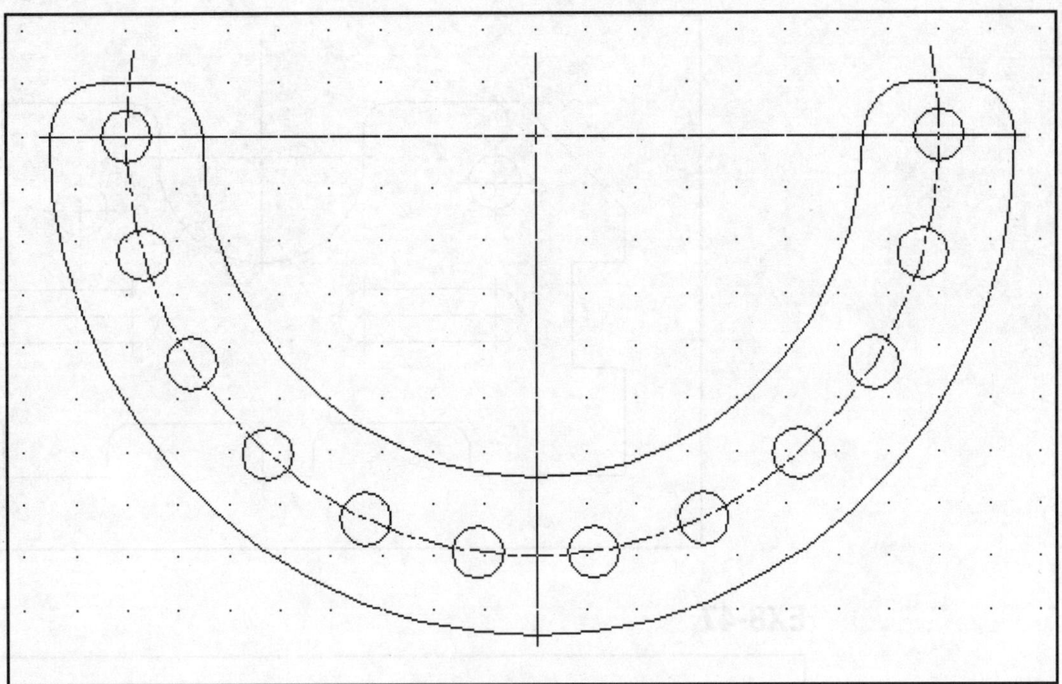

EX8-45

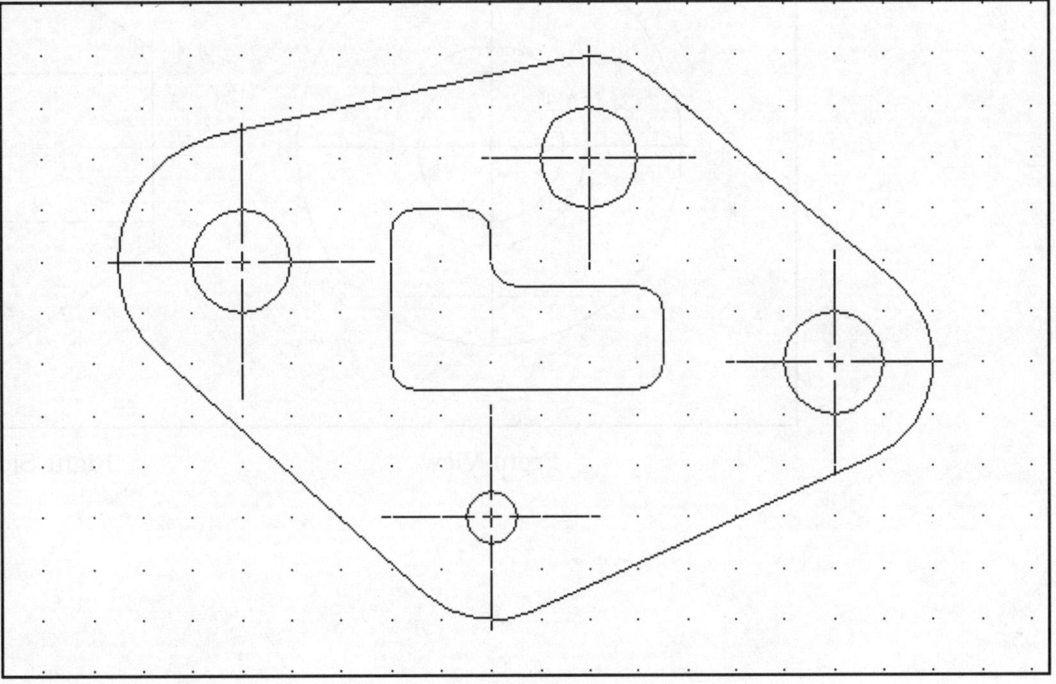

EX8-46

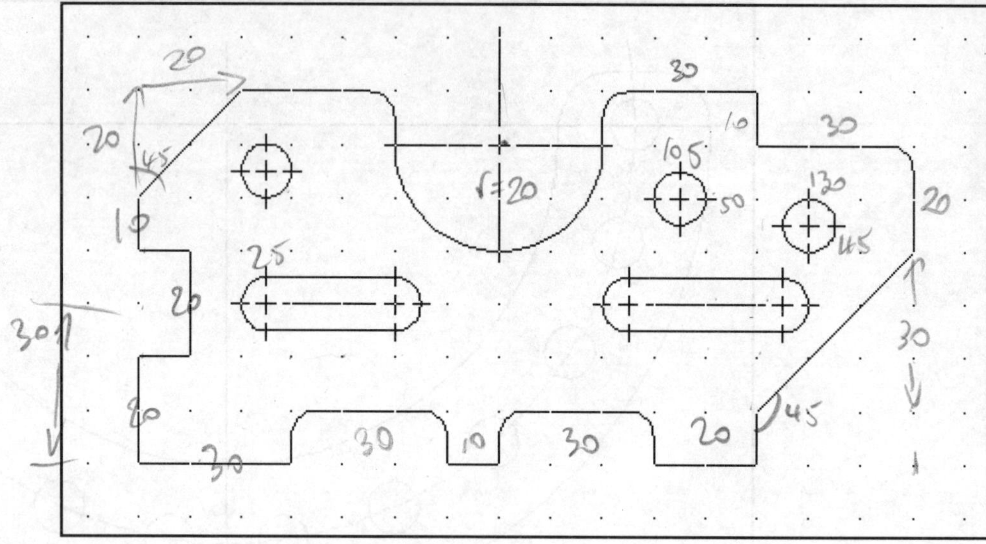

EX8-47

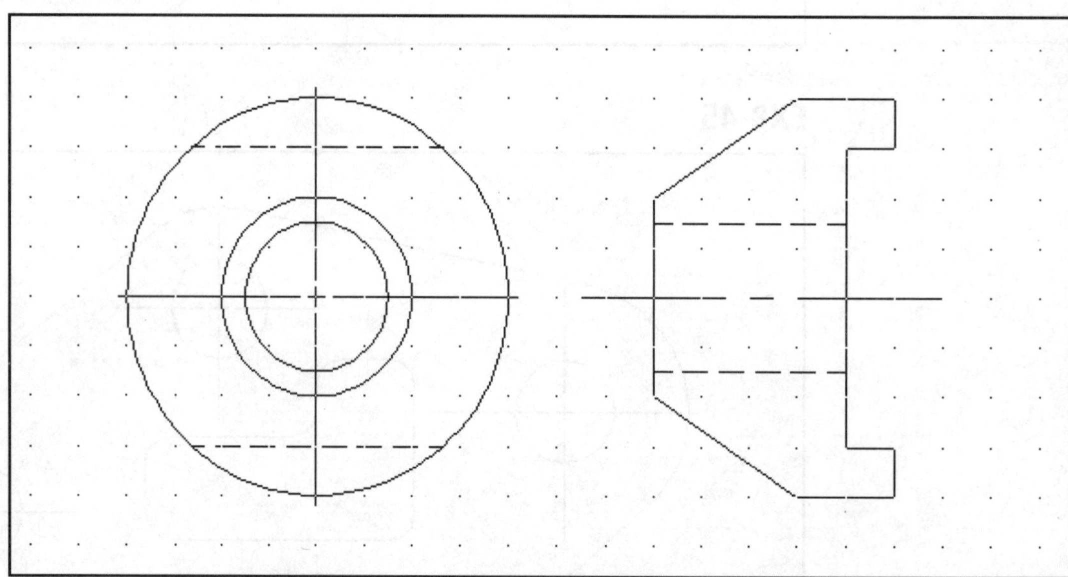

Front View   Right Side View

EX8-48

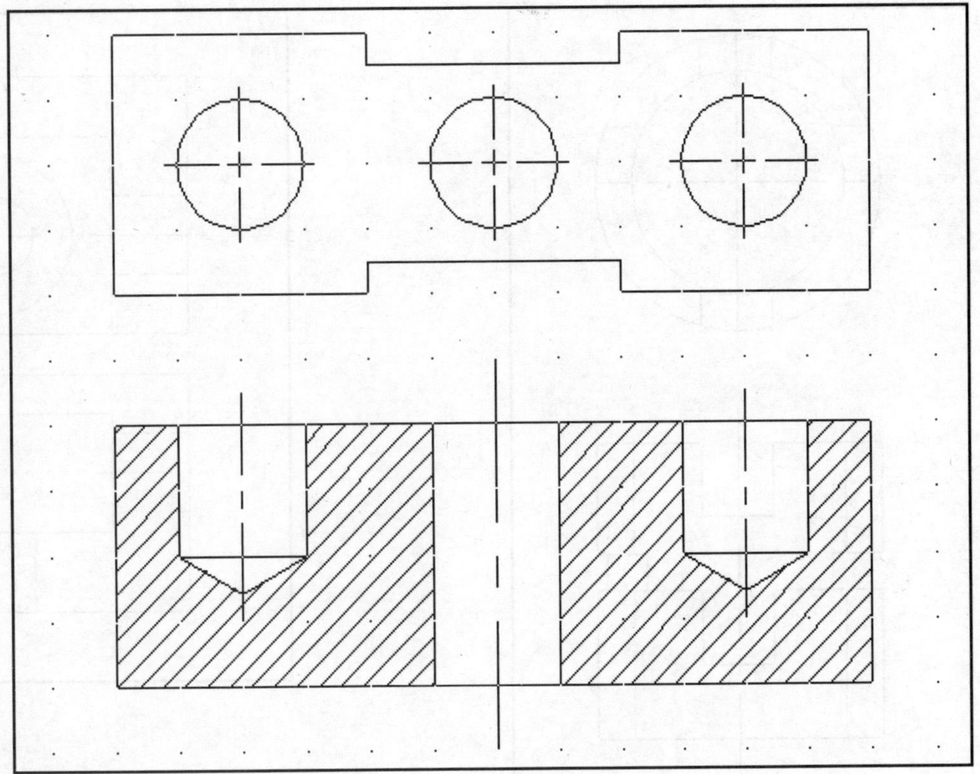

EX8-49

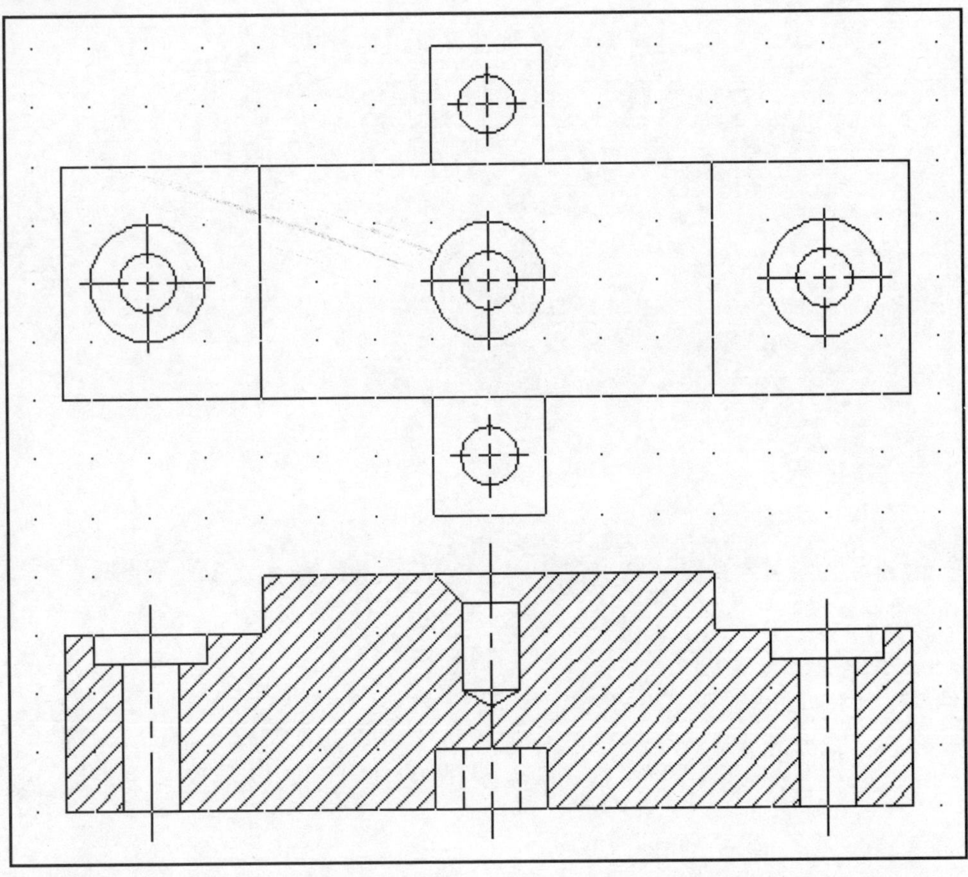

EX8-50

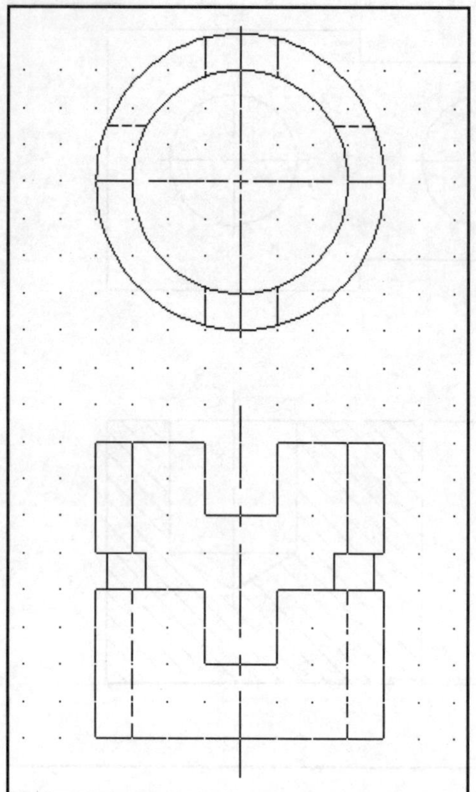

EX8-51

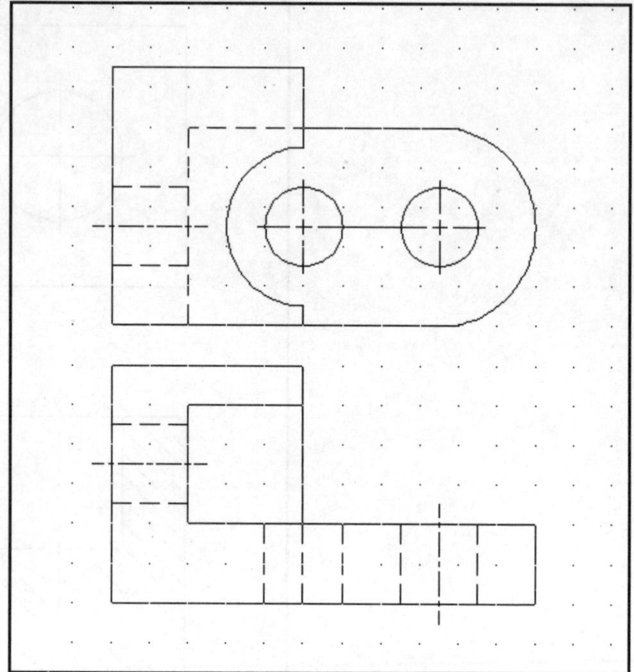

EX8-52

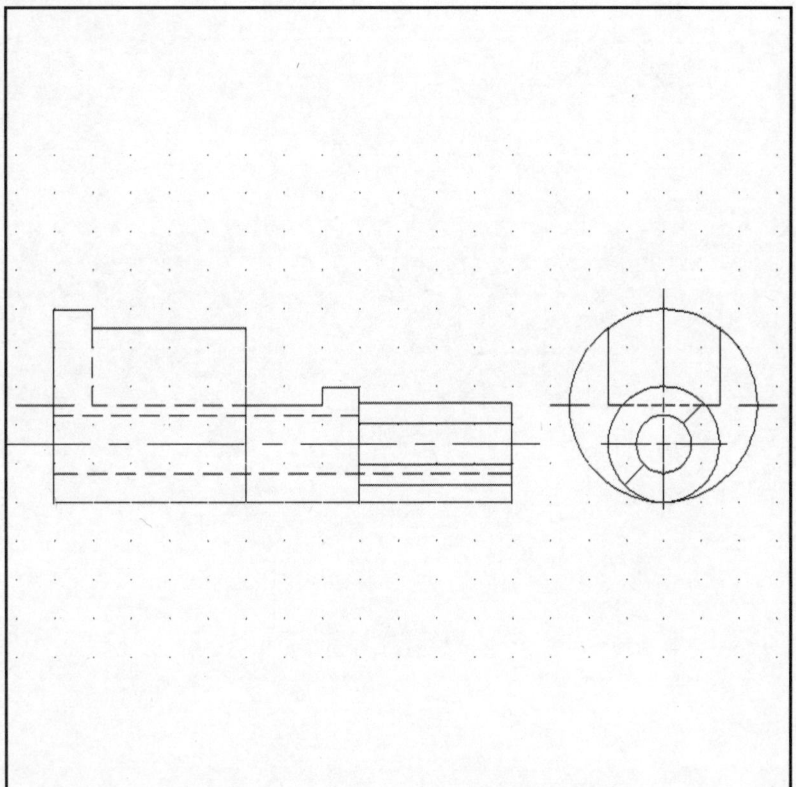

EX8-53

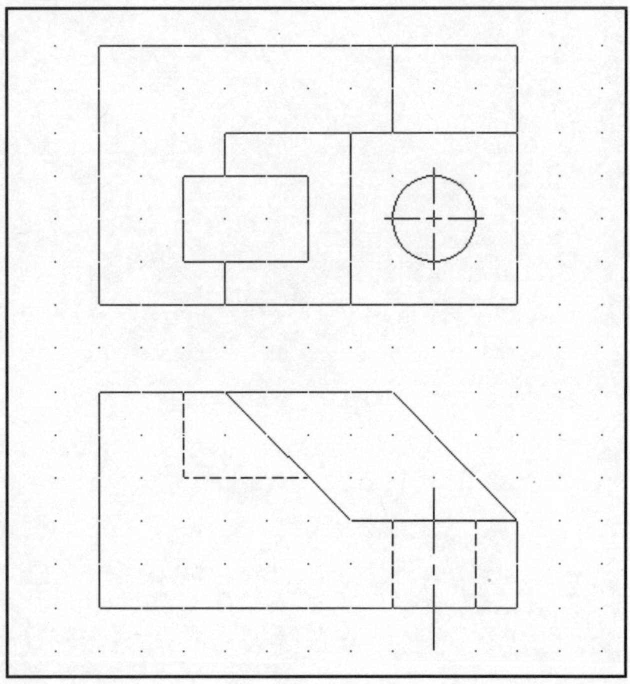

chapter nine
Tolerancing

9-1 Introduction

Tolerances define the manufacturing limits for dimensions. All dimensions have tolerances either written directly on the drawing as part of the dimension or implied by a predefined set of standard tolerances that apply to any dimension that does not have a stated tolerance.

This chapter explains general tolerance conventions and how they are applied by using AutoCAD. It includes a sample tolerance study and an explanation of standard fits and surface finishes.

Chapter 10 explains geometric tolerances.

9-2 Direct Tolerance Methods

There are two methods used to include tolerances as part of a dimension: plus and minus, and limits. Plus and minus tolerances can be expressed in either bilateral or unilateral forms.

A bilateral tolerance has both a plus and a minus value. A unilateral tolerance has either the plus or minus value equal to 0. Figure 9-1 shows a horizontal dimension of 60 millimeters that includes a bilateral tolerance of plus or minus 1 and another dimension of 60 millimeters that includes a bilateral tolerance of plus .20 or minus .10. Figure 9-1 also shows a dimension of 65 millimeters that includes a unilateral tolerance of plus 1 or minus 0.

Plus or minus tolerances define a range for manufacturing. If inspection shows that all dimensioned distances on an object fall within their specified tolerance range, the object is considered acceptable; that is, it has been manufactured correctly.

The dimension and tolerance 60 ± 0.1 means that the distance must be manufactured within a range no greater than 60.1 nor less than 59.9. The dimension and tolerance $65 + 1/-0$ defines the tolerance range as 65 to 66.

Figure 9-2 shows some bilateral and unilateral tolerances applied by using decimal inch values. Inch dimensions and tolerances are written in a

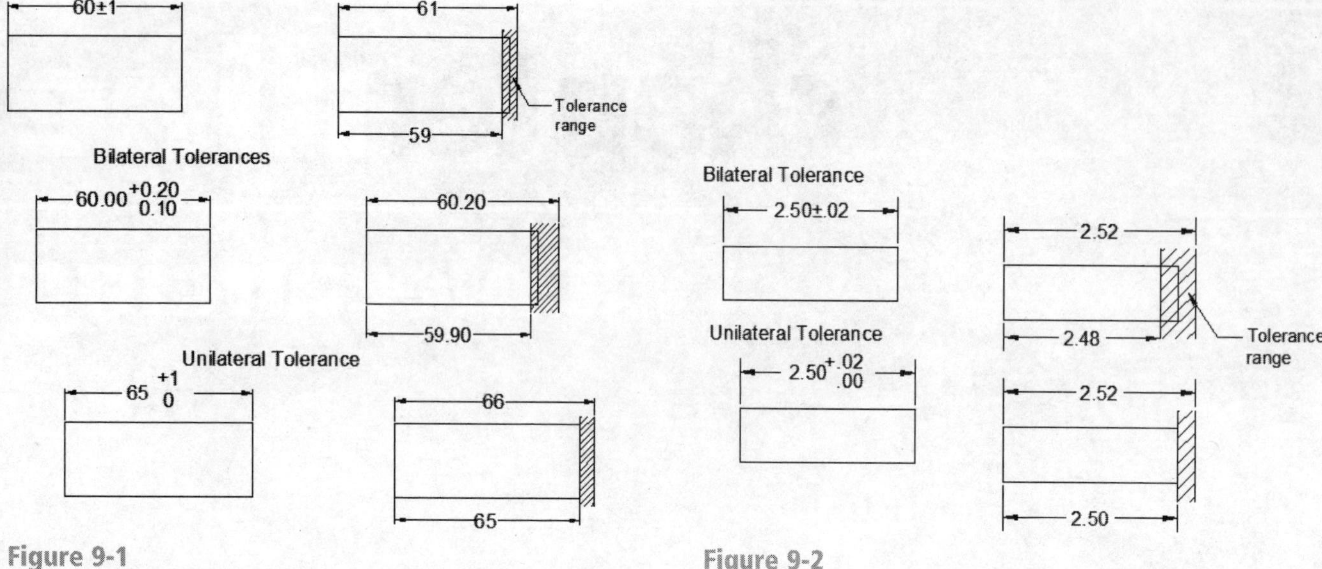

Figure 9-1

Figure 9-2

slightly different format from that used for millimeter dimensions and tolerances, but they also define manufacturing ranges for dimension values. The horizontal bilateral dimension and tolerance 2.50 ± .02 defines the longest acceptable distance as 2.52 inches and the shortest as 2.48. The unilateral dimension 2.50 + .02/−.00 defines the longest acceptable distance as 2.52 and the shortest as 2.50.

9-3 Tolerance Expressions

Dimension and tolerance values are written differently for inch and millimeter values. See Figure 9-3. Unilateral dimensions for millimeter values specify a zero limit with a single 0. A zero limit for inch values must include the same number of decimal places given for the dimension value. In the example shown in Figure 9-3, the dimension value .500 has a unilateral tolerance with minus zero tolerance. The zero limit is written as .000, three decimal places for both the dimension and the tolerance.

Figure 9-3

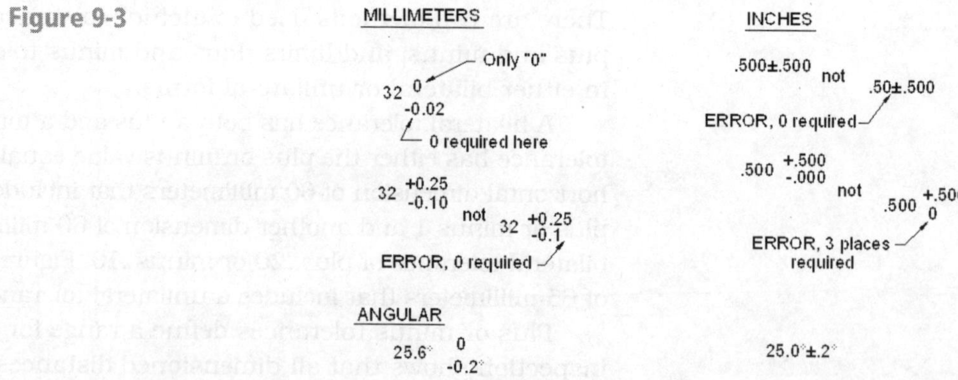

Both values in a bilateral tolerance must contain the same number of decimal places, although for millimeter values the tolerance values need not include the same number of decimal places as the dimension value. In Figure 9-3, the dimension value 32 is accompanied by tolerances of +0.25 and –0.10. This form is not acceptable for inch dimensions and tolerances. An equivalent inch dimension and tolerance would be written as 32.00 + 0.25/−0.10.

Degree values must include the same number of decimal places in both the dimension value and the tolerance values for bilateral tolerances. A single 0 may be used for a unilateral tolerance.

9-4 Understanding Plus and Minus Tolerances

A millimeter dimension and tolerance of 12.0 + 0.2/−0.1 means that the longest acceptable distance is 12.2000 . . . 0 and the shortest is 11.9000 . . . 0. The total range is 0.3000 . . . 0.

After an object is manufactured, it is inspected to ensure that the object has been manufactured correctly. Each dimensioned distance is measured and, if it is within the specified tolerance, is accepted. If the measured distance is not within the specified tolerance, the part is rejected. Some rejected objects may be reworked to bring them into the specified tolerance range, whereas others are simply scrapped.

Figure 9-4 shows a dimension with a tolerance. Assume that five objects were manufactured by using the same 12 + 0.2/−0.1 dimension and tolerance. The objects were then inspected, and the results were as listed. Inspected measurements usually have at least one more decimal place than that specified in the tolerance. Which objects are acceptable and which are not? Object 3 is too long, and object 5 is too short, because their measured distances are not within the specified tolerances.

Figure 9-5 shows a dimension and tolerance of 3.50 ± 0.02 inches. Object 3 is not acceptable, because it is too short, and object 4 is too long.

GIVEN (mm)
12 +0.2 −0.1

MEANS
TOL MAX = 12.2
TOL MIN = 11.9
TOTAL TOL = 0.3

OBJECT	AS MEASURED	ACCEPTABLE?
1	12.160	OK
2	12.020	OK
3	12.203	TOO LONG
4	11.920	OK
5	11.895	TOO SHORT

Figure 9-4

GIVEN (inches)
3.50±.02

MEANS
TOL MAX = 3.52
TOL MIN = 3.48
TOTAL TOL = .04

OBJECT	AS MEASURED	ACCEPTABLE?
1	3.520	OK
2	3.486	OK
3	3.470	TOO SHORT
4	3.521	TOO LONG
5	3.515	OK

Figure 9-5

9-5 Creating Plus and Minus Tolerances with AutoCAD

Plus and minus tolerances may be created by using AutoCAD in one of four ways: using the **Text** option or the **Mtext** option; typing the tolerances directly by using **Dtext**; or by setting the plus and minus values by using the **Dimension Style** tool.

To Create Plus and Minus Tolerances by Using the Text Option

The example given is for a horizontal dimension, but the procedure is the same for any linear or radial dimension.

1. Select the **Linear** tool from the **Dimensions** panel.
2. Select the extension line origins as explained in Section 8-3 and locate the dimension line.
   Specify dimension line location or
   [Mtext Text Angle Horizontal Vertical Rotated]:

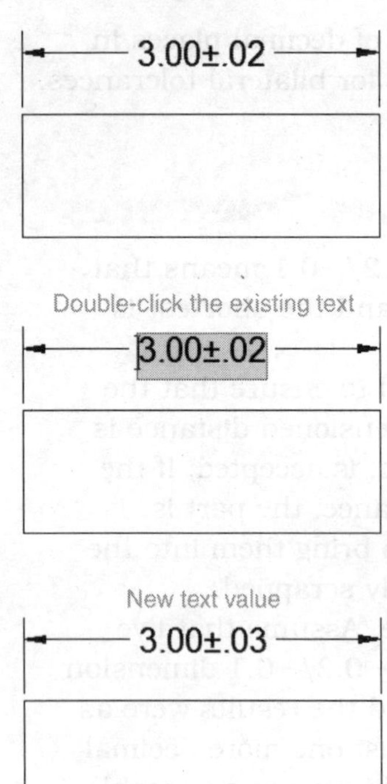

Figure 9-6

3 Type **t;** press **Enter.**

Dimension text <x.xxxx>:

4 Type the appropriate text value; press **Enter.**

Type the dimension value, then **%%p**, then the tolerance value.

Dimension text <x.xxxx>:5.00%%p.02.

In this example, the resulting dimension will be 3.00 ± 0.02. See Figure 9-6.

To Create Plus and Minus Tolerances with the Text Override Tool

Any existing text can be changed by using the **Text Override** tool. Figure 9-6 shows a 3.00 ± .02 dimension. Say, we wanted to change that tolerance to ±.03.

1 Double-click the dimension value.

A box with a shaded background will appear around the dimension value.

2 Delete the existing text, using the **Delete** key.

The value will disappear.

3 Type in the new value; press **Enter.**

> **NOTE**
>
> The symbol ± can also be created by use of the Windows character map by holding down the <Alt> key and typing **0177.**

The **Dimension Style Manager** on the **Dimensions** panel can be used to change the precision of the inital AutoCAD select dimension values. (The default value is four places: 1.0000.) If, for example, two decimal places are desired, use the **Precision** box on the **Primary Units** tab on the **Modify Dimension Style: Standard** dialog box to reset the system for two decimal places. See Section 8-5.

To Use Dtext to Create a Plus and Minus Tolerance

1 Type **Dtext** in response to a command prompt.

2 Place the starting point for the text; then define the appropriate height and angle.

3 Type the desired dimension.

Text: 5.00%%p.02

4 Press **Enter.**

In the example shown, the resulting dimension will be **5.00±.02.** The symbol will initially appear on the screen as %%p, but will change to ± when the last text line is entered.

To Use the Dimension Style Tool

1 Access the **Dimensions Style Manager** from the **Dimensions** panel.

2 Select the **Modify** option, then the **Tolerances** tab.

3 Select the arrow to the right of the **Method** box.

A list of available tolerancing methods will cascade. See Figure 9-7. AutoCAD offers two options for plus and minus tolerancing: **Symmetrical** and **Deviation.**

Figure 9-7

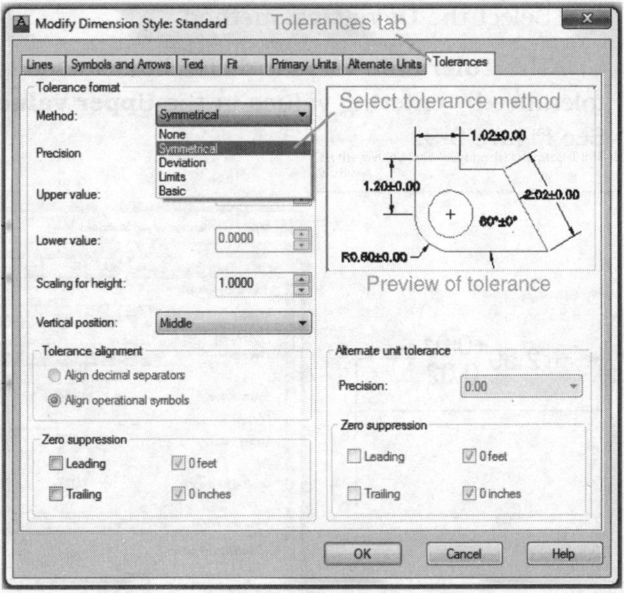

The Symmetrical Method

4a Select the **Symmetrical** method.

The **Tolerance format** box within the **Modify Dimension Style: Standard** dialog box is used to create a symmetrical tolerance by entering a value in the **Upper value** box. See Figure 9-8.

Figure 9-8

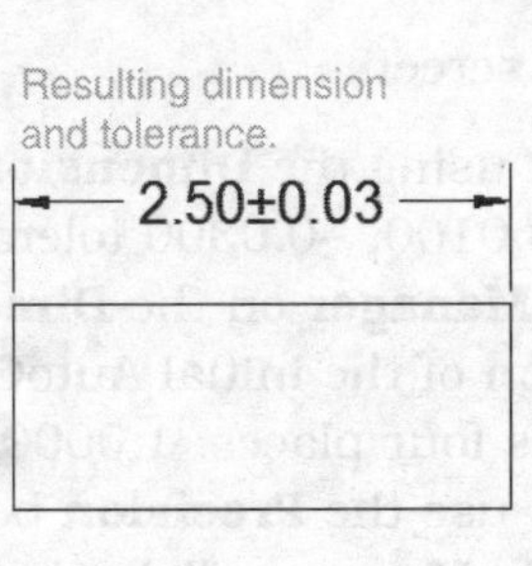

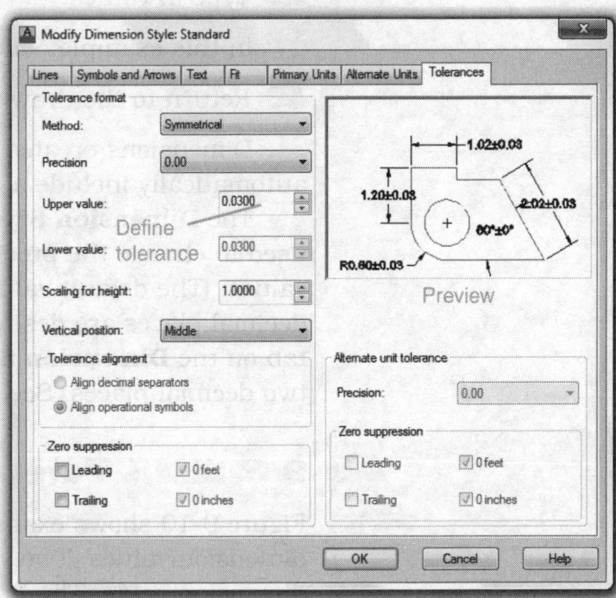

5a Type a value.

In this example, a value of **0.0300** was entered. Only an upper value needed to be entered, as the tolerance value is symmetrical.

6a Return to the drawing screen.

Dimensions created by using the **Dimensions** panel will now automatically include a ±0.0300 tolerance.

The Deviation Method

4b Select the **Deviation** method.

The **Tolerance format** dialog box is used to create a deviation tolerance by entering values in the **Upper value** and **Lower value** boxes. See Figure 9-9.

Figure 9-9

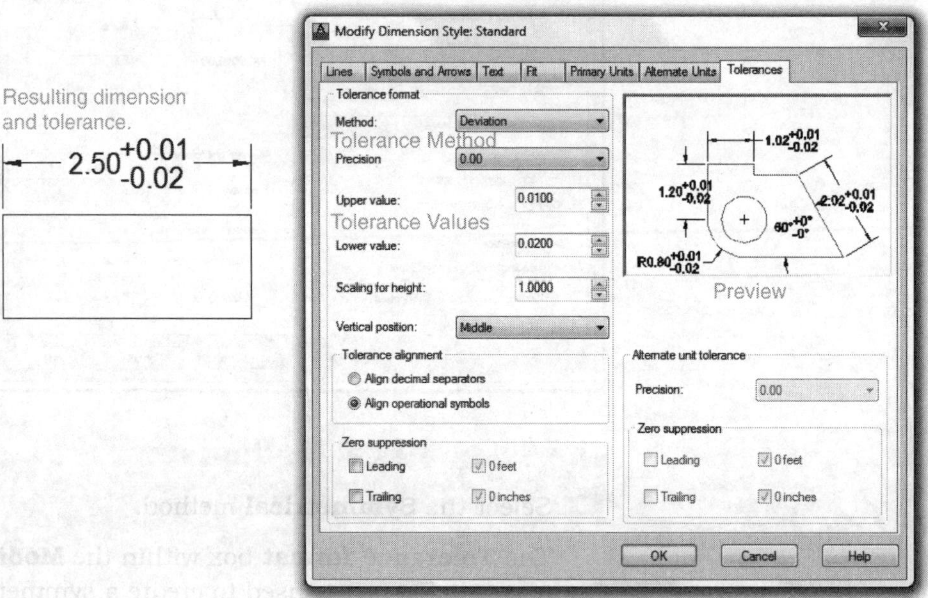

5b Type in values.

In this example, values of **0.0100** and **0.0200** were entered.

6b Return to the drawing screen.

Dimensions created by using the **Dimensions** panel will now automatically include a +0.0100, −0.0300 tolerance.

The **Dimension Style Manager** on the **Dimensions** panel can also be used to change the precision of the initial AutoCAD selected dimension values. (The default value is four places: 1.0000.) If, for example, two decimal places are desired, use the **Precision** box on the **Primary Units** tab on the **Dimension Style Manager** dialog box to reset the system for two decimal places. See Section 8-5.

9-6 Limit Tolerances

Figure 9-10 shows examples of limit tolerances. Limit tolerances replace dimension values. Two values are given: the upper and lower limits for the dimension value. The limit tolerance of 62.1 and 59.9 is mathematically

Figure 9-10

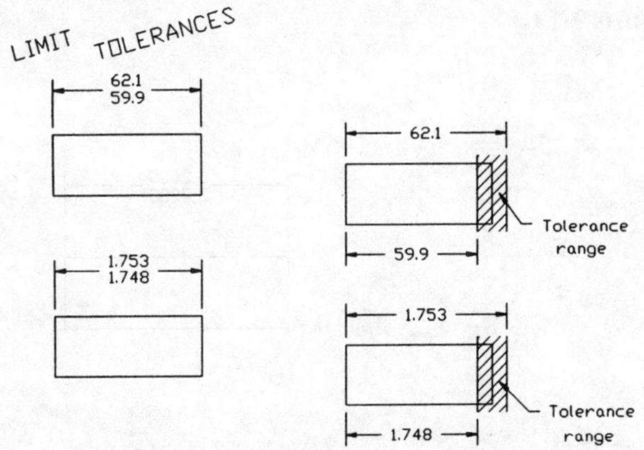

equal to 62 ± 0.1, but the stated limit tolerance is considered easier to read and understand.

Limit tolerances define a range for manufacture. Final distances on an object must fall within the specified range in order to be acceptable.

9-7 Creating Limit Tolerances by Using AutoCAD

Limit tolerances may be created by using AutoCAD in one of two ways: by using the **Dimension Style Manager,** or by modifying a given dimension by using the **Dimension Edit** tool.

To Create a Limit Tolerance by Using the Dimension Style Manager

1 Access the **Dimension Style Manager** from the **Dimensions** panel.

The **Dimension Style Manager** dialog box will appear.

2 Select the **Modify** option, then the **Tolerances** tab.

The **Modify Dimension Style: Standard** dialog box will appear.

3 Select the arrow to the right of the **Method** option box.

A list of available tolerance methods will cascade. See Figure 9-7.

4 Select the **Limits** option.

The **Tolerance format** dialog box will reappear with the headings **Upper value** and **Lower value** now in black letters, meaning that they can be accessed.

5 Type in the upper and lower values.

In this example, values of **0.01000** and **0.03000** were chosen. See Figure 9-11.

6 Return to the drawing screen.

Every dimension created by using the **Linear** dimension tool will now automatically create a limit tolerance on the basis of the selected distance and the selected upper and lower values. Figure 9-11 shows the results of the **Linear** dimension tool applied to a distance of 3.2500. The upper limit is 3.2500 + 0.0100, and the lower limit is 3.2500 – 0.0300.

Figure 9-11

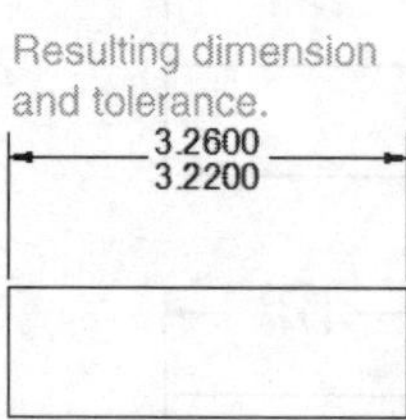

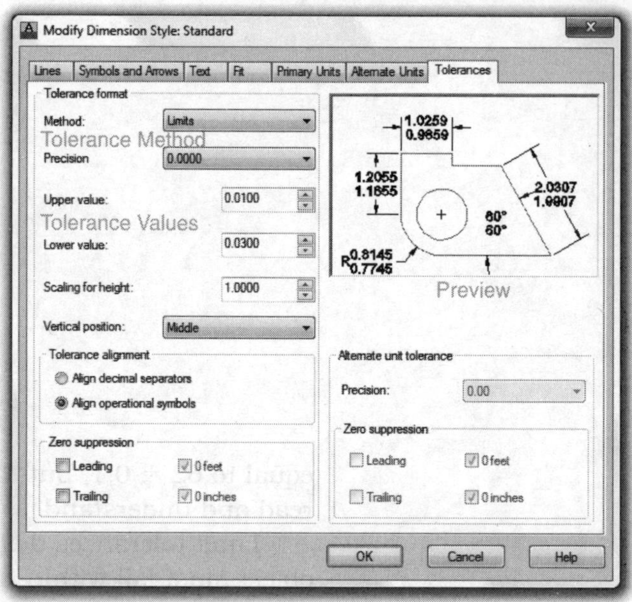

If only a few limit-type tolerances are to be used on a drawing, it is sometimes easier simply to modify an existing dimension rather than to change the **Tolerance** settings.

To Modify an Existing Dimension into a Limit Tolerance

1 Click the dimension.

See Figure 9-12.

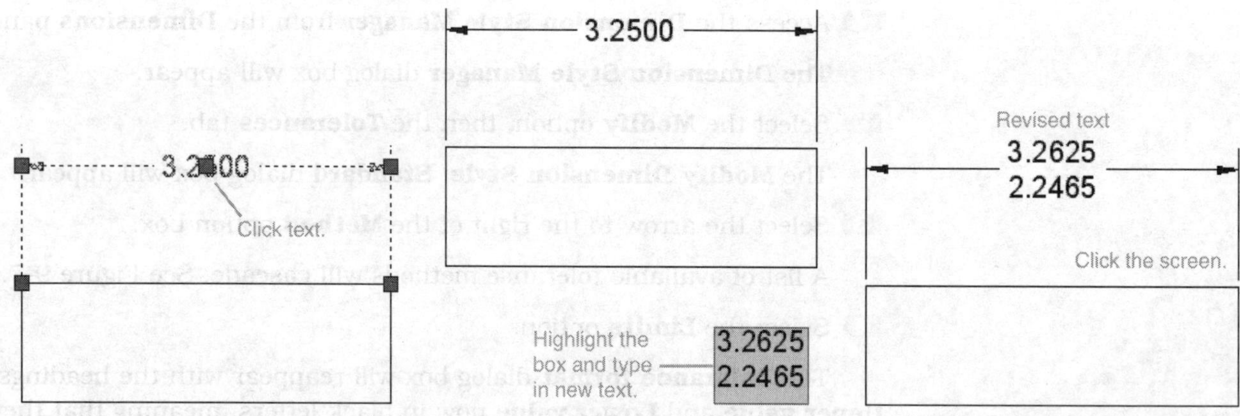

Figure 9-12

2 Type **dimedit** in response to a command prompt.

Enter type of dimension editing [Home New Rotate Oblique] <Home>:

3 Type **n;** press **Enter.**

A box containing the dimension text will appear.

4 Highlight the text in the box, and type in the new text.

5 Click the drawing screen.

Figure 9-12 shows the resulting changed dimension.

9-8 Angular Tolerances

Figure 9-13 shows an example of an angular dimension with a tolerance. The procedure explained for plus and minus tolerances applies to angular, as well as to linear, dimensions and tolerances.

Figure 9-13

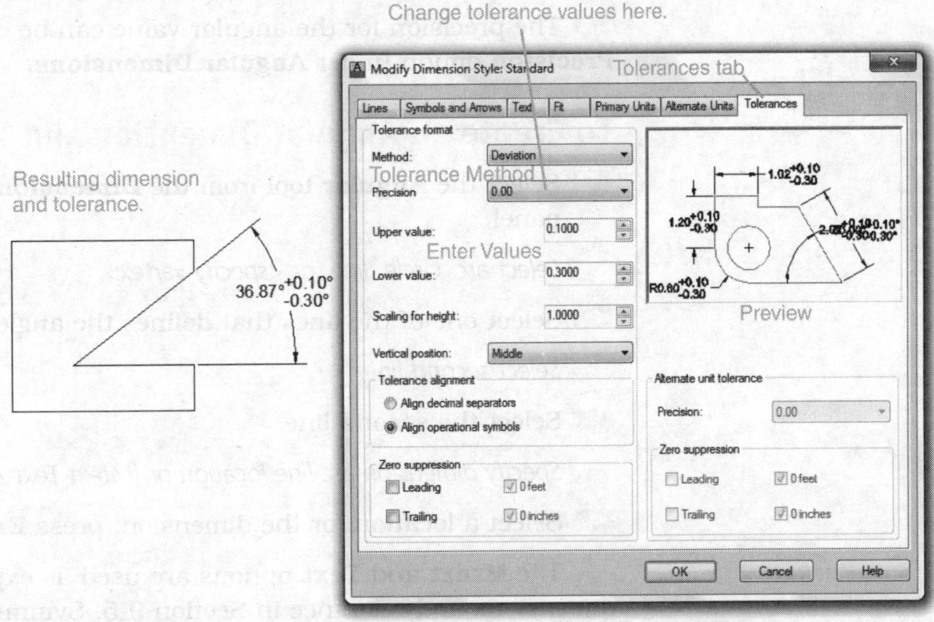

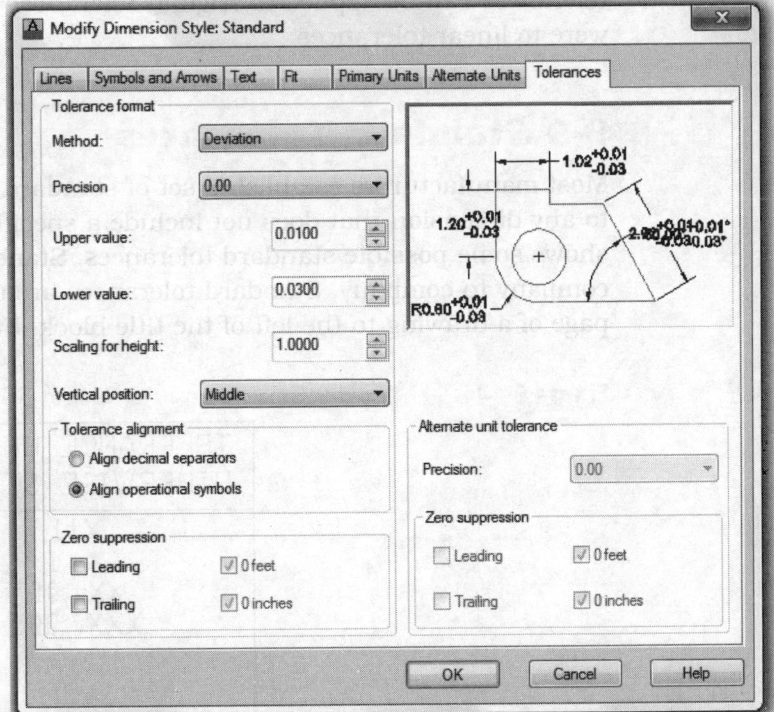

The precision of angular dimensions is set by using the **Primary Units** dialog box. In the example that follows, a deviation tolerance of +0.10, –0.30 was also specified.

To Set the Precision for Angular Dimensions and Tolerances

1. Access the **Dimension Style Manager,** then the **Modify** option, then the **Primary Units** option.

2 Select the arrow to the right of the **Precision** box.

A list of available precision factors will cascade.

3 Select two significant figures for both **Dimension** and **Tolerance**, and return to the drawing screen.

The precision for the angular value can be changed by using the **Precision** option under **Angular Dimensions.**

To Create an Angular Dimension and Tolerance

1 Select the **Angular** tool from the **Dimension** tool on the **Dimensions** panel.

Select arc, circle, line, or <specify vertex>:

2 Select one of the lines that defines the angle.

Select second line:

3 Select the second line.

Specify dimension arc line location or [Mtext Text Angle]:

4 Select a location for the dimension; press **Enter.**

The **Mtext** and **Text** options are used as explained for linear dimensions and tolerance in Section 9-5. Symmetrical, deviation, and limit tolerances can be applied to angular tolerances in the same way that they were to linear tolerances.

9-9 Standard Tolerances

Most manufacturers establish a set of standard tolerances that are applied to any dimension that does not include a specific tolerance. Figure 9-14 shows some possible standard tolerances. Standard tolerances vary from company to company. Standard tolerances are usually listed on the first page of a drawing to the left of the title block, but this location may vary.

Figure 9-14

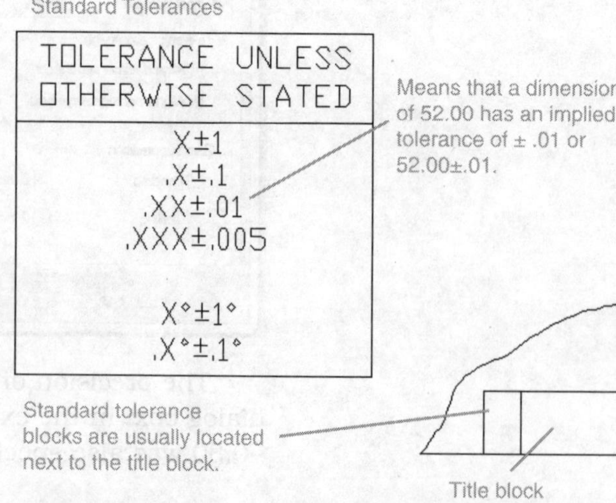

The X value used when specifying standard tolerances means any X stated in that format. A dimension value of 52.00 will have an implied tolerance of ±.01. This is because the stated standard tolerance is .XX ± .01, so any dimension value with two decimal places will have a standard implied tolerance of ±.01. A dimension value of 52.000 will have an implied tolerance of ±.005.

9-10 Double Dimensioning

It is an error, called ***double dimensioning***, to dimension the same distance twice. Double dimensioning is an error because it does not allow for tolerance buildup across a distance.

Figure 9-15 shows an object that has been dimensioned twice across its horizontal length: once by using three 30-millimeter dimensions, and a second time by using the 90-millimeter overall dimension. The two dimensions are mathematically equal, but are not equal when tolerances are considered. Assume that each dimension has a standard tolerance of ±1 millimeter. The three 30-millimeter dimensions could create an acceptable distance of 90 ± 3 millimeters, or a maximum distance of 93 and a minimum distance of 87. The overall dimension of 90 millimeters allows a maximum distance of 91 and a minimum distance of 89. The two dimensions yield different results when tolerances are considered.

Figure 9-15

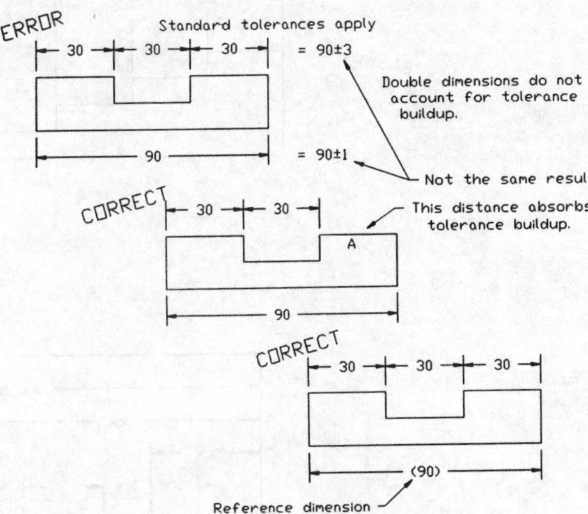

The size and location of a tolerance depends on the design objectives of the object, how it will be manufactured, and how it will be inspected. Even objects that have similar shapes may be dimensioned and toleranced very differently.

One possible solution to the double dimensioning shown in Figure 9-15 is to remove one of the 30-millimeter dimensions and to allow that distance to "float"—that is, absorb the cumulated tolerances. The choice of which 30-millimeter dimension to eliminate depends on the design objectives of the part. For this example, the far-right dimension was eliminated to remove the double-dimensioning error.

Another possible solution to the double-dimensioning error is to retain the three 30-millimeter dimensions and to change the 90-millimeter overall dimension to a reference dimension. A reference dimension is used only for mathematical convenience. It is not used during the manufacturing or inspection process. A reference dimension is designated on a drawing with parentheses (90).

If the 90-millimeter dimension were referenced, then only the three 30-millimeter dimensions would be used to manufacture and inspect the object. This would eliminate the double-dimensioning error.

9-11 Chain Dimensions and Baseline Dimensions

There are two systems used to apply dimensions and tolerances to a drawing: *chain* and *baseline.* Figure 9-16 shows examples of both systems. Chain dimensions relate each feature to the feature next to it; baseline dimensions relate all features to a single baseline or datum.

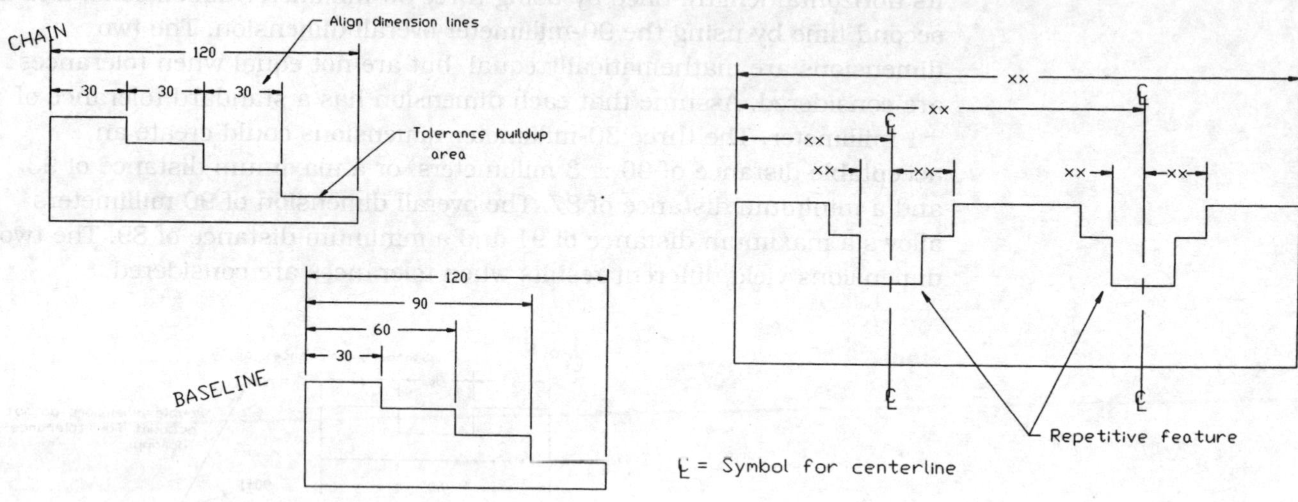

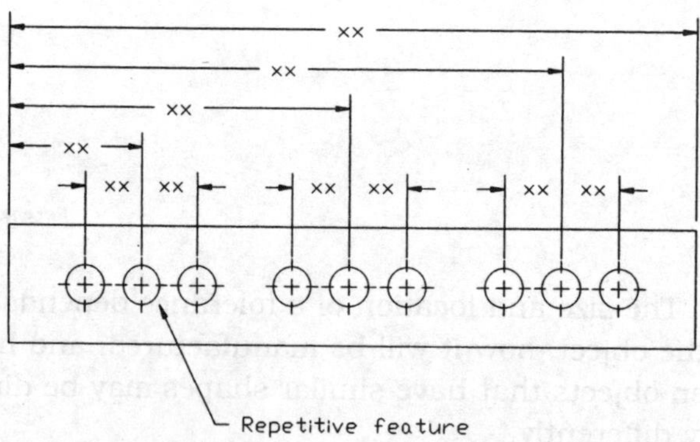

Figure 9-16

Chain and baseline dimensions may be used together. Figure 9-16 also shows two objects with repetitive features: one object includes two slots, and the other, three sets of three holes. In each example, the center of the repetitive feature is dimensioned to the left side of the object, which serves as a baseline. The sizes of the individual features are dimensioned by using chain dimensions referenced to centerlines.

Baseline dimensions eliminate tolerance buildup and can be related directly to the reference axis of many machines. They tend to take up much more area on a drawing than do chain dimensions.

Chain dimensions are useful in relating one feature to another, such as the repetitive hole pattern shown in Figure 9-16. In this example, the distance between the holes is more important than the distance of the individual hole from the baseline.

Figure 9-17 shows the same object dimensioned twice, once using chain dimensions and once using baseline dimensions. All distances are assigned a tolerance range of 2 millimeters stated in terms of limit tolerances. The maximum distance for surface A is 28 millimeters by the chain system and 27 millimeters by the baseline system. The 1-millimeter difference comes from the elimination of the first 26–24 limit dimension found on the chain example, but not on the baseline.

Figure 9-17

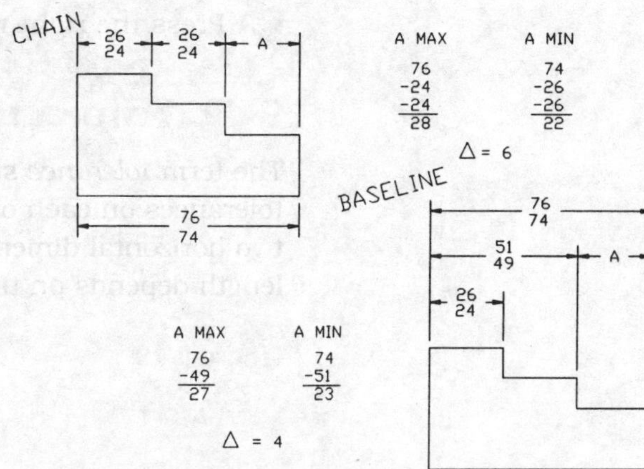

The total tolerance difference is 6 millimeters for the chain and 4 millimeters for the baseline. The baseline reduces the tolerance variations for the object simply because it applies the tolerances and dimensions differently. So why not always use baseline dimensions? For most applications, the baseline system is probably better, but if the distance between the individual features is more critical than the distance from the feature to the baseline, it is advisable to use the chain system.

To Create Baseline Dimensions by Using AutoCAD

The **Baseline** tool can be applied only after a linear dimension has been created. The object shown in Figure 9-18 was dimensioned by first creating the 1.00 dimension by use of the **Linear** dimension tool, then by using the **Baseline** tool as follows.

1. Create a linear dimension by using the **Linear** tool from the **Dimensions** panel.

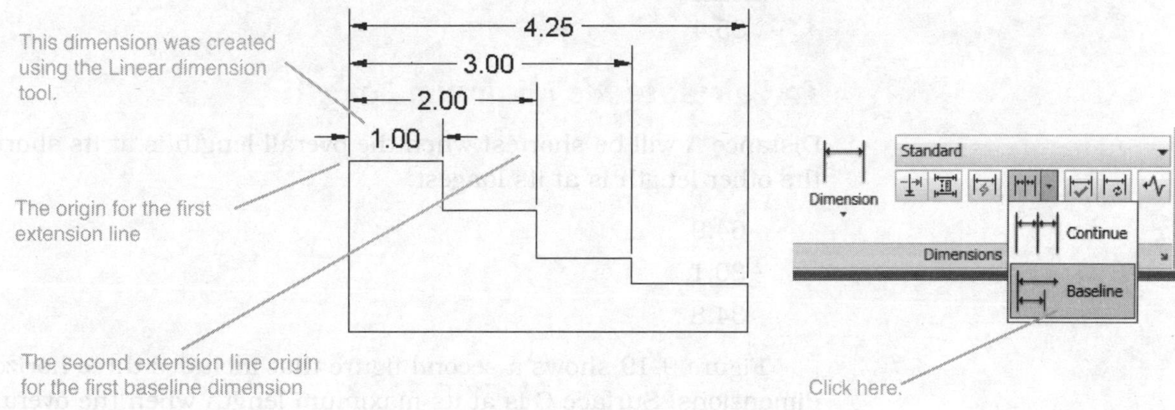

Figure 9-18

The point selected as the origin for the first extension line will become the origin of the baseline.

2. Select the **Baseline** tool from the **Dimensions** panel.

   Specify a second extension line origin or [Undo Select] <Select>:

3. Select the origin for the second extension line of the baseline dimension.

   Specify a second extension line origin or [Undo Select] <Select>:

4. Repeat the process until the baseline dimensioning is complete.

5. Press the right mouse button, and **Enter** the dimensions.

9-12 Tolerance Studies

The term *tolerance study* is used when analyzing the effects of a group of tolerances on each other and on an object. Figure 9-19 shows an object with two horizontal dimensions. The horizontal distance A is not dimensioned. Its length depends on the tolerances of the two horizontal dimensions.

Figure 9-19

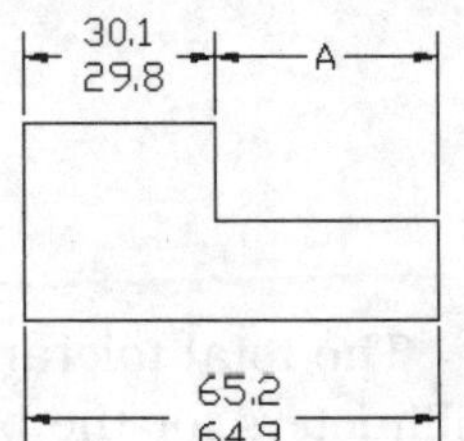

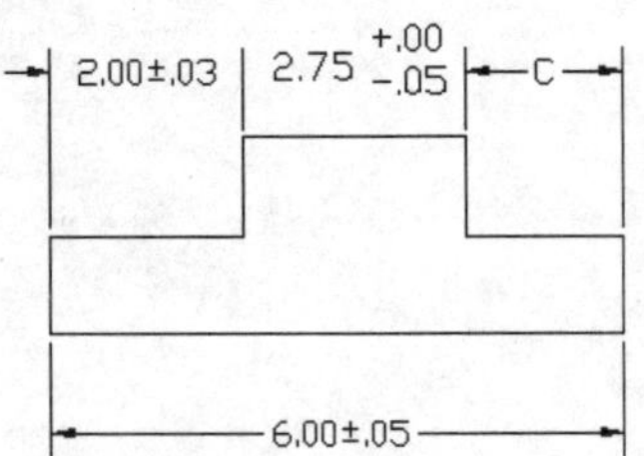

To Calculate A's Maximum Length

Distance A will be longest when the overall distance is at its longest and the other distance is at its shortest:

$$\begin{array}{r} 65.2 \\ -29.8 \\ \hline 35.4 \end{array}$$

To Calculate A's Minimum Length

Distance A will be shortest when the overall length is at its shortest and the other length is at its longest:

$$\begin{array}{r} 64.9 \\ -30.1 \\ \hline 34.8 \end{array}$$

Figure 9-19 shows a second figure that includes three horizontal dimensions. Surface C is at its maximum length when the overall dimension is at its longest and the other dimensions are at their shortest.

Surface C is at its minimum length when the overall length is at its shortest and the other dimensions are at their longest.

9-13 Rectangular Dimensions

Figure 9-20 shows an example of rectangular dimensions referenced to baselines. Figure 9-21 shows a circular object for which dimensions are referenced to a circle's centerlines. Dimensioning to a circle's centerline is critical to accurate hole location.

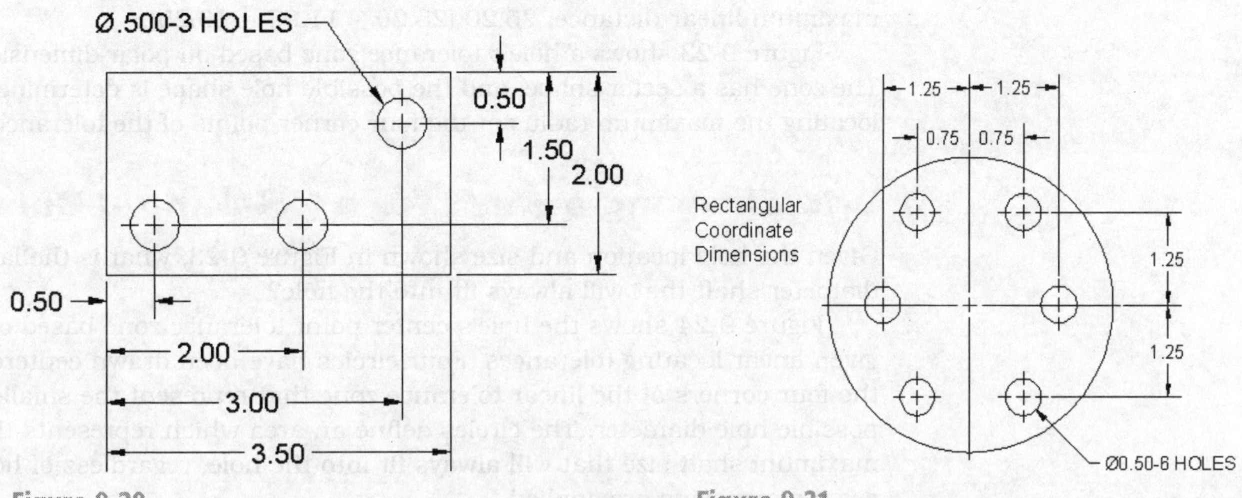

Figure 9-20

Figure 9-21

9-14 Hole Locations

When rectangular dimensions are used, the location of a hole's center point is defined by two linear dimensions. The result is a rectangular tolerance zone whose size is based on the linear dimension's tolerances. The shape of the center point's tolerance zone may be changed to circular by positional tolerancing, as described in Section 10-16.

Figure 9-22 shows the location and size dimensions for a hole. Also shown are the resulting tolerance zone and the overall possible hole shape. The center point's tolerance is ±0.2 by ±0.3, based on the given linear locating tolerances.

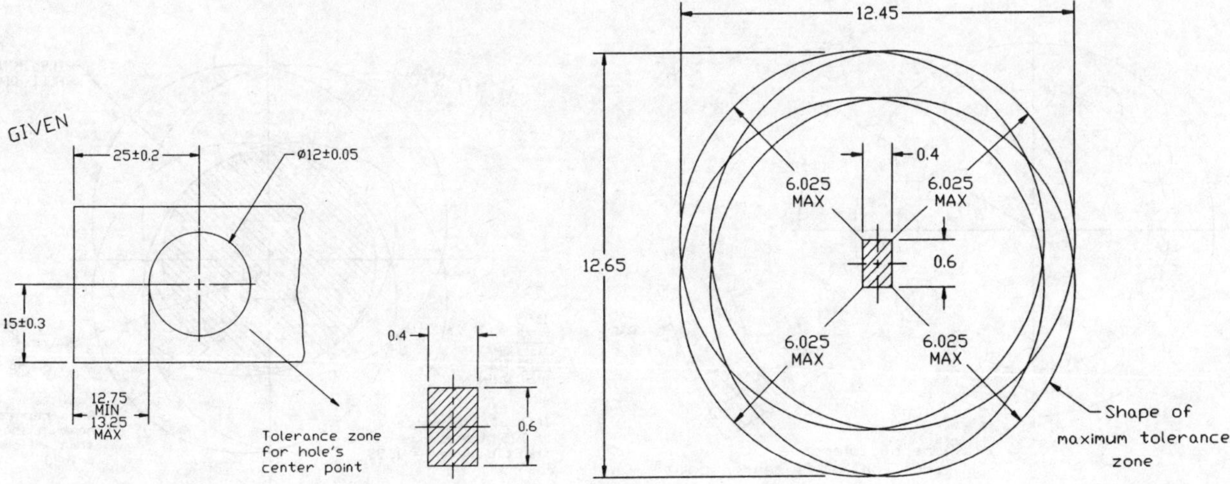

Figure 9-22

The hole diameter has a tolerance of ±0.05. This value must be added to the center point location tolerances to define the maximum possible overall shape of the hole. The maximum possible hole shape is determined by drawing the maximum radius from the four corner points of the tolerance zone.

This means that the left edge of the hole could be as close to the vertical baseline as 12.75 or as far as 13.25. The 12.75 value was derived by subtracting the maximum hole diameter value, 12.05, from the minimum linear distance, 24.80 (24.80 – 12.05 = 12.75). The 13.25 value was derived by subtracting the minimum hole diameter, 11.95, from the maximum linear distance, 25.20 (25.20 – 11.95 = 13.25).

Figure 9-23 shows a hole's tolerance zone based on polar dimensions. The zone has a sector shape, and the possible hole shape is determined by locating the maximum radius at the four corner points of the tolerance zone.

9-15 Choosing a Shaft for a Toleranced Hole

Given the hole location and size shown in Figure 9-23, what is the largest diameter shaft that will always fit into the hole?

Figure 9-24 shows the hole's center point tolerance zone based on the given linear locating tolerances. Four circles have been drawn centered at the four corners of the linear tolerance zone that represent the smallest possible hole diameter. The circles define an area which represents the maximum shaft size that will always fit into the hole, regardlcss of how the given dimensions are applied.

The diameter of this circular area can be calculated by subtracting the maximum diagonal distance across the linear tolerance zone (corner to corner) from the minimum hole diameter.

The results can be expressed as a formula.

For Linear Dimensions and Tolerances

$S_{max} = H_{min} - DTZ$

where

S_{max} = Maximum shaft diameter

H_{min} = Minimum hole diameter

DTZ = Diagonal distance across the tolerance zone

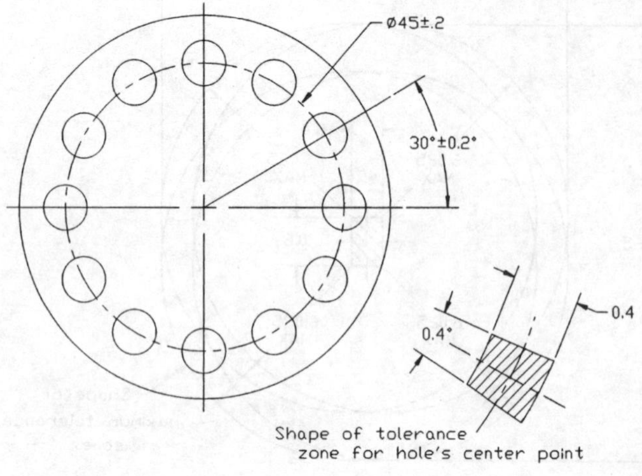

Figure 9-23

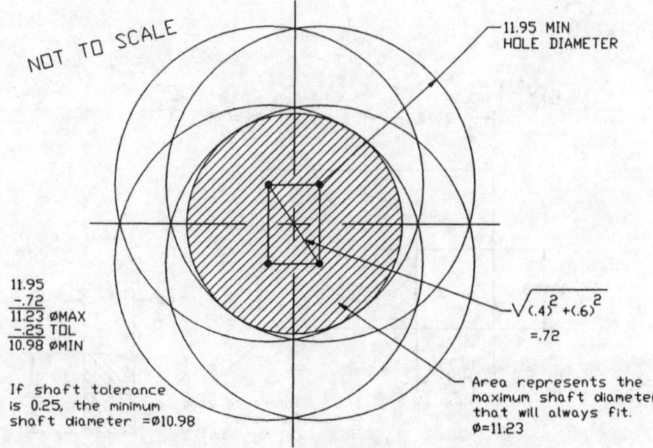

Figure 9-24

In the example shown, the diagonal distance is determined by the Pythagorean theorem:

$$DTZ = \sqrt{(.4)^2 + (.6)^2}$$
$$= \sqrt{.16 + .36}$$
$$DTZ = .72$$

This means that the maximum shaft diameter which will always fit into the given hole is 11.23.

$$S_{max} = H_{min} - DTZ$$
$$= 11.95 - .72$$
$$S_{max} = 11.23$$

This procedure represents a restricted application of the general formula for positional tolerances presented in Chapter 10. For a more complete discussion, see Section 10-16. Once the maximum shaft size has been established, a tolerance can be applied to the shaft. If the shaft had a total tolerance of 0.25, the minimum shaft diameter would be 11.23 – 0.25, or 10.98. Figure 9-24 shows a shaft dimensioned and toleranced according to these values.

The formula presented is based on the assumption that the shaft is perfectly placed on the hole's center point. This assumption is reasonable if two objects are joined by a fastener and both objects are free to move. When both objects are free to move about a common fastener, they are called *floating objects*.

9-16 Sample Problem SP9-1

Parts A and B in Figure 9-25 are to be joined by a common shaft. The total tolerance for the shaft is to be 0.05. What are the maximum and minimum shaft diameters?

Figure 9-25

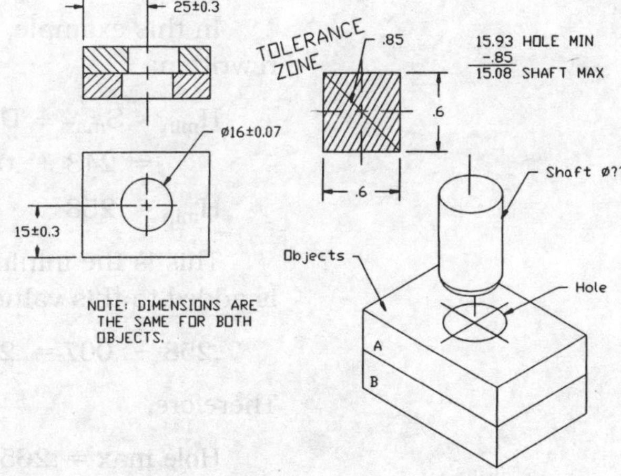

Both objects have the same dimensions and tolerances and are floating relative to each other.

$$S_{max} = H_{min} - DTZ$$
$$= 15.93 - .85$$
$$S_{max} = 15.08$$

The shaft's minimum diameter is found by subtracting the total tolerance requirement from the calculated maximum diameter.

$$15.08 - .05 = 15.03$$

Therefore,

Shaft max = 15.08

Shaft min = 15.03

9-17 Sample Problem SP9-2

The procedure presented in Sample Problem SP9-1 can be worked in reverse to determine the maximum and minimum hole size according to a given shaft size.

Objects AA and BB as shown in Figure 9-26 are to be joined by a bolt whose maximum diameter is 0.248. What is the minimum hole size for the objects that will always accept the bolt? What is the maximum hole size if the total hole tolerance is 0.007?

$$S_{max} = H_{min} - DZT$$

Figure 9-26

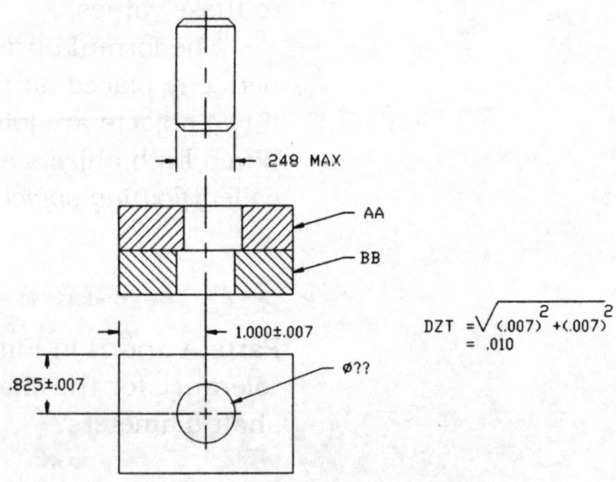

In this example, the H_{min} is the unknown factor, so the equation is rewritten:

$$H_{min} = S_{max} + DZT$$

$$= .248 + .010$$

$$H_{min} = .258$$

This is the minimum hole diameter, so the total tolerance requirement is added to this value:

$$.258 + .007 = .265$$

Therefore,

Hole max = .265

Hole min = .258

9-18 Standard Fits (Metric Values)

Calculating tolerances between holes and shafts that fit together is so common in engineering design that a group of standard values and notations has been established. These values are listed in tables in the appendix.

There are three possible types of fits between a shaft and a hole: clearance, interference, and transition. See Figure 9-27. There are several subclassifications within each of these categories.

Figure 9-27

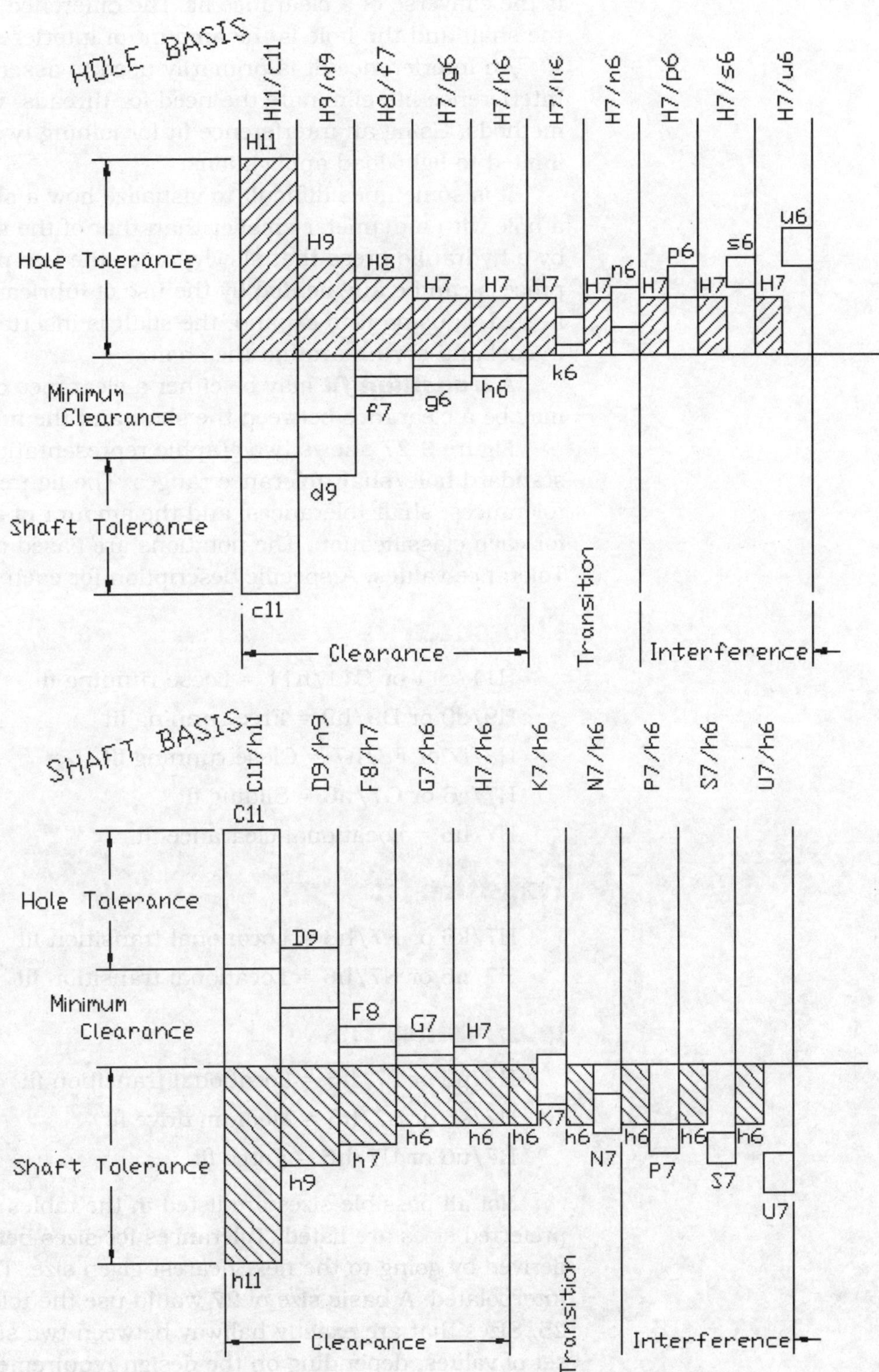

A ***clearance fit*** always defines the maximum shaft diameter as smaller than the minimum hole diameter. The difference between the two diameters is the amount of clearance. It is possible for a clearance fit to be defined with zero clearance; that is, the maximum shaft diameter is equal to the minimum hole diameter.

An ***interference fit*** always defines the minimum shaft diameter as larger than the maximum hole diameter, or more simply said, the shaft is always bigger than the hole. This definition means that an interference fit is the converse of a clearance fit. The difference between the diameter of the shaft and the hole is the amount of interference.

An interference fit is primarily used to assemble objects together. Interference fits eliminate the need for threads, welds, or other joining methods. Using an interference fit for joining two objects is generally limited to light-load applications.

It is sometimes difficult to visualize how a shaft can be assembled into a hole with a diameter smaller than that of the shaft. It is sometimes done by a hydraulic press that slowly forces the two parts together. The joining process can be augmented by the use of lubricants or heat. The hole is heated, causing it to expand, the shaft is inserted, and the hole is allowed to cool and shrink around the shaft.

A ***transition fit*** may be either a clearance or an interference fit. There may be a clearance between the shaft and the hole, or an interference.

Figure 9-27 shows two graphic representations of 20 different standard hole/shaft tolerance ranges. The figure shows ranges for hole tolerances, shaft tolerances, and the amount of clearance or interference for each classification. The notations are based on Standard International Tolerance values. A specific description for each category of fit follows.

Clearance Fits

H11/c11 or C11/h11 = Loose running fit

H9/d9 or D9/h9 = Free running fit

H8/f7 or F8/h7 = Close running fit

H7/g6 or G7/h6 = Sliding fit

H7/h6 = Locational clearance fit

Transition Fits

H7/k6 or K7/h6 = Locational transition fit

H7/n6 or N7/h6 = Locational transition fit

Interference Fits

H7/p6 or P7/h6 = Locational transition fit

H7/s6 or S7/h6 = Medium drive fit

H7/u6 or U7/h6 = Force fit

Not all possible sizes are listed in the tables in the appendix. Only preferred sizes are listed. Tolerances for sizes between the stated sizes are derived by going to the next nearest given size. The values are not interpolated. A basic size of 27 would use the tolerance values listed for 25. Sizes that are exactly halfway between two stated sizes may use either set of values, depending on the design requirements.

9-19 Nominal Sizes

The term *nominal* refers to the approximate size of an object that matches a common fraction or whole number. A shaft with a dimension of 1.500 ± 0.003 is said to have a nominal size of "one and a half inches." A dimension of 1.500 + 0.000/−0.005 is still said to have a nominal size of one and a half inches. In both examples, 1.5 is the closest common fraction.

9-20 Hole and Shaft Basis

One of the charts shown in Figure 9-27 applies tolerances starting with the nominal hole sizes, called ***hole basis tolerances***; the other applies tolerances starting with the shaft nominal sizes, called ***shaft basis tolerances.*** The choice of which set of values to use depends on the design application. In general, hole basis numbers are used more often because it is more difficult to vary hole diameters manufactured by the use of specific drill sizes than shaft sizes manufactured by the use of a lathe. Shaft sizes may be used when a specific fastener diameter is used to assemble several objects.

Figure 9-28 shows a hole, a shaft, and a set of sample values taken from the tables found in the appendix. One set of values is for hole basis tolerance, and the other for shaft basis tolerance. The fit values are the same for both sets of values. The hole basis values were derived starting with a nominal hole size of 20.000, whereas the shaft basis values were derived starting with a shaft nominal size of 20.000. The letters used to identify holes are always written in capital letters, and the letters for shaft values use lowercase.

Figure 9-28

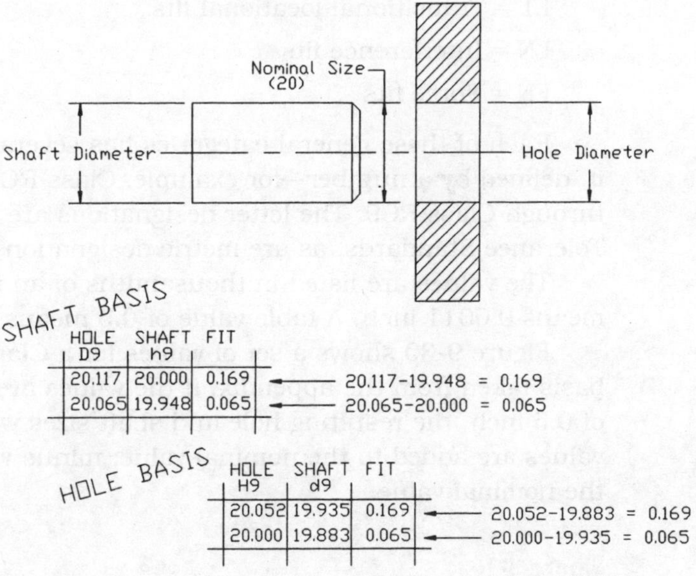

Additional fit tolerances may be found on the Web. Search for fits and tolerances.

9-21 Sample Problem SP9-3

Dimension a hole and a shaft that are to fit together, using a preferred clearance fit. Use hole basis values based on a nominal size of 12 mm.

Figure 9-29 shows values taken from the appropriate table in the appendix. The values may be applied directly to the shaft and hole as shown.

Figure 9-29

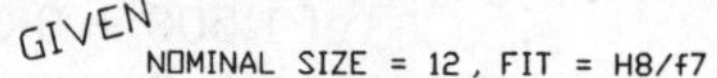

FROM CHART

NOMINAL SIZE	HOLE H8	SHAFT f7	FIT
12	12.027 12.000	11.984 11.966	0.061 0.016

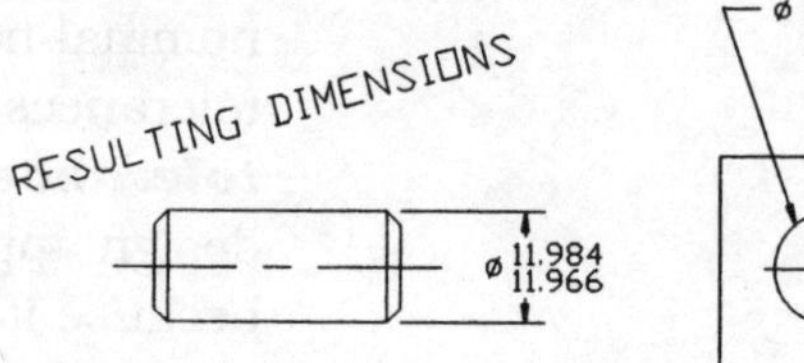

9-22 Standard Fits (Inch Values)

The appendix also includes tables of standard fit tolerances for inch values. The tables for inches are presented for a range of nominal values and are not for specific values, as are the metric value tables. The values may be on a hole or shaft basis.

Fits Defined by Using Inch Values Are Classified as Follows

RC = Running and sliding fits

LC = Clearance locational fits

LT = Transitional locational fits

LN = Interference fits

FN = Force fits

Each of these general categories has several subclassifications within it, defined by a number—for example, Class RC1, Class RC2, and so on through Class RC9. The letter designations are based on International Tolerance Standards, as are metric designations.

The values are listed in thousandths of an inch. A table value of 1.1 means 0.0011 inch. A table value of 0.5 means 0.0005 inch.

Figure 9-30 shows a set of values for a Class RC3 clearance fit hole basis taken from the appendix. If the values are applied to a nominal size of 0.5 inch, the resulting hole and shaft sizes will be as shown. Plus table values are added to the nominal value; minus values are subtracted from the nominal value.

Figure 9-30

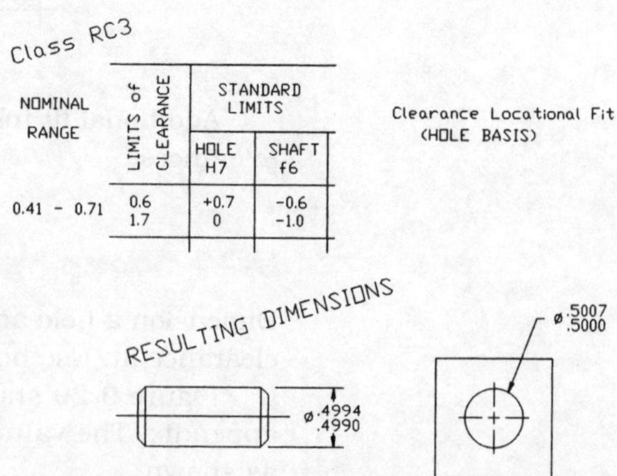

NOMINAL RANGE	LIMITS of CLEARANCE	STANDARD LIMITS	
		HOLE H7	SHAFT f6
0.41 - 0.71	0.6 1.7	+0.7 0	-0.6 -1.0

Nominal values that are common to two nominal ranges (0.71) may use values from either range.

9-23 Sample Problem SP9-4

Dimension a hole and shaft for a Class LN1 Interference fit based on a nominal diameter of 0.25 in. Use hole basis values.

Figure 9-31 shows the values for the 0.24–0.40 nominal range as listed in the appendix. The values are in thousandths of an inch. Plus values are added to the nominal size. The resulting shaft and hole dimensions are as shown. The diameter of the shaft is larger than that of the hole because this example calls for an interference fit.

Figure 9-31

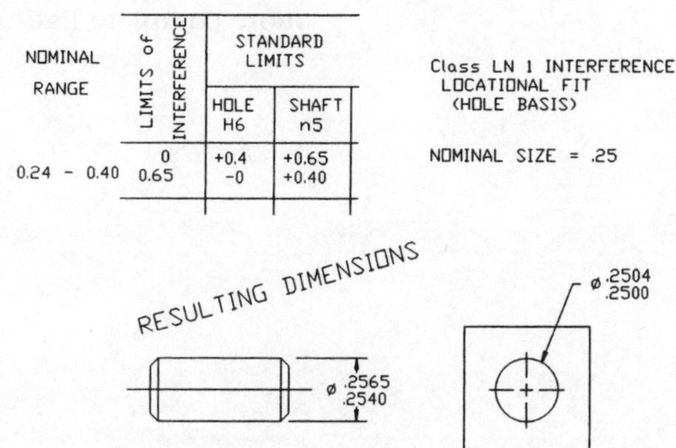

9-24 Preferred and Standard Sizes

It is important that designers always consider preferred and standard sizes when selecting sizes for designs. Most tooling is set up to match these sizes, so manufacturing is greatly simplified when preferred and standard sizes are specified. Figure 9-32 shows a list of preferred sizes for metric values.

Figure 9-32

PREFERRED SIZES (mm)			
First Choice	Second Choice	First Choice	Second Choice
1	1.1	12	14
1.2	1.4	16	18
1.6	1.8	20	22
2	2.2	25	28
2.5	2.8	30	35
3	3.5	40	45
4	4.5	50	55
5	5.5	60	70
6	7	80	90
8	9	100	110
10	11	120	140

Consider the case of design calculations that call for a 42-mm-diameter hole. A 42-mm-diameter hole is not a preferred size. A diameter of 40 mm is the closest preferred size, and a 45-mm diameter is a second choice. A 42-mm hole could be manufactured, but would require an unusual drill size that may not be available. It would be wise to reconsider the design to see whether a 40-mm diameter hole could be used, and if not, then a 45-mm diameter hole possibly could be used.

A very large-quantity production run could possibly justify the cost of special tooling, but for smaller runs, it is probably better to use preferred sizes. Machinists will have the required drills, and maintenance people will have the appropriate tools for these sizes.

Figure 9-33 shows a list of standard fractional drill sizes. Most companies now specify metric units or decimal inches; however, many standard items are still available in fractional sizes, and many older objects may still require fractional-sized tools and replacement parts. A more complete listing is available in the appendix.

Figure 9-33

Fraction	Decimal Equivalent	Fraction	Decimal Equivalent	Fraction	Decimal Equivalent
7/64	.1094	21/64	.3281	11/16	.6875
1/8	.1250	11/32	.3438	3/4	.7500
9/64	.1406	23/64	.3594	13/16	.8125
5/32	.1562	3/8	.3750	7/8	.8750
11/64	.1719	25/64	.3906	15/16	.9375
3/16	.1875	13/32	.4062	1	1.0000
13/64	.2031	27/64	.4219		
7/32	.2188	7/16	.4375	PARTIAL LIST of standard Twist Drill Sizes (Fractional Sizes)	
1/4	.2500	29/64	.4531		
17/64	.2656	15/32	.4688		
9/32	.2812	1/2	.5000		
19/64	.2969	9/16	.5625		
5/16	.3125	5/8	.6250		

9-25 Surface Finishes

The term ***surface finish*** refers to the accuracy (flatness) of a surface. Metric values are measured in micrometers (μm), and inch values are measured in microinches (μin.).

The accuracy of a surface depends on the manufacturing process used to produce the surface. Figure 9-34 shows a list of several manufacturing processes and the quality of the surface finish that they can be expected to produce.

Surface finishes have several design applications. ***Datum surfaces,*** or surfaces used for baseline dimensioning, should have fairly accurate surface finishes to help ensure accurate measurements, bearing surfaces should have good-quality surface finishes for better load distribution, and parts that operate at high speeds should have smooth finishes to help reduce friction.

Surface Roughness Average Obtained by Common Production Methods

Process

Roughness Height Rating Micrometers, Microinches

(μm) 50 25 12.5 6.3 3.2 1.6 0.8 0.4 0.2 0.1 0.05 0.025

(μin) 2000 1000 500 250 125 63 32 16 8 4 2 1

Flame Cutting
Snagging
Sawing
Planning, Shaping
Drilling
Chemical Milling
Elect Discharge Machine
Milling
Broaching
Reaming
Electron Beam
Laser

Surface Roughness Average Obtained by Common Production Methods

Process

Roughness Height Rating Micrometers, Microinches

(μm) 50 25 12.5 6.3 3.2 1.6 0.8 0.4 0.2 0.1 0.05 0.025

(μin) 2000 1000 500 250 125 63 32 16 8 4 2 1

Electrochemical
Boring, Turning
Barrel Finishing
Electronic Grinding
Roller Burnishing
Grinding
Honing
Electropolishing
Polishing
Lapping
Superfinish

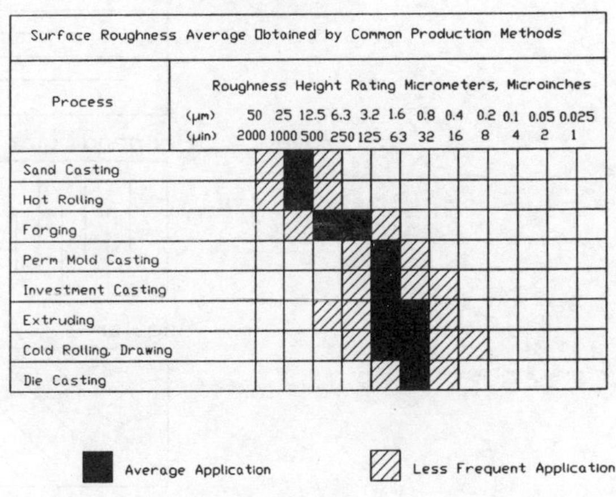

Figure 9-34

Figure 9-35 shows a screw head sitting on a very wavy surface. Note that the head of the screw is in contact with only two wave peaks, meaning that all the bearing load is concentrated on the two peaks. This situation could cause stress cracks and greatly weaken the surface. A better-quality surface finish would increase the bearing contact area.

Figure 9-35 also shows two very rough surfaces moving in contact with each other. The result will be excess wear to both surfaces because the surfaces touch only on the peaks, and these peaks will tend to wear faster than flatter areas. Excess vibration can also result when interfacing surfaces are too rough.

Surface finishes are classified into three categories: surface texture, roughness, and lay. ***Surface texture*** is a general term that refers to the overall quality and accuracy of a surface.

Roughness is a measure of the average deviation of a surface's peaks and valleys. See Figure 9-36.

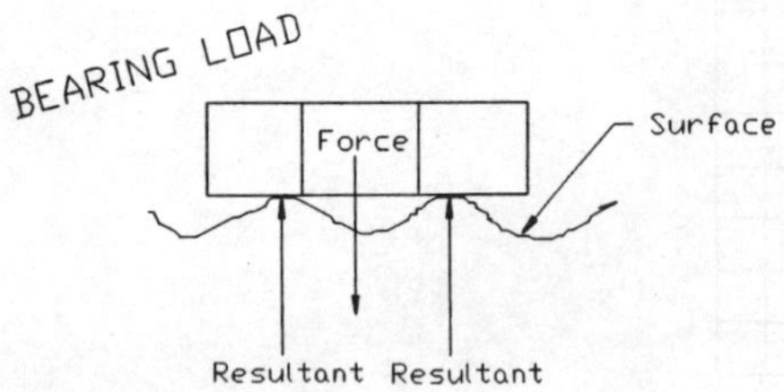

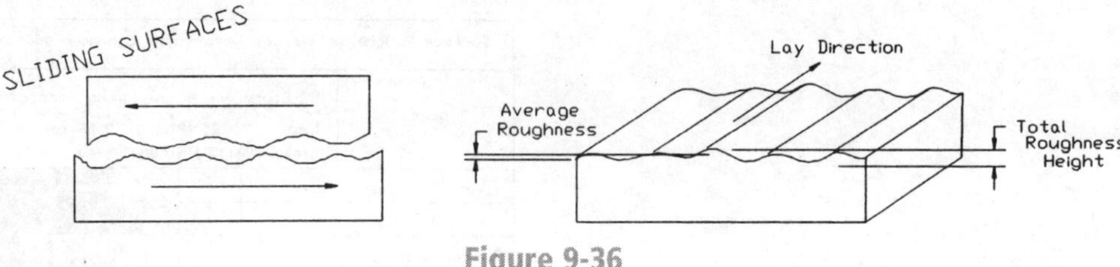

Figure 9-35

Figure 9-36

Lay refers to the direction of machine marks on a surface. See Figure 9-37. The lay of a surface is particularly important when two moving objects are in contact with each other, especially at high speeds.

Figure 9-37

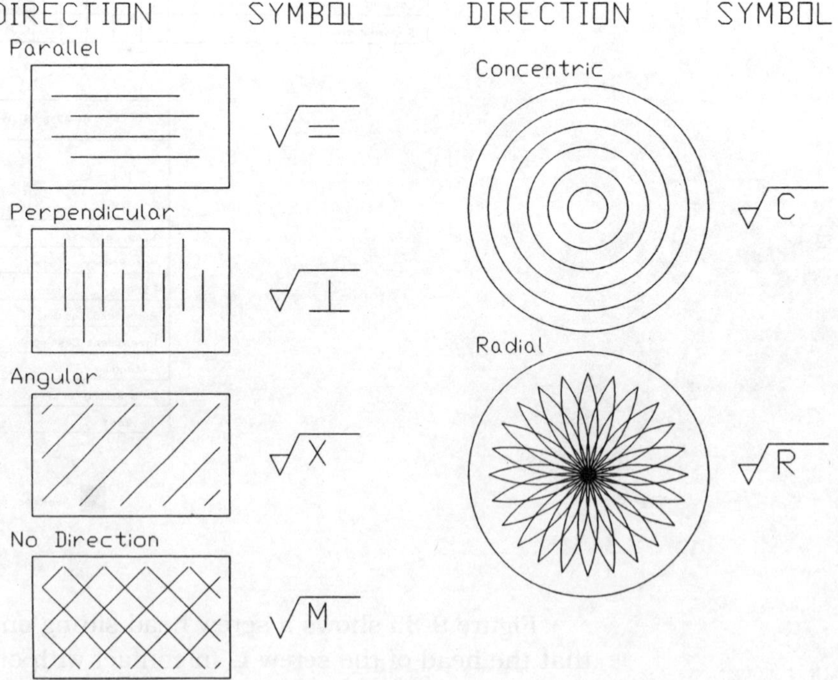

9-26 Surface Control Symbols

Surface finishes are indicated on a drawing with surface control symbols. See Figure 9-38. The general surface control symbol looks like a checkmark. Roughness values may be included with the symbol to specify the required accuracy. Surface control symbols can also be used to specify the manufacturing process that may or may not be used to produce a surface.

Figure 9-39 shows two applications of surface control symbols. In the first example, a 0.8-μm (32-μin.) surface finish is specified on the surface that serves as a datum for several horizontal dimensions. A 0.8-μm surface finish is generally considered the minimum acceptable finish for datums.

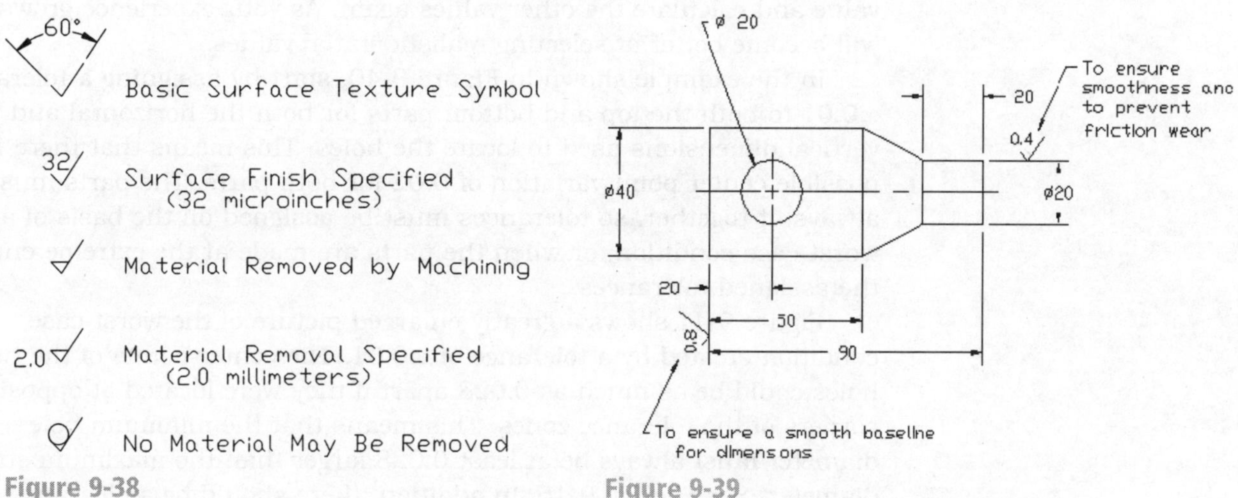

Figure 9-38

Figure 9-39

A second finish mark with a value of 0.4 μm is located on an extension line that refers to a surface that will be in contact with a moving object. The extra flatness will help prevent wear between the two surfaces.

It is suggested that a general finish mark be drawn and saved as a wblock so that it can be inserted as needed on future drawings. Add the machine mark "wblock" to any prototype drawings created.

9-27 Design Problems

Figure 9-40 shows two objects that are to be fitted together by a fastener such as a screw-and-nut combination. For this example, a cylinder will be used to represent a fastener. Only two nominal dimensions are given. The dimensions and tolerances were derived as follows.

Figure 9-40

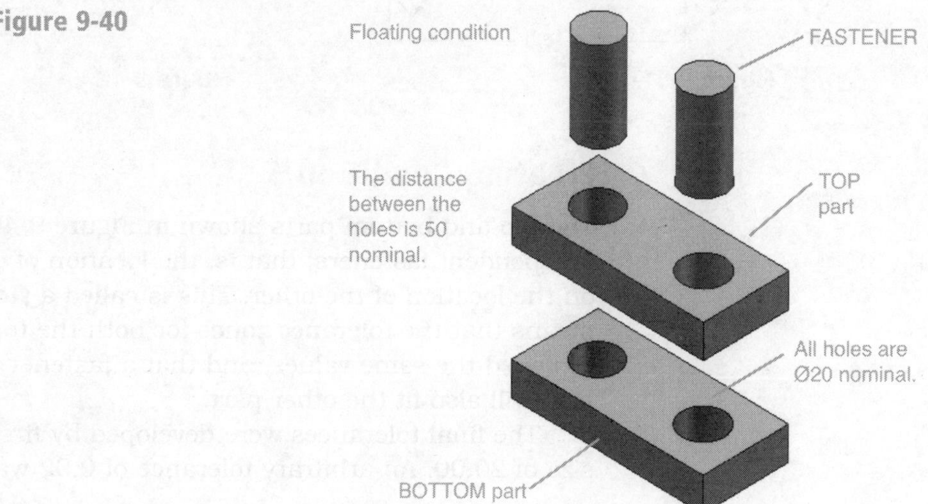

The distance between the centers of the holes is given as 50 nominal. The term *nominal* means that the stated value is only a starting point. The final dimensions will be close to the given value, but do not have to equal it.

Assigning tolerances is an iteration process; that is, a tolerance is selected, and other tolerance values are calculated, from the selected initial values. If the results are not satisfactory, go back and modify the initial value and calculate the other values again. As your experience grows, you will become better at selecting realistic initial values.

In the example shown in Figure 9-40, start by assigning a tolerance of ±0.01 to both the top and bottom parts for both the horizontal and vertical dimensions used to locate the holes. This means that there is a possible center point variation of 0.02 for both parts. The parts must always fit together, so tolerances must be assigned on the basis of a worst-case condition, or when the parts are made at the extreme ends of the assigned tolerances.

Figure 9-41 shows a greatly enlarged picture of the worst-case condition created by a tolerance of ±0.01. The center points of the two holes could be as much as 0.028 apart if they were located at opposite corners of the tolerance zones. This means that the minimum hole diameter must always be at least 0.028 larger than the maximum stud diameter. See Section 9-15. In addition, there should be a clearance tolerance assigned so that the hole and stud are never exactly the same size. Figure 9-42 shows the resulting tolerances.

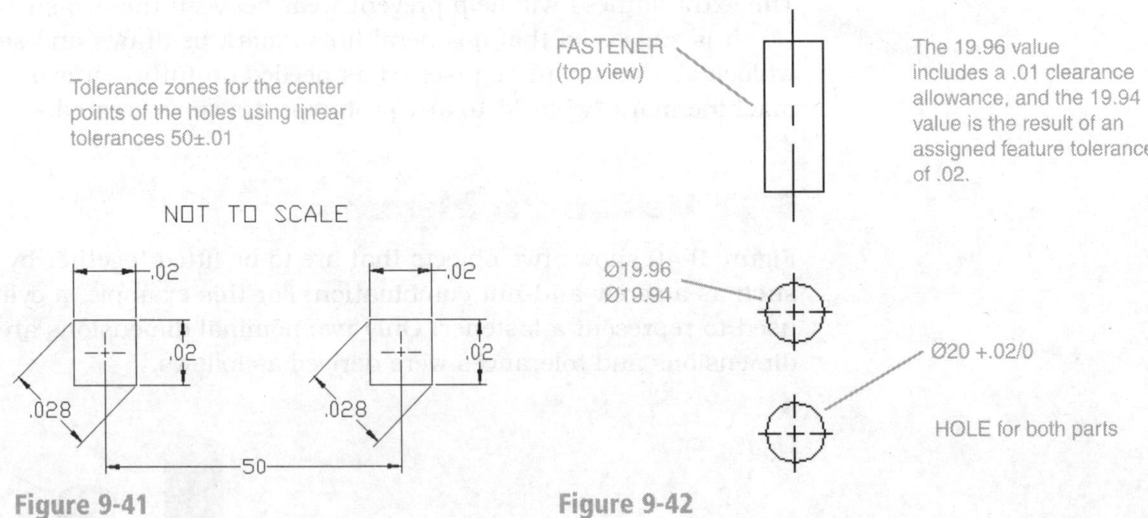

Figure 9-41

Figure 9-42

Floating Condition

The top and bottom parts shown in Figure 9-40 are to be joined by two independent fasteners; that is, the location of one fastener does not depend on the location of the other. This is called a ***floating condition.*** This means that the tolerance zones for both the top and bottom parts can be assigned the same values, and that a fastener diameter selected to fit one part will also fit the other part.

The final tolerances were developed by first defining a minimum hole size of 20.00. An arbitrary tolerance of 0.02 was assigned to the hole, and was expressed as 20.00 + 0.02/−0 so that the hole can never be any smaller than 20.00.

The 20.00 minimum hole diameter dictates that the maximum fastener diameter can be no greater than 19.97, or 0.03 (i.e., the rounded-off diagonal distance across the tolerance zone—0.028) less than the minimum hole diameter. A 0.01 clearance was assigned. The clearance ensures that the hole and fastener are never exactly the same diameter. The resulting maximum allowable diameter for the fastener is 19.96. Again, an arbitrary tolerance of 0.02 was assigned to the fastener. The final fastener dimensions are, therefore, 19.96 to 19.94.

The assigned tolerances ensure that there will always be at least 0.01 clearance between the fastener and the hole. The other extreme condition occurs when the hole is at its largest possible size (10.02) and the fastener is at its smallest (19.94). This means that there could be as much as 0.08 clearance between the parts. If this much clearance is not acceptable, then the assigned tolerances will have to be reevaluated.

Figure 9-43 shows the top and bottom parts dimensioned and toleranced. Any dimensions that do not have assigned tolerances are assumed to have standard tolerances. See Figure 9-14.

Note, in Figure 9-43, that the top edge of each part was assigned a surface finish. This was done to help ensure the accuracy of the 20 ± 0.01 dimension. If this edge surface were rough, it could affect the tolerance measurements.

Figure 9-43

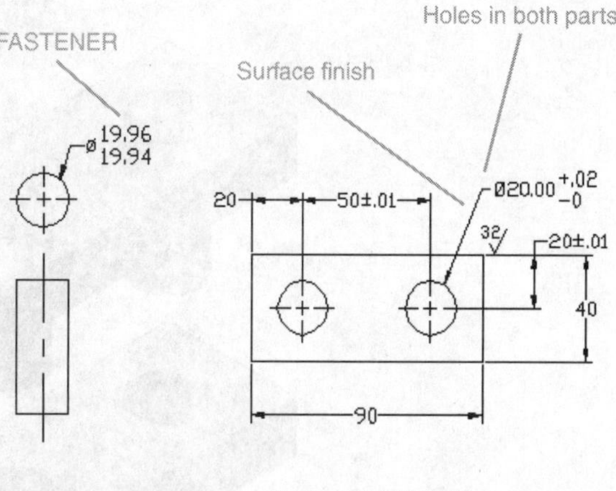

This example will be repeated in Chapter 10 with geometric tolerances. Geometric tolerance zones are circular rather than rectangular.

Fixed Condition

Figure 9-44 shows the same nominal conditions presented in Figure 9-40, but the fasteners are now fixed to the top part. This is called the ***fixed condition.*** In analyzing the tolerance zones for the fixed condition, one must consider two positional tolerances: the positional tolerances for the holes in the bottom part, and the positional tolerances for the fixed fasteners in the top part. This may be expressed in an equation as follows:

$$S_{max} + DTSZ = H_{min} - DTZ$$

where

S_{max} = Maximum shaft (fastener) diameter
H_{min} = Minimum hole diameter
DTSZ = Diagonal distance across the shaft's center point tolerance zone
DTZ = Diagonal distance across the hole's center point tolerance zone

If a dimension and tolerance of 50 ± 0.01 and 20 ± 0.01 are assigned to both the center distance between the holes and the center distance between the fixed fasteners, the values for DTSZ and DTZ will be equal. The formula can then be simplified as follows:

$$S_{max} = H_{min} - 2(DTZ)$$

Here, DTZ equals the diagonal distance across the tolerance zone. If a hole tolerance of 20.00 + 0.02/−0 is also defined, the resulting maximum shaft size can be determined, assuming that the calculated distance of 0.028 is rounded off to 0.03. See Figure 9-45.

$$S_{max} = 20.00 - 2(.03)$$
$$= 19.94$$

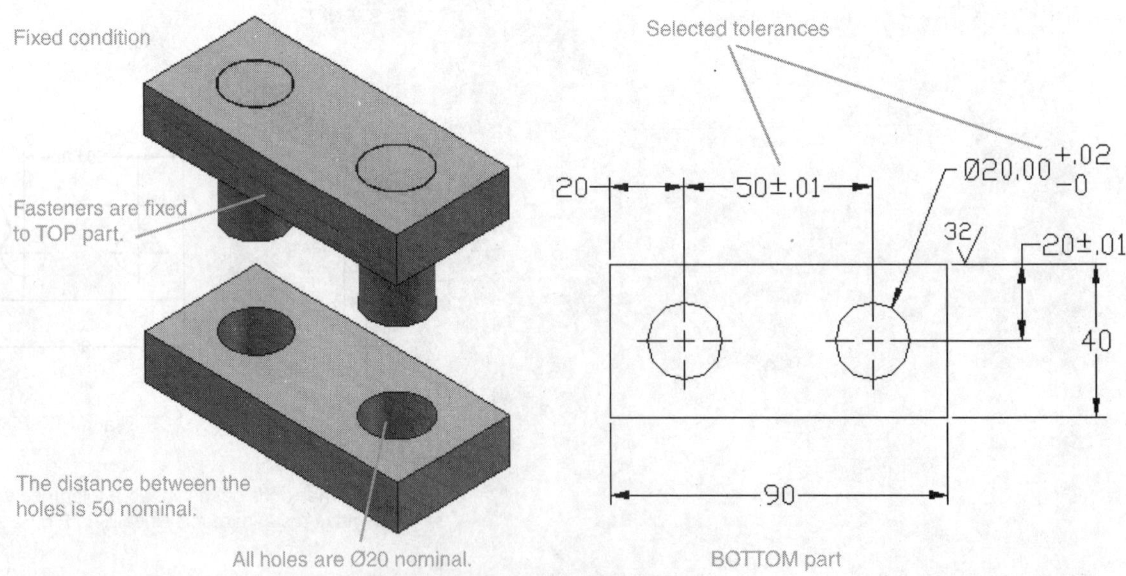

Figure 9-44

Figure 9-45

This means that the largest possible shaft diameter that will just fit equals 19.94. If a clearance tolerance of 0.01 is assumed to ensure that the shaft and hole are never exactly the same size, the maximum shaft diameter becomes 19.93. See Figure 9-46.

A feature tolerance of 0.02 on the shaft will result in a minimum shaft diameter of 19.91. Note that the 0.01 clearance tolerance and the 0.02 feature tolerance were arbitrarily chosen. Other possible values could have been used.

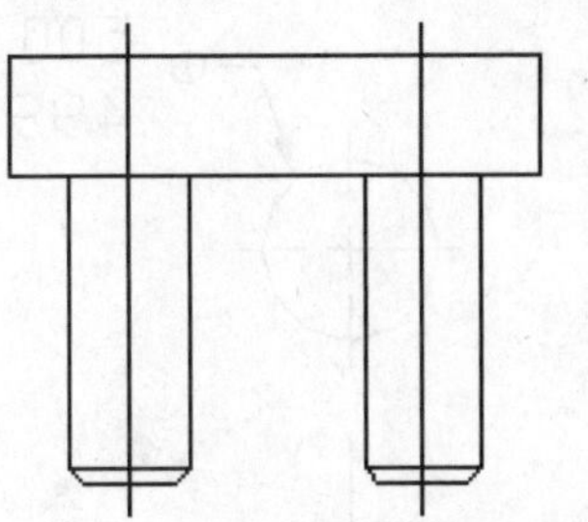

The shaft values were derived as follows.

20.00	The selected value for the minimum hole diameter
−.03	The rounded-off value for the hole positional tolerance
−.03	The rounded-off value for the shaft positional tolerance
−.01	The selected clearance value
19.93	The maximum shaft value
−.02	The selected tolerance value
19.91	The minimum shaft diameter

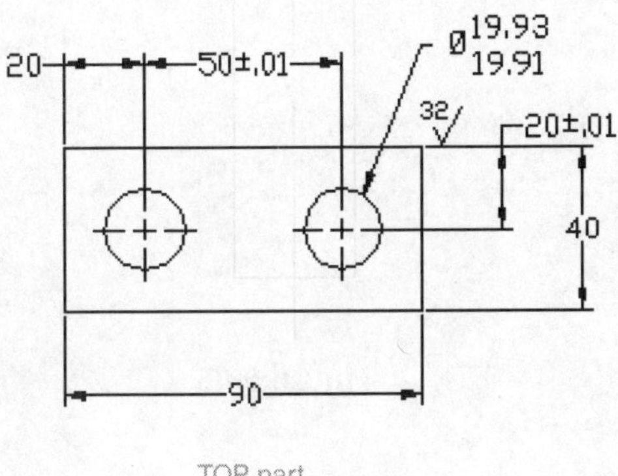

TOP part

Figure 9-46

To Design a Hole Given a Fastener Size

The previous two examples started by selecting a minimum hole diameter and then calculating the resulting fastener size. Figure 9-47 shows a situation in which the fastener size is defined and the problem is to determine the appropriate hole sizes. Figure 9-48 shows the dimensions and tolerances for both top and bottom parts.

Requirements:

Clearance, minimum = 0.003

Hole tolerances = 0.005

Positional tolerance = 0.002

Figure 9-47

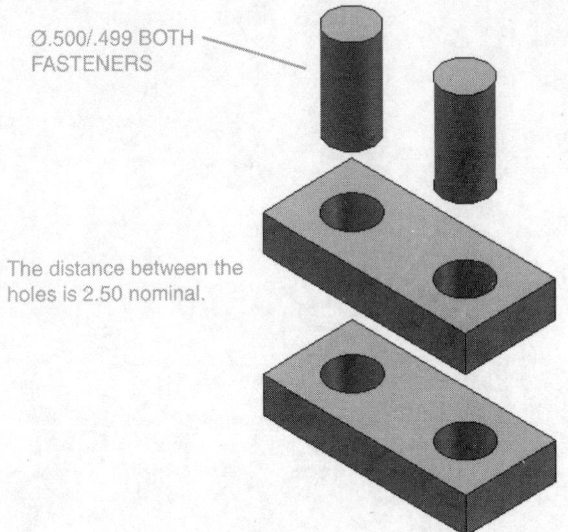

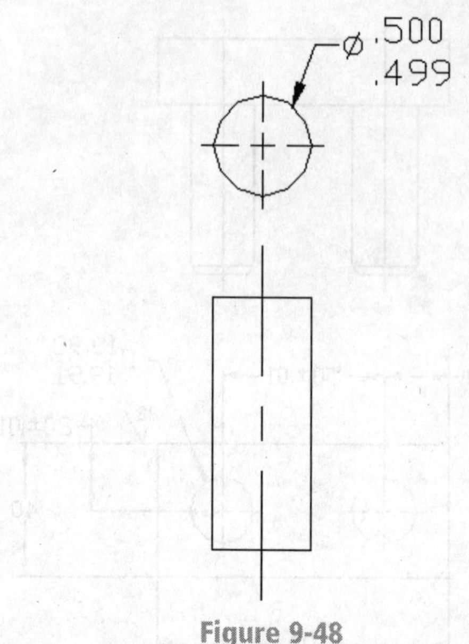

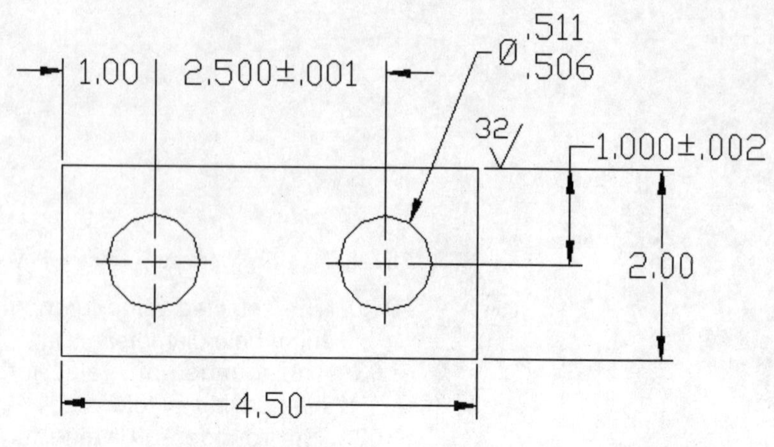

Figure 9-48

9-28 EXERCISE PROBLEMS

Redraw the objects shown in Exercise Problems EX9-1 through EX9-4, using the given dimensions. Include the listed tolerances.

EX9-1 Millimeters

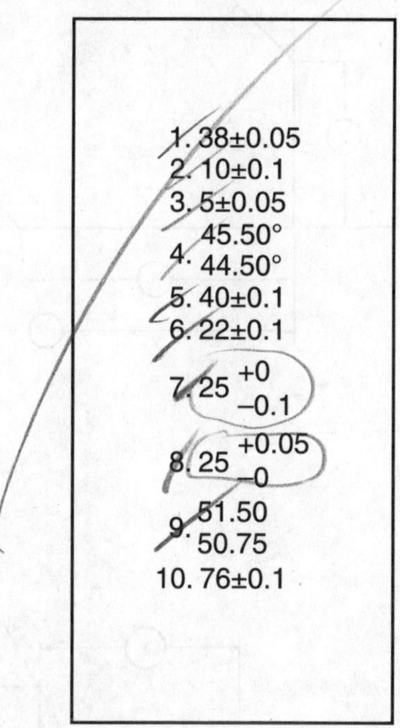

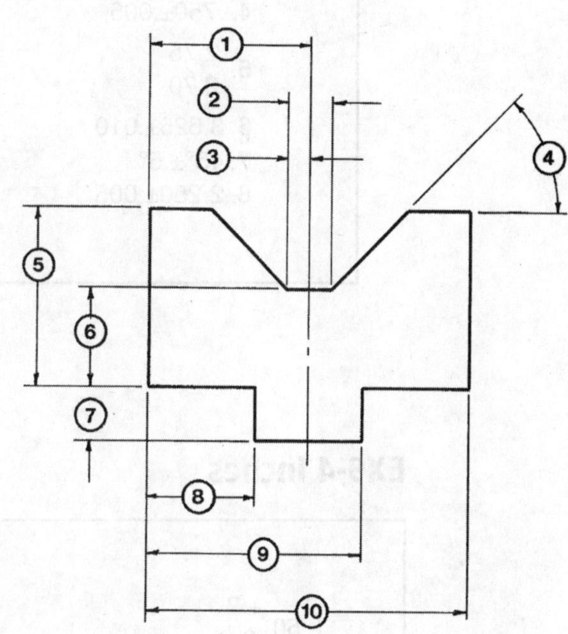

EX9-2 Millimeters

1. 34±0.25
2. 17±0.25
3. 25±0.05
4. 15.00 / 14.80
5. 50±0.05
6. 80±0.1
7. R5±0.1-8 PLACES
8. 45±0.25
9. 60±0.1
10. Ø14-3 HOLES
11. 15.00 / 14.80
12. 30.00 / 29.80

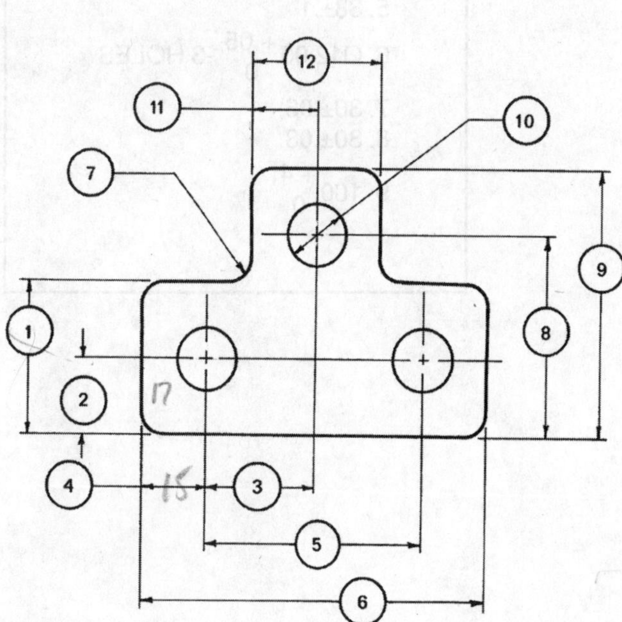

EX9-3 Inches

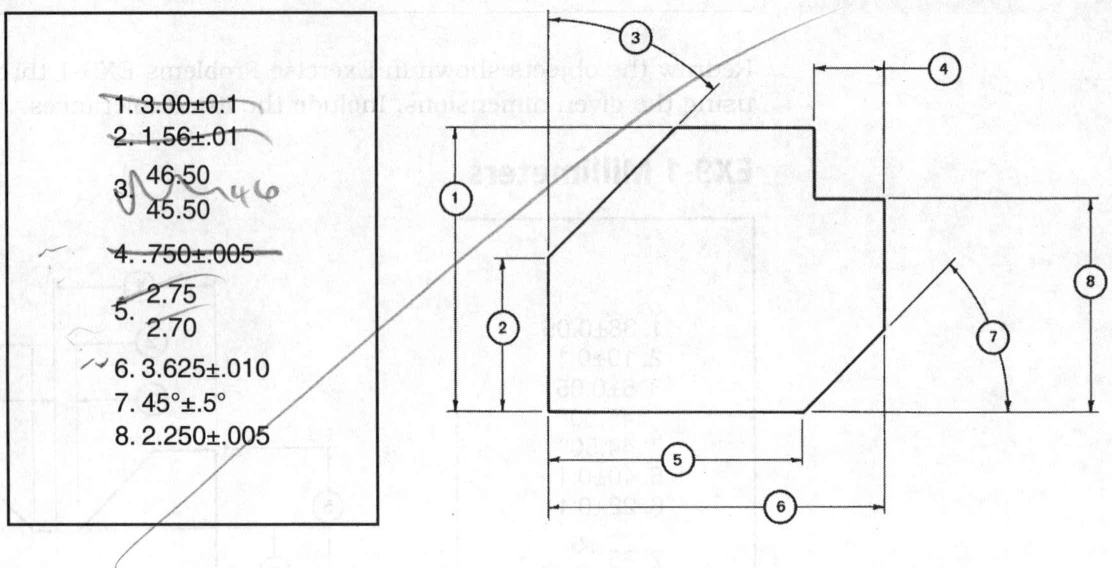

EX9-4 Inches

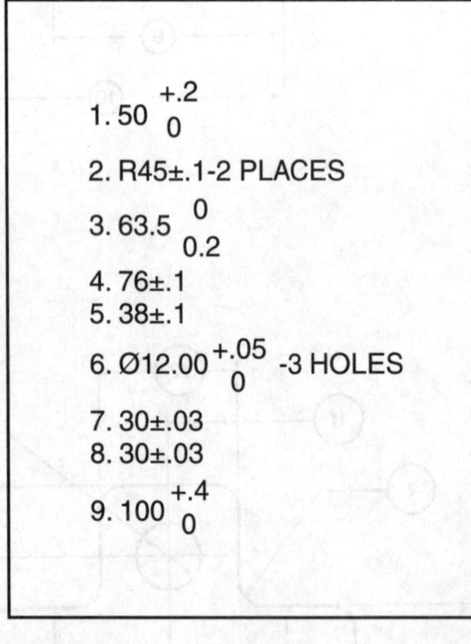

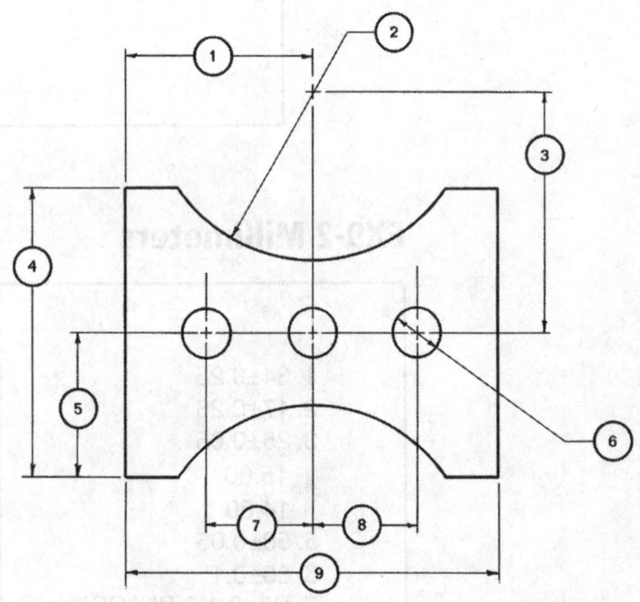

EX9-5 Millimeters

Redraw the following object, including the given dimensions and tolerances. Calculate and list the maximum and minimum distances for surface A.

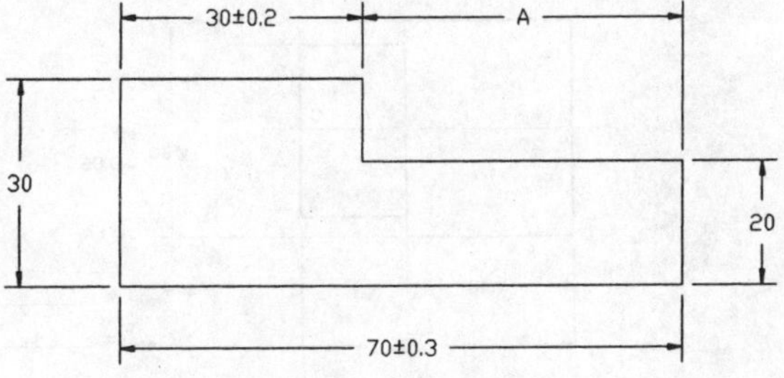

EX9-6 Inches

A. Redraw the following object, including the dimensions and tolerances. Calculate and list the maximum and minimum distances for surface A.

B. Redraw the given object and dimension it, using baseline dimensions. Calculate and list the maximum and minimum distances for surface A.

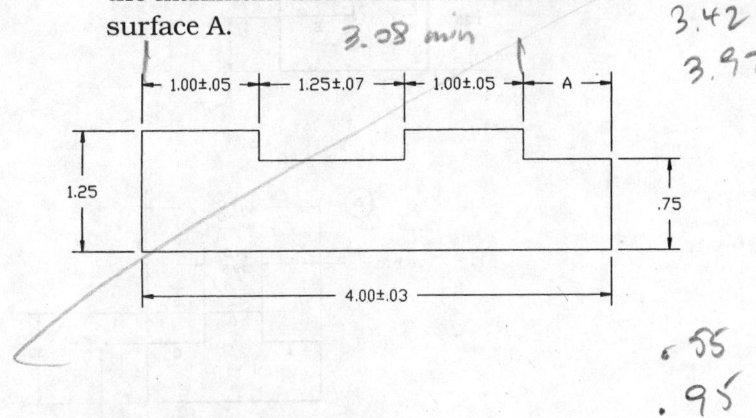

EX9-7 Millimeters

Redraw the following object, including the dimensions and tolerances. Calculate and list the maximum and minimum distances for surfaces D and E.

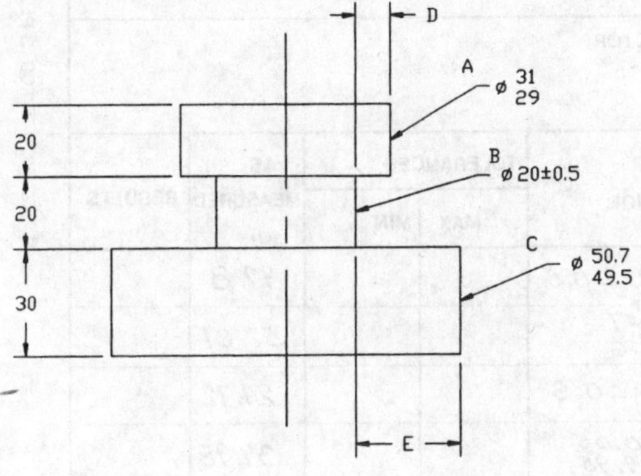

EX9-8 Millimeters

Dimension the following object twice: once using chain dimensions, and once using baseline dimensions. Calculate and list the maximum and minimum distances for surface D for both chain and baseline dimensions. Compare the results.

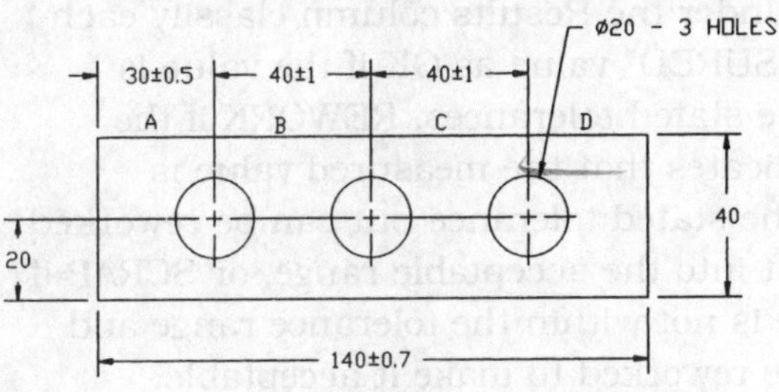

EX9-9 Inches

Redraw the following shapes, including the dimensions and tolerances. Also list the required minimum and maximum values for the specified distances.

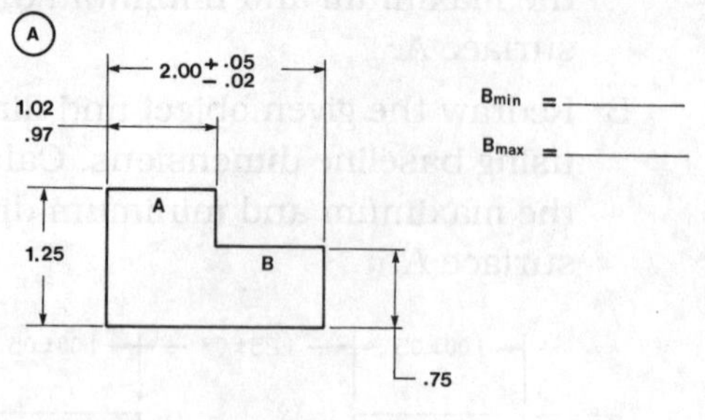

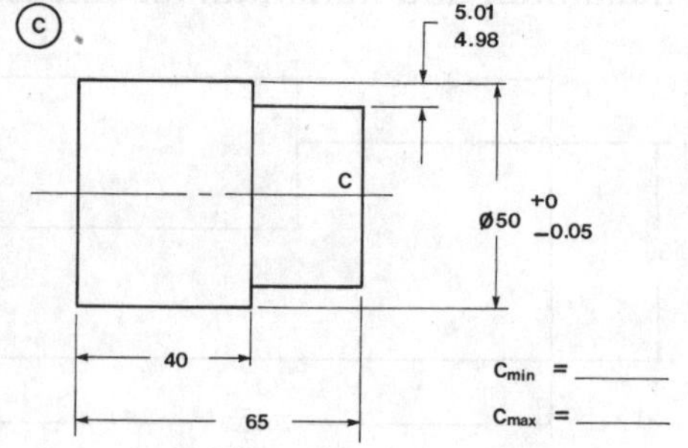

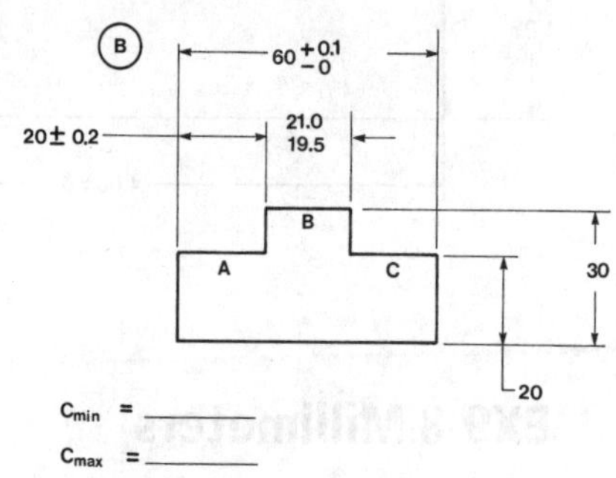

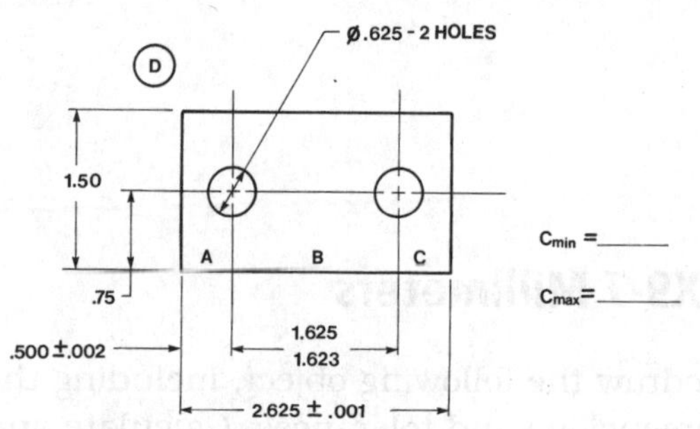

EX9-10

Redraw and complete the inspection report that follows. Under the Results column classify each "AS MEASURED" value as OK if the value is within the stated tolerances, REWORK if the value indicates that the measured value is beyond the stated tolerance but can be reworked to bring it into the acceptable range, or SCRAP if the value is not within the tolerance range and cannot be reworked to make it acceptable.

INSPECTION REPORT

PART NAME AND NO: 10755002

INSPECTOR:

DATE:

BASE DIMENSION	TOLERANCES MAX	TOLERANCES MIN	AS MEASURED	RESULTS
(1) 100±0.5			99.8	
(2) Ø 57 56			57.01	
(3) 22±0.3			21.72	
(4) 40.05 39.95			39.98	
(5) 22±0.3			21.68	
(6) R52 +0 −0.2			51.99	
(7) 35 +0.2 −0.3			35.20	
(8) 30 +0.4 0			30.27	
(9) 6.0 +.1 −.2			5.85	
(10) 12.0±0.2			11.90	

1.00 3 PLACES

.50—10 PLACES

EX9-11 Millimeters

Redraw the following charts and complete them on the basis of the following information:

A. Nominal = 16, Fit = H9/d9
B. Nominal = 30, Fit = H11/c11
C. Nominal = 22, Fit = H7/g6
D. Nominal = 10, Fit = C11/h11
E. Nominal = 25, Fit = F8/h7
F. Nominal = 12, Fit = H7/k6
G. Nominal = 3, Fit = H7/p6
H. Nominal = 19, Fit = H7/s6
I. Nominal = 27, Fit = H7/u6
J. Nominal = 30, Fit = N7/h6

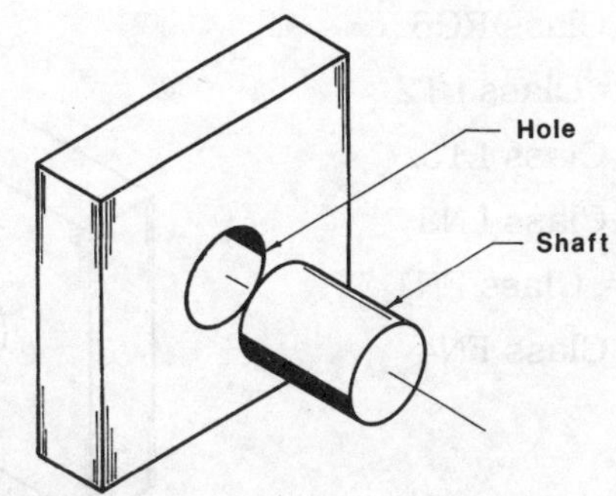

half space

NOMINAL	HOLE		SHAFT		CLEARANCE	
	MAX	MIN	MAX	MIN	MAX	MIN
A						
B						
C						
D						
E						

3.75 6 equal spaces

1.5 — 6.0 – 6 equal spaces

NOMINAL	HOLE		SHAFT		INTERFERENCE	
	MAX	MIN	MAX	MIN	MAX	MIN
F						
G						
H						
I						
J						

Use the same dimensions given above

EX9-12 Inches

Redraw the following charts, and complete them on the basis of the following information:

A. Nominal = 0.25, Fit = Class LC5
B. Nominal = 1.00, Fit = Class LC7
C. Nominal = 1.50, Fit = Class LC10
D. Nominal = 0.75, Fit = Class RC3
E. Nominal = 2.50, Fit = Class RC6
F. Nominal = 0.500, Fit = Class LT2
G. Nominal = 1.25, Fit = Class LT5
H. Nominal = 3.00, Fit = Class LN3
I. Nominal = 1.625, Fit = Class FN1
J. Nominal = 2.00, Fit = Class FN4

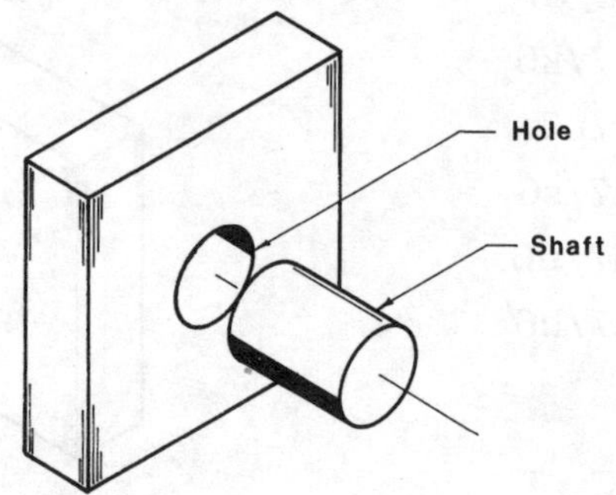

half space

3.75
6 equal
spaces

NOMINAL	HOLE		SHAFT		CLEARANCE	
	MAX	MIN	MAX	MIN	MAX	MIN
A						
B						
C						
D						
E						

1.5 6.0 – 6 equal spaces

NOMINAL	HOLE		SHAFT		INTERFERENCE	
	MAX	MIN	MAX	MIN	MAX	MIN
F						
G						
H						
I						
J						

Use the same dimensions given above

Draw the chart shown, and add the appropriate values according to the dimensions and tolerances given in Exercise Problems EX9-13 through EX9-16.

EX9-13 Millimeters

PART NO: 9-M53A

A. 20±0.1

B. 30±0.2

C. Ø20±0.05

D. 40

E. 60

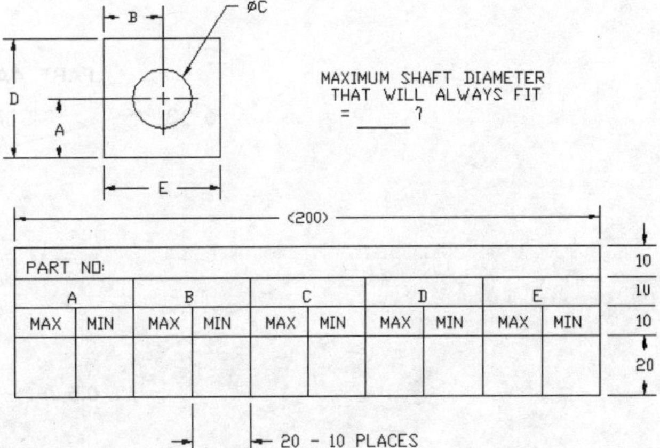

EX9-14 Millimeters

PART NO: 9-M53B

A. 32.02 / 31.97

B. 47.52 / 47.50

C. Ø18 +0.05 / 0

D. 64±0.05

E. 100±0.05

EX9-15 Millimeters

PART NO: 9-M53B

A. 32.02 / 31.97

B. 47.52 / 47.50

C. Ø18 +0.05 / 0

D. 64±0.05

E. 100±0.05

EX9-16 Millimeters

PART NO: 9-E47B

A. 18 +0 / −0.02

B. 26 +0 / −0.04

C. Ø 24.03 / 23.99

D. 52±0.04

E. 36±0.02

EX9-17 Millimeters

Prepare front and top views of Parts 4A and 4B on the basis of the given dimensions. Add tolerances to produce the stated clearances.

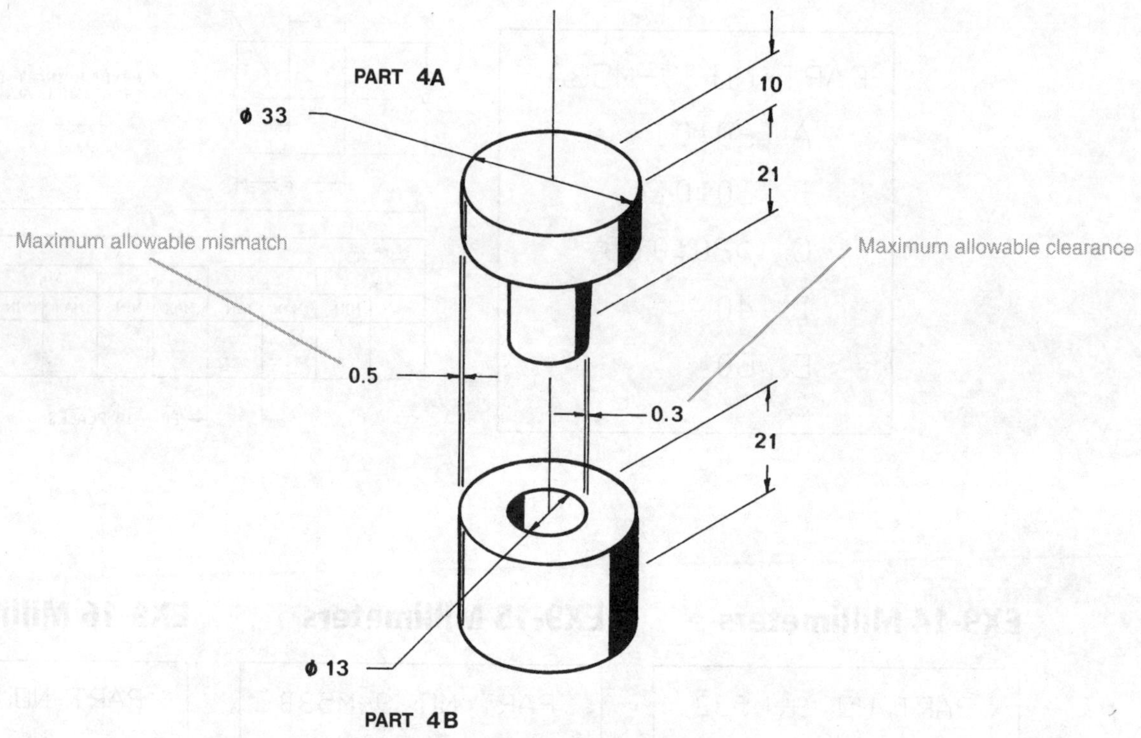

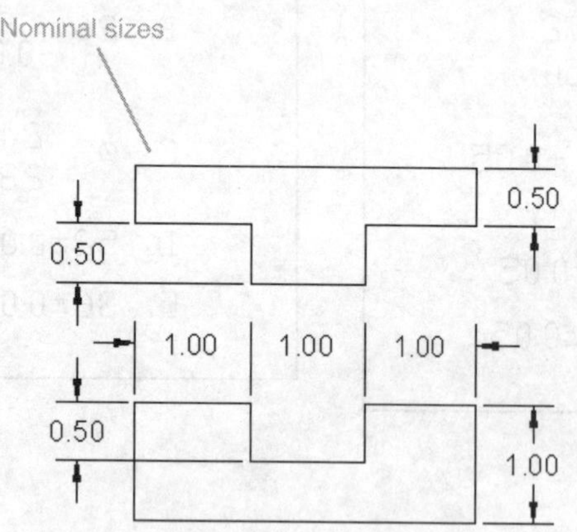

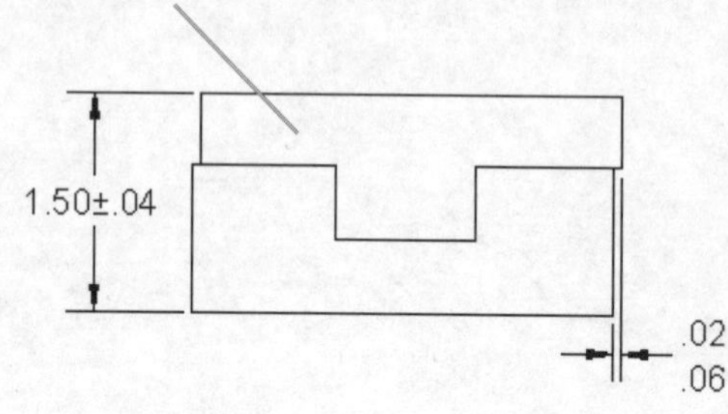

EX9-18 Inches

Redraw parts A and B, and add dimensions and tolerances to meet the "UPON ASSEMBLED" requirements.

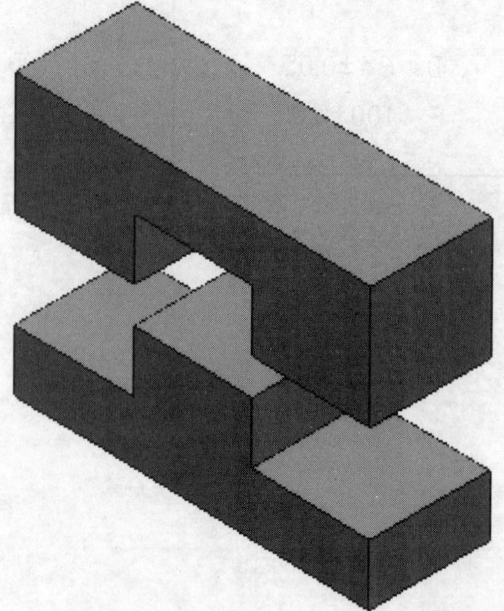

EX9-19 Millimeters

Draw a front and a top view of both given objects. Add dimensions and tolerances to meet the "FINAL CONDITION" requirements.

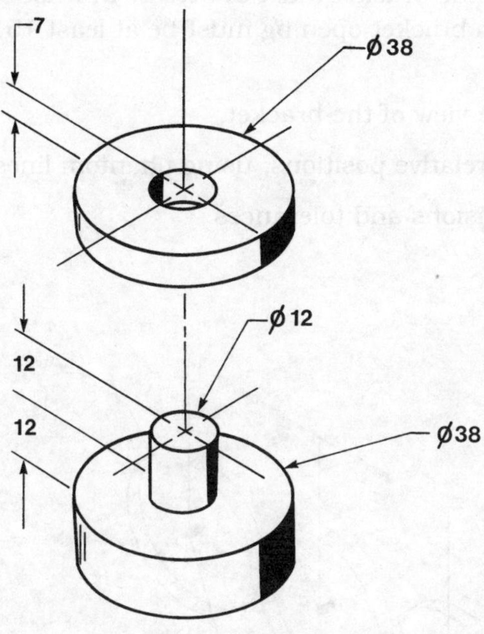

FINAL CONDITION

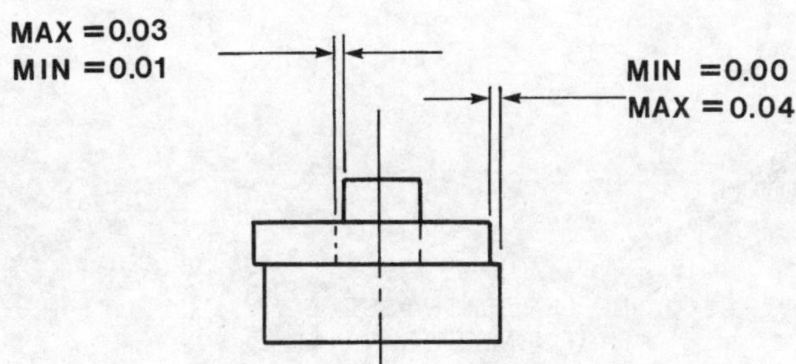

EX9-20 Inches

Given the nominal sizes that follow, dimension tolerance parts AM311 and AM312 so that they always fit together regardless of orientation. Further, dimension the overall lengths of each part so that, in the assembled condition, they will always pass through a clearance gauge with an opening of 90.00 ± 0.02.

In the assembled condition, both parts must always pass through the clearance gauge.

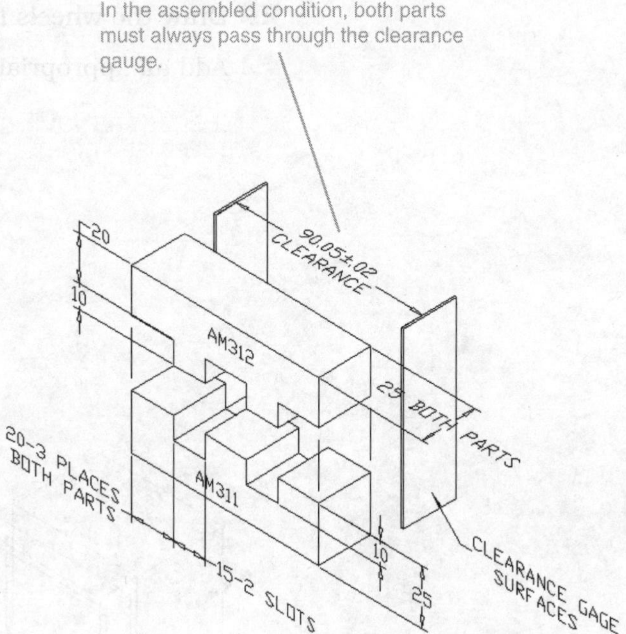

All given dimensions, except for the clearance gauge, are nominal.

EX9-21 Millimeters

Design a bracket that will support the three Ø100 wheels shown. The wheels will utilize three Ø5.00 ± 0.01 shafts attached to the bracket. The bottom of the bracket must have a minimum of 10 millimeters from the ground. The wall thickness of the bracket must always be at least 5 millimeters, and the minimum bracket opening must be at least 15 millimeters.

1. Prepare a front and a side view of the bracket.
2. Draw the wheels in their relative positions, using phantom lines.
3. Add all appropriate dimensions and tolerances.

ALL SIZES ARE NOMINAL, UNLESS OTHERWISE STATED.

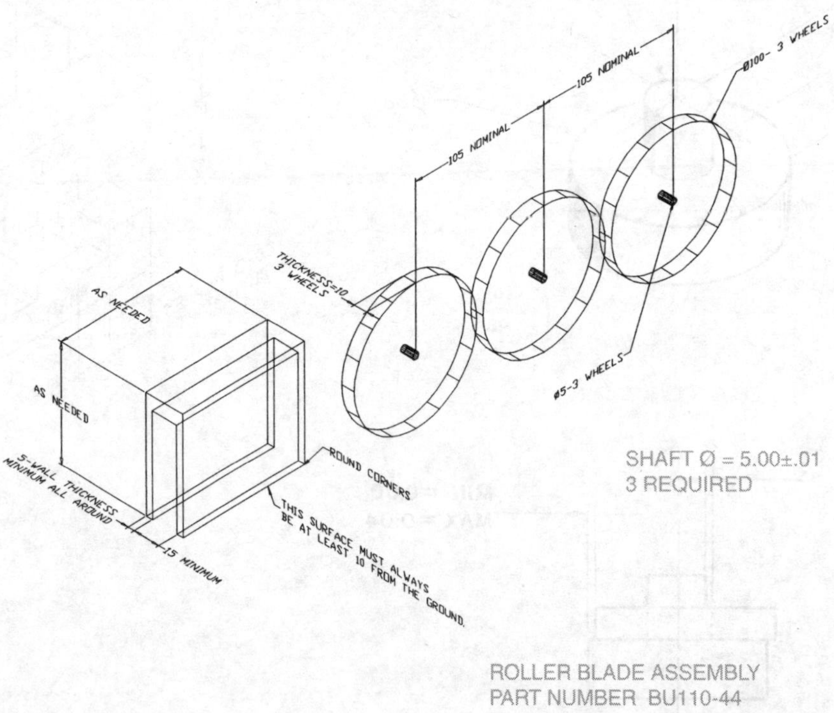

Given a top and bottom part in the floating condition, as shown in Figure EX9-22, add dimensions and tolerances to satisfy the given conditions. Size the top and bottom parts and fastener length as needed.

EX9-22 Inches–Clearance Fit

A. The distance between the holes is 2.00 nominal.

B. The diameter of the fasteners is Ø.375 nominal.

C. The fasteners have a total tolerance of 0.001.

D. The holes have a tolerance of 0.002.

E. The minimum allowable clearance between the fastener and the holes is 0.003.

F. The material is 0.375 inch thick.

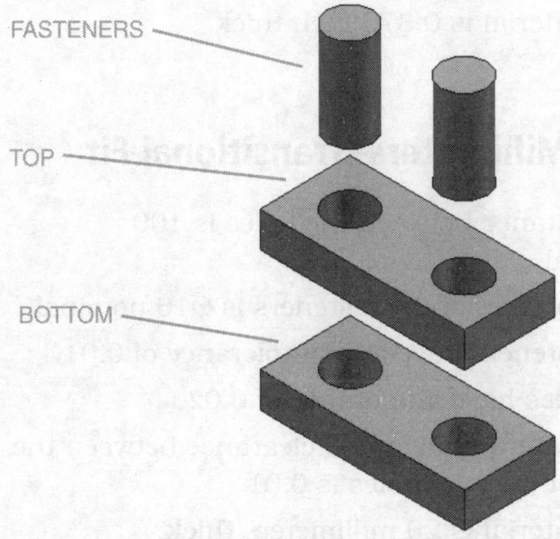

Figure EX9-22

EX9-23 Millimeters–Clearance Fit

A. The distance between the holes is 80 nominal.

B. The nominal diameter of the fasteners is Ø12.

C. The fasteners have a total tolerance of 0.05.

D. The holes have a tolerance of 0.03.

E. The minimum allowable clearance between the fastener and the holes is 0.02.

F. The material is 12 millimeters thick.

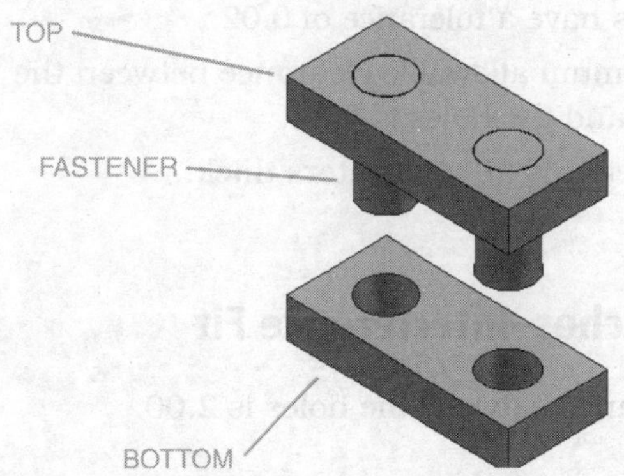

Figure EX9-23

EX9-24 Inches–Clearance Fit

A. The distance between the holes is 3.50 nominal.
B. The diameter of the fasteners is Ø.625.
C. The fasteners have a total tolerance of 0.005.
D. The holes have a tolerance of 0.003.
E. The minimum allowable clearance between the fastener and the holes is 0.002.
F. The material is 0.500 inch thick.

EX9-25 Millimeters–Clearance Fit

A. The distance between the holes is 120 nominal.
B. The diameter of the fasteners is Ø24 nominal.
C. The fasteners have a total tolerance of 0.01.
D. The holes have a tolerance of 0.02.
E. The minimum allowable clearance between the fastener and the holes is 0.04.
F. The material is 20 millimeters thick.

EX9-26 Inches–Interference Fit

A. The distance between the holes is 2.00 nominal.
B. The diameter of the fasteners is Ø.250 nominal.
C. The fasteners have a total tolerance of 0.001.
D. The holes have a tolerance of 0.002.
E. The maximum allowable interference between the fastener and the holes is 0.0065.
F. The material is 0.438 inch thick.

EX9-27 Millimeters–Interference Fit

A. The distance between the holes is 80 nominal.
B. The diameter of the fasteners is Ø10 nominal.
C. The fasteners have a total tolerance of 0.01.
D. The holes have a tolerance of 0.02.
E. The maximum allowable interference between the fastener and the holes is 0.032.
F. The material is 14 millimeters thick.

EX9-28 Inches–Locational Fit

A. The distance between the holes is 2.25 nominal.
B. The diameter of the fasteners is Ø.50 nominal.
C. The fasteners have a total tolerance of 0.001.
D. The holes have a tolerance of 0.002.
E. The minimum allowable clearance between the fastener and the holes is 0.0010.
F. The material is 0.370 inch thick.

EX9-29 Millimeters–Transitional Fit

A. The distance between the holes is 100 nominal.
B. The diameter of the fasteners is Ø16 nominal.
C. The fasteners have a total tolerance of 0.01.
D. The holes have a tolerance of 0.02.
E. The minimum allowable clearance between the fastener and the holes is 0.01.
F. The material is 20 millimeters thick.

Given a top and bottom part in the fixed condition, as shown in Figure EX9-23, add dimensions and tolerances to satisfy the given conditions. Size the top and bottom parts and fastener length as needed.

EX9-30 Inches–Clearance Fit

A. The distance between the holes is 2.00 nominal.
B. The diameter of the fasteners is Ø.375 nominal.
C. The fasteners have a total tolerance of 0.001.
D. The holes have a tolerance of 0.002.

E. The minimum allowable clearance between the fastener and the holes is 0.003.

F. The material is 0.375 inch thick.

EX9-31 Millimeters–Clearance Fit

A. The distance between the holes is 80 nominal.

B. The nominal diameter of the fasteners is Ø12.

C. The fasteners have a total tolerance of 0.05.

D. The holes have a tolerance of 0.03.

E. The minimum allowable clearance between the fastener and the holes is 0.02.

F. The material is 12 millimeters thick.

EX9-32 Inches–Clearance Fit

A. The distance between the holes is 3.50 nominal.

B. The diameter of the fasteners is Ø.625.

C. The fasteners have a total tolerance of 0.005.

D. The holes have a tolerance of 0.003.

E. The minimum allowable clearance between the fastener and the holes is 0.002.

F. The material is 0.500 inch thick.

EX9-33 Millimeters–Clearance Fit

A. The distance between the holes is 120 nominal.

B. The diameter of the fasteners is Ø24 nominal.

C. The fasteners have a total tolerance of 0.01.

D. The holes have a tolerance of 0.02.

E. The minimum allowable clearance between the fastener and the holes is 0.04.

F. The material is 20 millimeters thick.

EX9-34 Inches–Interference Fit

A. The distance between the holes is 2.00 nominal.

B. The diameter of the fasteners is Ø.250 nominal.

C. The fasteners have a total tolerance of 0.001.

D. The holes have a tolerance of 0.002.

E. The maximum allowable interference between the fastener and the holes is 0.0065.

F. The material is 0.438 inch thick.

EX9-35 Millimeters–Interference Fit

A. The distance between the holes is 80 nominal.

B. The diameter of the fasteners is Ø10 nominal.

C. The fasteners have a total tolerance of 0.01.

D. The holes have a tolerance of 0.02.

E. The maximum allowable interference between the fastener and the holes is 0.032.

F. The material is 14 millimeters thick.

EX9-36 Inches–Locational Fit

A. The distance between the holes is 2.25 nominal.

B. The diameter of the fasteners is Ø.50 nominal.

C. The fasteners have a total tolerance of 0.001.

D. The holes have a tolerance of 0.002.

E. The minimum allowable clearance between the fastener and the holes is 0.0010.

F. The material is 0.370 inch thick.

EX9-37 Millimeters–Transitional Fit

A. The distance between the holes is 100 nominal.

B. The diameter of the fasteners is Ø16 nominal.

C. The fasteners have a total tolerance of 0.01.

D. The holes have a tolerance of 0.02.

E. The minimum allowable clearance between the fastener and the holes is 0.01.

F. The material is 20 millimeters thick.

EX9-38 Millimeters

Given the following two assemblies, size the individual parts so that they always fit together. Create a drawing for each part, including dimensions and tolerances.

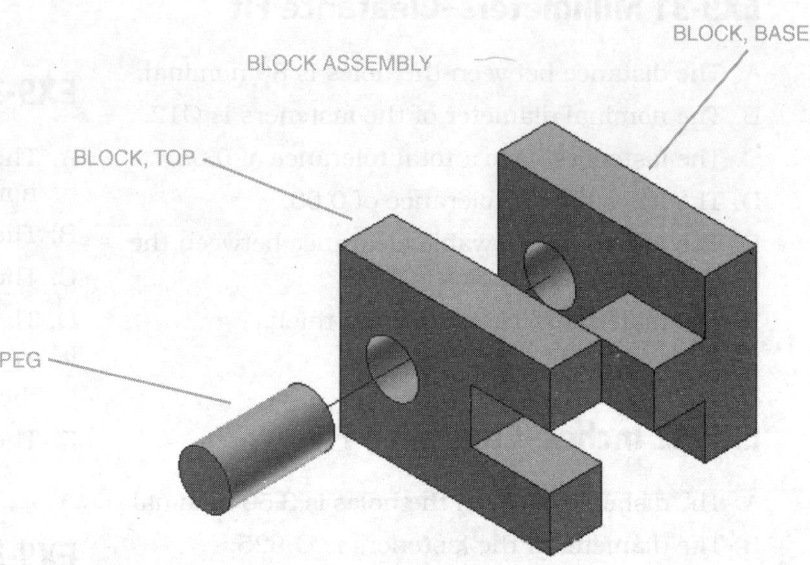

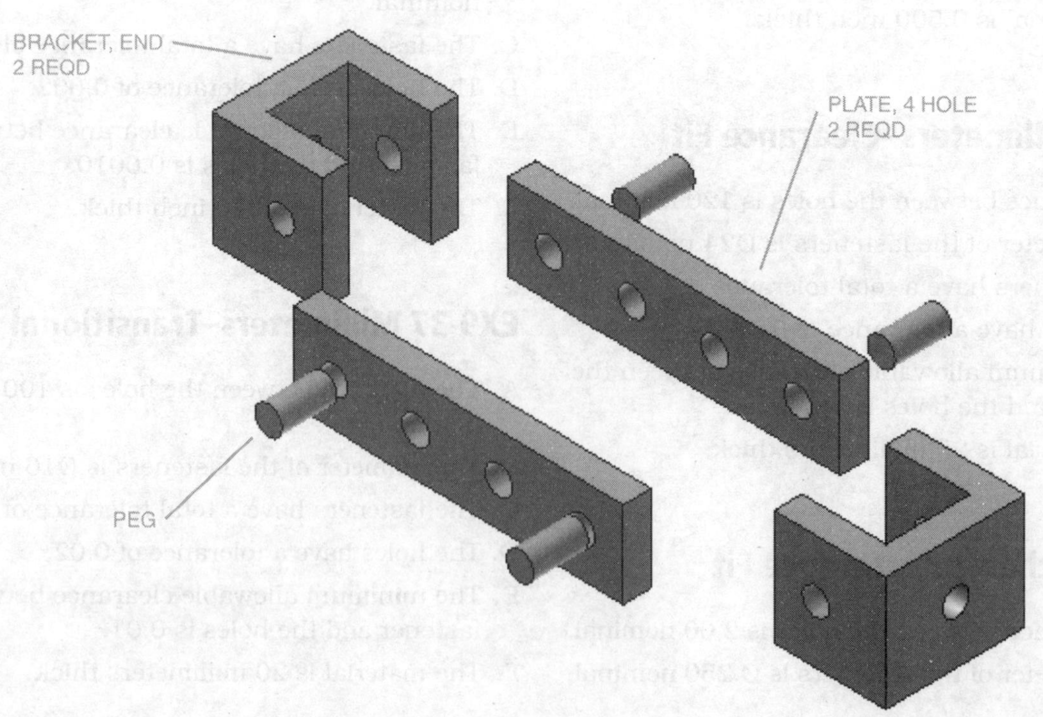

chapter ten
Geometric Tolerances

10-1 Introduction

Geometric tolerancing is a dimensioning and tolerancing system based on the geometric shape of an object. Surfaces may be defined in terms of their flatness or roundness, or in terms of how perpendicular or parallel they are to other surfaces.

Geometric tolerances allow a more exact definition of the shape of an object than do conventional coordinate-type tolerances. Objects can be toleranced in a manner more closely related to their design function, or so that their features and surfaces are more directly related to each other.

Figure 10-1 shows a square shape dimensioned and toleranced according to plus and minus tolerances. The resulting tolerance zone has an outside length of 51 and an inside length of 49 square. The defined tolerance zone allows any shape that falls within it to be deemed acceptable, or correctly manufactured. Figure 10-1 shows an exaggerated shape that fits within the defined tolerance zone and is not square, yet would be acceptable under the specified dimensions and tolerances. Geometric tolerancing can be used to more precisely define the tolerance zone when a more nearly square shape is required.

Figure 10-1

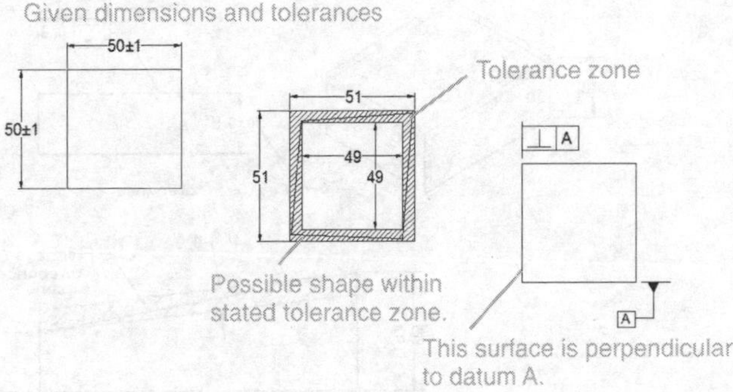

It should be pointed out that geometric tolerancing is not a panacea for all dimensioning and tolerancing problems. In many cases, coordinate tolerancing, as presented in Chapter 9, is sufficient to accurately define an object. Unnecessary or excessive use of geometric tolerances can increase production costs. Most objects are toleranced by using a combination of coordinate and geometric tolerances, depending on the design function of the object.

The key to using tolerances and selecting types of tolerances may be simply stated as, "Decimal points cost money." Every tolerance should be made as loose as possible while still maintaining the design integrity of the object. If a surface flatness is critical to the correct functioning of the object, then, of course, it will require a very close tolerance. But every tolerance should be considered individually and loosened wherever possible to make the object's manufacture easier and, therefore, less expensive.

10-2 Tolerances of Form

Tolerances of form are used to define the shape of a surface relative to itself. There are four classifications: flatness, straightness, roundness, and cylindricity. Tolerances of form are not related to other surfaces, but apply only to an individual surface.

10-3 Flatness

Flatness tolerances are used to define the amount of variation permitted in an individual surface. The surface is thought of as a plane not related to the rest of the object.

Figure 10-2 shows a rectangular object. How flat is the top surface? The given plus or minus tolerances allow a variation of ±0.5 across the surface. Without additional tolerances, the surface could look like a series of waves that vary between 30.5 and 29.5.

If the example in Figure 10-2 is assigned a flatness tolerance of 0.3, the height of the object, the feature tolerance could continue to vary according to the 30 ± 0.5 tolerance, but the surface itself could not vary by more than 0.3. In the most extreme condition, one end of the surface could be 30.5 above the bottom surface and the other end 29.5, but the surface would still be limited to within two parallel planes 0.3 apart, as shown.

To better understand the meaning of flatness, consider how the surface would be inspected. The surface would be acceptable if a gauge could be moved all around the surface and never varied by more than 0.3. See Figure 10-3. Every point in the plane must be within the specified tolerance.

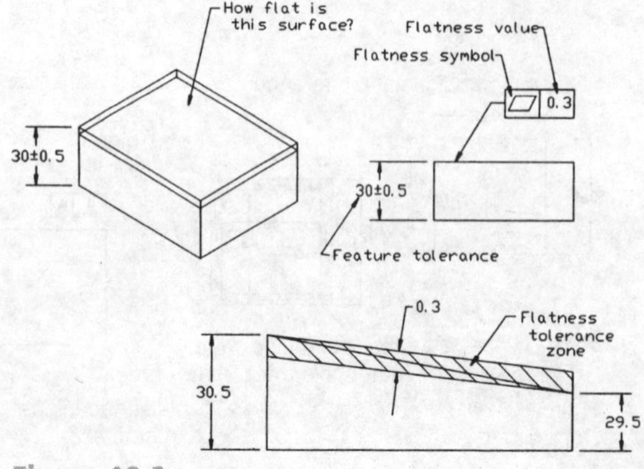

Figure 10-2

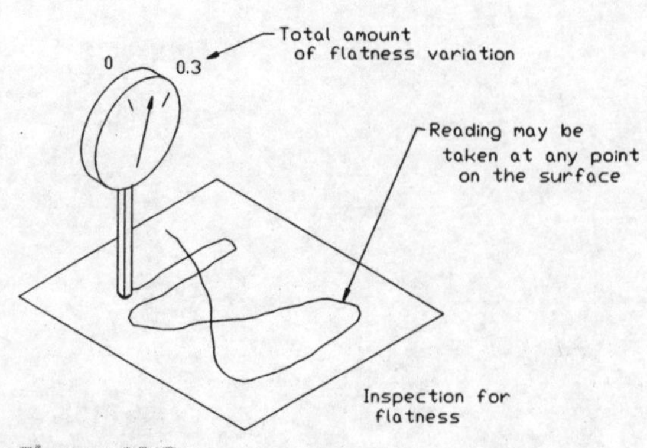

Figure 10-3

10-4 Straightness

Straightness tolerances are used to measure the variation of an individual feature along a straight line in a specified direction. Figure 10-4 shows an object with a straightness tolerance applied to its top surface. Straightness differs from flatness because straightness measurements are checked by moving a gauge directly across the surface in a single direction. The gauge is not moved randomly about the surface, as is required by flatness.

Straightness tolerances are most often applied to circular or matching objects to help ensure that the parts are not barreled or warped within the given feature tolerance range and therefore not fitted together well. Figure 10-5 shows a cylindrical object dimensioned and toleranced by the use of a standard feature tolerance. The surface of the cylinder may vary within the specified tolerance range, as shown.

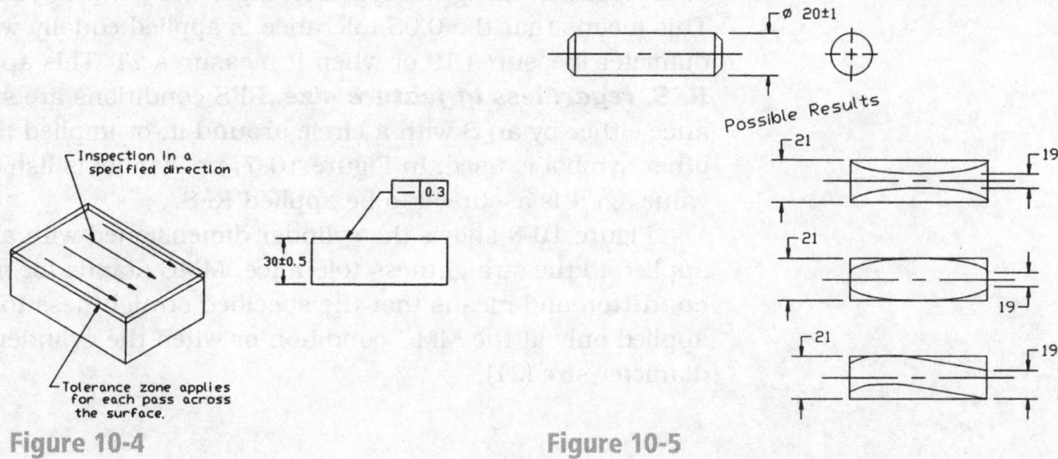

Figure 10-4

Figure 10-5

Figure 10-6 shows the same object shown in Figure 10-5, dimensioned and toleranced by use of the same feature tolerance, but also including a 0.05 straightness tolerance. The straightness tolerance limits the surface variation to 0.05, as shown.

Figure 10-6

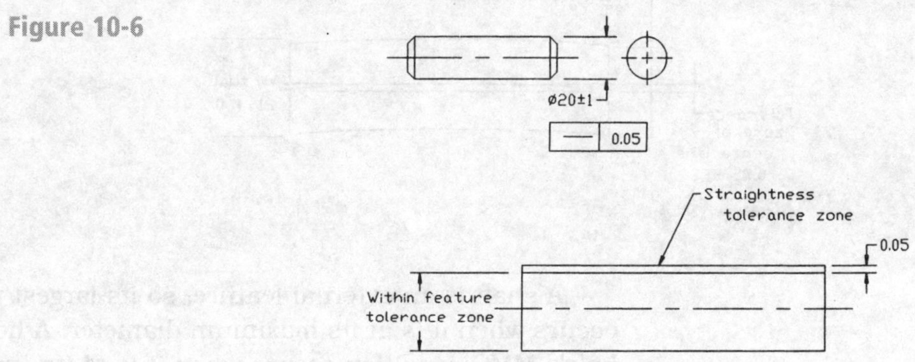

10-5 Straightness (RFS and MMC)

Figure 10-7 again shows the same cylinder shown in Figures 10-5 and 10-6. This time, the straightness tolerance is applied about the cylinder's centerline. This type of tolerance permits the feature tolerance and geometric tolerance to be used together to define a virtual condition. A virtual condition is used to determine the maximum possible size variation of the cylinder or

Figure 10-7

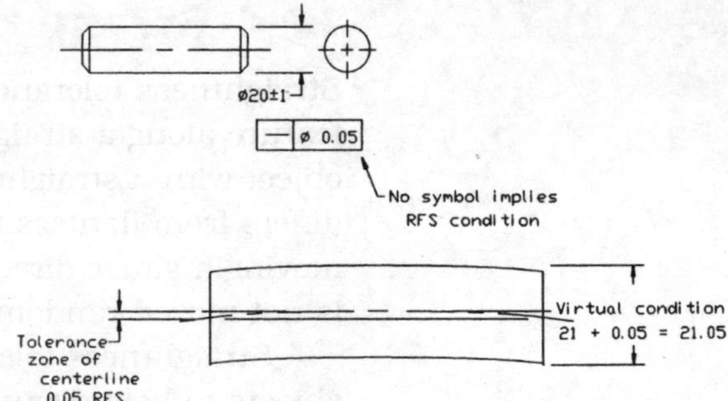

the smallest diameter hole that will always accept the cylinder. See Section 10-17.

The geometric tolerance specified in Figure 10-7 is applied to any circular segment along the cylinder, regardless of the cylinder's diameter. This means that the 0.05 tolerance is applied equally when the cylinder's diameter measures 19 or when it measures 21. This application is called ***RFS, regardless of feature size.*** RFS conditions are specified in a tolerance either by an S with a circle around it, or implied tacitly when no other symbol is used. In Figure 10-7, no symbol is listed after the 0.05 value, so it is assumed to be applied RFS.

Figure 10-8 shows the cylinder dimensioned with an ***MMC*** condition applied to the straightness tolerance. MMC stands for ***maximum material condition*** and means that the specified straightness tolerance (0.05) is applied only at the MMC condition or when the cylinder is at its maximum diameter size (21).

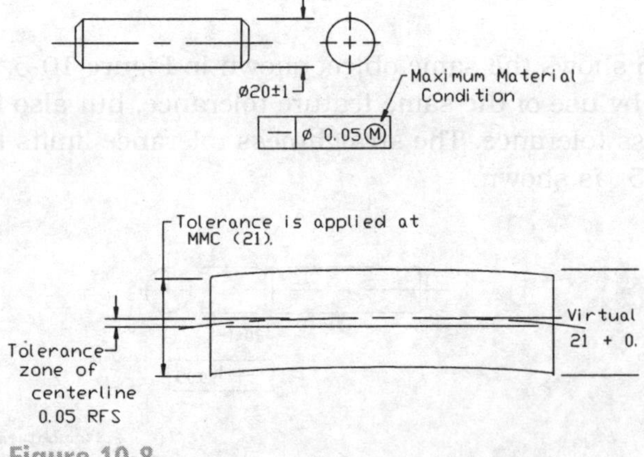

Measured Size	Allowable Tolerance Zone	Virtual Condition
21.0	0.05	21.05
20.9	0.15	21.15
20.8	0.25	21.25
⋮	⋮	⋮
20.0	1.05	22.05
⋮	⋮	⋮
19.0	2.05	23.05

Figure 10-8

A shaft is an external feature, so its largest possible size, or MMC, occurs when it is at its maximum diameter. A hole is an internal feature. A hole's MMC condition occurs when it is at its smallest diameter. The MMC condition for holes will be discussed later in the chapter, along with positional tolerances.

Applying a straightness tolerance at MMC allows for a variation in the resulting tolerance zone. Because the 0.05 flatness tolerance is applied at MMC, the virtual condition is still 21.05, the same as with the RFS condition; however, the tolerance is applied only at MMC. As the cylinder's diameter varies within the specified feature tolerance range, the acceptable tolerance zone may vary to maintain the same virtual condition.

Figure 10-8 lists ways in which the tolerance zone varies as the cylinder's diameter varies. When the cylinder is at its largest size, or MMC, the tolerance zone equals 0.05, or the specified flatness variation. When the cylinder is at its smallest diameter, the tolerance zone equals 2.05, or the total feature size plus the total flatness size. In all variations, the virtual size remains the same, so at any given cylinder diameter value, the size of the tolerance zone can be determined by subtracting the cylinder's diameter value from the virtual condition.

Figure 10-9 shows a comparison between different methods used to dimension and tolerance a .750 shaft. The first example uses only a feature tolerance. This tolerance sets an upper limit of .755 and a lower limit of .745. Any variations within that range are acceptable.

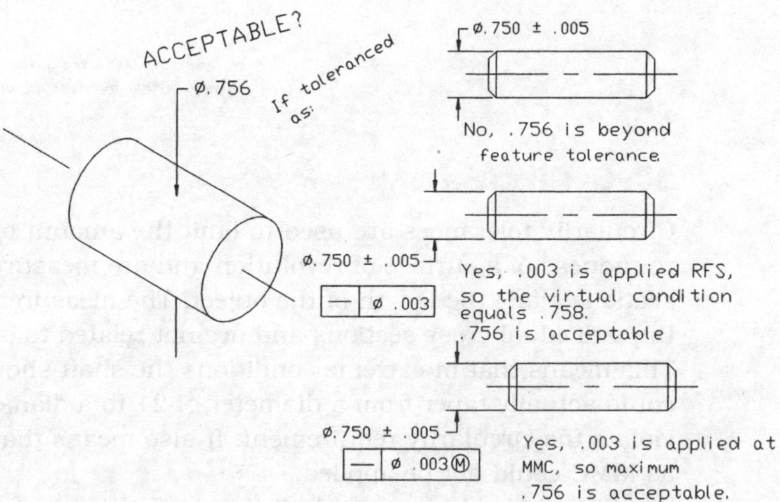

Figure 10-9

The RFS condition does not allow the tolerance zone to grow, as does the same tolerance applied at MMC.

The second example in Figure 10-9 sets a straightness tolerance of .003 about the cylinder's centerline. No conditions are defined, so the tolerance is applied RFS. This limits the variations in straightness to .003 at all feature sizes. For example, when the shaft is at its smallest possible feature size, .745, the .003 still applies. This means that a shaft measuring .745 that had a straightness variation greater than .003 would be rejected. If the tolerance has been applied at MMC, the part would be accepted. This does not mean that straightness tolerances should always be applied at MMC. If straightness is critical to the design integrity or function of the part, then straightness should be applied in the RFS condition.

The third example in Figure 10-9 applies the straightness tolerance about the centerline at MMC. This tolerance creates a virtual condition of .758. The MMC condition allows the tolerance to vary as the feature tolerance varies, so when the shaft is at its smallest feature size, .745, a straightness tolerance of .013 is acceptable (.010 feature tolerance +.003 straightness tolerance).

If the tolerance specification for the cylinder shown in Figure 10-9 were to have a 0.000 tolerance applied at MMC, it would mean that the shaft would have to be perfectly straight at MMC, or when the shaft was at its maximum value (.755); however, the straightness tolerance could vary as the feature size varied, as discussed for the other tolerance conditions. A 0.000 tolerance means that the MMC and the virtual conditions are equal.

Figure 10-10 shows a very long .750-diameter shaft. Its straightness tolerance includes a length qualifier that serves to limit the straightness variations over each inch of the shaft length and prevents excess waviness over the full length. The tolerance Ø.002/1.000 means that the total straightness may vary over the entire length of the shaft by .003 but that the variation is limited to .002 per 1.000 of shaft length.

Figure 10-10

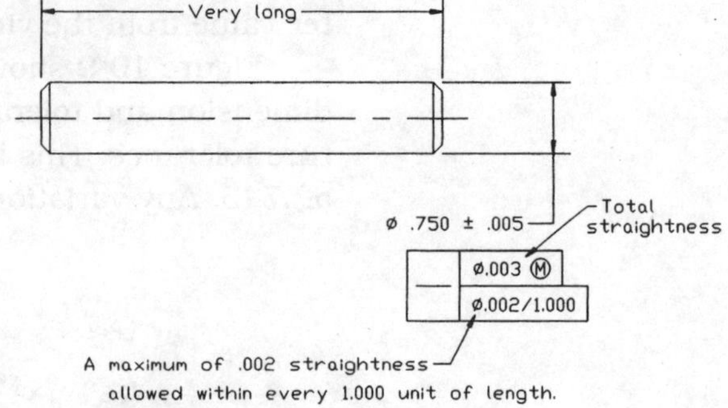

10-6 Circularity

Circularity tolerances are used to limit the amount of variation in the roundness of a surface of revolution and are measured at individual cross sections along the length of the object. The measurements are limited to the individual cross sections and are not related to other cross sections. This means that in extremc conditions the shaft shown in Figure 10-11 could actually taper from a diameter of 21 to a diameter of 19 and never violate the circularity requirement. It also means that qualifications such as MMC could not be applied.

Figure 10-11 shows a shaft that includes a feature tolerance and a circularity tolerance of 0.07. To understand circularity tolerances, consider an individual cross section, or slice, of the cylinder. The shape of the outside edge of the slice varies around the slice. The difference between the maximum diameter and the minimum diameter of the slice can never exceed the stated circularity tolerance.

Circularity tolerances can be applied to tapered sections and spheres, as shown in Figure 10-12. In both applications, circularity is measured around individual cross sections, as it was for the shaft shown in Figure 10-11.

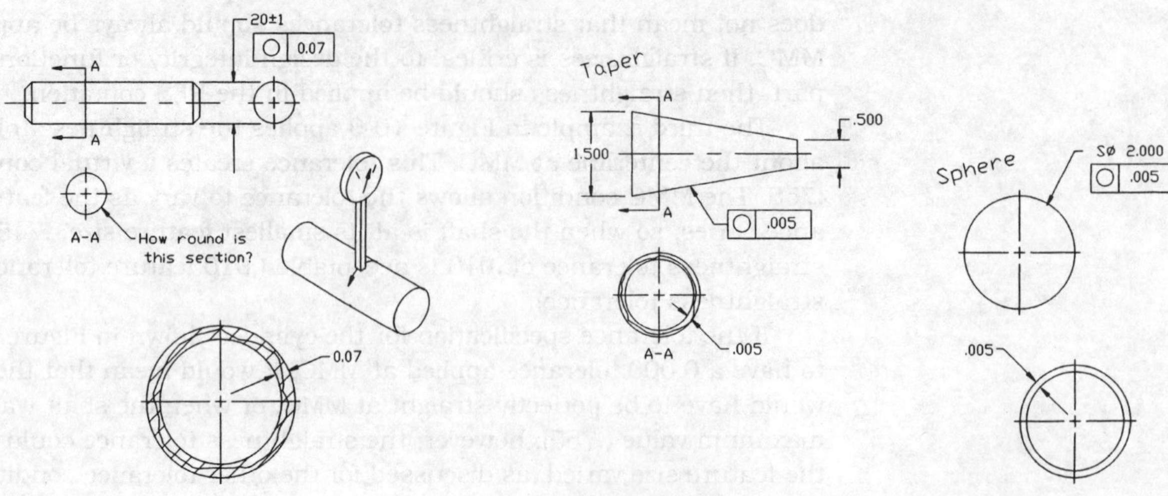

Figure 10-11 **Figure 10-12**

10-7 Cylindricity

Cylindricity tolerances are used to define a tolerance zone both around individual circular cross sections of an object and also along its length. The resulting tolerance zone looks like two concentric cylinders.

Figure 10-13 shows a shaft which includes a cylindricity tolerance that establishes a tolerance zone of .007. This means that if the maximum measured diameter is determined to be .755, the minimum diameter cannot be less than .748 anywhere on the cylindrical surface. Figure 10-14 shows how to draw the feature control frames that surround the tolerance symbol and size specifications.

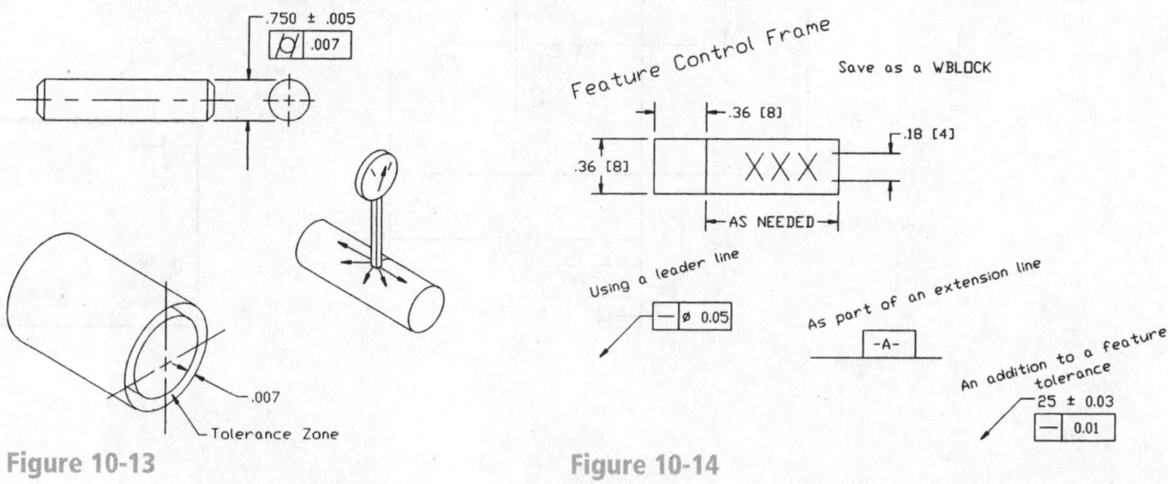

Figure 10-13

Figure 10-14

Cylindricity and circularity are somewhat analogous to flatness and straightness. Flatness and cylindricity are concerned with variations across an entire surface or plane. In the case of cylindricity, the plane is shaped like a cylinder. Straightness and circularity are concerned with variations of a single element of a surface—that is, a straight line across the plane in a specified direction for straightness, and a path around a single cross section for circularity.

10-8 Geometric Tolerances Created by Using AutoCAD

Geometric tolerances are tolerances that limit dimensional variations on the basis of geometric properties of an object. Figure 10-15 shows a list of

	TYPE OF TOLERANCE	CHARACTERISTIC	SYMBOL
FOR INDIVIDUAL FEATURES	FORM	STRAIGHTNESS	⏤
		FLATNESS	⏥
		CIRCULARITY	○
		CYLINDRICITY	⌭
INDIVIDUAL OR RELATED FEATURES	PROFILE	PROFILE OF A LINE	⌒
		PROFILE OF A SURFACE	⌓
RELATED FEATURES	ORIENTATION	ANGULARITY	∠
		PERPENDICULARITY	⊥
		PARALLELISM	//
	LOCATION	POSITION	⌖
		CONCENTRICITY	◎
	RUNOUT	CIRCULAR RUNOUT	↗
		TOTAL RUNOUT	⌰

TERM	SYMBOL
AT MAXIMUM MATERIAL CONDITION	Ⓜ
REGARDLESS OF FEATURE SIZE	Ⓢ
AT LEAST MATERIAL CONDITION	Ⓛ
PROJECTED TOLERANCE ZONE	Ⓟ
DIAMETER	⌀
SPHERICAL DIAMETER	S⌀
RADIUS	R
SPHERICAL RADIUS	SR
REFERENCE	( )
ARC LENGTH	⌒

Figure 10-15

geometric tolerance symbols. Figure 10-16 shows an object dimensioned by the use of geometric tolerances. The geometric tolerances were created as follows.

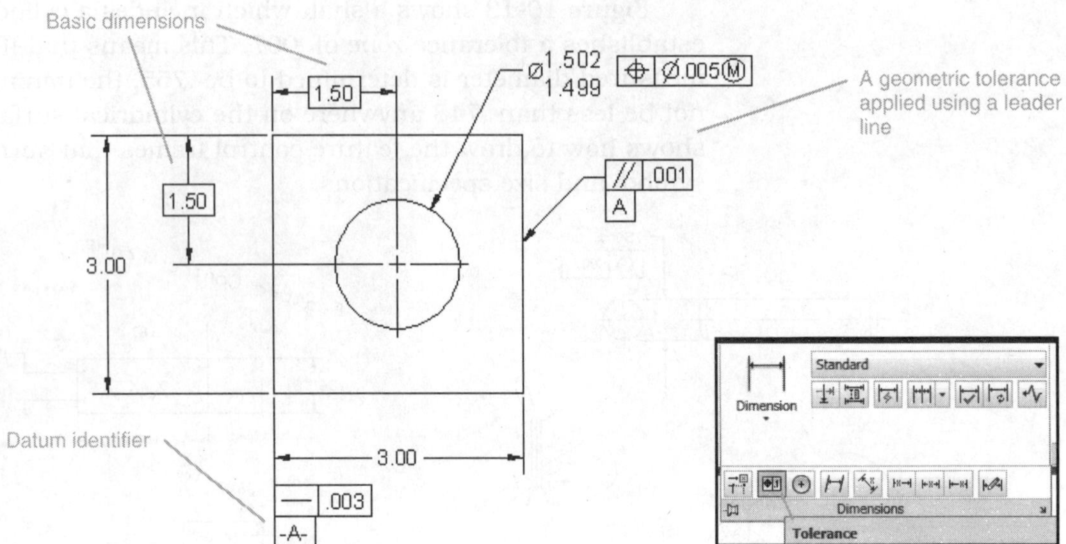

Figure 10-16

To Define a Datum

1 Select the **Tolerance** tool from the **Dimensions** panel.

The **Geometric Tolerance** dialog box will appear. See Figure 10-17.

Figure 10-17

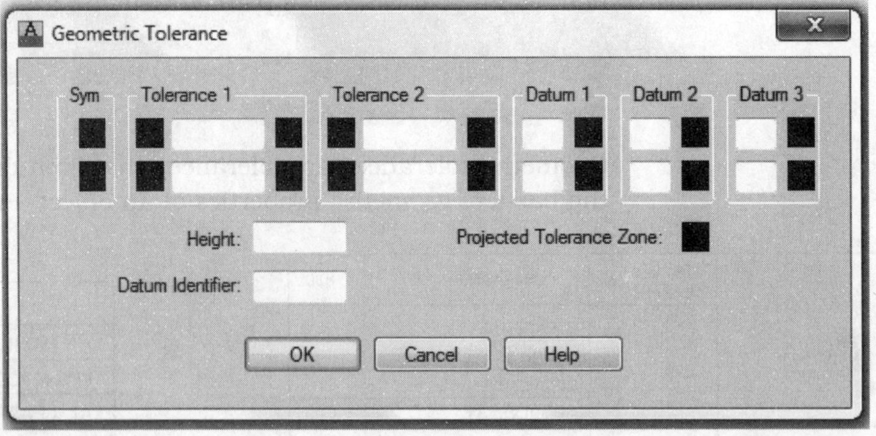

2 Click the **Datum Identifier** box and type **A**; then click **OK**.

Command: _tolerance
Enter tolerance location:

3 Position the datum identifier, and press the left mouse button. See Figure 10-16.

To Define a Straightness Value

1. Select the **Tolerance** tool from the **Dimensions** panel.

   The **Geometric Tolerance** dialog box will appear.

2. Select the top open box under the heading **Sym.**

   The **Symbol** dialog box will appear. See Figure 10-18.

Figure 10-18

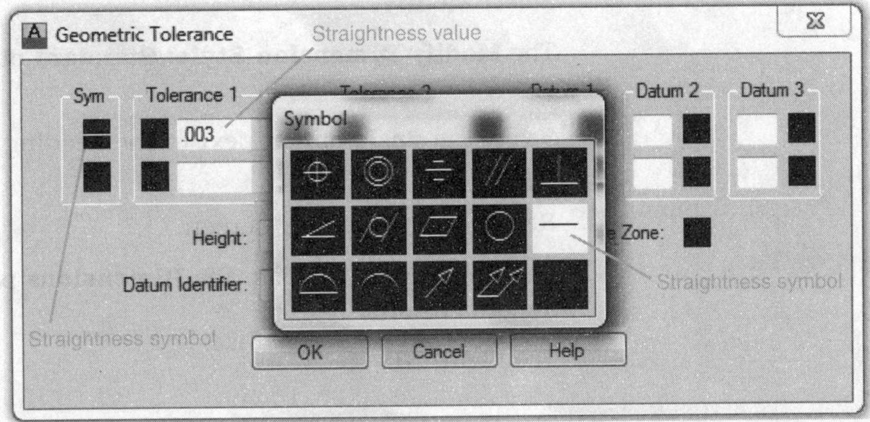

3. Select the straightness symbol, then **OK.**

   The **Geometric Tolerance** dialog box will reappear with the straightness symbol in the first box under the heading **Sym.**

4. Click the open **Tolerance 1** box, and type **.003;** click **OK.**

   Command: _tolerance
   Enter tolerance location:

5. Position the straightness tolerance, and press the left mouse button

   See Figure 10-19. Use the **Move** and **Osnap** tools if necessary to reposition the tolerance box. See Figure 10-16.

Figure 10-19

A straightness tolerance

.003

To Create a Positional Tolerance

A ***positional tolerance*** is used to locate and tolerance a hole in an object. Positional tolerances require base locating dimensions for the hole's center point. Positional tolerances also require a feature tolerance to define the diameter tolerances of the hole, and a geometric tolerance to define the position tolerance for the hole's center point.

To Create a Basic Dimension

See the two 1.50 dimensions in Figure 10-16 used to locate the center position of the hole.

1. Access the **Dimension Style Manager,** or type **DDIM** in response to a command prompt.

   The **Dimension Style Manager** dialog box will appear.

2. Select **Modify.**

   The **Modify Dimension Style: Standard** dialog box will appear. See Figure 9-7.

3. Select the **Basic** option next to the heading **Method** in the **Tolerance format** box.

4. Return to the drawing screen.

5. Use the **Linear** tool from the **Dimensions** panel, and add the appropriate dimensions.

   See Figure 10-16.

To Create Basic Dimensions from Existing Dimensions

Figure 10-20 shows a shape that includes dimensions. It has been decided to change two of the dimensions to basic dimensions. The procedure is as follows.

Figure 10-20

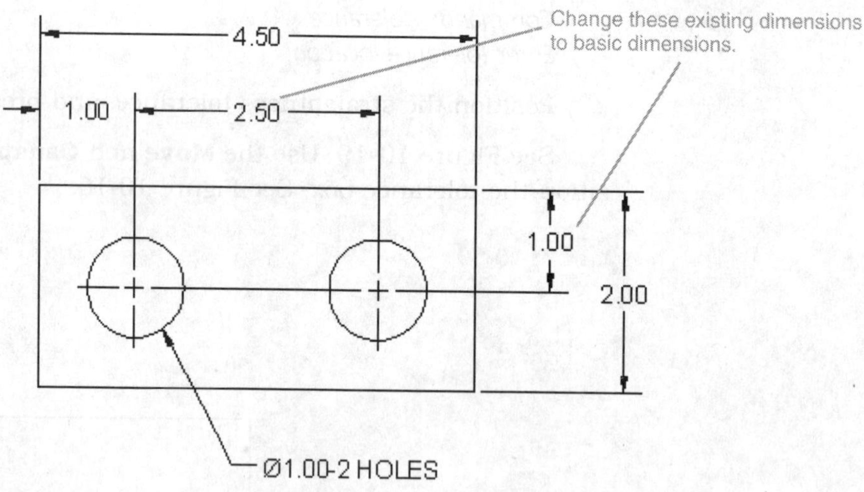

1. Click on the **2.50** dimension.

   Blue squares will appear on the dimension.

2. Right-click the mouse.

   A dialog box will appear.

3. Select the **Properties** option.

   The **Properties** dialog box will appear.

See Figure 10-21.

4 Use the scroll arrow next to the **P** in **Properties,** and locate the **Tolerances** options.

5 Click the open space next to the word **None,** and scroll down to the **Basic** option.
See Figure 10-22.

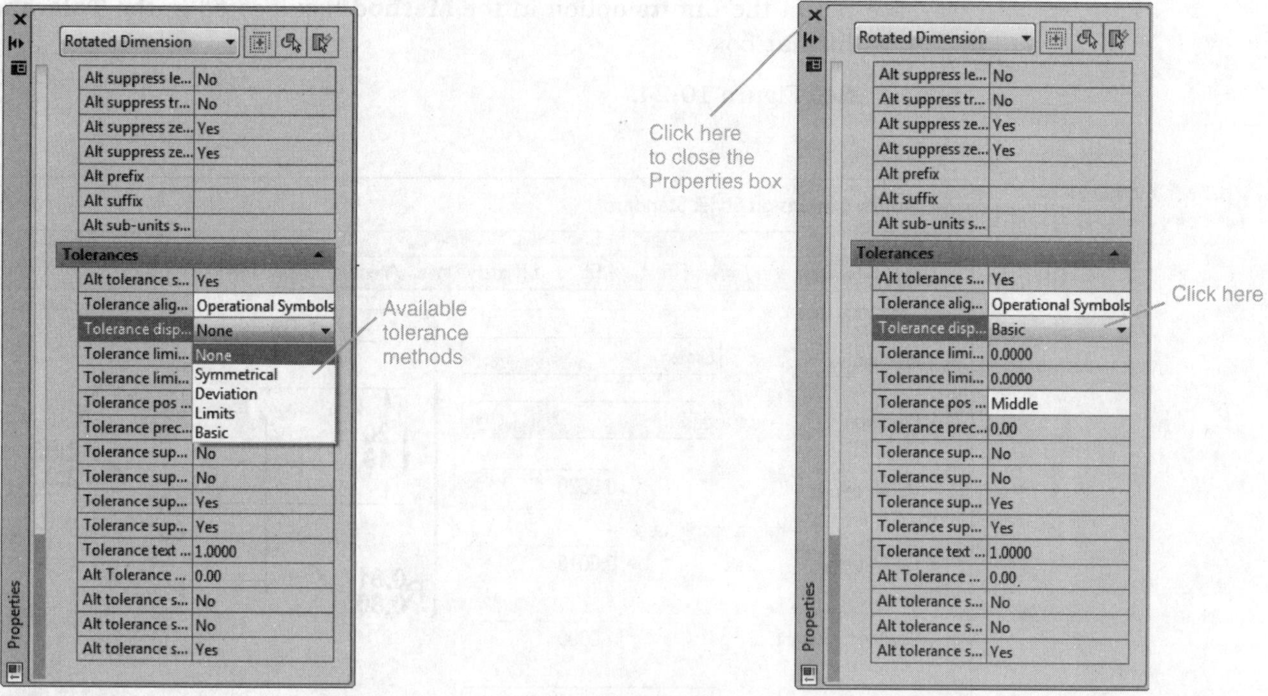

Figure 10-21 Figure 10-22

6 Scroll down the options, and select the **Basic** option; then click the close **X,** and press the **<Esc>** key.

7 Repeat the procedure for the vertical 1.00 dimension.

Figure 10-23 shows the final results.

Figure 10-23

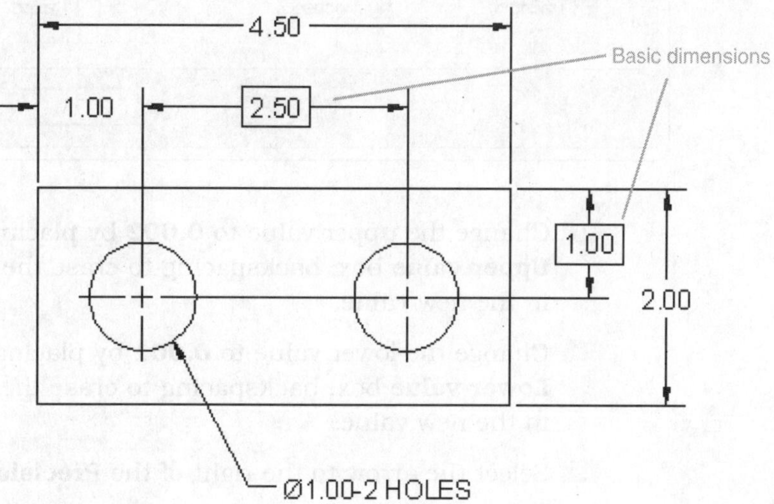

To Add a Limit Feature Tolerance to a Hole

1. Access the **Dimension Style Manager,** or type **DDIM** in response to a command prompt.

   The **Dimension Style Manager** dialog box will appear.

2. Select **Modify,** then the **Tolerances** tab.

   The **Modify Dimension Style: Standard** dialog box will appear.

3. Select the **Limits** option in the **Method** box located in the **Tolerance format** box.

   See Figure 10-24.

Figure 10-24

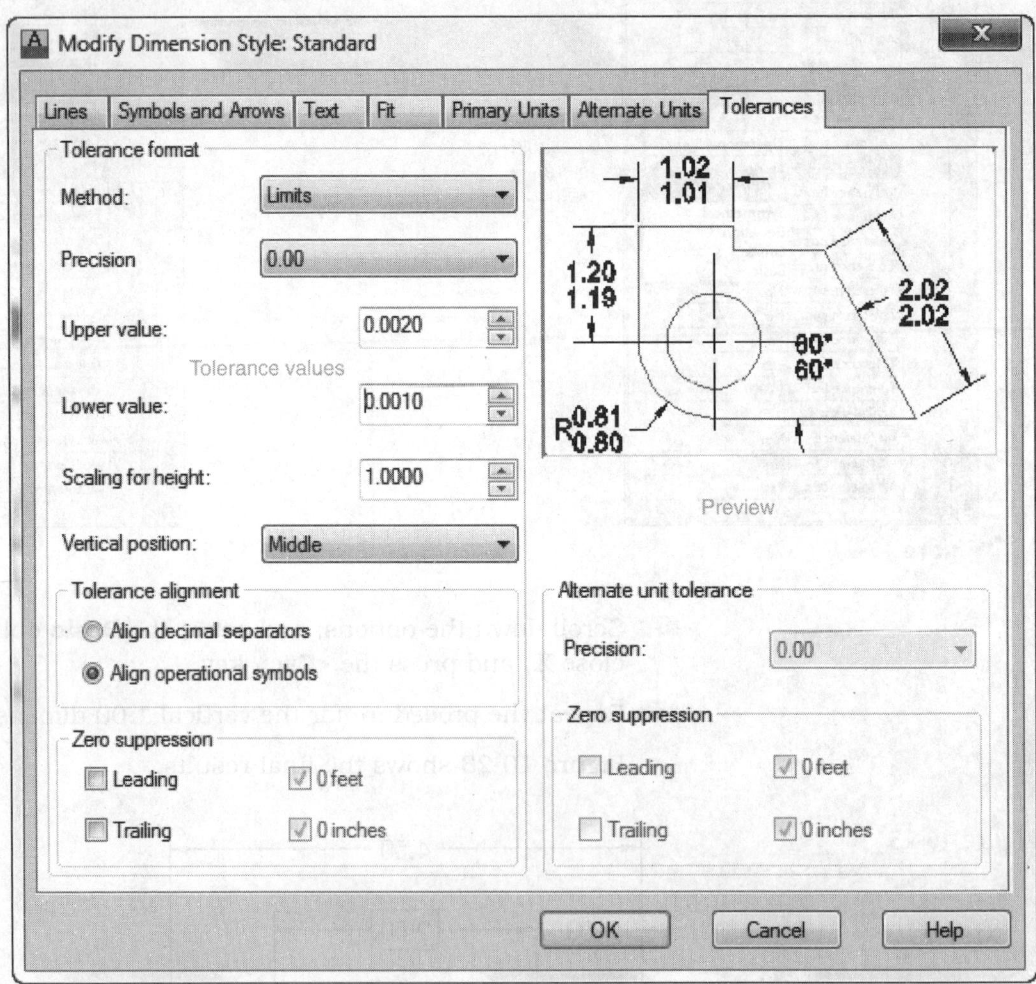

4. Change the upper value to **0.002** by placing the cursor within the **Upper value** box, backspacing to erase the existing value, and typing in the new value.

5. Change the lower value to **0.001** by placing the cursor within the **Lower value** box, backspacing to erase the existing value, and typing in the new value.

6. Select the arrow to the right of the **Precision** box.

   The **Precision** options will cascade down.

7 Change the precision for both **Dimension** and **Tolerance** boxes to three decimal places (**0.000**).

See Figure 10-24. AutoCAD will truncate any input according to the number of decimal places allowed by the precision settings. If the precision settings had been two decimal places (0.00), the resulting limit dimensions would have both been 1.50. The values defined in the third decimal place would have been ignored.

8 Return to the drawing screen.

9 Select the **Diameter** tool on the **Dimensions** panel.

Select arc or circle:

10 Select the hole.

Dimension line location (Text Angle):

11 Locate the diameter dimension.

To Add a Positional Tolerance to the Hole's Feature Tolerance

1 Select the **Tolerance** tool on the **Dimensions** panel.

The **Geometric Tolerance** dialog box will appear.

2 Select the top open box under the heading **Sym.**

The **Symbol** dialog box will appear with the positioning symbol highlighted. See Figure 10-25.

Figure 10-25

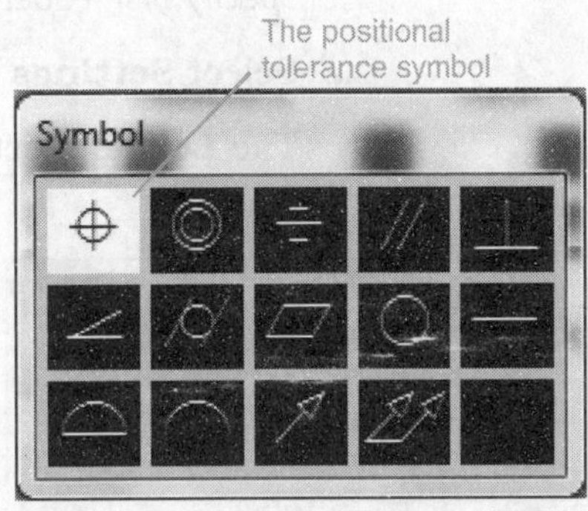

3 Select the top left open box under the heading **Tolerance 1.**

A diameter symbol will appear.

4 Select the **Value** box and type **0.0005.**

The numbers will appear in the box.

5 Select the top far-right open box under the heading **Tolerance 1.**

The **Material Condition** dialog box will appear.

6 Select the maximum material condition (MMC) symbol (the circle with an M in it).

7 Select **OK.**

The MMC symbol will appear in the material condition box in the **Geometric Tolerance** dialog box. Figure 10-26 shows the resulting **Geometric Tolerance** dialog box.

Figure 10-26

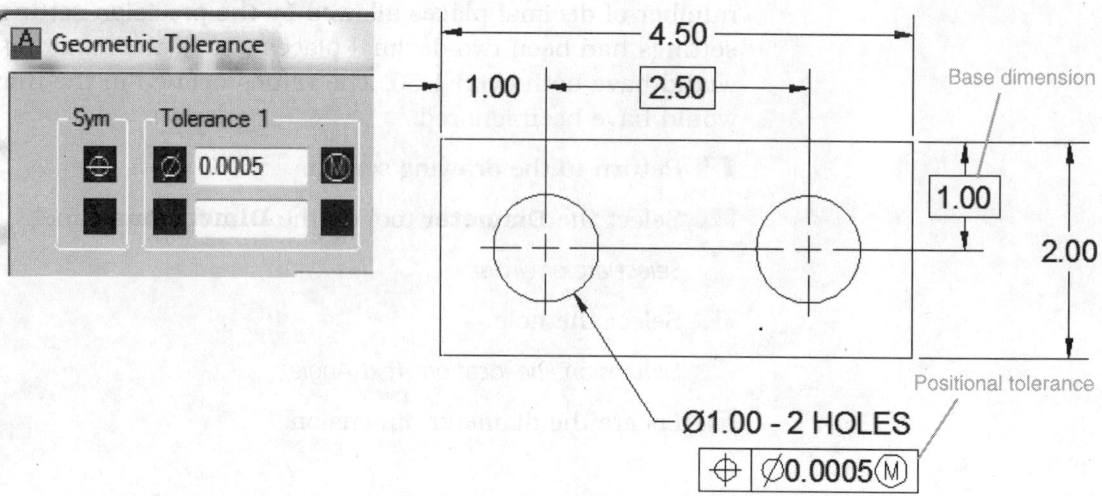

8 Select **OK.**

Enter tolerance location:

9 Locate the tolerance box.

Use the **Move** and **Osnap** commands to position the box, if necessary.

To Add a Geometric Tolerance with a Leader Line

1 Type **qleader** in response to a command prompt.

Specify first leader point, or [Settings] <Settings>:

2 Select **Settings** by pressing **Enter.**

The **Leader Settings** dialog box will appear. See Figure 10-27.

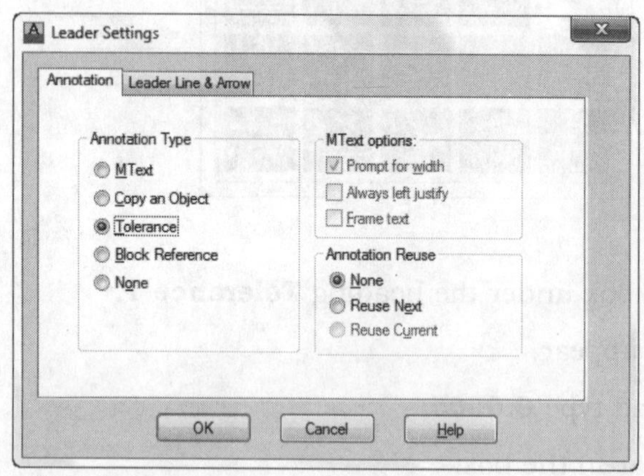

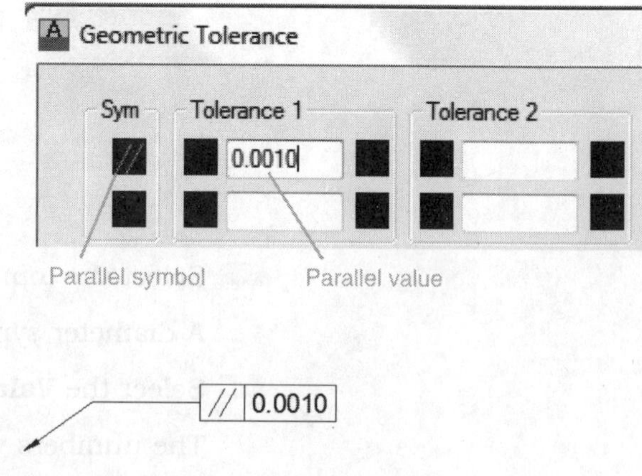

Figure 10-27

3 Select the **Tolerance** option in the **Annotation Type** box, then **OK.**

Specify first leader point, or [Settings] <Settings>:

4 Select a starting point for the leader line.

Specify next point:

5. Draw a short horizontal segment.

   The **Geometric Tolerance** dialog box will appear. See Figure 10-27.
6. Select the top **Sym** box.

   The **Symbol** dialog box will appear.
7. Select the parallel symbol.
8. Select the open box under the heading **Tolerance 1,** and type **0.0010.**
9. Select the open box under the heading **Datum 1;** type **A,** then **OK.**

   See Figure 10-27.

10-9 Tolerances of Orientation

Tolerances of orientation are used to relate a feature or surface to another feature or surface. Tolerances of orientation include perpendicularity, parallelism, and angularity. They may be applied under RFS or MMC conditions, but they cannot be applied to individual features by themselves. To define a surface as parallel to another surface is very much like assigning a flatness value to the surface. The difference is that flatness applies only within the surface; every point on the surface is related to a defined set of limiting parallel planes. Parallelism defines every point in the surface relative to another surface. The two surfaces are therefore directly related to each other, and the condition of one affects the other.

Orientation tolerances are used with locational tolerances. A feature is first located, and then it is oriented within the locational tolerances. This means that the orientation tolerance must always be less than the locational tolerances. The next four sections will further explain this requirement.

10-10 Datums

A ***datum*** is a point, axis, or surface used as a starting reference point for dimensions and tolerances. Figure 10-28 shows a rectangular object with three datum planes labeled A, B, and C. The three datum planes are called

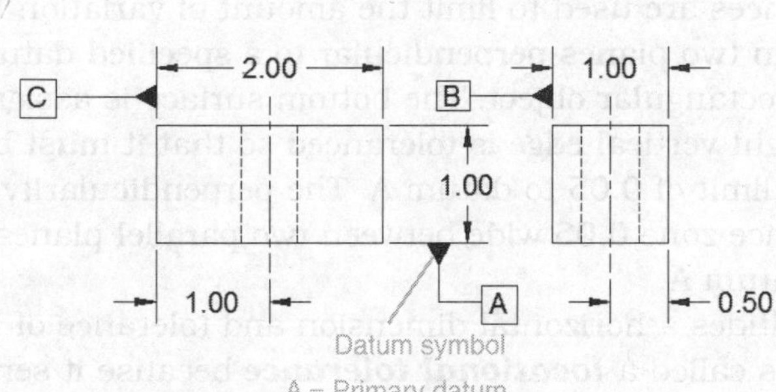

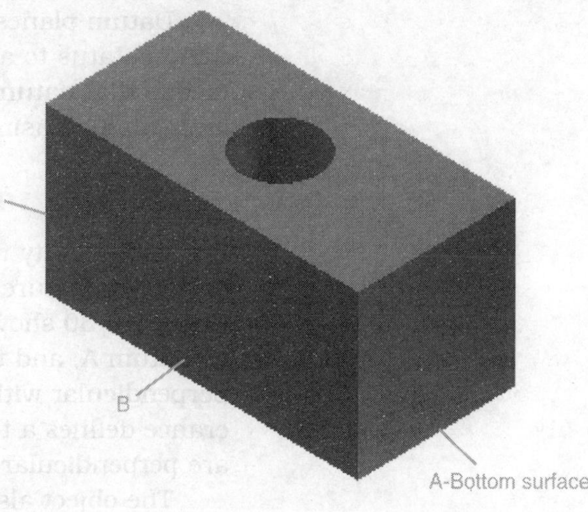

Figure 10-28

the primary, secondary, and tertiary datums, respectively. The three datum planes are, by definition, oriented exactly 90° to one another. A datum surface is defined by placing a filled datum triangle at the end of a leader line.

Figure 10-29 shows the A datum symbol. It is created as follows.

1. Access the **Multileader Style Manager** by clicking the arrowhead in the lower right corner of the **Leaders** panel under the **Annotate** tab.
2. Click the **Modify** option.
3. In the **Arrowhead** box, scroll down the symbols options and select the **Datum triangle filled** option.
4. Click OK.

Figure 10-29

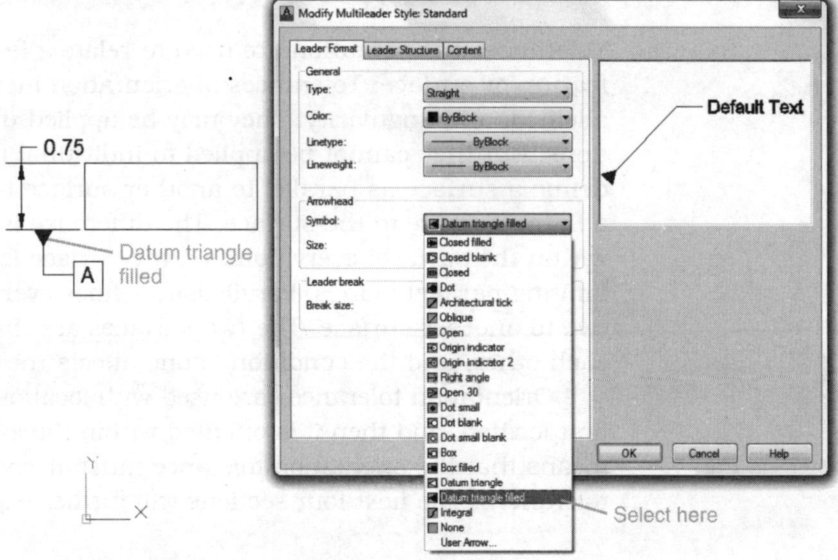

> **NOTE**
> Either Datum triangle filled or Datum triangle is acceptable.

Datum planes are assumed to be perfectly flat. When assigning a datum status to a surface, be sure that the surface is reasonably flat. This means that datum surfaces should be toleranced by using surface finishes, or created by using machine techniques that produce flat surfaces.

10-11 Perpendicularity

Perpendicularity tolerances are used to limit the amount of variation for a surface or feature within two planes perpendicular to a specified datum. Figure 10-30 shows a rectangular object. The bottom surface is assigned as datum A, and the right vertical edge is toleranced so that it must be perpendicular within a limit of 0.05 to datum A. The perpendicularity tolerance defines a tolerance zone 0.05 wide between two parallel planes that are perpendicular to datum A.

The object also includes a horizontal dimension and tolerance of 40 ± 1. This tolerance is called a ***locational tolerance*** because it serves to locate the right edge of the object. As with rectangular coordinate tolerances discussed in Chapter 9, the 40 ± 1 controls the location of the edge—that is, how far away or how close it can be to the left edge—but

Figure 10-30

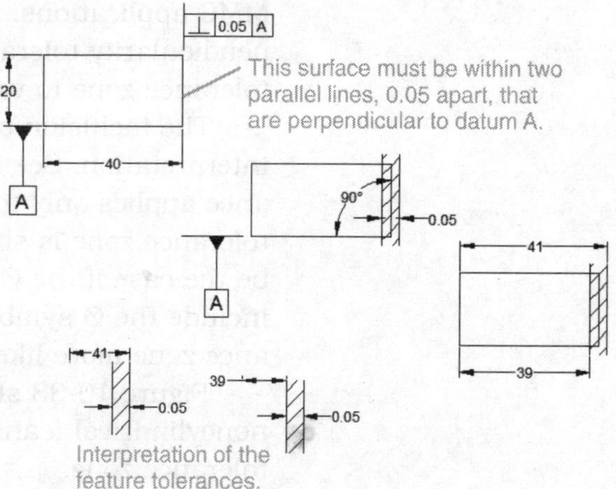

Interpretation of the feature tolerances.

does not directly control the shape of the edge. Any shape that falls within the specified tolerance range is acceptable. This may, in fact, be sufficient for a given design, but if a more controlled shape is required, a perpendicularity tolerance must be added. The perpendicularity tolerance works within the locational tolerance to ensure that the edge is not only within the locational tolerance but also is perpendicular to datum A.

Figure 10-30 shows the two extreme conditions for the 40 ± 1 locational tolerance. The perpendicularity tolerance is applied by first measuring the surface and determining its maximum and minimum lengths. The difference between these two measurements must be less than 0.05. Thus, if the measured maximum distance is 41, then no other part of the surface may be less than 41 − 0.05 = 40.95.

Tolerances of perpendicularity serve to complement locational tolerances, to make the shape more exact, so that tolerances of perpendicularity must always be smaller than tolerances of location. It would be of little use, for example, to assign a perpendicularity tolerance of 1.5 for the object shown in Figure 10-30. The locational tolerance would prevent the variation from ever reaching the limits specified by such a large perpendicularity tolerance.

Figure 10-31 shows a perpendicularity tolerance applied to cylindrical features: a shaft and a hole. The figure includes examples of both RFS and

Figure 10-31

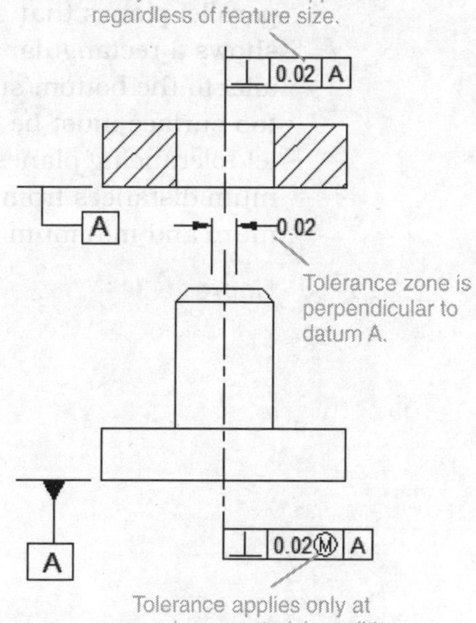

MMC applications. As with straightness tolerances applied at MMC, perpendicularity tolerances applied about a hole or shaft's centerline allow the tolerance zone to vary as the feature size varies.

The inclusion of the Ø symbol in a geometric tolerance is critical to its interpretation. See Figure 10-32. If the Ø symbol is not included, the tolerance applies only to the view in which it is written. This means that the tolerance zone is shaped like a rectangular slice, not a cylinder, as would be the case if the Ø symbol were included. In general, it is better always to include the Ø symbol for cylindrical features because it generates a tolerance zone more like that used in positional tolerancing.

Figure 10-33 shows a perpendicularity tolerance applied to a slot, a noncylindrical feature. The MMC specification is for variations in the tolerance zone.

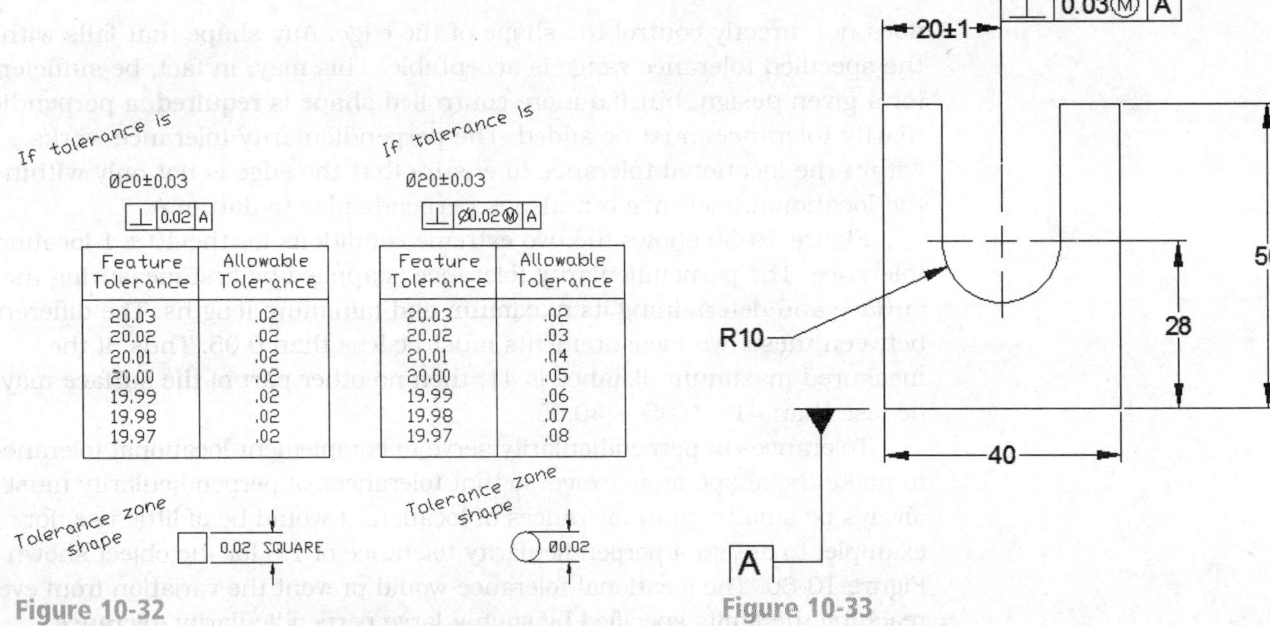

Feature Tolerance	Allowable Tolerance
20.03	.02
20.02	.02
20.01	.02
20.00	.02
19.99	.02
19.98	.02
19.97	.02

Feature Tolerance	Allowable Tolerance
20.03	.02
20.02	.03
20.01	.04
20.00	.05
19.99	.06
19.98	.07
19.97	.08

Figure 10-32

Figure 10-33

10-12 Parallelism

Parallelism is used to ensure that all points within a plane are within two parallel planes that are parallel to a referenced datum plane. Figure 10-34 shows a rectangular object that is toleranced so that its top surface is parallel to the bottom surface within 0.02. This means that every point on the top surface must be within a set of parallel planes 0.02 apart. These parallel tolerancing planes are located by determining the maximum and minimum distances from the datum surface. The difference between the maximum and minimum values may not exceed the stated 0.02 tolerance.

Figure 10-34

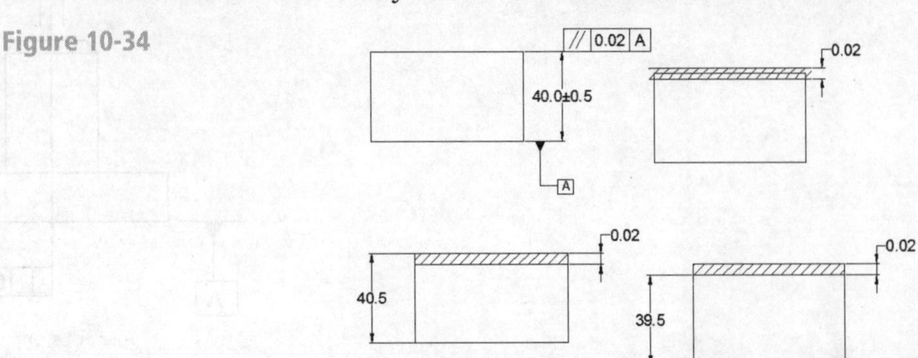

In the extreme condition of maximum feature size, the top surface is located 40.5 above the datum plane. The parallelism tolerance is then applied, meaning that no point on the surface may be closer than 40.3 to the datum. This is an RFS condition. The MMC condition may also be applied, thereby allowing the tolerance zone to vary as the feature size varies.

10-13 Angularism

Angularism tolerances are used to limit the variance of surfaces and axes that are at an angle relative to a datum. Angularism tolerances are applied, like perpendicularity and parallelism tolerances, as a way to better control the shape of locational tolerances.

Figure 10-35 shows an angularism tolerance and several ways in which it is interpreted at extreme conditions.

Figure 10-35

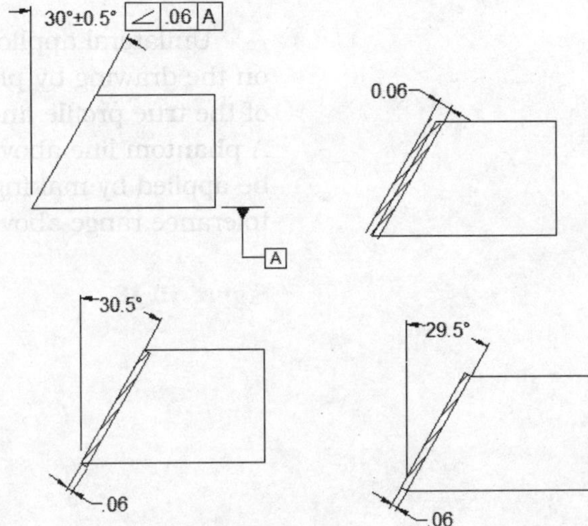

10-14 Profiles

Profile tolerances are used to limit the variations of irregular surfaces. They may be assigned as either bilateral or unilateral tolerances. There are two types of profile tolerances: surface and line. ***Surface profile tolerances*** limit the variation of an entire surface, whereas a ***line profile tolerance*** limits the variations along a single line across a surface.

Figure 10-36 shows an object that includes a surface profile tolerance referenced to an irregular surface. The tolerance is considered a bilateral

Figure 10-36

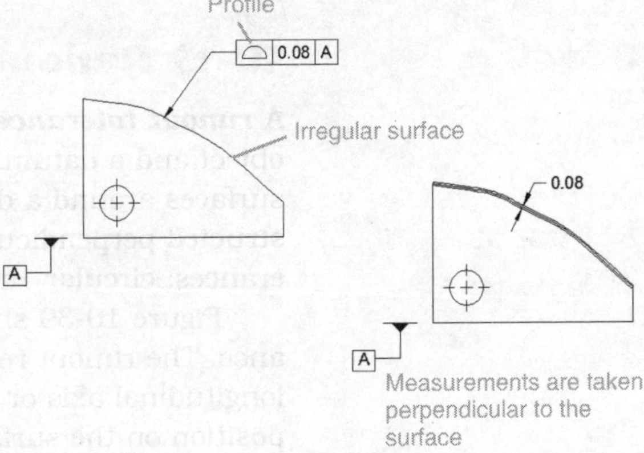

tolerance because no other specification is given. This means that all points on the surface must be located between two parallel planes 0.08 apart that are centered about the irregular surface. The measurements are taken perpendicular to the surface.

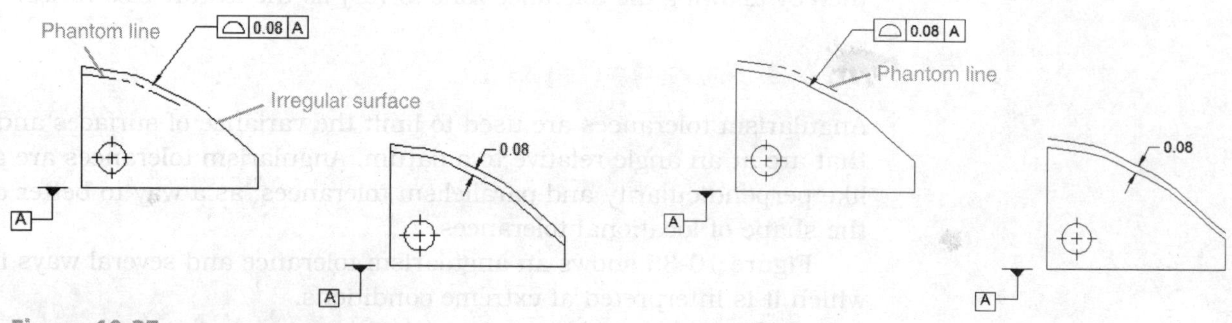

Figure 10-37

Unilateral applications of surface profile tolerances must be indicated on the drawing by phantom lines. The phantom line indicates on which side of the true profile line of the irregular surface the tolerance is to be applied. A phantom line above the irregular surface indicates that the tolerance is to be applied by making the true profile line 0, and then adding a specified tolerance range above that line. See Figures 10-37 and Figure 10-38.

Figure 10-38

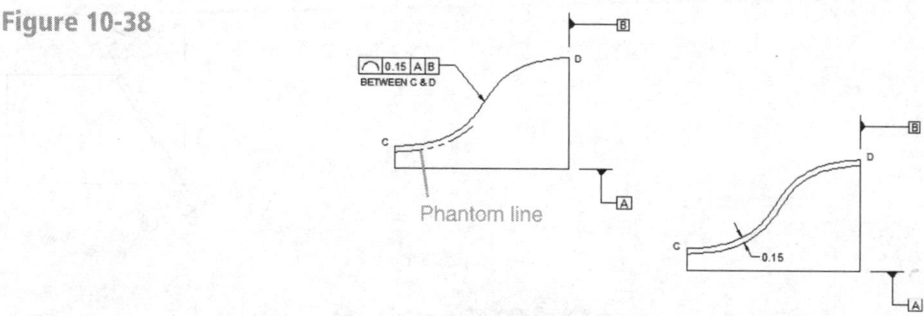

Profiles of line tolerances are applied to irregular surfaces, as shown in Figure 10-37. Profiles of line tolerances are particularly helpful for tolerancing an irregular surface that is constantly changing, such as the surface of an airplane wing.

Surface and line profile tolerances are somewhat analogous to flatness and straightness tolerances. Flatness and surface profile tolerances are applied across an entire surface; straightness and line profile tolerances are applied only along a single line across the surface.

10-15 Runouts

A ***runout tolerance*** is used to limit the variations between features of an object and a datum. More specifically, runout tolerances are applied to surfaces around a datum axis such as a cylinder or to a surface constructed perpendicular to a datum axis. There are two types of runout tolerances: circular and total.

Figure 10-39 shows a cylinder that includes a circular runout tolerance. The runout requirements are checked by rotating the object about its longitudinal axis or datum axis while holding an indicator gauge in a fixed position on the surface of the object.

Figure 10-39

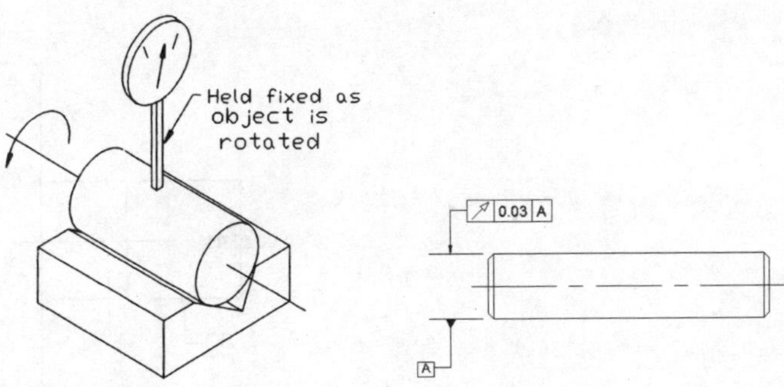

Runout tolerances may be either bilateral or unilateral. A runout tolerance is assumed to be bilateral unless otherwise indicated. If a runout tolerance is to be unilateral, a phantom line is used to indicate to which side of the object's true surface the tolerance is to be applied. See Figure 10-40.

Figure 10-40

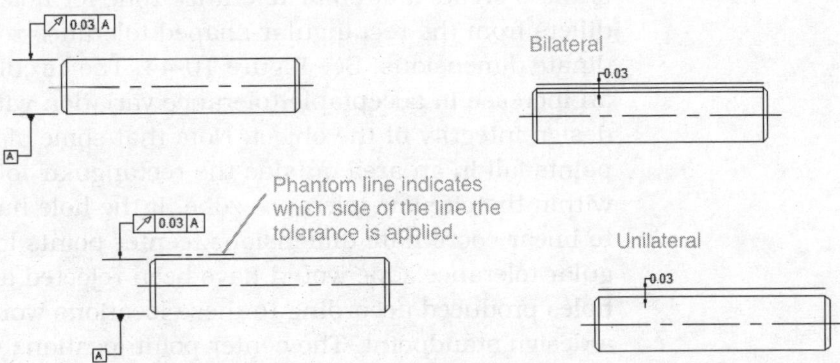

Runout tolerances may be applied to tapered areas of cylindrical objects, as shown in Figure 10-41. The tolerance is checked by rotating the object about a datum axis while holding an indicator gauge in place.

A total runout tolerance limits the variation across an entire surface. See Figure 10-42. An indicator gauge is not held in place while the object is rotated, as it is for circular runout tolerances, but is moved about the rotating surface.

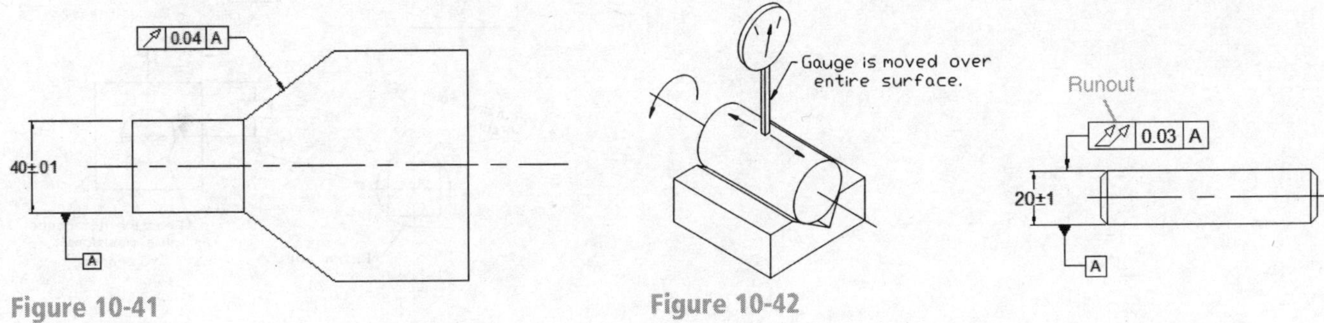

Figure 10-41

Figure 10-42

Figure 10-43 shows a circular runout tolerance that references two datums. The two datums serve as one datum. The object can then be rotated about both datums simultaneously as the runout tolerances are checked.

Figure 10-43

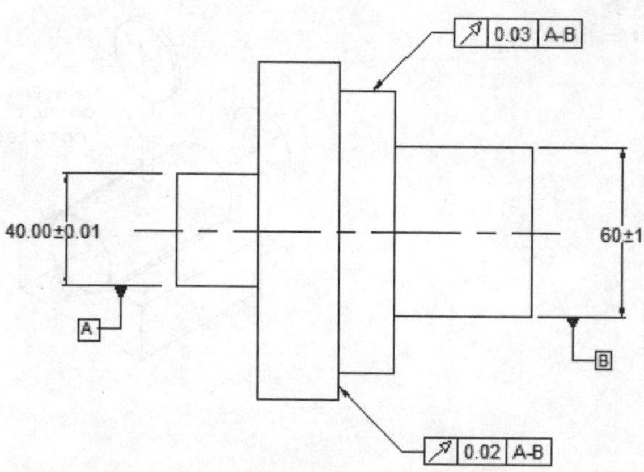

10-16 Positional Tolerances

Positional tolerances are used to locate and tolerance holes. Positional tolerances create a circular tolerance zone for hole center point locations that differs from the rectangular-shaped tolerance zone created by linear coordinate dimensions. See Figure 10-44. The circular tolerance zone allows for an increase in acceptable tolerance variation without compromising the design integrity of the object. Note that some of the possible hole center points fall in an area outside the rectangular tolerance zone, but are still within the circular tolerance zone. If the hole had been located according to linear coordinate dimensions, center points located beyond the rectangular tolerance zone would have been rejected as beyond tolerance, and yet holes produced according to these locations would function correctly, from a design standpoint. The center point locations would be acceptable if positional tolerances had been specified. The finished hole is round, so a round tolerance zone is appropriate. The rectangular tolerance zone rejects some holes unnecessarily.

Figure 10-44

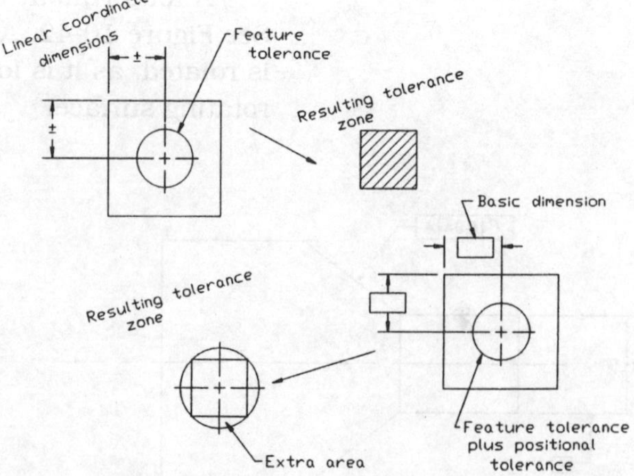

Holes are dimensioned and toleranced by the use of geometric tolerances by a combination of locating dimensions, feature dimensions and tolerances, and positional tolerances. See Figure 10-45. The locating dimensions are enclosed in rectangular boxes and are called ***basic dimensions.*** Basic dimensions are assumed to be exact.

Figure 10-45

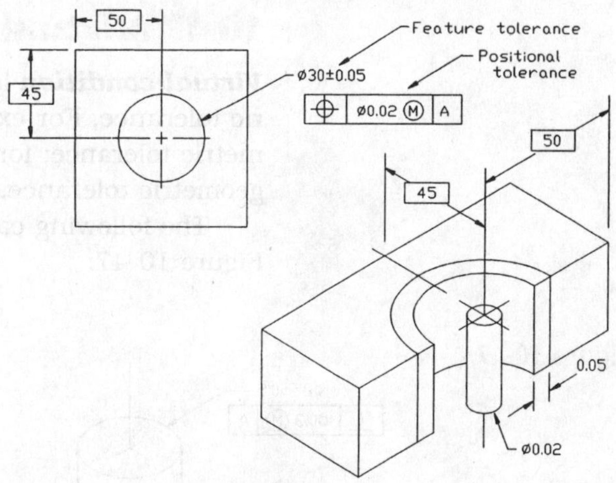

The feature tolerances for the hole are as presented in Chapter 9. They can be presented by using plus or minus, or limit-type, tolerances. In the example shown in Figure 10-45, the diameter of the hole is toleranced by a plus and minus 0.05 tolerance.

The basic locating dimensions of 45 and 50 are assumed to be exact. The tolerances that would normally accompany linear locational dimensions are replaced by the positional tolerance. The positional tolerance also specifies that the tolerance be applied at the centerline at maximum material condition. The resulting tolerance zones are as shown in Figure 10-45.

Figure 10-46 shows an object containing two holes that are dimensioned and toleranced by using positional tolerances. There are two consecutive horizontal basic dimensions. Because basic dimensions are exact, they do not have tolerances that accumulate; that is, there is no tolerance buildup.

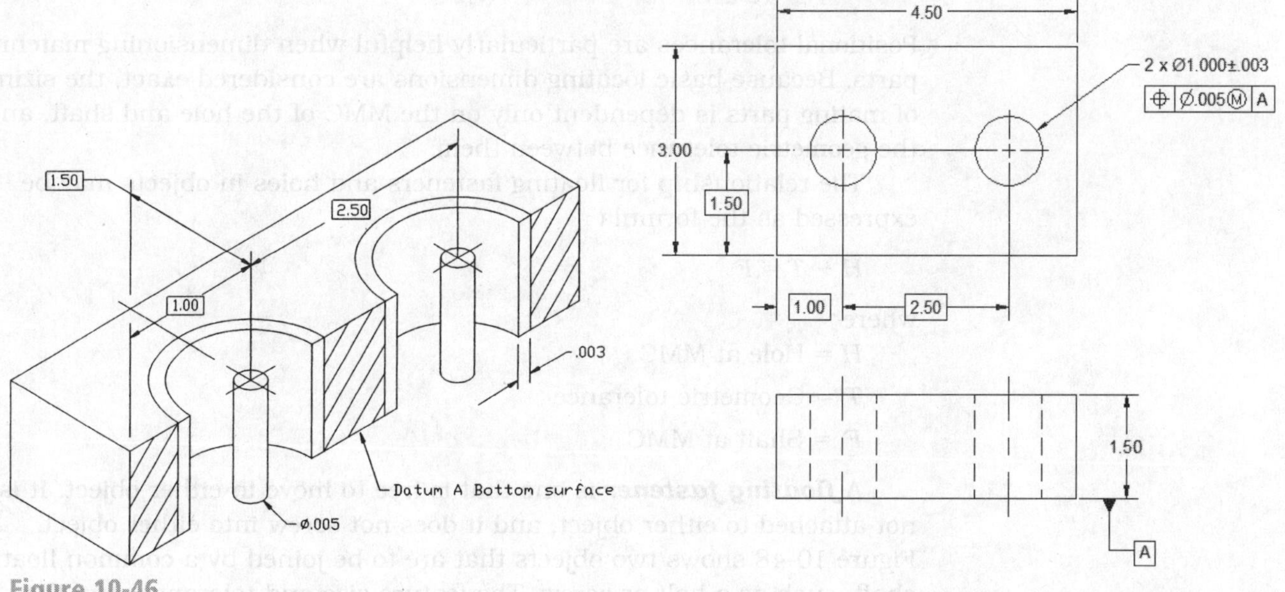

Figure 10-46

10-17 Virtual Condition

Virtual condition is a combination of a feature's MMC and its geometric tolerance. For external features (shafts), it is the MMC plus the geometric tolerance; for internal features (holes), it is the MMC minus the geometric tolerance.

The following calculations are based on the dimensions shown in Figure 10-47:

Figure 10-47

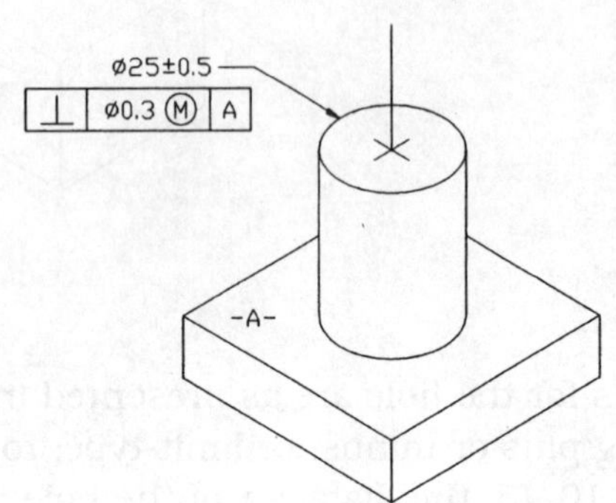

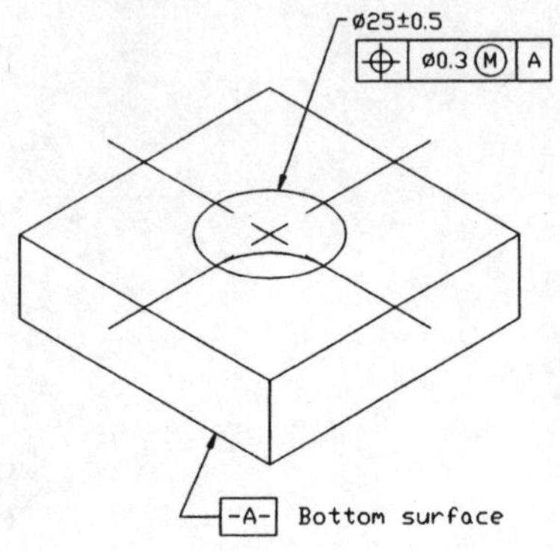

To Calculate the Virtual Condition for a Shaft

25.5 MMC for shaft—maximum diameter
+0.3 Geometric tolerance
25.8 Virtual condition

To Calculate the Virtual Condition for a Hole

24.5 MMC for hole—minimum diameter
−0.3 Geometric tolerance
24.2 Virtual condition

10-18 Floating Fasteners

Positional tolerances are particularly helpful when dimensioning matching parts. Because basic locating dimensions are considered exact, the sizing of mating parts is dependent only on the MMC of the hole and shaft, and the geometric tolerance between them.

The relationship for floating fasteners and holes in objects may be expressed as the formula

$$H - T = F$$

where

H = Hole at MMC

T = Geometric tolerance

F = Shaft at MMC

A ***floating fastener*** is one that is free to move in either object. It is not attached to either object, and it does not screw into either object. Figure 10-48 shows two objects that are to be joined by a common floating shaft, such as a bolt or screw. The feature size and tolerance, and the positional geometric tolerance, are both given. The minimum size hole that will always just fit is determined by the preceding formula:

$$H - T = F$$

$$11.97 - 0.02 = 11.95$$

Therefore, the shaft's diameter at MMC, the shaft's maximum diameter, equals 11.95. Any required tolerance would have to be subtracted from this shaft size.

The 0.02 geometric tolerance is applied at the hole's MMC. Thus, as the hole's size expands within its feature tolerance, the tolerance zone for the acceptable matching parts also expands. See the table in Figure 10-48.

Figure 10-48

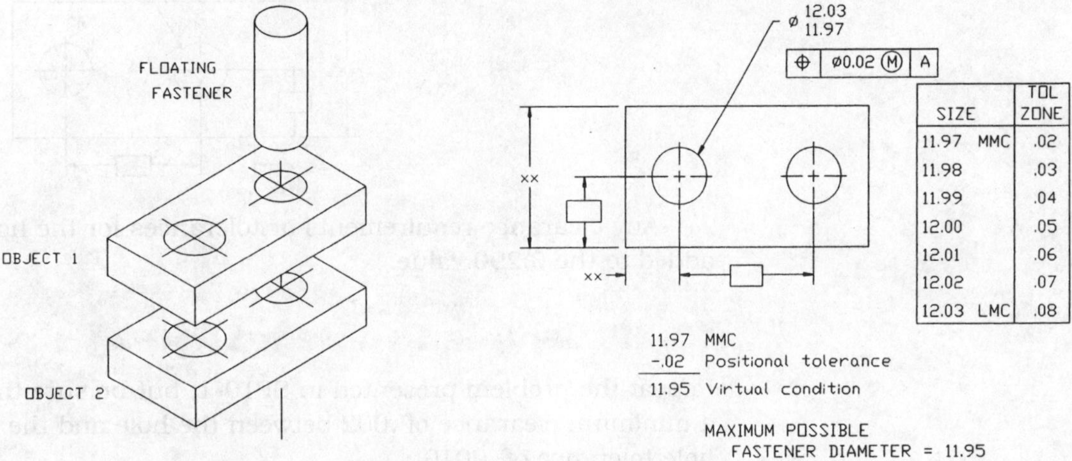

10-19 Sample Problem SP10-1

The situation presented in Figure 10-48 can be worked in reverse; that is, hole sizes can be derived from given shaft sizes.

The two objects shown in Figure 10-49 are to be joined by a .250-inch bolt. The parts are floating; that is, they are both free to move, and the fastener is not joined to either object. What is the MMC of the holes if the positional tolerance is to be .030?

Figure 10-49

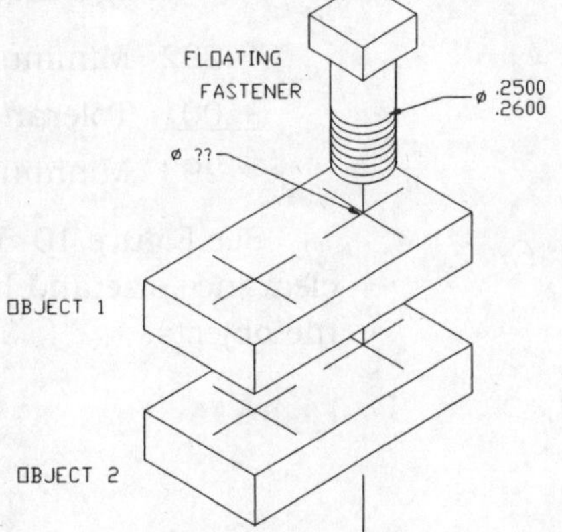

A manufacturer's catalog specifies that the tolerance for a .250 bolt is .2500 to .2600.

Rewriting the formula

$$H - T = F$$

to isolate the H, we have

$$H = F + T$$
$$= 0.260 + 0.030$$
$$= 0.290$$

The 0.290 value represents the minimum hole diameter, MMC, for all four holes, that will always accept the 0.250 bolt. Figure 10-50 shows the resulting drawing callout.

Figure 10-50

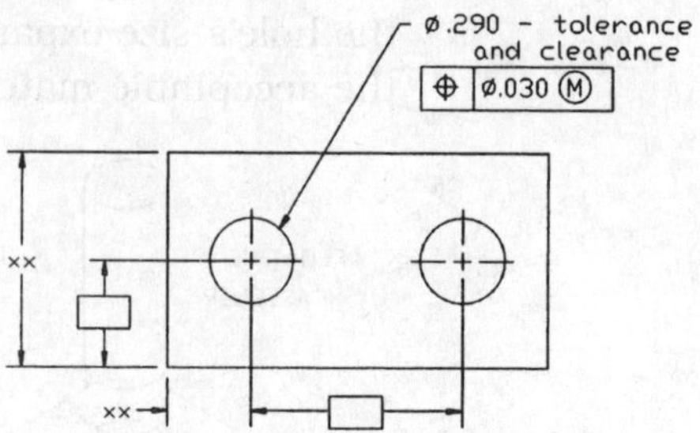

Any clearance requirements or tolerances for the hole would have to be added to the 0.290 value.

10-20 Sample Problem SP10-2

Repeat the problem presented in SP10-1, but be sure that there is always a minimum clearance of .002 between the hole and the shaft, and assign a hole tolerance of .0010.

Sample Problem SP10-1 determined that the maximum hole diameter that would always accept the .250 bolt was .290, according to the .030 positional tolerance. If the minimum clearance is to be .002, the maximum hole diameter is found as follows:

.290	Minimum hole diameter that will always accept the bolt (0 clearance at MMC)
+.002	Minimum clearance
.292	Min'mum hole diameter including clearance

Now assign the tolerance to the hole:

.292	Minimum hole diameter
+.001	Tolerance
.293	Minimum hole diameter

See Figure 10-51 for the appropriate drawing callout. The choice of clearance size and hole tolerance varies with the design requirements for the objects.

Figure 10-51

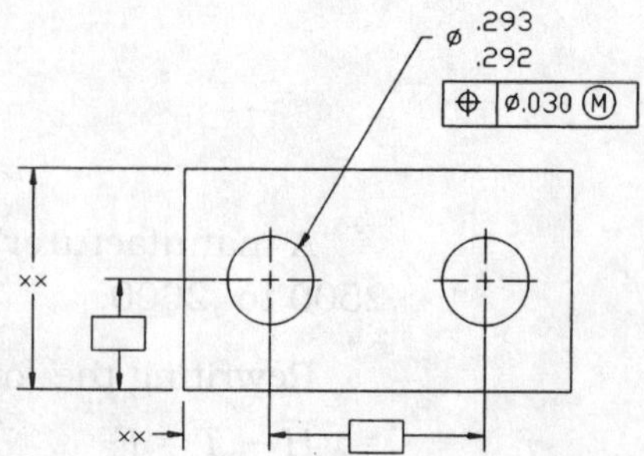

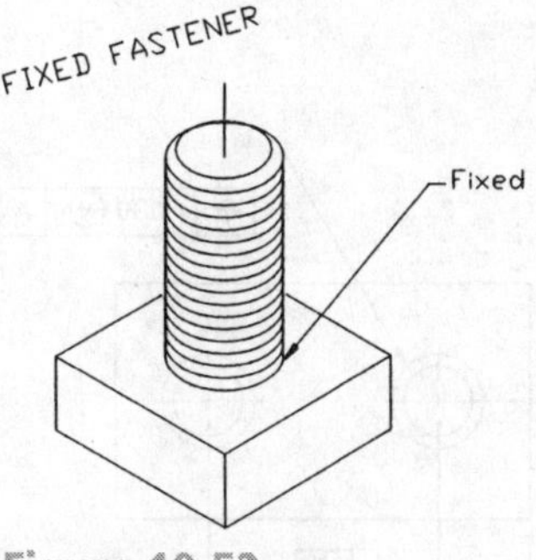

Figure 10-52

10-21 Fixed Fasteners

A ***fixed fastener*** is one that is attached to one of the mating objects. See Figure 10-52. Because the fastener is fixed to one of the objects, the geometric tolerance zone must be smaller than that used for floating fasteners. The fixed fastener cannot move without moving the object it is attached to. The relationship between fixed fasteners and holes in mating objects is defined by the following formula:

$$H - 2T = F$$

The tolerance zone is cut in half, as can be demonstrated by the objects shown in Figure 10-53. The same feature sizes that were used in Figure 10-48 are assigned, but in this example, the fasteners are fixed. Solving for the geometric tolerance, we obtain the following value:

$$H - F = 2T$$
$$11.97 - 11.95 = 2T$$
$$.02 = 2T$$
$$.01 = T$$

Figure 10-53

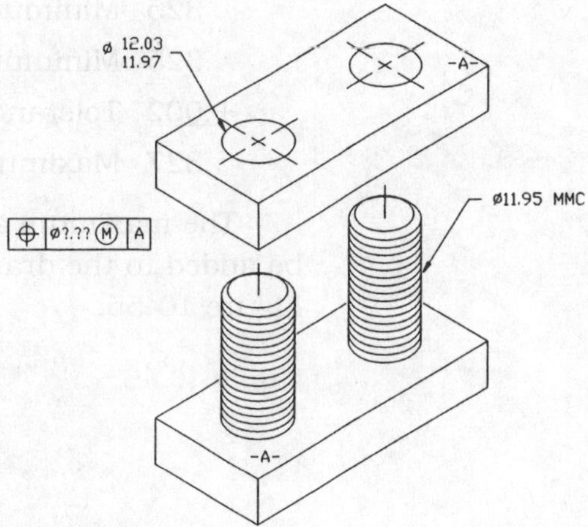

The resulting positional tolerance is half of that obtained for floating fasteners.

10-22 Sample Problem SP10-3

This problem is similar to Sample Problem SP10-1, but the given conditions are applied to fixed fasteners rather than to floating fasteners. Compare the resulting shaft diameters for the two problems. See Figure 10-54.

A. What is the minimum-diameter hole that will always accept the fixed fasteners?
B. If the minimum clearance is .005 and the hole is to have a tolerance of .002, what are the maximum and minimum diameters of the hole?

$$H - 2T = F$$
$$H = F + 2T$$
$$= .260 + 2(.030)$$
$$= .260 + .060$$
$$= .320$$ Minimum diameter that will always accept the fixed fastener

Figure 10-54

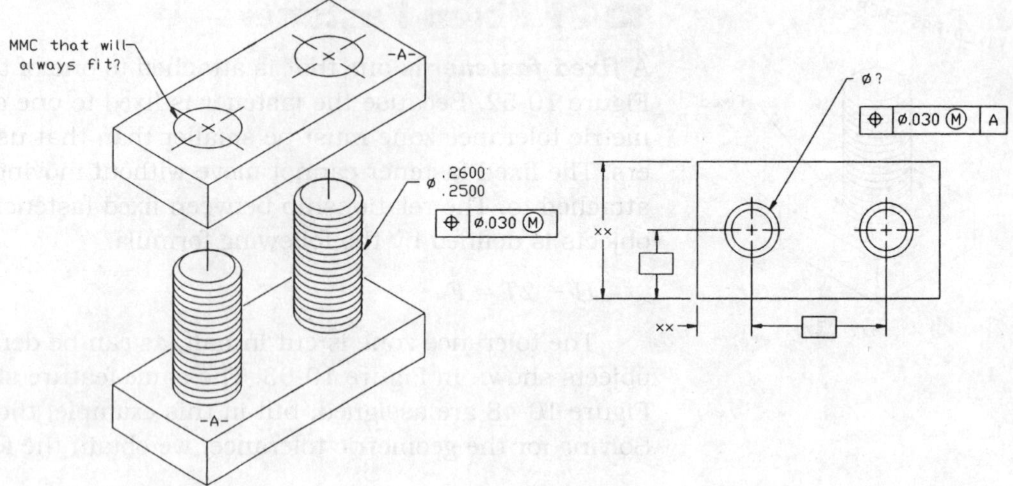

If the minimum clearance = .005 and the hole tolerance is .002,

.320	Virtual condition
+.005	Clearance
.325	Minimum hole diameter
.325	Minimum hole diameter
+.002	Tolerance
.327	Maximum hole diameter

The maximum and minimum values for the hole's diameter can then be added to the drawing of the object that fits over the fixed fasteners. See Figure 10-55.

Figure 10-55

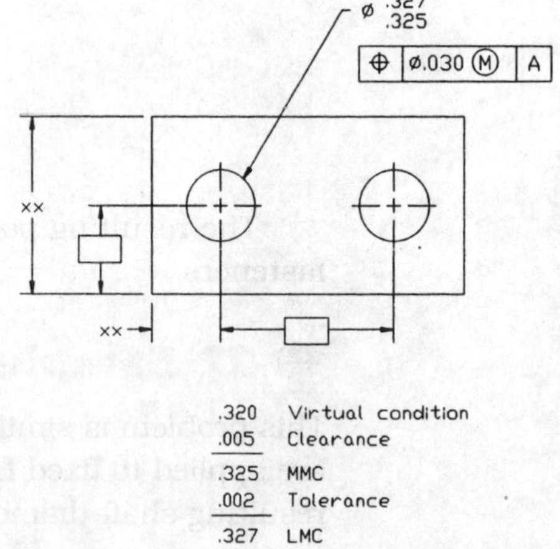

10-23 Design Problems

This problem was originally done in Section 9-27 using rectangular tolerances. It is done in this section by using positional geometric tolerances so that the two systems can be compared. It is suggested that you review Section 9-27 before reading this section.

Figure 10-56 shows top and bottom parts that are to be joined in the floating condition. A nominal distance of 50 between hole centers and 20 for the holes has been assigned. In Section 9-27, a rectangular tolerance of ±0.01 was selected and there was a minimum hole diameter of 20.00. Figure 10-57 shows the resulting tolerance zones.

Figure 10-56

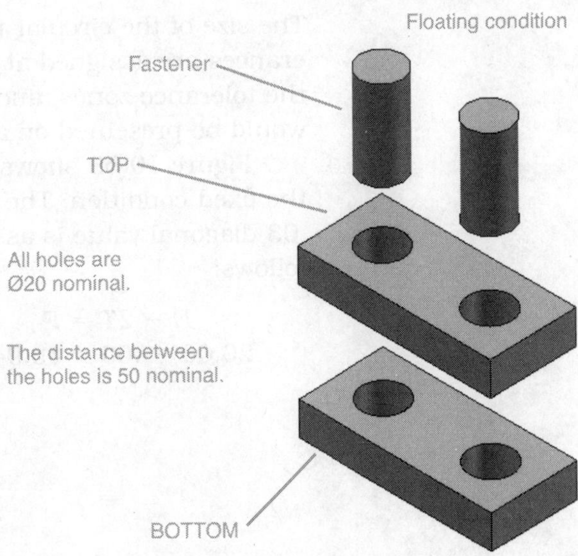

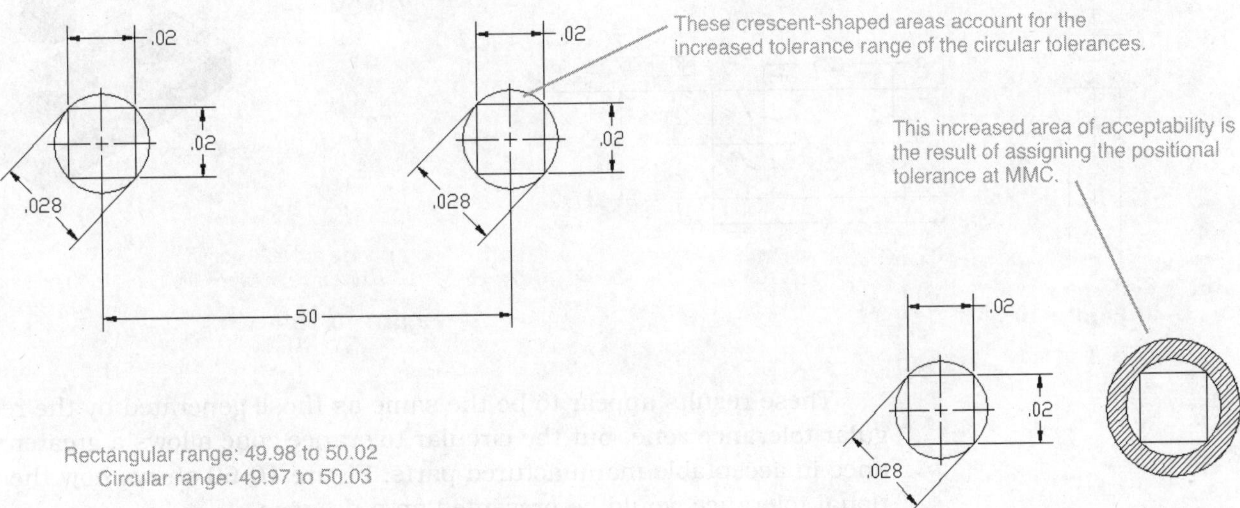

Figure 10-57

The diagonal distance across the rectangular tolerance zone is .028 and was rounded off to .03 to yield a maximum possible fastener diameter of 19.97. If the same .03 value is used to calculate the fastener diameter by using positional tolerance, the results will be as follows:

$$H - T = F$$

$$20.00 - 0.03 = 19.97$$

The results seem to be the same, but because of the circular shape of the positional tolerance zone, the manufactured results are not the same. The minimum distance between the inside edges of the rectangular zones is 49.98, or .01 from the center point of each hole. The minimum distance from the innermost points of the circular tolerance zones is 49.97, or .015 (half of the rounded-off .03 value) from the center point of each hole. The same value difference also occurs for the maximum distance between center points, where 50.02 is the maximum distance for the rectangular tolerances and 50.03 is the maximum distance for the circular tolerances.

The size of the circular tolerance zone increased more because the hole tolerances are assigned at MMC. Figure 10-57 shows a comparison between the tolerance zones, and Figure 10-58 shows how the positional tolerances would be presented on a drawing of either the top or bottom part.

Figure 10-59 shows the same top and bottom parts joined together in the fixed condition. The initial nominal values are the same. If the same .03 diagonal value is assigned as a positional tolerance, the results are as follows:

$$H - 2T = F$$
$$20.00 - .06 = 19.94$$

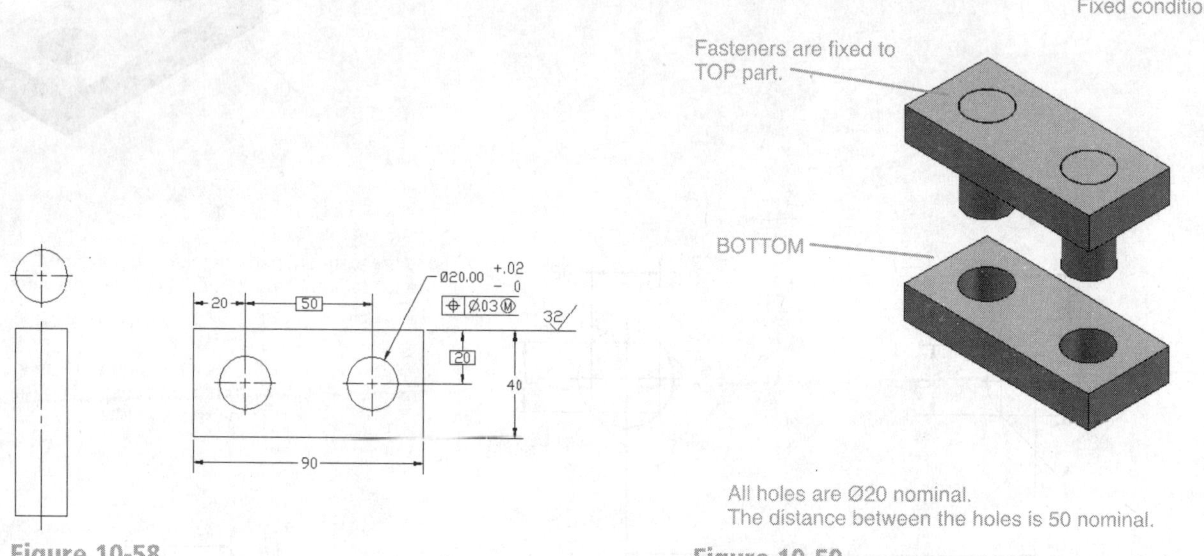

Figure 10-58

Figure 10-59

These results appear to be the same as those generated by the rectangular tolerance zone, but the circular tolerance zone allows a greater variance in acceptable manufactured parts. Figure 10-60 shows how the positional tolerance would be presented on a drawing.

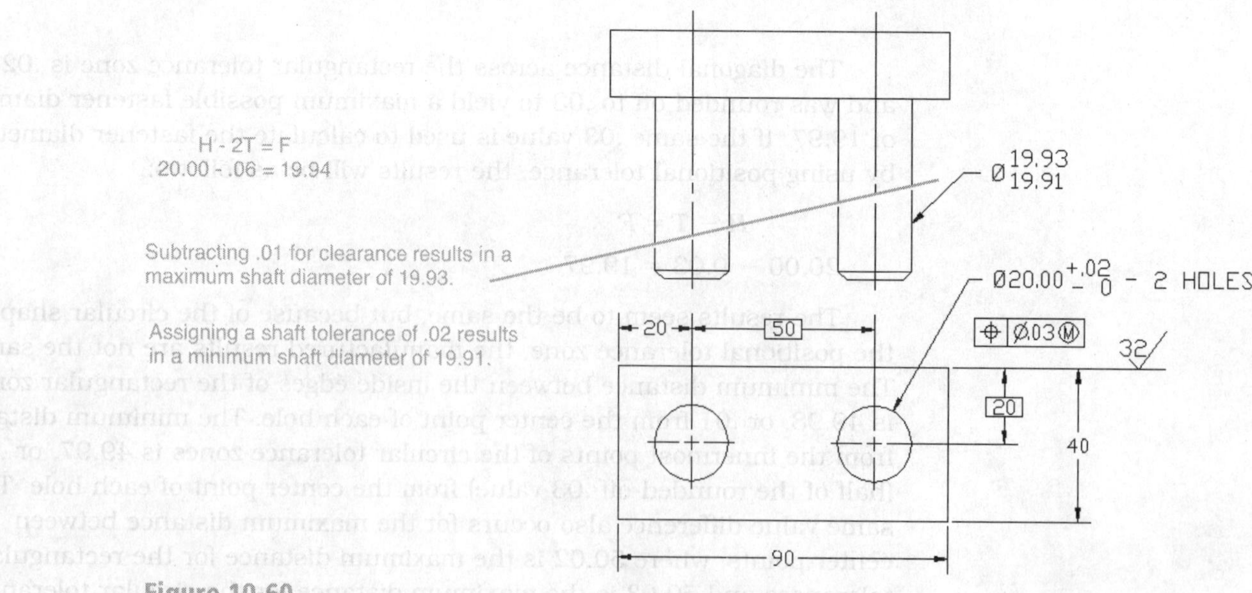

Figure 10-60

10-24 EXERCISE PROBLEMS

EX10-1

Redraw the object shown. Include all dimensions and tolerances.

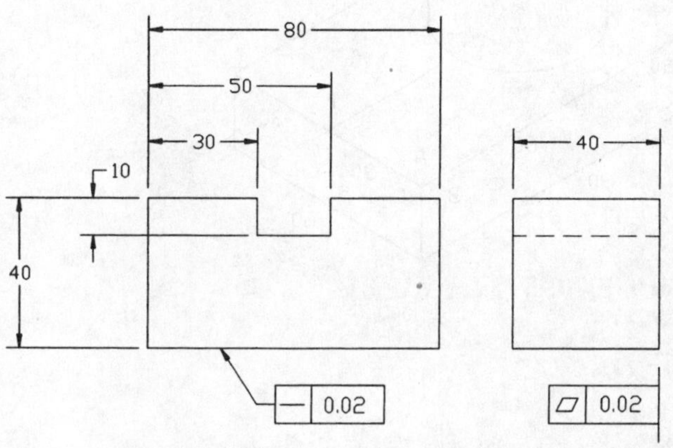

EX10-2

Redraw the following shaft, and add a feature dimension and tolerance of 36 ± 0.1 and a straightness tolerance of 0.07 about the centerline at MMC:

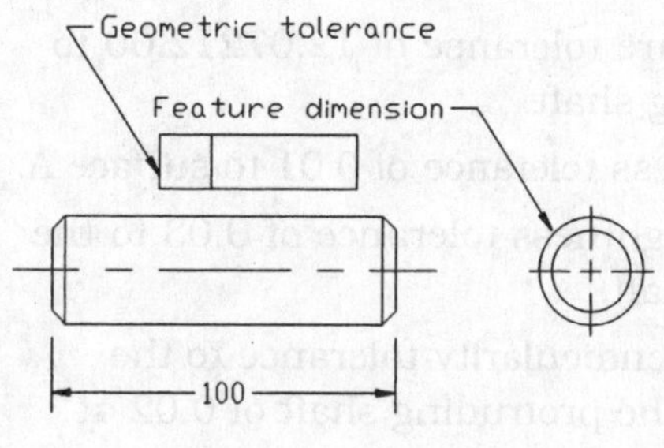

EX10-3

A. Given the shaft shown, what is the minimum hole diameter that will always accept the shaft?

B. If the minimum clearance between the shaft and a hole is equal to 0.02 and the tolerance on the hole is to be 0.6, what are the maximum and minimum diameters for the hole?

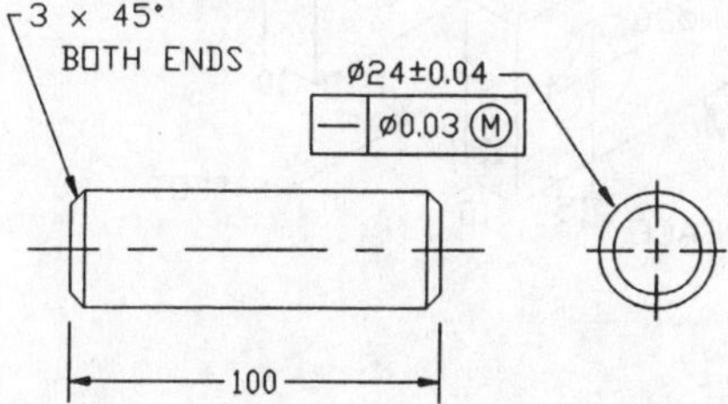

EX10-4

A. Given the shaft shown, what is the minimum hole diameter that will always accept the shaft?

B. If the minimum clearance between the shaft and a hole is equal to .005 and the tolerance on the hole is to be .007, what are the maximum and minimum diameters for the hole?

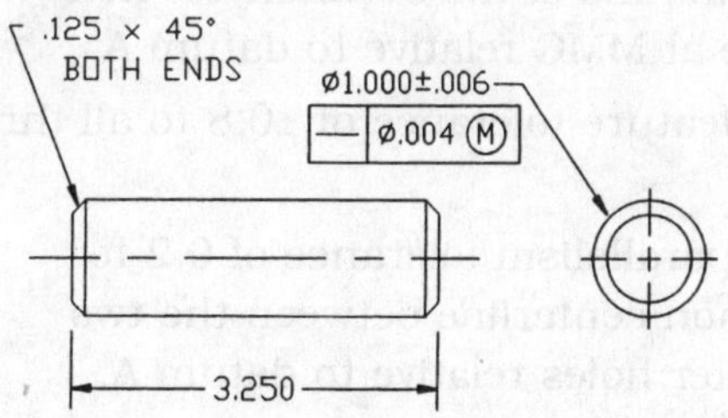

EX10-5

Draw a front and a right-side view of the object shown in Figure EX10-5, and add the appropriate dimensions and tolerances on the basis of the information that follows. Numbers located next to an edge line indicate the length of the edge.

A. Define surfaces A, B, and C as primary, secondary, and tertiary datums, respectively.

B. Assign a tolerance of ±0.5 to all linear dimensions.

C. Assign a feature tolerance of 12.07212.00 to the protruding shaft.

D. Assign a flatness tolerance of 0.01 to surface A.

E. Assign a straightness tolerance of 0.03 to the protruding shaft.

F. Assign a perpendicularity tolerance to the centerline of the protruding shaft of 0.02 at MMC relative to datum A.

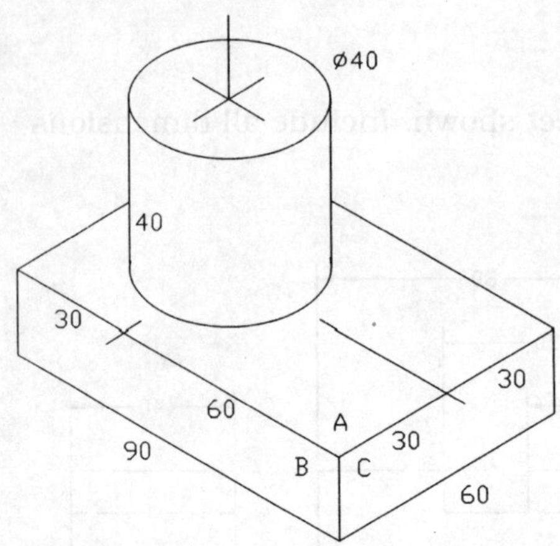

Figure EX10-5

EX10-6

Draw a front and a right-side view of the object shown in Figure EX10-6, and add the following dimensions and tolerances:

A. Define the bottom surface as datum A.

B. Assign a perpendicularity tolerance of 0.4 to both sides of the slot relative to datum A.

C. Assign a perpendicularity tolerance of 0.2 to the centerline of the 30-diameter hole centerline at MMC relative to datum A.

D. Assign a feature tolerance of ±0.8 to all three holes.

E. Assign a parallelism tolerance of 0.2 to the common centerline between the two 20-diameter holes relative to datum A.

F. Assign a tolerance of ±0.5 to all linear dimensions.

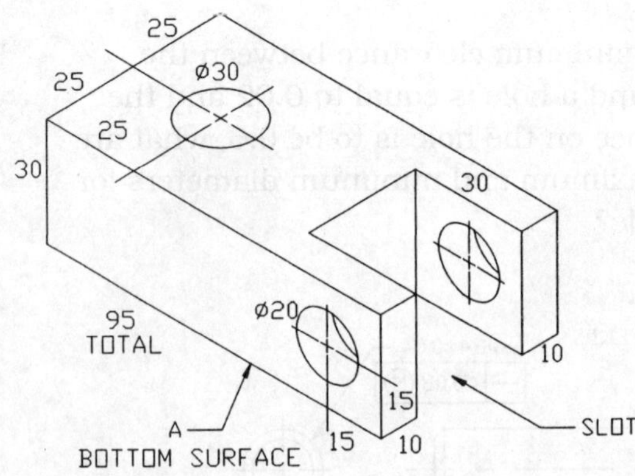

Figure EX10-6

EX10-7

Draw a circular front and the appropriate right-side view of the object shown in Figure EX10-7, and add the following dimensions and tolerances:

A. Assign datum A as indicated.

B. Assign the object's longitudinal axis as datum B.

C. Assign the object's centerline through the slot as datum C.

D. Assign a tolerance of ±0.5 to all linear tolerances.

E. Assign a tolerance of ±0.5 to all circular-shaped features.

F. Assign a parallelism tolerance of 0.01 to both edges of the slot.

G. Assign a perpendicularity tolerance of 0.01 to the outside edge of the protruding shaft.

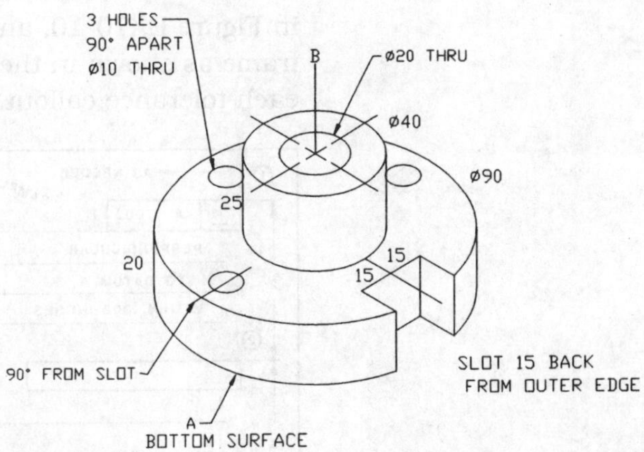

Figure EX10-7

EX10-8

Given the two objects shown in Figure EX10-8, draw a front and a side view of each. Assign a tolerance of ±0.5 to all linear dimensions. Assign a feature tolerance of ±0.4 to the shaft, and also assign a straightness tolerance of 0.2 to the shaft's centerline at MMC.

Tolerance the hole so that it will always accept the shaft with a minimum clearance of 0.1 and a feature tolerance of 0.2. Assign a perpendicularity tolerance of 0.05 to the centerline of the hole at MMC.

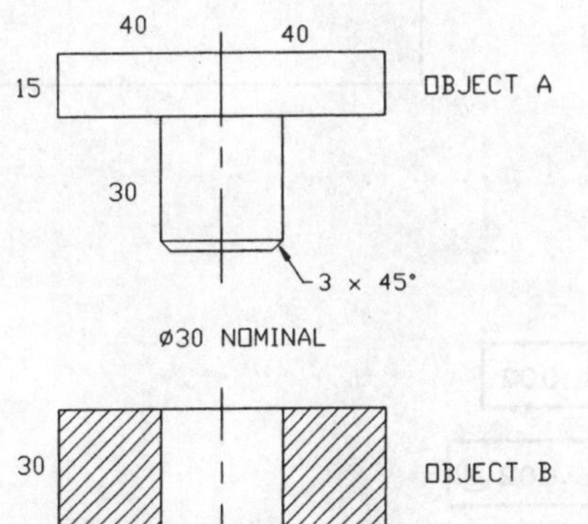

Figure EX10-8

EX10-9

Given the two objects shown in Figure EX10-9, draw a front and a side view of each. Assign a tolerance of ±.005 to all linear dimensions. Assign a feature tolerance of ±.004 to the shaft, and also assign a straightness tolerance of .002 to the shaft's centerline at MMC.

Tolerance the hole so that it will always accept the shaft with a minimum clearance of .001 and a feature tolerance of .002.

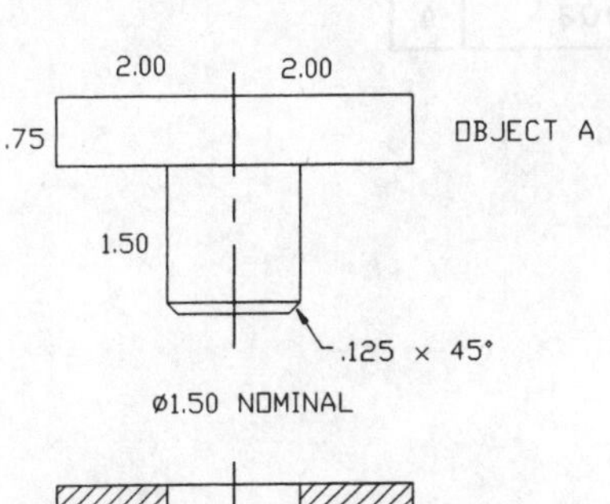

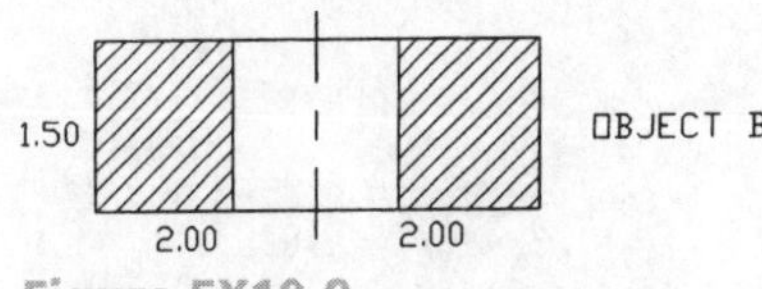

Figure EX10-9

EX10-10

Refer to parts A through G for this exercise problem. Use the format shown in Figure EX10-10, and redraw the given geometric tolerance symbols and frame as shown in the sample. Express in words **(Dtext)** the meaning of each tolerance callout.

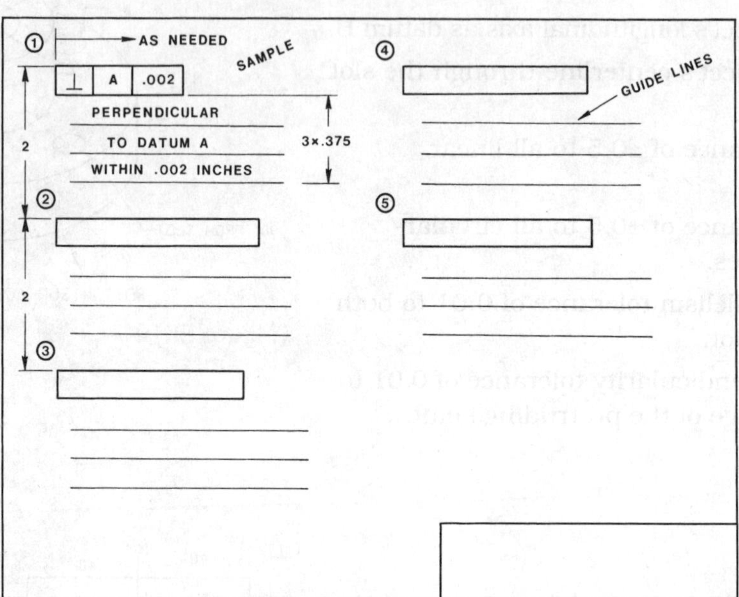

Figure EX10-10

A.

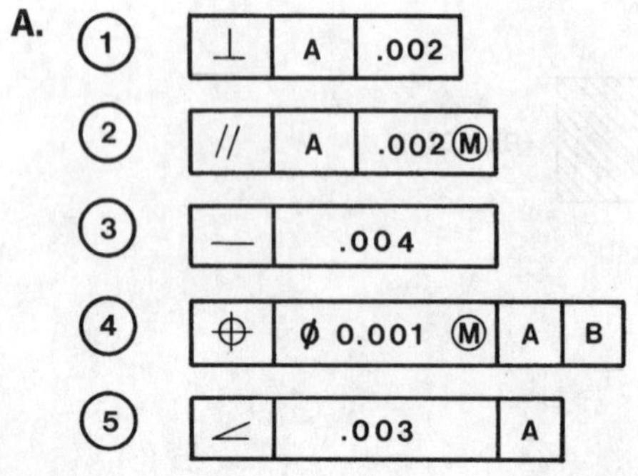

B.

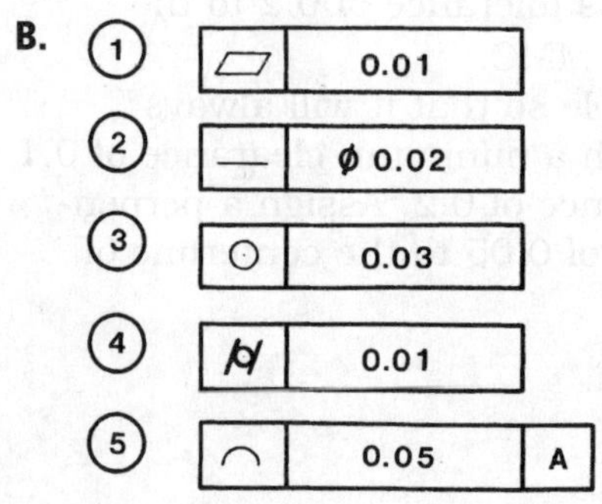

EX10-10, continued

C.

1. 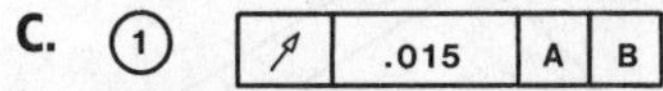

2. 

3. 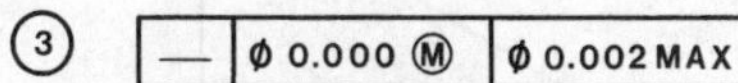

4. 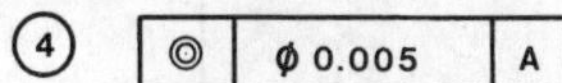

5. 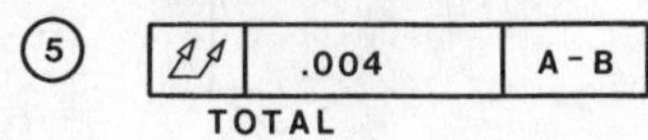

D.

1. ⌖ | 0.25 Ⓜ | A | B | C
2. ⌖ | 0.8 Ⓜ | A | B Ⓜ
3. ⌖ | ϕ 0.4 Ⓜ | A | B | C
4. ⌖ | ϕ 0.3 Ⓜ | A | B Ⓜ | C Ⓜ
5. ⌖ | ϕ 0.1 Ⓜ

E.

1. 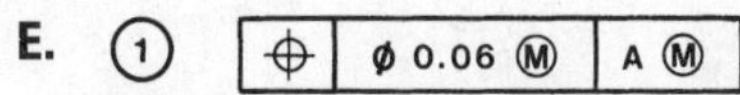

2. 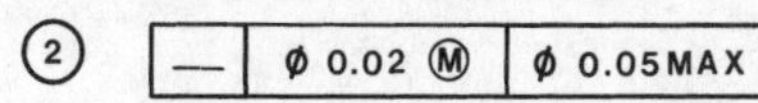

3. ⌖ | ϕ 0.0 Ⓜ | A | ϕ .05MAX

4. 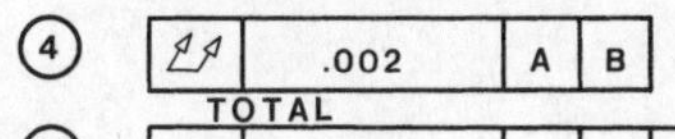

5. ⌓ | .003 | A | B | C
ALL AROUND

F.

1. ∠ | 0.04 Ⓜ | C | A Ⓜ | B Ⓜ
2. ↗ | 0.02 | A
3. ⊥ | 0.03 | A | B
4. // | ϕ 0.01 | A | B Ⓜ
5. ⌓ | 0.03 | A | B
ALL AROUND

G.

1. ⌖ | ϕ .002 Ⓜ
2. ⌖ | .005 Ⓜ | A | B | C
3. ⌖ | .002 | A | B Ⓜ
4. ⌖ | ϕ .003 Ⓜ | A | B Ⓜ | C Ⓜ
5. ⌖ | ϕ .015 Ⓜ | A | B

EX10-11 Millimeters

Draw front, top, and right-side views of the object in Figure EX10-11, including dimensions. Add the following tolerances and specifications to the drawing:

A. Surface 1 is datum A.

B. Surface 2 is datum B and is perpendicular to datum A within 0.1 millimeter.

C. Surface 3 is datum C and is parallel to datum A within 0.3 millimeter.

D. Locate a 16-millimeter-diameter hole in the center of the front surface that goes completely through the object. Use positional tolerances to locate the hole. Assign a positional tolerance of 0.02 at MMC perpendicular to datum A.

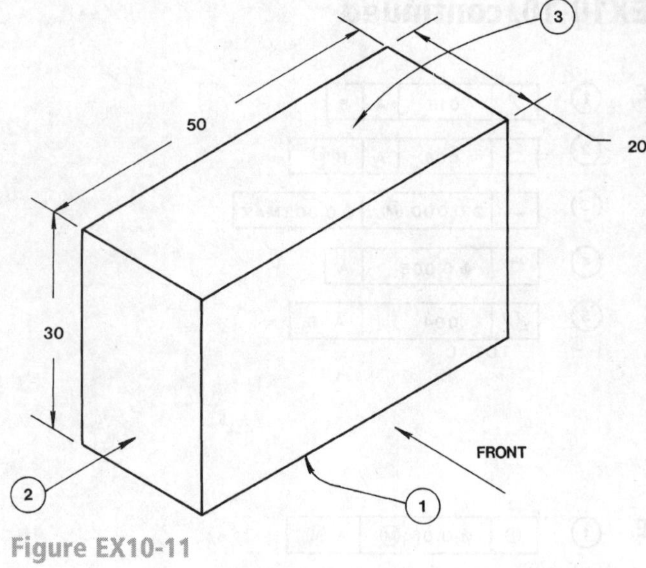

Figure EX10-11

EX10-12 Inches

Draw front, top, and right-side views of the object in Figure EX10-12, including dimensions. Add the following tolerances and specifications to the drawing:

A. Surface 1 is datum A.

B. Surface 2 is datum B and is perpendicular to datum A within .003 inch.

C. Surface 3 is parallel to datum A within .005 inch.

D. The cylinder's longitudinal centerline is to be straight within .001 inch at MMC.

E. Surface 2 is to have circular accuracy within .002 inch.

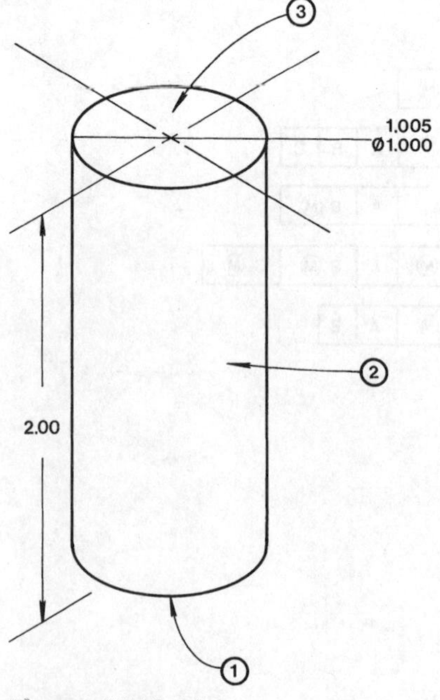

Figure EX10-12

EX10-13 Millimeters

Draw front, top, and right-side views of the object in Figure EX10-13, including dimensions. Add the following tolerances and specifications to the drawing:

A. Surface 1 is datum A.
B. Surface 4 is datum B and is perpendicular to datum A within .08 millimeter.
C. Surface 3 is flat within .03 millimeter.
D. Surface 5 is parallel to datum A within .01 millimeter.
E. Surface 2 has a runout tolerance of .2 millimeter relative to surface 4.
F. Surface 1 is flat within .02 millimeter.
G. The longitudinal centerline is to be straight within .02 millimeter at MMC and perpendicular to datum A.

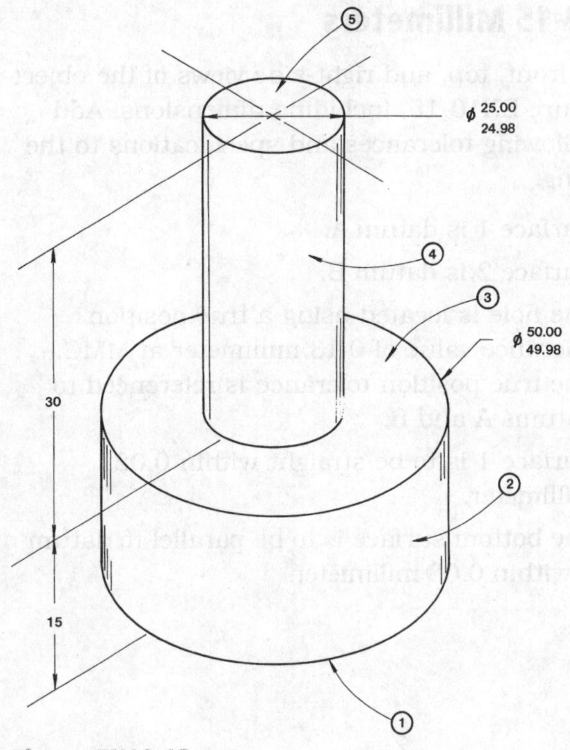

Figure EX10-13

EX10-14 Inches

Draw front, **Inches** top, and right-side views of the object in Figure EX10-14, including dimensions. Add the following tolerances and specifications to the drawing:

A. Surface 2 is datum A.
B. Surface 6 is perpendicular to datum A with .000 allowable variance at MMC, but with a .002-inch MAX variance limit beyond MMC.
C. Surface 1 is parallel to datum A within .005 inch.
D. Surface 4 is perpendicular to datum A within .004 inch.

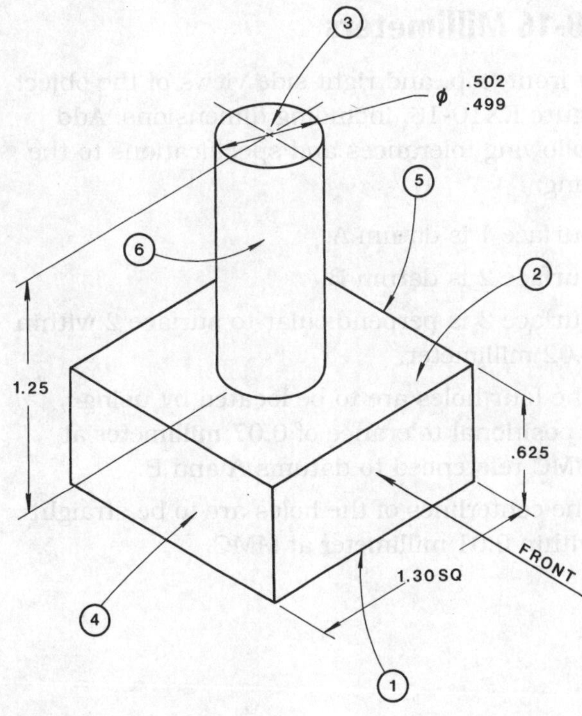

Figure EX10-14

EX10-15 Millimeters

Draw front, top, and right-side views of the object in Figure EX10-15, including dimensions. Add the following tolerances and specifications to the drawing:

A. Surface 1 is datum A.

B. Surface 2 is datum B.

C. The hole is located using a true position tolerance value of 0.13 millimeter at MMC. The true position tolerance is referenced to datums A and B.

D. Surface 1 is to be straight within 0.02 millimeter.

E. The bottom surface is to be parallel to datum A within 0.03 millimeter.

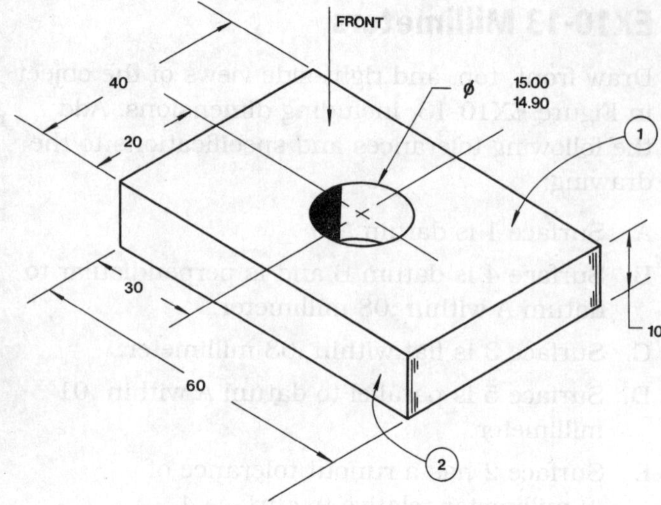

Figure EX10-15

EX10-16 Millimeters

Draw front, top, and right-side views of the object in Figure EX10-16, including dimensions. Add the following tolerances and specifications to the drawing:

A. Surface 1 is datum A.

B. Surface 2 is datum B.

C. Surface 3 is perpendicular to surface 2 within 0.02 millimeter.

D. The four holes are to be located by using a positional tolerance of 0.07 millimeter at MMC referenced to datums A and B.

E. The centerlines of the holes are to be straight within 0.01 millimeter at MMC.

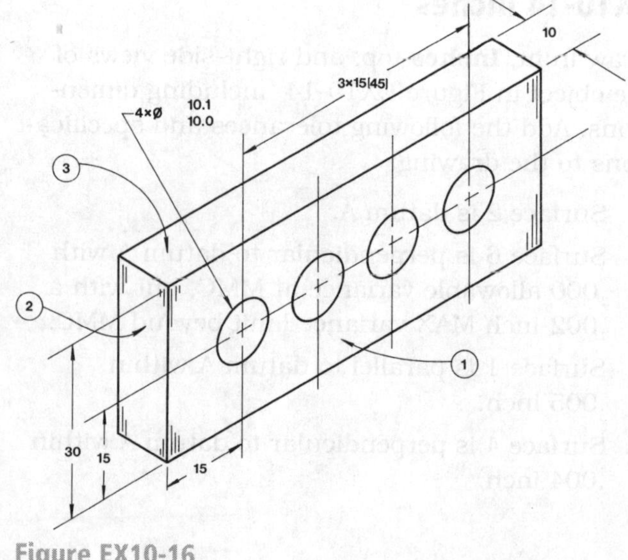

Figure EX10-16

EX10-17 Inches

Draw front, top, and right-side views of the object in Figure EX10-17, including dimensions. Add the following tolerances and specifications to the drawing:

A. Surface 1 has a dimension of .3782.375 inch and is datum A. The surface has a dual primary runout with datum B to within .005 inch. The runout is total.

B. Surface 2 has a dimension of 1.505 – 1.495 inch. Its runout relative to the dual primary datums A and B is .008 inch. The runout is total.

C. Surface 3 has a dimension of 1.000 ± .005 and has no geometric tolerance.

D. Surface 4 has no circular dimension, but has a total runout tolerance of .006 inch relative to the dual datums A and B.

E. Surface 5 has a dimension of .500 – .495 inch and is datum B. It has a dual primary runout with datum A within .005 inch. The runout is total.

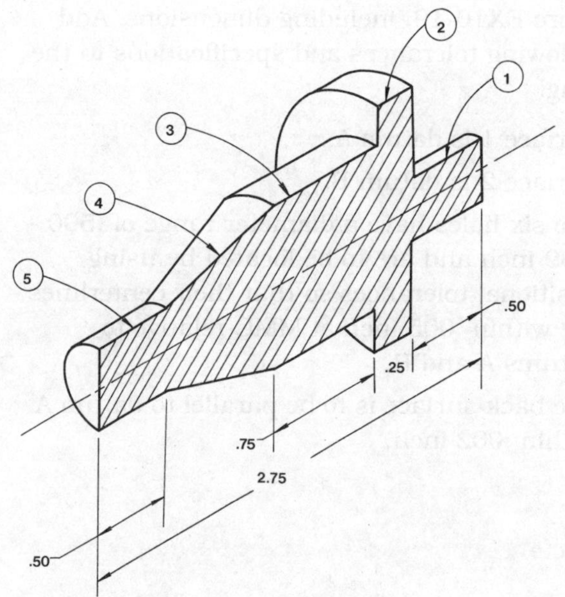

Figure EX10-17

EX10-18 Millimeters

Draw front, top, and right-side views of the object in Figure EX10-18, including dimensions. Add the following tolerances and specifications to the drawing:

A. Hole 1 is datum A.

B. Hole 2 is to have its circular centerline parallel to datum A within 0.2 millimeter at MMC when datum A is at MMC.

C. Assign a positional tolerance of 0.01 to each hole's centerline at MMC.

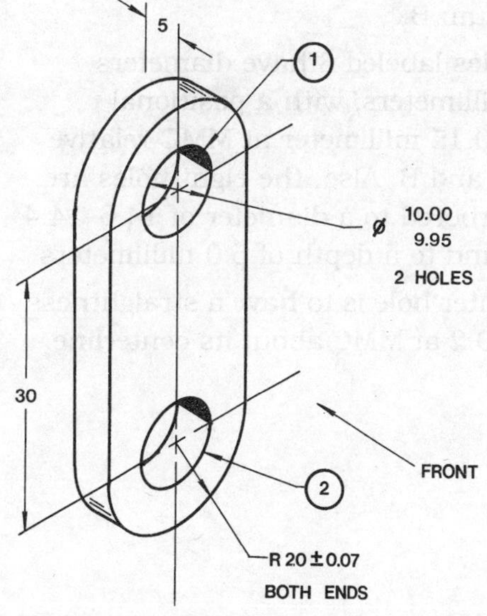

Figure EX10-18

EX10-19 Inches

Draw front, top, and right-side views of the object in Figure EX10-19, including dimensions. Add the following tolerances and specifications to the drawing:

A. Surface 1 is datum A.

B. Surface 2 is datum B.

C. The six holes have a diameter range of .500 – .499 inch and are to be located by using positional tolerances so that their centerlines are within .005 inch at MMC relative to datums A and B.

D. The back surface is to be parallel to datum A within .002 inch.

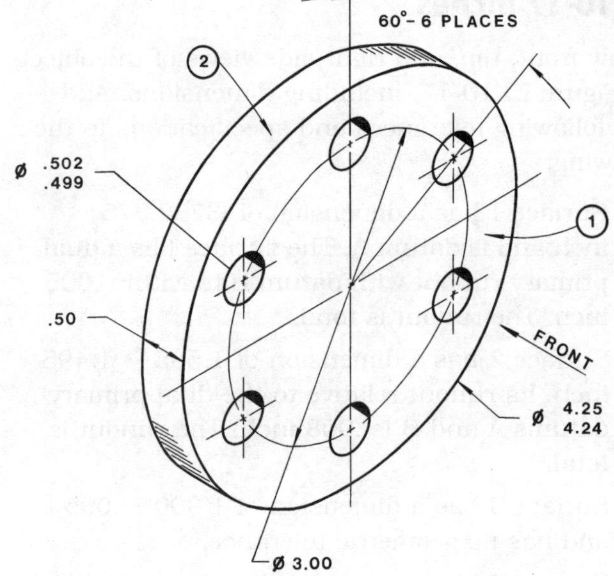

Figure EX10-19

EX10-20 Millimeters

Draw front, top, and right-side views of the object in Figure EX10-20, including dimensions. Add the following tolerances and specifications to the drawing:

A. Surface 1 is datum A.

B. Hole 2 is datum B.

C. The eight holes labeled 3 have diameters of 8.4–8.3 millimeters, with a positional tolerance of 0.15 millimeter at MMC relative to datums A and B. Also, the eight holes are to be counterbored to a diameter of 14.6–14.4 millimeters and to a depth of 5.0 millimeters.

D. The large center hole is to have a straightness tolerance of 0.2 at MMC about its centerline.

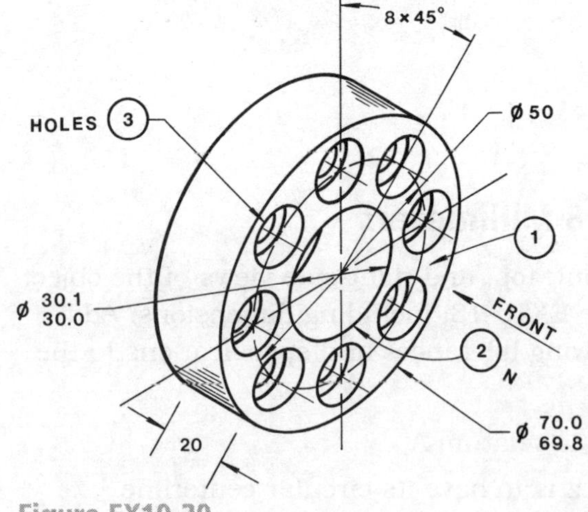

Figure EX10-20

EX10-21 Millimeters

Draw front, top, and right-side views of the object in Figure EX10-21, including dimensions. Add the following tolerances and specifications to the drawing:

A. Surface 1 is datum A.

B. Surface 2 is datum B.

C. Surface 3 is datum C.

D. The four holes labeled 4 have a dimension and tolerance of 8 + 0.3, –0 millimeters. The holes are to be located by using a positional tolerance of 0.05 millimeter at MMC relative to datums A, B, and C.

E. The six holes labeled 5 have a dimension and tolerance of 6 + 0.2, –0 millimeters. The holes are to be located by using a positional tolerance of 0.01 millimeter at MMC relative to datums A, B, and C.

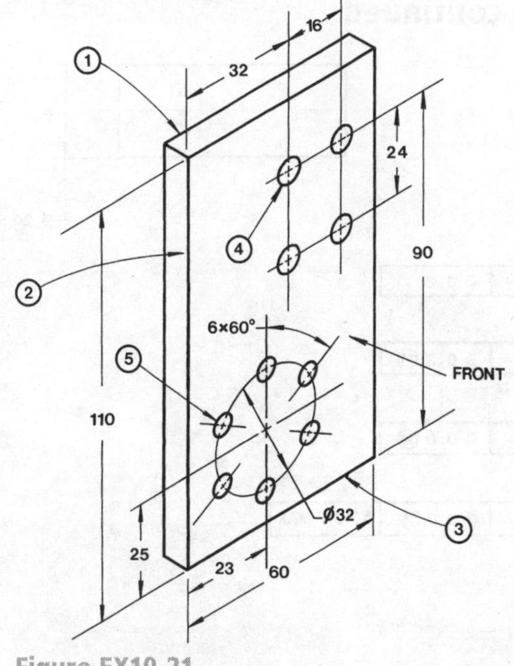

Figure EX10-21

EX10-22

The objects on the next page labeled A and B are to be toleranced by four different tolerances as shown. Redraw the charts shown in Figure EX10-22, and list the appropriate allowable tolerance for "as measured" increments of 0.1 millimeter or .001 inch. Also include the appropriate geometric tolerance drawing called out above each chart.

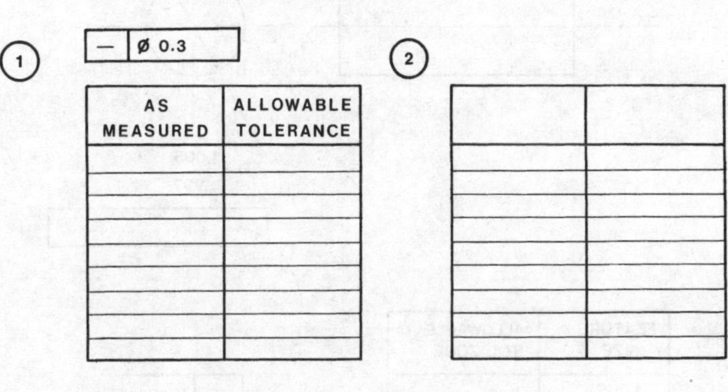

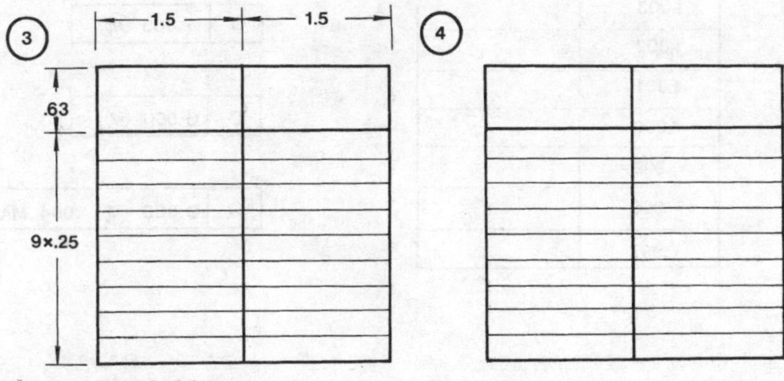

Figure EX10-22

EX10-22, continued

A.

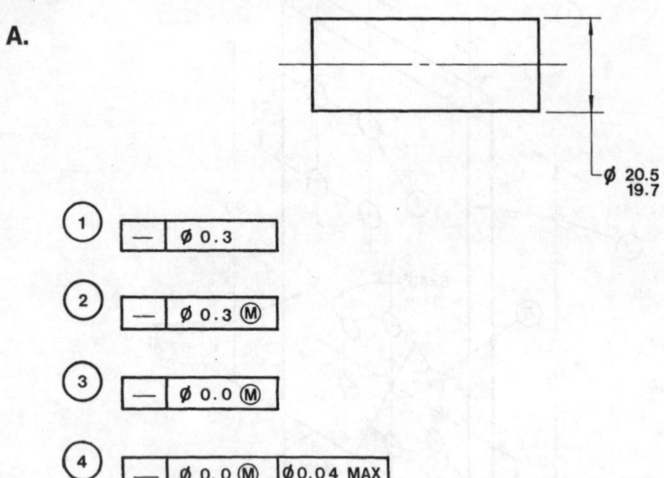

B.

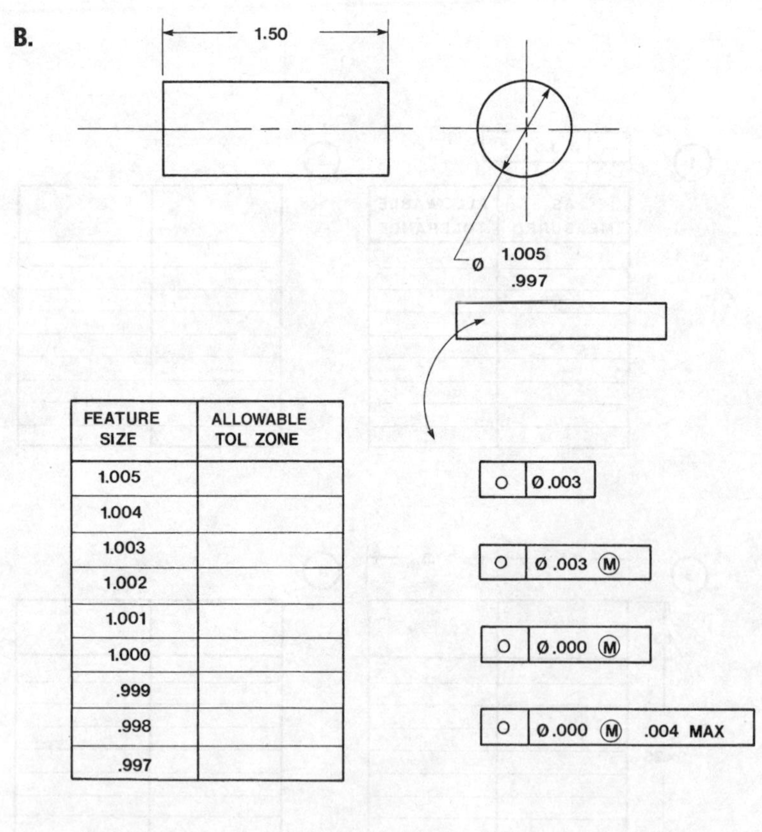

FEATURE SIZE	ALLOWABLE TOL ZONE
1.005	
1.004	
1.003	
1.002	
1.001	
1.000	
.999	
.998	
.997	

EX10-23

Dimension and tolerance parts 1 and 2 of Figure EX10-23 so that part 1 always fits into part 2 with a minimum clearance of .005 inch. The tolerance for part 1's outer matching surface is .006 inch.

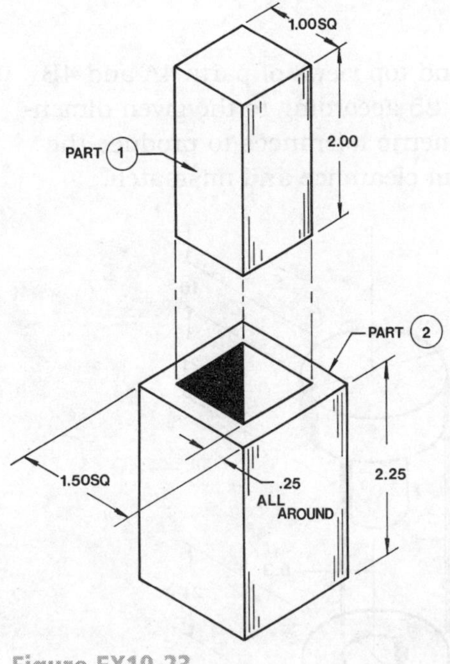

Figure EX10-23

EX10-24

Dimension and tolerance parts 1 and 2 of Figure EX10-24 so that part 1 always fits into part 2 with a minimum clearance of 0.03 millimeter. The tolerance for part 1's diameter is 0.05 millimeter. Take into account the fact that the interface is long relative to the diameters.

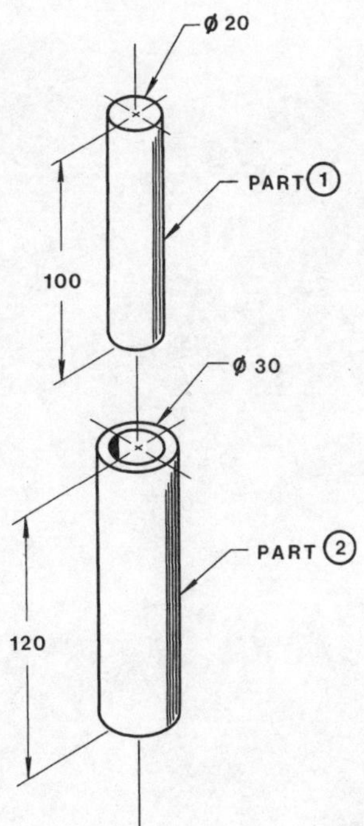

Figure EX10-24

EX10-25

Prepare front and top views of parts 4A and 4B of Figure EX10-25 according to the given dimensions. Add geometric tolerances to produce the stated maximum clearance and mismatch.

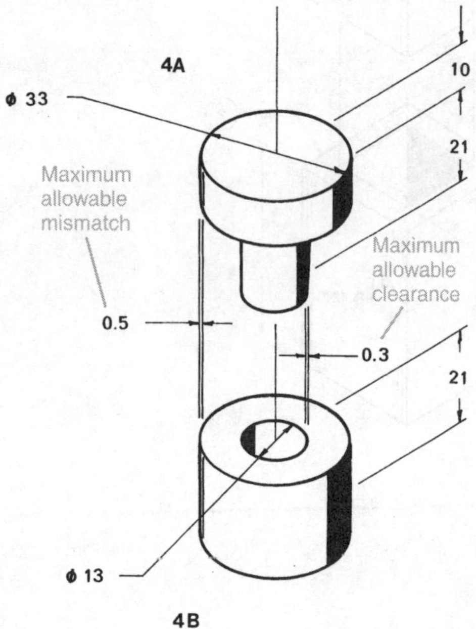

Figure EX10-25

EX10-26

Redraw parts A and B of Figure EX10-26, and add dimensions and tolerances to meet the "UPON ASSEMBLY" requirements.

The UPON ASSEMBLY condition.

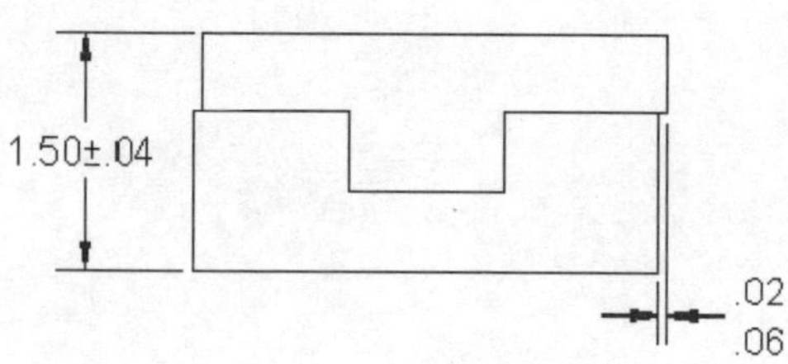

Nominal sizes

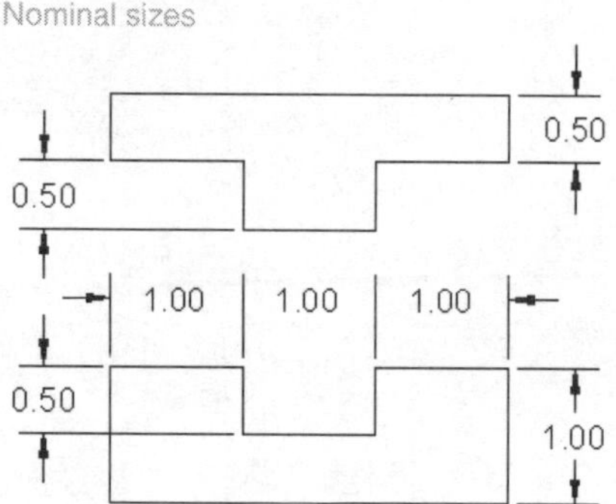

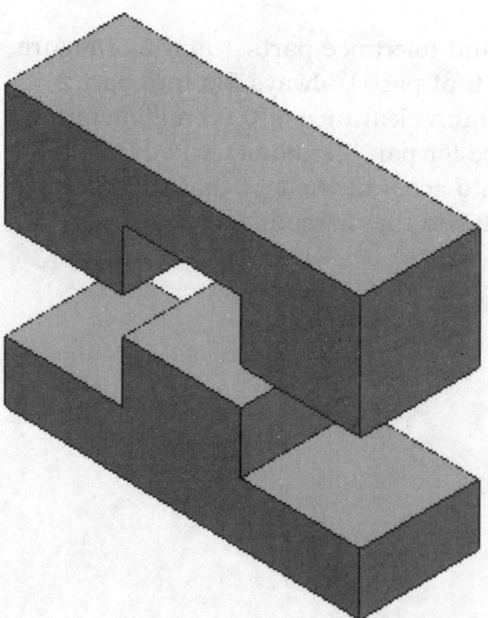

Figure EX10-26

EX10-27

Draw front and top views of both objects in Figure EX10-27. Add dimensions and geometric tolerances to meet the "FINAL CONDITION" requirements.

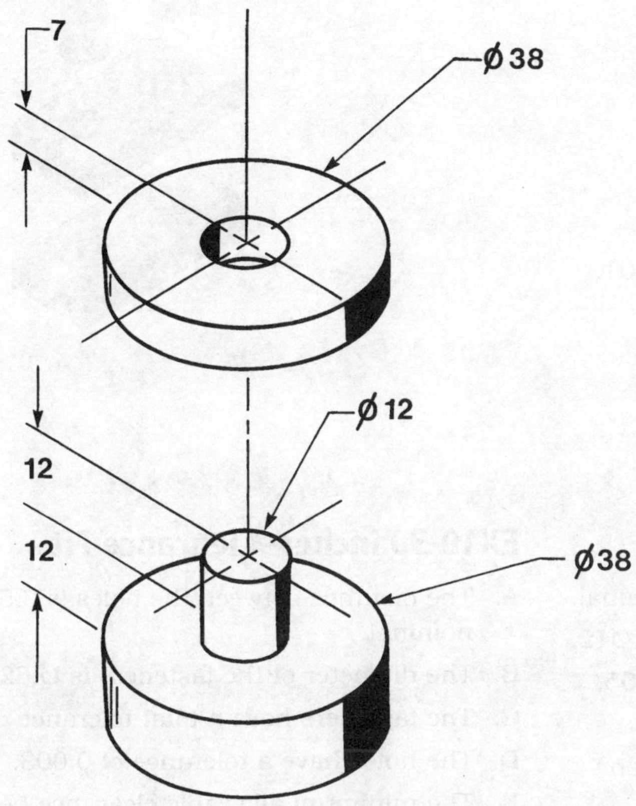

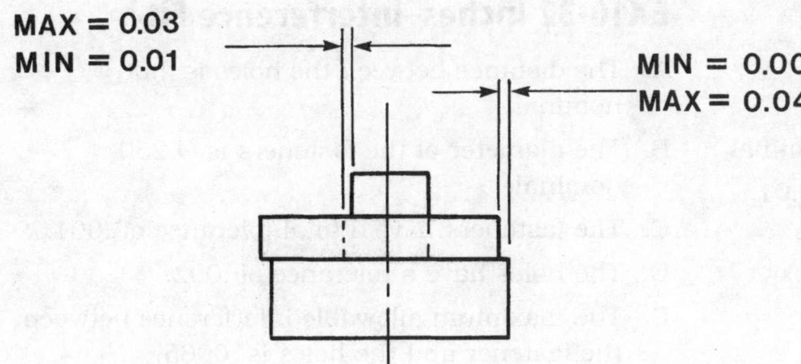

Figure EX10-27

Given a top and bottom part in the floating condition, as shown in Figure EX10-28, add dimensions and tolerances to satisfy the given conditions. Size the top and bottom parts and fastener length as needed. Use geometric and positional tolerances.

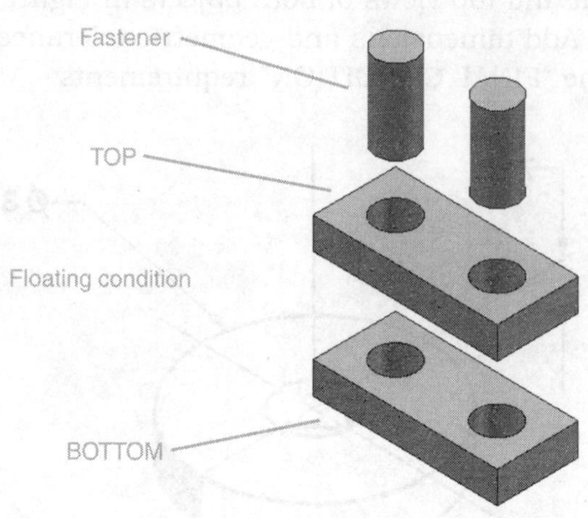

Figure EX10-28

EX10-28 Inches–Clearance Fit

A. The distance between the holes is 2.00 nominal.
B. The diameter of the fasteners is Ø.375 nominal.
C. The fasteners have a total tolerance of .001.
D. The holes have a tolerance of .002.
E. The minimum allowable clearance between the fastener and the holes is .003.
F. The material is .375 inch thick.

EX10-29 Millimeters–Clearance Fit

A. The distance between the holes is 80 nominal.
B. The nominal diameter of the fasteners is Ø12.
C. The fasteners have a total tolerance of 0.05.
D. The holes have a tolerance of 0.03.
E. The minimum allowable clearance between the fastener and the holes is 0.02.
F. The material is 12 millimeters thick.

EX10-30 Inches–Clearance Fit

A. The distance between the holes is 3.50 nominal.
B. The diameter of the fasteners is Ø.625.
C. The fasteners have a total tolerance of 0.005.
D. The holes have a tolerance of 0.003.
E. The minimum allowable clearance between the fastener and the holes is 0.002.
F. The material is 0.500 inch thick.

EX10-31 Millimeters–Clearance Fit

A. The distance between the holes is 120 nominal.
B. The diameter of the fasteners is Ø24 nominal.
C. The fasteners have a total tolerance of 0.01.
D. The holes have a tolerance of 0.02.
E. The minimum allowable clearance between the fastener and the holes is 0.04.
F. The material is 20 millimeters thick.

EX10-32 Inches–Interference Fit

A. The distance between the holes is 2.00 nominal.
B. The diameter of the fasteners is Ø.250 nominal.
C. The fasteners have a total tolerance of .001.
D. The holes have a tolerance of .002.
E. The maximum allowable interference between the fastener and the holes is .0065.
F. The material is .438 inch thick.

EX10-33 Millimeters–Interference Fit

A. The distance between the holes is 80 nominal.
B. The diameter of the fasteners is Ø10 nominal.
C. The fasteners have a total tolerance of 0.01.
D. The holes have a tolerance of 0.02.
E. The maximum allowable interference between the fastener and the holes is 0.032.
F. The material is 14 millimeters thick.

EX10-34 Inches–Locational Fit

A. The distance between the holes is 2.25 nominal.
B. The diameter of the fasteners is Ø.50 nominal.
C. The fasteners have a total tolerance of .001.
D. The holes have a tolerance of .002.
E. The minimum allowable clearance between the fastener and the holes is .0010.
F. The material is .370 inch thick.

EX10-35 Millimeters–Transitional Fit

A. The distance between the holes is 100 nominal.
B. The diameter of the fasteners is Ø16 nominal.
C. The fasteners have a total tolerance of 0.01.
D. The holes are to have a tolerance of 0.02.
E. The minimum allowable clearance between the fastener and the holes is 0.01.
F. The material is 20 millimeters thick.

Given a top and bottom part in the fixed condition, as shown in Figure EX10-36, add dimensions and tolerances to satisfy the given conditions. Size the top and bottom parts and fastener length as needed. Use geometric and positional tolerances.

EX10-36 Inches–Clearance Fit

A. The distance between the holes is 2.00 nominal.
B. The diameter of the fasteners is Ø.375 nominal.
C. The fasteners have a total tolerance of .001.
D. The holes have a tolerance of .002.
E. The minimum allowable clearance between the fastener and the holes is .003.
F. The material is .375 inch thick.

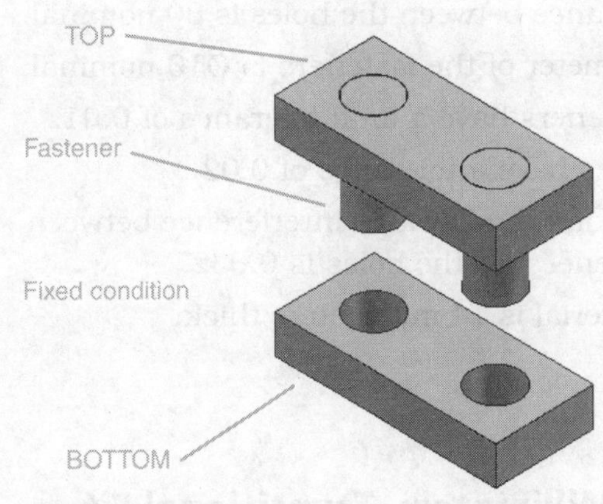

Figure EX10-36

EX10-37 Millimeters–Clearance Fit

A. The distance between the holes is 80 nominal.
B. The nominal diameter of the fasteners is Ø12.
C. The fasteners have a total tolerance of 0.05.
D. The holes have a tolerance of 0.03.
E. The minimum allowable clearance between the fastener and the holes is 0.02.
F. The material is 12 millimeters thick.

EX10-38 Inches–Clearance Fit

A. The distance between the holes is 3.50 nominal.
B. The diameter of the fasteners is Ø.625.
C. The fasteners have a total tolerance of .005.
D. The holes have a tolerance of .003.
E. The minimum allowable clearance between the fastener and the holes is .002.
F. The material is .500 inch thick.

EX10-39 Millimeters–Clearance Fit

A. The distance between the holes is 120 nominal.
B. The diameter of the fasteners is Ø24 nominal.
C. The fasteners have a total tolerance of 0.01.
D. The holes have a tolerance of 0.02.
E. The minimum allowable clearance between the fastener and the holes is 0.04.
F. The material is 20 millimeters thick.

EX10-40 Inches–Interference Fit

A. The distance between the holes is 2.00 nominal.
B. The diameter of the fasteners is Ø.250 nominal.
C. The fasteners have a total tolerance of .001.
D. The holes have a tolerance of .002.
E. The maximum allowable interference between the fastener and the holes is .0065.
F. The material is .438 inch thick.

EX10-41 Millimeters–Interference Fit

A. The distance between the holes is 80 nominal.
B. The diameter of the fasteners is Ø10 nominal.
C. The fasteners have a total tolerance of 0.01.
D. The holes have a tolerance of 0.02.
E. The maximum allowable interference between the fastener and the holes is 0.032.
F. The material is 14 millimeters thick.

EX10-42 Inches–Locational Fit

A. The distance between the holes is 2.25 nominal.
B. The diameter of the fasteners is Ø.50 nominal.
C. The fasteners have a total tolerance of .001.
D. The holes have a tolerance of .002.
E. The minimum allowable clearance between the fastener and the holes is .0010.
F. The material is .370 inch thick.

EX10-43 Millimeters–Transitional Fit

A. The distance between the holes is 100 nominal.
B. The diameter of the fasteners is Ø16 nominal.
C. The fasteners have a total tolerance of 0.01.
D. The holes are to have a tolerance of 0.02.
E. The minimum allowable clearance between the fastener and the holes is 0.001.
F. The material is 20 millimeters thick.

EX10-44

Given the two assemblies that follow, size the parts so that they always fit together. Create individual drawings of each part, including dimensions and tolerances. Use geometric and positional tolerances.

SUPPORT ASSEMBLY

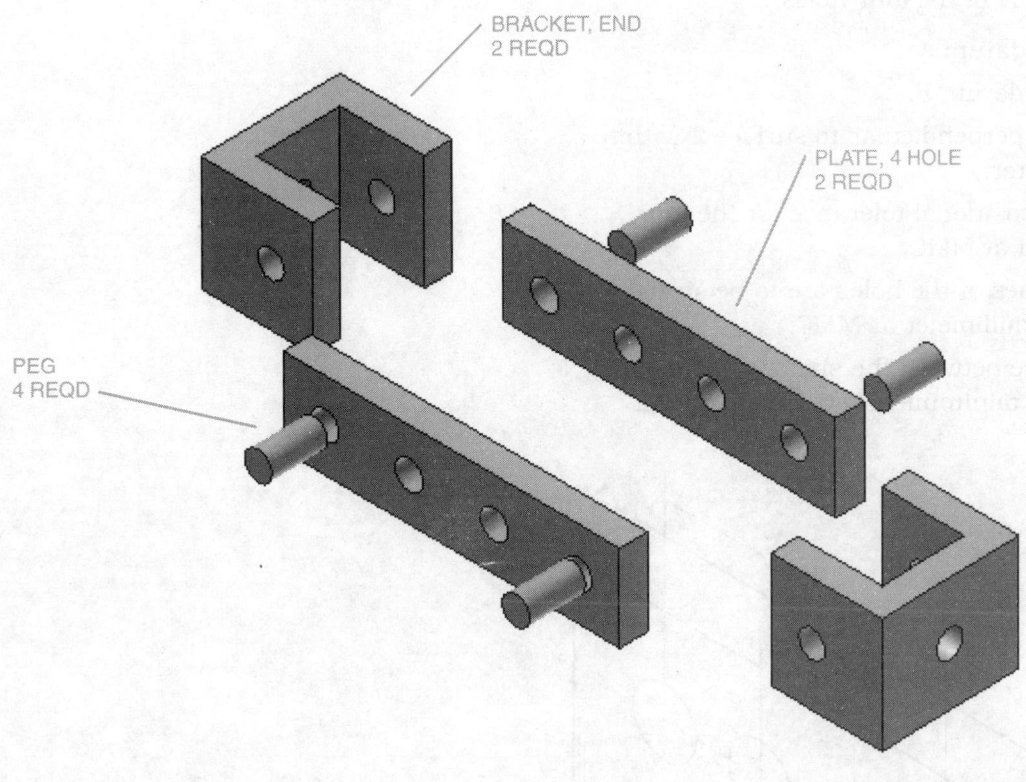

EX10-45

Assume that there are two copies of the part in Figure EX10-45 and that these parts are to be joined together by four fasteners in the floating condition. Draw front and top views of the object, including dimensions and tolerances. Add the given tolerances and specifications to the drawing, and then draw front and top views of a shaft that can be used to join the two objects. The shaft should be able to fit into any of the four holes.

A. Surface 1 is datum A.

B. Surface 2 is datum B.

C. Surface 3 is perpendicular to surface 2 within 0.02 millimeter.

D. Specify the positional tolerance for the four holes applied at MMC.

E. The centerlines of the holes are to be straight within 0.01 millimeter at MMC.

F. The clearance between the shafts and the holes is to be 0.05 minimum and 0.10 maximum.

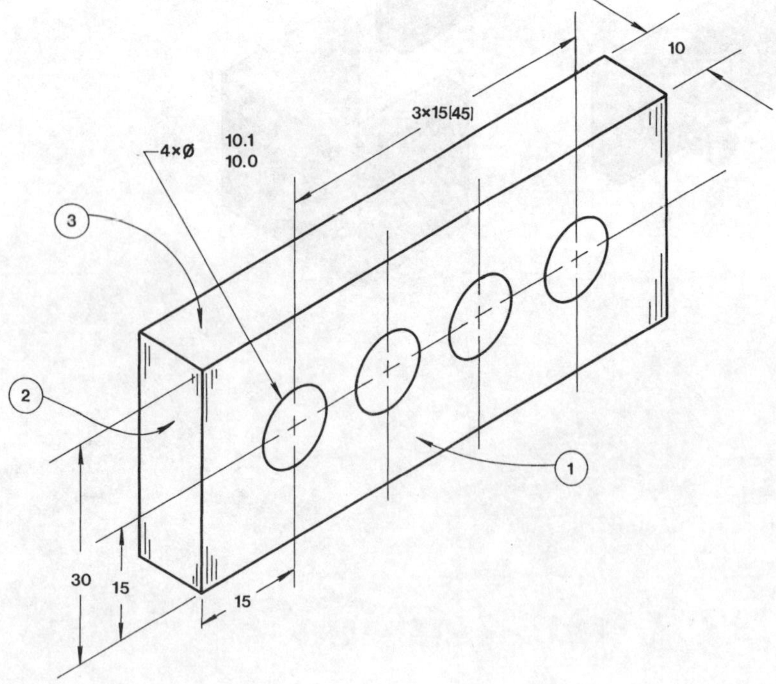

Figure EX10-45

EX10-46

Assume that there are two copies of the part in Figure EX10-46 and that these parts are to be joined together by six fasteners in the floating condition. Draw front and top views of the object, including dimensions and tolerances. Add the given tolerances and specifications to the drawing, and then draw front and top views of a shaft that can be used to join the two objects. The shaft should be able to fit into any of the six holes.

A. Surface 1 is datum A.

B. Surface 2 is round within .003.

C. Specify the positional tolerance for the six holes applied at MMC.

D. The clearance between the shafts and the holes is to be .001 minimum and .003 maximum.

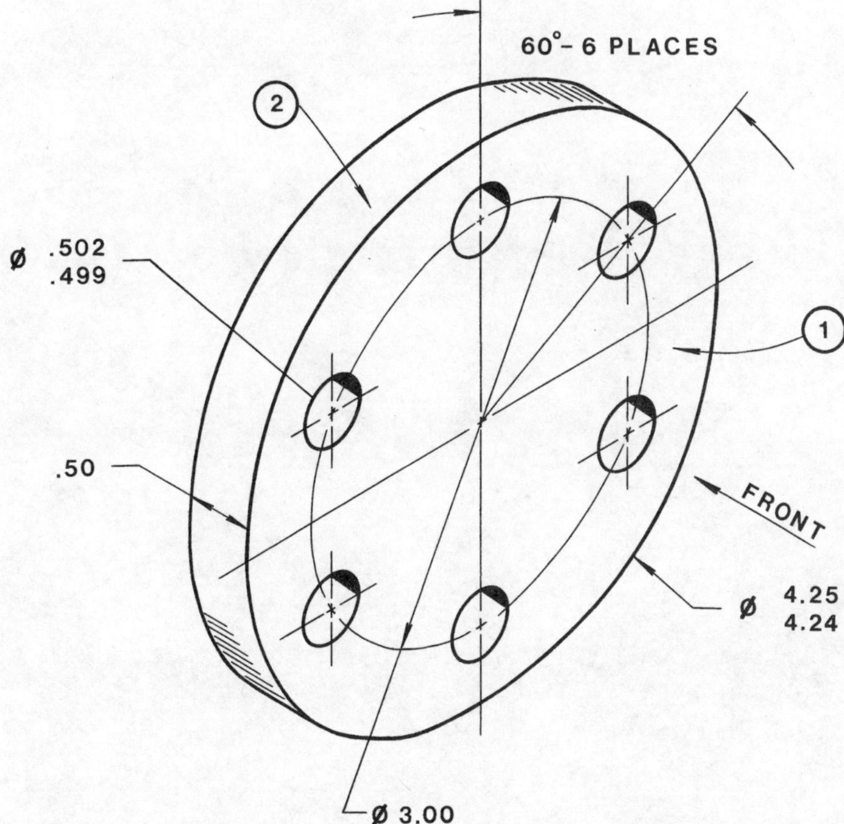

Figure EX10-46

11

chapter eleven

Threads and Fasteners

11-1 Introduction

This chapter explains how to draw threads, washers, keys, and springs. It explains how to use fasteners to join parts together and design uses for washers, keys, and springs.

Throughout the chapter, it will be suggested that blocks and wblocks be created of the various thread and fastener shapes. Thread representations, fastener head shapes, setscrews, and both internal and external thread representations for orthographic views and sectional views are so common in technical drawings that it is good practice to create a set of wblocks that can be used on future drawings in order to avoid having to redraw a thread shape every time it is needed.

See Chapter 3 for an explanation of the **Block** command.

11-2 Thread Terminology

Figure 11-1 shows a thread. The peak of a thread is called the ***crest***, and the valley portion is called the ***root***. The ***major diameter*** of a thread is the distance across the thread from crest to crest. The ***minor diameter*** is the distance across the thread from root to root.

Figure 11-1 Detailed representation

The ***pitch*** of a thread is the linear distance along the thread from crest to crest. Thread pitch is usually referred to in terms of a unit of length, such as 20 threads per inch or 1.5 threads per millimeter.

11-3 Thread Callouts (Metric Units)

Threads are specified on a drawing by drawing callouts. See Figure 11-2. The M preceding a drawing callout specifies that the callout is for a metric thread. Holes that are not threaded use the Ø symbol.

Figure 11-2

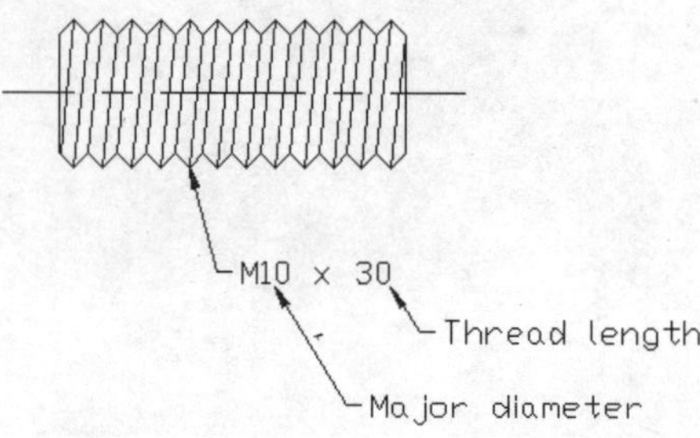

Major Dia	Coarse		Fine	
	Pitch	Tap Drill Dia	Pitch	Tap Drill Dia
1.6	0.35	1.25		
2	0.4	1.6		
2.5	0.45	2.05		
3	0.5	2.5		
4	.7	3.3		
5	0.8	4.2		
6	1	5.0		
8	1.25	6.7	1	7.0
10	1.5	8.5	1.25	8.7
12	1.75	10.2	1.25	10.8
16	2	14	1.5	14.5
20	2.5	17.5	1.5	18.5
24	3	21	2	22
30	3.5	26.5	2	28
36	4	32	3	33
42	4.5	37.5	3	39
48	5	43	3	45

Figure 11-3

The number following the M is the major diameter of the thread; for example, an M10 thread has a major diameter of 10 millimeters. The pitch of a metric thread is assumed to be a coarse thread unless otherwise stated. The callout M10 × 30 assumes a coarse thread, or 1.5 threads per millimeter. The number 30 is the thread length in millimeters. The "×" is read as "by," so the thread is called a "ten by thirty."

The callout M10 × 1.25 × 30 specifies a pitch of 1.25 threads per millimeter. This is not a standard coarse thread size, so the pitch must be specified.

Figure 11-3 shows a list of preferred thread sizes. These sizes are similar to the standard sizes shown in Figure 9-32. A list of other metric thread sizes is included in the appendix.

Whenever possible, use preferred thread sizes for designing. Preferred thread sizes are readily available and are usually cheaper than nonstandard sizes. In addition, tooling such as wrenches is also readily available for preferred sizes.

11-4 Thread Callouts (English Units)

English unit threads always include a thread form specification. Thread form specifications are designated by capital letters, as shown in Figure 11-4, and are defined as follows:

UNC—Unified National Coarse

UNF—Unified National Fine

UNEF—Unified National Extra Fine

UN—Unified National, or constant pitch threads

Figure 11-4

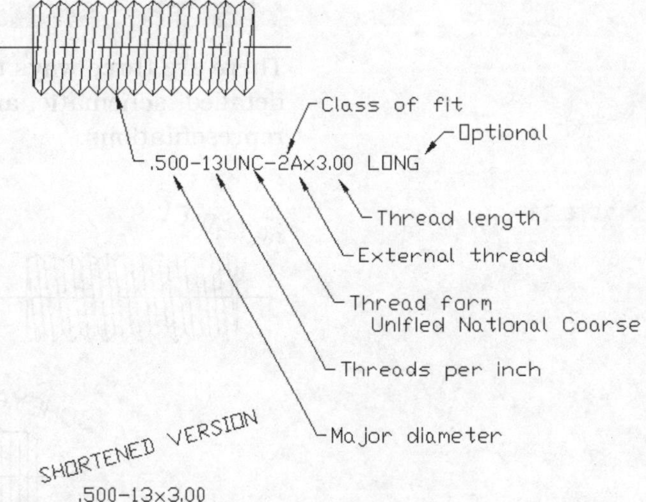

An English unit thread callout starts by defining the major diameter of the thread, followed by the pitch specification. The callout .500 –13 UNC means a thread whose major diameter is .500 inch, with 13 threads per inch, manufactured to the Unified National Coarse standards.

There are three possible classes of fit for a thread: 1, 2, and 3. The different classes specify a set of manufacturing tolerances. A class 1 thread is the loosest, and a class 3, the most exact. A class 2 fit is the most common.

The letter A designates an external thread, B an internal thread. The symbol × means "by," as in 2 × 4, or "two by four." The thread length (3.00) may be followed by the word LONG to prevent confusion about which value represents the length.

Drawing callouts for English unit threads are sometimes shortened, as shown in Figure 11-4. The callout .500–13UNC–2A × 3.00 LONG is shortened to .500–13 × 3.00. Only a coarse thread has 13 threads per inch, and it should be obvious whether a thread is internal or external, so these specifications may be dropped. Most threads are class 2, so it is tacitly accepted that all threads are class 2 unless otherwise specified. The shortened callout form is not universally accepted. When in doubt, use a complete thread callout.

A partial list of standard English unit threads is shown in Figure 11-5. A more complete list is included in the appendix. Some of the drill sizes listed use numbers and letters. The decimal equivalents to the numbers and letters are listed in the appendix.

Figure 11-5

		UNC		UNF		UNEF	
Major Dia	Decimal	Thread/in	Tap drill Dia.	Thread/in	Tap drill Dia.	Thread/in	Tap drill Dia.
#6	.138	40	#38	44	#37		
#8	.164	32	#29	36	#29		
#10	.190	24	#25	32	#21		
1/4	.250	20	7	28	3	32	.219
5/16	.312	18	F	24	1	32	.281
3/8	.375	16	.312	24	Q	32	.344
7/16	.438	14	U	20	.391	28	Y
1/2	.500	13	.422	20	.453	28	.469
9/16	.562	12	.484	18	.516	24	.516
5/8	.625	11	.531	18	.578	24	.578
3/4	.750	10	.656	16	.688	20	.703
7/8	.875	9	.766	14	.812	20	.828
1	1.000	8	.875	12	.922	20	.953
1 1/4	1.250	7	1.109	12	1.172	18	1.188
1 1/2	1.500	6	1.344	12	1.422	18	1.438

UNC = Unified National Coarse

UNF = Unified National Fine

UNEF = Unified National Extra Fine

11-5 Thread Representations

There are three ways to graphically represent threads on a drawing: detailed, schematic, and simplified. Figure 11-6 shows the three representations.

Figure 11-6

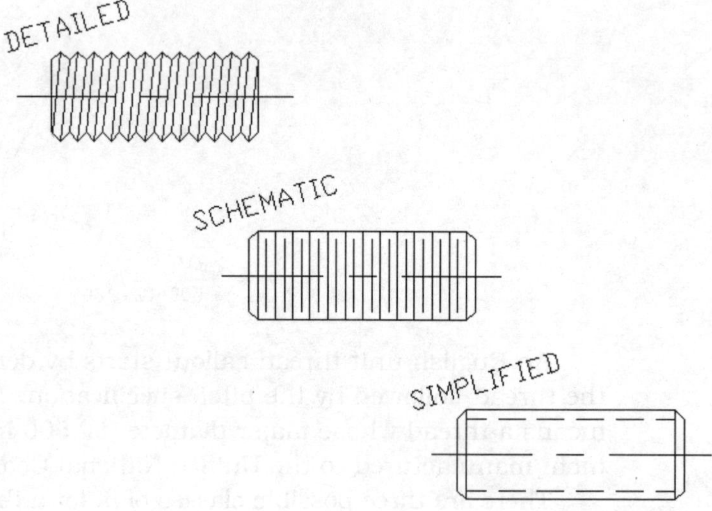

Detailed representations look the most like actual threads, but are time consuming to draw. Creating a wblock of a detailed shape will help eliminate this time constraint.

Schematic and simplified thread representations are created by drawing a series of straight lines. The simplified representation uses only two hidden lines and can be mistaken for an internal hole if it is not accompanied by a thread specification callout. The choice of which representation to use depends on individual preferences. The resulting drawing should be clear and easy to understand. All three representations may be used on the same drawing, but in general, only very large threads (those over 1.00 in., or 25 mm) are drawn for the detailed representation.

Ideally, thread representations should be drawn with each thread equal to the actual pitch size. This is not practical for smaller threads and not necessary for larger ones. Thread representations are not meant to be exact duplications of the threads, but representations, so convenient drawing distances are acceptable.

To Draw a Detailed Thread Representation

Draw a detailed thread representation for a 1.00-inch-diameter thread that is 3.00 inches long. See Figure 11-7.

1. Set **Grid** = **.5** and **Snap** = **.125.**
2. Draw a **4.00-inch** centerline near the center of the screen.
3. Zoom the area around the centerline.
4. Draw a zigzag pattern **.375** above the centerline using the 0.125 snap points. Start the zigzag line **.50** from the left end of the centerline.

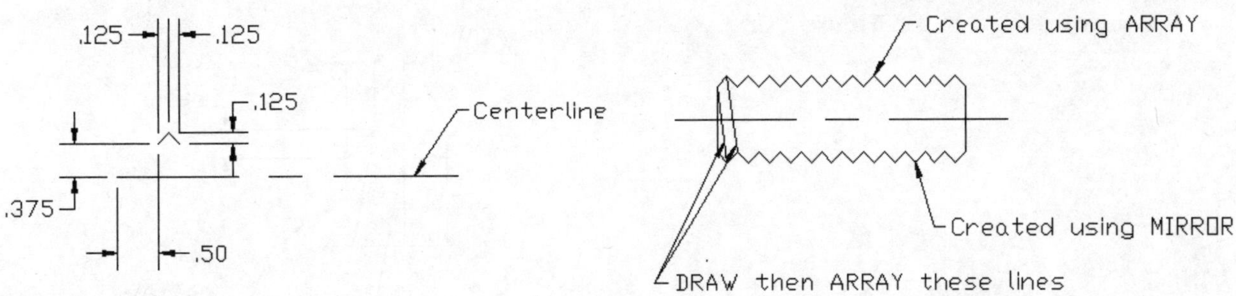

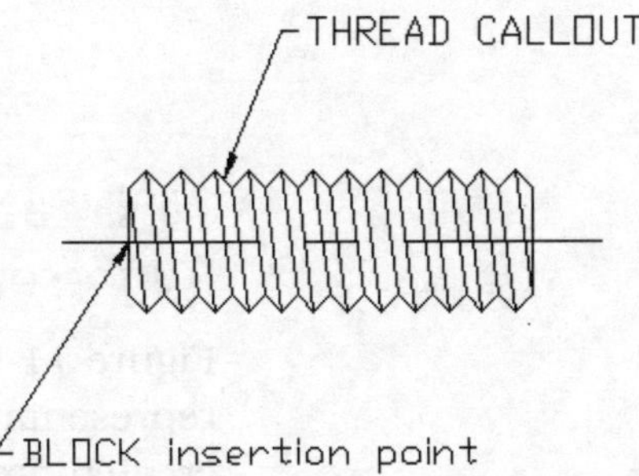

Figure 11-7

5 Access the **Array** command.

The **Array** dialog box will appear.

6 Select the **Rectangular** option.

7 Click the **Select objects** button, and then select the zigzag pattern.

8 Set the **Row value** for **1** and the **Column value** for **12.**

9 Set the **Row offset** for **0.0000.**

10 Set the **Column offset** for **0.25;** then select the **OK** button.

11 Mirror the arrayed zigzag line about the centerline.

12 Draw vertical lines at both ends of the thread and two slanted lines between the thread's roots and crests, as shown.

13 Array both slanted lines, using the same array parameters used for the zigzag line: **12** columns **.25** apart.

14 Save the thread representation as a block and wblock named **DETLIN.** Define the insertion point as shown.

Creating blocks is explained in Chapter 3.

Another technique for drawing a detailed thread representation is to draw a single thread completely and then use the **Copy** or **Array** command to generate as many additional threads as are necessary.

It is recommended that you save all thread wblocks on a separate disk. This disk will become a reference disk that you can use when creating other drawings that require threads.

Figure 11-8 shows a metric unit detailed thread representation. It was created by the procedure outlined. **Grid** was set at **10, Snap** was set at **2.5,** and the distance from the centerline to the zigzag pattern was **10.** Draw and save the metric detailed thread representation shown in Figure 11-8 as a wblock named **DETLMM.**

Figure 11-8

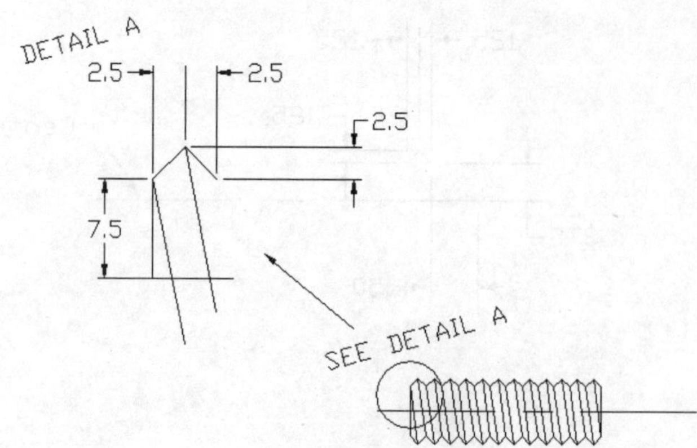

To Create an Internal Detailed Thread Representation in a Sectional View

Figure 11-9 shows how to create a 1.00-inch internal detailed thread representation from the wblock **DETLIN** of the external detailed thread created previously.

Figure 11-9

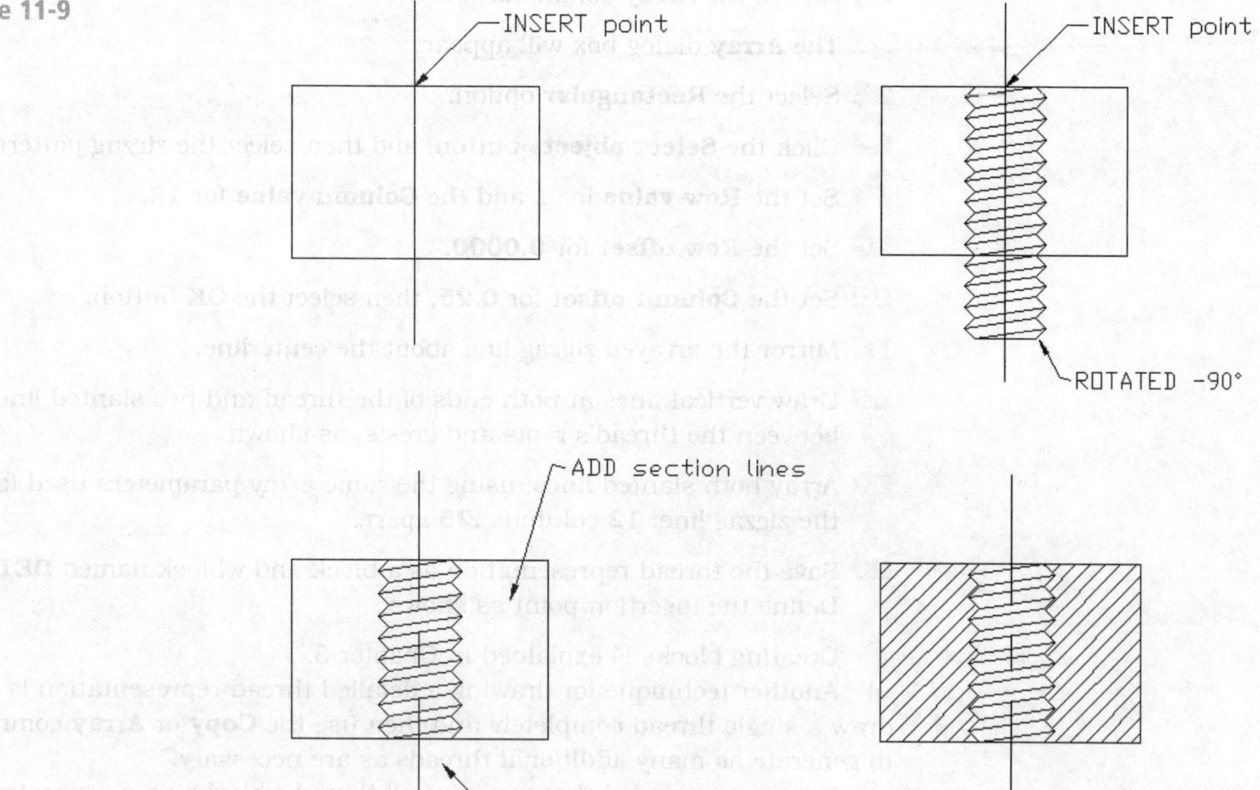

1. Use **Insert,** and locate the detailed wblock on the drawing screen at the indicated insert point. In this example, the thread is to be drawn in a vertical orientation, so the block is rotated **90°** when it is inserted. The same scale size is used for the wblock as was drawn for a 1.00-inch diameter thread.

2. The thread created from wblock **DETLIN** is longer than needed, so explode the block and then erase the excess lines.
3. Define the hatch pattern as **ANSI31,** and apply hatching to the areas outside of the thread, as shown.

To Create a Schematic Thread Representation

Draw a schematic representation of a 1.00-inch-diameter thread. See Figure 11-10.

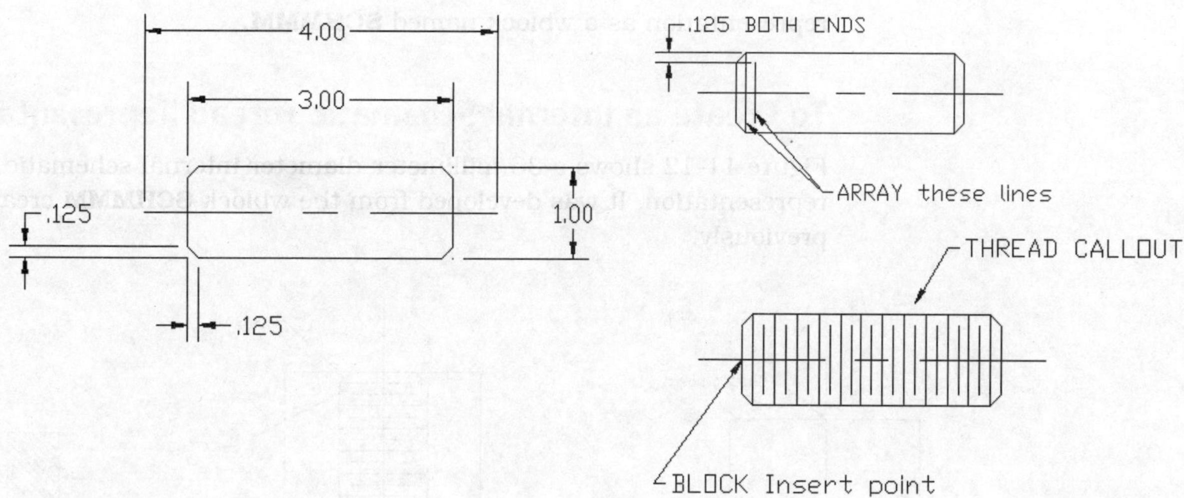

Figure 11-10

1. Set **Grid** to **.50** and **Snap** to **.125.**
2. Draw a **4.00-inch** centerline near the middle of the drawing screen.
3. Draw the outline of the thread, including a chamfer, using the dimensions shown.

The chamfer was drawn in this example by using the 0.125 snap points, but the **Chamfer** command could also have been used.

The 1.00 diameter was chosen because it will make it easier to determine scale factors for the wblock when inserting the representation into other drawings.

4. Draw three vertical lines as shown.
5. Use the **Array, Rectangular** command to draw **11** vertical lines across the thread. The distance between the 11 lines (COLUMNS) is **.25.**

   A distance of –.25 would create lines to the left of the original line.

6. Save the representation as a wblock named **SCHMINCH.** Define the insertion point as shown.

Figure 11-11 shows a metric unit version of a schematic thread representation in a sectional view. The procedure used to create the representation is the same as that explained previously, but with different drawing limits and different values. The major diameter is **20,** and the

Figure 11-11

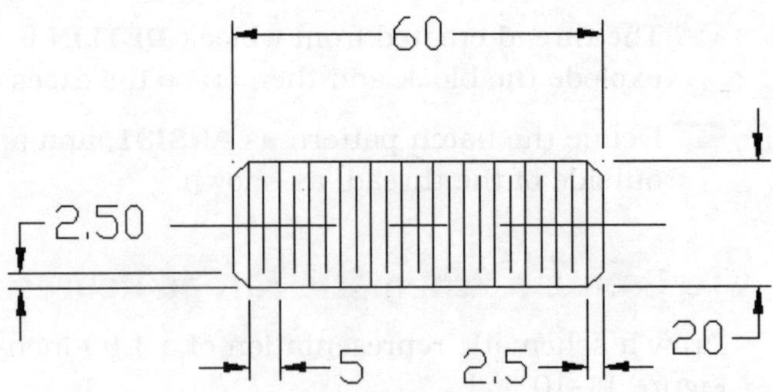

spacing between lines is **2.5** and **5,** as shown. Draw and save the representation as a wblock named **SCHMMM.**

To Create an Internal Schematic Thread Representation

Figure 11-12 shows a 36-millimeter-diameter internal schematic thread representation. It was developed from the wblock **SCHMMM** created previously.

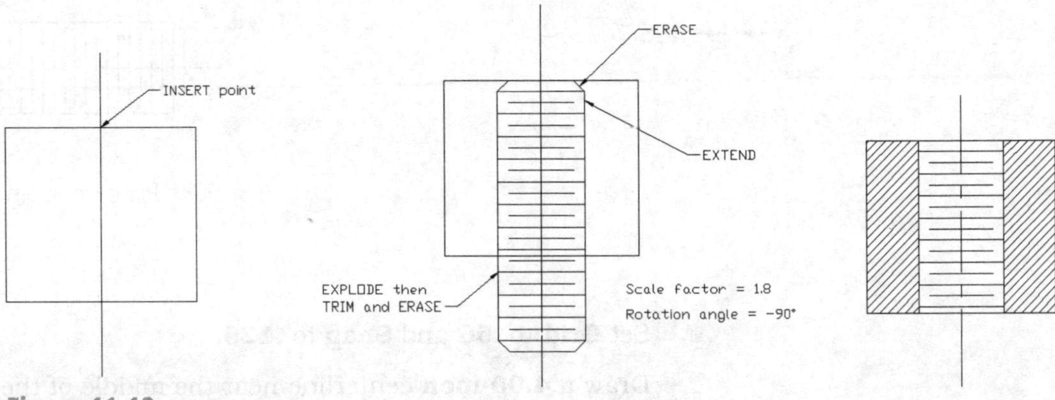

Figure 11-12

1 Set **Grid = 10**
Snap = 5
Limits = 297,210
Zoom = ALL

2 Insert the wblock **SCHMMM** at the indicated insertion point.

The required thread diameter is **36** millimeters. The wblock **SCHMMM** was drawn with a diameter of **20** millimeters. This means that the block must be enlarged by using a scale factor. The scale factor is determined by dividing the desired diameter by the wblock's diameter.

36/20 = 1.8

The wblock must also be rotated **90°** to give it the correct orientation.

3 The inserted thread shape is longer than desired, so first explode the wblock and then use the **Erase, Trim,** and **Extend** commands as needed.

4 Draw the sectional lines, using **Hatch ANSI31.**

5 Save the drawing as a wblock if desired.

To Create a Simplified Thread Representation

The simplified representation looks very similar to the orthographic view of an internal hole, so it is important to always include a thread callout with the representation. In the example shown, a leader line was included with the representation. See Figure 11-13. The leader serves as a reminder to add the appropriate drawing callout. If the leader line is in an inconvenient location when the wblock is inserted into a drawing, the leader line can be moved or simply erased.

1 Set **Grid = .5**

Snap = .125

2 Draw a **4.00** centerline near the center of the screen.

3 Draw the thread outline, using the given dimensions.

4 Draw the hidden lines, using the given dimensions.

5 Save the thread representation as a wblock named **SIMPIN.** Define the insertion point as shown.

Figure 11-14 shows an internal simplified thread representation in a sectional view. Note how hidden lines that cross over the sectional lines are used. The hatch must be drawn first, and the hidden lines added over the pattern. If the hidden lines are drawn first, the **Hatch** command may not add section lines to the portion between the hidden line and the solid line that represents the edge of the threaded hole.

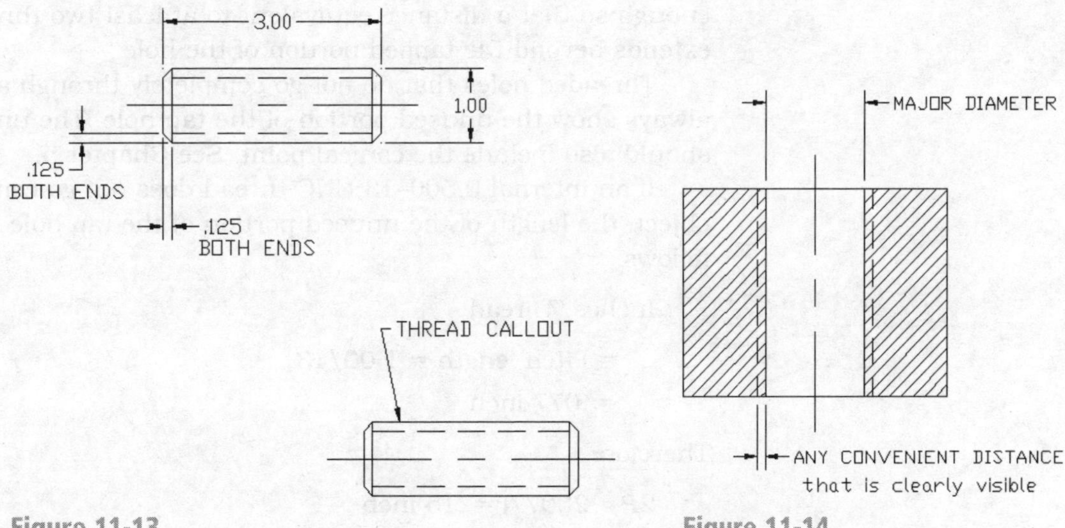

Figure 11-13

Figure 11-14

11-6 Orthographic Views of Internal Threads

Figure 11-15 shows top and front orthographic views of internal threads. One thread goes completely through the object, the other only partially.

Figure 11-15

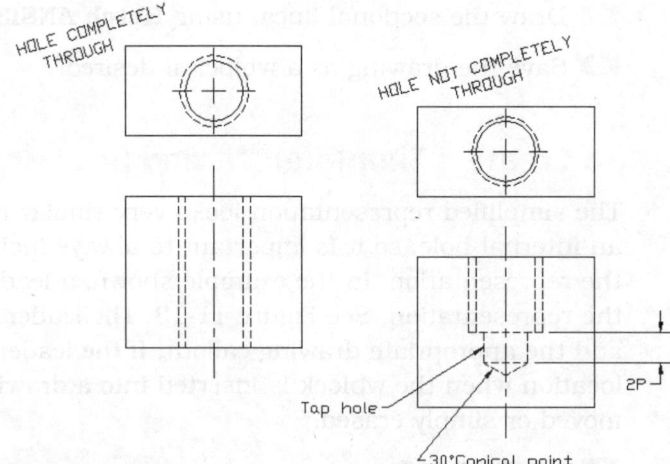

Internal threads are represented in orthographic views by parallel hidden lines. The distance between the lines should be large enough so that there is a clear distinction between the lines; that is, the lines should not appear to blend together or become a single, very thick line.

Circular orthographic views of threaded holes are represented by two circles: one drawn by using a continuous line and the other drawn by using a hidden line. The distance between the circles should be large enough to be visually distinctive. The two circles shown should both be clearly visible.

Threaded holes are created by first drilling a tap hole and then tapping (cutting) the threads with a tapping bit. Tapping bits have cutting surfaces on their side surfaces, not on the bottom. This means that if the tapping bit were forced all the way to the bottom of the tap hole, the bit could be damaged or broken. It is good design practice to make the tap hole deep enough so that a distance equivalent to at least two thread lengths ($2P$) extends beyond the tapped portion of the hole.

Threaded holes that do not go completely through an object must always show the unused portion of the tap hole. The unused portion should also include the conical point. See Chapter 5.

If an internal 0.500–13 UNC thread does not go completely through an object, the length of the unused portion of the tap hole is determined as follows:

Inches/Thread

= Pitch length = 1.00/13

= .077 inch

Therefore,

$2P = 2(.077) = .15$ inch

The distance .15 represents a minimum. It would be acceptable to specify a pilot hole depth greater than .15, depending on the specific design requirements.

If an internal M12 × 1.75 thread does not go completely through an object, the length of the unused portion of the tap hole is determined as follows:

2(Pitch length) = 2(1.75) = 3.50 mm

11-7 Sectional Views of Internal Thread Representations

Figure 11-16 shows sectional views of internal threads that do not go completely through an object. Each example was created from wblocks of the representations. The hatch pattern used was ANSI32. Each example includes both a threaded portion and an untapped pilot hole that extends approximately 2*P* beyond the end of the tapped portion of the hole.

Figure 11-16

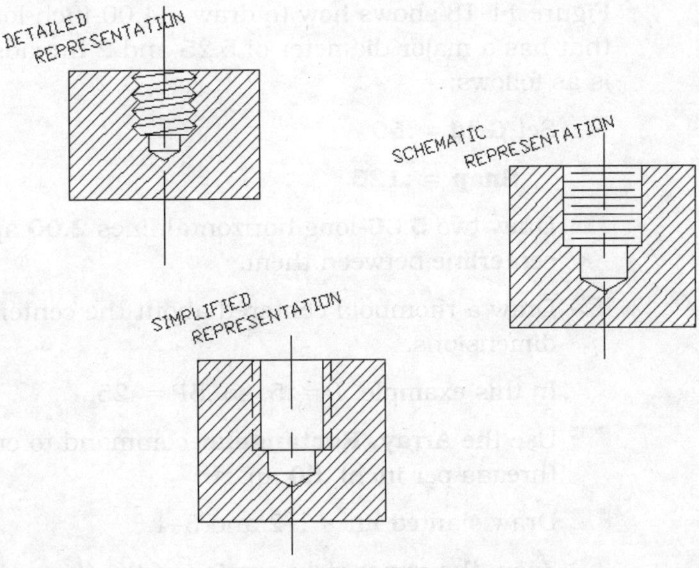

When drawing a simplified representation in a sectional view, draw the hidden lines that represent the outside edges of the threads after the section lines have been added. If the lines are drawn before the section lines are added, the section lines will stop at the outside line. Section lines should be drawn up to the solid line, as shown.

11-8 Types of Threads

Figure 11-17 shows the profiles of four different types of thread: American National, square, acme, and knuckle. There are many other types of

Figure 11-17

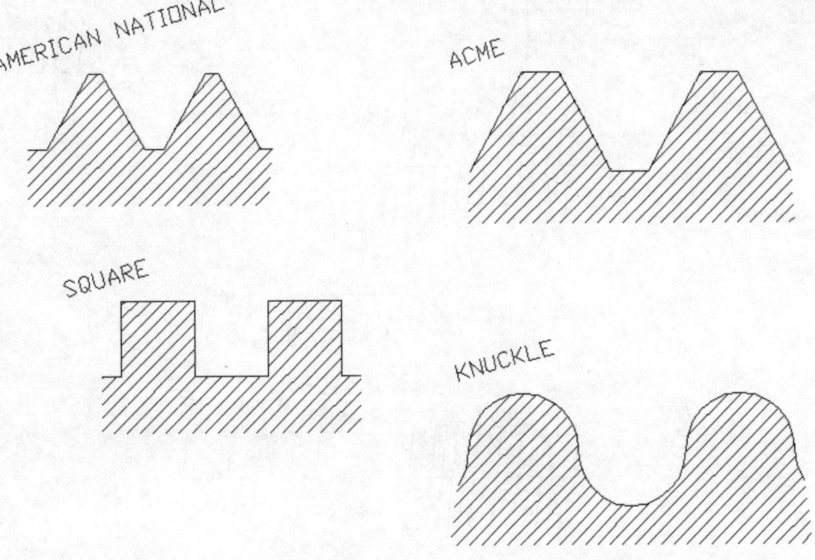

threads. In general, square and acme threads are used when heavy loading is involved. A knuckle thread can be manufactured from sheet metal and is most commonly found on a lightbulb.

The American National thread is the thread shape most often used in mechanical design work. All threads in this chapter are assumed to be American National threads unless otherwise stated.

11-9 How to Draw an External Square Thread

Figure 11-18 shows how to draw a 4.00-inch-long external square thread that has a major diameter of 5.25 and 2 threads per inch. The procedure is as follows:

1. Set **Grid = .50**

   Snap = .125

2. Draw two **5.00**-long horizontal lines **2.00** apart, and draw a **4.50** centerline between them.

3. Draw a rhomboid centered about the centerline according to the given dimensions.

   In this example, $P \doteq .5$, so $.5P = .25$.

4. Use the **Array, Rectangular** command to create eight columns (2 threads per inch) **.50** apart.

5. Draw slanted lines 1–2 and 3–4.

6. Zoom the upper right portion of the thread as needed.

7. Draw a horizontal line **.25** (.5*P*) from the outside edge of the thread as shown.

8. Draw line 5–6 from the intersection of the horizontal line drawn in step 7 with line 1–2, labeled point 5, to the intersection of the toothline 1–6 and the thread's centerline.

Figure 11-18

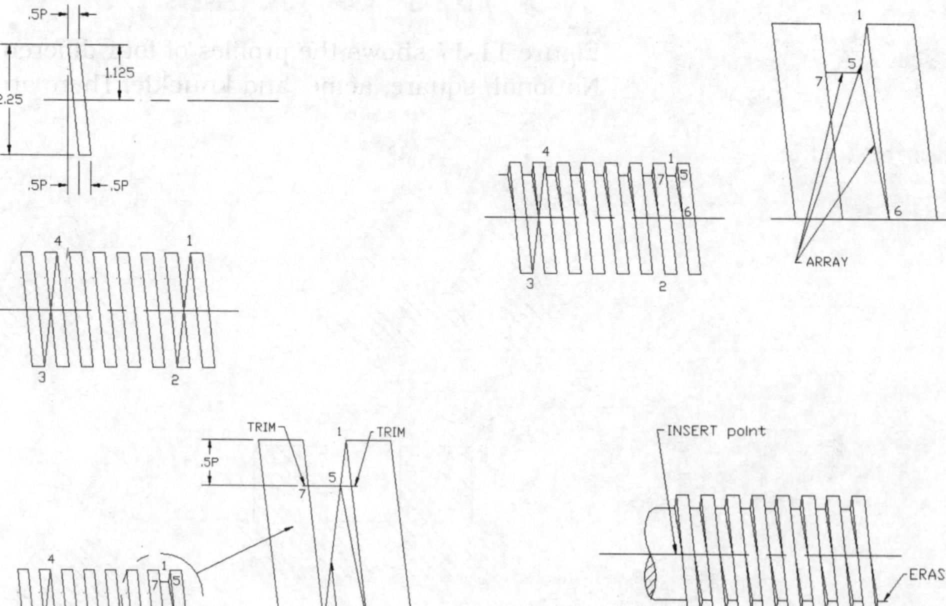

9. Trim the horizontal line to create line 5–7, and trim line 1–2 below point 5.
10. Array lines 1–5, 5–6, and 5–7 by using **Array, Rectangular** with eight columns **−.25** apart.

    The minus sign will generate a right-to-left array.
11. Repeat steps 7 through 10 for the lower portion of the thread. Array eight columns, **+.25** apart. The plus sign generates a left-to-right array.
12. Erase any excess lines, and add any necessary shaft information to the drawing.
13. Save the drawing as a wblock named **SQIN,** using the indicated insertion point.

11-10 How to Draw an Internal Square Thread

Figure 11-19 shows an external 2.25 × 2 square thread. The drawing was developed from wblock **SQIN** created in Section 11-9. The wblock was rotated to the correct orientation. **Erase** and **Trim** were used to fit the thread within the required depth. No scale factor was needed.

Figure 11-19

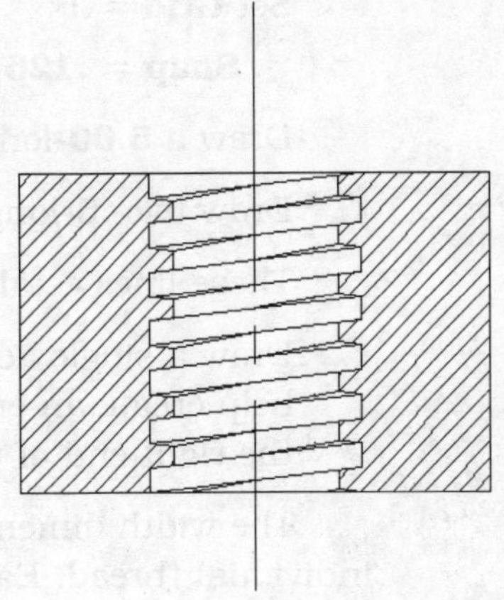

11-11 How to Draw an External Acme Thread

Draw a 2.25 × 2 × 4.00-long external acme thread. The procedure is as follows. See Figure 11-20.

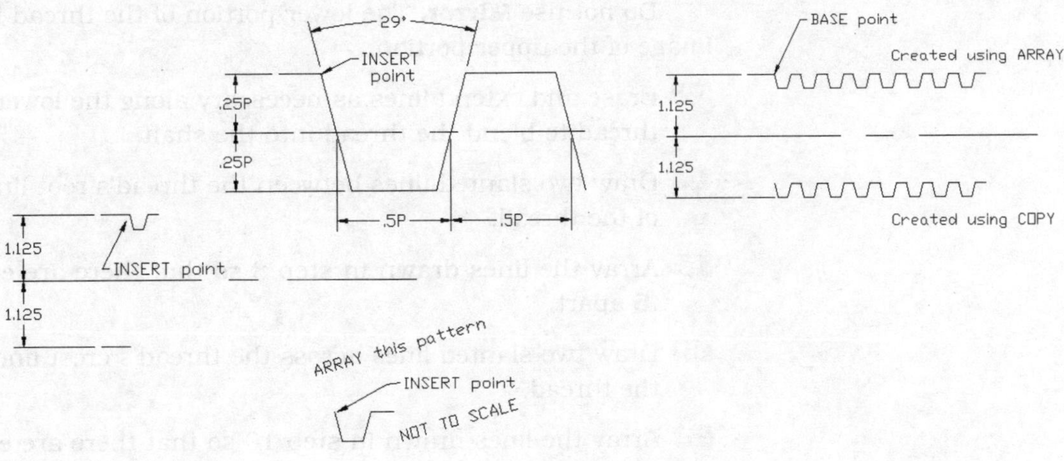

Figure 11-20, Part 1

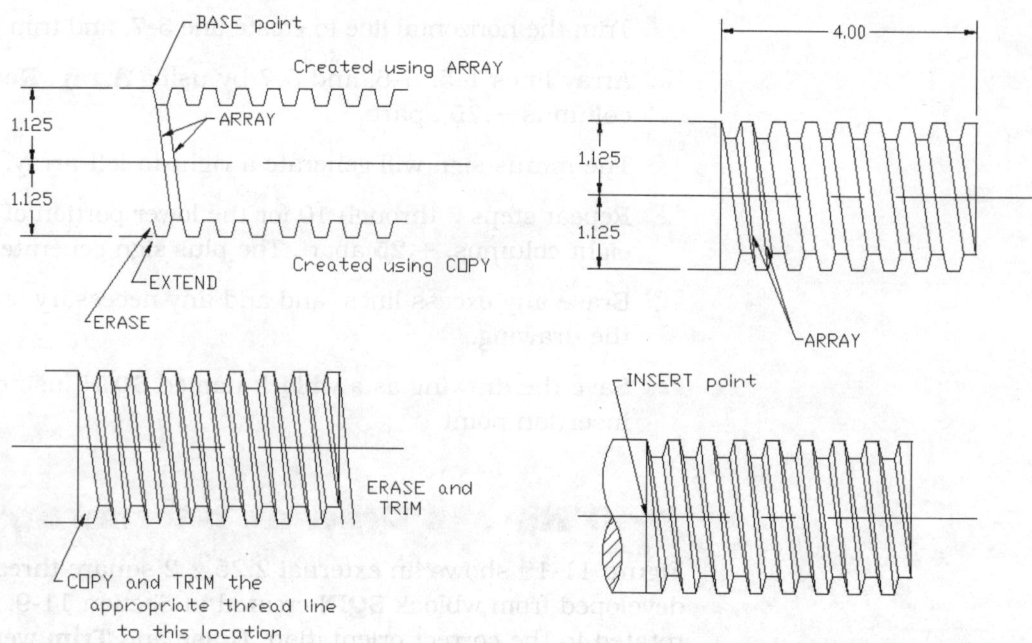

Figure 11-20, Part 2

1. Set **Grid = .5**

   Snap = .125

2. Draw a **5.00**-long horizontal centerline.

3. Draw two **.5**-long horizontal lines **1.125** above and below.

   These lines establish the major diameter of the thread.

4. Draw a single acme thread, using the given dimensions. Use **Zoom** to help create an enlarged working area. The first thread should start at the right end of the short horizontal line above the centerline.

   The width dimensions are taken along the horizontal centerline of the individual thread. Each side of the thread is slanted at **14.5°** [.5(29)]. In this example, $P = .5$, so $.5P = .25$, and $.25P = .125$.

5. Use the **Array** command, and draw eight columns (two threads per inch) **.5** apart to develop the top portion of the thread.

6. Copy and move the top portion of the thread to create the lower portion.

   Do not use **Mirror.** The lower portion of the thread is not a mirror image of the upper portion.

7. Erase and extend lines as necessary along the lower left portion of the thread to blend the thread into the shaft.

8. Draw two slanted lines between the thread's root lines at the left end of the thread.

9. Array the lines drawn in step 8 so that there are eight columns, **.5** apart.

10. Draw two slanted lines across the thread's crest lines at the left end of the thread.

11. Array the lines drawn in step 10 so that there are eight columns, **.5** apart.

12 Draw a vertical line at each end of the thread, establishing the thread's 4.00-inch length.

13 Erase and trim the excess lines from the left end of the thread.

14 Copy and trim a crest-to-crest line to complete the left end of the thread.

15 Save the drawing as a wblock named **ACMEIN,** using the indicated insertion point.

11-12 Bolts and Nuts

A ***bolt*** is a fastener that passes through a clearance hole in an object and is joined to a nut. There are no threads in the object. See Figure 11-21. Note that there are no hidden lines within the nut to indicate that the bolt is passing through. Drawing convention allows for nuts to be drawn without hidden lines.

Figure 11-21

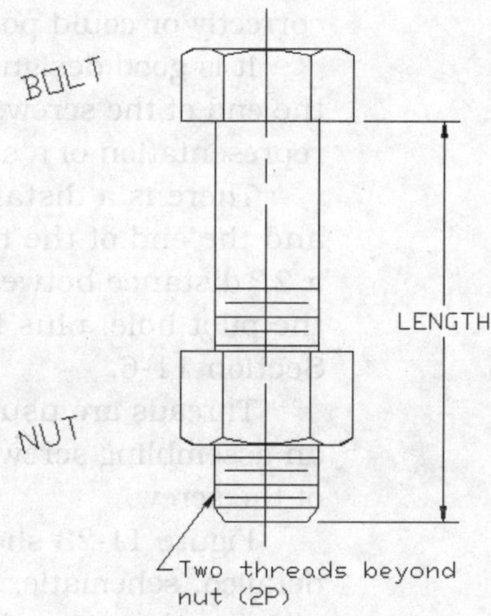

Threads on a bolt are usually made just long enough to correctly accept a nut. This is done to minimize the amount of contact between the edges of threads and the inside surfaces of the clearance holes. The sharp, knifelike thread edges could cut into the object, particularly if the application involves vibrations.

It is considered good design practice to specify a bolt length long enough to allow at least two threads to extend beyond the end of the nut. This ensures that the nut is fully attached to the bolt.

Bolt drawings can be created from wblocks of threads. Remember that a block must be exploded before it can be edited.

11-13 Screws

A ***screw*** is a fastener that assembles into an object. It does not use a nut. The joining threads are cut into the assembling object. See Figure 11-22.

Screws may or may not be threaded over their entire length. If a screw passes through a clearance hole in an object before it assembles into another object, it is good design practice to minimize the number of threads that contact the sides of the clearance hole.

Figure 11-22

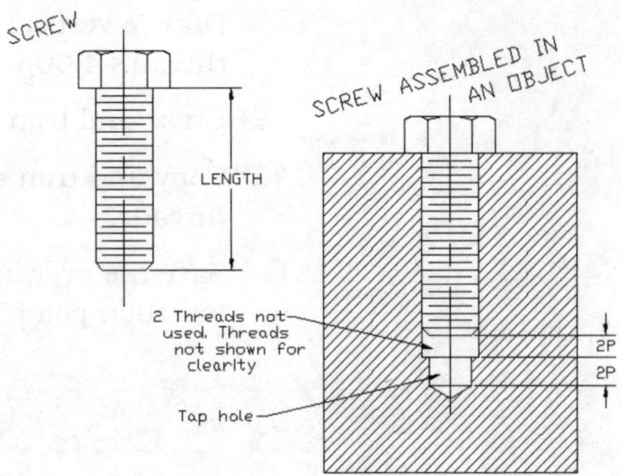

It is also considered good design practice to allow a few unused threads in the threaded hole beyond the end of an assembled screw. If a screw were forced to the bottom of a tapped hole, it might not assemble correctly or could possibly be damaged.

It is good design practice to allow at least two unused threads beyond the end of the screw. Figure 11-22 shows a schematic thread representation of a screw correctly mounted in a threaded hole.

There is a distance of $2P$ (two threads) between the end of the screw and the end of the threaded portion of the hole. There should also be a $2P$ distance between the end of the threaded hole and the end of the pilot hole, plus the conical point of the tap hole, as described in Section 11-6.

Threads are usually not drawn in a threaded hole beyond the end of an assembling screw. This makes it easier to visually distinguish the end of the screw.

Figure 11-23 shows a screw assembled into a hole drawn by using the detailed, schematic, and simplified representations in a sectional view. An orthographic view of a screw in a threaded hole is also shown.

The top view shown in Figure 11-23 applies to all three representations and the orthographic view.

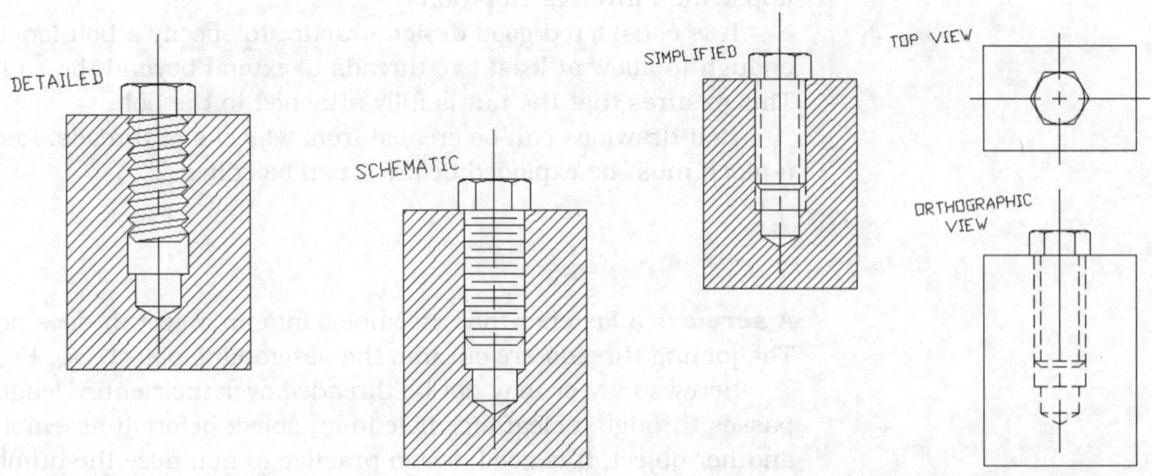

Figure 11-23

11-14 Studs

A ***stud*** is a threaded fastener that both screws into an object and accepts a nut. See Figure 11-24. The thread callouts and representations for studs are the same as they are for bolts and screws.

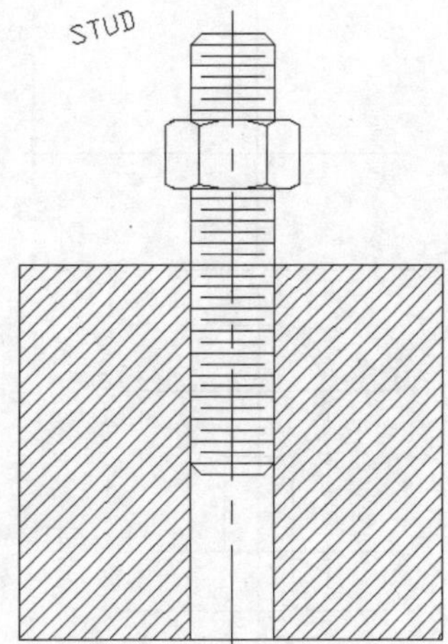

Figure 11-24

11-15 Head Shapes

Bolts and screws are manufactured with a variety of different head shapes, but hexagon (hex) and square head shapes are the most common. There are many different head sizes available for different applications. Extra-thick heads are used for heavy-load applications, and very thin heads are used for applications where space is limited. The exact head size specifications are available from fastener manufacturers.

This section shows how to draw hex and square heads according to accepted average sizes that are functions of the major diameters of both the bolt and the screw. It is suggested that hexagon and square head drawings be saved as wblocks for both inch and millimeter values so that they can be combined with the thread wblocks to form fasteners.

To Draw a Hexagon (Hex) Shaped Head

Draw front and top orthographic views of a hex head based on a thread with an M24 major diameter. See Figure 11-25.

1. Set **Limits = 297,210**
   Grid = 10
   Snap = 5

2. Draw a vertical line and two horizontal lines according to the given dimensions.

The two horizontal lines are used to locate the center of the head in the top view and the bottom of the head in the front view.

3. Use **Polygon,** and draw a hexagon distance across the flats equal to **1.5*D*,** where ***D*** is the major diameter of the thread.

In this example, a radius of **18** was used to draw the hexagon. $1.5D = 1.5(24) = 36$ is the distance across the flats of the hexagon. Use the **Polygon** command to circumscribe a six-sided polygon around a circle of radius 18.

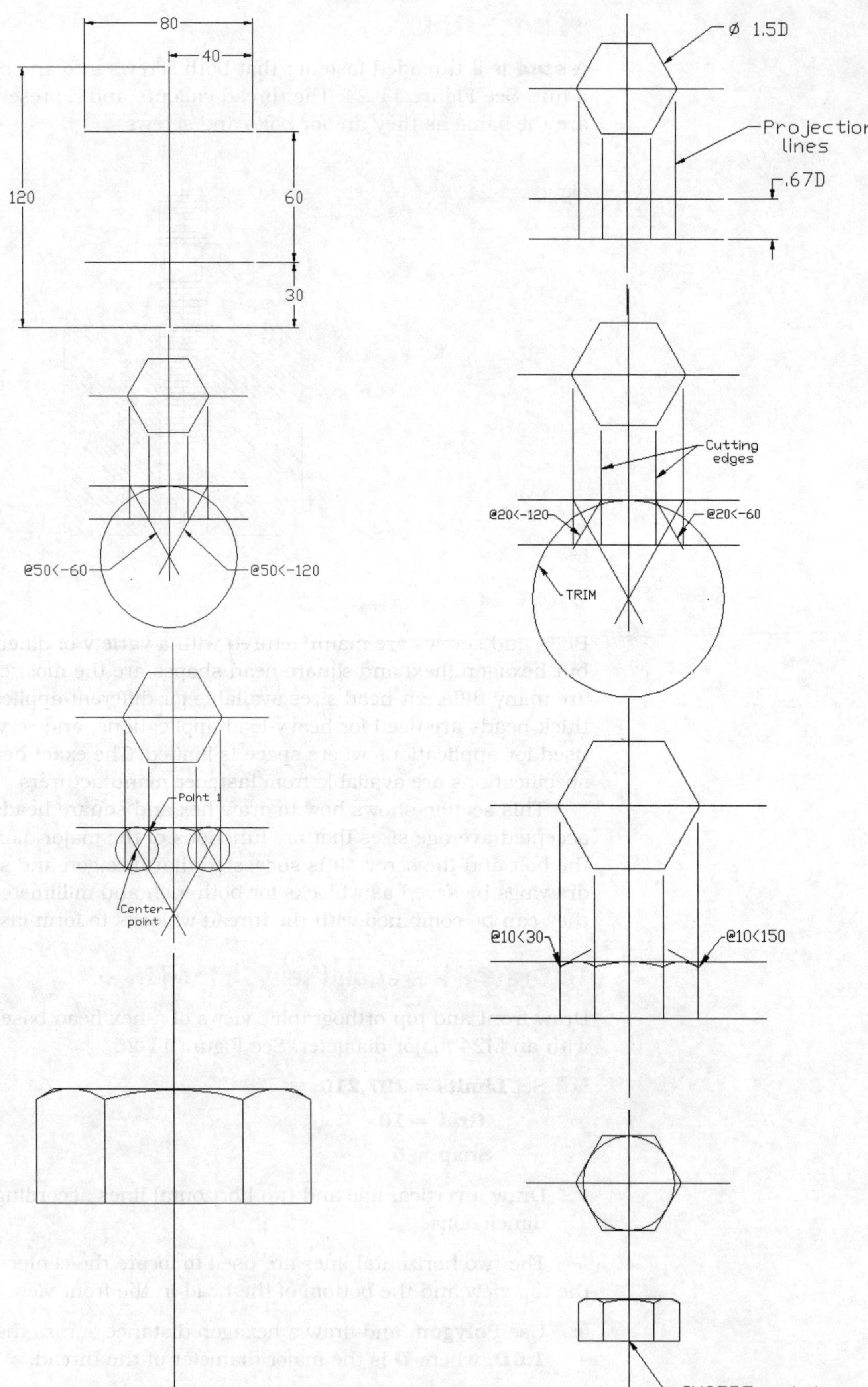

Figure 11-25

4 Offset a line **.67*D*** from the lower horizontal.

This line defines the thickness of the head. The head thickness is 0.67*D*, where *D* is the major diameter of the thread. In this example $D = 24$, so $0.67D = 0.67(24) = 16.08$, which can be rounded off to 16.

5 Draw projection lines from the corners of the hexagon in the top view into the front view.

6 Zoom in the front view portion of the drawing if necessary. Draw two **60°** lines from the corners of the front view as shown so that they intersect on the vertical centerline.

Use **Osnap Intersection** to accurately locate the corner points. The line from the left corner uses an input of @50,–60; the line from the right corner uses the input @50,–120.

7 Draw a circle whose center point is the intersection of the two 60° lines drawn in step 6 and the vertical centerline, and whose radius equals the distance from the center point to the line at the top of the front view.

8 Trim the circle so that only the arc between the inside projection lines remains.

9 Draw two **60°** lines as shown, using the inputs **@20,–120** and **@20,–60.**

10 Draw two circles centered about the intersection of the slanted lines drawn in steps 6 and 8. The radius of each circle equals the distance from the center point to the intersection of the circle drawn in step 7 and the inside projection lines labeled point 1.

11 Trim and erase as needed.

12 Draw two lines from the intersections of the smaller arcs with the outside edge of the head. The input for the lines is **@10,30** and **@10,150.**

These lines could have been generated by the **Chamfer** command.

13 Trim the chamfer lines to the top of the head.

14 Use **Zoom All,** and draw a circle that is circumscribed within the hexagon, as shown.

15 Save the drawing as a wblock named **HEXHEAD,** using the indicated insertion point.

To Draw a Square-Shaped Head

Draw front and top orthographic views of a hex head on the basis of a thread with a 1.00-inch major diameter. See Figure 11-26.

1 Set **Grid = .50**
Snap = .25

2 Draw two horizontal lines and a vertical line, using the given dimensions.

The intersection of the top horizontal line and the vertical line will be the center point of the top view, and the lower horizontal line will be the bottom edge of the head.

Figure 11-26

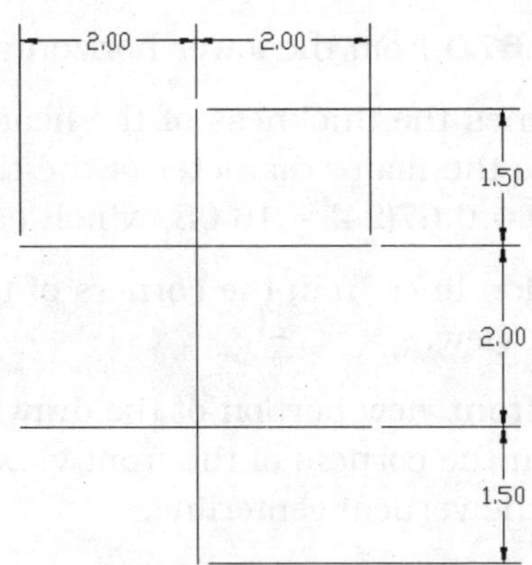

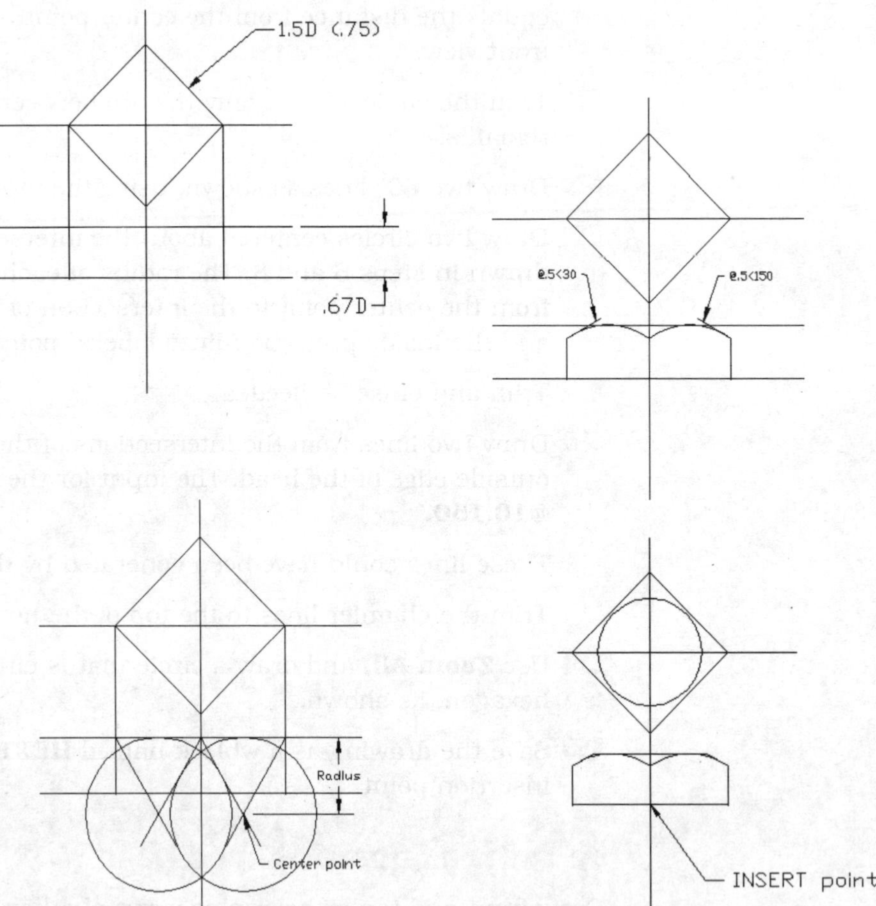

3. Use **Draw, Polygon** and **Modify, Rotate (45°)** to create a square oriented as shown.

   The distance across the square equals 1.50*D*, or 1.50 inches. This means that the radius for the polygon is **.75.**

4. Offset a line **.67 (.67D)** from the lower horizontal line.

   The offset distance is equal to the thickness of the head.

5 Project the corners of the square in the top view into the front view.

6 Zoom the front view, and draw four **60°** lines from the head's upper corners and the intersection of the centerline and the top surface of the head, as shown. The inputs for the lines are @**1.5,–120** and @**1.5,–60.** Use **Osnap Intersection** to ensure accuracy.

7 Use **Draw, Circle, Center, Radius,** and draw two circles about the center points created in step 6. Trim the excess portions of the circle.

8 Trim and erase any excess lines.

9 Add the **30°** chamfer lines as shown. The line inputs are @**.5,150** and @**.5,30.** Use **Osnap Intersection** to accurately locate the intersection between the arc and the vertical side line of the head.

10 Trim any excess lines.

11 Zoom the drawing back to its original size, and draw a circle in the top view tangent to the inside edges of the square.

12 Save the drawing as a wblock named **SQHEAD,** using the insertion point indicated.

11-16 Nuts

This section explains how to draw hexagon- and square-shaped nuts. Both construction methods are based on the head shape wblocks created in Section 11-15.

There are many different styles of nuts. A ***finished nut*** has a flat surface on one side that acts as a bearing surface when the nut is tightened against an object. A finished nut has a thickness equal to .88*D*, where *D* is the major diameter of the nut's thread size.

A ***locknut*** is symmetrical, with the top and bottom surfaces identical. A locknut has a thickness equal to .5*D*, where *D* is the major diameter of the nut's thread size.

To Draw a Hexagon-Shaped Finished Nut

Draw a hexagon-shaped finished nut for an M36 thread. See Figure 11-27.

1 Set **Limits = 297,210**

Grid = 10

Snap = 2.5

2 Construct a vertical line that is intersected by two horizontal lines **32** millimeters apart.

The thickness of a finished nut is 0.88*D*. In this example, 0.88(36) = 31.68, or 32.

3 Use **Insert,** and insert the **HEXHEAD** wblock created in Section 11-15.

The wblock **HEXHEAD** was created for an M24 thread, so the X and Y scale factors must be increased to accommodate the larger thread size. The scale factor is determined by dividing the desired size by the wblock size. In this example, 36/24 = 1.5. The scale factor is **1.5.** Respond to the command prompts as follows:

Command: INSERT

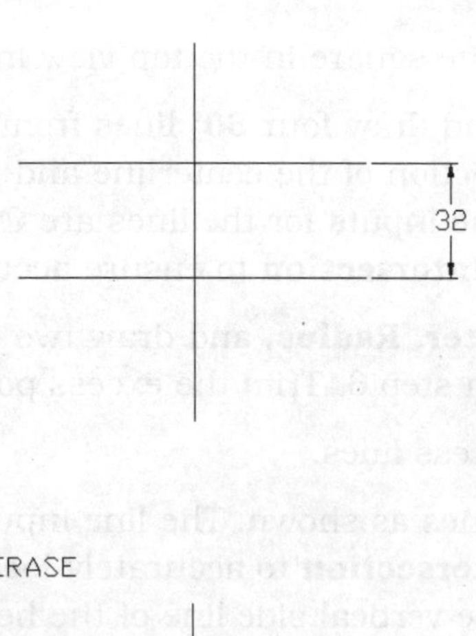

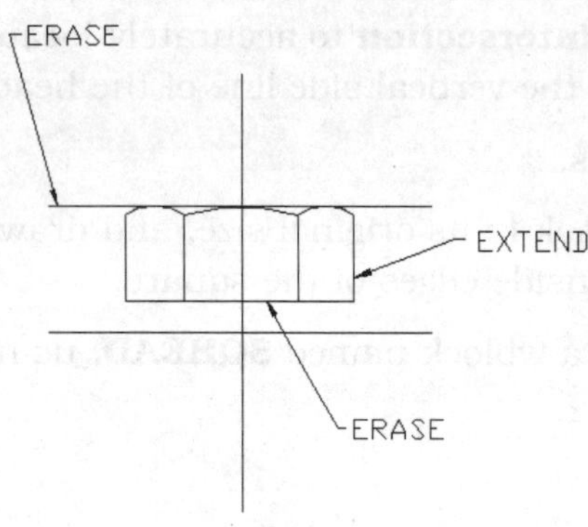

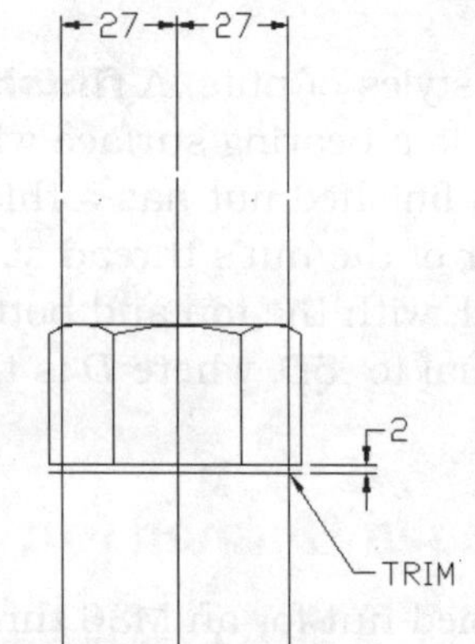

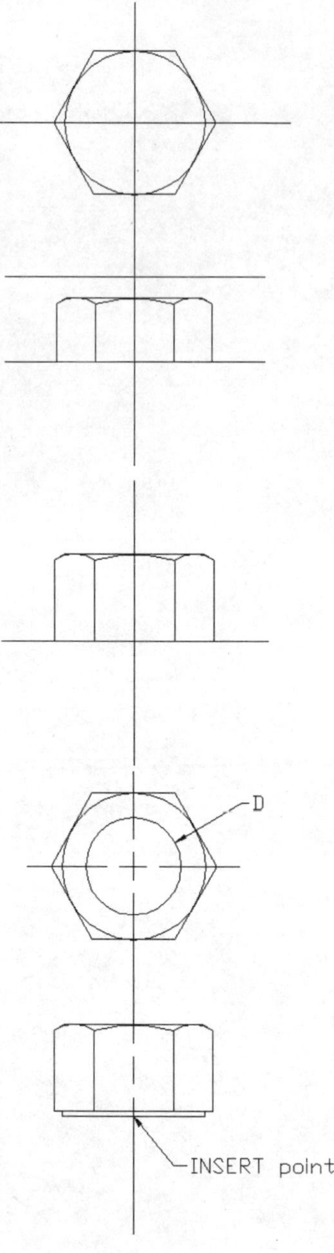

Figure 11-27

The **Insert** dialog box will appear.

4. Type or select **HEXHEAD;** press **Enter.**
5. Select the indicated insertion point.
6. Specify an X and Y scale of **1.5** and a **0** rotation angle; select **OK.**

   Specify insertion point or [Scale X Y Z Rotate PScale PX PY PZ PRotate]:

7. Press **Enter.**

   If you have not created a wblock, refer to Section 11-15 and draw a hexagon-shaped head.

8. Explode the wblock.
9. Move the front view of the nut so that the top surface aligns with the top parallel horizontal line.

10 Erase the bottom line of the front view of the nut, and extend the vertical line to the lower horizontal line. Erase the top horizontal line in the front view.

11 Use **Offset** to draw a horizontal line **2** millimeters below the bottom of the nut.

This line defines the shoulder surface of the nut. Any offset distance may be used as long as the line is clearly visible. The actual shoulder surface is less than 1 millimeter deep and would not appear clearly on the drawing. The shoulder surface has a diameter equal to 1.5*D* [1.5(36) = 54] or, in this example, 54.

12 Offset the centerline **27** (half of 54) to each side, and trim the excess lines.

13 Save the drawing as a wblock named **FNUTHEX.** Define the insertion point as shown.

To Draw a Locking Nut

Draw a locking nut for an M24 thread. See Figure 11-28. The **HEXHEAD** wblock was originally drawn for an M24 thread, so no scale factor is needed.

1 Set **Limits = 297,210**

Grid = 10

Snap = 5

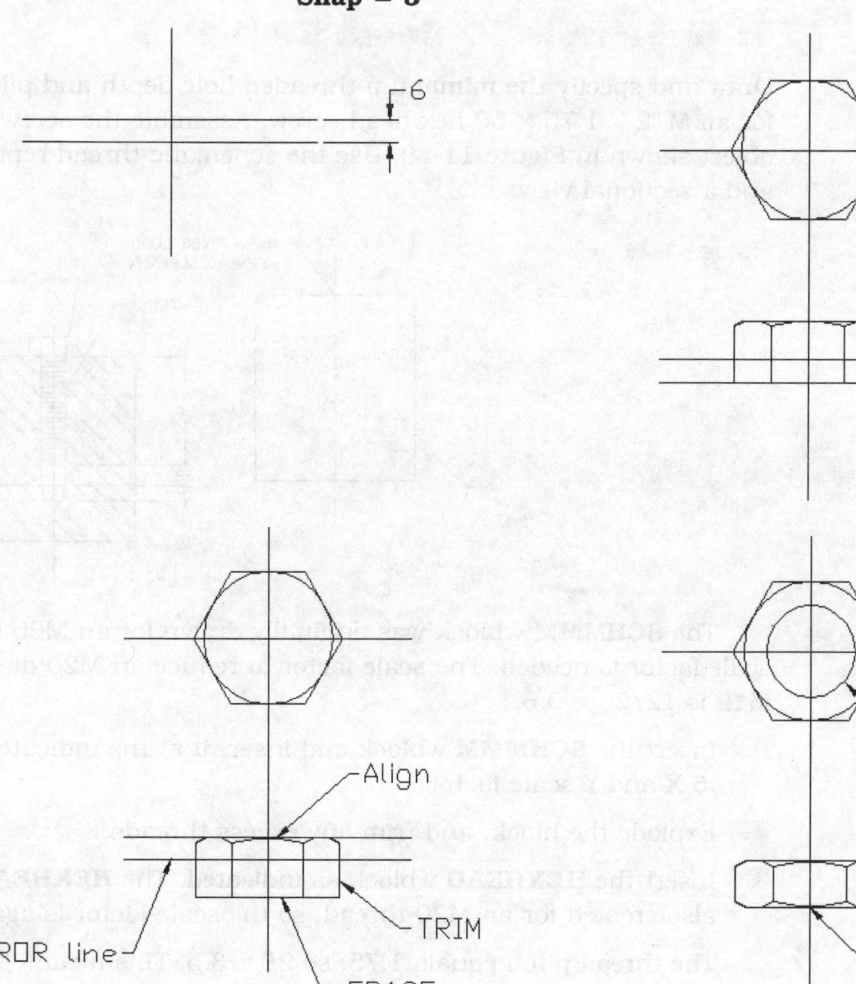

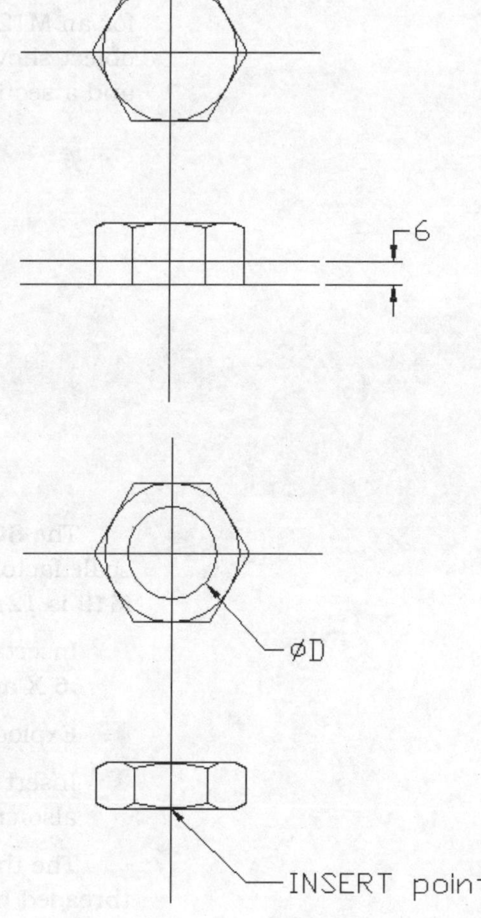

Figure 11-28

2. Draw a vertical line and two horizontal lines according to the given dimensions.

The 6 distance is half the $0.5D$ [0.5(24) = 12] thickness distance recommended for locknuts. Locknuts are symmetrical, so half of the nut will be drawn and then mirrored.

3. Insert the **HEXHEAD** wblock at the indicated insert point.
4. Explode the wblock.
5. Move the front view of the hex head so that it aligns with the horizontal line, as shown.
6. Trim and erase the lines that extend beyond the lower horizontal line.
7. Mirror the remaining portion of the front view about the lower horizontal line, and then erase the horizontal line.
8. Draw a circle of diameter ***D*** in the top view, as shown.
9. Save the drawing as a wblock named **LNUTHEX,** using the indicated insertion point.

The procedure explained previously for hexagon-shaped finish nuts and locknuts is the same as that for square-shaped nuts. Use the wblock **SQHEAD** in place of the **HEXHEAD** wblock.

11-17 Sample Problem SP11-1

Draw and specify the mimimum threaded hole depth and pilot hole depth for an M12 × 1.75 × 50 hex head screw. Assemble the screw into the object shown in Figure 11-29. Use the schematic thread representation and a sectional view.

Figure 11-29

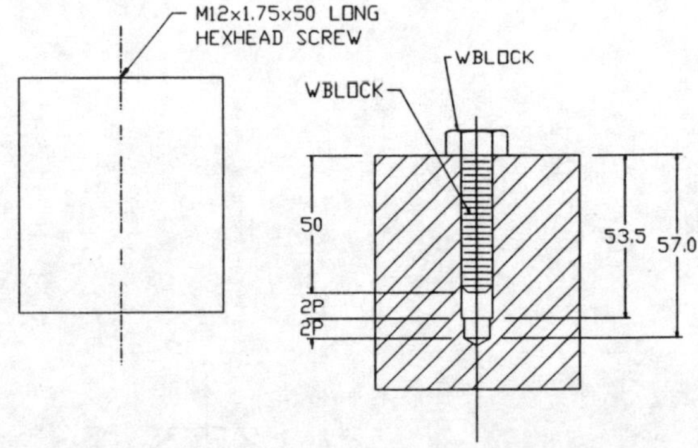

The **SCHMMM** wblock was originally drawn for an M20 thread, so a scale factor is needed. The scale factor to reduce an M20 diameter to an M12 is 12/20 = 0.6.

1. Insert the **SCHMMM** wblock and insert it at the indicated point. Use a **.6** X and Y scale factor.
2. Explode the block, and trim any excess threads.
3. Insert the **HEXHEAD** wblock as indicated. The **HEXHEAD** wblock was also created for an M20 thread, so the scale factor is again **.6.**

The thread pitch equals 1.75, so $2P = 3.5$. This means that the threaded hole should be at least 50 + 3.5, or 53.5, deep to allow for two unused threads beyond the end of the screw.

The unused portion of the pilot hole should also extend $2P$ beyond the end of the threaded portion of the hole, so the minimum pilot hole depth equals 53.5 + 3.5 = 57.

The diameter of the tap hole for the thread is given in a table in the appendix as 10.3. For this example, a diameter of 10 was used for drawing purposes. If required, the value of 10.3 would be given in the hole's drawing callout.

4 Draw the unused portion of the thread hole and pilot hole, as shown. Omit the thread representation in the portion of the threaded hole beyond the end of the screw, for clarity.

11-18 Sample Problem SP11-2

Determine the length of a .750–10UNC square head bolt needed to pass through objects 1 and 2 as shown in Figure 11-30. Include a hexagon-shaped locknut on the end of the bolt. Allow at least two threads beyond the end of the nut. Use the closest standard bolt length, and draw a schematic representation as a sectional view.

Figure 11-30

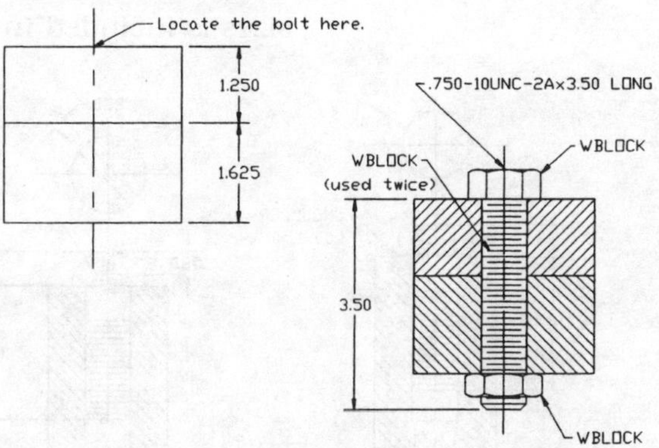

This construction is based on the wblocks **SCHMINCH, HEXHEAD,** and **LNUTHEX** created in Sections 11-5, 11-15, and 11-16. If no wblocks are available, refer to these sections for an explanation of how to create the required shapes.

The wblocks **SCHMINCH, HEXHEAD,** and **LNUTHEX** were created for a major diameter of 1.00 inch, so the scale factor needed to create a major diameter of .750 is .75.

1 Insert the **SCHMINCH** wblock at the indicated point. Use an X and Y scale factor of **.75.** Rotate the block **–90°** to the correct orientation.

The wblock **SCHMINCH** is not long enough to go completely through the objects, so a second wblock is inserted below the first.

2 Insert the **SQHEAD** wblock at the indicated point. Use an X and Y scale factor of **.75.**

3 Insert the wblock **LNUTHEX** at the indicated point. Use an X and Y scale factor of **.75.**

4 Explode the wblocks.

5 Trim the excess lines within the nut.

6 Calculate the minimum length for the bolt.

The total depth of objects 1 and 2 equals 1.250 + 1.625 = 2.875.

The thickness of the nut equals .88*D*, or .88(.75) = .375.

The pitch length of the thread equals 1.00/10 = .1, so 2*P* = .2.

The minimum bolt length equals 2.875 + .375 + .200 = 3.450.

From the table of standard bolt lengths in the appendix, the standard bolt length that is greater than 3.45 is 3.50, so the bolt callout can now be completed:

0.750 − 10UNC − 2 A × 3.50 LONG

The completed drawing with the appropriate bolt callout is shown in Figure 11-30.

11-19 Standard Screws

Figure 11-31 shows a group of standard screw shapes. The proportions given in Figure 11-30 are acceptable for general drawing purposes and represent average values. The exact dimensions for specific screws are available from manufacturers' catalogs. A partial listing of standard screw sizes is included in the appendix.

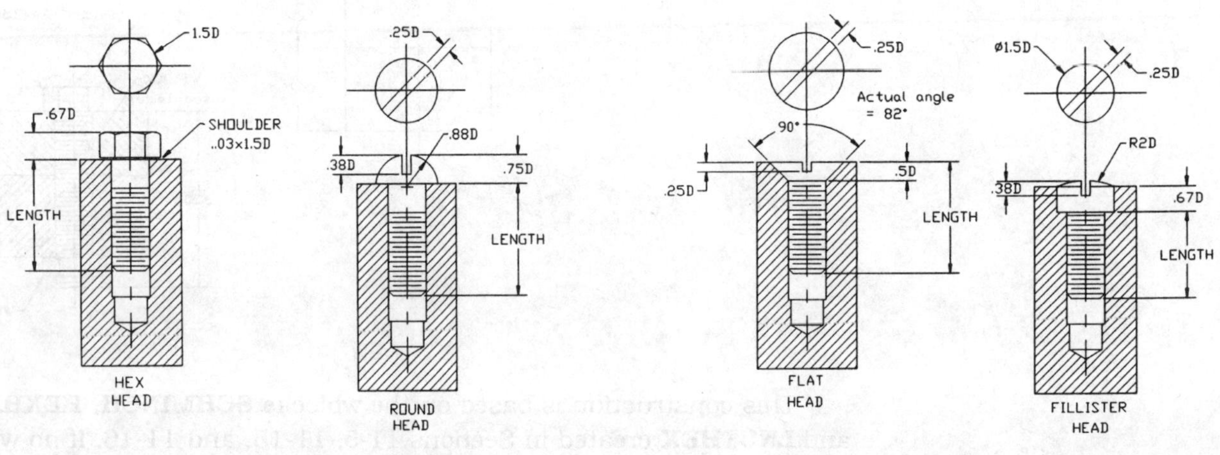

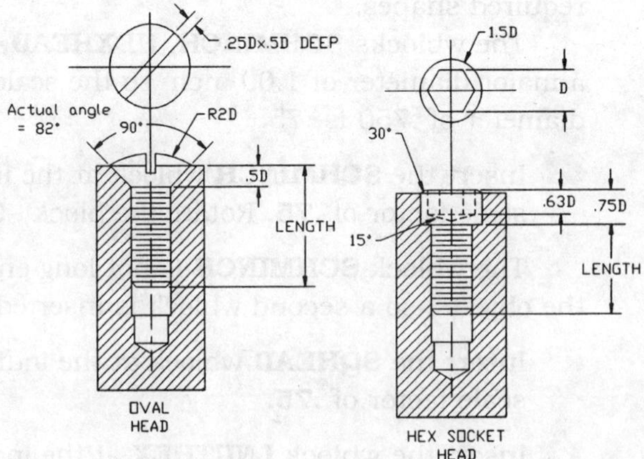

Figure 11-31

The given head shape dimensions are all in terms of *D*, the major diameter of the screw's thread. Information about the available standard major diameters and lengths is included in the appendix.

The choice of head shape is determined by the specific design requirements. For example, a flat head mounted flush with the top surface is a good choice when space is critical, when two parts butt against each other, or when aerodynamic considerations are involved. A round head can be assembled by using a common blade screwdriver, but it is more susceptible to damage than a hex head. The hex head, however, requires a specific wrench for assembly.

11-20 Setscrews

Setscrews are fasteners used to hold parts like gears and pulleys to rotating shafts or other objects in order to prevent slippage between the two objects. See Figure 11-32.

Figure 11-32

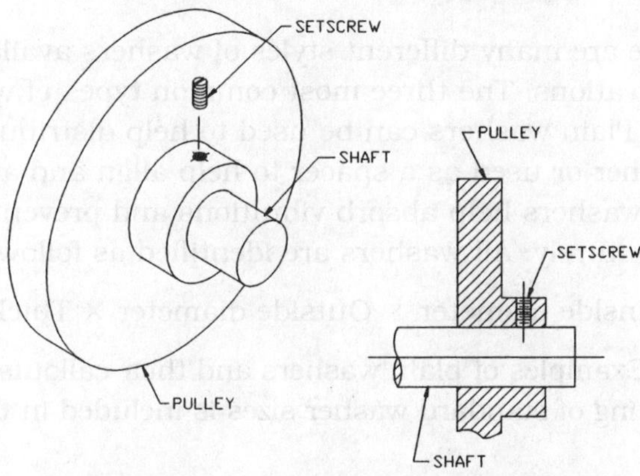

Most setscrews have recessed heads to help prevent interference with other parts. Many different head styles and point styles are available. See Figure 11-33.

Figure 11-33

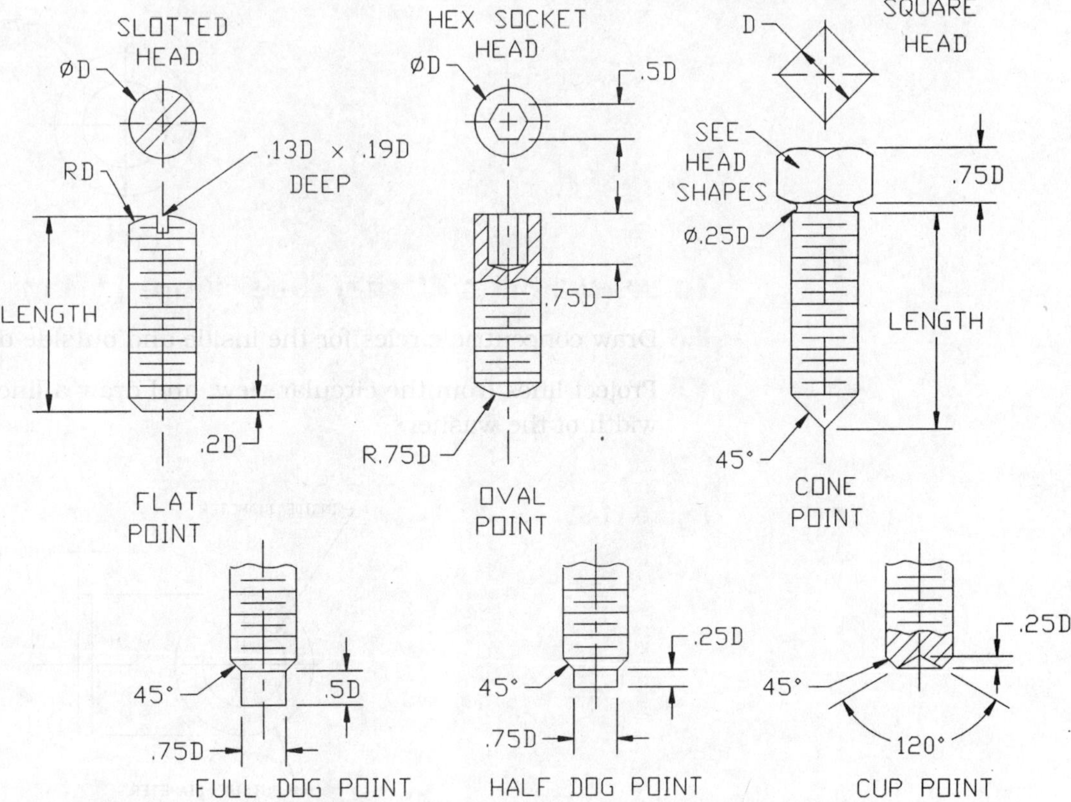

Setscrews are referenced on a drawing by the following format:

THREAD SPECIFICATION
HEAD SPECIFICATION POINT SPECIFICATION
SET SCREW
.250 – 20 UNC – 2 A 1.00 LONG
SLOT HEAD FLAT POINT
SET SCREW

The words "LONG," "HEAD," and "POINT" are optional.

11-21 Washers

There are many different styles of washers available for different design applications. The three most common types of washers are *plain, lock,* and *star.* Plain washers can be used to help distribute the bearing load of a fastener or used as a spacer to help align and assemble objects. Lock and star washers help absorb vibrations and prevent fasteners from loosening prematurely. All washers are identified as follows:

Inside diameter × Outside diameter × Thickness

Examples of plain washers and their callouts are shown in Figure 11-34. A listing of standard washer sizes is included in the appendix.

Figure 11-34

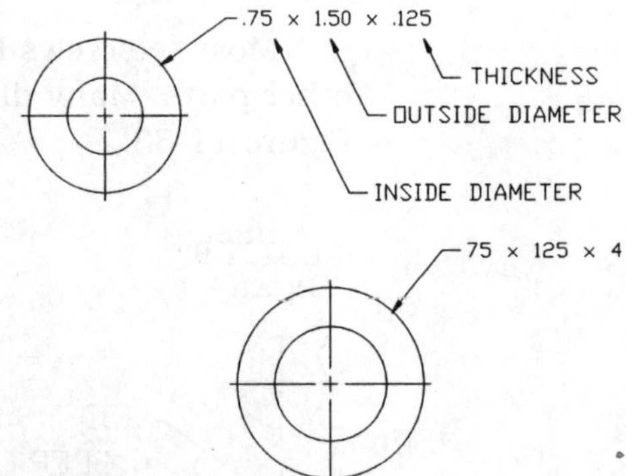

To Draw a Plain Washer (See Figure 11-35.)

1. Draw concentric circles for the inside and outside diameters.
2. Project lines from the circular view, and draw a line that defines the width of the washer.

Figure 11-35

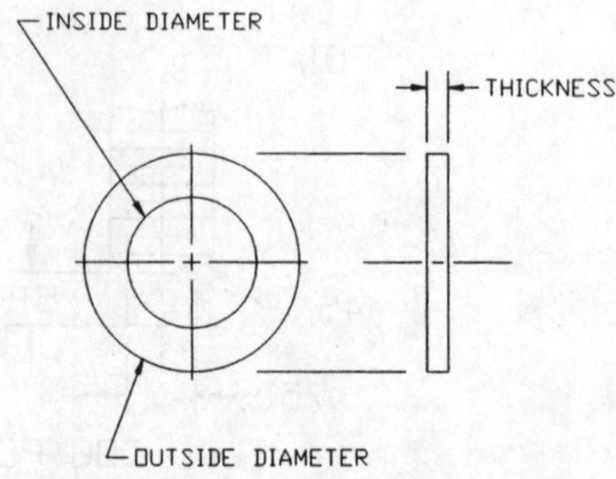

3 Use **Offset** to define the thickness.

Figure 11-36 shows two views of a lock washer. As the lock washer is compressed during assembly, it tends to flatten so that the slanted end portions are not usually included on the drawing. The drawing callout should include the words "LOCK WASHER."

Figure 11-37 shows an internal and an external tooth lock-type washer. They may also be called *star washers.*

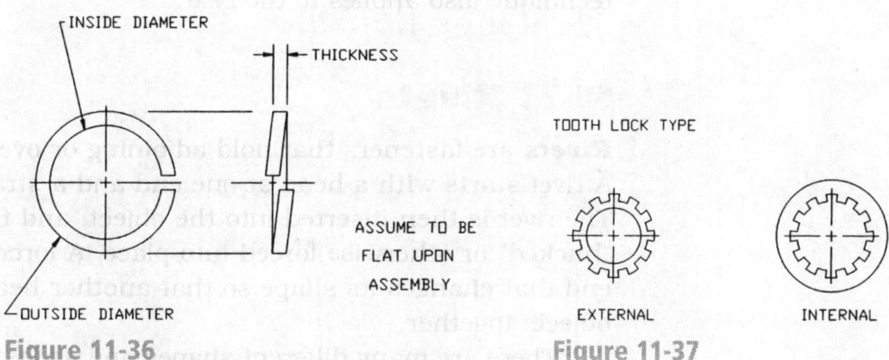

Figure 11-36

Figure 11-37

These washers are best drawn by first drawing an individual tooth, then using **Array** to draw a total of 12 teeth. Because there are 12 teeth, each tooth and the space between it and the next tooth require a total of 30°—that is, 15° for the tooth and 15° for the space between each tooth.

11-22 Keys

Keys are used to help prevent slippage in power transmission between parts—for example, a gear and a drive shaft. Grooves called ***keyways***, or ***keyseats***, are cut into both the gear and the drive shaft, and a key is inserted between, as shown in Figure 11-38.

There are four common types of keys: *square, Pratt & Whitney, Woodruff,* and *gib head.* Each has design advantages and disadvantages. See Figure 11-39. A list of standard key sizes is included in the appendix.

Square keys are called out on a drawing by specifying the length of one side of the square cross section and the overall length, Pratt &

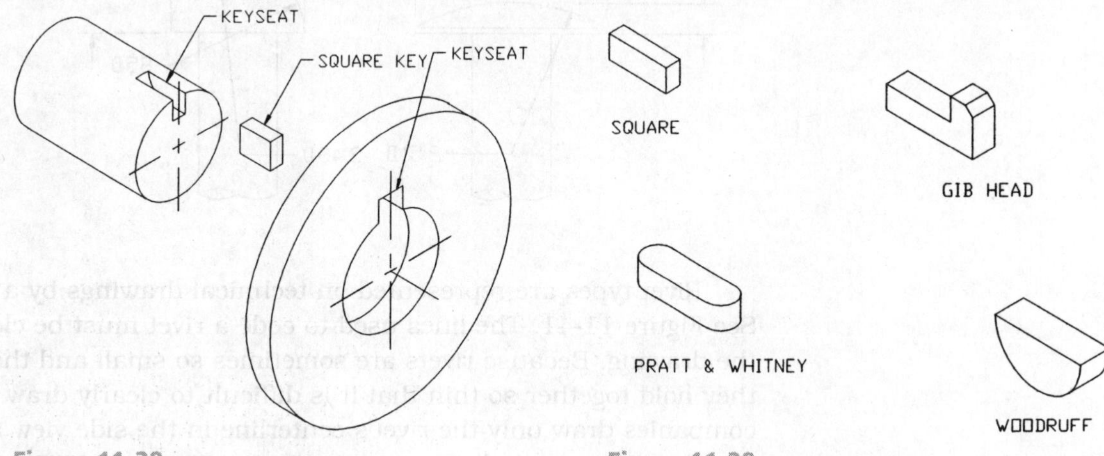

Figure 11-38

Figure 11-39

Whitney and Woodruff keys are specified by numbers, and gib head keys are defined by a group of dimensions. See the appendix for the appropriate tables and charts of standard key sizes.

Keyways are dimensioned as shown in Figure 8-78. Note that the depth of a keyway in a shaft is dimensioned from the bottom of the shaft. Because material has been cut away, the intersection between the shaft's centerline and top outside edge does not exist. It is better to dimension from a real surface than from a theoretical one. The same dimensioning technique also applies to the gear.

11-23 Rivets

Rivets are fasteners that hold adjoining or overlapping objects together. A rivet starts with a head at one end and a straight shaft at the other. The rivet is then inserted into the object, and the headless end is "bucked" or otherwise forced into place. A force is applied to the headless end that changes its shape so that another head is formed, holding the objects together.

There are many different shapes and styles of rivets. Figure 11-40 shows five common head shapes for rivets. Aircraft use hollow rivets because they are very lightweight. A design advantage for the use of rivets is that they can be drilled out, and removed or replaced, without damaging the objects that they hold together.

Figure 11-40

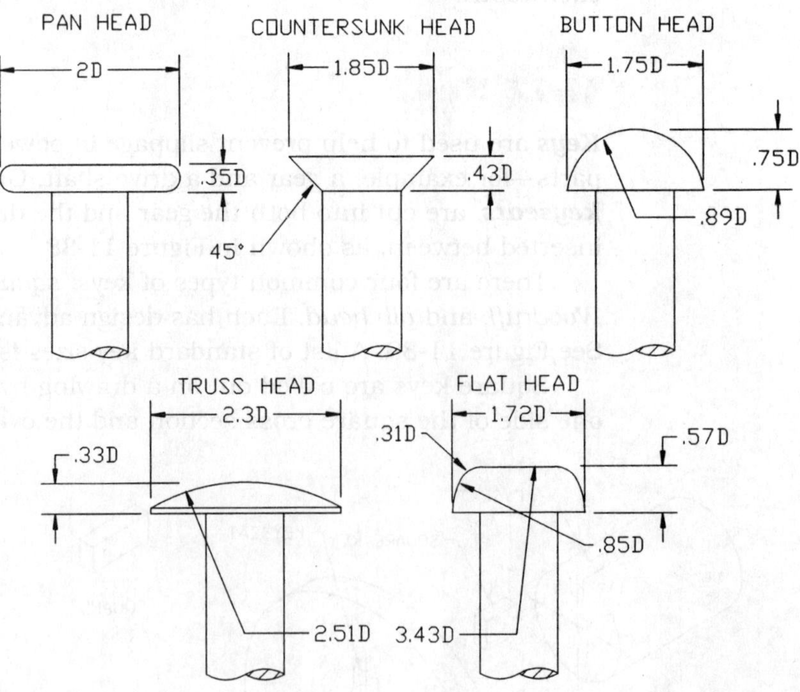

Rivet types are represented on technical drawings by a coding system. See Figure 11-41. The lines used to code a rivet must be clearly visible on the drawing. Because rivets are sometimes so small and the material that they hold together so thin that it is difficult to clearly draw the rivets, companies draw only the rivet's centerline in the side view and identify the rivet by a drawing callout.

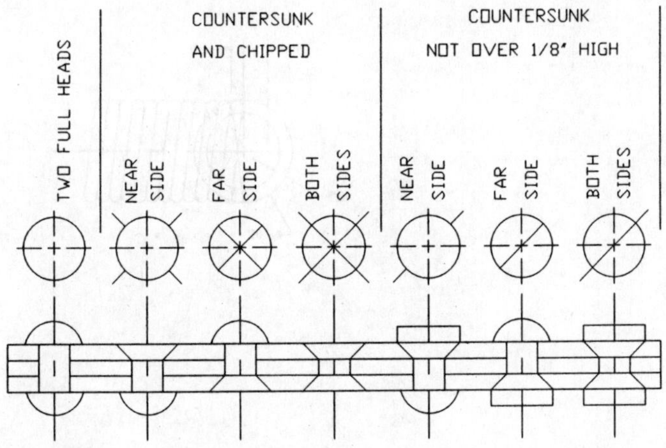

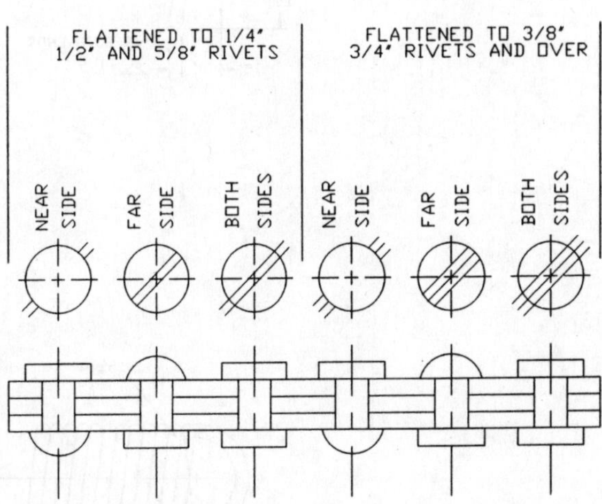

Figure 11-41

11-24 Springs

The most common types of springs used on technical drawings are compression, extension, and torsional. This section explains how to draw detailed and schematic representations of springs. Springs are drawn in their relaxed position (not expanded or compressed). Phantom lines may be used to show several different positions for springs as they are expanded or compressed.

Springs are defined by the diameter of their wire, the direction of their coils, their outside diameter, their total number of coils, and their total relaxed length. Information about their loading properties may also be included. The pitch of a spring equals the distance from the center of one coil to the center of the next coil.

As with threads, the detailed representations of springs are difficult and time consuming to draw, but the **Array** command shortens the drawing time considerably. Saving the representation as a wblock also helps avoid the necessity of having to redraw the representation for each new drawing.

Ideally, the distance between coils should be exactly equal to the pitch of the spring, but this is not always practical for smaller springs. Any convenient distance between coils may be used that presents a clear easy-to-understand representation of the spring.

To Draw a Detailed Representation of an Extension Spring

Draw an extension spring 2.00 inches in diameter with right-hand coils made from 0.250-inch wire. The spring's pitch equals .25, and the total length of the coils is 3.00 inches. See Figure 11-42.

Because the pitch of the spring equals the wire diameter, the coils will touch each other.

1 Set **Grid = .5**
Snap = .25

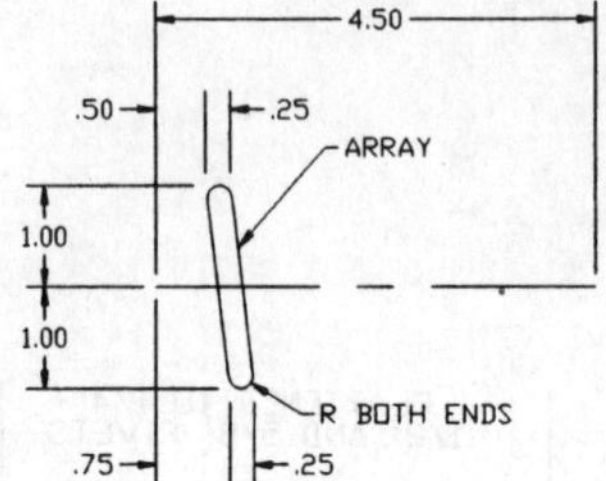

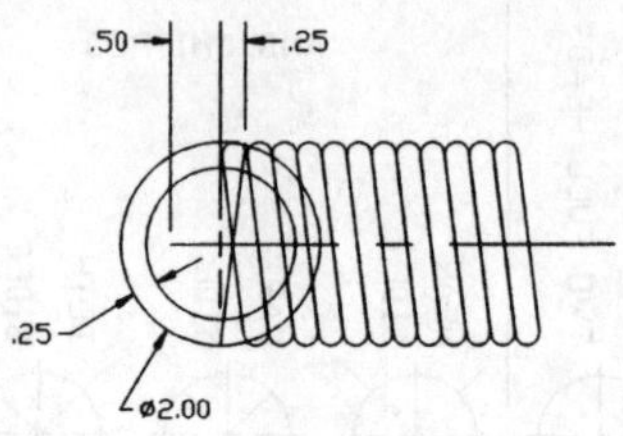

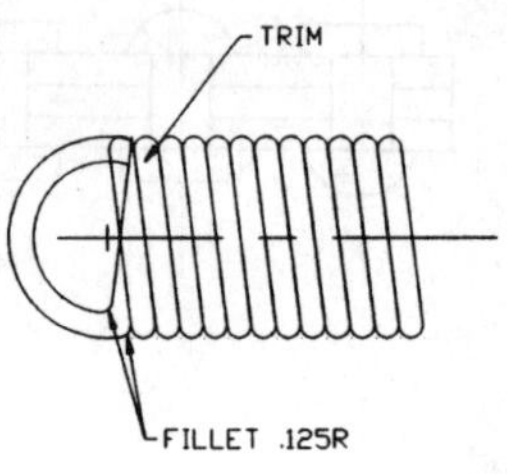

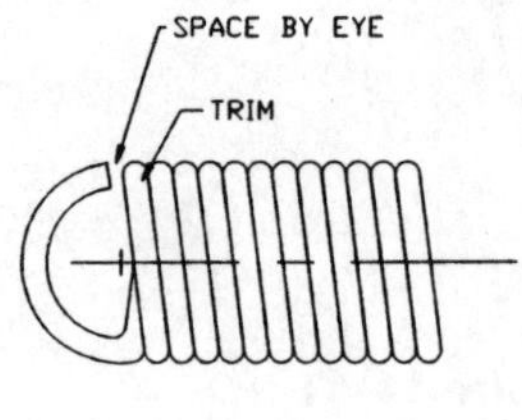

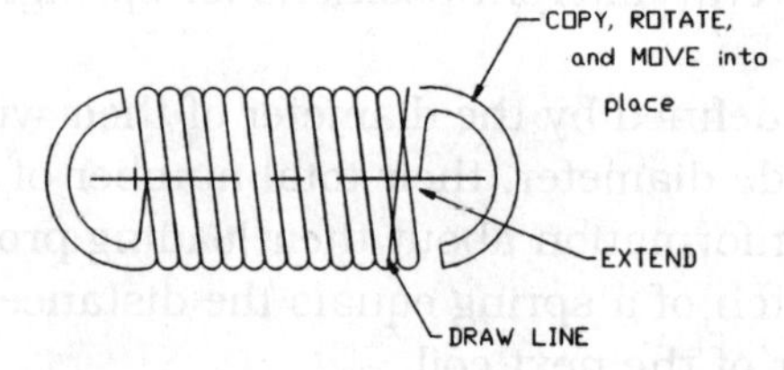

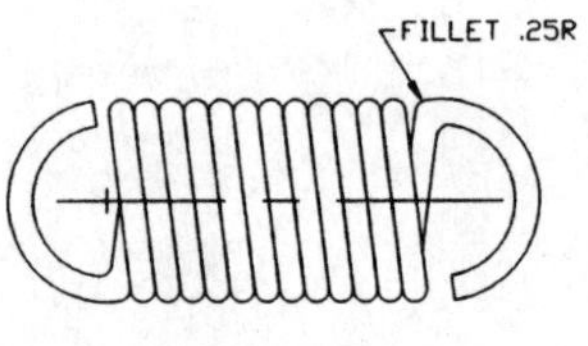

Figure 11-42

2. Draw the rounded shape of one of the coils.

    The distance between the lines equals the diameter of the spring wire. The diameter of the rounded ends also equals the diameter of the wire. The coil's offset equals the spring's pitch.

3. Array the coil shape.

    A rectangular array was used with one row, and 12 columns **.25** apart.

4. Draw two concentric circles at the left end of the spring so that the larger circle's diameter equals the spring's diameter. The vertical centerline of the circles is tangent to the left edge of the first coil.

5. Draw a line across the thread offset a distance equal to one pitch. The endpoints of the line are on snap points.

6. Trim the excess portion of the circles, and fillet the circles as shown.
7. Trim the excess portion of the slanted line, and cut back the end of the circles so that there is a noticeable gap between the first coil and the end of the circles. The gap distance is determined by eye.
8. Copy, rotate, and move the circular end portion to the right end of the spring.
9. Draw a slanted line across the farthest right coil, as shown.
10. Trim and extend the lines as necessary, and add the **FILLET .25R** as shown.
11. Save the drawing as a wblock named **EXTSPRNG.**

To Draw a Detailed Representation of a Compression Spring

Draw a compression spring with six right-hand coils made from .25-inch-diameter wire. The pitch of the spring equals .50 inch. The diameter of the spring is 2.00 inches. See Figure 11-43.

1. Set **Grid = .50**
   Snap = .25
2. Draw the rounded shape of the first left coil, as shown. The diameter of the rounded ends of the coil equals the diameter of the spring's wire.
3. Array the coil shape.

   In this example, a rectangular array was used to draw one row, and six columns **.50** inch apart.
4. Draw two slanted lines as shown.

   These lines represent the back portion of the coil. They are most easily drawn from a snap point next to the rounded portion of the coil shape (this point would be the corner point of the coil if the coil were not rounded) to a point tangent to the opposite rounded end of the coil.
5. Trim and array the slanted lines as shown.

   Use a rectangular array with one row, and six columns **.50** inch apart.
6. Draw the right end of the spring so that it appears to end just short of the spring's centerline. Any convenient distance may be used.
7. Draw the left end of the spring using **Copy,** and copy one of the existing slanted lines. Use **Zoom,** if necessary, to align the copied line with the coil. Draw the left end of the spring so that it appears to end just short of the centerline.
8. Save the drawing as a wblock named **COMPSPNG.**

   Figure 11-44 shows schematic representations of a compression and an extension spring. The distance between the peaks of the slanted lines should equal the pitch of the spring.

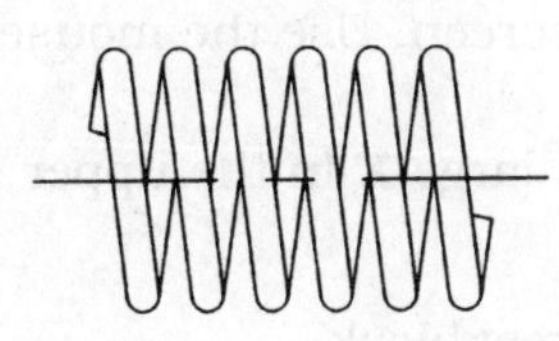

Figure 11-43

Figure 11-44

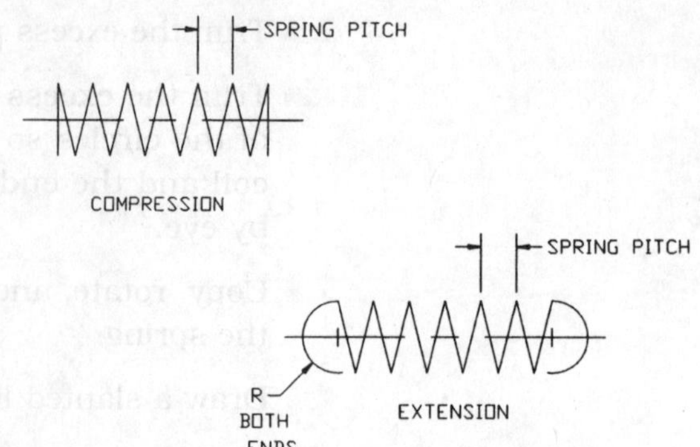

11-25 Tool Palettes

AutoCAD includes a Tool Palette that has, among other features, a set of fastener blocks. (See Section 3-21 for an explanation of Blocks.) The Tool Palette is accessed by using the **Tool Palettes** tool located on the Palettes panel under the **View** tab. See Figure 11-45.

Figure 11-45

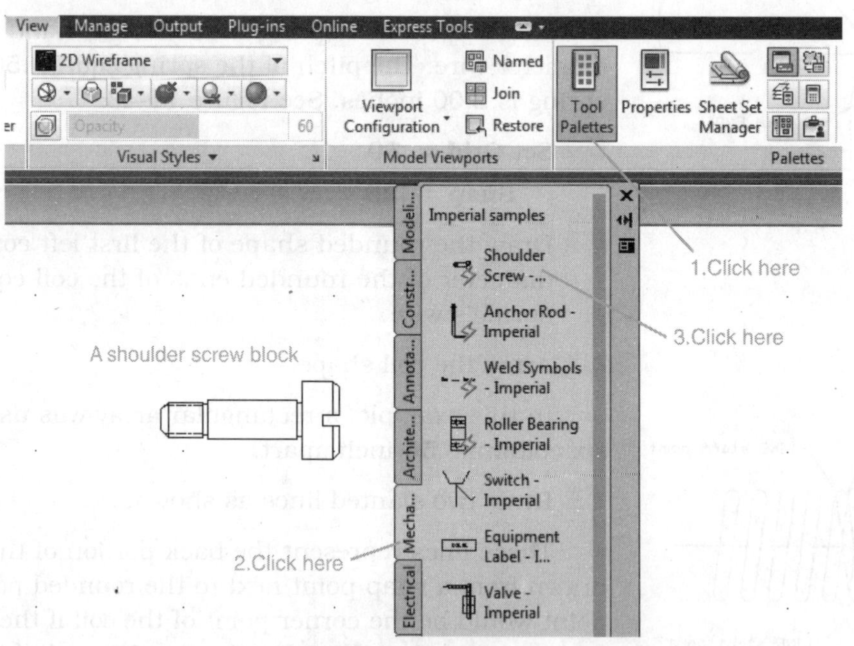

To Create a Shoulder Screw

1. Click the **Tool Palettes** tool on the **Palettes** panel under the **View** tab.

   The **Palettes** dialog box will appear.

2. Select the **Mechanical** tab.

   A listing of available blocks will appear.

3. Click the **Shoulder screw – Imperial block** icon.

   The shoulder screw block will appear on the screen. Use the mouse wheel to increase the viewing size of the screw.

   Remove the **Tool Palettes** box by clicking the large **X** in the upper right corner of the box.

4. Use the **Erase** tool and erase the shoulder screw block.

   Like any other block, the shoulder screw block can be scaled or edited.

To Change the Scale of a Tool Palette Block

1. Click the **Insert** tool on the **Block** panel under the **Home** tab.

   See Figure 11-46.

2. Change the X and Y scale factors to 2.00 and the rotation angle to 90°.

   The Z scale need not be changed, as this is a 2D (two-dimensional) drawing; that is, only the X and Y axes are being used. See Figure 11-47.

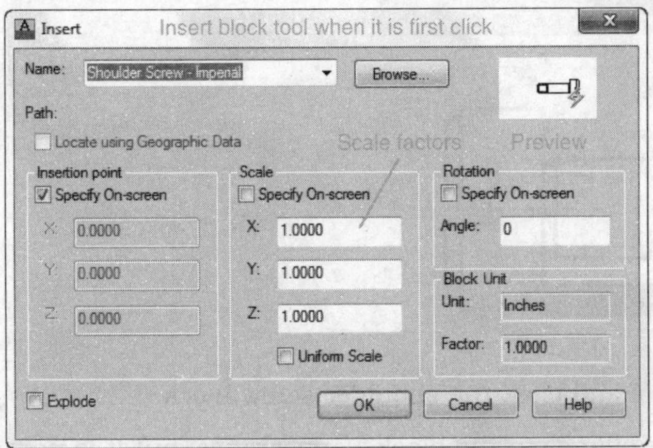

Figure 11-46

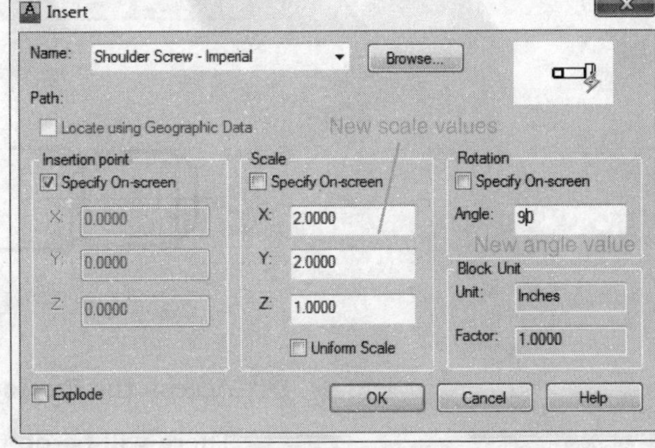

Figure 11-47

3. Click **OK.**

   Figure 11-48 shows the original shoulder screw next to the scaled one. Centerlines were added with the **Osnap Midpoint** option. The **Insert** dialog box can be used to change the screw's proportions—that is, scale the X direction to one value and the Y direction to a different value.

Figure 11-48

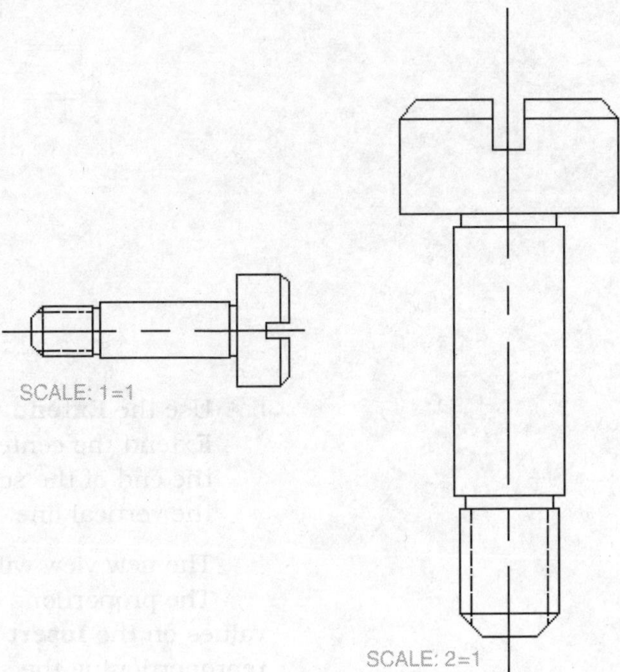

To Modify the Block

The shoulder screw block can be modified by using the **Explode** tool located on the **Modify** panel under the **Home** tab. See Figure 11-49.

Figure 11-49

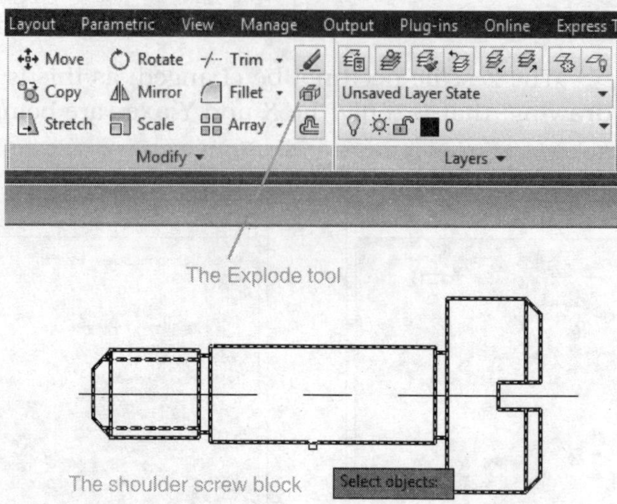

1 Access the **Explode** tool and click the shoulder screw block.

There will be no visible change in the block's appearance, but it is now composed of individual lines that can be erased or edited.

2 Use the **Move** tool, and move the threaded portion of the screw.

See Figure 11-50.

Figure 11-50

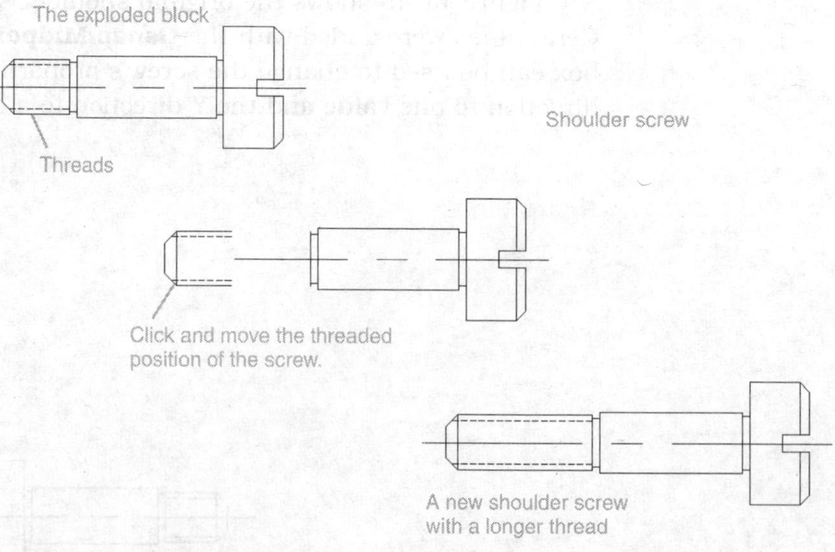

3 Use the **Extend** tool, and increase the thread length of the screw. Extend the centerline by adding a vertical line to the left and beyond the end of the screw. Extend the center to the vertical line, and erase the vertical line.

The new view will show a shoulder screw with a longer thread.

The proportions of the screw may be changed by using either the scale values on the **Insert** dialog box or the **Explode** tool and then reproportioning the screw.

11-26 EXERCISE PROBLEMS

EX11-1

Create wblocks for the following thread major diameters:

A. 1.00-in. detailed representation

B. 1.00-in. schematic thread representation

C. 1.00-in. simplified thread representation

D. 100-mm detailed representation

E. 100-mm schematic thread representation

F. 100-mm simplified thread representation

EX11-2

Draw a .750–10UNC–2_ × ___ LONG thread. Include the thread callout.

A. External –3.00 LONG.

B. Internal to fit into the object shown in Figure EX11-2.

C. Use a detailed representation.

D. Use a schematic representation.

E. Use a simplified representation.

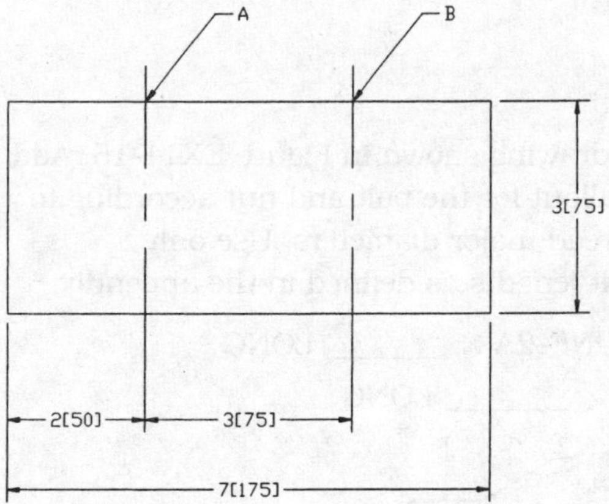

Figure EX11-2

EX11-3

Draw a .250–28UNF–2_ × ___ LONG thread. Include the thread callout.

A. External –1.50 LONG.

B. Internal to fit into the object shown in Figure EX11-2.

C. Use a detailed representation.

D. Use a schematic representation.

E. Use a simplified representation.

EX11-4

Draw an M36 × 4 × ___ LONG thread. Include the thread callout.

A. External –100 LONG.

B. Internal to fit into the object shown in Figure EX11-2.

C. Use a detailed representation.

D. Use a schematic representation.

E. Use a simplified representation.

EX11-5

Draw an M12 × 1.75 × ___ LONG thread. Include the thread callout.

A. External –40 LONG.

B. Internal to fit into the object shown in Figure EX11-2.

C. Use a detailed representation.

D. Use a schematic representation.

E. Use a simplified representation.

EX11-6

Draw a 2.75 × 2 × 5.00 inch-long external square thread.

EX11-7

Draw a 50 × 2 × 100 millimeter-long external square thread.

EX11-8

Draw a 3 × 1.5 × 6 inch-long external acme thread.

EX11-9

Draw an 80 × 1.5 × 200 millimeter-long external acme thread.

For Exercise Problems EX11-10 through EX11-13, draw the bolts, nuts, and screws assembled into the object shown in Figure EX11-2. If not given, determine the length of the fasteners, using the tables given in this chapter or in the appendix. Include the appropriate drawing callout.

EX11-10

A. .500–13UNC × ____ LONG HEX HEAD BOLT. Include a finished nut on the end of the bolt.

B. 5/8(.625)–18UNF × 1.5 LONG HEX HEAD SCREW. Specify the diameter and length of the tap hole.

C. Draw a detailed representation.

D. Draw a schematic representation.

E. Draw a simplified representation.

F. Draw an orthographic view.

G. Draw a sectional view.

EX11-11

A. M24– ____ LONG HEX HEAD BOLT. Include a finished nut on the end of the bolt.

B. M16–30 LONG HEX HEAD SCREW. Specify the diameter and length of the tap hole.

C. Draw a detailed representation.

D. Draw a schematic representation.

E. Draw a simplified representation.

F. Draw an orthographic view.

G. Draw a sectional view.

EX11-12

A. M30 × ____ LONG SQUARE HEAD BOLT. Include two locknuts on the end of the bolt.

B. M12 × 1.4 × 24 LONG SQUARE HEAD SCREW. Specify the diameter and length of the tap hole.

C. Draw a detailed representation.

D. Draw a schematic representation.

E. Draw a simplified representation.

F. Draw an orthographic view.

G. Draw a sectional view.

EX11-13

A. 1.25–7UNC × ____ LONG SQUARE HEAD BOLT. Include two locknuts on the end of the bolt.

B. .375–32UNEF × 1.5 LONG SQUARE HEAD SCREW. Specify the diameter and length of the tap hole.

C. Draw a detailed representation.

D. Draw a schematic representation.

E. Draw a simplified representation.

F. Draw an orthographic view.

G. Draw a sectional view.

EX11-14

Redraw the sectional view shown in Figure EX11-14. Include a drawing callout that defines the threads as M12. Specify the depth of the threaded hole, and the diameter and depth of the tap hole.

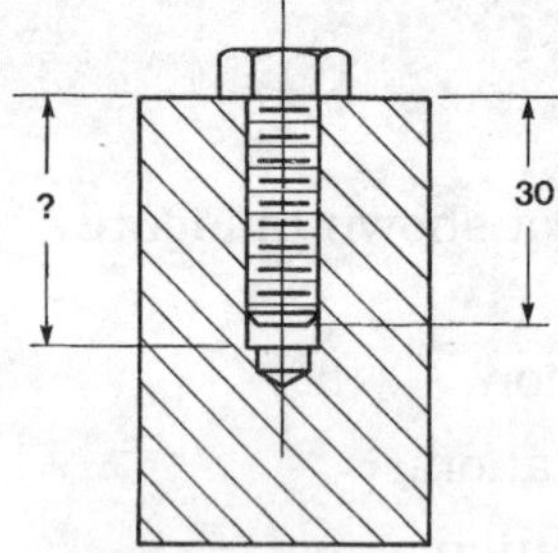

Figure EX11-14

EX11-15

Redraw the drawing shown in Figure EX11-15. Add a drawing callout for the bolt and nut according to the given thread major diameters. Use only standard bolt lengths as defined in the appendix.

A. .375–24UNF–2A × ________ LONG

B. M16 × 2 × ________ LONG

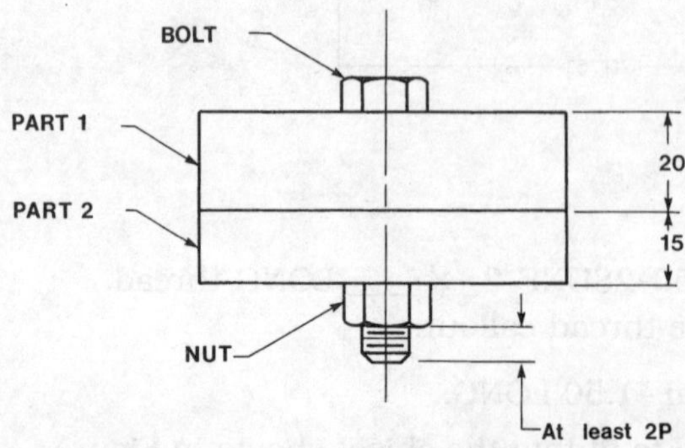

Figure EX11-15

EX11-16

Draw a front sectional view and a top orthographic view according to the given drawing and table information. Include the setscrews in the indicated holes. Include the appropriate drawing callout for each setscrew.

FOR INCH VALUES:

1 0.250–20UNC–2A × 1.00
SLOT HEAD, FLAT POINT
SET SCREW

2 .375–24UNF–2A × .750
HEX SOCKET, FULL DOG
SET SCREW

3 #10–28UNF–2A × .625
SQUARE, OVAL
SET SCREW

4 #6–32UNC–2A × .50
SLOT, CONE POINT
SET SCREW

FOR MILLIMETER VALUES:

1 M12 × 20
SLOT HEAD, FLAT POINT
SET SCREW

2 M16 × 2 × 30
SQUARE HEAD, HALF DOG
SET SCREW

3 M6 × 20
HEX SOCKET, CONE
SET SCREW

4 M10 × 1.5 × 20
CUP, SLOT
SET SCREW

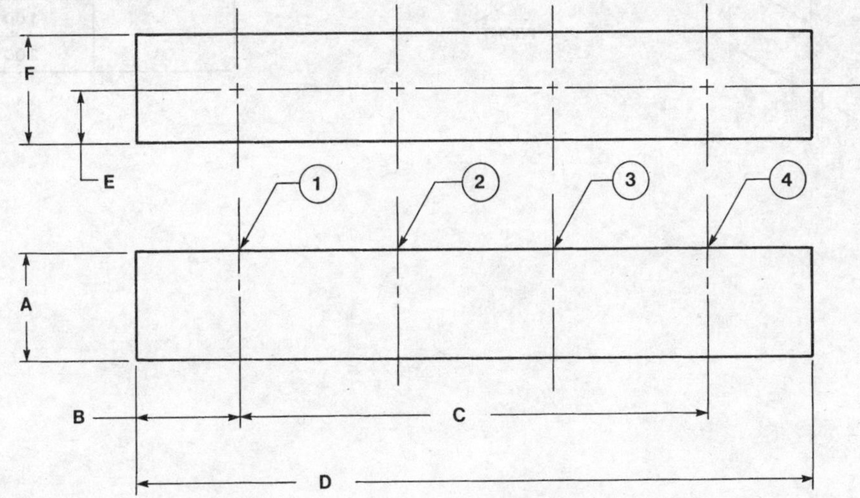

DIMENSION	INCHES	mm
A	2.00	50
B	1.00	25
C	3 X 1.00	3 X 40
D	6.5	170
E	.75	20
F	1.50	40

EX11-17

Draw a front sectional view and a top orthographic view according to the following drawing and table information:

A. Use inch values.

B. Use millimeter values.

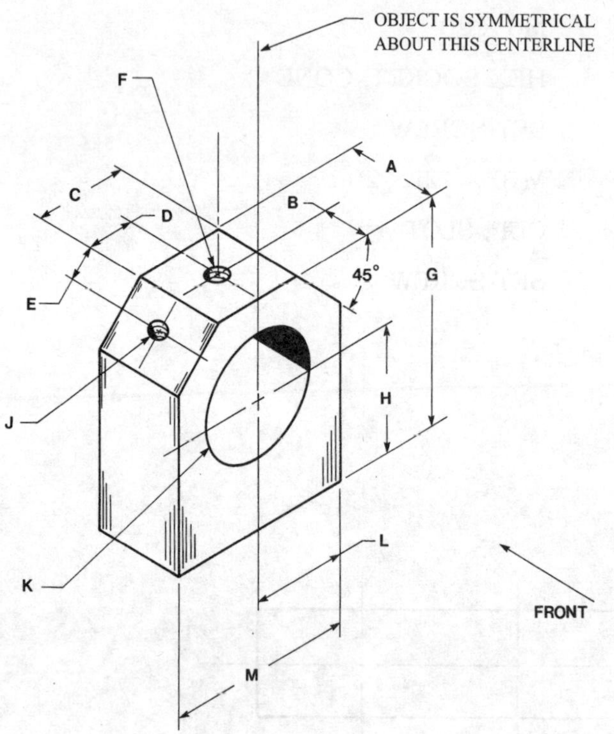

DIMENSION	INCHES	mm
A	1.00	26
B	.50	13
C	1.00	26
D	.50	13
E	.38	10
F	.190-32 UNF	M8 X 1
G	2.38	60
H	1.38	34
J	.164-36 UNF	M6
K	Ø1.25	Ø30
L	1.00	26
M	2.00	52

EX11-18

Redraw the drawing that follows as a sectional view. Select and include the drawing callouts for the nut and washer according to the given bolts. Specify the bolt lengths according to standard lengths listed in the appendix.

A. .625–11UNC–2A × ___ LONG HEX HEAD BOLT

B. M16 × 2 × ___ LONG HEX HEAD

C. .500-20 UNF × ___ LONG SQUARE HEAD

D. M20 × ___ SQUARE HEAD

E. .438-28 UNEF × ___ LONG HEX HEAD

F. M12 × 1.25 × ___ LONG HEX HEAD

G. .750-10 UNC × ___ LONG HEX HEAD

H. M24 × 3 × ___ LONG HEX HEAD

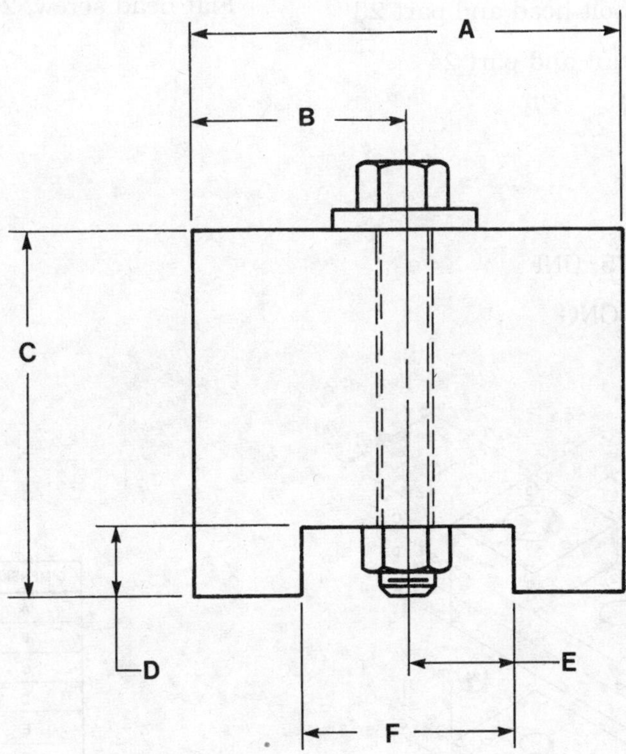

DIMENSION	INCHES	mm
A	3.00	76
B	1.50	38
C	2.50	64
D	.50	13
E	.75	19
F	1.50	38

EX11-19

Draw a front sectional view and a top orthographic view according to the given drawing and table information. Add fasteners to the labeled holes according to the information here. Include the appropriate drawing callouts. Use only standard sizes as listed in the appendix.

FOR INCH VALUES:

1. Nominal diameter = .250, UNC

   Square head bolt and nut

   A washer between the bolt head and part 23

   A washer between the nut and part 24

2. .375–24UNF–2A × 1.00

   SLOT, OVAL

   SETSCREW

3. Nominal diameter = .375, UNF

   Flat head screw, 1.25 LONG

FOR MILLIMETER VALUES:

1. Nominal diameter = 12, coarse

   Square head bolt and nut

   A washer between the bolt head and part 23

   A washer between the nut and part 24

2. M10 × .5 × 20

   SQUARE HEAD, FULL DOG

   SET SCREW

3. Nominal diameter = 12, fine

   Flat head screw, 20 LONG

NOTE: HOLES IN PART 24 ALIGN WITH THOSE IN PART 23.

DIMENSION	INCHES	mm
A	1.25	32
B	.63	16
C	.50	13
D	.38	10
E	.25	7
F	.63	16

EX11-20

Redraw the sectional view that follows, and include the appropriate bolts and nuts at locations W, X, Y, and Z so that the selected bolt heads sit flat on their bearing surfaces. Select the bolts from the standard sizes listed in the appendix.

(W) (X) (Y) (Z) INDICATES FASTENER LOCATIONS

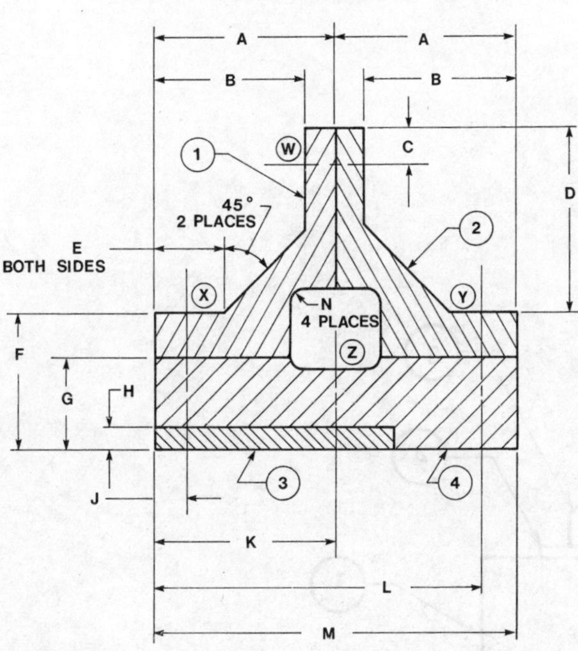

DIMENSION	INCHES	mm
A	1.00	50
B	1.63	41
C	.38	10
D	2.00	50
E	.75	19
F	1.50	38
G	1.00	25
H	.25	6
J	.38	10
K	2.00	50
L	3.63	92
M	4.00	100
N	R.13	3

EX11-21

Redraw the given drawing based on the information that follows. Include all bolt, nut, washer, and spring callouts. Use only standard sizes as listed in the appendix.

FOR INCH VALUES:

A. Major diameter of bolt = .375 coarse thread.

B. Add the appropriate nut.

C. Washer is .125 thick and allows a minimum clearance from the bolt of at least .125.

D. Compression springs are made from .125-diameter wire and are 1.00 long. They have an inside diameter that always clears the bolt by at least .125.

E. Parts 1 and 2 are 1.00 high and 4.00 wide.

F. Locate the bolts at least 1.00 from each end.

FOR MILLIMETER VALUES:

A. Major diameter of bolt = 12 coarse thread.

B. Add the appropriate nut.

C. Washer is 3 thick and allows a minimum clearance from the bolt of at least 2.

D. Compression springs are made from 4-diameter wire and are 24 long. They have an inside diameter that always clears the bolt by at least 3.

E. Parts 1 and 2 are 25 high and 100 wide.

F. Locate the bolts at least 25 from each end.

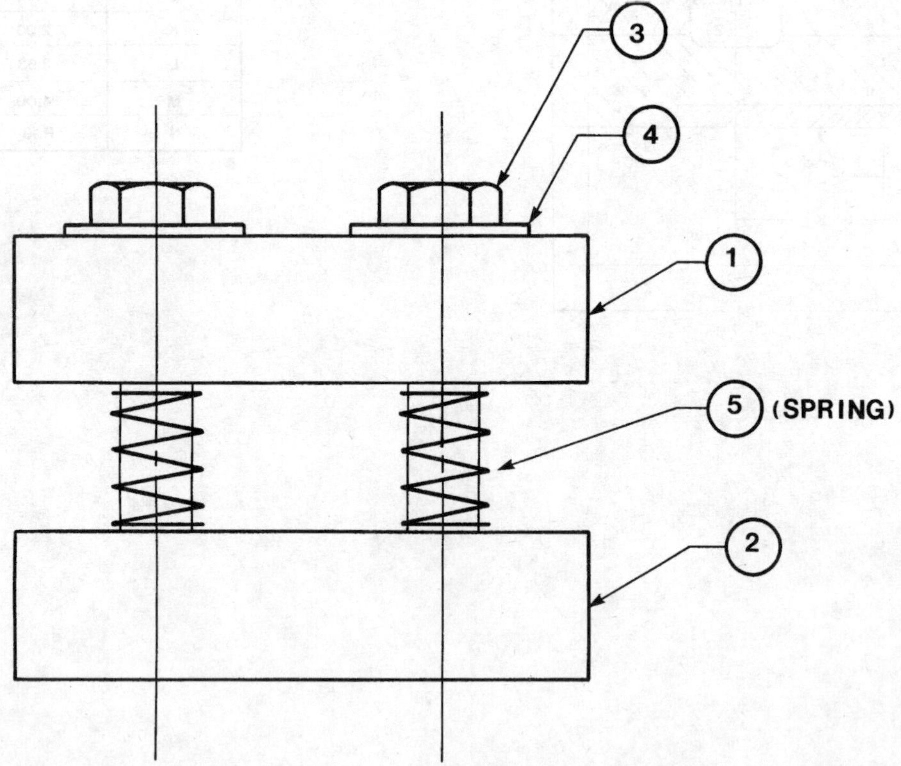

EX11-22

Figure EX11-22 shows two identical blocks that are to be held together by a bolt and a nut. Two washers are also used. Specify the appropriate fastener, nut, and washer for the following block sizes:

Block and nominal hole sizes:

A. 1.50 × 1.50 × 0.75 inches: Ø.375 inch

B. 20 × 20 × 12 mm; Ø8 mm

C. 2.00 × 2.00 × 0.625 inches; Ø.500 inch

D. 30 × 30 × 15 mm; Ø10 mm

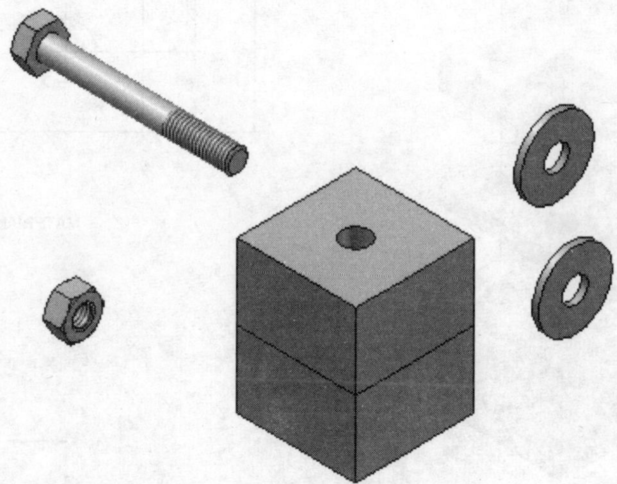

Figure EX11-22

EX11-23

Figure EX11-23 shows three parts that are to be held together by six screws. Given the part sizes, specify the six fasteners needed to assemble the parts.

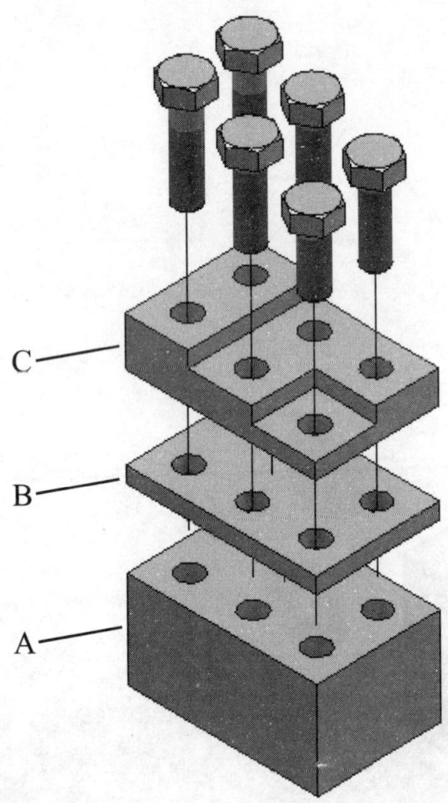

Figure EX11-23

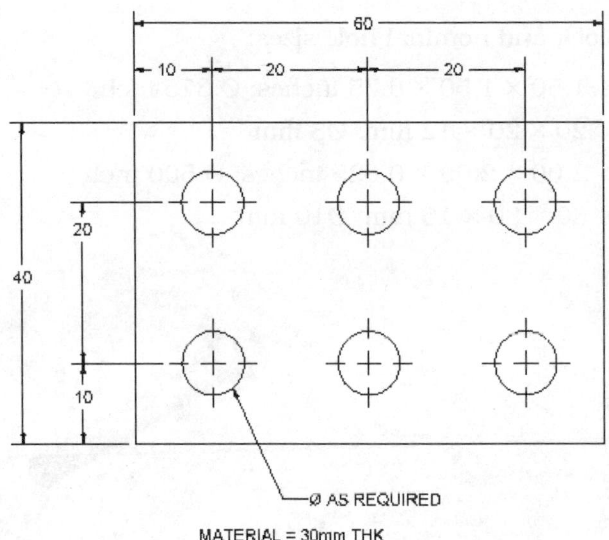

A

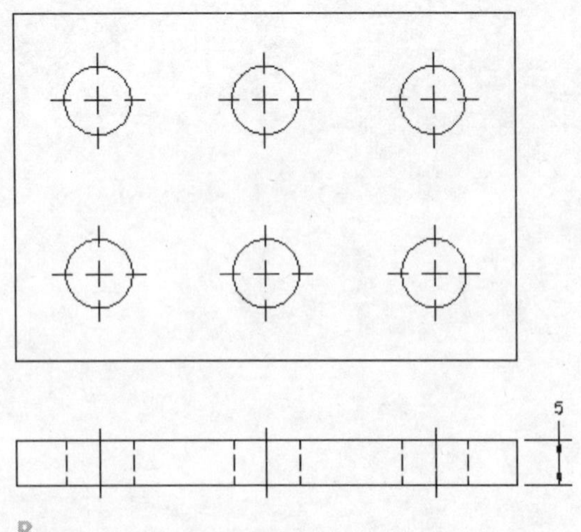

B

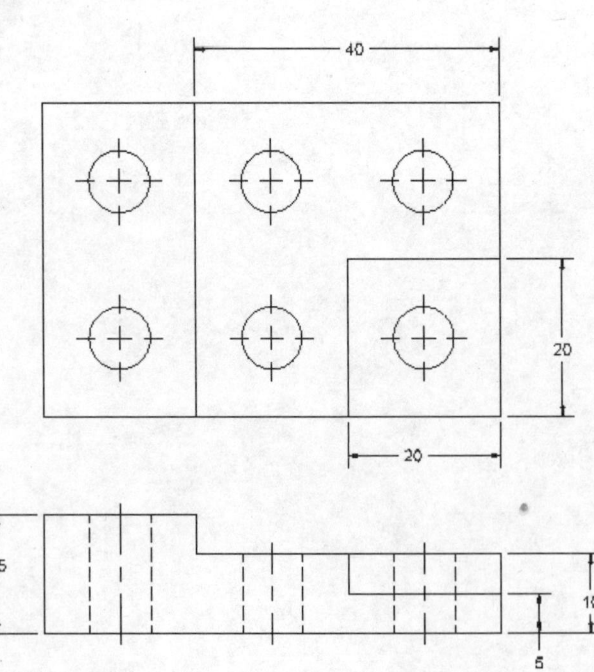

C

chapter twelve

Working Drawings

12-1 Introduction

This chapter explains how to create assembly drawings, parts lists, and detail drawings. It includes guidelines for titles, revisions, tolerances, and release blocks. The chapter shows how to create a design layout and then use the layout to create assembly and detail drawings through the **Layer** command.

12-2 Assembly Drawings

Assembly drawings show how objects fit together. See Figure 12-1. All information necessary to complete the assembly must be included on the drawing. This information may include specific assembly dimensions, torque requirements for bolts, finishing and shipping instructions, and any other appropriate company or customer specifications.

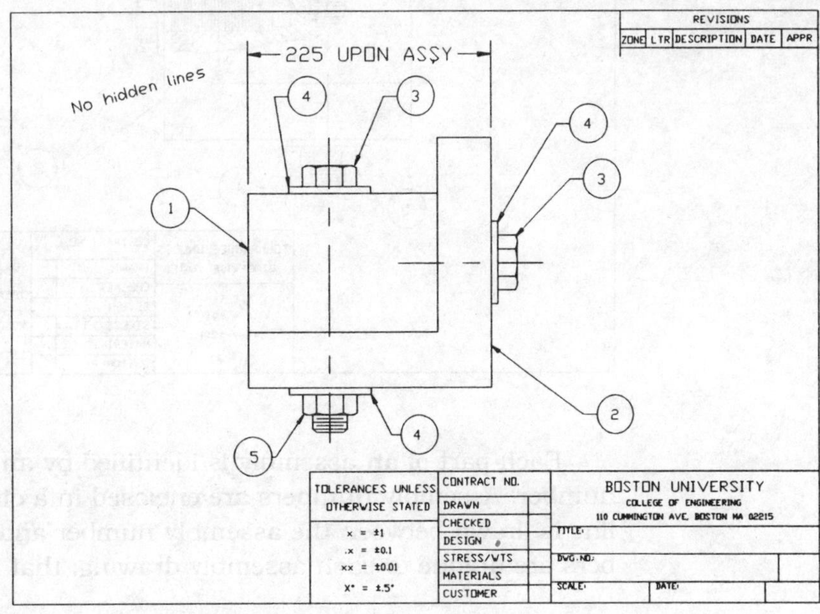

Figure 12-1

Assembly drawings are sometimes called *top drawings* because they are the first of a series of drawings used to define a group of parts that are to be assembled together. The group of drawings, referred to as a *family of drawings*, may include subassemblies, modification drawings, detail drawings, and a parts list. See Figure 12-2.

Figure 12-2

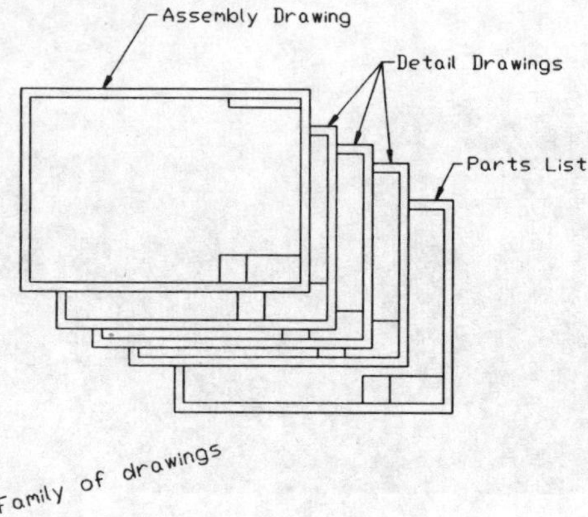

Assembly drawings do *not* contain hidden lines. A sectional view may be used to show internal areas critical to the assembly. Specific information about the internal surfaces of objects that make up the assembly can be found on the detail drawings of the individual objects. See Figure 12-3.

Figure 12-3

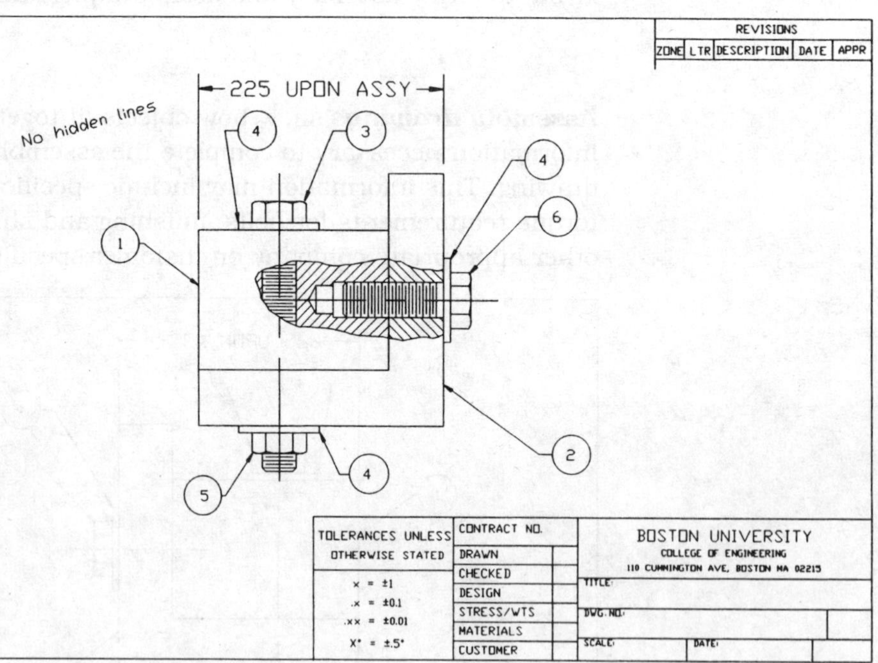

Each part of an assembly is identified by an assembly, or item, number. Assembly numbers are enclosed in a circle or ellipse, and a leader line is drawn between the assembly number and the part. Assembly numbers are unique to each assembly drawing; that is, a part that is used in several different assemblies may have a different assembly number on each assembly drawing.

If several of the same part are used in the same assembly, each part should be assigned the same assembly number. A leader line should be used to identify each part unless the differences between the parts are obvious. In Figure 12-4, the difference between head sizes for the fasteners is obvious, so all parts need not be identified.

Assemblies should be shown in their natural, or neutral, positions. Figure 12-5 shows a clamp in a slightly open position. It is best to show the clamp jaws partially open, not fully closed or fully open. In general, a drawing should show an assembly in its most common position.

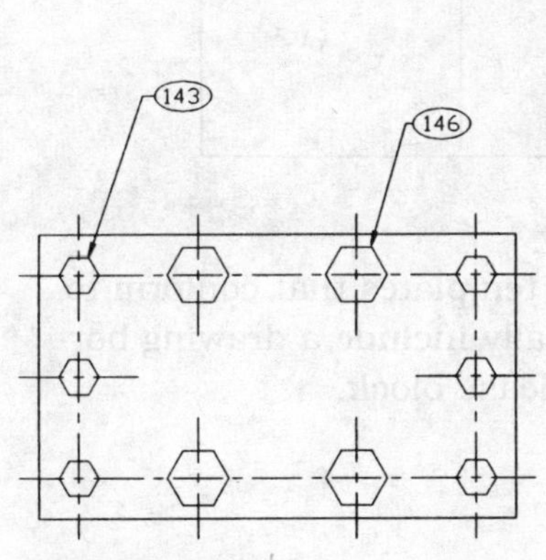

Figure 12-4

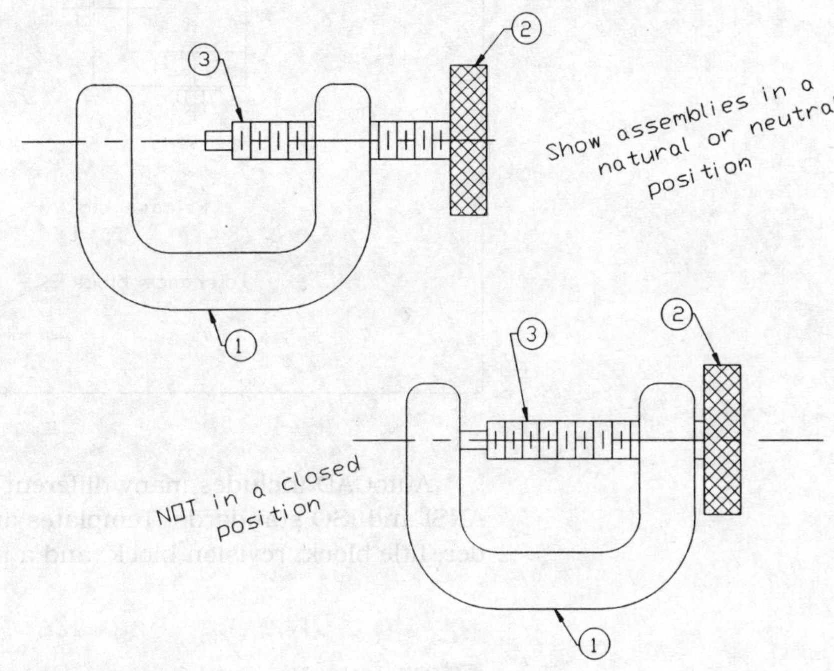

Figure 12-5

The range of motion for an assembly is shown by the use of phantom lines. See Figure 12-6. Note how the range of motion for the hinged top piece is displayed by using phantom lines.

Figure 12-6

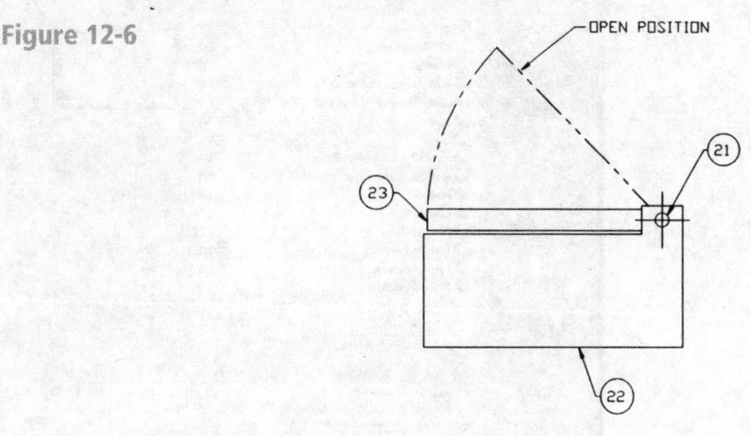

12-3 Drawing Formats (Templates)

Figure 12-7 shows a general format for an assembly drawing. The format varies from company to company and with the size of the drawing paper.

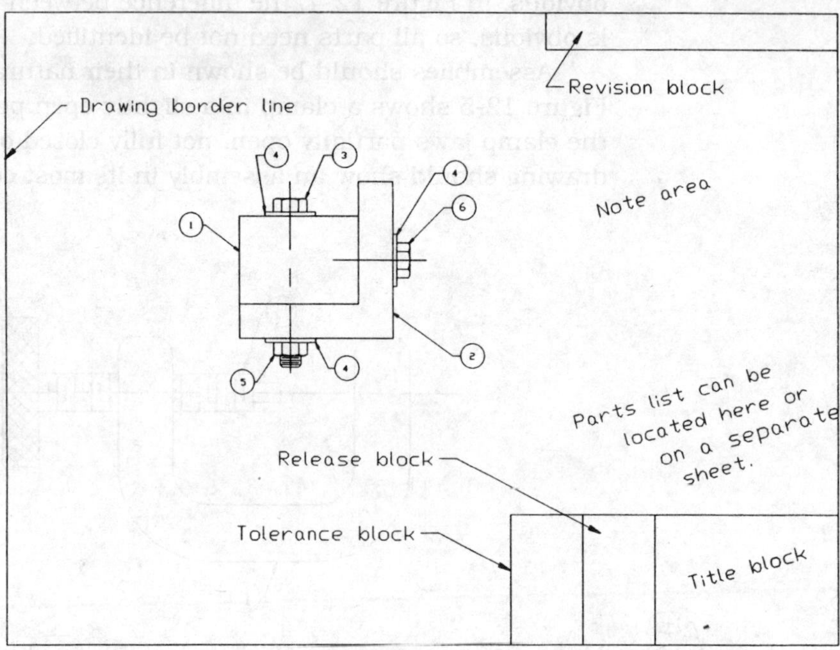

Figure 12-7

AutoCAD includes many different drawing templates that conform to ANSI and ISO standards. Templates automatically include a drawing border, title block, revision block, and a partial release block.

To Add a Drawing Template

1. Click the **New** tool.

   The **Select template** dialog box will appear. See Figure 12-8.

2. Select the **Tutorial-iMfg** template; click the **Open** box.

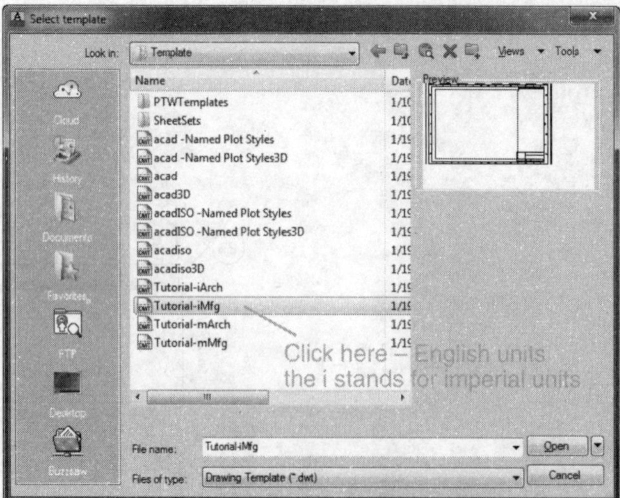

Figure 12-8

The template will appear on the screen. See Figure 12-9. Drawings may be created on the template just as they are with a blank no-template drawing screen.

Figure 12-9

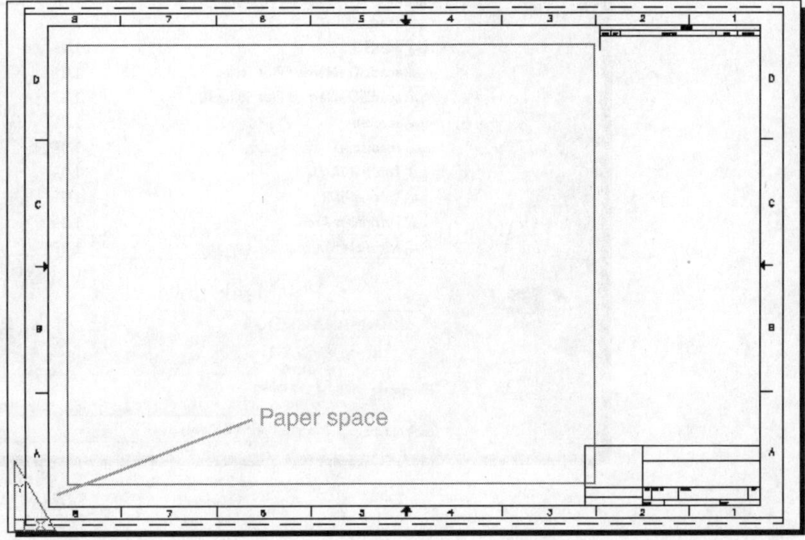

Figure 12-10 shows a completed title block for an iMfg template. It was completed by use of the **Text** tool. A listing of standard drawing sheet sizes is included in Section 1-8, Drawing Limits. An A-size drawing sheet is 8.5 × 11 inches. If an A-size template is selected, the screen units will automatically be fitted to the sheet size and will be in inches.

Figure 12-10

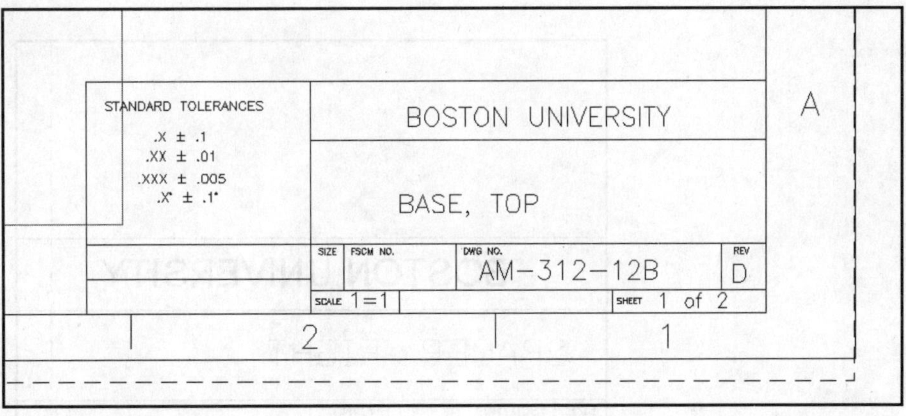

Standard metric drawing sheet sizes are also listed in Section 1-8. The closest equivalent to an A-size inch drawing is an A4-size drawing, which is 210 × 297 millimeters. Figure 12-11 shows the **Select template** dialog box set to select a **Tutorial-mMfg** template. The screen units will be in millimeters.

Figure 12-11

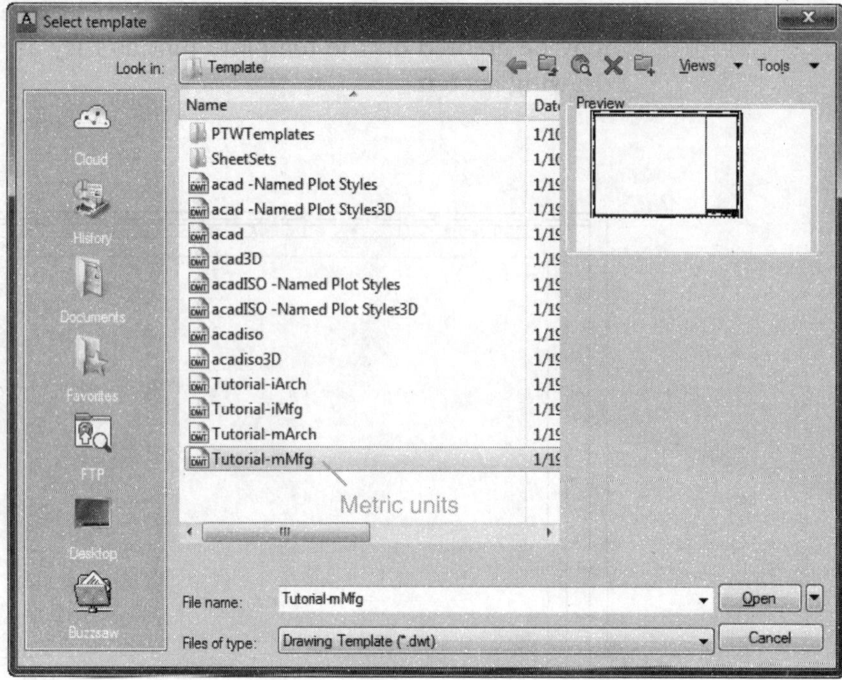

12-4 Title Block

Title blocks are located in the lower right corner of a drawing and include, at a minimum, the drawing's name and number, the company's name, the drawing scale, the release date of the drawing, and the sheet number of the drawing. Other information may be included. Figure 12-12 shows a sample title block created from an iMfg layout template. The text was added by use of the **Multiline Text** tool and positioned by use of the **Move** tool.

Figure 12-12

Figure 12-13 shows the title block from an mMfg layout template. The title block will appear with a series of XXX inputs. Use the **Explode** command and explode the title block.

Figure 12-13

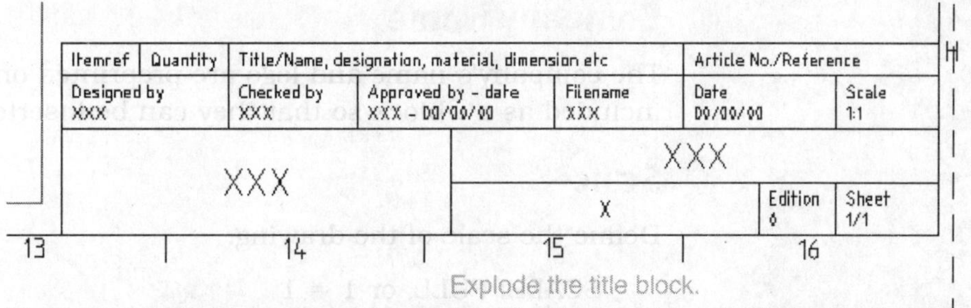

Explode the title block.

Itemref	Quantity	Title/Name, designation, material, dimension etc		Article No./Reference	
Designed by DESIGNED_BY	Checked by CHECKED_BY	Approved by - date APPROVED_BY_DATE	Filename FILENAME	Date DATE	Scale SCALE
OWNER			TITLE		
		DRAWING_NUMBER		Edition EDITION	Sheet SHEET

14 15 16

Erase unwanted words and type in new text.

Itemref	Quantity	Title/Name, designation, material, dimension etc		Article No./Reference	
Designed by BETHUNE,J	Checked by KELLEY,C	Approved by - date 4-15-10	Filename ME311-1	Date	Scale 1 = 1
Boston University			BRACKET, GUIDE		
		ME311-1			Sheet 1 of 3

14 15 16

Revised title block

The XXX inputs will be replaced with words. Erase the unwanted words and replace them with the appropriate names and numbers.

Drawing Titles (Names)

Drawing titles should be chosen so that they clearly define the function of the part. They should be presented in the following word sequence:

Noun, modifier, modifying phrase

For example,

SHAFT, HIGH SPEED, LEFT HAND

GASKET, LOWER

Noun names may be two words if normal usage includes the two words:

GEAR BOX, COMPOSITE

SHOCK ABSORBER, LEFT

Drawing Numbers

Drawing numbers are assigned by companies according to their usage requirement. The numbering system varies greatly. Usually, drawing numbers are recorded in a log book to prevent duplication of numbers.

Company Name

The company's name and logo are preprinted on drawing paper or are included as a wblock so that they can be inserted on each drawing.

Scale

Define the scale of the drawing.

SCALE: FULL, or 1 = 1

When the drawing size is the same as the object size, define the scale as follows:

SCALE: 2 = 1

When the drawing size is twice as large as the object size, the scale is defined like this:

SCALE: 1 = 2

When the drawing size is half as large as the object size, the scale is defined as follows:

Release Date

A drawing is released only after all persons required by the company's policy to review it have reviewed it and added their signatures to the release block. Once released, a drawing becomes a legal document. Drawings that have not been officially released are often stamped with a statement such as "NOT RELEASED" or "FOR REFERENCE ONLY."

Sheet

The number of the sheet relative to the total number of sheets that make up the drawing should be stated clearly.

SHEET 2 OF 3

or

SH 2 OF 3

12-5 Revision Block

Drawings used in industry are constantly being changed. Products are improved or corrected, and drawings must be changed to reflect and document these changes. Figure 12-14 shows a sample revision block.

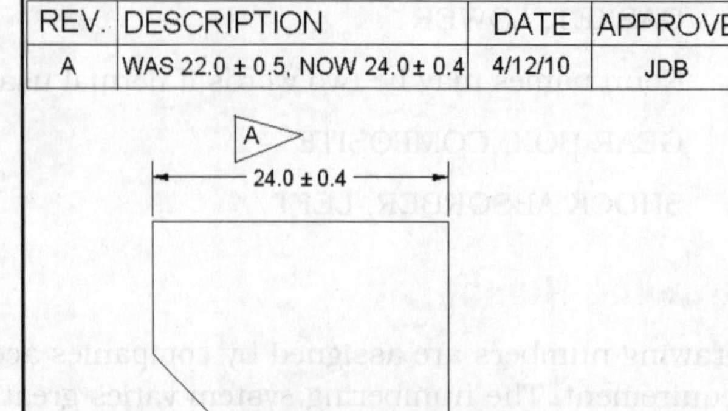

REV.	DESCRIPTION	DATE	APPROVED
A	WAS 22.0 ± 0.5, NOW 24.0± 0.4	4/12/10	JDB

Figure 12-14

Drawing changes are listed in the revision block by letter. Revision blocks are located in the upper right corner of the drawing. See Figure 12-7. Figure 12-15 shows a revision block from an mMfg template. The text was added by using **Mtext,** and the chart lines by using **Line.**

Figure 12-15

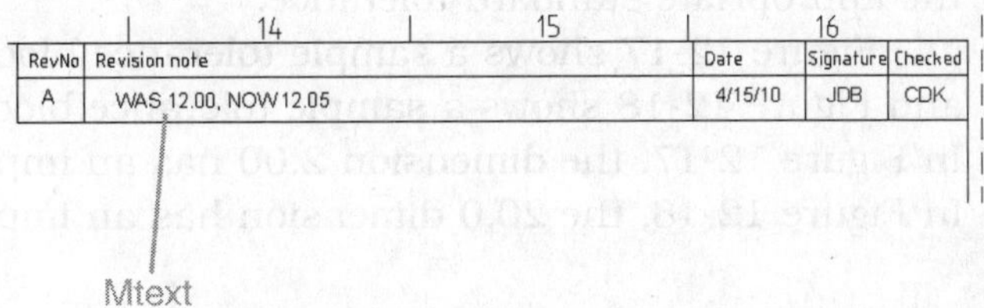

Each drawing revision is listed by letter in the revision block. A brief description of the change is also included. It is important that the description be as accurate and complete as possible. Revisions are often used to check drawing requirements on parts manufactured before the revisions were introduced.

The revision letter is also added to the field of the drawing in the area where the change was made. The letter is located within a "flag" to distinguish it from dimensions and drawing notes. The flag serves to notify anyone reading the drawing that revisions have been made.

Most companies have systems in place that allow engineers and designers to make quick changes to drawings. These change orders are called ***engineering change orders*** (ECOs), ***change orders*** (COs), or ***engineering orders*** (EOs), depending on the company's preference. Change orders are documented on special drawing sheets that are usually stapled to a print of the drawing. Figure 12-16 shows a change order attached to a drawing.

Figure 12-16

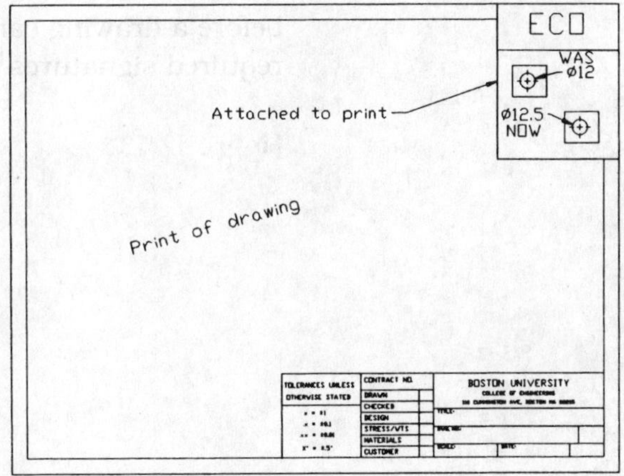

After a group of change orders accumulates, the change orders are incorporated into the drawing. This process is called a ***drawing revision,*** which is different from a revision to the drawing. Drawing revisions are usually indicated by a letter located somewhere in the title block. The revision letters may be included as part of the drawing number or in a separate box in the title block. Whenever you are working on a drawing, make sure that you have the latest revision and all appropriate change orders. Companies have recording and referencing systems for listing all drawing revisions and drawing changes.

12-6 Tolerance Block

Most drawings include a ***tolerance block*** next to the title block, which lists the standard tolerances that apply to the dimensions on the drawing. A dimension that does not include a specific tolerance is assumed to have the appropriate standard tolerance.

Figure 12-17 shows a sample tolerance block for inch values, and Figure 12-18 shows a sample tolerance block for millimeter values. In Figure 12-17, the dimension 2.00 has an implied tolerance of ±.01. In Figure 12-18, the 20.0 dimension has an implied tolerance of ±0.1.

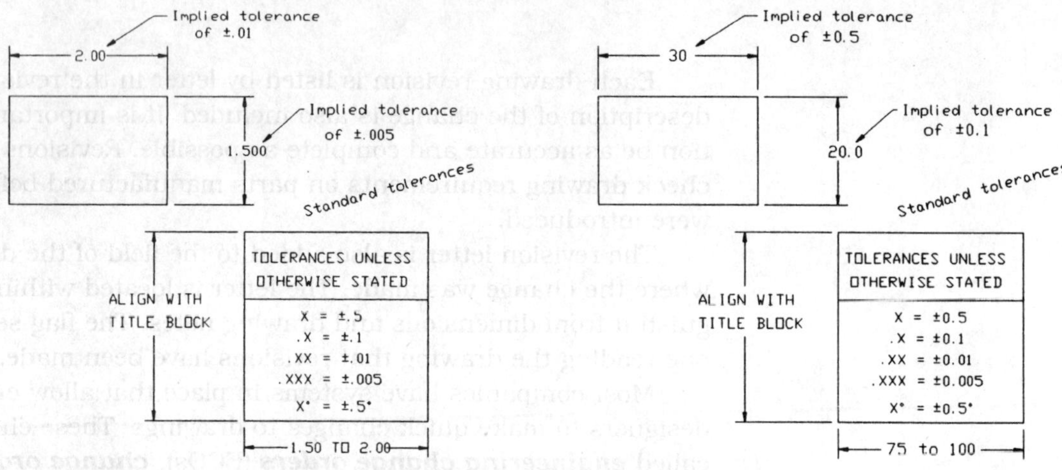

Figure 12-17 **Figure 12-18**

12-7 Release Block

A ***release block*** contains a list of approval signatures or initials required before a drawing can be released for production. See Figure 12-19. The required signatures are generally as follows.

Figure 12-19

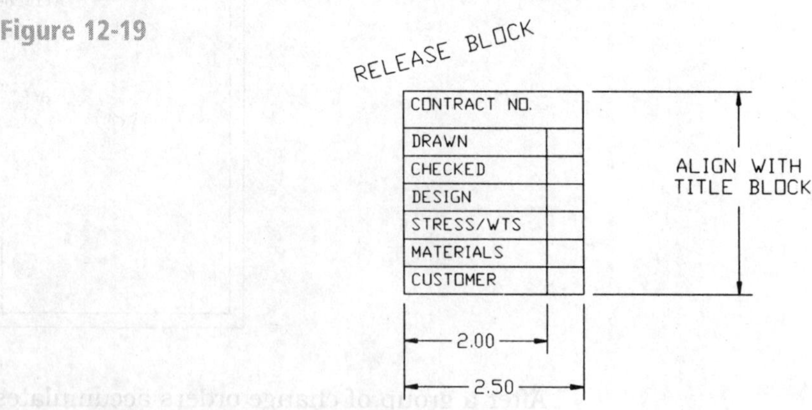

Drawn

Person that created the drawing.

Checked

Drawings are checked for errors and compliance with company procedures and conventions. Some large companies have checking departments, whereas smaller companies have drawings checked by a senior person or the drafting supervisor.

Design

The engineer in charge of the design project. The designer and the drafter may be the same person.

Stress/Wts

The department or person responsible for the stress analysis of the design.

Materials

Usually, a person in the production department checks the design and makes sure that the necessary materials and the machine times for the design are available. This person may also schedule production time.

Customer

The customer for the design may have a representative on site at the production facility to check that its design requirements are being met. For example, it is not unusual for the Air Force to assign an officer to a plant that manufactures its fighter aircraft.

12-8 Parts List (Bill of Materials—BOM)

A ***parts list*** is a listing of all parts used on an assembly. See Figure 12-20. The parts list was created by using the **Table** tool. See Section 2-27. The terms *parts list* and ***Bill of Materials*** are interchangeable. See Figure 12-21.

Figure 12-20

PARTS LIST					
NO.	DESCRIPTION	PART NO.	MATL	NOTE	QTY
1	BLOCK, TOP	BU311S1	SAE 1020		1
2	BLOCK, BOTTOM	BU311S2	SAE 1020		1
3	M16×24 HEX HEAD BOLT	SPM16H	STEEL	2	1
4	20×40×3 PLAIN WASHER		STEEL		3
5	M16 HEX NUT	2PM16N	STEEL		1
6	M16×20 HEX HEAD SCREW		STEEL		1

Figure 12-21

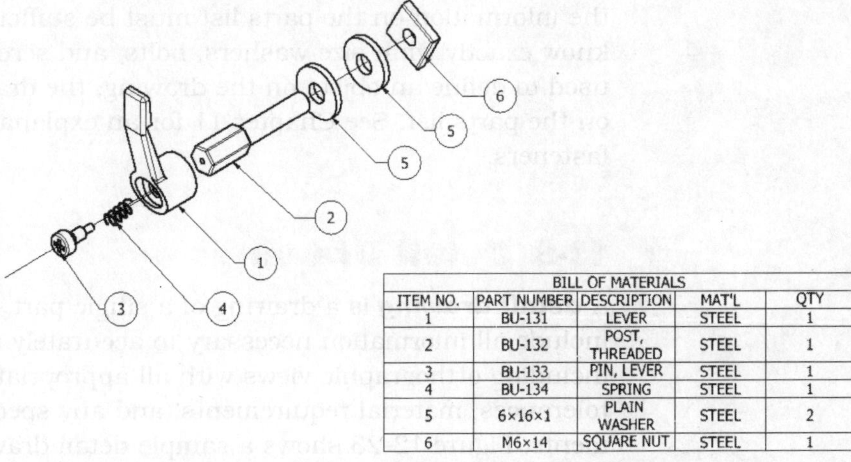

BILL OF MATERIALS				
ITEM NO.	PART NUMBER	DESCRIPTION	MAT'L	QTY
1	BU-131	LEVER	STEEL	1
2	BU-132	POST, THREADED	STEEL	1
3	BU-133	PIN, LEVER	STEEL	1
4	BU-134	SPRING	STEEL	1
5	6×16×1	PLAIN WASHER	STEEL	2
6	M6×14	SQUARE NUT	STEEL	1

Parts lists may be located on an assembly drawing above the title block or on a separate sheet of paper. Assembly drawings made by using AutoCAD often include the parts list on a separate layer within the drawing. Use only capital letters on a parts list.

Figure 12-22 shows two sample parts list formats, including dimensions. Parts list formats vary greatly from company to company. The dimensions are given in inches. They may be converted to millimeters by the conversion factor 1.00 inch = 25.4 millimeters. The AutoCAD template includes a parts list format that is automatically sized to the sheet size.

Figure 12-22

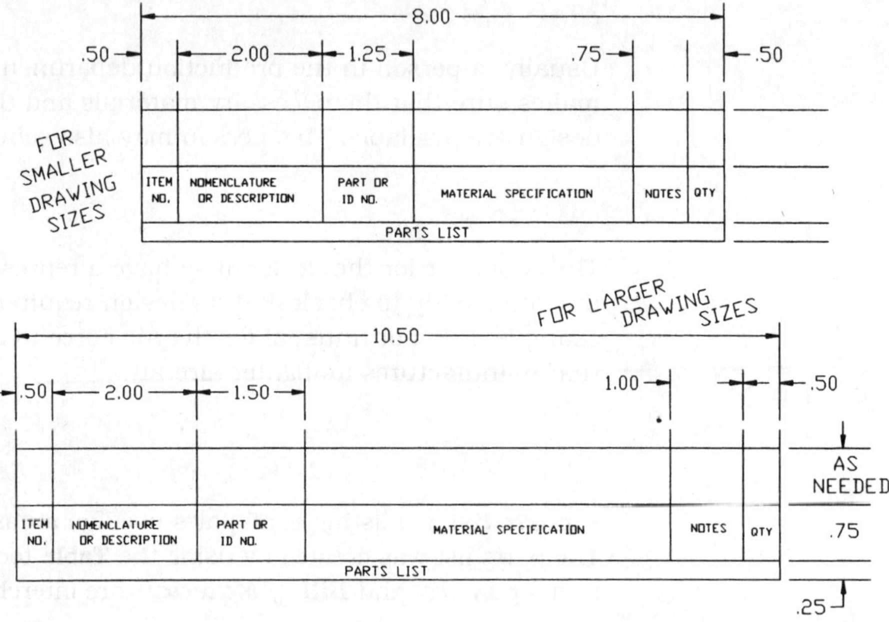

A parts list serves as a way to cross-reference detail drawing numbers to assembly item numbers. It also provides a list of the materials needed for production and is very helpful for scheduling and materials purchasing.

Parts purchased from a vendor and used exactly as they are supplied, without any modification, will not have detail drawings, but are included on the parts list. The washers, bolts, and screws listed on the parts list shown in Figure 12-21 would not have detail drawings. This means that the information on the parts list must be sufficient for a purchaser to know exactly what size washers, bolts, and screws to buy. The information used to define an object on the drawing, the drawing callout, is also used on the parts list. See Chapter 11 for an explanation of drawing callouts for fasteners.

12-9 Detail Drawings

A ***detail drawing*** is a drawing of a single part. The drawing should include all information necessary to accurately manufacture the part, including orthographic views with all appropriate hidden lines, dimensions, tolerances, material requirements, and any special manufacturing requirements. Figure 12-23 shows a sample detail drawing.

Figure 12-23

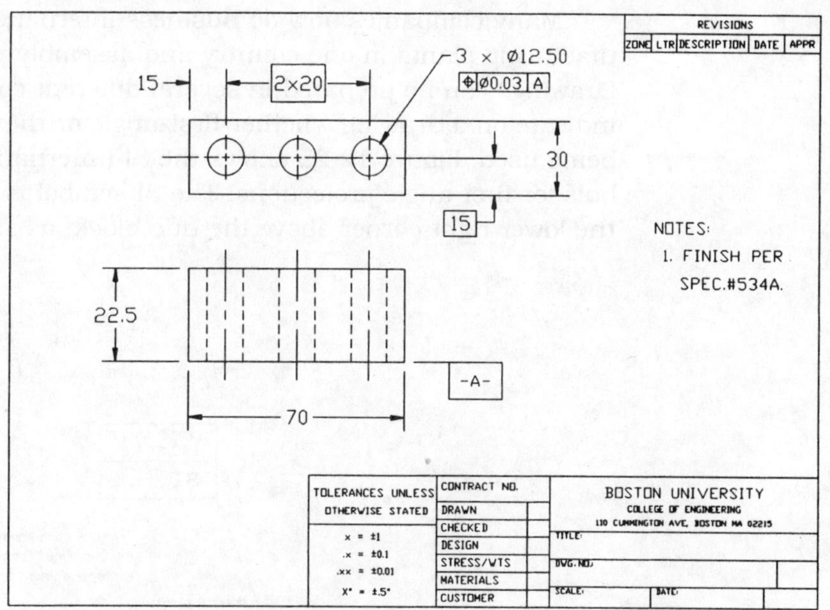

Detail drawings include title, release, tolerance, and revision blocks located on the drawing in the same places as they are found on assembly drawings.

12-10 First-Angle Projection

The instructions for the creation of orthographic views as presented in this book are based on third-angle projection. See Chapter 5. Third-angle projection is used in the United States, Canada, and Great Britain, among other countries. Many other countries such as Japan use first-angle projection to create orthographic views.

Figure 12-24 shows an object and the orthographic views of the object created in first-angle projection. Note that the top view in the first-angle projection is the same as the top view in the third-angle projection, but is located below the front view, not above the front view as in the third-angle projection. Right-side views are also the same, but are located to the left of the front view in first-angle projections and to the right in third-angle projections.

Figure 12-24

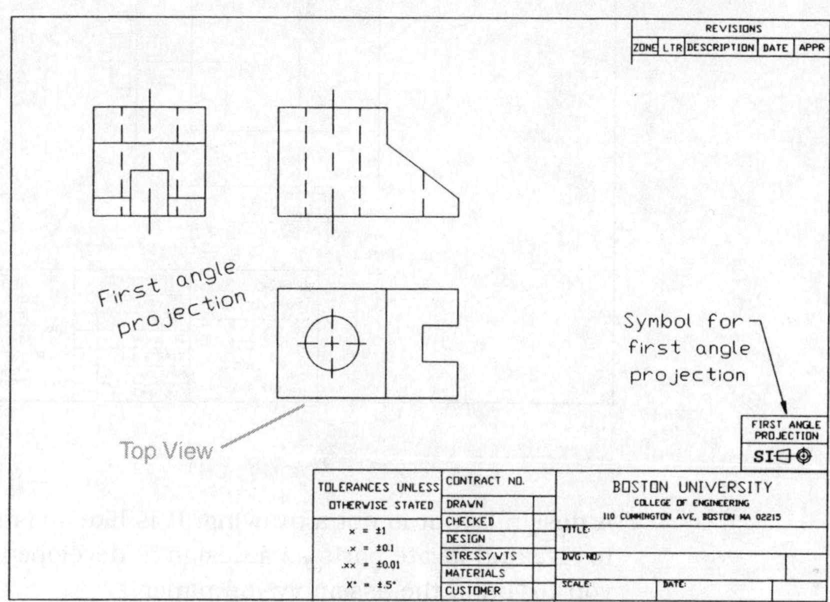

Many companies now do business internationally. They can have manufacturing plants in one country and assembly plants in another. Drawings can be prepared in several different countries. It is important to indicate on a drawing whether first-angle or third-angle projections are being used. Figure 12-25 shows the SI (International System of Units) symbols for first-angle projections. The SI symbol is included on a drawing in the lower right corner above the title block, as shown in Figure 12-24.

Figure 12-25

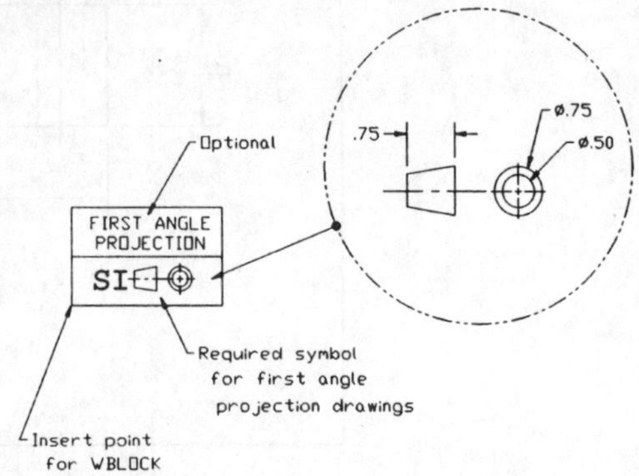

12-11 Drawing Notes

Drawing notes are used to provide manufacturing information that is not visual—for example, finishing instructions, torque requirements for bolts, and shipping instructions.

Drawing notes are usually located above the title block on the right side of the drawing. See Figure 12-26. Drawing notes are listed by number. If a note applies to a specific part of the drawing, the note number is enclosed in a triangle. The note numbers enclosed in triangles are also drawn next to the corresponding areas of the drawing.

Figure 12-26

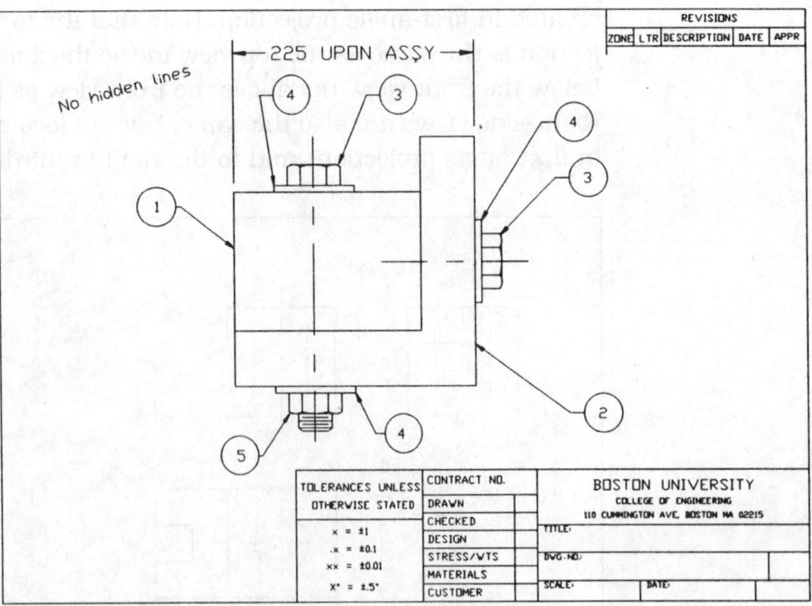

12-12 Design Layouts

A design layout is not a drawing. It is like a visual calculation sheet used to size and locate parts as a design is developed. A design layout allows you to "build the assembly" on paper.

When drawings are created on a drawing board, an initial layout is made to locate and size the parts. Then the individual detail drawings and the assembly drawing are traced from the layout.

The same procedure can be followed by using AutoCAD. First, create a design layout on one layer, then either transfer the individual parts and assembly drawing to other layers or create a new drawing from the layout drawing by using the **Save As** command.

The sample problem in the next section demonstrates how to create a design layout and then use the layout to create the required detail and assembly drawings.

12-13 Sample Problem SP12-1

Figure 12-27 shows an engineer's sketch for a design problem. Prepare an assembly drawing and a detail drawing of the PN123 base and PN124 center plate on the basis of the following information:

Figure 12-27

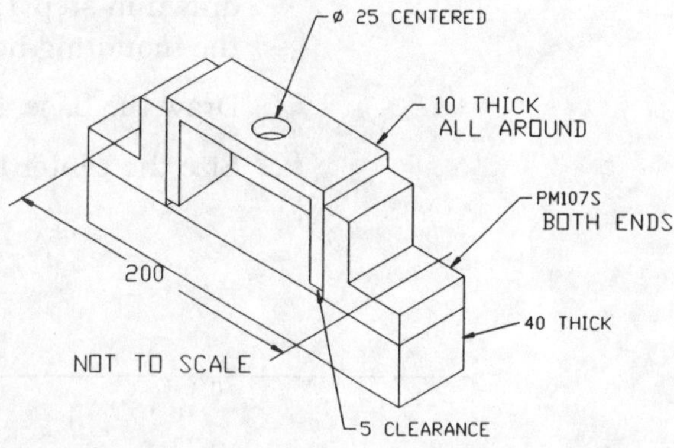

1. Parts PM107S end brackets are existing parts and can be used as is. Figure 12-28 shows a detail drawing of the part.

Figure 12-28

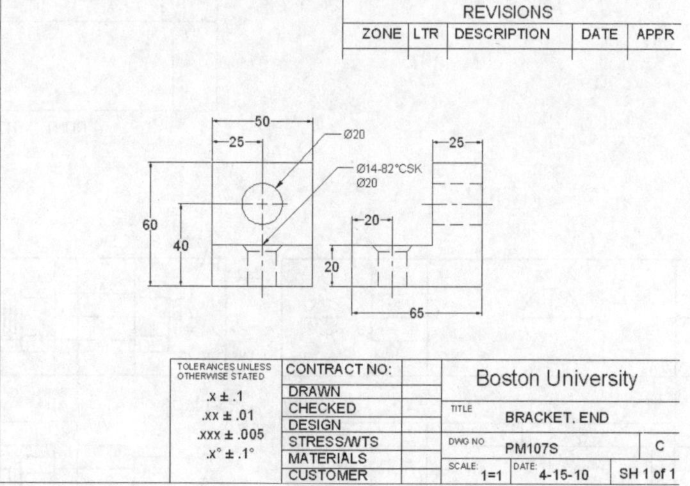

2. Place the mounting holes for the two end brackets 200 millimeters apart, as shown in the engineer's sketch.

3. Establish the size of the base so that it aligns with the end brackets and is 40 millimeters thick.

4. Determine the sizes for the center bracket so that it just fits between the end plates and has a 25-millimeter-diameter hole centered in its top surface. The center bracket should extend 10 millimeters above the end brackets and 5 millimeters above the base. The center bracket should be 10 millimeters thick all around.
5. Mount the end brackets to the base, using M12 flat head screws, and attach the end brackets to the center brackets by M20 bolts with appropriate nuts.
6. Use only standard-length fasteners.

To Create the Design Layout (See Figure 12-29.)

1. Draw horizontal and vertical lines that define the top of the base and the distance between the mounting holes in the end brackets.
2. Draw front and top views of the end brackets, using the vertical lines drawn in step 1. The vertical lines should align with the centerlines of the mounting holes.
3. Draw the base 40 millimeters thick.
4. Size the center brackets.

Figure 12-29

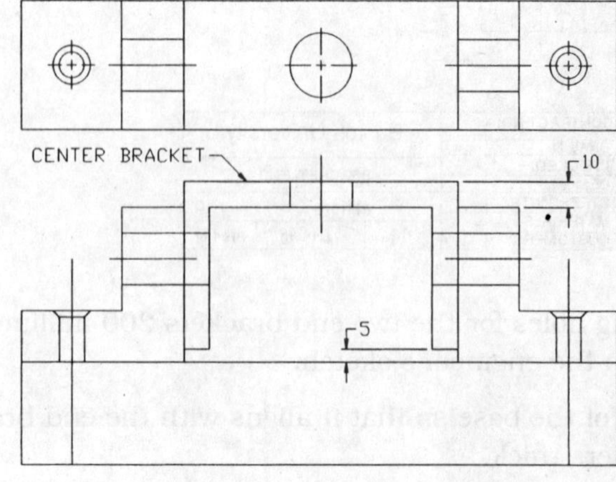

Note that at this stage of the layout, all lines are drawn according to the same pattern. Lines can be changed to hidden lines or centerlines when the detail and assembly drawings are created.

5 Add the M12 flat head screws. A length of 20 millimeters was chosen from the tables in the appendix. The threaded holes in the base are M12 to match the screws. The tap drill size is included on the layout for reference.

6 Add the M20 × 60 bolts and nuts.

The bolt length is determined by adding 25 (end bracket) + 10 (center bracket) + 15 (nut thickness = .75D) + 2 thread pitches = 52 millimeters. The next-largest standard bolt length, as listed in the appendix, is 60, so an M20 × 60 bolt is specified.

7 The diameter of the clearance holes was chosen as 14 and 22 and is listed on the layout.

The design layout is complete. It may be used to create the required assembly drawing and detail drawings in one of two ways: by using the **Layer** command and including all of the drawings under one file name, or by using the **Save As** command to create separate drawings.

To Create a Drawing Using Layers

When lines are moved from one layer to another, the lines will disappear from the original layer. This will, in essence, erase the layout drawing because all the lines will have been moved to other layers. The layout may be preserved by first making a copy of the layout, or that part of the layout that you wish to transfer, and then using the copy for the transfers.

To make a copy of the layout, use the **Copy** command. Select the entire screen, and select a base point. Select the exact same point as the second point of displacement, and AutoCAD will copy the layout exactly over itself. You can then move the appropriate lines to different layers.

NOTE

Explode all blocks before transferring them between layers. A block cannot be edited once it is moved from its original layer.

Create a detail drawing of the base by transferring the base from the design layout. Respond to the prompts as follows.

1 Copy the layout onto itself.

COMMAND:_Copy

Select objects:

2 Window the entire layout; press **Enter.**

<Base point or displacement>/Multiple:

3 Select a point on the screen.

Second point of displacement:

4 Select exactly the same point as that used in the previous step.

5 Create the given layers. See Section 3-24.

ASSEMBLY

END

END-DIM

BASE

BASE-DIM

CENTER

CENTER-DIM

PARTSLIST

The "DIM" layers will be used for the dimensions for the detail drawings. This will allow the dimensions to be shut off if they are not needed.

6 Transfer the base to a layer called **BASE.** See Section 3-24. Turn off all of the other layers. The resulting transfer should look like Figure 12-30.

Figure 12-30

It will be difficult to make a perfectly clean transfer—that is, a transfer of only the lines of the base. If other lines appear on the transferred base, erase and trim them as necessary.

7 Move the views closer together, if necessary.

8 Turn on the **BASE-DIM** layer, and make it the current layer. Add the appropriate dimensions, tolerances, and callouts.

9 Create the drawing format, and add the necessary information (drawing title, etc.).

The title block, and so forth, may be saved as a block or as part of a prototype drawing. Figure 12-31 shows the resulting drawing.

Figure 12-31

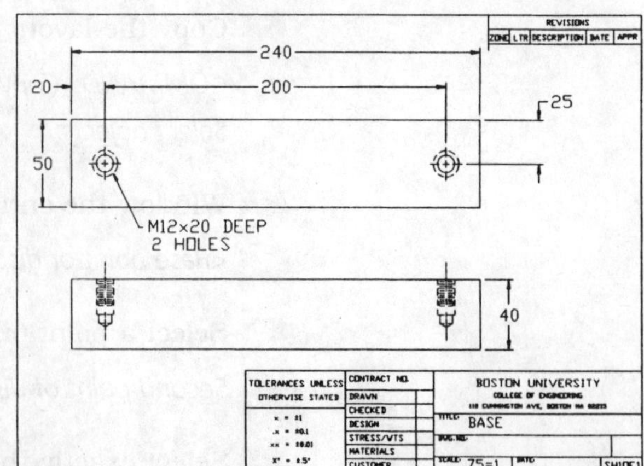

To Create a Drawing from a Layout

Figure 12-32 shows an assembly drawing that was created from the design layout. The procedure is as follows.

1. Save the design layout.
2. Create the assembly drawing from the layout drawing, but use the **Save As** command to save it under a different drawing name.
3. Add the appropriate drawing format and notes.
4. Save the assembly drawing, using its new name.

Figure 12-33 shows a parts list for the assembly.

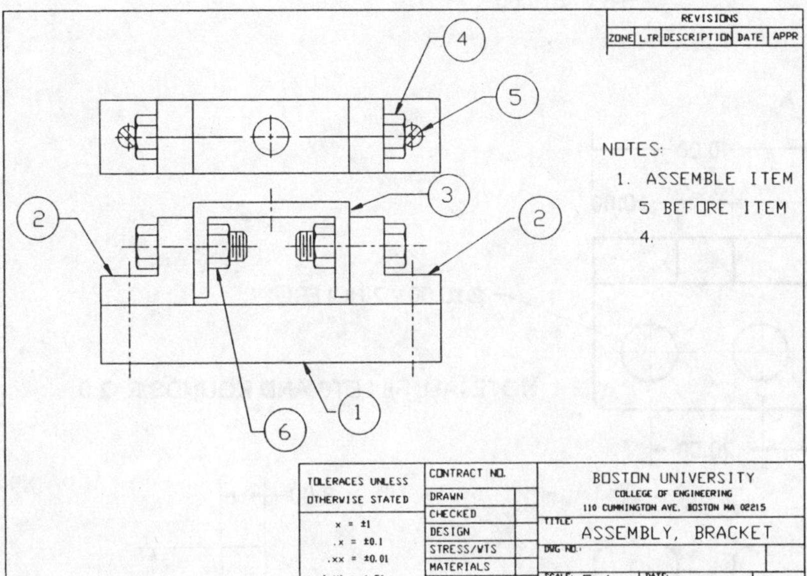

Figure 12-32

PARTS LIST			
ITEM NO	DESCRIPTION	MATL	QTY
1	BASE	STEEL	1
2	END BRACKET - PM107S	STEEL	2
3	CENTER PLATE	STEEL	1
4	M20x60 HEX HEAD BOLT	STEEL	2
5	M12x36 FLAT HEAD SCREW	STEEL	2
6	M20 NUT	STEEL	2

Figure 12-33

12-14 Sample Problem SP12-2

Figure 12-34 shows an assembly made from four different parts: a base, a bracket, and two posts. The detail drawing of each part is shown in Figure 12-35.

Figure 12-34

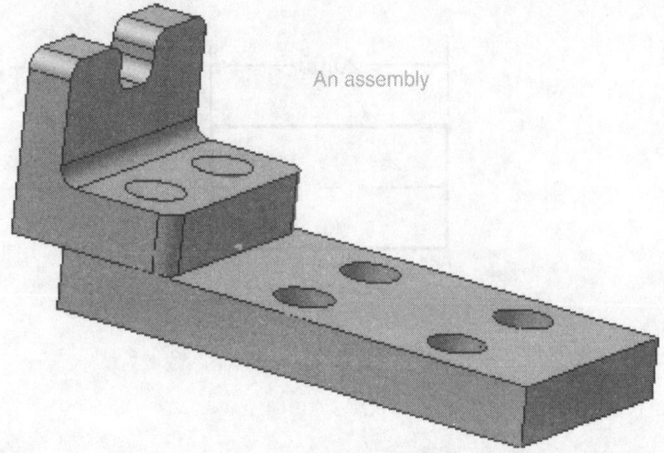

Figure 12-35

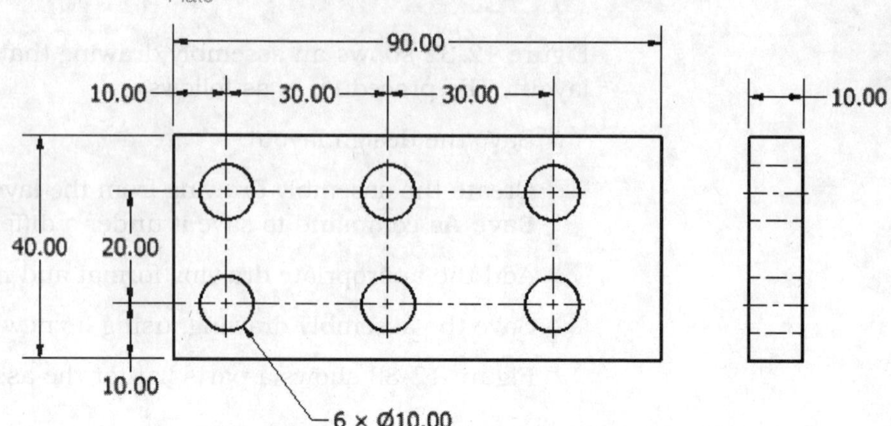

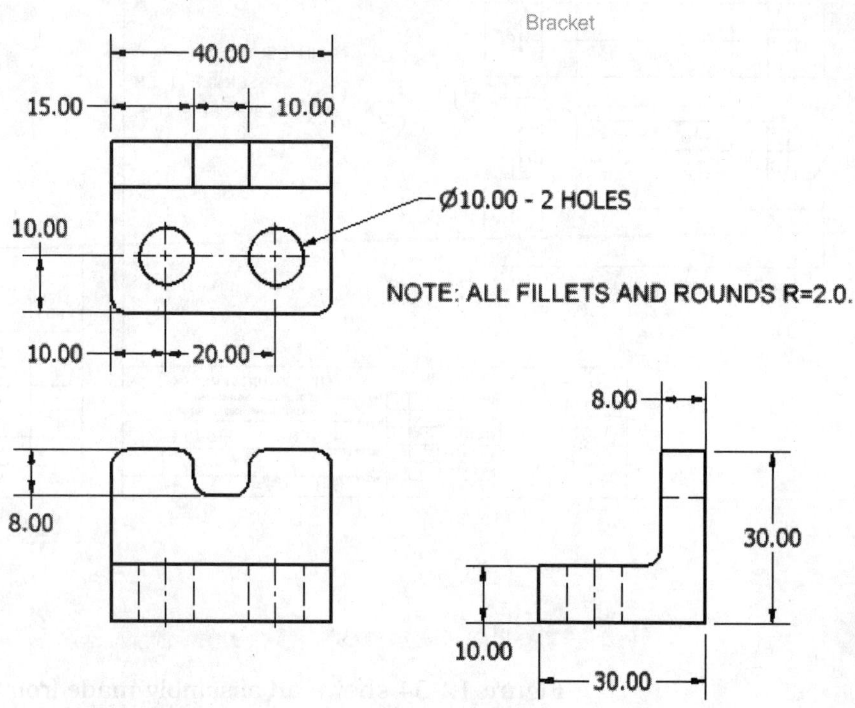

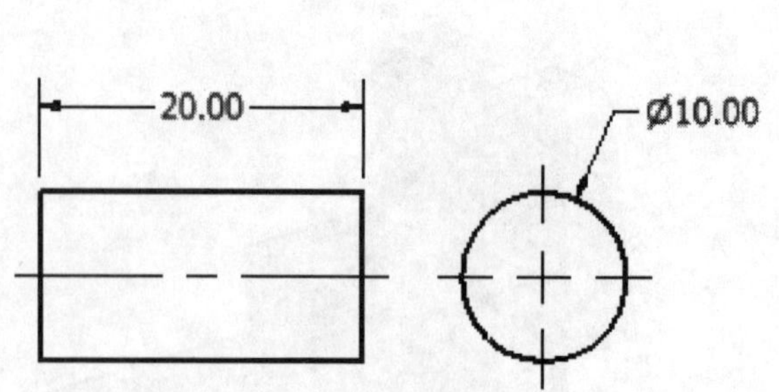

To Create an Assembly Drawing

1 Draw orthographic views of the parts in their assembled position.

See Figure 12-36. In this example, only a front and top view were drawn, as that is sufficient to define the assembly. The front view orientation was selected to display the profile of the assembled parts. Note that there are no hidden lines in assembly drawings.

2 Add assembly numbers to the drawing.

Remember that assembly numbers are different from part numbers. A part number is a number assigned to an individual part and remains with that part regardless of what assembly uses the part. An assembly number is unique to each assembly and does not transfer to other assemblies.

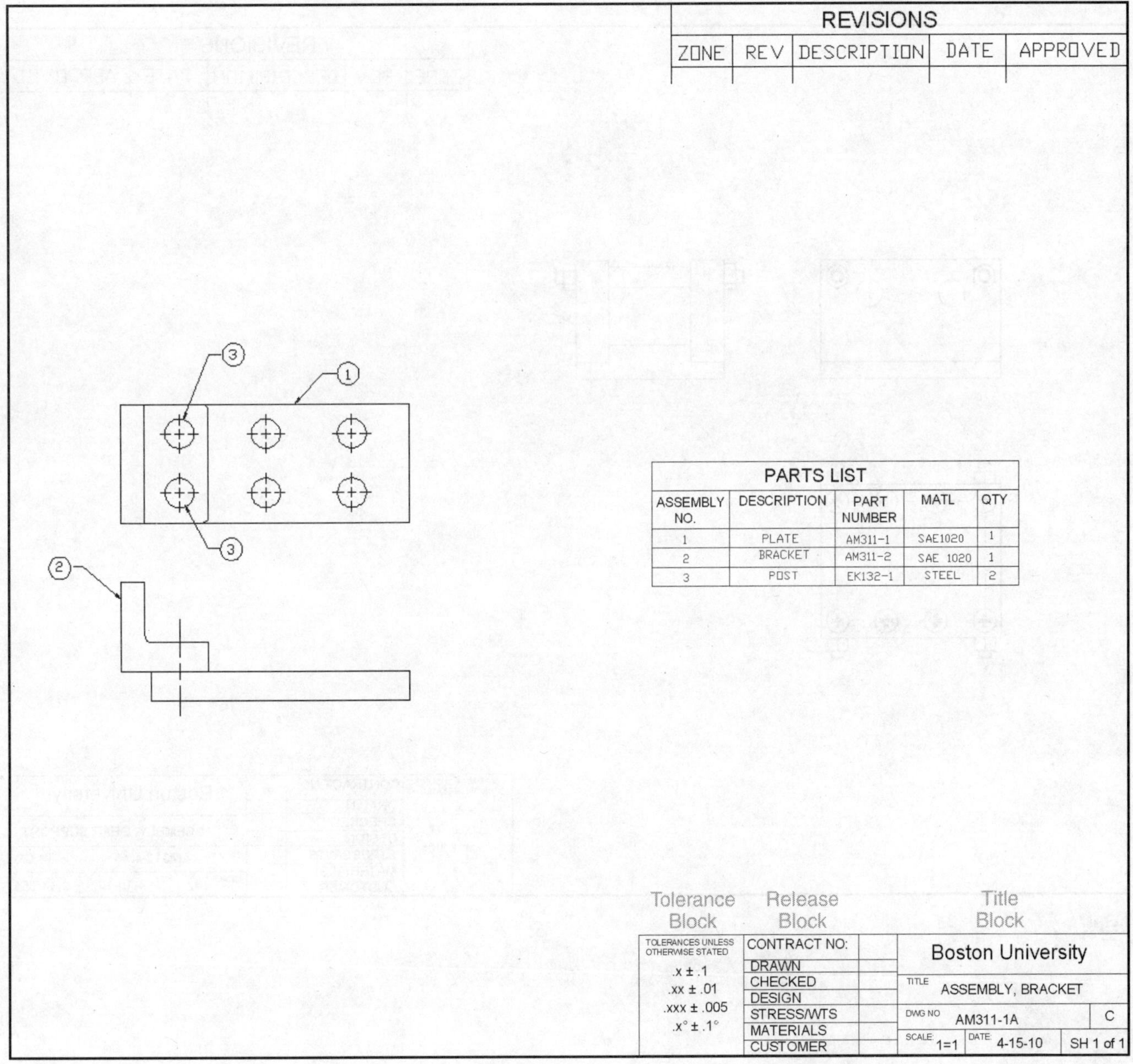

Figure 12-36

3 Create a parts list for the assembly.

As stated earlier, there is no standard format for parts lists. The example shown represents an average approach. Note the use of assembly numbers and part numbers.

4 Add a title block, a release block, and a tolerance block.

12-15 Sample Problem SP12-3

Figure 12-37 shows another example of an assembly drawing. In this example, a front, a right-side, and a bottom view were used to define the assembly. The parts list is located on a second sheet. In general, drawings should not be overcrowded. Parts lists, sectional views, and other drawing information are often located on second or third sheets.

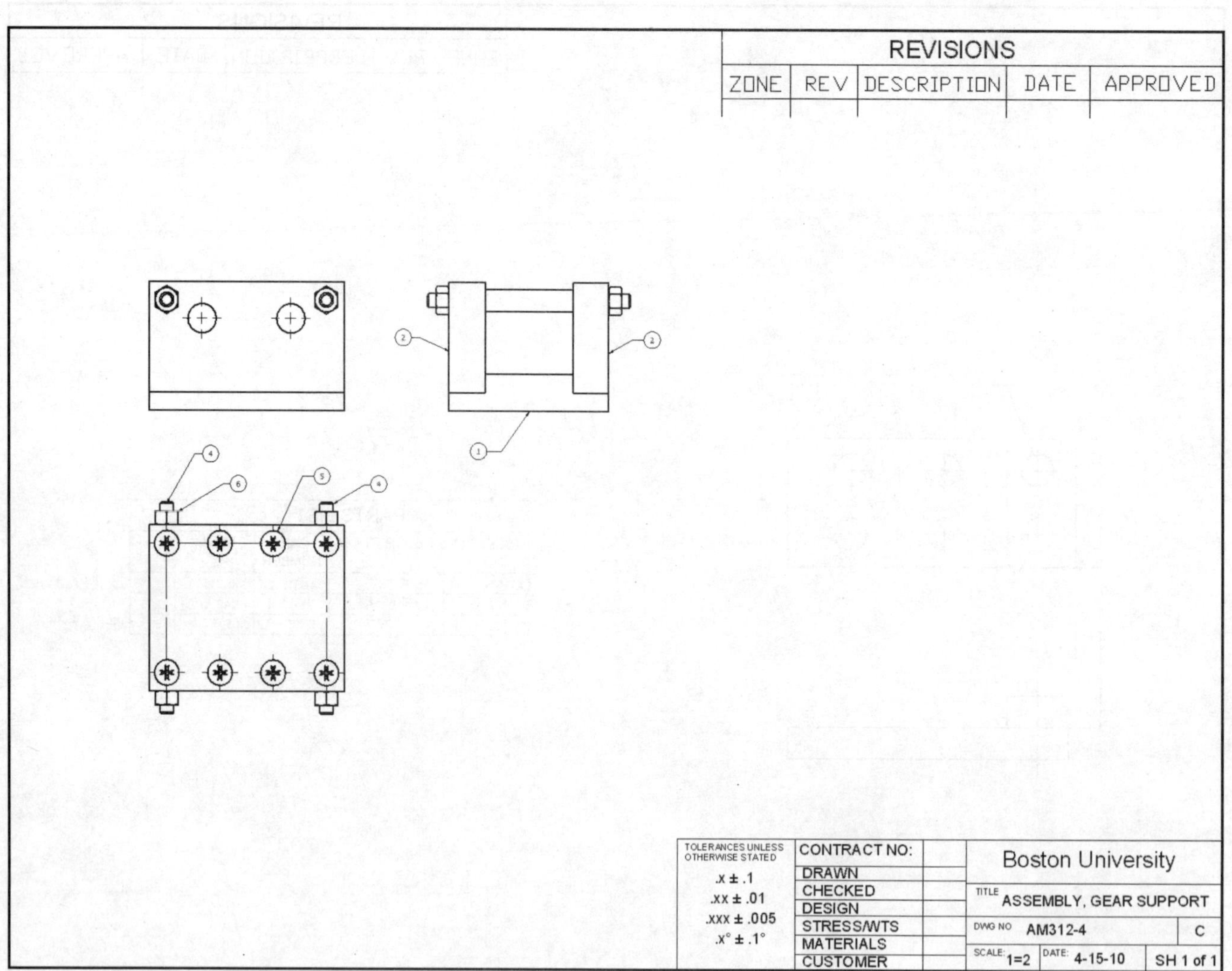

Figure 12-37

REVISIONS				
ZONE	REV	DESCRIPTION	DATE	APPROVED

Parts List				
ITEM	DESCRIPTION	PART NUMBER	MATERIAL	QTY
1	PLATE, BASE	BU-311-A	Plexiglas	1
2	PLATE, SIDE	BU-311-B	Plexiglas	2
3	POST, GUIDE	BU-311-C	Steel	2
4	POST, THREADED	BU-311-D	Steel	2
5	Pozidriv ISO metric machine screws	AS 1427 - M8 x 20	Steel, Mild	8
6	Metric Hex Nuts Styles 2	ANSI B18.2.4.2M - M8x1.25	Steel, Mild	4

TOLERANCES UNLESS OTHERWISE STATED	CONTRACT NO:		Boston University		
.x ± .1	DRAWN				
.xx ± .01	CHECKED		TITLE ASSEMBLY, GEAR SUPPORT		
.xxx ± .005	DESIGN				
.x° ± .1°	STRESS/WTS		DWG NO AM312-4		C
	MATERIALS				
	CUSTOMER		SCALE: 1=2	DATE: 4-15-10	SH 1 of 1

Figure 12-37 continued

12-16 EXERCISE PROBLEMS

EX12-1

A. Draw an assembly drawing of the given objects.

B. Draw detail drawings for all nonstandard parts.

C. Prepare a parts list. Specify the length for the M10 hex head screw.

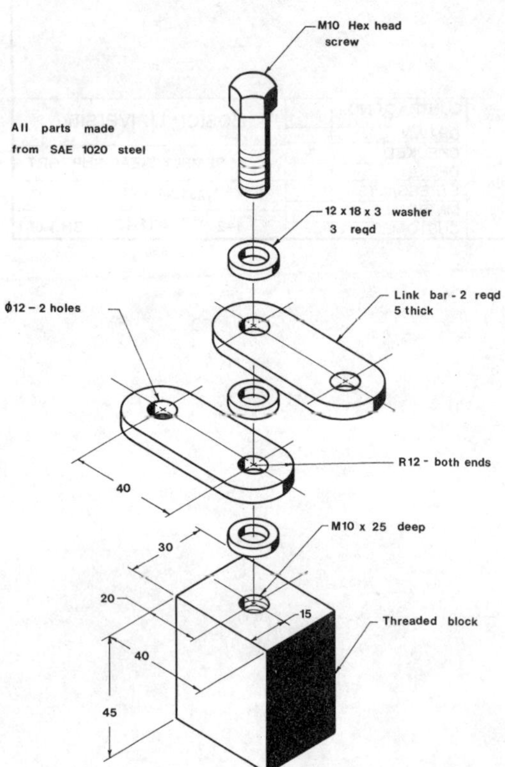

EX12-2

A. Draw an assembly drawing of the given objects.

B. Draw detail drawings for all nonstandard parts.

C. Prepare a parts list.

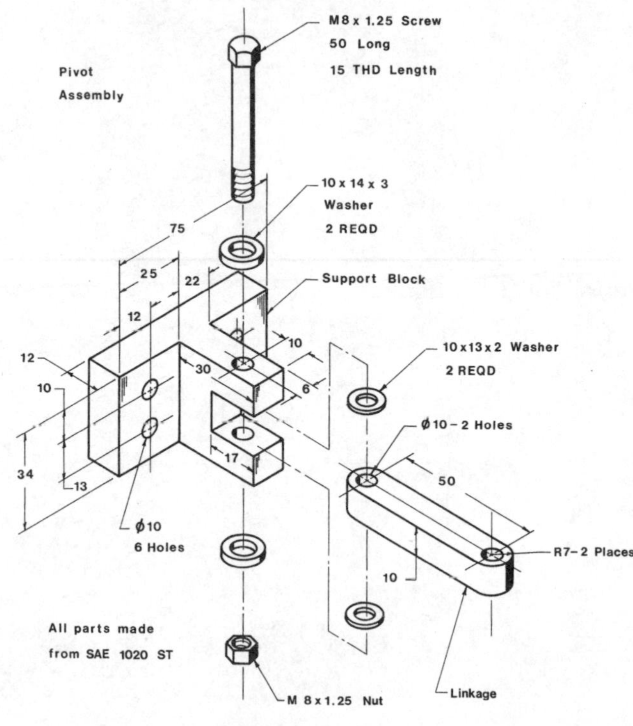

EX12-3

A. Draw an assembly drawing of the given objects.

B. Draw detail drawings for all nonstandard parts.

C. Prepare a parts list.

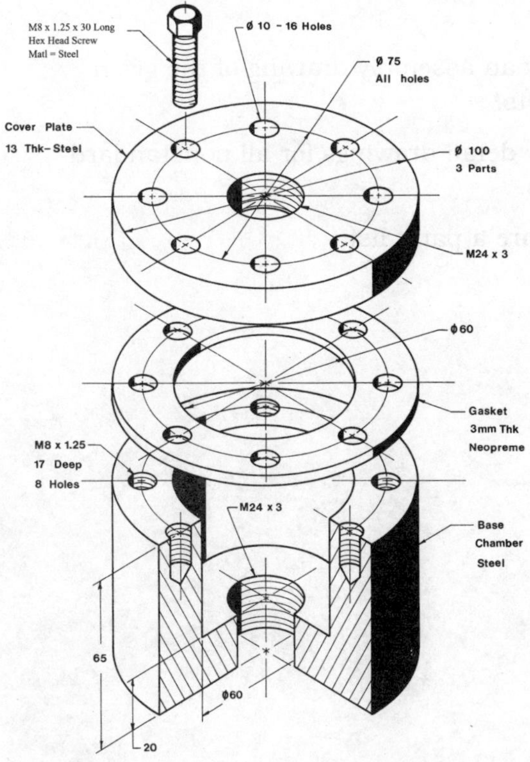

EX12-4

A. Draw an assembly drawing of the given objects.

B. Draw detail drawings for all nonstandard parts.

C. Prepare a parts list.

Design

D. Replace part 3 with a bolt and appropriate nut. Add four washers.

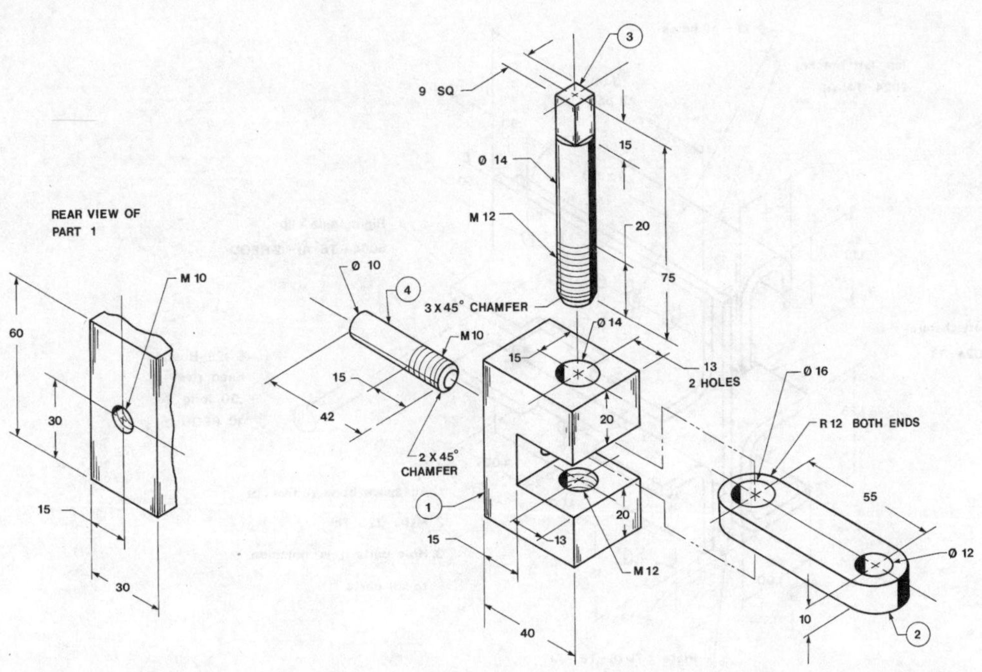

EX12-5

A. Draw an assembly drawing of the given objects.

B. Draw detail drawings for all nonstandard parts.

C. Prepare a parts list.

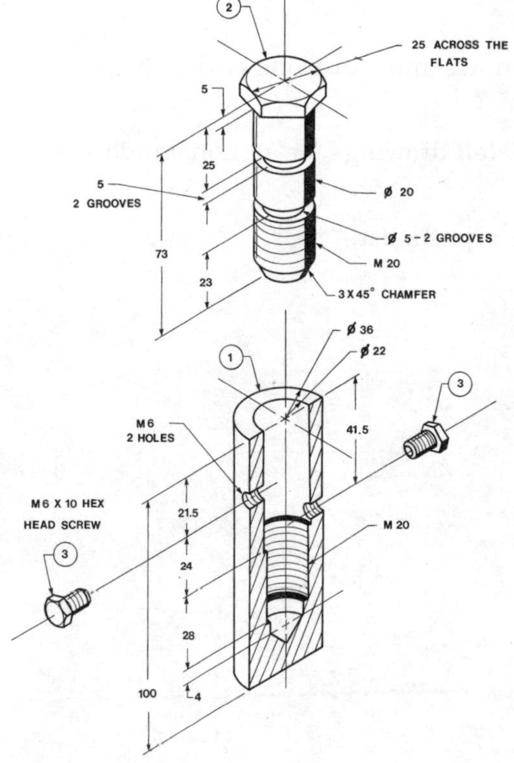

EX12-6

A. Draw an assembly drawing of the given objects.

B. Draw detail drawings for all nonstandard parts.

C. Prepare a parts list.

Design

D. Replace the rivets with the appropriate screws and nuts.

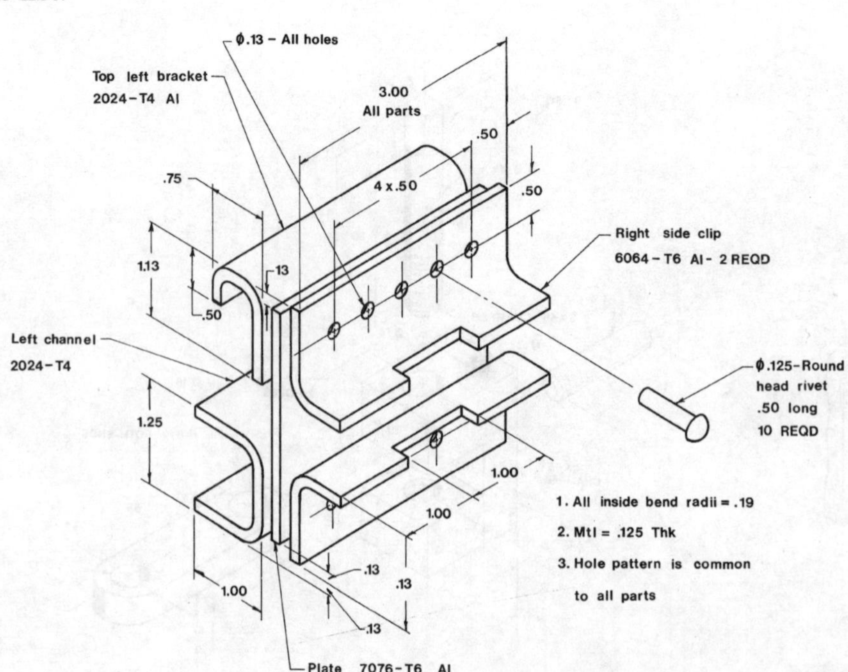

EX12-7 Millimeters

A. Draw an assembly drawing of the given objects.
B. Prepare a parts list.

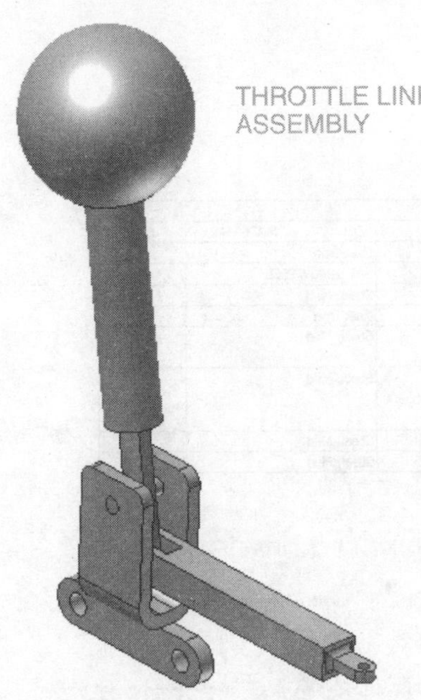

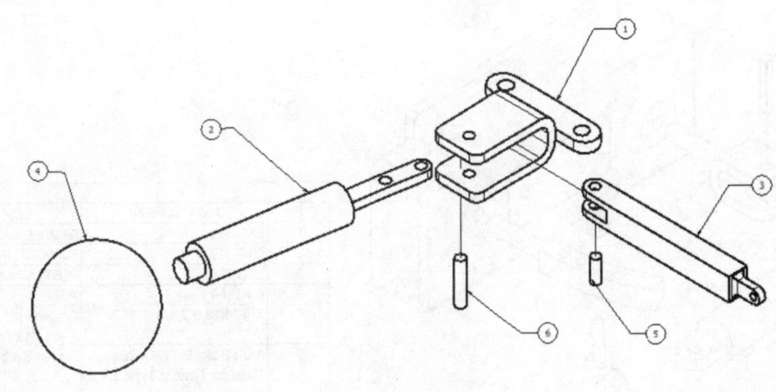

Parts List				
ITEM	PART NUMBER	DESCRIPTION	MATERIAL	QTY
1	ENG-A43	BOX,PIVOT	SAE1020	1
2	ENG-A44	POST,HANDLE	SAE1020	1
3	ENG-A45	LINK	SAE1020	1
4	AM300-1	HANDLE	STEEL	1
5	EK-132	POST-Ø6x14	STEEL	1
6	EK-131	POST-Ø6x26	STEEL	1

PIVOT BOX

30.00
15.00
R5.00
5.00
ALL AROUND
16.00
10.00
Ø6.00
47.00
R8.00
Ø8.00
2 HOLES
6.00
10.00
50.00
70.00

HANDLE

R30.00
26.00
Ø12.00 ↧ 12.00

HANDLE POST

45.00
5.00
2.50
25.00
80.00
10.00
Ø20.00
Ø12.00
10.00
5.00
R5.00
Ø6.00 THRU
2 HOLES

LINK

94.00
16.00
R6.00
Ø6.00 THRU
12.00
3.50
20.00
R4.00
4.00
BOTH
SIDES
14.00
3.50
R2 - ALL AROUND
Ø4.00 THRU
3.00
BOTH
SIDES

EX12-8 Inches

A. Draw an assembly drawing and parts list for the guide assembly.

ADJUSTABLE ASSEMBLY

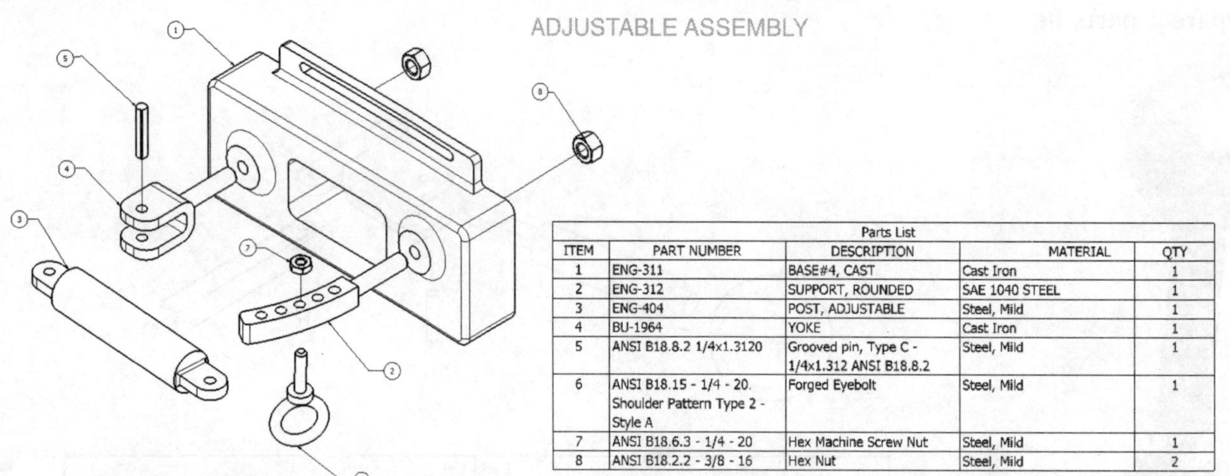

Parts List				
ITEM	PART NUMBER	DESCRIPTION	MATERIAL	QTY
1	ENG-311	BASE#4, CAST	Cast Iron	1
2	ENG-312	SUPPORT, ROUNDED	SAE 1040 STEEL	1
3	ENG-404	POST, ADJUSTABLE	Steel, Mild	1
4	BU-1964	YOKE	Cast Iron	1
5	ANSI B18.8.2 1/4x1.3120	Grooved pin, Type C - 1/4x1.312 ANSI B18.8.2	Steel, Mild	1
6	ANSI B18.15 - 1/4 - 20. Shoulder Pattern Type 2 - Style A	Forged Eyebolt	Steel, Mild	1
7	ANSI B18.6.3 - 1/4 - 20	Hex Machine Screw Nut	Steel, Mild	1
8	ANSI B18.2.2 - 3/8 - 16	Hex Nut	Steel, Mild	2

CAST BASE #4

NOTE: ALL FILLETS AND ROUNDS = R0.125 UNLESS OTHERWISE STATED.

ROUNDED SUPPORT

NOTE: ALL FILLETS = R0.125

ADJUSTABLE POST

NOTE: ALL FILLETS = R 0.125

YOKE

FORGED EYEBOLT

Thread = 1/4 = 20 UNC
0.03 X 45° Chamfer

EX12-9

Redraw the given objects as an assembly drawing, and add bolts with the appropriate nuts at the L and H holes. Add the appropriate drawing callouts. Specify standard bolt lengths.

A. Use inch values.

B. Use millimeter values.

C. Draw the front assembly view, using a sectional view.

D. Draw the fasteners, using schematic representations.

E. Draw the fasteners, using simplified representations.

F. Prepare a parts list.

G. Prepare detail drawings for each part.

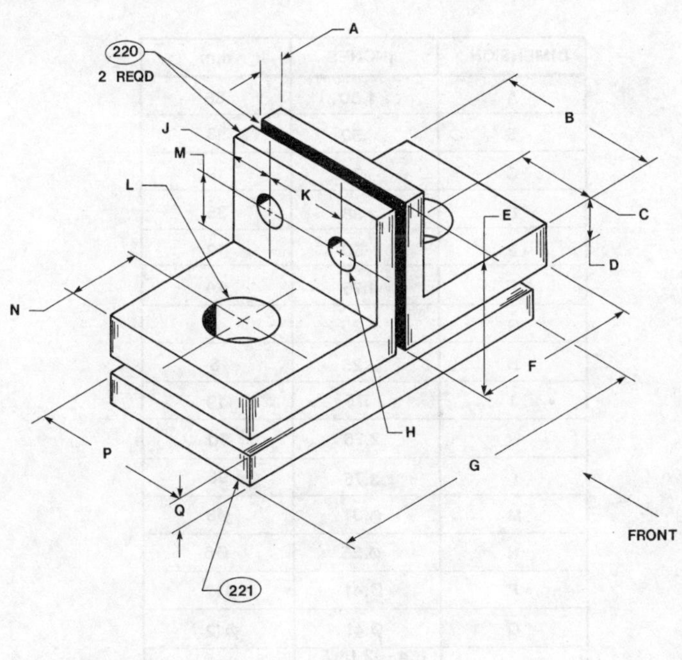

DIMENSION	INCHES	mm
A	.25	6
B	2.00	50
C	1.00	25
D	.50	13
E	1.75	45
F	2.00	50
G	4.00	100
H	Ø.438	Ø11
J	.50	12.5
K	1.00	25
L	Ø.781	Ø19
M	.63	16
N	.88	22
P	2.00	50
Q	.25	6

EX12-10

Redraw the given views, and add the appropriate hex head machine screws at M and N. Use standard length screws, and allow at least two unused threads at the bottom of each threaded hole. Add a bolt with the appropriate nut at hole P.

A. Use inch values.

B. Use millimeter values.

C. Draw the front assembly view, using a sectional view.

D. Draw the fasteners, using schematic representations.

E. Draw the fasteners, using simplified representations.

F. Prepare a parts list.

G. Prepare detail drawings for each part.

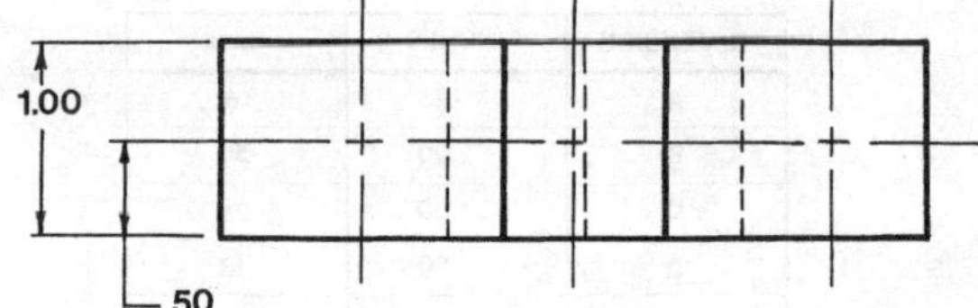

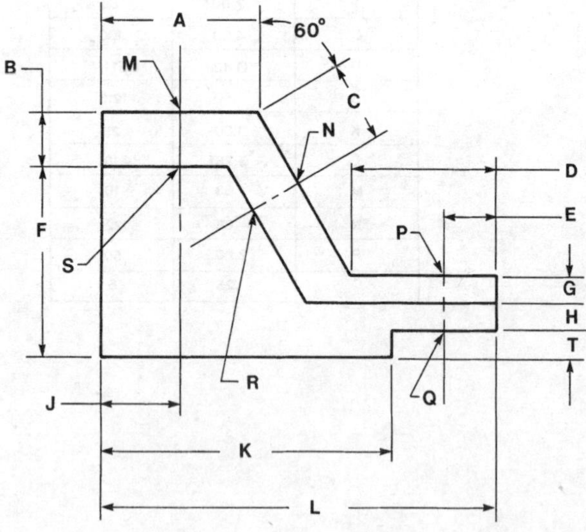

DIMENSION	INCHES	mm
A	1.50	38
B	.50	13
C	.75	19
D	1.38	35
E	.50	13
F	1.75	44
G	.25	6
H	.25	6
J	.75	19
K	2.75	70
L	3.75	96
M	Ø.31	Ø8
N	Ø.25	Ø6
P	Ø.41	Ø12
Q	Ø.41	Ø12
R	.164-32 UNF X .50 DEEP	M4 X 14 DEEP
S	.250-20 UNC X 1.63 DEEP	M6 X 14 DEEP
T	.25	6

EX12-11 Millimeters

Draw an assembly drawing and parts list for the circular damper assembly shown.

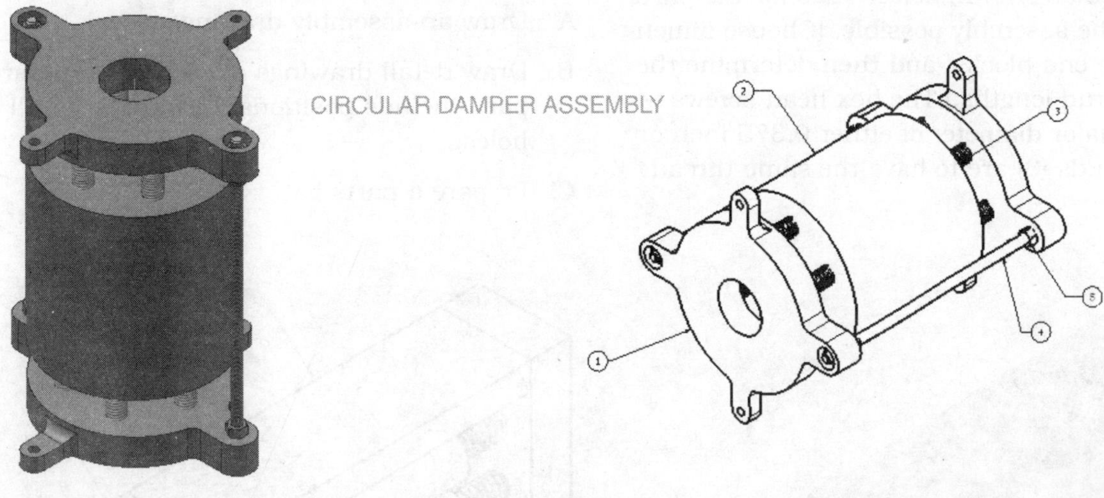

Parts List				
ITEM	PART NUMBER	DESCRIPTION	MATERIAL	QTY
1	BU2008-1	BASE, HOLDER	Steel	2
3	BU2008-2	SPRING, COMPRESSION	Steel, Mild	12
2	BU2008-3	COUNTERWEIGHT	Steel	1
4	AM312-12	POST, THREADED	Steel	2
5	AS 1112 - M18 Type	HEX NUT	Steel, Mild	8

Note: AM-312-12 Threaded Post is M18 x 560 long with 1 x 45° chamfers at each end

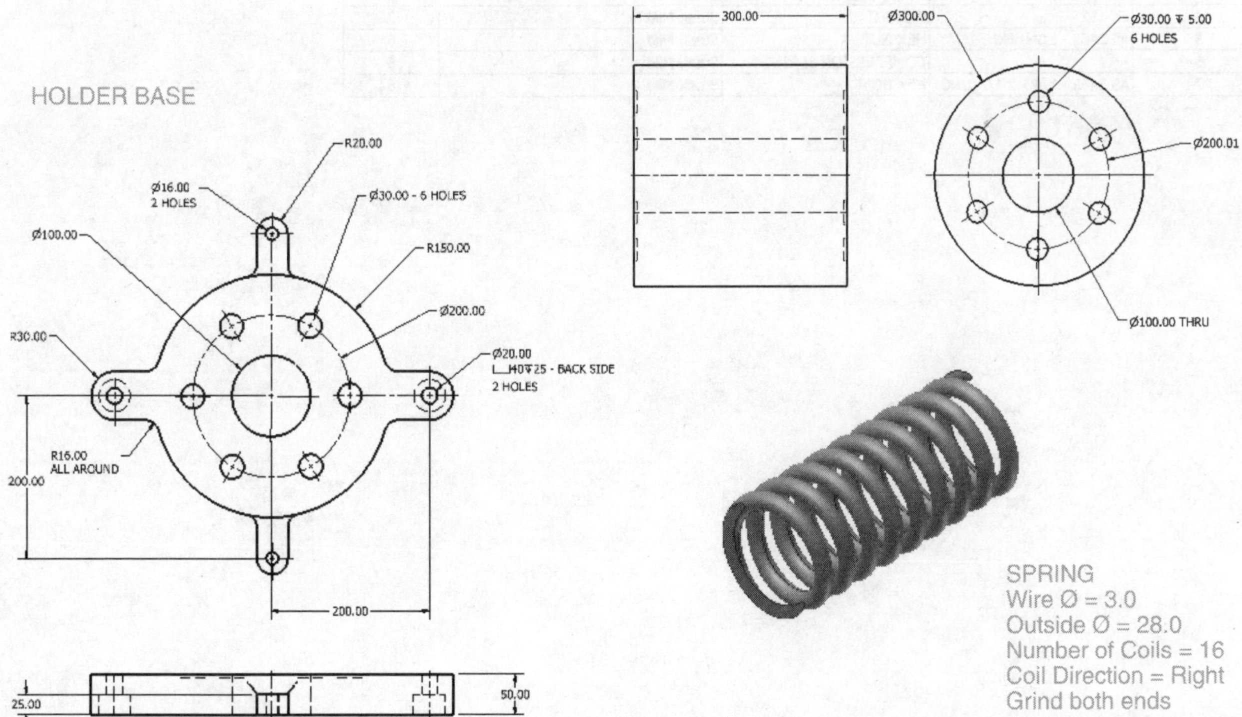

EX12-12 Inches

The objects given on the pages that follow are to be assembled as shown. Select sizes for the parts that make the assembly possible. (Choose dimensions for the end blocks, and then determine the screw and stud lengths.) The hex head screws (5) have a major diameter of either 0.375 inch or M10. The studs (3) are to have the same thread sizes as the screws and are to be screwed into the top part (2). The holes in the lower part (1) that accept the studs are to be clearance holes.

A. Draw an assembly drawing.

B. Draw detail drawings of each nonstandard part. Include positional tolerances for all holes.

C. Prepare a parts list.

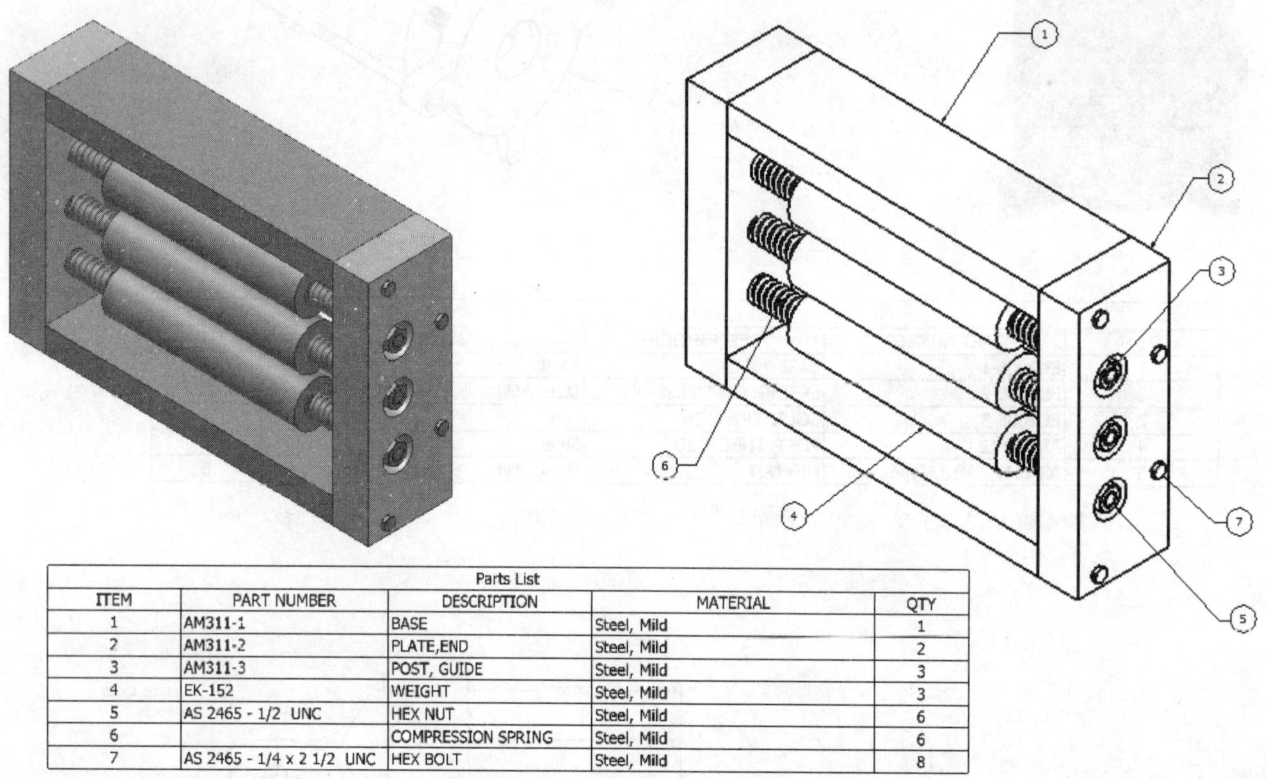

Parts List

ITEM	PART NUMBER	DESCRIPTION	MATERIAL	QTY
1	AM311-1	BASE	Steel, Mild	1
2	AM311-2	PLATE,END	Steel, Mild	2
3	AM311-3	POST, GUIDE	Steel, Mild	3
4	EK-152	WEIGHT	Steel, Mild	3
5	AS 2465 - 1/2 UNC	HEX NUT	Steel, Mild	6
6		COMPRESSION SPRING	Steel, Mild	6
7	AS 2465 - 1/4 x 2 1/2 UNC	HEX BOLT	Steel, Mild	8

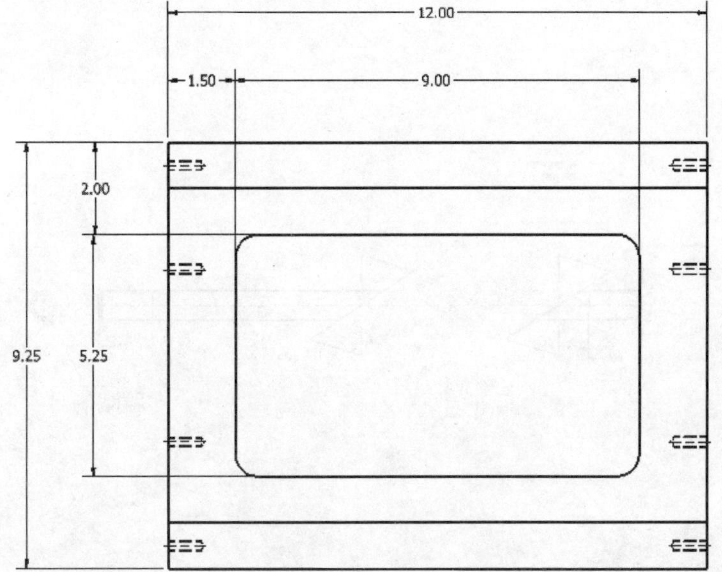
12.00
1.50
9.00
2.00
9.25
5.25

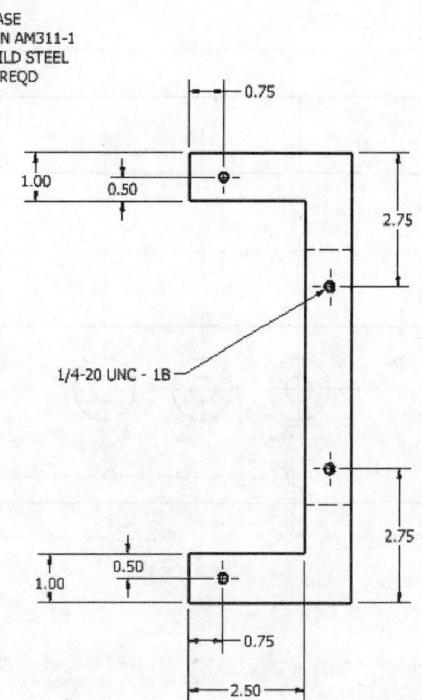
BASE
P/N AM311-1
MILD STEEL
1 REQD
0.75
1.00
0.50
2.75
1/4-20 UNC - 1B
2.75
0.50
1.00
0.75
2.50

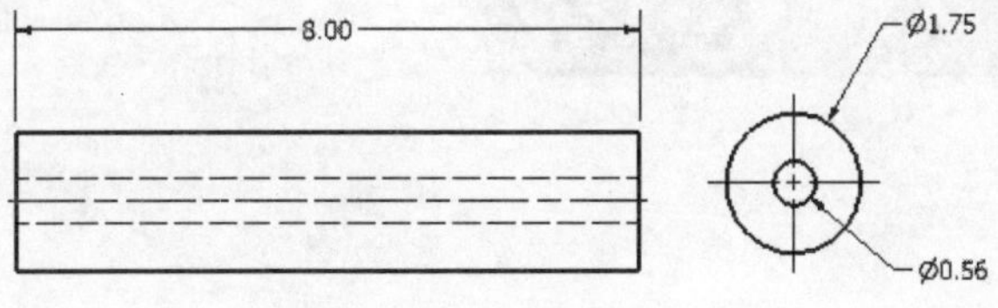
WEIGHT
P/N EK-152
MILD STEEL
3 REQD
8.00
Ø1.75
Ø0.56

END

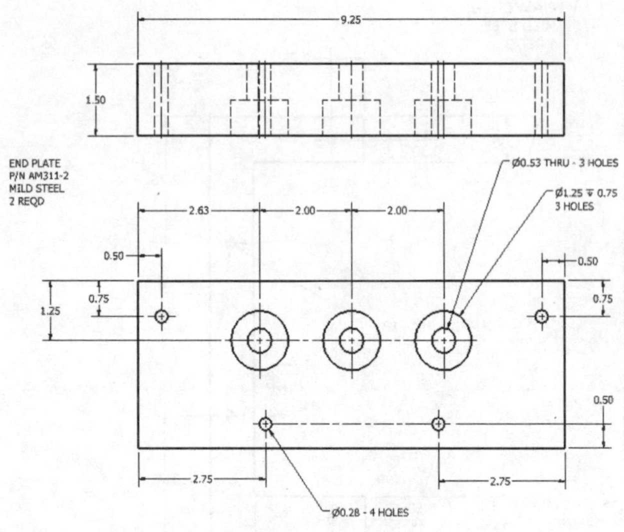

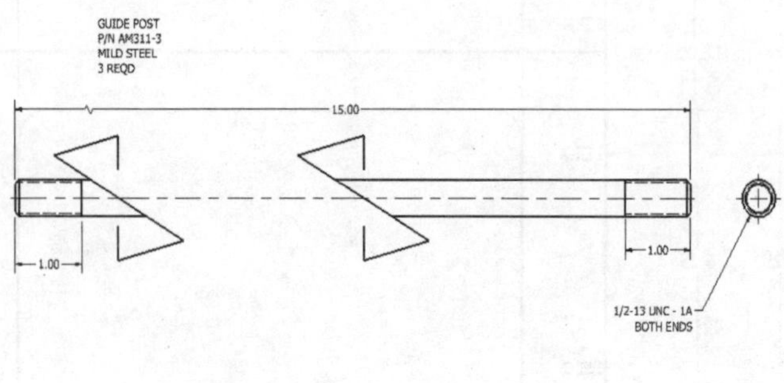

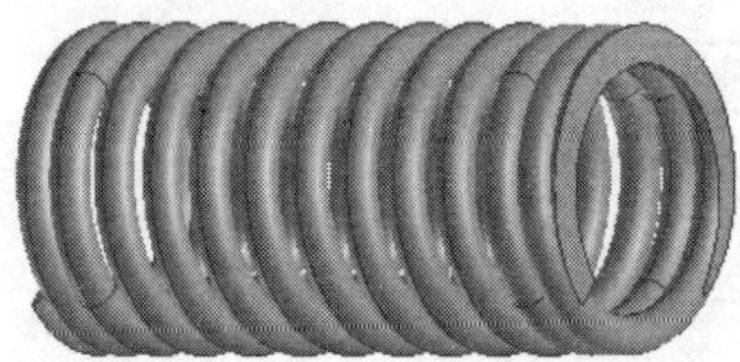

SPRING
Wire Ø = 0.125
Outside Ø = 1.000
Length = 2.00
Coil direction = light
Number of coils = 10
Grind both ends.

EX12-13 Inches

Draw an assembly drawing and parts list for the winding assembly.

WINDING ASSEMBLY

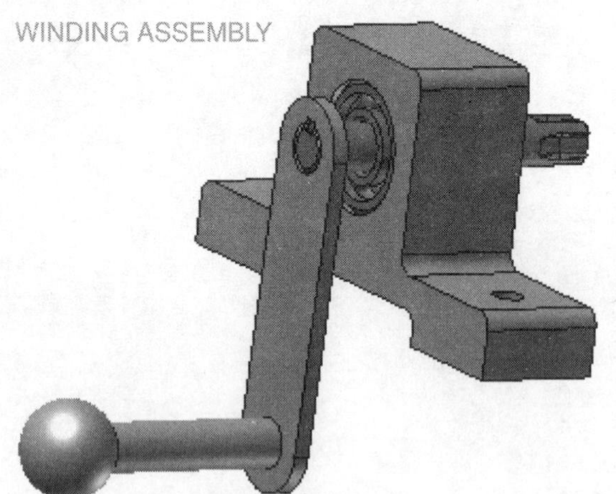

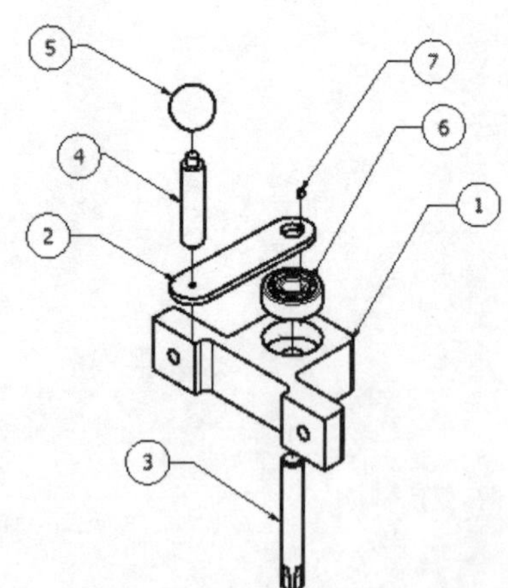

Parts List				
ITEM	PART NUMBER	DESCRIPTION	MATERIAL	QTY
1	EK131-1	SUPPORT	STEEL	1
2	EK131-2	LINK	STEEL	1
3	EK131-3	SHAFT,DRIVE	STEEL	1
4	EK131-4	POST, THREADED	STEEL	1
5	EK131-5	BALL	STEEL	1
6	BS 292 - BRM 3/4	Deep Groove Ball Bearings	STEEL,MILD	1
7	3/16x1/8x1/4	RECTANGULAR KEY	STEEL	1

SUPPORT

8.00
1.00
1.00
2.00
1.00
1.00

NOTE: ALL FILLETS AND ROUNDS R=0.250
UNLESS OTHERWISE STATED.

2.50
1.50
1.50
Ø.75 THRU
⌴ Ø2.00 ↧ .69
4.00
2.50
1.00
2.00
2.00

DRIVE SHAFT

Size and dimension for
a 3/16 × 1/8 × 0.25
Rectangular Key

SAE Series B
4 × 0.562 × 0.750 × 0.375
Spline

Ø.75
5.00

THREADED POST

.25
3.00
.38
Ø.75
1/4-20 UNC - 1A
3/8-16 UNC - 1A

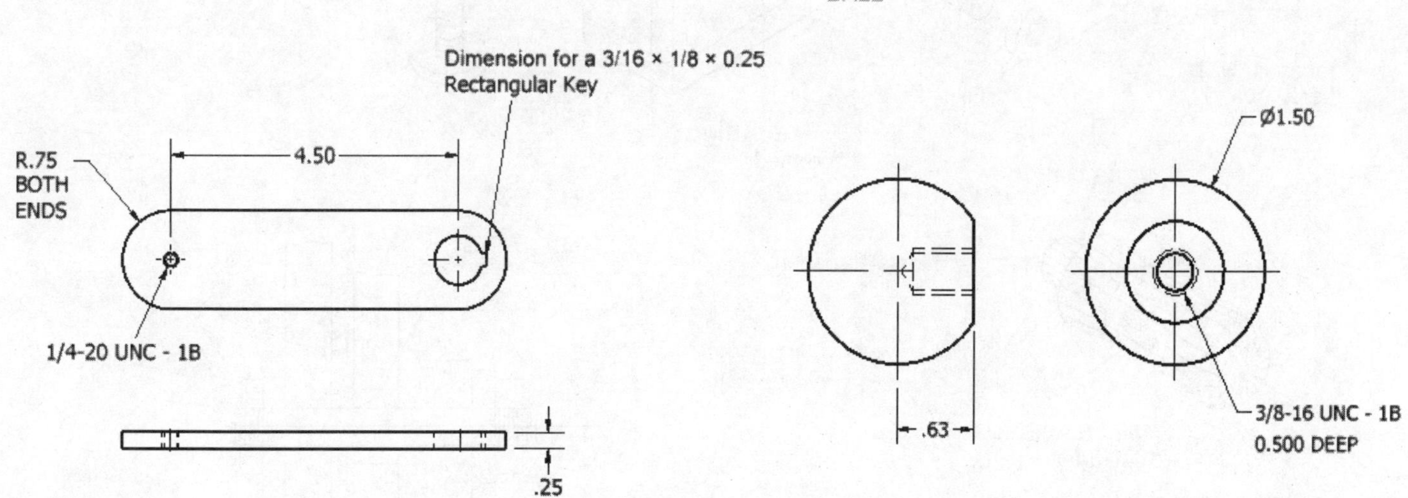

EX12-14 Inches

Design a hand-operated grinding wheel specifically for sharpening a chisel. The chisel is to be located on an adjustable rest while it is being sharpened. The mechanism should be able to be clamped to a table during operation by the use of two thumbscrews.

A standard grinding wheel is Ø6.00 inch and 1/2 inch thick, and has an internal mounting hole with a 50 ± 0.03 millimeter bore.

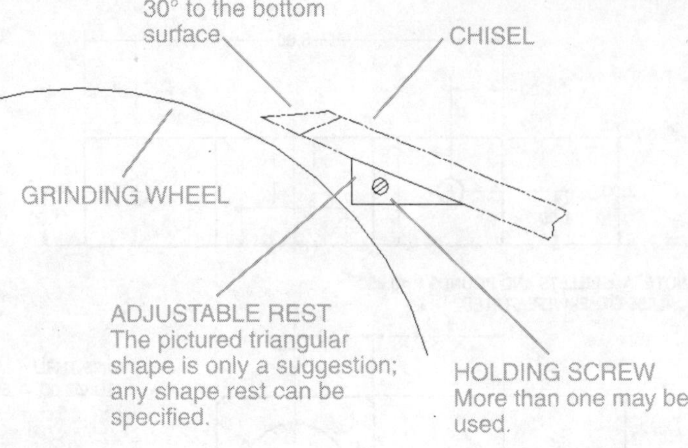

Prepare the Following Drawings:

A. Draw an assembly drawing.

B. Draw detail drawings of each nonstandard part. Include positional tolerances for all holes.

C. Prepare a parts list.

This is a nominal setup. It may be improved. Consider how the spacers rub against the stationary support, and consider double nuts at each end of the shaft.

EX12-15 Millimeters

A. Draw an assembly drawing of the given object.

B. Prepare a parts list.

C. Select appropriate fasteners to hold the object together.

D. Define the appropriate tolerances.

E. Define an assembly sequence, considering the size of any screw heads and nuts, and the tooling required for assembly.

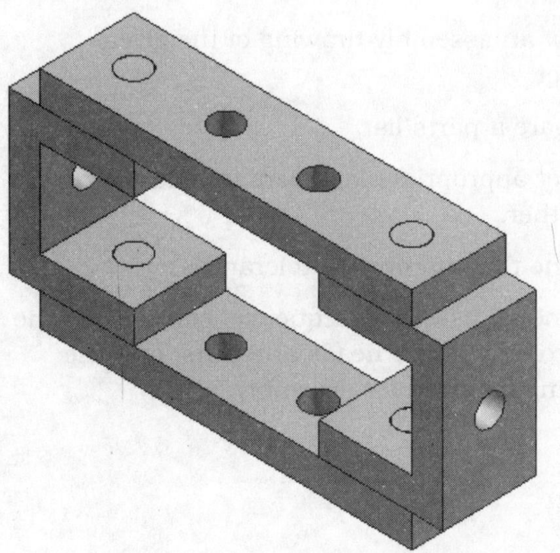

C-BRACKET, SAE1020 STEEL, 2 REQD
Part Number: AM311-1

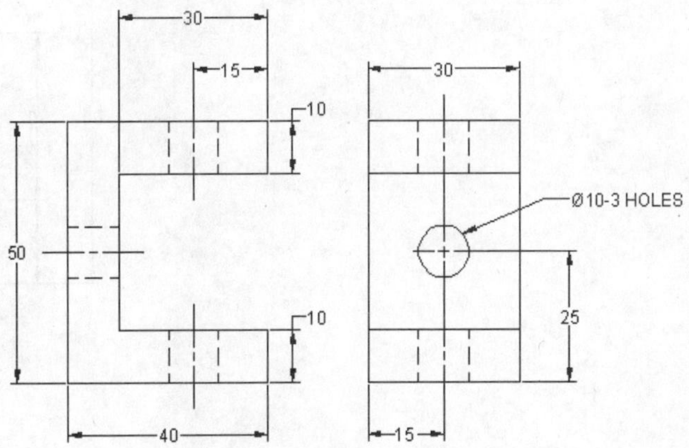

QUAD SPACER, SAE 1020 STEEL
2 REQD, Part Number: AM311-2

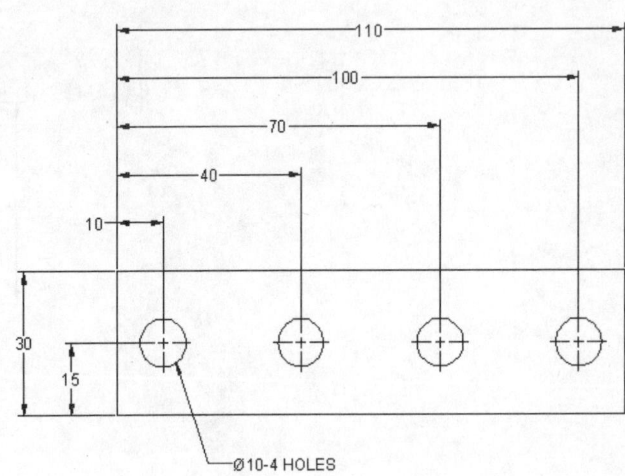

EX12-16 Millimeters

A. Draw an assembly drawing of the given object.

B. Prepare a parts list.

C. Select appropriate fasteners to hold the object together.

D. Define the appropriate tolerances.

E. Define an assembly sequence, considering the size of any screw heads and nuts, and the tooling required for assembly.

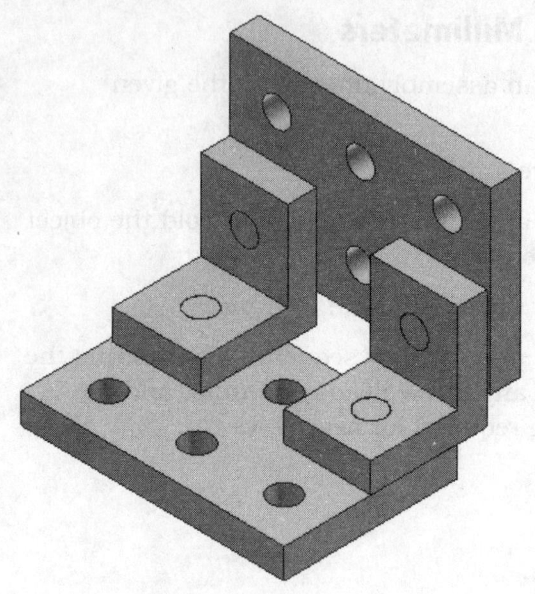

CLIP ASSEMBLY

SUPPORT PLATE
SAE 1040 STEEL, 2 REQD
Part Number: AM312-3

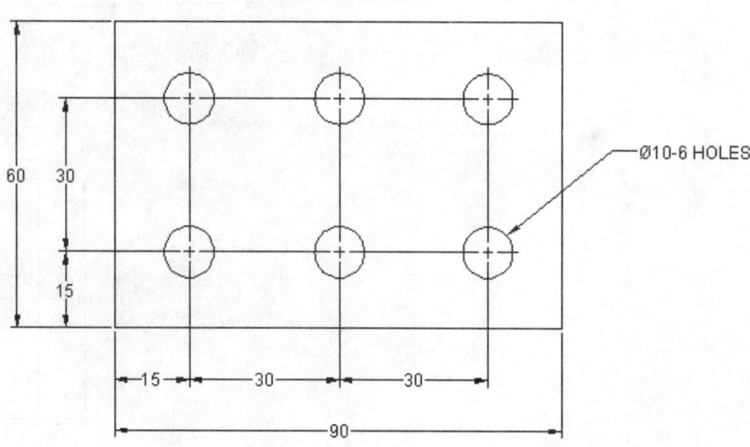

L-CLIP
SAE 1040 STEEL, 2 REQD
Part Number: AM312-4

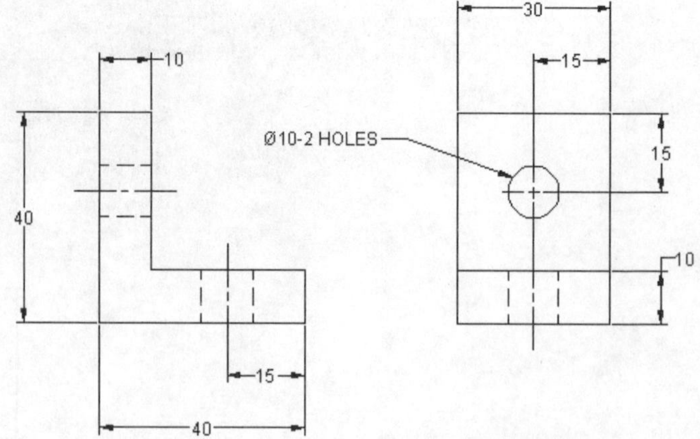

EX12-17 Millimeters

A. Draw an assembly drawing of the given object.

B. Prepare a parts list.

C. Select appropriate fasteners to hold the object together.

D. Define the appropriate tolerances.

E. Define an assembly sequence, considering the size of any screw heads and nuts, and the tooling required for assembly.

C-BRACKET
SAE 1020 STEEL, 4 REQD
Part Number: AM311-1

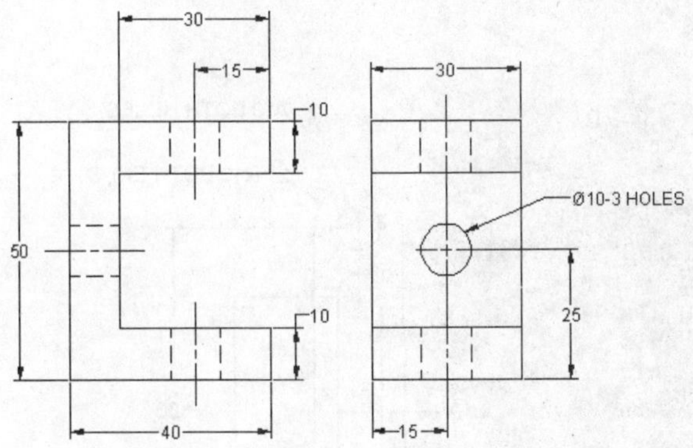

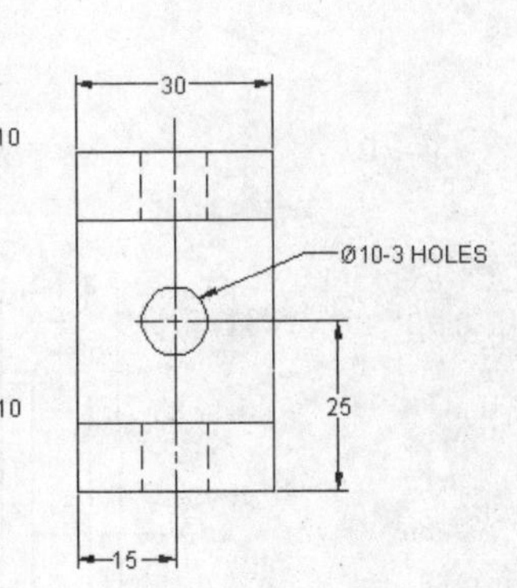

L-CLIP
SAE 1040 STEEL, 2 REQD
Part Number: AM312-4

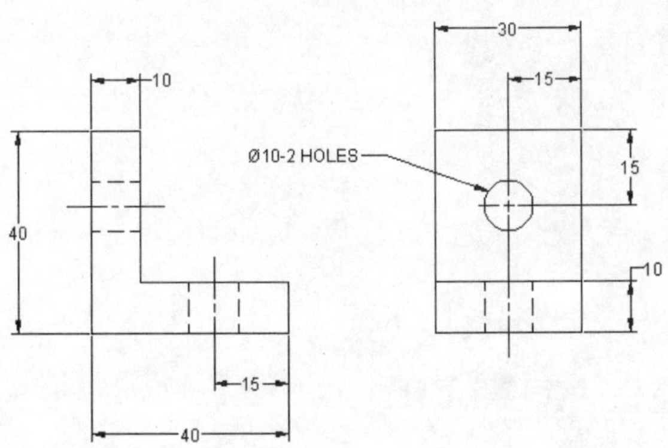

SUPPORT PLATE
SAE 1040 STEEL, 2 REQD
Part Number: AM312-3

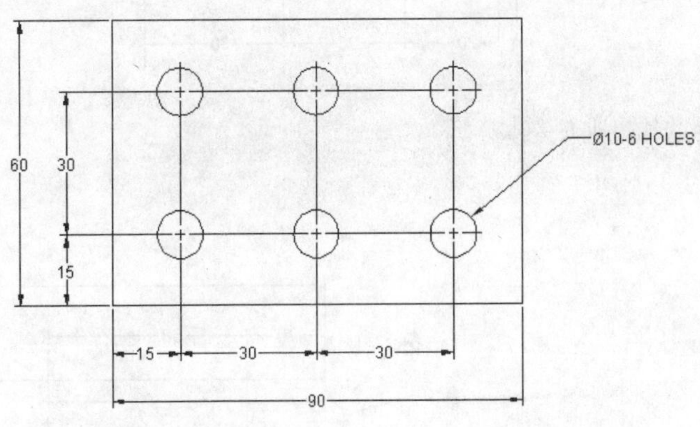

EX12-18 Millimeters

A. Draw an assembly drawing of the given object.

B. Prepare a parts list.

C. Select appropriate fasteners to hold the object together. Note that the fastener used to join the center link and the drive link passes over the web plate as the drive link rotates.

D. Define the appropriate tolerances.

E. Use phantom lines, and define the motion of the center link and the rocker link if the drive link rotates 360°.

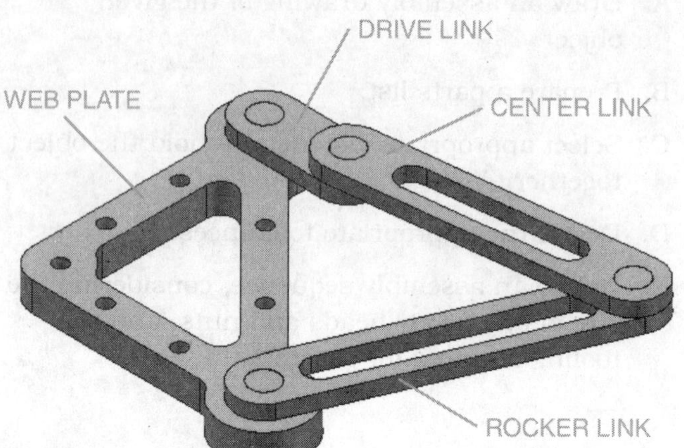

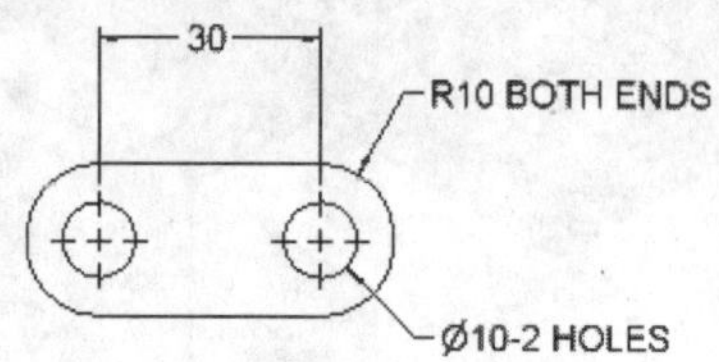

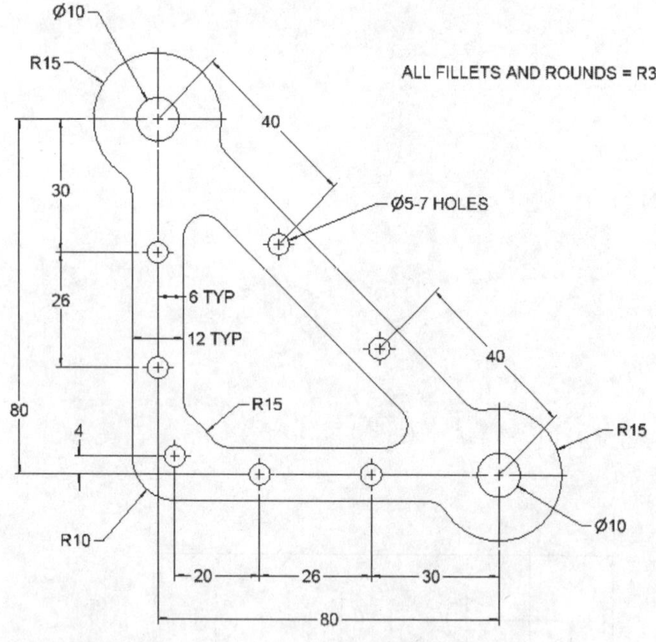

WEB PLATE
Part Number: AM311-22B
SAE 1040 STEEL
10mm THK

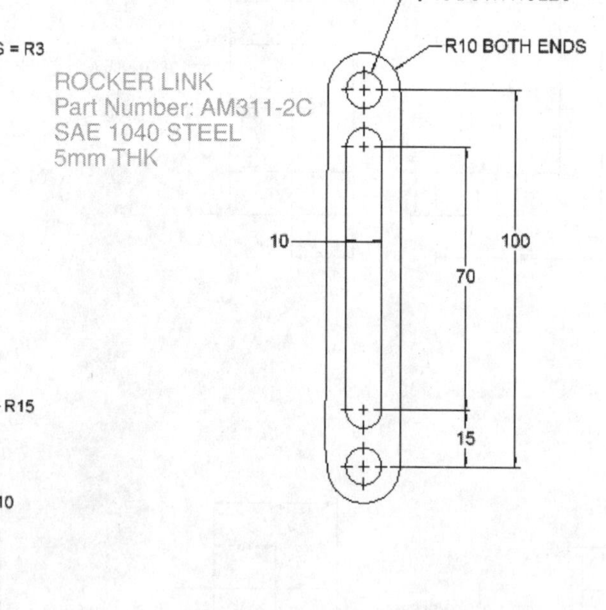

CENTER LINK
Part Number: AM311-22D
SAE 1040 STEEL
5mm THK

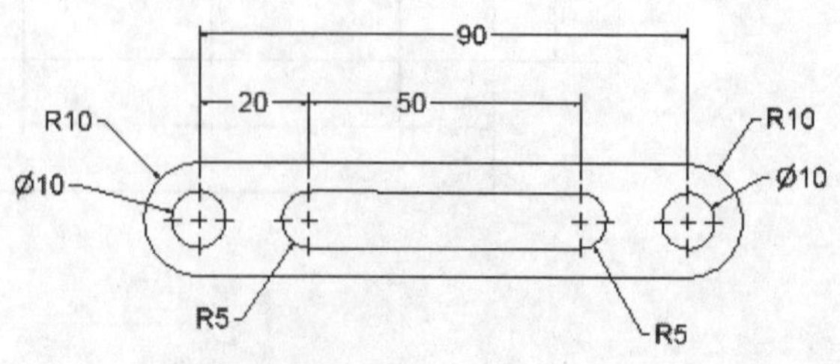

EX12-19 Millimeters

A. Draw an assembly drawing of the given object.

B. Prepare a parts list.

C. Select appropriate fasteners to hold the object together. Note that the fasteners used to join the side links to the holder arm pass over the holder base.

D. Define the appropriate tolerances. Use an H7/p6 tolerance between bushing-A and the holder base.

E. Use phantom lines to define the motion of the holder arm, side links, and cross link if the holder arm rotates between +30° and −30°.

LINK ASSEMBLY

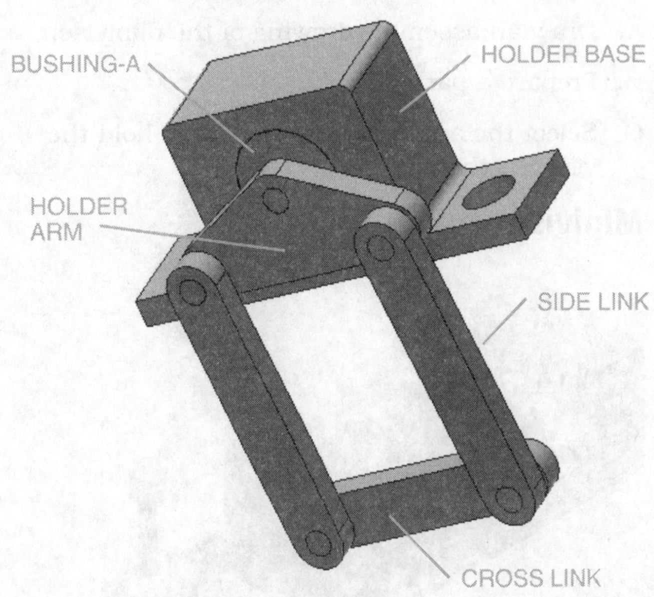

HOLDER BASE

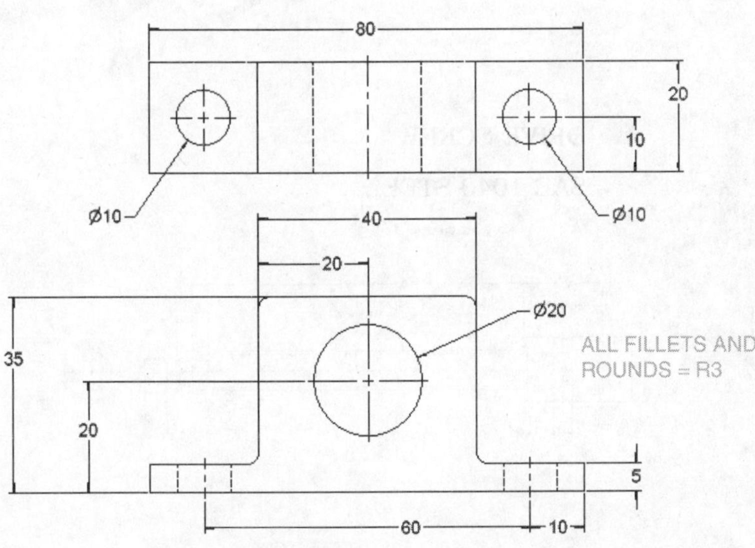

SIDE LINK
BU100-4
7075-T6 AL
5mm THK
2 REQD

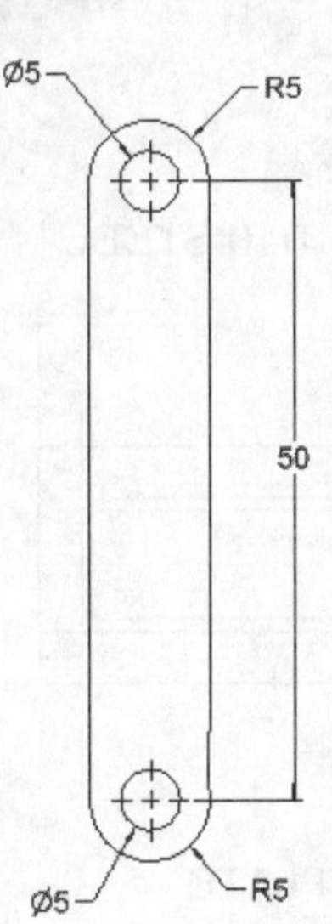

HOLDER ARM, BU100-2, 7075-T6, AL, 5mm THK

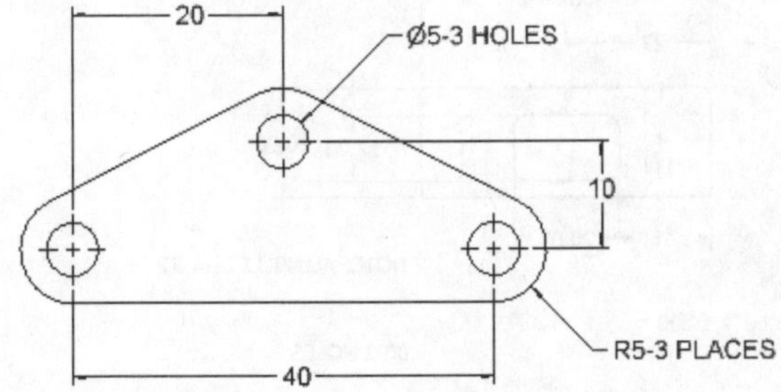

BUSHING-A
A/M CORP - B20-AD
TEFLON

CROSS LINK, BU100-3, 7075-T6, AL, 5mm THK

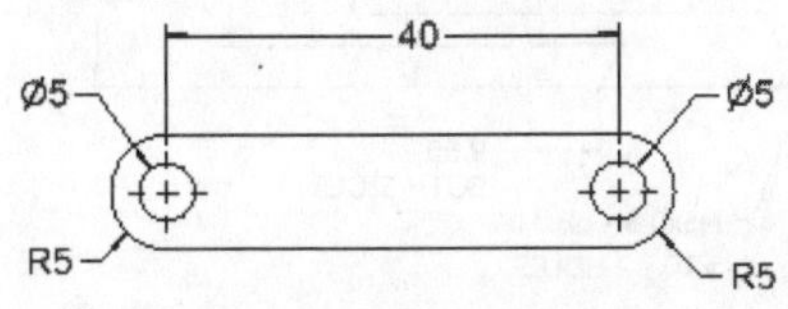

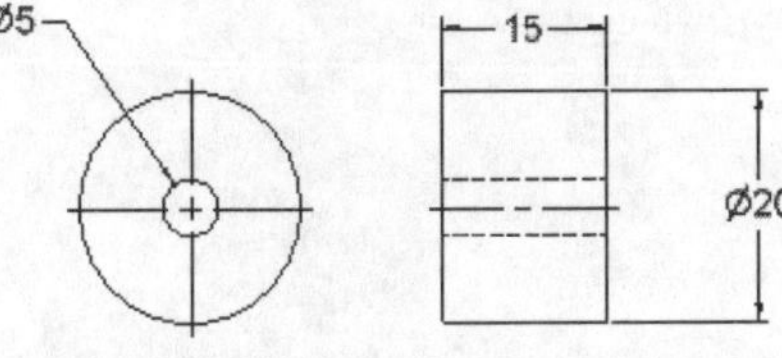

EX12-20 Millimeters

A. Draw an assembly drawing of the minivise.

B. Prepare a parts list.

C. Select the appropriate fasteners to hold the vise together.

D. Redesign the interface between the drive screw and the holder plate.

Minivise

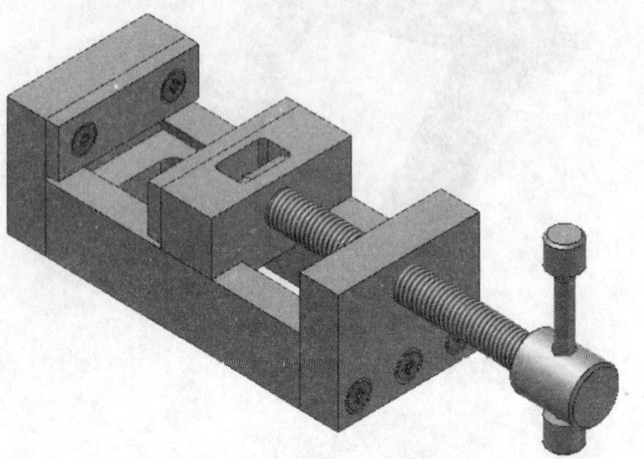

Minivise

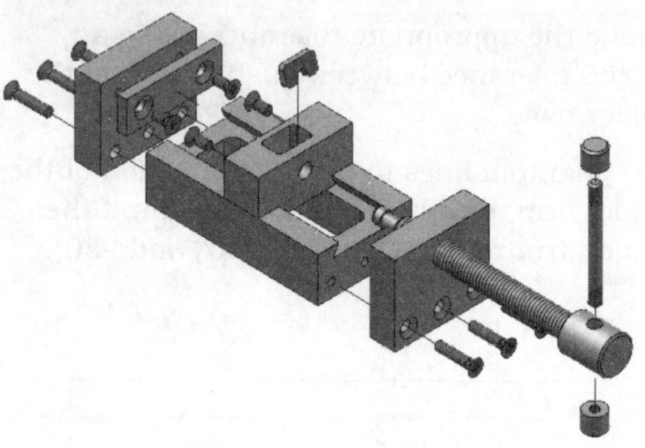

1 BASE

SAE 1040 STEEL

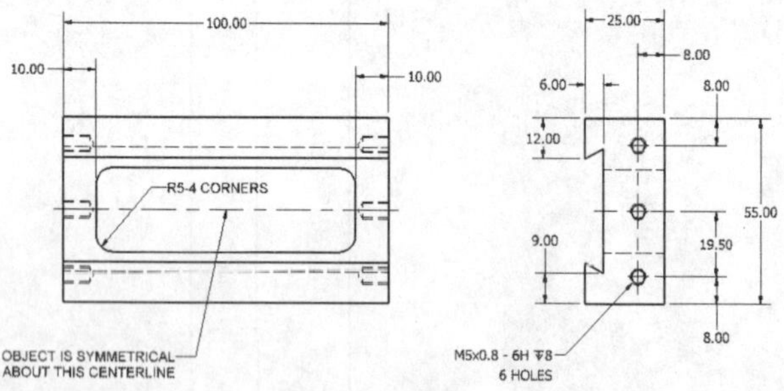

2 DRIVE SCREW

SAE 1040 STEEL

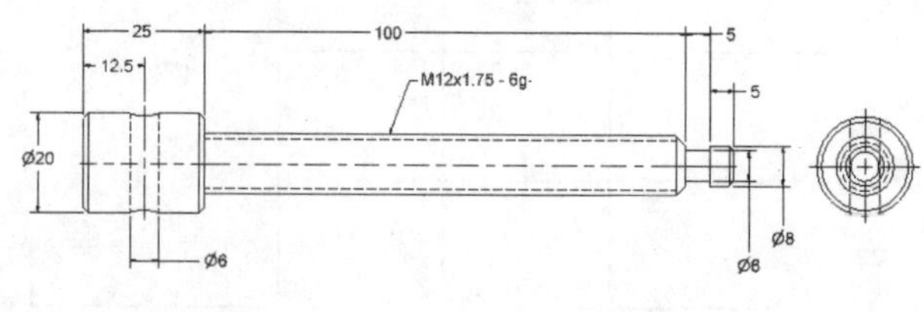

3 END PLATE

SAE 1040 STEEL

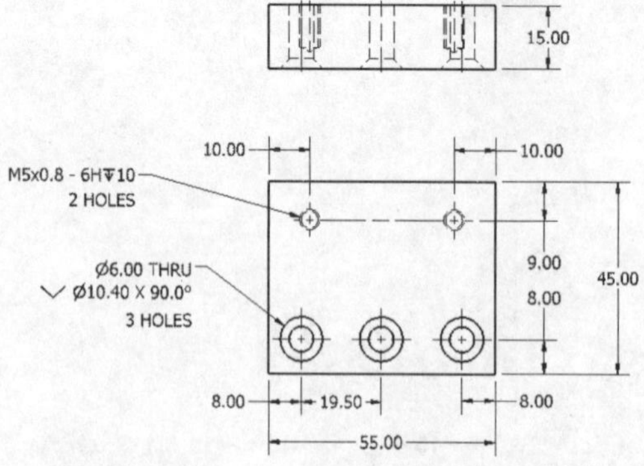

4 SLIDER

SAE 1040 STEEL

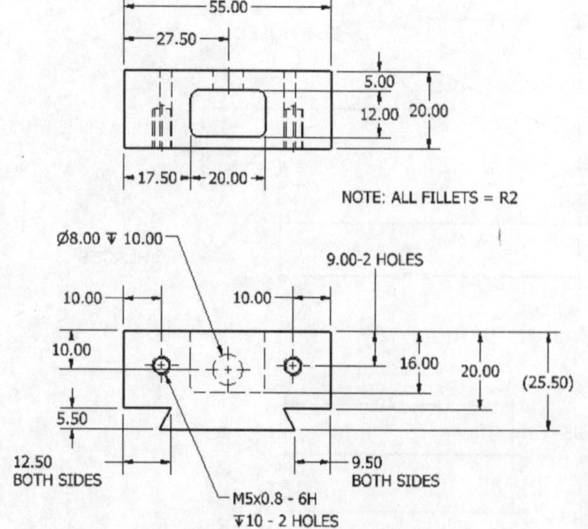

5 HOLDER PLATE

SAE 1040 STEEL

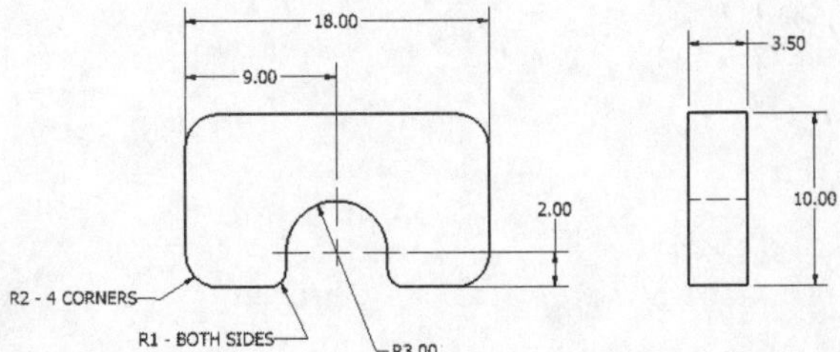

6 FACE PLATE

SAE 1040 STEEL

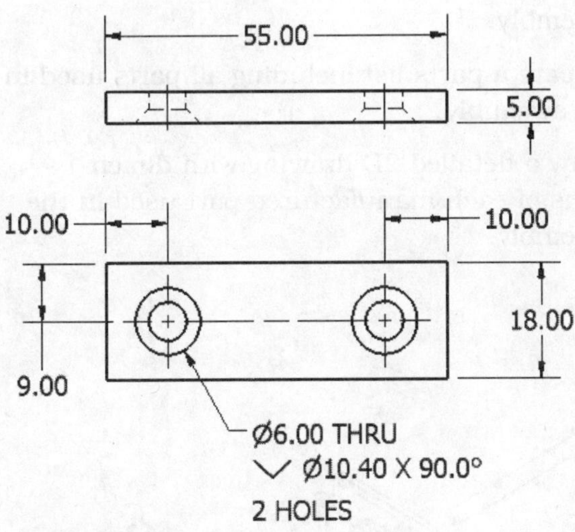

7 HANDLE

SAE 1040 STEEL

60.00

10.00 10.00

Ø6.00

M6x1 - 6g
BOTH ENDS

1×1 CHAMFER
BOTH ENDS

8 END CAP

SAE 1040 STEEL

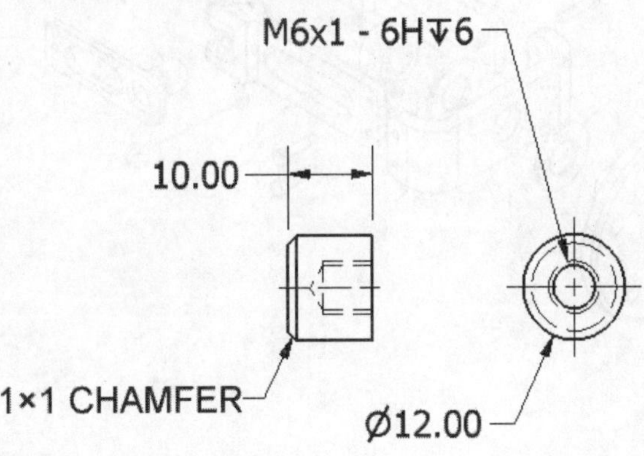

9 DRIVE PLATE

SAE 1040 STEEL

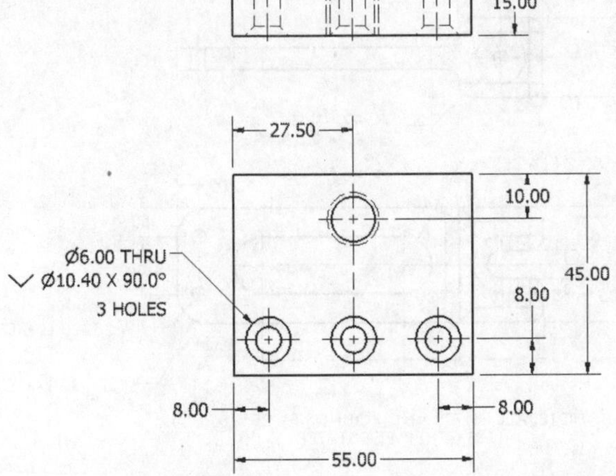

10 M5 × 10 RECESSED COUNTERSUNK HEAD-STEEL

11 M5 × 22 RECESSED COUNTERSUNK HEAD-STEEL

EX12-21 Inches

A. Draw an assembly drawing of the rocker assembly.

B. Prepare a parts list including all parts used in the assembly.

C. Draw a detailed 2D drawing with dimensions of each manufactured part used in the assembly.

Do not create drawings of purchased parts, screws, nuts, washers, or bearings.

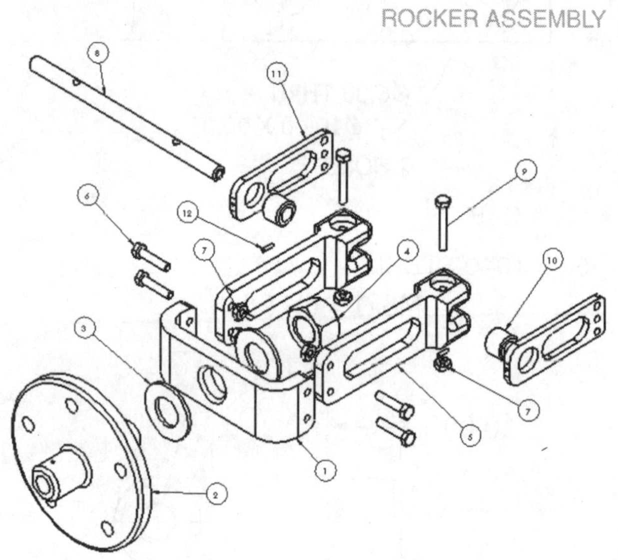

ITEM NO.	PART NUMBER	DESCRIPTION	QTY.
1	ME311-1	WHEEL BRACKET	1
2	ME311-2	WHEEL SUPPORT	1
3		1.00 × 1.75 × .06 PLAIN WASHER	2
4		1 × 8 UNC HEX NUT	1
5	ME311-3	SUPPORT ARM	2
6		1/4 - 28 UNF ×1.25 HEX HEAD	4
7		1/4 - 28 UNF × 1.75 HEX HEAD	2
8		1/4 - 28 UNF HEX NUT	6
9	ME311-4	PIVOT SHAFT	1
10		.500 × .875 .750 BEARING	2
11	ME311-5	STATIONARY ARM	2
12		#6-32 × .560 UNC SET SCREW CONE POINT	2

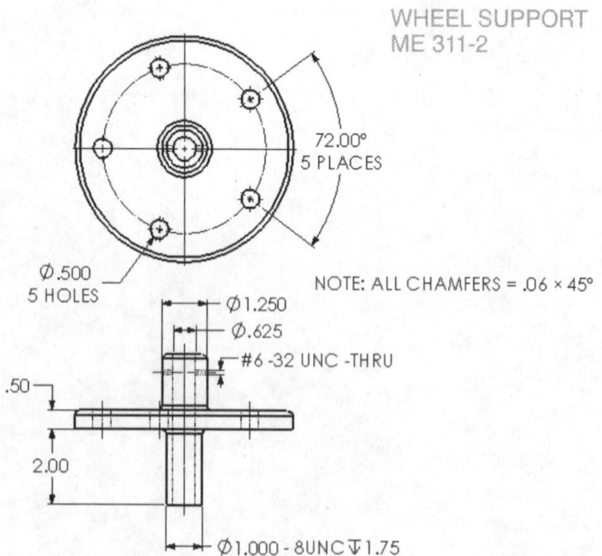

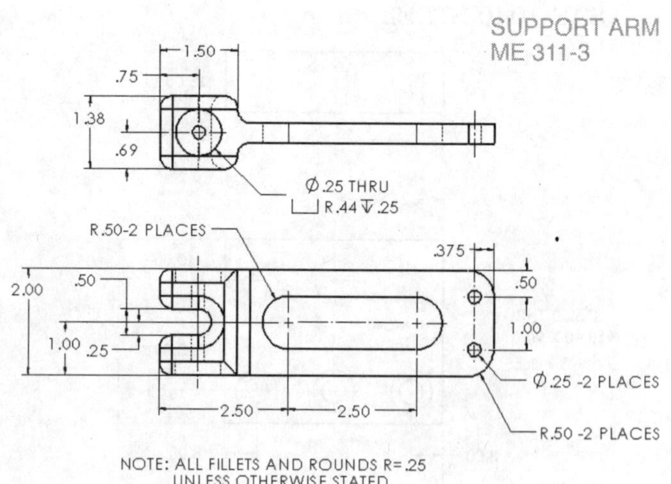

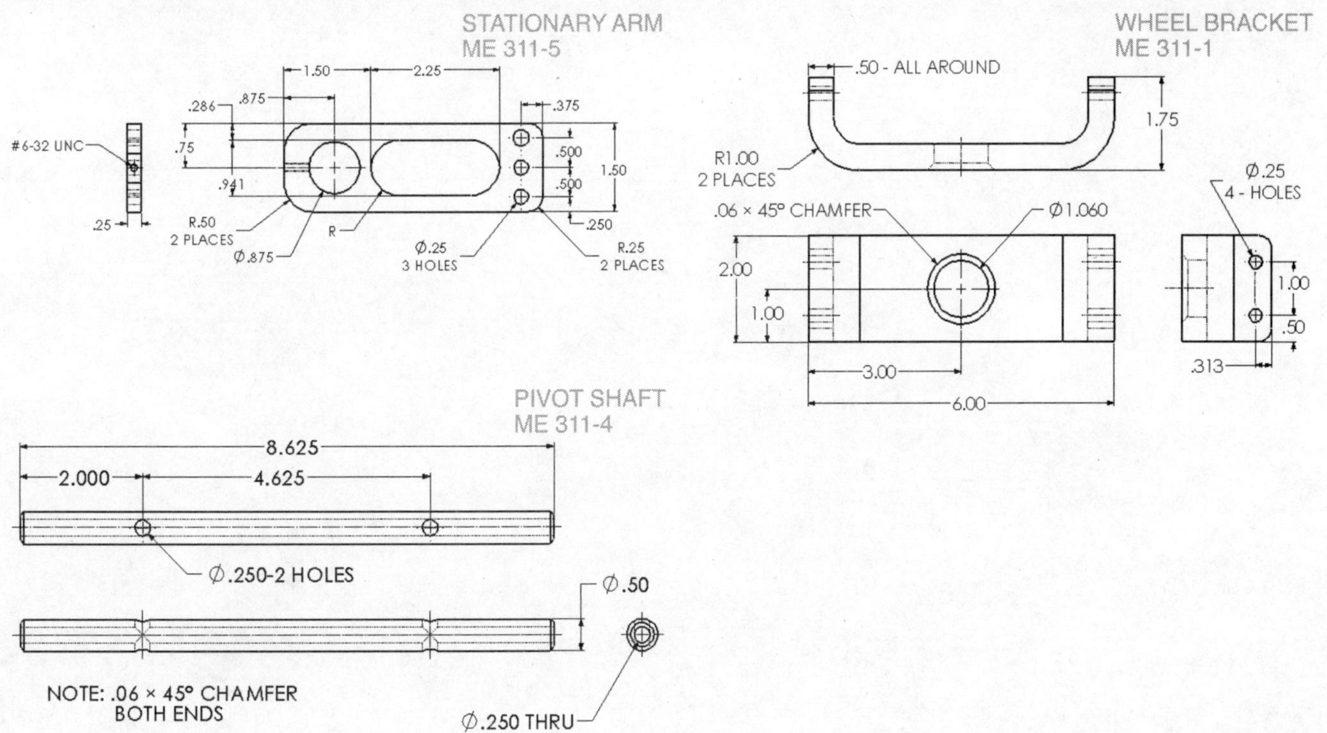
STATIONARY ARM
ME 311-5
1.50
2.25
.286
.875
.375
#6-32 UNC
.75
.500
.500
1.50
.941
.25
R.50
2 PLACES
R
.250
Ø.875
Ø.25
3 HOLES
R.25
2 PLACES
WHEEL BRACKET
ME 311-1
.50 - ALL AROUND
1.75
R1.00
2 PLACES
Ø.25
4 - HOLES
.06 × 45° CHAMFER
Ø1.060
2.00
1.00
1.00
.50
.313
3.00
6.00
PIVOT SHAFT
ME 311-4
8.625
2.000
4.625
Ø.250-2 HOLES
Ø.50
NOTE: .06 × 45° CHAMFER
BOTH ENDS
Ø.250 THRU

chapter thirteen

Gears, Bearings, and Cams

13-1 Introduction

This chapter explains how to draw and design with gears and bearings. The chapter does not discuss how to design specific gears and bearings, but how to design by using existing parts selected from manufacturers' catalogs. Various gear terms are defined, and design applications demonstrated.

The chapter also discusses how to design and draw a cam according to a displacement diagram. Different types of follower motion are explained, as well as different types of followers.

13-2 Types of Gears

There are many types of gears, including spur, bevel, worm, helical, and rack. See Figure 13-1. Each type has its own terminology, drawing requirements, and design considerations.

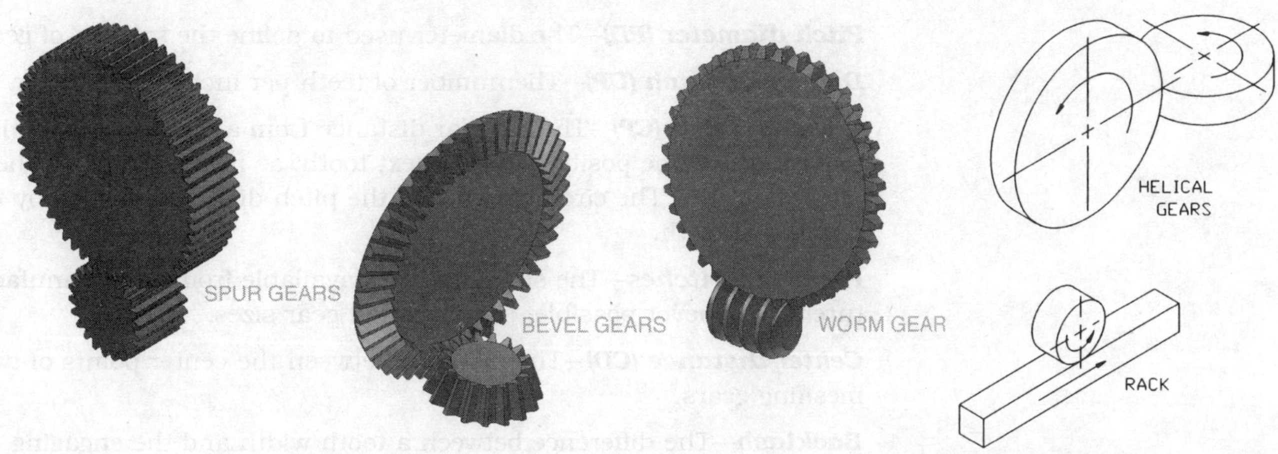

Figure 13-1

13-3 Gear Terminology—Spur

Following is a list of common spur gear terms and their meanings. Figure 13-2 illustrates the terms, and Figure 13-3 shows a listing of relative formulas.

Figure 13-2

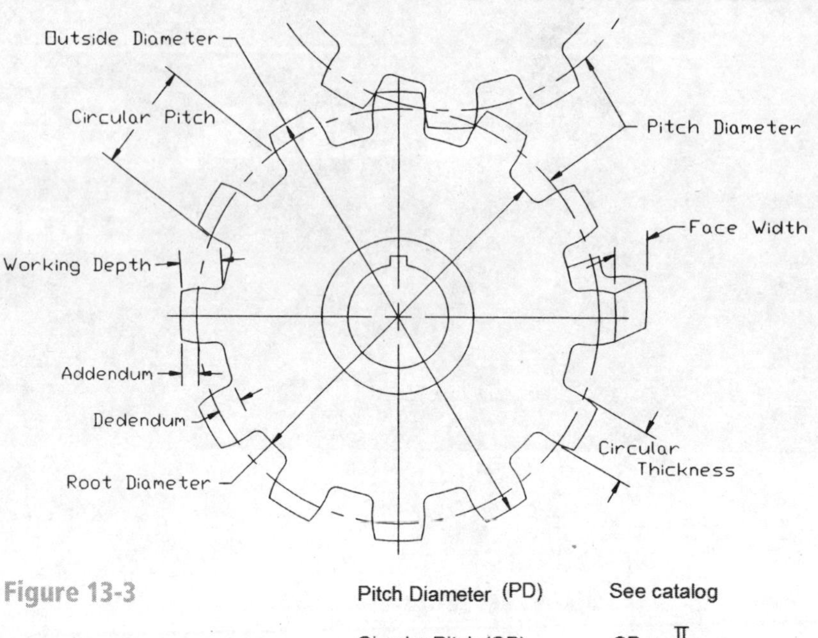

Figure 13-3

Pitch Diameter (PD)	See catalog
Circular Pitch (CP)	$CP = \frac{\pi}{DP}$
Diametral Pitch (DP)	$DP = \frac{\pi}{CP}$
Number of Teeth (N)	N = (PD)(DP)
Outside Diameter (OD)	See catalogs
Addendum (a)	$a = \frac{1}{DP}$
Dedendum (d)	d = a + .125 (For drawing purposes ONLY)
Root Diameter (RD)	RD = PD -d
Circular Thickness (CT)	$CT = \frac{PD}{2N}$
Face Width (F)	See catalogs

For Spur Gears Using English Units

Pitch diameter (PD)—The diameter used to define the spacing of gears.

Diametral pitch (DP)—The number of teeth per inch or millimeter.

Circular pitch (CP)—The circular distance from a fixed point on one tooth to the same position on the next tooth, as measured along the pitch diameter. The circumference of the pitch diameter divided by the number of teeth.

Preferred pitches—The standard sizes available from gear manufacturers. Whenever possible, use preferred gear sizes.

Center distance (CD)—The distance between the center points of two meshing gears.

Backlash—The difference between a tooth width and the engaging space on a meshing gear.

Addendum (a)—The height of a tooth above the pitch diameter.

Dedendum (d)—The depth of a tooth below the pitch diameter.

Whole depth—The total depth of a tooth. The addendum plus the dedendum.

Working depth—The depth of engagement of one gear into another. Equal to the sum of the two gear addendums.

Circular thickness—The distance across a tooth as measured along the pitch diameter.

Face width (FW)—The distance from front to back along a tooth, as measured perpendicular to the pitch diameter.

Outside diameter (OD)—The largest diameter of the gear. Equals the pitch diameter plus the addendum.

Root diameter (RD)—The diameter of the base of the teeth. The pitch diameter minus the dedendum.

Clearance—The distance between the addendum of a meshing gear and the dedendum of the mating gears.

Pressure angle—The angle between the line of action and a line tangent to the pitch diameter. Most gears have pressure angles of either 14.5° or 20°.

For Spur Gears Using Metric Units

The preceding definitions apply to both English unit and metric unit spur gears, with the exception of pitch. For English unit gears, pitch is defined as the number of teeth per inch relative to the pitch diameter and is expressed by the formula shown in Figure 13-4. Gears made to metric specifications are defined in terms of the amount of pitch diameter per tooth, called the gear's ***module.*** Figure 13-4 shows the formula for calculating a gear's module. Metric gears also have a slightly different tooth shape that makes them incompatible with English unit gears.

Figure 13-4

ENGLISH UNITS

$$\text{Pitch} = \frac{\text{Number of Teeth (N)}}{\text{Pitch Diameter (PD)}} = \frac{N}{PD}$$

METRIC UNITS

$$\text{Module} = \frac{\text{Number of Teeth (N)}}{\text{Pitch Diameter (PD)}} = \frac{PD}{N}$$

13-4 Spur Gear Drawings

Figure 13-5 shows a representation of spur gears. The individual teeth are not included in the front view, but are represented by three phantom lines. The diameters of the three lines represent the outside diameter, the pitch diameter, and the root diameter.

The outside diameter and the pitch diameter are usually given in manufacturers' catalogs. The root diameter can be calculated from the pitch diameter by the formula presented in Figure 13-3.

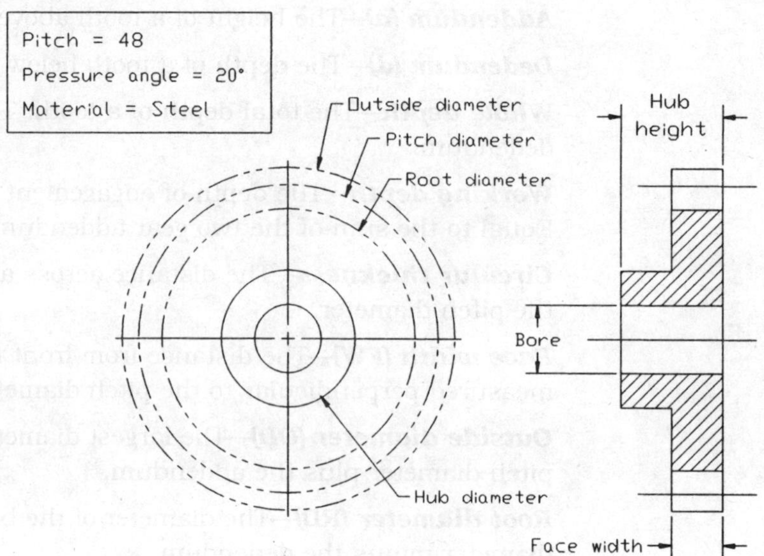

Figure 13-5

The side view of the gear is drawn as a sectional view taken along the vertical centerline. The gear size is defined by using the manufacturer's stock number, dimensions, and a list of appropriate design information.

Figure 13-6 shows the front representation view of three meshing gears. The gears are positioned so that the pitch circle diameters are tangent. Ideally, mating gears always should mesh exactly tangent to their pitch circles.

Gear representations were developed because it was both difficult and time consuming to accurately draw individual teeth when creating drawings on a drawing board. The AutoCAD **Array** and **Block** commands, among others, can be used to create detailed gear drawings that include all teeth; however, it is usually sufficient to show a few meshing teeth and use the representative centerlines for the remaining portions of both gears. See Figure 13-7.

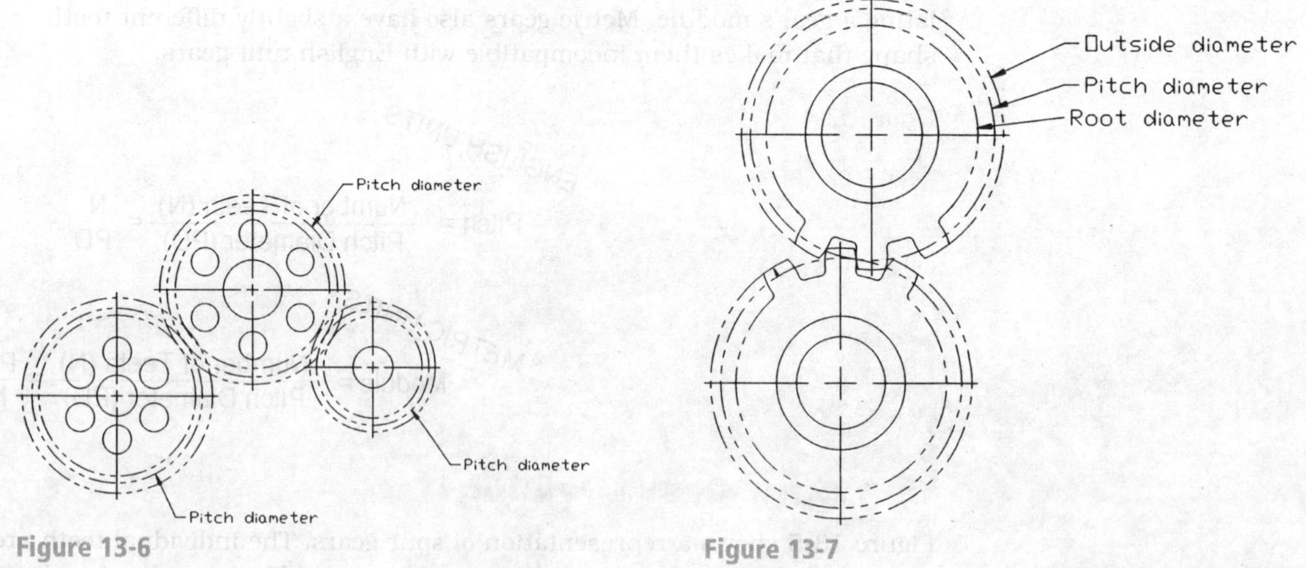

Figure 13-6

Figure 13-7

Most gear tooth shapes are based on an involute curve. Involute-based teeth fit together well, transfer forces smoothly, and can use one cutter to generate all gear tooth variations within the same pitch. Standards for tooth proportions have been established by the American National Standards Institute (ANSI) and the American Gear Manufacturers Association (AGMA).

13-5 Sample Problem SP13-1

Draw a front view of a spur gear that has an outside diameter of 6.50 inches, a pitch diameter of 6.00 inches, and a root diameter of 5.25 inches. The gear has 12 teeth.

The method presented is a simplified method and is an acceptable representation for most drawing applications. See Figure 13-8.

Figure 13-8

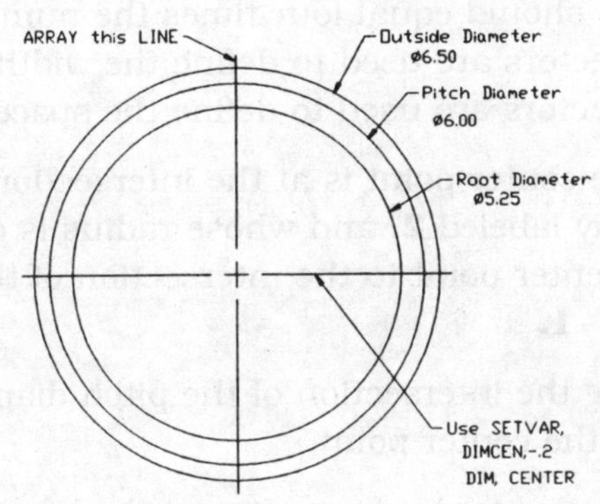

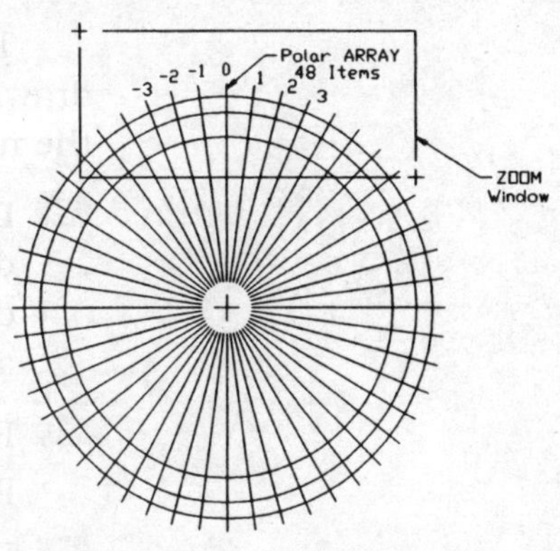

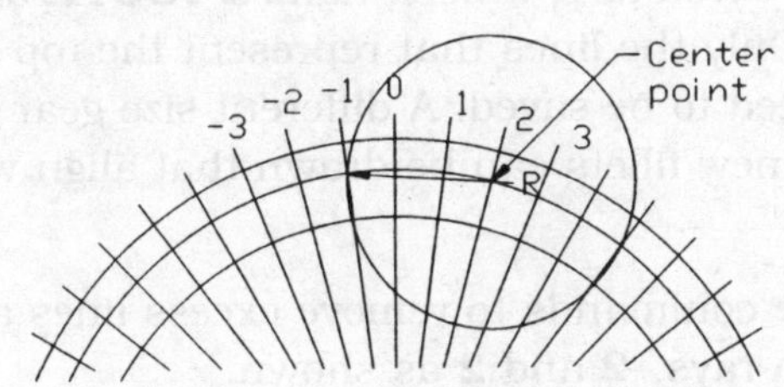

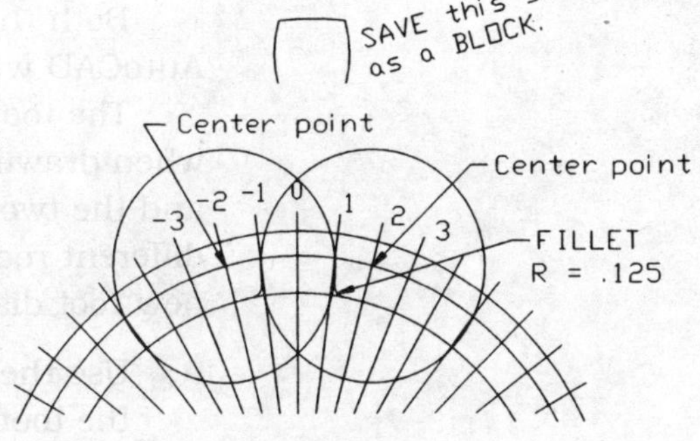

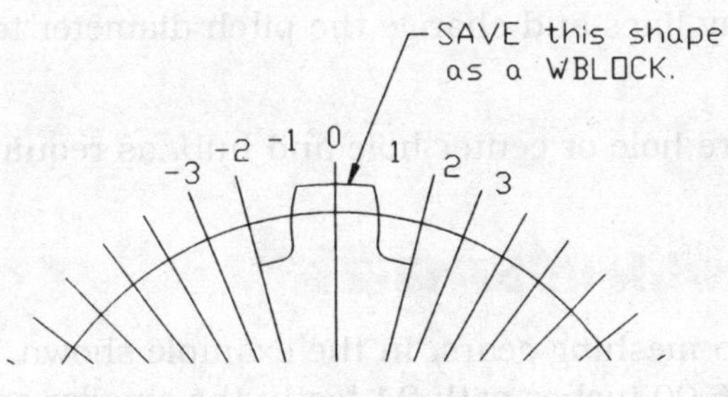

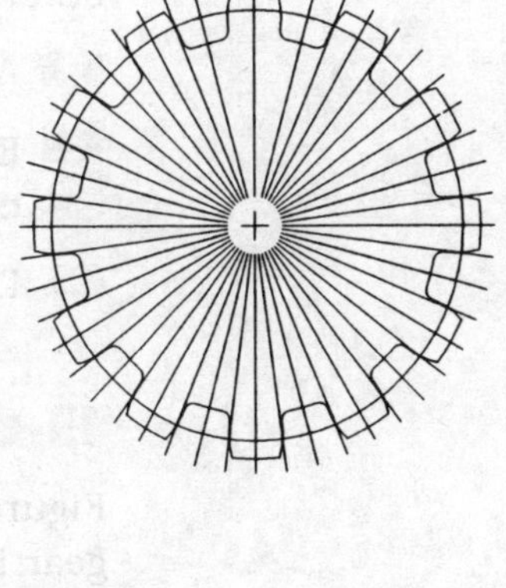

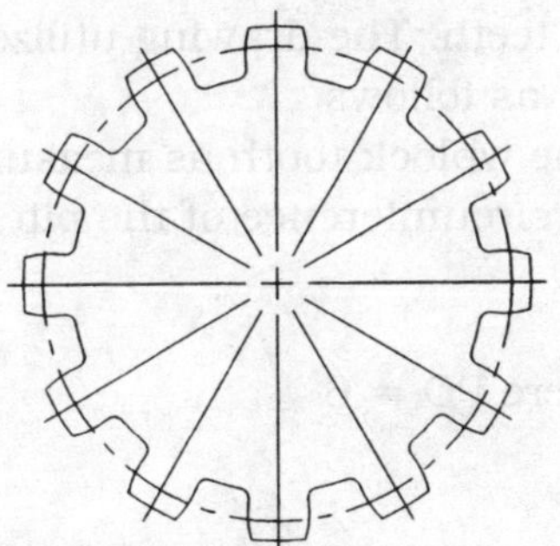

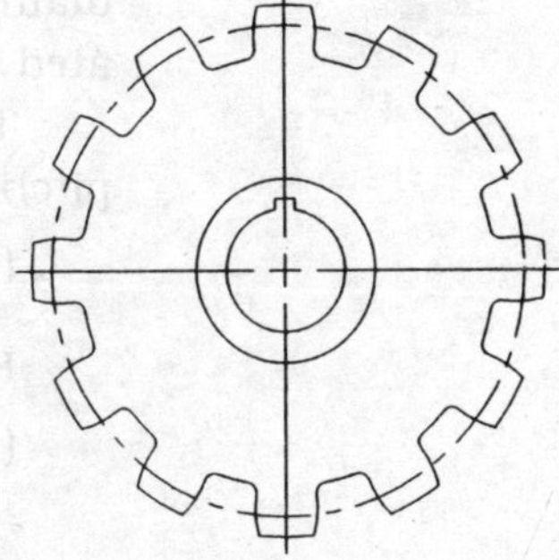

1. Draw three concentric circles of diameter **6.50, 6.00,** and **5.25.** Use the **Center Mark** command modified to draw a centerline for the circles.

2. Use the **Array** command and create **48** ray lines as shown. Label three rays on each side of the top vertical centerline as shown. Zoom the labeled area.

The number of rays should equal four times the number of teeth to be drawn. Two adjoining sectors are used to define the width of the tooth, and the next two adjacent sectors are used to define the space between teeth.

3. Draw a circle whose center point is at the intersection of the pitch diameter and the ray labeled **2,** and whose radius is determined by the distance from the center point to the intersection of the pitch diameter and the ray labeled **–1.**

4. Repeat step 3, using the intersection of the pitch diameter and the point labeled **–2** as the center point.

5. Use the **Fillet** command to draw a radius at the base of the tooth. Select the side of the tooth as one of the lines for the fillet, and the root diameter as the other line.

Both the circle and ray line will be within the selected cursor, but AutoCAD will select the last entity drawn, so the diameter will be selected.

The tooth shape can be saved as a wblock named **TOOTH** and used when drawing other gears. Only the lines that represent the top of the gear and the two side sections need to be saved. A different size gear will have a different root diameter, and new fillets can be drawn that align with the new root diameter.

6. Use the **Trim** and **Erase** commands to remove excess lines and create the tooth shape between rays **–2** and **2** as shown.

This tooth shape may be saved as a wblock and used when drawing other gears.

7. Array the tooth shape about the gear's center point.

8. Erase the excess ray lines and change the pitch diameter to a centerline.

9. Draw the gear's bore hole or center hole and hub, as required.

13-6 Sample Problem SP13-2

Figure 13-9A shows two meshing gears. In the example shown, the larger gear has a diameter of 6.00 inches with 24 teeth; the smaller gear has a diameter of 3.00 inches and 12 teeth. The drawing utilizes the wblock created in Sample Problem SP13-1 as follows.

The circular thickness of the wblock tooth as measured along the pitch diameter equals 1/12 the circumference of the pitch diameter.

$(1/12)(\pi\ PD)$

For the gear in SP13-1, where PD = 6

$(1/12)(\pi\ 6) = \pi/2$

$= 1.57$ inches

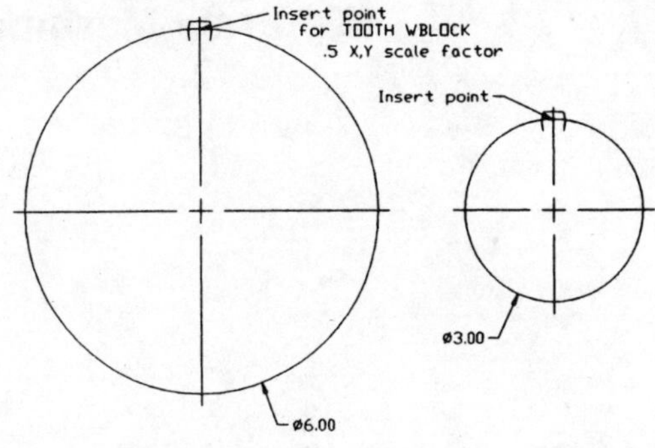

Figure 13-9A

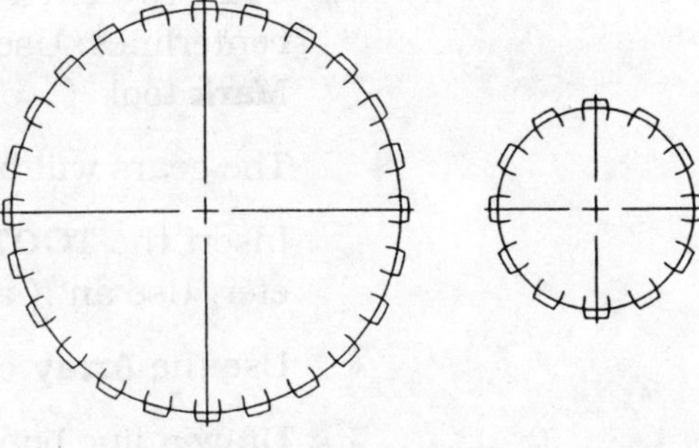

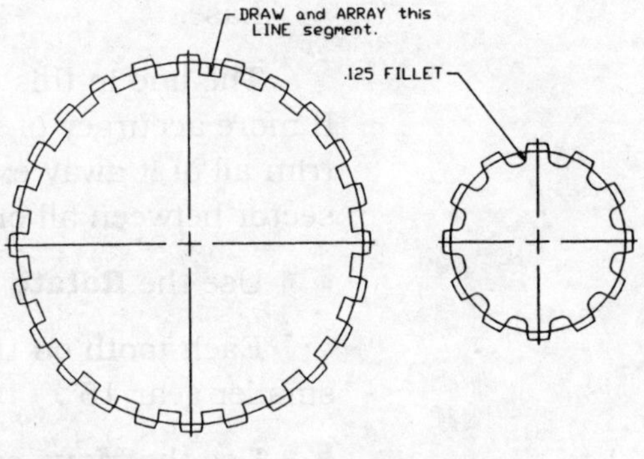

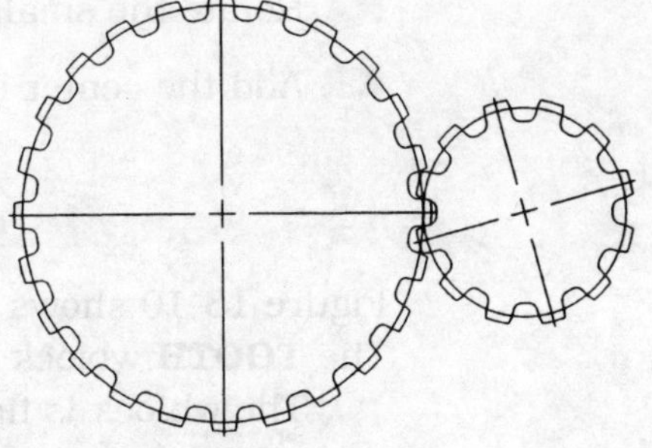

The large gear requires 24 teeth on a pitch diameter of 6, or twice as many teeth as the gear used to create the wblock. The teeth on the 24-tooth gear must be half the size of the tooth created in the wblock. The teeth on the smaller gear must be the same size as the teeth on the larger gear.

To Draw Meshing Spur Gears (See Figure 13-9B.)

Figure 13-9B

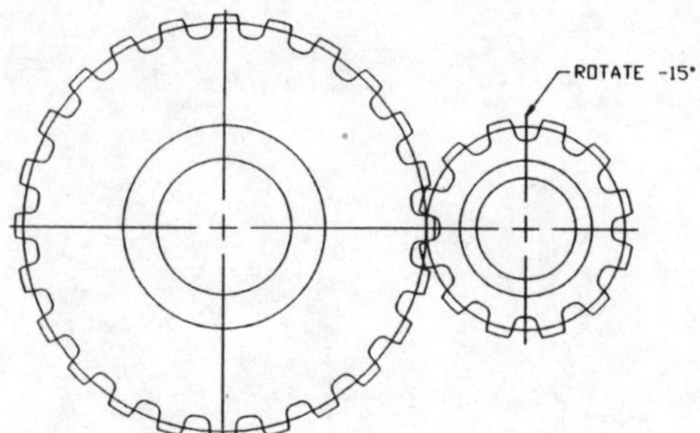

1 Draw two circles of diameter **6.00** and **3.00** inches. Include the circles' centerlines. Use **Setvar, Dimcen,** set to –**.2,** or use a modified **Center Mark** tool.

The gears will be drawn separately and then meshed.

2 Insert the **TOOTH** wblock on both gears as shown on the pitch diameter. Use an X and Y scale factor of **.5.** Explode the wblock.

3 Use the **Array** command to create the required 24 and 12 teeth.

4 Draw a line between the roots of two of the teeth as shown. Use the **Array** command to create the root circle. Add the fillet to each tooth base.

The line in this example is a straight line acceptable for smaller gears. If more accuracy of shape is required, draw a complete root circle and then trim all of it away except the portion between two tooth roots. Array this sector between all of the other teeth.

5 Use the **Rotate** command to orient the small gear with the large gear.

Each tooth on the large gear requires 360/24 = 15°. Rotate the smaller gear 15°.

6 Use the **Move** command to position the small gear.

The pitch circles of the two gears should be tangent.

7 Rotate the smaller gear's centerline **–15°.**

8 Add the center hubs to both gears as shown.

13-7 Sample Problem SP13-3

Figure 13-10 shows a gear that has a pitch diameter of 4.00 with 18 teeth. The **TOOTH** wblock can be used as follows.

The wblock is first reduced to accommodate the smaller diameter.

1 Draw a circle with a **4.00**-inch diameter. Include centerlines.

2 Insert the wblock, using an X and Y scale factor of **.4445.**

The scale factor was derived by considering the ratio between the number of teeth on the gear used to create the **TOOTH** wblock (12) and the number of teeth on the desired gear, 18, or 12/18 = .6667. The ratio between the diameters is also considered: 4.00/6.00 = .6667. The two ratios are multiplied together: (.6667)(.6667) = .4445.

Figure 13-10

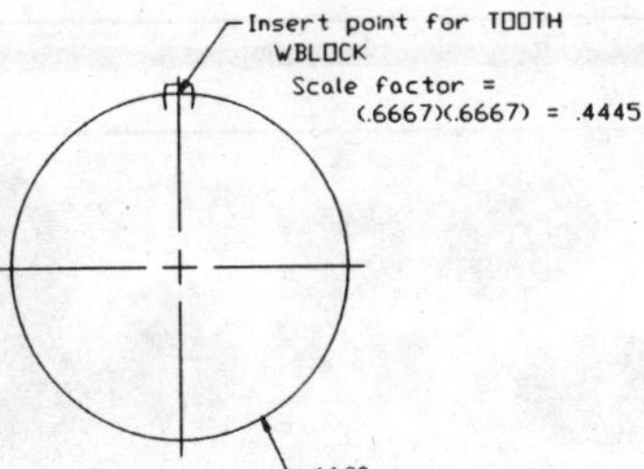

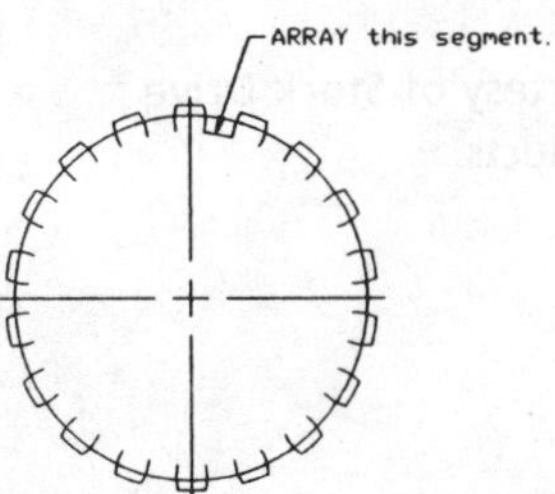

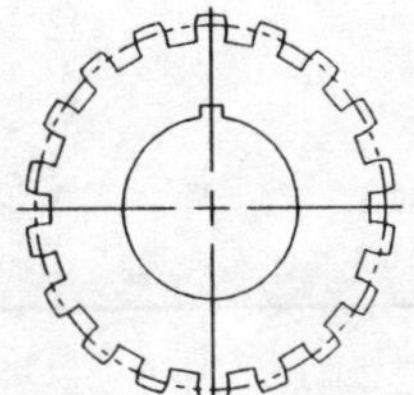

3 Use the **Array** command to create the required 18 teeth.

4 Draw a line between the end lines of two of the teeth, and array the line **18** times around the gear.

The line may be drawn as a straight line for small gears or as an arc for larger gears. The arc may be created by drawing a circle, then using the **Trim** command to create the desired length.

5 Add the center hub as required.

The same wblock can be used for metric gears, using the conversion factor 1.00 inch = 25.4 millimeters. It is probably easier to create a separate wblock for a metric tooth.

13-8 Selecting Spur Gears

When two spur gears are engaged, the smaller gear is called the *pinion gear* and the larger gear is called simply the *gear*. The relationship between the relative speed of two mating gears is directly proportional to the gears' pitch diameters. Also, the number of teeth on a gear is proportional to the gear's pitch diameter. This means that the ratio of speed between two meshing gears is equal to the ratio of the number of teeth on the two gears. If one gear has 40 teeth and the other 20, the speed ratio between the two gears is 2:1.

For gears to mesh properly, they must have the same pitch and pressure angle. Gear manufacturers present their gears in charts that include a selection of gears with common pitches and pressure angles. Figure 13-11 shows a sample spur gear listing from the website of Stock Drive Products. The site allows you to select a diametral pitch and all other appropriate product details. Once a gear is selected, the gear information will be displayed. You may be able to generate an AutoCAD drawing of the gear if you have a compatible setup. Many manufacturers offer free product catalogs.

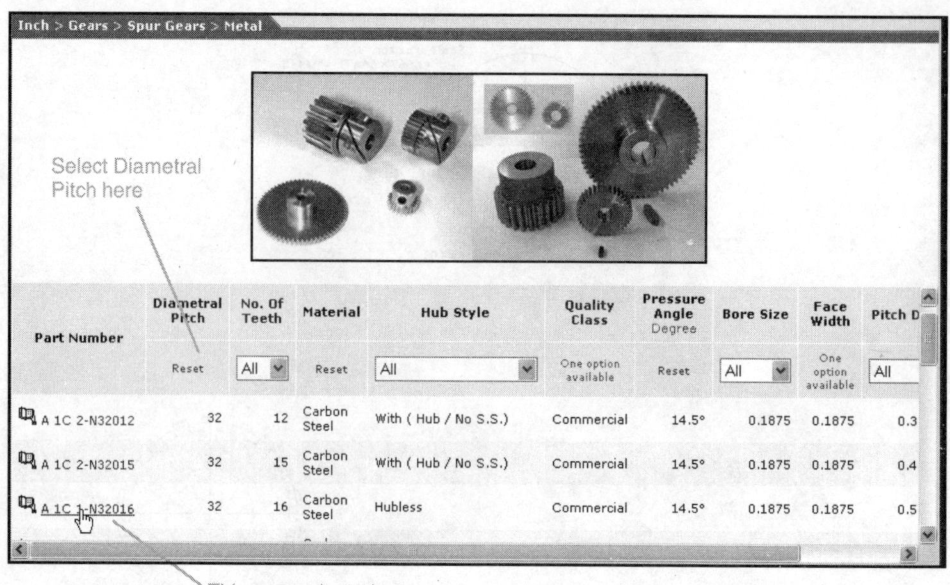

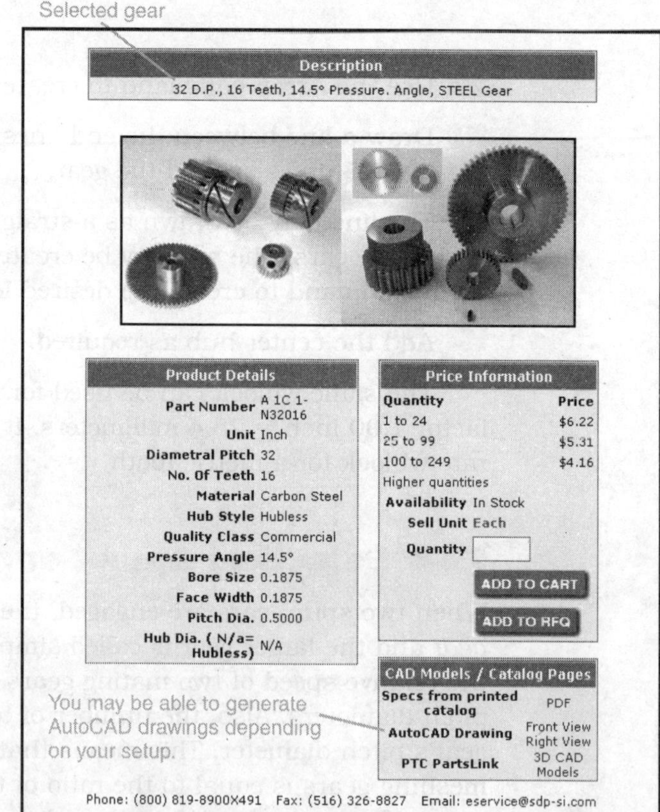

Figure 13-11
Courtesy of Stock Drive Products.

13-9 Center Distance Between Gears

The center distance between meshing spur gears is needed to align the gears properly. Ideally, gears mesh exactly on their pitch diameters, so the ideal center distance between two meshing gears is equal to the sum of the two pitch radii, or the sum of the two diameters divided by 2:

$$CD1 = (PD1 + PD2)/2$$

If two gears were chosen from the chart in Figure 13-11, and one had 30 teeth and a pitch diameter of .9375 and the other had 60 teeth and a pitch diameter of 1.8750, the center distance between the gears would be

$$CD1 = (.9375 + 1.8750)/2 = 1.4062$$

The center distance of gears is dependent on the tolerance of the gears' bores, the tolerance of the supporting shafts, and the feature and positional tolerance of the holes in the shaft's supporting structure. The following sample problem shows how these tolerances are considered and applied when matching two spur gears.

13-10 Sample Problem SP13-4

An electric motor generates power at 1750 rpm. Reduce this speed by a factor of 2, using steel metric gears with a module of 1.5 and a pressure angle of 20°. Figure 13-12 shows a list of gears. Determine the center distance between the gears, and specify the shaft sizes required for both gears.

Gear number A 1C22MYKW150 50A and number A 1C22MKYW150 100A were selected from the chart shown in Figure 13-12. The pinion gear has 50 teeth, and the large gear has 100, so if the pinion gear is mounted on the motor shaft, the larger gear will turn at 875 rpm, or half of the 1750 motor speed.

$$\frac{1}{2} = \frac{x}{1750}$$

$$x = \frac{1750}{2} = 875 \text{ rpm}$$

The specific design information for the selected gears is as follows:

PINION GEAR

PD = 75

OD = 78

N = 50

Bore = $20^{+0.021}_{-0.000}$

Tolerance = H7

LARGE GEAR

PD = 150

OD = 153

N = 100

Bore = $25^{+0.021}_{-0.000}$

Tolerance = H7

The center distance between the gears is equal to the sum of the two pitch diameters divided by 2:

$$\frac{PD1 + PD2}{2} =$$

$$\frac{75 + 150}{2} = 112.5$$

Figure 13-12
Courtesy of Stock Drive Products.

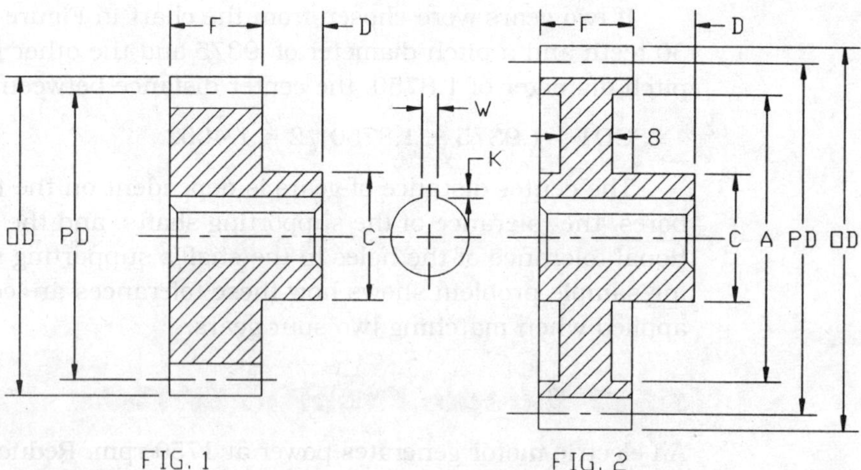

This information is available from the Stock Drive Products catalog or website.

Catalog Number	Fig No.	No. of Teeth	P.D.	O.D.	B* Bore (H7)	F Face Width	C Hub Dia	D Hub Proj	A Dia	W Dim	K Dim
A 1C22MYKW150 20A		20	30	33	14		25				
A 1C22MYKW150 24A		24	36	39	16		30			5	2.3
A 1C22MYKW150 25A		25	37.5	40.5		18	32				
A 1C22MYKW150 28A		28	42	45	18		36				
A 1C22MYKW150 30A		30	45	48							
A 1C22MYKW150 32A	1	32	48	51							
A 1C22MYKW150 36A		36	54	57							
A 1C22MYKW150 40A		40	60	63							
A 1C22MYKW150 48A		48	72	75				14		6	2.8
A 1C22MYKW150 50A		50	75	78	20		40				
A 1C22MYKW150 56A		56	84	87		16					
A 1C22MYKW150 60A		60	90	93					76		
A 1C22MYKW150 64A		64	96	99					82		
A 1C22MYKW150 70A		70	105	108					91		
A 1C22MYKW150 72A	2	72	108	111					94		
A 1C22MYKW150 80A		80	120	123	25		50		106	8	3.3
A 1C22MYKW150 100A		100	150	153					136		

* Gears with 14, 16, and 18mm bores have a tolerance of +.018, +.000.
20 and 25mm bores have a tolerance of +0.021/- 0

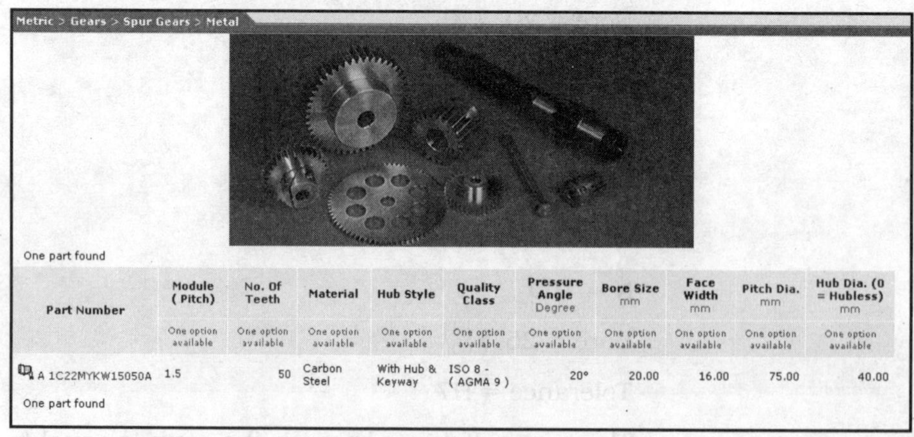

Metric > Gears > Spur Gears > Metal

One part found

Part Number	Module (Pitch)	No. Of Teeth	Material	Hub Style	Quality Class	Pressure Angle Degree	Bore Size mm	Face Width mm	Pitch Dia. mm	Hub Dia. (0 = Hubless) mm
	One option available	One option available	One option available	One option available	One option available	One option available	One option available	One option available	One option available	One option available
A 1C22MYKW15050A	1.5	50	Carbon Steel	With Hub & Keyway	ISO 8 - (AGMA 9)	20°	20.00	16.00	75.00	40.00

One part found

From the website www.SDP-SI.com

The manufacturer's catalog lists the bore tolerance as an H7. One gear has a nominal bore diameter of 20, and the other one of 25. Standard fit tolerances for metric values are discussed in Chapter 9, and appropriate tables are included in the appendix.

Tolerance values for a sliding fit (H7/g6) hole basis were selected for this design application. This means that the shaft tolerances are 19.993 and 19.980 for the pinion gear and 24.993 and 24.980 for the large gear.

13-11 Combining Spur Gears

Gears may be mounted on the same shaft. Gears on a common shaft have the same turning speed. Combining gears on the same shaft enables the designer to develop larger gear ratios within a smaller space.

Combining gears can also be used to help reduce the size of gear ratios between individual gears and the amount of space needed to create the reductions. Figure 13-13 shows a four-gear setup. Gears B and C are mounted on the same shaft. Gear A is the driver gear and is turning at a speed of 1750 rpm. The speed of gear D is determined as follows.

The ratio between gears A and B is

$$\frac{48}{72} = 0.6667$$

The speed of gear B is therefore

$$1750 \times .6667 = 1166.7 \text{ rpm}$$

Gears B and C are on the same shaft, so they have the same speed. Gear C is turning at 1166.7 rpm.

The ratio between gears C and D is

$$\frac{24}{48} = 0.5000$$

The speed of gear D is therefore

$$1166.7 \times .5000 = 583 \text{ rpm}$$

The ratio between gears A and D is 3:1.

13-12 Gear Terminology—Bevel

Bevel gears align at an angle with each other. An angle of 90° is most common. Bevel gears use much of the same terminology as spur gears, but with the addition of several terms related to the angles between the gears and the shape and position of the teeth. Figure 13-14 defines the related terminology.

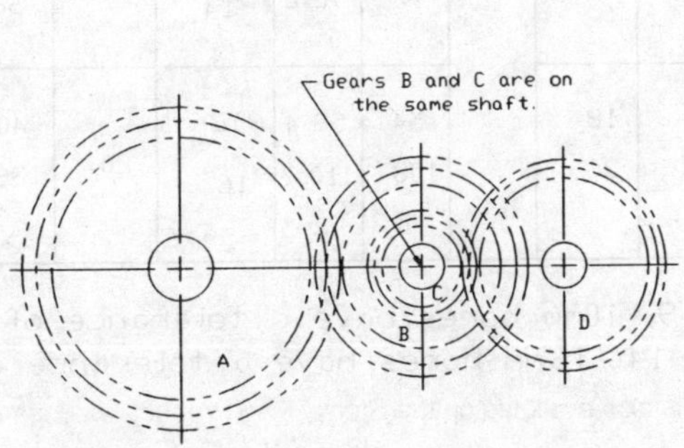

Figure 13-13

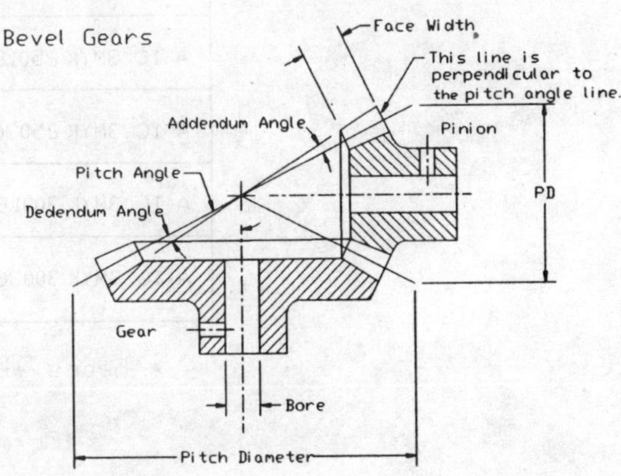

Figure 13-14
Courtesy of Stock Drive Products.

Bevel gears must have the same pitch or module value and have the same pressure angle for them to mesh properly. Manufacturers' catalogs usually list bevel gears in matched sets designated by ratios that have been predetermined to fit together correctly. Figure 13-15 shows a sample list of matched set bevel gears with millimeter values, and Figure 13-16 shows a list for inch values.

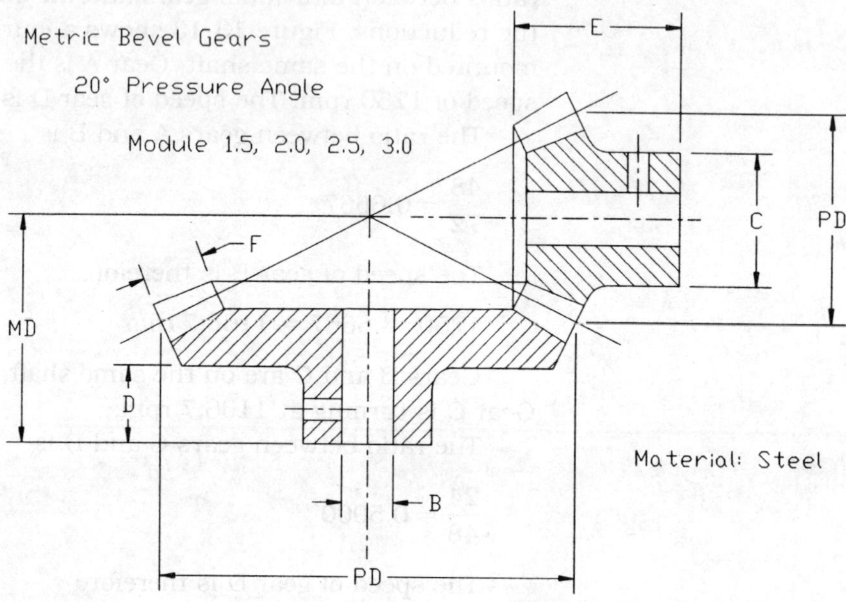

Catalog Number	Module	No. of Teeth	Ratio	PD	OD	B* Bore (H8)	F Face Width	E Length	C Hub Dia	D Hub Proj	MD Dim
A 1C 3MYK 15018	1:5	18	1:2	27	29.7	8	9.8	23	22	12.5	40.74
A 1C 3MYK 15036		36		54	55.4	10		18.5	30	10	26.75
A 1C 3MYK 20018	2:0	18		36	39.6	9	12.6	29	28	15	53.12
A 1C 3MYK 20036		36		72	73.8	12		24	36	13	35.21
A 1C 3MYK 25018	2.5	18		45	49.5	12	16.7	35	36	17	64.29
A 1C 3MYK 25036H		36		90	92.2	14		29	50	15	42.55
A 1C 3MYK 30018	3.0	18		54	59.4	12	20	40	41	18	75.27
A 1C 3MYK 30036H		36		108	110.7	16		36	60	19	52.32

* Gears with: 8, 9, 10mm bores have a tolerance of +0.022/-0
12, 14, 16mm bores have a tolerance of +0.027/-0

This information is also available on the Stock Drive Products website www.SDP-SI.com.

Figure 13-15
Courtesy of Stock Drive Products.

Figure 13-16
Courtesy of Stock Drive Products.

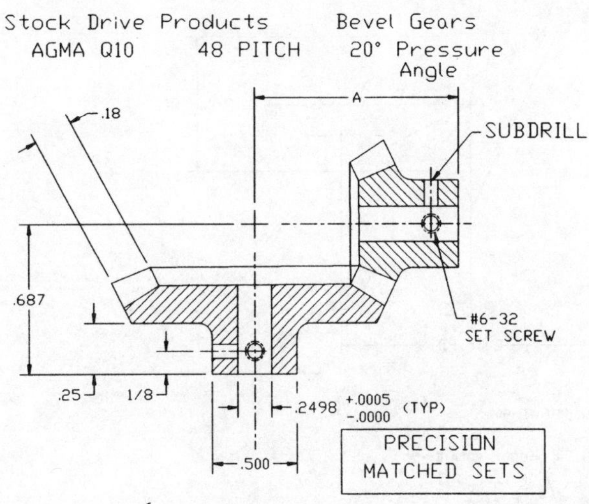

Catalog Number	Ratio	No. of Teeth	PD	A	Material
S1346Z-48S30A030	1:1	30 30	.625	.687	St Steel Aluminum
S1346Z-48S30S030	1:1	30 30	.625	.687	St Steel
S1346Z-48A30A030	1:1	30 30	.625	.687	Aluminum
S1346Z-48S30A045	1:1-1/2	30 45	.625 .937	.812	St Steel Aluminum
S1346Z-48S30S045	1:1-1/2	30 45	.625 .937	.812	St Steel
S1346Z-48A30A045	1:1-1/2	30 45	.625 .937	.812	Aluminum
S1346Z-48S30A060	1:2	30 60	.625 1.250	:937	St Steel Aluminum
S1346Z-48S30S060	1:2	30 60	.625 1.250	.937	St Steel
S1346Z-48A30A060	1:2	30 60	.625 1.250	.937	Aluminum
S1346Z-48S30A090	1:3	30 90	.625 1.875	1.250	St Steel Aluminum
S1346Z-48S30S090	1:3	30 90	.625 1.875	1.250	St Steel
S1346Z-48S30A090	1:3	30 90	.625 1.875	1.250	Aluminum
S1346Z-48S30A120	1:4	30 120	.625 2.500	1.531	St Steel Aluminum
S1346Z-48S30S120	1:4	30 120	.625 2.500	1.531	St Steel
S1346Z-48A30A120	1:4	30 120	.625 2.500	1.531	Aluminum

13-13 How to Draw Bevel Gears

Bevel gears are usually drawn by working from dimensions listed in manufacturers' catalogs for specific matching sets. The gears are drawn by using either a sectional view or a half-sectional view that shows the profiles of the two gears. Figure 13-17 shows a matching set of bevel gears that were drawn from the information given in Figure 13-15.

The procedure used to draw the gears, based on information given in manufacturers' catalogs, is as follows.

To Draw a Matched Set of Beveled Gears

1. Draw a perpendicular centerline pattern, and use the **Offset** command to define the pitch diameters of the pinion and gear.

2. Extend the pitch diameter lines, and draw lines from the center point to the intersections as shown.

Figure 13-17

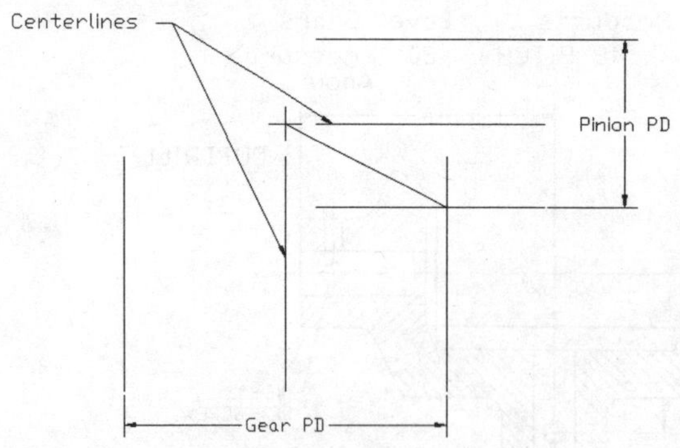

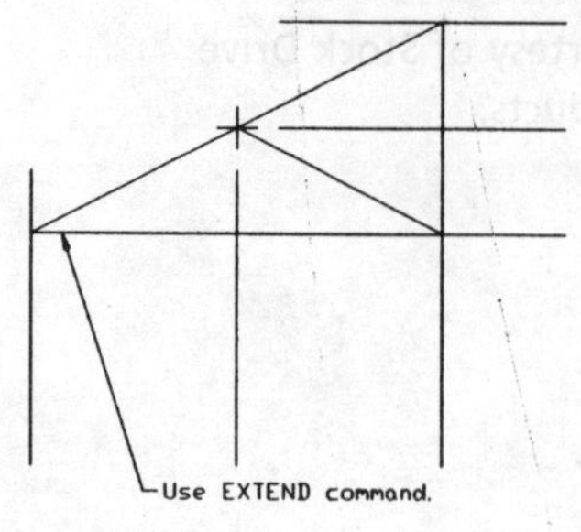

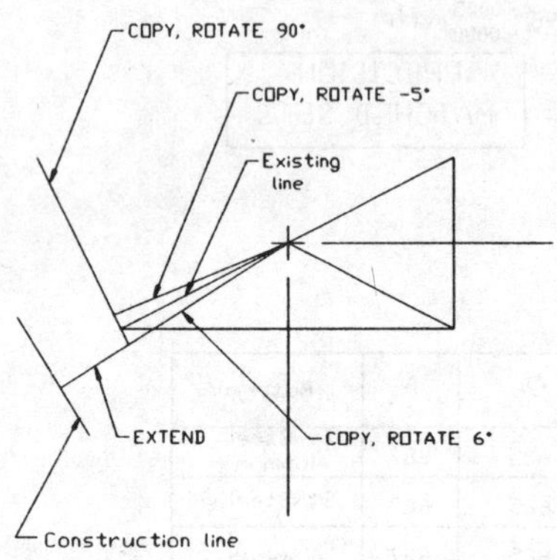

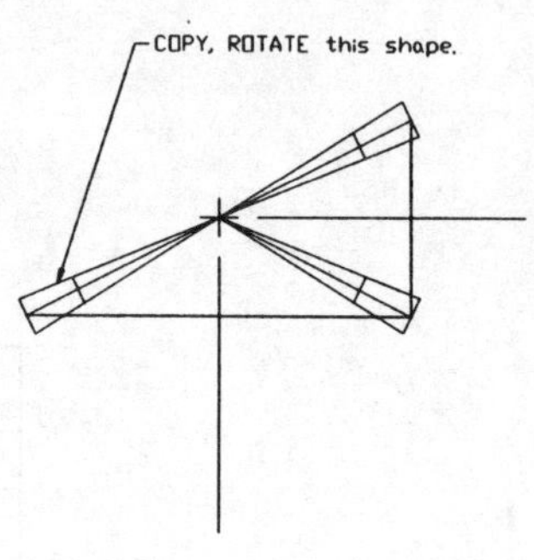

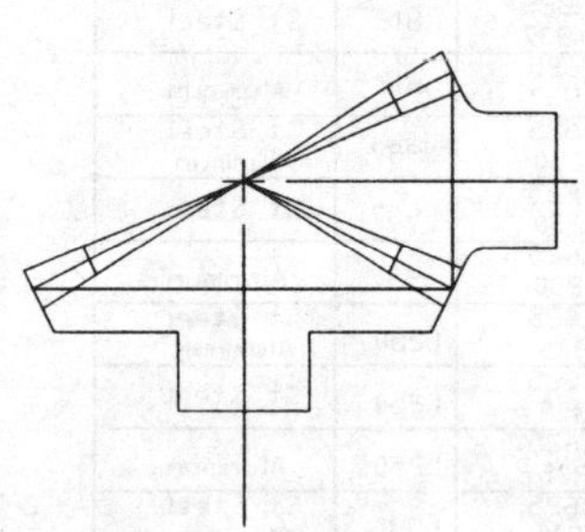

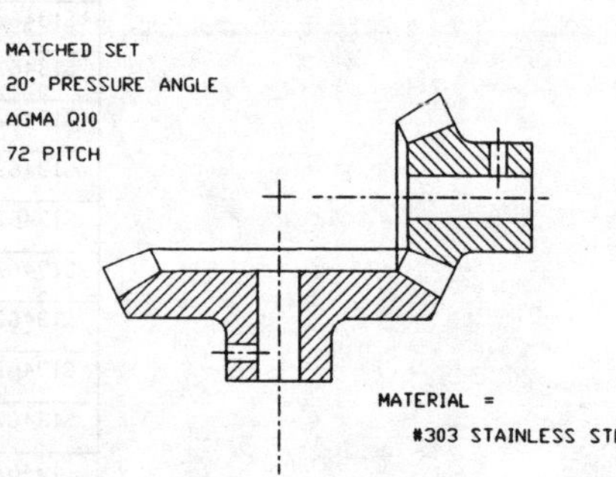

These lines are called the *face angle lines*. The ends of beveled gears are drawn perpendicular to the face angle lines. Gear manufacturers do not always include the outside diameter values with matching sets of gears. The values are sometimes listed, with data for the individual gears elsewhere in the catalog. If the outside diameter values are not given, they can be conservatively estimated by drawing the addendum angle approximately –5.0° from the face angle and the dedendum 6.0° from the face angle.

The perpendicular end lines may be constructed by use of the **Copy** and **Rotate** commands. Copy the existing face angle line directly over the existing line, and rotate the line 90° from the face angle line.

Use the **Extend** command to extend the rotated lines as needed. Add a construction line to help define an intersection between the dedendum ray line and the face line perpendicular to the face angle line. Trim and erase any excess lines.

3 Use the **Copy** and **Rotate** commands to copy the face shape and rotate it into the two other positions shown.

4 Use the given dimensions to complete the profiles. Erase and trim lines as necessary.

5 Draw the bore holes and holes for the setscrews according to the manufacturer's specifications.

6 Use the **Hatch** command to draw the appropriate hatch lines.

The two gears should have hatch patterns at different angles. In this example, the hatch pattern on the pinion is at 90° to the pattern on the gear.

13-14 Worm Gears

A worm gear setup is created by using a cylindrical gear called a ***worm*** and a circular matching gear called a ***worm gear.*** See Figure 13-18. As with other types of gears, worm gears must have the same pitch and pressure angle in order to mesh correctly. Manufacturers list matching worms and worm gears together in their catalogs. Figure 13-20 shows a gear manufacturer's listing for a worm gear and the appropriate worms.

Figure 13-18

Worm gears are drawn according to the representation shown in Figure 13-20 or by using sectional views as shown in Figure 13-19. The worm teeth shown can be drawn by the procedure for acme threads explained in Chapter 11.

Figure 13-19

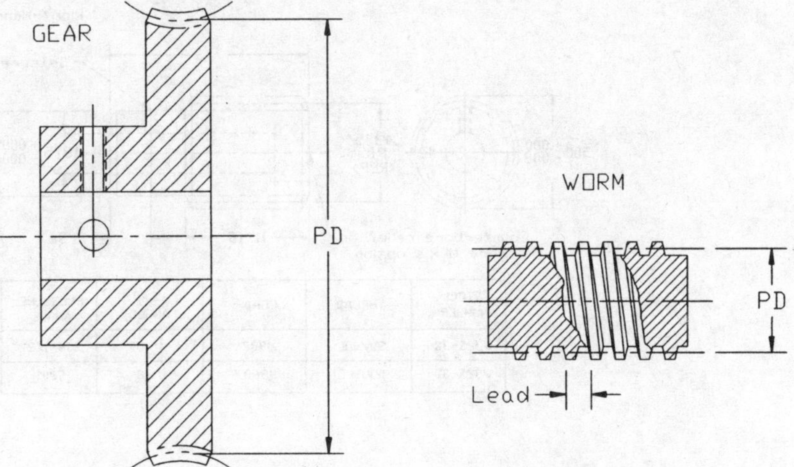

The relationship between worm gears is determined by the *lead* of the worm thread. The lead of a worm thread is similar to the pitch of a thread discussed in Chapter 11. Worm threads may be single, double, or quadruple. If a worm has a double thread, it will advance the gear twice as fast as a worm with a single thread.

Figure 13-20
Courtesy of W. M. Berg Inc.

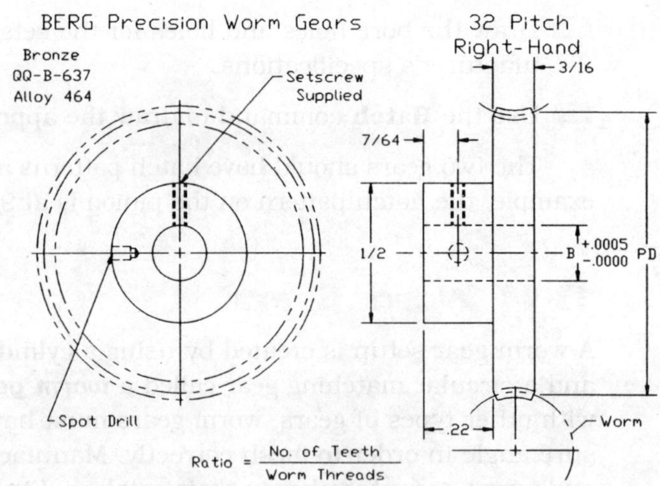

FOR SINGLE THREAD WORM CIRCULAR PITCH .0982 HELIX ANGLE 4° - 5' PRESSURE ANGLE 14-1/2°	FOR DOUBLE THREAD WORM CIRCULAR PITCH .1963 HELIX ANGLE 8° - 8' PRESSURE ANGLE 20°	NO. OF TEETH	PITCH DIA
STOCK NUMBER	STOCK NUMBER		
W32B29-S20	W32B29-D20	20	.625
W32B29-S30	W32B29-D30	30	.938
W32B29-S40	W32B29-D40	40	1.250
W32B29-S50	W32B29-D50	50	1.562
W32B29-S60	W32B29-D60	60	1.875
W32B29-S80	W32B29-D80	80	2.500
W32B29-S96	W32B29-D96	96	3.000
W32B29-S100	W32B29-D100	100	3.125
W32B29-S120	W32B29-D120	120	3.750
W32B29-S180	W32B29-D180	180	5.625

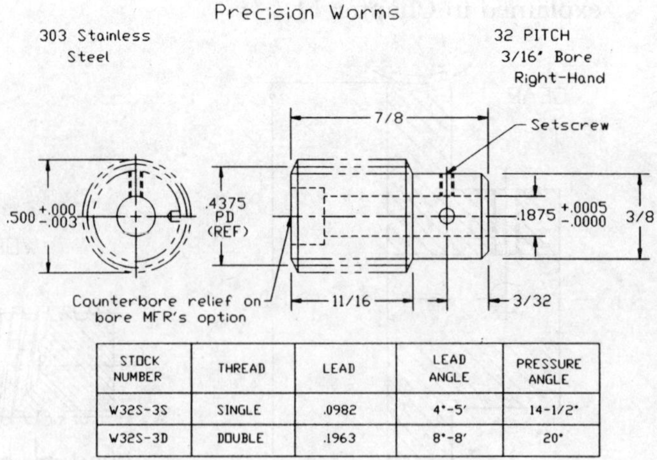

STOCK NUMBER	THREAD	LEAD	LEAD ANGLE	PRESSURE ANGLE
W32S-3S	SINGLE	.0982	4°-5'	14-1/2°
W32S-3D	DOUBLE	.1963	8°-8'	20°

13-15 Helical Gears

Helical gears are drawn as shown in Figure 13-21. The two gears are called the ***driver*** and the ***driven,*** as indicated. Figure 13-22 shows a manufacturer's listing of compatible helical gears.

Figure 13-21
Courtesy of Stock Drive Products.

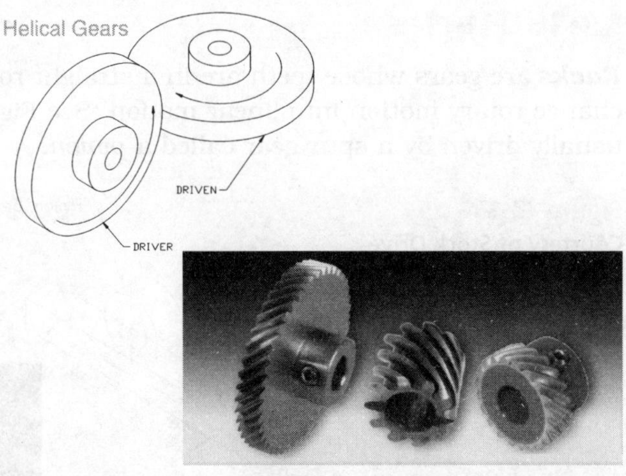

Figure 13-22
Courtesy of W. M. Berg Inc.

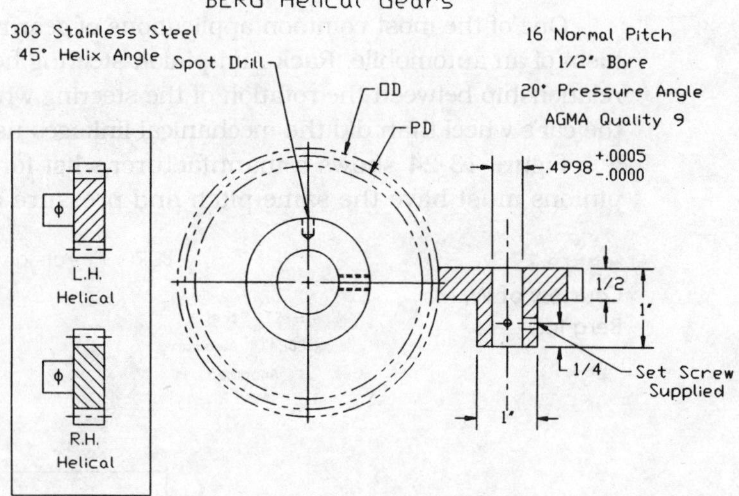

STOCK NUMBER				
RIGHT-HAND	LEFT-HAND	NO. OF TEETH	PITCH DIAMETER	OUTSIDE DIAMETER
H16S38-R12	H16S38-L12	12	1.060	1.185
H16S38-R16	H16S38-L16	16	1.4142	1.539
H16S38-R20	H16S38-L20	20	1.7677	1.892
H16S38-R24	H16S38-L24	24	2.1213	2.246
H16S38-R32	H16S38-L32	32	2.8284	2.953
H16S38-R40	H16S38-L40	40	3.5355	3.660
H16S38-R48	H16S38-L48	48	4.2426	4.367

Helical gears may be manufactured with either left- or right-hand threads. Left- and right-hand threads are used to determine the relative rotation direction of the gears.

13-16 Racks

Racks are gears whose teeth are in a straight row. Racks are used to change rotary motion into linear motion. See Figure 13-23. Racks are usually driven by a spur gear called a *pinion*.

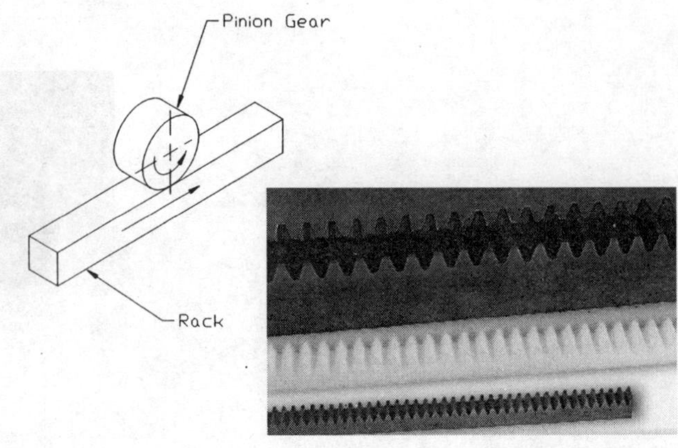

Figure 13-23
Courtesy of Stock Drive Products.

One of the most common applications of gear racks is the steering mechanism of an automobile. Rack-and-pinion steering helps create a more positive relationship between the rotation of the steering wheel and the linear input to the car's wheel than did the mechanical linkages used on older-model cars.

Figure 13-24 shows a manufacturer's list for racks. The rack and pinions must have the same pitch and pressure angle to mesh correctly.

Figure 13-24
Courtesy of W. M. Berg Inc.

BERG Precision Racks

416 ST. Steel &
2024T4 Aluminum
Anodized

24 to 120 Pitch
20° Pressure Angle
AGMA Quality 10

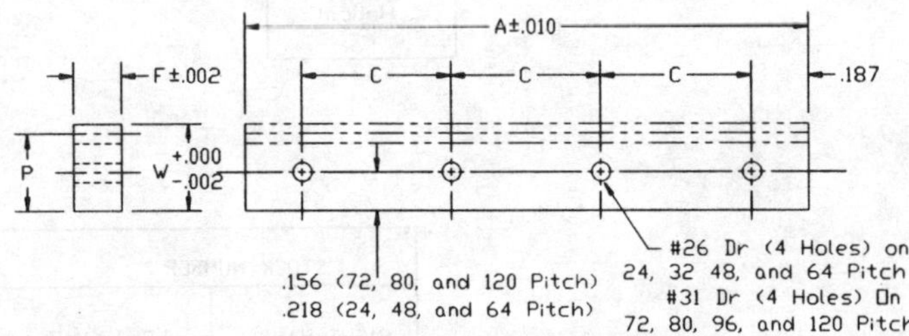

STOCK NUMBER	MATERIAL	PITCH	A	P	W	F	C
R4-5 R4-6	STAINLESS ST ALUMINUM	24	10"	.4383	.480	.230	3.208
R4-9 R4-10	STAINLESS ST ALUMINUM	32	10"	.4487	.480	.230	3.208
R4-11 R4-12	STAINLESS ST ALUMINUM	48	9"	.4592	.480	.230	2.879
R4-15 R4-16	STAINLESS ST ALUMINUM	64	7"	.4644	.480	.230	2.208
R4-17 R4-18	STAINLESS ST ALUMINUM	72	5"	.3411	.355	.167	1.541
R4-19 R4-20	STAINLESS ST ALUMINUM	80	5"	.3425	.355	.167	1.541
R4-21 R4-22	STAINLESS ST ALUMINUM	96	3"	.3446	.355	.167	.875
R4-23 R4-24	STAINLESS ST ALUMINUM	120	3"	.3467	.355	.167	.875

13-17 Ball Bearings

Ball bearings are used to help eliminate friction between moving and stationary parts. The moving and stationary parts are separated by a series of balls that ride in a *race*.

Figure 13-25 shows a listing for ball bearings that includes applicable dimensions and tolerances, which is from the Stock Drive Products website. There are many other types and sizes of ball bearings available.

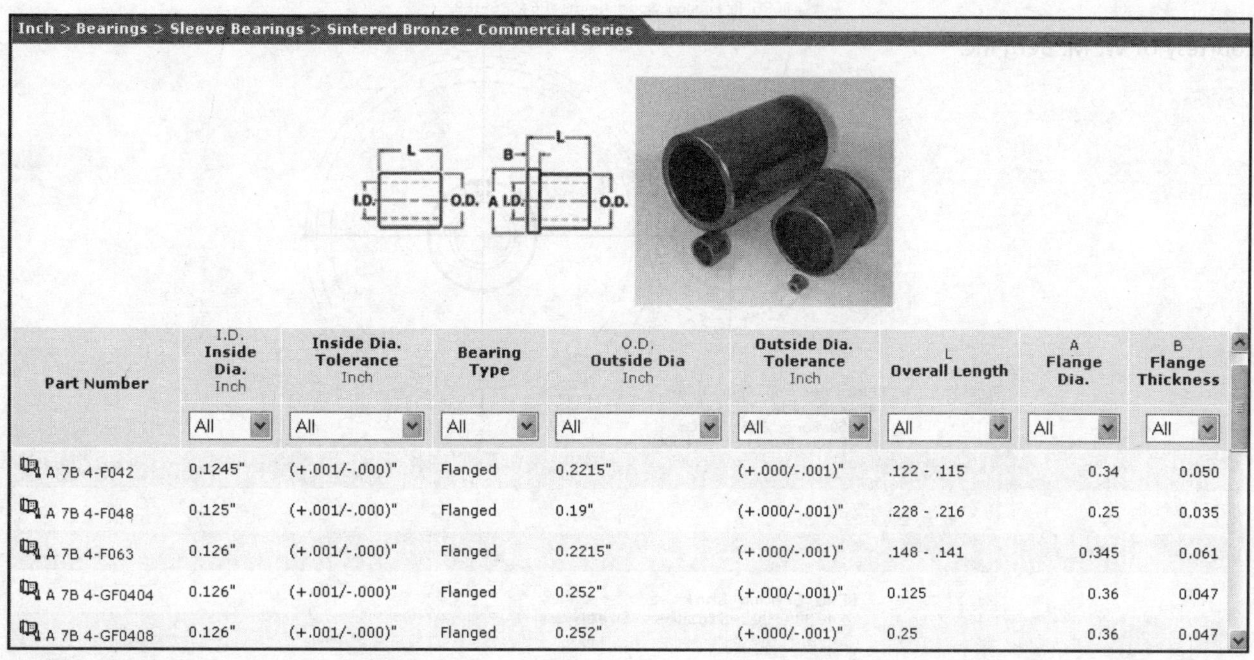

Inch > Bearings > Sleeve Bearings > Sintered Bronze - Commercial Series

Part Number	I.D. Inside Dia. Inch	Inside Dia. Tolerance Inch	Bearing Type	O.D. Outside Dia Inch	Outside Dia. Tolerance Inch	L Overall Length	A Flange Dia.	B Flange Thickness
	All	All	All	All	All	All	All	All
A 7B 4-F042	0.1245"	(+.001/-.000)"	Flanged	0.2215"	(+.000/-.001)"	.122 - .115	0.34	0.050
A 7B 4-F048	0.125"	(+.001/-.000)"	Flanged	0.19"	(+.000/-.001)"	.228 - .216	0.25	0.035
A 7B 4-F063	0.126"	(+.001/-.000)"	Flanged	0.2215"	(+.000/-.001)"	.148 - .141	0.345	0.061
A 7B 4-GF0404	0.126"	(+.001/-.000)"	Flanged	0.252"	(+.000/-.001)"	0.125	0.36	0.047
A 7B 4-GF0408	0.126"	(+.001/-.000)"	Flanged	0.252"	(+.000/-.001)"	0.25	0.36	0.047

Figure 13-25
Courtesy of Stock Drive Products.

Ball bearings may be drawn as shown in Figure 13-25 or by using one of the representations shown in Figure 13-26. It is recommended that the representations be drawn and saved as wblocks for use on future drawings.

Figure 13-26

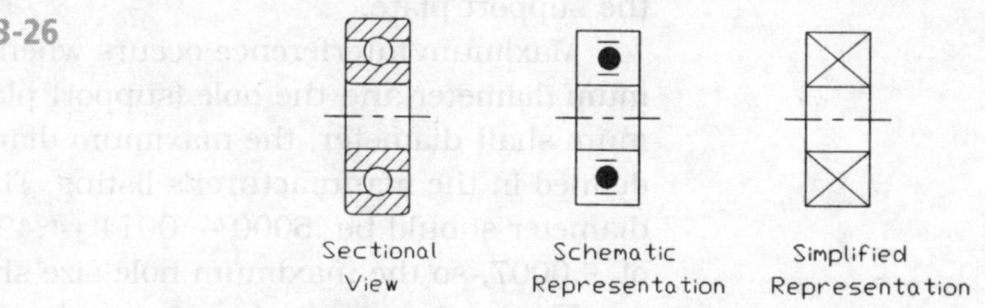

The outside diameter of the bearings listed in Figure 13-25 has a tolerance of +.0000/−.0002. The same tolerance range applies to the center hole. These tight tolerances are manufactured because this type of ball bearing is usually assembled by using a force fit. See Chapter 9 for an explanation of fits. Ball bearings are available that do not assemble by the use of force fits.

The following sample problem shows how ball bearings can be used to support the gear's shafts.

13-18 Sample Problem SP13-5

Figure 13-27 shows two spur gears and a dimensioned drawing of a shaft used to support both gears. Design a support plate for the shafts. Use ball bearings to support the shafts. Specify dimensions and tolerances for the support plate, and assume that the bearings are to be fitted into the support plate by the use of an LN2 medium press fit. The tolerance for the center distance between the gears is to be +.001, −.000.

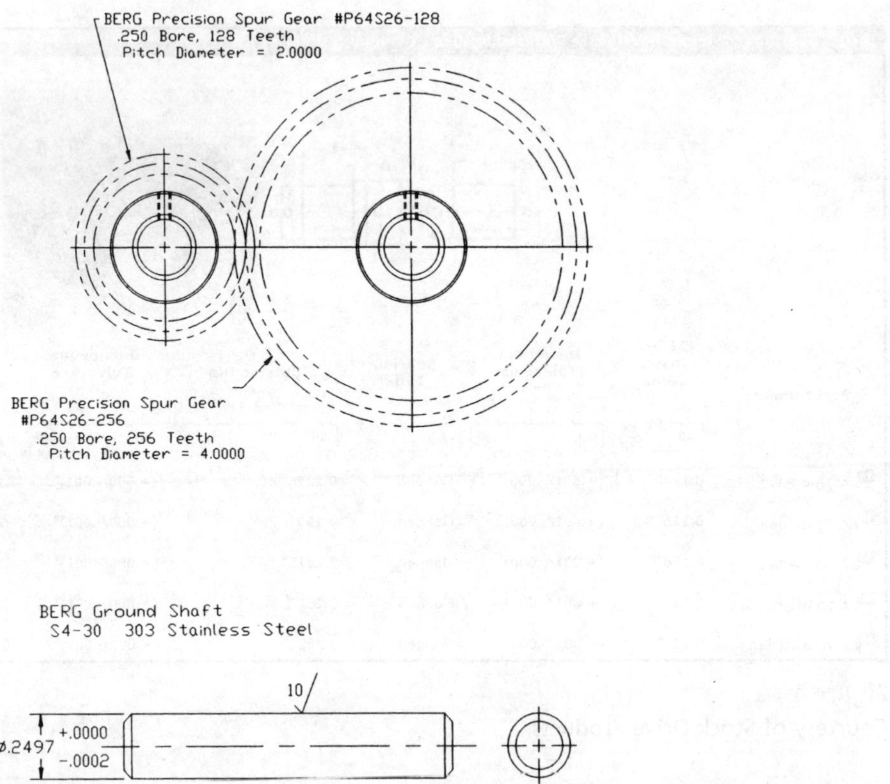

Figure 13-27
Courtesy of W. M. Berg Inc.

The maximum interference permitted for an LN2 medium press fit is .0011. See the fits tables in the appendix. For purposes of calculation, the bearing is considered to be the combination of the shaft and the holes in the support plate.

Maximum interference occurs when the shaft (bearing) is at its maximum diameter and the hole (support plate) is at its minimum. The maximum shaft diameter, the maximum diameter of the bearing, is .5000, as defined in the manufacturer's listing. This means that the minimum hole diameter should be .5000 − .0011 = .4989. An LN2 fit has a hole tolerance of +.0007, so the maximum hole size should be .4989 + .0007 = .4996.

The minimum interference, or the difference between the minimum shaft diameter and the maximum hole diameter, is .4998 − .4996 = .0002. There will always be at least .0002 interference between the ball bearing and the hole.

The bore of the selected bearing, listed in Figure 13-25, has a limit tolerance of .2500 − .2498. The shafts specified in Figure 13-27 have a limit tolerance of .2497 − .2495. This means that there will always be a slight clearance between the shaft and the bore hole.

The nominal center distance between the two gears is 3.000 inches. The given tolerance for the center distance is +.001, −.000. This tolerance can be ensured by assigning a positional tolerance of .0005 to each of the two holes applied at maximum material condition at the centerline. The base distance between the two holes is defined as 3.0000. The maximum center distance, including the positional tolerance, is 3.0000 + .0005 = 3.0005, and the minimum is 3.0000 – .0005 = 2.9995, or a total maximum tolerance of .001.

Figure 13-28 shows a detail drawing of the support plate.

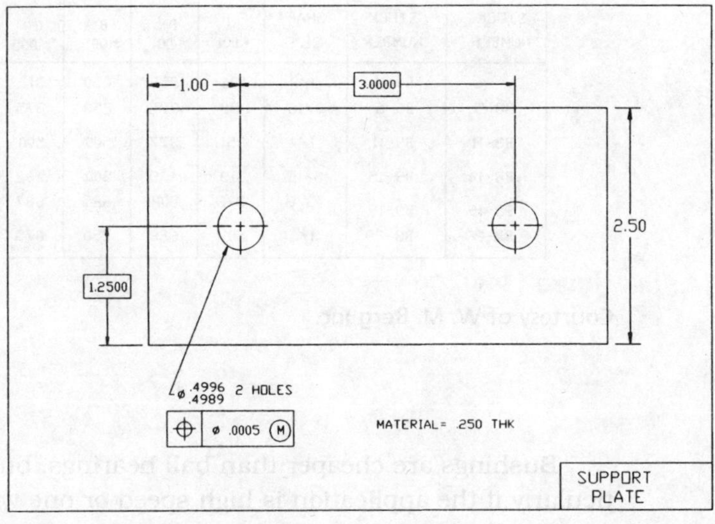

Figure 13-28

13-19 Bushings

A ***bushing*** is a cylindrically shaped bearing that helps reduce friction between a moving part and a stationary part. Bushings, unlike ball bearings, have no moving parts. Bushings are usually made from oil-impregnated bronze or Teflon. Figure 13-29 shows a manufacturer's list of bronze bushings, and Figure 13-30 shows a list for Teflon bushings.

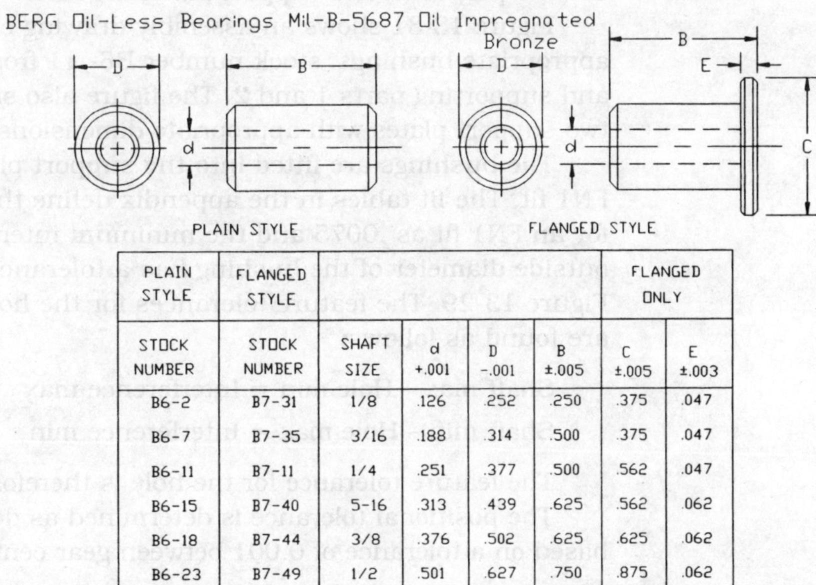

PLAIN STYLE STOCK NUMBER	FLANGED STYLE STOCK NUMBER	SHAFT SIZE	d +.001	D –.001	B ±.005	FLANGED ONLY C ±.005	FLANGED ONLY E ±.003
B6-2	B7-31	1/8	.126	.252	.250	.375	.047
B6-7	B7-35	3/16	.188	.314	.500	.375	.047
B6-11	B7-11	1/4	.251	.377	.500	.562	.047
B6-15	B7-40	5-16	.313	.439	.625	.562	.062
B6-18	B7-44	3/8	.376	.502	.625	.625	.062
B6-23	B7-49	1/2	.501	.627	.750	.875	.062

Figure 13-29
Courtesy of W. M. Berg Inc.

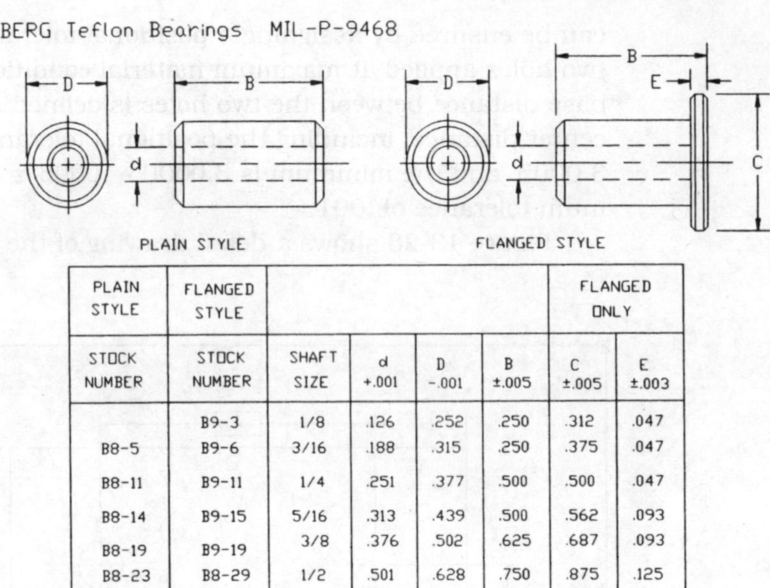

PLAIN STYLE	FLANGED STYLE					FLANGED ONLY	
STOCK NUMBER	STOCK NUMBER	SHAFT SIZE	d +.001	D -.001	B ±.005	C ±.005	E ±.003
	B9-3	1/8	.126	.252	.250	.312	.047
B8-5	B9-6	3/16	.188	.315	.250	.375	.047
B8-11	B9-11	1/4	.251	.377	.500	.500	.047
B8-14	B9-15	5/16	.313	.439	.500	.562	.093
B8-19	B9-19	3/8	.376	.502	.625	.687	.093
B8-23	B8-29	1/2	.501	.628	.750	.875	.125

Figure 13-30
Courtesy of W. M. Berg Inc.

Bushings are cheaper than ball bearings, but they wear over time, particularly if the application is high speed or one with heavy loading. Bushings are usually pressed into a supporting plate. Gear shafts must always have clearance from the inside diameters of bushings.

13-20 Sample Problem SP13-6

Figure 13-31 shows two support plates used to support and align a matched set of bevel gears. The gears selected are numbered S1346Z–48S30S60 in the Berg listings presented in Figure 13-16. The calculations are similar to those presented earlier for Sample Problem SP13-5, but with the addition of tolerances for the holes and machine screws used to join the two perpendicular support plates together.

Figure 13-31 shows an assembly drawing of the two gears along with appropriate bushings, stock number B6- 11 from Figure 13-29, and shafts and supporting parts 1 and 2. The figure also shows detail drawings of the two support plates with appropriate dimensions and tolerances.

The bushings are fitted into the support plates by the use of an FN1 fit. The fit tables in the appendix define the maximum interference for an FN1 fit as .0075 and the minimum interference as .0001. The outside diameter of the bushing has a tolerance of .3770 – .3760, per Figure 13-29. The feature tolerances for the holes in the support parts are found as follows:

Shaft max – Hole min = Interference max

Shaft min – Hole max = Interference min

The feature tolerance for the hole is therefore .3750 – .3695.

The positional tolerance is determined as described in SP13-5 and is based on a tolerance of 0.001 between gear centers.

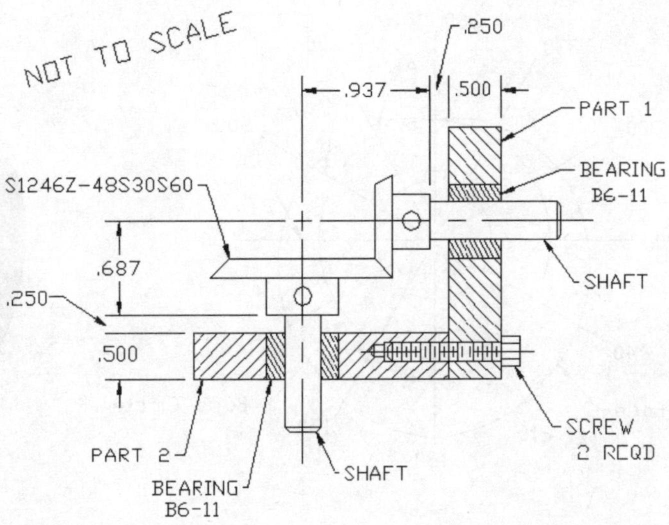

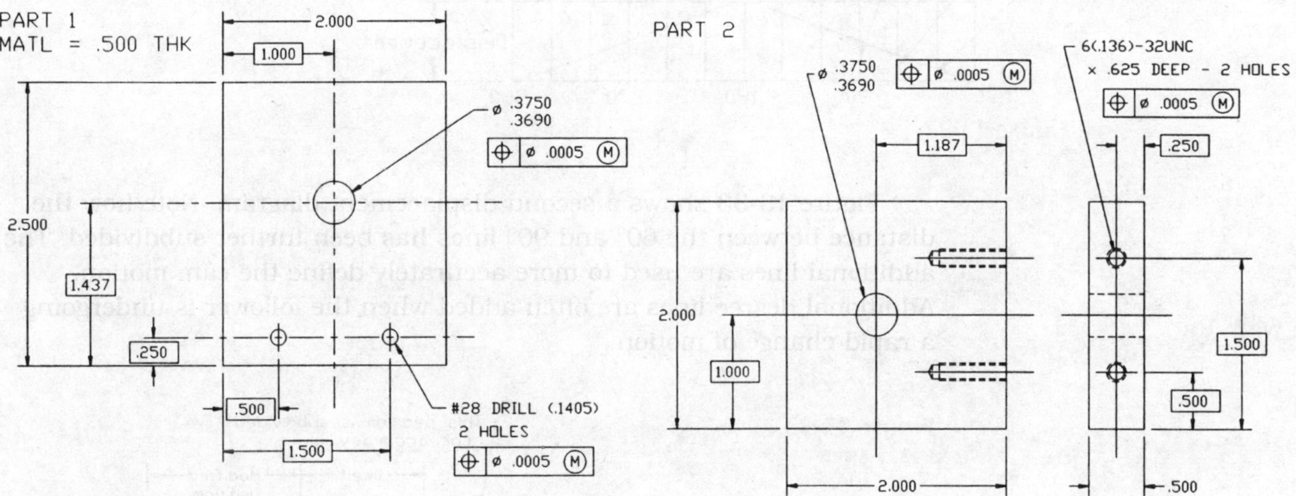

Figure 13-31

13-21 Cam Displacement Diagrams

A ***displacement diagram*** is used to define the motion of a cam follower. Displacement diagrams are set up as shown in Figure 13-32. The horizontal axis is marked off in 12 equal spaces that represent 30° on the cam. The vertical axis is used to define the linear displacement of the follower and is defined either in inches or in millimeters.

The vertical axis of a displacement diagram must be drawn to scale because, once defined, the vertical distances are transferred to the cam's base circle to define the cam's shape. Figure 13-32 shows distances A, B, and C on both the displacement diagram and cam. The distances define the follower displacement at the 30°, 60°, and 90° marks, respectively.

The horizontal axis may use any equal spacing to indicate the angle because the vertical distances will be transferred to the cam along ray lines. The lower horizontal line represents the circumference of the base circle.

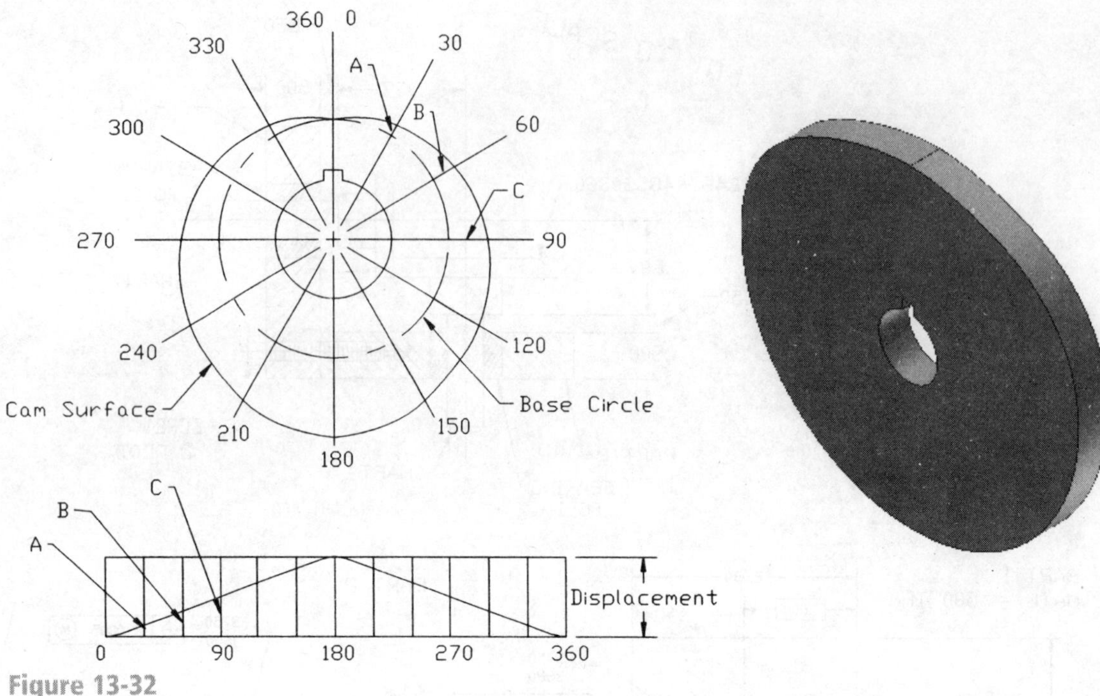

Figure 13-32

Figure 13-33 shows a second displacement diagram. Note how the distance between the 60° and 90° lines has been further subdivided. The additional lines are used to more accurately define the cam motion. Additional degree lines are often added when the follower is undergoing a rapid change of motion.

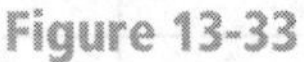

Figure 13-33

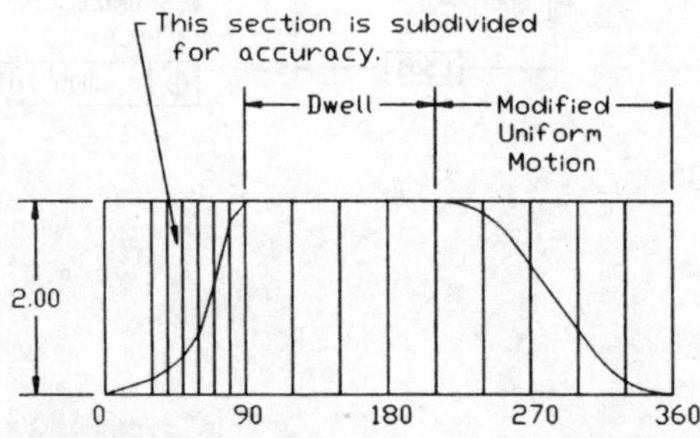

The term *dwell* means that the cam follower does not move either up or down as the cam turns. Dwells are drawn as straight horizontal lines on a displacement diagram. Note the horizontal line between the 90° and 210° lines on the displacement diagram shown in Figure 13-33. Dwells are drawn as sectors of constant radius on the cam.

To Set Up a Displacement Diagram

See Figure 13-34. The given dimensions are in inches. The values in the brackets, [ ], are in millimeters.

1. Set **Grid = .5 [10]**
   Snap = .25 [5]
2. Draw a horizontal line **6 [120]** long.
3. Draw a vertical line **2 [40]** from the left end of the horizontal line as shown.

Figure 13-34

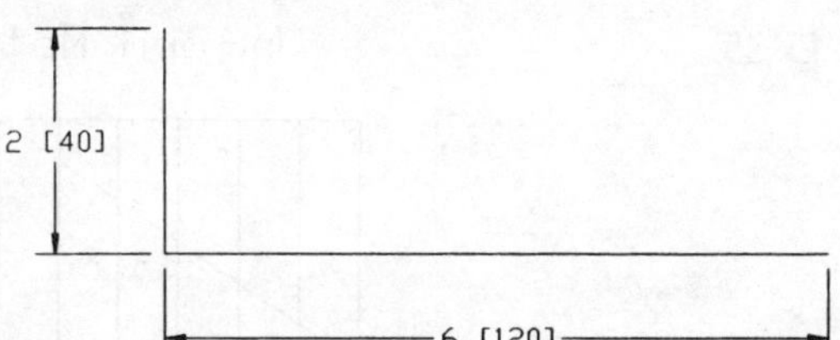

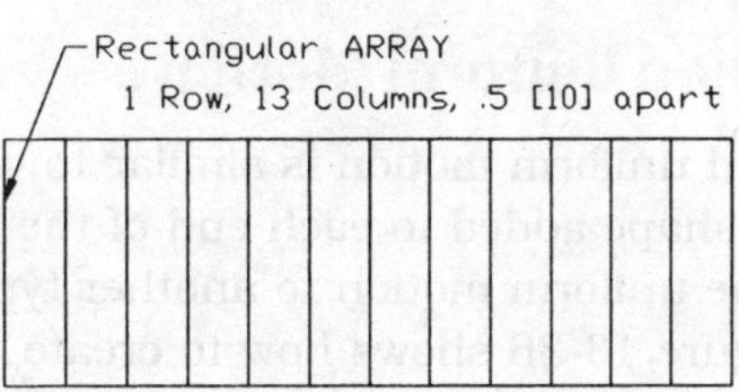

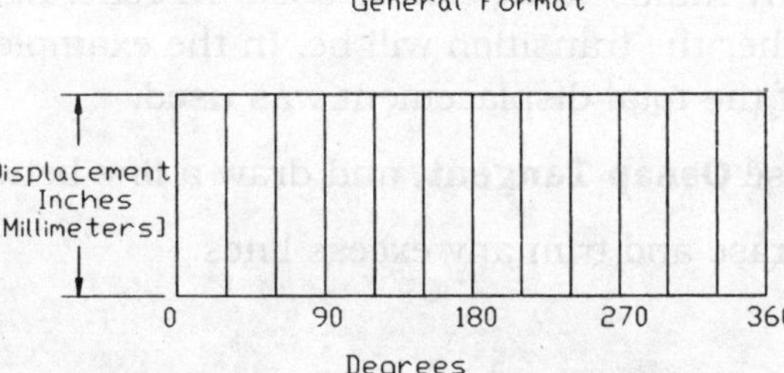

The length 2 [40] was chosen arbitrarily for this example. The vertical distance should be equal to the total displacement of the follower.

4 Use the **Array** command to create a rectangular array with **12** columns **.5 [10]** apart. Draw a horizontal line across the top of the diagram.

5 Label the horizontal axis in degrees, with each vertical line representing **30**°, and the vertical axis in inches [millimeters] of displacement.

13-22 Cam Motions

The shape of a cam surface is designed to move a follower through a specific distance. The surface also determines the acceleration, deceleration, and smoothness of motion of the follower. It is important that a cam surface be shaped to maintain continuous contact with the follower. Several standard cam motions are defined next.

Uniform Motion

Uniform motion is drawn as a straight line on a displacement diagram. See Figure 13-35. The follower rises the same distance for each degree of rotation by the cam.

Figure 13-35

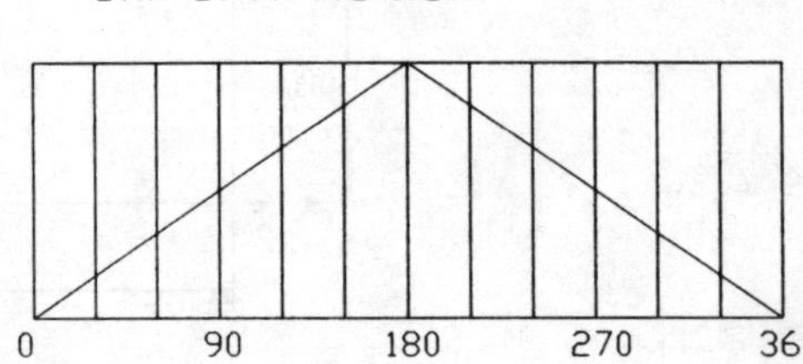

Modified Uniform Motion

Modified uniform motion is similar to uniform motion, but has a curved radius shape added to each end of the line to facilitate a smooth transition from the uniform motion to another type of motion or to a dwell section.

Figure 13-36 shows how to create a modified uniform motion on a displacement diagram. The procedure is as follows:

1. Set up a displacement diagram, as presented in the preceding section.
2. Draw two arcs or circles of radius no greater than half of the required displacement.

Any radius value can be used. In general, the larger the radius is, the smoother the transition will be. In the example shown, a radius equal to half of the total displacement was used.

3. Use **Osnap Tangent,** and draw a line between the two arcs.
4. Erase and trim any excess lines.

Figure 13-36

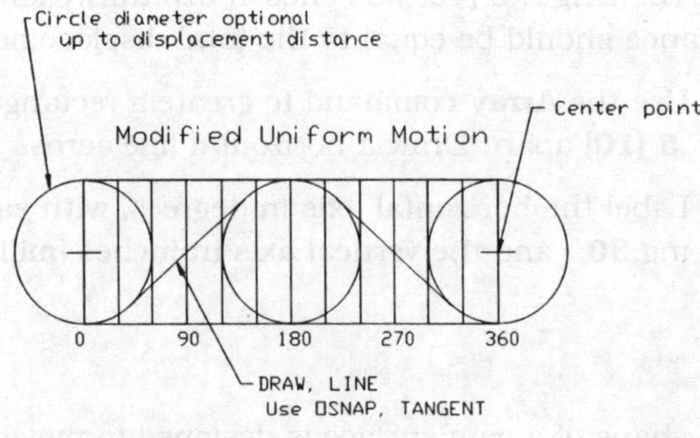

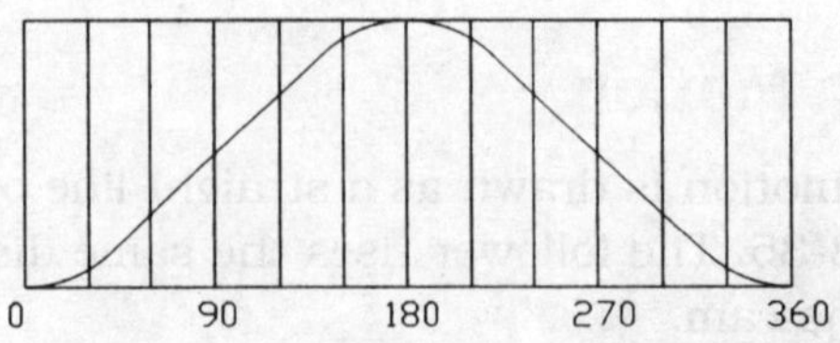

Harmonic Motion

Figure 13-37 shows how to create a harmonic cam motion. The procedure is as follows:

1. Set up a displacement diagram as presented in Section 13-21.
2. Draw a semicircle aligned with the left side of the displacement diagram. The diameter of the semicircle equals the total height of the displacement.

Figure 13-37

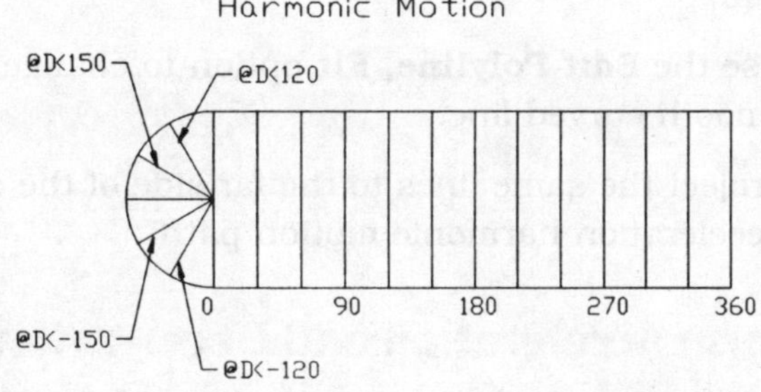

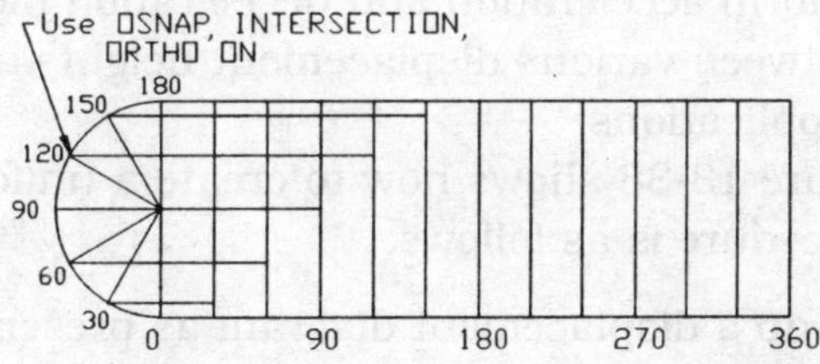

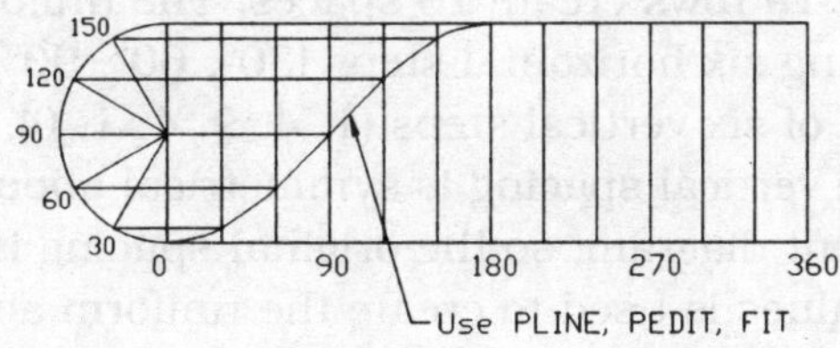

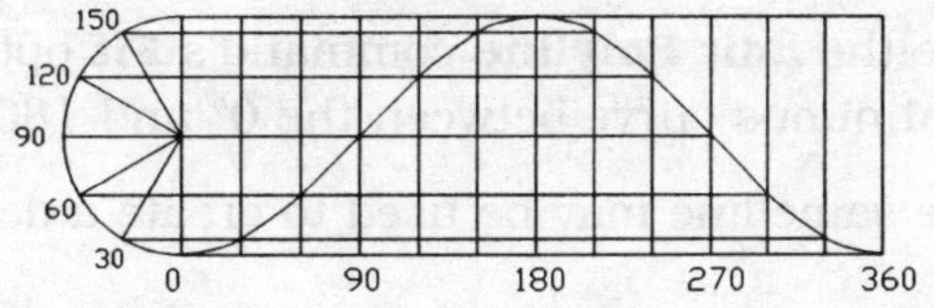

3. Use the **Array** command or the **Line** command with relative coordinate inputs, and draw rays every **30**° on the circle, as shown. Label the rays from 0° to 180° in 30° segments.

4. Use **Osnap Intersection** with **Ortho** on, **<F8>**, and draw projection lines from the intersections of the rays with the circumference of the circle across the displacement diagram.

5. Draw a polyline that starts at the lower left corner of the diagram and connects the intersections of like angle lines.

For this example, the horizontal line from the circle's 30° increment intersects with the vertical line from the 30° mark on the displacement diagram.

6. Use the **Edit Polyline, Fit** option to change the straight polyline into a smooth curved line.

7. Project the same lines to the far side of the diagram to define the deceleration harmonic motion path.

Uniform Acceleration and Deceleration

Uniform acceleration and deceleration are based on the knowledge that acceleration is related to distance by the square of the distance. Acceleration is measured in distance per second squared. Distances of units 1, 2, and 3 may be expressed as 1, 4, and 9, respectively.

Uniform acceleration and deceleration motions create smooth transitions between various displacement heights and are often used in high-speed applications.

Figure 13-38 shows how to create a uniform acceleration cam motion. The procedure is as follows:

1. Set up a displacement diagram as presented in Section 13-21.

2. Draw a horizontal construction line to the left, and align it with the bottom horizontal line of the displacement diagram.

3. Use the **Array** command, and create **1** column and **19** rows, **.1111** apart.

The 19 rows create 18 spaces. The uniform motion shape is created by combining six horizontal steps (30°, 60°, 90°, 120°, 150°, 180°) and the squares of six vertical steps (1, 4, 9, 4, 1, 0).

The vertical spacing is symmetrical about the centerline of the displacement diagram, so the original spacing is 1, 2, 3, 2, 1. The square of these values is used to create the uniform acceleration and deceleration.

The .1111 value was derived by dividing the displacement distance by the number of spaces, 2.00/18 = .1111.

4. Label the stack of vertical construction lines as shown.

5. Use the **Extend** command to extend the horizontal construction lines so that they intersect with the appropriate vertical degree line.

6. Use the **Edit Polyline** command's **Fit** option to create a smooth, continuous curve between the 0° and 180° lines.

The same line may be used to create a deceleration curve as shown.

Figure 13-38

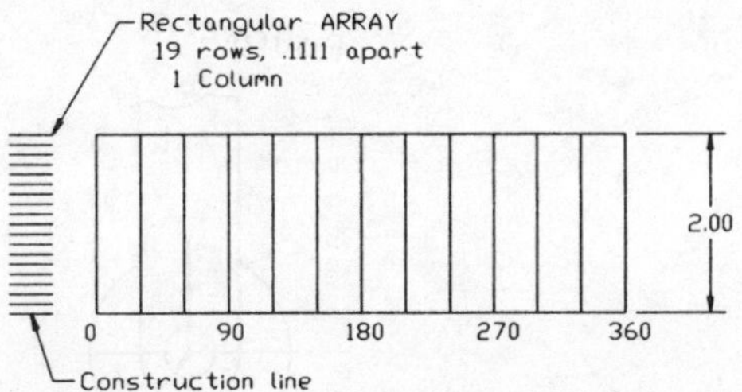

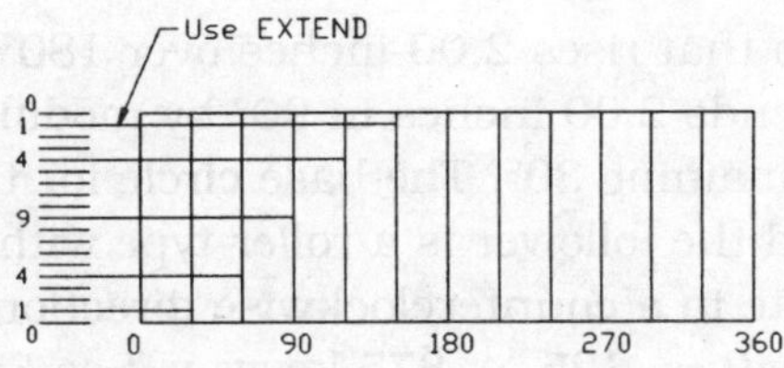

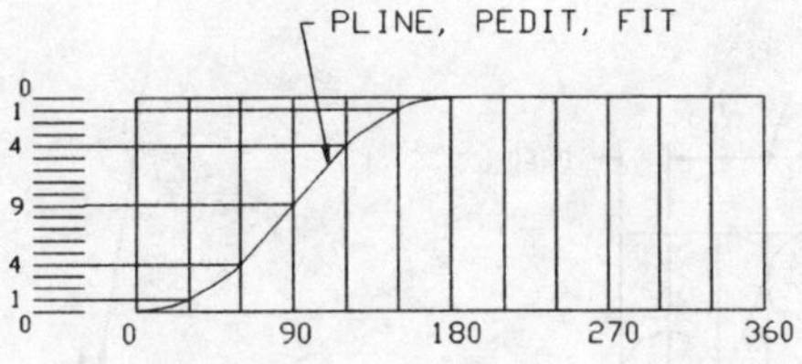

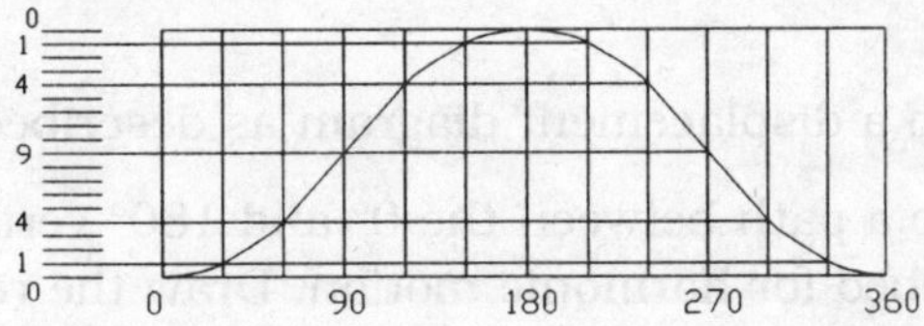

13-23 Cam Followers

There are two basic types of cam followers: those that roll as they follow the cam's surface, and those that have a fixed surface which slides in contact with the cam surface. Figure 13-39 shows an example of a roller follower and a fixed- or flat-surface follower. The flat-surface-type followers are limited to slow-moving cams with low force requirements.

Followers are usually spring loaded to keep them in contact with the cam surface during operation. Springs were discussed in Section 11-24.

Figure 13-39

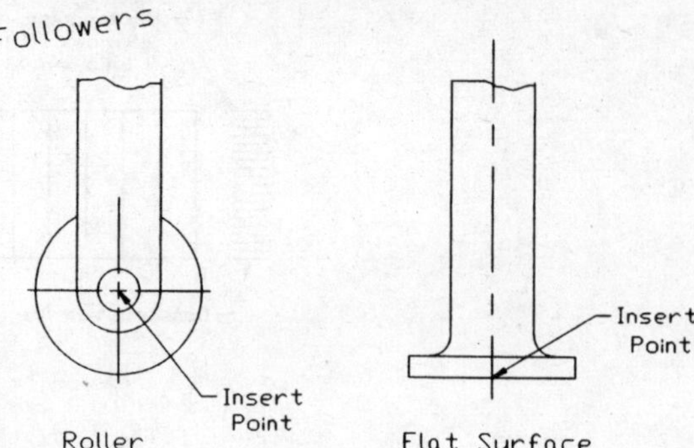

13-24 Sample Problem SP13-7

Design a cam that rises 2.00 inches over 180° by harmonic motion, dwells for 60°, descends 2.00 inches in 90° by modified uniform motion, and dwells the remaining 30°. The base circle for the cam is 3.00 inches in diameter, and the follower is a roller type with a 1.00-inch diameter. The cam will rotate in a counterclockwise direction. The center hole is .75 inch in diameter with a .125 × .875 keyway. See Figures 13-40 and 13-41.

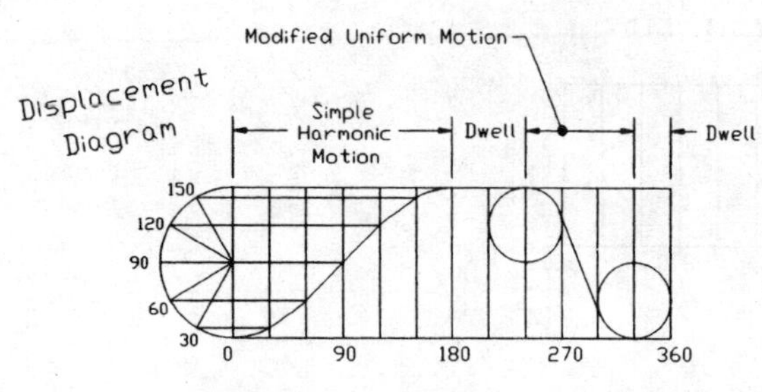

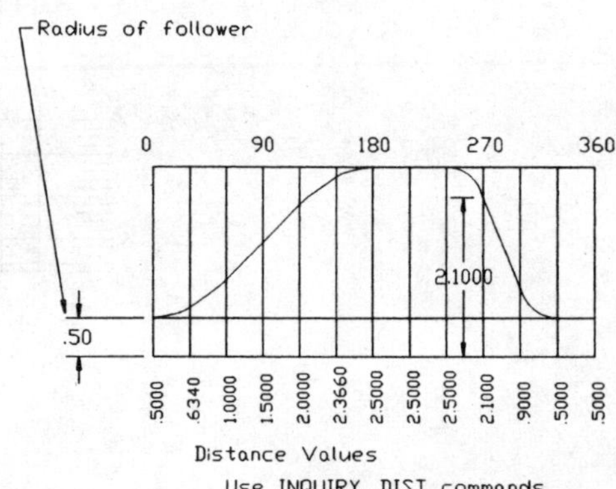

Figure 13-40

1. Set up a displacement diagram as described in Section 13-21.
2. Define a path between the 0° and 180° vertical lines, using the method described for harmonic motion. Draw the required circle on the left end of the diagram as shown.
3. Draw a horizontal line from the 180° to the 240° line.

   This line defines the follower's dwell.
4. Draw two arcs of **.50** radius, one tangent to the top horizontal line of the displacement diagram and the second tangent to the bottom line.

Draw one arc on the 240° line and the other on the 330° line as shown. In this example, the arcs have a radius equal to .25 of the total displacement. Any convenient radius value may be used.

5. Use the **Osnap Tangent** command, and draw a line tangent to the two arcs.
6. Erase and trim any excess lines and constructions.

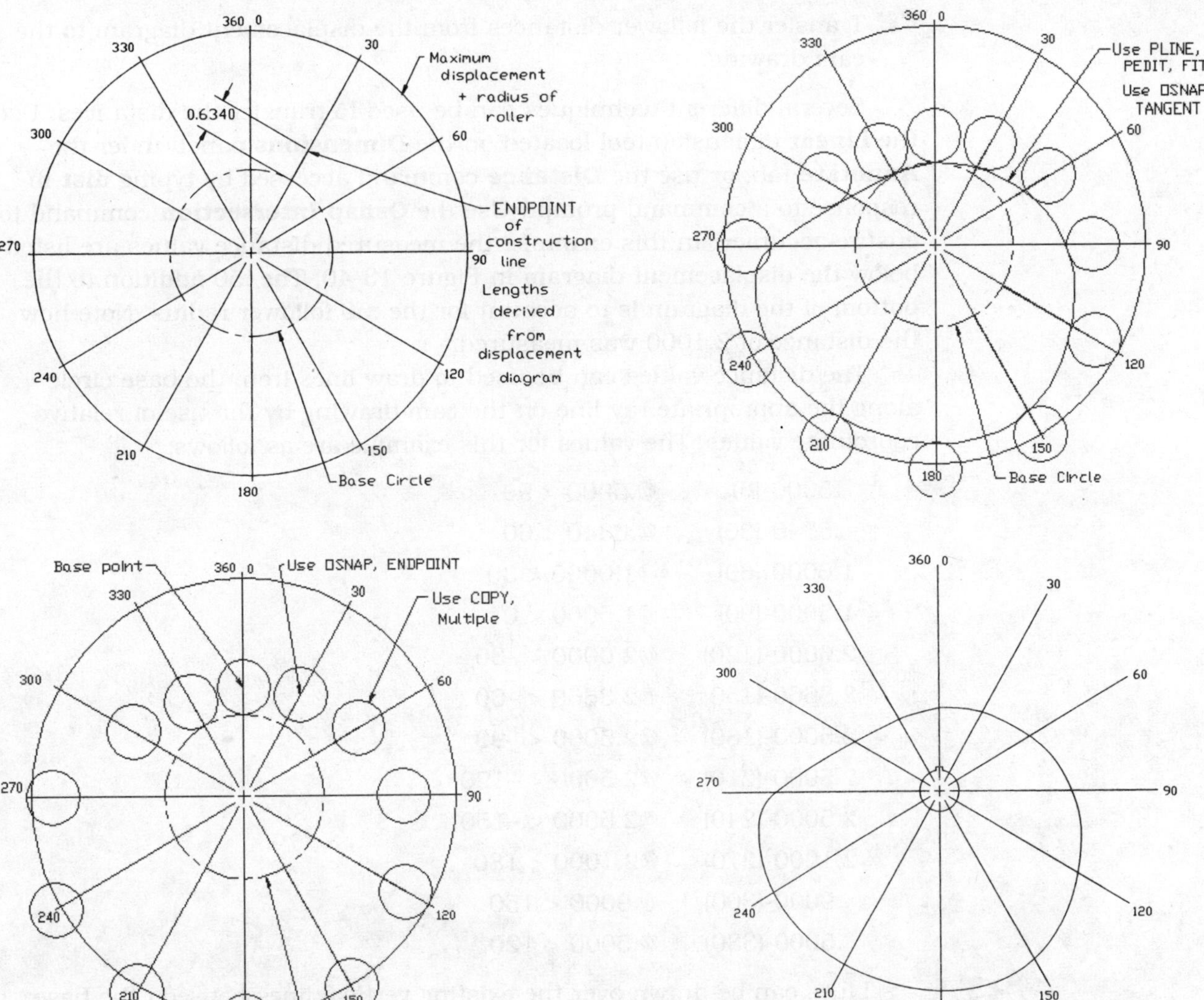

Figure 13-41

This completes the displacement diagram. The follower distances are now transferred to the cam's base circle to define the surface shape. See Figure 13-41.

7 Draw two concentric circles of **3.00** diameter and **8.00** diameter, respectively.

The 3.00 diameter is the base circle. The 8.00-diameter-circle value is derived from the radius of the base circle, plus the maximum displacement, plus the radius of the follower: 1.50 + 2 + .5 = 4.00 radius, or 8.00 diameter.

8 Use the **Setvar, Dimcen, -.2, Dim, Center** commands, or a modified **Center Mark** tool, to draw the centerlines for the 8.00 circle.

9 Use the **Array** command, and polar array the top portion of the vertical centerline **12** times around the full 360°.

10 Label the ray lines as shown.

Note that the top vertical ray line is labeled as both 0 and 360.

11 Transfer the follower distances from the displacement diagram to the cam drawing.

Several different techniques can be used to transfer the distances: Use the **Linear** dimension tool located on the **Dimensions** panel under the **Annotate** tab, or use the **Distance** command accessed by typing **dist** in response to a command prompt. Use the **Osnap Intersection** command to ensure accuracy. In this example, the measured distance values are listed below the displacement diagram in Figure 13-40. The .50 addition to the bottom of the diagram is to account for the .50 follower radius. Note how the distance of 2.1000 was measured.

The distance values can be used to draw lines from the base circle along the appropriate ray line on the cam drawing by the use of relative coordinate values. The values for this example are as follows:

.5000-(0)	@.5000 < 90
.6340-(30)	@.6340 < 60
1.0000-(60)	@1.0000 < 30
1.5000-(90)	@1.5000 < 0
2.0000-(120)	@2.0000 < –30
2.3660-(150)	@2.3660 < –60
2.5000-(180)	@2.5000 < –90
2.5000-(210)	@2.5000 < –120
2.5000-(240)	@2.5000 < –150
2.1000-(270)	@2.1000 < 180
.9000-(300)	@.9000 < 150
.5000-(330)	@.5000 < 120

Lines can be drawn over the existing vertical lines between the base line and the displacement path on the displacement diagram. The **Move, Rotate** or **Grips, Rotate** command can be used to transfer the lines to the base circle and appropriate ray line.

12 Draw circles of diameter **.50,** representing the roller follower, with their center points on the ends of the lines created in step 11.

Note that these lines and their endpoints are not visible on the screen, because they are drawn directly over the existing ray lines. The **Osnap Endpoint** command should be used to locate the circle's center point.

13 Use the **Draw, Polyline** command, and draw a line tangent to the follower at each ray line.

The tangent point for each ray may not be exactly on the ray line.

14 Use the **Edit Polyline, Spline** command to create the cam surface.

15 Draw the center hole and keyway according to the given dimensions.

16 Save the drawings, if desired.

13-25 EXERCISE PROBLEMS

EX13-1 Inches

Draw a spur gear with 24 teeth on a 4.00-pitch circle. The fillets at the base of each tooth have a radius of .0625. Locate a 1.00-diameter mounting hole in the center of the gear.

EX13-2 Millimeters

Draw a spur gear with 36 teeth on a 100-pitch circle. The fillets at the base of each tooth have a radius of 3. Locate a 20-diameter mounting hole in the center of the gear.

EX13-3

Use the information presented in Figure 13-12, and draw front and side sectional views of gear number A 1C22MYKW150 32A.

EX13-4

Use the information presented in Figure 13-12, and draw front and side sectional views of gear number A 1C22MYKW150 64A.

EX13-5

Use the information presented in Figure 13-15, and draw a sectional view of bevel gears A 1C3MYK 30018 and A 1C3MYK 30036H.

EX13-6

Use the information presented in Figure 13-15, and draw a sectional view of bevel gears A 1C3MYK 15018 and A 1C3MYK 15036.

EX13-7

Use the information presented in Figure 13-16, and draw a sectional view of the matched set of bevel gears S1346Z–48S30A120.

EX13-8

Use the information presented in Figure 13-20, and draw front and side views of a set of worm gears.

EX13-9

Use the information presented in Figure 13-22, and draw a front view of a matched set of helical gears.

EX13-10

Use the information presented in Figure 13-24, and draw a front view of a set of rack-and-pinion gears. Select a pinion gear from Figure 13-12.

EX13-11 Inches

Draw a displacement diagram and appropriate cam on the basis of the following information:

Dwell for 60°, rise 1.00 inch by harmonic motion over 180°, dwell for 30°, then descend 1.00 inch by harmonic motion over 90°.

The cam's base circle is 4.00 inches in diameter. Include a 1.25-inch center mounting hole.

EX13-12 Millimeters

Draw a displacement diagram and appropriate cam on the basis of the following information:

Dwell for 60°, rise 30 millimeters by harmonic motion over 180°, dwell for 30°, and then descend 30 millimeters by harmonic motion over 90°.

The cam's base circle is 120 millimeters in diameter. Include a 20-millimeter center mounting hole.

EX13-13 Inches

Draw a displacement diagram and appropriate cam on the basis of the following information:

Rise 1.25 inches over 180° by uniform acceleration motion, dwell for 60°, descend 1.25 inches over 90° by modified uniform motion, dwell for 30°.

The cam's base circle is 3.25 inches in diameter. Include a .75-inch-diameter center mounting hole.

EX13-14 Millimeters

Draw a displacement diagram and appropriate cam on the basis of the following information:

Rise 20 millimeters over 180° by uniform acceleration motion, dwell for 60°, descend 20 millimeters over 90° by modified uniform motion, dwell for 30°.

The cam's base circle is 80 millimeters in diameter. Include a 16-millimeter-diameter center mounting hole.

EX13-15 Inches

Draw a displacement diagram and appropriate cam on the basis of the following information:

Rise 0.60 inch in 90° by harmonic motion, dwell for 30°, rise .60 inch in 60° by modified uniform motion, dwell 60°, descend 1.20 inches by uniform deceleration in 120°.

The cam's base circle is 3.20 inches in diameter. Include a 1.75-inch-diameter center mounting hole.

EX13-16 Millimeters

Draw a displacement diagram and appropriate cam on the basis of the following information:

Rise 16 millimeters in 90° by harmonic motion, dwell for 30°, rise 16 millimeters in 60° by modified uniform motion, dwell 60°, descend 32 millimeters by uniform deceleration in 120°.

The cam's base circle is 84 millimeters in diameter. Include a 20-millimeter-diameter center mounting hole.

EX13-17 Inches

Draw a displacement diagram and appropriate cam on the basis of the following information: The cam's base circle is 2.00 inches. Include a Ø 0.625 center mounting hole. Rise 0.375 inch in 90° by harmonic motion, dwell for 90°, rise 0.375 inch in 90° by harmonic motion, descend 0.750 inch by harmonic motion in 90°.

EX13-18 Millimeters

Draw a displacement diagram and appropriate cam on the basis of the following information: The cam's base circle is 98 millimeters. Include a Ø 18 center mounting hole. Rise 15 millimeters in 90° by harmonic motion, dwell for 90°, rise 15 millimeters in 90° by harmonic motion, descend 30 millimeters by harmonic motion in 90°.

EX13-19 Inches

Draw a displacement diagram and appropriate cam on the basis of the following information: The cam's base circle is 2.00 inches. Include a Ø 0.625 center mounting hole. Rise 0.375 inch in 90° by uniform acceleration and deceleration motion, dwell for 90°, rise 0.375 inch in 90° by uniform acceleration and deceleration motion, descend 0.750 inch by harmonic motion in 90°.

EX13-20 Millimeters

Draw a displacement diagram and appropriate cam on the basis of the following information: The cam's base circle is 98 millimeters. Include a Ø 18 millimeter center mounting hole. Rise 15 millimeters in 90° by uniform acceleration and deceleration motion, dwell for 90°, rise 15 millimeters in 90° by uniform acceleration and deceleration motion, descend 30 millimeters by harmonic motion in 90°.

EX13-21 Inches

Draw an assembly drawing and parts list for the 2-gear assembly shown.

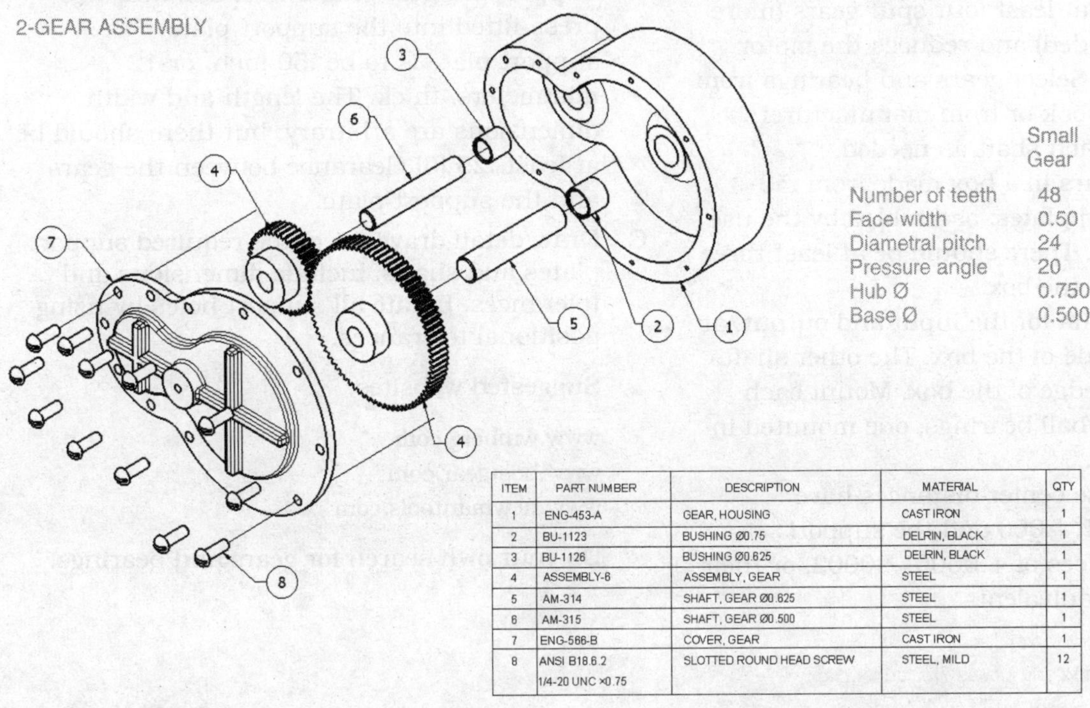

ITEM	PART NUMBER	DESCRIPTION	MATERIAL	QTY
1	ENG-453-A	GEAR, HOUSING	CAST IRON	1
2	BU-1123	BUSHING Ø0.75	DELRIN, BLACK	1
3	BU-1126	BUSHING Ø0.625	DELRIN, BLACK	1
4	ASSEMBLY-6	ASSEMBLY, GEAR	STEEL	1
5	AM-314	SHAFT, GEAR Ø0.625	STEEL	1
6	AM-315	SHAFT, GEAR Ø0.500	STEEL	1
7	ENG-566-B	COVER, GEAR	CAST IRON	1
8	ANSI B18.6.2 1/4-20 UNC ×0.75	SLOTTED ROUND HEAD SCREW	STEEL, MILD	12

	Small Gear	Large Gear
Number of teeth	48	96
Face width	0.50	0.50
Diametral pitch	24	24
Pressure angle	20	20
Hub Ø	0.750	1.00
Base Ø	0.500	0.625

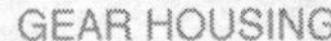

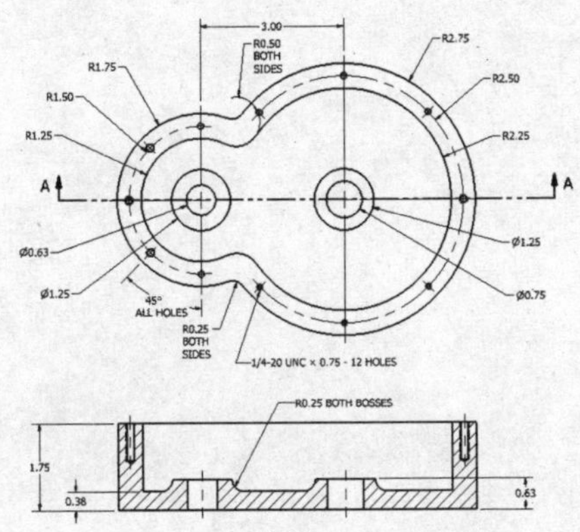

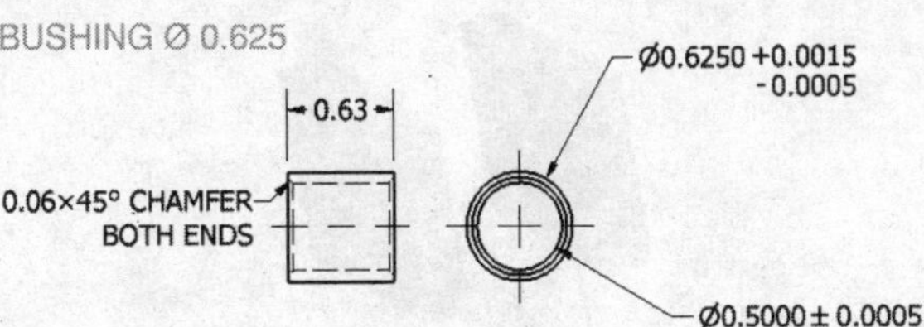

GEAR COVER

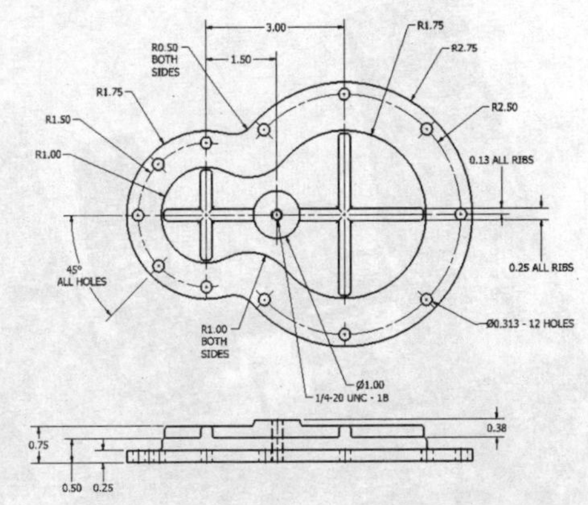

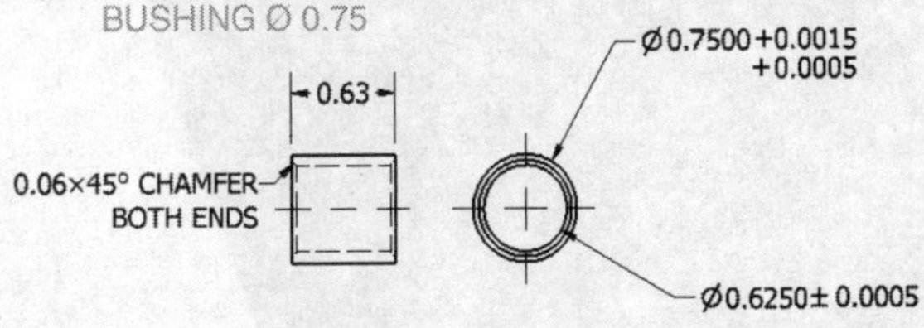

BUSHING Ø 0.625

BUSHING Ø 0.75

SHAFT, GEAR Ø 0.625

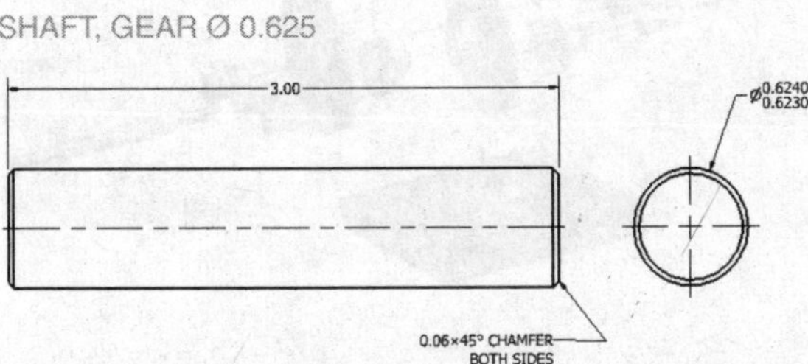

SHAFT, GEAR Ø 0.500

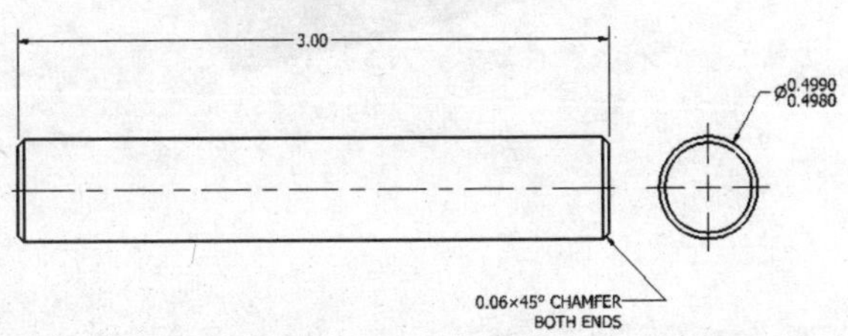

EX13-22

An electric motor operates at 3600 rpm. Design a gear that includes at least four spur gears (more may be used if needed) and reduces the motor speed to 200 rpm. Select gears and bearings from the tables in this book or from manufacturers' websites. Design each shaft as needed.

Enclose the gears in a box made from .50-inch [12-millimeter] plates, assembled by the use of flat head screws. There should be at least three screws per edge on the box.

Extend the shafts for the input and output, at least .50 [12] outside of the box. The other shafts should end at the edge of the box. Mount each shaft by using two ball bearings, one mounted in each support plate.

Assume that the center distances have tolerances of +.001, −.000 and the support shafts have tolerances of +.0000, −.0002, or their respective metric equivalents.

A. Draw an assembly drawing, showing the gears in their assembled positions.
B. Support the gear shafts with ball bearings press-fitted into the support plate. The support plate is to be .50 inch, or 12 millimeters, thick. The length and width dimensions are arbitrary, but there should be at least .25 [6] clearance between the gears and the support plate.
C. Draw detail drawings of the required support plates and shafts. Include dimensions and tolerances. Locate all support holes by using positional tolerances.

Suggested websites:

www.wmberg.com
www.bostgear.com
www.newmantools.com

Do your own search for gears and bearings.

Top and end pieces omitted for clarity

EX13-23

The accompanying figure shows a general setup for matched bevel gears. Complete the design for a gear box with a ratio of 3:1 between the two gears. Select appropriate bearings and fasteners. Dimension and tolerance the shaft sizes and each of the six supporting plates. Extend the input and output shafts by at least 1.00 inch [24 millimeters] beyond the surface of the box.

Assume that the center distances have tolerances of +.001, −.000 and the support shafts have tolerances of +.0000, −.0002, or their respective metric equivalents.

The figure shown represents half of the gear box. The other half includes another three plates without the holes for the shafts. There should be at least three screws in each edge of the box.

A. Draw an assembly drawing that shows the gears in their assembled positions.
B. Support the gear shafts with ball bearings press-fitted into the support plate. The support plate is to be .50 inch, or 12 millimeters, thick. The length and width dimensions are arbitrary, but there should be at least .375 [10] clearance between the gears and the support plates.
C. Draw detail drawings of the required support plates. Include dimensions and tolerances. Locate all support holes, using positional tolerances.

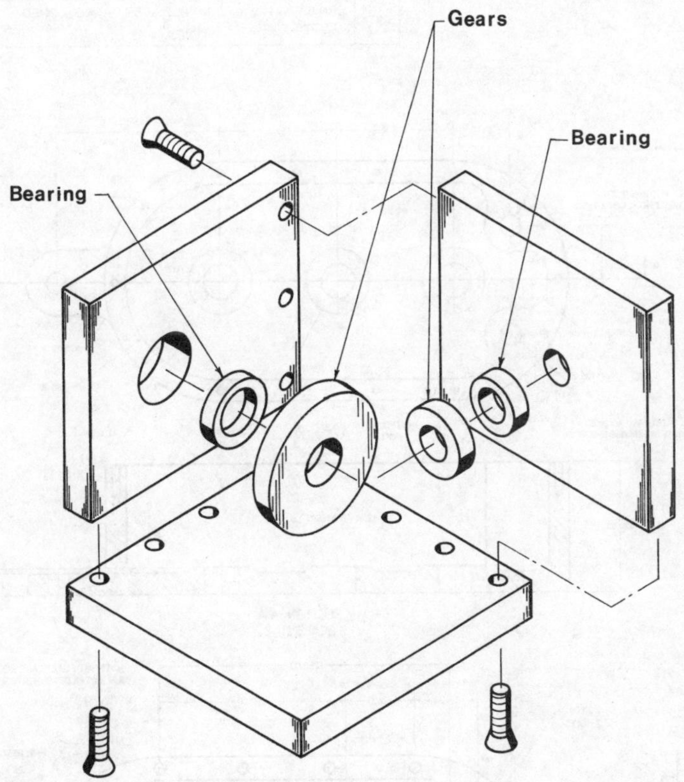

EX13-24 Millimeters

Draw an assembly drawing and parts list for the 4-gear assembly shown.

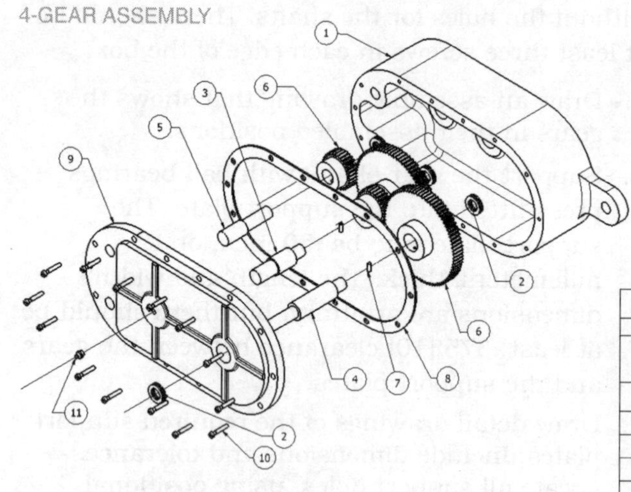

ITEM	PART NUMBER	DESCRIPTION	MATERIAL	QTY
1	ENG-311-1	HOUSING, 4 GEAR	CAST IRON	1
2	BS 5989; PART 1 010 - 20×32×8	BALL BEARING, THRUST	STEEL, MILD	4
3	SH-4002	SHAFT, NEUTRAL	STEEL	1
4	SH-4003	SHAFT, OUTPUT	STEEL	1
5	SH-4004A	SHAFT, INPUT	STEEL	1
6		ASSEMBLY, 4-GEAR	STEEL	2
7	CSN 02 1181 M6 × 16	SET SCREW, SLOTTED HEADLESS - FLAT POINT	STEEL, MILD	2
8	ENG-312-1	GASKET	BRASS, SOFT YELLOW	1
9	ENG-312-2	COVER	CAST IRON	1
10	CNS 4355-M6×35	SCREW, SLOTTED CHEESE HEAD	STEEL, MILD	14
11	CSN 02 7421- M10 x 1 coned short	NIPPLE, LUBRICATING, CONED TYPE A	STEEL, MILD	1

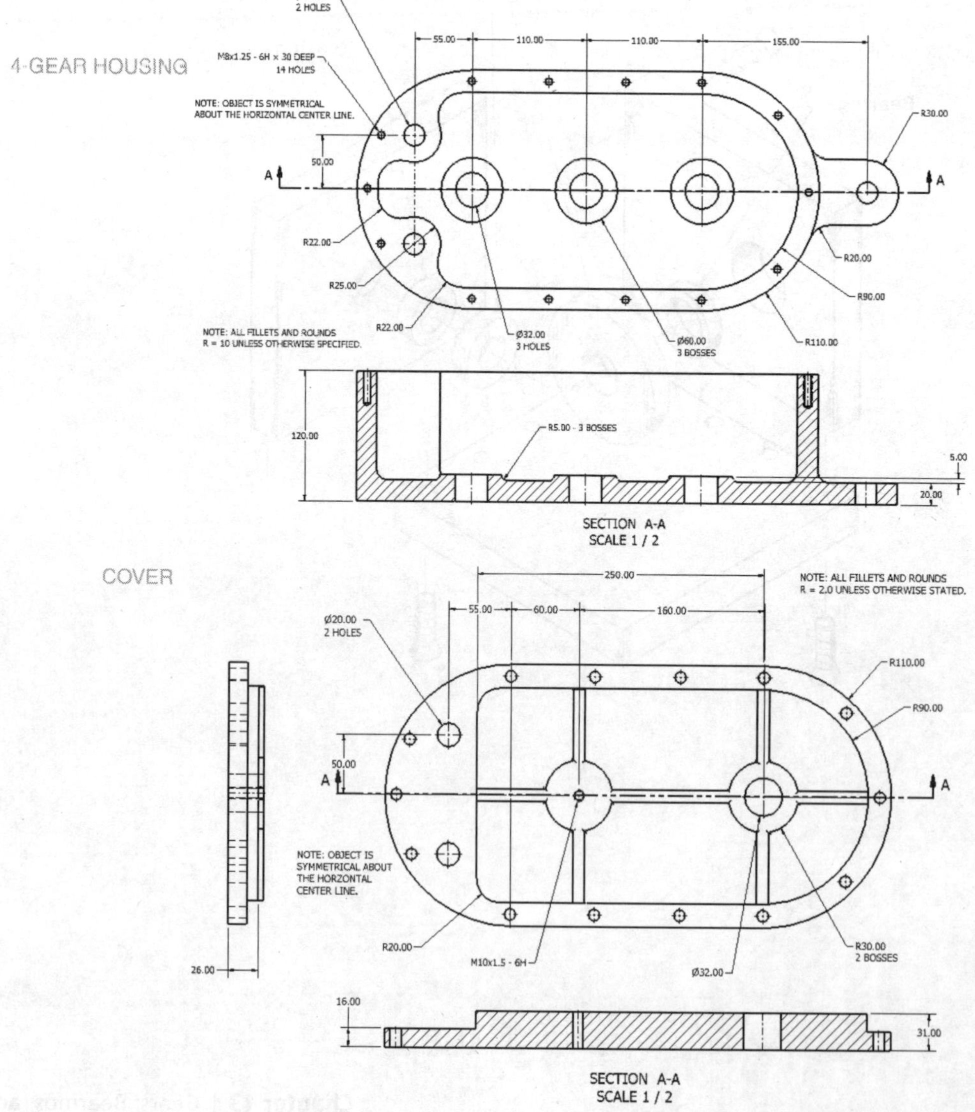

GASKET

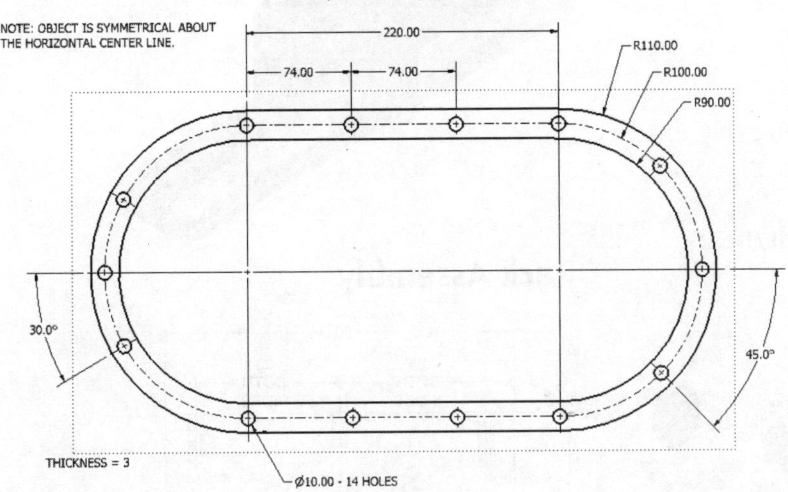

GEAR ASSEMBLY

Large Gear
Module = 2
Pitch Ø = 160
Number of teeth = 80

Small Gear
Module = 2
Pitch Ø = 60
Number of teeth = 30

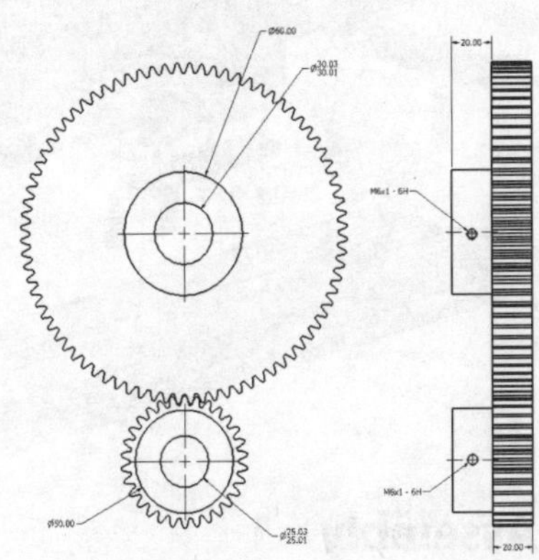

INPUT SHAFT

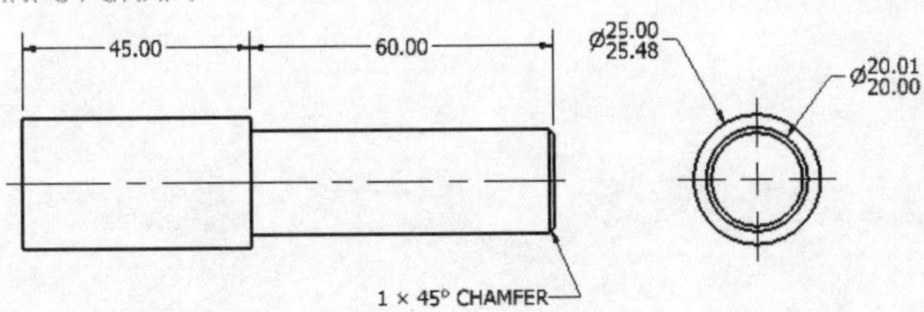

OUTPUT SHAFT

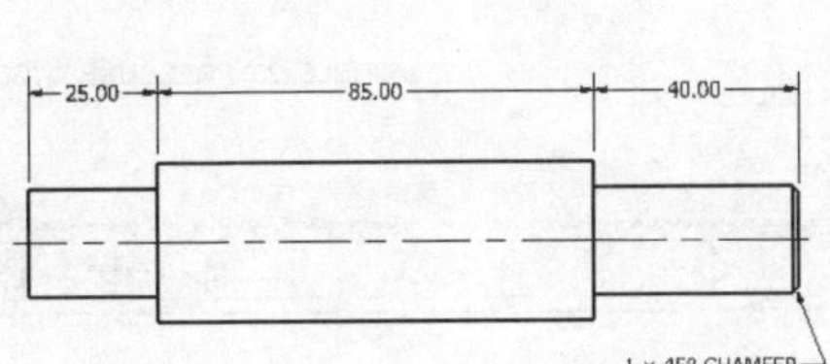

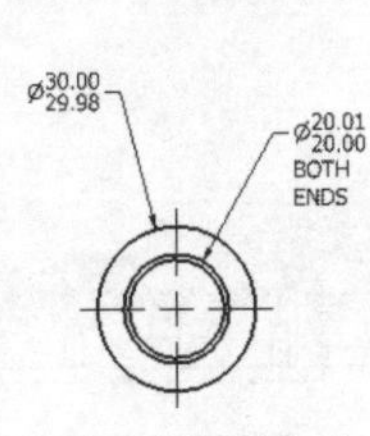

NEUTRAL SHAFT

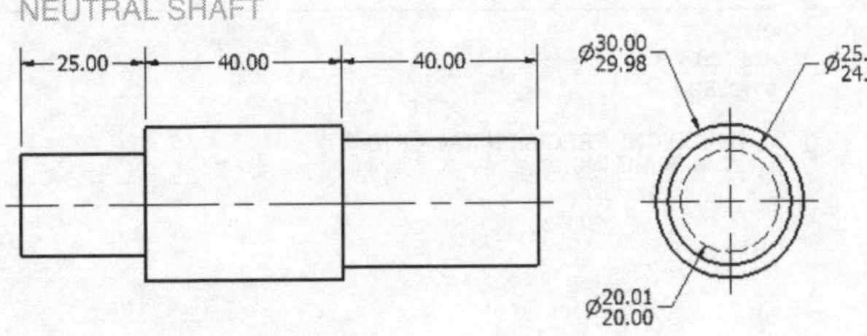

LUBRICATING NIPPLE

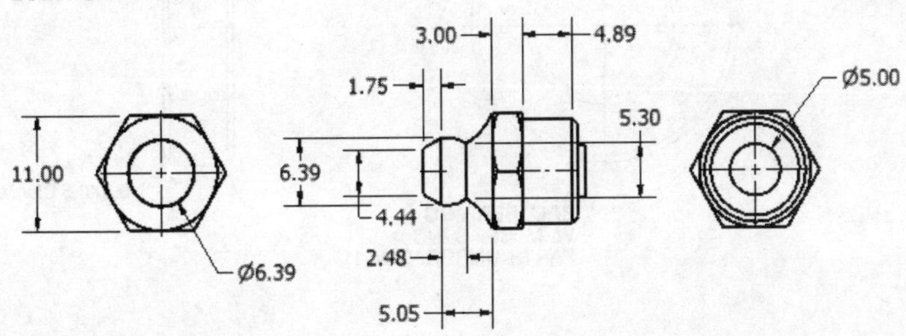

EX13-25

Perform the following functions for the slider assembly shown:

1. Select the appropriate fasteners.
2. Create an assembly drawing.
3. Create a parts list.
4. Specify the tolerance for the guide shaft/bearings interface.

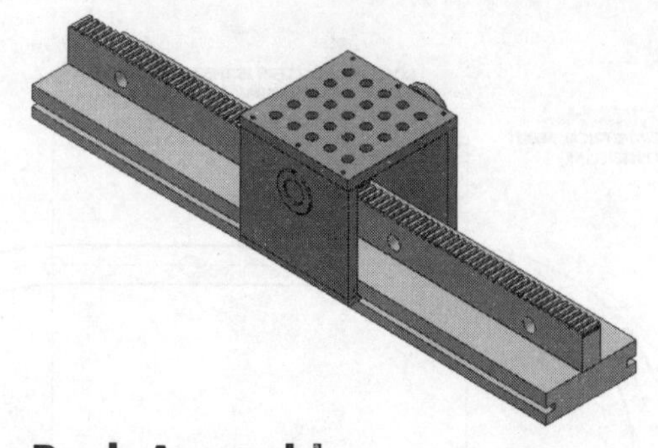

Rack Assembly

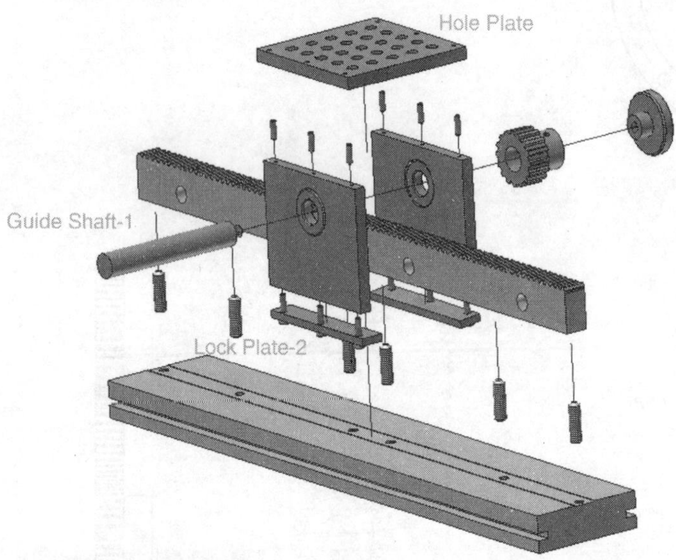

Rack Assembly - 1

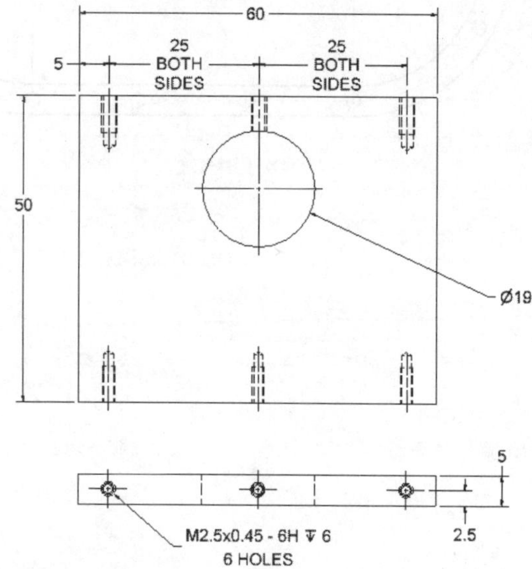

Side Plate

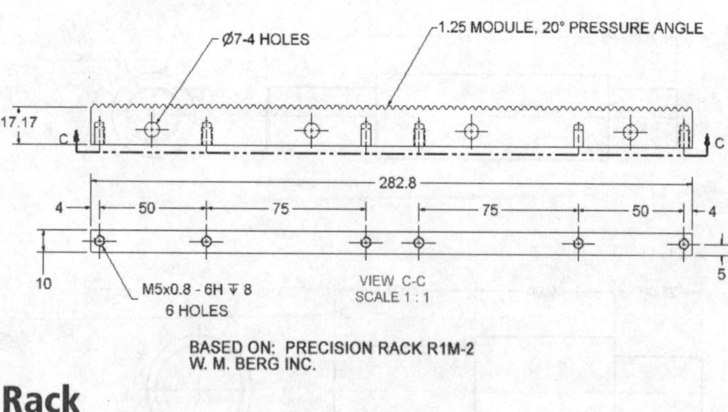

Rack

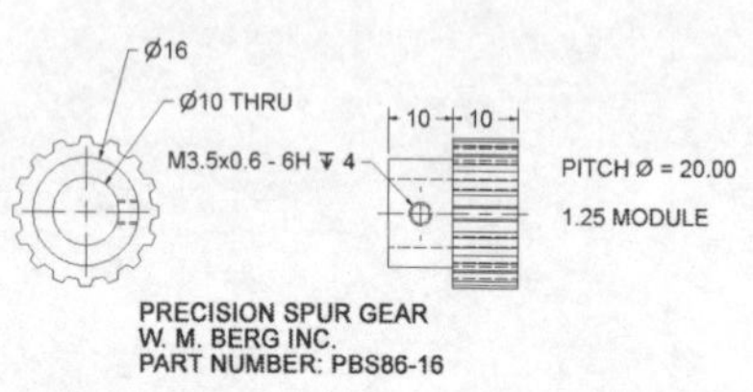

Gear 16

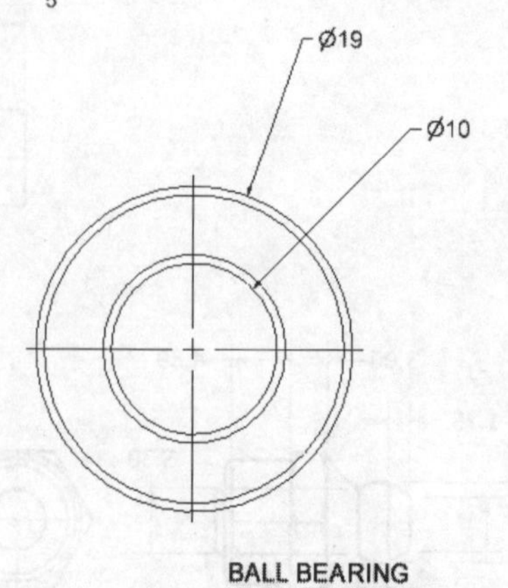

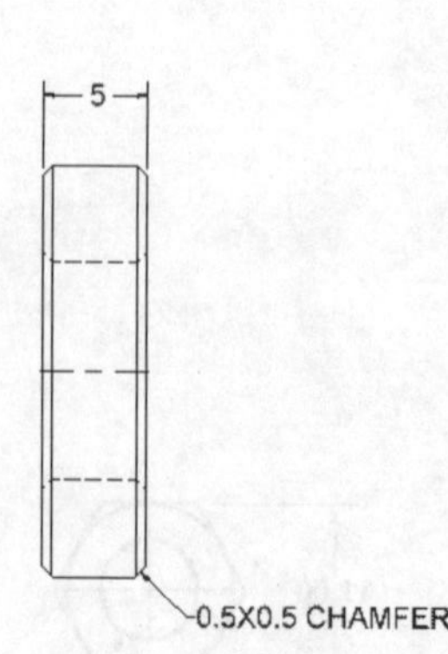

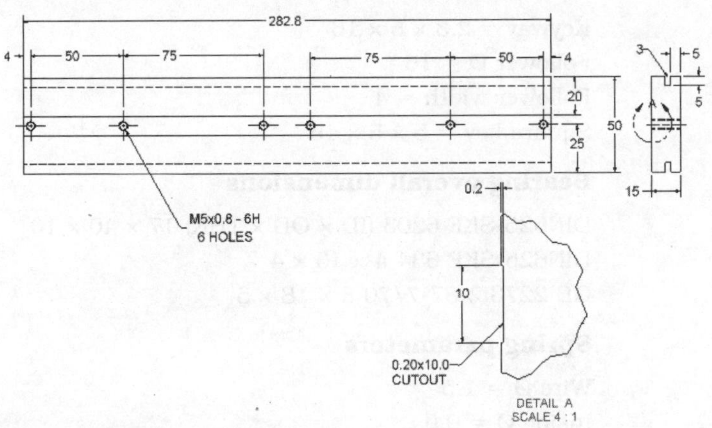

Base Slider

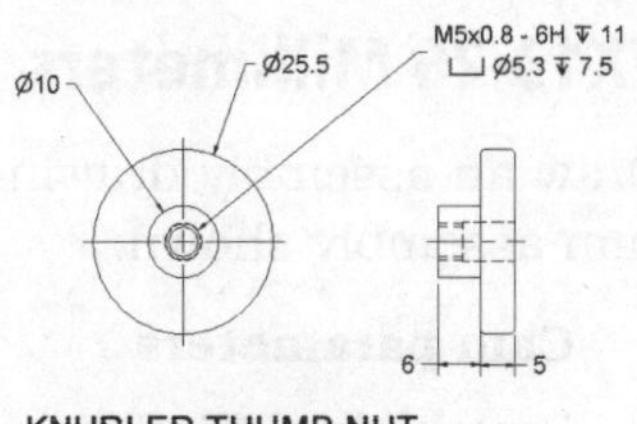

Thumb Nut

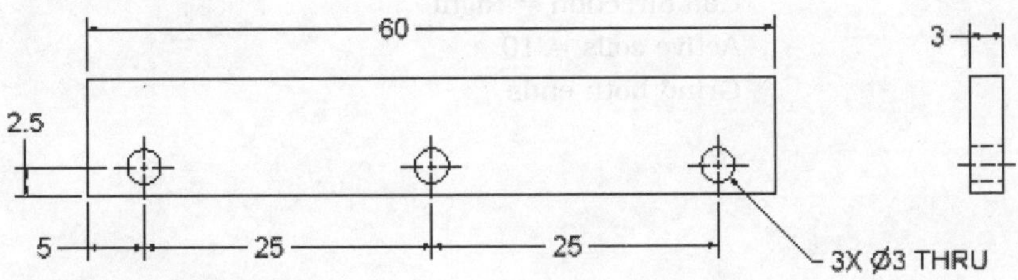

Lock Plate - 2

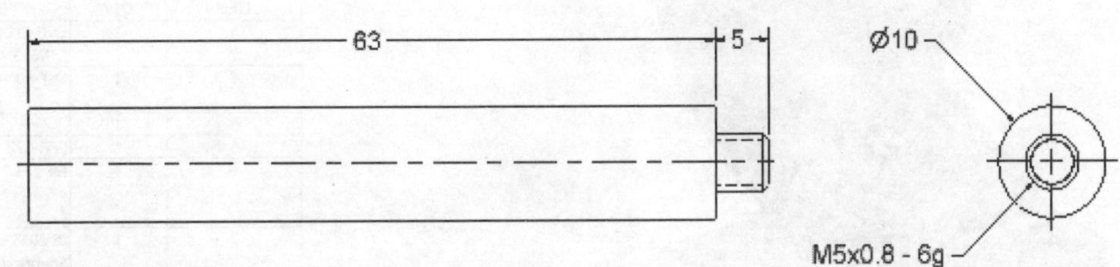

Guide Shaft - 1

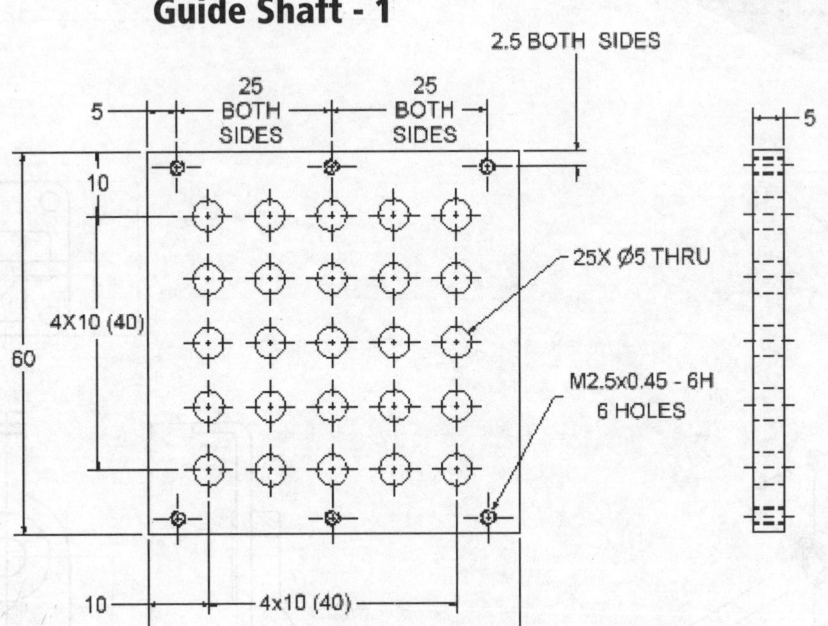

Hole Plate

EX13-26 Millimeters

Draw an assembly drawing and parts list for the cam assembly shown.

Cam parameters

Base circle = Ø146
Face width = 16
Motion: rise 10 by harmonic motion in 90°, dwell for 180°, fall 10 in 90°
Bore = Ø 16.0

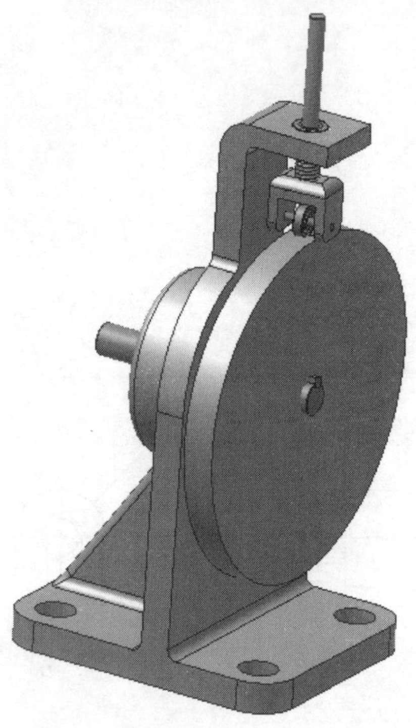

Keyway = 2.3 × 5 × 16
Follower Ø = 16
Follower width = 4
Square key = 5 × 5 × 16

Bearing overall dimensions

DIN625-SKF 6203 (ID × OD × THK) 17 × 40 × 10
DIN625-SKF 634 4 × 13 × 4
GB 2273.2-87-7/70 8 × 18 × 5

Spring parameters

Wire Ø = 1.5
Inside Ø = 9.0
Length = 20
Coil direction = Right
Active coils = 10
Grind both ends

Parts List			
ITEM	QTY	PART NUMBER	DESCRIPTION
1	1	ENG-2008-A	BASE, CAST
2	1	DIN625 - SKF 6203	Single row ball bearings
3	1	SHF-4004-16	SHAFT: Ø16×120,WITH 2.3×5×16 KEYWAY
4	1		SUB-ASSEMBLY, FOLLOWER
5	1	SPR-C22	SPRING,COMPRESSION
6	1	GB 273.2-87 - 7/70 - 8 x 18 x 5	Rolling bearings - Thrust bearings - Plan of boundary dimensions
7	1	IS 2048 - 1983 - Specification for Parallel Keys and Keyways B 5 x 5 x 16	Specification for Parallel Keys and Keyways

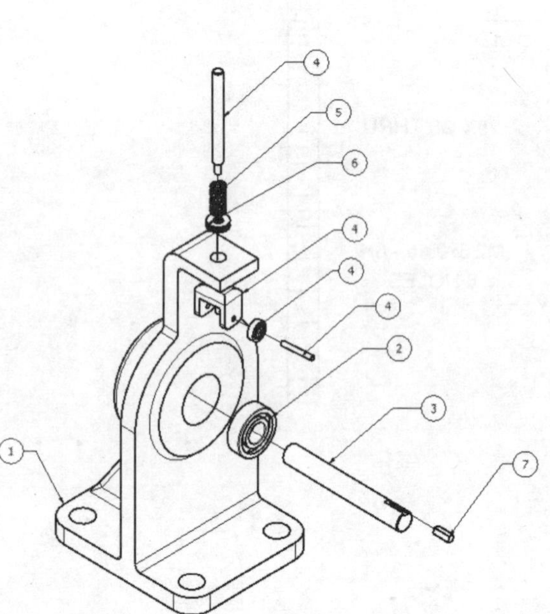

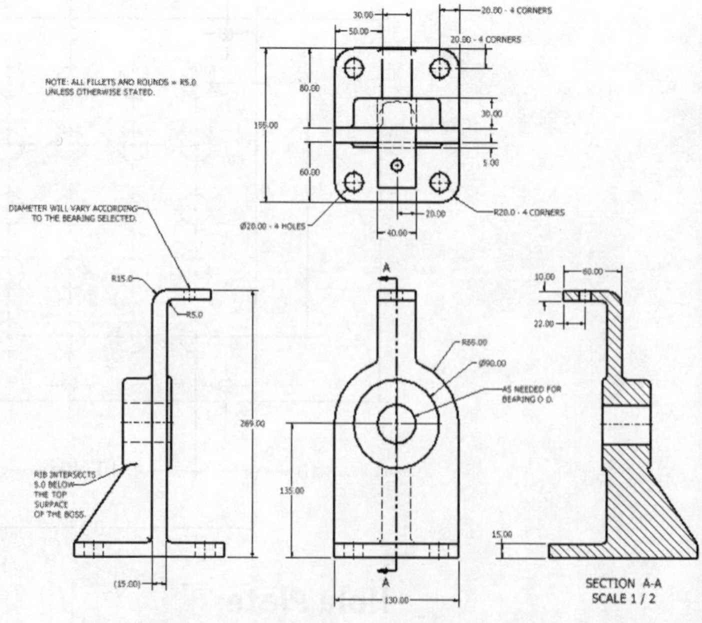

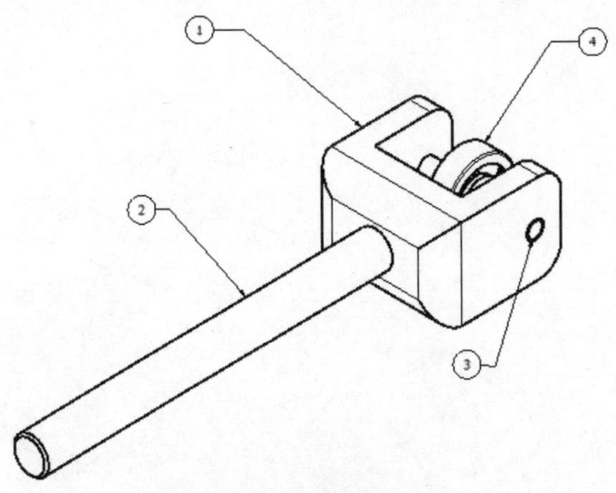

Parts List				
ITEM	PART NUMBER	DESCRIPTION	MATERIAL	QTY
1	AM-232	HOLDER	STEEL	1
2	AM-256	POST, FOLLOWER	STEEL	1
3	BS 1804-2 - 4 x 30	Parallel steel dowel pins - metric series	Steel, Mild	1
4	DIN625- SKF 634	Single row ball bearings	Steel, Mild	1

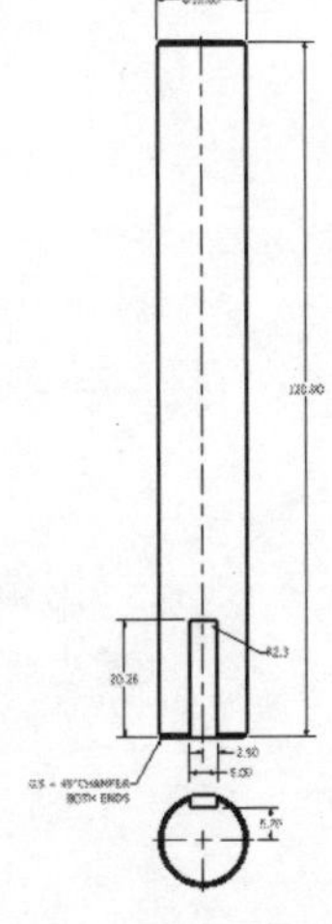

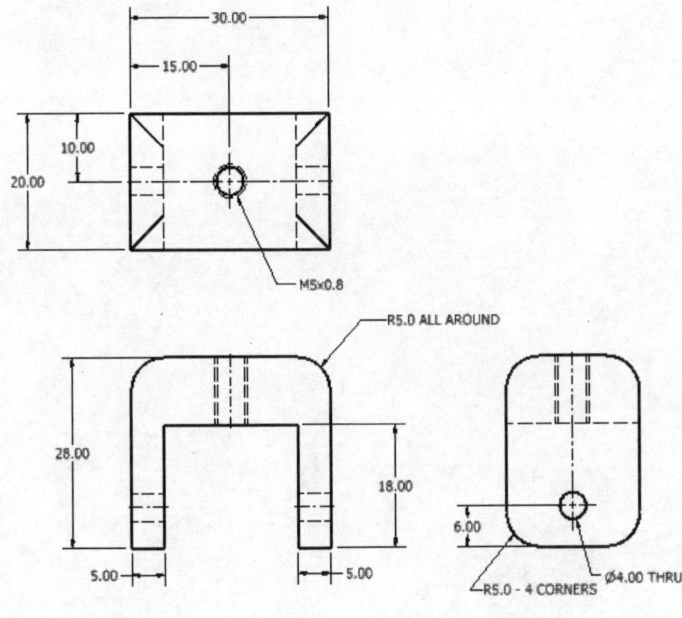

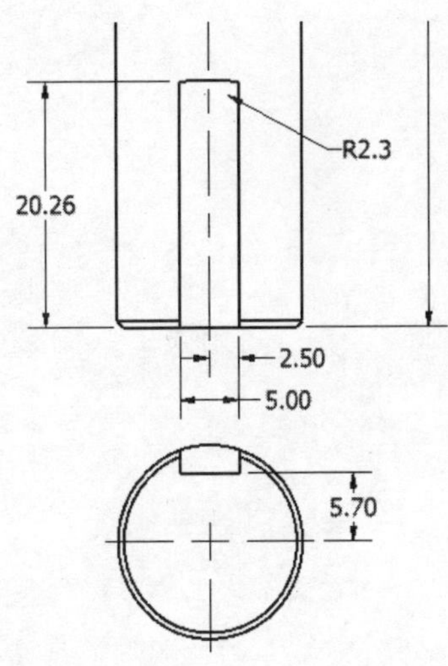

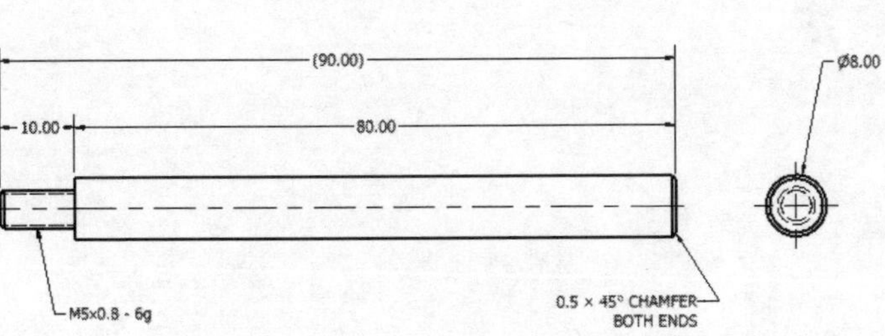

chapter fourteen Fundamentals of 3D Drawing

14-1 Introduction

This chapter introduces the fundamental concepts needed to produce 3D drawings in AutoCAD by use of the **View** command and the **acad3D** and **acadiso 3D** templates. The chapter shows how to change viewpoints and how to create, save, and work with user-defined coordinate systems called ***user coordinate systems,*** or UCSs.

The chapter demonstrates how to use both the **Viewports** and **Coordinates** panels. It also shows how to create orthographic views from given 3D objects by using the **View** panel tools.

14-2 The World Coordinate System

AutoCAD's absolute coordinate system is called the ***world coordinate system*** (WCS). The default setting for the WCS is a viewing position located so that you are looking at the system 90° to its X,Y plane. See Figure 14-1.

Figure 14-1

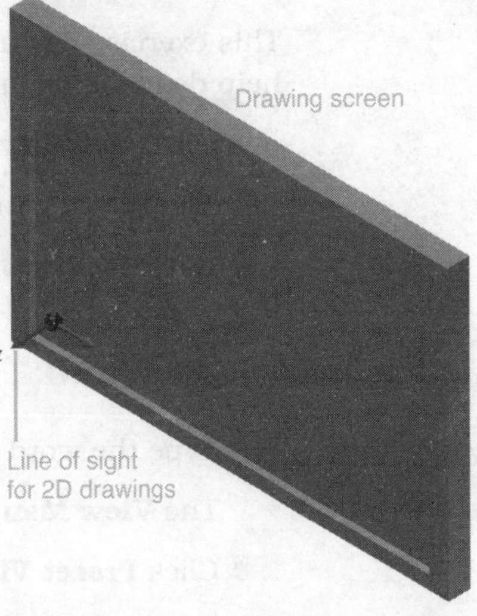

The Z axis is perpendicular to the X,Y plane, or directly aligned with your viewpoint. This setup is ideal for 2D drawings and is called a ***plan view.*** All of your drawings up to now have been done in this orientation.

Figure 14-2 shows a standard drawing screen created by using the acad template manager oriented so that you are looking directly down on the X,Y plane of the world coordinate system. The XY icon in the lower left corner of the screen is located on the origin of the world coordinate system (WCS). The WCS is a fixed coordinate system and is the basic system of AutoCAD. The user coordinate system (UCS) is a movable coordinate system.

Figure 14-2

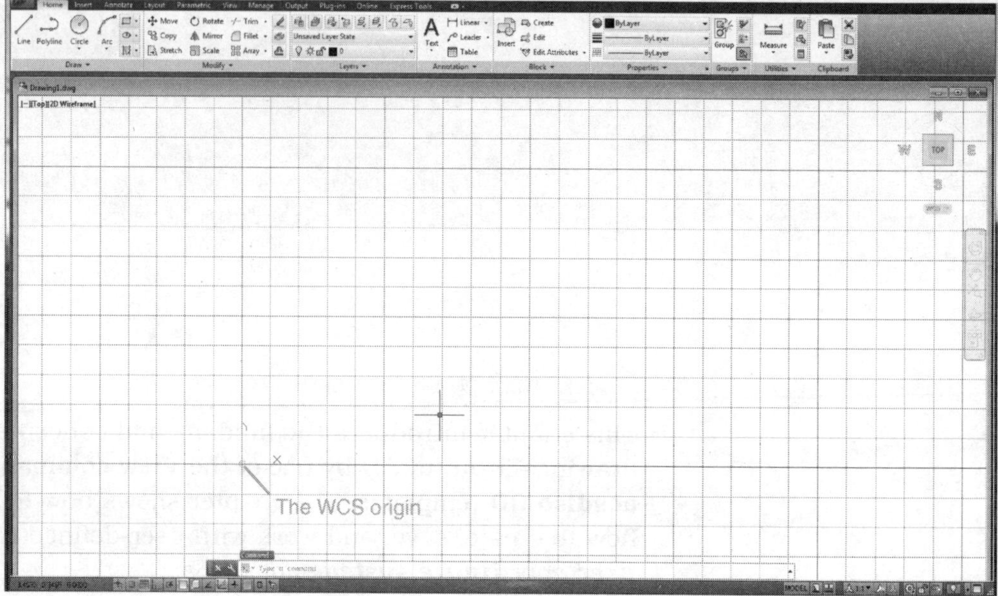

14-3 Viewpoints

The orientation of the WCS may be changed by changing the drawing's viewpoint. There are two ways to change the viewpoint: Use the **Views** tool on the **Views** panel under the **View** tab, or type the word **view** and access the **View Manager**.

To Change the Viewpoint by Using the Views Panel

This exercise assumes that the screen includes a grid. The grid serves to help define a visual orientation.

1. Click the **View** tab.

   The **Views** panel will appear. See Figure 14-3.

2. Click the **Views** tool, and select **SE Isometric**.

To Change the Viewpoint by Using the View Command

1. Type the word **view** in response to a command prompt.

   The **View Manager** dialog box will appear. See Figure 14-4.

2. Click **Preset Views;** then select **SE Isometric,** click **Apply**, and click **OK.**

Figure 14-3

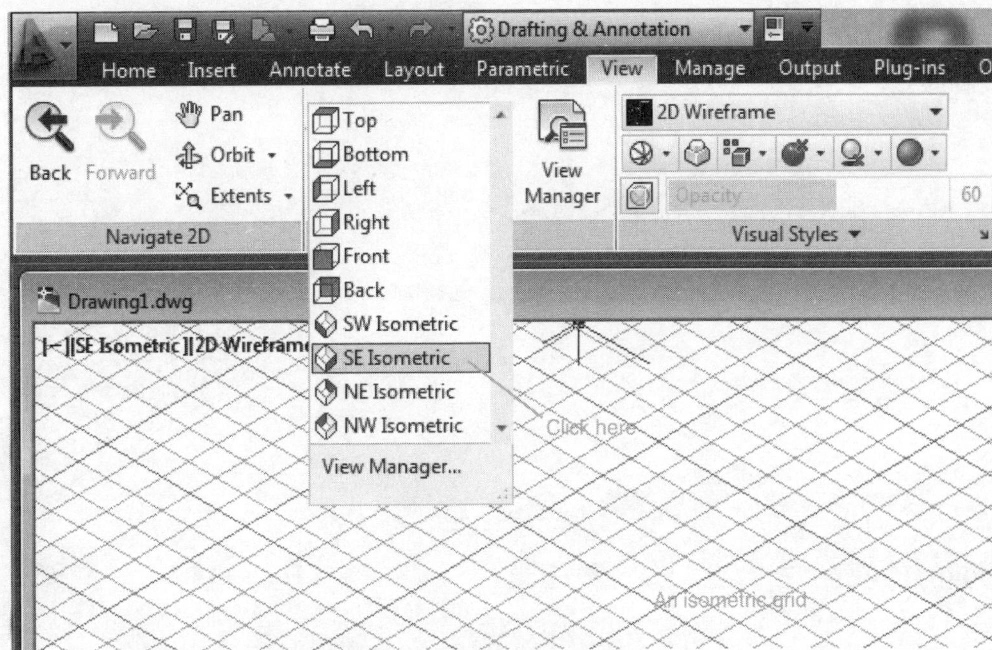

Figure 14-4

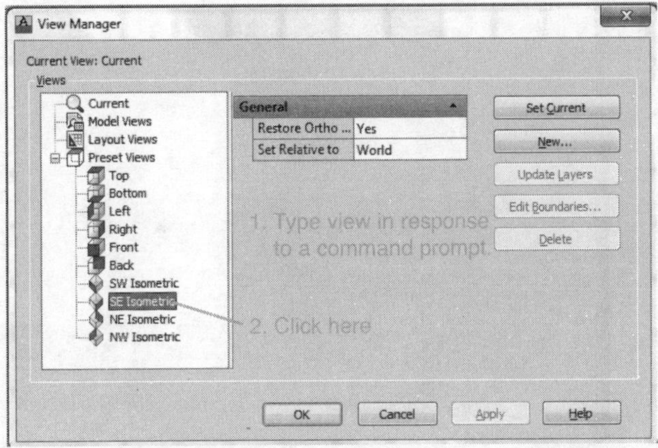

The drawing will now be oriented as shown in Figure 14-5. Note the change in the WCS icon. It now includes a Z axis. It is important to remember that you are still in the WCS, but are merely looking at it from a different perspective. This concept may be verified by drawing some simple shapes. Figure 14-6 shows a rectangular shape created by using the **Line** command, and a circle created by using the **Circle** command. These shapes are 2D shapes drawn in the WCS.

To Return to the Original WCS Orientation

Click **Top** on the **View** cube.

See Figure 14-7.

You can also return to the original WCS orientation by selecting **Top** from the **Views** tool.

Use the **Zoom** command at a scale value of **0.50** to return the figures to their approximate original view size. See Figure 14-8.

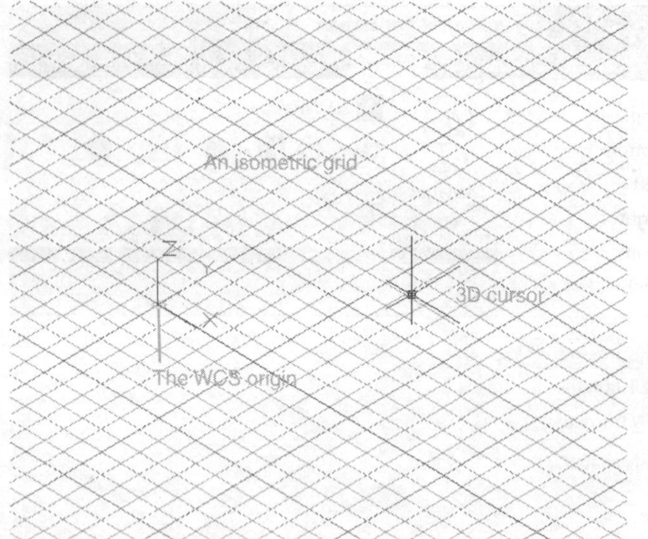

Figure 14-5

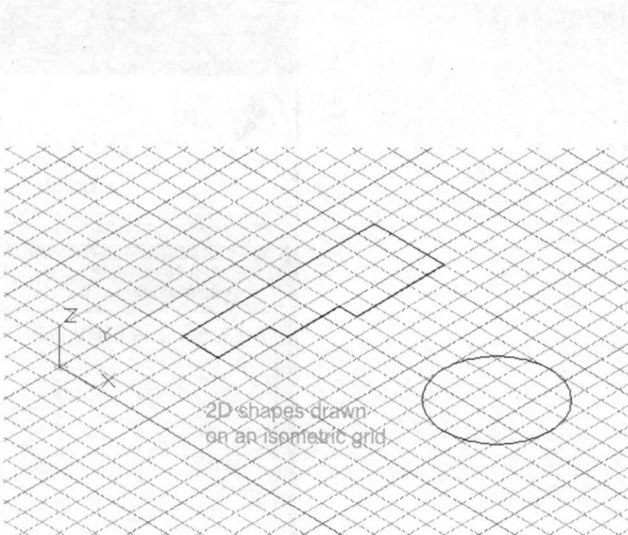

Figure 14-6

The View cube

WCS

Figure 14-7

A top view of the shapes shown in Figure 14-6.

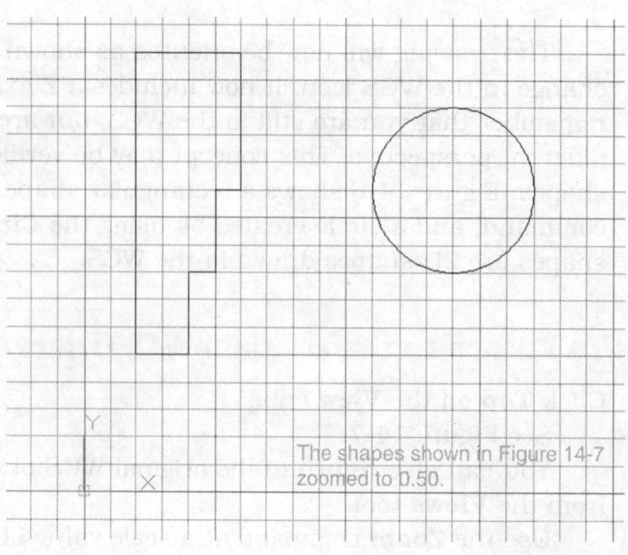

Figure 14-8

14-4 Perspective and Parallel Grids

Figure 14-9 shows both a perspective and a parallel grid background. Note the differences in the shape of the box shown against both backgrounds. The top back corner of the box on the parallel grid appears higher than the same corner of the box on the perspective grid.

Figure 14-9

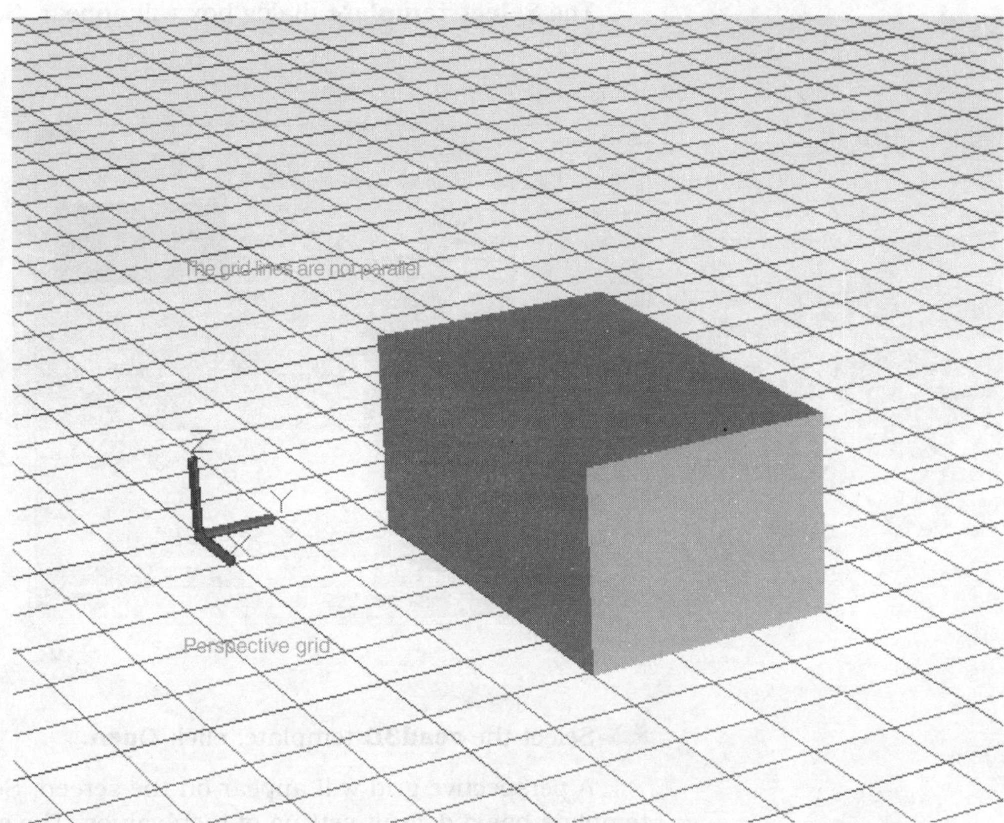

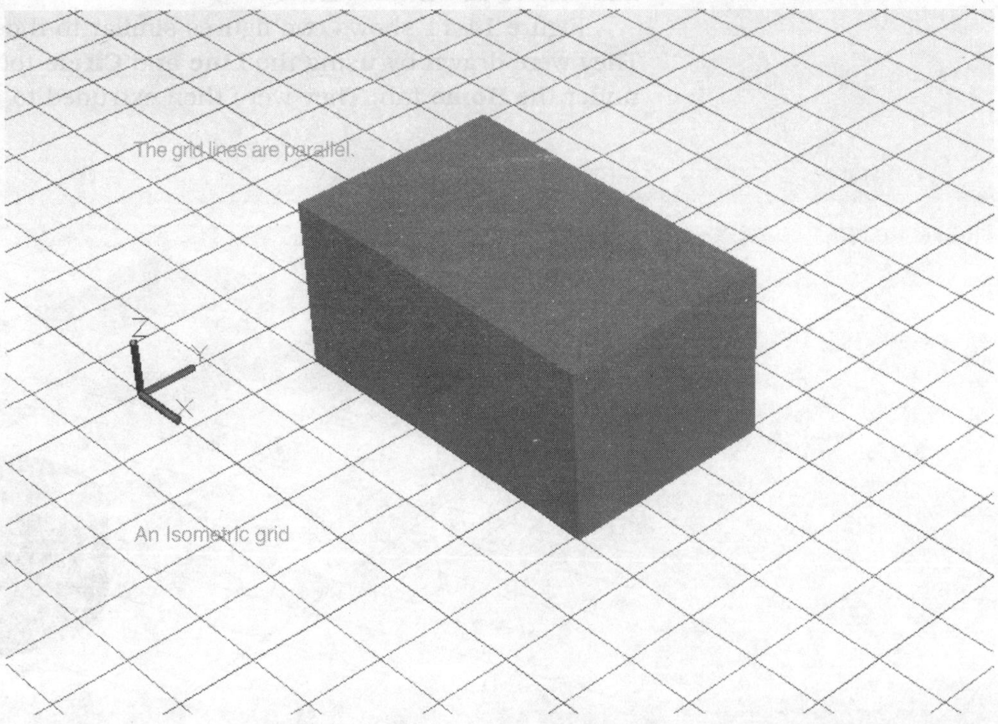

Perspective grid lines recede to a vanishing point or a series of vanishing points. Parallel grid lines always remain parallel. AutoCAD uses a 3-point perspective system.

To Create a Drawing with a Perspective Grid

1. Click the **New** tool.

The **Select template** dialog box will appear. See Figure 14-10.

Figure 14-10

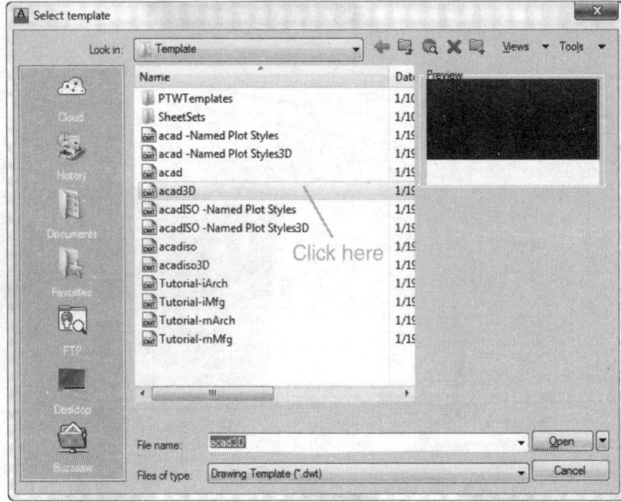

2. Select the **acad3D** template; click **Open.**

A perspective grid will appear on the screen. See Figure 14-11. This template has a default setting of inch values. The **acadiso3D** template has millimeters as default values.

Figure 14-11 shows two figures similar to those drawn in Figure 14-8. They were drawn by using the **Line** and **Circle** tools from the **Draw** panel under the **Home** tab. They were then extruded to create the 3D shapes.

Figure 14-11

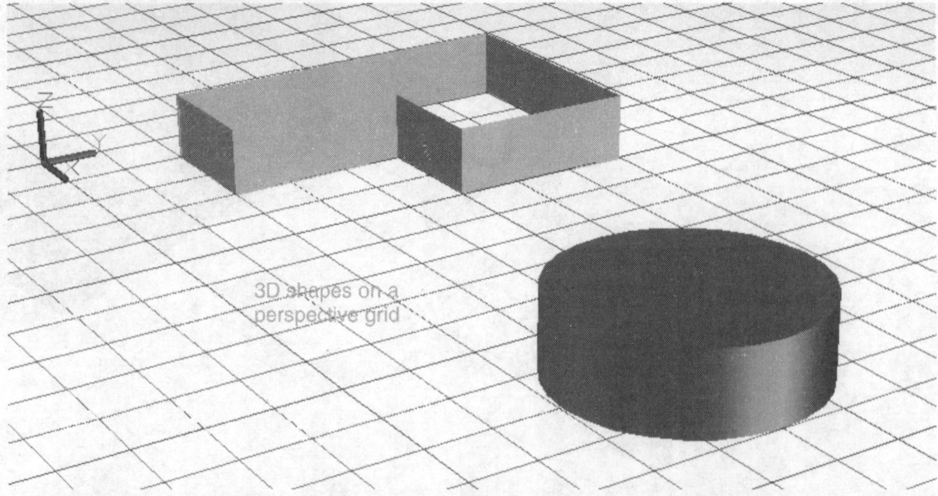

To Return to the 2D WCS

1. Click the **Top** view on the **View** cube.
2. Use the mouse wheel, and zoom the drawing as necessary.

Figure 14-12 shows the resulting top view. Note that the Z axis is not exactly perpendicular to the XY axis. This is because the shapes were created on a perspective grid.

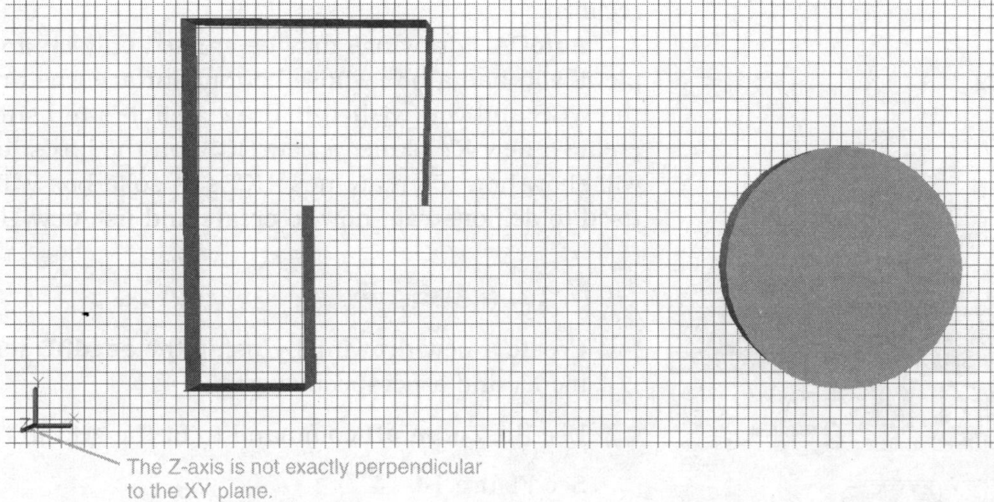

Figure 14-12

14-5 3D Modeling

AutoCAD has several drawing modes, including **2D Drafting & Annotation, 3D Modeling, 3D Basics,** and **AutoCAD Classic.**

To Access the 3D Modeling Mode

1. Start a new drawing, and select an **acad3D** template.

   See Figure 14-13.

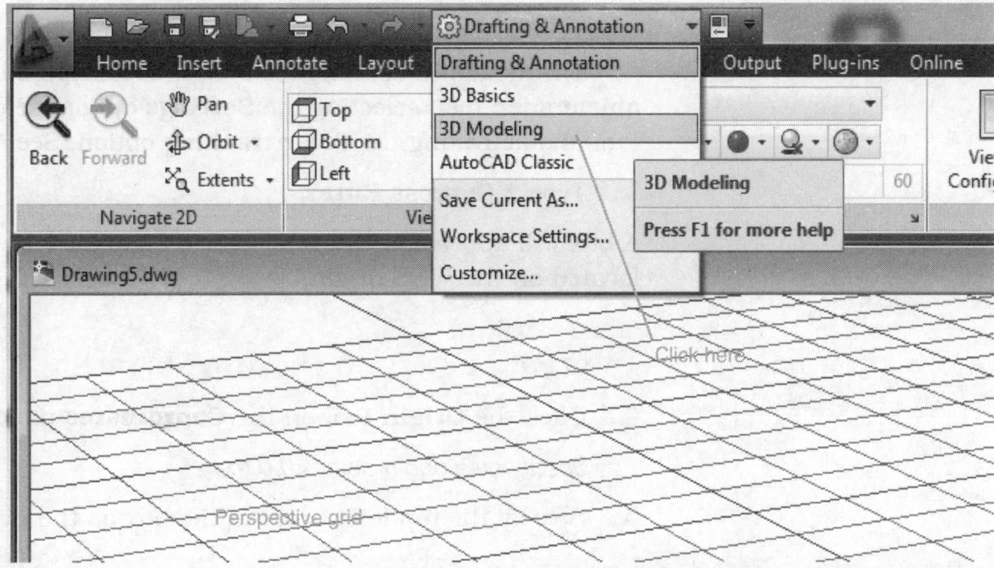

Figure 14-13

2. Move the cursor to the upper left corner of the screen, and select the **3D Modeling** option.

The remainder of this chapter will use the **3D Modeling** mode.

14-6 User Coordinate System (UCS)

User coordinate systems are coordinate systems that you define relative to the WCS. Drawings often contain several UCSs. UCSs can be saved and recalled.

AutoCAD drawings may be created only on an XY plane. So, for example, if you had a box whose bottom surface was drawn on the XY plane of the WCS and you wished to draw a circle's top surface, you would have to create a new XY plane, a new UCS, on the box's top surface. This section will show how to create new UCSs. A solid box will be drawn and then used to demonstrate how to create and use new UCSs.

To Draw a Solid Box

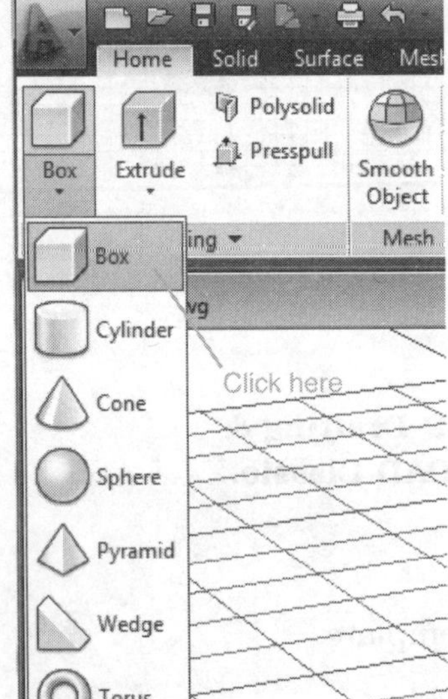

Figure 14-14

1. Create a new drawing by using the **acad3D** template, the **3D Modeling** mode, and a perspective grid.
2. Use the **Zoom all** command to fit the grid to the screen.

   See Figure 14-14.
3. Click the **Box** tool on the **Modeling** panel.

   Command:_box

   Specify first corner or [Center]:
4. Type **0,0,0;** press **Enter.**

   Specify other corner or [Cube Length]:

   These coordinates will locate the box's corner on the XYZ origin. The corner could have been located anywhere on the grid.
5. Type **5,5,0,** or use the **Snap** tool with dynamic coordinates. Press **Enter.**

   Specify height:

   The dynamics coordinates system is activated by right-clicking the **3D object snap** tool, selecting the **Settings** option, selecting the **Polar tracking** tab, and activating the **Polar tracking** option. See Figure 14-15.
6. Type **2.0;** press **Enter.**

A box will appear on the screen. See Figure 14-16. The corner of the box is located on the WCS origin.

To Create a UCS on the Top Surface

1. Click the **Origin** tool on the **Coordinates** panel under the **View** tab.

   Specify new origin point <0,0,0>:
2. Specify the top left corner of the box as the new origin.

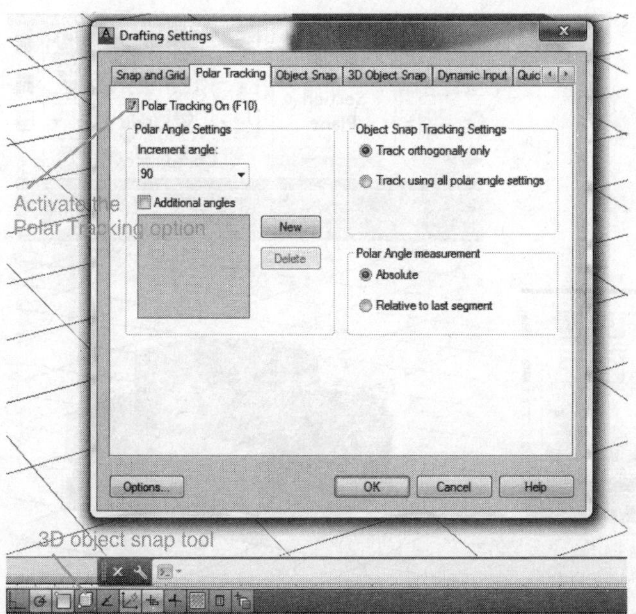

Figure 14-15

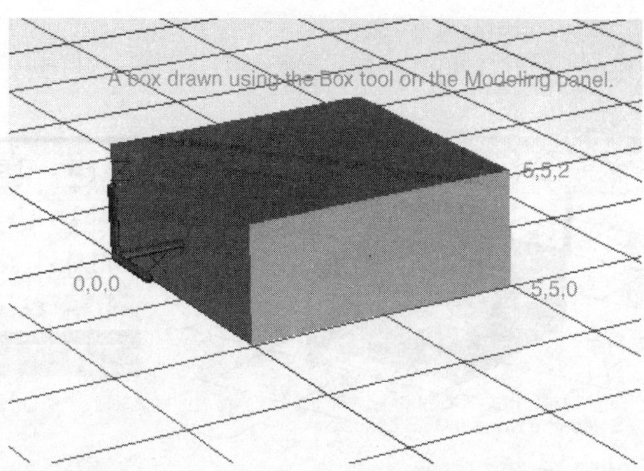

Figure 14-16

See Figure 14-17. You must use the **Osnap Endpoint** option (accessed by pressing **<Shift>**/right mouse button) to define the corner. The cursor moves only in the XY plane. If you locate the cursor on the corner without using the **Endpoint** option, the cursor may appear to be on the corner, but, in fact, it will be located on the XY plane at a point behind the corner point.

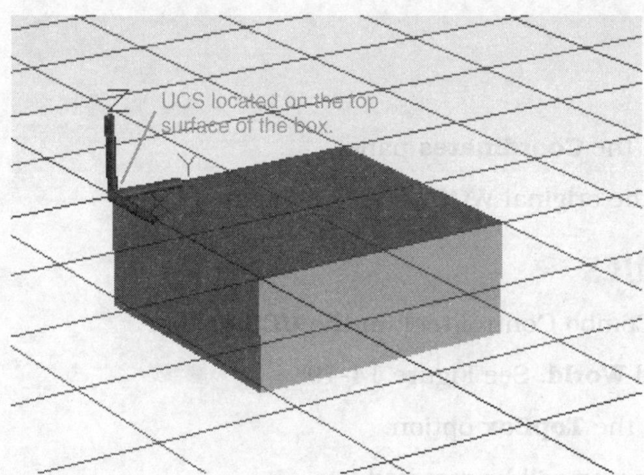

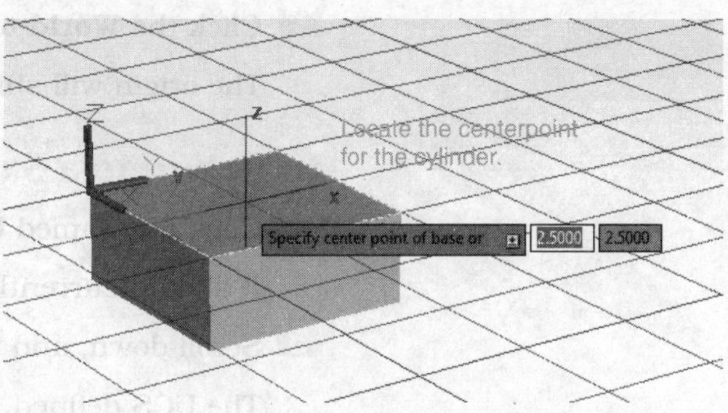

Figure 14-17

The origin is now located on the top left corner of the box. This is a new UCS.

3 Use the **Cylinder** command, and draw a cylinder on the top surface of the box. Locate the cylinder's center point at **2.5,2.5,0;** make the Ø = **4.00** and the height = **1.00.**

To Save a UCS

The UCS created in Figure 14-17 can be saved and later restored without having to redefine it.

1 Right-click the **Origin** icon.

See Figure 14-18. The **UCS** dialog box will appear.

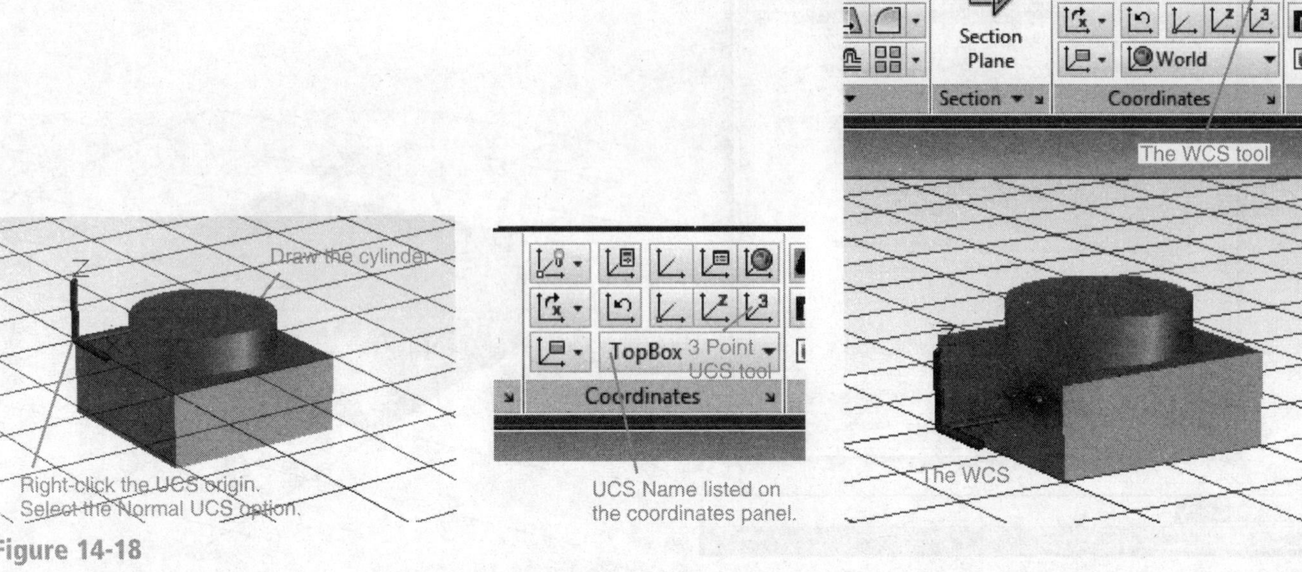

Figure 14-18

2 Click the **Named UCS** option.

3 Click **Save**.

4 In this example, the name **TopBox** was entered.

5 Press **Enter**. The UCS is now saved. The name should appear on the **Coordinates** panel.

To Return to the WCS

1 Click the **World** tool on the **Coordinates** panel.

The origin will shift to the original WCS axis. See Figure 14-18.

To Return to a Saved UCS

1 Click the Named **UCS** Combo Control tool on the **UCS** toolbar.

It should currently read **World**. See Figure 14-19.

2 Scroll down, and select the **TopBox** option.

The UCS defined in this way will be restored.

To Define a UCS by Using the 3 Point Tool

Use the **3 Point** tool to define a UCS on the front right surface of the box. See Figure 14-19.

1 Click the **3 Point** tool on the **Coordinates** panel.

Specify new origin point <0,0,0>:

2 Click the lower corner of the box.

This step assumes that the **Snap** option is on and set to match the grid. Also, you can use **Osnap** settings to ensure that you are grabbing end points. Press **Shift** and the right mouse button to access the dialog box.

Specify point on the positive portion of the X-axis <x,x,x>:

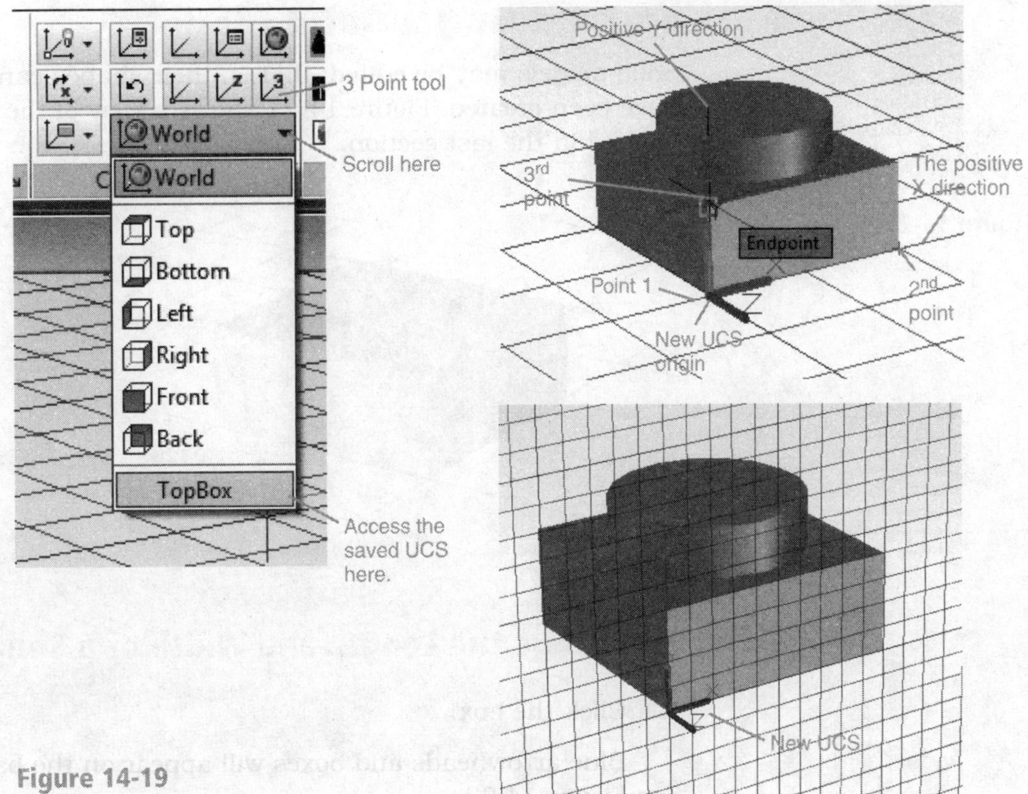

Figure 14-19

3. Click the lower, far right corner of the box.

Specify point on the positive portion of the Y-axis <x,x,x>:

The upper front corner of the box, just above the new origin, will be specified, but it cannot simply be clicked. The corner is not on the current XY plane.

4. Use **Osnap Endpoint**, and click the corner.

5. Click the **Origin** tool, and then click the new origin created by using the **3 Point** tool.

6. Use the **Cylinder** command on the **Modeling** panel, and draw a Ø2.00 × 1.00 cylinder centered about the **2.5,1,0** point on the new UCS.

See Figure 14-20.

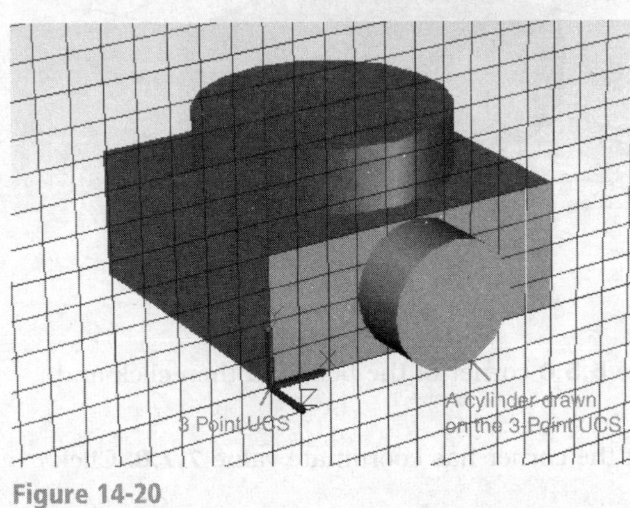

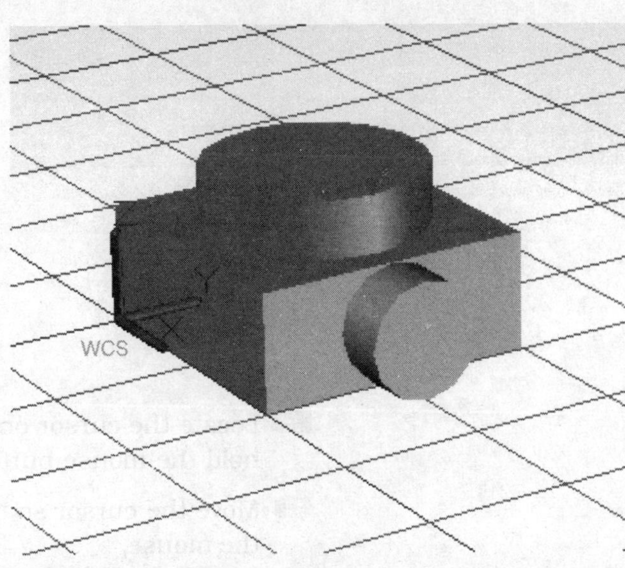

Figure 14-20

14-7 Editing a Solid Model

Solid models may be edited; that is, their shapes can be changed after they have been created. Figure 14-21 shows a view of the 5 × 5 × 2 solid model created in the last section.

Figure 14-21

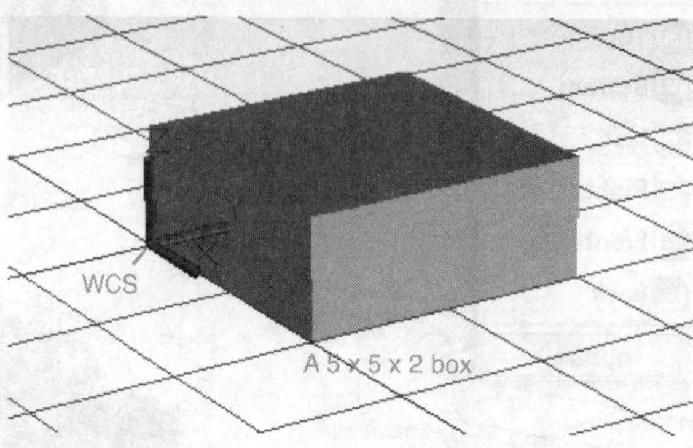

To Change the Length and Width of a Solid Model

1. Click the box.

   Blue arrowheads and boxes will appear on the base plane of the box. See Figure 14-22.

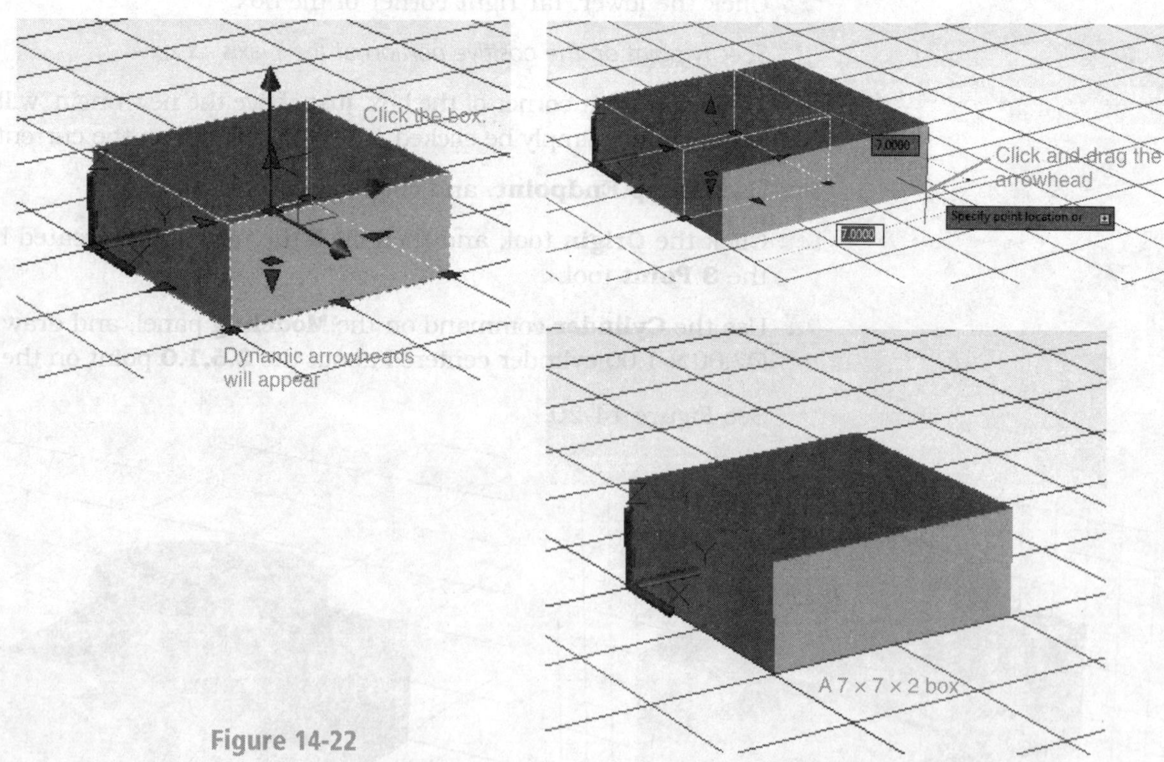

Figure 14-22

2. Locate the cursor on the **5,5,0** corner of the box, and then click and hold the mouse button.
3. Move the cursor so that the corner has coordinate value **7,7,0.** Click the mouse.

Use the **Snap** tool to locate the new corner point, or enter the new values for the corner **(7,7,0).**

4 Press the **<Esc>** key.

14-8 Creating UCSs on a Perspective Grid

The procedures just defined for creating and saving UCSs are exactly the same for objects created on a perspective grid. Figure 14-23 shows the same 5 × 5 × 2 solid model in Figure 14-15 drawn on a perspective grid. The box was drawn by using the **Box** tool on the **Modeling** panel and an **acad3D** template.

Figure 14-23

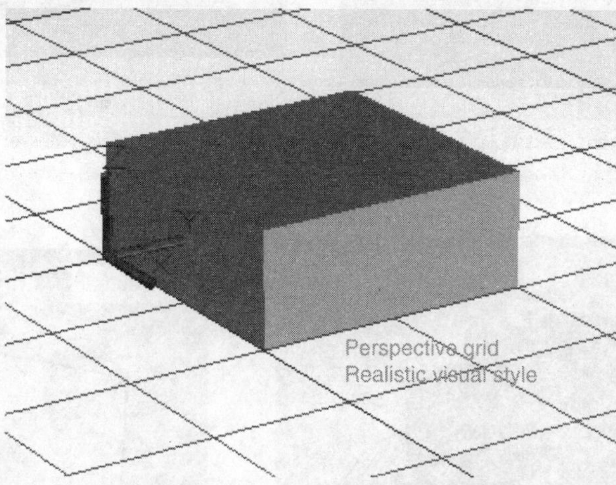

The solid model will appear as a solid gray object that is difficult to see. This is the **Realistic** visual style.

To Change Visual Styles

1 Click the **View** tab; then click the arrowhead on the **Visual Styles** tool, and select the **Wireframe** option.

See Figure 14-24.

Figure 14-24

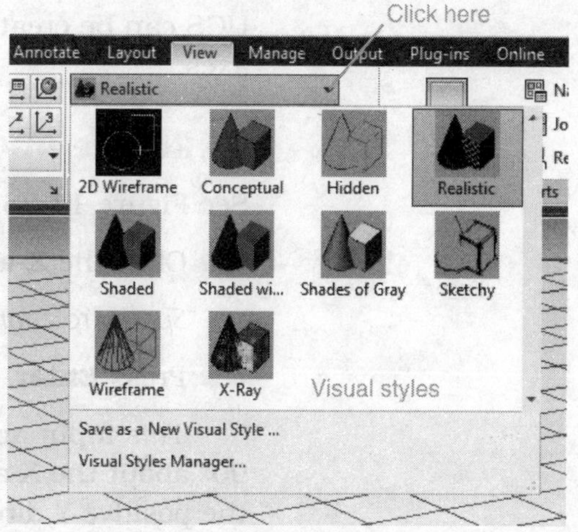

The model will change to the wireframe format.

Figure 14-25 shows the block displayed by using four of the available options.

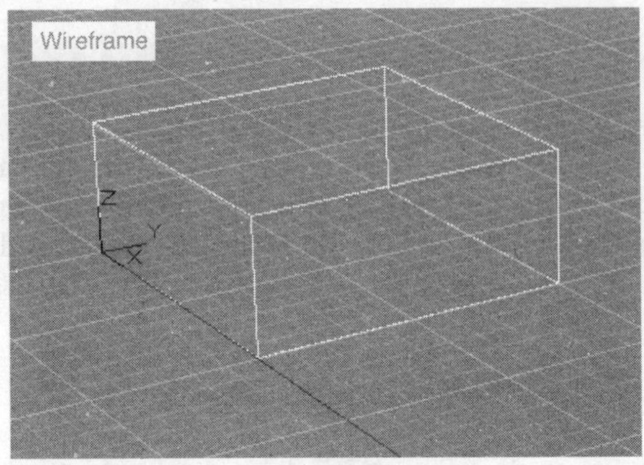

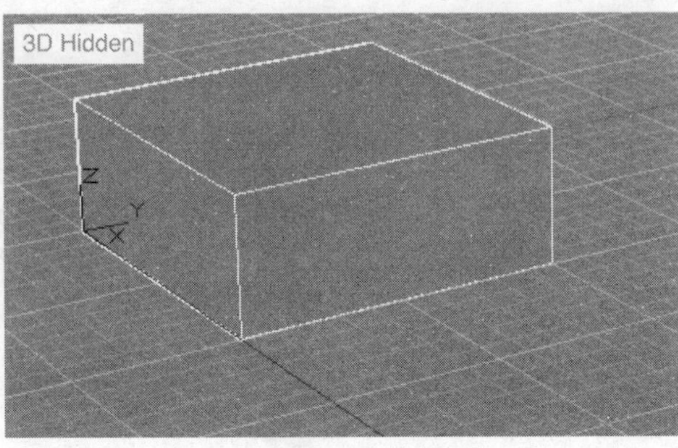

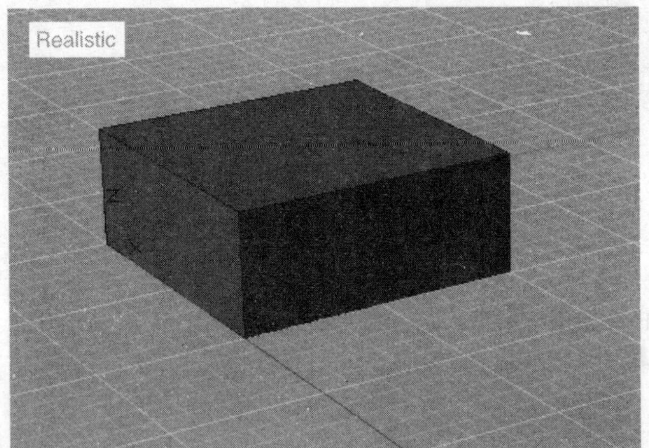

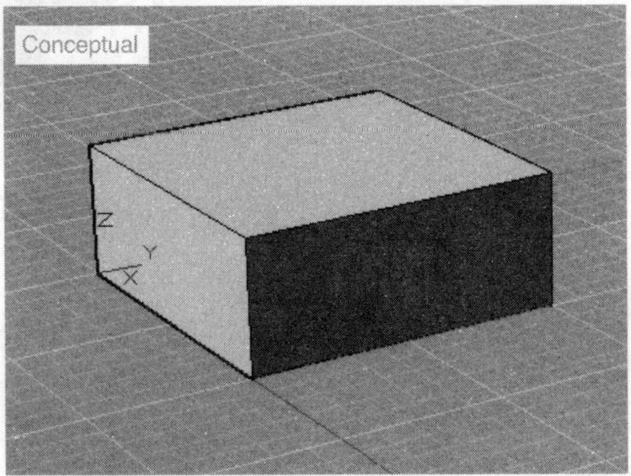

Figure 14-25

14-9 Rotating a UCS Axis

Figure 14-26 shows a 5 × 5 × 2 box drawn on the WCS axis with its origin on the 0,0,0 point. It is displayed in the Conceptual visual style. A new UCS can be created by rotating the coordinates about one of the major axes.

To Rotate About the X Axis

See Figure 14-26.

1. Click the **X-axis** tool on the **Coordinates** panel.

   Specify rotation axis about the X-axis <90>:90° is the default value.

2. Press **Enter**.

This input accepts the 90° default value. The axis and grid will rotate 90° about the X axis. You can now draw on the new XY axis, which has the positive Y direction in the vertical direction.

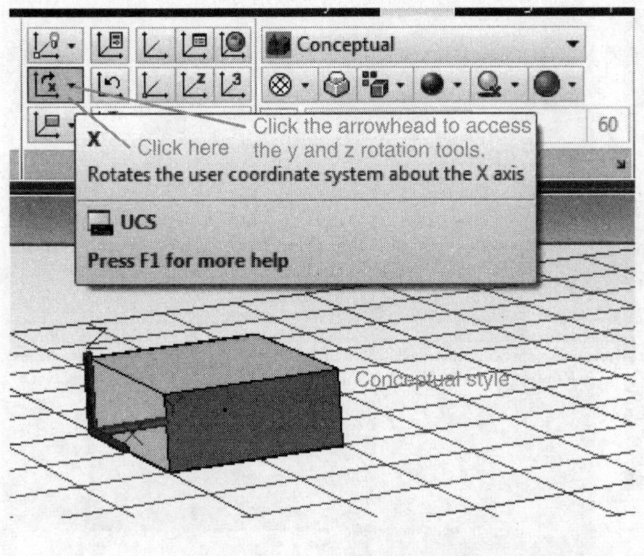

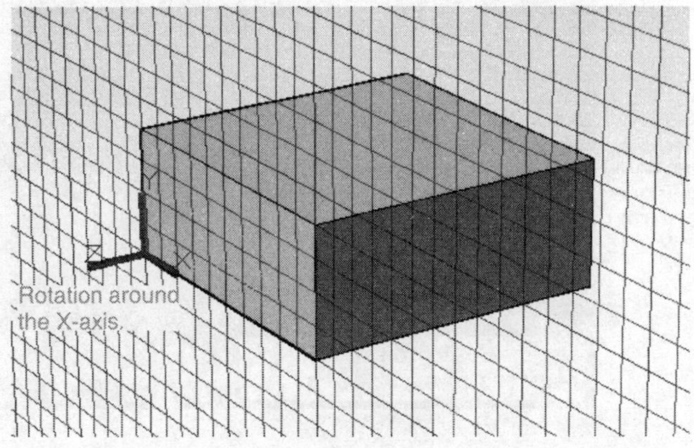

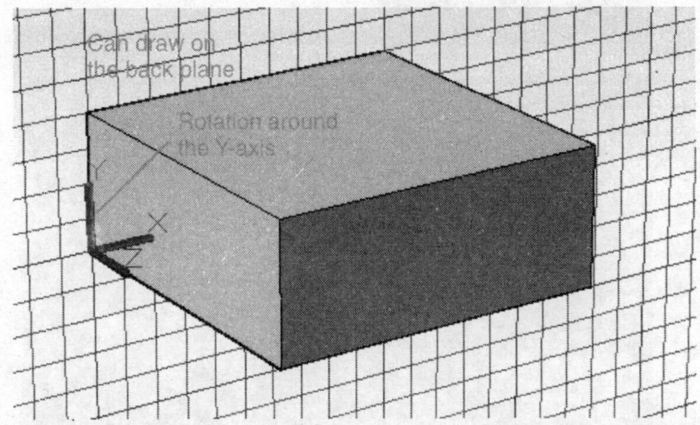

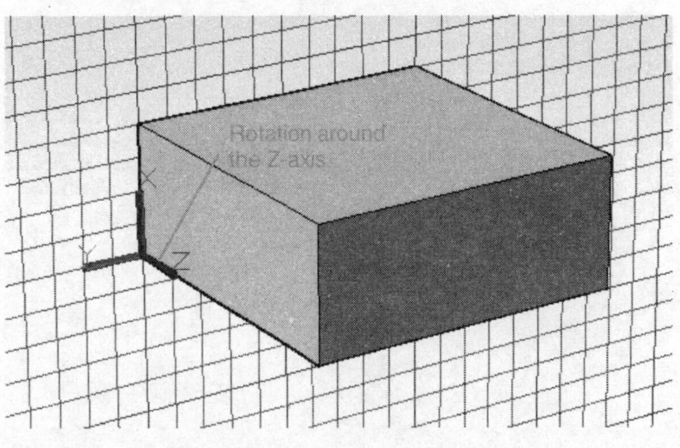

Figure 14-26

3. Click the **Y-axis** tool on the **Coordinates** panel.

   Specify rotation axis about the Y-axis <90°>:

4. Press **Enter**.

   The XZ axis and grid will have rotated 90°. You can now draw on the back plane of the box.

5. Click the **Z-axis** tool.

   Specify rotation angle about the Z-axis <90>:

6. Press **Enter**.

   The axis will have rotated 90°.
   Use the **Undo** tool to return to the original WCS orientation.

14-10 Sample Problem SP14-1

Draw an L-shaped bracket. The bracket will be used to demonstrate how to use UCSs.

1. Start a new drawing by using the **acad3D** template with a perspective grid.

2. Use the **Box** tool on the **Modeling** panel, and draw a **5, 5, 2 box** in the **3D Wireframe** visual style.

   See Figure 14-27.

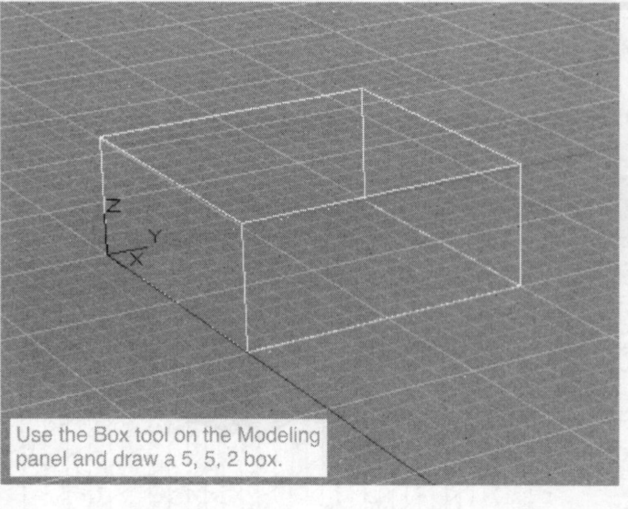

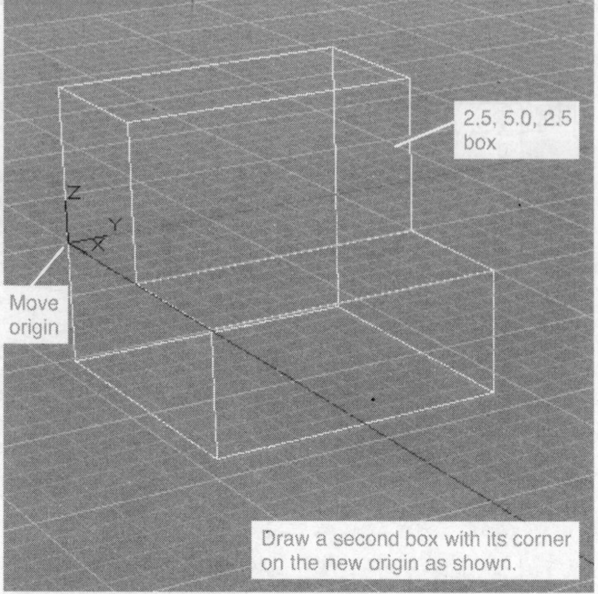

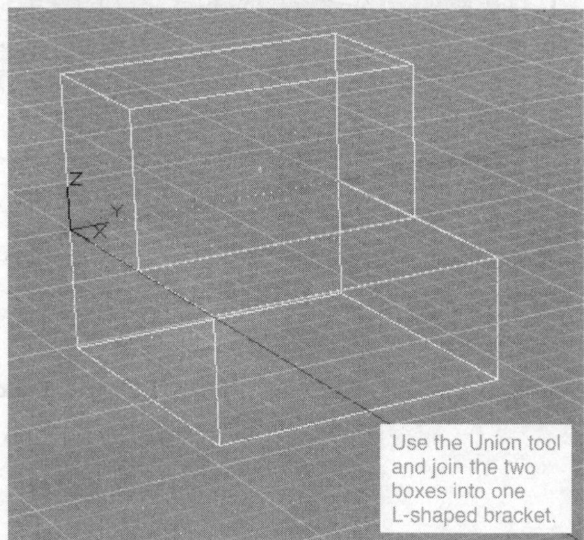

Figure 14-27

3. Use the **Origin** tool on the **Coordinates** panel, and move the origin to the top surface of the box as shown. Use **Osnap Endpoint** (press and hold the **<Shift>** key; click the right mouse button) to locate the new origin.

4. Use the new origin, and create a box whose base is located from the new origin (0,0,0) to a new corner (2.5,5.0,0). Make the height **2.5.**

5. Click the **Solid** tab, and then click the **Union** tool located on the **Boolean** panel.

The **Union** tool will join the two boxes together to form one object. Notice which lines are removed by the **Union** tool.

14-11 Visual Errors

When working in 3D, it is important to remember that you cannot rely on visual inputs to locate shapes. What you see may be misleading. For example, Figure 14-28 shows a circle that appears to be drawn on the upper

Figure 14-28

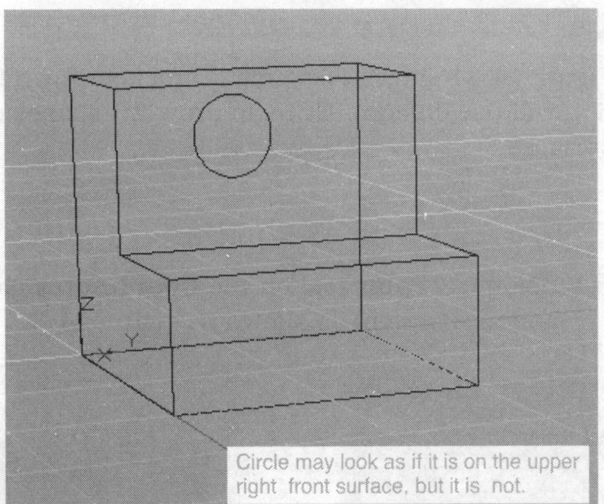

right surface of an L-shaped bracket. In fact, the circle is not located on the surface. This visual distortion is due to the line of sight of the view. The fact that the circle is on the back surface can be verified by changing the point of view from perspective to **Top.**

To Change Views

1 Click the **View** tab, and select the **Top** option from the **Views** panel.

See Figure 14-29.

The top view is shown in Figure 14-30. This view clearly shows that the circle is drawn on the back surface.

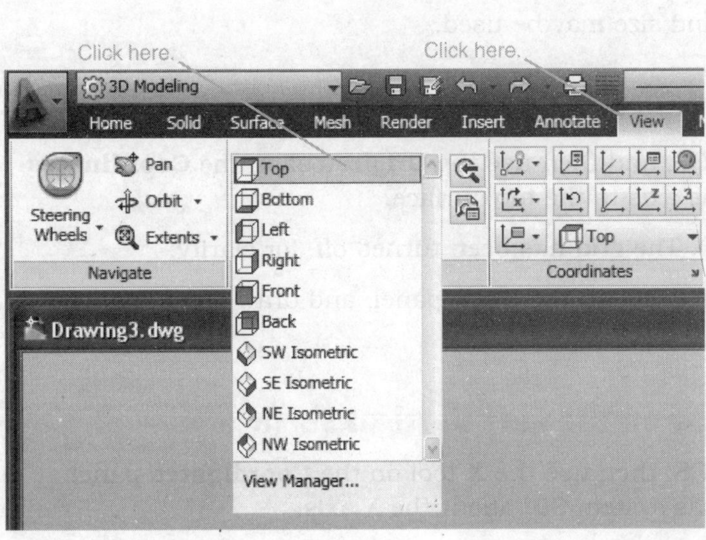

Figure 14-29

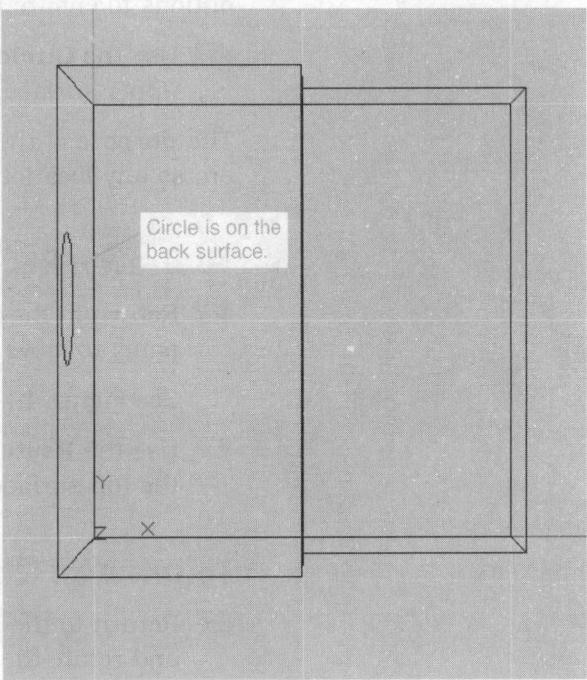

Figure 14-30

14-12 Sample Problem SP14-2

Figure 14-31 shows the same L-bracket drawn for Figure 14-27. This section will use different UCSs to draw 2D shapes on three of the L-bracket's surfaces.

To Draw a Circle on the Upper Front Surface

1. Use the **3 Point** tool on the **Coordinates** panel, and locate the origin and axis system as shown in Figure 14-32.

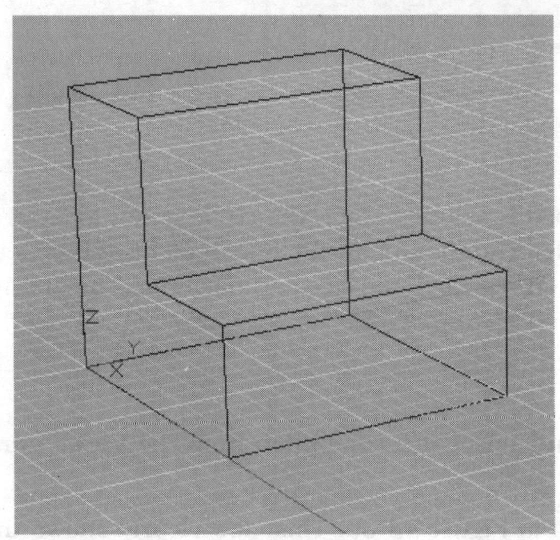

Figure 14-31

Point in the positive Y direction

Point in the positive X direction

New origin

Figure 14-32

Remember, you can draw only on the XY plane. Use the **Object Snap** options to ensure that the correct origin location is selected.

2. Use the **Circle** tool on the **Draw** panel, and draw a circle on the front upper surface, as shown.

The purpose of the circle is to help visually identify the surface that it is on, so any location and size may be used.

To Draw a Rectangle on the Top Surface

1. Return to the WCS, and then use the **Origin** tool on the **Coordinates** panel to move the axis to the top surface.

   See Figure 14-33. The grid has been turned off, for clarity.

2. Use the **Rectangle** tool on the **Draw** panel, and draw a rectangle on the top surface.

To Draw an Ellipse on the Left Vertical Surface

1. Return to the WCS; then use the **X** tool on the **Coordinates** panel, and rotate the axis system **90**° about the X axis.

   See Figure 14-34. The XY axis is now aligned with the left vertical axis.

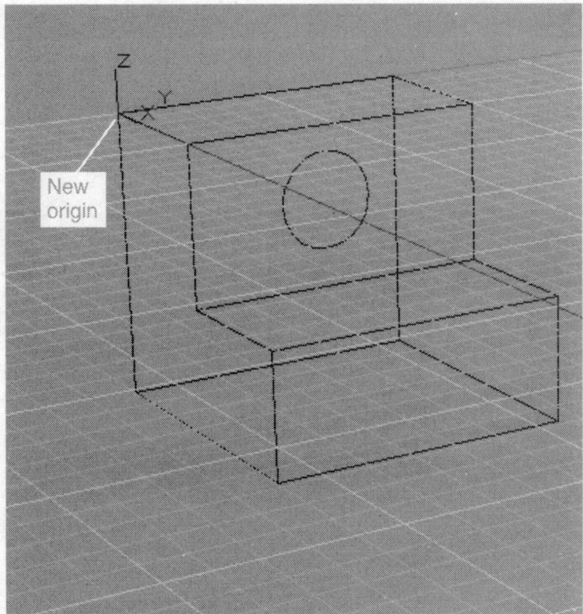

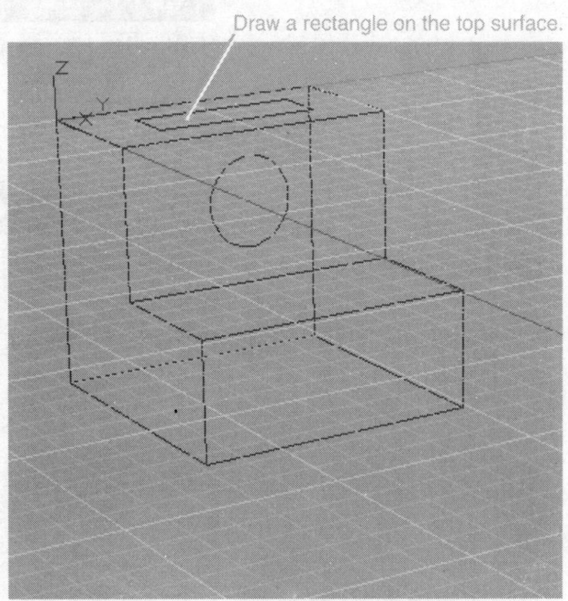

Figure 14-33

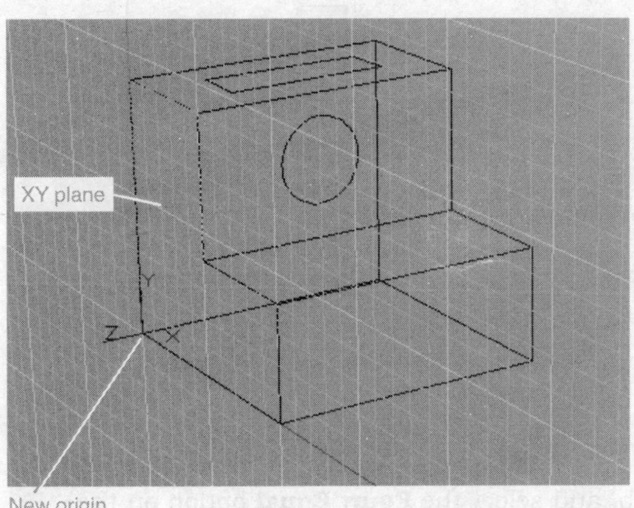

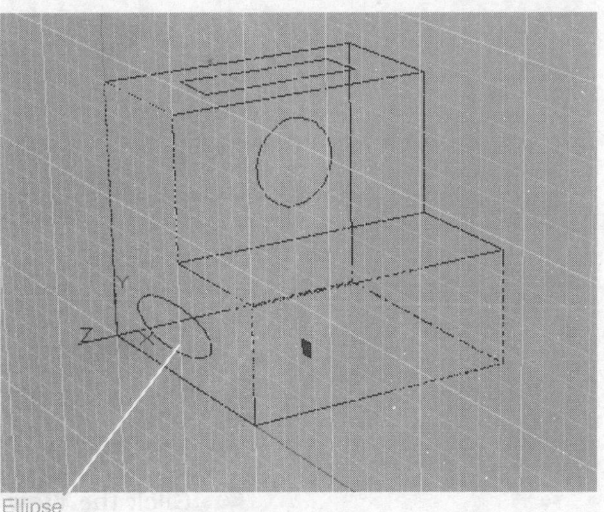

Figure 14-34

2. Use the **Ellipse** tool on the **Draw** panel, and draw an ellipse on the left vertical surface.
3. Save the L-bracket.

14-13 Orthographic Views

Once a 3D object has been created, orthographic views may be taken directly from the object. The screen is first split into four ports, each showing the 3D object. The viewpoint of three of the ports will be changed to create the front, top, and right-side views of the object.

For this example, the L-bracket was redrawn by using the same dimension as presented in Figure 14-15, but using an acad template. The SE Isometric view was used in Figure 14-35.

Figure 14-35

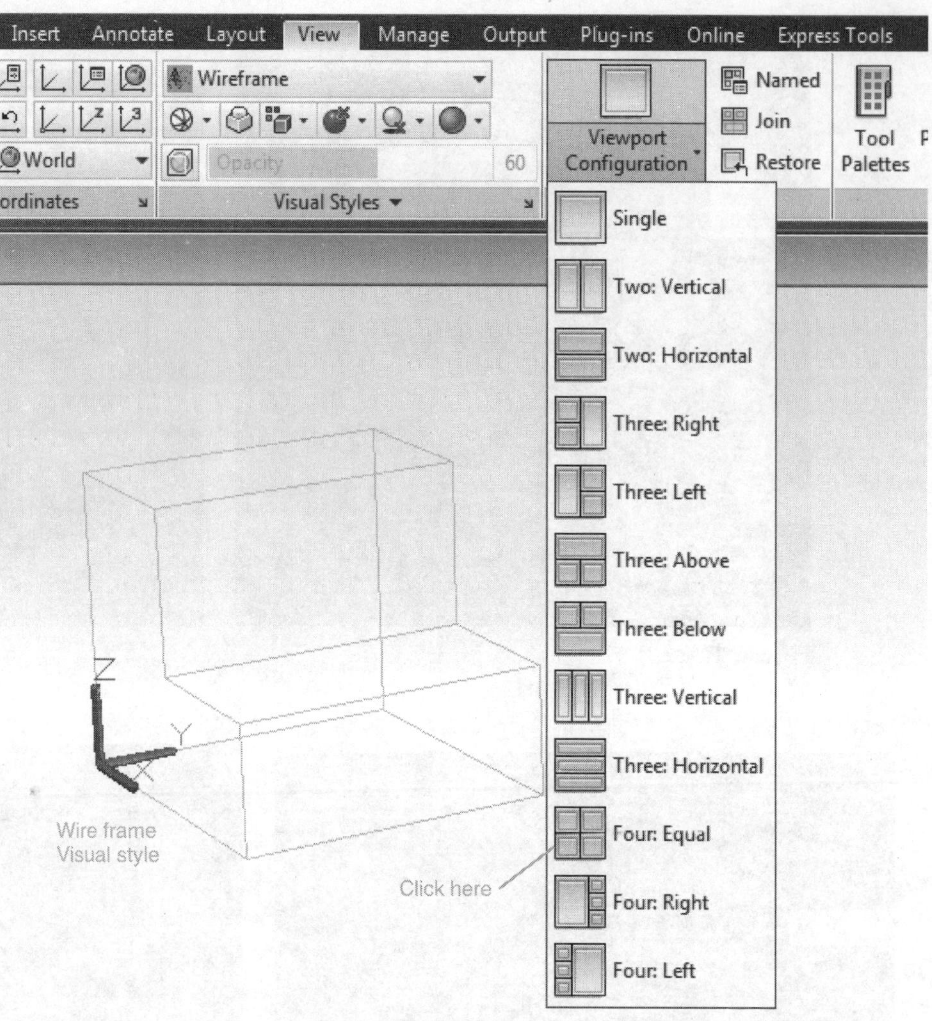

To Create Four Viewports

1. Click the **View** tab, and select the **Four: Equal** option on the **Viewports** panel.

See Figure 14-35.

Viewports can also be created by using the **Viewports** dialog box.

2. Type the word **viewports** in response to a command prompt.

3. Select the **Four: Equal** option.

See Figure 14-36.

Figure 14-37 shows the L-bracket in four equal ports. Note that the cursor is visible in only one port at a time—the active port. To change active ports, move the cursor into the port and click the mouse.

To Create Orthographic Views

1. Move the cursor into the top left port, and press the left mouse button.

This will make this viewport the current viewport, and the cursor will appear in the port.

Figure 14-36

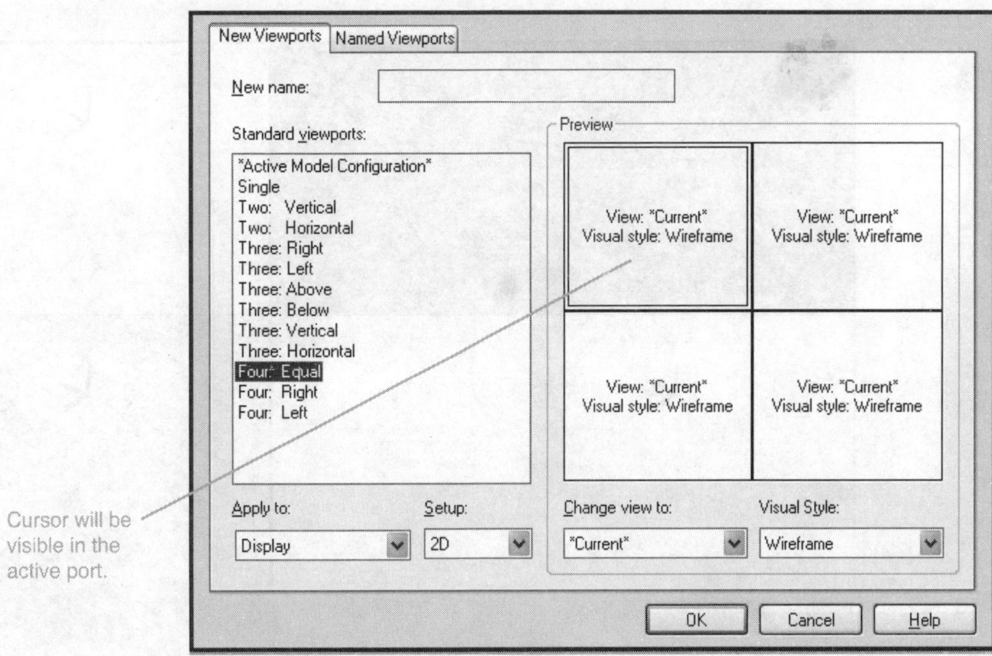

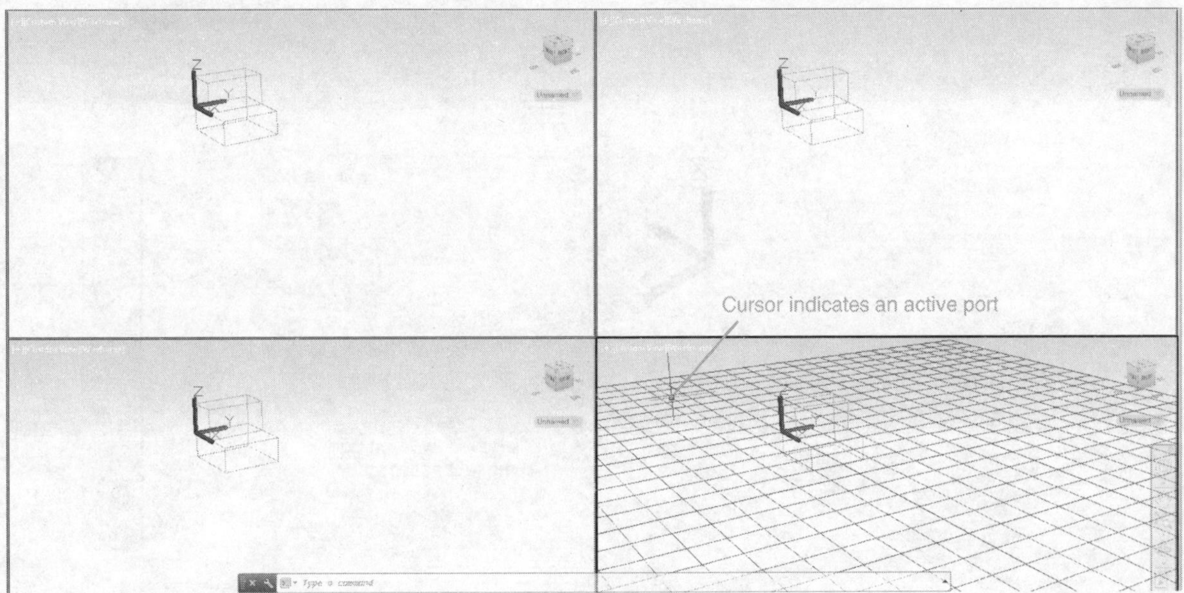

Figure 14-37

2. Select the **Top** tool from the **View** cube.

   A top view of the object will appear in the port.

See Figure 14-38.

3. Move the cursor into the lower left viewport, and click the mouse to make this viewport the current viewport.

   Note the world space icon faintly appearing in the upper right corner of the viewport. See Figure 14-39.

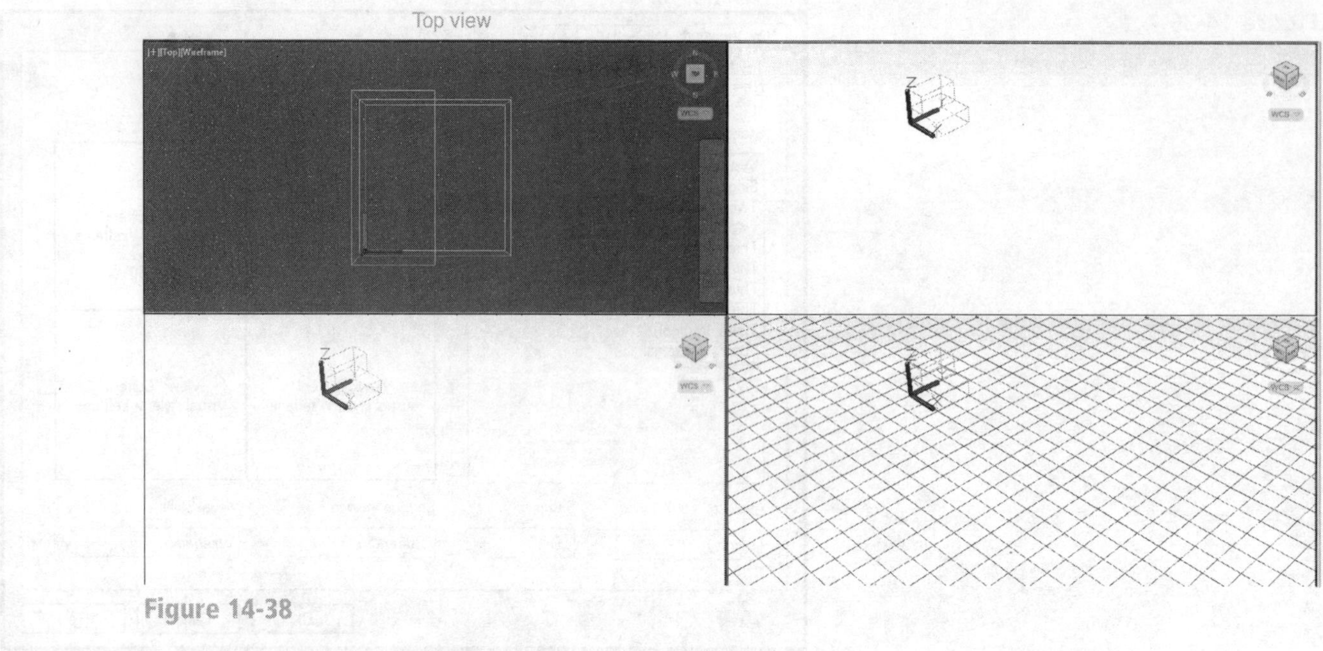

Figure 14-38

Figure 14-39

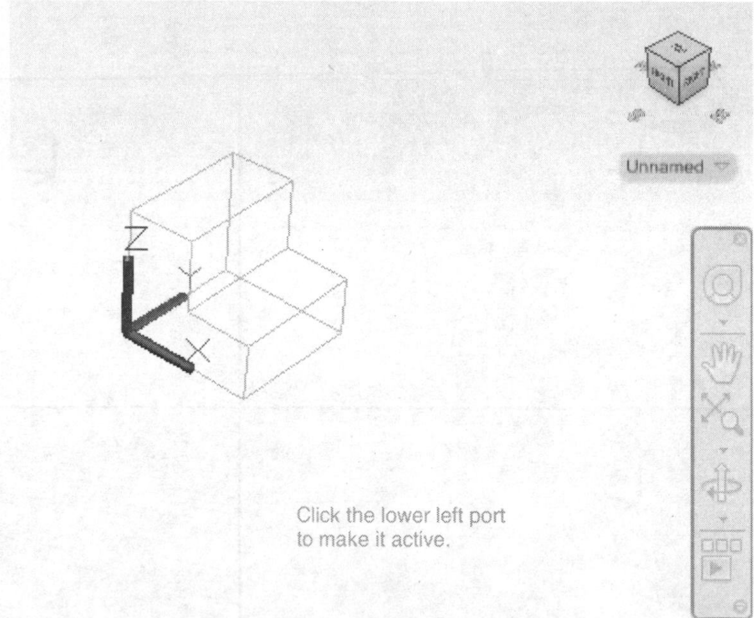

4. Locate the cursor on the **S** on the **world space** icon, hold the mouse button down, and move the cursor around. Note the changes in the view's orientation. Click the **Undo** tool to return to the original view orientation.
5. Click the word **FRONT** on the icon.

   The view orientation will change to a front view. See Figure 14-40.
6. Use the **Right** option on the **View** panel, and create a right-side view of the object.

See Figure 14-41.

Figure 14-40

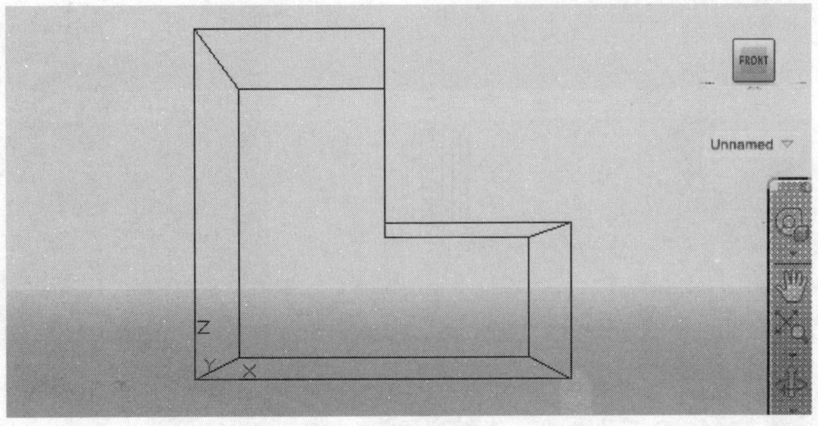

Front view

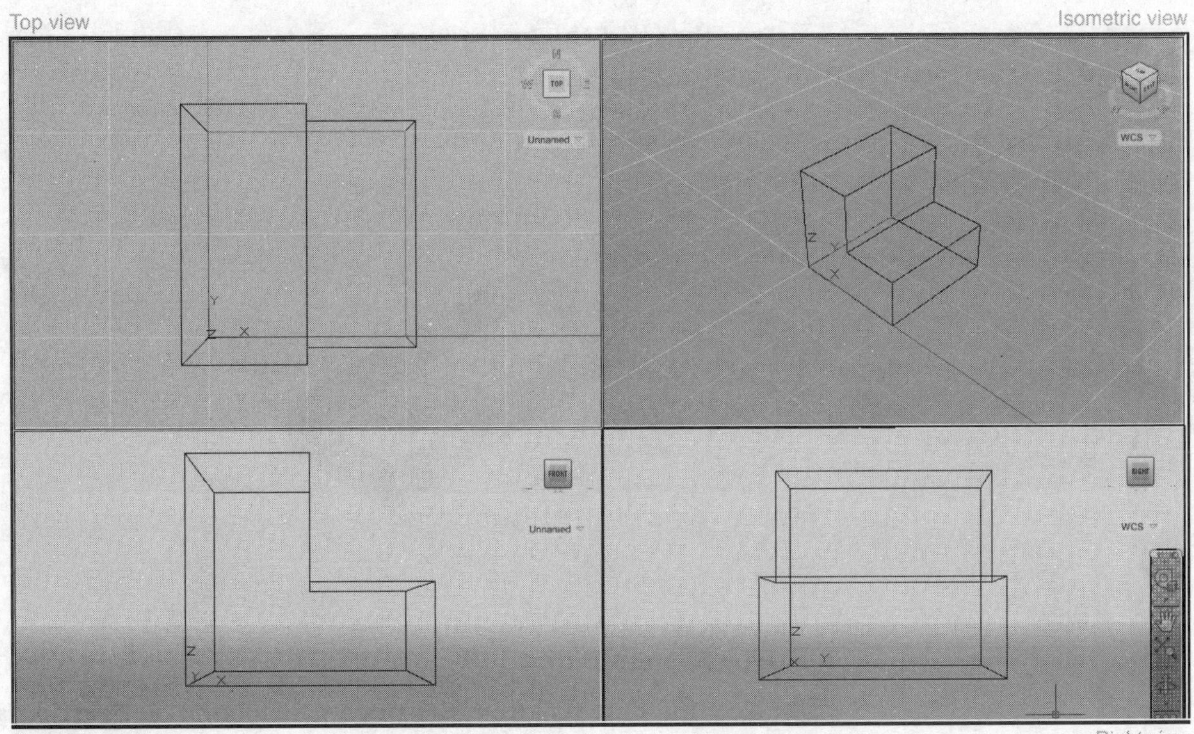

Figure 14-41

14-14 Line Thickness

The **Thickness** command is used to create 3D surfaces from 2D drawing commands. Figure 14-42 shows a line and a circle drawn as normal 2D entities and then drawn a second time with the **Thickness** command set for 2 and 3, respectively. The figures were drawn with a 3D perspective grid background. The **Line** command generates a plane perpendicular to the plane of the original line, and the **Circle** command generates a cylinder perpendicular to the plane of the base circle.

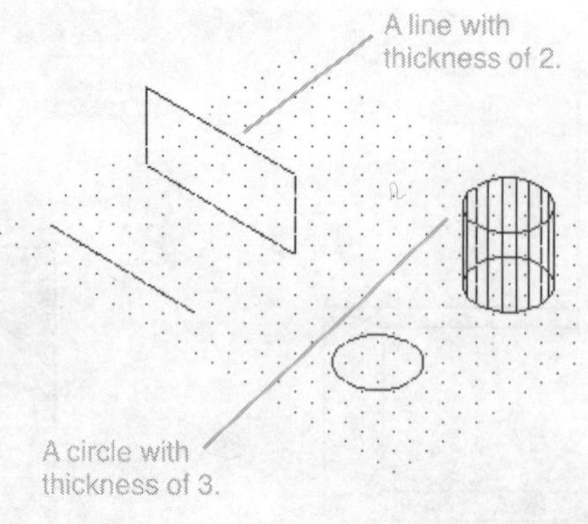

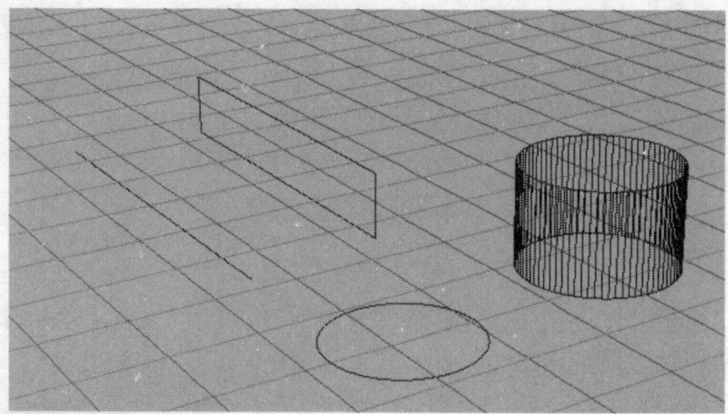

Figure 14-42

To Use the Thickness Command

In the following example, an **acad3D** template was created. Grid and snap spacing is **.5**, with decimal units, and the viewpoint is **SE Isometric**.

1. Type the word **thickness** in response to a command prompt.

   See Figure 14-43.

   Enter new value for THICKNESS <0.0000>:

Figure 14-43

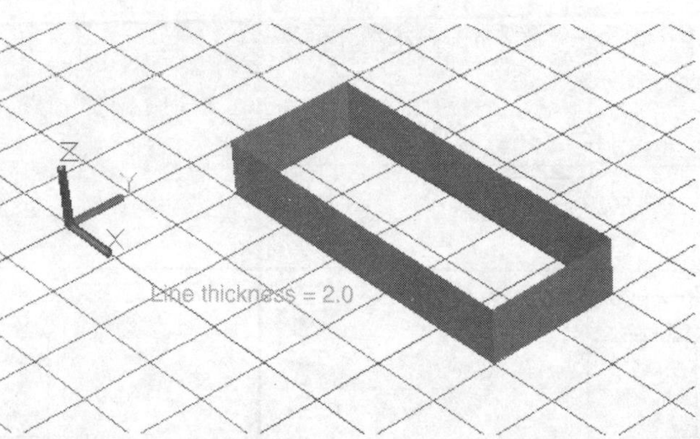

2. Type **2;** press **Enter.**
3. Select the **Line** tool from the **Draw** panel found on **Drafting and annotation**.

   Command: _line

   From point:
4. Continue using the **Line** tool, and draw the box shape shown in Figure 14-43.
5. Press the right mouse button; click **Enter**.

   The shape shown in the figure is not a box, but is four perpendicular planes. There is no top or bottom surface.

The default thickness value may also be defined by using the **Properties** command on the **Modify** menu. The **Modify** menu is accessed by windowing the entire box, right-clicking the mouse, and selecting the **Properties** option. The **Properties** dialog box will appear. See Figure 14-44. Change the thickness value to **2.0000.**

Figure 14-45 shows a hexagon and an arc drawn with the **Thickness** command set at values of 2 and 4, respectively.

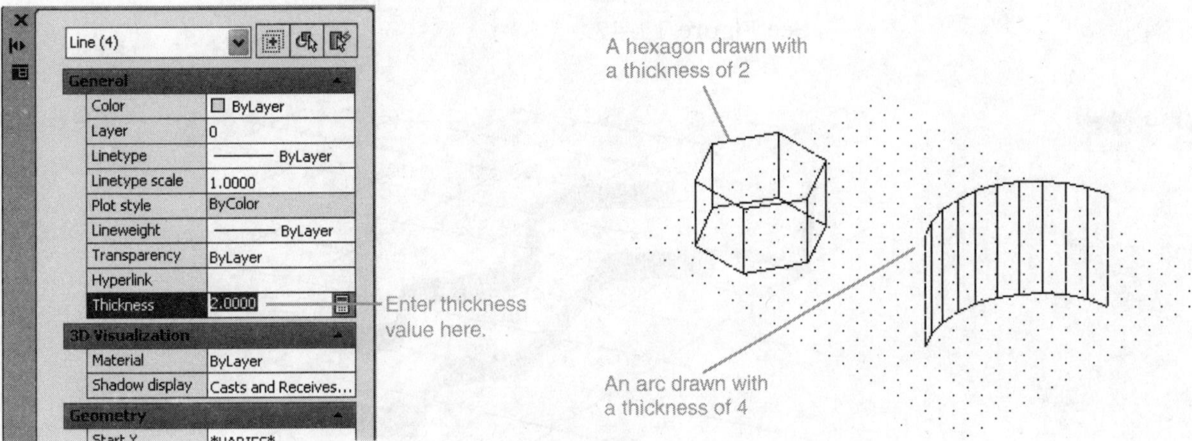

Figure 14-44

Figure 14-45

To Draw a Curve by Using Thickness (See Figure 14-46.)

Use the **acad3D** template.

1. Access the **Thickness** command.

   Specify new default elevation <0.0000>:

2. Type **3.5;** press **Enter**.
3. Select the **Polyline** tool from the **Draw** panel.

   Command: _pline
   Specify start point:

4. Draw a polyline approximately like the one shown in Figure 14-46.

Figure 14-46

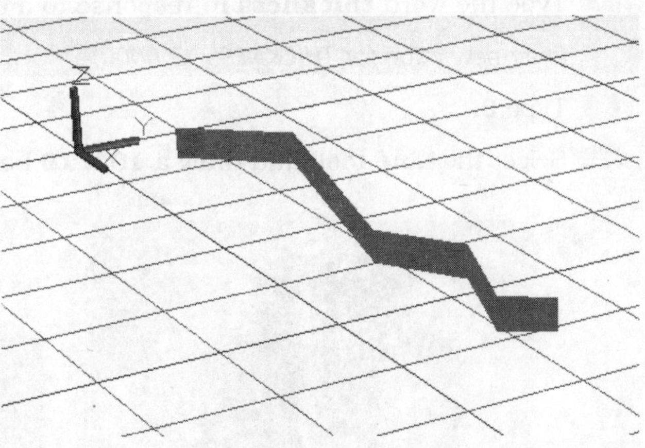

5. Select the **Edit Polyline** tool from the **Modify** panel.

   Command: _pedit
   Select polyline or [Multiple]:

6. Select the polyline.

   Enter an option [Close Join Width Edit vertex Fit Spline Decurve Ltype gen Undo]:

7. Select the **Fit** option.

   See Figure 14-47.

Figure 14-47

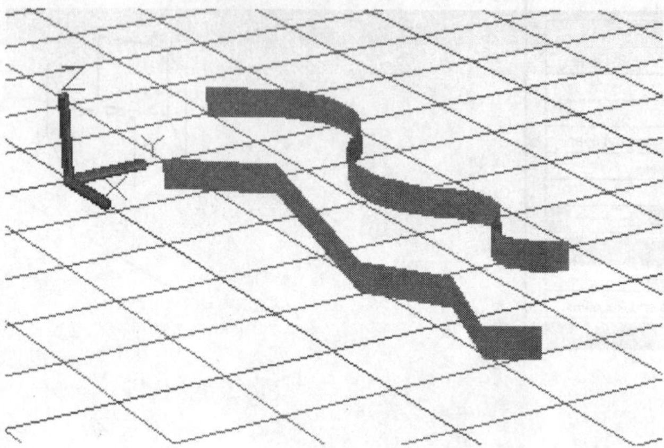

8. Right-click the mouse, and click **Enter**.

14-15 Using the Thickness Command to Create Objects

The **Thickness** command can be used with different UCSs to create simulated 3D objects. The objects will actually be open-ended plane structures. The procedure that follows shows how to create the object shown in Figure 14-48. The drawing was created with **Grid** and **Snap** set to **.5,** with decimal units, and with an **SE Isometric** viewpoint.

To Draw the Box

1. Type the word **thickness** in response to a command prompt.

   Enter new value for THICKNESS <2.0000>:

2. Type **6.**

3. Select the **Line** tool, and draw a **10 × 10** box as shown in Figure 14-49.

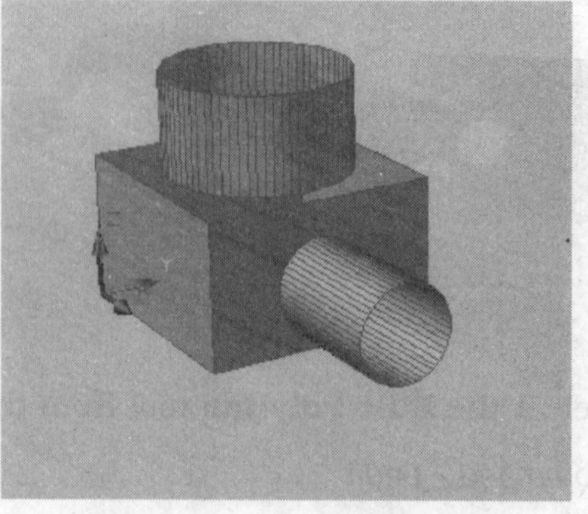

Figure 14-48

The box is drawn so that its corner is on the origin of the WCS.

Figure 14-49

To Create a New UCS

1 Click the **3 Point** UCS tool on the **Coordinates** panel under the **View** tab.

Specify new origin point <0,0,0>:

2 Select the lower left corner of the box as shown in Figure 14-50.

Figure 14-50

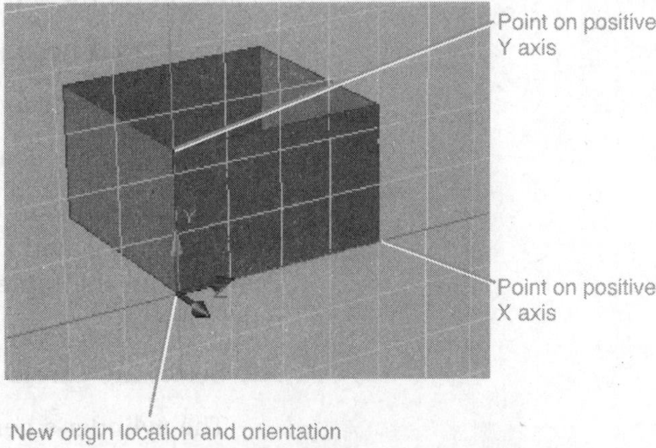

> **NOTE**
> Use **Osnap Endpoint** to select the corner point.

Specify point on the positive portion of X-axis:

3 Click the lower right corner as shown.

Specify point on the positive portion of Y-axis:

4 Pick the corner on the Y axis above the origin.

To Draw the Right Cylinder

This cylinder will be 6 units long, so there is no need to change the thickness setting.

1 Select the **Circle** tool, and draw a cylinder centered on the right face of the box.

The coordinate value for the cylinder's center point is **5,3,** and the radius value is **2.00.** See Figure 14-51.

Figure 14-51

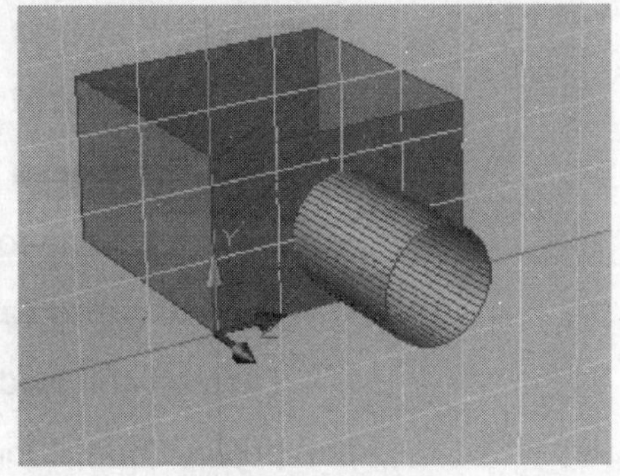

To Draw the Top Cylinder

First, return the drawing to the original WCS X,Y axes; then, change the location of the X,Y plane so that the top cylinder can be drawn in the correct position.

1. Select the **World** tool from the **Coordinates** panel.
2. Click the **Origin** tool on the **Coordinates panel**, and locate a new origin on the left corner of the top surface of the box.
3. Type **thickness** in response to a command prompt.

   Enter new value for THICKNESS <0.0000>:

4. Type **4;** press **Enter.**

   Note the shift in the grid pattern. The WCS origin icon is still located at the same place, but the grid origin is on the top surface. See Figure 14-52. Positions on the top surface may be located by using the displayed coordinate values.

5. Select the **Circle** tool, and draw the cylinder as shown in Figure 14-53.

   The cylinder's center point is at **5,5** and its radius = **4.**

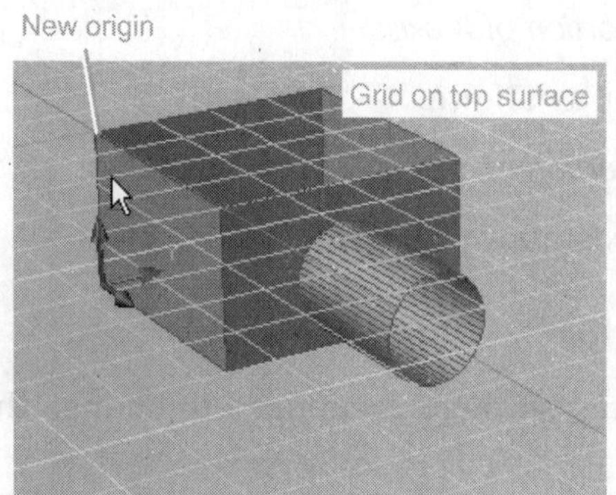

Figure 14-52

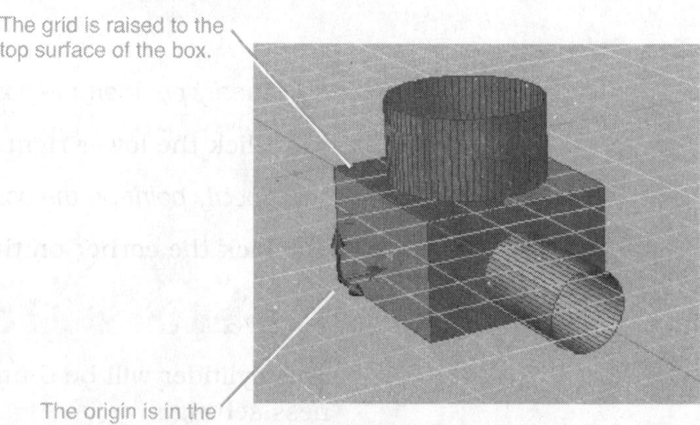

Figure 14-53

To Return the Drawing to Its Original Settings

1. Click the **World** tool on the **Coordinates** panel.
2. Type **thickness** in response to a command prompt.

   Enter new value for THICKNESS <0.0000>:

3. Type **0;** press **Enter.**
4. Turn off the grid.

The object should look like the one shown in Figure 14-48.

14-16 EXERCISE PROBLEMS

Exercise problems EX14-1 through EX14-4 require you to draw 2D shapes on various surfaces of 3D objects created by use of the **Thickness** command. All 2D shapes should be drawn at the center of the surfaces on which they appear. Either the acad or acad3D template may be used.

A. Draw the 2D shapes as shown.

B. Divide the screen into four viewports, and create front, top, and right-side orthographic views for each object.

EX14-1 Inches

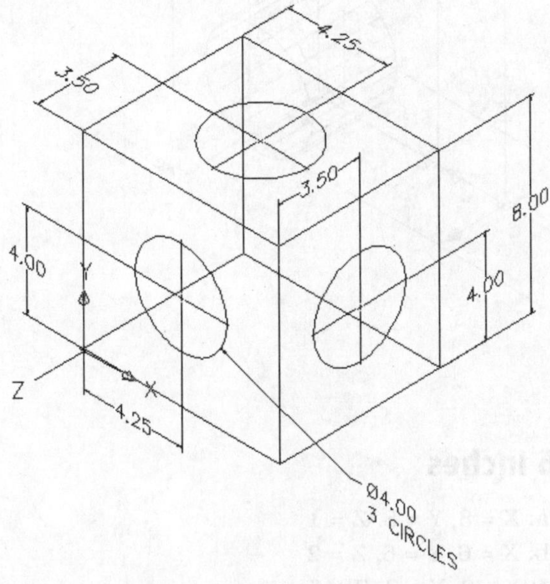

EX14-2 Millimeters

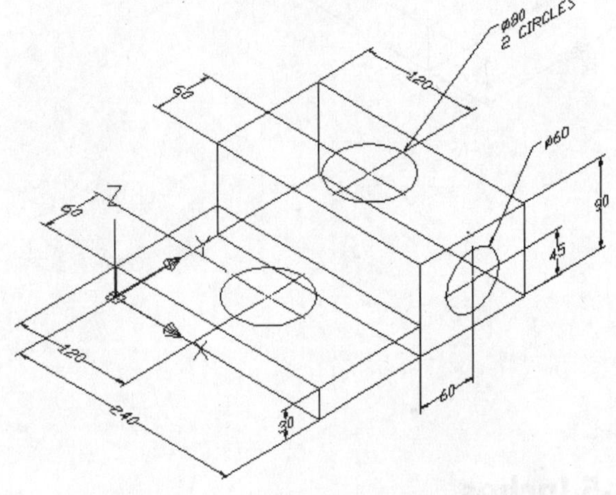

EX14-3 Millimeters

Both cylinders are centered on the top surfaces as shown.

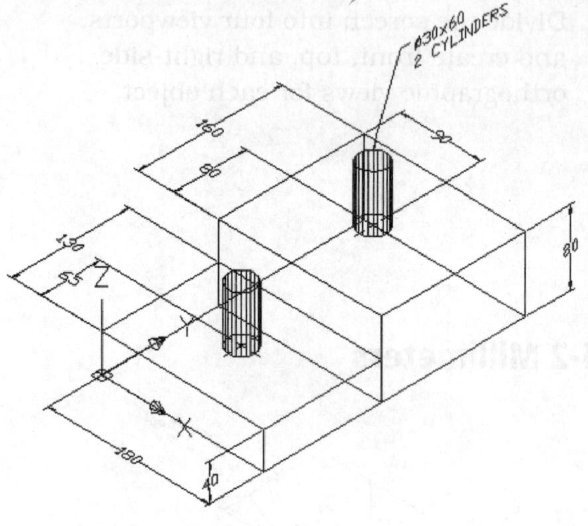

EX14-4 Millimeters

Redraw the figures presented in Exercise Problems EX14-5 through EX14-17 as wireframe models, using the **Thickness** command. Divide the screen into four viewports, and create front, top, and right-side orthographic views and one isometric view, as shown in Figure 14-38.

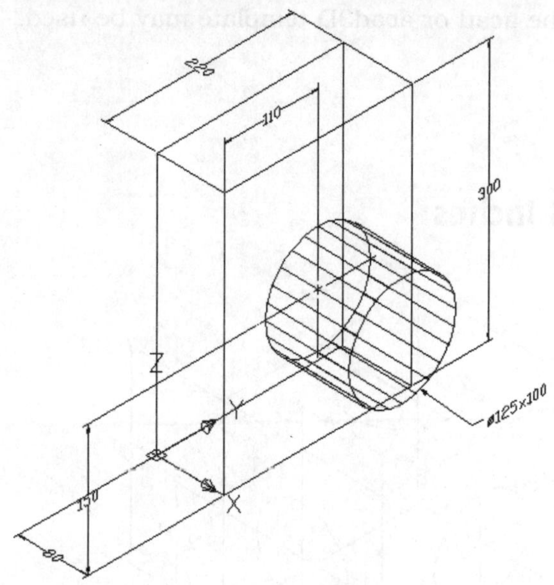

EX14-5 Inches

Box a: X = 6, Y = 5, Z = 2
Box b: X = 4, Y = 4, Z = 4
Box c: X = 5, Y = 2, Z = 1

Hint: Consider a modified version of the NE Isometric viewpoint.

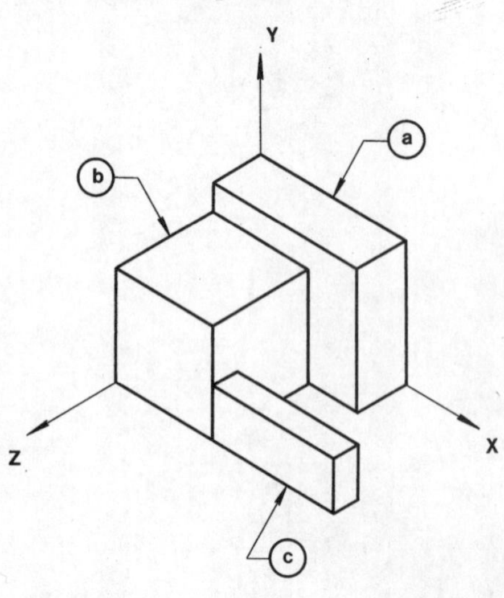

EX14-6 Inches

Box a: X = 8, Y = 8, Z = 1
Box b: X = 6, Y = 6, Z = 2
Box c: X = 2, Y = 2, Z = 6

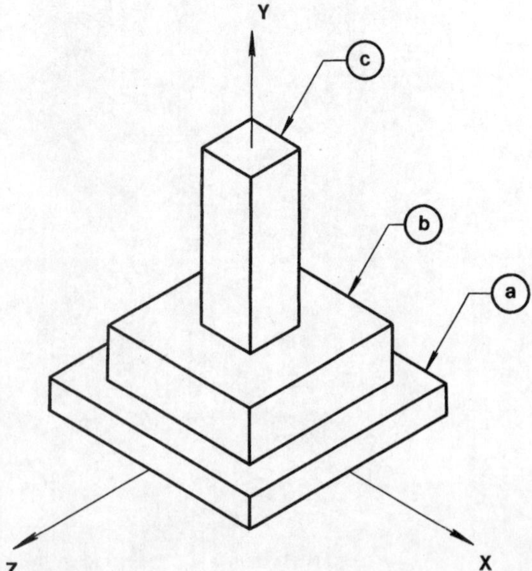

EX14-7 Millimeters

Each box is 2 × 2 × 5.

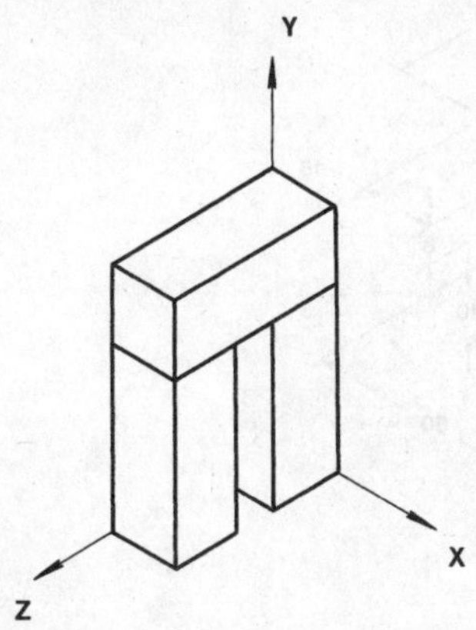

EX14-8 Millimeters

Cylinder a: Ø10 × 30 LONG
Cylinder b: Ø20 × 8 LONG
Cylinder c: Ø35 × 18 LONG

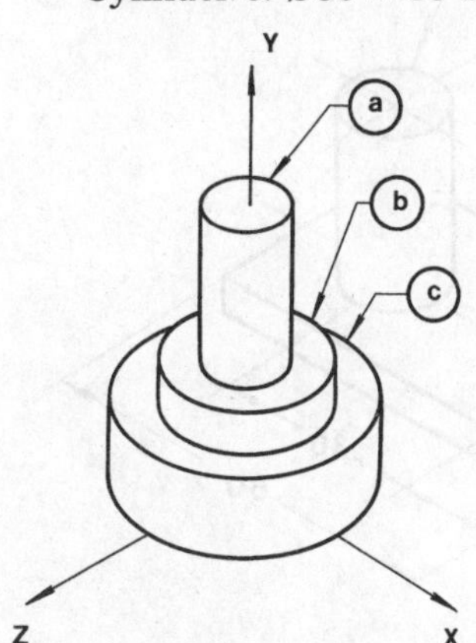

EX14-9 Millimeters

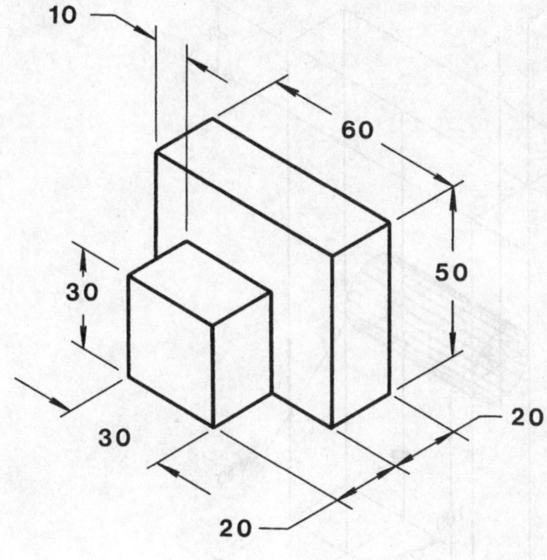

EX14-10 Millimeters

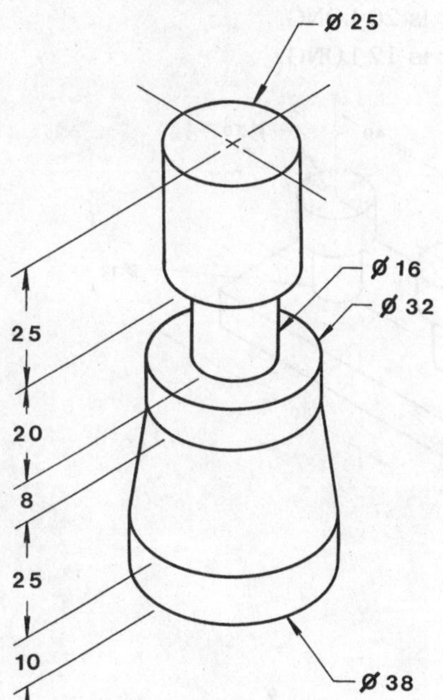

EX14-11 Millimeters

Cylinders are 30 LONG.

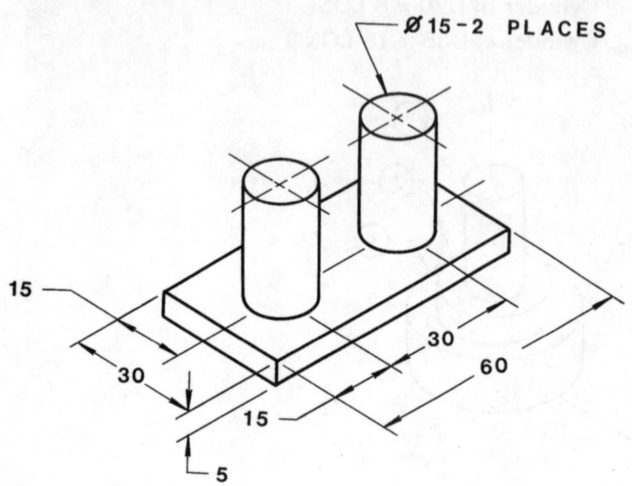

EX14-12 Millimeters

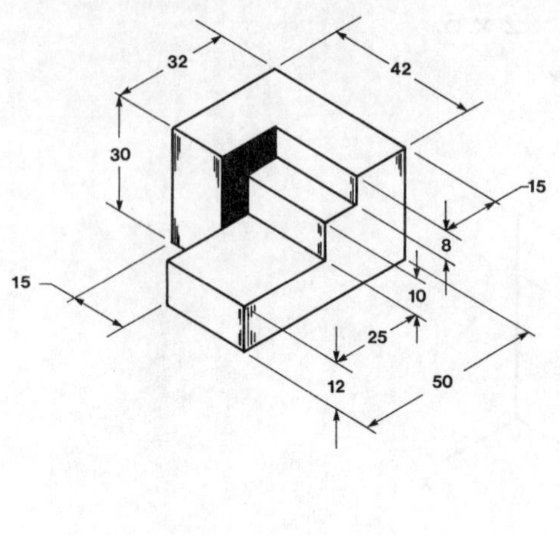

EX14-13 Millimeters

The Ø12 cylinder is 20 LONG.
The Ø20 cylinder is 12 LONG.

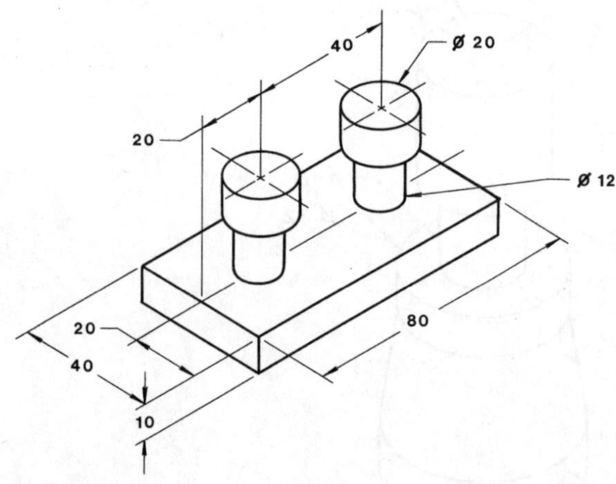

EX14-14 Millimeters

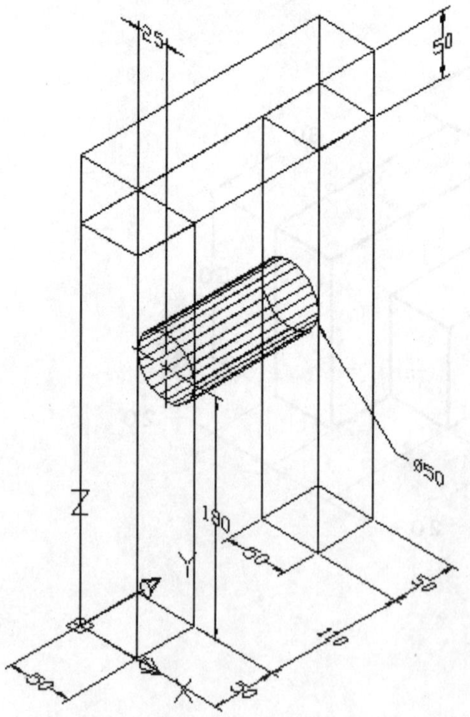

EX14-15 Millimeters

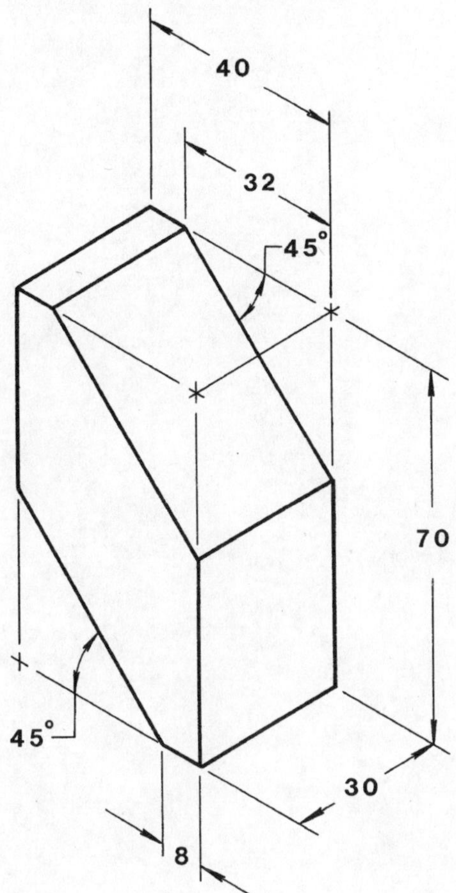

EX14-16 Millimeters

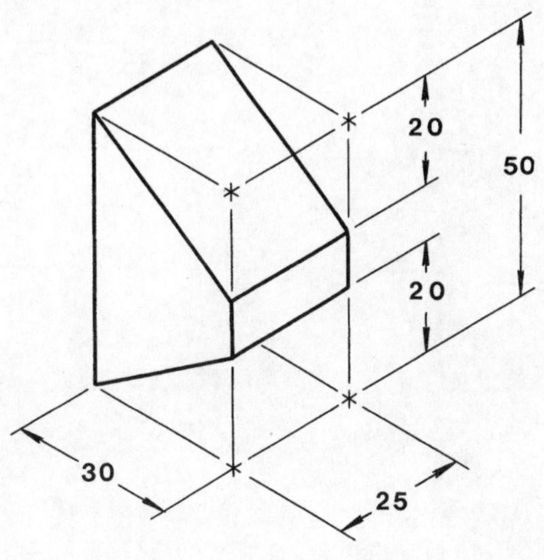

EX14-17 Millimeters

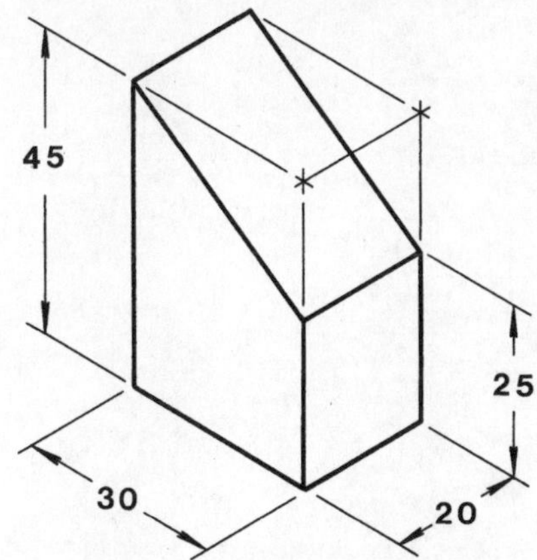

chapter fifteen
Modeling

15-1 Introduction

This chapter introduces solid modeling. The solid modeling commands can be accessed through the **3D Modeling** workspace or the **3D Basics** workspace. Figure 15-1 shows the panels and tabs associated with both workspaces. Chapter 14 introduced many commands from the **3D Modeling** workspace. The current chapter builds on that introduction and also introduces some of the **3D Basics** commands.

Solid modeling allows you to create objects as solid entities. Solid models differ from surface models in that solid models have density and are not merely joined surfaces.

Solid models are created by joining together, or *unioning*, basic primitive shapes—boxes, cylinders, wedges, and so on—or by defining a shape as a polyline and extruding it into a solid shape. Solid primitives may also be subtracted from one another. For example, to create a hole in a solid box, draw a solid cylinder and then subtract the cylinder from the box. The result will be an open volume in the shape of a hole.

The first part of the chapter deals with the individual tools of the **Modeling** panel under the **Home** tab in the **3D Modeling** workspace. The second part gives examples of how to create solid objects by joining primitive shapes and changing UCSs. The chapter ends with a discussion of the **Solid Editing** panel.

The **acad3D** template set to an **SE Isometric** view will be used throughout the chapter as a background grid.

3D Basis

3D Modeling

Figure 15-1

15-2 Box

The **Box** tool on the **Create** panel has two options: **Center** and **Corner. Corner** is the default option. The **Center** tool is used to draw a box by first locating its center point. The **Corner** tool is used to draw a box by first locating one of its corner points.

Use the **acad3D** template, access the **3D Modeling** workspace, and set the drawing for an **SE Isometric** 3D view. The SE Isometric 3D comment is located on the **View** panel under the **Home** tab.

To Draw a Box by Using the Corner Option (See Figure 15-2.)

1. Select the **Box** tool from the **Create** panel.

Command: _box

Specify corner of box or [Center]:

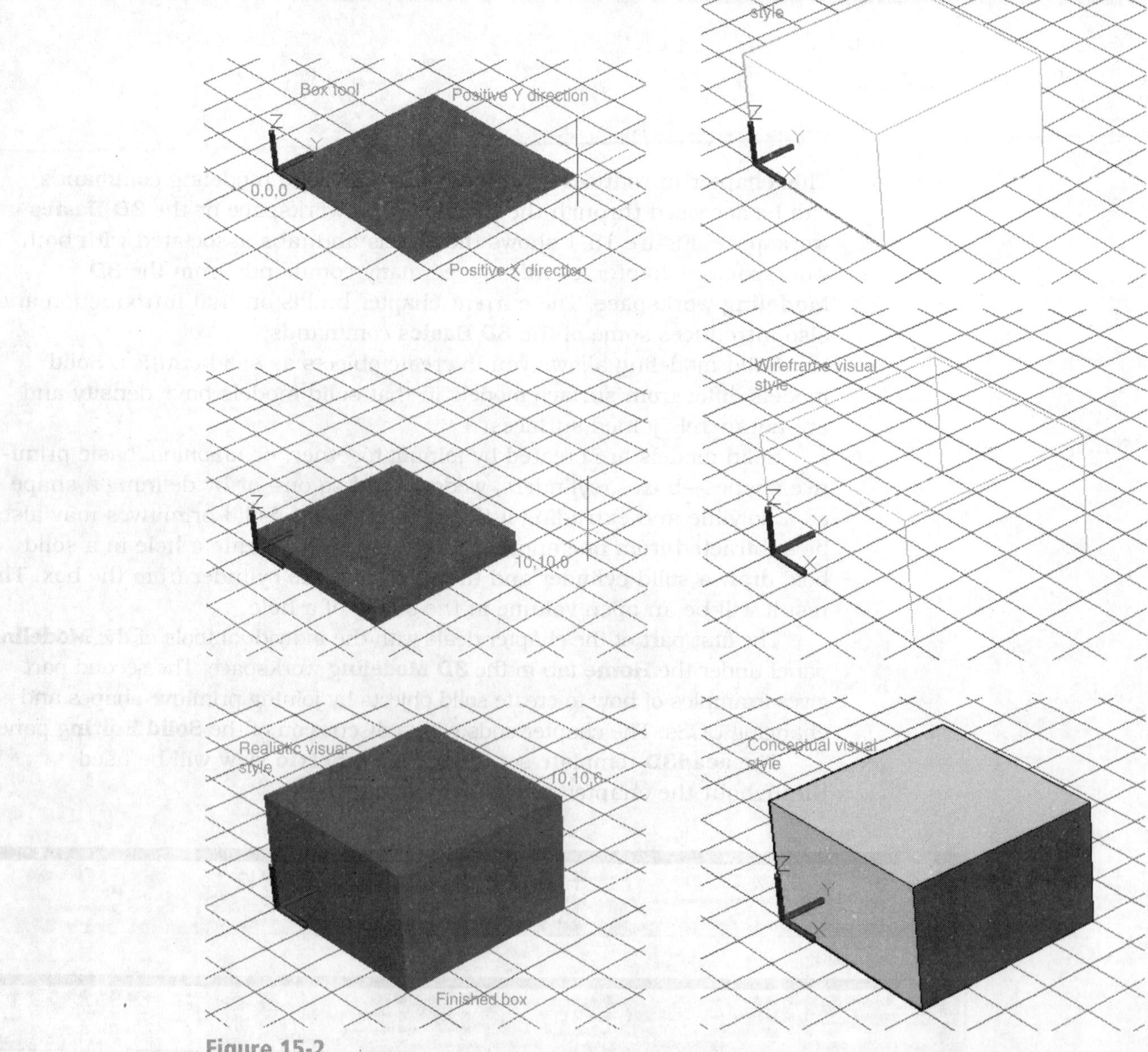

Figure 15-2

2. Type **0,0,0;** press **Enter.**

   This means that the corner of the box will be located on the 0,0,0 (the origins) point of the XY plane.

   Specify other corner or [Cube Length]:

3. Locate the cursor in a positive X direction, and type **10,10,0;** press **Enter.**

   Specify height or [2 points] <0.9396>:

4. Locate the cursor in a positive Z direction, and type **6;** press **Enter.**

To Change the Visual Style

Figure 15-2 shows the generated box with four different visual styles: realistic, wireframe, hidden, and conceptual. The **Visual Styles** command is located on the **Visual Styles** panel under the **View** tab. See Figure 15-3. To change the visual style of an object, click on the desired new style.

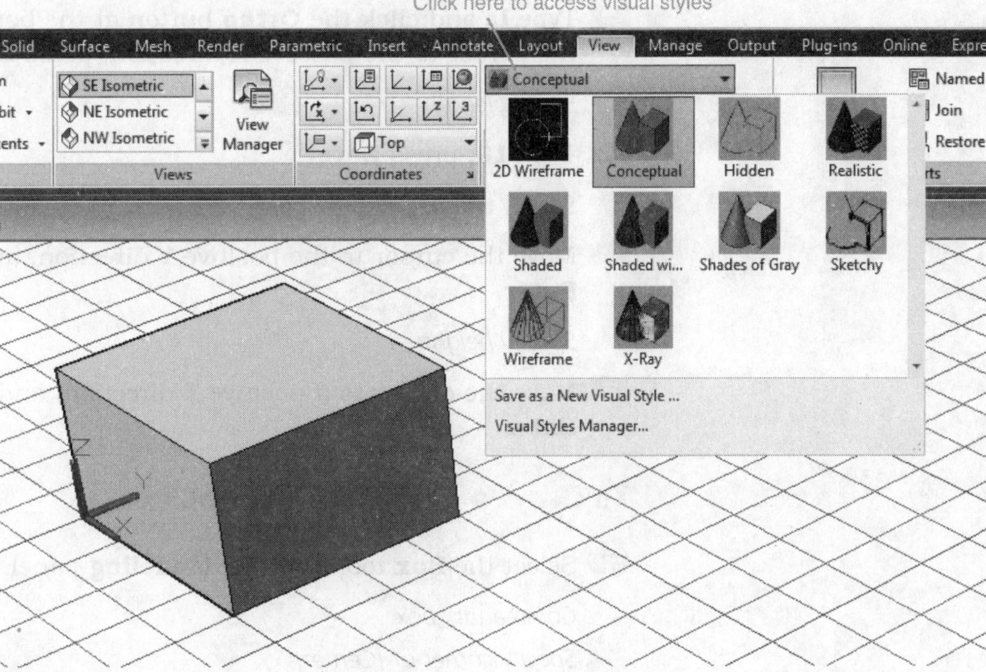

Figure 15-3

To Draw a Box from Given Dimensions

See Figure 15-4. Draw a box with a length of **10,** a width of **8,** and a height of **4,** with its corner at the **2,2,0** point. Use the cursor to define a positive X direction.

1. Select the **Box** tool from the **Modeling** panel.

   Command: _box
   Specify corner or [Center]:

Figure 15-4

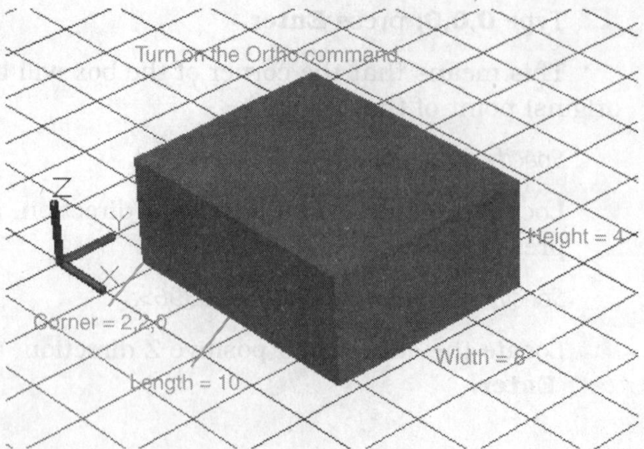

2. Type **2,2,0;** press **Enter.**

   Specify corner or [Cube Length]:

   There are three different ways to define the next point for the box: Enter coordinate values (10,0); activate the **Snap** command and use the dynamic screen coordinate display to select the point; or activate the **Ortho** command and enter a length value, as will be defined in this example.

3. Type **L**, and click the **Ortho** button at the bottom of the screen. Move the cursor to the positive X direction; press **Enter.**

   Specify length:

4. Type **10;** press **Enter.**

   Specify width:

5. Move the cursor to the positive Y direction, and type **8;** press **Enter.**

   Specify height:

6. Move the cursor to a positive Z direction, and type **4;** press **Enter.**

To Draw a Cube (See Figure 15-5.)

1. Select the **Box** tool from the **Modeling** panel.

   Command: _box

   Specify corner of [Center]:

Figure 15-5

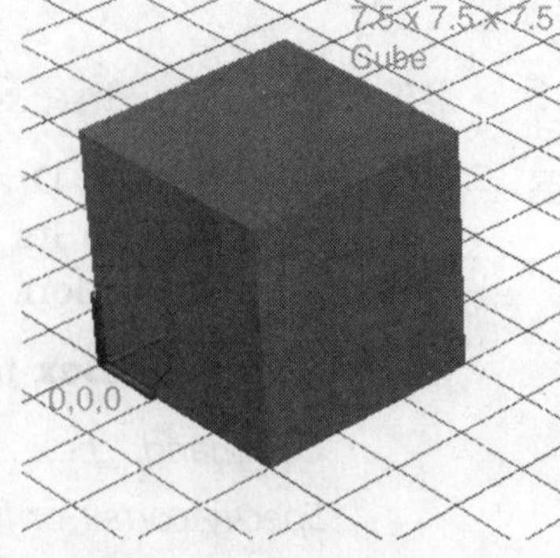

2. Type **0,0,0;** press **Enter.**

Specify corner or [Cube Length]:

3. Type **c;** press **Enter.**

Specify length:

4. Type **7.5;** press **Enter.**

AutoCAD automatically makes all three edges of the box equal lengths of 7.5.

NOTE

Use the **Ortho** tool to align the edge of the cube with the X axis.

To Use Dynamic Grips

This example will use the 7.5 × 7.5 × 7.5 cube just drawn.

1. Click any port of the box.

Blue arrowheads will appear on the XY plane of the box. See Figure 15-6.

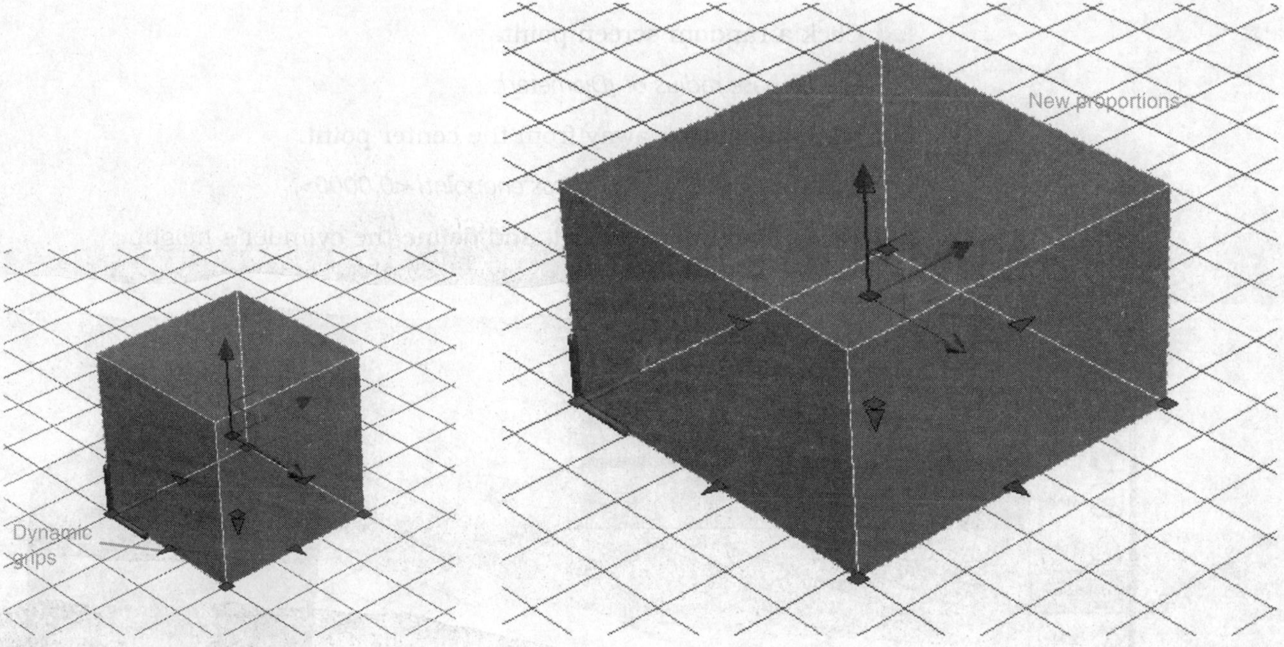

Figure 15-6

2. Click and hold one of the arrowheads, and drag the cursor away from the box.

Note how the box changes shape. Try moving different arrows to see how the cube responds.

15-3 Sphere

To Draw a Sphere (See Figure 15-7.)

1. Select the **Sphere** tool. The **Sphere** tool is a flyout from the **Box** tool on the **Modeling** panel under the **Home** tab.

   Specify center of sphere or [3P 2P Ttr]:

2. Type **5,5,0; press Enter.**

   Specify radius or [Diameter]:

3. Type **4;** press **Enter.**

The sphere shown in Figure 15-7 uses the **Realistic** visual style.

15-4 Cylinder

There are two options associated with the **Cylinder** command: circular and elliptical. This means that cylinders may be drawn with either elliptical or circular base planes. The base elliptical shape is drawn by the same procedure as was outlined for the **Ellipse** command in Chapter 2.

To Draw a Cylinder with a Circular Base

The **Cylinder** tool is a flyout from the **Box** tool. See Figure 15-8.

1. Select the **Cylinder** tool from the **Modeling** panel under the **Home** tab.

   Command: _cylinder

   Specify center point or base or [3P 2P Ttr Elliptical] <0,0,0>:

2. Click a random screen point.

   Specify base radius or [Diameter]:

3. Move the cursor away from the center point.

   Specify height or [2 Point/Axis endpoint] <0,0000>:

4. Move the cursor upward, and define the cylinder's height.

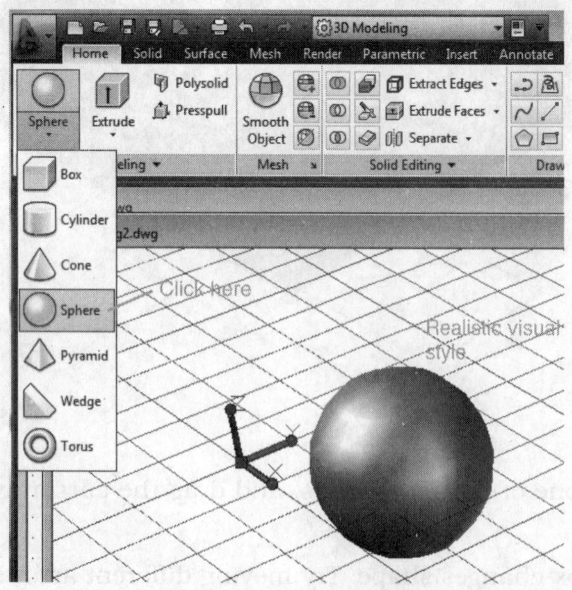

Figure 15-7

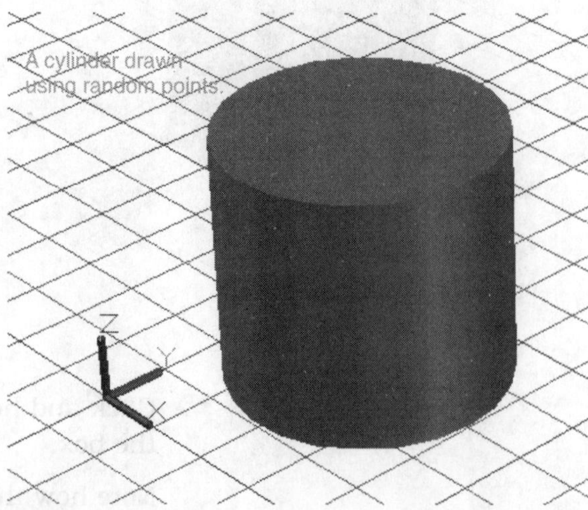

Figure 15-8

To Draw a Cylinder with an Elliptical Base

See Figure 15-9. The sequence that follows uses coordinate value input. The same points could have been selected by moving the crosshairs and pressing the left mouse button.

Figure 15-9

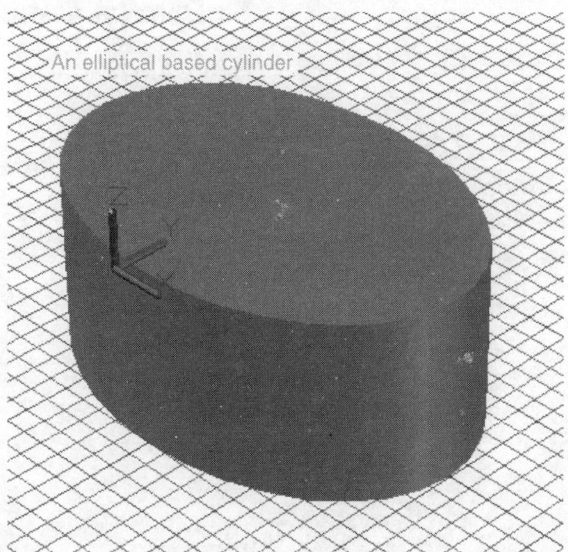

1. Select the **Cylinder** tool from the **Modeling** panel.

   Command: _cylinder

   Specify center point or base or [3P 2P Ttr Elliptical] <0,0,0>:

2. Type **e;** press **Enter.**

   Specify endpoint of first axis or [center]:

3. Type **0,0,0;** press **Enter.**

This input locates one end of the base axis on the 0,0,0 point of the XY plane.

Specify other endpoint of first axis:

4. Type **10,0,0;** press **Enter.**

   This input locates the axis line along the X axis. Use the **Ortho** tool if necessary.

   Specify endpoint of second axis:

   Note that the line dragging from the crosshairs has one end centered on the axis just defined.

5. Type **5,3.5,0;** press **Enter.**

   Specify height or [2 Point Axis endpoint]

6. Type **4;** press **Enter.**

   An elliptical base can also be defined by first defining a center point for the ellipse and then defining the length of the radii of the major and minor axes.

15-5 Cone

There are two options associated with the **Cone** tool: circular and elliptical. This means that cones can be drawn with either an elliptical or circular base plane. The base elliptical shape is drawn by the same procedure as was outlined for the **Ellipse** command in Chapter 2.

To Draw a Cone with an Elliptical Base (See Figure 15-10.)

Figure 15-10

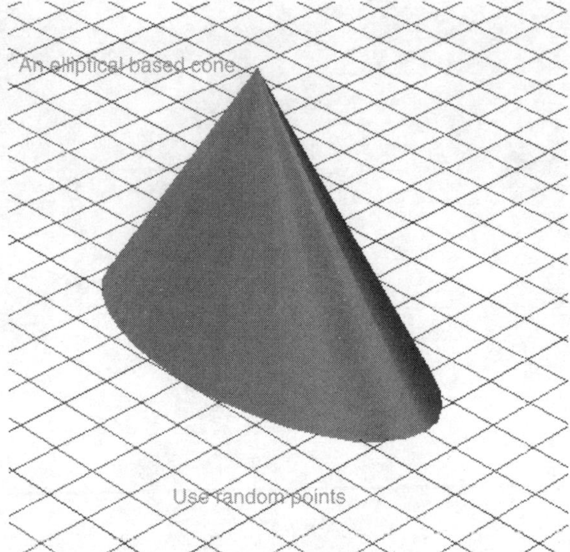

1 Select the **Cone** tool from the **Modeling** panel.

Command: _cone

Specify center point or base or [3P 2P Ttr Elliptical] <0,0,0>:

2 Type **e**; press **Enter.**

Specify endpoint of first axis or [Center]:

3 Pick a random point.

This input will locate one end of the ellipse axis at the 0,0,0 point of the XY plane.

Specify other endpoint of first axis:

4 Move the cursor away from the center point, and select a second point.

Specify endpoint of second axis:

5 Move the cursor, creating an elliptical shape, and pick a point.

Specify height or [2 Point Axis endpoint Top radius]:

6 Move the cursor to the positive Z direction, and select a point; press **Enter.**

A response of **A** to the *Apex/<Height>:* prompt allows you to select the height of the cone by using the crosshairs.

To Draw a Cone with a Circular Base (See Figure 15-11.)

1 Select the **Cone** tool from the **Modeling** panel toolbar.

Command: _cone

Specify center point [3P 2P Ttr Elliptical] <0,0,0>:

2. Type **5,5,0;** press **Enter.**

   Specify base radius or [Diameter]:

3. Type **3;** press **Enter.**

   Specify height or [2 Point Axis endpoint Top radius]:

4. Move the cursor to the positive Z direction, and type **7;** press **Enter.**

Figure 15-12 shows a cone with a top radius of 2.00 and height of 5.00. To create a top radius on the cone, type **T** in response to the *Specify height* prompt and enter a radius value.

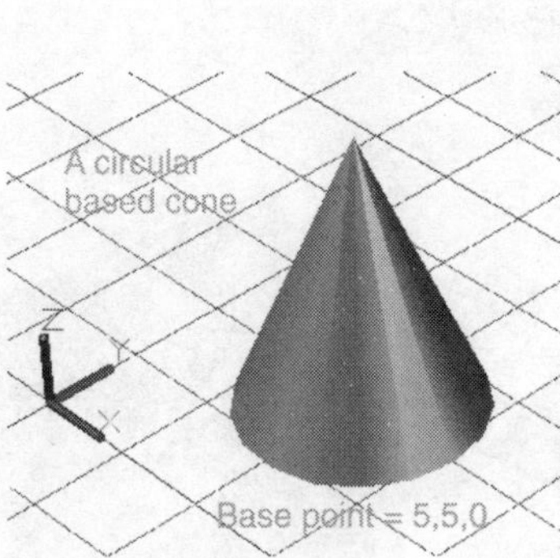

Figure 15-11

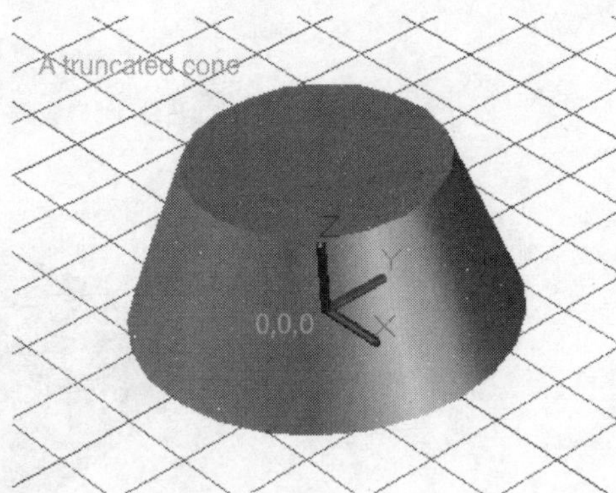

Figure 15-12

15-6 Wedge

There are two options associated with the **Wedge** command: center and corner.

To Draw a Wedge by Defining Its Corner Point (See Figure 15-13.)

1. Select the **Wedge** tool from the **Modeling** panel.

   Command: _wedge
   Specify first corner or [Center]:

2. Type **0,0,0;** press **Enter.**

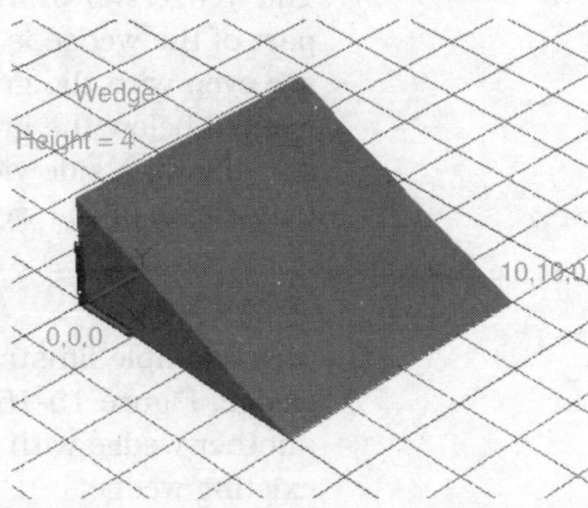

Figure 15-13

This input will locate the corner of the wedge on the 0,0,0 point of the XY plane.

Specify other corner or [Cube Length]:

The default response to this command defines the diagonal corner of the wedge's base.

3 Type **10,10,0;** press **Enter.**

Specify height:

4 Locate the cursor in the positive Z direction, and type **4;** press **Enter.**

A wedge shape can be drawn by using random points.

To Draw a Wedge by Defining Its Center Point (See Figure 15-14.)

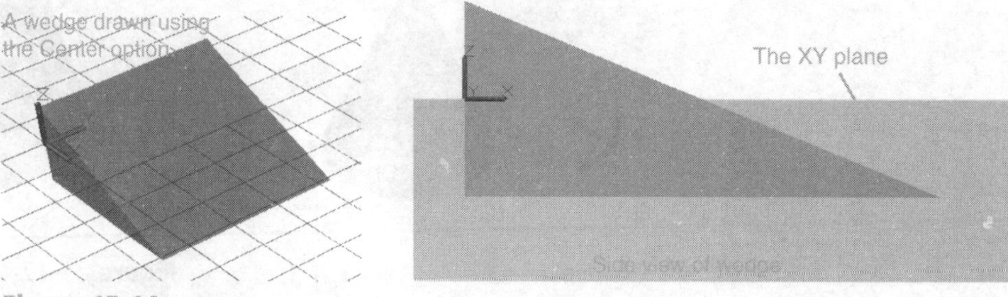

Figure 15-14

1 Select the **Wedge** tool from the **Modeling** panel.

Command: _wedge

Specify first corner or [Center] <0,0,0>

2 Type **c;** press **Enter.**

Specify center:

3 Type **5,5,0;** press **Enter.**

Specify corner or [Cube Length]:

4 Type **10,10,0;** press **Enter.**

Specify height or [2 Point] <4.000>:

5 Locate the cursor in the positive Z direction, and type **4;** press **Enter.**

The wedge shown in Figure 15-14 is centered about the XY plane; that is, part of the wedge is above the plane, and part is below. This is not easy to see even with the grid shown. The far right corner of the wedge is actually located below the grid at the 10,10 point on the XY plane. Figure 15-14 also shows a side view of the same wedge. Note how the line bisects the height line of the wedge.

To Align a Wedge with an Existing Wedge

This example illustrates how you can use different inputs to position a wedge. Figure 15-15 shows a $10 \times 8 \times 4$ wedge. The problem is to draw another wedge with its back surface aligned with the back surface of the existing wedge.

Figure 15-15

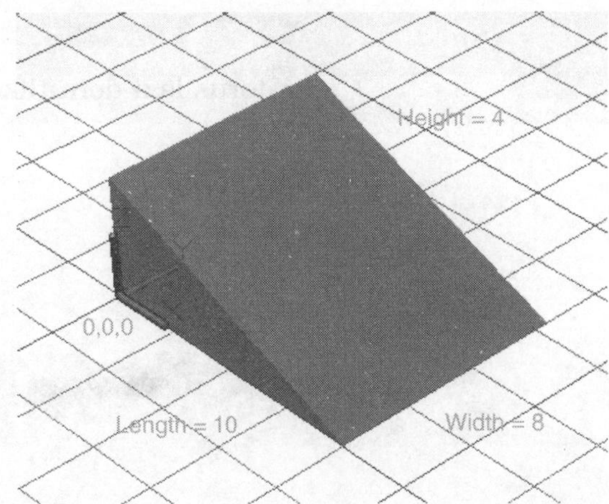

1. Select the **Wedge** tool from the **Modeling** panel.

   Command: _wedge

   Specify first corner or [Center]:

2. Type **0,0,0;** press **Enter.**

   Specify other corner or [Cube Length]:

3. Specify length. Type **L;** press **Enter.**

   Move the cursor so that it is located in the negative X direction.

4. Type = **–10;** press **Enter.**

   Specify width:

5. Move the cursor so that it is located in a positive Y direction. Type **8.00;** press **Enter.**

   Specify height or [2 Point] <4.0000>:

6. Use **Osnap Endpoint**, and select the Z-axis corner point of the existing wedge.

   See Figure 15-16. The model could also have been constructed by using the **Copy** command to create a second wedge, the **Rotate** command to rotate the new wedge 180°, and the **Move** command to align the wedge with the existing wedge. Use **Osnap Endpoint** to ensure exact alignment.

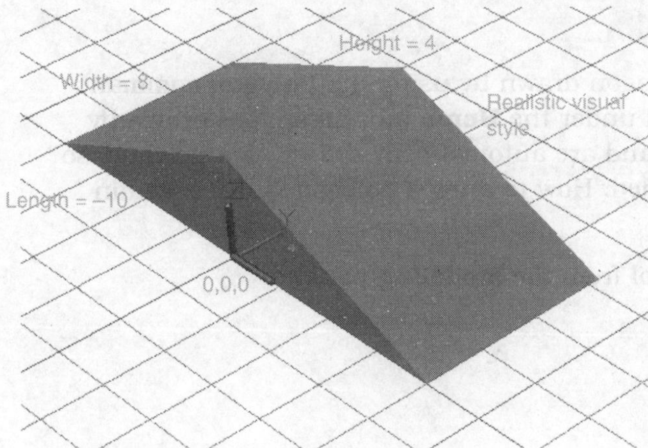

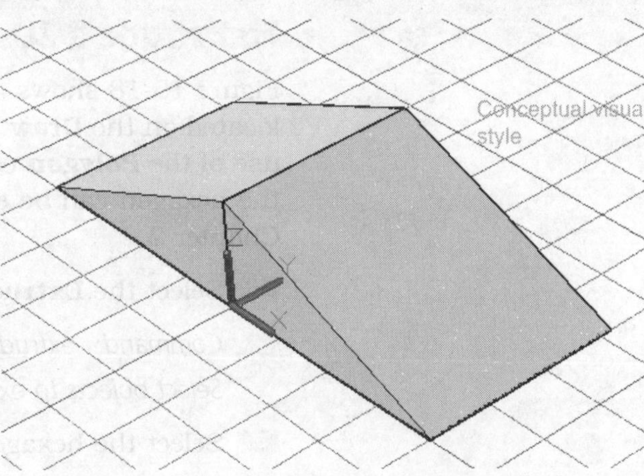

Figure 15-16

15-7 Torus

A torus is a donutlike shape. See Figure 15-17.

Figure 15-17

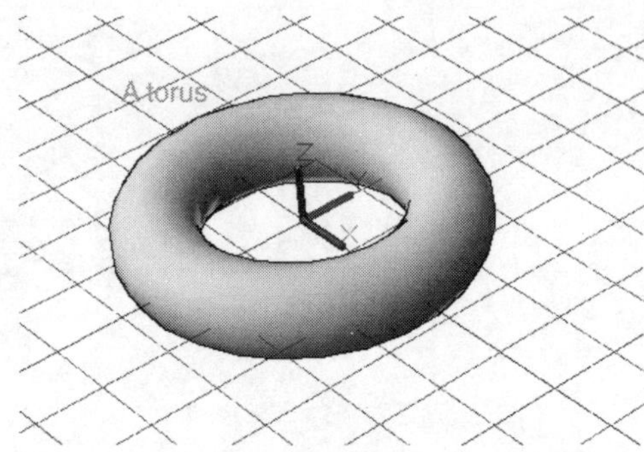

To Draw a Torus

1 Select the **Torus** tool from the **Modeling** panel.

Command: _torus

Specify center point or [3P 2P Ttr]:

2 Type **0,0,0;** press **Enter.**

This input will locate the center of the torus at the 0,0,0 point on the XY plane.

Specify radius or [Diameter] <3.0000>:

3 Type **5;** press **Enter.**

Specify tube radius or [2 Point Diameter]:

4 Type **1.5;** press **Enter.**

The finished torus is shown in Figure 15-17.

15-8 Extrude

The **Extrude** command is used to extend existing 2D shapes into 3D shapes. The **Extrude** tool can be applied only to a polyline.

To Extrude a 2D Polyline

Figure 15-18 shows a hexagon drawn by using the **Polygon** command located on the **Draw** panel under the **Home** tab. All shapes drawn by use of the **Polygon** command are automatically drawn as a polyline, so the hexagon can be extruded. How to draw a polygon is discussed in Chapter 2.

1 Select the **Extrude** tool from the **Modeling** panel.

Command: _extrude

Select objects to extrude:

2 Select the hexagon.

Select objects:

Figure 15-18

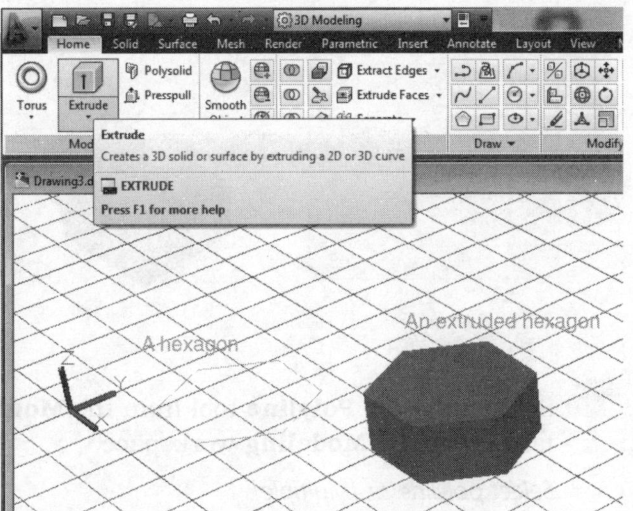

3 Press **Enter.**

Specify height of extrusion or [Direction Path Taper angle] <4.0000>:

4 Locate the cursor in a positive Z direction, and then type **6;** press **Enter.**

Specify angle of taper for extrusion <0>:

5 Press **Enter.**

Figure 15-19 shows a closed spline created by using **Polyline,** the **Fit** option on the **Polyline Edit** tool. The **Extrude** command was applied specifying a height of **5.**

Figure 15-19

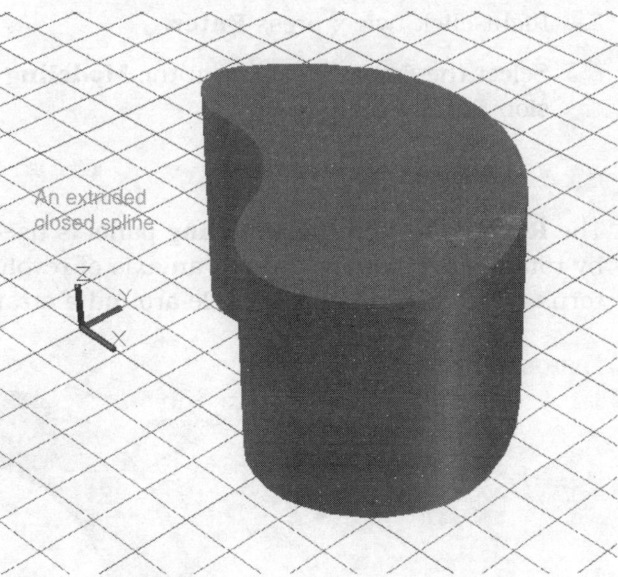

To Create a Polyline from Line Segments

Figure 15-20 shows a 2D shape that was created by using the **Line** tool from the **Draw** panel. The object must be converted to a polyline before it can be extruded. For visual purposes, the shape was windowed.

Figure 15-20

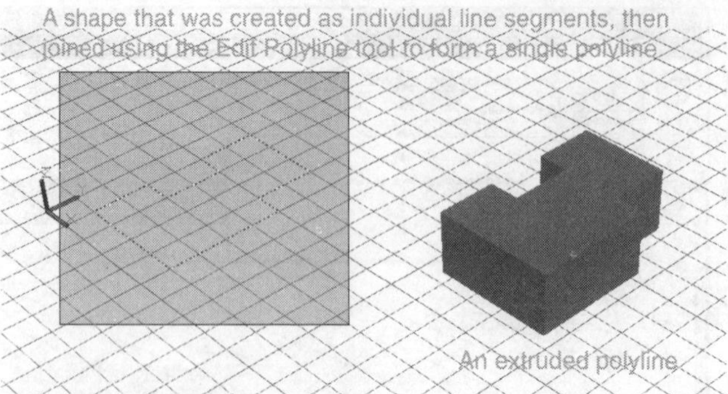

1. Select the **Edit Polyline** tool from the **Modify** panel under the **Home** tab on the **3D Modeling** workspace.

   Select polyline or [Multiple]:

2. Select any one of the lines in the 2D shape.

   Object selected is not a polyline

   Do you want to turn it into one? <Y>:

3. Press **Enter.**

   Enter an option [Close Join Width Edit vertex Fit Spline Decurve Ltype gen Undo]:

4. Select the **Join** option.

   The polyline will be defined by joining together all of the line segments to form a polyline. A curve is considered to be a line segment.

   Select objects:

5. Window the entire object.

   Enter an option [Close Join Width Edit vertex Fit Spline Decurve Ltype gen Undo]:

6. Right-click twice; press **Enter.**

7. Select the **Extrude** tool from the **Modeling** panel, and create an extrusion **5** units high.

15-9 Revolve

The **Revolve** tool on the **Modeling** panel is used to create a solid 3D object by rotating a 2D shape around an axis of revolution. Figure 15-21 shows a torus created by rotating a circle around a straight line.

Figure 15-21

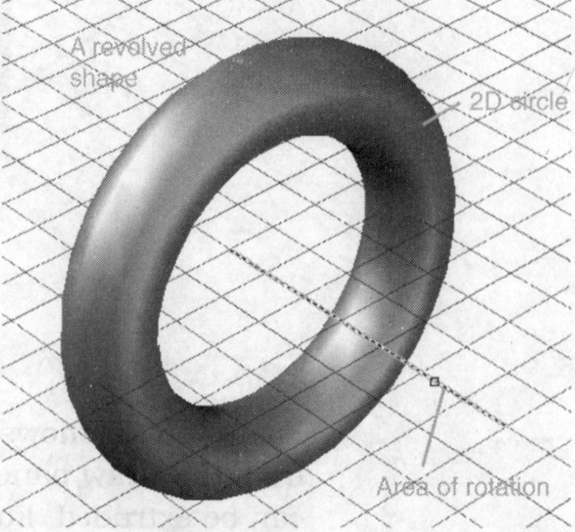

To Create a Revolved Solid Object

This procedure assumes that the curve path (2D shape) and the line that will be used as the axis of revolution already exist on the drawing.

1. Select the **Revolve** tool from the **Modeling** panel.

   Command: _revolve

   Select objects to revolve:

2. Select the circle.

   Select objects to revolve:

3. Press **Enter.**

   Specify start point for axis of revolution or define axis by [Object X Y Z] <object>:

4. Select one end of the line to be used as the axis of revolution. Use **Osnap Endpoint** if necessary.

   Specify axis endpoint:

5. Select the other end of the axis line.

   Specify angle of revolution or [Start angle] <360>:

6. Press **Enter.**

15-10 Helix

See Figure 15-22.

Figure 15-22

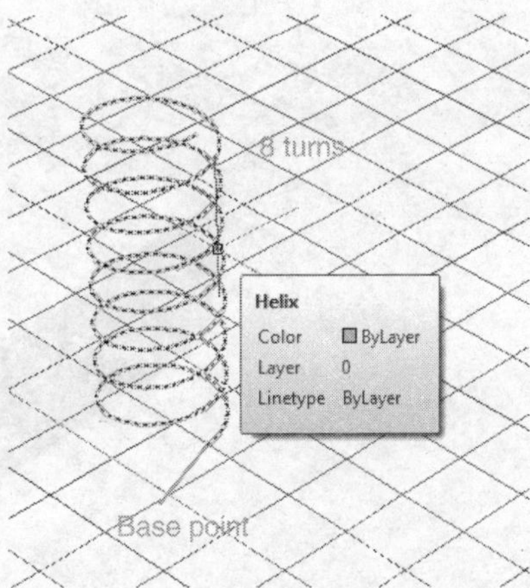

1. Type **helix** in response to a command prompt.

   Number of turns = 3, Twist = CCW.

   Specify center point of base:

2. Select a point on the screen; press the left mouse button.

   Specify base radius or [Diameter] <1.0000>:

3. Type **2;** press **Enter.**

   Specify top radius or [Diameter] <2.0000>:

4. Press **Enter.**

   Specify helix height or [Axis endpoint Turns turn Height tWist] <6.3885>:

5. Type **t;** press **Enter.**

Enter number of turns <3.0000>:

6. Type **8;** press **Enter.**

Specify helix height or [Axis endpoint Turns turn Height tWist] <1.0000>:

7. Use the dynamic input option, and select a helix height by moving the cursor.

8. Press the left mouse button.

15-11 Polysolid

See Figures 15-23 and 15-24.

Figure 15-23

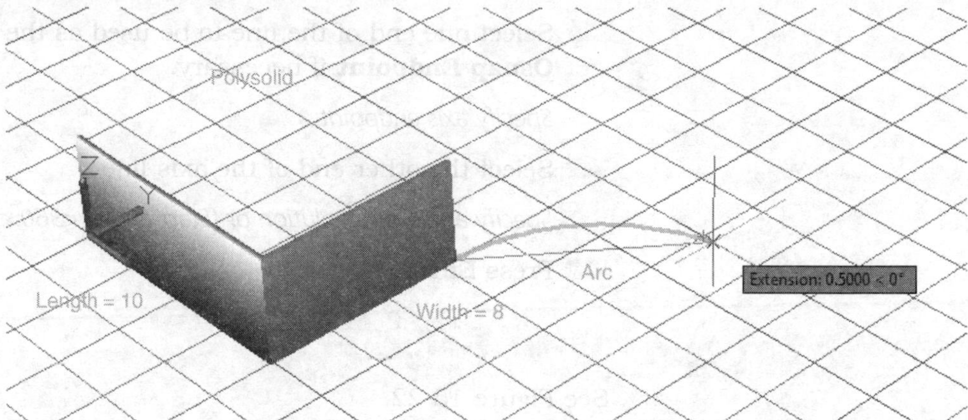

Figure 15-24

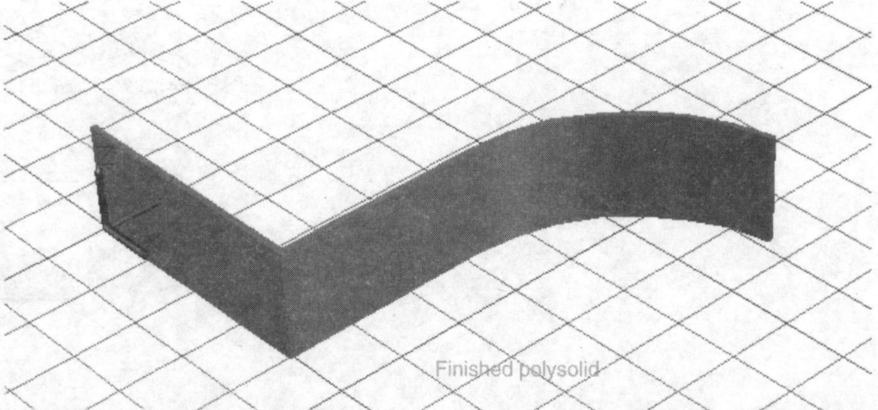

1. Select the **Polysolid** tool from the **Modeling** panel.

Polysolid Specify start point or [Object Height Width Justified] <object>:

2. Type **0,0,0;** press **Enter.**

Specify next point or [Arc Close Undo]:

3. Position the cursor in the positive X direction, and then type **10;** press **Enter.**

> **NOTE**
> Turn the **Ortho** command on to align the polysolid with the X axis.

Specify next point or [Arc Close Undo]:

4. Position the cursor in the positive Y direction, and then type **8;** press **Enter.**

   Specify next point or [Arc Close Undo]:

   Turn the **Ortho** command off.

5. Type **a;** press **Enter.**

   The polysolid will now generate an arc.

6. Create an arc, press the right mouse button, and select the **Enter** option.

15-12 Loft

See Figure 15-25.

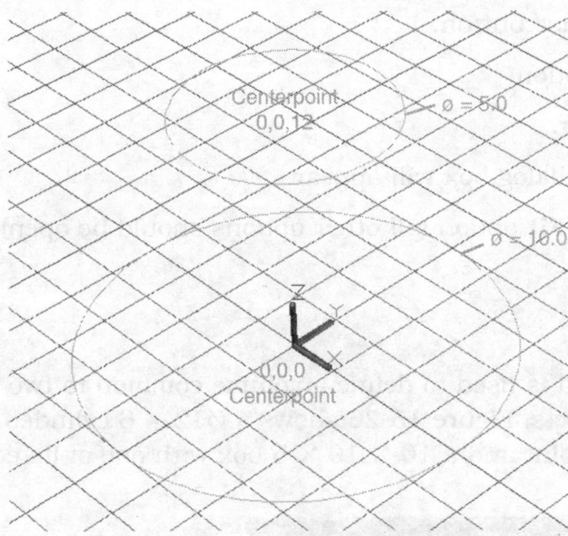

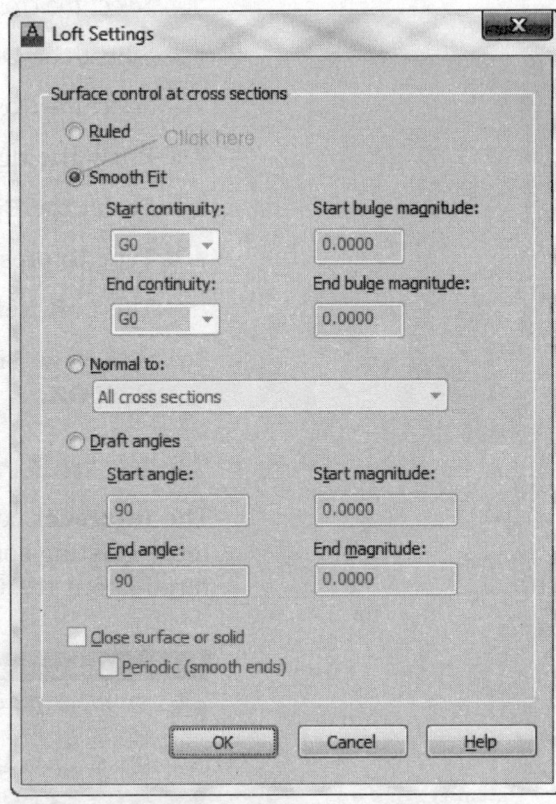

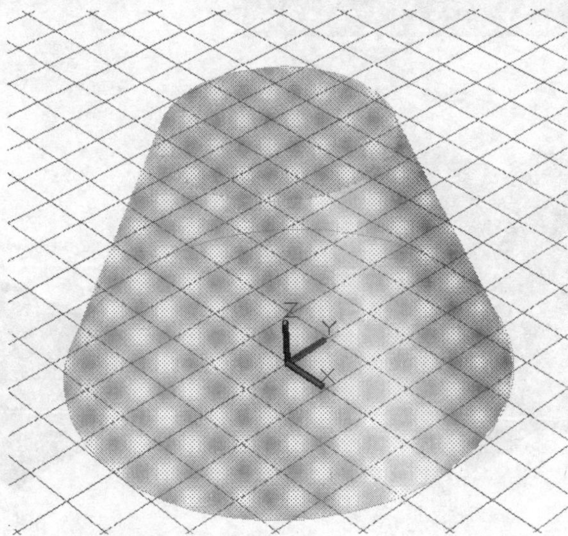

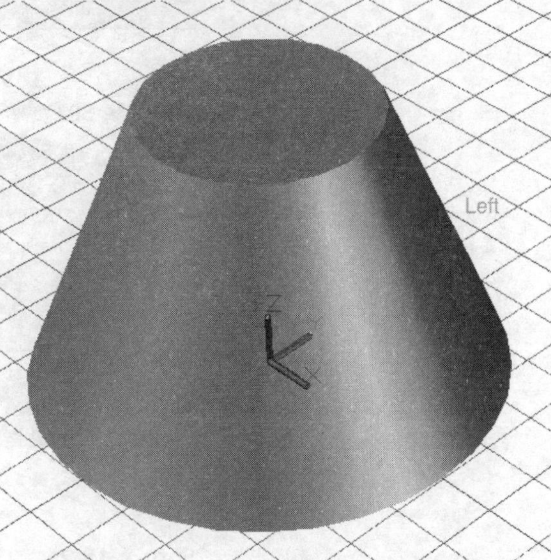

Figure 15-25

1. Use the **Circle** tool on the **Draw** panel, and draw a **Ø10** circle centered about the 0,0,0 origin.

2. Use the **Circle** tool on the **Draw** panel to draw a Ø5 circle centered about 0,0,12.

The Z value of 12 will locate the Ø5 circle's center point above the Ø10 circle's center point.

3. Select the **Loft** tool from the **Modeling** panel.

Select the cross sections in lofting order:

4. Select the **Ø10** circle.

Select the cross sections in lofting order:

5. Select the **Ø5** circle.

Select the cross sections in lofting order:

6. Press the right mouse button.

7. Select the **Enter** option.

8. Type **5**; press **Enter.**

The **Loft Settings** dialog box will appear.

9. Select the **Smooth Fit** option (all other options should be open); click **OK.**

15-13 Intersect

The **Intersect** command is used to define a volume common to two or more existing solid objects. Figure 15-26 shows a Ø12 × 6 cylinder centered about the 0,0,0 point and a 10 × 10 × 5 box with one of its corners

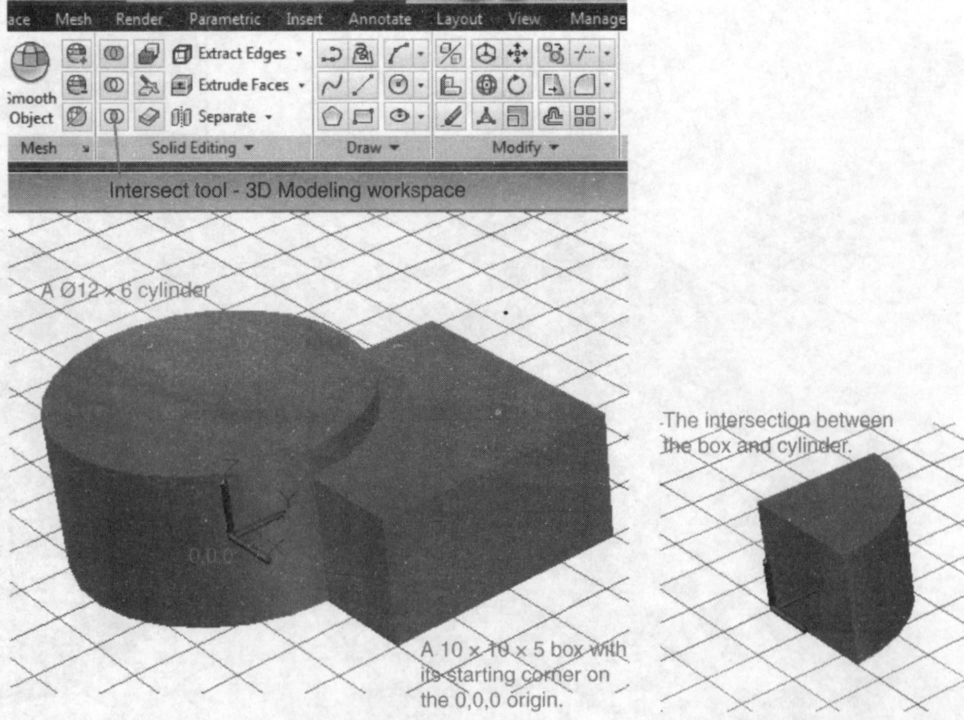

Figure 15-26

located on the 0,0,0 point. They were both drawn on the XY plane. The following procedure will define the volume common to both of them:

1. Select the **Intersect** tool from the **Solid Editing** panel under the **Home** tab.

   Command: _intersect

   Select objects:

2. Select the box.

   Select objects:

3. Select the cylinder.

   Select objects:

4. Press **Enter.**

   Figure 15-26 shows the resulting common volume.

15-14 Union and Subtract

Solid objects may be combined to form more complex objects. Objects can be added together by the **Union** command and subtracted from each other by the **Subtract** command. A volume common to two or more objects may be defined by the **Intersect** command. The tools for these three commands are located on the **Solid Editing** panel under the **Home** tab in the **3D Modeling** workspace, and on the **Edit** panel under the **Home** tab in the **3D Basics** workspace. This section will use the **3D Basics** workspace. See Figure 15-27.

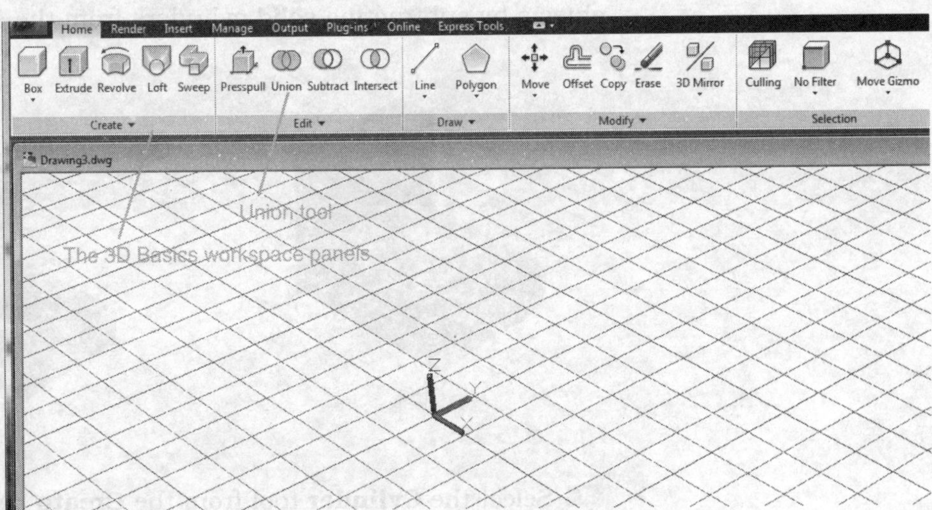

Figure 15-27

To Union Two Objects

Figure 15-28 shows two 10 × 10 × 3 solid boxes drawn with adjoining surfaces.

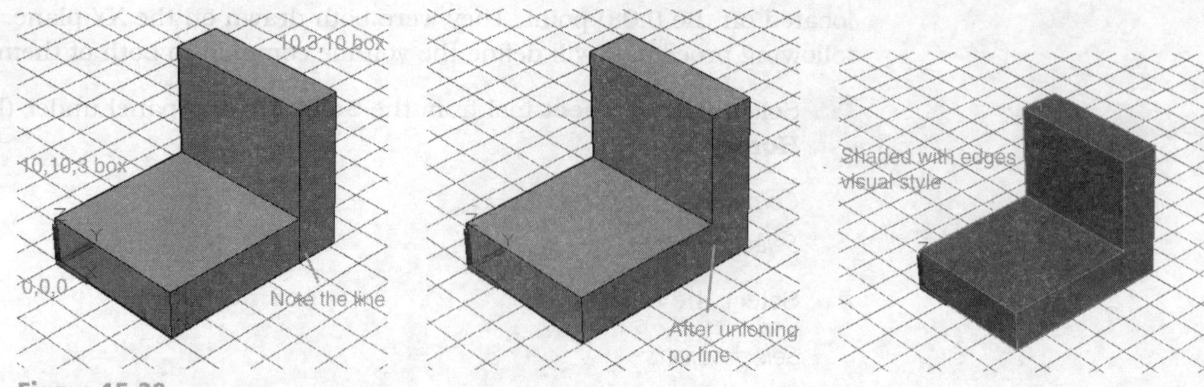

Figure 15-28

1. Select the **Union** tool from the **Edit** panel.

   Command: _union

   Select objects:

2. Select a box.

   Select objects:

3. Select the other box.

   Select objects:

4. Press **Enter.**

Note the changes in the boxes after they have been unioned. The solid object is no longer two boxes, but an L-shaped object.

To Subtract an Object

Figure 15-29 shows the L-shaped bracket formed in Figure 15-28. This exercise will add a hole to the front surface. Holes are created in solid objects by subtracting solid cylinders from the existing objects.

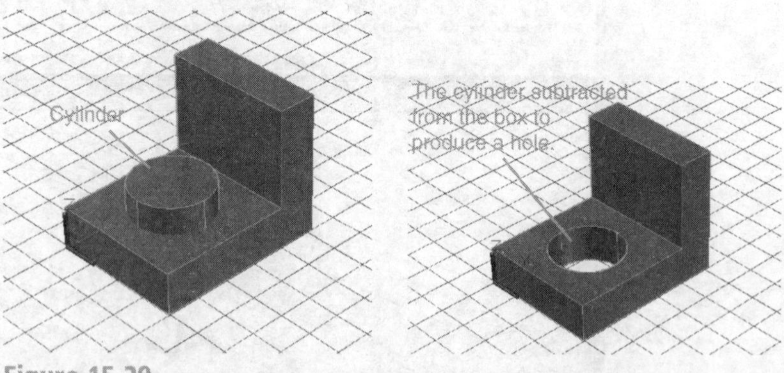

Figure 15-29

1. Select the **Cylinder** tool from the **Create** panel.

   Command: _cylinder

   Specify center point of base or [3P 2P Ttr Elliptical]:

2. Type **5,5,0;** press **Enter.**

   Remember, we are still working on the XY plane.

   Specify base radius or [2 Point Axis endpoint] <5.0000>:

3. Type **3;** press **Enter.**

Specify height or [2 Point Axis endpoint] <10.0000>:

4. Type **5;** press **Enter.**

The height of the cylinder was deliberately drawn higher than the top surface of the bracket to illustrate that the two heights need not be equal for the **Subtract** command to work. The only requirement is that the cylinder be equal to, or greater than, the height of the box surface. See Figure 15-29.

5. Select the **Subtract** tool from the **Edit** panel.

Command: _subtract
Select solids and regions to subtract from . . .
Select objects:

This prompt is asking you to define the main object—that is, the object that you want to remain after the subtraction.

6. Select the L-shaped bracket.

Select objects:

7. Press **Enter.**

Select solids and regions to subtract ...
Select objects:

This prompt is asking you to define the object that you want removed by the subtraction.

8. Select the cylinder.

Select objects:

9. Press **Enter.**

15-15 Solid Modeling and UCSs

In this section, we will again work with the L-shaped bracket and add a hole to the upper surface. The procedure is to create a new UCS with its origin at the left intersection of the two perpendicular surfaces, and then create and subtract a cylinder. See Figure 15-30.

1. Select the **3 Point** tool from the **Coordinates** panel under the **Home tab** on the **3D Basics** workspace.

Specify new origin point <0.0000>:

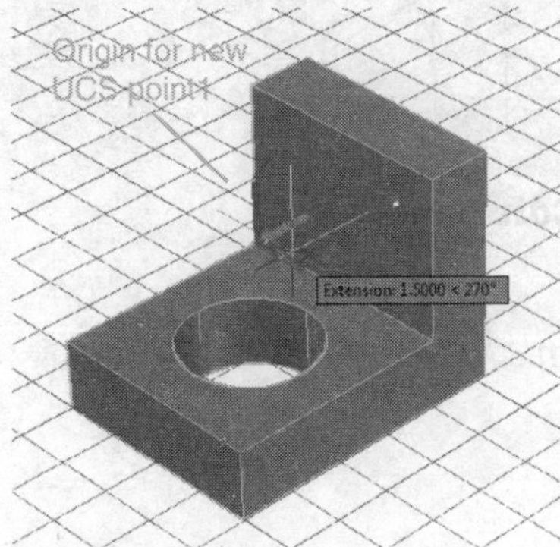

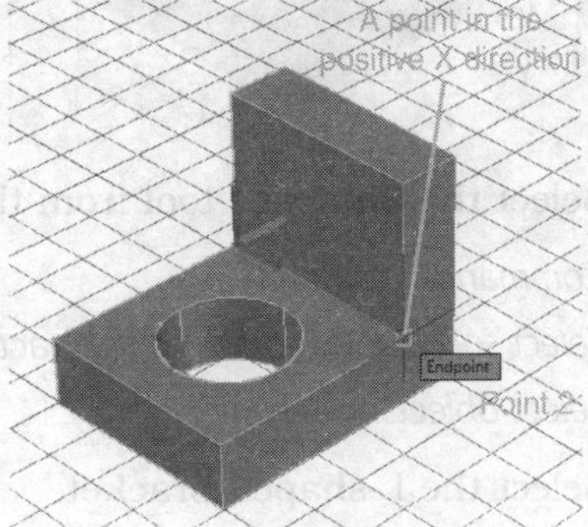

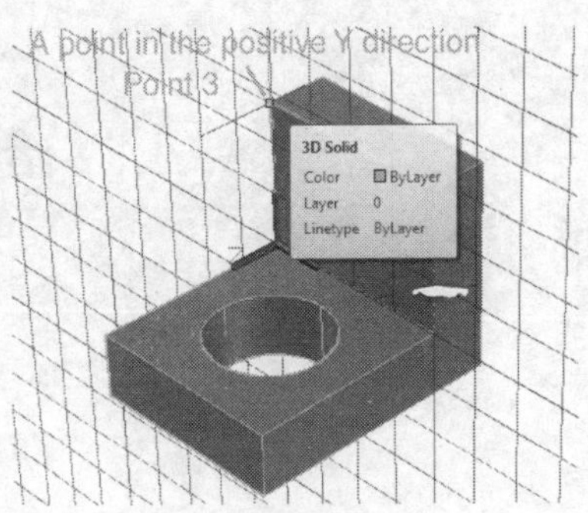

Figure 15-30

2 Use **Osnap Endpoint** (<shift>/right button), and select the corner as shown.

The coordinate system will move to the new location.

UCS Specify point on positive portion of X = Axis <1.0000, 0.0000, 0,0000>:

3 Use the **Osnap Endpoint** tool, and select the corner, as shown.

UCS Specify point on positive –1 portion of the USC XY plan <1.0000, 0.0000, 0.0000>:

4 Use the **Osnap Endpoint** tool, and select the corner, as shown.

5 Select the **Cylinder** tool from the **Create** panel.

Specify center point of the base or [3P 2P Ttr Elliptical]:

6 Type **5,3.5,0;** press **Enter.**

We are now drawing on the new UCS.

Specify base radius or [Diameter] <1.5000>:

7 Type **2.50;** press **Enter.**

Specify height or [2 Point Axis endpoint] <5.0000>:

8 Use the dynamic input options, and move the cursor in the negative Z direction.

The cylinder height will increase as the cursor is moved.

9 Define the cylinder height at any distance greater than 3, the thickness of the L-bracket; press **Enter.**

See Figure 15-31.

Figure 15-31

10 Select the **Subtract** tool from the **Edit** panel.

Command: _subtract

Select solids and regions to subtract from . . .

Select objects:

11 Select the L-shaped bracket.

Select objects:

12 Press **Enter.**

Select solids and regions to subtract ...
Select objects:

13 Select the cylinder.

Select objects:

14 Press **Enter.**

15 Click the **World** tool on the **Coordinates** panel under the **Home** tab.

Figure 15-32 shows the resulting solid object.

Figure 15-32

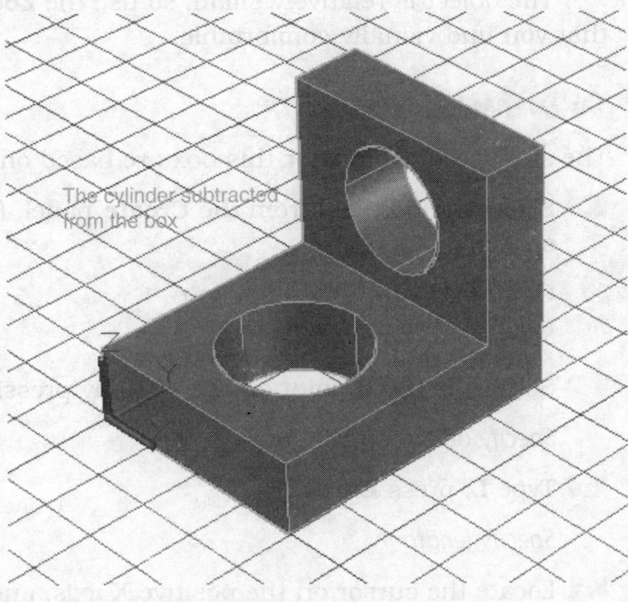

15-16 Combining Solid Objects

Figure 15-33 shows a dimensioned object. The following section explains how to create the object as a solid model. There are many different ways to create a solid model. The sequence presented here was selected to demonstrate several different input options.

Figure 15-33

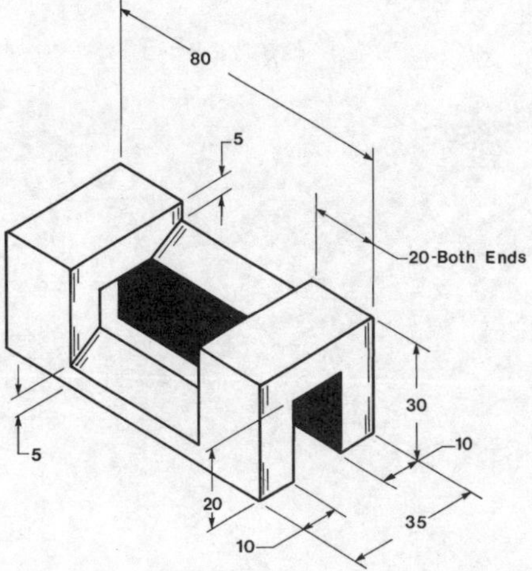

To Set Up the Drawing

Set up the drawing as follows:

Acadiso3D template

Units = Decimal (millimeters)

Drawing Limits = 297,210

Grid = 10 × 10 parallel

Snap = 10

View = SE Isometric

The object is relatively small, so use the **Zoom** tool to create a size that you find visually comfortable.

To Draw the First Box

The size specifications for this box are based on the given dimensions.

1. Select the **Box** tool from the **Create** panel. (Use the **3D Basics** workspace.)

   Command: _box
   Specify first corner or [Center]:

2. Select the **0,0,0** point on the WCS by pressing **Enter.**

   Specify other or [Cube Length]:

3. Type **L;** press **Enter.**

   Specify length:

4. Locate the cursor on the positive X axis, and type **80;** press **Enter.**

   Turn **Ortho** on, if needed.

   Specify width:

5. Locate the cursor in the positive Y direction, and type **36;** press **Enter.**

   Specify height:

6. Locate the cursor in the positive Z direction, and type **30;** press **Enter.**

   See Figure 15-34.

Figure 15-34

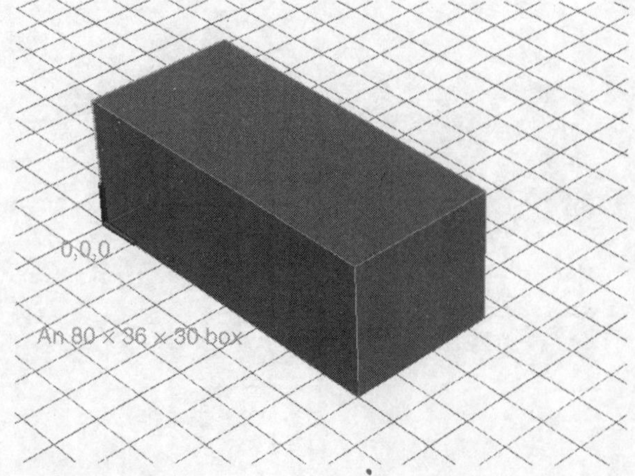

To Create the Internal Open Volume

The volume will be created by subtracting a second box from the first box.

1. Select the **Box** tool from the **Create** panel.

   Command: _box
   Specify corner of box or [Center]:

2. Select the **0,10,0** point on the WCS.

   The point 0,10,0 was selected on the basis of the given 10-millimeter dimension. The point can be selected by using the crosshairs because it is on the grid located on the XY plane.

   Specify corner or [Cube Length]:

3. Type **L;** press **Enter.**

   Specify length:

4. Locate the cursor in the positive X direction, and type **80;** press **Enter.**

   Specify width:

5. Locate the cursor in the positive Y direction, and type **15;** press **Enter.**

   Specify height:

6. Locate the cursor in the positive Z direction, and type **20;** press **Enter.**

   Figure 15-35 shows the second box within the first box.

Figure 15-35

7. Select the **Subtract** tool from the **Edit** panel.

   Command: _subtract
   Select solids and regions to subtract from . . .
   Select objects:

8. Select the first box.

   Select objects:

9. Press **Enter.**

   Select solids and regions to subtract . . .
   Select objects:

10. Press **Enter.**

    See Figure 15-36.

To Create the Top Cutout

See Figure 15-37.

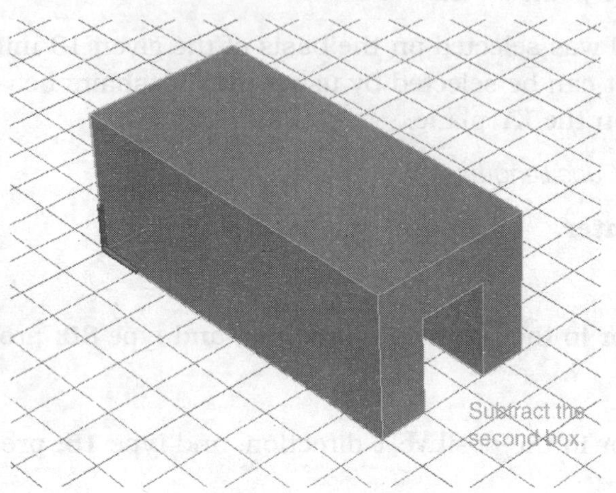

Figure 15-36

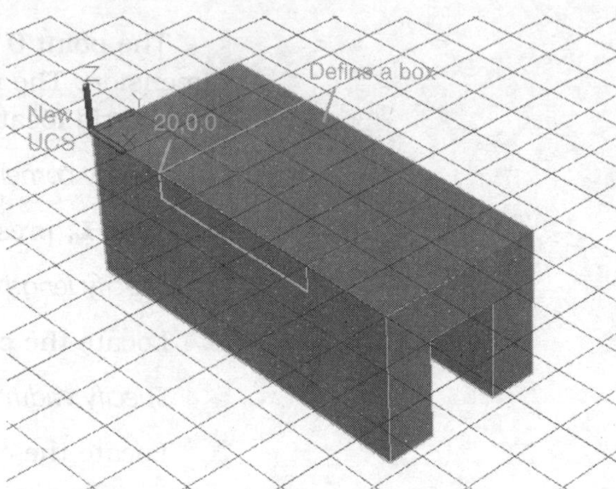

Figure 15-37

The cutout will be created by drawing a box and wedge and subtracting them from the existing object.

To Create a Box

1. Move the origin to the top surface of the box, using the **3-Point** tool located on the **Coordinates** panel. Define the origin, second point, and third point, as shown. Use the **Endpoint** option of the **Osnap** tool to define the point.
2. Select the **Box** tool from the **Create** panel.

   Specify first corner or [Center]:
3. Type **20,0,0;** press **Enter.**

   Specify other corner or [Cube Length]:
4. Position the cursor in the positive X and Y directions, and type **60,35,0;** press **Enter.**

   Specify height or [2 Point]<0.0000>:
5. Position the cursor in the negative Z direction, and type **–5;** press **Enter.**
6. Use the **Subtract** tool from the **Edit** panel, and subtract the box from the existing object.

See Figure 15-38.

To Create a Wedge

See Figure 15-39.

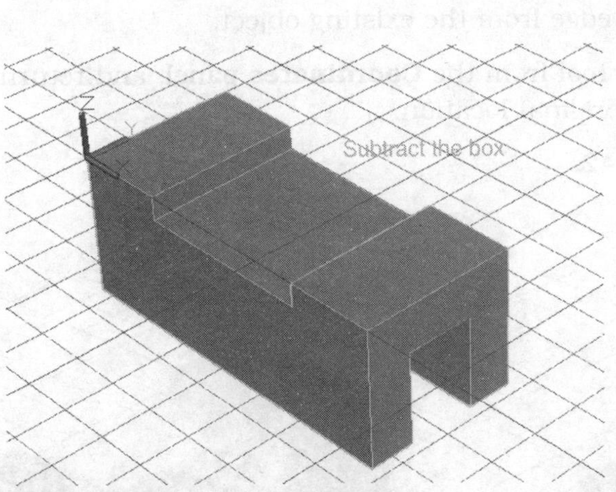

Figure 15-38

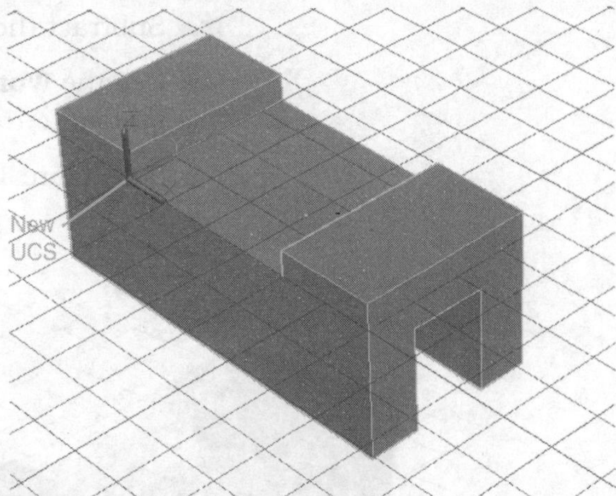

Figure 15-39

1. Define a new UCS, as shown. Use the **3-Point** tool, or use the **Origin** tool located on the **Coordinates** panel in the **3D Modeling** workspace.

2. Select the **Z** tool from the **Coordinates** panel, and rotate the axis **90°** around the Z axis.

   See Figure 15-40.

3. Select the **Wedge** tool from the **Create** panel.

   Specify first corner or (Center):

4. Select the **0,0,0** point of the current UCS.

   Specify other corner or [Cube Length]:

5. Use **Osnap Endpoint**, and select the opposite diagonal corner of the box cutout, as shown.

   Specify height or [2 Point]<0.0000>:

6. Locate the cursor in the negative Z direction, and type –**20;** press **Enter.**

   See Figure 15-41.

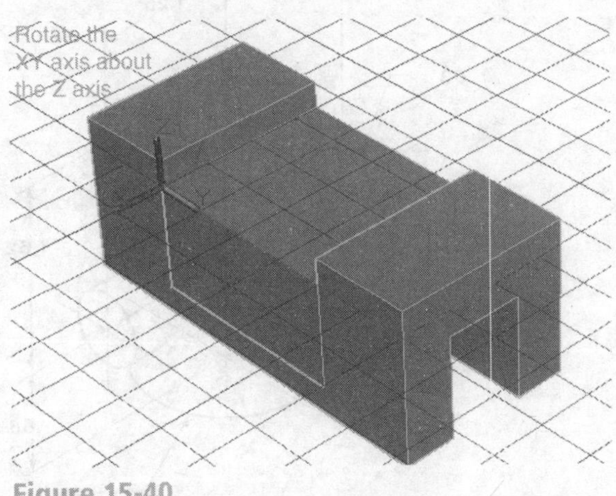

Figure 15-40

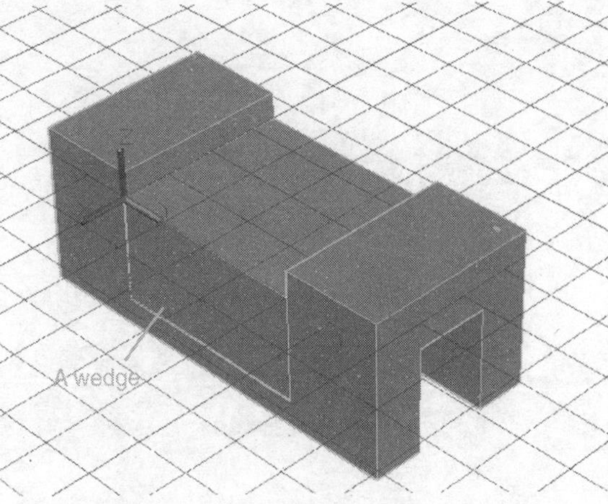

Figure 15-41

7. Subtract the wedge from the existing object.

8. Use the **World** tool from the **Coordinates** panel, and return the axis system to the original location.

   See Figure 15-42.

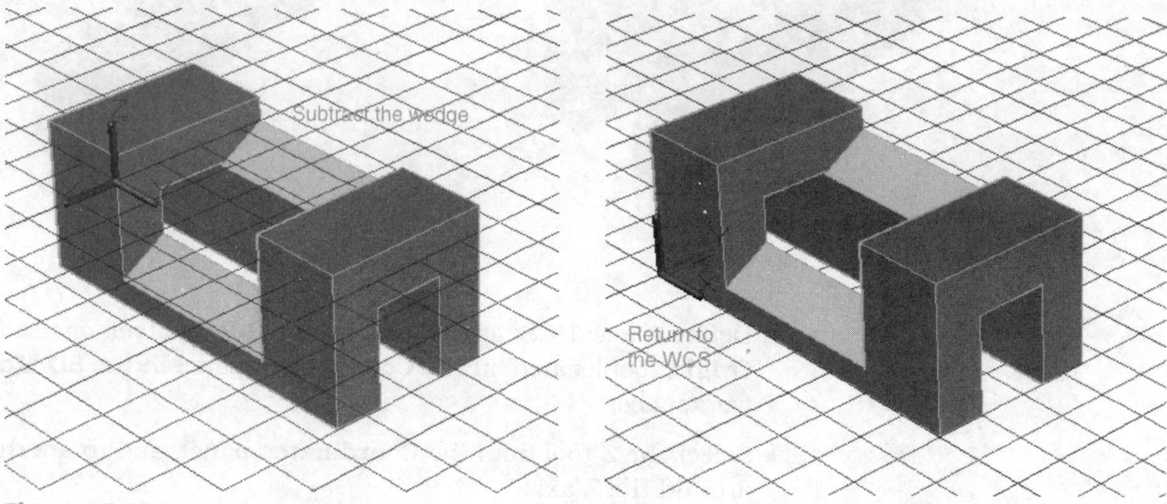

Figure 15-42

15-17 Intersecting Solids

Figure 15-43 shows an incomplete 3D drawing of a cone and a cylinder. The problem is to complete the drawing in 3D and show the front, top, and right-side orthographic views of the intersecting objects. If this problem were to be done by hand on a drawing board, it would require extensive projection between views, as well as a high degree of precision in the line work. Drawn as a solid model, the problem is much simpler and serves to show the strength of solid modeling as a design tool.

Figure 15-43

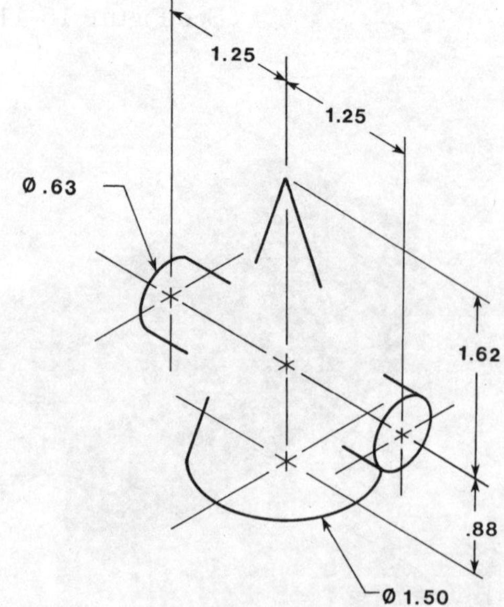

To Set Up the Drawing

Set up the drawing screen as follows:

Grid = 0.50 × 0.50

Snap = .50

Units = Decimal

View = SE Isometric

Template = acad3D

3D Modeling workspace

See Figure 15-44. The objects are small, so use the **Zoom** command to create a comfortable visual size.

Figure 15-44

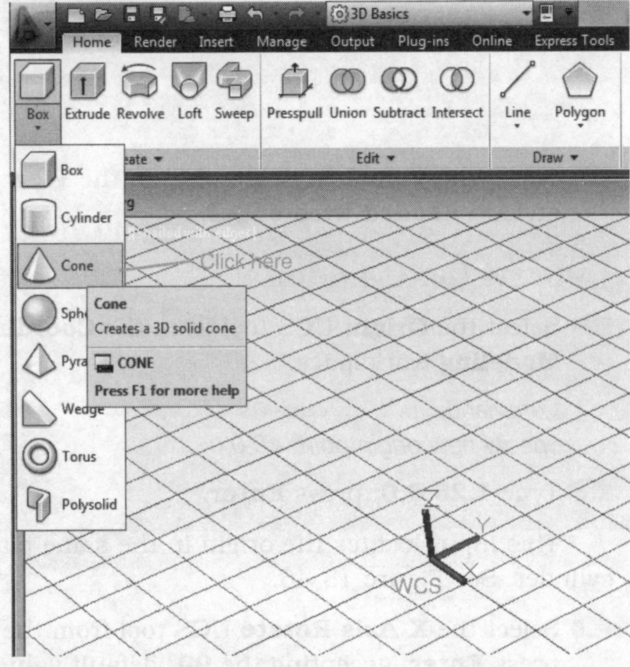

To Draw the Cone

1. Select the **Cone** tool from the **Modeling** panel under the **Home** tab in the **3D Modeling** workspace.

   Command: _cone

   Specify center point of base or [3P 2P Ttr Elliptical]

2. Type **0,0,0;** press **Enter.**

   The center point of the cone will be located on the origin of the WCS.

   Specify base radius or [Diameter] <0,0000>:

3. Type **d;** press **Enter.**

   Specify diameter:

4. Type **1.50.**

   Specify height or [2 Point Axis endpoint Top radius]<1.0000>:

5. Locate the cursor in the positive Z direction, and type **2.50;** press **Enter.**

See Figure 15-45.

Figure 15-45

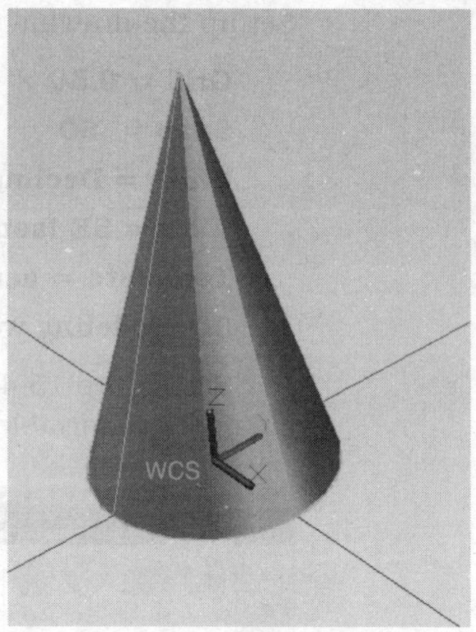

6 Select the **Visual Styles** tool from the **View** panel, and change the style to **Shaded with edges.**

To Draw the Cylinder

1 Select the **Origin** UCS tool from the **Coordinates** panel on the **3D Modeling** workspace.

Command: _ucs
Specify new origin point <0,0,0>:

2 Type **1.25,0,0;** press **Enter.**

This input locates the origin in the same plane as the end of the cylinder. See Figure 15-46.

3 Select the **X Axis Rotate** UCS tool from the **Coordinates** panel, and press **Enter,** accepting the **90**° default value. Then select the **Y Axis Rotate** UCS tool, type **–90**, and press **Enter.**

See Figure 15-46.

Figure 15-46

4. Select the **Cylinder** tool from the **Modeling** panel under the **Home** tab.

   Command: _cylinder

   Specify center point of base or [3P 2P Elliptical]:

5. Type **0, .88, 0.**

   Specify base radius or [Diameter] <0.0000>:

6. Type **d;** press **Enter.**

   Specify diameter <1.0000>:

7. Type **.63;** press **Enter.**

   Specify height or [2Point Axis endpoint] <1.0000>:

8. Locate the cursor in the negative Z direction, and type **2.50;** press **Enter.**

   See Figure 15-47.

To Complete the 3D Drawing

1. Select the **Union** tool from the **Solid Editing** panel.

   Command: _union

   Select objects:

2. Select the cone.

   Select objects:

3. Select the cylinder.

   Select objects:

4. Press **Enter.**

   Command:

5. Select the **World** tool from the **Coordinates** panel.
6. Turn off **Grid.**

See Figure 15-48.

Figure 15-47

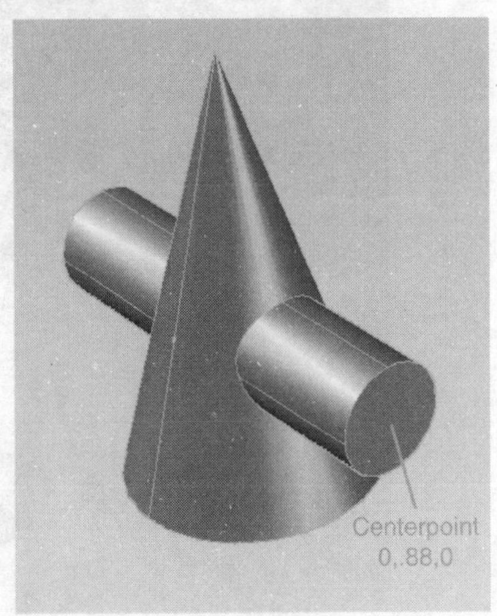

Figure 15-48

To Create the Viewports for the Orthographic Views

Click the **View** tab in the **3D Modeling** workspace, access the **Viewports Configuration** panel, and select the **Four: Equal** option.

See Figure 15-49. AutoCAD will automatically create three orthographic views of the object, plus an isometric view. See Figure 15-50. These views

Figure 15-49

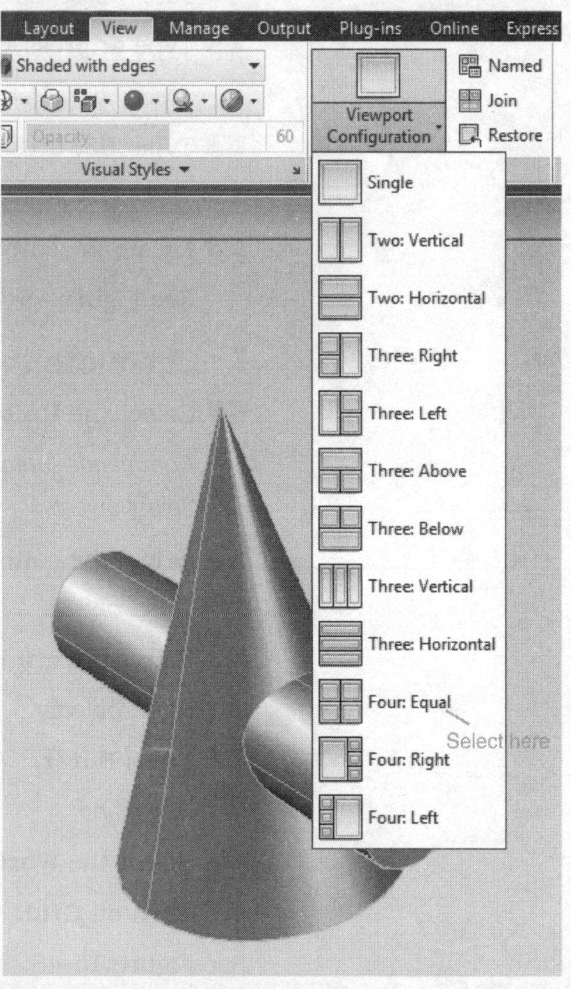

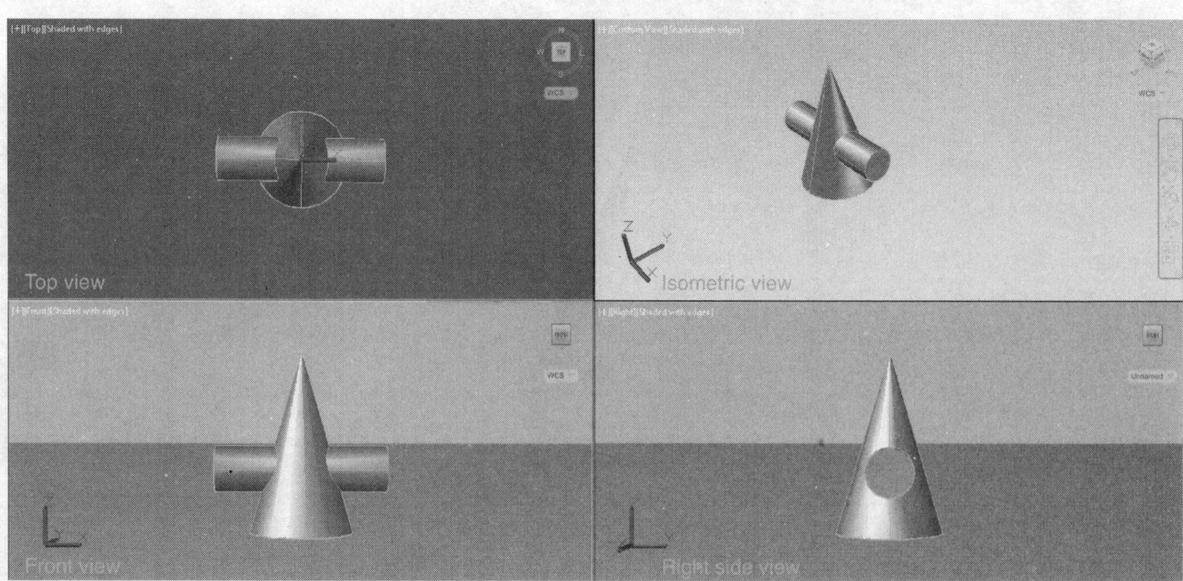

Figure 15-50

may be modified, as explained in Section 14-13, to show a front, top, and right side orthographic view of the object.

15-18 Solid Models of Castings

Figure 15-51 shows a casting. Note that the object includes rounded edges. These rounded edges can be created on a solid model by using the **Fillet** command. The **Fillet** command was explained in Chapter 2.

Decimal inches are used for all dimensions.

To Draw the Basic Shape

The basic shape will first be drawn in 2D, then extruded into the 3D solid model.

1 Set up the drawing screen as needed.

In this example, the **acad3D** template was used, and a top view was created by using the **Top** tool from the **Views** panel or by clicking the word **Top** on the **View** icon.

2 Draw the basic shape by using first the **Circle** tool, and then the **Line** tool along with the **Osnap Tangent** option.

See Figure 15-52. It is important to know the center point locations for the two circles in terms of their X,Y components. In this example, the center point location for the large circle is 0,0, and the location for the small circle is 4,0. The large circle's diameter equals 3.00 inches, and the small circle's diameter equals 1.25 inches. The circles are 4.0 inches apart.

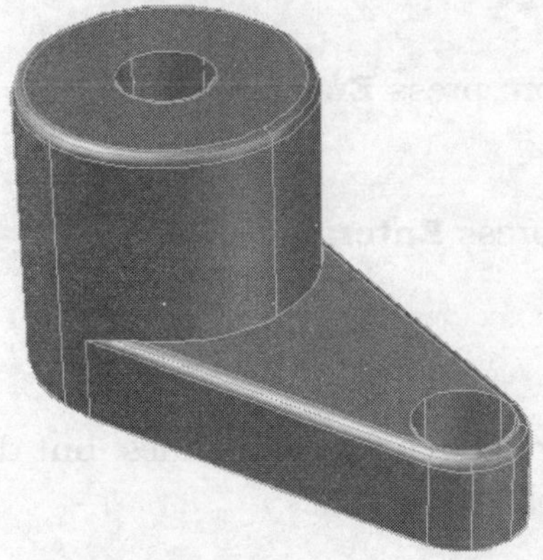

Figure 15-51

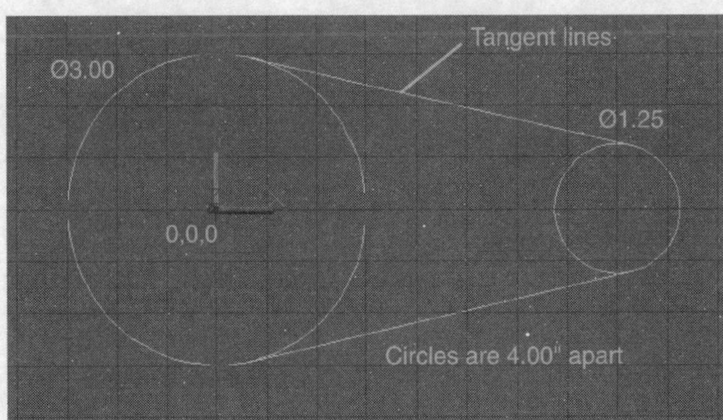

Figure 15-52

To Create a Polyline from the Basic Shape

Because only polylines can be extruded, some of the lines in the basic shape must be formed into a polyline. The large circle can be extruded, so it need not be included as part of the polyline; however, the polyline must be a closed area, so it will need part of the circle. The needed circular segment can be created by drawing a second large circle directly over the existing circle and then using the **Trim** command to remove the excess portion. Remember that two lines can occupy the same space in AutoCAD drawings. If there is difficulty in working with the two large circles, trim the circles and then add another larger circle, if needed.

Figure 15-53 shows the resulting shape that will be joined to form a polyline.

Figure 15-53

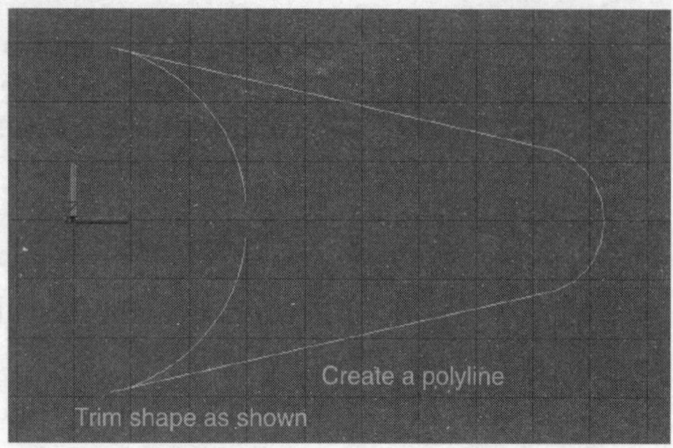

1. Select the **Edit Polyline** tool from the **Modify** panel.

   Command: _pedit
   Select polyline or [Multiple]:

2. Select the remaining portion of the small circle.

   Object selected is not a polyline
   Do you want to turn it into one? <Y>

3. Press **Enter**.

   Enter an option [Close Join Width Edit vertex Fit/Spline Decurve Ltype gen Undo eXit] <X>:

4. Select the **Join** option; press **Enter**.

   Select objects:

5. Window the object; press **Enter**.

   Select objects:

6. Press **Enter** twice.

   There will be no visible changes to the lines, but they have been combined to form a single polyline.

To Extrude the Shape

1. Select the **SE Isometric** tool from the **Views** panel under the **View** tab, and make it the current view.

2. Use the **Zoom** tool, if needed, to present the figure at a comfortable visual size.

   See Figure 15-54.

3. Select the **Extrude** tool from the **Modeling** panel under the **Home** tab.

   Command: _extrude
   Select objects to extrude:

4. Select the polyline.

In this example, a height of 1.00 was assigned. See Figure 15-55.

Command:

The shape is presented in the **Hidden with edges** visual style.

5. Select the **Cylinder** tool from the **Modeling** panel under the **Home** tab, and create a cylinder whose diameter equals the original large-circle diameter (Ø3.00) and whose height is **3**, with a center point of **0,0,0.**

   See Figure 15-56.

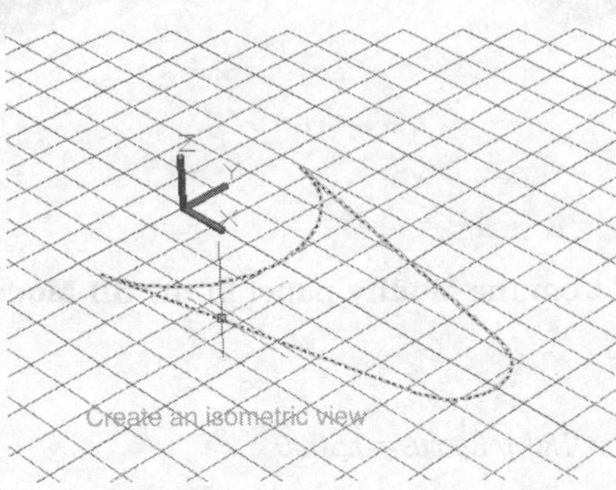

Figure 15-54

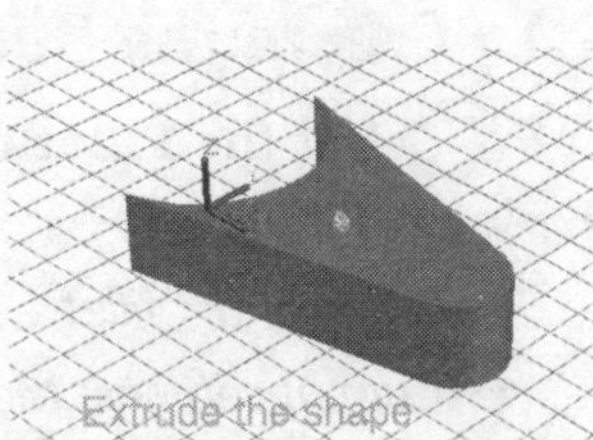

Figure 15-55

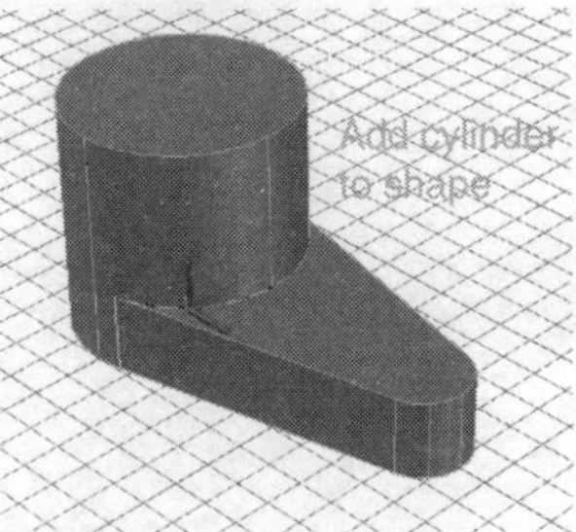

Figure 15-56

To Add the Holes

Create the holes by subtracting cylinders from the object.

1. Select the **Cylinder** tool from the **Modeling** panel under the **Home** tab.

   Command: _cylinder

   Specify center point for base of cylinder or [Elliptical] <0,0,0>:

2. Type **0,0,0;** press **Enter.**
   This value came from the original circle's center point location.

3. Enter the appropriate diameter and height values. In this example, a radius of **0.50** inch and a height of **3.5** were selected.

   Command:

4. Repeat the **Cylinder** command.

   Specify center point for base of cylinder or [Elliptical] <0,0,0>:

5. Type **4,0,0.**

6. Draw a Ø**1.00** × **1.25** cylinder.

   See Figure 15-57.

7. Select the **Union** tool from the **Solid Editing** panel, and join the large cylinder portion of the object to the polyline portion.

8. Select the **Subtract** tool from the **Solid Editing** panel, and subtract the cylinders from the basic shape.

   See Figure 15-58.

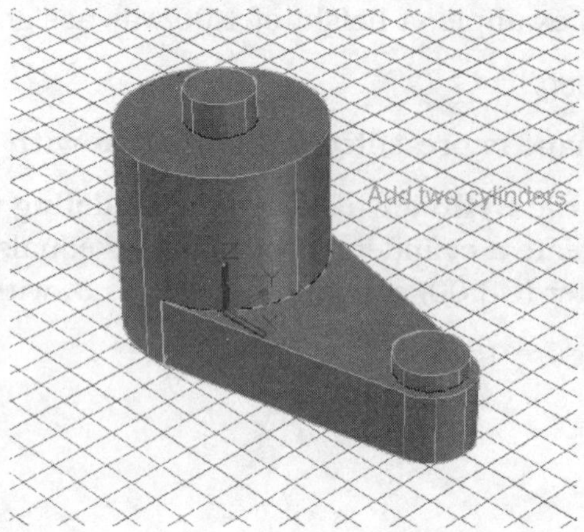

Figure 15-57

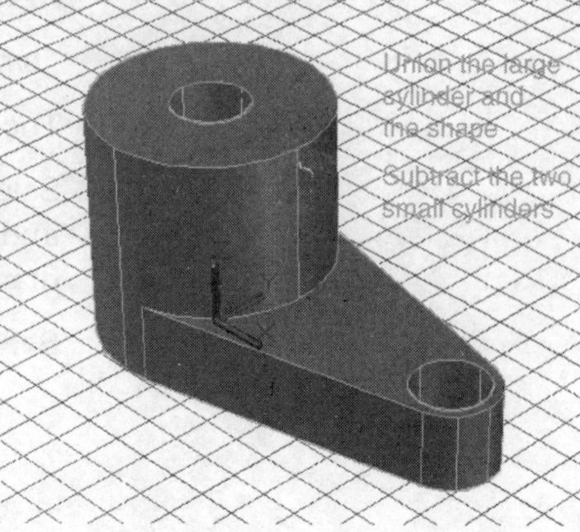

Figure 15-58

To Create the Rounded Edges

1. Select the **Fillet** tool from the **Modify** panel in the **3D Modeling** workspace.

   Command: _fillet

   Current settings: Mode = TRIM, Radius=0.5000.

   Select first object or [Undo Polyline Radius Trim Multiple]:

2. Type **r**, and enter a value of **.125**.
3. Repeat the **Fillet** command, and select the outside edge of the top surface of the large cylindrical portion of the object.

   Enter fillet radius <0.1250>:

4. Press **Enter.**

   Select first object or [Undo Polyline Radius Trim Multiple]:

5. Press **Enter.**

   See Figure 15-59.

6. Use the **Fillet** tool to create a fillet along the top edges of the object as shown in Figure 15-60.

   Note that the arc edge line between the large cylindrical portion of the object and the extended flat area cannot be filleted.

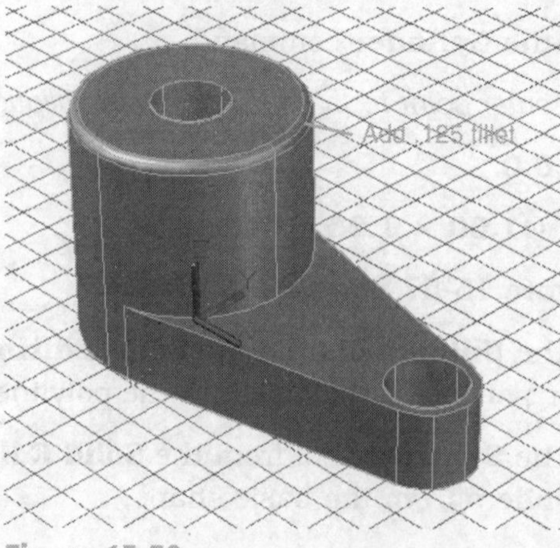

Figure 15-59

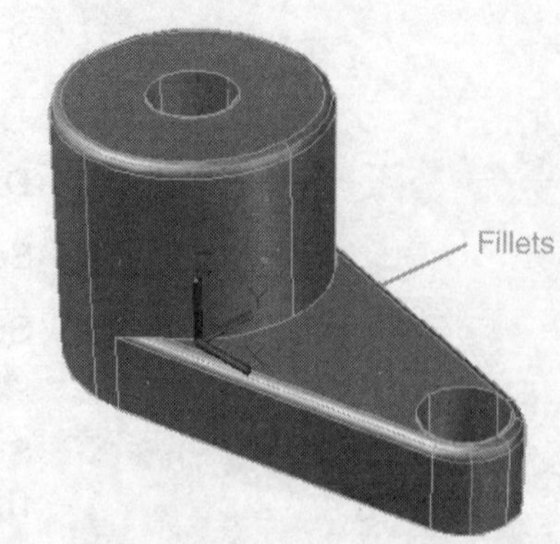

Figure 15-60

15-19 Thread Representations in Solid Models

This section explains how to draw thread representations for solid models. The procedure presented only broadly represents a thread. It is not an actual detailed solid drawing of a thread. As with the thread representations presented in Chapter 11 for 2D drawings, 3D representations are acceptable for most applications.

1. Select the **Cylinder** tool from the **Modeling** panel under the **Home** tab, and draw a cylinder.

   In the example shown, a cylinder of diameter **3** and a height of **6** was drawn centered about the **0,0,0** point of the WCS. See Figure 15-61. It is presented on the **acad3D** template with a **Wireframe** visual style.

Draw a cylinder to represent the body of the thread and arrayed circles to represent the threads.

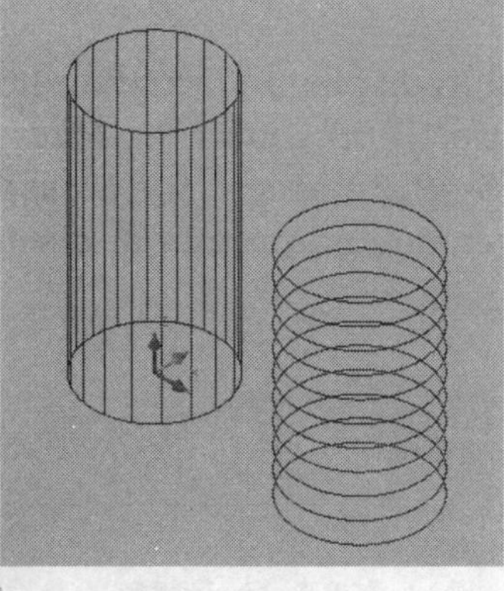

Chamfer the top surface of the thread.

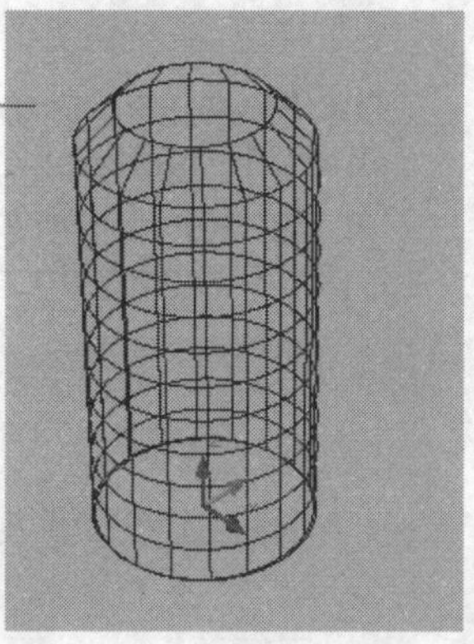

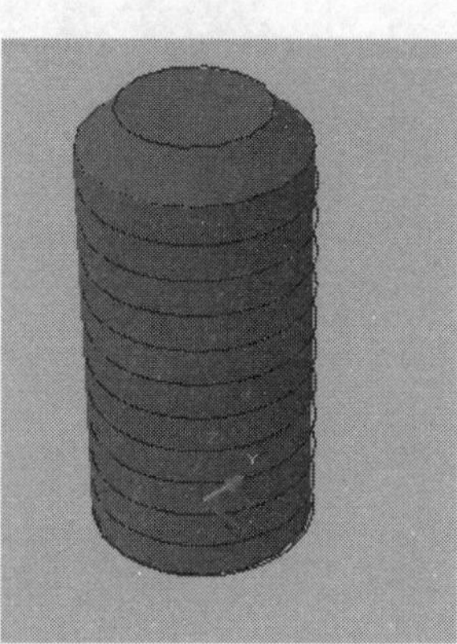

Figure 15-61

2. Draw a circle with a diameter equal to the diameter of the cylinder. In this example, use Ø3.00.

3. Select the **3D Array** command from the **Modify** panel, located under the **Home** tab. The **3D Array** tool is a flyout from the **3D Mirror** tool.

   Select object:

4. Select the circle; press **Enter.**

   Enter the type of array [Rectangular or Polar array] <e>:

5. Type **r**; press **Enter.**

   Enter the number of rows (---)<1>:

6. Press **Enter.**

   Enter the number of columns: (|||)<1>:

7. Press **Enter.**

   Enter the number of levels:

8. Type **11**; press **Enter.**

   The number 11 is used because the cylinder is 6 units high, and in this example circles representing threads will be spaced 0.5 apart. The top edge of the thread will be chamfered.

   Specify the distance between levels: (...):

9. Type **.5**; press **Enter.**

10 Select the **Move** tool from the **Modify** panel, and move the arrayed circles' center points to the **0,0,0** origin.

11 Select the **Chamfer** tool from the **Modify** panel, and draw a **.5 × .5** chamfer around the top edge of the cylinder.

15-20 List

The **List** command is used to display database information for a drawn solid object. Figure 15-62 shows a list for the cone-cylinder object shown in Figure 15-48. There is no icon for the **List** command. Type **list** in response to a command prompt, and select the object.

15-21 Massprop

The **Massprop** command is used to display information about the structural characteristics of an object. Figure 15-63 shows the **Massprop** information for the object shown in Figure 15-48. To access the **Massprop** command, type **Massprop** in response to a command prompt and select the object.

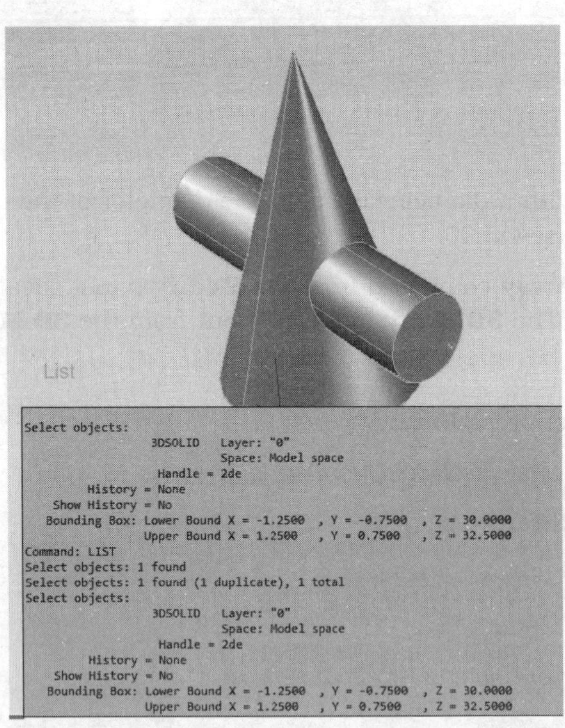

Figure 15-62

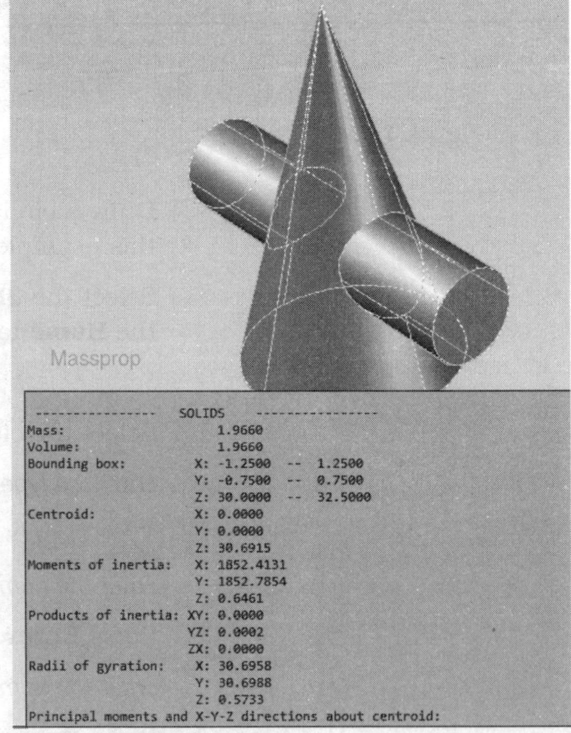

Figure 15-63

15-22 Face and Edge Editing

AutoCAD has the capability to edit faces and edges of existing solids. The **Solid Editing** commands are located on the **Solid Editing** panel under the **Home** tab in the **3D Modeling** workspace. See Figure 15-64. The following examples are based on a solid box of dimensions 4 × 2 × 3 drawn in the **Shaded with edges** visual style:

Figure 15-64

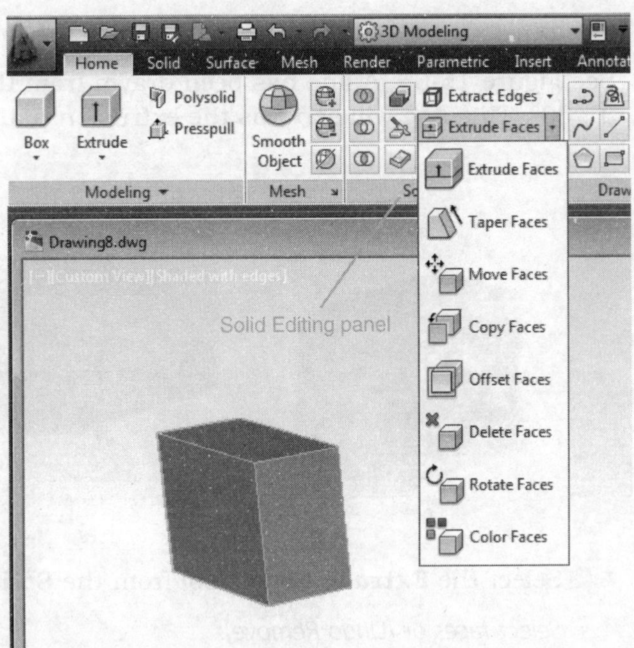

To Extrude a Face (See Figure 15-65.)

Figure 15-65

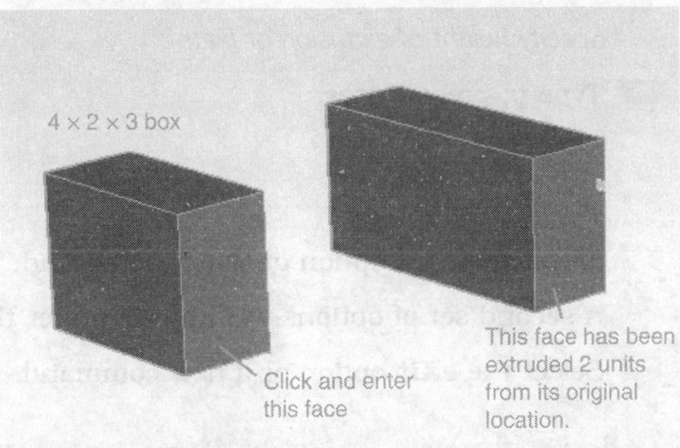

1. Select the **Extrude Faces** tool from the **Solid Editing** panel on the **3D Modeling** workspace.

   Select faces or [Undo Remove]:

2. Select the right face by moving the cursor to the center of the face and left-clicking.

   Select faces or [Undo Remove]:

3. Press the right mouse button, and enter the face.

   Specify height of extrusion or [Path]:

4. Type **2;** press **Enter.**

   Specify angle of taper for extrusion <0>:

5. Press **Enter.**

6. Select the **eXit** option or a new command.

To Extrude a Face Along a Path

See Figure 15-66. A line has been drawn from the right corner of the box 3", 30°. This line will serve as the extrusion path.

Figure 15-66

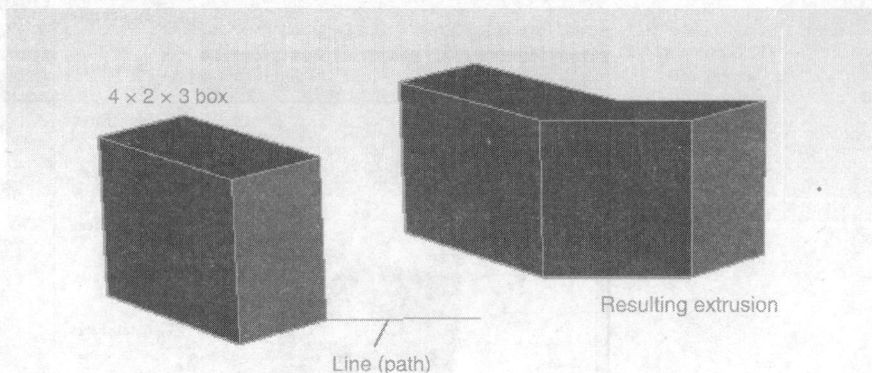

1. Select the **Extrude Faces** tool from the **Solid Editing** panel.

   Select faces or [Undo Remove]:

2. Click the right face.

   Select faces or [Undo Remove]:

3. Press the right mouse button, and enter the face.

   Specify height of extrusion or [Path]:

4. Type **p;** press **Enter.**

   Select extrusion path:

5. Select the line.
6. Select the **eXit** option or a new command.

   A second set of options will appear under the same heading.

7. Select the **eXit** option or a new command.

To Extrude Two Faces at the Same Time (See Figure 15-67.)

1. Select the **Extrude Faces** tool from the **Solid Editing** panel.

   Select faces or [Undo Remove]:

Figure 15-67

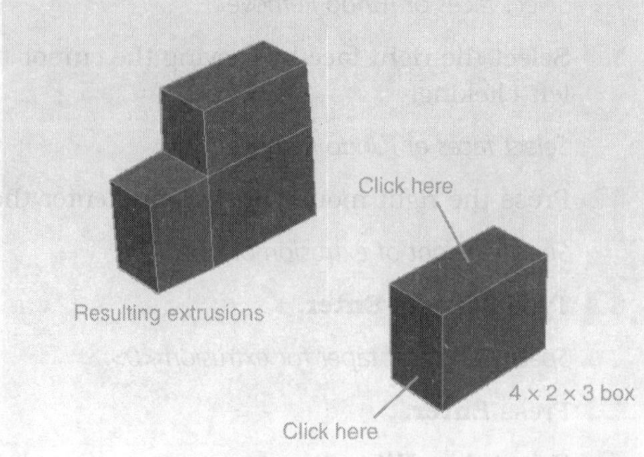

2. Select the right face, and then select the top face.

   Select faces or [Undo Remove]:

3. Press the right mouse button, and enter the face.

   Specify height of extrusion or [Path]:

4. Type **2;** press **Enter.**

5. Select the **eXit** option or a new command.

   A second set of options will appear under the same heading.

6. Select the **eXit** option or a new command.

To Move a Face (See Figure 15-68.)

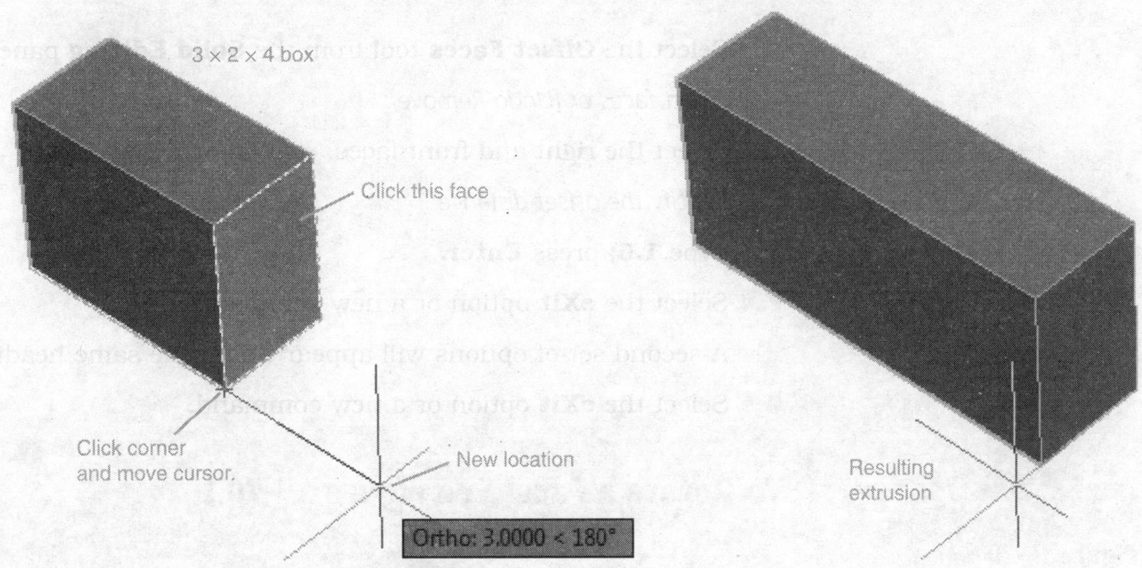

Figure 15-68

1. Select the **Move Faces** tool from the **Solid Editing** panel.

   Select faces or [Undo Remove]:

2. Select the right face, and enter it.

   Specify a base point or displacement:

3. Select the corner of the box as shown.

   Use the **Endpoint** option of the **Object snap** toolbar.

   Specify a second point of displacement.

4. Select a second point along the X axis.

5. Press **Enter.**

6. Select the **eXit** option or a new command.

   A second set of options will appear under the same heading.

7. Select the **eXit** option or a new command.

To Offset Faces (See Figure 15-69.)

Figure 15-69

1. Select the **Offset Faces** tool from the **Solid Editing** panel.

   Select faces or [Undo Remove]:

2. Select the right and front faces, and enter them.

   Specify the offset distance:

3. Type **1.5;** press **Enter.**
4. Select the **eXit** option or a new command.

   A second set of options will appear under the same heading.

5. Select the **eXit** option or a new command.

To Rotate a Face (See Figure 15-70.)

Figure 15-70

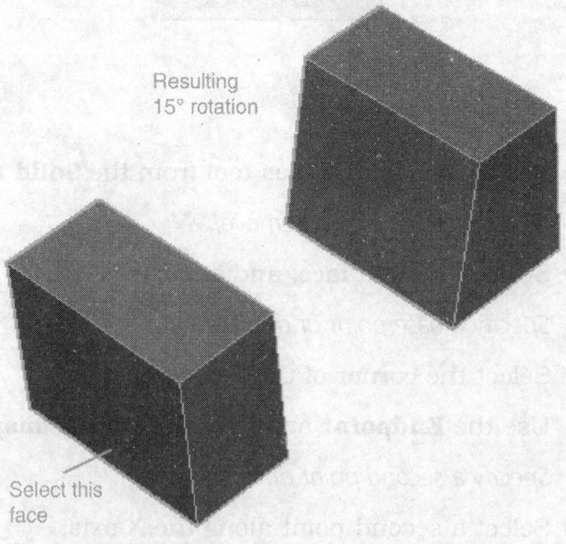

1. Select the **Rotate Faces** tool from the **Solid Editing** panel.

   Select faces or [Undo Remove]:

2. Select the front face, and enter it.

   Specify an axis point or [Axis by object View Xaxis Yaxis Zaxis]<2 points>:

3. Type **x;** press **Enter.**

   Specify the origin of the rotation <0,0,0>:

4. Press **Enter.**

   Specify the rotation angle or [Reference]:

5. Type **15;** press **Enter.**

   An input of **–15** would have rotated the face in the opposite direction.

6. Select the **eXit** option or a new command.

   A second set of options will appear under the same heading.

7. Select the **eXit** option or a new command.

To Taper a Face

See Figure 15-71.

Figure 15-71

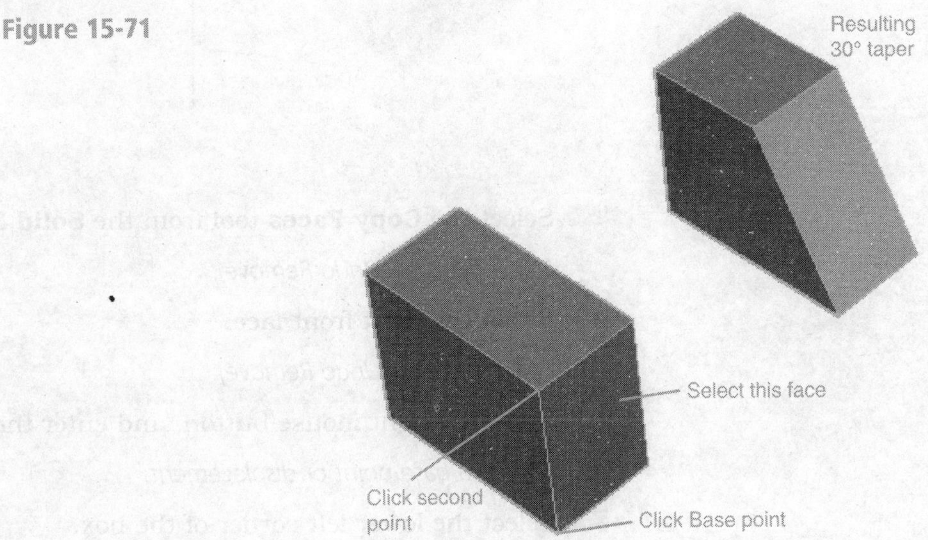

1. Select the **Taper Faces** tool from the **Solid Editing** toolbar.

   Select faces or [Undo Remove]:

2. Select the right front face.

   Select faces or [Undo Remove]:

3. Press the right mouse button, and enter the face.

   Specify the base point:

4. Select the lower left corner of the box.

   Specify another point along the axis of tapering:

5. Use **Osnap Endpoint**, and specify the top corner, as shown in Figure 15-74.

   Specify the taper angle:

6. Type **30;** press **Enter.**

   [Extrude Move Rotate Offset Taper Delete Copy coLor Undo eXit]<eXit>:

7. Select the **eXit** option or a new command.

A second set of options will appear under the same heading.

8. Select the **eXit** option or a new command.

To Copy a Face

See Figure 15-72.

Figure 15-72

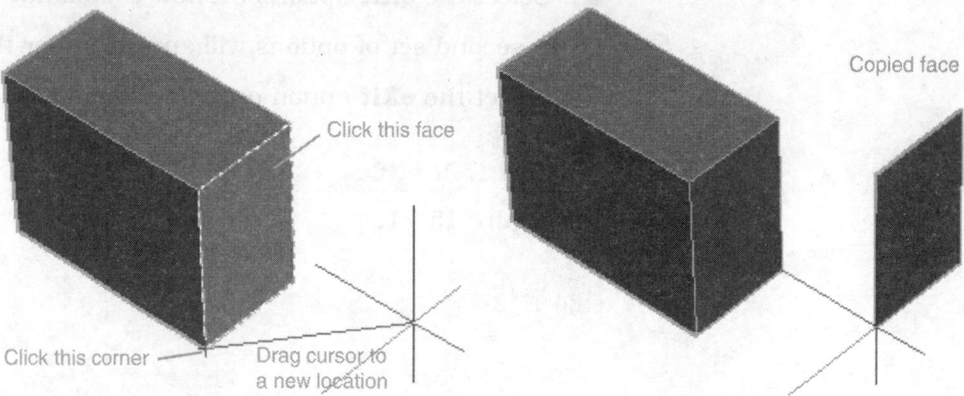

1. Select the **Copy Faces** tool from the **Solid Editing** panel.

   Select faces or [Undo Remove]:

2. Select the right front face.

   Select faces or [Undo Remove]:

3. Press the right mouse button, and enter the face.

   Specify a base point or displacement:

4. Select the lower left corner of the box.

   Specify a second point of displacement:

5. Select the location for the copied face.

   [Extrude Move Rotate Offset Taper Delete Copy coLor Undo eXit]<eXit>:

6. Select the **eXit** option or a new command.

   A second set of options will appear under the same heading.

7. Select the **eXit** option or a new command.

To Copy Edges (See Figure 15-73.)

1. Select the **Copy Edges** tool from the **Solid Editing** panel.

   The **Copy Edges** is a flyout from the **Extract Edges** tool on the **Solid Editing** panel.

   Select edges or [Undo Remove]:

2. Select two edges.

   Select edges or [Undo Remove]:

Figure 15-73

3. Press the right mouse button, and enter the edges.

   Specify a base point or displacement:

4. Select the lower endpoint of the vertical line.

   Specify a second point of displacement:

5. Select a second point.

   Enter an edge editing option [Copy coLor Undo eXit] <eXit>:

6. Type **x;** press **Enter.**

To Imprint an Object (See Figure 15-74.)

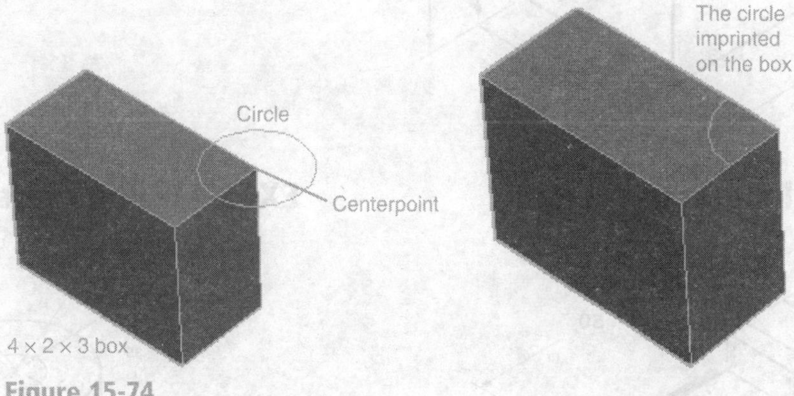

Figure 15-74

1. Draw a solid box **(4 × 2 × 3)**, then a **Ø1.00** circle with its center point on the upper right corner of the box, as shown.

2. Select the **Imprint** tool from the **Solid Editing** panel.

   The **Imprint** tool is a flyout from the **Extract Edges** tool.

   Select a 3D solid

3. Select the box.

   Select an object to imprint:

4. Select the circle.

   Select the source object <N>:

5. Type **y;** press **Enter** twice.

15-23 EXERCISE PROBLEMS

Draw the objects in Exercise Problems EX15-1 through EX15-45 as follows:

A. Draw each as a solid model.
B. Create front, top, and right-side orthographic views from the solid models.
C. Dimension the orthographic views.

EX15-1 Inches

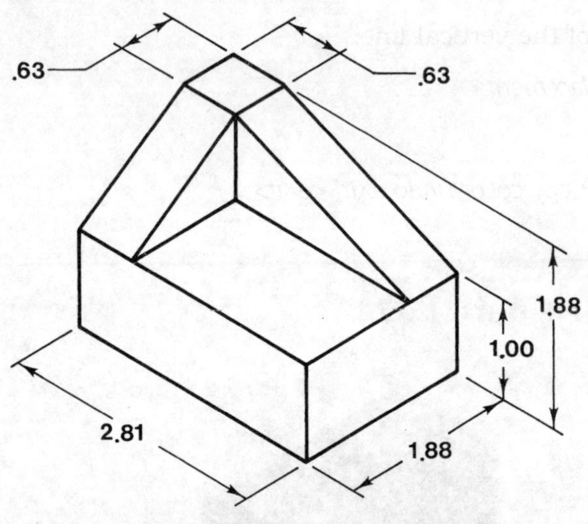

EX15-2 Inches

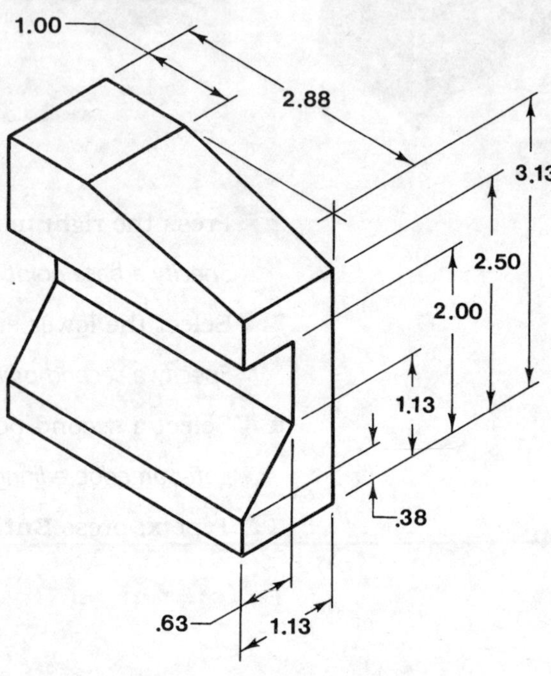

EX15-3 Millimeters

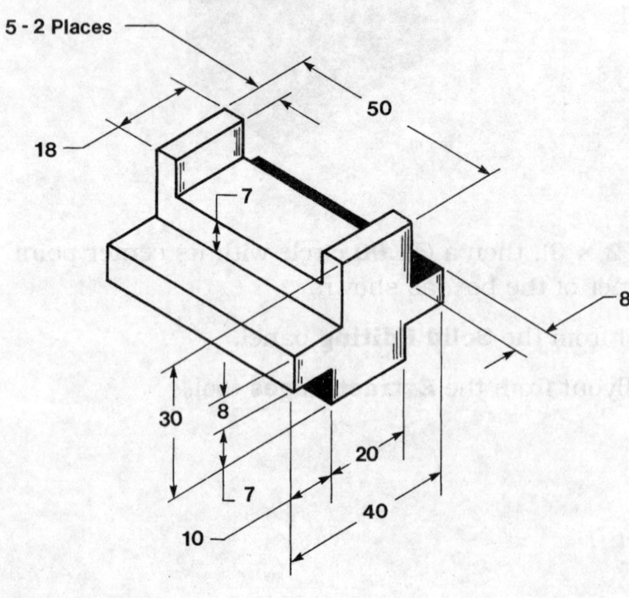

EX15-4 Millimeters

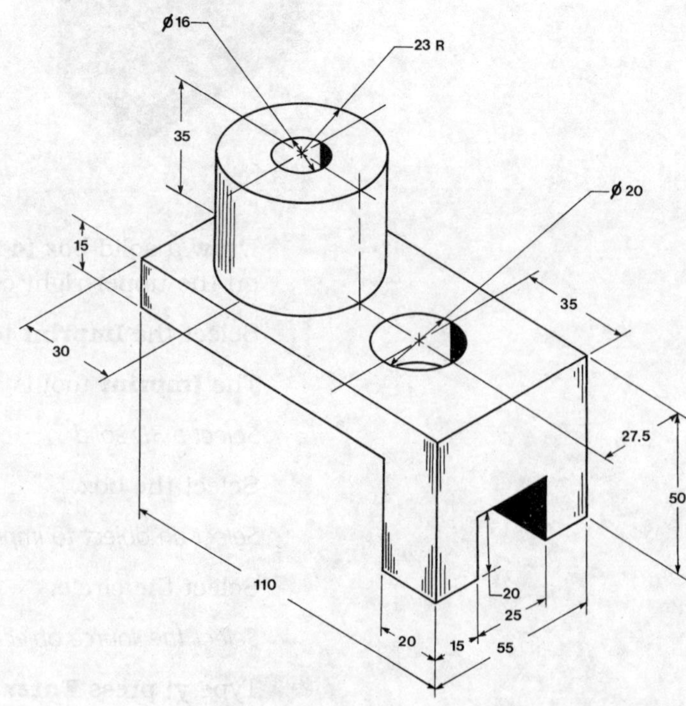

EX15-5 Inches

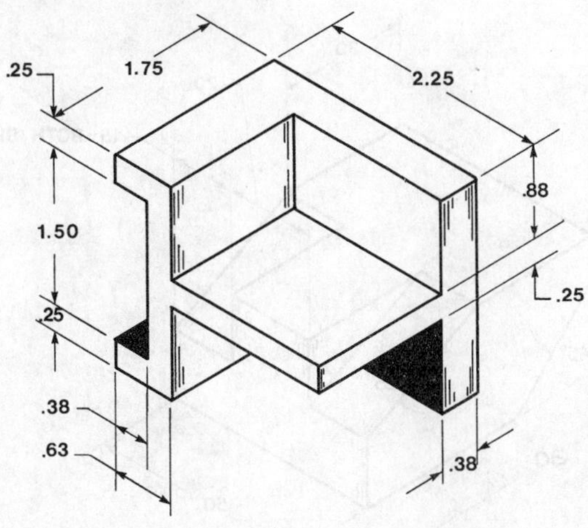

EX15-6 Millimeters

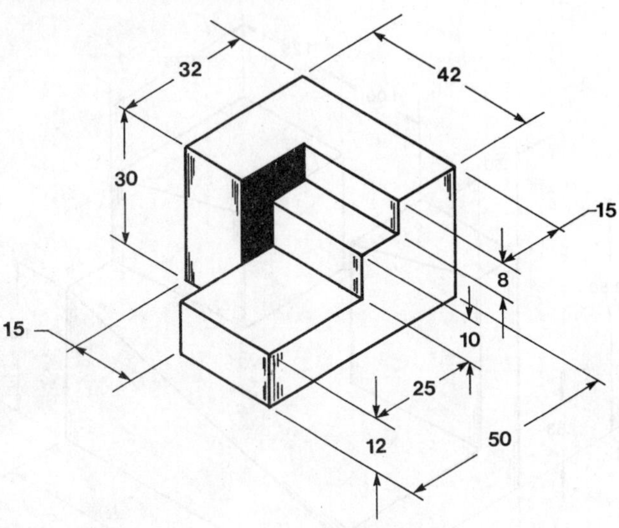

EX15-7 Millimeters

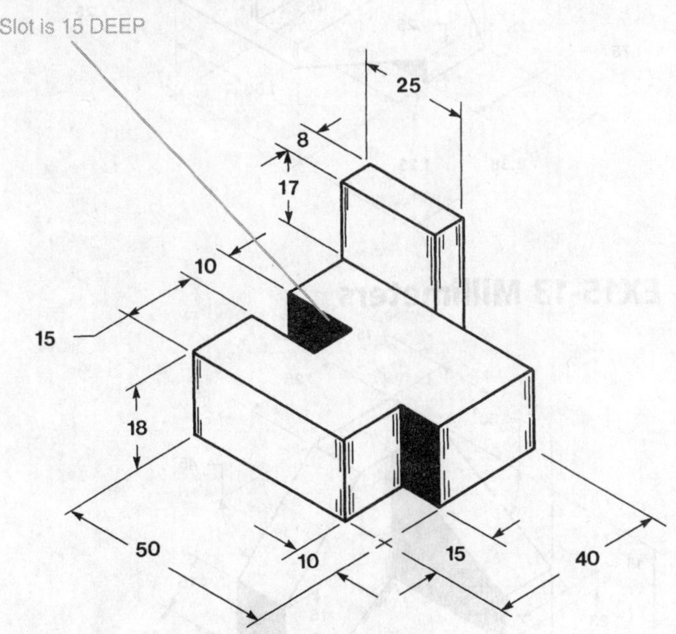

EX15-8 Millimeters

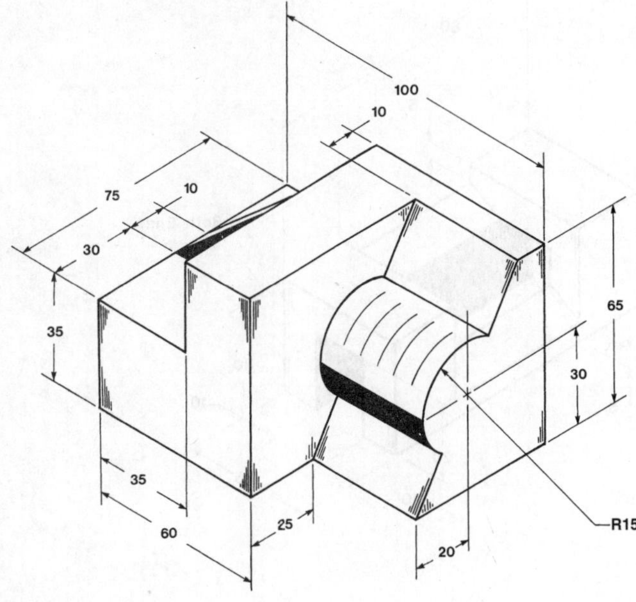

EX15-9 Inches

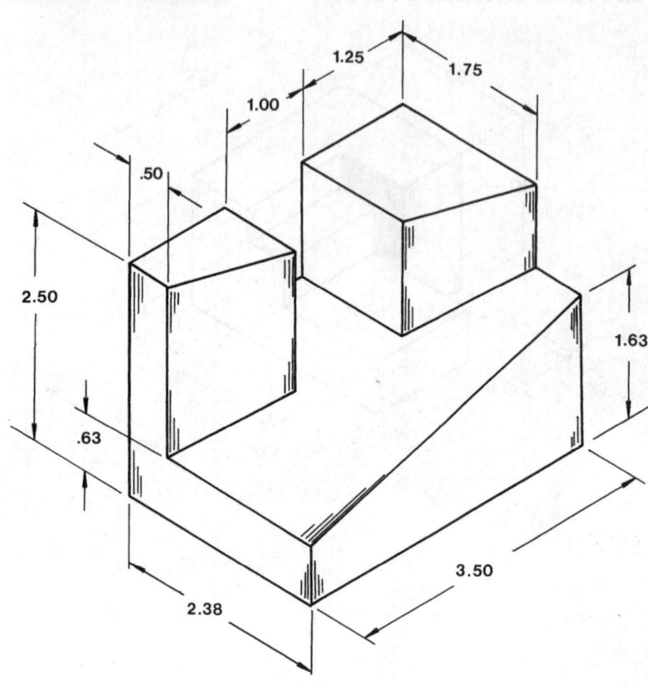

EX15-10 Millimeters

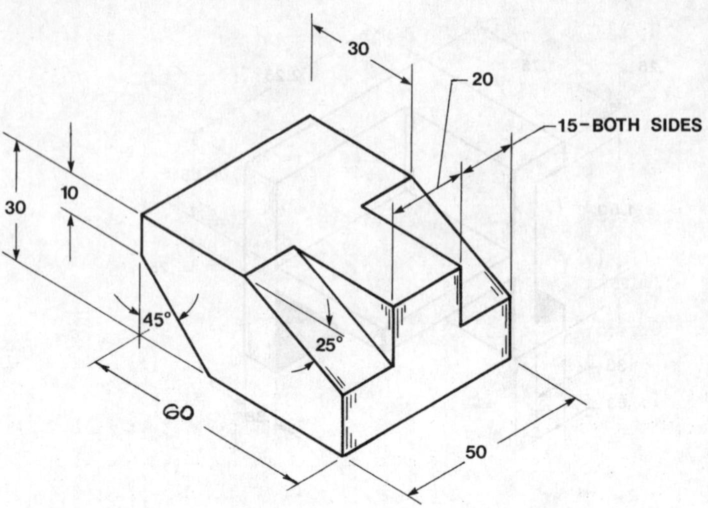

EX15-11 Millimeters

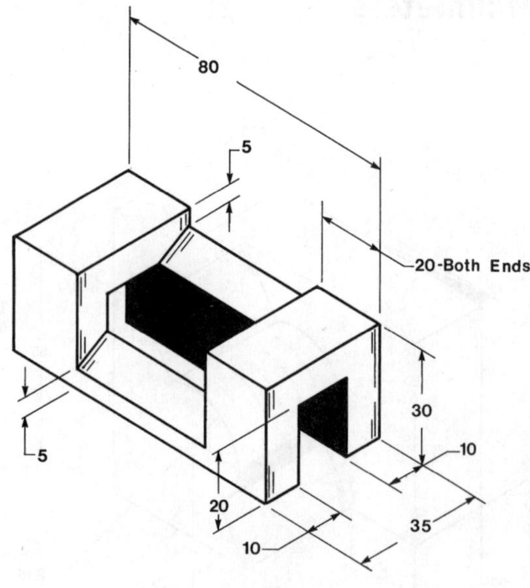

EX15-12 Inches

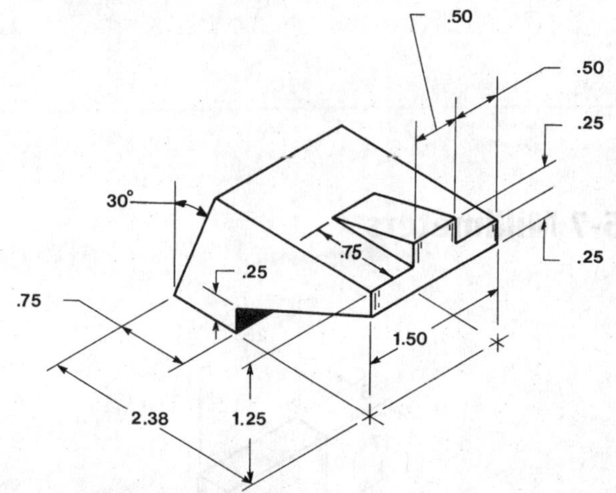

EX15-13 Millimeters

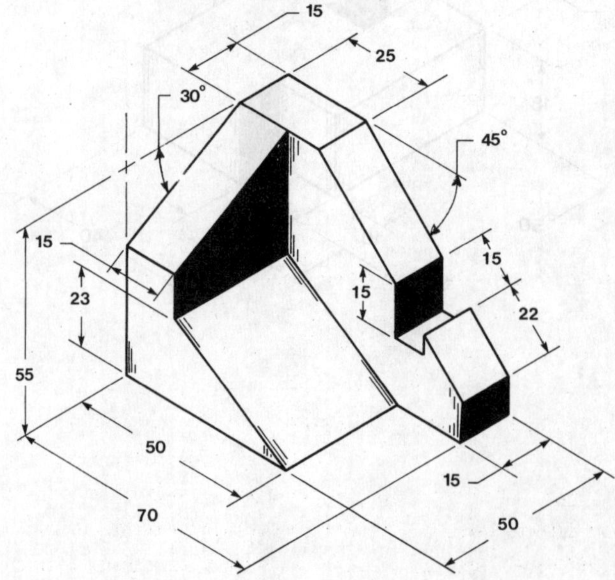

EX15-14 Inches

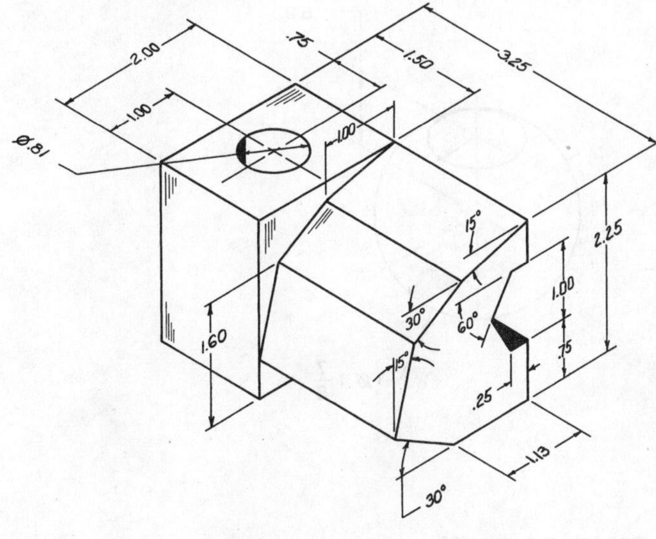

EX15-15 Millimeters

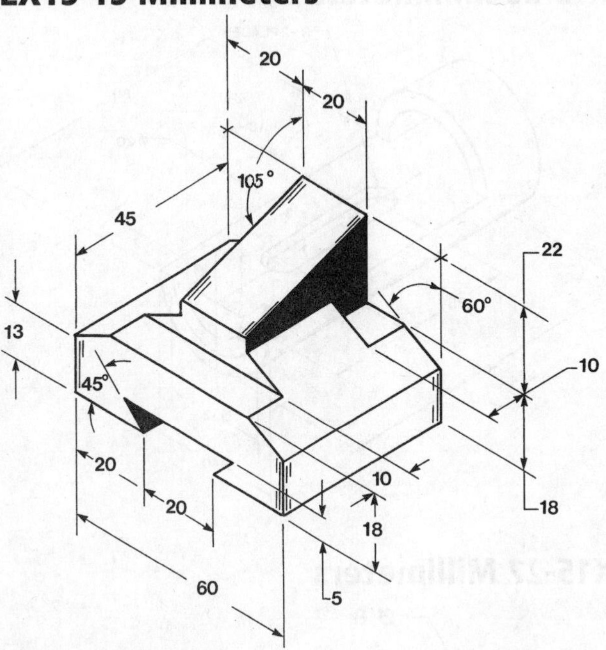

EX15-16 Millimeters

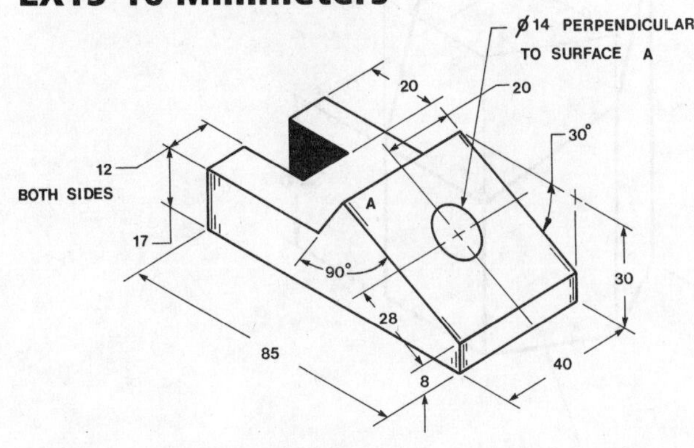

EX15-17 Inches

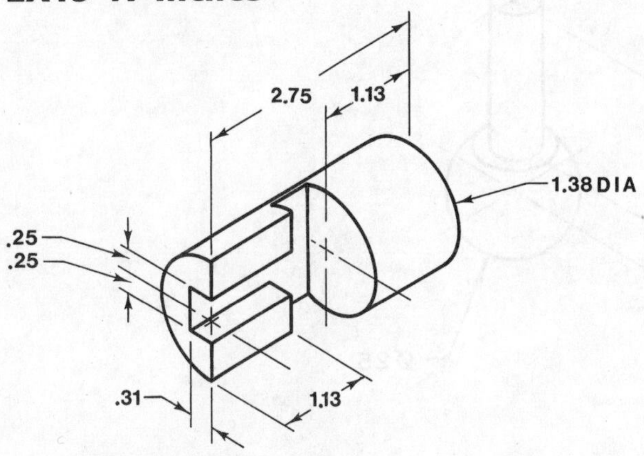

EX15-18 Millimeters

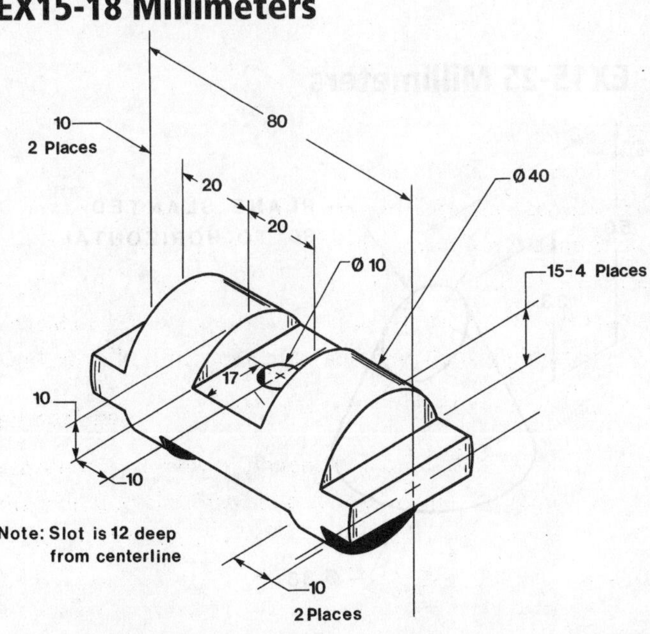

EX15-19 Millimeters

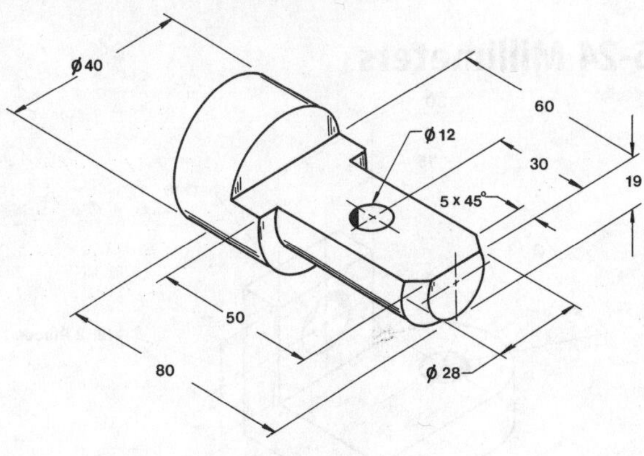

EX15-20 Millimeters

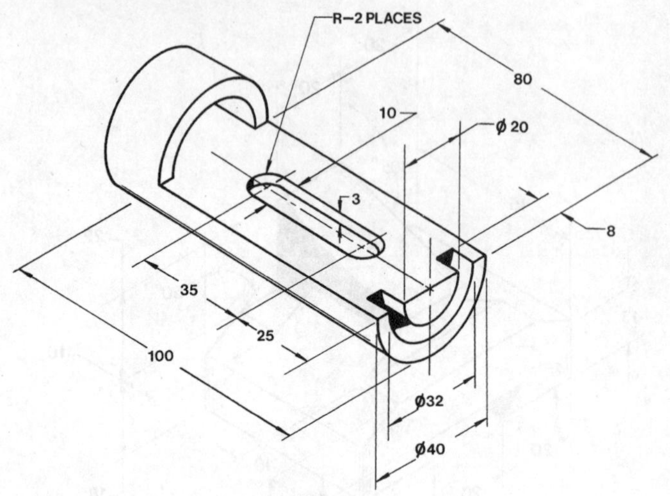

EX15-21 Inches

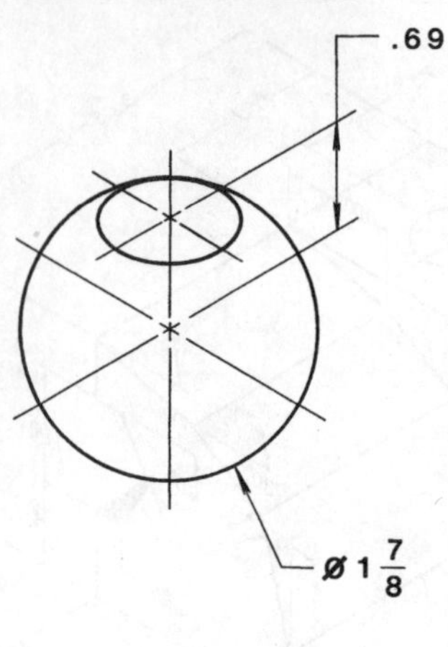

EX15-22 Millimeters

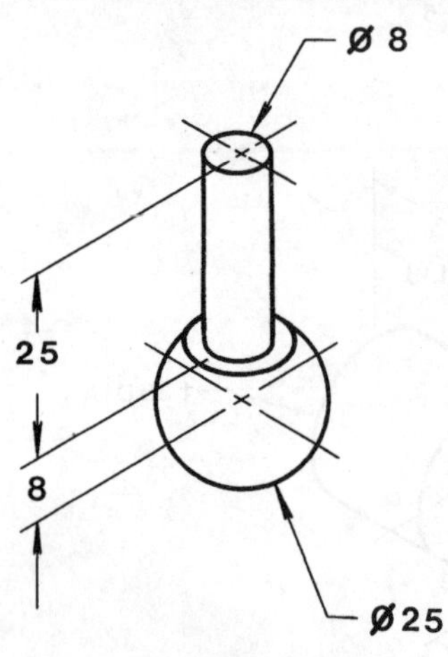

EX15-23 Millimeters

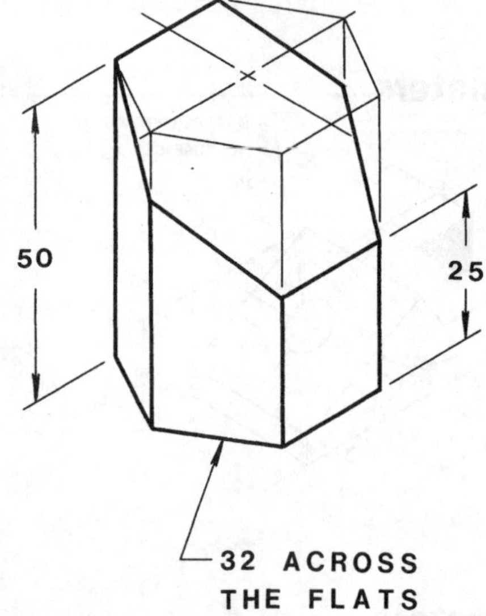

EX15-24 Millimeters

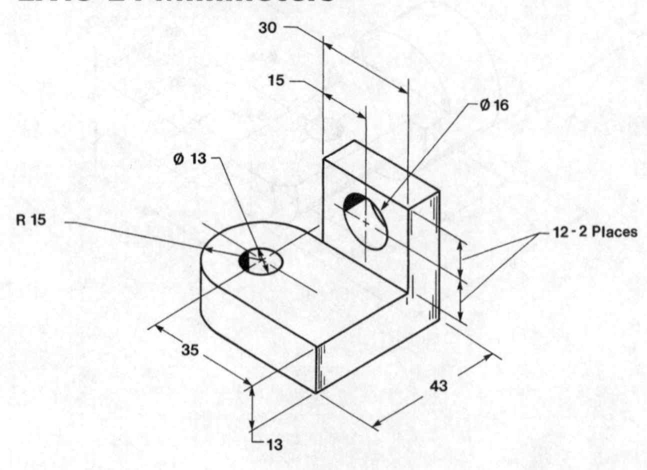

EX15-25 Millimeters

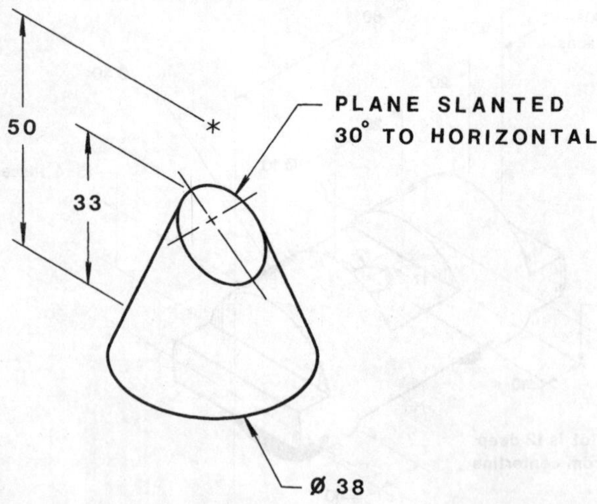

EX15-26 Millimeters (Scale 2:1)

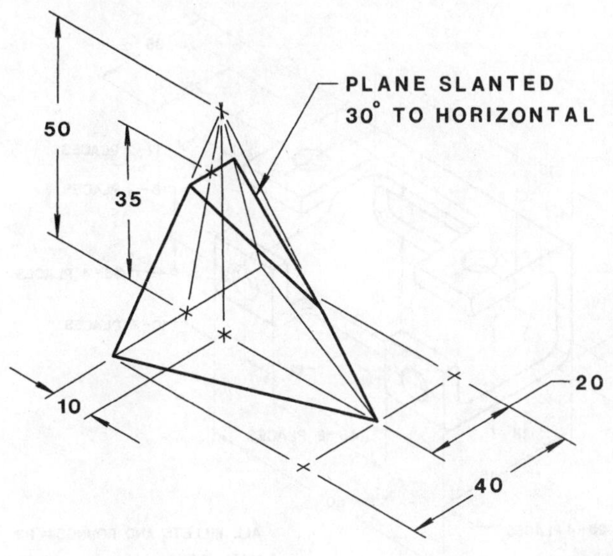

EX15-27 Millimeters

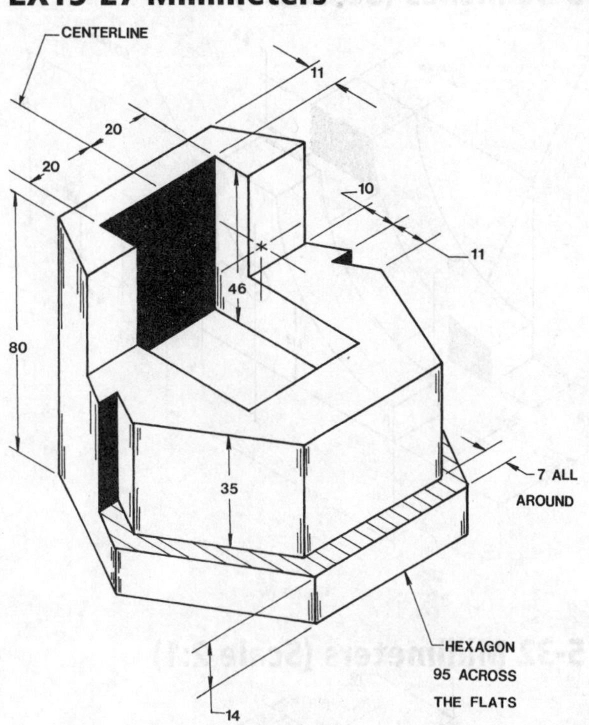

EX15-28 Inches

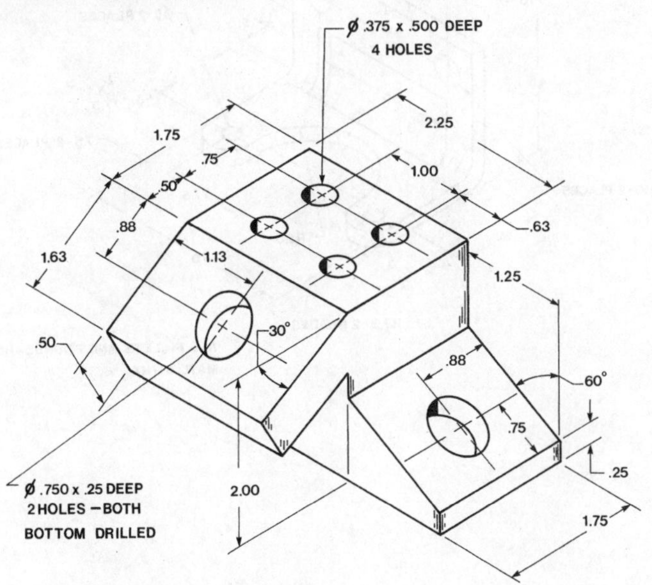

EX15-29 Millimeters

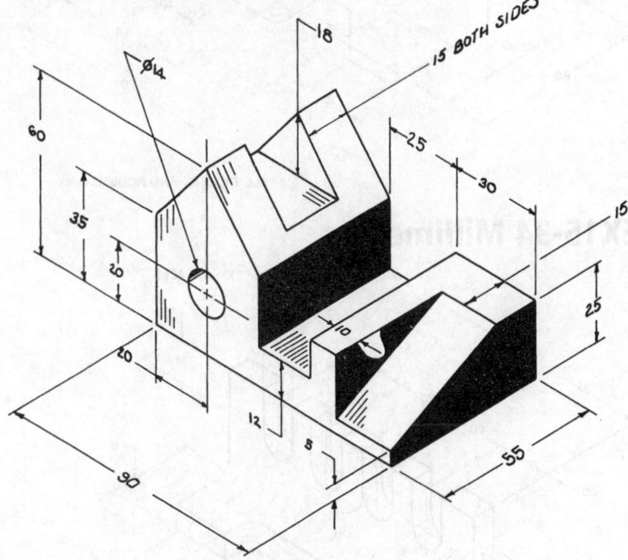

EX15-30 Inches (Scale 2:1)

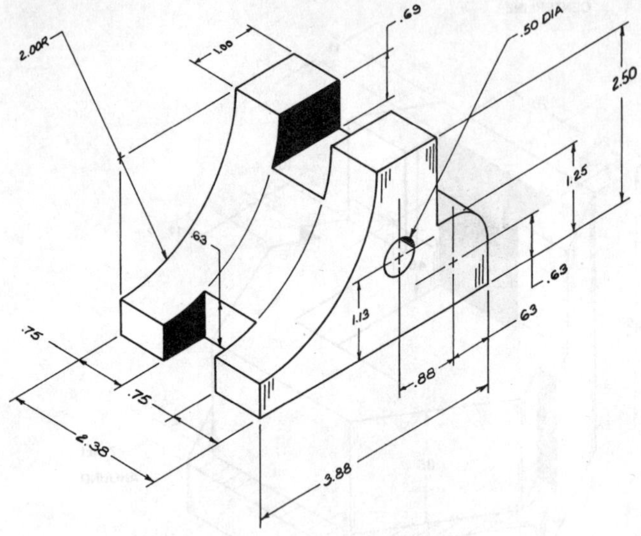

EX15-31 Millimeters

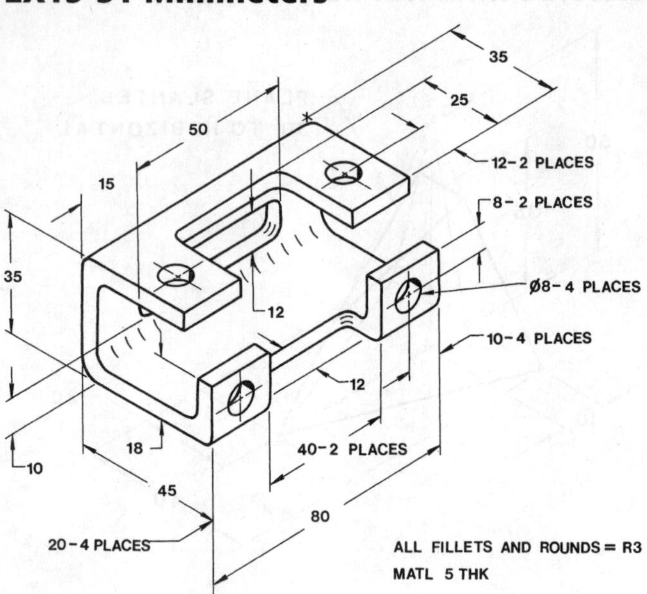

EX15-32 Millimeters (Scale 2:1)

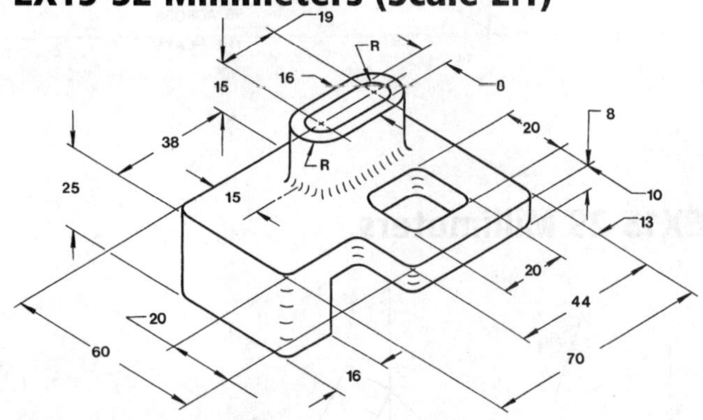

EX15-33 Millimeters

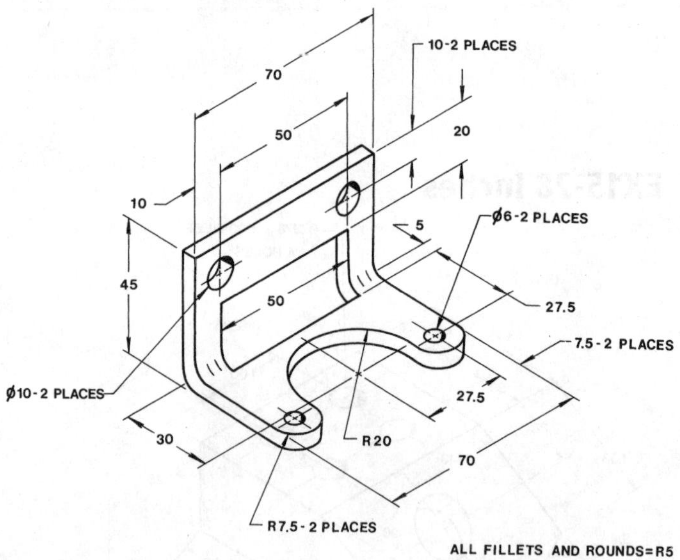

EX15-34 Millimeters

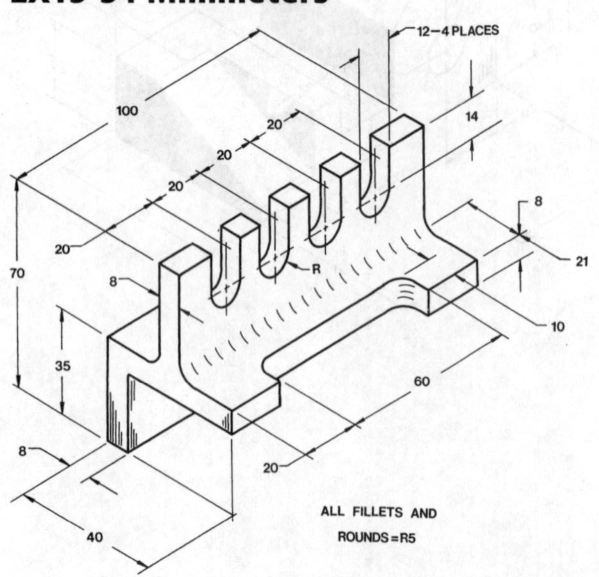

EX15-35 Inches (Scale 2:1)

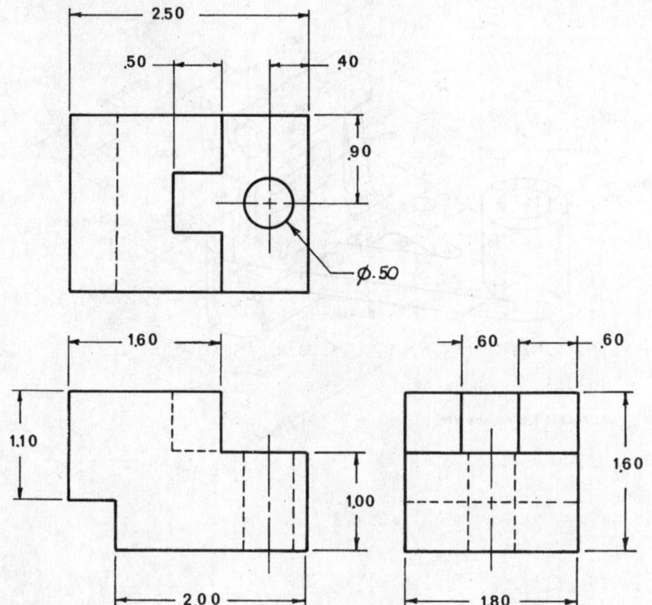

EX15-36 Inches (Scale 4:1)

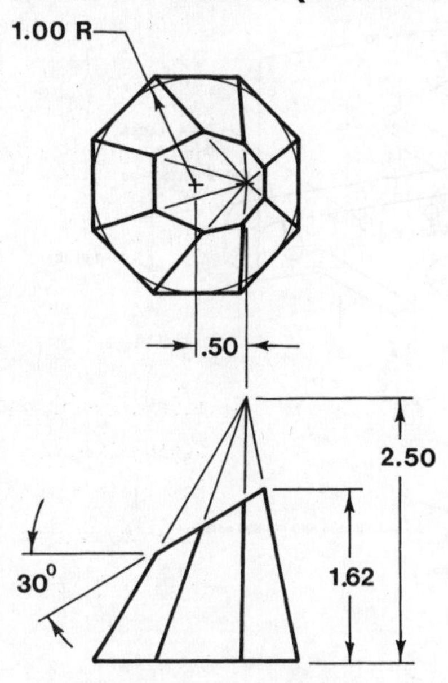

EX15-37 Inches

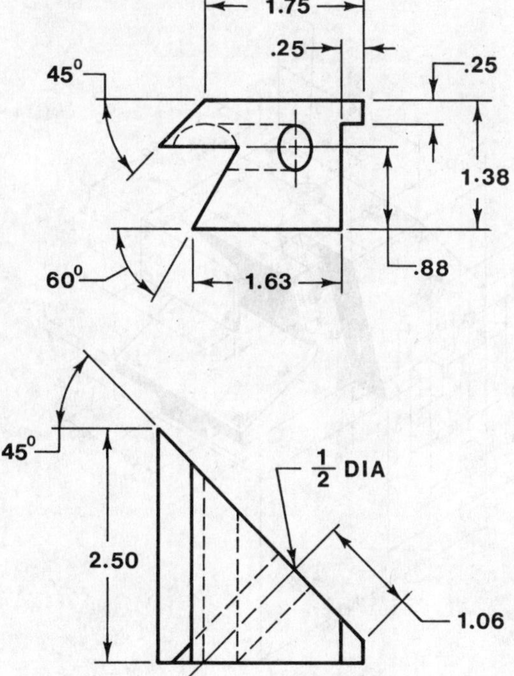

EX15-38 Inches

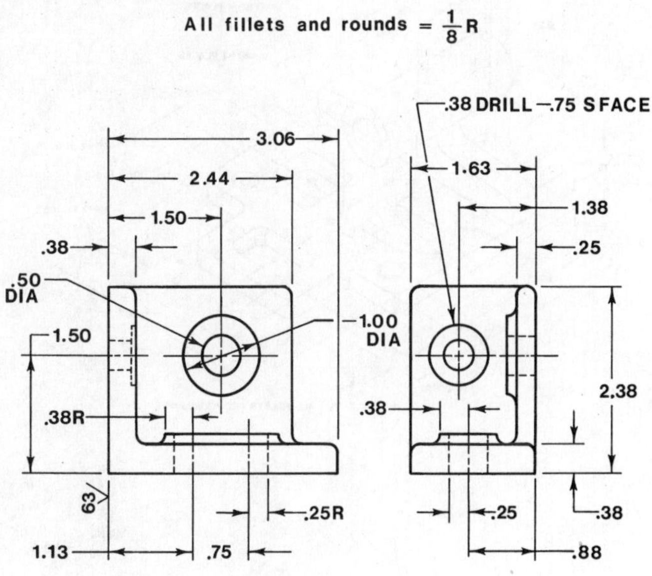

EX15-39 Millimeters

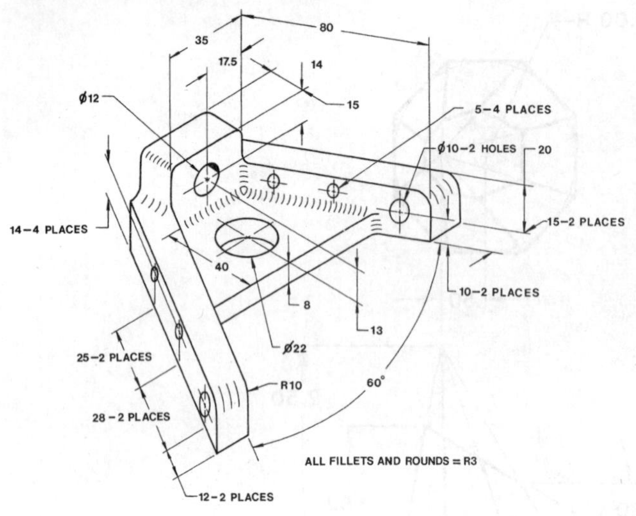

EX15-40 Millimeters

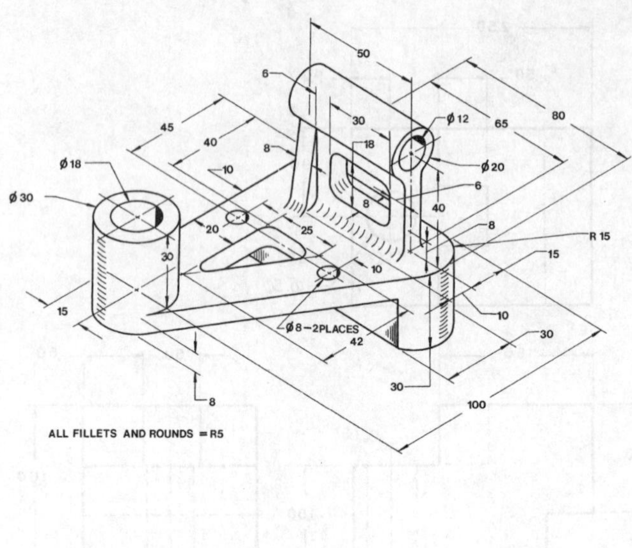

EX15-41 Millimeters

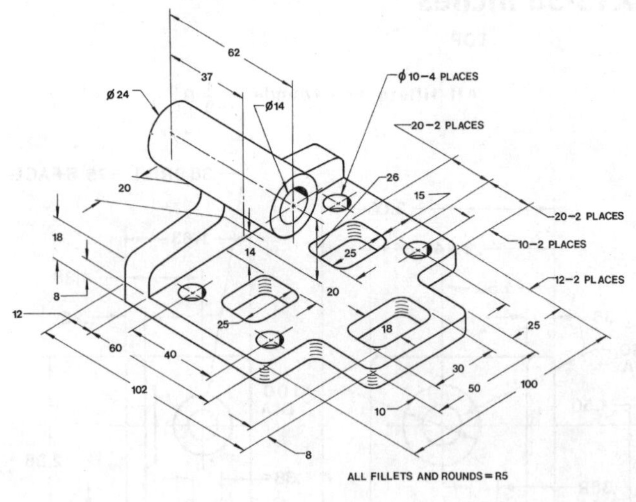

EX15-42 Millimeters

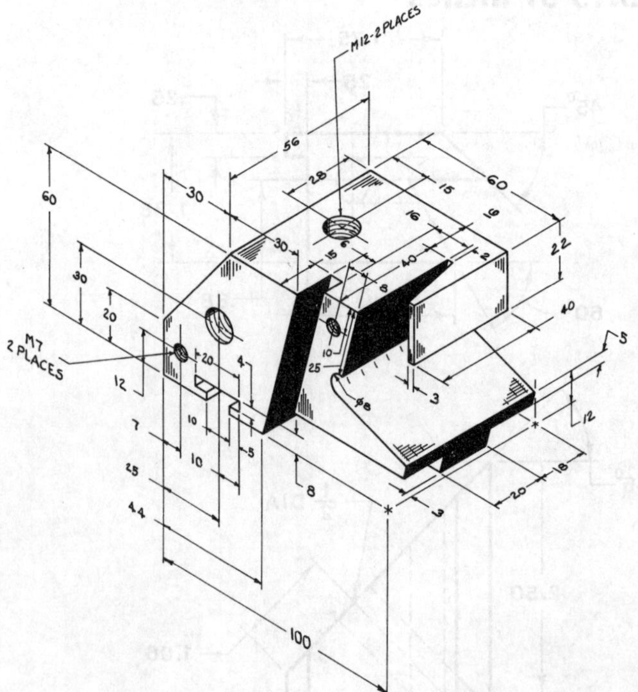

EX15-43 Millimeters

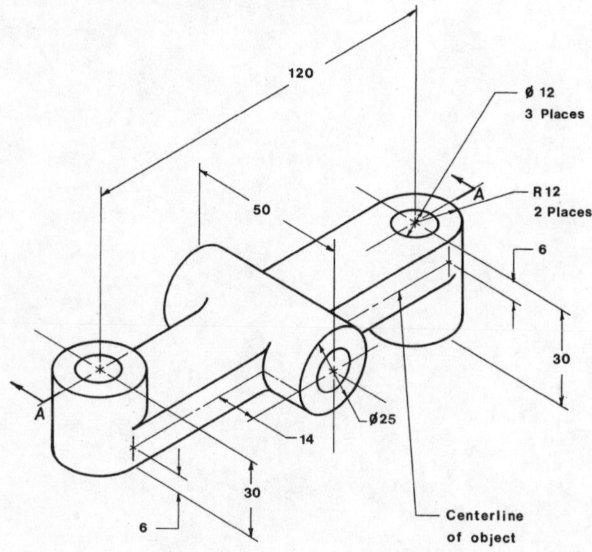

EX15-45 Millimeters

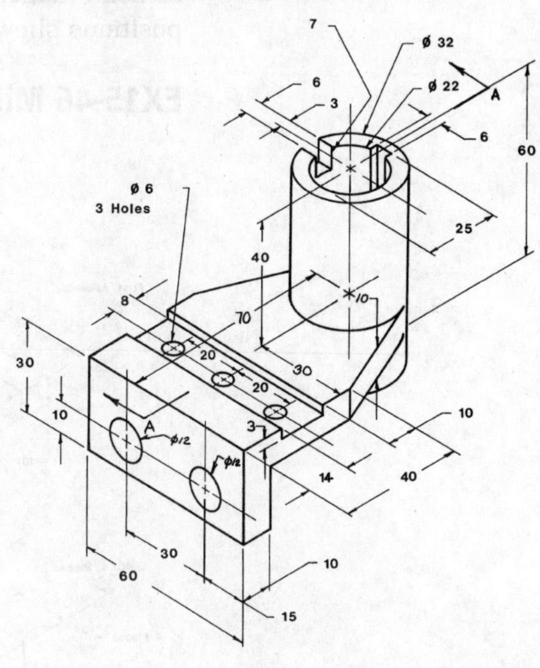

EX15-44 Inches

Draw a solid model of the object, and then create the three indicated sectional views from the model.

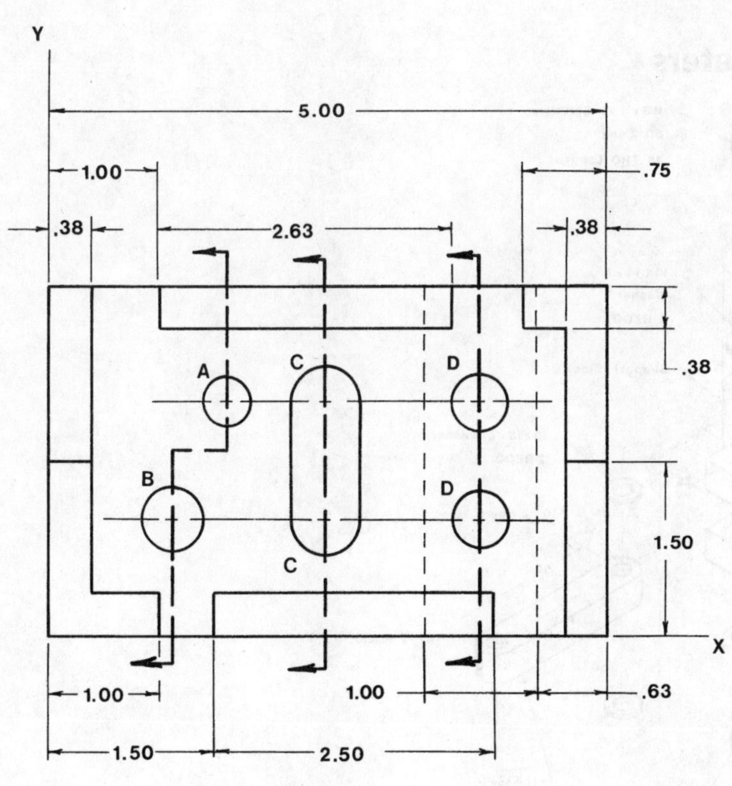

HOLE	X	Y	DIA
A	1.63	2.00	.44
B	1.13	1.00	.56
C	2.50	2.00 1.00	.63
D	3.88	2.00 1.00	.50

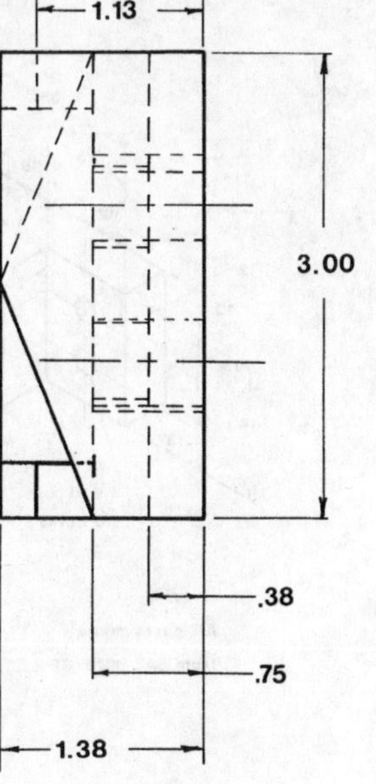

Redraw the assemblies in Exercise Problems EX15-46 through EX15-48 as solid models with the individual parts located in approximately the positions shown.

EX15-46 Millimeters

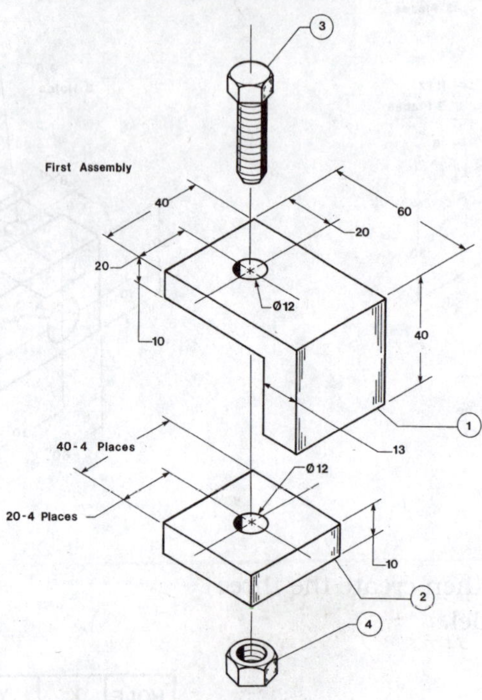

EX15-47 Millimeters

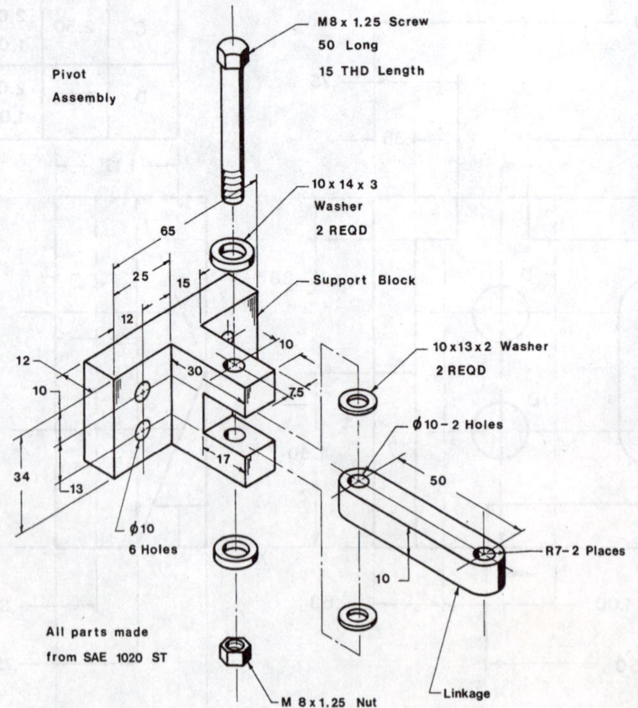

EX15-48 Millimeters

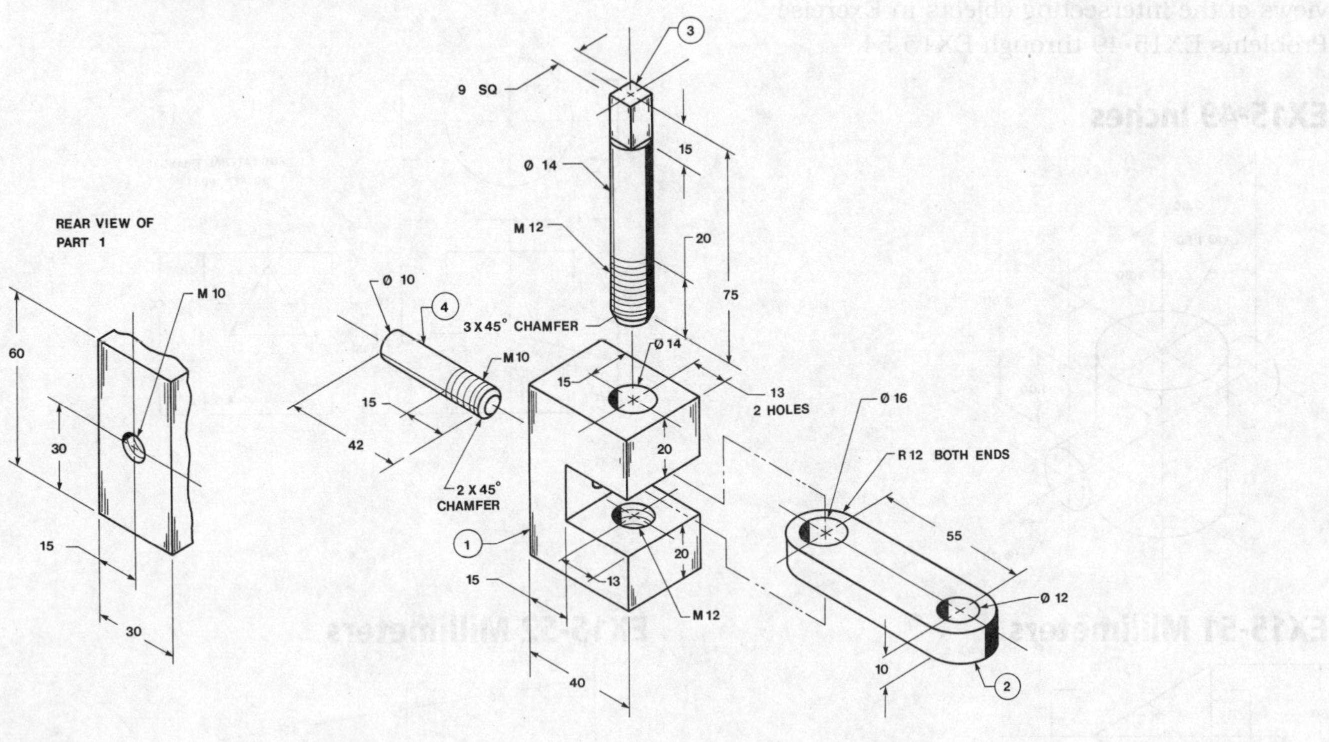

Prepare solid models and 3D orthographic views of the intersecting objects in Exercise Problems EX15-49 through EX15-54.

EX15-49 Inches

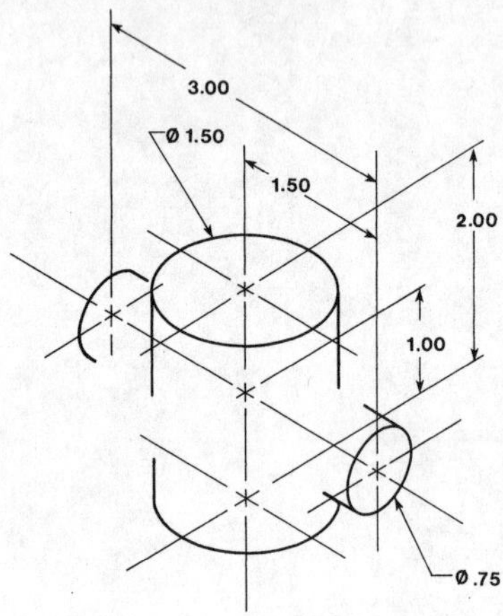

EX15-50 Millimeters

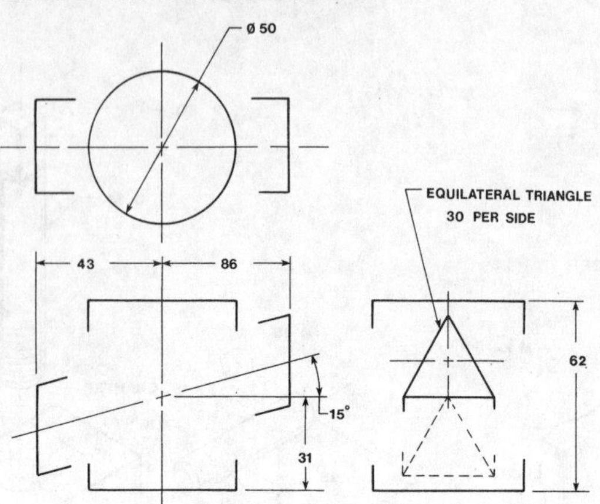

EX15-51 Millimeters

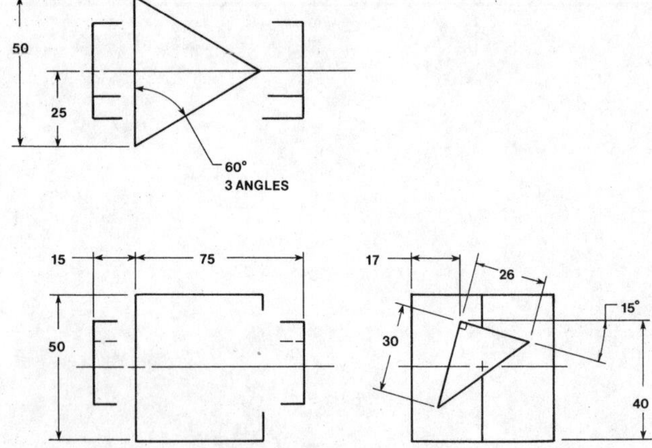

EX15-52 Millimeters

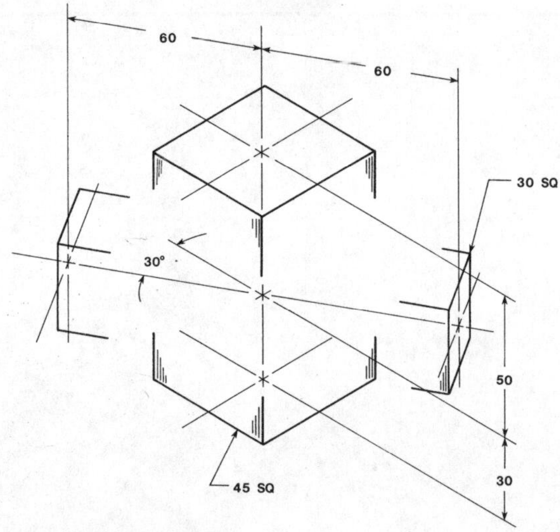

EX15-53 Millimeters

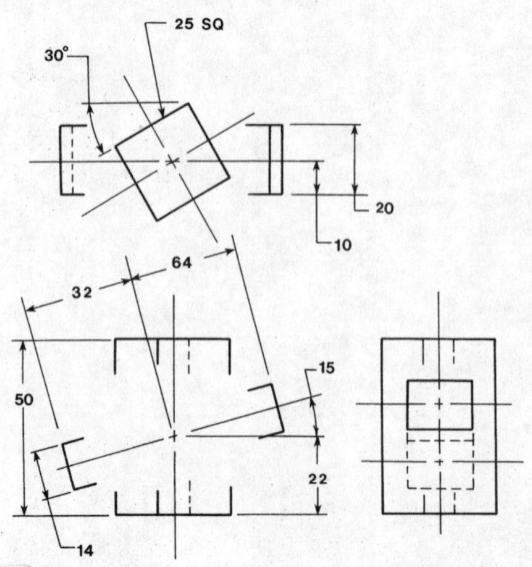

EX15-54 Inches

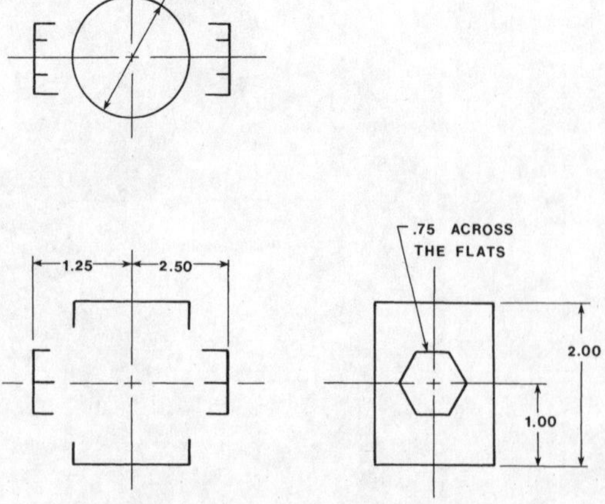

EX15-55 Millimeters

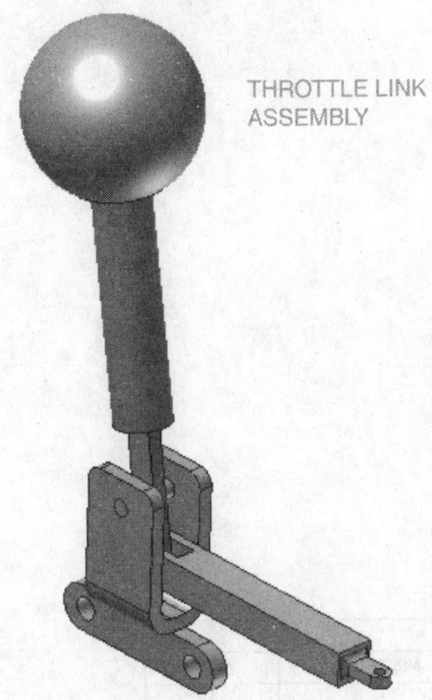

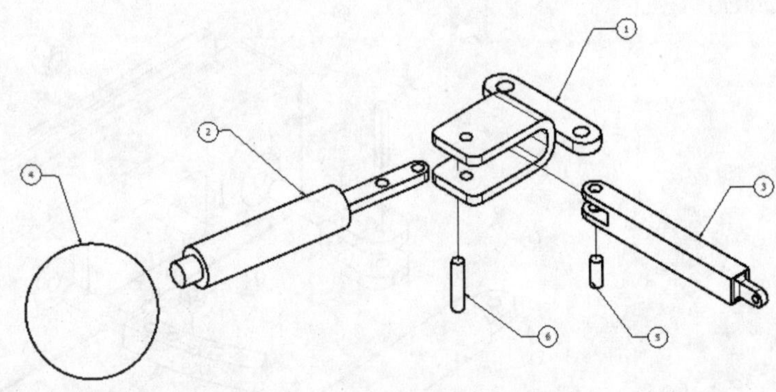

Parts List				
ITEM	PART NUMBER	DESCRIPTION	MATERIAL	QTY
1	ENG-A43	BOX,PIVOT	SAE1020	1
2	ENG-A44	POST,HANDLE	SAE1020	1
3	ENG-A45	LINK	SAE1020	1
4	AM300-1	HANDLE	STEEL	1
5	EK-132	POST-Ø6x14	STEEL	1
6	EK-131	POST-Ø6x26	STEEL	1

PIVOT BOX

30.00 15.00 R5.00 10.00 Ø6.00 47.00 R8.00 Ø8.00 2 HOLES 10.00 50.00 70.00 5.00 ALL AROUND 16.00 6.00

HANDLE

R30.00 26.00 Ø12.00 ▾ 12.00

HANDLE POST

5.00 2.50 10.00 5.00 45.00 25.00 80.00 10.00 Ø20.00 Ø12.00 R5.00 Ø6.00 THRU 2 HOLES

LINK

94.00 16.00 R6.00 Ø6.00 THRU 12.00 3.50 20.00 R4.00 14.00 3.50 R2 - ALL AROUND Ø4.00 THRU 4.00 BOTH SIDES 3.00 BOTH SIDES

EX15-56

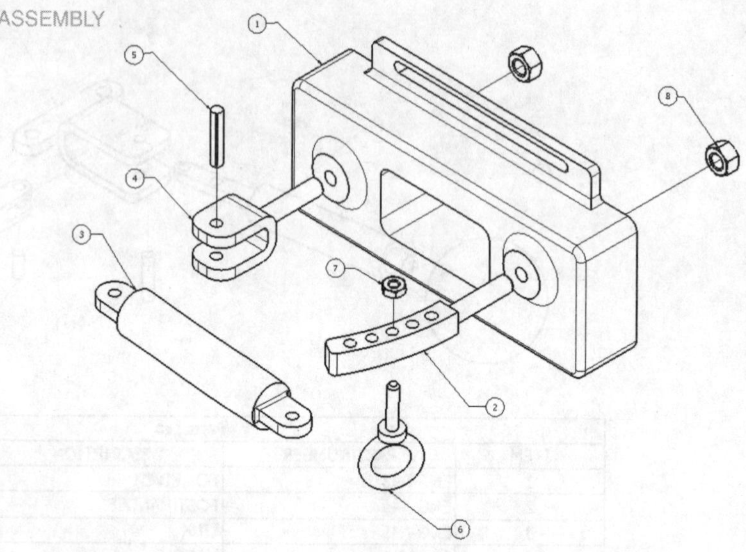

Parts List				
ITEM	PART NUMBER	DESCRIPTION	MATERIAL	QTY
1	ENG-311	BASE#4, CAST	Cast Iron	1
2	ENG-312	SUPPORT, ROUNDED	SAE 1040 STEEL	1
3	ENG-404	POST, ADJUSTABLE	Steel, Mild	1
4	BU-1964	YOKE	Cast Iron	1
5	ANSI B18.8.2 1/4x1.3120	Grooved pin, Type C - 1/4x1.312 ANSI B18.8.2	Steel, Mild	1
6	ANSI B18.15 - 1/4 - 20. Shoulder Pattern Type 2 - Style A	Forged Eyebolt	Steel, Mild	1
7	ANSI B18.6.3 - 1/4 - 20	Hex Machine Screw Nut	Steel, Mild	1
8	ANSI B18.2.2 - 3/8 - 16	Hex Nut	Steel, Mild	2

CAST BASE #4

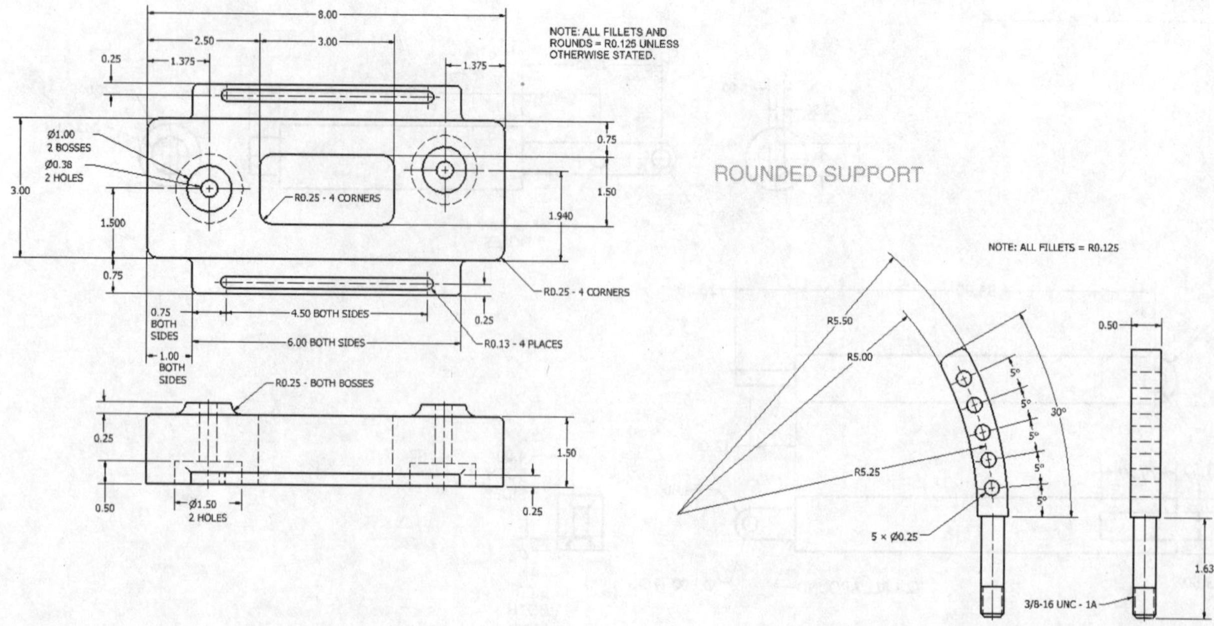

EX15-56, continued

ADJUSTABLE POST

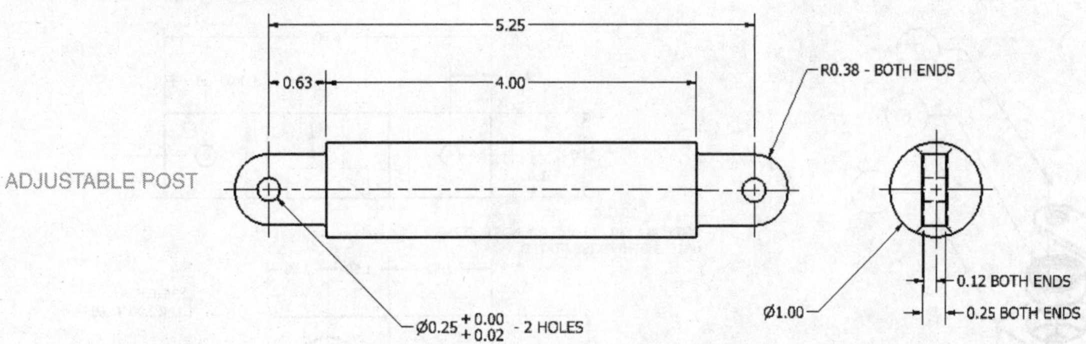

YOKE

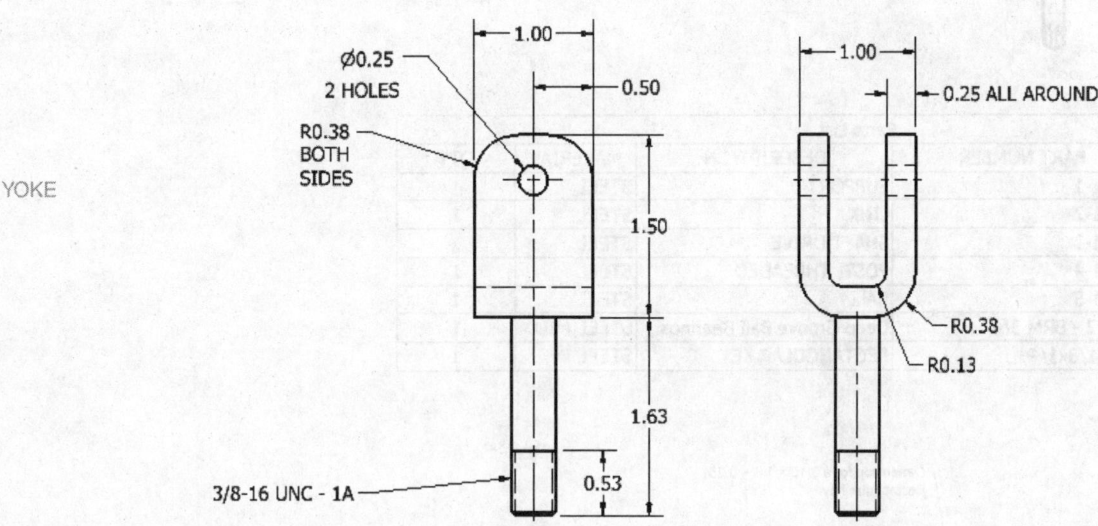

FORGED EYEBOLT

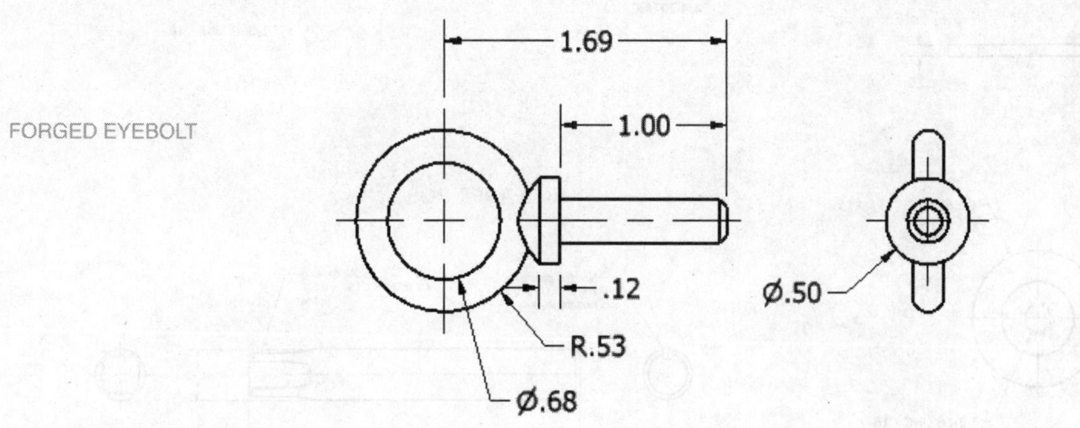

EX15-57

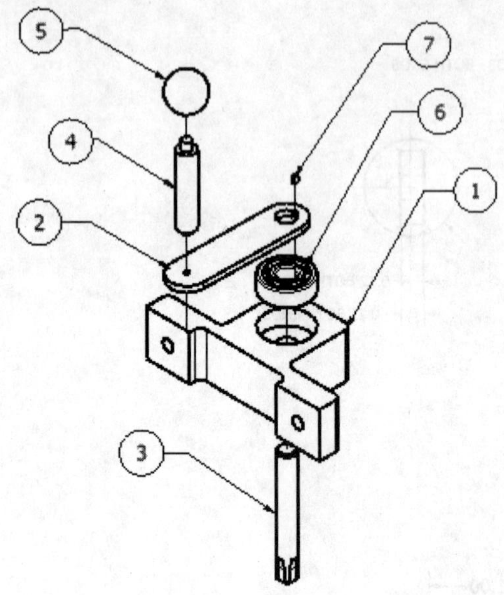

SUPPORT

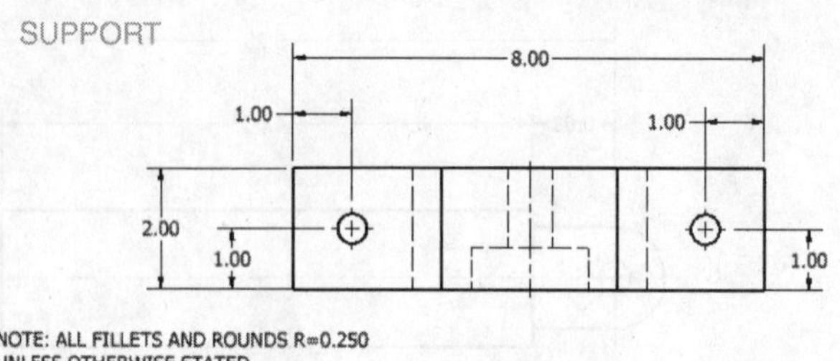

NOTE: ALL FILLETS AND ROUNDS R=0.250
UNLESS OTHERWISE STATED.

Parts List				
ITEM	PART NUMBER	DESCRIPTION	MATERIAL	QTY
1	EK131-1	SUPPORT	STEEL	1
2	EK131-2	LINK	STEEL	1
3	EK131-3	SHAFT,DRIVE	STEEL	1
4	EK131-4	POST, THREADED	STEEL	1
5	EK131-5	BALL	STEEL	1
6	BS 292 - BRM 3/4	Deep Groove Ball Bearings	STEEL,MILD	1
7	3/16x1/8x1/4	RECTANGULAR KEY	STEEL	1

LINK

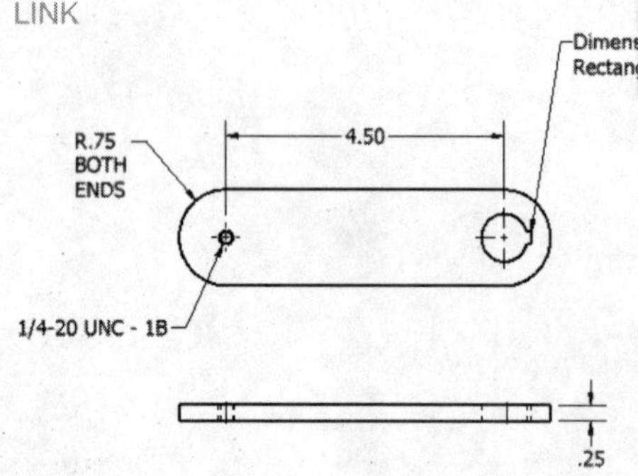

DRIVE SHAFT

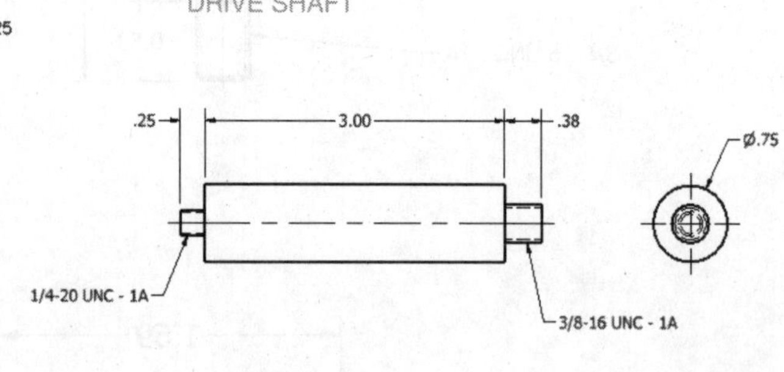

BALL

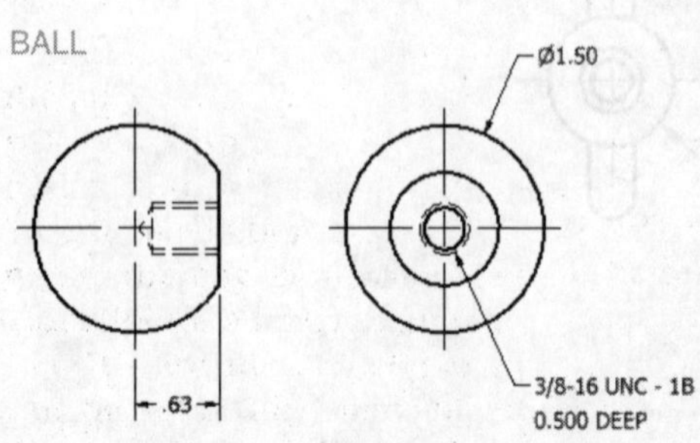

THREADED POST

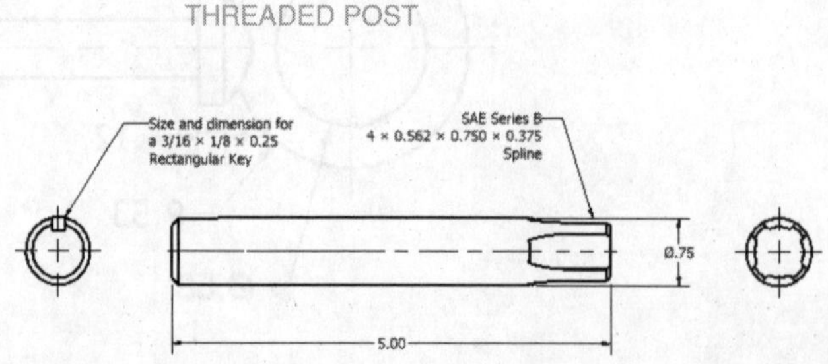

EX15-58

Parts List			
ITEM	QTY	PART NUMBER	DESCRIPTION
1	1	ENG-2008-A	BASE, CAST
2	1	DIN625 - SKF 6203	Single row ball bearings
3	1	SHF-4004-16	SHAFT: Ø16×120,WITH 2.3×5×16 KEYWAY
4	1		SUB-ASSEMBLY, FOLLOWER
5	1	SPR-C22	SPRING,COMPRESSION
6	1	GB 273.2-87 - 7/70 - 8 x 18 x 5	Rolling bearings - Thrust bearings - Plan of boundary dimensions
7	1	IS 2048 - 1983 - Specification for Parallel Keys and Keyways B 5 x 5 x 16	KEY, SQUARE

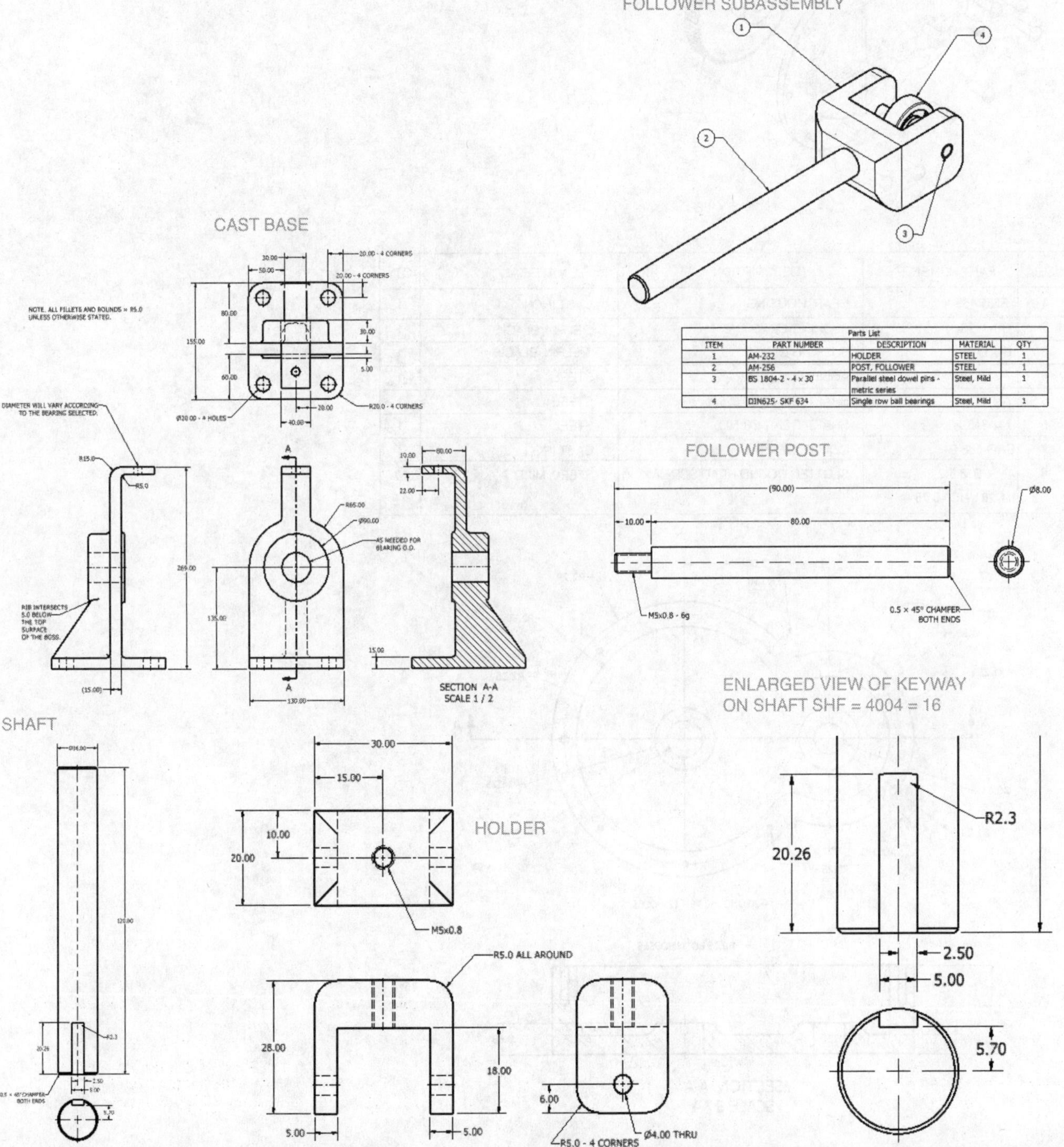

Parts List				
ITEM	PART NUMBER	DESCRIPTION	MATERIAL	QTY
1	AM-232	HOLDER	STEEL	1
2	AM-256	POST, FOLLOWER	STEEL	1
3	BS 1804-2 - 4 x 30	Parallel steel dowel pins - metric series	Steel, Mild	1
4	DIN625- SKF 634	Single row ball bearings	Steel, Mild	1

EX15-59

2-GEAR ASSEMBLY

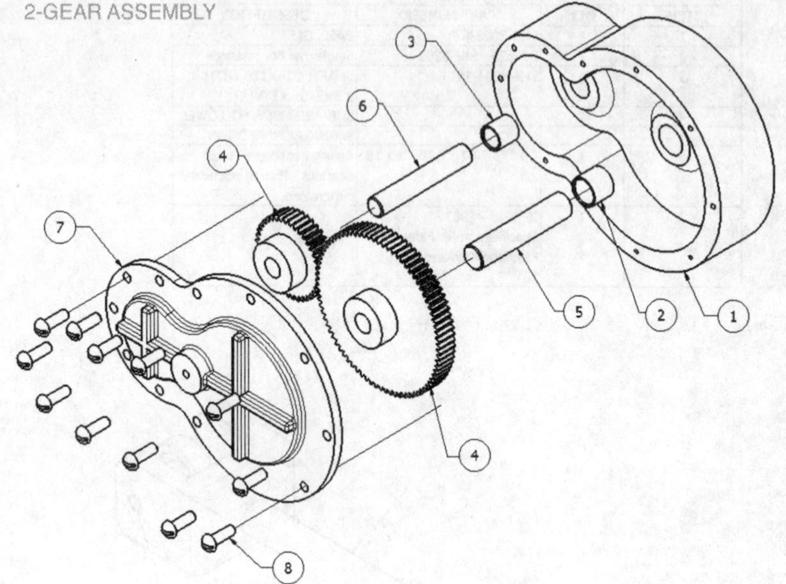

	Small Gear	Large Gear
Number of teeth	48	96
Face width	0.50	0.50
Diametral pitch	24	24
Pressure angle	20	20
Hub Ø	0.750	1.00
Base Ø	0.500	0.625

ITEM	PART NUMBER	DESCRIPTION	MATERIAL	QTY
1	ENG-453-A	GEAR, HOUSING	CAST IRON	1
2	BU-1123	BUSHING Ø0.75	DELRIN, BLACK	1
3	BU-1126	BUSHING Ø0.625	DELRIN, BLACK	1
4	ASSEMBLY-6	ASSEMBLY, GEAR	STEEL	1
5	AM-314	SHAFT, GEAR Ø0.625	STEEL	1
6	AM-315	SHAFT, GEAR Ø0.500	STEEL	1
7	ENG-566-B	COVER, GEAR	CAST IRON	1
8	ANSI B18.6.2 1/4-20 UNC ×0.75	SLOTTED ROUND HEAD SCREW	STEEL, MILD	12

GEAR HOUSING

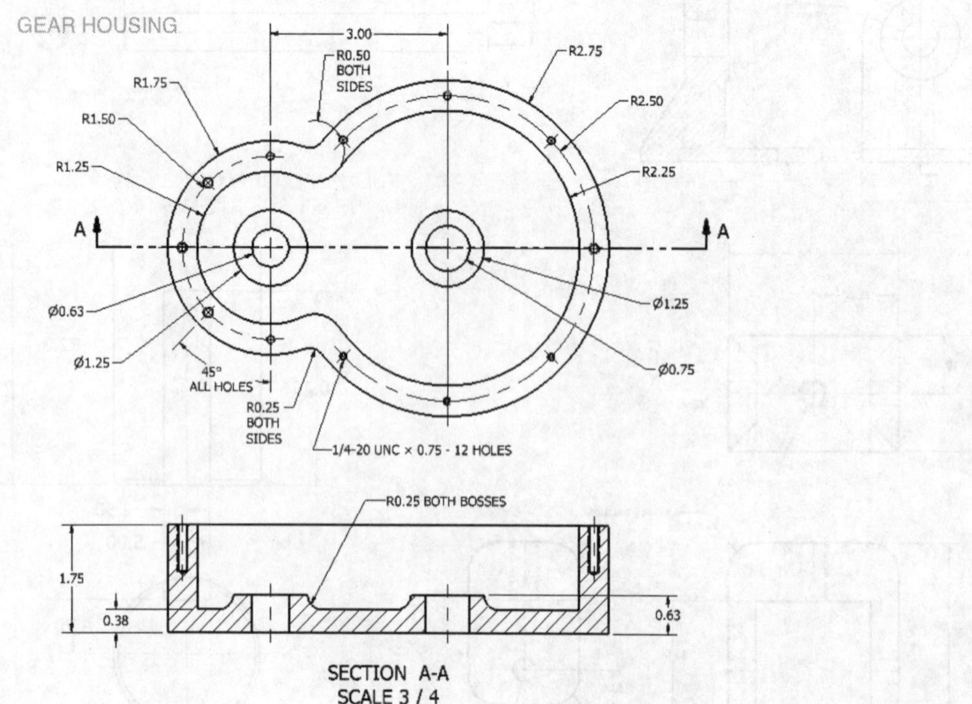

EX15-59, continued

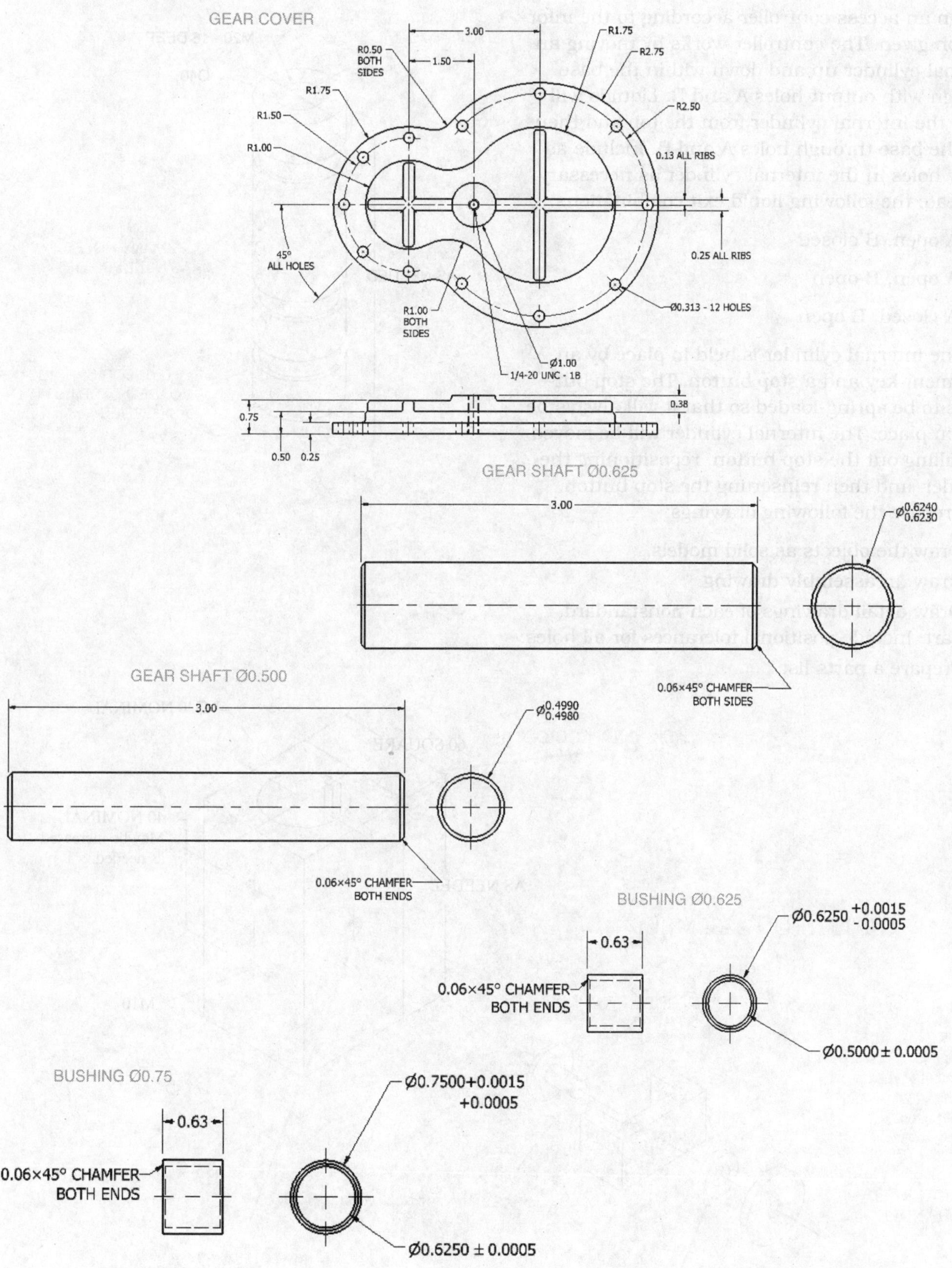

EX15-60

Design an access controller according to the information given. The controller works by moving an internal cylinder up and down within the base to align with output holes A and B. Liquids will enter the internal cylinder from the top and then exit the base through holes A and B. Include as many holes in the internal cylinder as necessary to create the following liquid exit combinations:

1 A open, B closed

2 A open, B open

3 A closed, B open

The internal cylinder is held in place by an alignment key and a stop button. The stop button is to be spring-loaded so that it will always be held in place. The internal cylinder will be moved by pulling out the stop button, repositioning the cylinder, and then reinserting the stop button.

Prepare the following drawings:

A. Draw the objects as solid models.
B. Draw an assembly drawing.
C. Draw detail drawings of each nonstandard part. Include positional tolerances for all holes.
D. Prepare a parts list.

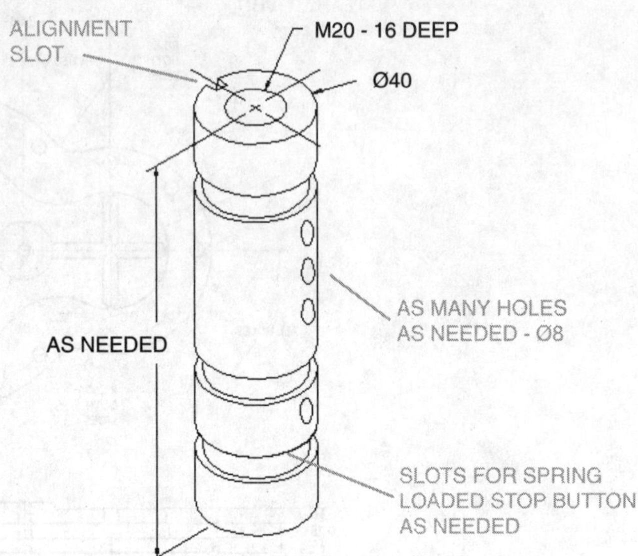

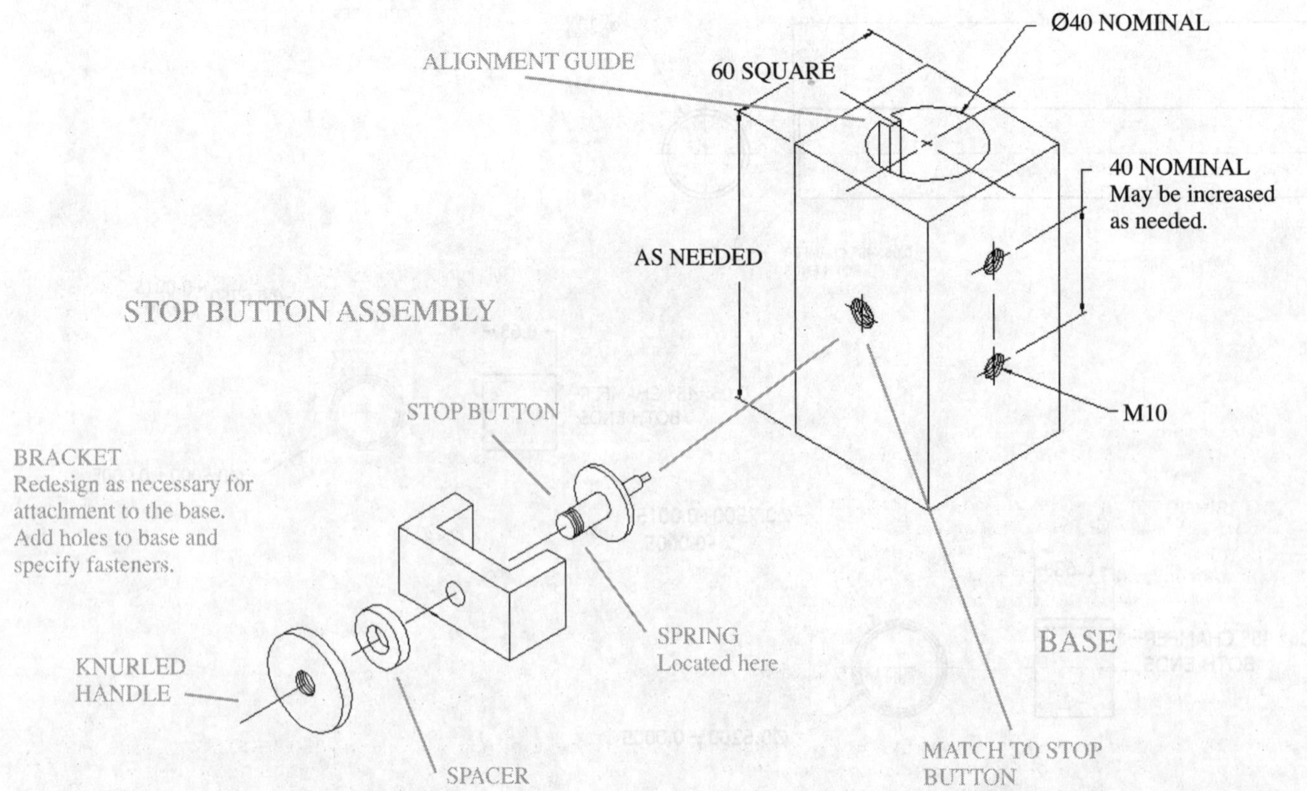

EX15-61

Design a hand-operated grinding wheel specifically for sharpening a chisel. The chisel is to be located on an adjustable rest while it is being sharpened. The mechanism should be able to be clamped to a table during operation by two thumbscrews.

A standard grinding wheel is Ø 6.00 inch, is ½ inch thick, and has an internal mounting hole with a 50.00 ± 0.3 millimeter bore.

Prepare the following drawings:

A. Draw the objects as solid models.
B. Draw an assembly drawing.
C. Draw detail drawings of each nonstandard part.
D. Prepare a parts list.

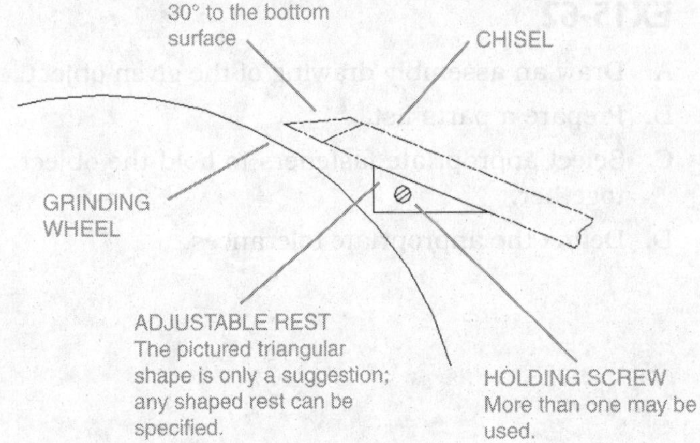

SUPPORT

This support may be designed as a casting.

GRINDING WHEEL
1/2" Thick, Ø6".
Ø50.00±.03mm bore

SHAFT

Insert handle here.

LINK

Locate bearing here, if specified.

THUMBSCREWS

GRINDING WHEEL

BEARING

SPACER

SPACER

Metal threaded end

NUT

NUT

SHAFT

This is a nominal setup. It may be improved. Consider how the spacers rub against the stationary support, and consider double nuts at each end of the shaft.

HANDLE ASSEMBLY
Wooden with threaded metal insert

LINK

SUPPORT

EX15-62

A. Draw an assembly drawing of the given object.
B. Prepare a parts list.
C. Select appropriate fasteners to hold the object together.
D. Define the appropriate tolerances.

C-BRACKET
SAE 1020 STEEL, 4 REQD
Part Number: AM311-1

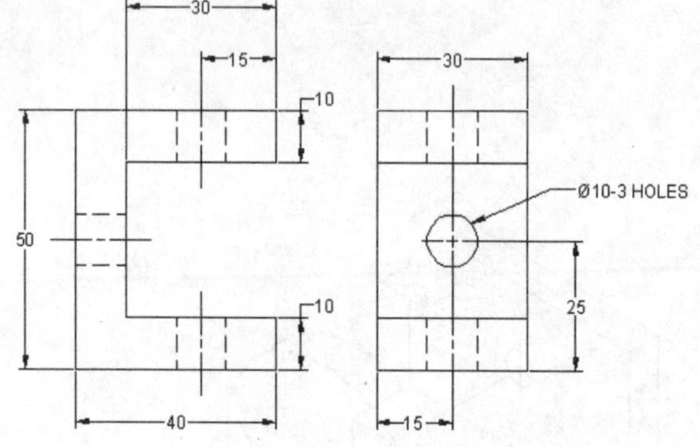

SUPPORT PLATE
SAE 1040 STEEL, 2 REQD
Part Number: AM312-3

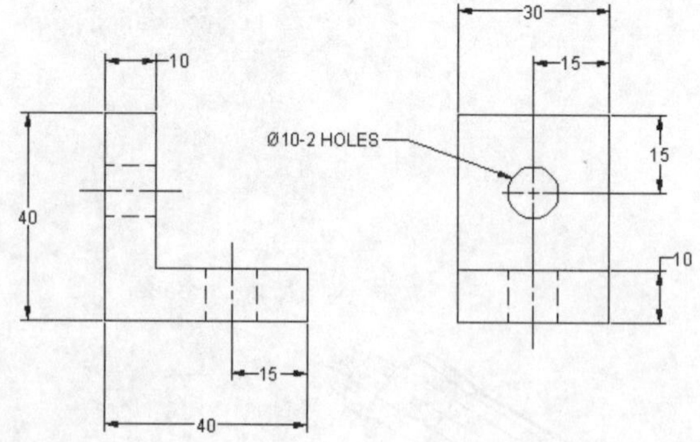

L-CLIP
SAE 1040 STEEL, 2 REQD
Part Number: AM312-4

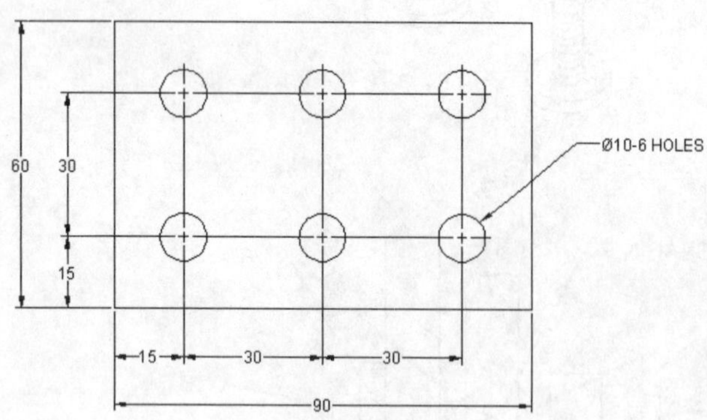

EX15-63

A. Draw an assembly drawing of the given object.
B. Prepare a parts list.
C. Select appropriate fasteners to hold the object together.
D. Define the appropriate tolerances.
E. Use phantom lines, and define the motion of the center link and the rocker link if the drive link rotates 360°.

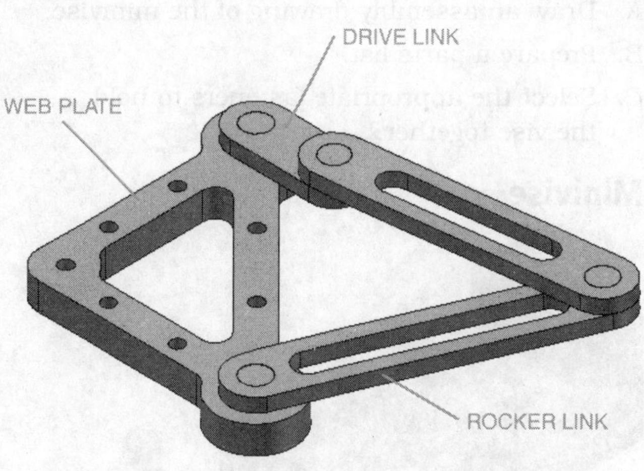

DRIVE LINK, SAE 1040 STEEL
Part Number: AM311-22A
5mm THK

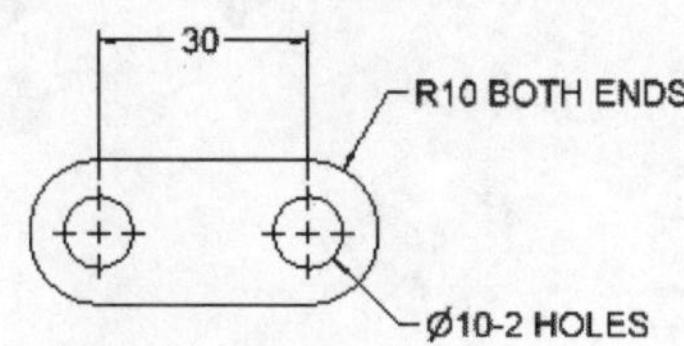

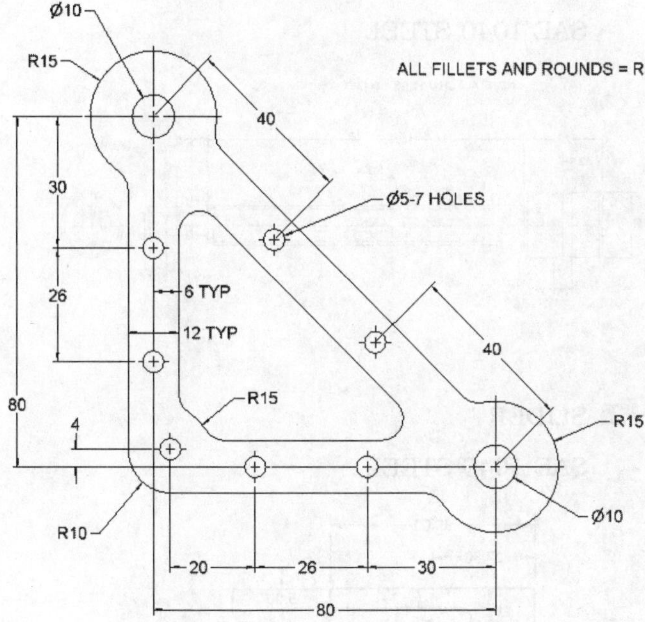

WEB PLATE, SAE 1040 STEEL
Part Number: AM311-22B
10mm THK

ROCKER LINK, SAE 1040 STEEL
Part Number: AM311-22C
5mm THK

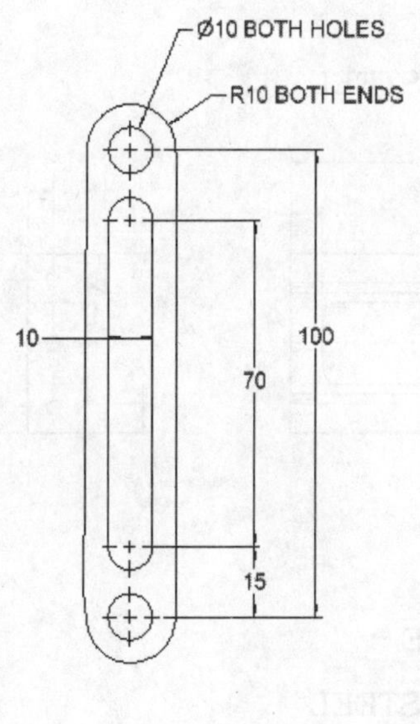

CENTER LINK, SAE 1040 STEEL
Part Number: AM311-22D
5mm THK

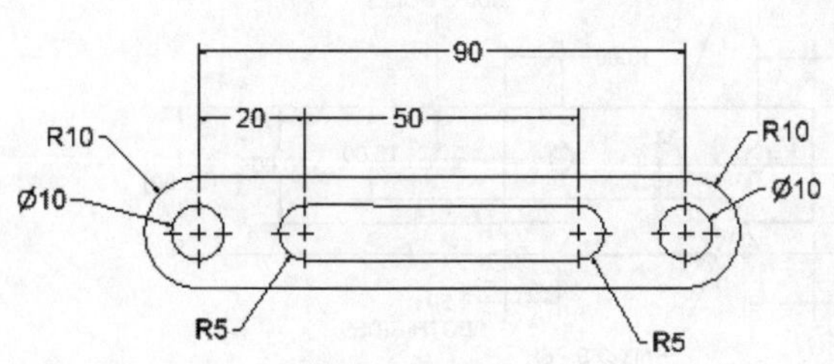

EX15-64

A. Draw an assembly drawing of the minivise.

B. Prepare a parts list.

C. Select the appropriate fasteners to hold the vise together.

D. Redesign the interface between the drive screw and the holder plate.

Minivise

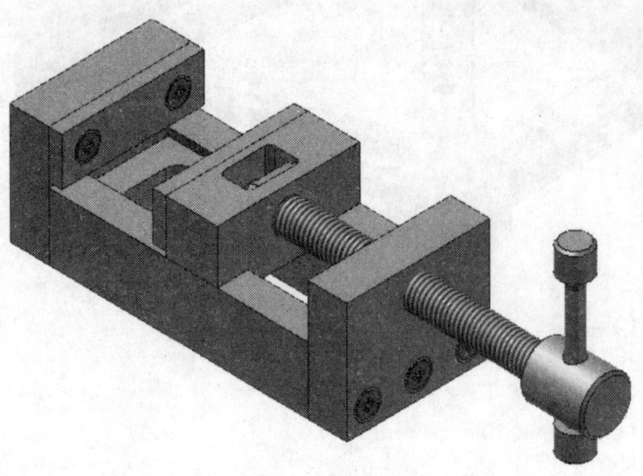

Minivise -ISO

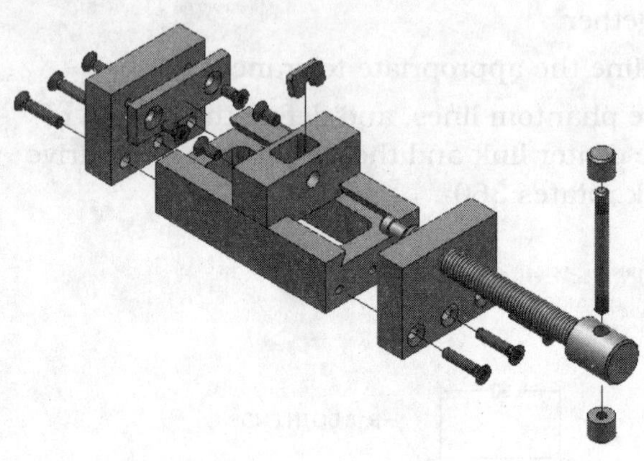

1 BASE

SAE 1040 STEEL

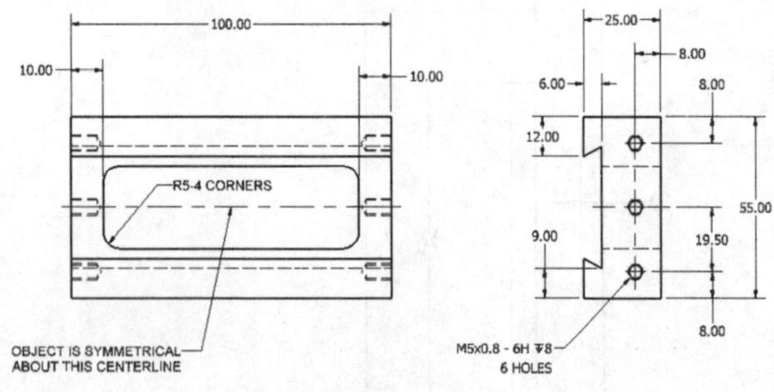

2 DRIVE SCREW

SAE 1040 STEEL

NOTE: ALL CHAMFERS = 1x45

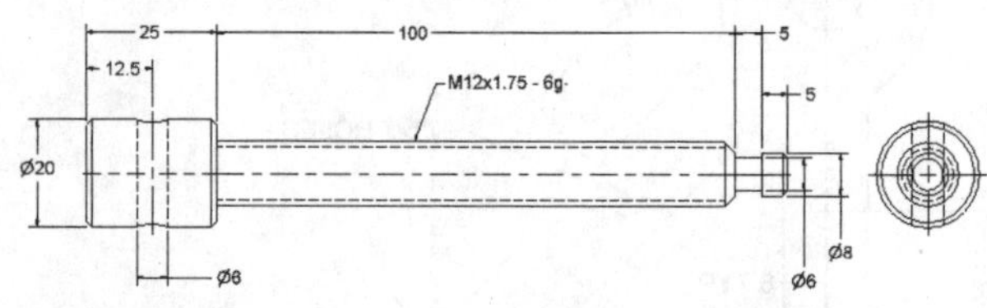

3 END PLATE

SAE 1040 STEEL

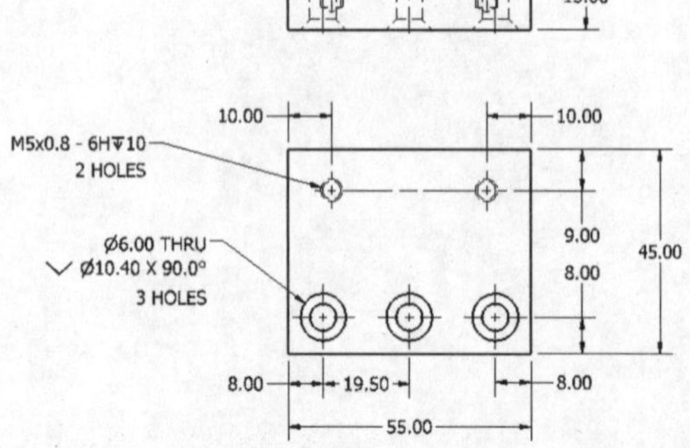

4 SLIDER

SAE 1040 STEEL

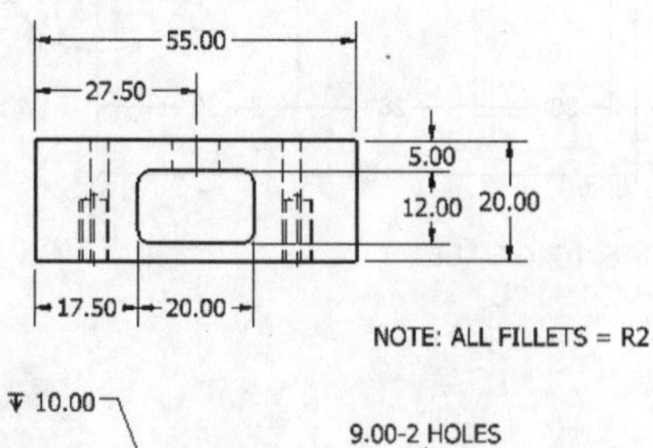

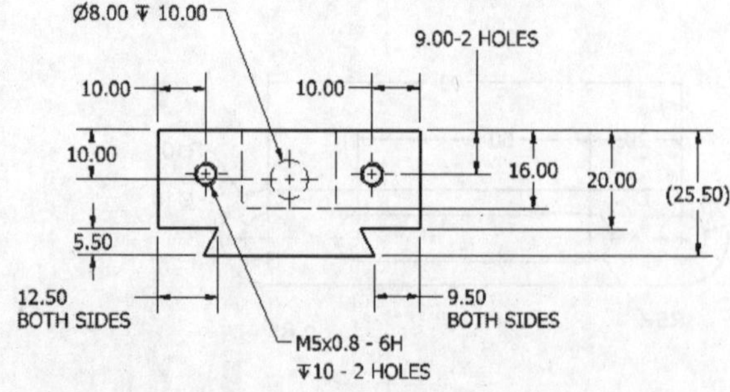

EX15-64, continued

5 HOLDER PLATE

SAE 1040 STEEL

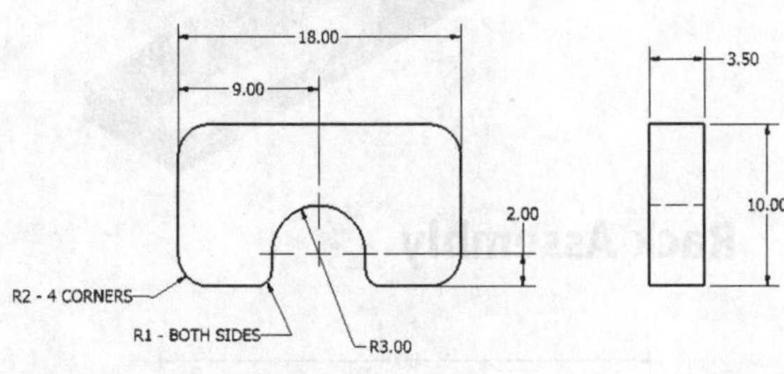

6 FACE PLATE

SAE 1040 STEEL

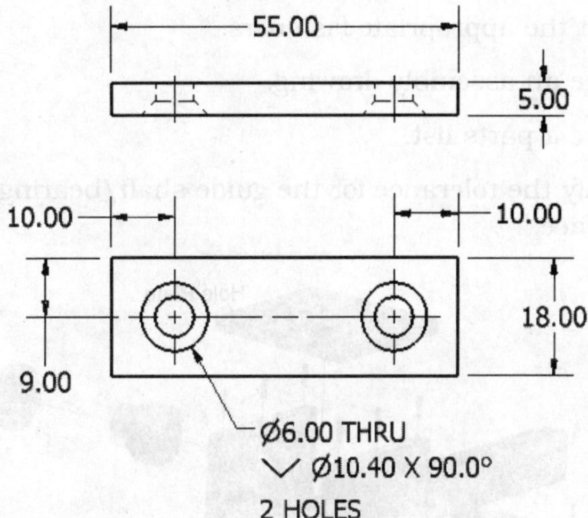

7 HANDLE

SAE 1040 STEEL

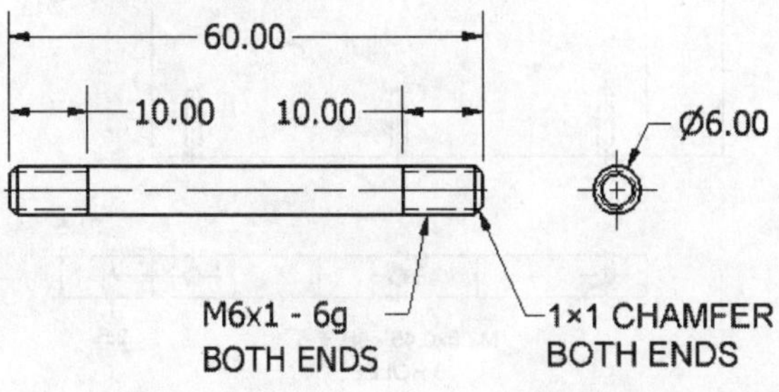

8 END CAP

SAE 1040 STEEL

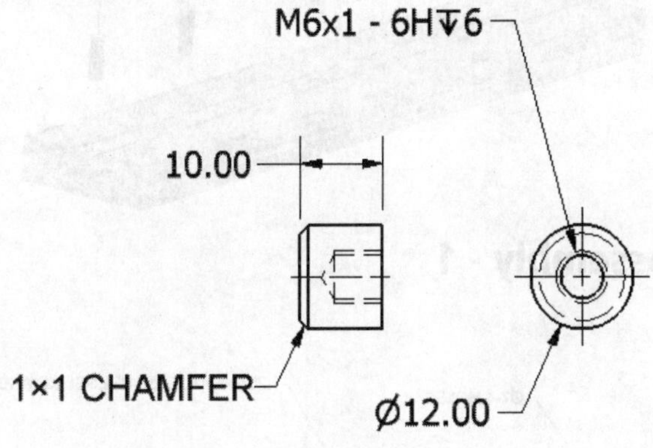

9 DRIVE PLATE

SAE 1040 STEEL

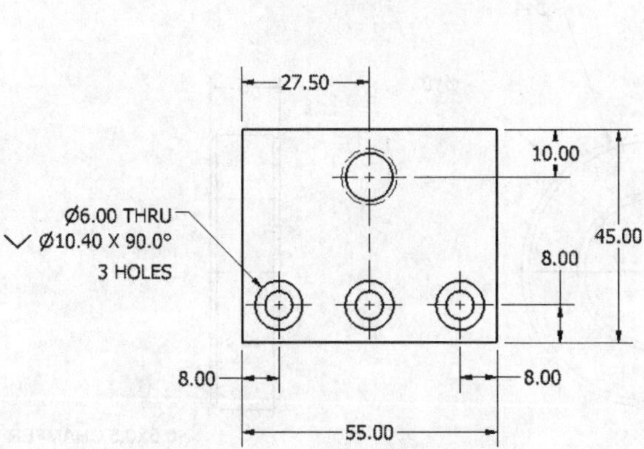

10 M5 × 10 RECESSED COUNTERSUNK HEAD-STEEL

11 M5 × 22 RECESSED COUNTERSUNK HEAD-STEEL

EX15-65

Create the following for the slider assembly shown:

1. Select the appropriate fasteners.
2. Create an assembly drawing.
3. Create a parts list.
4. Specify the tolerance for the guide shaft/bearings interface.

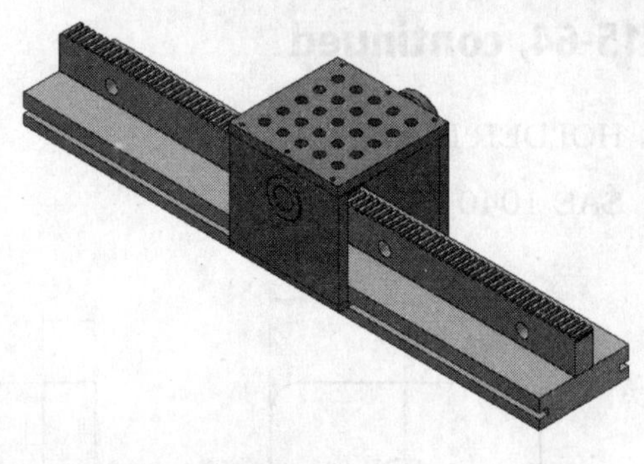

Rack Assembly

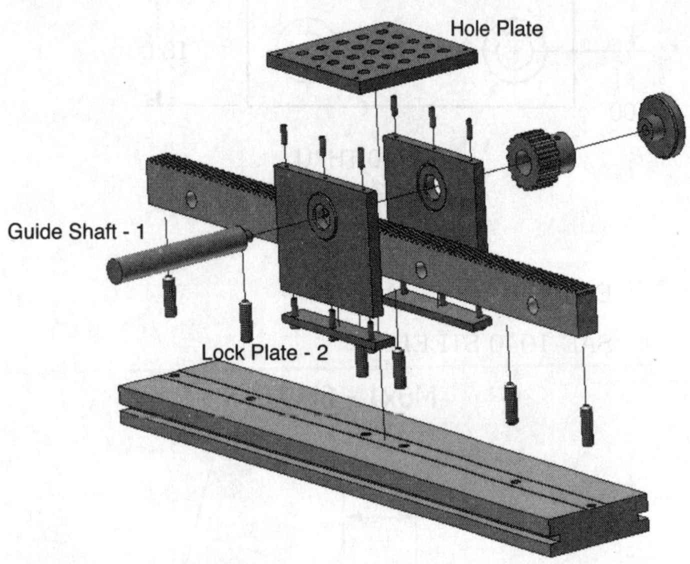

Rack Assembly - 1

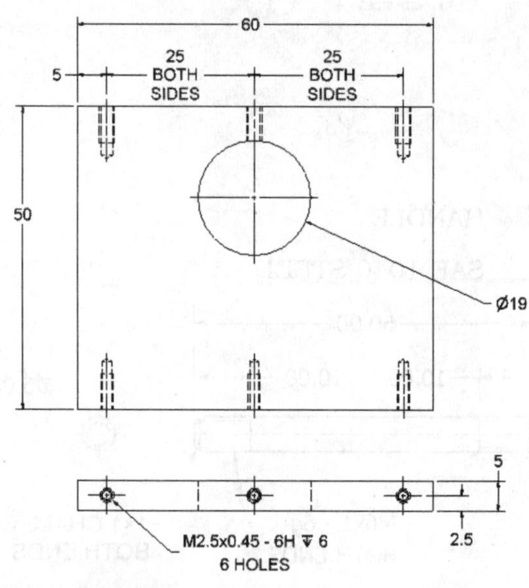

Side Plate

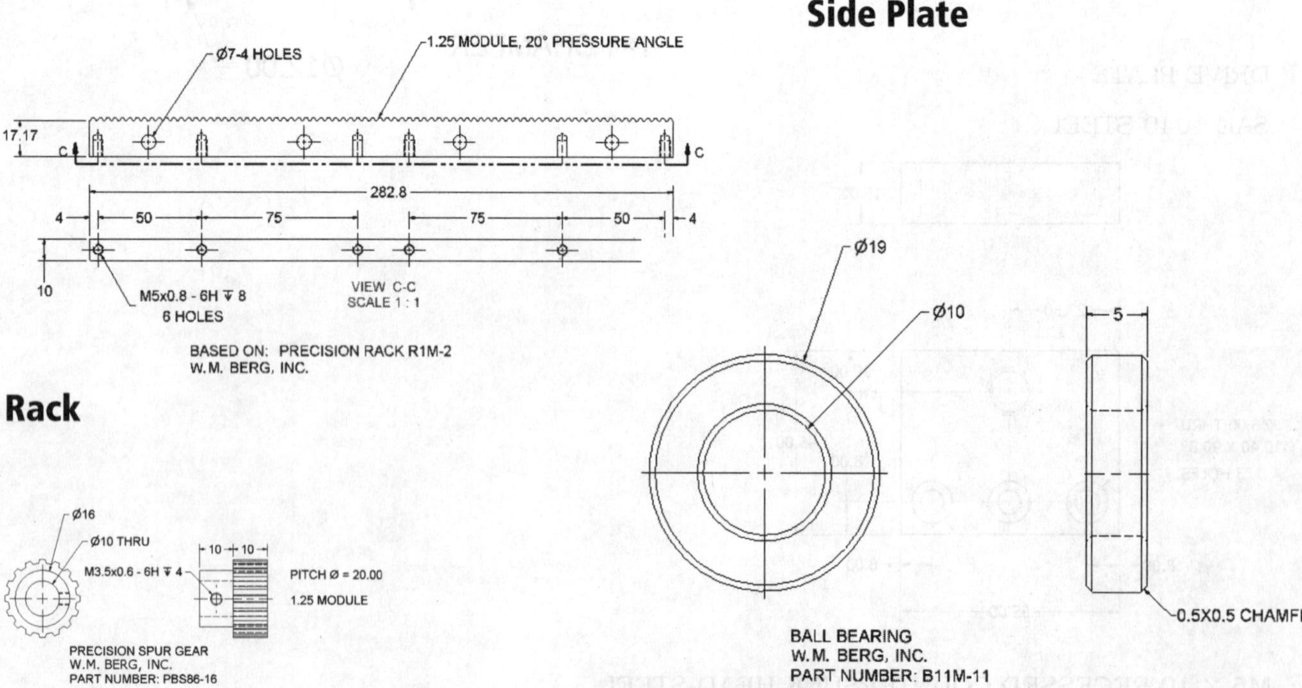

Rack

Gear 16

Bearing

EX15-65, continued

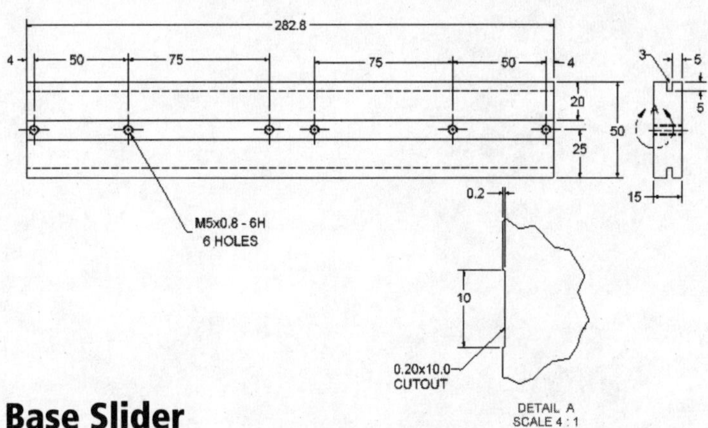

Base Slider

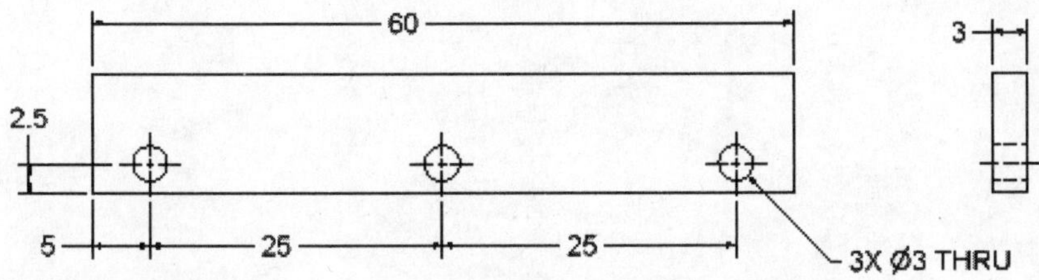

Lock Plate - 2

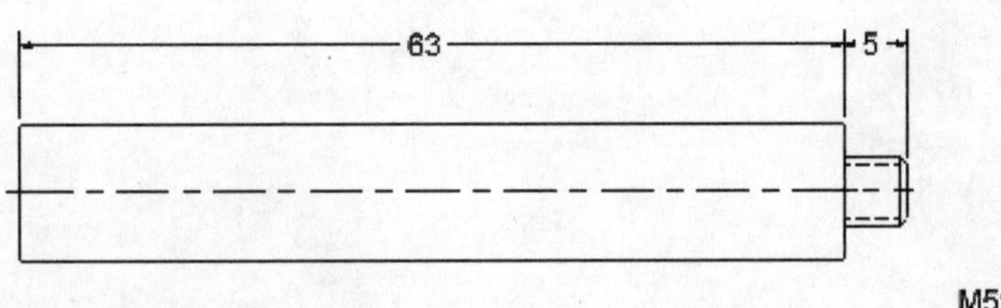

Guide Shaft - 1

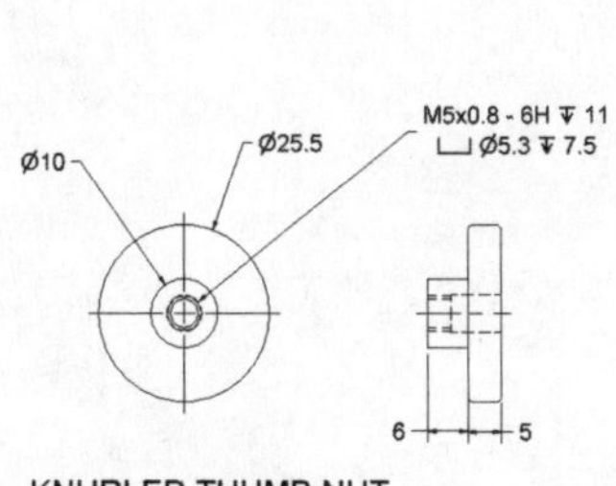

Thumb Nut

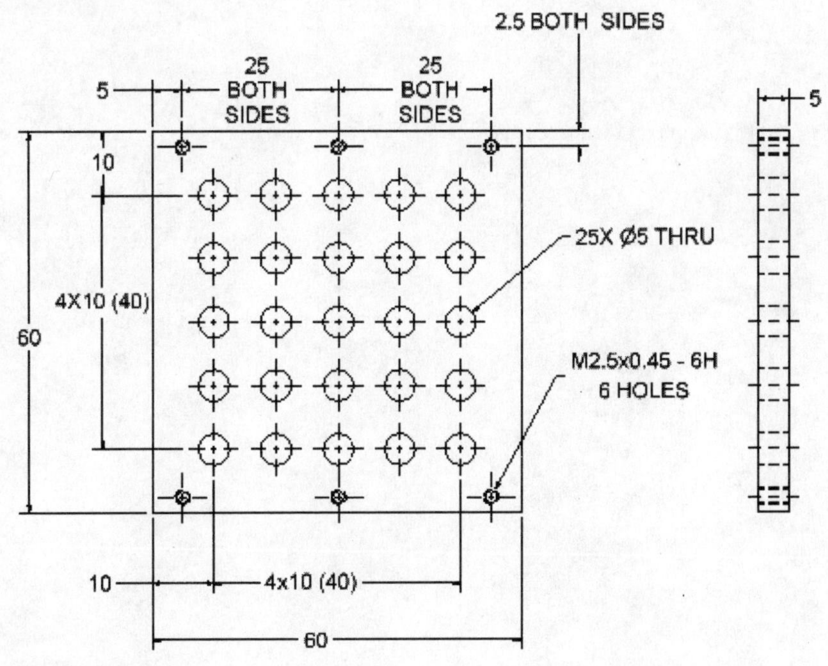

Hole Plate

chapter sixteen Projects

16-1 Introduction

This chapter presents two large projects: the Milling Vise and the Tenon Jig. The projects are intended to serve as group projects or as large individual projects.

16-2 Project 1: Milling Vise

Figure 16-1 shows a milling vise. The subassemblies, detailed drawings, and BOMs are included.

Complete the following or as it is assigned by your instructor.

1 The Milling Vise

See Figure 16-1.

A. An assembly drawing.

B. A BOM; include Item Numbers, Part Numbers, Descriptions, and Quantities

Figure 16-1
Milling Vise

2 Base Subassembly

See Figure 16-2.

A. An assembly drawing

B. A BOM

C. Dimensioned drawings of each part that is used in the subassembly.

Figure 16-2 Base Subassembly

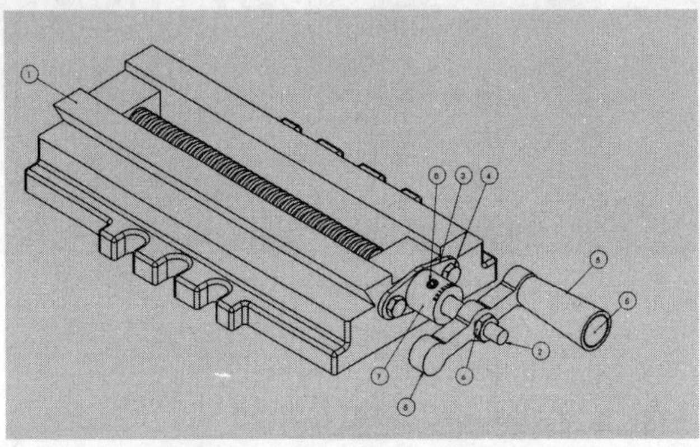

ITEM NO.	PART NUMBER	DESCRIPTION	QTY.
1	BU2012-B	BASE	1
2	P100-20A	ACME, BASE	1
3	BU-313	PLATE, COVER, BASE	1
4	M6 × 1.0 ×16	SCREW, SLOTTED CAP	2
5	PN311-1A	HANDLE, SUBASSEMBLY	1
6	M8 ×1.25	NUT, HEX	1
7	ENG-2	COLLAR	1
8	M6 × 1.0 ×10	SET SCREW-CONE	1

Dimensioned and tolerance drawings of the parts that make up the base subassembly are as follows.

Base

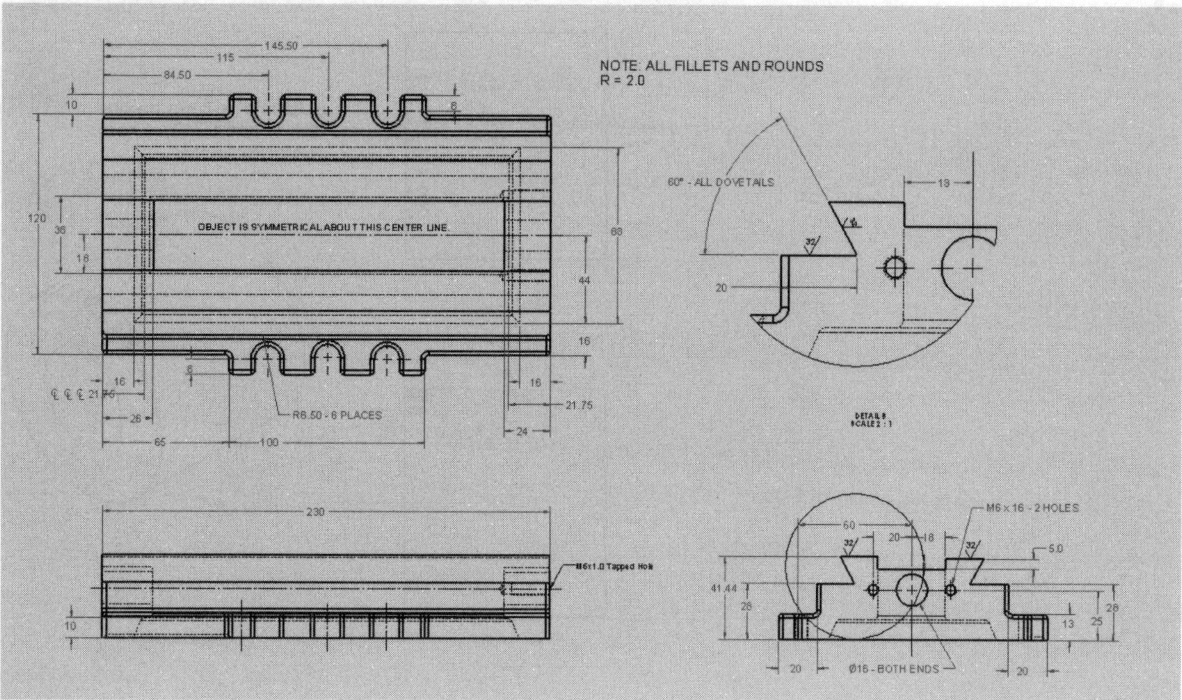

Figure 16-3

Figure 16-4

ACME, Base

M16x4 ACME
293
10
57
93
12
M8
DETAIL A
SCALE 1 : 1
Ø16
R5
8SQ
4
SECTION B-B
SCALE 1 : 1

Figure 16-5 Collar

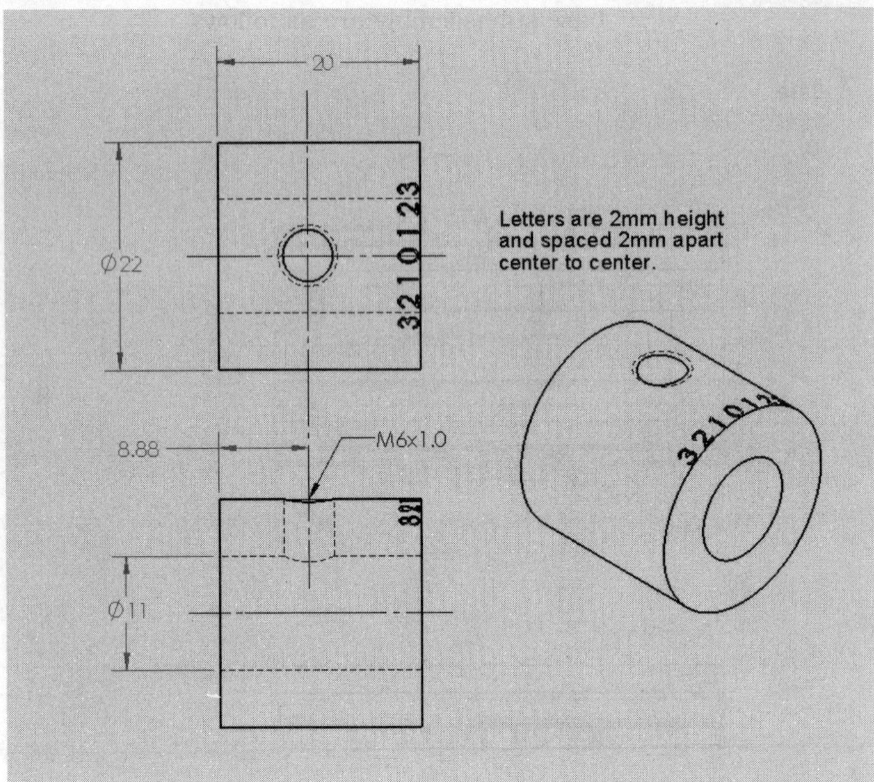

Figure 16-6 Plate, Cover, Base

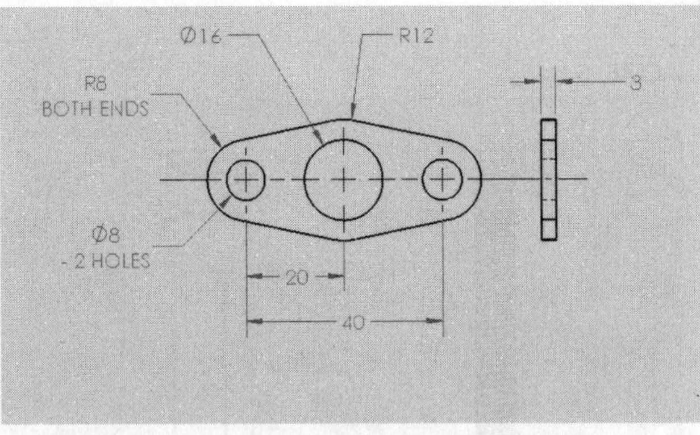

Figure 16-7 Handle Subassembly

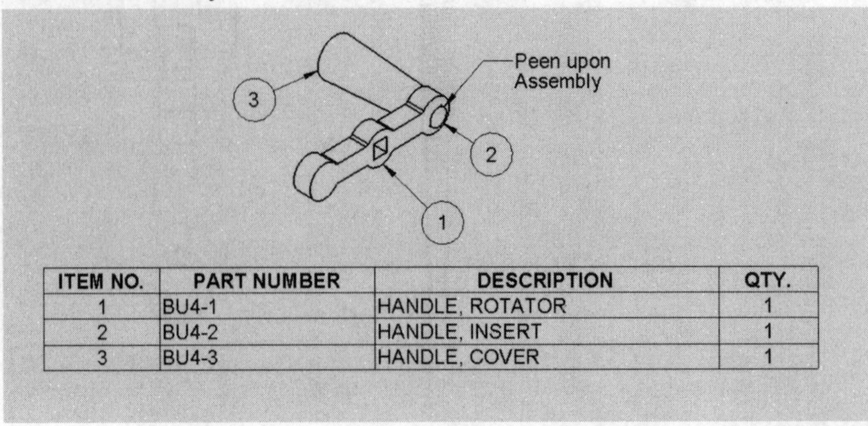

ITEM NO.	PART NUMBER	DESCRIPTION	QTY.
1	BU4-1	HANDLE, ROTATOR	1
2	BU4-2	HANDLE, INSERT	1
3	BU4-3	HANDLE, COVER	1

Figure 16-8 Handle, Rotater

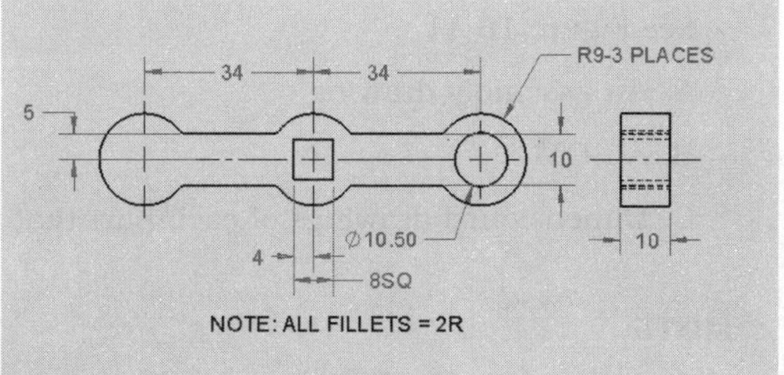

Figure 16-9 Handle, Insert

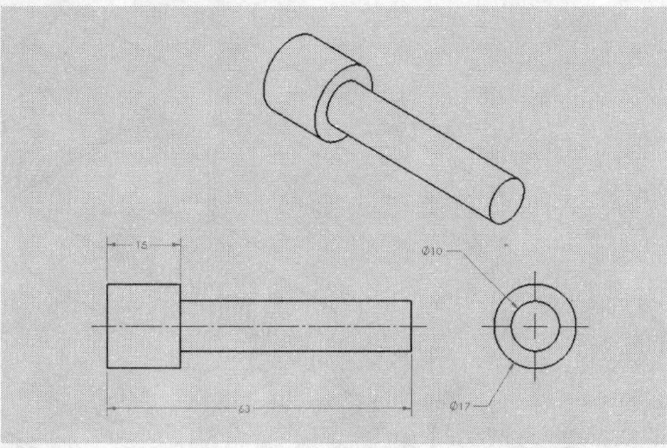

Figure 16-10 Handle, Cover

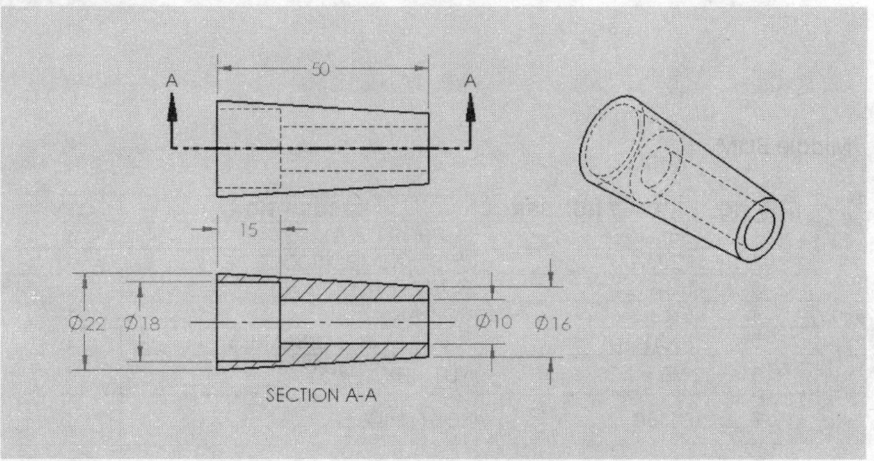

> **NOTE**
> Standard parts do not need drawings, but require manufacturer's part numbers listed in the BOM.

3 Middle Subassembly

See Figure 16-11.

A. An assembly drawing

B. A BOM

C. Dimensioned drawings of each part that is used in the Subassembly

> **NOTE**
>
> Standard parts do not need drawings, but require manufacturer's part numbers listed in the BOM.

Middle Subassembly

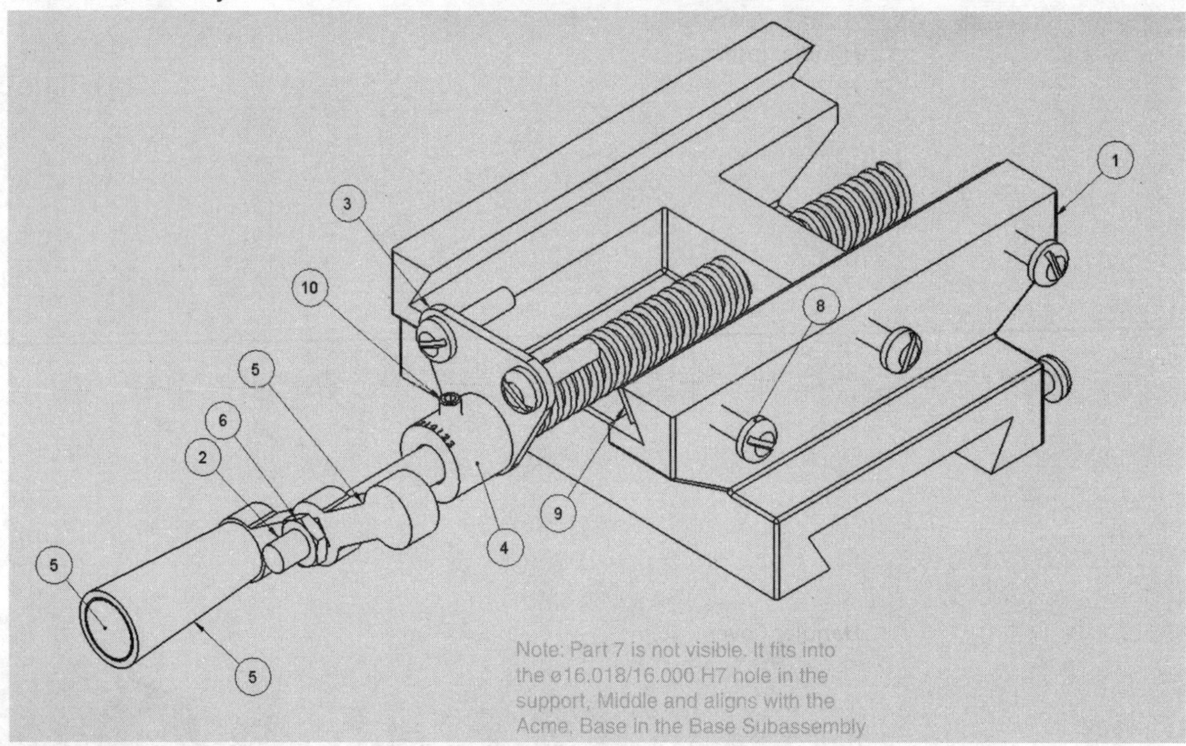

Middle BOM

ITEM NO.	PART NUMBER	DESCRIPTION	QTY.
1	S51-2A	SUPPORT, MIDDLE	1
2	P200-24	POST, ACME, MIDDLE	1
3	BU-312	PLATE, END	1
4	ENG-2	COLLAR	1
5	PN311-1A	HANDLE, SUBASSEMBLY	1
6	M8 × 1.25	NUT,HEX	1
7	P155B	POST, MIDDLE	1
8	M6 × 1.0 ×25	SCREW, PAN	8
9	SP-33	BAR, SPACER	1
10	M6 × 1.0 × 16	SET SCREW, SOCKET	1

Figure 16-11

Dimensioned and tolerance drawings of the parts that make up the Base Subassembly are as follows:

Figure 16-12a and 16-12b Middle Subassembly

Note that Figure 16-12a shows a dimensioned drawing of the Support, Middle, but does not include any fillets. Fillets were omitted for clarity. Figure 16-12b is a 3D of the Support, Middle, that shows the fillets. Use the fillets shown in Figure 16-12b as a guide to applying fillets.

Middle Subassembly

M16x4 ACME

Support, Middle
see 3D drawing
for fillet locations.

ϕ 16.018 / 16.000 H7

60° ALL DOVETAILS

DETAIL A
SCALE 2 : 1

Fillets not shown for clarity

M6x1-6 HOLES
6 HOLES

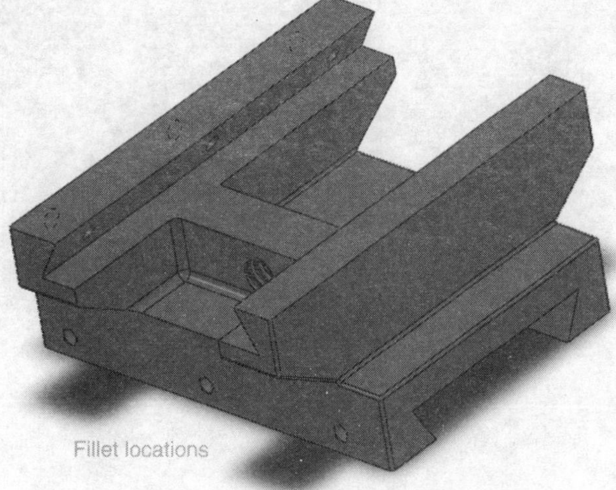

Fillet locations

Figure 16-12

Post, Acme, Middle

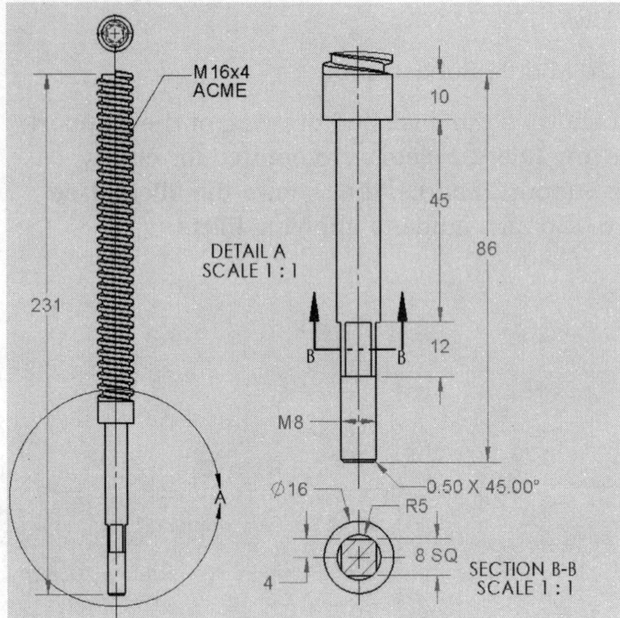

Figure 16-13

Plate, End

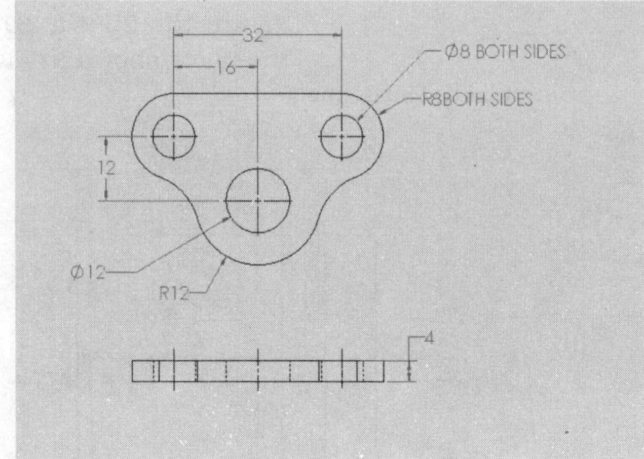

Figure 16-14

Figure 16-15

Post, Middle

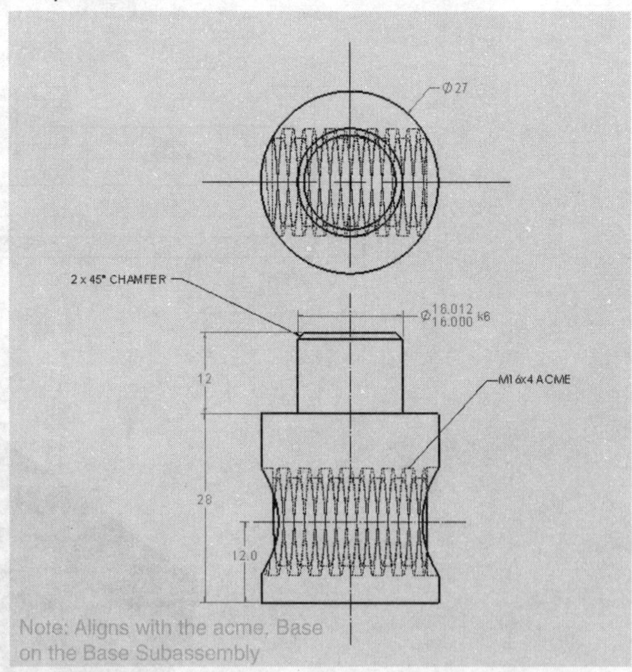

4 Top Subassembly

A. An assembly drawing

B. A BOM

C. Dimensioned drawings of each part that is used in the Subassembly

NOTE

Standard parts do not need drawings, but require manufacturer's part numbers listed in the BOM.

Bar, Spacer

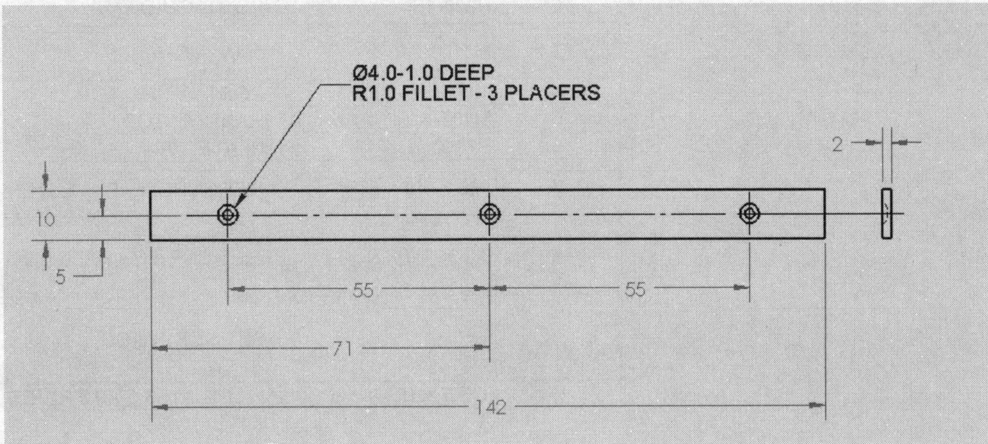

Figure 16-16

Dimensioned and tolerance drawings of the parts that make up the base subassembly are as follows:

Figure 16-17a and Figure 16-17b Top Subassembly

Figure 16-17

Top Subassembly

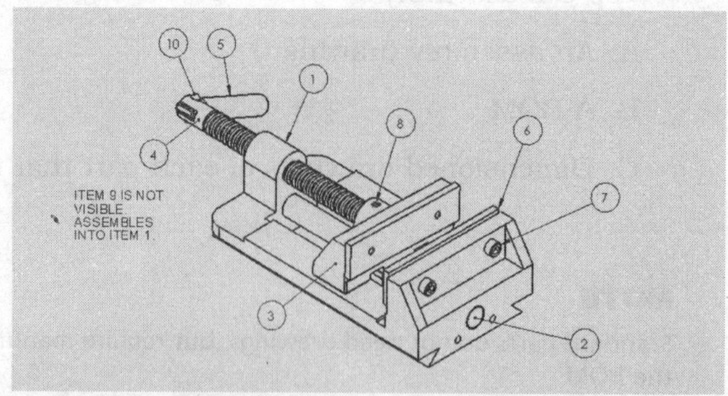

ITEM NO.	PART NUMBER	DESCRIPTION	QTY.
1	S50-1	SUPPORT, TOP	1
2	P200-16	POST, GUIDE	1
3	MJ100-2A	JAW, MOVABLE	1
4	M16x4	POST, ACME, TOP	1
5	M407-A	HANDLE, TOP	1
6	PT100	PLATE, JAW	2
7	M6 × 1.0 × 8	SET SCREW - FILLESTER HEAD	4
8	M6 × 1.0 × 8	SET SCREW - HALF DOG	1
9	M6 × 1.0 × 6	SET SCREW-CUP	1
10	Ø3.5 × 16	3.5 × 16 RIVET	1

Support, Top

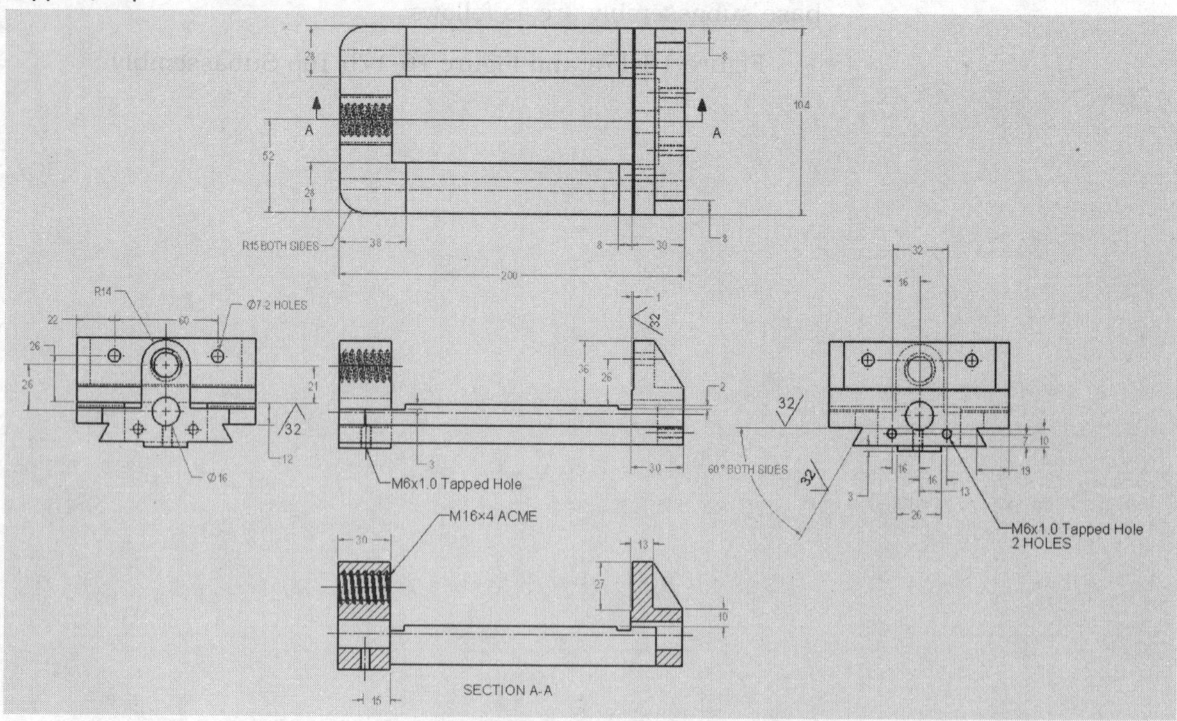

Figure 16-18

Post, Acme, Top

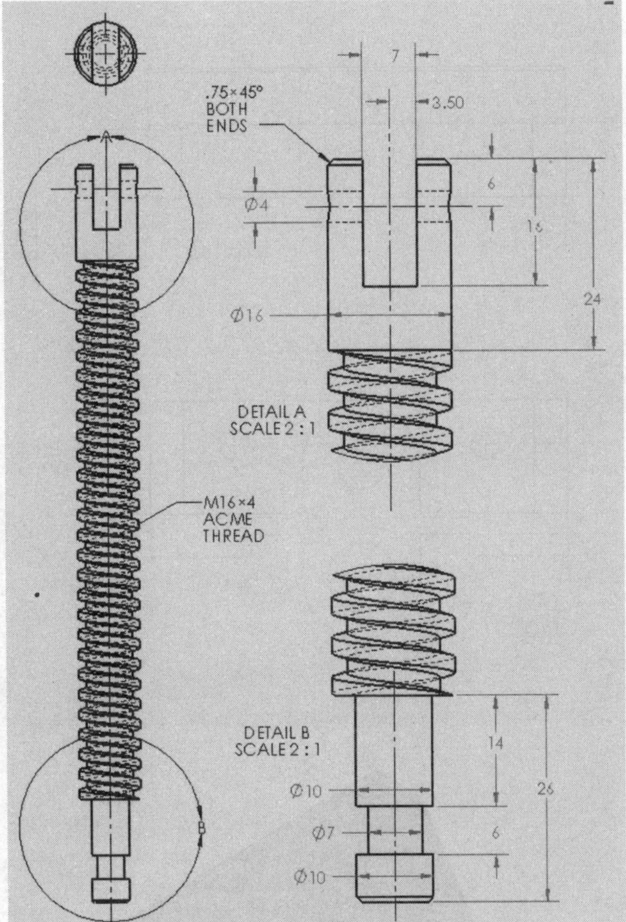

Figure 16-19

Post, Guide

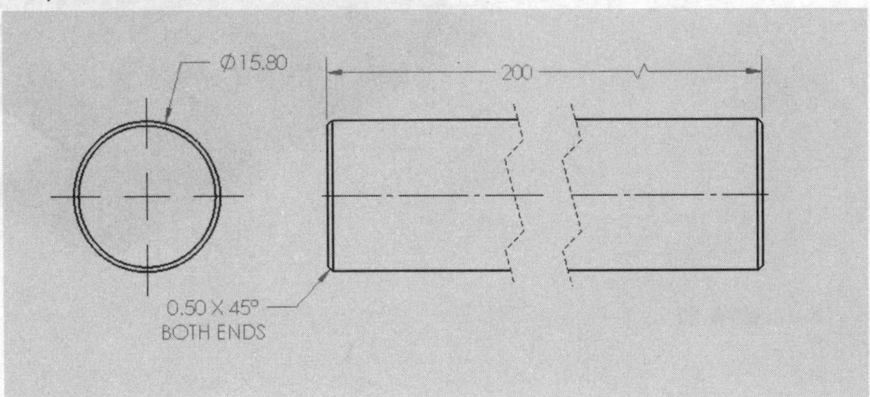

Figure 16-20

Figure 16-21a and 16-21b Jaw, Movable

Note that Figure 16-21a shows a dimensioned drawing of the Jaw, Movable, but does not include any fillets. Fillets were omitted for clarity. Figure 16-21b is a 3D of the Jaw, Movable, that shows the fillets. Use the fillets shown in Figure 16-21b as a guide to applying fillets.

Jaw, Movable

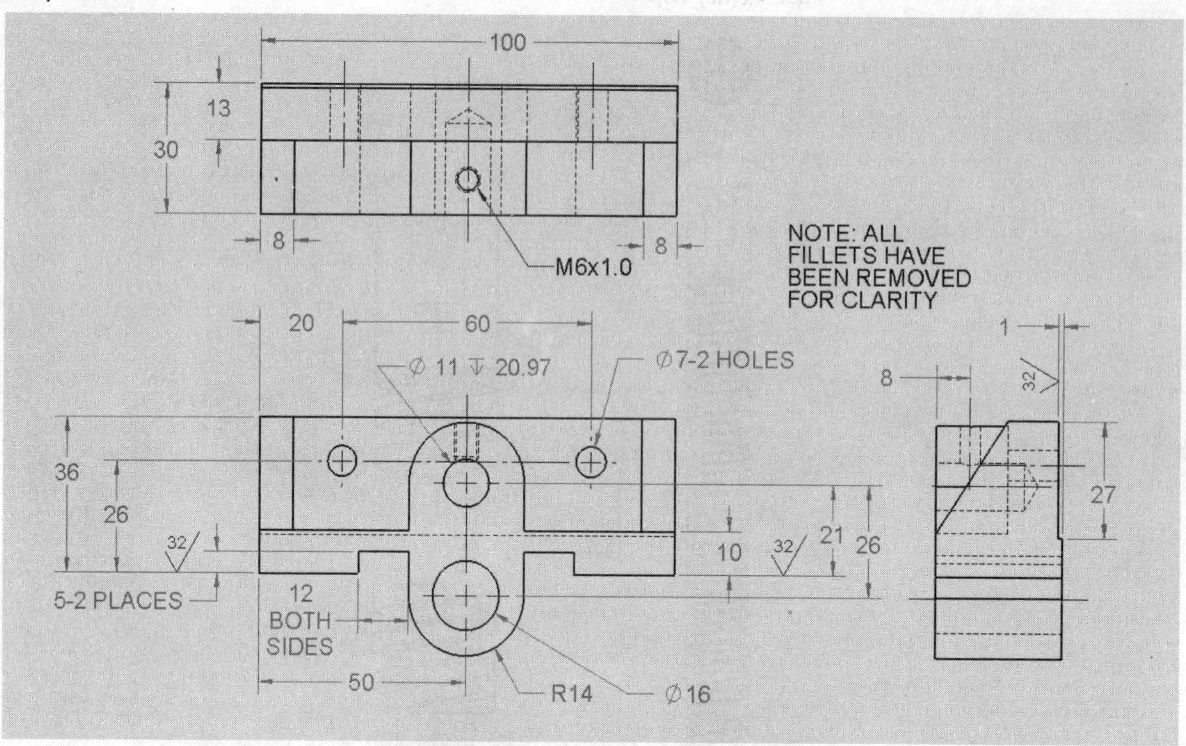

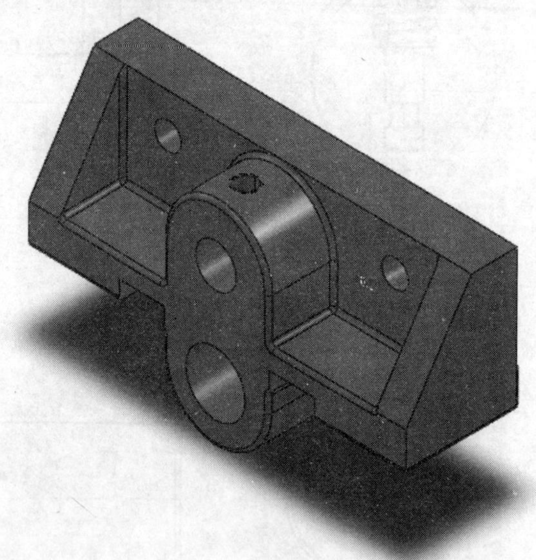

Figure 16-21

Figure 16-22 Handle

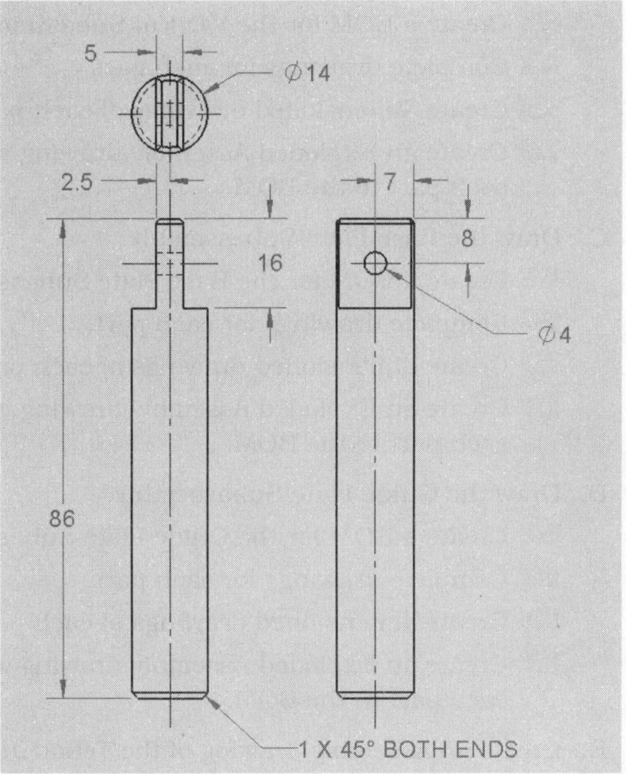

Figure 16-23 Plate, Jaw

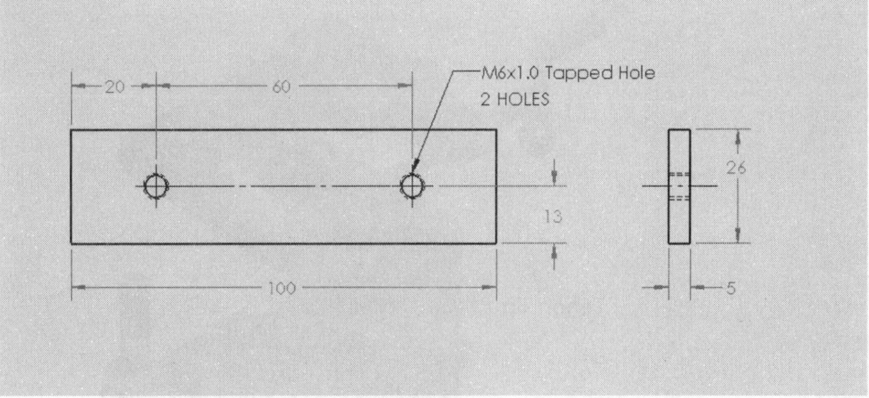

16-3 Project 2: Tenon Jig

The Tenon Jig has four main subassemblies: Clamping, Vertical, Base Plate, and Guide Plate. There are other parts that are used in the final assembly. This is intended to be a group project, but could be done by one person. Complete the following assignments:

A. Draw the Clamping Subassembly.

1. Create a BOM for the Clamping Subassembly.
2. Complete drawings for each part.
3. Create dimensioned drawings of each part.
4. Create an Exploded Assembly drawing with balloons referencing each part to the BOM.

B. Draw the Vertical Subassembly.

1. Create a BOM for the Vertical Subassembly.
2. Complete drawings for each part.
3. Create dimensioned drawings of each part.
4. Create an Exploded Assembly drawing with balloons referencing each part to the BOM.

C. Draw the Base Plate Subassembly.

1. Create a BOM for the Base Plate Subassembly.
2. Complete drawings for each part.
3. Create dimensioned drawings of each part.
4. Create an Exploded Assembly drawing with balloons referencing each part to the BOM.

D. Draw the Guide Plate Subassembly.

1. Create a BOM for the Guide Plate Subassembly.
2. Complete drawings for each part.
3. Create dimensioned drawings of each part.
4. Create an Exploded Assembly drawing with balloons referencing each part to the BOM.

E. Create an Assembly drawing of the Tenon Jig.

1. Create a BOM for the Tenon Jig.

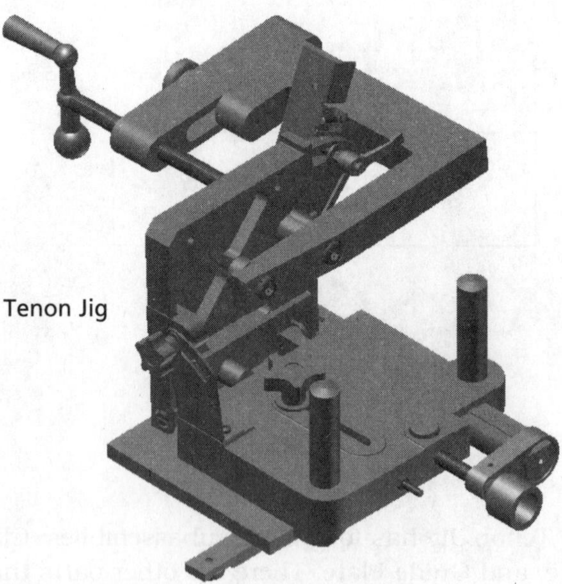

Tenon Jig

Figure 16-24a

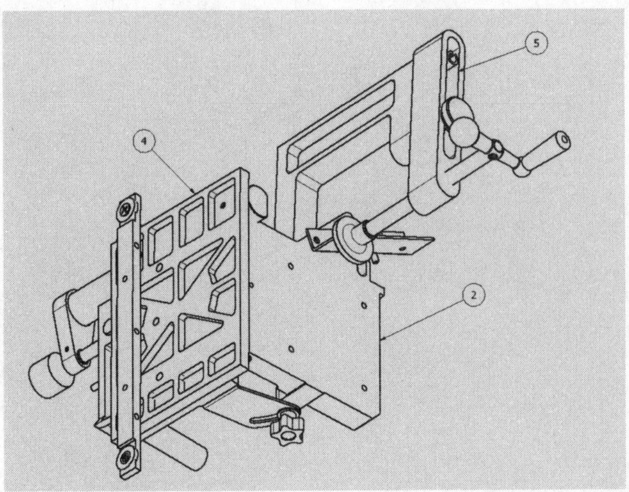

Figure 16-24b

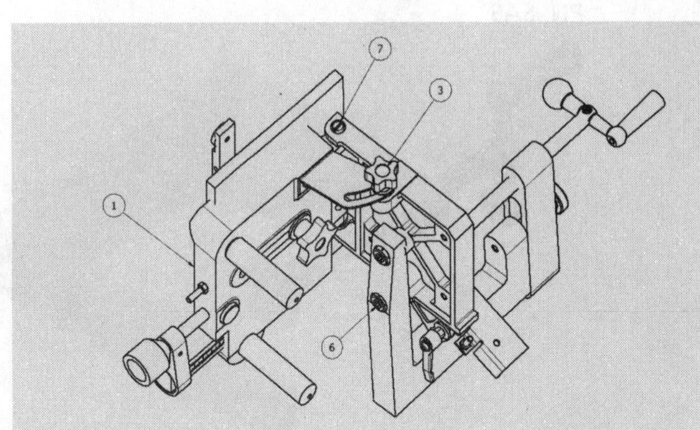

Figure 16-24c

PARTS LIST				
ITEM	PART NUMBER	DESCRIPTION	MATERIAL	QTY
1	SA-1	BASE SUB-ASSEMBLY		1
2	SA-2	VERTICAL SUB-ASSEMBLY		1
3	SA-3	ADJUSTER SUB-ASSEMBLY		1
4	SA-4	GUIDE SUB-ASSEMBLY		1
5	SA-5	CLAMP SUB-ASSEMBLY		1
6	M10x1.5 x 25	DRILLED FORGED HEAXAGON SOCKET HEAD CAP SCREW	MILD STEEL	2
7	SA-6B	SLOTTED HEAD MACHINE SCREW	MILD STEEL	2

Figure 16-24d

Slotted Head Machine Screw
PN: SA-6B

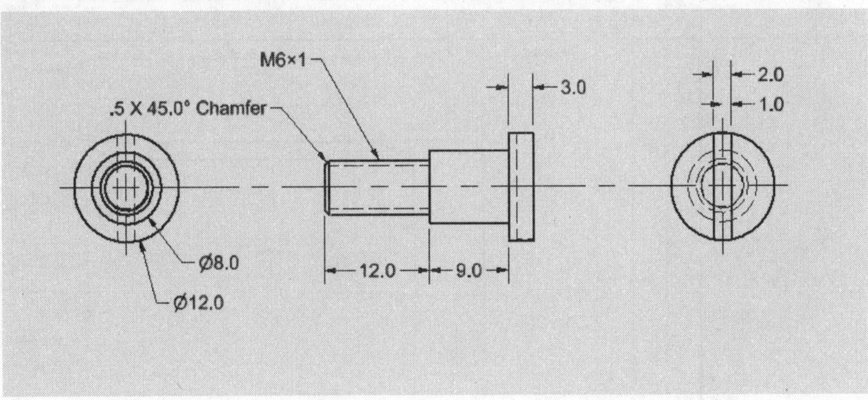

Figure 16-24e

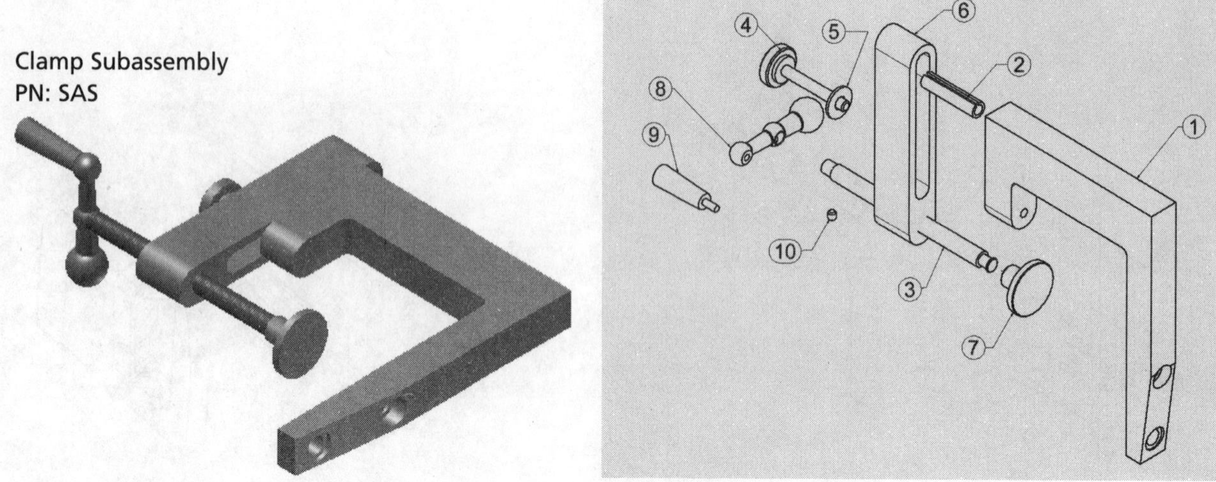

PARTS LIST				
ITEM NO.	PART NUMBER	DESCRIPTION	MAT'L	QTY
1	BU-121	C-BRACKET	CASTING	1
2	BU-122	PIN	STEEL	1
3	BU-123	POST, THREADED	STEEL	1
4	BU-124	SCREW, THUMB	STEEL	1
5	10×24×2	PLAIN WASHER	STEEL	1
6	BU-125	SLIDER	CASTING	1
7	BU-126	HOLDER	STEEL	1
8	BU-127	PIVOT, HANDLE	CASTING	1
9	BU-128	POST, HANDLE	STEEL	1
10	M6×6	SET SCREW, SOCKET HEAD, FLAT POINT	STEEL	1

Figure 16-25

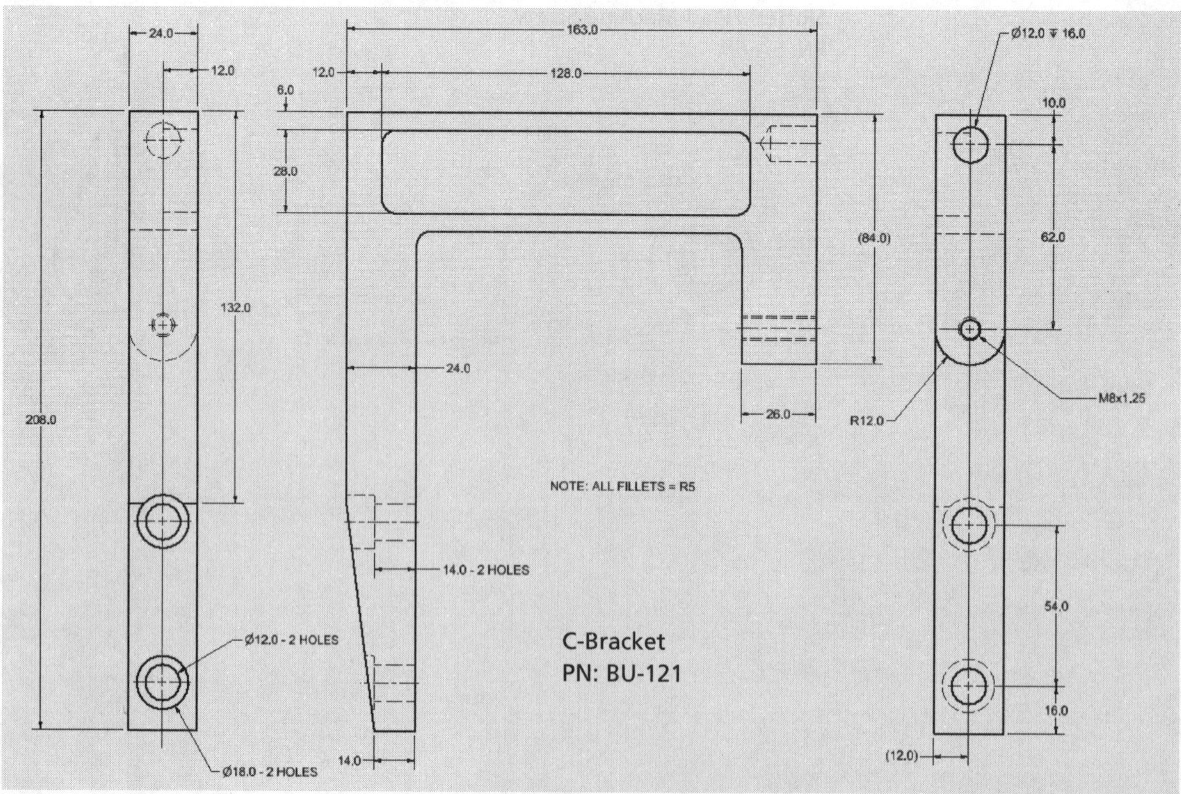

Figure 16-26

Pin
PN: BU-122

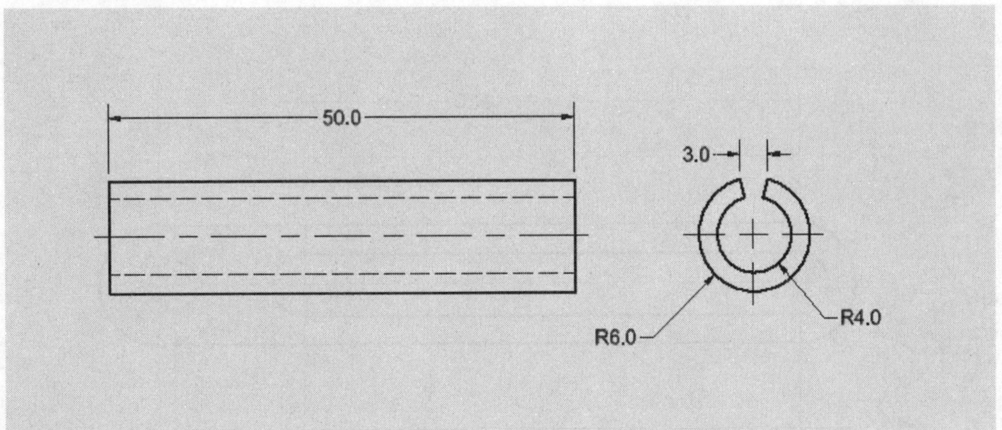

Figure 16-27

Post Threaded
PN: BU-123

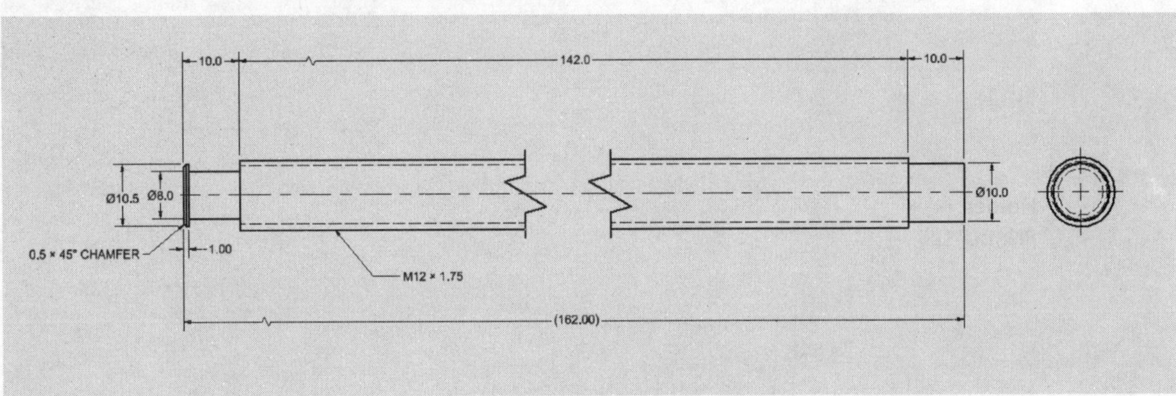

Figure 16-28

Screw, Thumb
PN: BU-124

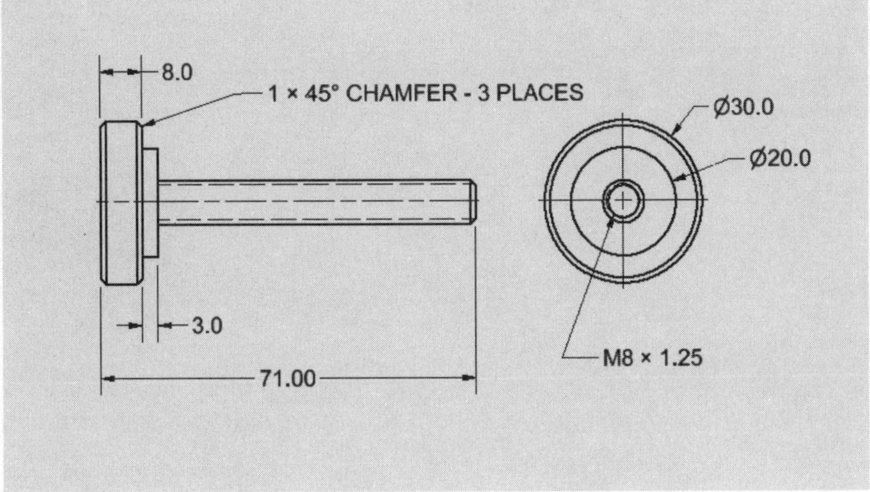

Figure 16-29

Slider
PN: BU-125

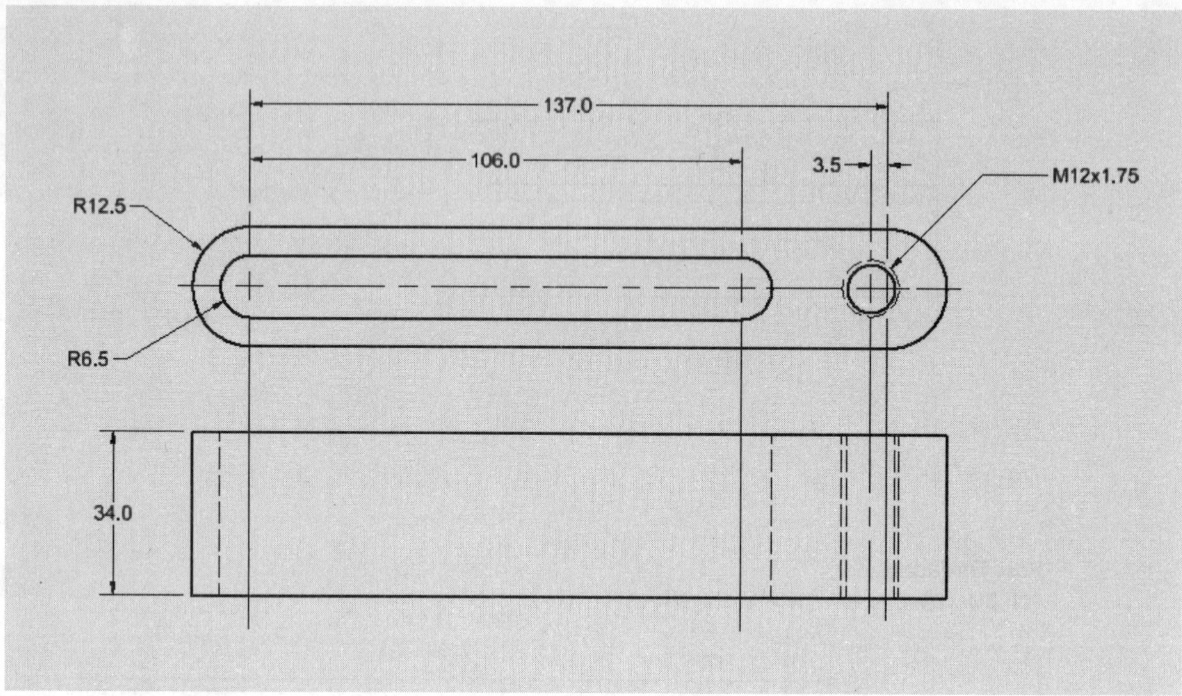

Figure 16-30

Holder
PN: BU-126

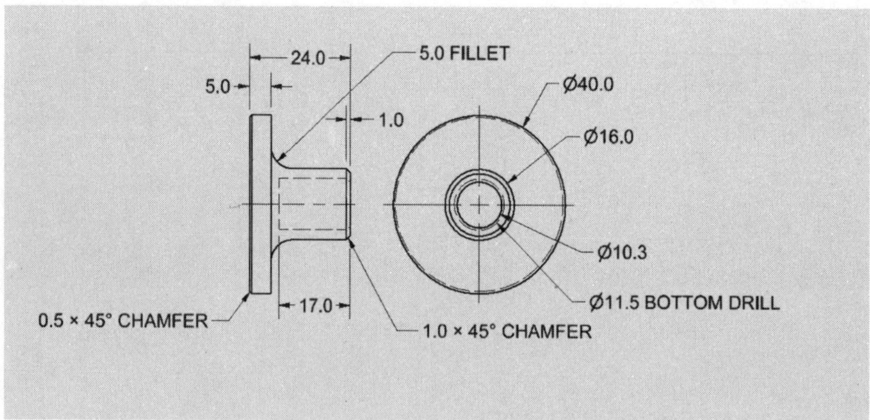

Figure 16-31

Pivot, Handle
PN: BU-127

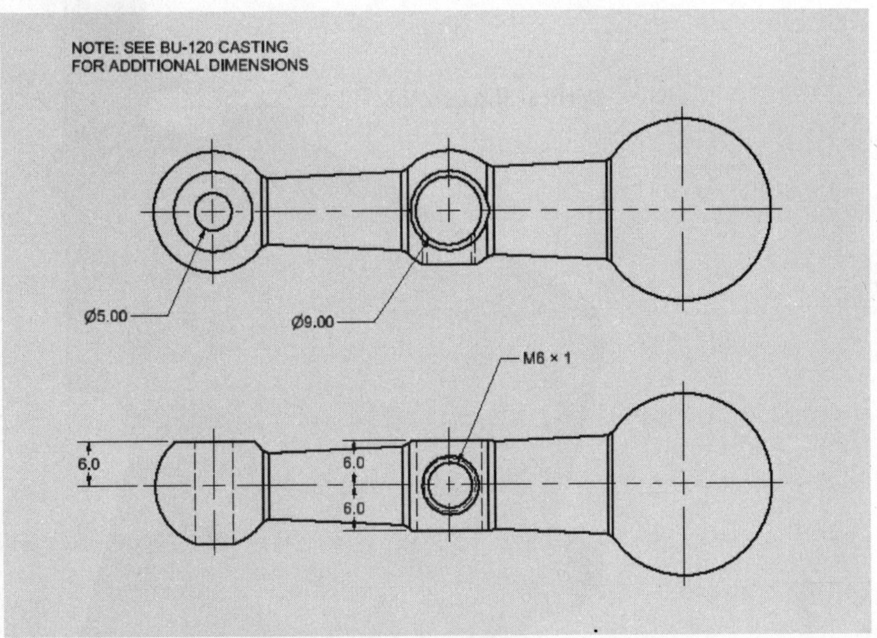

Casting for Pivot, Handle

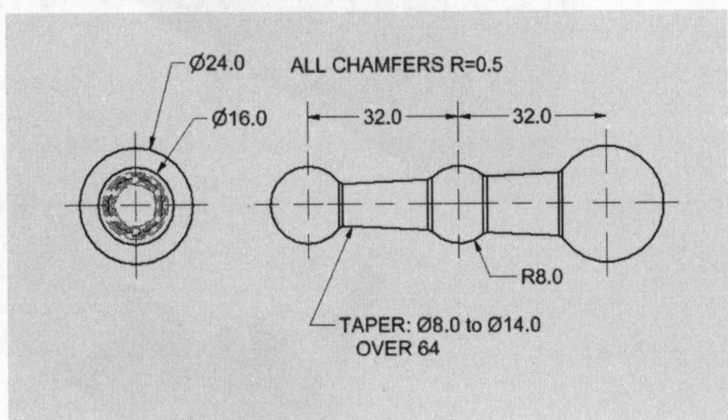

Figure 16-32

Post, Handle
PN: BU-128

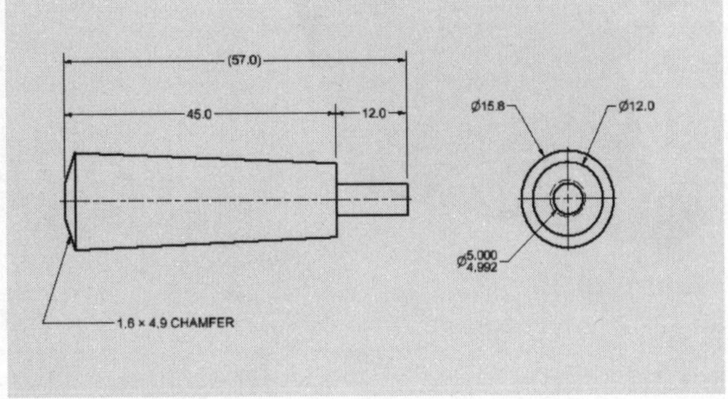

Figure 16-33

Vertical Subassembly

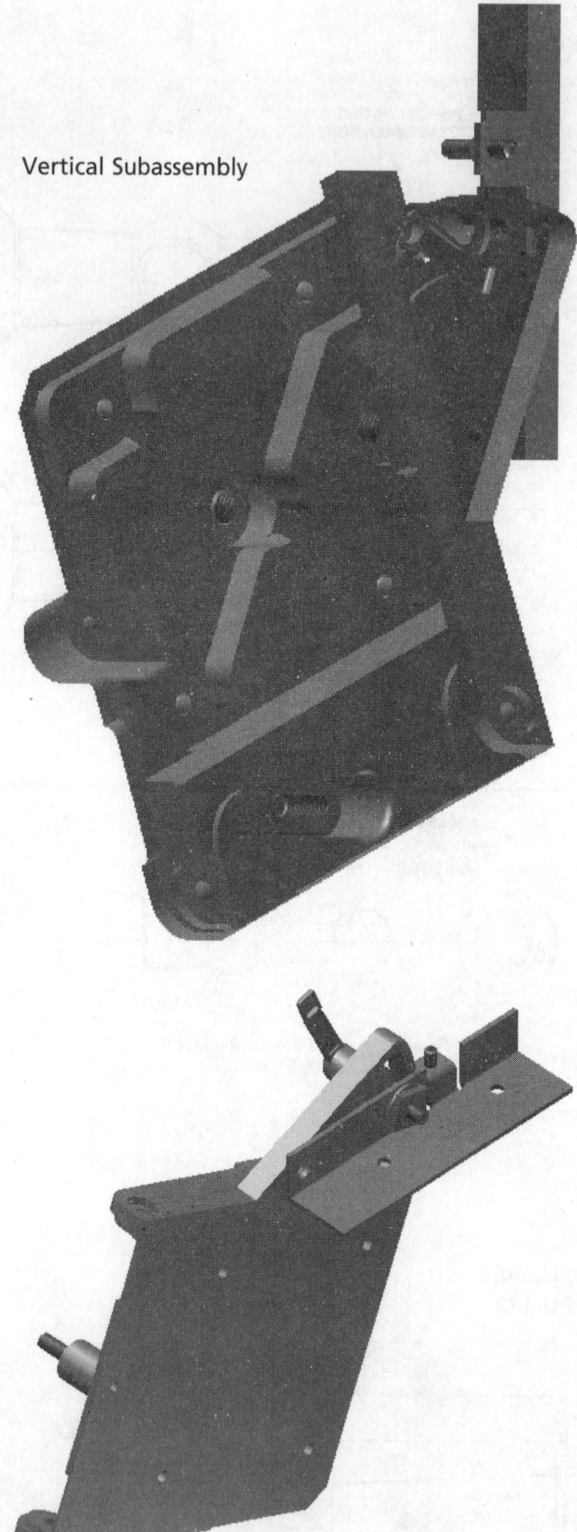

Figure 16-34

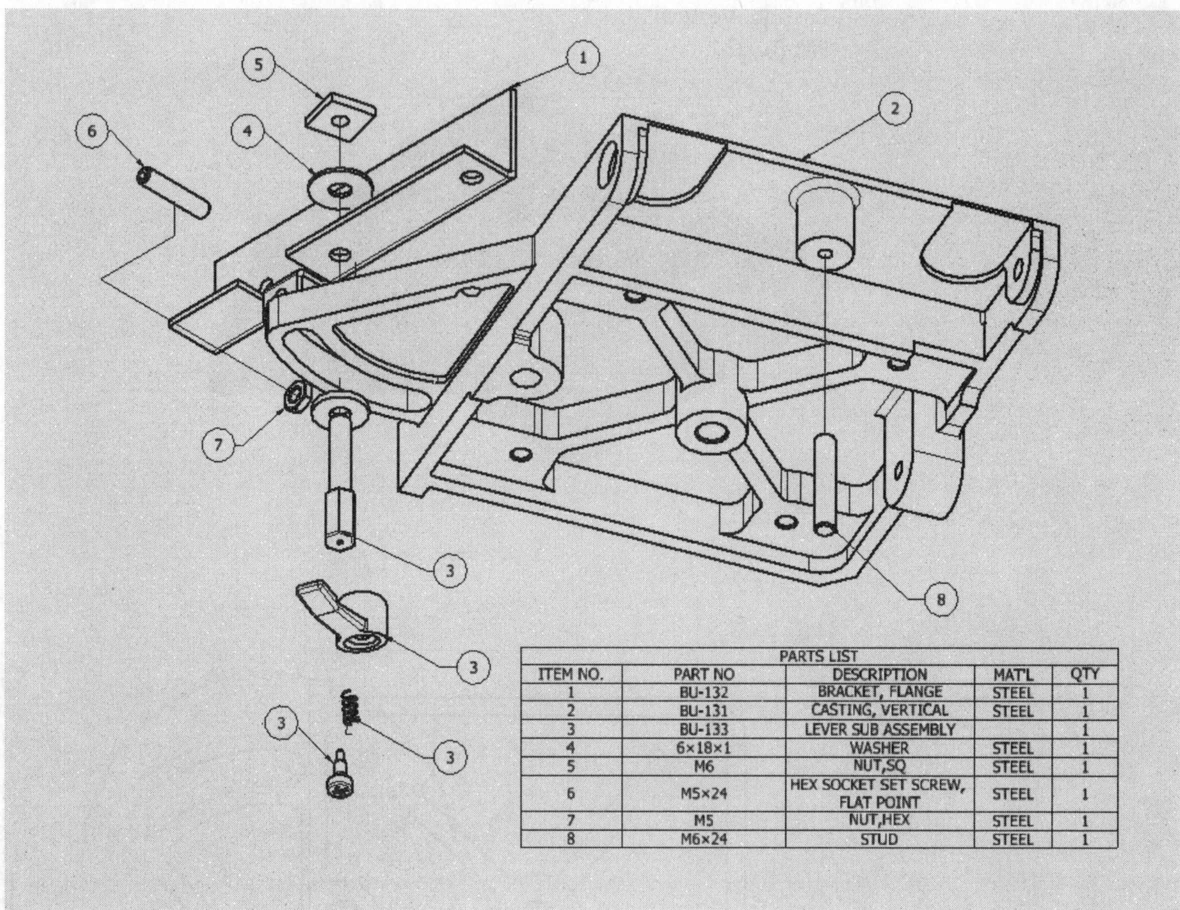

PARTS LIST				
ITEM NO.	PART NO	DESCRIPTION	MAT'L	QTY
1	BU-132	BRACKET, FLANGE	STEEL	1
2	BU-131	CASTING, VERTICAL	STEEL	1
3	BU-133	LEVER SUB ASSEMBLY		1
4	6×18×1	WASHER	STEEL	1
5	M6	NUT,SQ	STEEL	1
6	M5×24	HEX SOCKET SET SCREW, FLAT POINT	STEEL	1
7	M5	NUT,HEX	STEEL	1
8	M6×24	STUD	STEEL	1

Figure 16-35

Bracket, Flange
PN: BU-132

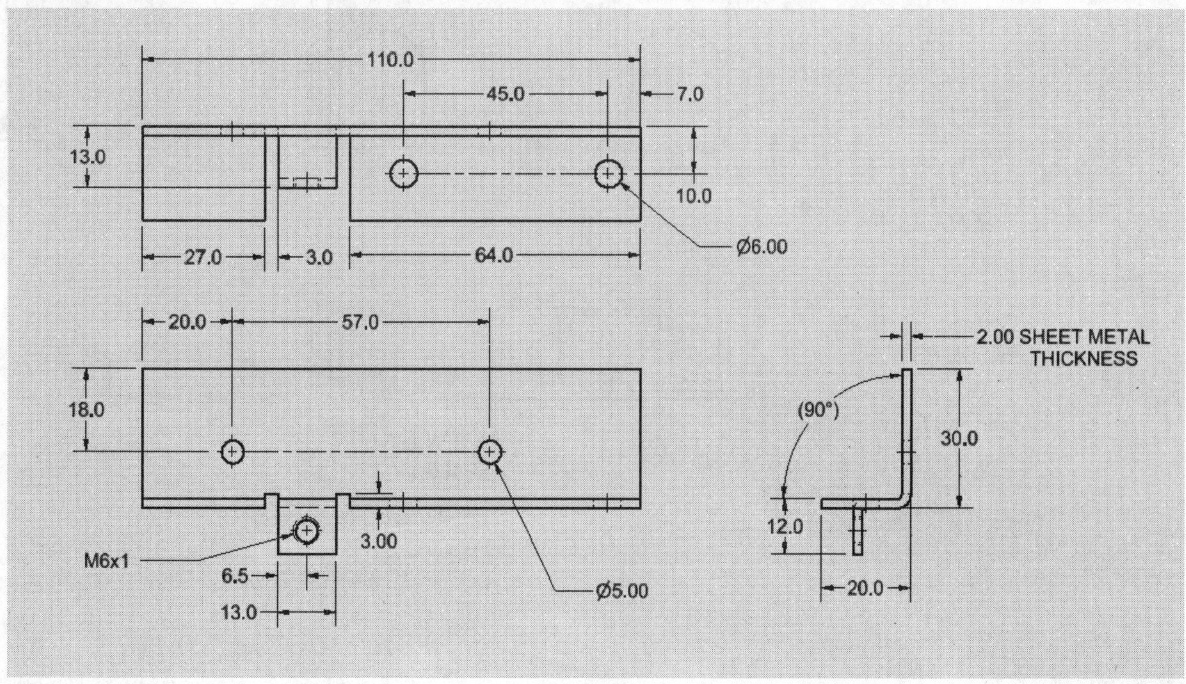

Figure 16-36

Casting, Vertical
PN: BU-131

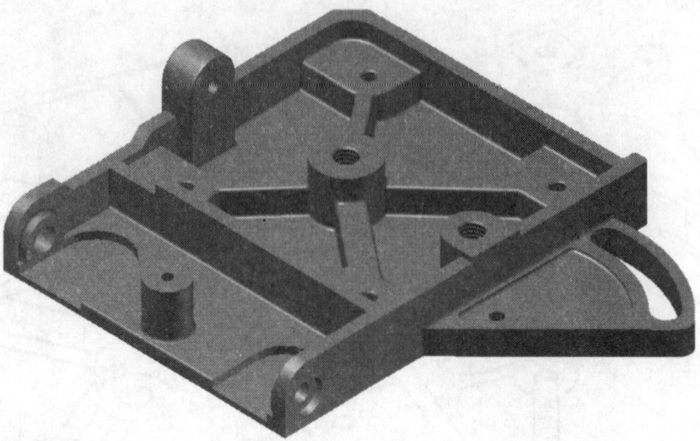

Figure 16-37a

B

C

A A

VIEW B-B
SCALE 1 : 1

B

Casting, Vertical
PN: BU-131

VIEW A-A
SCALE 1 : 1

Figure 16-37b

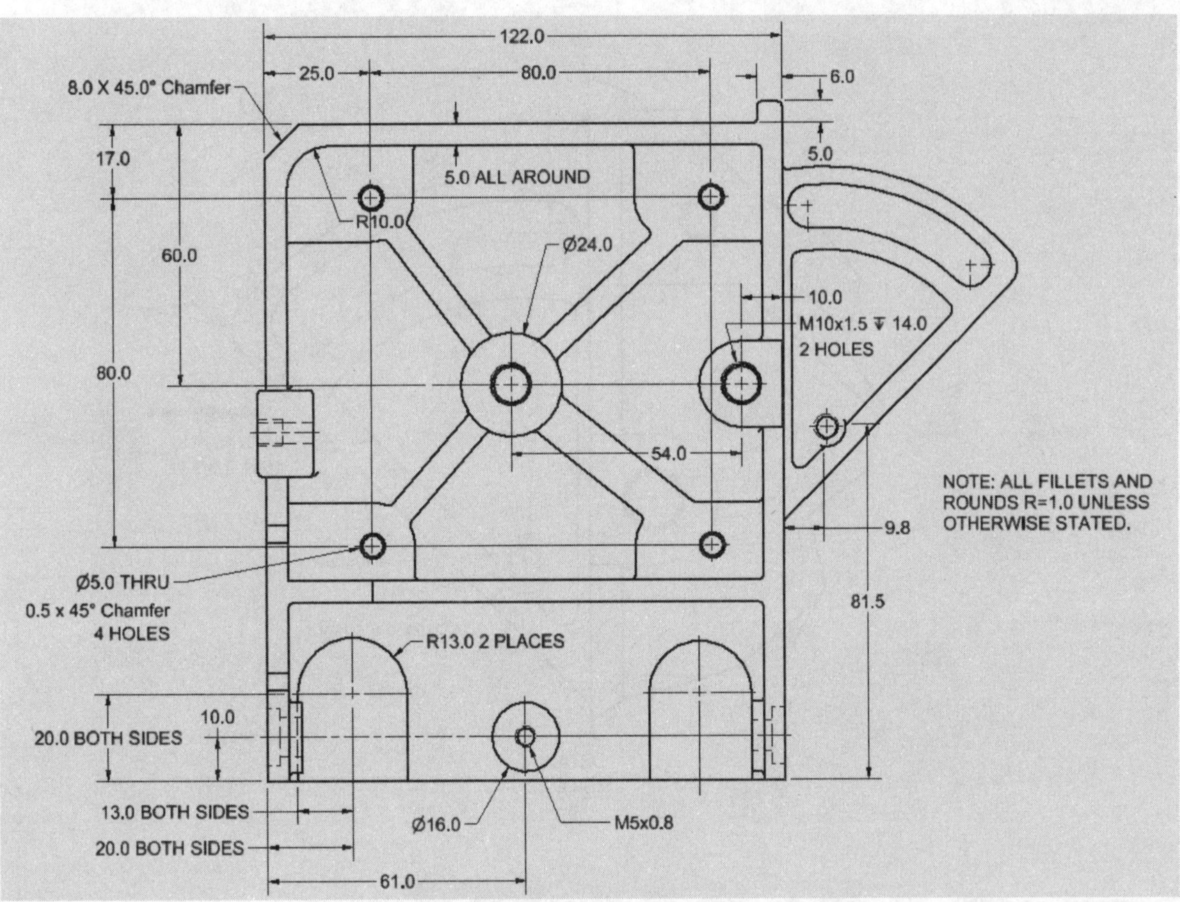

Figure 16-37c

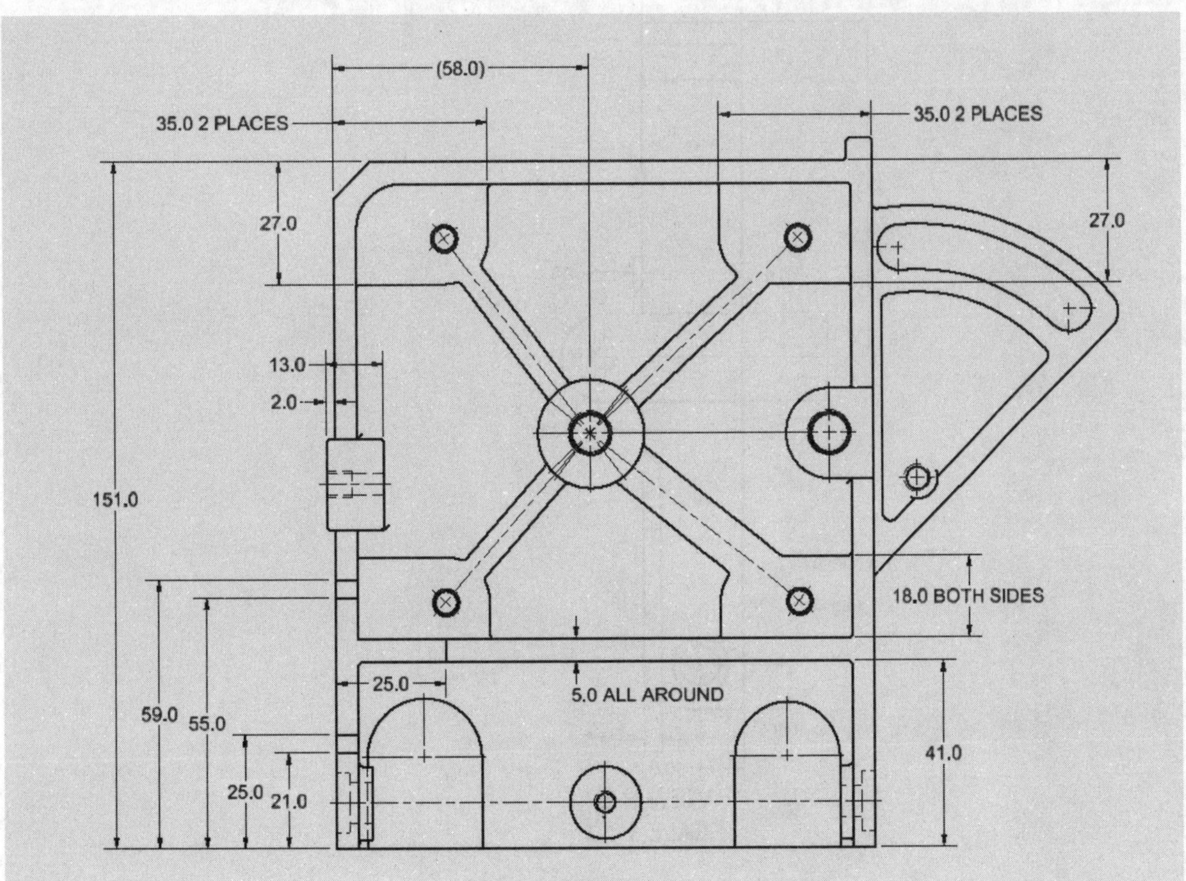

Figure 16-37d

Figure 16-37e

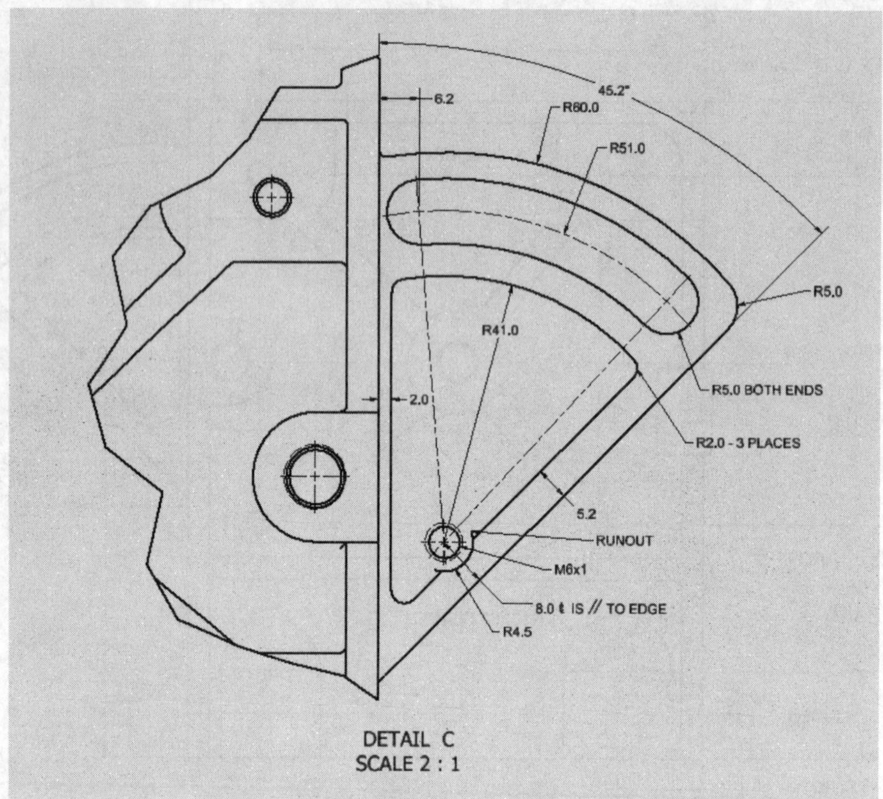

Figure 16-37f

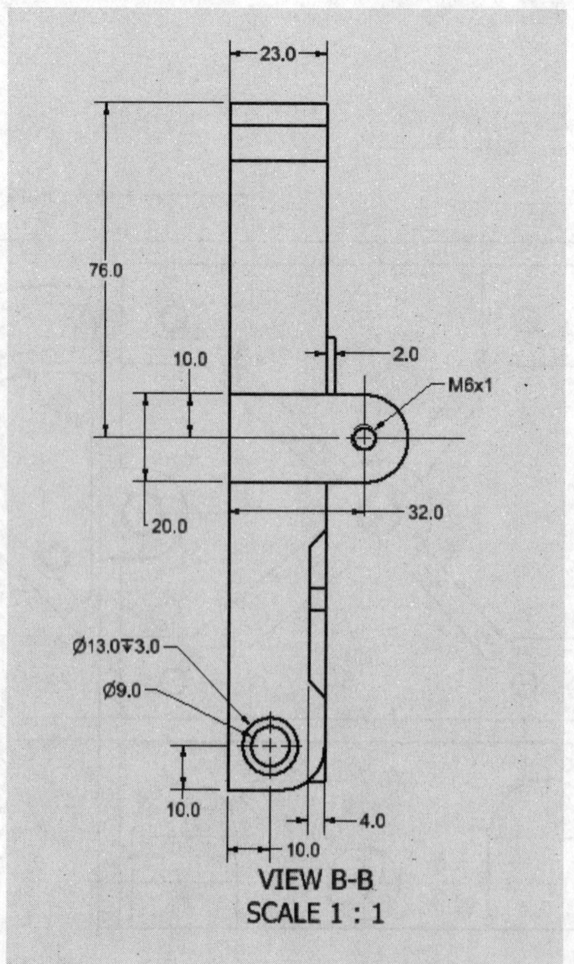

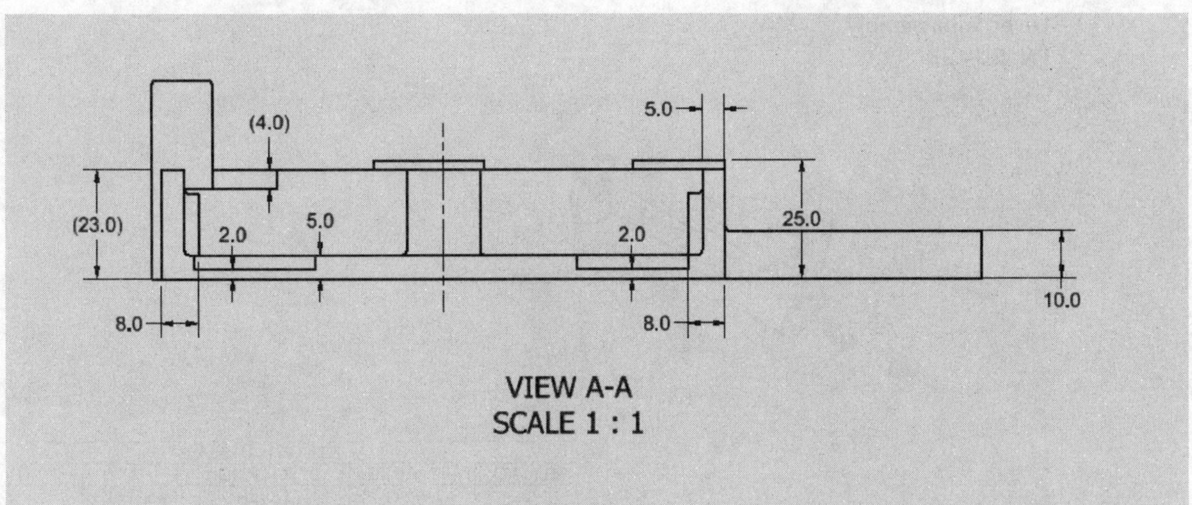

Figure 16-37g

Right Side View

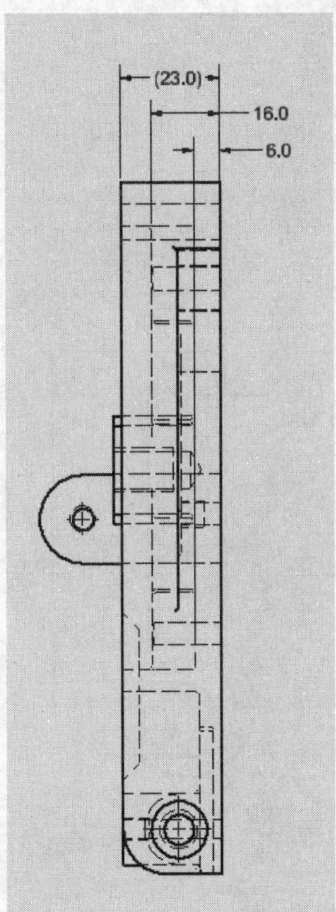

Figure 16-37h

Lever Subassembly
PN: BU-133

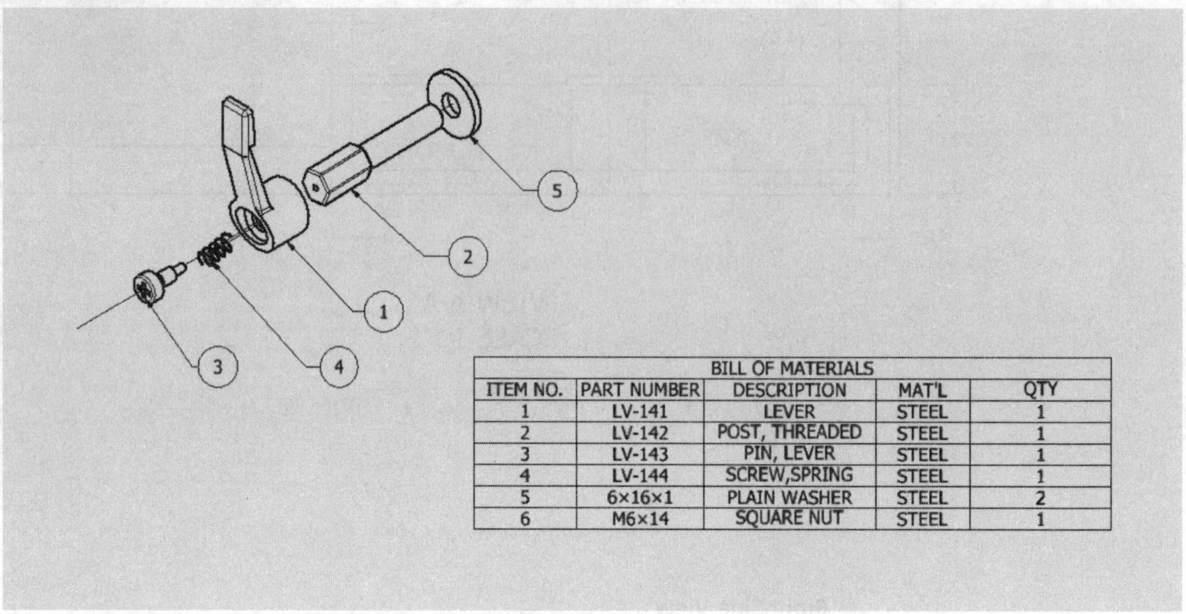

BILL OF MATERIALS				
ITEM NO.	PART NUMBER	DESCRIPTION	MAT'L	QTY
1	LV-141	LEVER	STEEL	1
2	LV-142	POST, THREADED	STEEL	1
3	LV-143	PIN, LEVER	STEEL	1
4	LV-144	SCREW,SPRING	STEEL	1
5	6×16×1	PLAIN WASHER	STEEL	2
6	M6×14	SQUARE NUT	STEEL	1

Figure 16-38a

Lever
PN: LV-141

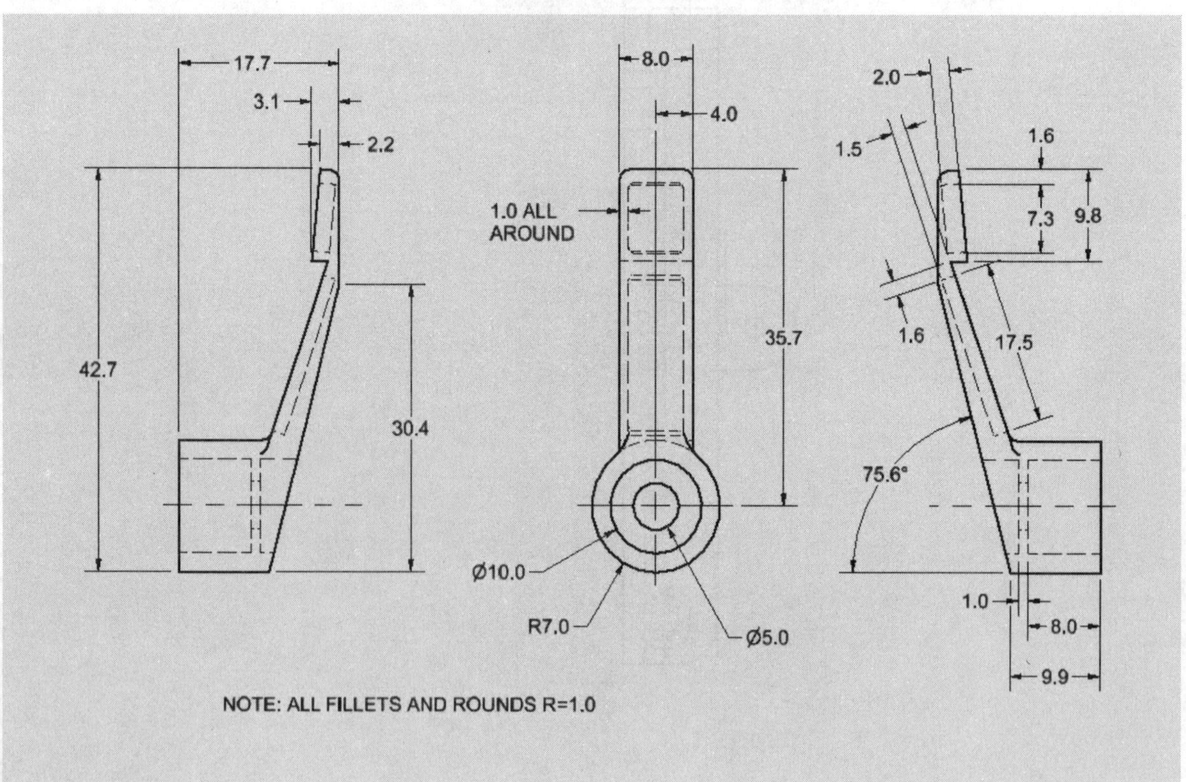

Figure 16-38b

Post, Threaded
PN: LV-142

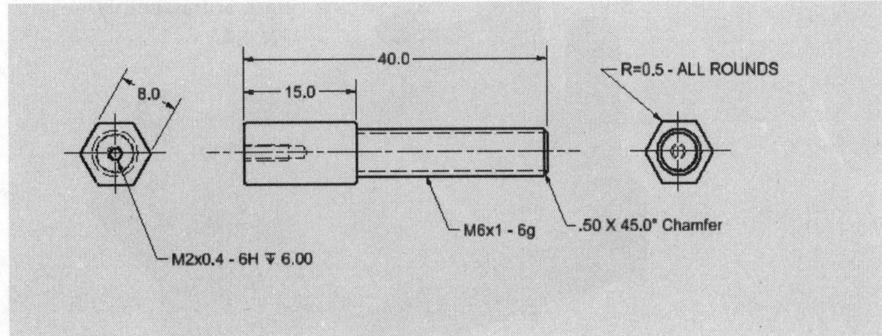

Figure 16-38c

Pin, Lever
PN: LV-143

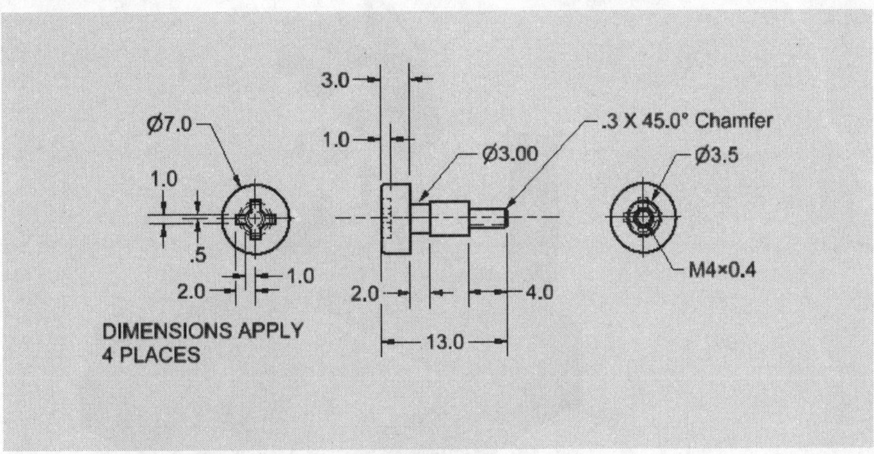

Figure 16-38d

Screw, Spring
PN: LV-144

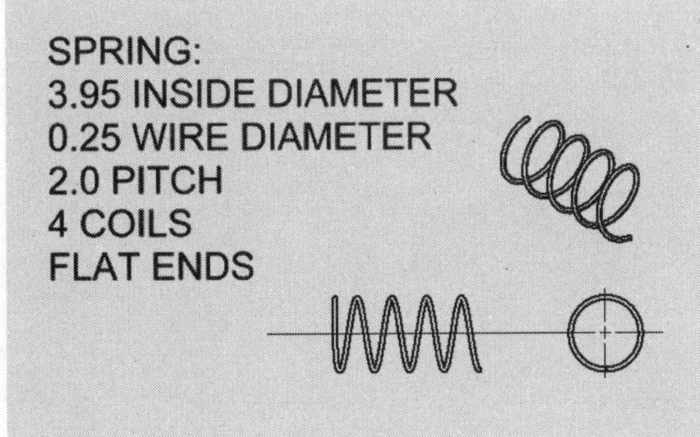

Figure 16-38e

Figure 16-39a

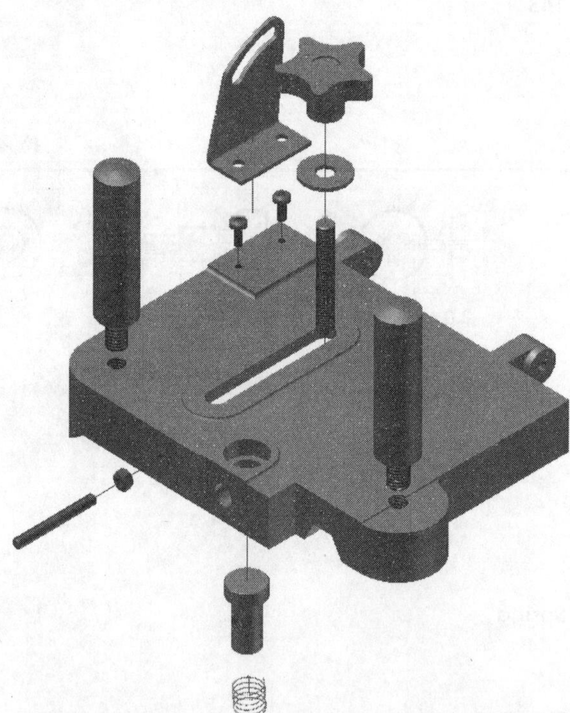

Figure 16-39b

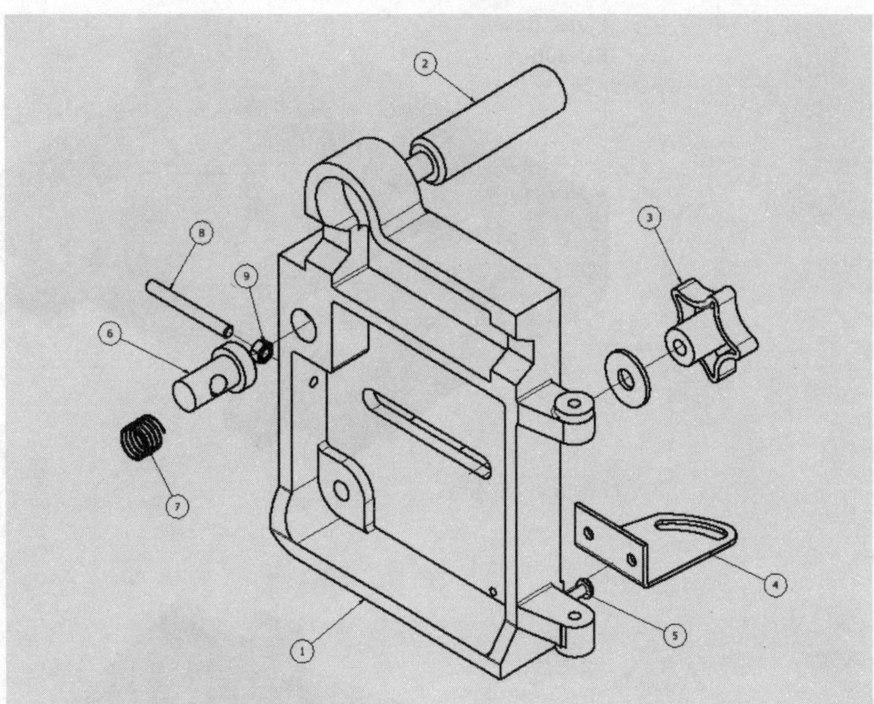

Figure 16-39c

PARTS LIST				
ITEM	PART NUMBER	DESCRIPTION	MATERIAL	QTY
1	BU-306-A	PLATE,BASE	CAST STEEL	1
2	P53-A2	POST, HANDLE, LARGE	STEEL	2
3	H5-21	LARGE KNOB SUB-ASSEMBLY		1
4	BU202	CLIP, BASE	STEEL	1
5	M4x0.7 x 10	Cross Recessed Pan Head Machine Screw	STEEL, MILD	2
6	P23-402	POST, RELEASE	STEEL	1
7	BU-003	SPRING	PIANO WIRE	1
8	M5x45	STUD	STEEL	1
9	M5	HEX NUT	Steel	1

Figure 16-39d

Plate, Base
BU-306-A

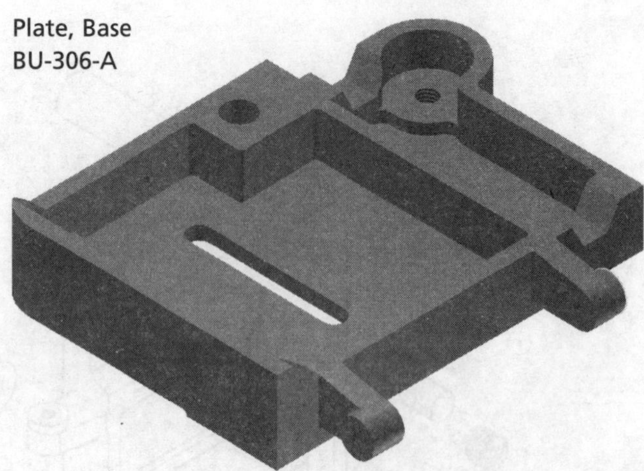

Figure 16-40a

Figure 16-40b

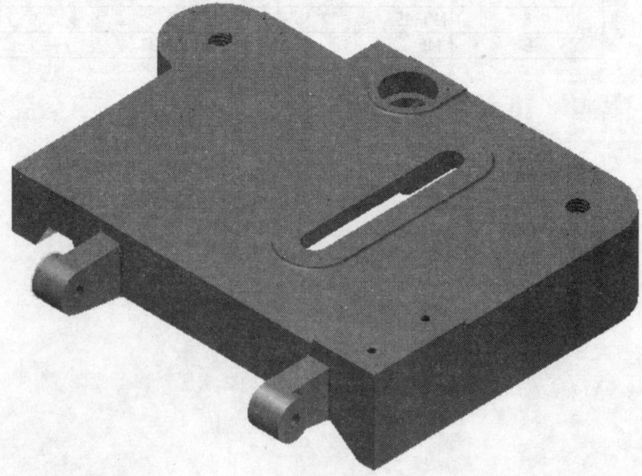

Figure 16-40c

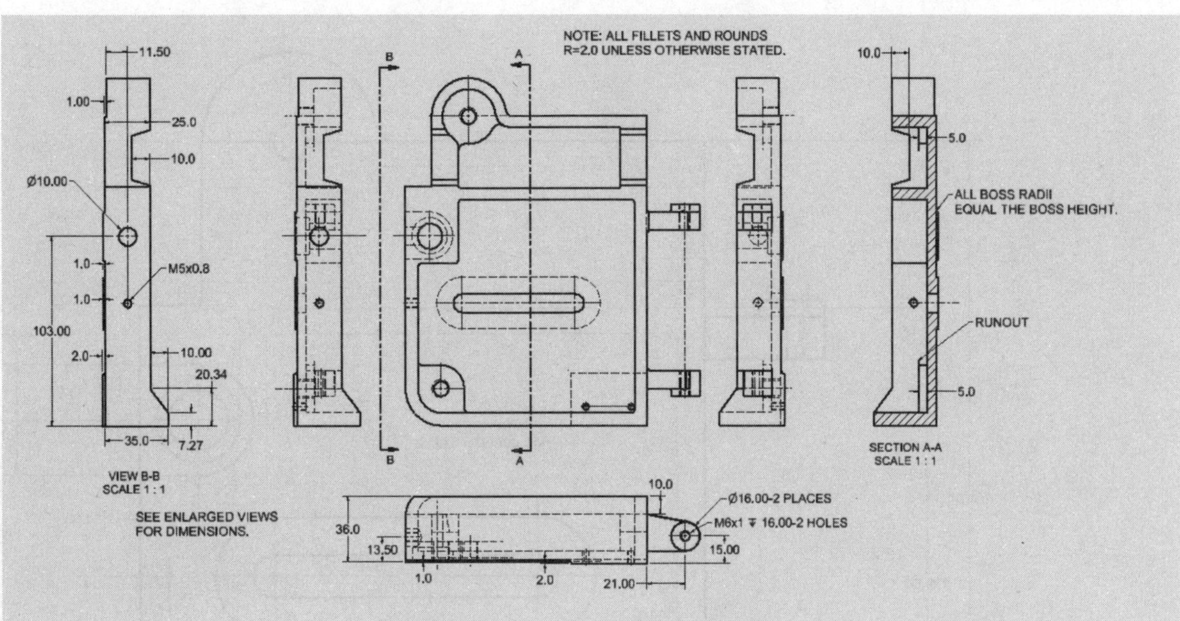

Figure 16-40d

99.00
R21.00
M10x1.5 ⊽ 16.00
15.00
11.00
17.00
27.54
33.00
6.00
R4.0-2 PLACES
15.00
R15.00
6.00
30.00
14.00
Ø14.00
Ø20.00 ⊽ 7.00
35.00
15.00
R5.00
87.00
130.00
103.00
R13.00
14.00
10.00
30.00
7.00 - ALL AROUND
10.00
R20.00
M4x0.7 -2 HOLES
25.00
9.00
M10x1.5
115.00

Figure 16-40e

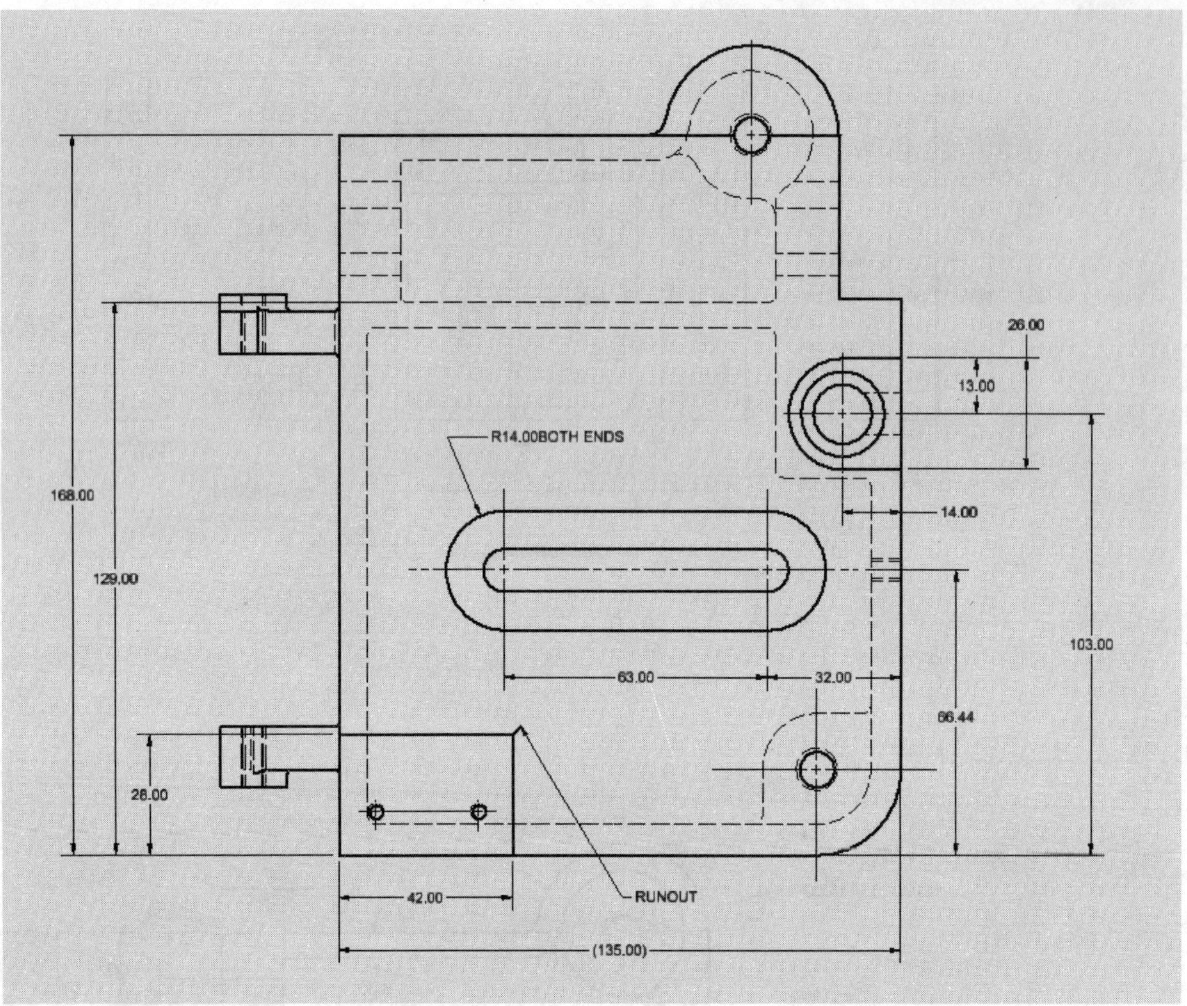

Figure 16-40f

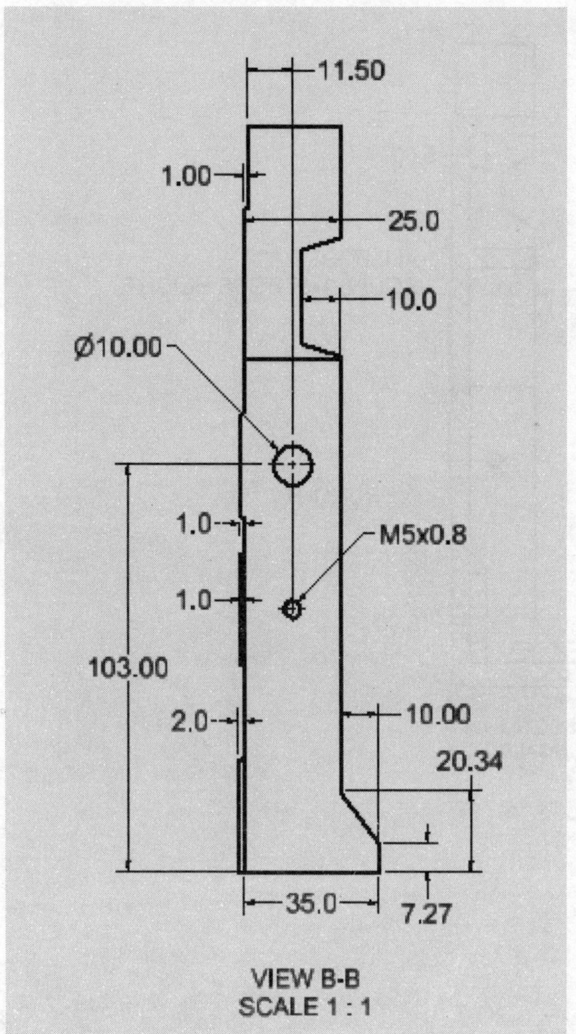

Figure 16-40g

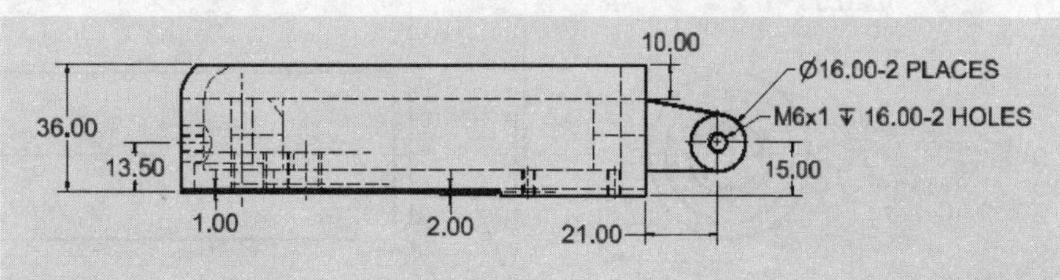

Figure 16-40h

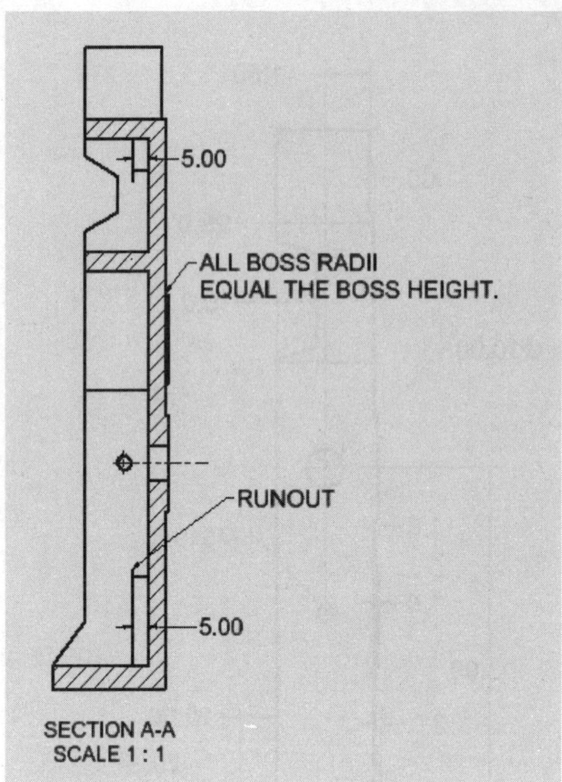

Figure 16-40i

Post Handle, Large
PS3-A2

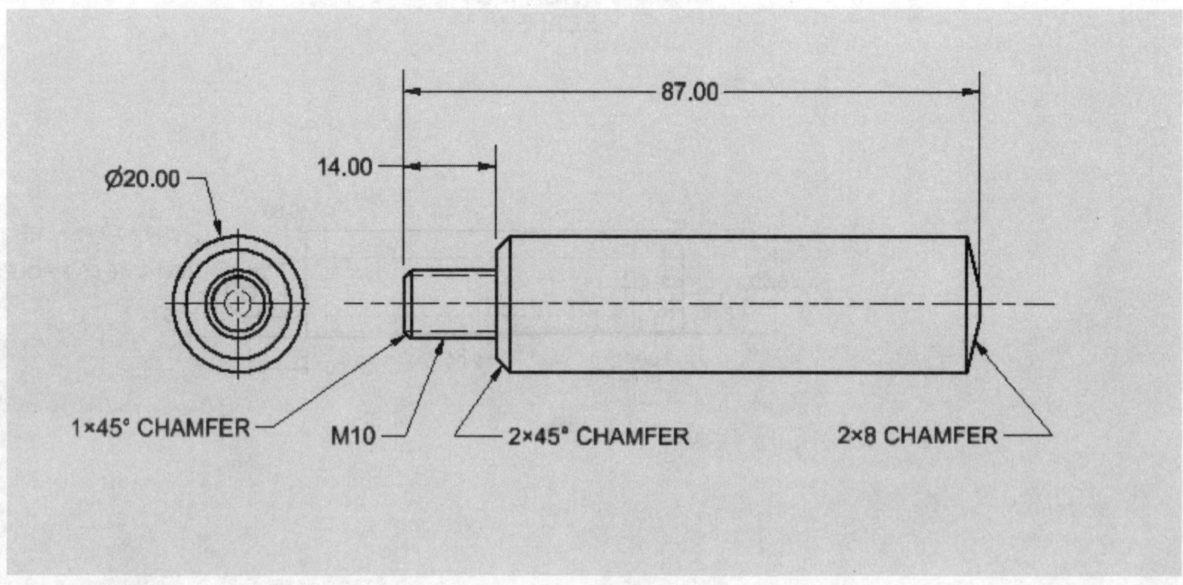

Figure 16-41

Large Knob Subassembly
PN: HS-21

Figure 16-42a

Large Knob Subassembly
PN: HS-21

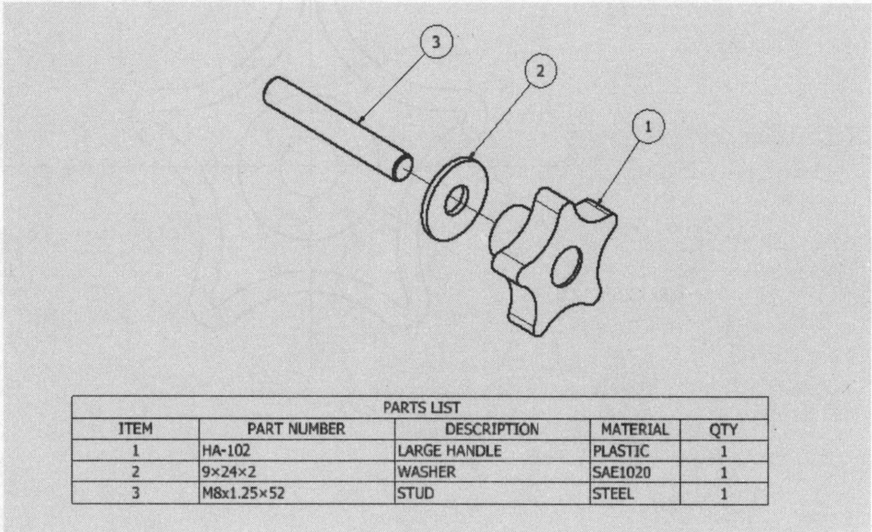

PARTS LIST				
ITEM	PART NUMBER	DESCRIPTION	MATERIAL	QTY
1	HA-102	LARGE HANDLE	PLASTIC	1
2	9×24×2	WASHER	SAE1020	1
3	M8x1.25×52	STUD	STEEL	1

Figure 16-42b

Washer
9 × 24 × 2

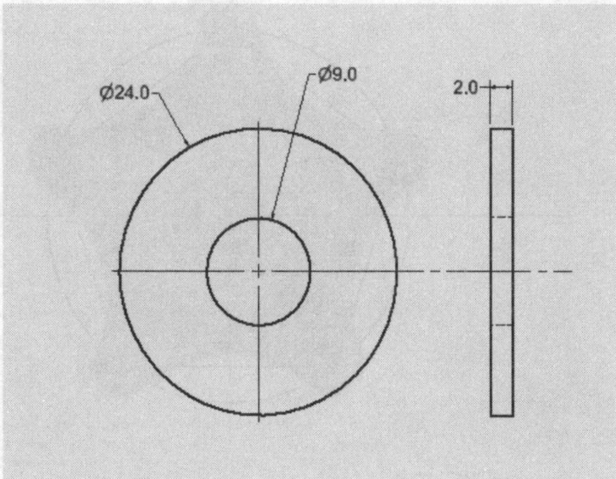

Figure 16-42c

Large Handle
PN: HA-102

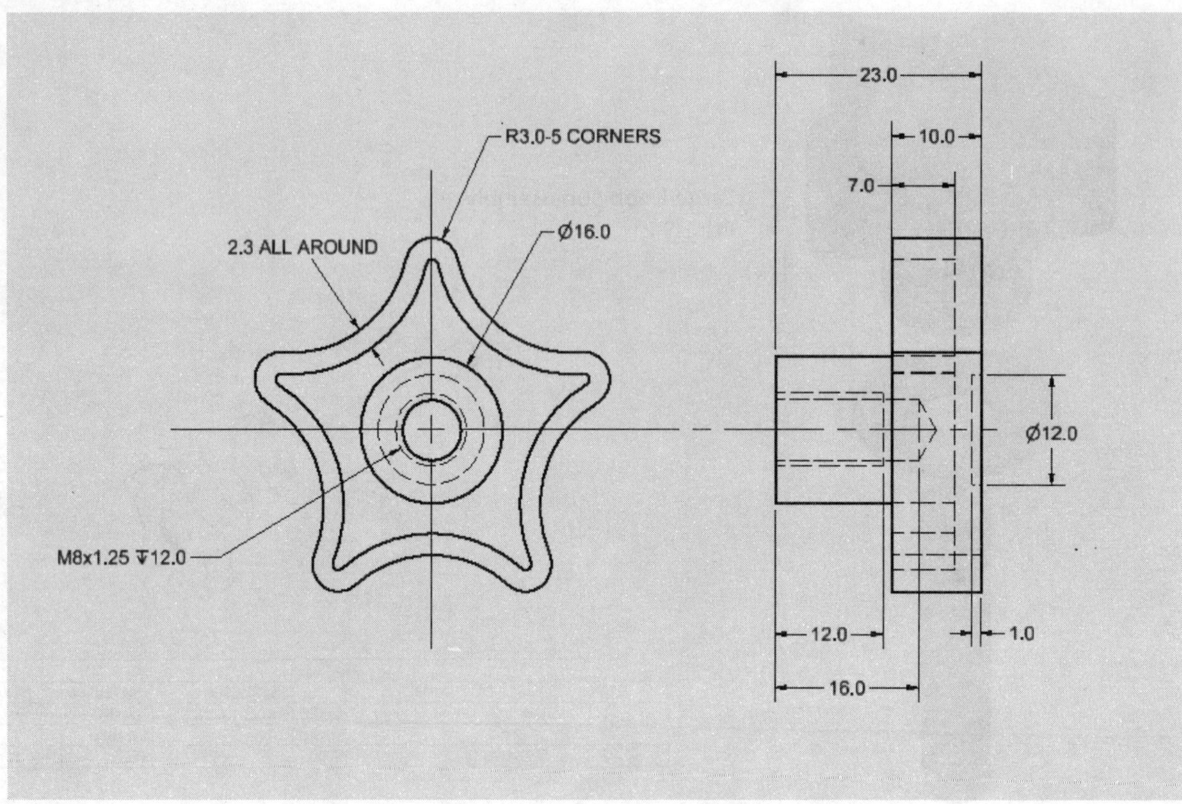

Figure 16-42d

Layout for Large Handle

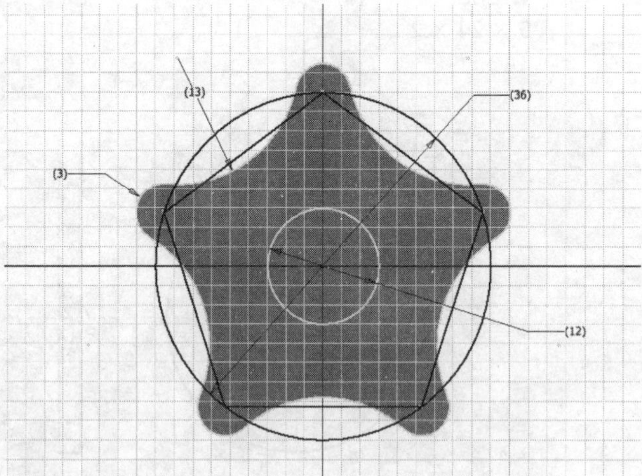

Figure 16-42e

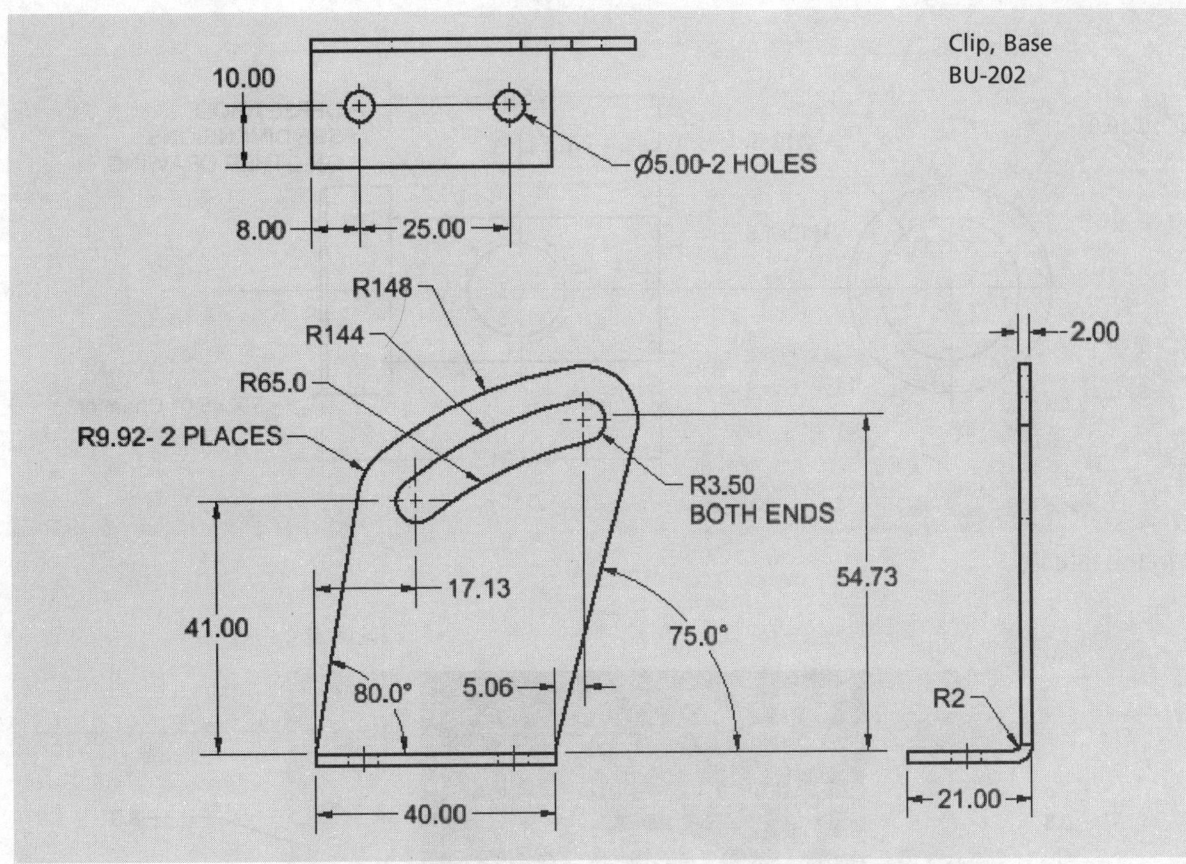

Figure 16-43

Figure 16-44

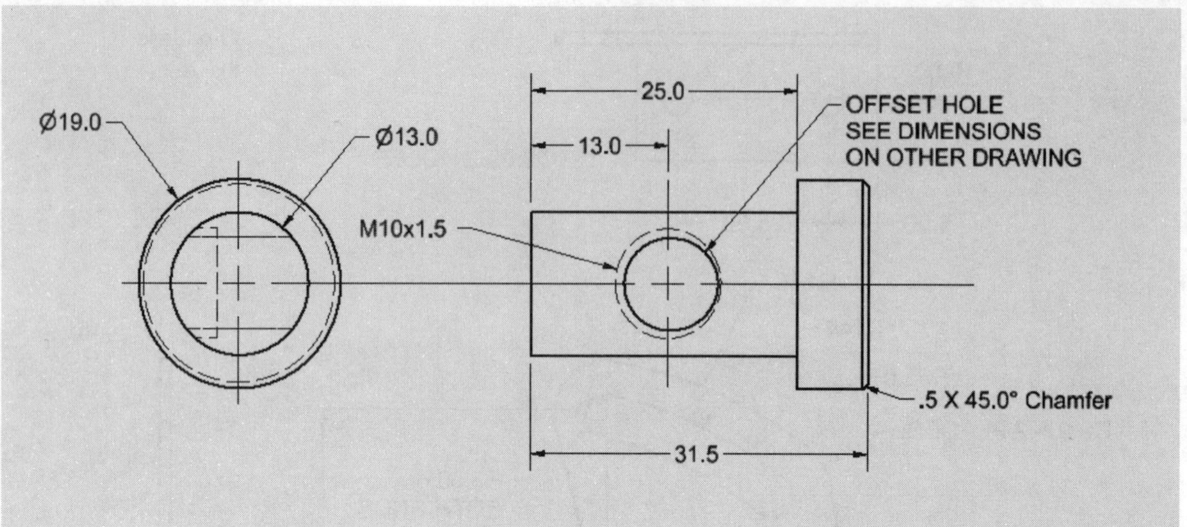

Figure 16-44b

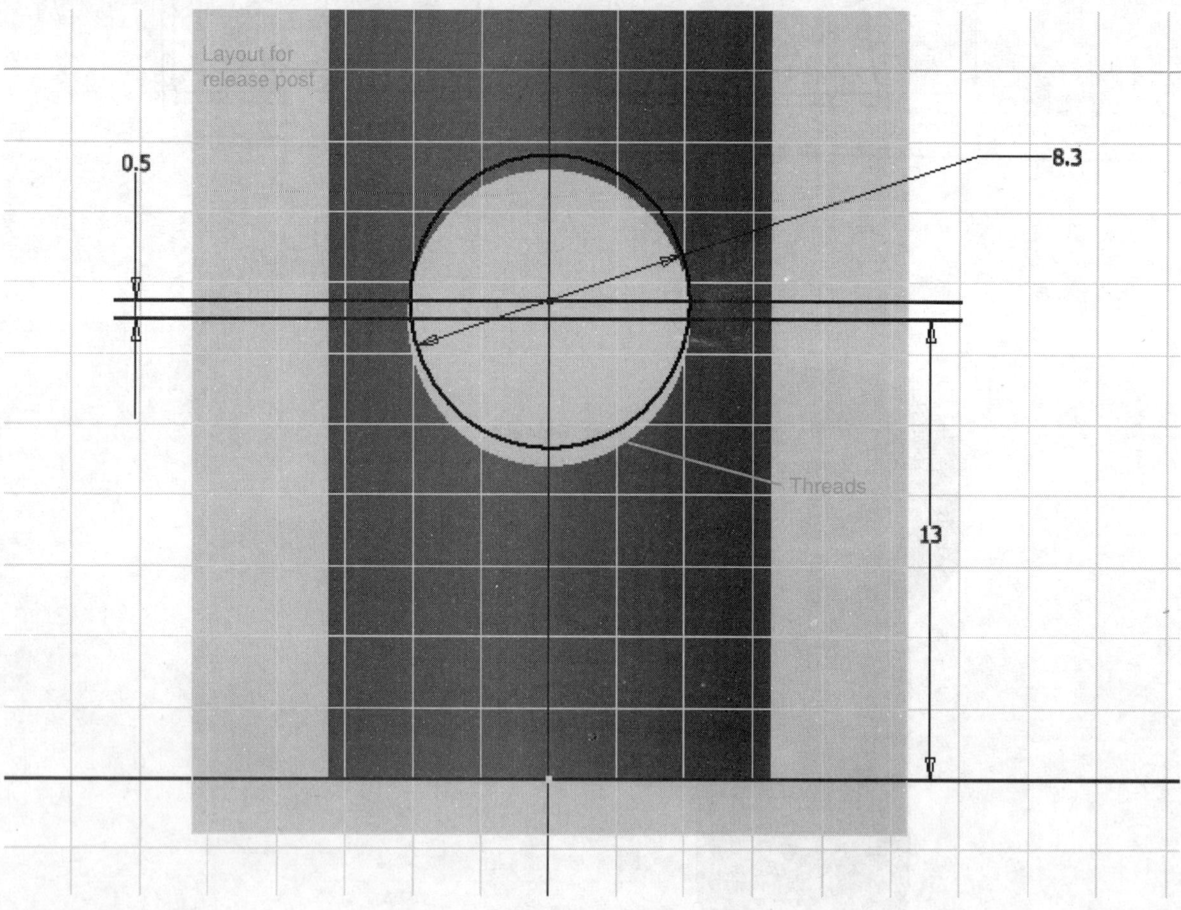

Figure 16-44c

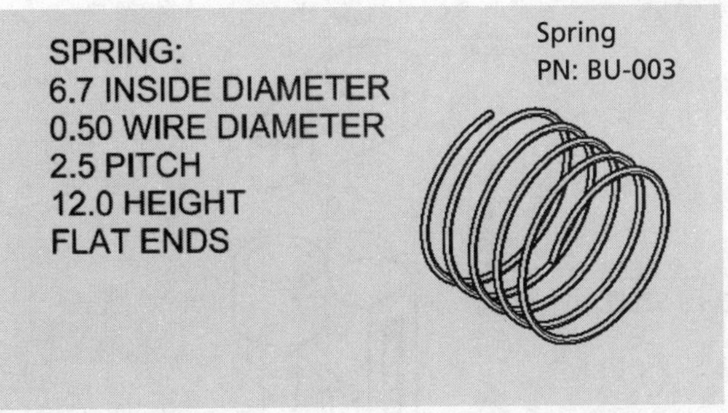

Figure 16-45

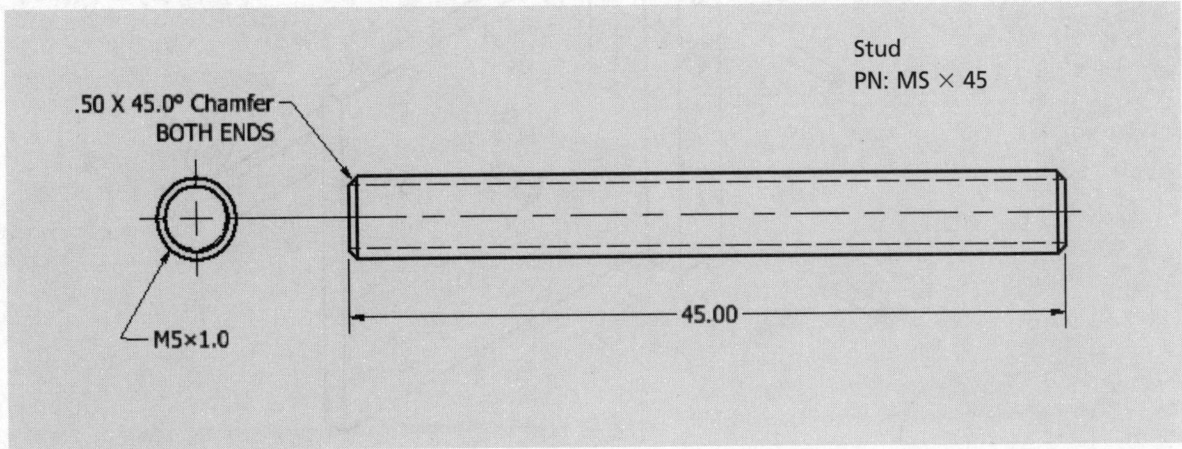

Figure 16-46

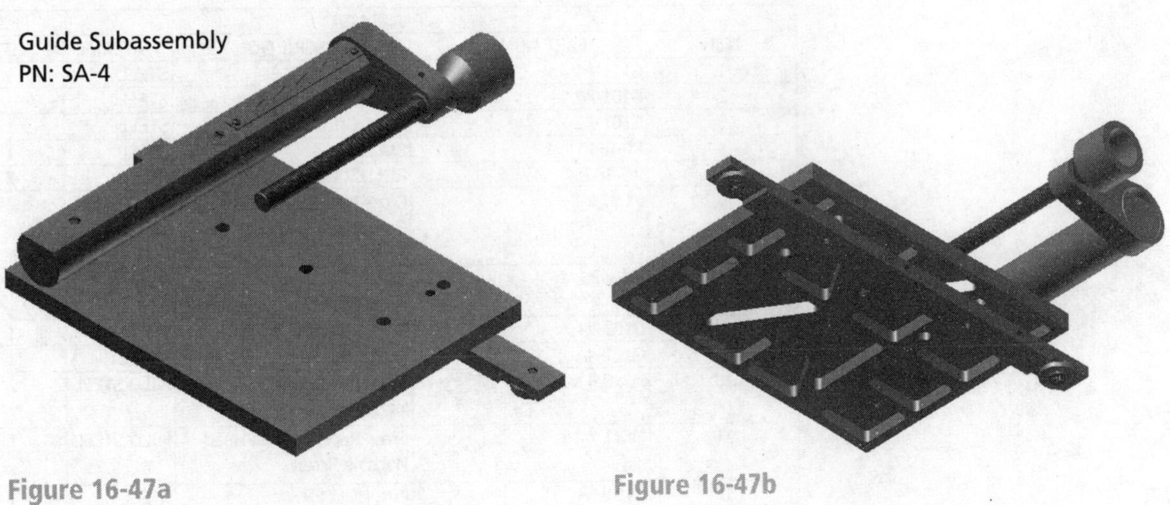

Figure 16-47a

Figure 16-47b

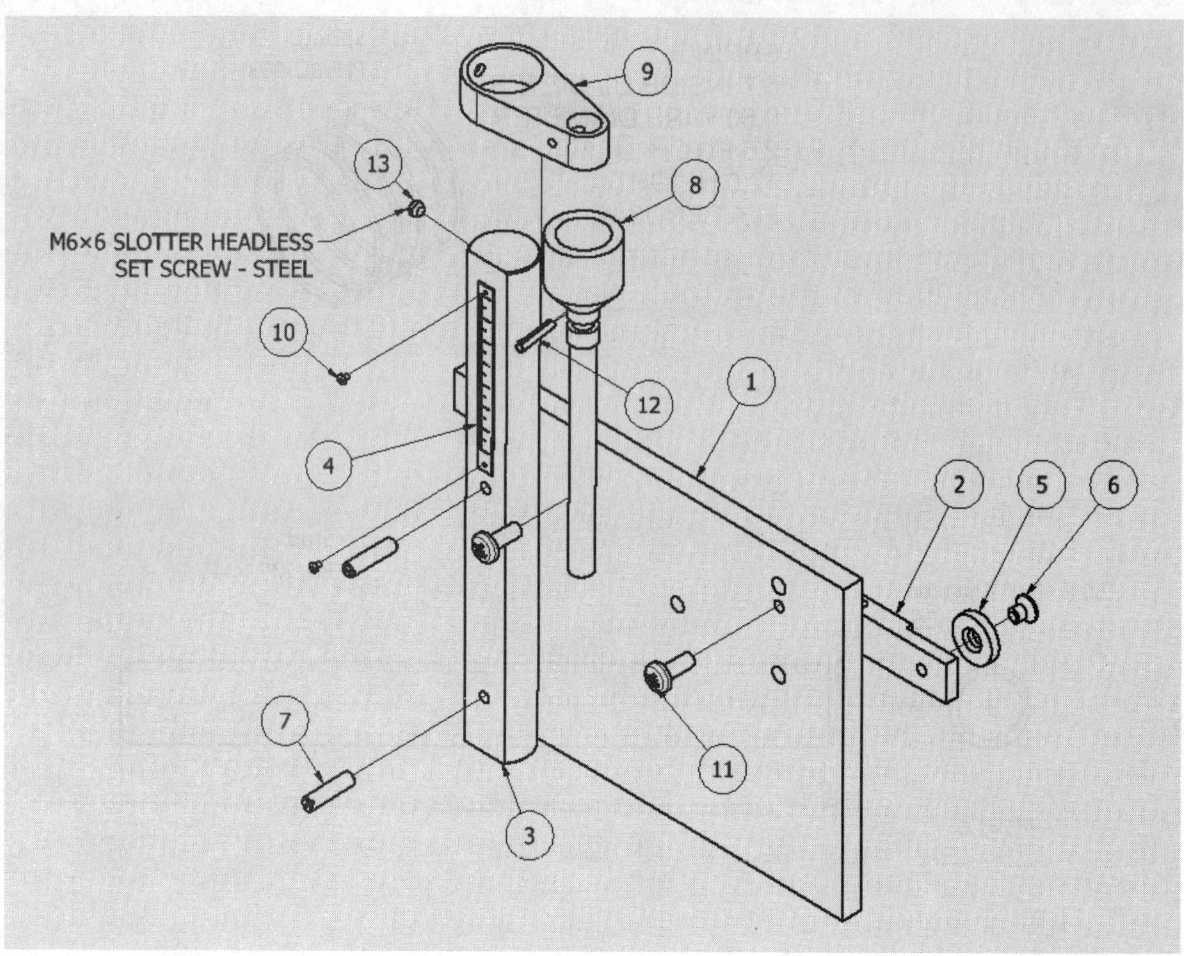

Figure 16-47c

PARTS LIST				
ITEM	PART NUMBER	DESCRIPTION	MATERIAL	QTY
1	G101-A1	PLATE, GUIDE	STEEL	1
2	G101-A2	BAR, GUIDE	STEEL	1
3	G101-A3	POST,GUIDE	STEEL	1
4	RR-6-40	RULER	STEEL	1
5	RG-1005	ROLLER,GUIDE	STEEL	2
6	M6x1 x 8	Cross Recessed Flat Countersunk Head Machine Screw	MILD STEEL	2
7	M6 x 25	Slotted Headless Set Screw - Flat Point	Steel	2
8	G103-2	SCREW,GUIDE	Steel	1
9	G101-4A	PLATE,GUIDE	STEEL	1
10	M2x0.4 x 3	Cross Recessed Pan Head Machine Screw	MILD STEEL	2
11	M6x1 x 16	Cross Recessed Pan Head Machine Screw	MILD STEEL	2
12	G101-63	PIN, HOLDER	STEEL	1

Figure 16-47d

Plate, Guide
PN: G101-A1

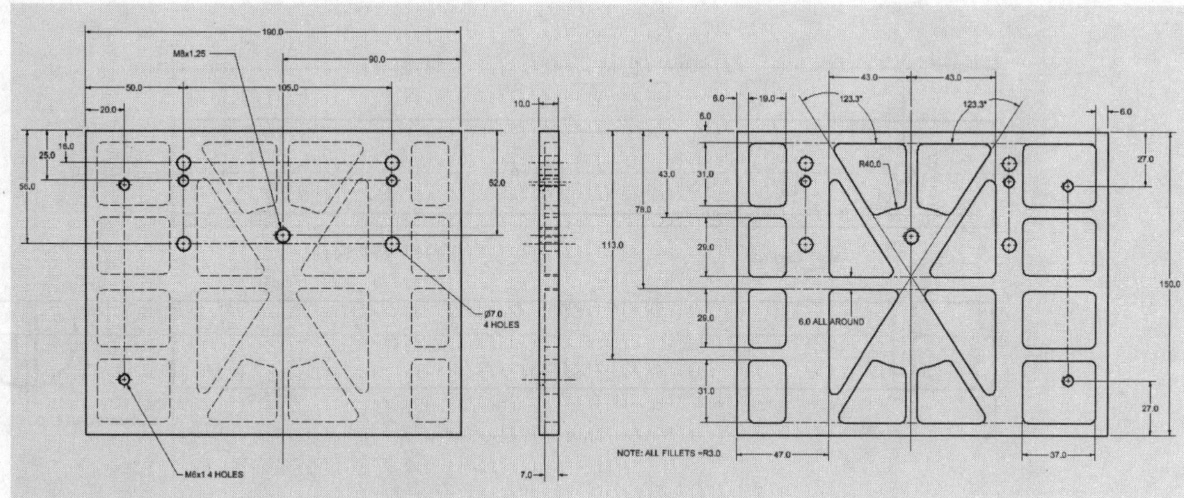

Figure 16-48

Bar, Guide
PN: G101-A2

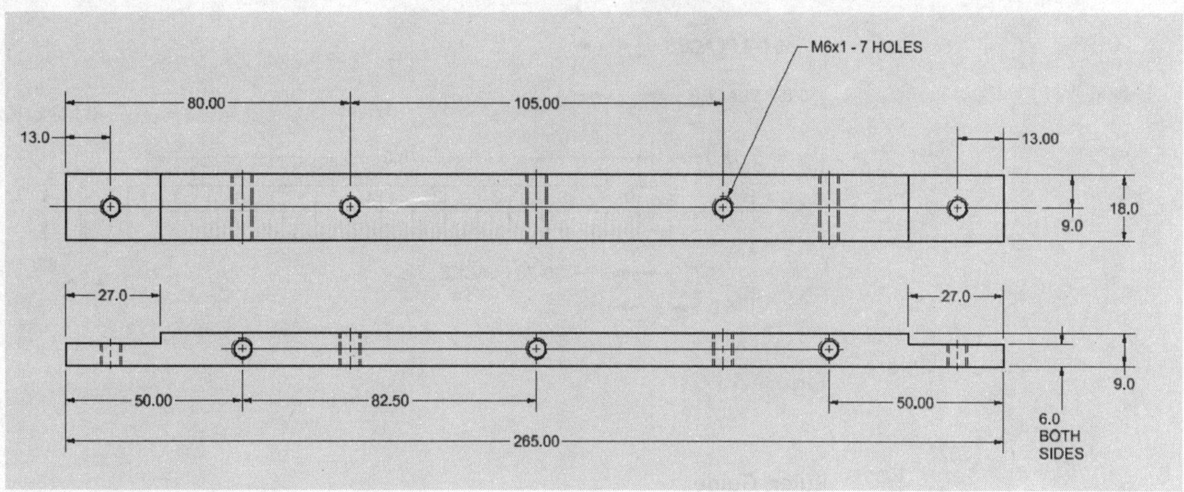

Figure 16-49

Post Guide
PN: G101-A3

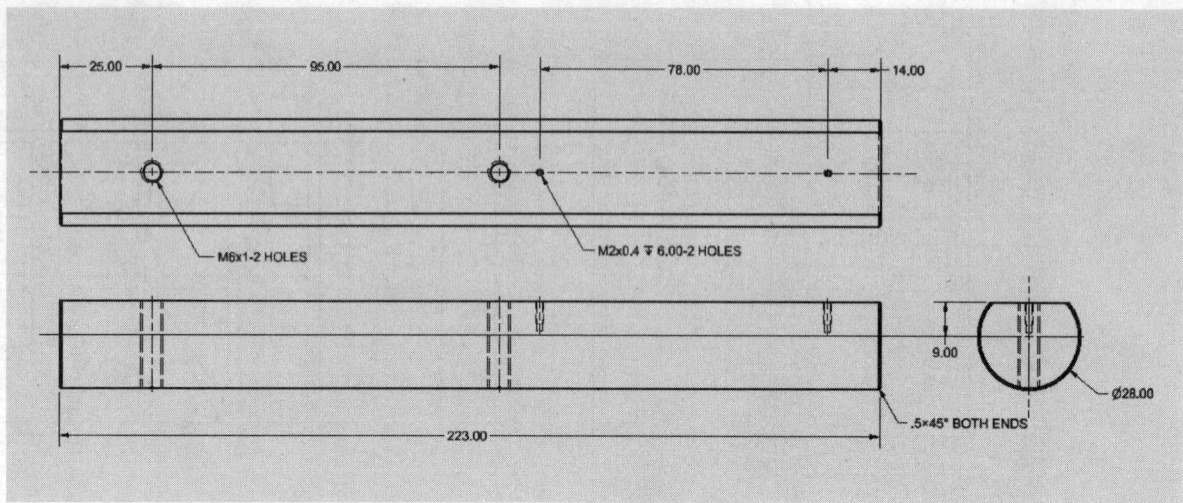

Figure 16-50

Ruler
PN: RR-6-40

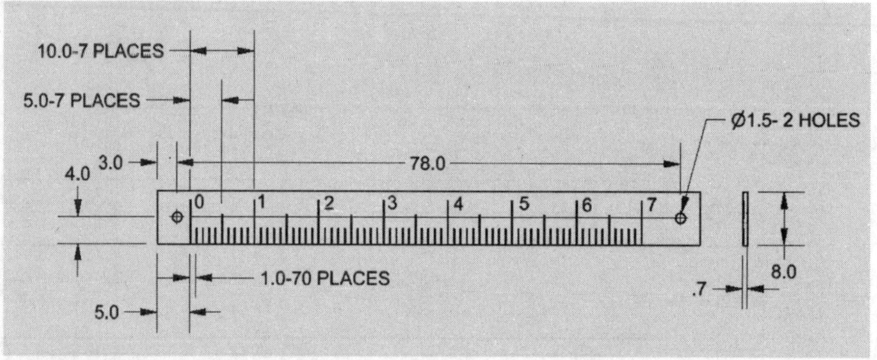

Figure 16-51

Ruler, Guide
PN: RG-1005

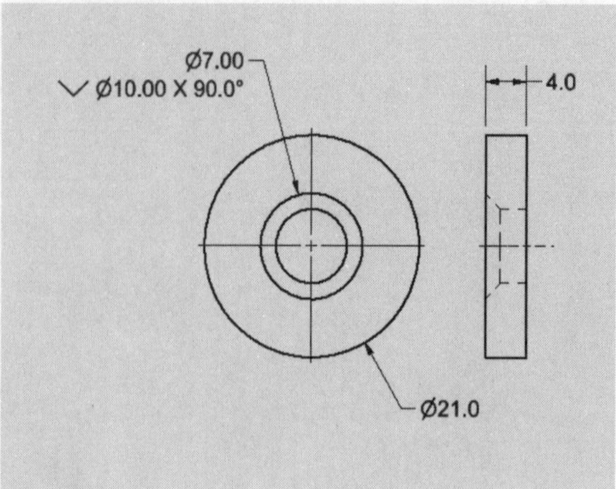

Figure 16-52

Screw, Guide
PN: G103-2

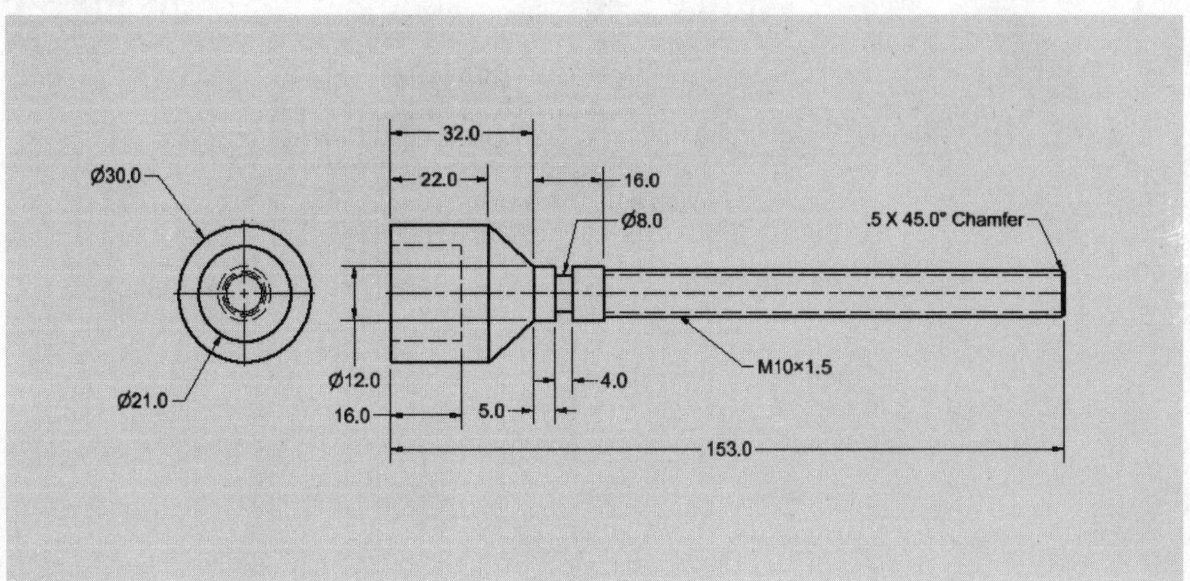

Figure 16-53

Plate, Guide
PN: G101-4A

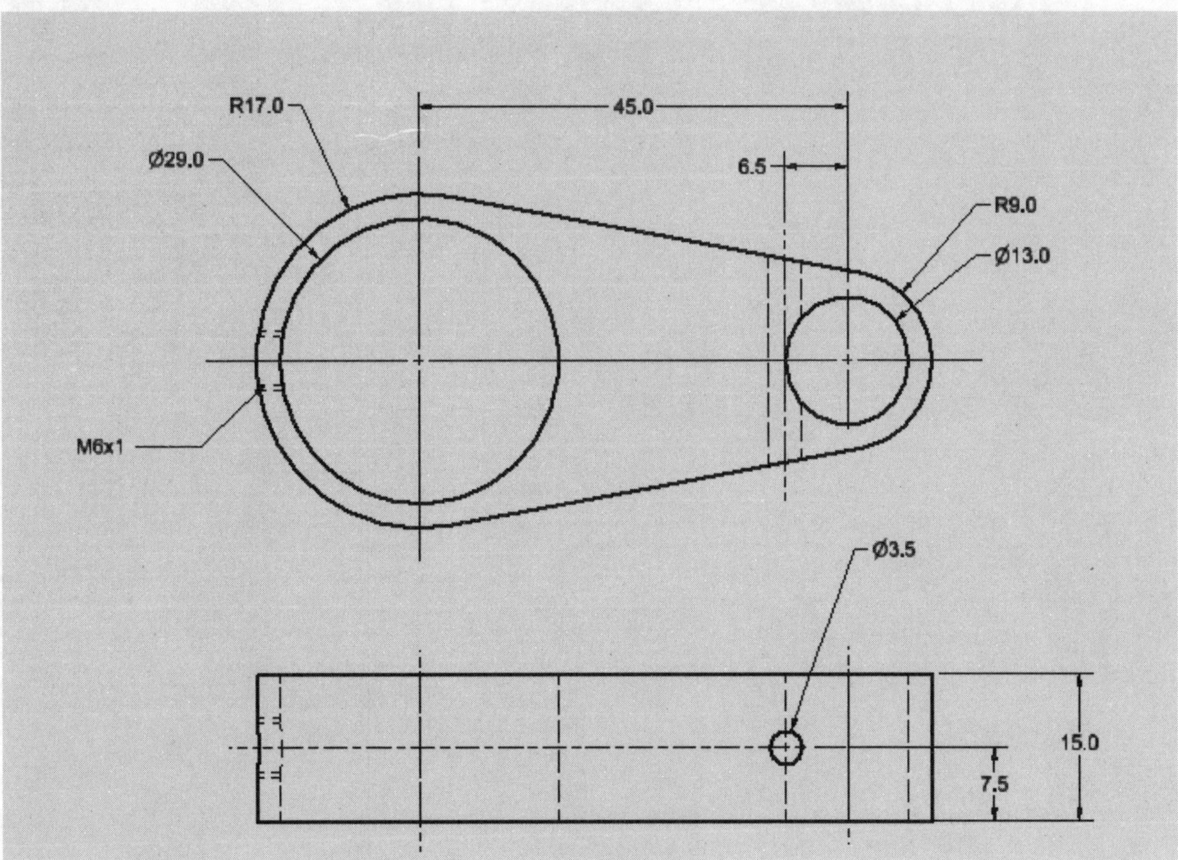

Figure 16-54

Pin, Holder
PN: G101-63

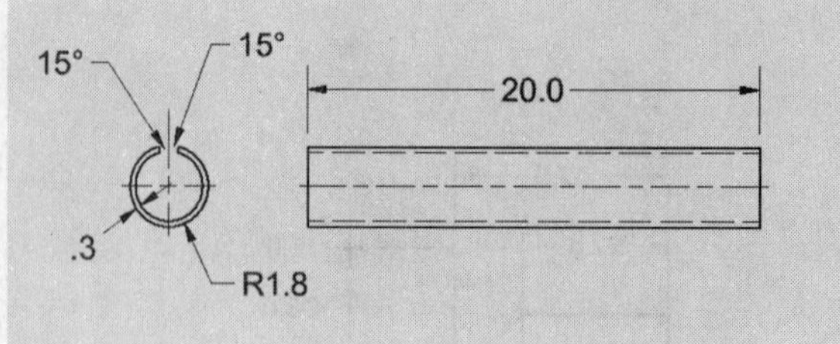

Figure 16-55

appendix

Wire and Sheet Metal Gauges

Gauge	Thickness	Gauge	Thickness
000 000	0.5800	18	0.0403
00 000	0.5165	19	0.0359
0 000	0.4600	20	0.0320
000	0.4096	21	0.0285
00	0.3648	22	0.0253
0	0.3249	23	0.0226
1	0.2893	24	0.0201
2	0.2576	25	0.0179
3	0.2294	26	0.0159
4	0.2043	27	0.0142
5	0.1819	28	0.0126
6	0.1620	29	0.0113
7	0.1443	30	0.0100
8	0.1285	31	0.0089
9	0.1144	32	0.0080
10	0.1019	33	0.0071
11	0.0907	34	0.0063
12	0.0808	35	0.0056
13	0.0720	36	0.0050
14	0.0641	37	0.0045
15	0.0571	38	0.0040
16	0.0508	39	0.0035
17	0.0453	40	0.0031

Figure A-1

American Standard Clearance Locational Fits

Nominal Size Range Inches Over – To	Class LC1 Limits of Clearance	Class LC1 Standard Limits Hole H6	Class LC1 Standard Limits Shaft h5	Class LC2 Limits of Clearance	Class LC2 Standard Limits Hole H7	Class LC2 Standard Limits Shaft h6	Class LC3 Limits of Clearance	Class LC3 Standard Limits Hole H8	Class LC3 Standard Limits Shaft h7	Class LC4 Limits of Clearance	Class LC4 Standard Limits Hole H10	Class LC4 Standard Limits Shaft h9
0 – 0.12	0 0.45	+0.25 0	0 -0.2	0 0.65	+0.4 0	0 -0.25	0 1	+0.6 0	0 -0.4	0 2.6	+1.6 0	0 -1.0
0.12 – 0.24	0 0.5	+0.3 0	0 -0.2	0 0.8	+0.5 0	0 -0.3	0 1.2	+0.7 0	0 -0.5	0 3.0	+1.8 0	0 -1.2
0.24 – 0.40	0 0.65	+0.4 0	0 -0.25	0 1.0	+0.6 0	0 -0.4	0 1.5	+0.9 0	0 -0.6	0 3.6	+2.2 0	0 -1.4
0.40 – 0.71	0 0.7	+0.4 0	0 -0.3	0 1.1	+0.7 0	0 -0.4	0 1.7	+1.0 0	0 -0.7	0 4.4	+2.8 0	0 -1.6
0.71 – 1.19	0 0.9	+0.5 0	0 -0.4	0 1.3	+0.8 0	0 -0.5	0 2	+1.2 0	0 -0.8	0 5.5	+3.5 0	0 -2.0
1.19 – 1.97	0 1.0	+0.6 0	0 -0.4	0 1.6	+1.0 0	0 -0.6	0 2.6	+1.6 0	0 -1.0	0 6.5	+4.0 0	0 -2.5

Figure A-2A

Nominal Size Range Inches Over – To	Class LC5 Limits of Clearance	Class LC5 Standard Limits Hole H7	Class LC5 Standard Limits Shaft g6	Class LC6 Limits of Clearance	Class LC6 Standard Limits Hole H9	Class LC6 Standard Limits Shaft f8	Class LC7 Limits of Clearance	Class LC7 Standard Limits Hole H10	Class LC7 Standard Limits Shaft e9	Class LC8 Limits of Clearance	Class LC8 Standard Limits Hole H10	Class LC8 Standard Limits Shaft d9
0 – 0.12	0.1 0.75	+0..4 0	-0.1 -0.35	0.3 1.9	+1.0 0	-0.3 -0.9	0.6 3.2	+1.6 0	-0.6 -1.6	1.0 3.6	+1.6 0	-1.0 -2.0
0.12 – 0.24	0.15 0.95	+0.5 0	-0.15 -0.45	0.4 2.3	+1.2 0	-0.4 -1.1	0.8 3.8	+1.8 0	-0.8 -2.0	1.2 4.2	+1.8 0	-1.2 -2.4
0.24 – 0.40	0.2 1.2	+0.6 0	-0.2 -0.6	0.5 2.8	+1.4 0	-0.5 -1.4	1.0 4.6	+2.2 0	-1.0 -2.4	1.6 5.2	+2.2 0	-1.6 -3.0
0.40 – 0.71	0.25 1.35	+0.7 0	-0.25 -0.65	0.6 3.2	+1.6 0	-0.6 -1.6	1.2 5.6	+2.8 0	-1.2 -2.8	2.0 6.4	+2.8 0	-2.0 -3.6
0.71 – 1.19	0.3 1.6	+0.8 0	-0.3 -0.8	0.8 4.0	+2.0 0	-0.8 -2.0	1.6 7.1	+3.5 0	-1.6 -3.6	2.5 8.0	+3.5 0	-2.5 -4.5
1.19 – 1.97	0.4 2.0	+1.0 0	-0.4 -1.0	1.0 5.1	+2.5 0	-1.0 -2.6	2.0 8.5	+4.0 0	-2.0 -4.5	3.0 9.5	+4.0 0	-3.0 -5.5

Figure A-2B

American Standard Running and Sliding Fits

(Hole Basis)

Nominal Size Range Inches		Class RC1			Class RC2			Class RC3			Class RC4		
		Limits of Clearance	Standard Limits		Limits of Clearance	Standard Limits		Limits of Clearance	Standard Limits		Limits of Clearance	Standard Limits	
Over	To		Hole H5	Shaft g4		Hole H6	Shaft g5		Hole H7	Shaft f6		Hole H8	Shaft f7
0	0.12	0.1	+0.2	-0.1	0.1	+0.25	-0.1	0.3	+0.4	-0.3	0.3	+0.6	-0.3
		0.45	0	-0.25	0.55	0	-0.3	0.95	0	-0.55	1.3	0	-0.7
0.12	0.24	0.15	+0.2	-0.15	0.15	+0.3	-0.15	0.4	+0.5	-0.4	0.4	+0.7	-0.4
		0.5	0	-0.3	0.65	0	-0.35	1.12	0	-0.7	1.5	0	-0.0
0.24	0.40	0.2	+0.25	-0.2	0.2	+0.4	-0.2	0.5	+0.6	-0.5	0.5	+0.9	-0.5
		0.6	0	-0.35	0.85	0	-0.45	1.5	0	-0.9	2.0	0	-1.1
0.40	0.71	0.25	+0.3	-0.25	0.25	+0.4	-0.25	0.6	+0.7	-0.6	0.6	+1.0	-0.6
		0.75	0	-0.45	0.95	0	-0.55	1.7	0	-1.0	2.3	0	-1.3
0.71	1.19	0.3	+0.4	-0.3	0.3	+0.5	-0.3	0.8	+0.8	-0.8	0.8	+1.2	-0.8
		0.95	0	-0.55	1.2	0	-0.7	2.1	0	-1.3	2.8	0	-1.6
1.19	1.97	0.4	+0.4	-0.4	0.4	+0.6	-0.4	1.0	+1.0	-1.0	1.0	+1.6	-1.0
		1.1	0	-0.7	1.4	0	-0.8	2.6	0	-1.6	3.6	0	-2.0

Figure A-3A

Nominal Size Range Inches		Class RC5			Class RC6			Class RC7			Class RC8		
		Limits of Clearance	Standard Limits		Limits of Clearance	Standard Limits		Limits of Clearance	Standard Limits		Limits of Clearance	Standard Limits	
Over	To		Hole H8	Shaft e7		Hole H9	Shaft e8		Hole H9	Shaft d8		Hole H10	Shaft c9
0	0.12	0.6	+0.6	-0.6	0.6	+1.0	-0.6	1.0	+1.0	-1.0	2.5	+1.6	-2.5
		1.6	0	-1.0	2.2	0	-1.2	2.6	0	-1.6	5.1	0	-3.5
0.12	0.24	0.8	+0.7	-0.8	0.8	+1.2	-0.8	1.2	+1.2	-1.2	2.8	+1.8	-2.8
		2.0	0	-1.3	2.7	0	-1.5	3.1	0	-1.9	5.8	0	-4.0
0.24	0.40	1.0	+0.9	-1.0	1.0	+1.4	-1.0	1.6	+1.4	-1.6	3.0	+2.2	-3.0
		2.5	0	-1.6	3.3	0	-1.9	3.9	0	-2.5	6.6	0	-4.4
0.40	0.71	1.2	+1.0	-1.2	1.2	+1.6	-1.2	2.0	+1.6	-2.0	3.5	+2.8	-3.5
		2.9	0	-1.9	3.8	0	-2.2	4.6	0	-3.0	7.9	0	-5.1
0.71	1.19	1.6	+1.2	-1.6	1.6	+2.0	-1.6	2.5	+2.0	-2.5	4.5	+3.5	-4.5
		3.6	0	-2.4	4.8	0	-2.8	5.7	0	-3.7	10.0	0	-6.5
1.19	1.97	2.0	+1.6	-2.0	2.0	+2.5	-2.0	3.0	+2.5	-3.0	5.0	+4.0	-5.0
		4.6	0	-3.0	6.1	0	-3.6	7.1	0	-4.6	11.5	0	-7.5

Figure A-3B

American Standard Transition Locational Fits

Nominal Size Range Inches		Class LT1			Class LT2			Class LT3		
		Fit	Standard Limits		Fit	Standard Limits		Fit	Standard Limits	
Over	To		Hole H7	Shaft js6		Hole H8	Shaft js7		Hole H7	Shaft k6
0	0.12	-0.10 +0.50	+0.4 0	+0.10 -0.10	-0.2 +0.8	+0.6 0	+0.2 -0.2			
0.12	0.24	-0.15 -0.65	+0.5 0	+0.15 -0.15	-0.25 +0.95	+0.7 0	+0.25 -0.25			
0.24	0.40	-0.2 +0.5	+0.6 0	+0.2 -0.2	-0.3 +1.2	+0.9 0	+0.3 -0.3	-0.5 +0.5	+0.6 0	+0.5 +0.1
0.40	0.71	-0.2 +0.9	+0.7 0	+0.2 -0.2	-0.35 +1.35	+1.0 0	+0.35 -0.35	-0.5 +0.6	+0.7 0	+0.5 +0.1
0.71	1.19	-0.25 +1.05	+0.8 0	+0.25 -0.25	-0.4 +1.6	+1.2 0	+0.4 -0.4	-0.6 +0.7	+0.8 0	+0.6 +0.1
1.19	1.97	-0.3 +1.3	+1.0 0	+0.3 -0.3	-0.5 +2.1	+1.6 0	+0.5 -0.5	+0.7 +0.1	+1.0 0	+0.7 +0.1

Figure A-4A

Nominal Size Range Inches		Class LT4			Class LT5			Class LT6		
		Fit	Standard Limits		Fit	Standard Limits		Fit	Standard Limits	
Over	To		Hole H8	Shaft k7		Hole H7	Shaft n6		Hole H7	Shaft n7
0	0.12				-0.5 +0.15	+0.4 0	+0.5 +0.25	-0.65 +0.15	+0.4 0	+0.65 +0.25
0.12	0.24				-0.6 +0.2	+0.5 0	+0.6 +0.3	-0.8 +0.2	+0.5 0	+0.8 +0.3
0.24	0.40	-0.7 +0.8	+0.9 0	+0.7 +0.1	-0.8 +0.2	+0.6 0	+0.8 +0.4	-1.0 +0.2	+0.6 0	+1.0 +0.4
0.40	0.71	-0.8 +0.9	+1.0 0	+0.8 +0.1	-0.9 +0.2	+0.7 0	+0.9 +0.5	-1.2 +0.2	+0.7 0	+1.2 +0.5
0.71	1.19	-0.9 +1.1	+1.2 0	+0.9 +0.1	-1.1 +0.2	+0.8 0	+1.1 +0.6	-1.4 +0.2	+0.8 0	+1.4 +0.6
1.19	1.97	-1.1 +1.5	+1.6 0	+1.1 +0.1	-1.3 +0.3	+1.0 0	+1.3 +0.7	-1.7 +0.3	+1.0 0	+1.7 +0.7

Figure A-4B

American Standard Interference Locational Fits

Nominal Size Range Inches Over	To	Limits of Interference	Class LN1 Standard Limits Hole H6	Shaft n5	Limits of Interference	Class LN2 Standard Limits Hole H7	Shaft p6	Limits of Interference	Class LN3 Standard Limits Hole H7	Shaft r6
0	0.12	0	+0.25	+0.45	0	+0.4	+0.63	0.1	+0.4	+0.75
		0.45	0	+0.25	0.65	0	+0.4	0.75	0	+0.5
0.12	0.24	0	+0.3	+0.5	0	+0.5	+0.8	0.1	+0.5	+0.9
		0.5	0	+0.3	0.8	0	+0.5	0.9	0	+0.6
0.24	0.40	0	+0.4	+0.65	0	+0.6	+1.0	0.2	+0.6	+1.2
		0.65	0	+0.4	1.0	0	+0.6	1.2	0	+0.8
0.40	0.71	0	+0.4	+0.8	0	+0.7	+1.1	0.3	+0.7	+1.4
		0.8	0	+0.4	1.1	0	+0.7	1.4	0	+1.0
0.71	1.19	0	+0.5	+1.0	0	+0.8	+1.3	0.4	+0.8	+1.7
		1.0	0	+0.5	1.3	0	+0.8	1.7	0	+1.2
1.19	1.97	0	+0.6	+1.1	0	+1.0	+1.6	0.4	+1.0	+2.0
		1.1	0	+0.6	1.6	0	+1.0	2.0	0	+1.4

Figure A-5

American Standard Force and Shrink Fits

Nominal Size Range Inches Over	To	Limits of Interference	Class FN 1 Standard Limits Hole	Shaft	Limits of Interference	Class FN 2 Standard Limits Hole	Shaft	Limits of Interference	Class FN 3 Standard Limits Hole	Shaft	Limits of Interference	Class FN 4 Standard Limits Hole	Shaft
0	0.12	0.05	+0.25	+0.5	0.2	+0.4	+0.85				0.3	+0.4	+0.95
		0.5	0	+0.3	0.85	0	+0.6				0.95	0	+0.7
0.12	0.24	0.1	+0.3	+0.6	0.2	+0.5	+1.0				0.4	+0.5	+1.2
		0.6	0	+0.4	1.0	0	+0.7				1.2	0	+0.9
0.24	0.40	0.1	+0.4	+0.75	0.4	+0.6	+1.4				0.6	+0.6	+1.6
		0.75	0	+0.5	1.4	0	+1.0				1.6	0	+1.2
0.40	0.56	0.1	+0.4	+0.8	0.5	+0.7	+1.6				0.7	+0.7	+1.8
		0.8	0	+0.5	1.6	0	+1.2				1.8	0	+1.4
0.56	0.71	0.2	+0.4	+0.9	0.5	+0.7	+1.6				0.7	+0.7	+1.8
		0.9	0	+0.6	1.6	0	+1.2				1.8	0	+1.4
0.71	0.95	0.2	+0.5	+1.1	0.6	+0.8	+1.9				0.8	+0.8	+2.1
		1.1	0	+0.7	1.9	0	+1.4				2.1	0	+1.6
0.95	1.19	0.3	+0.5	+1.2	0.6	+0.8	+1.9	0.8	+0.8	+2.1	1.0	+0.8	+2.1
		1.2	0	+0.8	1.9	0	+1.4	2.1	0	+1.6	2.3	0	+1.8
1.19	1.58	0.3	+0.6	+1.3	0.8	+1.0	+2.4	1.0	+1.0	+2.6	1.5	+1.0	+3.1
		1.3	0	+0.9	2.4	0	+1.8	2.6	0	+2.0	3.1	0	+2.5
1.58	1.97	0.4	+0.6	+1.4	0.8	+1.0	+2.4	1.2	+1.0	+2.8	1.8	+1.0	+3.4
		1.4	0	+1.0	2.4	0	+1.8	2.8	0	+2.2	3.4	0	+2.8

Figure A-6

Preferred Clearance Fits — Cylindrical Fits
(Hole Basis; ANSI B4.2)

Basic Size		Loose Running			Free Running			Close Running			Sliding			Locational Clear.		
		Hole H11	Shaft c11	Fit	Hole H9	Shaft d9	Fit	Hole H8	Shaft f7	Fit	Hole H7	Shaft g6	Fit	Hole H7	Shaft h6	Fit
4	Max	4.075	3.930	0.220	4.030	3.970	0.090	4.018	3.990	0.040	4.012	3.996	0.024	4.012	4.000	0.020
	Min	4.000	3.855	0.070	4.000	3.940	0.030	4.000	3.978	0.010	4.000	3.988	0.004	4.000	3.992	0.000
5	Max	5.075	4.930	0.220	5.030	4.970	0.090	5.018	4.990	0.040	5.012	4.996	0.024	5.012	5.000	0.020
	Min	5.000	4.855	0.070	5.000	4.940	0.030	5.000	4.978	0.010	5.000	4.988	0.004	5.000	4.992	0.000
6	Max	6.075	5.930	0.220	6.030	5.970	0.090	6.018	5.990	0.040	6.012	5.996	0.024	6.012	6.000	0.020
	Min	6.000	5.885	0.070	6.000	5.940	0.030	6.000	5.978	0.010	6.000	5.988	0.004	6.000	5.992	0.000
8	Max	8.090	7.920	0.260	8.036	7.960	0.112	8.022	7.987	0.050	8.015	7.995	0.029	8.015	8.000	0.024
	Min	8.000	7.830	0.080	8.000	7.924	0.040	8.000	7.972	0.013	8.000	7.986	0.005	8.000	7.991	0.000
10	Max	10.090	9.920	0.026	10.036	9.960	0.112	10.022	9.987	0.050	10.015	9.995	0.029	10.015	10.000	0.024
	Min	10.000	9.830	0.080	10.000	9.924	0.040	10.000	9.972	0.013	10.000	9.986	0.005	10.000	9.991	0.000
12	Max	12.112	11.905	0.315	12.043	11.950	0.136	12.027	11.984	0.061	12.018	11.994	0.035	12.018	12.000	0.029
	Min	12.000	11.795	0.095	12.000	11.907	0.050	12.000	11.966	0.016	12.000	11.983	0.006	12.000	11.989	0.000
16	Max	16.110	15.905	0.315	16.043	15.950	0.136	16.027	15.984	0.061	16.018	15.994	0.035	16.018	16.000	0.029
	Min	16.000	15.795	0.095	16.000	15.907	0.050	16.000	15.966	0.016	16.000	19.983	0.006	16.000	15.989	0.000
20	Max	20.130	19.890	0.370	20.052	19.935	0.169	20.033	19.980	0.074	20.021	19.993	0.041	20.021	20.000	0.034
	Min	20.000	19.760	0.110	20.000	19.883	0.065	20.000	19.959	0.020	20.000	19.980	0.007	20.000	19.987	0.000
25	Max	25.130	24.890	0.370	25.052	24.935	0.169	25.033	24.980	0.074	25.021	24.993	0.041	25.021	25.000	0.034
	Min	25.000	24.760	0.110	25.000	24.883	0.065	25.000	24.959	0.020	25.000	24.980	0.007	25.000	24.987	0.000
30	Max	30.130	29.890	0.370	30.052	29.935	0.169	30.033	29.980	0.074	30.021	29.993	0.041	30.021	30.000	0.034
	Min	30.000	29.760	0.110	30.000	29.883	0.065	30.000	29.959	0.020	30.000	29.980	0.007	30.000	29.987	0.000

Figure A-7

Preferred Transition and Interference Fits — Cylindrical Fits
(Hole Basis; ANSI B4.2)

Basic Size		Locational Trans.			Locational Trans.			Locational Inter.			Medium Drive			Force		
		Hole H7	Shaft k6	Fit	Hole H7	Shaft n6	Fit	Hole H7	Shaft p6	Fit	Hole H7	Shaft s6	Fit	Hole H7	Shaft u6	Fit
4	Max	4.012	4.009	0.011	4.012	4.016	0.004	4.012	4.020	0.000	4.012	4.027	-0.007	4.012	4.031	-0.011
	Min	4.000	4.001	-0.009	4.000	4.008	-0.016	4.000	4.012	-0.020	4.000	4.019	-0.027	4.000	4.023	-0.031
5	Max	5.012	5.009	0.011	5.012	5.016	0.004	5.012	5.020	0.000	5.012	5.027	-0.007	5.012	5.031	-0.011
	Min	5.000	5.001	-0.009	5.000	5.008	-0.016	5.000	5.012	-0.020	5.000	5.019	-0.027	5.000	5.023	-0.031
6	Max	6.012	6.009	0.011	6.012	6.016	0.004	6.012	6.020	0.000	6.012	6.027	-0.007	6.012	6.031	-0.011
	Min	6.000	6.001	-0.009	6.000	6.008	-0.016	6.000	6.012	-0.020	6.000	6.019	-0.027	6.000	6.023	-0.031
8	Max	8.015	8.010	0.014	8.015	8.019	0.005	8.015	8.024	0.000	8.015	8.032	-0.008	8.015	8.037	-0.013
	Min	8.000	8.001	-0.010	8.000	8.010	-0.019	8.000	8.015	-0.024	8.000	8.023	-0.032	8.000	8.028	-0.037
10	Max	10.015	10.010	0.014	10.015	10.019	0.005	10.015	10.024	0.000	10.015	10.032	-0.008	10.015	10.037	-0.013
	Min	10.000	10.001	-0.010	10.000	10.010	-0.019	10.000	10.015	-0.024	10.000	10.023	-0.032	10.000	10.028	-0.037
12	Max	12.018	12.012	0.017	12.018	12.023	0.006	12.018	12.029	0.000	12.018	12.039	-0.010	12.018	12.044	-0.015
	Min	12.000	12.001	-0.012	12.000	12.012	-0.023	12.000	12.018	-0.029	12.000	12.028	-0.039	12.000	12.033	-0.044
16	Max	16.018	16.012	0.017	16.018	16.023	0.006	16.018	16.029	0.000	16.018	16.039	-0.010	16.018	16.044	-0.015
	Min	16.000	16.001	-0.012	16.000	16.012	-0.023	16.000	16.018	-0.029	16.000	16.028	-0.039	16.000	16.033	-0.044
20	Max	20.021	20.015	0.019	20.021	20.028	0.006	20.021	20.035	-0.001	20.021	20.048	-0.014	20.021	20.054	-0.020
	Min	20.000	20.002	-0.015	20.000	20.015	-0.028	20.000	20.022	-0.035	20.000	20.035	-0.048	20.000	20.041	-0.054
25	Max	25.021	25.015	0.019	25.021	25.028	0.006	25.021	25.035	-0.001	25.021	25.048	-0.014	25.021	25.061	-0.027
	Min	25.000	25.002	-0.015	25.000	25.015	-0.028	25.000	25.022	-0.035	25.000	25.035	-0.048	25.000	25.048	-0.061
30	Max	30.021	30.015	0.019	30.021	30.028	0.006	30.021	30.035	-0.001	30.021	30.048	-0.014	30.021	30.061	-0.027
	Min	30.000	30.002	-0.015	30.000	30.015	-0.028	30.000	30.022	-0.035	30.000	30.035	-0.048	30.000	30.048	-0.061

Figure A-8

Preferred Clearance Fits — Cylindrical Fits
(Shaft Basis; ANSI B4.2)

Basic Size		Loose Running Hole C11	Loose Running Shaft h11	Loose Running Fit	Free Running Hole D9	Free Running Shaft h9	Free Running Fit	Close Running Hole F8	Close Running Shaft h7	Close Running Fit	Sliding Hole G7	Sliding Shaft h6	Sliding Fit	Locational Clear. Hole H7	Locational Clear. Shaft h6	Locational Clear. Fit
4	Max	4.145	4.000	0.220	4.060	4.000	0.090	4.028	4.000	0.040	4.016	4.000	0.024	4.012	4.000	0.020
	Min	4.070	3.925	0.070	4.030	3.970	0.030	4.010	3.988	0.010	4.004	3.992	0.004	4.000	3.992	0.000
5	Max	5.145	5.000	0.220	5.060	5.000	0.090	5.028	5.000	0.040	5.016	5.000	0.024	5.012	5.000	0.020
	Min	5.070	4.925	0.070	5.030	4.970	0.030	5.010	4.988	0.010	5.004	4.992	0.004	5.000	4.992	0.000
6	Max	6.145	6.000	0.220	6.060	6.000	0.090	6.028	6.000	0.040	6.016	6.000	0.024	6.012	6.000	0.020
	Min	6.070	5.925	0.070	6.030	5.970	0.030	6.010	5.988	0.010	6.004	5.992	0.004	6.000	5.992	0.000
8	Max	8.170	8.000	0.260	8.076	8.000	0.112	8.035	8.000	0.050	8.020	8.000	0.029	8.015	8.000	0.024
	Min	8.080	7.910	0.080	8.040	7.964	0.040	8.013	7.985	0.013	8.005	7.991	0.005	8.000	7.991	0.000
10	Max	10.170	10.000	0.260	10.076	10.000	0.112	10.035	10.000	0.050	10.020	10.000	0.029	10.015	10.000	0.024
	Min	10.080	9.910	0.080	10.040	9.964	0.040	10.013	9.985	0.013	10.005	9.991	0.005	10.000	9.991	0.000
12	Max	12.205	12.000	0.315	12.093	12.000	0.136	12.043	12.000	0.061	12.024	12.000	0.035	12.018	12.000	0.029
	Min	12.095	11.890	0.095	12.050	11.957	0.050	12.016	11.982	0.016	12.006	11.989	0.006	12.000	11.989	0.000
16	Max	16.205	16.000	0.315	16.093	16.000	0.136	16.043	16.000	0.061	16.024	16.000	0.035	16.018	16.000	0.029
	Min	16.095	15.890	0.095	16.050	15.957	0.050	16.016	15.982	0.016	06.006	15.989	0.006	16.000	15.989	0.000
20	Max	20.240	20.000	0.370	20.117	20.000	0.169	20.053	20.000	0.074	20.028	20.000	0.041	20.021	20.000	0.034
	Min	20.110	19.870	0.110	20.065	19.948	0.065	20.020	19.979	0.020	20.007	19.987	0.007	20.000	19.987	0.000
25	Max	25.240	25.000	0.370	25.117	25.000	0.169	25.053	25.000	0.074	25.028	25.000	0.041	25.021	25.000	0.034
	Min	25.110	24.870	0.110	25.065	24.948	0.065	25.020	24.979	0.020	25.007	24.987	0.007	25.000	24.987	0.000
30	Max	30.240	30.000	0.370	30.117	30.000	0.169	30.053	30.000	0.074	30.028	30.000	0.041	30.021	30.000	0.034
	Min	30.110	29.870	0.110	30.065	29.948	0.065	30.020	29.979	0.020	30.007	29.987	0.007	30.000	29.987	0.000

Figure A-9

Preferred Transition and Interference Fits — Cylindrical Fits
(Shaft Basis; ANSI B4.2)

Basic Size		Locational Trans. Hole K7	Locational Trans. Shaft h6	Locational Trans. Fit	Locational Trans. Hole N7	Locational Trans. Shaft h6	Locational Trans. Fit	Locational Inter. Hole F7	Locational Inter. Shaft h6	Locational Inter. Fit	Medium Drive Hole S7	Medium Drive Shaft h6	Medium Drive Fit	Force Hole U7	Force Shaft h6	Force Fit
4	Max	4.003	4.000	0.011	3.996	4.000	0.004	3.992	4.000	0.000	3.985	4.000	-0.007	3.981	4.000	-0.011
	Min	3.991	3.992	-0.009	3.984	3.992	-0.016	3.980	3.992	-0.020	3.973	3.992	-0.027	3.969	3.992	-0.031
5	Max	5.003	5.000	0.011	4.996	5.000	0.004	4.992	5.000	0.000	4.985	5.000	-0.007	4.981	5.000	-0.011
	Min	4.991	4.992	-0.009	4.984	4.992	-0.016	4.980	4.992	-0.020	4.973	4.992	-0.027	4.969	4.992	-0.031
6	Max	6.003	6.000	0.011	5.996	6.000	0.004	5.992	6.000	0.000	5.985	6.000	-0.007	5.981	6.000	-0.011
	Min	5.991	5.991	-0.009	5.984	5.992	-0.016	5.980	5.992	-0.020	5.973	5.992	-0.027	5.969	5.992	-0.031
8	Max	8.005	8.000	0.014	7.996	8.000	0.005	7.991	8.000	0.000	7.983	8.000	-0.008	7.978	8.000	-0.013
	Min	7.990	7.991	-0.010	7.981	7.991	-0.019	7.976	7.991	-0.024	7.968	7.991	-0.032	7.963	7.991	-0.037
10	Max	10.005	10.000	0.014	9.996	10.000	0.005	9.991	10.000	0.000	9.983	10.000	-0.008	9.978	10.000	-0.013
	Min	9.990	9.991	-0.010	9.981	9.991	-0.019	9.976	9.991	-0.024	9.968	9.991	-0.032	9.963	9.991	-0.037
12	Max	12.006	12.000	0.017	11.995	12.000	0.006	11.989	12.000	0.000	11.979	12.000	-0.010	11.974	12.000	-0.015
	Min	11.988	11.989	-0.012	11.977	11.989	-0.023	11.971	11.989	-0.029	11.961	11.989	-0.039	11.956	11.989	-0.044
16	Max	16.006	16.000	0.017	15.995	16.000	0.006	15.989	16.000	0.000	15.979	16.000	-0.010	15.974	16.000	-0.015
	Min	15.988	15.989	-0.012	15.977	15.989	-0.023	15.971	15.989	-0.029	15.961	15.989	-0.039	15.956	15.989	-0.044
20	Max	20.006	20.000	0.019	19.993	20.000	0.006	19.986	20.000	-0.001	19.973	20.000	-0.014	19.967	20.000	-0.020
	Min	19.985	19.987	-0.015	19.972	19.987	-0.028	19.965	19.987	-0.035	19.952	19.987	-0.048	19.946	19.987	-0.054
25	Max	25.006	25.000	0.019	24.993	25.000	0.006	24.986	25.000	-0.001	24.973	25.000	-0.014	24.960	25.000	-0.027
	Min	24.985	24.987	-0.015	24.972	24.987	-0.028	24.965	24.987	-0.035	24.952	24.987	-0.048	24.939	24.987	-0.061
30	Max	30.006	30.000	0.019	29.993	30.000	0.006	29.986	30.000	-0.001	29.973	30.000	-0.014	29.960	30.000	-0.027
	Min	29.985	29.987	-0.015	29.972	29.987	-0.028	29.987	29.987	-0.035	29.952	29.987	-0.048	29.939	29.987	-0.061

Figure A-10

American National Standard Type A Plain Washers
(ANSI B18.22.1-1965, R1975)

Nominal Washer Size		Series	Inside Diameter			Outside Diameter			Thickness		
			Basic	Tolerance		Basic	Tolerance		Basic	Max.	Min.
				Plus	Minus		Plus	Minus			
#6	.138		.156	.008	.005	.375	.015	.005	.049	.065	.036
#8	.164		.188	.008	.005	.438	.015	.005	.049	.065	.036
#10	.190		.219	.008	.005	.500	.015	.005	.049	.065	.036
1/4	.250	N	.281	.015	.005	.625	.015	.005	.065	.080	.051
1/4	.250	W	.312	.015	.005	.734	.015	.007	.065	.080	.051
5/16	.312	N	.344	.015	.005	.688	.015	.007	.065	.080	.051
5/16	.312	W	.375	.015	.005	.875	.030	.007	.083	.104	.064
3/8	.375	N	.406	.015	.005	.812	.015	.007	.065	.080	.051
3/8	.375	W	.438	.015	.005	1.000	.030	.007	.083	.104	.064
7/16	.438	N	.469	.015	.005	.922	.015	.007	.065	.080	.051
7/16	.438	W	.500	.015	.005	1.250	.030	.007	.083	.104	.064
1/2	.500	N	.531	.015	.005	1.062	.030	.007	.095	.121	.074
1/2	.500	W	.562	.015	.005	1.375	.030	.007	.109	.132	.086
9/16	.562	N	.594	.015	.005	1.156	.030	.007	.095	.121	.074
9/16	.562	W	.625	.015	.005	1.469	.030	.007	.109	.132	.086
5/8	.625	N	.656	.030	.007	1.312	.030	.007	.095	.121	.074
5/8	.625	W	.688	.030	.007	1.750	.030	.007	.134	.160	.108
3/4	.750	N	.812	.030	.007	1.469	.030	.007	.134	.160	.108
3/4	.750	W	.812	.030	.007	2.000	.030	.007	.148	.177	.122
7/8	.875	N	.938	.030	.007	1.750	.030	.007	.134	.160	.108
7/8	.875	W	.938	.030	.007	2.250	.030	.007	.165	.192	.136
1	1.000	N	1.062	.030	.007	2.000	.030	.007	.134	.160	.108
1	1.000	W	1.062	.030	.007	2.500	.030	.007	.165	.192	.136
1 1/8	1.125	N	1.250	.030	.007	2.250	.030	.007	.134	.160	.108
1 1/8	1.125	W	1.250	.030	.007	2.750	.030	.007	.165	.192	.136
1 1/4	1.250	N	1.375	.030	.007	2.500	.030	.007	.165	.192	.136
1 1/4	1.250	W	1.375	.030	.007	3.000	.030	.007	.165	.192	.136
1 3/8	1.375	N	1.500	.030	.007	2.750	.030	.007	.165	.192	.136
1 3/8	1.375	W	1.500	.045	.010	3.250	.045	.010	.180	.213	.153
1 1/2	1.500	N	1.625	.030	.007	3.000	.030	.007	.165	.192	.136
1 1/2	1.500	W	1.625	.045	.010	3.500	.045	.010	.180	.213	.153
1 5/8	1.625		1.750	.045	.010	3.750	.045	.010	.180	.213	.153
1 3/4	1.750		1.875	.045	.010	4.000	.045	.010	.180	.213	.153
1 7/8	1.875		2.000	.045	.010	4.250	.045	.010	.180	.213	.153
2	2.000		2.125	.045	.010	4.500	.045	.010	.180	.213	.153
2 1/4	2.250		2.375	.045	.010	4.750	.045	.010	.220	.248	.193
2 1/2	2.500		2.625	.045	.010	5.000	.045	.010	.238	.280	.210
2 3/4	2.750		2.875	.065	.010	5.250	.065	.010	.259	.310	.228
3	3.000		3.125	.065	.010	5.500	.065	.010	.284	.327	.249

Figure A-11

American National Standard Helical Spring Lock Washers (ANSI B18.21.1-1972)

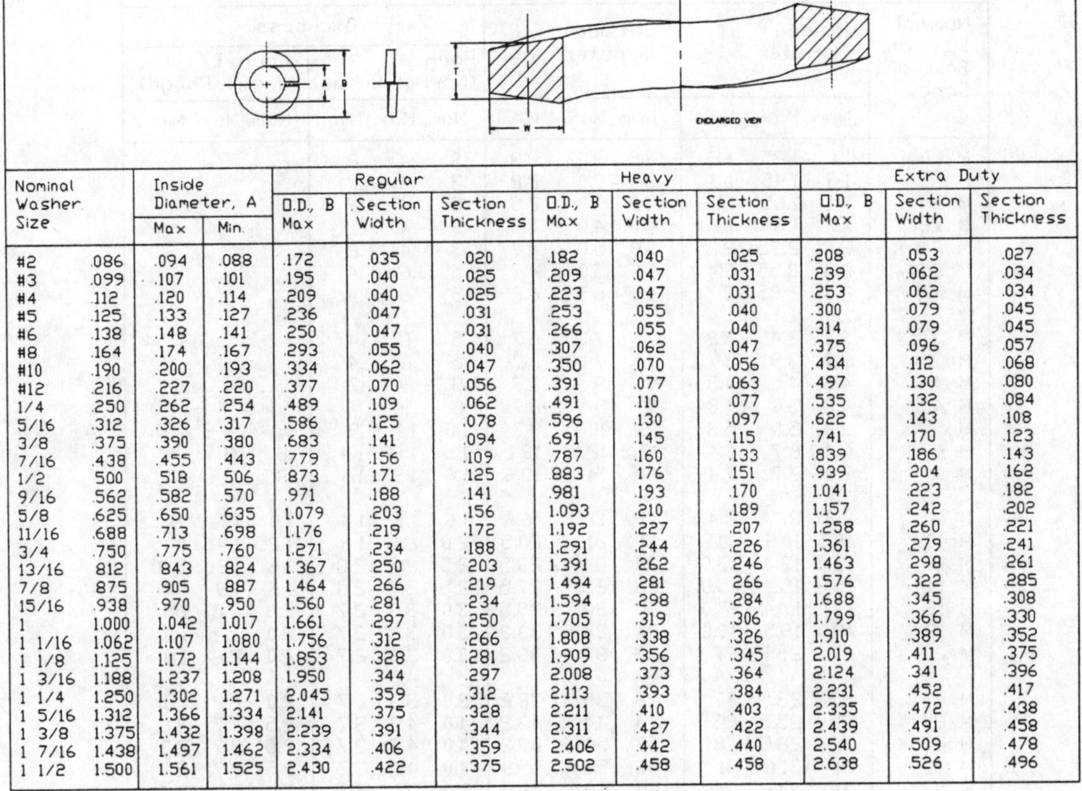

Nominal Washer Size		Inside Diameter, A		Regular			Heavy			Extra Duty		
		Max	Min.	O.D., B Max	Section Width	Section Thickness	O.D., B Max	Section Width	Section Thickness	O.D., B Max	Section Width	Section Thickness
#2	.086	.094	.088	.172	.035	.020	.182	.040	.025	.208	.053	.027
#3	.099	.107	.101	.195	.040	.025	.209	.047	.031	.239	.062	.034
#4	.112	.120	.114	.209	.040	.025	.223	.047	.031	.253	.062	.034
#5	.125	.133	.127	.236	.047	.031	.253	.055	.040	.300	.079	.045
#6	.138	.148	.141	.250	.047	.031	.266	.055	.040	.314	.079	.045
#8	.164	.174	.167	.293	.055	.040	.307	.062	.047	.375	.096	.057
#10	.190	.200	.193	.334	.062	.047	.350	.070	.056	.434	.112	.068
#12	.216	.227	.220	.377	.070	.056	.391	.077	.063	.497	.130	.080
1/4	.250	.262	.254	.489	.109	.062	.491	.110	.077	.535	.132	.084
5/16	.312	.326	.317	.586	.125	.078	.596	.130	.097	.622	.143	.108
3/8	.375	.390	.380	.683	.141	.094	.691	.145	.115	.741	.170	.123
7/16	.438	.455	.443	.779	.156	.109	.787	.160	.133	.839	.186	.143
1/2	500	518	506	873	171	.125	883	176	.151	.939	204	.162
9/16	.562	.582	.570	.971	.188	.141	.981	.193	.170	1.041	.223	.182
5/8	.625	.650	.635	1.079	.203	.156	1.093	.210	.189	1.157	.242	.202
11/16	.688	.713	.698	1.176	.219	.172	1.192	.227	.207	1.258	.260	.221
3/4	.750	.775	.760	1.271	.234	.188	1.291	.244	.226	1.361	.279	.241
13/16	812	843	824	1.367	.250	203	1.391	262	246	1.463	298	.261
7/8	875	.905	887	1.464	266	.219	1.494	281	266	1.576	.322	.285
15/16	.938	.970	.950	1.560	.281	.234	1.594	.298	.284	1.688	.345	.308
1	1.000	1.042	1.017	1.661	.297	.250	1.705	.319	.306	1.799	.366	.330
1 1/16	1.062	1.107	1.080	1.756	.312	.266	1.808	.338	.326	1.910	.389	.352
1 1/8	1.125	1.172	1.144	1.853	.328	.281	1.909	.356	.345	2.019	.411	.375
1 3/16	1.188	1.237	1.208	1.950	.344	.297	2.008	.373	.364	2.124	.341	.396
1 1/4	1.250	1.302	1.271	2.045	.359	.312	2.113	.393	.384	2.231	.452	.417
1 5/16	1.312	1.366	1.334	2.141	.375	.328	2.211	.410	.403	2.335	.472	.438
1 3/8	1.375	1.432	1.398	2.239	.391	.344	2.311	.427	.422	2.439	.491	.458
1 7/16	1.438	1.497	1.462	2.334	.406	.359	2.406	.442	.440	2.540	.509	.478
1 1/2	1.500	1.561	1.525	2.430	.422	.375	2.502	.458	.458	2.638	.526	.496

Figure A-12

American National Standard Internal-External Tooth Lock Washers (ANSI B18.21.1-1972)

Size	A Inside Diameter		B Outside Diameter		C Thickness		Size	A Inside Diameter		B Outside Diameter		C Thickness	
	Max.	Min.	Max.	Min.	Max.	Min.		Max.	Min.	Max.	Min.	Max.	Min.
#4	.123	.115	.475	.460	.021	.021	5/16	.332	.320	.900	.865	.040	.032
	.123	.115	.510	.495	.021	.017		.332	.320	.985	.965	.045	.037
			.610	.580				.332	.320	1.070	1.045	.050	.042
										1.155	1.130		
#6	.150	.141	.510	.495	.028	.023	3/8	.398	.384	.985	.965	.045	.037
			.610	.580				.398	.384	1.070	1.045	.050	.042
			.690	.670						1.155	1.130		
										1.260	1.220		
#8	.176	.168	.610	.580	.034	.028	7/16	.464	.448	1.070	1.045	.050	.042
			.690	.670						1.155	1.130		
			.760	.740				.464	.448	1.260	1.220	.055	.047
										1.315	1.290		
#10	.204	.195	.610	.580	.034	.028	1/2	.530	.512	1.260	1.220	.055	.047
	.204	.195	.690	.670	.040	.032				1.315	1.290		
			.760	.740				.530	.512	1.410	1.380	.060	.052
			.900	.880				.530	.512	1.620	1.590	.067	.059
#12	.231	.221	.690	.670	.040	.032	9/16	.596	.576	1.315	1.290	.055	.047
	.231	.221	.760	.725				.596	.576	1.430	1.380	.060	.052
			.900	.880				.596	.576	1.620	1.590	.067	.059
			.985	.965	.045	.037				1.830	1.797		
1/4	.267	.256	.760	.725	.040	.032	5/8	.663	.640	1.410	1.380	.060	.052
	.267	.256	.900	.880				.663	.640	1.620	1.590	.067	.059
			.985	.965	.045	.037				1.830	1.797		
			1.070	1.045						1.975	1.935		

Figure A-13

British Standard Bright Metal Washers - Metric Series (BS 4320:1968)

Nominal Size of Bolt or Screw	Inside Diameter			Outside Diameter			Thickness: Form A (Normal Range)			Thickness: Form B (Light Range)		
NORMAL DIAMETER SIZES	Nom.	Max.	Min.	Nom.	Max.	Min.	Nom.	Max.	Min.	Nom.	Max.	Min.
M 1.0	1.1	1.25	1.1	2.5	2.5	2.3	.3	.4	.2			
M 1.2	1.3	1.45	1.3	3.0	3.0	2.8	.3	.4	.2			
M 1.4	1.5	1.65	1.5	3.0	3.0	2.8	.3	.4	.2			
M 1.6	1.7	1.85	1.7	4.0	4.0	3.7	.3	.4	.2			
M 2.0	2.2	2.35	2.2	5.0	5.0	4.7	.3	.4	.2			
M 2.2	2.4	2.55	2.4	5.0	5.0	4.7	.5	.6	.4			
M 2.5	2.7	2.85	2.7	6.5	6.5	6.2	.5	.6	.4			
M 3	3.2	3.4	3.2	7	7	6.7	.5	.6	.4			
M 3.5	3.7	3.9	3.7	7	7	6.7	.5	.6	.4			
M 4	4.3	4.5	4.3	9	9	8.7	.8	.9	.7			
M 4.5	4.8	5.0	4.8	9	9	8.7	.8	.9	.7			
M 5	5.3	5.5	5.3	10	10	9.7	1.0	1.1	.9			
M 6	6.4	6.7	6.4	12.5	12.5	12.1	1.6	1.8	1.4	.8	.9	.7
M 7	7.4	7.7	7.4	14	14	13.6	1.6	1.8	1.4	.8	.9	.7
M 8	8.4	8.7	8.4	17	17	16.6	1.6	1.8	1.4	1.0	1.1	.9
M 10	10.5	10.9	10.5	21	21	20.5	2.0	2.2	1.8	1.25	1.45	1.05
M 12	13.0	13.4	13.0	24	24	23.5	2.5	2.7	2.3	1.6	1.80	1.40
M 14	15.0	15.4	15.0	28	28	27.5	2.5	2.7	2.3	1.6	1.8	1.4
M 16	17.0	17.4	17.0	30	30	29.5	3.0	3.3	2.7	2.0	2.2	1.8
M 18	19.0	19.5	19.0	34	34	33.2	3.0	3.3	2.7	2.0	2.2	1.8
M 20	21	21.5	21	37	37	36.2	3.0	3.3	2.7	2.0	2.2	1.8
M 22	23	23.5	23	39	39	38.2	3.0	3.3	2.7	2.0	2.2	1.8
M 24	25	25.5	25	44	44	43.2	4.0	4.3	3.7	2.5	2.7	2.3
M 27	28	28.5	28	50	50	49.2	4.0	4.3	3.7	2.5	2.7	2.3
M 30	31	31.6	31	56	56	55.0	4.0	4.3	3.7	2.5	2.7	2.3
M 33	34	34.6	34	60	60	59.0	5.0	5.6	4.4	3.0	3.3	2.7
M 36	37	37..6	37	66	66	65.0	5.0	5.6	4.4	3.0	3.3	2.7
M 39	40	40.6	40	72	72	71.0	6.0	6.6	5.4	3.0	3.3	2.7

Figure A-14

American National Standard and Unified Standard Square Bolts (ANSI B18.2.1-1972)

SQUARE BOLTS: Nominal Size or Basic Product Diameter		Body Diam., E	Width Across Flats, F			Width Across Corners, G		Height, H			Radius of Fillet, R
		Max.	Basic	Max.	Min.	Max.	Min.	Basic	Max.	Min.	Max.
1/4	.2500	.260	3/8	.375	.362	.530	.498	11/64	.188	.156	.03
5/16	.3125	.324	1/2	.500	.484	.707	.665	13/64	.220	.186	.03
3/8	.3750	.388	9/16	.562	.544	.795	.747	1/4	.268	.232	.03
7/16	.4375	.452	5/8	.625	.603	.884	.828	19/64	.316	.278	.03
1/2	.5000	.515	3/4	.750	.725	1.061	.995	21/64	.348	.308	.03
5/8	.6250	.642	15/16	.938	.906	1.326	1.244	37/64	.444	.400	.06
3/4	.7500	.768	1 1/8	1.125	1.088	1.591	1.494	1/2	.524	.476	.06
7/8	.8750	.895	1 5/16	1.312	1.269	1.856	1.742	19/32	.620	.568	.06
1	1.0000	1.022	1 1/2	1.500	1.450	2.121	1.991	21/32	.684	.628	.09
1 1/8	1.1250	1.149	1 11/16	1.688	1.631	2.386	2.239	3/4	.780	.720	.09
1 1/4	1.2500	1.277	1 7/8	1.875	1.812	2.652	2.489	27/32	.876	.812	.09
1 3/8	1.3750	1.404	2 1/16	2.062	1.994	2.917	2.738	29/32	.940	.872	.09
1 1/2	1.5000	1.531	2 1/4	2.250	2.175	3.182	2.986	1	1.036	.964	.09

Figure A-15

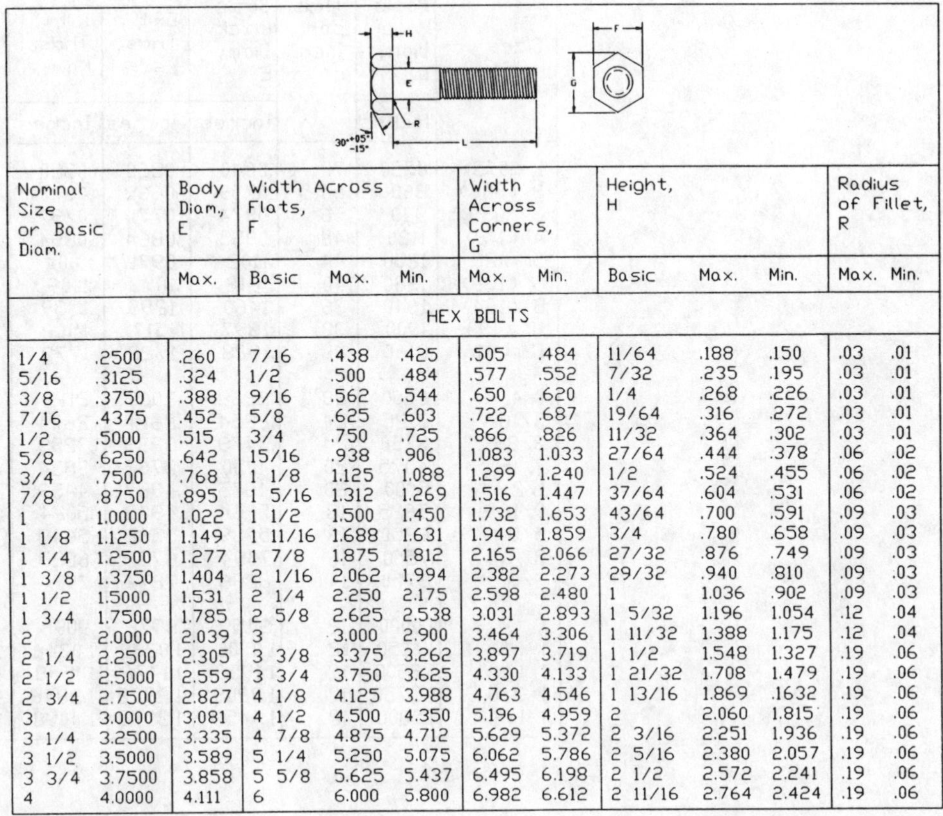

American National Standard and Unified Standard Hex Head Screws
(ANSI B18.2.1-1972)

Nominal Size or Basic Diam.		Body Diam, E	Width Across Flats, F			Width Across Corners, G		Height, H			Radius of Fillet, R	
		Max.	Basic	Max.	Min.	Max.	Min.	Basic	Max.	Min.	Max.	Min.
HEX BOLTS												
1/4	.2500	.260	7/16	.438	.425	.505	.484	11/64	.188	.150	.03	.01
5/16	.3125	.324	1/2	.500	.484	.577	.552	7/32	.235	.195	.03	.01
3/8	.3750	.388	9/16	.562	.544	.650	.620	1/4	.268	.226	.03	.01
7/16	.4375	.452	5/8	.625	.603	.722	.687	19/64	.316	.272	.03	.01
1/2	.5000	.515	3/4	.750	.725	.866	.826	11/32	.364	.302	.03	.01
5/8	.6250	.642	15/16	.938	.906	1.083	1.033	27/64	.444	.378	.06	.02
3/4	.7500	.768	1 1/8	1.125	1.088	1.299	1.240	1/2	.524	.455	.06	.02
7/8	.8750	.895	1 5/16	1.312	1.269	1.516	1.447	37/64	.604	.531	.06	.02
1	1.0000	1.022	1 1/2	1.500	1.450	1.732	1.653	43/64	.700	.591	.09	.03
1 1/8	1.1250	1.149	1 11/16	1.688	1.631	1.949	1.859	3/4	.780	.658	.09	.03
1 1/4	1.2500	1.277	1 7/8	1.875	1.812	2.165	2.066	27/32	.876	.749	.09	.03
1 3/8	1.3750	1.404	2 1/16	2.062	1.994	2.382	2.273	29/32	.940	.810	.09	.03
1 1/2	1.5000	1.531	2 1/4	2.250	2.175	2.598	2.480	1	1.036	.902	.09	.03
1 3/4	1.7500	1.785	2 5/8	2.625	2.538	3.031	2.893	1 5/32	1.196	1.054	.12	.04
2	2.0000	2.039	3	3.000	2.900	3.464	3.306	1 11/32	1.388	1.175	.12	.04
2 1/4	2.2500	2.305	3 3/8	3.375	3.262	3.897	3.719	1 1/2	1.548	1.327	.19	.06
2 1/2	2.5000	2.559	3 3/4	3.750	3.625	4.330	4.133	1 21/32	1.708	1.479	.19	.06
2 3/4	2.7500	2.827	4 1/8	4.125	3.988	4.763	4.546	1 13/16	1.869	.1632	.19	.06
3	3.0000	3.081	4 1/2	4.500	4.350	5.196	4.959	2	2.060	1.815	.19	.06
3 1/4	3.2500	3.335	4 7/8	4.875	4.712	5.629	5.372	2 3/16	2.251	1.936	.19	.06
3 1/2	3.5000	3.589	5 1/4	5.250	5.075	6.062	5.786	2 5/16	2.380	2.057	.19	.06
3 3/4	3.7500	3.858	5 5/8	5.625	5.437	6.495	6.198	2 1/2	2.572	2.241	.19	.06
4	4.0000	4.111	6	6.000	5.800	6.982	6.612	2 11/16	2.764	2.424	.19	.06

Figure A-16

Coarse-Thread Series, UNC, UNRC, and NC — Basic Dimensions

Sizes	Basic Major Diam., D	Thds. per Inch, n	Basic Pitch Diam., E	Minor Diameter		Lead Angle at Basic P.D.		Area of Minor Diam. at D-2h	Tensile Stress Area
				Ext. Thds., Ks	Int. Thds., Kn				
	Inches		Inches	Inches	Inches	Deg.	Min.	Sq. In.	Sq. In.
1 (.073)	.0730	64	.0629	.0538	.0561	4	31	.00218	.00263
2 (.086)	.0860	56	.0744	.0641	.0667	4	22	.00310	.00370
3 (.099)	.0990	48	.0855	.0734	.0764	4	26	.00406	.00487
4 (.112)	.1120	40	.0958	.0813	.0849	4	45	.00496	.00604
5 (.125)	.1250	40	.1088	.0943	.0979	4	11	.00672	.00796
6 (.138)	.1380	32	.1177	.0997	.1042	4	50	.00745	.00909
8 (.164)	1.640	32	.1437	.1257	.1302	3	58	.01196	.0140
10 (.190)	.1900	24	.1629	.1389	.1449	4	39	.01450	.0175
12 (.216)	.2160	24	.1889	.1649	.1709	4	1	.0206	.0242
1/4	.2500	20	.2175	.1887	.1959	4	11	.0269	.0318
5/16	.3125	18	.2764	.2443	.2524	3	40	.0454	.0524
3/8	.3750	16	.3344	.2983	.3073	3	24	.0678	.0775
7/16	.4375	14	.3911	.3499	.3602	3	20	.0933	.1063
1/2	.5000	13	.4500	.4056	.4167	3	7	.1257	.1419
9/16	.5625	12	.5084	.4603	.4723	2	59	.162	.182
5/8	.6250	11	.5660	.5135	.5266	2	56	.202	.226
3/4	.7500	10	.6850	.6273	.6417	2	40	.302	.334
7/8	.8750	9	.8028	.7387	.7547	2	31	.419	.462
1	1.0000	8	.9188	.8466	.8647	2	29	.551	.606
1 1/8	1.1250	7	1.032	.9497	.9704	2	31	.693	.763
1 1/4	1.2500	7	1.572	1.0747	1.0954	2	15	.890	.969
1 3/8	1.3750	6	1.2667	1.1705	1.1946	2	24	1.054	1.155
1 1/2	1.5000	6	1.3917	1.2955	1.3196	2	11	1.294	1.405

Figure A-17

Fine-Thread Series, UNC, UNRC, and NC — Basic Dimensions

Sizes	Basic Major Diam., D	Thds. per Inch, n	Basic Pitch Diam., E	Minor Diameter		Lead Angle at Basic P.D.		Area of Minor Diam. at D-2h	Tensile Stress Area
				Ext. Thds., Ks	Int. Thds., Kn				
	Inches		Inches	Inches	Inches	Deg.	Min.	Sq. In.	Sq. In.
1 (.073)	.0730	72	.0640	.0560	.0580	3	57	.00237	.00278
2 (.086)	.860	64	.0759	.0668	.0691	3	45	.00339	.00394
3 (.099)	.990	56	.0874	.0771	.0797	3	43	.00451	.00523
4 (.112)	.1120	48	.0985	.0864	.0894	3	51	.00566	.00661
5 (.125)	.1250	44	.1102	.0971	.1004	3	45	.00716	.00830
6 (.138)	.1380	40	.1218	.1073	.1109	3	44	.00874	.01015
8 (.164)	.1640	36	.1460	.1299	.1339	3	28	.01285	.01474
10 (.190)	.1900	32	.1697	.1517	.1562	3	21	.0175	.0200
12 (.216)	.2160	28	.1928	.1722	.1773	3	22	.0226	.0258
1/4	.2500	28	.2268	.2062	.2113	2	52	.0326	.0364
5/16	.3125	24	.2854	.2614	.2674	2	40	.0524	.0580
3/8	.3750	24	.3479	.3239	.3299	2	11	.0809	.0878
7/16	.4375	20	.4050	.3762	.3834	2	15	.1090	.1187
1/2	.5000	20	.4675	.4387	.4459	1	57	.1486	.1599
9/16	.5625	18	.5264	.4943	.5024	1	55	.189	.203
5/8	.6250	18	.5889	.5568	.5649	1	43	.240	.256
3/4	.7500	16	.7094	.6733	.6823	1	36	.351	.373
7/8	.8750	14	.8286	.7874	.7977	1	34	.480	.509
1	1.0000	12	.9459	.8978	.9098	1	36	.625	.663
1 1/8	1.1250	12	1.0709	1.0228	1.0348	1	25	.812	.856
1 1/4	1.2500	12	1.1959	1.1478	1.1598	1	16	1.024	1.073
1 3/8	1.3750	12	1.3209	1.2728	1.2848	1	9	1.260	1.315
1 1/2	1.5000	12	1.4459	1.3978	1.4098	1	3	1.521	1.581

Figure A-18

American National Standard General-Purpose Acme Screw Thread Form—Basic Dimensions (ANSI B1.5-1977)

Thds. per Inch	Pitch	Height of Thread (Basic)	Total Height of Thread	Thread Thickness (Basic)	Width of Flat	
					Crest of Internal Thread (Basic)	Root of Internal Thread
16	.06250	.03125	.0362	.03125	.0232	.0206
14	.07143	.03571	.0407	.03571	.0265	.0239
12	.08333	.04167	.0467	.04167	.0309	.0283
10	.10000	.05000	.0600	.05000	.0371	.0319
8	.12500	.06250	.0725	.06250	.0463	.0411
6	.16667	.08333	.0933	.08333	.0618	.0566
5	.20000	.10000	.1100	.10000	.0741	.0689
4	.25000	.12500	.1350	.12500	.0927	.0875
3	.33333	.16667	.1767	.16667	.1236	.1184
2 1/2	.40000	.20000	.2100	.20000	.1483	.1431
2	.50000	.25000	.2600	.25000	.1853	.1802
1 1/2	.66667	.33333	.3433	.33333	.2471	.2419
1 1/3	.75000	.37500	.3850	.37500	.2780	.2728
1	1.0000	.50000	.5100	.50000	.3707	.3655

Figure A-19

60° Stub Threads

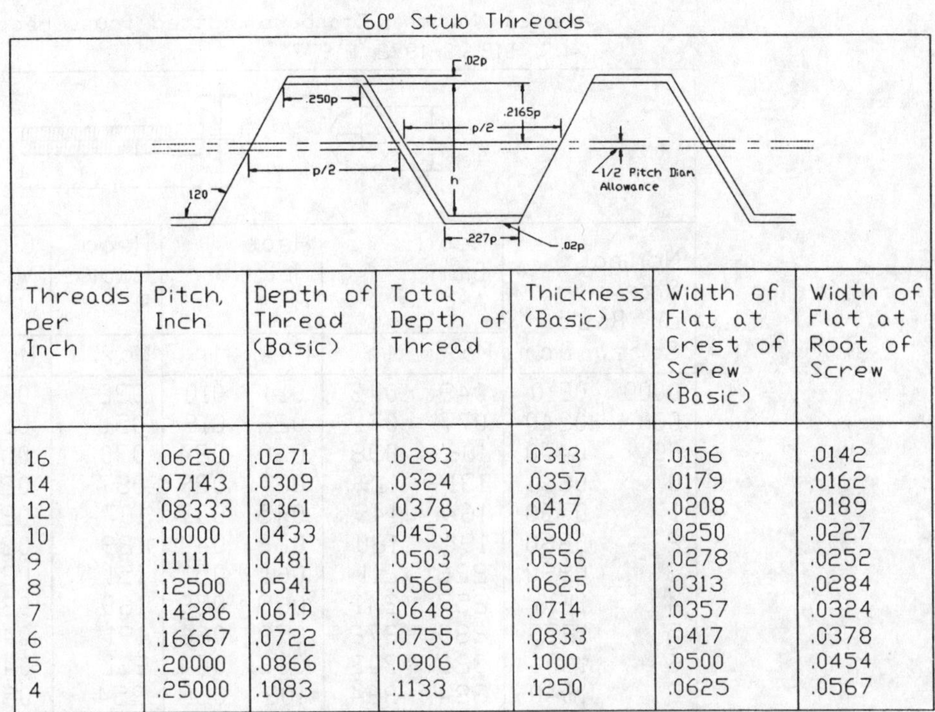

Threads per Inch	Pitch, Inch	Depth of Thread (Basic)	Total Depth of Thread	Thickness (Basic)	Width of Flat at Crest of Screw (Basic)	Width of Flat at Root of Screw
16	.06250	.0271	.0283	.0313	.0156	.0142
14	.07143	.0309	.0324	.0357	.0179	.0162
12	.08333	.0361	.0378	.0417	.0208	.0189
10	.10000	.0433	.0453	.0500	.0250	.0227
9	.11111	.0481	.0503	.0556	.0278	.0252
8	.12500	.0541	.0566	.0625	.0313	.0284
7	.14286	.0619	.0648	.0714	.0357	.0324
6	.16667	.0722	.0755	.0833	.0417	.0378
5	.20000	.0866	.0906	.1000	.0500	.0454
4	.25000	.1083	.1133	.1250	.0625	.0567

Figure A-20

American National Standard Slotted 100° Flat Countersunk Head Machine Screws (ANSI B18.6.3-1972, R1977)

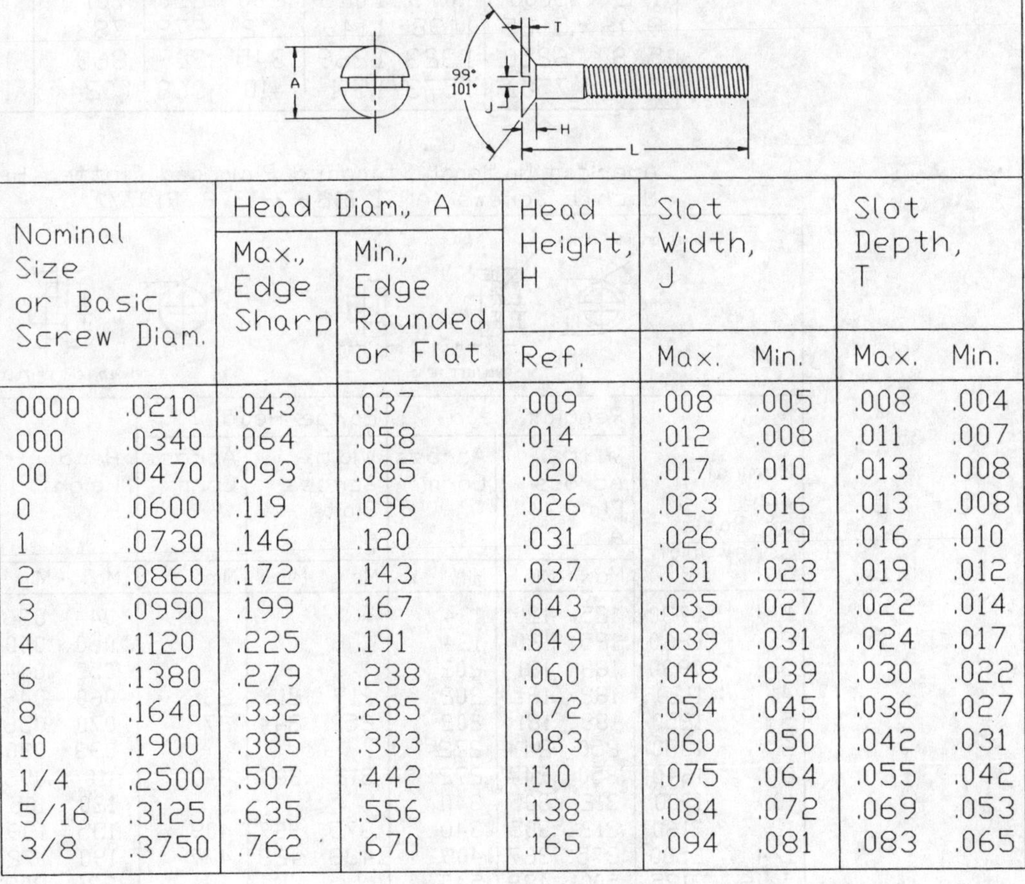

Nominal Size or Basic Screw Diam.		Head Diam., A		Head Height, H	Slot Width, J		Slot Depth, T	
		Max., Edge Sharp	Min., Edge Rounded or Flat	Ref.	Max.	Min.	Max.	Min.
0000	.0210	.043	.037	.009	.008	.005	.008	.004
000	.0340	.064	.058	.014	.012	.008	.011	.007
00	.0470	.093	.085	.020	.017	.010	.013	.008
0	.0600	.119	.096	.026	.023	.016	.013	.008
1	.0730	.146	.120	.031	.026	.019	.016	.010
2	.0860	.172	.143	.037	.031	.023	.019	.012
3	.0990	.199	.167	.043	.035	.027	.022	.014
4	.1120	.225	.191	.049	.039	.031	.024	.017
6	.1380	.279	.238	.060	.048	.039	.030	.022
8	.1640	.332	.285	.072	.054	.045	.036	.027
10	.1900	.385	.333	.083	.060	.050	.042	.031
1/4	.2500	.507	.442	.110	.075	.064	.055	.042
5/16	.3125	.635	.556	.138	.084	.072	.069	.053
3/8	.3750	.762	.670	.165	.094	.081	.083	.065

Figure A-21

Figure A-22 American National Standard Slotted Truss Head Machine Screws (ANSI B18.6.3-1972, R1977)

Nominal Size or Basic Screw Diam.		Head Diam., A		Head Height, H		Head Radius, R	Slot Width, J		Slot Depth, T	
		Max.	Min.	Max.	Min.	Max.	Max.	Min.	Max.	Min.
0000	.0210	.049	.043	.014	.010	.032	.009	.005	.009	.005
000	.0340	.077	.071	.022	.018	.051	.013	.009	.013	.009
00	.0470	.106	.098	.030	.024	.070	.017	.010	.018	.012
0	.0600	.131	.119	.037	.029	.087	.023	.016	.022	.014
1	.0730	.164	.149	.045	.037	.107	.026	.019	.027	.018
2	.0860	.194	.180	.053	.044	.129	.031	.023	.031	.022
3	.0990	.226	.211	.061	.051	.151	.035	.027	.036	.026
4	.1120	.257	.241	.069	.059	.169	.039	.031	.040	.030
5	.1250	.289	.272	.078	.066	.191	.043	.035	.045	.034
6	.1380	.321	.303	.086	.074	.211	.048	.039	.050	.037
8	.1640	.384	.364	.102	.088	.254	.054	.045	.058	.045
10	.1900	.448	.425	.118	.103	.283	.060	.050	.068	.053
12	.2160	.511	.487	.134	.118	.336	.067	.056	.077	.061
1/4	.2500	.573	.546	.150	.133	.375	.075	.064	.087	.070
5/16	.3125	.698	.666	.183	.162	.457	.084	.072	.106	.085
3/8	.3750	.823	.787	.215	.191	.538	.094	.081	.124	.100
7/16	.4375	.948	.907	.248	.221	.619	.094	.081	.142	.116
1/2	.5000	1.073	1.028	.280	.250	.701	.106	.091	.161	.131
9/16	.5625	1.198	1.149	.312	.279	.783	.118	.102	.179	.146
5/8	.6250	1.323	1.269	.345	.309	.863	.133	.116	.196	.162
3/4	.7500	1.573	1.511	.410	.368	1.024	.149	.131	.234	.182

Figure A-23 American National Standard Plain and Slotted Hexagon Head Machine Screws (ANSI B18.6.3-1972, R1977)

Nominal Size or Basic Screw Diam.		Regular Head			Large Head			Head Height H		Slot Width J		Slot Depth T	
		Width Across Flats A		Across Corn. W	Width Across Flats A		Across Corn. W						
		Max.	Min.	Min.	Max.	Min.	Min.	Max.	Min.	Max.	Min.	Max.	Min.
1	.0730	.125	.120	.134				.044	.036				
2	.0860	.125	.120	.134				.050	.040				
3	.0990	.188	.181	.202				.055	.044				
4	.1120	.188	.181	.202	.219	.213	.238	.060	.049	.039	.031	.036	.025
5	.1250	.188	.181	.202	.250	.244	.272	.070	.058	.043	.035	.042	.030
6	.1380	.250	.244	.272				.093	.080	.048	.039	.046	.033
8	.1640	.250	.244	.272	.312	.305	.340	.110	.096	.054	.045	.066	.052
10	.1900	.312	.305	.340				.120	.105	.060	.050	.072	.057
12	.2160	.312	.305	.340	.375	.367	.409	.155	.139	.067	.056	.093	.077
1/4	.2500	.375	.367	.409	.438	.428	.477	.190	.172	.075	.064	.101	.083
5/16	.3125	.500	.489	.545				.230	.208	.084	.072	.122	.100
3/8	.3750	.562	.551	.614				.295	.270	.094	.081	.156	.131

Figure A-24

Slotted Round Head Machine Screws
(ANSI B18.6.3-1972, R1977 Appendix)

Nominal Size or Basic Screw Diam.*		Head Diameter, A		Head Height, H		Slot Width, J		Slot Depth, T	
		Max.	Min.	Max.	Min.	Max.	Min.	Max.	Min.
0000	.0210	.041	.035	.022	.016	.008	.004	.017	.013
000	.0340	.062	.056	.031	.025	.012	.008	.018	.012
00	.0470	.089	.080	.045	.036	.017	.010	.026	.018
0	.0600	.113	.099	.053	.043	.023	.016	.039	.029
1	.0730	.138	.122	.061	.051	.026	.019	.044	.033
2	.0860	.162	.146	.069	.059	.031	.023	.048	.037
3	.0990	.187	.169	.078	.067	.035	.027	.053	.040
4	.1120	.211	.193	.086	.075	.039	.031	.058	.044
5	.1250	.236	.217	.095	.083	.043	.035	.063	.047
6	.1380	.260	.240	.103	.091	.048	.039	.068	.051
8	.1640	.309	.287	.120	.107	.054	.045	.077	.058
10	.1900	.359	.334	.137	.123	.060	.050	.087	.065
12	.2160	.408	.382	.153	.139	.067	.056	.096	.073
1/4	.2500	.472	.443	.175	.160	.075	.064	.109	.082
5/16	.3125	.590	.557	.216	.198	.084	.072	.132	.099
3/8	.3750	.708	.670	.256	.237	.094	.081	.155	.117
7/16	.4375	.750	.707	.328	.307	.094	.081	.196	.148
1/2	.5000	.813	.766	.355	.332	.106	.091	.211	.159
9/16	.5625	.938	.887	.410	.385	.118	.102	.242	.183
5/8	.6250	1.000	.944	.438	.411	.133	.116	.258	.195
3/4	.7500	1.250	1.185	.547	.516	.149	.131	.320	.242

Figure A-25

AMERICAN NATIONAL STANDARD SQUARE HEAD SETSCREWS
(ANSI B18.6.2)

Nominal Size of Basic Screw Diameter		Width Across Flats		Width Across Corners		Head Height		Neck Relief Diameter		Max Neck Relief Fillet Radius	Min Neck Relief Width	Min Head Radius
		Max.	Min.	Max.	Min.	Max.	Min.	Max.	Min.			
10	0.1900	0.188	0.180	0.265	0.247	0.148	0.134	0.145	0.140	0.027	0.083	0.48
1/4	0.2500	0.250	0.241	0.354	0.331	0.196	0.178	0.185	0.170	0.032	0.100	0.62
5/16	0.3125	0.312	0.302	0.442	0.415	0.245	0.224	0.240	0.225	0.036	0.111	0.78
3/8	0.3750	0.375	0.362	0.530	0.497	0.293	0.270	0.294	0.279	0.041	0.125	0.94
7/16	0.4375	0.438	0.423	0.619	0.581	0.341	0.315	0.345	0.330	0.046	0.143	1.09
1/2	0.5000	0.500	0.484	0.707	0.665	0.389	0.361	0.400	0.385	0.050	0.154	1.25
9/16	0.5625	0.562	0.545	0.795	0.748	0.437	0.407	0.454	0.439	0.054	0.167	1.41
5/8	0.6250	0.625	0.606	0.884	0.833	0.485	0.452	0.507	0.492	0.059	0.182	1.56
3/4	0.7500	0.750	0.729	1.060	1.001	0.582	0.544	0.620	0.605	0.065	0.200	1.88
7/8	0.8750	0.875	0.852	1.237	1.170	0.678	0.635	0.731	0.716	0.072	0.222	2.19
1	1.0000	1.000	0.974	1.414	1.337	0.774	0.726	0.838	0.823	0.081	0.250	2.50
1 1/8	1.1250	1.125	1.096	1.591	1.505	0.870	0.817	0.939	0.914	0.092	0.283	2.81
1 1/4	1.2500	1.250	1.219	1.768	1.674	0.966	0.908	1.064	1.039	0.092	0.283	3.12
1 3/8	1.3750	1.375	1.342	1.945	1.843	1.063	1.000	1.159	1.134	0.109	0.333	3.44
1 1/2	1.5000	1.500	1.464	2.121	2.010	1.159	1.091	1.284	1.259	0.109	0.333	3.75

AMERICAN NATIONAL STANDARD SQUARE HEAD SETSCREWS (ANSI B18.6.2)

Nominal Size or Basic Screw Diameter		Cup and Flat Point Diameters		Dog and Half-Dog Point Diameters		Point Length				Oval Point Radius +0.031 -0.000	Cone Point Angle 90° ± 2° for these Nominal Lengths or Longer, 118° ± 2° for Shorter Screws
						Dog		Half-Dog			
		Max.	Min.	Max.	Min.	Max.	Min.	Max.	Min.		
10	0.1900	0.102	0.088	0.127	0.120	0.095	0.085	0.050	0.040	0.142	1/4
1/4	0.2500	0.132	0.118	0.156	0.149	0.130	0.120	0.068	0.058	0.188	5/16
5/16	0.3125	0.172	0.156	0.203	0.195	0.161	0.151	0.083	0.073	0.234	3/8
3/8	0.3750	0.212	0.194	0.250	0.241	0.193	0.183	0.099	0.089	0.281	7/16
7/16	0.4375	0.252	0.232	0.297	0.287	0.224	0.214	0.114	0.104	0.328	1/2
1/2	0.5000	0.291	0.270	0.344	0.334	0.255	0.245	0.130	0.120	0.375	9/16
9/16	0.5625	0.332	0.309	0.391	0.379	0.287	0.275	0.146	0.134	0.422	5/8
5/8	0.6250	0.371	0.347	0.469	0.456	0.321	0.305	0.164	0.148	0.469	3/4
3/4	0.7500	0.450	0.425	0.562	0.549	0.383	0.367	0.196	0.180	0.562	7/8
7/8	0.8750	0.530	0.502	0.656	0.642	0.446	0.430	0.227	0.221	0.656	1
1	1.0000	0.609	0.579	0.750	0.734	0.510	0.490	0.260	0.240	0.750	1 1/8
1 1/8	1.1250	0.689	0.655	0.844	0.826	0.572	0.552	0.291	0.271	0.844	1 1/4
1 1/4	1.2500	0.767	0.733	0.938	0.920	0.635	0.615	0.323	0.303	0.938	1 1/2
1 3/8	1.3750	0.848	0.808	1.031	1.011	0.698	0.678	0354	0.334	1.031	1 5/8
1 1/2	1.5000	0.926	0.886	1.125	1.105	0.760	0.740	0.385	0.365	1.125	1 3/4

Figure A-26

American National Standard Slotted Headless Setscrews (ANSI B18.6.2)

Nominal Size or Basic Screw Diameter		Crown Radius Basic	Slot Width		Slot Depth		Cup and Flat Point Diameters		Dog Pont Diameters		Point Length				Oval Point Radius Basic	Cone Point Angle 90°±2° For These Nominal Lengths or Longer 118°±2° For Shorter
											Dog		Half-Dog			
			MAX	MIN	MAX	MIN	MAX	MIN	MAX	MIN	MAX	MIN	MAX	MIN		
0	0.0600	0.060	0.014	0.0010	0.020	0.016	0.033	0.027	0.040	0.037	0.032	0.028	0.017	0.013	0.045	5/64
1	0.0730	0.073	0.016	0.012	0.020	0.016	0.040	0.033	0.049	0.045	0.040	0.036	0.021	0.017	0.055	3/32
2	0.0860	0.086	0.018	0.014	0.025	0.019	0.047	0.039	0.057	0.053	0.046	0.042	0.024	0.020	0.064	7/64
3	0.0990	0.099	0.020	0.016	0.028	0.022	0.054	0.045	0.066	0.062	0.052	0.048	0.027	0.023	0.074	1/8
4	0.1120	0.112	0.024	0.018	0.031	0.025	0.061	0.051	0.075	0.070	0.058	0.054	0.030	0.026	0.084	5/32
5	0.1250	0.125	0.026	0.020	0.036	0.026	0.067	0.057	0.083	0.078	0.063	0.057	0.033	0.027	0.094	3/16
6	0.1380	0.138	0.028	0.022	0.040	0.030	0.074	0.064	0.092	0.087	0.073	0.067	0.038	0.032	0.104	3/16
8	0.1640	0.164	0.032	0.026	0.046	0.036	0.087	0.076	0.109	0.103	0.083	0.077	0.043	0.037	0.123	1/4
10	0.1900	0.190	0.035	0.029	0.053	0.043	0.102	0.088	0.127	0.120	0.095	0.085	0.050	0.040	0.142	1/4
12	0.2160	0.216	0.042	0.035	0.061	0.051	0.115	0.101	0.144	0.137	0.115	0.105	0.060	0.050	0.162	5/16
1/4	0.2500	0.250	0.049	0.041	0.068	0.058	0.132	0.118	0.156	0.149	0.130	0.120	0.068	0.058	0.188	5/16
5/16	0.3125	0.312	0.055	0.047	0.083	0.073	0.172	0.156	0.203	0.195	0.161	0.151	0.083	0.073	0.234	3/8
3/8	0.3750	0.375	0.068	0.060	0.099	0.089	0.212	0.194	0.250	0.241	0.193	0.183	0.099	0.089	0.281	7/16
7/16	0.4375	0.438	0.076	0.068	0.114	0.104	0.252	0.232	0.297	0.287	0.224	0.214	0.114	0.104	0.328	1/2
1/2	0.5000	0.500	0.086	0.078	0.130	0.120	0.291	0.270	0.344	0.334	0.255	0.245	0.130	0.120	0.375	9/16
9/16	0.5625	0.562	0.096	0.088	0.146	0.136	0.332	0.309	0.391	0.379	0.287	0.275	0.146	0.134	0.422	5/8
5/8	0.6250	0.625	0.107	0.097	0.161	0.151	0.371	0.347	0.469	0.456	0.321	0.305	0.164	0.148	0.469	3/4
3/4	0.7500	0.750	0.134	0.124	0.193	0.183	0.450	0.425	0.562	0.549	0.383	0.367	0.196	0.180	0.562	7/8

Figure A-27

Lengths for Threaded Fasteners

DIAMETER	.250	.313	.375	.438	.500	.563	.625	.750	.875	1.000	1.250	1.500	1.750	2.000	2.500	3.000	3.500	4.000
5(.125)	●	●	●	●	●	●	●	●	●	●		●						
6(.138)	●	●	●	●	●	●	●	●	●	●	●	●		●				
8(.164)	●	●	●	●	●	●	●	●	●	●	●	●		●				
10(.190)	●	●	●	●	●	●	●	●	●	●	●	●	●	●				
12(.216)	●	●	●	●	●	●	●	●	●	●		●		●				
.250	●	●	●	●	●	●	●	●	●	●	●	●	●	●	●			
.313	●	●	●	●	●	●	●	●	●	●	●	●	●	●	●			
.375	●	●	●	●	●	●	●	●	●	●	●	●		●	●	●		
.438	●	●	●	●	●	●	●	●	●	●	●	●		●	●	●		
.500	●	●	●	●	●	●	●	●	●	●	●	●		●	●	●	●	●
.563			●	●	●	●	●	●	●	●		●		●	●	●	●	●
.625			●	●	●	●	●	●	●	●		●		●		●		●
.750					●	●	●	●	●	●		●		●		●	●	●
.875							●	●	●	●		●		●		●	●	●
1.000												●		●	●	●		●

Figure A-28

Lengths for Metric Threaded Fasteners

DIAMETER	4	5	8	10	12	16	20	24	30	36	40	45	50	60	70
1.6	●	●	●												
2	●	●	●												
2.5	●	●	●	●	●										
3		●	●	●	●										
4			●	●	●	●	●								
5			●	●	●	●	●	●							
6				●	●	●	●	●							
8					●	●	●	●	●	●	●				
10						●	●	●	●	●	●	●	●	●	
12						●	●	●	●	●	●	●	●	●	●
16							●	●	●	●	●	●	●	●	●
20								●	●	●	●	●	●	●	●
24									●	●	●	●	●	●	●
30										●	●	●	●	●	●

Figure A-29

American National Standard Square and Hexagon Machine Screw Nuts
(ANSI B18.6.3-1972, R1977)

Nom. Size	Basic Diam.	Basic F	Max. F	Min. F	Max. G	Min. G	Max. G1	Min. G1	Max. H	Min. H
0	.0600	5/32	.156	.150	.221	.206	.180	.171	.050	.043
1	.0730	5/32	.156	.150	.221	.206	.180	.171	.050	.043
2	.0860	3/16	.188	.180	.265	.247	.217	.205	.066	.057
3	.0990	3/16	.188	.180	.265	.247	.217	.205	.066	.057
4	.1120	1/4	.250	.241	.354	.331	.289	.275	.098	.087
5	.1250	5/16	.312	.302	.442	.415	.361	.344	.114	.102
6	.1380	5/16	.312	.302	.442	.415	.361	.344	.114	.102
8	.1640	11/32	.344	.332	.486	.456	.397	.378	.130	.117
10	.1900	3/8	.375	.362	.530	.497	.433	.413	.130	.117
12	.2160	7/16	.438	.423	.619	.581	.505	.482	.161	.148
1/4	.2500	7/16	.438	.423	.619	.581	.505	.482	.193	.178
5/16	.3125	9/16	.562	.545	.795	.748	.650	.621	.225	.208
3/8	.3750	5/8	.625	.607	.884	.833	.722	.692	.257	.239

Figure A-30

Standard Twist Drill Sizes (Inches)

SIZE	DIAMETER	SIZE	DIAMETER	SIZE	DIAMETER	SIZE	DIAMETER
40	.098	19	.166	C	.242	U	.368
39	.0995	18	.1695	D	.246	3/8	.375
38	.1015	11/64	.1719	1/4(E)	.250	V	.377
37	.104	17	.173	F	.257	W	.386
36	.1065	16	.177	G	.261	25/64	.3906
7/16	.1094	15	.180	17/64	.2656	X	.397
35	.110	14	.182	H	.266	Y	.404
34	.111	13	.185	I	.272	13/32	.4062
33	.113	3/16	.1875	J	.277	Z	.413
32	.116	12	.189	K	.281	27/64	.4219
31	.120	11	.191	9/32	.2812	7/16	.4375
1/8	.125	10	.1935	L	.290	29/64	.4531
30	.1285	9	.196	M	.295	15/32	.4688
29	.136	8	.199	19/64	.2969	31/64	.4844
28	.1405	7	.201	N	.302	1/2	.5000
9/64	.1406	13/64	.2031	5/16	.3125	9/16	.5625
27	.144	6	.204	O	.316	5/8	.625
26	.147	5	.2055	P	.323	11/16	.6875
25	.1495	4	.209	21/64	.3281	3/4	.750
24	.152	3	.213	Q	.332	13/16	.8125
23	.154	7/32	.2188	R	.339	7/8	.875
5/32	.1562	2	.221	11/32	.3438	15/16	.9375
22	.157	1	.228	S	.348		
21	.159	A	.234	T	.358		
20	.161	B	.238	23/64	.3594		

NOTES FOR TWIST DRILL SIZES - INCHES

1. This is only a partial list of standard drill sizes.
2. Whenever possible, specify holes sizes that correspond to standard drill sizes.
3. Drill sizes are available in 1/64 increments between .5000 and 1.2500.
4. Drill sizes are available in 1/32 increments between 1.2500 and 1.500.

Figure A-31

Standard Twist Drill Sizes (Millimeters)					
0.40	2.05	5.10	8.60	15.25	30.00
0.42	2.10	5.20	8.70	15.50	30.50
0.45	2.15	5.30	8.80	15.75	31.00
0.48	2.20	5.40	8.90	16.00	31.50
0.50	2.25	5.50	9.00	16.25	32.00
0.55	2.30	5.60	9.10	16.50	32.50
0.60	2.35	5.70	9.20	16.75	33.00
0.65	2.40	5.80	9.30	17.00	33.50
0.70	2.45	5.90	9.40	17.25	34.00
0.75	2.50	6.00	9.50	17.50	34.50
0.80	2.60	6.10	9.60	17.75	35.00
0.85	2.70	6.20	9.70	18.00	35.50
0.90	2.80	6.30	9.80	18.50	36.00
0.95	2.90	6.40	9.90	19.00	36.50
1.00	3.00	6.50	10.00	19.50	37.00
1.05	3.10	6.60	10.20	20.00	37.50
1.10	3.20	6.70	10.50	20.50	38.00
1.15	3.30	6.80	10.80	21.00	40.00
1.20	3.40	6.90	11.00	21.50	42.00
1.25	3.50	7.00	11.20	22.00	44.00
1.30	3.60	7.10	11.50	22.50	46.00
1.35	3.70	7.20	11.80	23.00	48.00
1.40	3.80	7.30	12.00	23.50	50.00
1.45	3.90	7.40	12.20	24.00	
1.50	4.00	7.50	12.50	24.50	
1.55	4.10	7.60	12.80	25.00	
1.60	4.20	7.70	13.00	25.50	
1.65	4.30	7.80	13.20	26.00	
1.70	4.40	7.90	13.50	26.50	
1.75	4.50	8.00	13.80	27.00	
1.80	4.60	8.10	14.00	27.50	
1.85	4.70	8.20	14.25	28.00	
1.90	4.80	8.30	14.50	28.50	
1.95	4.90	8.40	14.75	29.00	
2.00	5.00	8.50	15.00	29.50	

Figure A-32

Standard Thread Sizes—Inches				
		Pitch		
Number or Fraction	Decimal	Coarse UNC	Fine UNF	Extra Fine UNEF
# 0	0.060		80	
# 2	0.088	56	64	
# 4	0.112	40	48	
# 6	0.138	32	40	
# 8	0.164	32	36	
# 10	0.190	24	32	
1/4	0.250	20	28	32
5/16	0.312	18	24	32
3/8	0.375	16	24	32
7/16	0.438	14	20	28
1/2	0.500	13	20	28
9/16	0.562	12	18	24
5/8	0.625	11	18	24
3/4	0.750	10	16	20
7/8	0.875	9	14	20
1	1.000	8	12	20

Figure A-33

Metric Threads—Preferred Sizes		
Nominal Diameter	Pitch	
	Coarse	Fine
1	0.25	
1.2	0.25	
1.6	0.35	
2	0.40	
2.5	0.45	
3	0.50	
4	0.70	
5	0.80	
6	1.00	
8	1.25	1.00
10	1.50	1.25
12	1.75	1.50
16	2.00	1.50
20	2.50	1.50
24	3.00	2.00
30	3.50	2.00

Figure A-34

Thread Length	3/16	1/4	3/8	1/2	5/8	3/4	7/8	1	1 1/4	1 1/2	1 3/4	2	2 1/2	3
#2 - 5	√	√	√	√	√	√	√	√						
#4 - 40		√	√	√	√	√	√	√	√	√				
#6 - 32		√	√	√	√	√		√	√	√	√	√	√	√
#8 - 32		√	√	√	√	√		√	√	√	√	√	√	√
#10 - 24		√	√	√	√	√		√	√	√	√	√	√	√
#10 - 32		√	√	√		√		√	√	√	√	√	√	√
#12 - 24			√	√	√	√		√	√	√	√	√	√	√
1/4 - 20				√	√	√	√	√	√	√	√	√	√	√
5/16 - I8				√	√	√	√	√	√	√	√	√	√	√
3/8 - 16				√	√	√	√	√	√	√	√	√	√	√
1/2 - 13						√	√	√	√	√	√	√	√	√
5/8 - 11							√	√	√	√	√	√	√	√
3/4 - 10										√		√		√

Figure A-35

Thread Specs	Fasteners—Standard Lengths										
	5	6	8	10	12	14	16	18	20	25	30	35
M3×.5	√	√	√	√	√	√	√	√	√	√	√	√
M4×.7		√	√	√	√	√	√	√	√	√	√	√
M5×.8		√	√	√	√	√	√	√	√	√	√	√
M6×1		√	√	√	√	√	√	√	√	√	√	√
M8× 1		√	√	√	√	√	√	√	√	√	√	√
M8× 1.25			√	√	√	√	√	√	√	√	√	√
M10×1			√	√	√	√	√	√	√	√	√	√
M10×1.5				√	√	√	√	√	√	√	√	√
M12×1.25					√	√	√	√	√	√	√	√
M12×1.5					√	√	√	√	√	√	√	√
M14×1.5						√	√	√	√	√	√	√
M16×1.5							√	√	√	√	√	√
M18×1.5								√	√	√	√	√
M20×1.5									√	√	√	√
M22×1.5										√	√	√
M24×2										√	√	√

Figure A-36

Figure A-37

American National Standard Plain Washers

Nominal Washer Size		Series	Inside Diameter	Outside Diameter	Thickness
No. 0	0.060	N	0.068	0.125	0.025
		R	0.068	0.188	0.025
		W	0.068	0.250	0.025
No. 1	0.073	N	0.084	0.155	0.025
		R	0.084	0.219	0.025
		W	0.084	0.281	0.032
No. 2	0.086	N	0.094	0.188	0.025
		R	0.094	0.250	0.032
		W	0.094	0.344	0.032
No. 3	0.099	N	0.109	0.219	0.025
		R	0.109	0.312	0.032
		W	0.109	0.406	0.040
No. 4	0.112	N	0.125	0.250	0.032
		R	0.125	0.375	0.040
		W	0.125	0.438	0.040
No. 5	0.125	N	0.141	0.281	0.032
		R	0.141	0.406	0.040
		W	0.141	0.500	0.040
No. 6	1.380	N	0.156	0.312	0.032
		R	0.156	0.438	0.040
		W	0.156	0.562	0.040
No. 8	0.164	N	0.188	0.375	0.040
		R	0.188	0.500	0.040
		W	0.188	0.633	0.063
No. 10	0.190	N	0.203	0.406	0.040
		R	0.203	0.562	0.040
		W	0.203	0.734	0.063
No. 12	0.216	N	0.234	0.438	0.040
		R	0.234	0.625	0.063
		W	0.234	0.875	0.063
1/4	0.250	N	0.281	0.500	0.063
		R	0.281	0.734	0.063
		W	0.281	1.000	0.063
5/16	0.312	N	0.344	0.625	0.063
		R	0.344	0.875	0.063
		W	0.344	1.125	0.063
3/8	0.375	N	0.406	0.734	0.063
		R	0.406	1.000	0.063
		W	0.406	1.250	0.100
7/16	0.438	N	0.469	0.875	0.063
		R	0.469	1.125	0.063
		W	0.469	1.469	0.100
1/2	0.500	N	0.531	1.000	0.063
		R	0.531	1.2.5	0.100
		W	0.531	1.125	0.100
9/16	0.562	N	0.594	1.125	0.063
		R	0.594	1.469	0.100
		W	0.594	2.000	0.100
5/8	0.625	N	0.656	1.250	0.100
		R	0.656	1.750	0.100
		W	0.656	2.250	0.160
3/4	0.750	N	0.812	1.375	0.100
		R	0.812	2.000	0.100
		W	0.812	2.500	0.160
7/8	0.875	N	0.938	1.469	0.100
		R	0.938	2.250	0.160
		W	0.938	2.750	0.160
1	1.000	N	1.062	1.750	0.100
		R	1.062	2.500	0.160
		W	1.062	3.000	0.160

Flat Washers—Metric Sizes			
Nominal	Inside ∅	Outside ∅	Thickness
16	1.7	4	0.35
2	2.2	5	0.35
2.5	2.7	6	0.55
3	3.2	7	0.55
3.5	3.7	8	0.55
4	4.3	9	0.9
5	5.3	10	1.1
6	6.4	12	1.8
8	8.4	16	1.8
10	10.5	20	2.2
12	13	24	2.7
14	15	28	2.7
16	17	30	3.3
20	21	37	3.3
24	25	44	4.3
30	31	56	4.3

Figure A-38

Index

H

I

K

L

M

N

O

W